Frommer's®
California 2012

by Harry Basch, Tara de Lis,
Mark Hiss, Erika Lenkert,
Kristin Luna & Matthew Poole

WILEY

John Wiley & Sons, Inc.

Published by:
John Wiley & Sons, Inc.
111 River St.
Hoboken, NJ 07030-5774

ISBN 978-1-118-01731-9 (paper); ISBN 978-1-118-09978-0 (ebk); ISBN 978-1-118-09979-7 (ebk); ISBN 978-1-118-09980-3 (ebk)

Editor: Stephen Bassman
Production Editor: Lindsay Conner
Cartographer: Andrew Dolan
Photo Editor: Alden Gewirtz
Cover Photo Editor: Richard Fox
Design and Layout by Vertigo Design
Graphics and Prepress by Wiley Indianapolis Composition Services

Front cover photo: Napa Valley vineyards © Dennis Frates/Alamy Images
Back cover photo: California surfing © Shotfile.com/Ultimate Group, LLC/Alamy Images

For information on our other products and services or to obtain technical support, please contact our Customer Care Department within the U.S. at 877/762-2974, outside the U.S. at 317/572-3993 or fax 317/572-4002.

Wiley also publishes its books in a variety of electronic formats. Some content that appears in print may not be available in electronic formats.

Manufactured in China

5 4 3 2 1

CONTENTS

4 SAN FRANCISCO 56

5 THE SAN FRANCISCO BAY AREA 159

6 THE WINE COUNTRY 201

LIST OF MAPS

ABOUT THE AUTHORS

Harry Basch is the author of *Frommer's Exploring America by RV* and *RV Vacations For Dummies* and a contributor to *Frommer's USA*. His books, articles, and photographs—many of which he produced in collaboration with his late wife, Shirley—have been published internationally for more than 25 years.

Tara de Lis is a native Angeleno. She spent six years as the L.A. City Editor for Citysearch.com and has been published in *L.A. Times Magazine, Gayot*, dineLA, AOL, and CitySpots. Never officially off-duty, she spends her "free time" seeking out new restaurants and hand-crafted cocktails.

A third-generation Southern Californian, **Mark Hiss** is a writer and photographer who has spent more than 25 years in San Diego. He was founding editor of both the visitor guide *Where San Diego* and *Performances,* the playbill magazine for the city's leading performing arts venues. He is also a recovering publicist who spent many years working for several of San Diego's top theater companies.

A native San Franciscan, **Erika Lenkert** spends her time traipsing around the Bay Area and across the globe in search of adventure and great food. She has written for *Travel + Leisure, Food & Wine, Bride's, Wine Country Living, San Francisco Magazine, Los Angeles Magazine,* and *Time Out*. Her latest work is an entertaining and cooking guide called *The Last-Minute Party Girl: Fashionable, Fearless, and Foolishly Simple Entertaining* (www. lastminutepartygirl.com).

Kristin Luna hopped around a bit before finding a permanent home in San Francisco. Her intrepid spirit has led her all over the globe in search of adventure, whether scuba diving cageless with sharks in the South Pacific or hurling herself out of a plane at 15,000 feet in the Pyrenees. Kristin has worked on other Frommer's guides and been a contributor to *Newsweek, Forbes Traveler,* and the Travel Channel. Her work has also appeared in the *San Francisco Chronicle, Islands, Real Simple, Sherman's Travel, Glamour, People,* and *Entertainment Weekly.*

Matthew Poole, a native Californian, has authored more than two dozen travel guides to California, Hawaii, and abroad. A regular contributor to radio and television travel programs, he has made numerous guest appearances on the award-winning *Bay Area Backroads* television show, among other broadcast outlets. Before becoming a full-time travel writer and photographer, he worked as an English tutor in Prague, ski instructor in the Swiss Alps, and scuba instructor in Maui and Thailand. Highly allergic to office buildings and mortgage payments, he spends most of his time traveling the globe in search of new adventures.

HOW TO CONTACT US

In researching this book, we discovered many wonderful places—hotels, restaurants, shops, and more. We're sure you'll find others. Please tell us about them, so we can share the information with your fellow travelers in upcoming editions. If you were disappointed with a recommendation, we'd love to know that, too. Please write to:

Frommer's California 2012
John Wiley & Sons, Inc. • 111 River St. • Hoboken, NJ 07030-5774
frommersfeedback@wiley.com

ADVISORY & DISCLAIMER

Travel information can change quickly and unexpectedly, and we strongly advise you to confirm important details locally before traveling, including information on visas, health and safety, traffic and transport, accommodations, shopping, and eating out. We also encourage you to stay alert while traveling and to remain aware of your surroundings. Avoid civil disturbances, and keep a close eye on cameras, purses, wallets, and other valuables.

While we have endeavored to ensure that the information contained within this guide is accurate and up-to-date at the time of publication, we make no representations or warranties with respect to the accuracy or completeness of the contents of this work and specifically disclaim all warranties, including without limitation warranties of fitness for a particular purpose. We accept no responsibility or liability for any inaccuracy or errors or omissions, or for any inconvenience, loss, damage, costs, or expenses of any nature whatsoever incurred or suffered by anyone as a result of any advice or information contained in this guide.

The inclusion of a company, organization, or website in this guide as a service provider and/or potential source of further information does not mean that we endorse them or the information they provide. Be aware that information provided through some websites may be unreliable and can change without notice. Neither the publisher nor author shall be liable for any damages arising herefrom.

FROMMER'S STAR RATINGS, ICONS & ABBREVIATIONS

Every hotel, restaurant, and attraction listing in this guide has been ranked for quality, value, service, amenities, and special features using a **star-rating system.** In country, state, and regional guides, we also rate towns and regions to help you narrow down your choices and budget your time accordingly. Hotels and restaurants are rated on a scale of zero (recommended) to three stars (exceptional). Attractions, shopping, nightlife, towns, and regions are rated according to the following scale: zero stars (recommended), one star (highly recommended), two stars (very highly recommended), and three stars (must-see).

In addition to the star-rating system, we also use **seven feature icons** that point you to the great deals, in-the-know advice, and unique experiences that separate travelers from tourists. Throughout the book, look for:

special finds—those places only insiders know about

fun facts—details that make travelers more informed and their trips more fun

kids—best bets for kids and advice for the whole family

special moments—those experiences that memories are made of

overrated—places or experiences not worth your time or money

insider tips—great ways to save time and money

great values—where to get the best deals

The following **abbreviations** are used for credit cards:

AE	American Express	**DISC**	Discover	**V**	Visa
DC	Diners Club	**MC**	MasterCard		

TRAVEL RESOURCES AT FROMMERS.COM

Frommer's travel resources don't end with this guide. Frommer's website, **www.frommers. com**, has travel information on more than 4,000 destinations. We update features regularly, giving you access to the most current trip-planning information and the best airfare, lodging, and car-rental bargains. You can also listen to podcasts, connect with other Frommers.com members through our active-reader forums, share your travel photos, read blogs from guidebook editors and fellow travelers, and much more.

THE BEST OF CALIFORNIA

by Harry Basch, Tara de Lis, Mark Hiss, Erika Lenkert, Kristin Luna & Matthew Poole

n my early 20s, I took the requisite college student's pilgrimage to Europe, exploring its finer train stations and sleeping on the premier park benches from London to Istanbul. I was relatively anonymous—just another tanned and skinny, blond and blue-eyed American with a backpack. That is, until I crossed into the former Eastern Bloc.

The reaction there was dramatic, almost palpable. Like Moses parting the sea, I wandered the crowded streets of Prague and citizens would stop, stare, and step aside as if I bore a scarlet letter *A* across my chest. It wasn't until a man with faltering English approached me that I discovered the reason for my newfound celebrity status.

"Eh, you. Where you from? No, no. Let me guess." He stepped back and gave a cursory examination, followed by a pregnant pause. "Ah, I've got it! California! You're from California, no?" His eyes gleamed as I told him that, yes, he was quite correct. "Wonderful! Wonderful!" A dozen or so pilsners later with my loquacious new friend, it all became clear to me: To him, I was a celebrity—a rich, convertible-driving surfer who spent most of his days lazing on the beach, fending off hordes of buxom blondes while arguing with his agent via cellphone. The myth is complete, I thought. I *am* the Beach Boys. I *am Baywatch.* Status by association. The tentacles of Hollywood have done what no NATO pact could achieve—they've leapfrogged the staid issues of capitalism versus communism by offering a far more potent narcotic: the mystique of sun-drenched California, of movie stars strolling down Sunset Boulevard, of beautiful women in tight shorts and bikini tops roller-skating along Venice Beach. In short, the world has bought what the movie industry is selling.

Of course, the allure is understandable. It *is* warm and sunny most days of the year, movie stars *do* abound in Los Angeles, and you can't swing a cat by its tail without hitting an in-line skater in Venice Beach. This part of the California mystique, however exaggerated, *does* exist, and it's not hard to find.

But there's more—a lot more—to California that isn't scripted, sanitized, and broadcasted to the world's millions of mesmerized masses. Beyond the Hollywood glitter is a wondrously diverse state that, if it ever seceded from the Union, would be one of the most productive, powerful nations in the world. We've got it all: misty redwood forests, an exceptionally verdant Central Valley teeming with agriculture, the mighty Sierra Nevada Mountain Range, eerily fascinating deserts, a host of world-renowned cities, and, of course, hundreds of miles of stunning coastline.

And despite the endemic crime, pollution, traffic, and bowel-shaking earthquakes for which California is famous, we're still the golden child of the United States, America's spoiled rich kid, either loved or loathed by everyone else. (Neighboring Oregon, for example, sells lots of license-plate rims that proudly state, "I hate California.") Truth be told, however, we don't care what anyone thinks of us. Californians *know* they live in one of the most diverse and interesting places in the world, and we're proud of the state we call home.

PREVIOUS PAGE: **Golden Gate Bridge from Baker Beach.**

Granted, we can't guarantee that you'll bump into Arnold Schwarzenegger or learn to surf, but if you have a little time, a little money, and an adventurous spirit, then Harry, Mark, Erika, Kristin, Tara and I can help guide you through one of the most fulfilling vacations of your life. The five of us travel the world for a living, but we *choose* to live in California—because no other place on earth has so much to offer.

—*Matthew Poole*

THE best OF NATURAL CALIFORNIA

- **Redwood National and State Parks:** Acres of inconceivably massive redwood trees, up to 350 feet tall, tower over thick, lush, oversize ferns, mosses, and wild orchids in the old-growth forests along the Northern California coast. Walking through these groves is an unforgettably humbling, serene experience. See "Redwood National & State Parks," in chapter 7.

- **Point Reyes National Seashore:** This extraordinarily scenic stretch of coast and wetlands is one of the state's best bird-watching spots for waterfowl, shorebirds, songbirds, osprey, and red-shouldered hawks. You might even catch a glimpse of a whale from the Point Reyes Lighthouse. See "Point Reyes National Seashore," in chapter 7.

- **Lake Tahoe:** One of the world's most magnificent bodies of fresh water, sparkling Lake Tahoe contains close to 40 trillion gallons—enough to cover the entire state of California to a depth of 15 inches. See "Lake Tahoe," in chapter 8.

- **Mount Shasta:** The mighty volcano Mount Shasta, a solitary tower of rock and snow, rises thousands of feet above the valley floor. If you're fit, it makes for an exhilarating climb as well. See "Mount Shasta & the Cascades," in chapter 8.

- **Yosemite National Park:** You're in for the ultimate treat at Yosemite. Nothing in the state—maybe even the world—compares to this vast wilderness and its

Pfeiffer Beach, Big Sur.

miles of rivers, lakes, peaks, and valleys. With 3 of the 10 tallest waterfalls on Earth, the largest granite monolith anywhere, and some of the world's largest trees, Yosemite is one of the most superlative natural places on the planet. See "Yosemite National Park," in chapter 9.

o **Big Sur:** Sloping redwood forests and towering cliffs pounded by the Pacific create one of the world's most dramatic coastal panoramas. See "The Big Sur Coast," in chapter 11.

o **Channel Islands National Park:** This is California in its most virginal state. Paddle a kayak into sea caves; camp among indigenous island fox and seabirds; and swim, snorkel, or scuba dive tide pools and kelp forests teeming with

Joshua Tree National Park.

wildlife. The channel waters are prime for whale-watching, and winter brings elephant-seal mating season, when you'll see them and their sea lion cousins sunbathing on cove beaches. See "Channel Islands National Park," in chapter 12.

o **Joshua Tree National Park:** You'll find awesome rock formations; groves of flowering cactuses and gnarly, eerily beautiful Joshua trees; ancient Native American petroglyphs; and shifting sand dunes in this desert wonderland. If you choose to camp here, you'll sleep under a brilliant night sky. See "Joshua Tree National Park," in chapter 15.

o **Anza-Borrego Desert State Park:** California's largest state park attracts most of its visitors during the spring wildflower season, when a kaleidoscopic carpet blankets the desert floor. Others come year-round to hike more than 100 miles of trails. See "Anza-Borrego Desert State Park," in chapter 15.

o **Torrey Pines State Reserve:** This pristine park is named for the rare, dramatic little species of pine that grows only here and on a tiny island off the coast. Eight miles of trails immerse hikers in a delicate and beautiful coastal environment featuring mesas, canyons, and marshes. One of San Diego's best beaches awaits at the foot of the sandstone cliffs. See chapter 16.

THE best BEACHES

o **Sonoma Coast State Beaches:** Stretching 10 miles from Bodega Bay to Jenner, these sands draw 300 bird species. Look for osprey from December to September, seal pups from March to June, and gray whales from December to April. See "Along the Sonoma Coast," in chapter 7.

- **Santa Cruz's Beaches:** Santa Cruz has 29 miles of beaches, varied enough to please surfers, swimmers, fishers, sailboarders, the sand-pail-and-shovel set, and the bikini-and-biceps crowd. For starters, walk down the steps from the famous Santa Cruz Beach Boardwalk to the mile-long Main Beach, complete with summer lifeguards and golden-oldie tunes drifting over the sand. See "Santa Cruz," in chapter 11.

- **Pismo Beach:** Pismo's 23-mile stretch of prime beachfront has been an annual destination for generations of California families. Fishing, shopping, surfing, and renting dune buggies are just a few of the many outdoor activities here. Even dogs are welcome to play on the beach. See "Pismo Beach," in chapter 12.

- **Santa Barbara's East Beach:** This wide swath of white sand hosts beach umbrellas, sand-castle builders, and volleyball games. On Sundays, local artists display their work beneath the palm trees. See "Santa Barbara," in chapter 12.

- **Malibu's Legendary Beaches:** Zuma and Surfrider beaches inspired the 1960s surf music that embodies the Southern California coast culture. Surfrider is home to L.A.'s best waves. Zuma is loaded with snack bars, restrooms, jungle gyms, and other amenities. The beach affords some of the state's best sunbathing, in front of the Malibu Colony, a star-studded enclave of multimillion-dollar homes. See "Beaches," in chapter 13.

- **La Jolla's Beaches:** *La Jolla* may be misspelled Spanish for "the jewel," but *this* is no mistake: The bluff-lined beaches here are among the state's most beautiful. Each has a distinct personality: Surfers love Windansea's waves; harbor seals have adopted the Children's Pool; La Jolla Shores is popular for swimming, sunbathing, and kayaking; and the Cove is a top snorkeling spot— and the best place to spot the electric-orange California state fish, the garibaldi. See "Beaches," in chapter 16.

THE best GOLF COURSES

- **Pebble Beach Golf Links:** The famous 17-Mile Drive is the site of 10 national championships and the celebrity-laden AT&T Pebble Beach National Pro-Am. The nearby Pacific and a backdrop of the Del Monte Forest *almost* justify the astronomical greens fees. See "Pebble Beach & 17-Mile Drive," in chapter 11.

- **Poppy Hills** (Pebble Beach): *Golf Digest* has called this Robert Trent Jones, Jr.–designed course one of the world's top 20. Cutting through the Del Monte Forest pines, it is kept in state-of-the-art condition. Unlike many competitors, it's rarely crowded. See "Pebble Beach & 17-Mile Drive," in chapter 11.

- **PGA West TPC Stadium Course** (La Quinta): The par-3 17th hole has a tiny island where Lee Trevino made Skins Game history with a hole in one. The rest of Pete Dye's 7,261-yard design is flat with huge bunkers, lots of water, and severe mounding throughout. See "The Palm Springs Desert Resorts," in chapter 15.

- **Torrey Pines Golf Course** (La Jolla): Two 18-hole championship courses overlook the ocean and give players plenty of challenges—and distractions. In January, the Farmers Insurance Open (formerly known as the Buick Invitational) takes place here; the rest of the year, these gorgeous municipal courses are open to everyone. See "Outdoor Pursuits," in chapter 16.

PGA West TPC Stadium golf course.

THE best CALIFORNIA TRAVEL EXPERIENCES

o **Riding a Cable Car:** It's the quintessential San Francisco experience, taking the Powell-Hyde cable car down to Fisherman's Wharf. When you reach the top of Nob Hill, grab the rail with one hand and hold your camera with the other, because you're about to see a view of the bay that'll make you all weepy. See chapter 4.

o **Exploring Alcatraz Island:** Even if you loathe tourist attractions, you'll dig Alcatraz. Just looking at the Rock from across the bay is enough to give you the heebie-jeebies—and the park rangers have put together an excellent audio tour. Heck, even the boat ride across the bay is worth the price. See chapter 4.

o **Hot-Air Ballooning over Napa Valley:** Sure, you have to rise at dawn to do it, but drifting over the Napa Valley's vineyards in a balloon is the best way to view the verdant, undulating hills, meticulously striped with vines and bordered by mountains. Flights run in the morning on clear days, when the air is calm and cool. You can book a trip through your hotel or with **Bonaventura Balloon Company** (© **800/FLY-NAPA** [359-6272]) or **Adventures Aloft** (© **800/627-2759**). See "Hot-Air Ballooning over the Valley," in chapter 6.

o **Wine Tasting in Napa or Sonoma:** You don't have to be a connoisseur to appreciate the wine trail. All you need is a decadent streak and a designated driver. Sniff and sip at a few wineries, take in the bucolic views, and see why this region is one of the hottest destinations in the country—a place to sample some of the world's best wines right at the source. See chapter 6.

o **Taking a Train Ride Through the Redwoods:** Where else on this planet would you get an opportunity to ride a historic steam train through a remote coastal redwood forest? The **Skunk Train** (℗ 866/457-5865), in Fort Bragg, once lugged logs and now takes tourists on an all-day outing through a redwood forest, an 80-mile journey that crosses over 31 bridges and trestles and through two deep tunnels. They even offer a Sunset Dinner Barbecue excursion. See chapter 7.

o **Rafting Scenic Northern California Rivers:** You can white-water raft through cascades of raging Class 4 waters or float under blue skies, through deep forests, past all sorts of wildlife. Depending on the river and the time of year, some trips are okay for children over age 6. See chapters 9 and 10.

o **Spelunking a Real Gold Mine** (Sutter Creek): Don your hard hat, "tag in," board the mine shuttle, and experience what it's like to be a gold miner. The **Sutter Gold Mine** tour (℗ 866/762-2837) takes you deep into a mine that's loaded with gold deposits. You'll have the chance to sluice for some real gold. See chapter 10.

o **Panning for Gold in the Gold Country:** In southern Gold Country, you can dig into living history and pan for gold. Several companies, including **Gold Prospecting Adventures** (℗ 800/596-0009) in Jamestown, offer dredging lessons and gold-panning tours. You'll quickly learn that this is backbreaking labor, although an adventure. And who knows? You might get lucky and launch a new gold rush. See chapter 10.

o **Taking a Studio Tour** (Los Angeles): Studio tours are opportunities to see actual stage sets for shows, past and present, such as *Desperate Housewives* and

Powell-Hyde cable car.   Ballooning in Napa.

The Skunk Train, Redwood Forest.

Panning for gold, Sutter Gold Mine.

The Tonight Show with Jay Leno, and you never know who you're going to spot emerging from his or her star wagon. See "Exploring the City," in chapter 13.

o **Learning How to Surf:** What could be a better experience during your California vacation than learning how to surf on the same breaks that the Beach Boys surfed? Surfing schools, such as **Learn to Surf L.A.** (𝄐 **310/663-2479**), in Manhattan Beach, will guarantee you'll get up on a longboard and be surfing the easy waves in one short lesson. See "Surfing," in the "Outdoor Pursuits" section in chapter 13.

o **Cruising Sunset Boulevard:** It's a must for first-time visitors because you'll see a cross section of everything that is L.A.: legendary clubs, studios, hotels, and zip codes that you'll instantly recognize from the silver screen and TV shows. The journey ends with a trip to Malibu's fabled beaches, where those classy *Baywatch* episodes were filmed (how perfect). See "L.A.'s Top Attractions," in chapter 13.

o **Skating Venice Beach:** You haven't visited Southern California properly until you've rented some skates at Venice Beach and taken in the human carnival around you. Get a head start on people-watching from your seat at the Sidewalk Cafe; buy some cheap sunglasses, silver jewelry, or ethnic garb; and relish the wide beach, blue sea, and performers along the boardwalk. See "L.A.'s Top Attractions," in chapter 13.

o **Flying a World War II Fighter Aircraft:** Strap yourself into a vintage 600-horsepower fighter aircraft and prepare to blow your mind as you (yes, *you*) perform aerobatic maneuvers—loops, rolls, and lazy-eights—above the San Diego coastline, accompanied (but not flown) by a pilot from **Barnstorming Adventures** (𝄐 **800/759-5667**). It's an experience you'll never forget. See "Outdoor Pursuits," in chapter 16.

o **Explore Wreck Alley:** Several scuttled vessels sit on the ocean floor, about 1 mile off Mission Beach, providing certified divers the chance to investigate a nautical graveyard teeming with sea life. The artificial reef includes a 366-foot Canadian destroyer, the *Yukon,* as well as the remnants of a research station toppled by a storm in 1988. See "Outdoor Pursuits," in chapter 16.

Surf lessons.

THE best OF SMALL-TOWN CALIFORNIA

o **St. Helena:** In the heart of the Napa Valley, St. Helena is known for its Main Street. In a horse and buggy, Robert Louis Stevenson and his bride once made their way down this thoroughfare lined with Victorian homes. The Victorians remain, but now they're stores for designer clothing, hardware, bath products, you name it. Come for the old-time, tranquil mood and the food. See "Napa Valley," in chapter 6.

o **Healdsburg:** An exceptional destination within the vast wine country region of Sonoma, this charming town is centered on its historic square, which maintains old-fashioned charm despite being home to world-class hotels, restaurants, and shopping. And did we mention that it's a 5-minute drive to some of the state's best wineries? See "Healdsburg," in chapter 6.

o **Mendocino:** An artists' colony with a New England flavor, Mendocino has doubled as Cabot Cove, Maine, as the backdrop for *Murder, She Wrote.* On the cliffs above the Pacific Ocean, it has small art galleries, general stores, weathered wooden homes, and organic restaurants. See "Mendocino," in chapter 7.

o **Arcata:** If you're losing faith in America, restore it by spending a few days in this Northern California coastal town. Arcata has it all: its own redwood forest and bird marsh, a charming town square, great family-owned restaurants, and even its own minor-league baseball team, which draws the entire town together on many an afternoon. See "Eureka & Environs," in chapter 7.

o **Nevada City:** The entire town is a national historic landmark and the best place to understand Gold Rush fever. Settled in 1849, it offers fine dining and shopping and a stock of the multigabled Victorian frame houses of the Old West. Relics of the Donner Party are on display at the 1861 Firehouse No. 1. See "The Gold Country," in chapter 10.

ABOVE: **Malakoff Diggins State Historic park, Nevada City.** LEFT: **Ojai Valley.**

- **Pacific Grove:** Escape beach crowds just 2 miles west of Monterey, in Pacific Grove, known for its tranquil waterfront and clean air. It draws thousands of monarch butterflies between October and March. See "Pacific Grove," in chapter 11.

- **Ojai:** When filmmakers needed a Shangri-La for the movie *Lost Horizon,* they drove to Ojai Valley, with its unspoiled eucalyptus groves and small ranches in soft, green hills. Ojai is the amiable village at the valley's heart—a mecca for artists, free spirits, and city folk in need of a restful weekend in the country. See "The Ojai Valley," in chapter 12.

- **Santa Catalina Island:** A day trip to the small town of Catalina makes for a most indulgent day: Take a scenic boat ride, shop, snorkel and dive, golf, hike, lick ice cream, get a sunburn, and barhop sans fear of a DUI. *Tip:* The helicopter taxi is cheaper than you'd expect. See "Santa Catalina Island," in chapter 14.

- **Julian:** This old mining town in the Cuyamaca Mountains near San Diego is now known for a different kind of mother lode: apples (and the ensuing apple pies). The pioneer legacy here includes a local-history museum, an Old West cemetery, and some of the town's original gold mines. See "Julian: Gold, Apple Pies & a Slice of Small-Town California," in chapter 16.

THE best FAMILY VACATION EXPERIENCES

- **San Francisco:** The City by the Bay will entertain every member of the family. If you're traveling with kids, ride the cable cars that "climb halfway to the stars," and visit the Exploratorium, the Metreon, the zoo, the ships at the National Maritime Museum, Golden Gate Park, and more. See chapter 4.

Yosemite National Park.

o **Lake Tahoe:** Lake Tahoe has fun activities galore for families: skiing, snowboarding, hiking, tobogganing, swimming, fishing, boating, water-skiing, mountain biking, and so on. The possibilities seem endless. See "Lake Tahoe," in chapter 8.

o **Yosemite National Park:** Camping or sleeping in a cabin in Yosemite is one of California's top family attractions. Sites lie scattered over 17 campgrounds, ringed by the Sierra Nevada. By day, families can pack their schedule with hiking, bicycling, white-water rafting, climbs up snowy peaks, and more. See "Yosemite National Park," in chapter 9.

o **Santa Cruz:** This funky bayside town has the stuff of an ideal family trip: surfing, sea kayaking, hiking, fishing, and shopping. And those fantastic beaches and the legendary amusement park on the boardwalk will please travelers of all ages. See "Santa Cruz," in chapter 11.

o **Monterey:** It's been called Disneyland-by-the-Sea because of all its tourist activities, including those on Cannery Row and Fisherman's Wharf. The state-of-the-art Monterey Bay Aquarium, however, is a class act, the best in the world. See chapter 11.

o **Disneyland Resort:** "The Happiest Place on Earth" is enhanced by its sister theme park, **Disney's California Adventure.** Whether you're wowed by the animation, thrilled by the coasters,

Cannery Row.

Knott's Berry Farm, another side trip from L.A.

or interested in the history and secrets of this pop-culture juggernaut, you won't leave disappointed. Get a FASTPASS to skip those long lines! See "Side Trips from Los Angeles," in chapter 14.

o **San Diego Zoo, Zoo Safari Park & SeaWorld:** San Diego boasts three of the world's best animal attractions. At the zoo, animals live in naturalistic habitats, and it's one of only four zoos in the U.S. with giant pandas. At the Zoo Safari Park, most of the 3,500 animals roam freely over an 1,800-acre spread. And SeaWorld, with its water-themed rides, flashy animal shows, and detailed exhibits, is an aquatic wonderland of pirouetting dolphins and 4-ton killer whales with a penchant for drenching visitors. See "The Three Major Animal Parks," in chapter 16.

THE best ARCHITECTURAL LANDMARKS

o **The Golden Gate Bridge** (San Francisco): More tomato red than golden, the famous bridge remains the cheery hallmark of the San Francisco skyline. It's also an excellent expanse to walk. See "The Top Attractions," in chapter 4.

o **The Painted Ladies** (San Francisco): The so-called "Painted Ladies" are San Francisco's famous, ornately decorated Victorian homes. Check out the brilliant beauties around Alamo Square. Most of the extant 14,000 structures date from the second half of the 19th century. See chapter 4.

o **Winchester Mystery House** (San Jose): The heiress to the Winchester rifle fortune, Sarah Winchester, created one of the major "Believe It or Not!" curiosities of California, a 160-room Victorian mansion. When a fortuneteller told Sarah she wouldn't die if she'd continue to build onto her house, her mansion underwent construction day and night from 1884 to 1922. She did die eventually, and the hammers were silenced. See chapter 5.

Golden Gate Bridge.

- **The Carson Mansion** (Eureka): This ornate Victorian is one of the state's most photographed and flamboyant Queen Anne-style structures. It was built in 1885 by the Newsom brothers for William Carson, the local timber baron. Today it's the headquarters of a men's club. See chapter 7.

- **The California State Capitol Building** (Sacramento): The Golden State's dazzling white capitol was built in 1869 and renovated in 1976. Its dome—which looks like a Fabergé egg from inside—and original statuary along its eaves remain, and antiques from the original offices furnish its historic rooms. The collection of California governors' portraits is strangely compelling. See "Sacramento," in chapter 10.

- **Mission San Carlos Borromèo del Río Carmelo** (Carmel): The second mission founded in California, in 1770 by Father Junípero Serra, is perhaps the most beautiful. Its stone church and tower dome have been carefully restored, and a garden of poppies adjoins the church. See "Carmel-by-the-Sea," in chapter 11.

- **Hearst Castle** (San Simeon): William Randolph Hearst's 165-room abode is one of the last great estates of America's Gilded Age. It's an astounding, over-the-top monument to unbridled wealth and power. See "San Simeon: Hearst Castle," in chapter 12.

- **Walt Disney Concert Hall** (Los Angeles): You would have to fly to Spain to see Frank Gehry's other architectural masterpiece, the Guggenheim Museum in Bilbao, and this one is sufficiently awe-inspiring. And the dramatically curvaceous stainless-steel exterior houses one of the most acoustically perfect concert halls in the world. See chapter 13.

- **The Gamble House** (Pasadena): The Smithsonian Institution calls this 1908 Arts and Crafts landmark one of the nation's most important houses. Visitors can tour the spectacular interior, designed and impeccably executed, down to the last teak armchair, by Charles and Henry Greene. See chapter 13.

THE best MUSEUMS

- **De Young Museum** (San Francisco): The city's oldest museum was rebuilt from the ground up, and in late 2005 debuted as one of San Francisco's top attractions. Anchored in beautiful Golden Gate Park, surrounded by stunning flora, and shimmering in its fabulous copper exterior, it has a fantastic collection of American paintings; decorative arts and crafts; and arts from Africa, Oceania, and the Americas. Topping it off is a tower with great city views and a surprisingly good cafe with outdoor tables overlooking the sculpture garden. See "Exploring the City," in chapter 4.

- **California Academy of Sciences** (San Francisco): With an aquarium, planetarium, and museum all rolled into one, the Academy stays packed with families perusing the Rainforests of the World annex (a four-level glass tower comprising four countries' native species) and taunting Claude, the resident albino alligator. See "Exploring the City," in chapter 4.

- **Walt Disney Family Museum** (San Francisco): A chronological history of the Disney family, this new Presidio collection chronicles the span of Walt's life and career. Surprisingly, the museum caters more to adults than children, since history is its focus. See "Golden Gate National Park & the Presidio," in chapter 4.

- **The Exploratorium** (San Francisco): The hands-on, interactive Exploratorium boasts 650 exhibits that help show how things work. See "Exploring the City," in chapter 4.

- **California State Railroad Mu-seum** (Sacramento): Old Sacramento's biggest attraction, the 100,000-square-foot museum was once the terminus of the transcontinental and Sacramento Valley railways. It displays dozens of locomotives and railroad cars, among other attractions. See "Sacramento," in chapter 10.

De Young Museum.

Railroad Museum.

Getty Museum.

o **Getty Museum at the Getty Center** (Los Angeles): Designed by Richard Meier and completed in 1997 to the tune of $1 billion, the Getty Center is a striking, starkly futuristic architectural landmark, with panoramic views of the city and ocean. The building itself is enough reason to visit, but so is the permanent collection, the crown jewel of which is van Gogh's "Irises," which the museum paid $54 million to acquire. The gardens and vistas are beautiful as well. See "L.A.'s Top Attractions," in chapter 13.

o **Petersen Automotive Museum** (Los Angeles): This museum is a natural for Los Angeles, a city

Petersen Automotive Museum.

whose personality and history are so entwined with the popularity of the automobile. Impeccably restored vintage autos are displayed in life-size dioramas accurate to the last period detail. Upstairs galleries house celebrity vehicles, car-related artwork, and exhibits. See "Exploring the City," in chapter 13.

o **Museum of Contemporary Art San Diego:** San Diego's internationally respected contemporary art museum operates three facilities, including the downtown Jacobs Building which transformed a portion of the historic train station into one of the city's cultural icons. Together with its other downtown annex and the flagship space that overlooks the ocean in La Jolla, MCASD stakes its claim as the boldest, most important museum in San Diego. See "Exploring the Area," in chapter 16.

THE best LUXURY HOTELS & RESORTS

○ **The Ritz-Carlton, San Francisco** (Nob Hill; ✆ **800/241-3333**): This is the sine qua non of luxury hotels, offering near-perfect service and every possible amenity. Even if you can't afford a guest room, come for the mind-blowing Sunday brunch. See p. 80.

○ **The Mandarin Oriental** (San Francisco; ✆ **800/622-0404**): The Mandarin Oriental is perched so high above the city that the fog rolls in *below* you. It's surreal. Maybe you really did die and go to heaven? See p. 75.

○ **Calistoga Ranch** (Calistoga; ✆ **707/254-2800**): Napa Valley's latest upscale hotel blows away the competition, with individual luxury cabins stocked with every imaginable luxury. In a secluded canyon, it's where nature meets nurture, with a fabulous pool, spa, gym, and guest-only restaurant overlooking a lake. See p. 217.

○ **The Ritz-Carlton Highlands** (Truckee; ✆ **800/241-3333**): The most anticipated opening of the past year was the chateaulike Ritz-Carlton, perched high in the Sierra Nevada Mountains alongside Lake Tahoe. The sprawling resort began welcoming guests just in time for the 2010 ski season, and with ski-in, ski-out access to the Northstar slopes, a lavish spa and fitness center (17,000 sq. ft., to be exact), two outdoor swimming pools and hot tubs, and even a golf course, it didn't disappoint. See p. 319.

○ **Château du Sureau** (Oakhurst; ✆ **559/683-6860**): Near Yosemite, the Château du Sureau and Erna's Elderberry House restaurant stand out for their European attention to quality and detail. Room furnishings are exquisite, and the cuisine is worthy of the stars. See p. 352.

○ **Casa Palmero Resort** (Pebble Beach; ✆ **800/654-9300**): A small, ultraluxury resort on the first tee of the Pebble Beach Golf Course, Casa Palmero has 24 intimate and private cottages and suites. Is $2,550 per night okay with you?

○ **Post Ranch Inn** (Big Sur; ✆ **800/527-2200**): Twelve hundred feet above the sea, the elevated wood-and-glass guest cottages at this romantic cliffside retreat give guests the illusion that they're living at cloud level. See p. 473.

○ **Four Seasons Resort** (Santa Barbara; ✆ **800/819-5053**): Open since 1927, this Four Seasons operation, on the grounds of the historic Biltmore Hotel, has palm-studded formal gardens and prime beachfront along "America's Riviera." Wander the elegant Spanish-Moorish arcades and walkways, accented by exquisite Mexican tile, and then play croquet on manicured lawns or relax at the Coral Casino Beach and Cabana Club. The rooms are the epitome of refined luxury. See p. 522.

○ **Shutters on the Beach** (Santa Monica; ✆ **800/334-9000**) and **Casa del Mar** (Santa Monica; ✆ **800/898-6999**): If an oceanfront room at either of these hotels doesn't put a spring in your love life, we don't know what will. Shutters is dressed up like a rich friend's contemporary-chic beach house, while glamorous Casa del Mar is an impeccably restored Art Deco–era delight. See p. 559 and 558.

○ **Beverly Hills Hotel and Bungalows** (Beverly Hills; ✆ **800/283-8885**): A deep dent in your credit card is a small price to pay for the chance to take afternoon tea next to Ozzy Osbourne, swim laps in the same pool Katharine Hepburn once dove into fully clothed, and eat pancakes in the fabled Fountain Coffee Shop. See p. 563.

- **La Quinta Resort & Club** (La Quinta; ℂ **800/598-3828**): This mecca for serious golfers has morphed into an upscale family hotel without disturbing the quality of service. While Dad is putting away, Mom can luxuriate in one of more than 35 spa treatment rooms, and the kids can splash in one of the 41 outdoor pools and Jacuzzis or exercise on one of the 23 tennis courts. The property is designed to reduce the feeling of a megaresort, and the service exceeds expectations. Fido is welcome also, for a fee ($100 a night). See p. 744.

- **The Grand Del Mar** (Del Mar; ℂ **888/314-2030**): This resort nestled in the foothills of San Diego's North County is a faux Tuscan villa padded with ornate, Vegas-style luxury. Liberally accented with fountains, courtyards, sweeping staircases, and outdoor fireplaces, it's so grandly European that you'll feel as if you are visiting the doge at his country estate. Its signature restaurant, Addison, is one of the city's most sumptuous dining rooms, with cuisine to match. See p. 841.

THE best AFFORDABLE SMALL HOTELS & INNS

- **Hotel Bohème** (San Francisco; ℂ **415/433-9111**): This hotel is the perfect mixture of art, style, class, romance, and location—just steps from the sidewalk cafes of North Beach. If Bette Davis were alive today, this is where she'd stay. See p. 81.

- **St. Orres** (Gualala; ℂ **707/884-3303**): Designed in a Russian style—complete with two Kremlinesque, onion-domed towers—St. Orres offers secluded accommodations constructed from century-old timbers salvaged from a nearby mill. One of the most eye-catching inns on California's North Coast. See p. 261.

- **Albion River Inn** (Albion; ℂ **800/479-7944**): One of the best rooms with a view on the coast, the Albion River Inn is on a cliff overlooking a rugged stretch of shoreline. Most of the luxuriously appointed rooms have Jacuzzi tubs for two, elevated to window level. Add champagne, and you're guaranteed to have a night you won't soon forget. See p. 272.

- **River Ranch Lodge** (Lake Tahoe; ℂ **866/991-9912**): Alongside the Truckee River, the River Ranch has long been one of our favorite affordable inns around Lake Tahoe. It has everything you'd want in a mountain lodge: rustic decor, a great bar and outdoor deck overlooking the river, and a restaurant serving wood-oven-roasted Montana elk loin and other hearty dishes. See p. 320.

- **Gunn House Hotel** (Sonora; ℂ **209/532-3421**): Built in 1850 by Dr. Lewis C. Gunn, this was the first two-story adobe structure in Sonora and is now one of the best moderately priced hotels in the Gold Country. It's easy to catch the forty-niner spirit here, as the entire hotel and grounds are brimming with quality antiques and turn-of-the-20th-century artifacts. See p. 420.

○ **Mount Shasta Ranch B&B** (Mount Shasta; ✆ **530/926-3870**): Built in 1923 as a private retreat and thoroughbred horse ranch for one of the country's most famous horse trainers and racing tycoons, this B&B offers one of the best deals anywhere. Rates start at $60 a night and include a full country breakfast. See p. 336.

○ **Evergreen Lodge** (Yosemite; ✆ **800/935-6343**): Scattered through a grove of towering pines near the entrance to Yosemite, Evergreen's rustic cabins, with a beautiful old bar and restaurant, afford easy access to dozens of outdoor adventures. Enjoy a pitcher of beer and a game of Ping-Pong on the patio, or sit around the campfire telling stories and roasting marshmallows. See p. 349.

○ **The Mosaic** (Beverly Hills; ✆ **800/463-4466**): This Beverly Hills boutique is an ideal blend of art, luxury, service, location, and value. Huge rainforest shower heads, Frette linens, Bulgari bath products, Wolfgang Puck refreshments, and piles of pillows will leave you wondering if you checked in at the pearly gates. See p. 568.

○ **Huntley Santa Monica Beach** (Santa Monica; ✆ **310/394-5454**): Tucked away on the edge of a quiet Santa Monica neighborhood is my favorite Santa Monica hotel, one that combines a superb location with excellent service and strikingly stylish decor. The Huntley's 18th-floor **Penthouse** restaurant, bar, and lounge has one of the best views in Santa Monica. See p. 560.

○ **Casa Malibu** (Malibu; ✆ **800/831-0858**): This beachfront motel will fool you from the front; its humble entrance on Pacific Coast Highway belies the quiet, restful haven within. Bougainvillea vines festoon the rooftops and balconies of the motel's 21 rooms around a courtyard garden. Many rooms have private decks above the sand, and one suite was reportedly Lana Turner's favorite. See p. 562.

○ **Olallieberry Inn** (Cambria; ✆ **888/927-3222**): This 1873 Greek Revival house, furnished in Victorian style, is an ideal base for exploring Hearst Castle. The gracious innkeepers will provide directions to Moonstone Beach, restaurant recommendations, a scrumptious breakfast, and more. See p. 488.

○ **Marriott's Desert Springs Resort & Spa** (Palm Desert; ✆ **800/331-3112**): In the spirit of Disney-esque resorts, this oasis welcomes guests with a lobby featuring a 60-foot bar, tropical birds, and gondolas that tour the fairways and gardens. Once settled, kids will revel in the lagoonlike pools and play areas (with supervised children's programs). And grown-ups can luxuriate on the golf course, tennis court, or 30,000-square-foot day spa. See p. 743.

○ **Casa Cody** (Palm Springs; ✆ **800/231-2639**): You'll feel more like a houseguest than a client at this 1920s Spanish-style *casa,* blessed with peaceful, blossoming grounds and two pools. The southwestern-style rooms are large and equipped for extended stays, and the hotel is just a couple of easy blocks from the heart of the action. See p. 742.

○ **La Pensione Hotel** (San Diego; ✆ **800/232-4683**): In Little Italy, on the fringe of downtown San Diego, this find feels like a small, modern European hotel, with tidy lodgings at bargain prices. Great dining options abound in the surrounding blocks, and you'll be perfectly situated to explore the rest of the city and region by car or trolley. The immediate neighborhood is filled with boutiques and some of the city's most dashing new architecture. See p. 784.

THE best PLACES TO STAY WITH THE KIDS

- **KOA Kamping Kabins** (Point Arena; ☏ **800/562-4188**): Once you see the adorable log cabins at this KOA campground, you'll have to admit that this is one cool way to spend the weekend on the coast. Primitive is the key word: mattresses, a heater, and a light bulb are the standard amenities. All you need is some bedding (or sleeping bags), cooking and eating utensils, and charcoal for the barbecue. See p. 265.

- **Camping at Yosemite's Tuolumne Meadows** (☏ **800/436-7275**): At an elevation of 8,600 feet, this is the largest alpine meadow in the High Sierra. A gateway to the "high country," it's especially memorable in late spring, when it's carpeted with wildflowers. Park authorities run the large campground and a full-scale naturalist program, but hard-core adventurers can backpack into the wilderness. See p. 366.

- **Disneyland Resort Hotels** (Anaheim; ☏ **714/956-MICKEY** [956-6425]): The Holy Grail of Disney lovers has always been the "Official Hotel of the Magic Kingdom," the original **Disneyland Hotel** (p. 698). The newer **Paradise Pier Hotel** (p. 700) and **Grand Californian** (p. 699) are also an easy monorail or tram ride to Disneyland's gates (the Grand Californian opens directly into California Adventure).

- **Marriott's Desert Springs Resort & Spa** (Palm Desert; ☏ **800/331-3112**): In the spirit of Disney-esque resorts, this oasis welcomes guests with a lobby featuring a 60-foot bar, tropical birds, and gondolas that tour the fairways and gardens. Once settled, kids will revel in the lagoonlike pools and play areas (with supervised children's programs). And grown-ups can luxuriate on the golf course, tennis court, or 30,000-square-foot day spa. See p. 743.

THE best RESTAURANTS

- **Restaurant Gary Danko** (San Francisco; ☏ **415/749-2060**), is always a sure bet for a perfect contemporary French meal complete with polished service and flambéed finales. See p. 99.

- **Chez Panisse** (Berkeley; ☏ **510/548-5525**): This is the domain of Alice Waters, "the queen of California cuisine." Originally inspired by the Mediterranean, her kitchen has found its own style, captivating the imagination as well as the senses. Chez Panisse's delicacies include grilled fish wrapped in fig leaves with red-wine sauce, and Seckel pears poached in red wine with burnt caramel. See p. 166.

- **Bistro Don Giovanni** (Napa; ☏ **707/224-3300**): In this large, cheery Napa Valley dining room, you can get an incredible Italian meal without a reservation. Just drop in and wait at the bar for a seat. See p. 223.

- **Restaurant 301** (Eureka; ☏ **800/404-1390**): A recipient of *Wine Spectator's* Grand Award, Mark Carter is passionate about food and wine, and it shows: His hotel restaurant is considered the best on the Northern Coast. Most of the herbs and many vegetables come fresh from the hotel's organic gardens. Indulge in the five-course fixed-price dinner menu; Carter pairs each course with an excellent wine, available by the glass or as part of a wine flight. See p. 283.

- **Erna's Elderberry House** (Oakhurst; ☏ **559/683-6800**): Erna's shines like a beacon across the culinary wasteland around Yosemite. The six-course menu, which changes nightly, is an ideal blend of Continental and California cuisine. Portions are bountiful, served in an elegant European setting. See p. 353.

- **French Laundry** (Yountville; ☏ **707/944-2380**): Foodies already know that one of the top restaurants in the world is in Napa Valley's tiny town of Yountville. For this culinary magic carpet ride from Thomas Keller you'll need to fight for reservations 2 months in advance. See p. 221.

- **The Bazaar by José Andrés** (Beverly Hills; ☏ **310/246-5555**): The Bazaar is the Disneyland of culinary adventure; the whimsical Philippe Starck design augments celebrity chef Jose Andres's hybrid menu, which is half traditional Spanish tapas, the other half all avant-garde, molecular gastronomy technique. Be it a dish as simple as rare, imported Spanish *jamon Iberico,* or a juice-filled olive "skin" that melts in your mouth like salty candy, the experience is truly one of a kind. See p. 584.

- **Hatfield's** (Los Angeles; ☏ **323/935-2977**): Husband-and-wife team Quinn and Karen Hatfield split duties at this elegant Melrose eatery between savory and pastry. His yellowtail croque-madame and her off-menu chocolate-peanut-butter truffle cake have become sought-after signature dishes. It doesn't hurt that they round out their trifecta with one of the city's best sommeliers and cocktail specialists, Peter Birmingham. See p. 591.

- **Koi** (West Hollywood; ☏ **310/659-9449**): One of L.A.'s hottest restaurants has celebrities arriving nightly for addictive dishes such as baked crab rolls with edible rice paper. Koi is a killer combo of good feng shui and superb Asian fusion cuisine. See p. 589.

- **The Marine Room** (La Jolla; ☏ **866/644-2351**): It has been around for 60-plus years, but chef Bernard Guillas keeps this senior citizen in tiptop shape. Those who come for the smashing beachside view (waves sometimes slam into the windows) may be surprised by the inventive, French-inspired food. See p. 809.

THE best PERFORMING ARTS & SPECIAL EVENTS

- **The San Francisco Opera** (☏ **415/864-3330**): The first municipal opera in the U.S., with world-renowned productions and members, performs at the War Memorial Opera House, modeled after the Opéra Garnier in Paris. The season opens with a gala in September and runs through December. See chapter 4.

- **The San Francisco Symphony** (☏ **415/864-6000**): The symphony is such a hot ticket, it's hard to get a seat in advance. If your concierge doesn't have any tricks up his sleeve, you can try to buy tickets at the door or from someone attempting to sell his at the last second. See chapter 4.

- **The American Conservatory Theater** (San Francisco; ☏ **415/749-2-ACT** [749-2228]): The A.C.T. is one of the nation's leading regional theaters—the American equivalent of the British National Theatre, the Berliner Ensemble, or the Comédie Française in Paris. See chapter 4.

Performance at the San Francisco Opera House.

Getting cheeky at Coachella music festival.

o **The Monterey Jazz Festival** (✆ 831/373-3366): The third weekend of September, the Monterey Fairgrounds draws jazz fans from around the world. The 3-day festival, known for the sweetest jazz west of the Mississippi, usually sells out a month in advance. See "Calendar of Events," in chapter 2.

o **The Hollywood Bowl** (Los Angeles; ✆ 323/850-2000): This iconic outdoor amphitheater is the summer home of the Los Angeles Philharmonic, a stage for visiting virtuosos—including the occasional pop star—and the setting for splendid fireworks shows. See chapter 13.

o **Festival of Arts/Pageant of the Masters** (Laguna Beach): These events draw crowds to the Orange County coast every July and August. Begun in 1932 by a handful of painters, the festival has grown to showcase hundreds of artists. In the evening, crowds marvel at the Pageant of the Masters' *tableaux vivants,* in which costumed townsfolk pose inside a giant frame and depict famous works of art, accompanied by music. See "The South Coast," in chapter 14.

o **The Old Globe Theatre** (San Diego; ✆ 619/234-5623): This Tony Award–winning theater company has launched such Broadway hits as *Dirty Rotten Scoundrels, The Full Monty,* and *Into the Woods.*

o **Coachella Valley Music & Arts Festival** (Indio): This festival rocks for 3 days in April and draws crowds for its diverse lineup of over 180 acts, everyone from Kanye West and Arcade Fire to Lauryn Hill, Cut Copy, Robyn, and the Drums in 2011 alone. See www.coachella.com.

2

CALIFORNIA IN DEPTH

by Matthew Poole

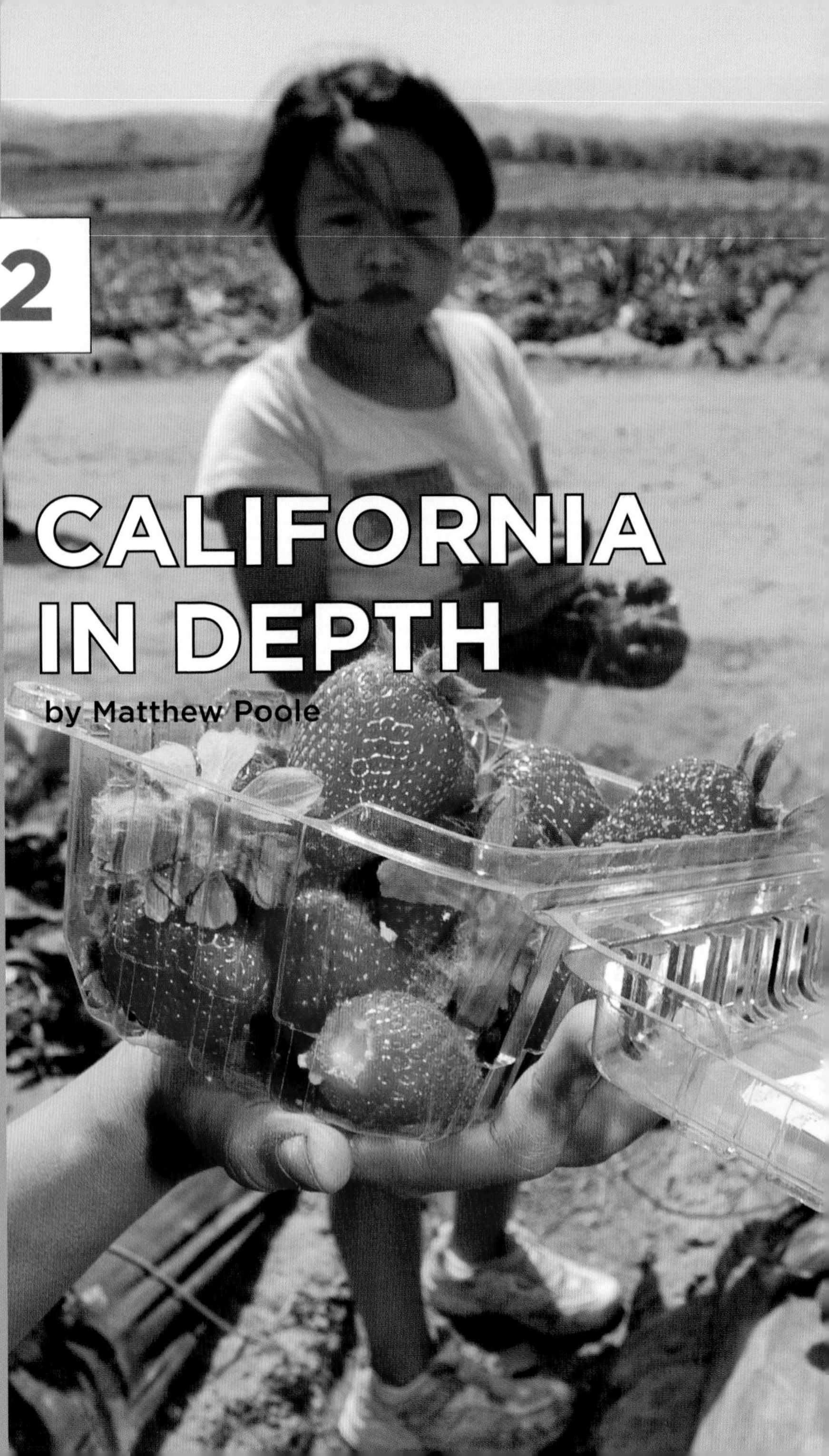

The more you know about California, the more you're likely to enjoy and appreciate everything the state has to offer. In fact, it's California's incredible diversity and rough-'n'-tumble history that make it one of the most popular travel destinations in the world. With two of the nation's largest megalopolises—the San Francisco Bay Area and the greater Los Angeles basin—California has the largest, wealthiest, and most urbanized population of any state in the nation. Yet it's also an agricultural wonderland with a bounty that runs the gamut from artichokes, raisins, garlic, and asparagus to some of the finest wine-making grapes in the world. And it still manages to be home to much of the country's most striking and varied wilderness—from purple mountains' majesty to arid, marvelously barren desert to coastlines of unsurpassed beauty.

The pages that follow include a brief enlightening tale of how California came to be the most plentiful and powerful state in the nation, but the best advice we can give you about California is to just go. Bring an open mind and a sense of adventure—the rest is waiting for you.

CALIFORNIA TODAY

Much of California's current prosperity and popularity can be attributed to deft restructuring of the economy during the post–Cold War era. A classic example is the numerous Air Force and Naval bases that were shut down, leaving thousands of civilians unemployed. Yet thanks to an unprecedented collaboration between government and private enterprise, many of the former bases were reopened as business parks (McClellan Air Force Base in Sacramento), tourist attractions (San Francisco's Presidio is a prime example), and, in some cases, even movie studios (Treasure Island Naval Base on the San Francisco Bay). California high-tech industries, once employed to build better bombs, have also earned healthy dividends by retooling their trade toward computer and information-based enterprises. Meanwhile, the industries that have always bolstered California's economy—agriculture, tourism, entertainment, and manufacturing—continue to thrive and profit.

So what's in California's future? A recent survey of the most popular name given to California's newborns says a lot about the direction in which the Golden State is headed. You probably didn't guess José, but then again, you may not have known that California is the most racially diverse state in the nation, playing host to every race, ethnic heritage, language group, and religion in the *world*. So if you're prone to xenophobia, you might want to spend your vacation elsewhere,

PREVIOUS PAGE: **Tanaka Farms, Irvine, California.**

because California will soon be the mother of all melting pots, where no single race or ethnic group will constitute a majority of the state's population.

The numbers are already bewildering: 37 million people, a whopping one-third of whom live in the Los Angeles basin. California already receives the highest numbers of immigrants in America each year—more than 200,000 annually. Whether this is a potential boon or a time bomb for California's future is impossible to predict, but it makes for a very interesting place to live and visit. How long this social boom will last is anyone's guess, but, in the meantime, California is living up to its legacy as the land of golden promise.

A TALE OF TWO states

It doesn't take a psychiatrist to figure out that California suffers from an acute identity crisis. We Californians may, on the surface, appear to be one big *Happy Days* family, but in reality we've divided our state into separate factions worthy of Montague and Capulet. That is, you're either a Northern Californian or a Southern Californian, two opposing tribes that have little in common. In fact, which side you even choose to visit may reveal something about you.

All the California glamour, wealth, fame, fast cars, surf scenes, and buxom blondes you see on television are pure southern invention. If this is the California you're looking for, head due south, dude: Assuming you're not terribly interested in intellectual stimulation, you won't be disappointed. In fact, it's nearly impossible not to be immediately swept up by the energy and excitement that places like West Hollywood and Venice Beach exude. It's a narcotic effect, the allure of flashy wealth, gorgeous bodies, and celebrity status. Even watching it all as a bystander imparts a heady mixture of thrill and envy.

Northern California may be frightfully demure in comparison, but in the long run, its subdued charms and natural beauty prevail. Wealth is certainly in abundance, but rarely displayed. The few hard bodies that exist are usually swathed in loose jeans and shirts. The few celebrities who live here keep very low profiles and are more likely to be on their ranches than in a Rolls Royce. Ostentation in any form is looked down upon (of course, it's okay to *own* a BMW, as long as it's slightly dirty), and unlike in Los Angeles, you can actually explore smog-free San Francisco on foot.

Ironically, it's the Northern Californians who think of themselves as superior for having prudently eschewed the trappings of wealth and status (in fact, L.A.-bashing is a popular pastime). Southern Californians, on the other hand, couldn't care less what the Northerners think of them; it's all sour grapes as they bask poolside 300 sunny days of the year. In fact, most Southern Californians would be perfectly content to form their own state. The idea has been bandied about the state capital for years, but it consistently meets its Waterloo when it comes to water rights, always a hotly contested issue in California politics. Northern California holds two-thirds of the state's watershed, and without the incredibly complex system of aqueducts, reservoirs, and dams that keep huge flows moving southward, Southern California's 15 million citizens would be in a world of hurt.

But regardless of our polarized views and lifestyles, most Californians do agree on one thing: We're still the best damn dysfunctional state in America.

—Matthew R. Poole

LOOKING BACK: CALIFORNIA HISTORY
European Discovery & Colonization

Although very little remains to mark the existence of West Coast Native Americans, anthropologists estimate that as many as half a million aborigines flourished on this naturally abundant land for thousands of years before the arrival of Europeans in the mid–16th century. Sailing from a small colony, established 10 years before, on the southern tip of Baja California, Portuguese explorer Juan Rodríguez Cabrillo is credited with being the first European to "discover" California, in 1542. Over the next 200 years, dozens of sailors mapped the coast, including British explorer Sir Francis Drake.

European colonial competition and Catholic missionary zeal prompted Spain to establish settlements along the Alta (upper) California coast and claim the lands as its own. In 1769, Father Junípero Serra, accompanied by 300 soldiers and clergy, began forging a path from Mexico to Monterey. A small mission and presidio (fort) were established that year at San Diego. Most of the solidly built missions still remain—Mission Delores, Mission San Juan Bautista, Mission San Diego de Alcala, to name just a few—and they offer public tours.

During that time, thousands of Native Americans were converted to Christianity and coerced into labor. Many others died from imported diseases. Because not all the natives welcomed their conquerors with open arms, many missions and pueblos (small towns) suffered repeated attacks, leading to the construction of California's now ubiquitous—and fireproof—red-tile roofs.

No settlement had more than 100 inhabitants when Spain's sovereignty was compromised by an 1812 Russian outpost called Fort Ross, 60 miles north of San Francisco (open to the public). But the biggest threat came from the British and their last-ditch effort to win back their territories in the War of 1812.

Juan Bautista de Anza and Sir Francis Drake.

Embattled at home as well as abroad, the Spanish finally relinquished their claim to Mexico and California in 1821. Under Mexican rule, Alta California's Spanish missionaries lost much of their land to the increasingly wealthy *Californios,* Mexican immigrants who were granted vast land tracts.

American Expansion

Beginning in the late 1820s, Americans from the East began to make their way to California via a 3-month sail around Cape Horn. Most of them settled in the territorial capital of Monterey and in Northern California.

From the 1830s on, more and more settlers headed west. Along with them came daring explorers. In 1843, Marcus Whitman, a missionary seeking to prove that settlers could travel overland through the Oregon Territory's Blue Mountains, helped blaze the Oregon Trail; the first covered-wagon train made the 4-month crossing in 1844. Over the next few years, several hundred Americans made the trek to California over the Sierra Nevada range via Truckee Pass, just north of Lake Tahoe.

As the drive to the west increased, the U.S. government sought to extend its control over Mexican territory north of the Rio Grande, the river that now divides the United States and Mexico. In 1846, President James Polk offered Mexico $40 million for California and New Mexico. The offer might have been accepted, but America's simultaneous annexation of Texas, to which Mexico still laid claim, resulted in a war between the two countries. Within months, the United States overcame Mexico and took possession of the entire West Coast.

Historical map shows California as an island.

Gold Rush of 1849.

Gold & Statehood

In 1848, California's non–Native American population was around 7,000. That same year, flakes of gold were discovered by workers building a sawmill along the American River. Word of the find spread quickly, bringing more than 300,000 men and women into California between 1849 and 1851, one of the largest mass migrations in American history. Of course, very few prospectors unearthed a gold mine, and within 15 years the gold had dissipated, though many of the new residents remained. In fact, much of the mining equipment and Gold Rush–era buildings remain today and are on display throughout the Gold Country.

In 1850, California was admitted to the Union as the 31st state. The state constitution on which California applied for admission included several noteworthy features. To protect the miners, slavery was prohibited. To attract women from the East Coast, legal recognition was given to the separate property of a married woman (California was the first state to offer such recognition). By 1870, almost 90% of the state's Native American population had been wiped out, and the bulk of the rest was removed to undesirable inland reservations.

Mexican and Chinese laborers were brought in to help local farmers and to work on the transcontinental railroad, which was completed in 1869. The new rail line transported Easterners to California in just 5 days, marking a turning point in the settlement of the West. Many of these original steam engines are on display at the California State Railroad Museum in Sacramento.

Growth & Industry

In 1875, when the Santa Fe Railroad reached Los Angeles, Southern California's population of just 10,000 was divided equally between Los Angeles and San Diego. Los Angeles, however, began to grow rapidly in 1911, when the film industry moved here from the East Coast to take advantage of cheap land and a warm climate that enabled movies to be shot outdoors year-round. The movies' glamorous, idyllic portrayal of California boosted the region's popularity and population, especially during the Great Depression of the 1930s, when thousands of families (like the Joads in John Steinbeck's *The Grapes of Wrath*) packed up their belongings and headed west in search of a better life.

World War II brought heavy industry to California, in the form of munitions factories, shipyards, and airplane manufacturing. Freeways were built, military bases were opened, and suburbs were developed. In the 1950s, California in general, and San Francisco in particular, became popular among artists and intellectuals. The so-called Beat Generation appeared, later to inspire alternative-culture groups, most notably the "flower children" of the 1960s, in San Francisco's

Hollywood, 1920s.

1930s ad to promote tourism in California.

Haight-Ashbury district. During the "Summer of Love" in 1967, as the war in Vietnam escalated, student protests increased at Berkeley and elsewhere in California, as they did across the country. A year later, amid rising racial tensions, Martin Luther King, Jr., was killed, setting off riots in the Watts section of Los Angeles and in other cities. Soon thereafter, Robert F. Kennedy was fatally shot in Los Angeles after winning the California Democratic Party presidential primary. Antiwar protests continued into the 1970s.

Perhaps in response to an increasingly violent society, the 1970s also gave rise to several exotic religions and cults, which found eager adherents in California. The spiritual "New Age" continued into the 1980s, along with a growing population, environmental pollution, and escalating social ills, especially in Los Angeles. California also became very rich. Real estate values soared, the computer industry—centered in "Silicon Valley" south of San Francisco—boomed, and banks and businesses prospered.

Recession, Redemption & Terrorism

The late 1980s and early 1990s, however, brought a devastating recession to the state. Californians, like many other Americans, became increasingly conservative. Though they remained concerned about the nation's problems—economic competition from abroad, the environment, drugs, and the blight of homelessness—their fascination with alternative lifestyles ebbed as the former campus rebels among them settled into comfortable positions in industry and politics. In short, the baby boomers were growing up and settling down.

AIDS also became a major issue of the 1990s, particularly in San Francisco, where it quickly became the number-one killer of young men. Los Angeles had its problems as well, most notably the race riots spurred by the videotaped beating of black motorist Rodney King, by four white police officers, who were subsequently acquitted. Two years later, a major earthquake caused billions of dollars in damage to L.A.'s buildings and freeways, leaving thousands injured and homeless. Oakland's hills became a raging inferno, killing 26 people and destroying 3,000 homes.

Midway through the 1990s, America's economy slowly yet surely began to improve, a welcome relief to recession-battered Californians. Crime and unemployment began to drop, while public schools received millions for much-needed improvements. Computer- and Internet-related industries flourished in the Bay Area, with entrepreneurialism fueling much of the explosive growth. As the stock market continued its record-setting pace through the end of the decade, no state reaped more benefits than California, which gained new millionaires by the day.

At the millennium, optimism in the state's strong economy and quality of life was at an all-time high. Unemployment rates were still low, and property rates still rising. Then came three out-of-the-blue sucker punches to California's rosy economy: (1) the rapid demise of many, if not most, of the dot.coms in the stock market slump (new websites, gleefully chronicling the death throes of the fledgling enterprises, popped up to amuse the formerly envious); (2) an energy deregulation scheme gone awry, leaving irate residents with periodic rolling blackouts and escalating energy bills (never have so many taken such a sudden, intense interest in ways to save and create energy); and (3) the September 11, 2001, terrorist attacks that left Californians, along with the rest of the country, stunned and added a near-deathblow to an already reeling economy.

Oil production in California, turn of the century.

Modern California.

Migrant workers.

Google is based in San Francisco. Many other tech companies are based in Silicon Valley, south of the city.

But even the darkest clouds had a silver lining. The dot.com bomb led to a massive rise in vacancies and declines in rent (though it's still outrageous) as the thousands of itinerant gold diggers hitched up and moved out. We solved our energy crisis by outing those greedy Enron execs living in the empire of Texas. And since 9/11 we've even surprised ourselves by how patriotic we still are. Every Californian was knocked senseless by the shocking deeds of religious fanatics, but we quickly fought back—both literally and economically—to regain our national pride and enviable lifestyle. Oh, California—if the world hands us a lemon, we'll slice it into our imported sparkling water.

> **Impressions**
>
> *California is not so much a state of the Union as it is an imagination that seceded from our reality a long time ago. . . . California became the first to discover that it was fantasy that led reality, not the other way around.*
> —William Irwin Thompson

CALIFORNIA IN BOOKS & FILM
Recommended Books

There's no shortage of reading material about the history and culture of California, one of the most romanticized places on Earth. Almost from the beginning, novelists and poets were an essential part of California's cultural mosaic, and the works they've created offer a fascinating window into the lives and legends that have greatly influenced California's inception and fervid growth.

HISTORY

Readers are spoiled for choices when it comes to historical accounts of California's pioneers. Salinas native John Steinbeck, one of the state's best-known authors, paints a vivid portrayal of proletarian life in the early to mid-1900s. His *Grapes of Wrath* remains the classic account of itinerant farm laborers coming to California in the midst of the Great Depression. *Cannery Row* has forever made the Monterey waterfront famous, and *East of Eden* brings a deep insight into the way of life in the Salinas Valley.

Famed humorist and storyteller Mark Twain penned vivid tales during California's Gold Rush era, including one of his most popular works, "The Celebrated Jumping Frog of Calaveras County" (an annual Gold Country competition that still has legs). Other good Gold Rush reads include Bret Harte's *The Luck of Roaring Camp,* a sentimental tale of hard-luck miners and their false toughness, and J. S. Holliday's *The World Rushed In,* one of the finest nonfiction accounts of the Gold Rush still in print.

San Francisco was also a popular setting for many early works, including Twain's *San Francisco,* a collection of articles that glorified "the liveliest, heartiest community on our continent." It was also the birthplace of Jack London, one of the best-known American writers, who wrote several short stories of his younger days as an oyster pirate on the San Francisco Bay, as well as *Martin Eden,* London's semiautobiographical account of his life along the Oakland shores.

A work of fiction featuring San Francisco during the Gold Rush is *Daughter of Fortune,* by acclaimed novelist and Marin resident Isabel Allende. The tale begins in Chile and follows the life of Eliza, an orphan adopted by a proper English spinster and her brother. In love with a boy who has sailed for the gold fields, a pregnant Eliza runs away from home to search for him and is befriended by a Chinese doctor. Allende's vivid depiction of life in California during the mid–19th century is one of the novel's strengths.

HOLLYWOOD

For what some critics consider the best novels ever written about Hollywood, turn to Nathanael West's *The Day of the Locust,* a savage and satirical look at 1930s life on the fringes of the film industry, and Bud Shulberg's *What Makes Sammy Run?* featuring everyone's favorite amoral, desperate agent Sammy Glick.

Lawrence Ferlinghetti reads at a house party, while Michael McClure reclines, 1957.

Following in these footsteps is Michael Tolkein's *The Player,* an unsentimental journey into the industry of filmmaking, and John Fante's 1939 *Ask The Dust,* wherein yet another young writer gets his hopes and dreams crushed.

And while we are recommending downer (if brilliant) books, follow Los Angeles's turbulent history and speculate on its future via Mark Davis's *City of Quartz;* equally lugubrious is Upton Sinclair's novel *Oil!* which is representative of 1920s Southern California. You can also relive some of the state's most infamous (and brutal) moments via Vincent Bugliosi's *Helter Skelter,* the best version of the Manson murders and the book most responsible for childhood nightmares among a certain generation, or one of the many books about San Francisco's Zodiac Killer or L.A.'s Hillside Strangler.

MYSTERY & MAYHEM

For all you mystery buffs headed to California, two must-reads include Frank Norris's *McTeague: A Story of San Francisco,* a violent tale of love and greed set in turn-of-the-20th-century San Francisco, and Dashiell Hammett's *The Maltese Falcon,* a steamy detective novel that captures the seedier side of San Francisco in the 1920s. Another favorite is Raymond Chandler's *The Big Sleep,* where private dick Philip Marlowe plies the seedier side of Los Angeles in the 1930s.

California has always been a hotbed for alternative—and, more often than not, controversial—literary styles. Joan Didion, in her novel *Slouching Toward Bethlehem,* and Hunter S. Thompson, in his columns for the *San Francisco Examiner* (brought together in the collection *Generation of Swine*), both used a "new journalistic" approach in their studies of 1960s San Francisco. Tom Wolfe's early work, *The Electric Kool-Aid Acid Test,* follows the Hell's Angels, the Grateful Dead, and Ken Kesey's Merry Pranksters as they ride through that hallucinogenic decade. Meanwhile, Jack Kerouac, Allen Ginsberg, and the rest of the "Beat" writers were penning protests against political conservatism—and promoting their bohemian lifestyle—via Ginsberg's controversial poem *Howl* (daringly published by Lawrence Ferlinghetti, poet and owner of City Lights Bookstore in San Francisco's North Beach district) and Kerouac's famous tale of American adventure, *On the Road.*

MODERN MATERIAL

If you're interested in a contemporary look back at four generations in the life of an American family, you can do no better than Wallace Stegner's *Angle of Repose.* The winner of the Pulitzer Prize in 1971, this work chronicles the lives of pioneers on the Western frontier. Among Stegner's many other works of fiction and nonfiction about the West is his novel *All the Little Live Things,* which explores the conflicts faced by retired literary agent Joe Allston; the book is set in the San Francisco Bay Area of the 1960s. *The Spectator Bird* (winner of the 1976 National Book Award) revisits Allston's character as he reflects on his life and his memories of a search for his roots.

Set in San Francisco, best-selling author Amy Tan's *The Joy Luck Club* is an enlightening account of bonds between Chinese-American mothers and their daughters. One of the more famous and beloved pieces of modern fiction based in San Francisco is Armistead Maupin's *Tales of the City.* Maupin is a Dickens for his time, and this is a must-read for a leisurely afternoon. His 1970s soap opera covers the residents of 28 Barbary Lane (Macondry Lane on Russian Hill was the inspiration), melding sex, drugs, and growing self-awareness with enormous warmth and humor.

SPECIAL-INTEREST READS

Geology buffs will want to pack a copy of *Assembling California,* John McPhee's fascinating observation of California's complex geological history. Most of this volume was previously published in the *New Yorker.*

Outdoor enthusiasts have literally dozens of sporting books to choose from, but most comprehensive is Foghorn Press's excellent outdoor series—*California Camping, California Fishing, California Golf, California Beaches,* and *California Hiking*—available at every major bookstore in the state.

Recommended Movies

The beauty and metaphor that is California (Gold Rush, Land of Opportunity, Go West Young Man, Silver Screen—the list goes on) has inspired far too many moviemakers to list in any comprehensive way, but I've compiled a short list of the California-based gems that have inspired generations of movie fans.

Vertigo (1958) is the work of possibly the greatest movie director of all time, Alfred Hitchcock, who always used locations well. Remember Mount Rushmore in *North by Northwest*? In *Vertigo,* the suspense master uses San Francisco to dizzying effect (pun intended).

Monterey Pop (1969), D. A. Pennebaker's first-rate rockumentary, chronicles the glorious 3-day music festival of the same name that was actually a better realization of the Summer of Love dream than Woodstock ever hoped to be. The film wonderfully captures '60s San Francisco's Haight-Ashbury vibe and the California sound, including groups such as the Mamas and the Papas (whose leader, the late John Phillips, was the brains behind the event), Jefferson Airplane, Janis Joplin with Big Brother and the Holding Company, Jimi Hendrix, Canned Heat, the Who, and others, including a stunning performance by Otis Redding.

Clint Eastwood made his directorial debut with *Play Misty for Me* (1971), a winningly creepy thriller costarring Jessica Walter (and Donna Mills, of quintessentially Californian *Knots Landing* fame). Young, studly Clint looks mighty fine, but the real star of the show is stunning Carmel, which Clint films with a genuine hometown love and a master's eye. (You may remember that Eastwood was elected mayor of Carmel-by-the-Sea in 1986; he still owns the Mission Ranch, an elegant country inn, and resides in town.) Watch for the great footage of Big Sur's Bixby Bridge too.

California in Books & Film

The iconic Valley Girl film *Clueless.*

What's Up, Doc? (1972) is a Peter Bogdanovich–directed, Buck Henry–scribed gem starring Barbra Streisand and Ryan O'Neal that shows off the hilly streets of San Francisco—especially Chinatown—at their most colorful and romantic.

A more lighthearted view of California comes from *Gidget* (1965). Perky Sally Field is the ultimate California beach girl in the ultimate California beach movie. This innocent romp is really a joy to watch—far superior to the Frankie Avalon/Annette Funicello beach movies—with excellent footage of Malibu Beach and Pacific Coast Highway (cruisin' with the top down, of course).

Staying South, *Chinatown* (1974) is possibly the finest noir ever committed to film, using L.A. in the '70s to re-create L.A. in the '30s impeccably. Not only did director Roman Polanski (pre-exile) capture the City of Angels masterfully, but writer Robert Towne worked in an essential slice of city history: the dirty dealing and power grabbing of water rights that allowed—for better or worse—the infant desert city to blossom into the sprawling metropolis you see today. And, of course, this true classic features Jack Nicholson as the hard-boiled detective embroiled with *femme fatale* Faye Dunaway, plus legendary Hollywood heavyweight John Huston as the evil genius behind the Chandleresque web of intrigue. Its modern-day noir and crime successor is the Oscar-winning *L.A. Confidential* (1997).

Valley Girl (1983), starring a teenage Nicolas Cage, is an underdog in a teen genre that includes *Fast Times at Ridgemont High* (1982) and *Clueless* (1995), but it comes out a winner because of its New-Wave-Boy-meets-mall-lovin'-Valley-Girl love story at the height of Valley Girl mania.

The Big Picture (1989) is director Christopher Guest's first feature, a dead-on and deadly satire of the movie industry, filmed presumably on a shoestring around Hollywood and just outside in the desert. It's hilarious, and we don't just mean the locations.

Steve Martin's *L.A. Story* (1991) is a romantic look at everything that's wonderfully silly about life in contemporary Tinseltown.

The Player (1992) all too realistically captures the seedy underbelly and soul-selling seductive power of Hollywood influence and celebrity. Everybody who's anybody in the movie industry knows how scarily close to home Tim Robbins's portrayal of beleaguered studio exec Griffin Mill hits.

And finally, there is the film version of *The Grapes of Wrath* (1940). The John Ford–directed, Academy Award–winning film of dispossessed "Okie" Dust Bowl farmers who migrate west to the promised land—California—wins a spot on this list not for its tremendous footage of the Golden State, but because it beautifully evokes California's agrarian story.

EATING & DRINKING IN CALIFORNIA

California's agriculture industry is not only the number-one producer in the nation, but the number one in the world. No other state in the union cultivates like the Golden State: California farmers and ranchers pump more than $30 billion a year into the California economy, employ more than a million people statewide, and export billions of dollars in goods each year to markets across the globe. In fact, California's farmers produce over half the country's fruit and vegetables on just a measly 3% of its farmland. Almonds, olives, lemons, artichokes, figs,

Dim sum from a Wok Wiz tour in San Francisco's Chinatown. See chapter 4.

dates, and truckloads of grapes and tomatoes are just some of the commercially produced consumables that thrive in the state's mellow Mediterranean climate.

But California's cuisine is greater than the sum of its parts. Along with a rich pantry, immigration has affected what and how Californians and its visitors eat. In Northern California, the Gold Rush attracted an enormous number of Chinese from Canton Province who stayed to work on the railroad and eventually settled into Chinatowns throughout the state. Chinese eateries opened to feed the largely male workforce, but by the 1920s, adventuresome Anglos found it fashionable to give Chinese food a try, and soon you could sample Cantonese sweet-and-sour pork in every city, big or small.

In Southern California, Latino immigrants brought their influence to bear, introducing unfamiliar spices and changing the tastes of a population to such an extent that fast food today means tacos and burritos as much as hamburgers and fries. Los Angeles, in fact, can make its strongest claim to culinary fame (beyond the first and still champion celebrity chef, the highly influential Wolfgang Puck of Beverly Hills's iconic **Spago;** p. 588), courtesy of its many hole-in-the-wall ethnic restaurants. Reflecting the dozens (if not hundreds) of cultures that have settled in the area, the curious can nosh on Armenian, Nicaraguan, Oaxacan, Ethiopian, Isan Thai, Romanian, and Hungarian food, to name a few—a veritable United Nations of dining experiences, and many of them within just a few blocks of each other. And that's not even discussing California rolls, which regrettably (in the minds of some purists) forever changed sushi eating from a meditative consideration on a choice slice of fish to a circus stunt wrapped in seaweed.

Perhaps the greatest modern influence on how tuned-in Californians eat can be traced to food gurus such as Alice Waters. Her restaurant, Berkeley-based **Chez Panisse** (p. 166), began as an outgrowth of Waters's desire to feed her friends and became a philosophical training ground for many of today's important chefs. Like French cooks—and Waters was profoundly changed by a year living in Paris—she is interested not in the quantity or cost of ingredients, but strictly in quality and freshness.

In Berkeley, Waters created an infrastructure in which her restaurant is dependent on a cadre of small farmers, and vice versa. It wasn't enough, however, to provide customers with the freshest heirloom tomatoes and organic baby lettuces: The breads must be crusty and fresh; the meats must be sourced from trusted ranchers; the cheese should complement the fruits and come from local producers as well.

So along with a generation of restaurateurs, Chez Panisse inspired such robust local artisan producers as Acme Bread and Cowgirl Creamery. California cuisine—which is really about showcasing the flavors of locally grown, seasonal bounty at its peak—has spread throughout and beyond California, thanks to Waters and to the chefs who have made her vision their own.

WHEN TO GO
Weather

California's weather is so varied that it's impossible to generalize about the state.

San Francisco's temperate marine climate means relatively mild weather year-round. In summer, temperatures rarely top 70°F (21°C; pack sweaters, even in Aug), and the city's famous fog rolls in most mornings and evenings. In winter, the mercury seldom falls below freezing, and snow is almost unheard of. Because of the fog, summer rarely sees more than a few hot days in a row. Head a few miles inland, though, and it's likely to be clear and hot.

The **Central Coast** shares San Francisco's climate, although it gets warmer as you get farther south. Seasonal changes are less pronounced south of San Luis Obispo, where temperatures remain relatively stable year-round. The Northern Coast is rainier and foggier; winters tend to be mild but wet.

Summers are cool around **Lake Tahoe** and in the **Shasta Cascades.** The climate is ideal for hiking, camping, and other outdoor activities, making these regions popular with residents of the state's sweltering deserts and valleys. From late November to early April, skiers also flock to this area, for terrific snowfall.

Southern California—including **Los Angeles** and **San Diego**—is usually much warmer than the Bay Area, and it gets significantly more sun. Even in winter, daytime temperatures regularly reach into the 60s (15°–20°C) and warmer. Summers can be stifling inland, but Southern California's coastal communities are comfortable. The area's limited rainfall is generally seen between December and mid-April, but it's rarely intense enough to be more than a slight inconvenience. It's possible to sunbathe throughout the year, but only die-hard enthusiasts and wet-suited surfers venture into the ocean in winter. The water is warmest in summer and fall, but even then, the Pacific is too chilly for many.

The **deserts,** including **Palm Springs** and the desert national parks, are sizzling hot in summer; temperatures regularly top 100°F (38°C). Winter is the time to visit the desert resorts (and remember, it gets surprisingly cold at night in the desert).

Avoiding the Crowds

Given California's pleasant summer weather (with relatively low humidity), the time between Memorial Day and Labor Day is **high tourist season** virtually everywhere—except for desert areas such as Palm Springs and Death Valley, where sizzling temperatures daunt all but the hardiest bargain hunters. Naturally, prices are highest at this time, and they can drop dramatically before and after that period. (Exceptions to this rule include the aforementioned deserts and winter ski resorts.) ***Insider tip:*** Many Californians think the best time to travel the state is autumn. From late September to early December, crowds drop off, shoulder-season rates kick in, and winter rains have yet to start looming.

Holidays

Banks, government offices, post offices, and many stores, restaurants, and museums are closed on the following legal national holidays: January 1 (New Year's Day), the third Monday in January (Martin Luther King Day), the third Monday in February (Presidents' Day), the last Monday in May (Memorial Day), July 4 (Independence Day), the first Monday in September (Labor Day), the second

Monday in October (Columbus Day), November 11 (Veterans Day/Armistice Day), the fourth Thursday in November (Thanksgiving Day), and December 25 (Christmas). The Tuesday after the first Monday in November is Election Day, a federal government holiday in presidential-election years (held every 4 years, and next in 2012).

Calendar of Events

For an exhaustive list of events, check **http://events.frommers.com**, where you'll find a searchable, up-to-the-minute roster of what's happening in cities all over the world.

JANUARY

Tournament of Roses, Pasadena. A spectacular parade marches down Colorado Boulevard, with lavish floats, music, and extraordinary equestrian entries, followed by the Rose Bowl football game and a nightlong party along Colorado Boulevard. Call ✆ **626/449-4100** or see **www.tournamentofroses.com** for details. January 1.

Santa Barbara International Film Festival. For 10 days, Santa Barbara does its best impression of Cannes. There's a flurry of foreign and independent film premieres, appearances by actors and directors, and symposiums on cinematic topics. For a rundown of events, call ✆ **805/963-0023,** or see **www.sbfilmfestival.org**. Late January to early February.

Chinese New Year and Golden Dragon Parade, Los Angeles. Dragon dancers and martial arts masters parade through the streets of downtown's Chinatown. Chinese opera and other events are scheduled. For this year's schedule, contact the Chinese Chamber of Commerce at ✆ **213/617-0396,** or visit **www.lachinesechamber.org**. Late January or early February.

FEBRUARY

AT&T Pebble Beach National Pro-Am, Pebble Beach. A PGA-sponsored tour where pros team up with celebrities to compete on three famous golf courses. Call ✆ **800/541-9091** or 831/649-1533, or visit **www.attpbgolf.com**. Early February.

National Date Festival, Indio. Crowds gather to celebrate the Coachella Valley desert's most beloved cash crop, with events such as camel and ostrich races, the Blessing of the Date Garden, and Arabian Nights pageants. Plenty of date-sampling booths are set up, along with rides, food vendors, and other county-fair trappings. Call ✆ **800/811-3247** or 760/863-8247, or visit **www.datefest.org**. Two weeks mid-February.

MARCH

Festival of Whales, Dana Point. The Dana Point community celebrates the return of the gray whales migrating off the coast with an annual street fair, food, games, entertainment, and "Majestic Migration" parade. It's great for families. Call ✆ **949/496-5794,** ext. 7, or go to **www.festivalofwhales.com** for details. Early March.

Return of the Swallows, San Juan Capistrano. Each St. Joseph's Day, visitors flock to this village for the arrival of the loyal flock of swallows that nest in the mission and remain until October. The celebration includes a parade, dances, and special programs. Call ✆ **949/234-1300,** or visit **www.missionsjc.com** for details. March 19.

Kraft Nabisco Championship, Rancho Mirage. This 33-year-old LPGA golf tournament takes place near Palm Springs. After the celebrity Pro-Am early in the week, the best female pros get down to business. For further information, call ✆ **760/324-4546** or visit **www.nabiscochampionship.com**. Other special-interest events for women usually take place around the tournament, including the country's largest annual lesbian gathering. Last week of March/first week of April.

Redwood Coast Dixieland Jazz Festival, Eureka. Four days of jazz featuring some of the best Dixieland, blues, and zydeco bands in the world. Call ✆ **707/445-3378,** or see **www.redwoodcoast musicfestivals.org**. Late March.

Flower Fields in Bloom at Carlsbad Ranch. One of the most spectacular sights in San Diego's North County is the ranunculus blossoms that create a striped, floral blanket in March and April. This is a working ranch, but visitors are welcome to tour the fields. For information, call ✆ **760/431-0352** or see **www.theflowerfields.com**. March and April.

APRIL

San Francisco International Film Festival. One of the nation's oldest film festivals, featuring more than 100 films and videos from 30-plus countries. Tickets are inexpensive, and screenings are open to the general public. Call ✆ **415/561-5000,** or visit **www.sffs.org**. Mid-April to early May.

Toyota Grand Prix, Long Beach. An exciting weekend of Indy-class auto racing and entertainment in downtown Long Beach draws world-class drivers from the United States and Europe, plus many celebrity contestants and spectators. Contact the Grand Prix Association at ✆ **888/82-SPEED** (827-7333) or **www.longbeachgp.com**. Mid-April.

Coachella Valley Music & Arts Festival, Indio. This music festival, at the Empire Polo Club in Indio, rocks hard for 3 days on multiple stages and tents, with nearly 180 acts. In 2011: Kanye West, Arcade Fire, Lauryn Hill, Cut Copy, Robyn, The Drums, Kings of Leon, and more. See **www.coachella.com** for tickets. Mid-April.

ArtWalk, San Diego. This free, 2-day festival in stylish Little Italy is the largest art event in the San Diego/Tijuana region, attracting some 70,000 people

each year. It features visual and performing arts—painting, sculpture, photography, music, and dance—in outdoor venues, galleries, artist studios, and businesses. The event also offers hands-on art experiences for kids. Call ✆ **619/615-1090,** or visit **www.missionfederal artwalk.org**. Late April.

MAY

Cinco de Mayo. A weeklong celebration of one of Mexico's most jubilant holidays takes place throughout **Los Angeles** near May 5. Large crowds, live music, dances, and food create a carnival-like atmosphere. The main festivities are held in El Pueblo de Los Angeles State Historic Park. Call ✆ **213/485-6855** for information.

The Cinco de Mayo celebration in Old Town, **San Diego,** features folkloric music, dance, food, and historical reenactments. Call ✆ **619/260-1700** for more information. Early May.

Calaveras County Fair and Jumping Frog Jubilee, Angels Camp. Inspired by Mark Twain's "The Celebrated Jumping Frog of Calaveras County," this race draws frog contestants and their guardians from all over. Call ✆ **209/736-2561,** or see **www.frogtown.org**. Third weekend in May.

Paso Robles Wine Festival. What began as a small, neighborly gathering has grown into the largest outdoor wine tasting in California. The 3-day event features winery open houses and tastings, a golf tournament, a 5K run and 10K bike ride, and concerts, plus a festival in downtown's City Park. For a schedule, call ✆ **805/239-8463** or visit **www.pasowine.com**. Third weekend in May.

Bay to Breakers Foot Race, San Francisco. One of the city's most popular annual events, it's more fun than run. Thousands of entrants show up dressed—or undressed—in their best costumes for the 7½-mile run. Call ✆ **415/359-2800,** or log on to **www.baytobreakers.com**. Third Sunday of May.

Carnaval, San Francisco. The Mission District's largest annual event is a 2-day series of festivities culminating with a parade on Mission Street. Half a million spectators line the route, and samba musicians and dancers continue playing on 14th Street, near Harrison, after the march. Call ✆ **415/920-0125,** or visit **www.carnavalsf.com**. Memorial Day weekend.

JUNE

Ojai Music Festival. This event has been drawing world-class classical and jazz personalities to the open-air Libbey Bowl since 1947. Past events have featured Igor Stravinsky, Aaron Copland, and the Juilliard String Quartet. Seats (and local lodgings) fill up quickly; call ✆ **805/646-2094** for more information, or log on to **www.ojaifestival.org**. Early June.

San Diego County Fair. Referred to as the Del Mar Fair by locals, this is the other big happening (besides horse racing) at the Del Mar Fairgrounds. The entire county turns out for the 3-week event, with livestock competitions, rides, flower and garden shows, food and craft booths, carnival games, and home-arts exhibits. There are also grandstand concerts by big-name performers. Call ✆ **858/793-5555,** or check **www.sdfair. com**. Mid-June through early July.

Mariachi USA Festival, Los Angeles. For this 2-day, family-oriented celebration of Mexican culture at the Hollywood Bowl, festivalgoers pack their picnic baskets and enjoy music, folkloric ballet, and related performances by top groups. The all-day, all-night celebration is one of the largest mariachi festivals in the world. For tickets, call ✆ **800/ MARIACHI** (627-4224) or 323/850-2000 (the Hollywood Bowl), or log on to **www.mariachiusa.com**. Late June.

Los Angeles Film Festival, Los Angeles. With an attendance of more than 60,000, the festival showcases more than 175 American and international indies, short films, and music videos during a 10-day event. Call ✆ **866/345-6337,** or log on to **www.lafilmfest.com**. Late June.

San Francisco Lesbian, Gay, Bisexual, Transgender Pride Parade. It's celebrated over various weekends throughout the state in June and July, but San Francisco's party draws up to half a million participants. The parade heads west from Market Street and Beale to Market and Eighth streets, where hundreds of food, art, and information booths are set up around several stages. Call ✆ **415/864-0831,** or visit **www. sfpride.org** for info. Late June.

JULY

Mammoth Lakes Jazz Jubilee. This 4-day festival features 20 bands on 10 different stages, plus food, drink, and dancing—all under the pine trees and stars. Call ✆ **760/934-2478,** or see **www.mammothjazz.org**. Second weekend in July.

World Championship Over-the-Line Tournament, San Diego. This beach softball event, dating from 1953, is renowned for boisterous, beer-soaked, anything-goes behavior. More than 1,000 three-person teams compete, and upwards of 50,000 people attend. It's a heap of fun for the open-minded but a bit much for small kids. It takes place on Fiesta Island in Mission Bay; admission is free. For more details, call ✆ **619/688-0817** or visit **www.ombac.org**. Mid-July.

Thoroughbred Racing Season, Del Mar. The "turf meets the surf" during the thoroughbred racing season at the Del Mar Race Track. Post time is 2pm most days; the track is dark on Tuesdays. Special events are held throughout the season, including Friday afternoon concerts by top bands. For this year's schedule, call ✆ **858/755-1141** or visit **www.dmtc.com**. Mid-July to mid-September.

Gilroy Garlic Festival. A gourmet food fair with more than 85 booths serving garlicky food from almost every ethnic background, plus close to 100 arts, crafts, and entertainment booths. Call ✆ **408/842-1625,** or visit **www.gilroy garlicfestival.com**. Last full weekend in July.

Beach Festival, Huntington Beach. Two weeks of fun in the sun featuring two surfing competitions—the U.S. Open of Surfing and the world-class Pro of Surfing—plus such extreme sports as BMX biking, skateboarding, and more. The festival includes entertainment, food, product booths, and giveaways—and plenty of tanned, swimsuit-clad bodies of both sexes. For more information, call ✆ **714/969-3492** or log on to **www. surfcityusa.com**. Late July.

Festival of Arts & Pageant of the Masters, Laguna Beach. A 60-plus-year tradition in artsy Laguna, this festival centers on a fantastic performance-art production in which actors re-create famous old masters paintings. Other festivities include live music, crafts sales, art demonstrations and workshops, and the grass-roots Sawdust Festival across the street. Call ✆ **800/487-FEST** (3378) or 949/494-1145; there's online info at **www.foapom.com**. July through August.

Comic-Con International, San Diego. Some 60,000 people attend America's largest comic book convention each year when it lands at the San Diego Convention Center for a weekend of auctions, dealers, autographs, and seminars focusing on graphic novels and fantasy/sci-fi movies and television shows. Past special guests include Hugh Jackman, Matt Groening, Halle Berry, Stan Lee, Angelina Jolie, and Quentin Tarantino. For further details, call ✆ **619/491-2475** or check **www. comic-con.org**. Late July.

U.S. Open Sandcastle Competition, Imperial Beach. The quintessential beach event: a parade and children's castle-building contest on Saturday, followed by the adult event on Sunday. Astounding creations are plundered after the awards ceremony. For details,

call ✆ **619/424-6663** or visit **www. usopensandcastle.com**. Late July.

Old Spanish Days Fiesta, Santa Barbara. The city's biggest annual event, this 5-day festival features a parade with horse-drawn carriages, music and dance performances, marketplaces, and a rodeo. Call ✆ **805/962-8101,** or visit **www.oldspanishdays-fiesta.org**. Early August.

La Jolla SummerFest, San Diego. This is perhaps San Diego's most prestigious annual music event. It features a range of classical and contemporary music, from tango to Tchaikovsky, with guest composers and musicians ranging from Chick Corea to Yo-Yo Ma. SummerFest also offers master classes, open rehearsals, and workshops. Contact the La Jolla Music Society at ✆ **858/459-3728,** or visit **www.ljms.org**. Early to mid-August.

Nisei Week Japanese Festival, Los Angeles. This weeklong celebration of Japanese culture and heritage is held in the Japanese American Cultural and Community Center Plaza in Little Tokyo. Festivities include parades, food, music, arts, and crafts. Call ✆ **213/687-7193,** or see **www.niseiweek.org**. Mid-August.

Los Angeles County Fair, Pomona. Horse racing, arts, agricultural displays, celebrity entertainment, and carnival rides are among the attractions at one of the largest county fairs in the world, at the Los Angeles County Fair and Exposition Center. Call ✆ **909/623-3111,** or visit **www.fairplex.com** for information. Throughout September.

Long Beach Blues Festival, Long Beach. Great performances by blues legends such as Etta James, Dr. John, and the Allman Brothers make this an event you won't want to miss. In the middle of the athletic field at Long Beach State, the event serves cold beer, wine, and food. Call ✆ **562/985-2899,** or log on to **www.kkjz.org**. Labor Day weekend.

Sausalito Art Festival, Sausalito. A juried exhibit of more than 180 artists. It's accompanied by music provided by Bay Area jazz, rock, and blues performers and international cuisine enhanced by wines from some 50 Napa and Sonoma producers. Call ☎ **415/331-3757,** or log on to **www.sausalitoartfestival.org** for information. Labor Day weekend.

Monterey Jazz Festival. Features top names in traditional and modern jazz. One of the oldest annual jazz festivals in the world. Call ☎ **831/373-3366,** or see **www.montereyjazzfest.com** for more info. Mid-September.

Danish Days, Solvang. Since 1936, this 3-day event has been celebrating old-world customs and pageantry with a parade, gymnastics exhibitions by local schoolchildren, demonstrations of Danish arts and crafts, and plenty of *aebleskivers* (Danish fritters) and *medisterpolse* (Danish sausage). Call ☎ **800/468-6765** for more information, or see **www.solvangusa.com**. Mid-September.

Fleet Week, San Diego. The name is a bit of a misnomer; the nation's largest military-appreciation event actually lasts a full month. It features navy ship tours, a college football game, an auto race of classic speedsters, the renowned Miramar air show, and more. For more info call ☎ **800/FLEET-WEEK** (353-3893), or log on to **www.fleetweeksandiego. org**. Mid-September to mid-October.

Simon Rodia Watts Towers Jazz Festival, Los Angeles. This event pays tribute to the roots of jazz in gospel and blues, as well as celebrating the avant-garde and Latin jazz scene. It's also a great opportunity to visit the Watts Towers. Call ☎ **213/847-4646,** or log on to **www.myspace.com/drumnjazz.** Late September.

OCTOBER
The Half Moon Bay Art & Pumpkin Festival, Half Moon Bay. The festival features a Great Pumpkin Parade,

pie-eating contests, a pumpkin-carving competition, arts and crafts, and all manner of squash cuisine. The highlight of the event is the Giant Pumpkin weigh-in. October (for exact date and details, call the Pumpkin Hot Line at ☎ **650/726-9652**).

Catalina Island Jazz Trax Festival, Catalina Island. Contemporary jazz artists travel to the island to play in the legendary Avalon Casino Ballroom. The festival is held over 2 consecutive 3-day weekends. Call ☎ **866/872-9849,** or visit **www.jazztrax.com** for advance ticket sales and a schedule of performers. Early October.

Sonoma County Harvest Fair, Sonoma County Fairgrounds. A 3-day celebration of the harvest with exhibitions, art shows, and annual judging of the local wines. Contact ☎ **707/545-4203** or **www.harvestfair.org**. Dates vary.

Hollywood Film Festival, Los Angeles. More than 50 films from the U.S. and abroad are screened, amid celebrities galore. Actors and filmmakers will find a variety of workshops and marketplaces. Call ☎ **310/288-1882,** or visit **www. hollywoodawards.com** for info and tickets. Mid-October.

West Hollywood Halloween Costume Carnaval, Los Angeles. This is one of the world's largest Halloween parties. More than 400,000 people, many dressed in outlandish drag couture, party all night along Santa Monica Boulevard. Call ☎ **310/289-2525,** or see **www.visit westhollywood.com** for info. October 31.

NOVEMBER
Catalina Island Triathlon, Catalina Island. This is one of the top triathlons in the world. Participants run on unpaved roads, swim in the cleanest bay on the West Coast, and bike on challenging trails. There's also a "kids' tri." Call Pacific Sports at ☎ **714/978-1528,** or visit **www.pacificsportsllc.com**. Early November.

Doo Dah Parade, Pasadena. This outrageous spoof of the Rose Parade features such participants as the Briefcase Precision Drill Team and a kazoo-playing marching band. Call ✆ **626/590-1134,** or visit **www.pasadenadoodahparade. info**. Near Thanksgiving.

Hollywood Christmas Parade, Los Angeles. This spectacular, star-studded parade marches through the heart of Hollywood. For information, call ✆ **323/469-2337.** Sunday after Thanksgiving.

DECEMBER

Balboa Park December Nights, San Diego. The city's urban park is decked out in holiday splendor for a weekend of evening events, including a candlelight procession, caroling and baroque music, craft displays, ethnic food, and hot cider. The event and the park's 13 museums are free these evenings. For more information, call ✆ **619/239-0512** or visit **www.balboapark.org**. First weekend in December.

Christmas Boat Parade of Lights. Following long-standing tradition, sailors decorate their crafts with colorful lights. Several Southern California harbors hold nighttime parades to showcase the creations, which range from tiny dinghies draped with a single strand of lights to showy yachts with entire Nativity scenes twinkling on deck. Contact the following for schedules and information: Ventura Harbor, ✆ **805/382-3001;** Long Beach, ✆ **562/435-4093;** Huntington Harbor, ✆ **714/840-7542;** and **San Diego Bay** (www.sdparadeoflights. org). December.

Whale-Watching Season, San Diego. From mid-December to mid-March,

more than 25,000 California gray whales make the trek from chilly Alaskan seas to the warm-water breeding lagoons of Baja California. Cabrillo National Monument, on the panoramic Point Loma peninsula, offers a glassed-in observatory from which to spot the whales, examine whale exhibits, and listen to taped narration describing these popular mammals. Many boating excursion companies offer whale-watching tours throughout the season. For more information, visit **www.sandiego. org**. Mid-December through mid-March.

College Bowl Games, San Diego. The city hosts two college football bowl games: the **Holiday Bowl** and the **Poinsettia Bowl.** The Holiday Bowl features top teams from the Pac 10 and Big 12 Conferences, while the Poinsettia Bowl pits a team from the Mountain West Conference against an at-large opponent. The fledgling Poinsettia Bowl (✆ **619/285-5061;** www.poinsettiabowl. net) was inaugurated in 2005; the Holiday Bowl (✆ **619/283-5808;** www. holidaybowl.com) has been played since 1978, augmented by several special events, including the nation's biggest balloon parade of giant inflatable characters. Late December.

New Year's Eve Torchlight Parade, Big Bear Lake. Watch dozens of nighttime skiers follow a serpentine path down Snow Summit's ski slopes bearing glowing torches—it's one of the state's loveliest traditions. Afterward, the party continues indoors with live bands, food, and drink. Call ✆ **909/866-5766,** or log on to **www.bigbearmountainresorts. com**. December 31.

RESPONSIBLE TRAVEL

California offers numerous ways to be an eco-friendly visitor. The biggest favor you can do for the environment is keeping your driving to a minimum, and in California there are numerous car-free adventures to choose from. Here are a few examples:

- Instead of driving though the Wine Country, consider a self-guided but fully supported 3-day biking tour with **Wine Country Bikes** (© **866/922-4537;** www.winecountrybikes.com).

- From San Francisco, you can take a bus to **Yosemite National Park** (p. 355) and join one of the numerous hiking, biking, and horseback riding trips that explore Yosemite Valley.

- Tour the state via **Amtrak** (www.amtrakcalifornia.com). Some of the most beautiful train routes in the U.S. wend along the California coast, stopping in such coastal cities as San Lois Obispo, Los Angeles, San Juan Capistrano, and San Diego. (At some train stops, such as Santa Barbara and Ventura, you can literally walk to your hotel from the station.)

In San Francisco there are numerous restaurants that purchase only organically grown foods (processing foods and manufacturing fertilizers and pesticides take significant amounts of energy), and the city's $25-million **Orchard Garden Hotel** (p. 72) is the only hotel in the state that was built to the nationally accepted standards for green buildings developed by the U.S. Green Building Council. San Francisco's extensive public transportation system makes it easy to get around without a car (in fact, we recommend not driving here).

For more information on ecologically responsible travel, visit **California Vagabond** at **www.californiavagabond.com**. Here you'll find tips on environmentally friendly accommodations, car rentals, and more. In addition to the resources listed above, see www.frommers.com/planning for more tips on responsible travel.

3

SUGGESTED CALIFORNIA ITINERARIES

by Matthew Poole, Erika Lenkert, Tara de Lis & Harry Basch

Because California is so vast and geographically varied—from misty redwood forests and eerily beautiful deserts to gold-sand beaches and rugged mountain ranges—it would take months to see all its major attractions. We're guessing your vacation hours are limited, so we're recommending these itineraries, to help you make the most of your time.

Essentially, we're divulging how we, the authors, would spend our own weeklong dream trips. We've divided the chapter into our favorite regions and singled out the best sites, hotels, restaurants, and scenic drives. We've allowed leeway to stray from each route, but we've also mapped out enough details to guide you through an entire journey.

As you choose a route, be sure to consider the importance of timing. If you don't care to learn what it's like to drive through an Easy-Bake oven, skip the Southern California desert route in mid-July. Yosemite and Lake Tahoe are best avoided in winter, when several access roads close down due to heavy snowfall. The Wine Country is best in spring, when the Napa and Sonoma valleys are abloom and the summer crowds haven't yet arrived, or during the heady fall grape crush. Pacific Coast Highway is great year-round, as long as the sun is out and the convertible top is down.

For all of the routes in this chapter, you'll need a car, so fly into the largest city near each itinerary region and rent a vehicle for a week. See "Getting There" and "Getting Around," in chapter 17, for information about airports, driving rules,

Heavenly gondola ride, Lake Tahoe. PREVIOUS PAGE: **Summer on Lake Tahoe.**

and rental-car companies. You'll also need a detailed map and some Dramamine if you're prone to road sickness, because most of these itineraries take you down winding roads. And since it's almost always sunny in California, splurge on a convertible Mustang—it will turn the mundane task of driving into one of the highlights of your vacation.

—Matthew Poole

PACIFIC COAST HIGHWAY IN 1 WEEK

If you've ever wondered why it's outrageously expensive to buy a home in California, this seaside journey by car will resolve the mystery: Superlatives don't do justice to the views you'll see while twisting and turning, climbing and descending along Pacific Coast Highway (Hwy. 1) from San Francisco to Big Sur. It's one of the nation's most thrilling roads, gripping the mountainside while it takes you past coastal redwood forests, ocean cliffs, and secluded coves battered by the dazzling, formidable Pacific.

The trek begins with a half-day's leisurely drive from San Francisco to Santa Cruz, and then continues south past Monterey and Carmel into thickly forested Big Sur. Not a single part of this drive lacks interesting sights; even the acres of artichokes around the farming town of Castroville are pretty, and it's a wonder the ocean views around Big Sur don't cause hundreds of car wrecks a day.

Heavy traffic can afflict Carmel and Big Sur on summer weekends. If you plan your trip to avoid the congestion, you can cruise at 55 miles per hour from town to town—with the top down and your spirits up.

DAY 1: Santa Cruz & Boardwalk

From San Francisco, take Hwy. 1 south and follow the signs to Pacifica. Continue along Hwy. 1 for about 60 miles to Santa Cruz. Check into the **Pleasure Point Inn ★★** (p. 431) and make a reservation for the

Kayaking Monterey Bay.

Bittersweet Bistro ★★ (p. 432). Spend some time on the **Santa Cruz Beach Boardwalk** ★★ (p. 424) and be sure to ride the wooden Giant Dipper roller coaster and the old-school carousel. The **Seymour Marine Discovery Center** (p. 426) is also worth a visit, especially for kids. Have dinner in Aptos at the **Bittersweet Bistro** ★★ (p. 432) and head back to the inn.

DAY 2: Monterey Bay Aquarium

Sleep in, sip coffee on the roof deck, and admire the ocean view until checkout (11am), or walk along the coastal path to **Capitola** ★ (p. 428) for a bloody mary. Back in the car, head south on Hwy. 1 to Monterey, about a 1-hour drive. Check into the **Seven Gables Inn** ★★★ (p. 450) or **Martine Inn** ★★ (p. 449) for 2 nights, and make a dinner reservation for **Montrio Bistro** ★★ (p. 444) for this evening, and **Fandango** restaurant ★★ (p. 452) and the **Monterey Bay Kayaks** tour (p. 439) for tomorrow. Drive to the **Monterey Bay Aquarium** ★★★ (p. 438), the world's finest. Spend 2 to 3 hours here, and then stroll **Cannery Row** (briefly if you loathe tourist schlock; p. 436). Drive or walk to **Montrio** for dinner.

DAY 3: Kayaking & Sea Otters

Breakfast at the inn, and then drive to Del Monte Beach for a leisurely **kayak tour of Monterey Bay.** Watching sea otters and sea lions play from the water is an unforgettable experience, requiring no kayaking expertise. Afterward, stroll along **Old Fisherman's Wharf** (p. 444) and snack on all those small cups of fresh seafood sold at one of many faux fish markets. Return to the car for an afternoon/sunset drive along **17-Mile Drive** ★★ (p. 454). Dine at **Fandango** and return to the B&B.

DAY 4: Seafood & Beer in Carmel

Eat breakfast, check out, and drive to Carmel. Check in to the **Mission Ranch** ★★ (p. 461) for 2 nights, and make a reservation for the **Flying**

Carmel.

Fish Grill ★★ (p. 464) for tonight and **Aubergine** ★★★ (p. 463) for tomorrow night. Apply sunscreen, pack a jacket, and walk along the coastal path to downtown **Carmel** for window-shopping—a beloved Carmel pastime—and a burger and beer at the **Hog's Breath Inn** (p. 465). If it's Saturday, take the 2pm **Carmel Walking Tour** (p. 460); otherwise, pick up a free map at the **Carmel**

Carmel Beach.

Business Association (p. 457) and check out the **Mission San Carlos** ★★ (p. 458) and **Tor House** ★ (p. 458) on your own. Have dinner at the **Flying Fish Grill,** and then stroll back to the **Mission Ranch bar** for an Irish whiskey and piano tunes.

DAY 5: Chillin' at the Beach

Take the day off. Sleep in, stock up on picnic stuff at **Nielsen Brothers Market** (p. 466), and devote the day to **Carmel Beach** ★★ (p. 457)—a welcoming stretch of pristine white sand and cypress trees. Head back to your hotel room in the late afternoon, clean up, and walk to the hotel restaurant for a fat steak dinner.

DAY 6: Big Sur

Check out, have breakfast at the **Little Swiss Cafe** (p. 466), and top off the fuel tank. Drive south on Hwy. 1 deep into **Big Sur** ★★★, and make various stops along the way to photograph the spectacular coastline. Have lunch at **Café Kevah** (p. 476), and then check into **Deetjen's Big Sur Inn** ★ (p. 472) if you like extrarustic lodgings; the **Treebones Resort** ★★ (p. 473) if you're on a budget; or the **Post Ranch Inn** ★★★ (p. 473) for a splurge.

DAY 7: Hiking & Home

Check out, then drive to **Julia Pfeiffer Burns State Park** ★★ (p. 472) and hit the trail from the parking area to **McWay Waterfall** (it's an easy trek). If you have time, you can return to San Francisco via Hwy. 1, though taking Hwy. 101 near Salinas is a much faster route.

TAHOE & YOSEMITE IN 1 WEEK

This weeklong excursion covers two of my favorite places on the planet: Lake Tahoe and Yosemite National Park. I've visited both these mountain regions countless times, yet each time I'm nonetheless awestruck by their beauty. I'd go so far as to credit them for my choice of career: The opportunity to explore natural wonders such as these is what compelled me to be a travel writer.

The trip starts in North Lake Tahoe, winds its way to South Lake Tahoe, and then veers southeast along Hwy. 395 to Mono Lake. From there, it cuts westward on Hwy. 120 and heads up, up, up to the famed Tioga Pass and into Yosemite National Park. In winter months, the scenery is even more spectacular, but

Tioga Pass is usually closed due to snow. The inland route, via Hwy. 49, will get you there in winter, but it adds about 4 hours' driving time.

The quickest way to cover this ground is to fly into Reno–Tahoe International Airport and rent a car; otherwise, take I-80 east from the San Francisco or Sacramento airports to Truckee. From there, it's a short drive southward on Hwy. 89 to the north shore of Lake Tahoe. From Yosemite National Park, it's about a 3½-hour drive back to San Francisco.

Be sure to pack comfortable hiking shoes, a swimsuit, a small backpack, plenty of sunscreen, a wide-brimmed hat, and spare cash for the casinos.

DAY 1: Bike Ride & Slot Machines

From Tahoe City, head south on West Lake Boulevard for a few miles to **Sunnyside Lodge ★★** (p. 321). Check in for 2 nights, make dinner reservations at **Gar Woods Grill & Pier ★** (p. 326) tonight and **Manzanita ★★** (p. 325) tomorrow night, and then have lunch on the deck at Sunnyside and soak in the view. Drive back to Tahoe City to the **Olympic Bike Shop** (p. 304). Rent a bike for a few hours and take the scenic paved bike path that follows West Lake Boulevard and the Truckee River. Return the bikes and then drive to **Gar Woods** (leave time to arrive before sunset). After dinner, drive to the **Cal-Neva Casino ★** (p. 319) for some evening entertainment, and then head back to the hotel.

DAY 2: Rafting & Lakeside Dining

Eat breakfast at the **Fire Sign Café ★** (p. 327) down the street, and then drive to **Truckee River Raft Rental** (p. 308) in Tahoe City. If you're not into rafting, go on a sailboat cruise instead with **Tahoe Sailing Charters** (p. 306). After a leisurely raft trip down the mostly calm, always beautiful Truckee River, have a burger and beers on the riverside deck at the **River Ranch Lodge & Restaurant ★★** (p. 320) while waiting for the return shuttle. Next, drive to **Squaw Valley ★★★** (p. 302) and ride the cable car to **High**

Mono Lake.

Camp ★★ (p. 305), where you can explore numerous hiking trails, ice-skate, or admire the view at the **Poolside Café.** Either walk or take the cable car back to the parking lot, and then walk over to **Manzanita** for dinner.

DAY 3: Picnic Lunch, Beachside Mai Tais & More Gambling

Sleep in, grab breakfast at the hotel, and check out. Stock up on sandwiches and drinks at the deli, stuff them into a backpack, and head south on Hwy. 89 toward South Lake Tahoe. Park at **Emerald Bay ★★** (p. 310) and walk to **Vikingsholm ★** (p. 310) for a lakeside picnic lunch. (I recommend the hike to **Eagle Lake** as well; p. 308.) Back in the car to **South Lake Tahoe,** drive through town (heading east on Lake Tahoe Blvd./Hwy. 50) into Nevada, and check into a lakeside cabin at **Zephyr Cove ★** (p. 316) for 2 nights. Drink a mai tai at the **beachside bar,** and then take a shuttle or taxi back toward the casinos for great sushi and *teriyaki chicken* at the **Naked Fish ★★** (p. 324). Spend the evening at the **casinos.**

DAY 4: Gondola Ride & Lobster

Sleep in, have breakfast at **Zephyr Cove Restaurant** (p. 316), and then walk to the pier and board the **MS *Dixie II*** (p. 309) for a 2-hour cruise to Emerald Bay. Return to the beachside bar for another mai tai, and then relax at the gold-sand beach in front of your cabin. If you can water-ski or wakeboard, consider renting a boat or jet ski. Around 4pm, hop in the car and head to the **Heavenly Resort ★★** (p. 300) for a **gondola** ride (p. 300) to the **viewing platform** before sunset (wow!). For dinner, drive to **Fresh Ketch ★** (p. 323) for oysters, steak, and lobster. Then win your money back at the **casinos** and/or see a **show.**

DAY 5: Mono Lake & Yosemite

Today's itinerary entails lots of driving, so rise early, eat breakfast at Zephyr Cove Restaurant, gas up the car, and take the Kingsbury Grade to Hwy. 395

John Muir Trail, Yosemite.

(it's a bit confusing to find, so bring a map). Head south to **Mono Lake ★** (p. 375), spend an hour or so at the excellent visitor center, and then head east on Hwy. 120 into **Yosemite National Park ★★★** (p. 355) toward **Yosemite Valley.** Be sure to stretch your legs at **Tuolumne Meadows ★★** (p. 363) and walk around a bit, admiring the view. If you can afford it, check into the legendary **Ahwahnee Hotel ★★★** (p. 367) for 2 nights; otherwise, stay either at the **Wawona Hotel ★** (p. 368) or at my favorite lodging in Yosemite, the **Evergreen Lodge ★★** (it's a bit of a drive from Yosemite Valley but worth the trip; p. 349). Dine at the hotel and call it a night.

DAY 6: Tours, Biking & Alpenglow

Sleep in, eat breakfast at the hotel, and take the 2-hour **Valley Floor Tour** (p. 358) in an open-air tram. Better yet, purchase the *Map and Guide to Yosemite Valley,* rent bikes at **Yosemite Lodge** or **Curry Village** (p. 367), and take your own tour along the paved trail that winds throughout the valley. When you return the bikes, use the *Map and Guide to Yosemite Valley*—which lists an assortment of hikes and short nature walks—to plan tomorrow's hike while you have lunch at one of the overpriced cafes in Curry Village. Save energy for the long hike on Day 7, and stroll eastward at a leisurely pace into the valley on the **John Muir Trail ★★** (p. 361), along the Merced River toward Vernal falls—it's one of the most scenic trails in Yosemite. Make sure you have a clear view of the valley at sunset to witness the **alpenglow.** Return to the hotel for dinner. If it's a summer Saturday, mosey over to the Wawona Hotel for their old-fashioned **barbecue dinner** on the front lawn (p. 368).

DAY 7: Hiking & Drive Home

Rise early, catch a light breakfast, check out (but leave your luggage at the hotel), and unfold your *Map and Guide to Yosemite Valley* to see which hike best fits your schedule and endurance level. Some of my favorites are the **Upper Yosemite Fall Trail ★** (a real thigh-burner but very rewarding; p. 360) and the **Mist Trail ★** (p. 361) to Nevada Falls. Alas, after your hike, it's time to head home. If you're heading to the Bay Area or Sacramento, take Hwy. 120 toward Groveland and follow the signs.

1 WEEK FOR FOOD & WINE LOVERS

The San Francisco Bay Area is one of the nation's top destinations for world-class food and wine. The region's culinary diversity began with the California Gold Rush of 1849, when more than 300,000 people from all over the world migrated to Northern California to strike it rich. When the gold no longer panned out, many of the immigrants remained in California and used their earnings to start small farms, dairy ranches, wineries, fisheries, and restaurants that served family recipes from around the world.

Today, California still harbors an impressive concentration of small, family-operated ranches, organic farms, and boutique wineries throughout Central and Northern California, providing local chefs with some of the nation's finest organic produce, artisan cheeses, hormone-free meats, and small-production wines. In fact, it was a Bay Area chef who *invented* California cuisine—the renowned Alice Waters. Even a full week of glorious gluttony won't begin to cover the range of cuisines and varietals available to serious epicureans as they indulge their inner cognoscenti, but with careful pacing and a little exercise worked into your route, you can savor the region's finest foods and still fit in your pants by the time you head home. Well, maybe.

Note: Because some of the following attractions operate only on certain days, you may need to rearrange the itinerary based on opening hours. It's also important to make restaurant reservations as far in advance as possible; the places recommended here are popular on the foodie circuit. Also, you'll need a car for the Berkeley and the Wine Country excursions.

DAY 1: Alfresco Noshing by Day & Fine Dining by Night

Start your movable feast in San Francisco at the **Ferry Building Marketplace Farmers' Market ★★★**, at the foot of Market Street in the Embarcadero (p. 119). From November to March, when produce is less abundant, the market takes place Tuesday and Saturday mornings; the rest of the year, it's open on Thursday and Sunday mornings as well. Join the throngs of locals as they browse the dozens of outdoor stalls filled with organic goods from local artisan farms, and snack on free samples of specialty foods. Inside, shop or simply gawk at delicacies from the city's finest gourmet chocolatiers, bakeries, fish and meat mongers, and tea merchants. If you haven't already filled up on free samples, have lunch at the **Slanted Door ★★** (p. 94; reservations a must), located at the north end of the Marketplace. Afterward, burn calories with a leisurely bayside walk along the Embarcadero to Fisherman's Wharf. If your feet are up for it, continue walking to Fort Mason and the **Marina** (a brisk 20- to 30-min. walk from Fisherman's Wharf) for more classic bay views. Rest in the late afternoon to revitalize yourself for a French feast at **Restaurant Gary Danko ★★★** (p. 99), one of the city's finest dining rooms, or for a more affordable but equally wonderful Italian meal at **A16 ★★** (p. 101). Both require advance reservations.

DAY 2: North Beach Treats & Chez Panisse

Pace yourself. Start the morning with coffee and a light breakfast at one of the sidewalk cafes in **North Beach,** such as **Caffè Greco.** Wander the streets suffused with Italian heritage and the aromas of roasting garlic and pizza. Drop by **Biordi Art Imports** to pick up some **Italian pottery** (p. 144). Enjoy a leisurely lunch at **L'Osteria del Forno ★★**—classic Italian fare at reasonable prices served in a shoebox-size dining room (p. 98)— or sample authentic Hong Kong–style dining at **Great Eastern ★**, where rare delicacies are available for the adventurous palate. After lunch, it's time to find your way to Berkeley to learn how artisan chocolate is made during **Scharffen Berger Chocolate Maker's 1-hour tour.** From the city, it's a 20-minute drive, traffic permitting (you can also take BART; call for directions, ⓒ **510/465-2278**); take Columbus Avenue south and follow signs to I-80 east, which will take you across the Bay Bridge toward Oakland and Berkeley. Take the Ashby Avenue exit heading east, turn left at Seventh Street (the first signal), go to the second light, and the factory is on your right, at the corner of Seventh and Heinz streets. After the tour, it's time to dine at one of the nation's most famous and influential restaurants: **Chez**

Panisse ★★★. Still owned and run by Alice Waters, the godmother of contemporary California cuisine, it's a requisite pilgrimage stop for serious gourmands (p. 166). If the skies are clear on the drive back to San Francisco, revel in the **city views** from the East Bay or Treasure Island.

DAY 3: Eating Your Way Through Chinatown

Kick off another gluttonous day in San Francisco with Wok Wiz's **"I Can't Believe I Ate My Way Through Chinatown"** excursion—established by the late, beloved icon Shirley Fong-Torres, who passed away in 2011 (*C* **650/**

Alice Waters of Chez Panisse.

355-9657; www.wokwiz.com). Part variety show, part feast, the Chinatown food tour takes place every Saturday and some Sundays; call for details. If you're visiting on a weekday, try Wok Wiz's standard Chinatown tour, another authentic introduction to delicacies hidden throughout

Chez Panisse.

Chinatown. Work off lunch (included in the tour price) with a visit to **Golden Gate Park** (p. 124), where you can visit the amazing **de Young Museum** ★★★ (p. 131), lounge in the grass, or ride a paddle boat. Head to the bustling Mission District for dinner at **Delfina** ★★, one of the city's best Italian restaurants, with its hip, young, fun patrons and casual setting (p. 112).

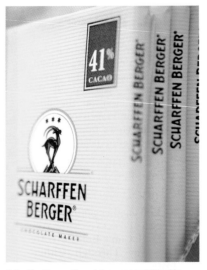

Scharffen Berger Chocolates was established in South San Francisco in 1997.

DAY 4: Union Square

Spend your last day in the city **shopping at Union Square** department stores and boutiques. Have a light lunch of antipasto and a salad at the **Emporio Armani Cafe,** and then spend the afternoon with a visit to **Alcatraz Island** ★★★ (p. 113) or the city's museums (p. 128). Or just pamper yourself with a spa treatment at the Huntington Hotel's **Nob Hill Spa** ★★. In the evening, either go for a multicourse affair with flambéed desserts at **Gary Danko** ★★★ (p. 99); a more relaxed Greek-inspired feast at one of my favorite restaurants in the city, **Kokkari** ★★ (p. 93); or some of the city's finest Mediterranean-influenced cuisine at the city's beloved **Zuni Café** ★★ (p. 106). If you've still got energy after dinner, head downtown for a gentleman's hour at **Bourbon & Branch** (p. 152); be sure to book online for your password, wine tasting at **First Crush** (p. 156), or champagne at the **Bubble Lounge** (p. 156).

DAY 5: Napa Wine Tasting

Get an early start to **Napa** on scenic Hwy. 101 (p. 202), which crosses the Golden Gate Bridge and is a far prettier drive than I-80. Make **Artesa Vineyards & Winery** ★★ your first wine-tasting stop, as it's known for its beautiful views and contemporary architecture, as well as for its Carneros District pinot noirs (p. 207). Next, stop at **Bistro Don Giovanni** ★★ for an excellent Italian lunch (don't skip the pasta); if the weather's warm, reserve a patio table overlooking the garden, whimsical fountain, and vineyards (p. 223). Next, take the scenic drive to the **Hess Collection** winery and art gallery ★★ (p. 207), indulge the senses with a private sit-down wine-tasting party at **Swanson Vineyards & Winery** ★ (p. 210), or tour Francis Ford Coppola's stunning historic winery with a tour at **Rubicon Estate** ★ (p. 211). Then you can satiate your appetite at celebrity chef Michael Chiarello's festive Italian hot spot, **Bottega Ristorante** ★ (p. 223). Stay the night at any of the recommended B&Bs or hotels in your price range (p. 233), but make sure you book a room as far in advance as possible.

DAY 6: Sparkling Wine, Hand-Dug Caves & Hot Springs

Take it easy on the morning meal and have just coffee and pastries (ask your concierge for the best place near you). Then head north on Hwy. 29 to **Schramsberg ★★** in Calistoga (about ½ hr. from downtown Napa and 15 min. from St. Helena) for a tour of their sparkling wine-making process and hand-dug caves, followed by a tasting (p. 214). Head back "down valley" for lunch at long-standing French favorite **Bistro Jeanty ★★** in Yountville (p. 223). Then spend the rest of the afternoon visiting other wineries in the area, including **Domaine Chandon ★★** (p. 209) and **Joseph Phelps Vineyards ★** (p. 213). Or relax with spa treatments at funky-cool **Dr. Wilkinson's Hot Springs ★**, one of Calistoga's numerous spas (p. 220). For an indulgent dinner, grab a bite at Iron Chef Morimoto's new **Morimoto Napa ★★** (p. 222).

DAY 7: Food & Wine Gifts & Picnic & Pétanque

Reserve the day for shopping. Start with a light breakfast near your hotel. Then head to St. Helena for the Main Street boutiques. Grab mementos and gifts from **Napa Valley Olive Oil Manufacturing Company** (p. 212), follow your nose at the culinary emporium **Dean & DeLuca** (p. 225), and buy a picnic lunch from **Oakville Grocery,** which has a few picnic tables on-site (p. 225). Taste wines and play the French lawn-bowling game *pétanque* at **St. Supéry** winery (p. 211). If you have time, you can stop in downtown **Sonoma** (p. 226) to meander around its square, or make one last stop at **Buena Vista Carneros Winery ★** (p. 230). Or extend your trip and head to Northern Sonoma for a truly unforgettable dinner at **Cyrus ★★★** (p. 245). Then it's back to San Francisco the same way you came, just in time to start your diet again.

4

SAN FRANCISCO

by Matthew Poole

San Francisco's reputation as a rollicking city where almost anything goes dates back to the boom-or-bust days of the California gold rush. It's always been this way: This city is so beautiful, exciting, diverse, and cosmopolitan that you can always find something new to see and do no matter if it's your first or fiftieth visit. Oh, and bring a warm jacket: Bob Hope once remarked that San Francisco is the city of four seasons—every day.

Things to Do   Consistently ranked as America's Favorite City (suck on that, New York), San Francisco never ceases to entertain. Enjoy the cool blast of salty air as you stroll across the **Golden Gate.** Stuff yourself with dim sum in **Chinatown.** Browse the secondhand shops along **Haight Street.** Recite poetry in a **North Beach** coffeehouse. Stroll **Ocean Beach,** skate through **Golden Gate Park,** ride the **cable cars** to **Fisherman's Wharf,** tour a **Victorian mansion,** explore **Alcatraz Island,** go to a **Giants** ball game—the list is endless.

Shopping   Oh baby, start polishing that credit card. Some of our favorites include strolling the hip boutiques in **Hayes Valley,** gourmet delicacies at the **Ferry Building Marketplace,** the wow factor of **Union Square** and **Westfield San Francisco Centre,** real vinyl at **Amoeba Records** on Haight Street, and the weird-to-wonderful shopping bazaar that is **Chinatown.**

Nightlife and Entertainment   It's true: San Francisco sells more theater tickets per capita than any major city in America. We love to watch our recycled Broadway musicals at the **A.C.T.** and transgender tragedies at **Theatre Rhinoceros.** The San Francisco **Symphony, Opera,** and **Ballet** are three great reasons to dress up. Sunday's are a Drag (show) at **Harry Denton's Starlight Room,** while anything goes down at **The Endup.** Maceo Parker's playing at **Yoshi's,** Stanton Moore is at the **Boom Boom Room,** and Tainted Love is sold out at **Bimbo's 365 Club.** Let's end the night with a Golden Gate Martini at **Top of the Mark.**

Restaurants and Dining   With more than 3,500 restaurants in San Francisco, you could eat at a different restaurant every night for 10 years and still not visit them all. Try **Afghan, Burmese, Cambodian, Cajun, Moroccan, Persian, Ethiopian**—or better yet, follow the **street food craze** at roaminghunger.com/sf in search of **Sam's Chowdermobile, Chairmain Bao,** and **Waffle Mania** food trucks.

ORIENTATION
Getting There
BY PLANE
Two major airports serve the Bay Area: San Francisco International and Oakland International.

PREVIOUS PAGE: **Route 1 and Highway 101 merge at the Golden Gate's entrance.**

SAN FRANCISCO INTERNATIONAL AIRPORT   Almost four dozen major scheduled carriers serve **San Francisco International Airport** (**SFO;** ☎ **650/821-8211;** www.flysfo.com), 14 miles directly south of downtown on U.S. 101. Drive time to downtown during commuter rush hour is about 40 minutes; at other times, it's about 20 to 25 minutes. You can also ride BART from the airport to downtown and the East Bay.

The fastest and cheapest way to get from SFO to the city is to take **BART** (Bay Area Rapid Transit; ☎ **415/989-2278;** www.bart.gov), which offers numerous stops within downtown San Francisco. This route, which takes about 35 minutes, avoids traffic on the way and costs a heck of a lot less than taxis or shuttles (about $8 each way, depending on exactly where you're going). Just jump on the airport's free shuttle bus to the International terminal, enter the BART station there, and you're on your way to San Francisco. Trains leave approximately every 15 minutes.

A **cab** from the airport to downtown costs $35 to $40, plus tip, and takes about 30 minutes, traffic permitting.

SuperShuttle (☎ **800/BLUE-VAN** [258-3826] or 415/558-8500; www.supershuttle.com) is a private shuttle company that offers door-to-door airport service, in which you share a van with a few other passengers. They will take you anywhere in the city, charging $17 per person to a residence or business. The shuttle stops at least every 20 minutes to pick up passengers from the marked areas outside the terminals' upper levels. Reservations are required for the return trip to the airport only and should be made 1 day before departure. These shuttles often demand they pick you up 2 hours before your domestic flight and 3 hours before international flights and during holidays. Keep in mind that you could be the first one on and the last one off, so this trip could take a while; you might want to ask before boarding. For $65, you can charter either the entire van for up to seven people or an Execucar private sedan for up to four people. For more info on the **Execucar,** call ☎ **800/410-4444.**

The San Mateo County Transit system, **SamTrans** (☎ **800/660-4287** in Northern CA, or 650/508-6200; www.samtrans.com), runs two buses between SFO and the Transbay Terminal at First and Mission streets. Bus no. 292 costs $2 and makes the trip in about 55 minutes. The KX bus costs $4 and takes just 35 minutes but permits only one carry-on bag. Both buses run daily. The schedule is available on www.samtrans.com.

You can also call ☎ **511** or visit www.511.org for up-to-the-minute information about public transportation and traffic.

OAKLAND INTERNATIONAL AIRPORT   About 5 miles south of downtown Oakland, at the Hegenberger Road exit of Calif. 17 (U.S. 880; if coming from the south, take 98th Ave.), **Oakland International Airport** (☎ **800/247-6255** or 510/563-3300; www.oaklandairport.com) primarily serves passengers with East Bay destinations.

Taxis from the Oakland airport to downtown San Francisco are expensive, costing approximately $50, plus tip.

Bayporter Express (☎ **877/467-1800** in the Bay Area, or 415/467-1800 elsewhere; www.bayporter.com) is a shuttle service that charges $34 for the first person and $15 for each additional person for the ride from the Oakland Airport to downtown San Francisco. Children 11 and under pay

money-saving **TOURIST PASSES**

If you're the type who loves to cram as many tourist attractions as possible into one trip, then you might want to consider purchasing a **San Francisco CityPass** or **GO San Francisco Card.** The **CityPass** includes 7 days of unlimited public transportation (including cable cars, Metro streetcars, and the entire bus system) and access to some of the city's major attractions: the California Palace of the Legion of Honor and de Young museums, Aquarium of the Bay, the Asian Art Museum, the San Francisco Museum of Modern Art, the Exploratorium, and a Blue & Gold Fleet bay cruise. Discounts and coupons to other tourist-related attractions and activities are included as well. You can buy a CityPass at any of the above attractions or online at **www.city pass.com**. Current rates are $64 for adults and $39 for kids 5 to 12. For more information, visit the CityPass website at **www.citypass.com** or send an e-mail to info@city pass.com. For recorded information, call © **888/330-5008.**

I think the better deal, however, is the **GO San Francisco Card** (© **800/887-9103;** www.gosanfranciscocard.com). It offers free or discounted admission to more than 45 of the most popular attractions, activities, and tours throughout the Bay Area and Wine Country; has far more flexibility (available in 1-, 2-, 3-, 5-, and 7-day increments over a 14-day period); and comes with a nifty little full-color guidebook that fits in your back pocket. In addition, some stores and restaurants offer discounts of up to 20% to Go San Francisco Card holders. The Go Cards are smart-technology enabled, which means they operate by calendar day and are activated the first time they are swiped, so you'll want to start your touring early in the morning to get the most value. The 2-day card costs $76 for adults ($53 for kids 3–12) and doesn't need to be used on consecutive days.

$10. The fare for outer areas of San Francisco is higher. The service accepts advance reservations. To the right of the Oakland Airport exit, there are usually shuttles that take you to San Francisco for around $20 per person. The shuttles in this fleet are independently owned, and prices vary.

The cheapest way to reach downtown San Francisco is to take the shuttle bus from the Oakland Airport to **BART** (© **510/465-2278;** www. bart.gov). The AirBART shuttle bus runs about every 15 minutes Monday through Saturday from 5am to 12:05am and Sunday from 8am to 12:05am. It makes pickups in front of terminals 1 and 2 near the ground transportation signs. Tickets must be purchased at the Oakland Airport's vending machines prior to boarding. The cost is $2 for the 10-minute ride to BART's Coliseum station in Oakland. BART fares vary, depending on your destination; the trip to downtown San Francisco costs $3.15 and takes 15 minutes once you're onboard. The entire excursion should take around 45 minutes.

BY CAR

If you drive from Los Angeles, you can take either the longer coastal route along Hwy. 1/U.S. 101 (437 miles, 11 hr.) or the inland route along I-5 to I-580 (389 miles, 6½ hr.). From Mendocino, it's a little more than 3 hours along Hwy. 1, and about 3¼ hours along U.S. 101; and from Sacramento, it's 88 miles, or 1½ hours, along I-80.

BY TRAIN

San Francisco–bound **Amtrak** (✆ **800/872-7245** or 800/USA-RAIL [872-7245]; www.amtrak.com) trains leave from New York and cross the country via Chicago. The journey takes about 3½ days, and seats sell quickly. At this writing, the lowest round-trip fare costs about $380 from New York and $290 from Chicago. Round-trip tickets from Los Angeles range from $104 to as much as $200. Trains arrive in Emeryville, just north of Oakland, and connect with regularly scheduled buses to San Francisco's Ferry Building and the Caltrain station in downtown San Francisco.

Caltrain (✆ **800/660-4287;** www.caltrain.com) operates train service between San Francisco and the towns of the peninsula. The city depot is at 700 Fourth St., at Townsend Street.

Visitor Information

The **San Francisco Visitor Information Center,** on the lower level of Hallidie Plaza, 900 Market St., at Powell Street (✆ **415/391-2000;** www.onlyinsanfrancisco.com), is the best source of specialized information about the city.

You can also get the latest on San Francisco at the following online addresses:

- The *Bay Guardian,* the city's free weekly paper: **www.sfbg.com**
- *SF Gate,* the city's *Chronicle* newspaper: **www.sfgate.com**
- CitySearch: **http://sanfrancisco.citysearch.com**

Neighborhoods in Brief

UNION SQUARE   Union Square is the commercial hub of San Francisco. Most major hotels and department stores are crammed into the area surrounding the actual square, which was named for a series of violent pro-union mass

Union Square.

x

4

Orientation

SAN FRANCISCO

A mural by Ray Patlan on the side of the Leonard R. Flynn Elementary School in the Mission.

demonstrations staged here on the eve of the Civil War. A plethora of upscale boutiques, restaurants, and galleries occupy the spaces tucked between the larger buildings. A few blocks west is the **Tenderloin** neighborhood, a patch of poverty and blight where you should keep your wits about you. The **Theater District** is 3 blocks west of Union Square.

THE FINANCIAL DISTRICT East of Union Square, this area, bordered by the Embarcadero and by Market, Third, Kearny, and Washington streets, is the city's business district and the stamping grounds for many major corporations. The pointy TransAmerica Pyramid, at Montgomery and Clay streets, is one of the district's most conspicuous architectural features. To its east sprawls the Embarcadero Center, an 8½-acre complex housing offices, shops, and restaurants. Farther east still is the old Ferry Building, the city's prebridge transportation hub. Ferries to Sausalito and Larkspur still leave from this point. However, in 2003, the building became an attraction in itself when it was completely renovated, jampacked with outstanding restaurants and gourmet food- and wine-related shops, and surrounded by a farmers' market a few days a week.

NOB HILL & RUSSIAN HILL Bounded by Bush, Larkin, Pacific, and Stockton streets, Nob Hill is a genteel, well-heeled district still occupied by the city's major power brokers and the neighborhood businesses they frequent. Russian Hill extends from Pacific to Bay and from Polk to Mason. It contains steep streets, lush gardens, and high-rises occupied by both the moneyed and the bohemian.

CHINATOWN A large red-and-green gate on Grant Avenue at Bush Street marks the official entrance to Chinatown. Beyond lies a 24-block labyrinth, bordered by Broadway, Bush, Kearny, and Stockton streets, filled with restaurants, markets, temples, shops, and, of course, a substantial percentage of

Cars on infamously crooked Lombard Street.

San Francisco's Chinese residents. Chinatown is a great place for exploration all along Stockton and Grant streets, Portsmouth Square, and the alleys that lead off them, such as Ross and Waverly. This district has a maddening combination of incessant traffic and horrible drivers, so don't even think about driving around here.

NORTH BEACH This Italian neighborhood, which stretches from Montgomery and Jackson to Bay Street, is one of the best places in the city to grab a coffee, pull up a cafe chair, and do some serious people-watching. Nightlife is equally happening in North Beach; restaurants, bars, and clubs along Columbus and Grant avenues attract folks from all over the Bay Area, who fight for a parking place and romp through the festive neighborhood. Down Columbus, toward the Financial District, are the remains of the city's Beat Generation landmarks, including Ferlinghetti's City Lights Bookstore and Vesuvio's Bar. Broadway—a short strip of sex joints—cuts through the heart of the district. **Telegraph Hill** looms over the east side of North Beach, topped by Coit Tower, one of San Francisco's best vantage points.

FISHERMAN'S WHARF North Beach runs into Fisherman's Wharf, which was once the busy heart of the city's great harbor and waterfront industries. Today it's a kitschy and mildly entertaining tourist area with little, if any, authentic waterfront life, except for a small fleet of fishing boats and some lethargic sea lions. What it does have going for it are activities for the entire family, with attractions, restaurants, trinket shops, and beautiful views and walkways everywhere you look.

THE MARINA DISTRICT Created on landfill for the Pan Pacific Exposition of 1915, the Marina District boasts some of the best views of the Golden Gate, as well as plenty of grassy fields alongside San Francisco Bay. Elegant Mediterranean-style homes and apartments, inhabited by the city's well-to-do singles and wealthy families, line the streets. Here, too, are the Palace of Fine Arts, the Exploratorium, and Fort Mason Center. The main street is Chestnut, between Franklin and Lyon, which abounds with shops, cafes, and boutiques. Because of its landfill foundation, the Marina was one of the hardest-hit districts in the 1989 quake.

COW HOLLOW West of Van Ness Avenue, between Russian Hill and the Presidio, this flat, grazeable area supported 30 dairy farms in 1861. Today Cow Hollow is largely residential and yuppie. Its two primary commercial thoroughfares are Lombard Street, known for its many relatively inexpensive motels, and Union Street, a flourishing shopping sector filled with restaurants, pubs, cafes, and shops.

4

SAN FRANCISCO | Orientation

PACIFIC HEIGHTS The ultraelite, such as the Gettys and Danielle Steel—and those lucky enough to buy before the real estate boom—reside in the mansions and homes in this neighborhood. When the rich meander out of their fortresses, they wander down to Union Street and join the pretty people who frequent the street's long stretch of chic boutiques and lively neighborhood restaurants, cafes, and bars.

JAPANTOWN Bounded by Octavia, Fillmore, California, and Geary, Japantown shelters only a small percentage of the city's Japanese population, but exploring these few square blocks is still a cultural experience.

CIVIC CENTER Although millions of dollars have gone toward brick sidewalks, ornate lampposts, and elaborate street plantings, the southwestern section of Market Street can still feel a little sketchy due to the large number of homeless who wander the area. The Civic Center at the "bottom" of Market Street, however, is a stunning beacon of culture and refinement. This large complex of buildings includes the domed and dapper City Hall, the Opera House, Davies Symphony Hall, and the Asian Art Museum. The landscaped plaza connecting the buildings is the staging area for San Francisco's frequent demonstrations for or against just about everything.

SOMA No part of San Francisco has been more affected by recent development than the area south of Market Street (dubbed "SoMa"), the area within the triangle of the Embarcadero, Hwy. 101, and Market Street. Until a decade ago, it was a district of old warehouses and industrial spaces, with a few scattered underground nightclubs, restaurants, and shoddy residential areas. But when it became the hub of dot-commercialization and half-million-dollar-plus lofts, its fate changed forever. Today, the area is jumping, thanks to fancy loft residents; the baseball stadium; and surrounding businesses, restaurants, and nightclubs, in addition to urban entertainment a la the Museum of Modern Art, Yerba Buena Gardens, Metreon, and a slew of big-bucks hotels that make tons of money from businesspeople. Though still gritty in some areas, it's growing more glittery by the year.

MISSION DISTRICT This is another area that was greatly affected by the city's new wealth. The Mexican and Latin American populations here, with their cuisine, traditions, and art, make the Mission District a vibrant area to visit. Some parts of the neighborhood are still poor and sprinkled with the homeless, gangs, and drug addicts, but young urbanites have also settled in the area, attracted by its "reasonably" (a relative term) priced rentals and endless oh-so-hot restaurants and bars that stretch from 16th and Valencia streets to 25th and Mission streets. Less adventurous tourists may just want to duck into Mission Dolores, cruise by a few of the 200-plus amazing murals, and head back downtown. But anyone who's interested in hanging with the hipsters and experiencing the hottest restaurant and bar nightlife should definitely beeline it here. Use caution at night.

THE CASTRO One of the liveliest streets in town, the Castro is practically synonymous with San Francisco's gay community (even though it is technically a street in the Noe Valley District). At the very end of Market Street, between 17th and 18th streets, the Castro has dozens of shops, restaurants, and bars catering to the gay community. Open-minded straight people are welcome, too.

HAIGHT-ASHBURY Part trendy, part nostalgic, part funky, the Haight, as it's most commonly known, was the soul of the psychedelic, free-loving 1960s and the center of the counterculture movement. Today the gritty neighborhood straddling upper Haight Street, on the eastern border of Golden Gate Park, is more gentrified, but the commercial area still harbors all walks of life. Leftover aging hippies mingle with grungy, begging street kids outside Ben & Jerry's Ice Cream Store (where they might still be talking about Jerry Garcia), nondescript marijuana dealers whisper "buds" as shoppers pass, and many people walking down the street have DayGlo hair. But you don't need to be a freak or wear tie-dye to enjoy the Haight—the ethnic food, trendy shops, and bars cover all tastes. From Haight Street, walk south on Cole Street for a more peaceful and quaint neighborhood experience.

RICHMOND & SUNSET DISTRICTS San Francisco's suburbs of sorts, these are the city's largest and most populous neighborhoods, consisting mainly of small (but expensive) homes, shops, and neighborhood restaurants. Although they border Golden Gate Park and Ocean Beach, few tourists venture into "The Avenues," as these areas are referred to locally, unless they're on their way to the Cliff House, the zoo, or the Palace of the Legion of Honor.

GETTING AROUND
By Public Transportation

The **San Francisco Municipal Transportation Agency,** 1 S. Van Ness Ave., better known as "Muni" (*©* **877/878-8883;** www.sfmta.com), operates the city's cable cars, buses, and streetcars. Together, these three services crisscross the entire city. Fares for buses and streetcars are $2 for adults; 75¢ for seniors over 65, children 5 to 17, and riders with disabilities. Cable cars, which run from 6:30am to 12:50am, cost a whopping $5 for all people over 5 ($2 for seniors and riders with disabilities 9pm–7am). Exact change is required on all vehicles except cable cars. Fares are subject to change. Muni's NextBus uses satellite technology to track vehicles on their routes; **www.nextmuni.com** provides up-to-the-minute information about when the next bus or streetcar is coming.

For detailed route information, phone Muni or consult the Muni map at the front of the San Francisco Yellow Pages. If you plan to use public transportation extensively, you might want to invest in a comprehensive transit and city map ($2), sold at the San Francisco Visitor Information Center (p. 60),

Walk, bike, or drive over an icon.

Powell/Market cable car booth, and many downtown retail outlets. Also see the "Money-Saving Tourist Passes" box for more information.

BY CABLE CAR San Francisco's cable cars might not be the most practical means of transport, but the rolling historic landmarks are a fun ride. The three lines are concentrated in the downtown area. The most scenic, and exciting, is the Pow-

Alternative transportation in the World Naked Bike Ride.

ell–Hyde line, which follows a zigzag route from the corner of Powell and Market streets, over both Nob Hill and Russian Hill, to a turntable at gaslit Victorian Square in front of Aquatic Park. The Powell–Mason line starts at the same intersection and climbs Nob Hill before descending to Bay Street, just 3 blocks from Fisherman's Wharf. The least scenic is the California Street line, which begins at the foot of Market Street and runs a straight course through Chinatown and over Nob Hill to Van Ness Avenue. All riders must exit at the last stop and wait in line for the return trip. The cable car system operates from approximately 6:30am to 12:50am, and each ride costs $5.

BY BUS Buses reach almost every corner of San Francisco and beyond—they even travel over the bridges to Marin County and Oakland. Overhead electric cables power some buses; others use conventional gas engines. All are numbered and display their destinations on the front. Signs, curb markings, and yellow bands on adjacent utility poles designate stops, and most bus shelters exhibit Muni's transportation map and schedule. Many buses travel along Market Street or pass near Union Square and run from about 6am to midnight. After midnight, there is infrequent all-night "Owl" service. For safety, avoid taking buses late at night.

Popular tourist routes include bus nos. 5, 7, and 71, all of which run to Golden Gate Park; 41 and 45, which travel along Union Street; and 30, which runs between Union Square and Ghirardelli Square. A bus ride costs $2 for adults and 75¢ for seniors over 65, children 5 to 17, and riders with disabilities.

BY STREETCAR Six of Muni's seven streetcar lines, designated J, K, L, M, N, and T, run underground downtown and on the streets in the outer neighborhoods. The sleek rail cars make the same stops as BART (see below) along Market Street, including Embarcadero Station (in the Financial District), Montgomery and Powell streets (both near Union Sq.), and the Civic Center (near City Hall). Past the Civic Center, the routes branch off: The J line takes you to Mission Dolores; the K, L, and M lines run to Castro Street; and the N line parallels Golden Gate Park and extends to the Embarcadero station. The newest one (called T-Third Street, opened in 2007) runs to AT&T Park and the San Francisco Caltrain station and then continues south along Third Street, ending near Monster (Candlestick) Park.

The most recent new line to this system is not a newcomer at all, but is, in fact, an encore performance of San Francisco's beloved rejuvenated 1930s streetcar. The beautiful, retro, multicolored F-Market streetcar runs from 17th and Castro streets to Beach and Jones streets; every other streetcar continues to Jones and Beach streets in Fisherman's Wharf. This is a quick and charming way to get up- and downtown without any hassle.

Curb Your Wheels!

When parking on a hill, drivers are required by law to apply the hand brake and curb their front wheels—toward the curb when facing downhill, away from it when facing uphill. Failure to curb your wheels, preventing a possible "runaway," will result in an expensive fine that is aggressively enforced.

BY BART BART, an acronym for **Bay Area Rapid Transit** (© **415/989-2278;** www. bart.gov), is a futuristic-looking, high-speed rail network that connects San Francisco with the East Bay and the San Francisco and Oakland airports. Four stations are on Market Street. Fares range from $1.75 to $11, depending on how far you go. Machines in the stations dispense tickets that are magnetically encoded with a dollar amount. Computerized exits automatically deduct the correct fare. Children 4 and under ride free. Trains run every 15 to 20 minutes Monday through Friday from 4am to midnight, Saturday from 6am to midnight, and Sunday from 8am to midnight. In keeping with its futuristic look, BART now offers online trip planners that you can download to your PDA, iPod, or cellphone.

By Taxi

This isn't New York, so don't expect a taxi to appear whenever you need one—if at all. If you're downtown during rush hour or leaving a major hotel, it won't be hard to hail a cab; just look for the lighted sign on the roof that indicates the vehicle is free. Otherwise, it's a good idea to call one of the following companies to arrange a ride: **Veteran's Cab** (© **415/552-1300**), **Luxor Cabs** (© **415/282-4141**), **De-Soto Cab** (© **415/970-1370**), or **Yellow Cab** (© **415/333-3333**). Rates are approximately $3.10 for the first mile and 45¢ each fifth of a mile thereafter.

By Car

You don't need a car to explore downtown San Francisco. In fact, with the city becoming more crowded by the minute, a car can be your worst nightmare—you're likely to end up stuck in traffic with lots of aggressive and frustrated drivers, pay upward of $30 a day to park (plus a whopping 14% parking lot tax), and spend a good portion of your vacation looking for a parking space. Don't bother. However, if you want to venture outside the city, driving is the best way to go.

Before heading outside the city, especially in winter, call © **800/427-7623** for California **road conditions** and for current traffic information.

CAR RENTALS All the major rental companies operate in the city and have desks at the airports. When we last checked, you could get a compact car for a week for anywhere from $165 to $315, including all taxes and other charges.

National car-rental companies operating in San Francisco include **Alamo** (© 877/222-9075; www.alamo.com), **Avis** (© 800/331-1212; www.avis.com), **Budget** (© 800/527-0700), **Dollar** (© 800/800-4000; www.dollar.com), **Enterprise** (© 800/261-7331; www.enterprise.com), **Hertz** (© 800/654-3131; www.hertz.com), **National** (© 877/222-9058; www.nationalcar.com), and **Thrifty** (© 800/367-2277; www.thrifty.com).

PARKING If you want a relaxing vacation, don't attempt to find street parking downtown or in Nob Hill, North Beach, or Chinatown; by Fisherman's Wharf; or on Telegraph Hill. Park in a garage or take a cab or a bus. If you do find street parking, read signs that explain when you can park and for how long. Be careful to avoid zones that become tow areas during rush hours.

[FastFACTS] SAN FRANCISCO

American Express For travel arrangements, traveler's checks, currency exchange, and other member services, an office is at 455 Market St., at First Street (☏ **415/536-2600**), in the Financial District, open Monday through Friday from 9am to 5:30pm and Saturday from 10am to 2pm. To report lost or stolen traveler's checks, call ☏ **800/221-7282.** For American Express Global Assist, call ☏ **800/554-2639.**

Area Codes The area code for San Francisco is **415;** for Oakland, Berkeley, and much of the East Bay, **510;** for the peninsula, generally **650.** Napa and Sonoma are **707.** Most phone numbers in this chapter are in San Francisco's 415 area code, but there's no need to dial it if you're within city limits.

Earthquakes There will always be earthquakes in California, most of which you'll never notice. However, in case of a significant shaker, there are a few basic precautionary measures you should know. When you are inside a building, seek cover; do not run outside. Stand under a doorway or against a wall, and stay away from windows. If you exit a building after a substantial quake, use stairwells, not elevators. If you are in your car, pull over to the side of the road and stop—but not until you are away from bridges, overpasses, telephone poles, and power lines. Stay in your car. If you're out walking, stay outside and away from trees, power lines, and the sides of buildings. If you're in an area with tall buildings, find a doorway in which to stand.

Emergencies Call ☏ **911** to report a fire, call the police, or get an ambulance anywhere in the United States. This is a toll-free call (no coins are required at public telephones).

Hospitals **Saint Francis Memorial Hospital,** 900 Hyde St., between Bush and Pine streets on Nob Hill (☏ **415/353-6000;** www.saintfrancismemorial. org), provides emergency service 24 hours a day; no appointment is necessary. The hospital also operates a **physician-referral service** (☏ **800/333-1355**).

Safety Few locals would recommend walking alone late at night in certain areas, particularly the Tenderloin, between Union Square and the Civic Center. Compared to dodgy neighborhoods in other cities, however, even this section of San Francisco is relatively tranquil. You should also be alert in the Mission District, around 16th and Mission streets; the lower Fillmore area, around lower Haight Street; and SoMa (south of Market St.).

Taxes The United States has no value-added tax (VAT) or other indirect tax at the national level. Every state, county, and city has the right to levy its own nonrefundable local tax on all purchases, including hotel and restaurant checks, airline tickets, and so on; this tax is not included in the price tags you'll see on merchandise. Sales tax in San Francisco is 8.5%. Hotel tax is charged on the room tariff only (which is not subject to sales tax) and is set by the city, ranging from 12% to 17% around Northern California.

Toilets Those weird, oval-shaped, olive-green kiosks on the sidewalks throughout San Francisco are high-tech self-cleaning public toilets. It costs 25¢ to enter, with no time limit, but I don't recommend using the ones in the sketchier neighborhoods, such as the Tenderloin and the Mission, because they're mostly used by crackheads and prostitutes.

WHERE TO STAY

San Francisco is an extensive—and expensive—hotel town, especially considering its relatively small size.

Most of the hotels listed below are within walking distance of Union Square and accessible via cable car. Union Square is near the city's major shops, the Financial District, and all transportation. Prices listed below do not include state and city taxes, which total 14%.

San Francisco Reservations, 360 22nd St., Ste. 300, Oakland, CA 94612 (www.hotelres.com; *℃* **800/677-1570** or 510/628-4450), arranges reservations for more than 150 of San Francisco's hotels and often offers discounted rates. Their nifty website allows Internet users to make reservations online. Other good online sites with discounted rates include **www.hotels.com** and **www.localgetaways.com**.

Union Square
VERY EXPENSIVE

Campton Place ★★ This luxury boutique hotel offers some of the most exclusive accommodations in town—not to mention the most expensive. Rooms are compact but comfy, with limestone, pear wood, and Italian-modern decor. The two executive suites and one luxury suite push the haute envelope to even more sumptuous heights. Discriminating returning guests will still find superlative service (including California king-size beds, exquisite bathrooms, bathrobes, top-notch toiletries, slippers, and every other necessity and extra that's made Campton Place a favored temporary address). A recent change in ownership also brought a new chef to the restaurant, which now offers local California cuisine with Mediterranean and Indian inspirations. The bar/bistro in front is a chic clubby spot for a dry martini.

340 Stockton St. (btw. Post and Sutter sts.), San Francisco, CA 94108. www.camptonplace.com. *℃* **866/332-1670** or 415/781-5555. Fax 415/955-5536. 110 units. $250–$685 double; $490–$3,000 suite. American breakfast $18. AE, DC, MC, V. Valet parking $45. Bus: 2, 3, 4, 30, 38, or 45. Cable car: Powell–Hyde or Powell–Mason line (1 block west). BART: Market St. **Amenities:** Restaurant; concierge; outdoor fitness terrace; room service. *In room:* A/C, TV w/pay movies, hair dryer, minibar, Wi-Fi ($13 per day).

Hotel Monaco ★★ This remodeled 1910 Beaux Arts building has plenty of atmosphere, thanks to a whimsically ethereal lobby with a two-story French inglenook fireplace. The guest rooms, which were upgraded in 2006, follow suit, with canopy beds, Asian-inspired armoires, bamboo writing desks, lively stripes, and vibrant color. Everything is bold but tasteful, and as playful as it is serious, with nifty extras like flatscreen TVs and complimentary Wi-Fi. The decor, combined with the truly grand neighboring Grand Café restaurant that's ideal for cocktails and mingling (but also serves breakfast and lunch), would put this place on my top-10 list if it weren't for rooms that tend to be too small (especially for the price) and the lack of a sizable gym. Your stay also includes a complimentary wine and cheese tasting accompanied by shoulder and neck massages. *Tip:* If you were/are a big fan of Jefferson Airplane, inquire about their Grace Slick Shrine Suite.

501 Geary St. (at Taylor St.), San Francisco, CA 94102. www.monaco-sf.com. ℂ **866/622-5284** or 415/292-0100. Fax 415/292-0111. 201 units. $139–$279 double; $279–$539 suite. Rates include evening wine and cheese tasting. Call for discounted rates. AE, DC, DISC, MC, V. Valet parking $49. Bus: 2, 3, 4, 27, or 38. Pets accepted. **Amenities:** Restaurant; concierge; exercise room; Jacuzzi; room service; spa; sauna and steam room. *In room:* A/C, TV, CD player, hair dryer, minibar, Wi-Fi.

Westin St. Francis ★★ ☺ At the turn of the 20th century, Charles T. Crocker and a few of his wealthy buddies decided that San Francisco needed a world-class hotel, and up went the St. Francis. Hordes of VIPs have hung their hats and hosiery here, including Emperor Hirohito of Japan, Queen Elizabeth II, Mother Teresa, King Juan Carlos of Spain, the shah of Iran, and the U.S. presidents from Taft to Clinton.

The hotel has done massive renovations, costing $185 million over the past decade, the most recent being a $40-million upgrade that was completed mid-2009—$12 million of which was delegated to the Main Building. The older rooms of the main building vary in size and have more old-world charm than the newer rooms, but the Tower is remarkable for its great views of the city from above the 18th floor. If you can swing a room in the Main Building overlooking Union Square, it's worth it. Although the St. Francis is too massive to offer the personal service you get at the smaller hotels on Nob Hill, few other hotels in San Francisco can match its majestic aura.

335 Powell St. (btw. Geary and Post sts.), San Francisco, CA 94102. www.westinstfrancis.com. ℂ **866/500-0038** or 415/397-7000. Fax 415/774-0124. 1,195 units. Main building: $229–$529 double; Tower (Grand View): $179–$559 double; from $650 suite (in either building). Extra person $30. Continental breakfast $15–$18. AE, DC, DISC, MC, V. Valet parking $42. Bus: 2, 3, 4, 30, 38, 45, or 76. Cable car: Powell–Hyde or Powell–Mason lines (direct stop). Pets under 40 lb. accepted (dog beds available on request). **Amenities:** 2 restaurants; concierge; elaborate health club and spa; room service. *In room:* A/C, TV, fridge (some rooms), hair dryer, minibar, Wi-Fi ($9.95 per day).

EXPENSIVE

Hotel Adagio ★★ ✦ Our local hip-hotel company, Joie de Vivre, revamped every one of this 1929 Spanish Revival hotel's 171 large, bright guest rooms in gorgeous modern style. Other plusses include firm mattresses, double-paned windows that open, quiet surroundings, MP3 docking station, Wi-Fi, and flatscreen TVs. Executive floors (7–16) also come with robes, upscale amenities, makeup mirrors, and stereos with iPod ports. Bathrooms are old but spotless and have resurfaced tubs. Feel like splurging? Go for one of the two penthouse-level suites; one has lovely terraces with a New York vibe. Adjacent **Bar Adagio** is a hip spot for cocktails, wines by the glass, and pizzettas, panini, and burgers. *Tip:* Rooms above the eighth floor have good, but not great, views of the city.

550 Geary St., San Francisco, CA 94102. www.thehoteladagio.com. ℂ **800/228-8830** or 415/775-5000. Fax 415/775-9388. 171 units. $139–$349 double. AE, DISC, MC, V. Valet parking $39. **Amenities:** Restaurant; bar; concierge; fitness center; room service. *In room:* TV w/Nintendo and pay movies, CD player and/or MP3 docking station, fridge, hair dryer, free high-speed Internet, minibar.

Marina Green
Marina Blvd
MARINA
Fort
Mason
Cervantes Blvd
North Point St.
Bay St.
Francisco St.
Exploratorium
Richardson Ave.
Divisadero St.
Pierce St.
Avila St.
Moscone
Rec. Ctr.
Chestnut St.
101
8
6
Lombard St.
7
Greenwich St.
COW HOLLOW
Filbert St.
Union St.
Green St.
Vallejo St.
Broadway
Pacific Ave.
Jackson St.
5
Alta
Plaza
**PACIFIC
HEIGHTS**
Lafayette
Park
Washington St.
Clay St.
Sacramento St.
**PRESIDIO
HEIGHTS**
California St.
Pine St.
Bush St.
4
Sutter St.
Post St.
Japan Center
Hamilton Sq. Geary Blvd.
**WESTERN
ADDITION**
Collins St.
Wood St.
O'Farrell St.
Ellis St.
Eddy St.
Jefferson
Square
Anza St.
**UNIVERSITY OF
SAN FRANCISCO**
Turk Blvd.
Golden Gate Ave.
Fulton St.
McAllister St.
U.S.F.
Alamo
Square
Cabrillo St.
Grove St.
Hayes St.
**HAYES
VALLEY**
Fell St.
Fulton St.
**Conservatory
of Flowers**
Oak St.
John F. Kennedy Dr.
The Panhandle
Page St.
Waller St.
**HAIGHT-
ASHBURY**
Haight St.
Hermann St.
GOLDEN GATE PARK
Buena
Vista
Park
Duboce
Park Duboce Ave.
1
3
Kezar Dr.
**Kezar
Stadium**
Frederick St.
14th St.
Lincoln Wy.
Carl St.
15th St.
Hugo St.
Corona
Heights
Park
CASTRO
16th St.
**Mission
Dolores**
**INNER
SUNSET**
Parnassus Ave.
States St.
17th St.
Castro Theatre
2
**UNIVERSITY OF
CALIFORNIA–
SAN FRANCISCO**
Carmel St.
Market St.
18th St.
Mission
Dolores
Park

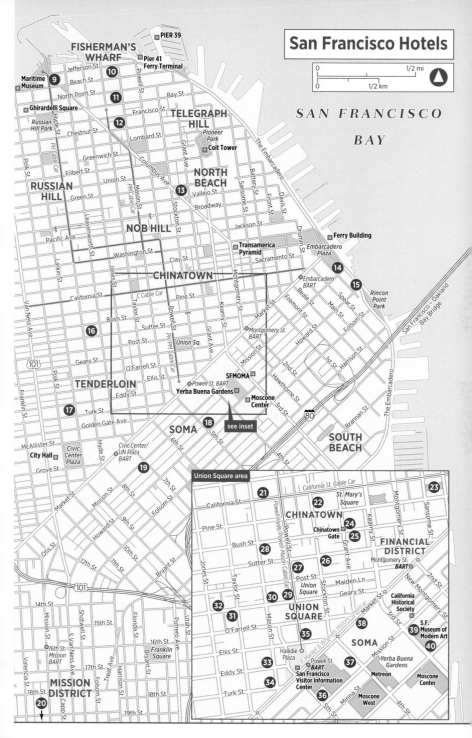

The Orchard Garden Hotel ★★   If Al Gore were a hotelier, this would be his hotel. The Orchard Garden is California's first generation of truly "green" hotels and the only hotel in the state that was built to the nationally accepted standards for green buildings developed by the U.S. Green Building Council (USGBC). It's the first hotel in the city to use the European-style key-card system that turns power off each time you leave, saving about 20% in energy consumption. But going green doesn't mean you have to cut back on comfort—yes, that's Egyptian cotton linen on the king-size bed, real feather down in the pillows, Aveda bath products, and plush spa-style robes in the closet. Rooms are superinsulated (and very quiet). The hotel also has a pleasant rooftop garden and **Roots Restaurant,** serving contemporary American cuisine made from locally sourced organic products. *Note:* If the hotel is booked, inquire about their sister property—the Orchard Hotel—up the street.

466 Bush St. (at Grant Ave.), San Francisco, CA 94108. www.theorchardgardenhotel.com. ℂ **888/717-2881** or 415/399-9807. Fax 415/393-9917. 86 units. $169–$499 double. AE, DC, DISC, MC, V. Valet parking $40. Cable car: Powell–Hyde or Powell–Mason line. **Amenities:** Restaurant; concierge; fitness center (and $15 passes to Club One); free DVD library. *In room:* A/C, flatscreen HDTV, hair dryer, minibar, MP3 docking station, Wi-Fi.

Sir Francis Drake ★★   This landmark hotel is one of San Francisco's grande dames, operating continuously since 1928 in the heart of Union Square. The Kimpton Hotel company has done a wonderful job renovating the hotel (which has been sorely needed since I was a kid), giving this elegant lady a much-needed makeover. It's always a pleasure to have Tom Sweeny, the ebullient (and legendary) beefeater doorman, handle your bags as you enter the elegant, captivating lobby, with its gilded high ceilings, glittering crystal chandeliers, and massive marble staircase that leads to a mezzanine overlooking bustling Powell Street.

　　Scala's Bistro (p. 89), one of the most festive restaurants downtown, serves good Mediterranean cuisine in a stylish setting on the first floor; the Italian-style **Caffe Espresso** does an equally commendable job serving coffees, pastries, and sandwiches daily. **Harry Denton's Starlight Room** (p. 156), on the 21st floor, offers cocktails, entertainment, and dancing nightly with a panoramic view of the city.

450 Powell St. (at Sutter St.), San Francisco, CA 94102. www.sirfrancisdrake.com. ℂ **800/795-7129** or 415/392-7755. Fax 415/391-8719. 416 units. $183–$303 double; from $5,200 suite. AE, DC, DISC, MC, V. Valet parking $44. Bus: 2, 3, 4, 45, or 76. Cable car: Powell–Hyde or Powell–Mason line (direct stop). Pets welcome. **Amenities:** 2 restaurants; bar; concierge; exercise room; room service. *In room:* A/C, TV w/movies on demand, hair dryer, minibar, free Wi-Fi.

MODERATE

Hotel Frank ★★   Only a block from Union Square, this former Maxwell Hotel is the new darling among hip business travelers and serious shoppers. A major renovation was finished in the spring of 2009, bringing the hotel to an even more upscale, boutique-hotel standard. A clever interior makeover by one of the country's most cutting-edge designers incorporates a blend of popular design trends through the decades; check out the Art Deco light fixtures and bold color scheme throughout. The guest rooms exude a custom-designed look: houndstooth-patterned carpeting, elongated emerald green headboards in crocodile-patterned leather, sleek white leather couches, vintage 1930s artwork. Even the bathrooms are outfitted in floor-to-ceiling Carrara marble. The hotel's 28 roomy junior suites offer excellent value despite the slightly audible elevator noise, but best of all are the pair of one-bedroom penthouses that offer separate living rooms and exceptional views of the city.

386 Geary St. (at Mason St.), San Francisco, CA 94102. www.hotelfranksf.com. ✆ **877/828-4478** or 415/986-2000. 153 units. $169–$399 double; $209–$469 junior suite; from $699 penthouse suite. AE, DC, DISC, MC, V. Valet parking $35, an additional $5 for oversized cars. Bus: 2, 3, 4, 30, 38, or 45. Cable car: Powell–Hyde or Powell–Mason lines (1 block east). **Amenities:** Concierge; room service. *In room:* A/C, flatscreen TV w/pay movies, hair dryer, minibar, MP3 docking station, free Wi-Fi.

Hotel Metropolis ★ ☺ 🎁 On a slightly sketchy block just off of Market Street, a few blocks from Union Square, the Hotel Metropolis is ideal for people who dread staying at a boring, corporate McHotel. As with most downtown hotels, the rooms are on the small side, but all are vibrant and cheery, with vivid colors, custom African Limba–wood furnishings, and comfy beds with wave-shaped headboards with portholes. The six Executive Rooms on the 10th floor are upgraded with feather beds and pillows, iPod alarm clocks, and robes, while the three-room Urban Explorers Kids Suite, which sleeps up to six adults and three children, is filled with pint-size furniture, bunk beds, a computer, a chalk-board wall, toys, and rubber ducky decor in the bathroom.

25 Mason St. (at Turk and Market sts.), San Francisco, CA 94102. www.hotelmetropolis.com. ✆ **877/628-4412** or 415/775-4600. 105 units. $99–$289 double; $159–$369 suite. AE, DC, DISC, MC, V. Valet parking $30. Bus: All Market St. buses. Streetcar: Powell St. station. **Amenities:** Exercise room; room service. *In room:* TV w/pay-per-view, hair dryer, free Wi-Fi.

Hotel Milano ★ Neoclassical Italian design patterned after Giorgio Armani's villa in Milan, elegantly streamlined rooms (with double-paned soundproof windows), moderate prices, and a central location next to the San Francisco Centre make Hotel Milano a popular choice for tourists and businesspeople alike. The hotel also has a film-production facility and private screening room to entice media types. Corporate travelers come for the spacious guest rooms, which feature everything an executive could want, from Wi-Fi to video game systems and work desks. Suites have spa tubs and bidets.

55 Fifth St. (btw. Market and Mission sts.), San Francisco, CA 94103. www.hotelmilanosf.com. ✆ **415/543-8555.** Fax 415/543-5885. 108 units. $109–$199 double. Extra person $20. AE, DC, DISC, MC, V. Valet parking $45. Bus: All Market St. buses. **Amenities:** Concierge; fitness room; spa; steam room and sauna. *In room:* A/C, TV w/video games, fridge, hair dryer, Wi-Fi ($9.95 per day).

Hotel Union Square ★★ The Hotel Union Square has achieved that rare hat trick of history, location, and style. It's San Francisco's first boutique hotel, built in 1913 for the 1915 Pan Pacific Exposition, and it's only a half-block from Union Square, in the heart of the city with the cable cars passing by your window. Its 2008 renovation has juxtaposed contemporary and classic San Francisco with original 1915 Egyptian mosaic murals and opulent moldings contrasted by sleek furnishings and state-of-the-art technology. The guest rooms are like urban apartments, each outfitted with platform beds with custom-made leather headboards, velvety chaise longues, and flatscreen televisions. Many have an open, loftlike layout with exposed brick walls and floating ceiling installations, while the two rooftop penthouses are the ultimate in chic, with expansive redwood decks with city views. There's also a custom Kids Suite, a Dashiell Hammett–themed suite, and "Sleep & Soak" rooms on each floor that feature spalike bathrooms.

114 Powell St. (btw. O'Farrell and Ellis sts.), San Francisco, CA 94102. www.hotelunionsquare.com. ✆ **800/553-1900** or 415/397-3000. 131 units. $149–$349 double; $199–$499 suite; $229–$799 penthouse suite. Rates include morning coffee and tea and weekday wine reception. AE, DC, DISC, MC, V. Valet parking $30. Bus: 2, 3, 4, 30, 38, 45, or 76. Cable car: Powell–Hyde or Powell–Mason line. Streetcar: Powell St. station. **Amenities:** Room service (from the adjacent Tad's Steakhouse), fitness center access. *In room:* TV w/pay-per-view, hair dryer, free Wi-Fi.

Hotel Vertigo ★★ Formerly the York Hotel, the Hotel Vertigo opened its doors in fall 2008 to much pressure after being dubbed *the* hot new place to stay and play in San Francisco by more than one jaded San Francisco critic (yours truly included). The good news: It lived up to the buzz, and its new stylistic design will undoubtedly attract tourists and business travelers looking for an alternative to the W Hotel. There's even some colorful history involved as well—the hotel occupies the former site of the Empire Hotel made famous in Alfred Hitchcock's *Vertigo,* hence the name. The movie plays 24/7 in the lobby and is available for free viewings in each room as well. Guest rooms feature playful, eclectic design features such as white tufted-leather headboards, custom wingback chairs in vibrant orange, and crocodile-patterned tiles in the bathrooms.

940 Sutter St. (btw. Leavenworth and Hyde sts.), San Francisco, CA 94109. www.hotelvertigosf. com. ✆ **888/444-4605** or 415/885-6800. 102 units. $169–$399 double; $350–$495 suite. Rates include morning beverages in lobby. AE, DISC, MC, V. Valet parking $35. Bus: 2, 3, or 4. Pets under 40 lb. accepted for a $25 cleaning fee. **Amenities:** Concierge. *In room:* TV w/pay movies, hair dryer, MP3 docking station, free Wi-Fi.

INEXPENSIVE

The Golden Gate Hotel ★ 🏷 San Francisco's stock of small hotels in historic turn-of-the-20th-century buildings includes some real gems—Golden Gate Hotel is one of them. It's 2 blocks north of Union Square and 2 blocks down (literally) from the crest of Nob Hill, with cable car stops at the corner for easy access to Fisherman's Wharf and Chinatown. The city's theaters and restaurants are also within walking distance. But the best thing about the 1913 Edwardian hotel is that it's family run: John and Renate Kenaston and daughter Gabriele are hospitable innkeepers who take obvious pleasure in making their guests comfortable. Each individually decorated room has been repainted and carpeted and has handsome antique furnishings from the early 1900s, quilted bedspreads, and fresh flowers. Request a room with a claw-foot tub if you enjoy a good, hot soak. Afternoon tea is served daily from 4 to 7pm, and guests are welcome to use the house fax and computer with Wi-Fi free of charge.

775 Bush St. (btw. Powell and Mason sts.), San Francisco, CA 94108. www.goldengatehotel.com. ✆ **800/835-1118** or 415/392-3702. Fax 415/392-6202. 25 units, 14 with bathroom. $95–$105 double without bathroom; $150–$165 double with bathroom. Rates include continental breakfast and afternoon tea. AE, DC, MC, V. Self-parking $25. Bus: 2, 4, 30, 38, or 45. Cable car: Powell–Hyde or Powell–Mason line (1 block east). BART: Powell and Market. **Amenities:** Access to health club 1 block away. *In room:* TV, hair dryer upon request, free Wi-Fi.

Hotel Bijou ★ 🏷 Although it's on the periphery of the gritty Tenderloin (just 3 blocks off Union Sq.), once inside this gussied-up 1911 hotel, all's cheery, bright, and perfect for budget travelers who want a little style with their savings. Joie de Vivre hotel group disguised the hotel's age with lively decor, a Deco theater theme, and a heck of a lot of vibrant paint. To the left of the small lobby is a "theater" where guests can watch San Francisco–based double features nightly (it has cute old-fashioned theater seating, though it's just a basic TV showing videos). Upstairs, rooms named after locally made films are small, clean, and colorful (think buttercup, burgundy, and purple) and have tiny bathrooms (one of which is so small you have to close the door to access the toilet). Alas, a few mattresses could be firmer, and the single elevator is small and slow. But considering the price, and perks like the continental breakfast and friendly service, you can't go wrong here.

111 Mason St., San Francisco, CA 94102. www.hotelbijou.com. ℂ **800/771-1022** or 415/771-1200. Fax 415/346-3196. 65 units. $99–$159 double. Rates include continental breakfast. AE, DC, DISC, MC, V. Valet parking $32. Bus: All Market St. buses. Streetcar: Powell St. station. **Amenities:** Concierge; room service. In room: TV, hair dryer, Wi-Fi ($7.95 per day).

Hotel des Arts ★★ 🍴   While this bargain find has the same small lobby, narrow hallways, and cramped rooms as San Francisco's numerous other Euro-style hotels, the des Arts distances itself from the competition by including a visually stimulating dose of artistic license. The lobby, for example, hosts a rotating art gallery featuring contemporary works by emerging local artists and is outfitted with groovy furnishings. You'll love the lively location as well: right across the street from the entrance to Chinatown and 2 blocks from Union Square. There's even a French brasserie right downstairs. Considering the price (rooms with a very clean shared bathroom start at $59), quality, and location, it's quite possibly the best budget hotel in the city. One suite can sleep up to four persons at no additional charge. *Tip:* Log on to the hotel's website to check out the "Painted Rooms" designed by local artists, and then call the hotel directly to book your favorite.

447 Bush St. (at Grant St.), San Francisco, CA 94108. www.sfhoteldesarts.com. ℂ **800/956-4322** or 415/956-3232. Fax 415/956-0399. 51 units, 26 with private bathroom. $79–$159 double with bathroom; $59–$79 double without bathroom. Rates include continental breakfast. AE, DC, MC, V. Nearby parking $18. Cable car: Powell–Hyde or Powell–Mason line. **Amenities:** Concierge. In room: TV, hair dryer, minifridge and microwave in many rooms, free Wi-Fi.

Financial District

VERY EXPENSIVE

The Mandarin Oriental ★★★   No hotel combines better ultraluxury digs with incredible views than this gem. Heaven begins after a rocketing ride on the elevators to the rooms, located between the 38th and 48th floors of a high-rise. The opulent rooms feature contemporary Asian-influenced decor, but the best details by far are the huge windows with superb city views, particularly when the fog rolls in. Not all rooms have bathtubside views (incredible and standard with the signature rooms), but every one does have a luxurious marble bathroom stocked with terry and cotton cloth robes, a makeup mirror, and silk slippers. The 2,000-square-foot Taipan suite—which has a kitchenette, living room, dining area, bedroom, roomy bathroom, and bayview balcony half the size of a football field—is twice as big as my entire house. An added bonus: The restaurant, **Silks,** has a kitchen crew working wonders with the Asian-influenced menu, though the dining room can be awkwardly empty.

222 Sansome St. (btw. Pine and California sts.), San Francisco, CA 94104. www.mandarinoriental. com/sanfrancisco. ℂ **800/622-0404** or 415/276-9888. Fax 415/276-9304. 158 units. $395–$640 double; from $875 suite. Continental breakfast $21; American breakfast $32. AE, DC, DISC, MC, V. Valet parking $36. Bus: All Market St. buses. Streetcar: J, K, L, or M to Montgomery. **Amenities:** Restaurant; bar; concierge; fitness center; room service. In room: A/C, TV w/pay movies, CD player, hair dryer, minibar, Wi-Fi ($13 per day).

SoMa

VERY EXPENSIVE

Four Seasons Hotel San Francisco ★★★ What makes this überluxury hotel one of my favorites is its perfect combination of elegance, trendiness, and modern luxury. The entrance, either off Market or through a narrow alley off Third Street, is deceptively underwhelming, although it does tip you off to the hotel's overall discreetness. Many of the oversize rooms (starting at 460 sq. ft. and including 46 suites) overlook Yerba Buena Gardens. Not too trendy, not too traditional, they're just right, with custom-made mattresses and pillows, beautiful works of art, and huge luxury marble bathrooms with deep tubs and L'Occitane toiletries. Adding to the perks are free access to the building's huge Sports Club L.A. (the best hotel gym in the city), a 2-block walk to Union Square, and a vibe that combines sophistication with a hipness far more refined than the W or the Clift. Its only contender in that department is the St. Regis.

757 Market St. (btw. Third and Fourth sts.), San Francisco, CA 94103. www.fourseasons.com/sanfrancisco. ℂ **800/819-5053** or 415/633-3000. Fax 415/633-3001. 277 units. $355–$855 double; $750 executive suite. AE, DC, DISC, MC, V. Parking $50. Bus: All Market St. buses. Streetcar: F, and all underground streetcars. BART: All trains. **Amenities:** Restaurant; bar; concierge; huge fitness center; room service; spa; Wi-Fi in lobby. *In room:* A/C, TV w/pay movies, hair dryer, high-speed Internet ($15 per day), minibar.

The St. Regis Hotel ★★★ The latest in full-blown high-tech luxury is yours at this überchic 40-story SoMa tower. Strategically near the Museum of Modern Art and Yerba Buena Gardens, this shrine to urban luxury welcomes guests (and residents willing to pay upward of $2 million for an apartment) with a 16-foot-long gas fireplace and streamlined lobby bar that's frequented by city socialites. A "personal butler" takes you to your room and shows you how to use its touch-screen control panel that works everything, from the temperature to the lights. Decor is minimalist, with sexy touches like Barcelona benches, 42-inch plasma TVs, and leather walls. Bathrooms beckon with deep soaking tubs, 13-inch LCD TVs, rainfall shower heads, and fancy toiletries, but definitely leave your room for an afternoon at the posh two-floor **Remède Spa,** the huge pool and fitness center, and restaurant **Ame,** where chef Hiro Sone, who also owns Terra in Napa Valley, presides over an Asian-influenced menu.

125 Third St. (at Mission St.), San Francisco, CA 94103. www.stregis.com/sanfrancisco. ℂ **877/787-3447** or 415/284-4000. Fax 415/284-4100. 260 units. $459–$679 double; $750–$8,500 suite. AE, DC, DISC, MC, V. Parking $45 per day. Bus: 15, 30, or 45. Streetcar: J, K, L, or M to Montgomery. **Amenities:** 2 restaurants; bar; 24-hr. concierge; health club w/heated lap pool; room service; sauna and steam room; giant spa; whirlpool; Wi-Fi ($15 per day). *In room:* A/C, 2 TVs w/pay movies, hair dryer, high-speed Internet access ($15 per day), minibar.

W San Francisco Hotel ★★ As modern and hip as its fashionable clientele, this 31-story property suits its neighbors, which include the Museum of Modern Art, the Moscone Center, and the Metreon entertainment center. The trendy, urban style extends to the guest rooms, which contain a feather bed with a goose-down comforter and pillows, an upholstered chaise longue, and louvered blinds that open to (usually) great city views. Bathrooms are supersleek and stocked with Bliss products. Whimsical touches like kaleidoscopes and mini Buddha statues make the place all the more homey. Furthering the cool vibe is the bi-level **XYZ** bar and restaurant, which serves wonderful Californian cuisine within a beautiful modern interior full of couches and heated by a massive fireplace. The W boasts a 5,000-square-foot outpost of NYC's **Bliss Spa,** and pets are allowed in guest rooms (in fact, they offer dog-walking and grooming services, as well as litter boxes, beds, bowls, and gifts; a $100 cleaning fee applies). All in all, this is one of the top places to stay in San Francisco, particularly if you enjoy the nightlife scene, which quite literally begins at the W's doorstep.

181 Third St. (btw. Mission and Howard sts.), San Francisco, CA 94103. www.wsanfrancisco.com. ℭ **877/822-0000** or 415/777-5300. Fax 415/817-7823. 410 units. From $359 double; $1,800–$2,500 suite. AE, DC, DISC, MC, V. Valet parking $49. Bus: 15, 30, or 45. Streetcar: J, K, L, or M to Montgomery. **Amenities:** Restaurant; 2 bars; concierge; fitness center; heated atrium pool and Jacuzzi; room service; spa; sun deck. In room: A/C, TV w/pay movies, CD/DVD player, hair dryer, minibar, free Wi-Fi.

EXPENSIVE

The Harbor Court ★★   When the Embarcadero Freeway was torn down after the Big One in 1989, one of the major benefactors was the "wellness-themed" Harbor Court hotel: The 1926 landmark building's backyard view went from a wall of cement to a dazzling vista of the Bay Bridge (be sure to request a bayview room, for an extra fee). Just off the Embarcadero at the edge of the Financial District and a few blocks from AT&T Park, this former YMCA books a lot of corporate travelers, but anyone who seeks stylish, high-quality accommodations—half-canopy beds, large armoires, soundproof windows, and 27-inch LCD TVs—with a superb view and lively scene will be perfectly content here. A major bonus is the free use of the adjoining fitness club, a top-quality YMCA facility with a grand indoor swimming pool. Two more reasons to stay here are the daily hosted evening wine reception and the adjacent **Ozumo Sushi Bar and Robata Grill,** which has a hugely popular happy hour, a cool vibe, and wonderful cuisine.

165 Steuart St. (btw. Mission and Howard sts.), San Francisco, CA 94105. www.harborcourthotel. com. ℭ **866/792-6283** or 415/882-1300. Fax 415/882-1313. 131 units. $87–$295 double; from $519 suite. Continental breakfast $10. AE, DC, DISC, MC, V. Parking $40. Bus: 14 or 80x. Streetcar: Embarcadero. Pets accepted. **Amenities:** Access to adjoining health club and large, heated indoor pool; room service. In room: A/C, TV, hair dryer, minibar, free Wi-Fi.

Hotel Vitale ★★   Perched at the foot of the Embarcadero with outstanding waterfront and Bay Bridge views from east-facing rooms, this 199-unit hotel opened in early 2005 to instant popularity. In addition to its prime location across from the Ferry Building Marketplace (p. 119), Hotel Vitale looks pretty darn chic, from the clean-lined lobby, lounge, and **Americano** restaurant (with a hopping after-work bar scene), to the modern and masculine rooms armed with contemporary perks like flatscreen TVs, CD players with groovy compilations, gourmet minibars, huge bathrooms with walk-in showers (in some), and nature-themed pop art. Despite excellent service from the well-trained staff, a few subtleties separate Vitale from true luxury-hotel status: For example, the fitness room is pretty basic. However, they offer complimentary access to the nearby fancy YMCA, which has all the workout essentials, including a full-size pool—and the penthouse spa with outdoor soaking tubs makes up for a lot. If you can live with a few quirks, it's a very attractive place to stay, especially if you book one of the suites with 270-degree San Francisco views.

8 Mission St. (at Embarcadero), San Francisco, CA 94105. www.hotelvitale.com. ℭ **888/890-8868** or 415/278-3700. Fax 415/278-3750. 199 units. $299–$499 double; from $799 suite. Rates

include morning paper, free morning yoga, and free courtesy car to downtown locations on weekdays. AE, DC, DISC, MC, V. Valet parking $48. Bus: 2, 7, 14, 21, 71, or 71L. **Amenities:** Restaurant; concierge; exercise room; spa. *In room:* A/C, TV w/pay movies, MP3/CD player, hair dryer, minibar, free Wi-Fi.

The InterContinental San Francisco ★★   You can't enter San Francisco from the south without wondering what the odd-but-pretty facade vaguely resembling a cross between a test tube and a larger-than-life aquarium looming in the distance is. But fear not: It's just the second InterContinental property to nab a San Francisco zip code. When the InterContinental began welcoming guests in February 2008, it was the first new lodging to open in the city in 3 whole years. Common spaces have a more neo-Japanese feel, but rooms are quite classic—ask for one on a top floor. Spanning 32 levels, this hotel has views of the city that are hard to beat this side of Market Street. One of the hotel's highlights is its posh lobby lounge, **Bar 888,** where the house specialty grappa is dispensed generously, and the adjoining restaurant, **Luce,** already the recipient of a Michelin star. Another is the luxe **I-Spa,** comprising a state-of-the-art gym and skylit lap pool. The InterContinental isn't the most unique place to stay in town—amenities are pretty much the same stuff you'd expect from any five-star—but it's still every bit as nice, and often cheaper, than its neighboring competitors.

888 Howard St. (at Fifth St.), San Francisco, CA 94105. www.intercontinentalsanfrancisco.com. ℂ **888/811-4273.** Fax 415/616-6501. 500 units. $139–$399 double; from $500 suite. AE, DC, DISC, MC, V. Valet parking $46. Bus: 6, 7, 9, 15, 19, 21, 27, 30, 31, 45, or 71. BART: Civic Center or Powell St. **Amenities:** Restaurant; concierge; fitness center; pool; room service; spa. *In room:* A/C, TV w/pay movies, CD player, hair dryer, minibar, MP3 docking station, Wi-Fi ($15 per day).

MODERATE

The Good Hotel ★   In 2008, this "socially conscious" budget became an affordable alternative to SoMa's traditionally pricey lineup of hotels. With an eco-friendly take on things—hybrid car drivers, for example, get free parking—the hotel is designed to give back to the environment. But the hotel definitely doesn't take itself too seriously. There's a fun-for-all photo booth in the lobby, where your photo outtake lives a long life as part of the hotel's wallpaper scheme, and you'll glimpse the glow-in-the-dark GOOD NIGHT sticker pasted on the ceiling only when you turn the lights off. The sometimes-tongue-in-cheek "Be Good" mantra is scribbled throughout the establishment even in the most unnecessary of places (such as the bedroom). The hotel has a yummy pizzeria on tap, too, **Good Pizza,** serving up artisan thin-crust pies with fresh, local ingredients. *Note:* The neighborhood is one of San Francisco's more interesting (to put it delicately). While as a resident I don't think twice about patrolling the Seventh Street corridor solo, visitors are often a bit more reluctant.

112 Seventh St. (btw. Minna and Mission sts.), San Francisco, CA 94103. www.thegoodhotel.com. ℂ **800/444-5819** or 415/621-7001. Fax 415/621-4069. 117 units. $89–$139 double. AE, DC, DISC, MC, V. Parking free for hybrid cars, $20 for nonhybrids. Bus: 6, 7, 9, 19, 21, 27, 31, or 71. BART: Civic Center or Powell St. Cable car: Powell–Hyde or Powell–Mason line (2 blocks west). **Amenities:** Restaurant; access to heated pool across the street; ZipCar for member use. *In room:* TV, hair dryer, MP3 docking station, free Wi-Fi.

The Mosser ★ 🌿   "Hip on the Cheap" might best sum up the Mosser, a highly atypical budget hotel that incorporates Victorian architecture with modern interior design. It originally opened in 1913 as a luxury hotel, only to be dwarfed by

Elements: A Hip Mission District Hotel

Bad credit? No problem. There's finally a place for the perpetually young and broke to stay and play in the heart of the Mission District. The **Elements Hotel** is sort of a cross between a boutique hotel and a hostel, offering both private rooms and shared dorms, all with private bathrooms. Add to that Wi-Fi access throughout the hotel, a free Internet lounge, rooftop parties, free movie nights, lockers, free continental breakfast, luggage storage, laundry facilities, free linens, TVs (in private rooms), a lively restaurant and lounge called Medjool, and a plethora of inexpensive ethnic cafes in the neighborhood, and, baby, you've got it made. The hotel is at 2524 Mission St., between 21st and 22nd streets (www.elementssf. com; ℂ **866/327-8407** or 415/647-4100). Rates per person are between $25 and $30; expect higher rates and minimum stays during holidays.

the far more modern high-rise hotels that surround it. But a major multimillion-dollar renovation a few years back transformed this aging charmer into a sophisticated, stylish, and surprisingly affordable SoMa lodging. Guest rooms are replete with original Victorian flourishes—bay windows and hand-carved moldings—that juxtapose well with the contemporary custom-designed furnishings, granite showers, stainless-steel fixtures, ceiling fans, Frette linens, double-paned windows, and modern electronics. The least expensive rooms are quite small and share a bathroom, but are an incredible deal for such a central location—3 blocks from Union Square, 2 blocks from the MOMA, and half a block from the cable car turnaround. It also borders on a "sketchy" street, but so do most hotels a few blocks west of Union Square. The hotel's restaurant, **Annabelle's Bar & Bistro,** serves lunch and dinner.

54 Fourth St. (at Market St.), San Francisco, CA 94103. www.themosser.com. ℂ **800/227-3804** or 415/986-4400. Fax 415/495-7653. 166 units, 112 with bathroom. $79–$209 double with bathroom; $47–$119 double without bathroom; $143–$359 suite. Rates include safe-deposit boxes at front desk. AE, DC, DISC, MC, V. Parking $29, plus $8 for oversize vehicles. Streetcar: F, and all underground Muni. BART: All trains. **Amenities:** Restaurant; bar; 24-hr. concierge. *In room:* Ceiling fan, TV, AM/FM stereo w/CD player, hair dryer, Wi-Fi ($9.95 per day).

Nob Hill
VERY EXPENSIVE

The Fairmont San Francisco ★★★ ☺   The granddaddy of Nob Hill's elite cadre of ritzy hotels, the century-old Fairmont is a must-visit if only to marvel at the incredibly glamorous lobby with its vaulted ceilings, Corinthian columns, spectacular spiral staircase, and rococo furniture. Such decadence carries to the guest rooms, where luxuries abound: oversize marble bathrooms, thick down blankets, goose-down king pillows, extralong mattresses, and large walk-in closets. Its perch atop Nob Hill affords spectacular city views from every room—though the panoramics from the Tower Suites are the best. It's fun to indulge in afternoon tea (daily 2:30–4:30pm) in the ornate **Laurel Court** restaurant and lounge, which serves as the hotel's centerpiece. A local institution that's been around since I was a kid is the hotel's **Tonga Room,** a Disneyland-like tropical bar and restaurant where happy hour hops with bands playing on a floating island in a pool, and there's a "rain storm" every 30 minutes.

950 Mason St. (at California St.), San Francisco, CA 94108. www.fairmont.com/sanfrancisco. © **866/540-4491** or 415/772-5000. Fax 415/772-5013. 591 units. Main building $229–$349 double; from $500 suite. Tower $289–$469 double; from $750 suite. Penthouse $12,500. Extra person $30. AE, DC, DISC, MC, V. Parking $50. Cable car: California St. line (direct stop). **Amenities:** 2 restaurants/bars; babysitting; concierge; health club (free for Fairmont President's Club members; $15 per day or $20 per 2 days, nonmembers); room service; Wi-Fi in lobby. *In room:* A/C, TV w/pay movies and video games available, hair dryer, high-speed Internet, kitchenette in some units, minibar.

The Ritz-Carlton, San Francisco ★★★   The Ritz-Carlton, San Francisco has been the benchmark for the city's luxury hotels since it opened in 1991 in the former Metropolitan Insurance headquarters. The interior was restored with fine furnishings, fabrics, and artwork, including a pair of Louis XVI blue marble urns with gilt mountings, and 19th-century Waterford candelabras. Rooms were completely upgraded in 2008 to the tune of $12.5 million. Club rooms, on the top floors, have a dedicated concierge, separate elevator-key access, and complimentary small plates throughout the day. No restaurant in town has more formal service than **Dining Room,** which serves exquisite modern French cuisine with Japanese influence by famed chef Ron Siegel (a veteran of French Laundry and Charles Nob Hill, and one of the only non-Japanese chefs to win the Iron Chef competition). The less formal **Terrace Restaurant** offers contemporary Mediterranean cuisine and the city's most lavish Sunday champagne/jazz brunch. The **Lobby lounge** serves classic afternoon tea and cocktails with low-key live entertainment daily, and sushi Wednesday through Saturday.

600 Stockton St. (btw. Pine and California sts.), San Francisco, CA 94108. www.ritzcarlton.com. © **800/241-3333** or 415/296-7465. Fax 415/291-0288. 336 units. $445–$480 double; $499–$629 club-level double; $579–$699 executive suite. Buffet breakfast $32; Sun champagne brunch $65. Weekend discounts and packages available. AE, DC, DISC, MC, V. Parking $62. Cable car: California St. cable car line (direct stop). **Amenities:** 2 restaurants; 3 bars; concierge; outstanding fitness center; Jacuzzi; indoor pool; room service; steam room. *In room:* A/C, TV w/ pay movies, hair dryer, minibar, Wi-Fi ($13 per day).

North Beach & Fisherman's Wharf

EXPENSIVE

Argonaut Hotel ★★ ☺   The four-story timber-and-brick landmark building, the Argonaut Hotel, was originally built in 1908 as a warehouse for the California Fruit Canners Association. Its rooms are whimsically decorated to emulate a luxury cruise ship in cheerful nautical colors (though evidence of its modest past appears in original brick walls, large timbers, and steel warehouse doors). Suites have wonderful views and come fully loaded with telescopes and spa tubs, and "view" rooms overlook the wharf or bay (some offer fabulous views of Alcatraz and the Golden Gate Bridge). The friendly staff goes out of their way to make little ones feel at home and allows each pint-size guest to pick a new plaything from the hotel's "treasure chest." The hotel is attached to the **Blue Mermaid Chowder House & Bar,** a friendly casual eatery. *Tip:* The concierge seems to be able to work wonders when you need tickets to Alcatraz—even when the trips are officially sold out.

495 Jefferson St. (at Hyde St.), San Francisco, CA 94109. www.argonauthotel.com. © **866/415-0704** or 415/563-0800. Fax 415/563-2800. 252 units. $189–$389 double; $489–$1,089 suite. Rates include evening wine in the lobby, daily newspaper, and child-friendly perks like cribs and

strollers. AE, DC, DISC, MC, V. Parking $39. Bus: 10, 30, or 47. Streetcar: F. Cable car: Powell–Hyde line. **Amenities:** Restaurant; bar; concierge; fitness center; Wi-Fi in public areas; yoga video and mats. *In room:* A/C, flatscreen TV w/Nintendo and pay movies, Web TV, DVD and CD players, hair dryer, free high-speed Internet access, minibar.

MODERATE

Best Western Tuscan Inn at Fisherman's Wharf ★★   Like an island of
respectability in a sea of touristy schlock, this boutique Best Western is one of the best midrange hotels at Fisherman's Wharf. It continues to exude a level of style and comfort far beyond that of its neighboring competitors. For example, every evening in the plush lobby warmed by a grand fireplace, a wine reception is hosted by the manager, and the adjoining **Café Pescatore** serves wonderful pizzas and grilled meats from their wood-burning oven. The rooms are a definite cut above competing Fisherman's Wharf hotels: All are handsomely decorated and have writing desks and armchairs. The only caveat is the lack of scenic views—a small price to pay for a good hotel in a prime location.

425 North Point St. (at Mason St.), San Francisco, CA 94133. www.tuscaninn.com. ℂ **800/648-4626** or 415/561-1100. Fax 415/561-1199. 221 units. $149–$269. Rates include coffee, tea, and evening wine reception. AE, DC, DISC, MC, V. Parking $42. Bus: 10, 15, or 47. Cable car: Powell–Mason line. Pets welcome for $50. **Amenities:** Concierge; access to nearby gym; room service. *In room:* A/C, TV w/video games and pay movies, hair dryer, minibar, free Wi-Fi.

The Hotel Bohème ★★ 🏠   Romance awaits at the intimate Hotel Bohème.
Although it's on the busiest avenue in North Beach, once you climb the staircase to this narrow second-floor boutique hotel, you'll discover a style and demeanor reminiscent of a home on Russian Hill. Beat-era jazz photos decorate the hallways and, while there are no common areas other than a little booth for check-in and concierge, rooms are truly sweet, with gauze-draped canopies, stylish decor such as ornate parasols shading ceiling lights, and dramatically colored walls. Although the bathrooms are spiffy, they're tiny and have showers only. The staff is ultrahospitable, and bonuses include sherry in the lobby each afternoon. Some fabulous cafes, restaurants, bars, and shops along Columbus Avenue are just a few steps away, and Chinatown and Union Square are within easy walking distance. *Tip:* Request a room off the street side, which is quieter.

444 Columbus Ave. (btw. Vallejo and Green sts.), San Francisco, CA 94133. www.hotelboheme. com. ℂ **415/433-9111.** Fax 415/362-6292. 15 units. $174–$214 double. Rates include afternoon sherry. AE, DC, DISC, MC, V. Parking $12–$31 at nearby public garages. Bus: 12, 15, 30, 41, 45, or 83. Cable car: Powell–Mason line. **Amenities:** Concierge. *In room:* TV, hair dryer, free Wi-Fi.

INEXPENSIVE

The San Remo Hotel ★ 🖉   This small, European-style *pensione* is one of the
best budget hotels in San Francisco. In a quiet North Beach neighborhood, within walking distance of Fisherman's Wharf, the Italianate Victorian structure originally served as a boardinghouse for dockworkers displaced by the great fire of 1906. As a result, the rooms are small and bathrooms are shared, but all is forgiven when it comes time to pay the bill. Rooms are decorated in cozy country style, with brass and iron beds; oak, maple, or pine armoires; and wicker furnishings. The immaculate shared bathrooms feature tubs and brass pull-chain toilets with oak tanks and brass fixtures. If the penthouse—which has its own bathroom, TV, fridge, and patio—is available, book it: You won't find a more romantic place to stay in San Francisco for so little money.

2237 Mason St. (at Chestnut St.), San Francisco, CA 94133. www.sanremohotel.com. ☎ **800/352-7366** or 415/776-8688. Fax 415/776-2811. 62 units, 61 with shared bathroom. $75–$99 double; $175–$185 penthouse suite. AE, DC, MC, V. Self-parking $13–$14. Bus: 10, 15, 30, or 47. Streetcar: F. Cable car: Powell–Mason line. **Amenities:** Access to nearby health club; Internet kiosk in lobby; 2 massage chairs; TV room. *In room:* Ceiling fan.

The Wharf Inn 🗡 This is my top choice for good-value/great-location lodging at Fisherman's Wharf. The inn offers your standard no-frills motel accommodations, but it's the location—right next to the one of the most popular tourist attractions in the world—that counts. The rooms are done in pleasant tones of earth, muted greens, and burnt orange, but more important, they are smack-dab in the middle of the wharf, a mere 2 blocks from PIER 39 and the cable car turn-around, and within walking distance of the Embarcadero and North Beach. The inn is ideal for car-bound families because parking is free (that saves at least $30 a day right off the bat).

2601 Mason St. (at Beach St.), San Francisco, CA 94133. www.wharfinn.com. ☎ **877/275-7889** or 415/673-7411. Fax 415/776-2181. 51 units. $125–$159 double; $299–$439 penthouse. AE, DC, DISC, MC, V. Free parking. Bus: 10, 15, 39, or 47. Streetcar: F. Cable car: Powell–Mason or Powell–Hyde line. **Amenities:** Access to nearby health club ($10 per day). *In room:* TV, hair dryer (upon request), free Wi-Fi.

Cow Hollow & Pacific Heights

EXPENSIVE

Hotel Del Sol ★★ ☺ 🗡 The cheeriest motel in town is just 2 blocks off the Marina District's bustling section of Lombard. Three-level Hotel del Sol is all about festive flair: The sunshine theme extends from the Miami Beach–style use of vibrant color, as in the yellow, red, orange, and blue exterior, to the heated courtyard pool, which beckons the youngish clientele as they head for their cars parked (for free!—unheard of in San Francisco) in cabana-like spaces. This is also one of the most family-friendly places to stay, with a "Kids are VIPs" program, including a family suite (with bunks and toys); a library of books, toys, and videos; childproofing kits; rooms that have been baby-proofed; bonded babysitting services; evening cookies and milk; pool toys; and kids' sunglasses and visors.

3100 Webster St. (at Greenwich St.), San Francisco, CA 94123. www.thehoteldelsol.com. ☎ **877/433-5765** or 415/921-5520. Fax 415/931-4137. 57 units. $139–$199 double; $179–$239 suite. Rates include continental breakfast and free newspapers in the lobby. AE, DC, DISC, MC, V. Free parking. Bus: 22, 28, 41, 43, 45, or 76. **Amenities:** Heated outdoor pool. *In room:* TV/VCR, CD player, fridge and DVD in suites only, kitchenette in 3 units, Wi-Fi ($7.95 per day).

Hotel Drisco ★★ 🎁 On one of the most sought-after blocks of residential property in all of San Francisco, the Drisco, built in 1903, is one of the city's best small hotels. Refinements are evident, from the welcoming lobby to the calming ambience of the cream, yellow, and light green guest rooms. As in the neighboring mansions, traditional custom-made furnishings and thick, luxurious fabrics abound here. The hotel's comfy beds will make you want to loll late into the morning before primping in the large marble bathrooms, complete with robes and slippers, and then enjoying a leisurely breakfast in the newly redecorated dining room. Each suite has a couch that unfolds into a bed (although you would never guess from the looks of it), 2 HDTVs, and superior views. A 24-hour coffee and tea service is available in the sitting room just off the lobby. Street parking is at no cost and the hotel's staff will help you find a convenient spot.

2901 Pacific Ave. (at Broderick St.), San Francisco, CA 94115. www.hoteldrisco.com. © **800/634-7277** or 415/346-2880. Fax 415/567-5537. 48 units. $169–$259 deluxe king; $351–$519 suite. Rates include gourmet continental breakfast and evening wine and cheese. AE, DC, DISC, MC, V. Street parking available. Bus: 3 or 24. **Amenities:** Concierge; exercise room and free pass to YMCA; room service. *In room:* TV/DVD, CD player, fridge, hair dryer, minibar, free Wi-Fi.

INEXPENSIVE

Marina Inn ★ 🔥 Marina Inn is one of the best low-priced hotels in San Francisco. How it offers so much for so little is mystifying. Each guest room in the 1924 four-story Victorian looks like something from a country-furnishings catalog, complete with rustic pinewood furniture, a four-poster bed with silky-soft comforter, pretty wallpaper, and soothing tones of rose, hunter green, and pale yellow. You also get remote-control televisions discreetly hidden in pine cabinetry—all for as little as $60 a night. Combined with continental breakfast, friendly service, free Wi-Fi, and an armada of shops and restaurants within easy walking distance, it is one of my top choices for best overall value. *Note:* Traffic can be a bit noisy here, so the hotel added double panes on windows facing the street.

3110 Octavia St. (at Lombard St.), San Francisco, CA 94123. www.marinainn.com. © **800/274-1420** or 415/928-1000. Fax 415/928-5909. 40 units. $59–$69. Rates include continental breakfast. AE, DC, DISC, MC, V. Bus: 28, 30, 43, or 76. *In room:* TV, hair dryer (upon request), free Wi-Fi.

Marina Motel Established in 1939, the Marina Motel is one of San Francisco's first motels, built for the opening of the Golden Gate Bridge. The same family has owned this peach-colored, Spanish-style stucco building for three generations, and they've taken exquisite care of it. All rooms look out onto an inner courtyard, which is awash with beautiful flowering plants and wall paintings by local artists. Though the rooms show minor signs of wear and tear, they're all quite clean, bright, quiet, and pleasantly decorated with framed lithographs of old San Francisco. Two-bedroom suites come with fully equipped kitchens. The Presidio and Marina Green are mere blocks away, and you can easily catch a bus downtown. The only downside is the street noise, which is likely to burden light sleepers. *Bonus:* All rooms include a breakfast coupon valid for two entrees for the price of one at nearby **Judy's Restaurant.**

2576 Lombard St. (btw. Divisadero and Broderick sts.), San Francisco, CA 94123. www.marina motel.com. © **800/346-6118** or 415/921-9406. Fax 415/921-0364. 38 units. $75–$165 double; $109–$199 suite. Lower rates in winter. Rates include 2-for-1 breakfast coupon at nearby cafe. AE, DISC, MC, V. Free covered parking. Bus: 28, 29, 30, 43, or 45. Dogs accepted ($10 nightly fee). *In room:* Fridge, hair dryer.

Civic Center & Environs

MODERATE

The Phoenix Hotel ★★ If you'd like to tell your friends you stayed in the same hotel as David Bowie, Keanu Reeves, Moby, Franz Ferdinand, and Interpol, this is the place to go. On the fringes of San Francisco's aromatic Tenderloin District (rife with the homeless and addicts), this well-sheltered retro 1950s-style hotel is a gathering place for visiting rock musicians, writers, and filmmakers who crave a dose of Southern California—hence the palm trees and pastel colors. The focal point of the Palm Springs–style hotel is a small, heated outdoor pool adorned with a mural by artist Francis Forlenza and ensconced in a modern sculpture garden. Rooms are more pop than plush, with bright island-inspired furnishings and original local art; each faces the pool. If you want luxury and quiet, stay elsewhere, but if you're looking for a great scene, head to the Phoenix.

601 Eddy St. (at Larkin St.), San Francisco, CA 94109. www.thephoenixhotel.com. (C) **800/248-9466** or 415/776-1380. Fax 415/885-3109. 44 units. $119–$149 double; $219–$399 suite. Rates include continental breakfast and free passes to Kabuki Springs & Spa. AE, DC, MC, V. Free parking. Bus: 19, 31, 38, or 47. **Amenities:** Bar; concierge; heated outdoor pool. *In room:* TV, VCR (upon request), fridge and microwave (some rooms), hair dryer, free Wi-Fi.

The Queen Anne Hotel ★★ 🛡 This majestic 1890 Victorian charmer was once a grooming school for upper-class young women. Restored in 1980 and renovated in early 2006, the four-story building recalls San Francisco's golden days. Walk under rich red draperies to the lavish "grand salon" lobby replete with English oak wainscoting and period antiques, and it feels like a different era. Guest rooms also contain a profusion of antiques—armoires, marble-top dressers, and other Victorian-era pieces. Some have corner turret bay windows that look out on tree-lined streets, as well as separate parlor areas and wet bars; others have cozy reading nooks and fireplaces. All rooms have phones and nice bath amenities in their marble-tiled bathrooms. Guests can relax in the parlor, with two fireplaces, or in the hotel library. If you don't mind staying outside the downtown area, this hotel is highly recommended and very classic San Francisco.

1590 Sutter St. (btw. Laguna and Webster sts.), San Francisco, CA 94115. www.queenanne.com. (C) **800/277-3970** or 415/441-2828. Fax 415/775-5212. 48 units. $110–$199 double; $169–$350 suite. Extra person $10. Rates include continental breakfast on weekday mornings, afternoon tea and sherry, and morning newspaper. AE, DC, DISC, MC, V. Parking $14. Bus: 2, 3, or 4. **Amenities:** 24-hr. concierge; access to nearby health club for $10. *In room:* TV, hair dryer, free Wi-Fi.

Haight-Ashbury & the Castro

The Parker Guest House ★★ This is the best B&B option in the Castro, and one of the best in the entire city. In fact, even some of the better hotels could learn a thing or two from this fashionable, gay-friendly, 5,000-square-foot, 1909 beautifully restored Edwardian home and adjacent annex a few blocks from the heart of the Castro's action. Within the bright, cheery urban compound, period antiques abound. But thankfully, the spacious guest rooms are wonderfully updated with smart patterned furnishings, voice mail, robes, and spotless private bathrooms (plus amenities) en suite or, in two cases, across the hall. A fire burns nightly in the cozy living room, and guests are also welcome to make themselves at home in the wood-paneled common library (with fireplace and piano), sunny breakfast room overlooking the garden, and spacious garden with fountains and a steam room. Animal lovers will appreciate the companionship of the house pugs, Porter, Patsy, and Perry.

520 Church St. (btw. 17th and 18th sts.), San Francisco, CA 94114. www.parkerguesthouse.com. (C) **888/520-7275** or 415/621-3222. Fax 415/621-4139. 21 units. $129–$199 double; $219 junior suite. Rates include extended continental breakfast and evening wine and cheese. AE, DISC, MC, V. Self-parking $17. Bus: 22 or 33. Streetcar: J Church. **Amenities:** Concierge; access to nearby health club; steam room. *In room:* TV, hair dryer, free Wi-Fi.

Stanyan Park Hotel ★★ ☺ 🛡 The only real hotel on the east end of Golden Gate Park and the west end of funky-chic Haight Street, this small inn offers classic San Francisco–style living at a very affordable price. The Victorian structure, which has operated as a hotel under a variety of names since the turn of the 20th century and is on the National Register of Historic Places, offers good-size rooms all done in period decor. Its three stories are decorated with antique furnishings; Victorian wallpaper; and pastel quilts, curtains, and carpets. Families will appreciate the six one- and two-bedroom suites, each of which has a full kitchen and formal dining and living rooms and can sleep up to six comfortably. Tea is served each afternoon from 4 to 6pm. Continental breakfast is served in the dining room off the lobby from 6 to 10am. All rooms are nonsmoking.

750 Stanyan St. (at Waller St.), San Francisco, CA 94117. www.stanyanpark.com. © **415/751-1000.** Fax 415/668-5454. 36 units. $139–$225 double; $275–$350 suite. Rates include continental breakfast and afternoon and evening tea service. Rollaway $20; cribs free. AE, DISC, MC, V. Off-site parking $14. Bus: 7, 33, 43, 66, or 71. Streetcar: N. *In room:* TV, hair dryer, kitchen (in suites only), free Wi-Fi.

The Willows Inn ★ Right in the heart of the Castro, the all-nonsmoking Willows Inn employs a staff eager to greet and attend to their mostly gay and lesbian guests. The country and antique willow furnishings don't strictly suit a 1903 Edwardian home, but everything's quite comfortable—especially considering the extras, which include an expanded continental breakfast (fresh fruit, yogurt, baked goods, gourmet coffee, eggs, and orange juice), the morning paper, nightly cocktails, a sitting room (with a DVD player), and a pantry with limited kitchen facilities. The homey rooms vary in size from large (queen-size bed) to smaller (double bed) and are priced accordingly. Each room has a vanity sink, and all the rooms share eight water closets and shower rooms.

710 14th St. (near Church and Market sts.), San Francisco, CA 94114. www.willowssf.com. © **800/431-0277** or 415/431-4770. Fax 415/431-5295. 12 units, none with bathroom. $99–$140 double; $160 suite. Rates include continental breakfast. AE, DC, DISC, MC, V. Bus: 22 or 37. Streetcar: Church St. station (across the street) or F. *In room:* TV/VCR, fridge, free Wi-Fi.

WHERE TO EAT

San Francisco's dining scene is one of the best in the world. Below is a cross section of the city's best restaurants, in every price range. For a greater selection of reviews, pick up a copy of *Frommer's San Francisco* (John Wiley & Sons, Inc.).

Union Square

EXPENSIVE

Grand Café ★ FRENCH If you aren't interested in exploring restaurants beyond those in Union Square and want a huge dose of atmosphere with your seared salmon, Grand Café is your best bet. Its claims to fame? The grandest dining room in San Francisco, an enormous 156-seat, turn-of-the-20th-century ballroomlike dining oasis whose whimsical Art Nouveau sensibility combines with a Parisian train station. To match the surroundings, the menu features such extravagant French-inspired California dishes as *carre d'agneau á la forestiere* (Sonoma rack of lamb crusted with herbed mixed-vegetable tian, in wild mushroom and pearl onion sauce) or *cassolette de la mer* (lobster tail, prawns, sea bass, mussels, littleneck clams, and savoy cabbage in tomato Pastis lobster broth). You can also drop by for a lighter meal or an après-theater drink in the more casual bar, which offers similar dishes for about half the price. There's also a wonderful selection of small-batch American whiskeys and single-malt Scotches.

THE PRESIDIO

MARINA

Marina Green
Marina Blvd.

Fort
Mason

Cervantes Blvd.

North Point St.

Bay St.

Divisadero St.

Avila St.

Pierce St.

Moscone
Rec. Ctr.

Francisco St.

Chestnut St.

COW
HOLLOW

Lombard St.

101

Greenwich St.

Franklin St.

Octavia St.

Filbert St.

Broderick St.

Union St.

Fillmore St.

Green St.

Vallejo St.

Gough St.

Broadway

Pacific Ave.

Laguna St.

PACIFIC
HEIGHTS

Jackson St.

Scott St.

Alta
Plaza

Lafayette
Park

Buchanan St.

Washington St.

Clay St.

Sacramento St.

PRESIDIO
HEIGHTS

Lake St.

Cornwall St.

Clement St.

California St.

Pine St.

Bush St.

5th Ave.
2nd Ave.

Cherry St.

Maple St.

Laurel St.

Walnut St.

Presidio Ave.

Lyon St.

Baker St.

Sutter St.

Post St.

Japan Center

WESTERN
ADDITION

Palm Ave.

Jordan Ave.

Commonwealth Ave.

Parker Ave.

Spruce St.

Collins St.

Wood St.

Euclid Ave.

Hamilton Sq.

Geary Blvd.

O'Farrell St.

Steiner St.

Webster St.

6th Ave.
4th Ave.
3rd Ave.

Arguello Blvd.

Anza St.

UNIVERSITY OF
SAN FRANCISCO

Masonic Ave.

Turk Blvd.

Golden Gate Ave.

Ellis St.

Eddy St.

Jefferson
Square

RICHMOND

Balboa St.

Fulton St.

Cabrillo St.

U.S.F.

McAllister St.

Grove St.

Alamo
Square

Fulton St.

Divisadero St.

HAYES
VALLEY

Octavia St.

Fell St.

Laguna St.

Willard St.

Conservatory
of Flowers

John F. Kennedy Dr.

Stanyan St.

Cole St.

Central Ave.

Lyon St.

Hayes St.

Pierce St.

Fillmore St.

GOLDEN GATE PARK

The Panhandle

Fell St.

Clayton St.

HAIGHT-
ASHBURY

Oak St.

Page St.

Haight St.

Buena
Vista
Park

Duboce
Park

Duboce Ave.

Waller St.

Hermann St.

Kezar Dr.

Ashbury St.

Alpine Terr.

Sanchez St.

Kezar
Stadium

Frederick St.

Downey St.

Buena Vista Ave.

14th St.

Noe St.

Lincoln Wy.

Hugo St.

Carl St.

Belvedere St.

15th St.

Corona
Heights
Park

Castro St.

Dolores St.

Guerrero St.

INNER
SUNSET

UNIVERSITY OF
CALIFORNIA–
SAN FRANCISCO

Shrader St.

Cole St.

States St.

CASTRO

16th St.

Church St.

Mission
Dolores

5th Ave.
6th Ave.

Parnassus Ave.

Carmel St.

Market St.

Castro Theatre

17th St.

18th St.

Mission
Dolores
Park

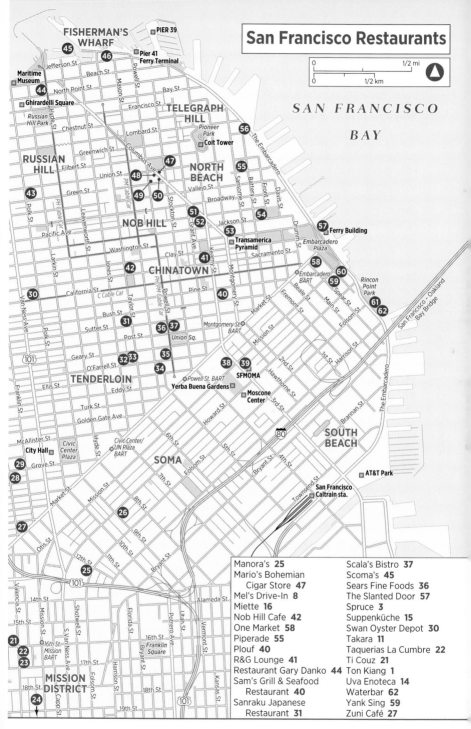

San Francisco Restaurants

FISHERMAN'S WHARF
PIER 39
Pier 41 Ferry Terminal
Maritime Museum
Ghirardelli Square
Russian Hill Park
RUSSIAN HILL
TELEGRAPH HILL
Pioneer Park
Coit Tower
NORTH BEACH
NOB HILL
CHINATOWN
Transamerica Pyramid
Ferry Building
Embarcadero Plaza
Embarcadero BART
Rincon Point Park
SAN FRANCISCO BAY
TENDERLOIN
Union Sq.
Montgomery St. BART
Powell St. BART
Yerba Buena Gardens
SFMOMA
Moscone Center
SOUTH BEACH
City Hall
Civic Center/UN Plaza BART
Civic Center Plaza
SOMA
AT&T Park
San Francisco Caltrain sta.
MISSION DISTRICT
16th St. Mission BART
San Francisco-Oakland Bay Bridge

Manora's **25**
Mario's Bohemian
  Cigar Store **47**
Mel's Drive-In **8**
Miette **16**
Nob Hill Cafe **42**
One Market **58**
Piperade **55**
Plouf **40**
R&G Lounge **41**
Restaurant Gary Danko **44**
Sam's Grill & Seafood
  Restaurant **40**
Sanraku Japanese
  Restaurant **31**

Scala's Bistro **37**
Scoma's **45**
Sears Fine Foods **36**
The Slanted Door **57**
Spruce **3**
Suppenküche **15**
Swan Oyster Depot **30**
Takara **11**
Taquerias La Cumbre **22**
Ti Couz **21**
Ton Kiang **1**
Uva Enoteca **14**
Waterbar **62**
Yank Sing **59**
Zuni Café **27**

87

501 Geary St. (at Taylor St., adjacent to the Hotel Monaco). ✆ **415/292-0101.** www.grandcafe-sf. com. Reservations recommended. Main courses $18–$33. AE, DC, DISC, MC, V. Mon–Fri 7–10:30am and 11:30am–2:30pm; Sat–Sun 8am–2:30pm; Fri–Sat 5–11pm; Sun–Thurs 5–10pm. Valet parking free at brunch, $15 for 3 hr. at dinner, $3 each additional half-hour. Bus: 2, 3, 4, 27, or 38.

Wayfare Tavern ★★ AMERICAN   One of three recent restaurants to open in the Bay Area courtesy of *Food Network* celebrity chef Tyler Florence, Wayfare Tavern was the most buzzed-about dining spot to open in 2010. With upscale pub grub in a hunting lodgelike environment—animal heads adorn the walls, the color palette sticks to hues of khaki and black—this intimate experience added some much-needed juice to the Financial District's somewhat tired food scene.

Florence puts his own creative spin on classic comfort foods like mac and cheese, pot roast, and grits. The Wayfare Burger "Le Grand" may very well be the most popular item on the menu: a hunk of grass-fed proprietary grind, with local Mt. Tam cheese, roasted onion, and smoked back on brioche (with the option to add a Petaluma egg, sunny side up). More inventive fare like chicken liver mousse with pomelo marmalade and toasted brioche or poutine, that Canadian favorite of french fries with mozzarella curd, braised short rib and truffle gravy, round out the menu. The portion sizes are pretty generous; you'll best understand what Wayfare Tavern is all about if you order a combination of dishes for the table to share.

558 Sacramento St. (at Leidesdorff Alley). ✆ **415/772-9060.** www.wayfaretavern.com. Reservations recommended. Main courses $22–$28. AE, DC, DISC, MC, V. Mon–Fri 11am–11pm; Sat–Sun 5–11pm. Bus: 1, 10, 12, 30X, 41, or 82X.

MODERATE

Bocadillos ★★ 🏠 SPANISH/BASQUE TAPAS   The sister to Piperade (p. 98) is flat-out fabulous if you're in the mood for tapas or Spanish-influenced small plates and a seat at the communal table. Executive chef Gerald Hirigoyen celebrates his Basque roots with outstanding offerings such as warm octopus with confit potatoes and piquillos, scallops "mole cortado" with sherry and orange, cold poached foie gras with calamari and grape salpicon, and astounding warm chocolate cake with sautéed bananas. Just watch your budget—at up to $12 per plate, the tab can creep up on you. You might also want to check out their breakfast, which includes baked eggs with chorizo and manchego cheese. Don't come anticipating a formal dining environment or a cocktail: This small Financial District space is cafe-casual and serves beer and wine only.

710 Montgomery St. (at Washington St.). ✆ **415/982-2622.** www.bocasf.com. Breakfast items $2–$6; lunch and dinner small items $7–$15. AE, DC, DISC, MC, V. Mon–Wed 7am–10pm; Thurs–Fri 7am–10:30pm; Sat 5–10:30pm. Closed Sun. Bus: 15, 30X, or 41.

Hana Zen ★ 🏠 JAPANESE   Even most locals don't know about this Japanese restaurant, mistaking it for just another touristy sushi bar. Sure, they serve good sushi, but what makes this place special is the yakitori bar, which cranks out savory skewered and grilled meats and veggies cooked over 500-degree charcoal. It's all prepared Benihana-style, with acrobatic chefs whirling knives around and making lots of *"hai!"* "ahhh," and "ooohh" sounds. My favorite dishes are the asparagus spears wrapped in thinly sliced pork, and the grilled marinated shiitake mushrooms. A few tables are perched beside windows overlooking downtown, but the best seats are at the long, arched yakitori bar, where deft chefs spear nearly 30 versions of the meal on a stick. You can order either one pair at a time if you like the show, or all at once for a feast; about a half-dozen make a meal. The terminally indecisive can opt for the Yakitori Dinner Set for $32, which makes an interesting meal for two.

115 Cyril Magnin St. (at Ellis St.). © **415/421-2101.** www.hanazenrestaurant.com. Sushi/yakitori items $5–$10. AE, DC, MC, V. Sun–Thurs 11:30am–midnight; Fri–Sat 11:30am–1am. Bus: 27 or 38.

Kuleto's ★ ITALIAN   Kuleto's is one of downtown's Italian darlings. Muscle your way into a seat at the antipasto bar or at the chef's counter overlooking the kitchen and fill up on Italian specialties and selections from the wine list featuring 30 by-the-glass options. Partake in the likes of penne pasta drenched in tangy lamb-sausage marinara sauce, clam linguine (generously overloaded with fresh clams), or any of the grilled fresh-fish specials in the casually refined dining room. If you don't arrive by 6pm, expect to wait—this place fills up fast. Not to worry, though: You can always cross the hotel lobby to the wine bar, which also serves the full menu and is open from 6 to 10pm daily. Don't have time to sit down? Try **Caffè Kuleto's,** which is located just outside and serves panini, pastries, salads, and espresso to go, open daily from 7am to 8pm.

In the Villa Florence Hotel, 221 Powell St. (btw. Geary and O'Farrell sts.). © **415/397-7720.** www. kuletos.com. Reservations recommended. Breakfast $5–$15; main courses $16–$37. AE, DC, DISC, MC, V. Mon–Fri 7–10:30am and 11:30am–11pm; Sat–Sun 8:30–10:30am and 11:30am–11pm. Bus: 2, 3, 4, or 38. Streetcar: All streetcars. Cable car: Powell–Mason or Powell–Hyde line.

Scala's Bistro ★★ FRENCH/ITALIAN   Firmly entrenched at the base of the refurbished Sir Francis Drake hotel, this downtown favorite blends Italian bistro and old-world atmosphere with jovial and bustling results. Offering just the right balance of elegance and informality, this is a perfect place to stop in for a late-night bite. Of the tempting array of Italian and French dishes, it's de rigueur to start with the "Earth and Surf" calamari appetizer with grilled portobello mushrooms. Golden beet salad and garlic cream mussels are also good bets. Generous portions of moist, rich duck-leg confit will satisfy hungry appetites, but if you can order only one thing, make it Scala's signature dish: seared salmon. Resting on a bed of creamy buttermilk mashed potatoes and accented with a tomato, chive, and white-wine sauce, it's downright delicious. Finish with Bostini cream pie, a dreamy combo of vanilla custard and orange chiffon cake with a warm chocolate glaze.

In the Sir Francis Drake hotel, 432 Powell St. (at Sutter St.). © **415/395-8555.** www.scalasbistro. com. Reservations recommended. Breakfast $7–$10; main courses $12–$30 lunch and dinner. AE, DC, DISC, MC, V. Daily 7–10:30am and 11:30am–midnight. Bus: 2, 3, 4, 30, 45, or 76. Cable car: Powell–Hyde line.

INEXPENSIVE

Dottie's True Blue Café ★ ☺ AMERICAN/BREAKFAST   This family-owned breakfast restaurant is one of my favorite downtown diners. This is the kind of place you'd expect to see off Route 66, where most customers are on a first-name basis with the staff and everyone is welcomed with a hearty hello and steaming mug of coffee. Dottie's serves far-above-average American morning fare (big portions of French toast, pancakes, bacon and eggs, omelets, and the like), delivered to tables laminated with old movie-star photos on rugged, diner-quality plates. Whatever you order arrives with delicious homemade bread, muffins, or scones, as well as house-made jelly. There are also daily specials and vegetarian dishes.

In the Pacific Bay Inn, 522 Jones St. (at O'Farrell St.). ✆ **415/885-2767.** Reservations not accepted. Breakfast $5–$11. DISC, MC, V. Wed–Mon 7:30am–3pm (lunch 11:30am–3pm). Bus: 2, 3, 4, 27, or 38. Cable car: Powell–Mason line.

Sanraku Japanese Restaurant ★ 🍴 JAPANESE/SUSHI A perfect combination of great cooked dishes and sushi at bargain prices makes this straightforward, bright, and busy restaurant the best choice in the area for Japanese food. The friendly, hardworking staff does its best to keep up with diners' demands, but the restaurant gets quite busy during lunch, when a special box lunch of the likes of California roll, soup, salad, deep-fried salmon roll, and beef with noodles with steamed rice comes at a very digestible $11. The main menu, which is always available, features great sesame chicken with teriyaki sauce and rice; tempura; a vast selection of *nigiri* (raw fish sushi) and rolls; and delicious combination plates of sushi, sashimi, and teriyaki. Dinner sees brisk business, too, but a table always seems to be available.

704 Sutter St. (at Taylor St.). ✆ **415/771-0803.** www.sanraku.com. Main courses $7–$13 lunch, $10–$26 dinner; 7-course fixed-price dinner $55. AE, DC, DISC, MC, V. Mon–Sat lunch 11am–4pm, dinner 4–10pm; Sun dinner 4–10pm. Bus: 2, 3, 4, 27, or 38. Cable car: Powell–Mason line.

Sears Fine Foods ★ ☺ AMERICAN Sears is not just another downtown diner—it's an old-fashioned institution, famous for its crispy, dark-brown waffles; light sourdough French toast served with house-made strawberry preserves; and silver-dollar-size Swedish pancakes (18 per serving!). As the story goes, Ben Sears, a retired clown, founded the diner in 1938. His Swedish wife, Hilbur, was responsible for the legendary pancakes, which, although the restaurant is under new ownership, are still whipped up according to her family's secret recipe. Sears also offers classic lunch and dinner fare—try the Reuben for lunch and codfish and chips for dinner, followed by a big slice of pie for dessert. Breakfast is served until 3pm every day, and plan on a brief wait to be seated on weekends.

439 Powell St. (btw. Post and Sutter sts.). ✆ **415/986-0700.** www.searsfinefood.com. Reservations accepted for parties of 6 or more. Breakfast $3–$12; salads and soups $3–$8; main courses $14–$29. AE, DC, MC, V. Daily 6:30am–10pm (breakfast until 3pm). Bus: 2, 3, 4, or 38. Cable car: Powell–Mason or Powell–Hyde line.

SoMa

EXPENSIVE

Ame ★★★ NEW AMERICAN Restaurateurs Hiro Sone and Lissa Doumani, the owners of the sensational Napa Valley restaurant Terra, have blessed us foodies with an equally fantastic restaurant in the city. On the ground level of the *très* chic St. Regis Hotel, the L-shaped dining room with its mesquite flooring, red accents, and long striped curtains fits right in with the hotel's minimalist theme. Sone, a master of Japanese, French, and Italian cuisines, offers an array of exotic selections that are utterly tempting: ragout of sweetbreads with salsify and forest mushrooms; Japanese egg custard with lobster and urchin; mushroom risotto topped with foie gras; grilled Wagyu beef with fried Miyagi oysters and rémoulade sauce. If you can't figure out where to start on a menu where everything looks wonderful, opt for Sone's A Taste of Ame, an $85 five-course tasting menu that, for an additional $65, is paired with a bevy of wines by the glass. After dinner, be sure to enjoy an aperitif at the hotel's swank bar where the city's elite congregate nightly.

689 Mission St. (at Third St.). ℂ **415/284-4040.** www.amerestaurant.com. Reservations recommended. Main courses $22–$38. AE, DC, DISC, MC, V. Daily 5:30–10pm. Valet parking $15 for the 1st 3 hr. Bus: 15, 30, or 45. Streetcar: J, K, L, or M to Montgomery.

Boulevard ★★ AMERICAN   Master restaurant designer Pat Kuleto and chef Nancy Oakes are behind one of San Francisco's most beloved restaurants. Inside, the historic Belle Epoque interior with its vaulted brick ceilings, floral banquettes, mosaic floor, and tulip-shaped lamps sets the stage for Oakes's equally impressive sculptural and mouthwatering upscale American dishes. Starters alone could make a perfect meal, especially if you indulge in pan-seared day boat sea scallops with sautéed fresh hearts of palm, pomelo, basil, toasted shallots, and macadamia nuts, or the pan-seared foie gras with rhubarb syrup on wholegrain toast. The nine or so main courses are equally creative and might include grilled Pacific sea bass with fresh gulf prawns, grilled artichoke, spring asparagus, and green garlic purée; or fire-roasted Angus filet with crispy Yukon gold potatoes, béarnaise sauce, spinach, crimini mushrooms, and red wine *jus*. Finish with warm chocolate cake with a chocolate caramel center, caramel corn, and butterscotch ice cream. Three levels of formality—bar, open kitchen, and main dining room—keep things from getting too snobby. Although steep prices prevent most from making Boulevard a regular gig, you'd be hard-pressed to find a better place for a special, fun-filled occasion.

1 Mission St. (btw. the Embarcadero and Steuart sts.). ℂ **415/543-6084.** www.boulevardrestaurant. com. Reservations recommended. Main courses $14–$22 lunch, $29–$39 dinner. AE, DC, DISC, MC, V. Mon–Fri 11:30am–2pm; Sun–Thurs 5:30–10pm; Fri–Sat 5:30–10:30pm. Valet parking $12 lunch, $10 dinner. Bus: 12, 15, 30, 32, or 41. BART: Embarcadero.

Ducca ★★★ ITALIAN   Ducca delivers primo seasonal Italian dishes seasoned with a hint of California at this ode to Venice inside the Westin San Francisco Market Street hotel. Such offerings might include Berkshire pork scallopine with Parmesan mashed potatoes and sautéed Brussels sprout leaves, and Bellwether Farms ricotta ravioli with wine forest-mushroom ragu, erbette chard, and crème fraîche. A selection of *cichetti*—Italian-style bar snacks—makes happy hour a tasty undertaking. The room is smartly arranged into three inviting areas: a stylish bar and lounge, an alfresco terrace, and an airy dining room with embossed columns, cream-colored banquettes, and a bustling open kitchen. Be sure to arrive a bit early to enjoy a Campari and soda in the circular lounge or outdoors by the fireplace.

50 Third St. (btw. Market and Mission sts., adjacent to the Westin San Francisco Market St. hotel). ℂ **415/977-0271.** www.duccasf.com. Main courses $19–$32. AE, DISC, MC, V. Mon–Fri 6:30–10:30am and 11:30am–2:30pm; Sat–Sun 6:30–11am; Sun–Thurs 5:30–10pm; Fri–Sat 5:30–10:30pm. Valet parking $10. Bus: 15, 30, or 45. Streetcar: J, K, L, or M.

EPIC Roasthouse ★★ STEAKHOUSE   Location is everything, and the EPIC Roasthouse and its adjoining sister restaurant, Waterbar (see below), were both built from the ground up on perhaps the most prime piece of real estate in the city, with spectacular, glittering views of the Bay Bridge, Treasure Island, and the city skyline. At EPIC, it's all about steak—you'd be unwise to order anything but. Renowned chef and co-owner Jan Birnbaum, a New Orleans man who knows his meat, runs the show in his huge exhibition kitchen, overseeing the wood-fired hearth to make sure your $84 rib-eye for two is cooked to your specs. The restaurant's Pat Kuleto–designed interior makes for a grand entrance: Only when you're done marveling at the bold industrial elements of leather, stone, mahogany, and massive cast-iron gears do you notice the phenomenal view of the Bay Bridge from the two-story-tall wall of windows. Perhaps the only thing prettier than the scenery is Birnbaum's sizzling 26-ounce bone-in porterhouse on your plate ("Every steak comes with a handle," claims Jan). If you don't have a reservation, the upstairs Quiver Bar serves both bar and full menus, but the crowd often consists of obnoxious businessmen and Gucci-toting gold diggers from across the bridge. *Tip:* On sunny days, beg the hostess for a table on the bayview patio.

369 Embarcadero (at Harrison St.). ⓒ **415/369-9955.** www.epicroasthousesf.com. Reservations recommended. Main courses $19–$42. AE, DC, DISC, MC, V. Lunch Thurs–Fri 11:30am–2pm; dinner Sun–Thurs 5–9:30pm, Fri–Sat 5–10:30pm; brunch Sat–Sun 11am–3pm. Valet parking $12 lunch, $10 dinner. Bus: 1, 12, 14, or 41. Streetcar: F. BART: Embarcadero.

Waterbar ★★ SEAFOOD   Built in tandem with the EPIC Roasthouse (see above), Waterbar is the surf to EPIC's turf. As with EPIC, Waterbar was built just a few years ago from the ground up right on the Embarcadero waterfront. Whereas renowned restaurant designer Pat Kuleto went with a moderately conservative industrial look at the EPIC steakhouse, at Waterbar he unleashed his imagination and created the most visually playful decor since he opened Farallon in 1997. The focal point of the restaurant is a pair of radiant 19-foot floor-to-ceiling circular aquariums filled with fish and marine critters from the Pacific. The aquatic theme ebbs on with a beautiful glass "caviar" chandelier and a horse-shoe-shaped raw bar that has too few of the most coveted seats in town. Even the open kitchen is visually—and aromatically—pleasing. The menu offers a wide selection of market-driven, sustainable seafood such as oak-roasted Maine haddock with smoked butterball potatoes, ancho chili butter, and oyster broth; and local halibut poached in milk with grilled asparagus—but more fun can be had at the raw bar noshing on oysters and small plates. Either way, be sure to start off with the superb mahimahi ceviche with plantain tostones. If the weather is agreeable, ask the hostess for a table on the patio, which affords spectacular waterfront views. If the coastal chill has set in, opt for a table by the soaring windows inside instead to see San Francisco lit up in all her glory. *Note:* When bustling with the after-work crowd, Waterbar can get quite noisy; bear that in mind if you're seeking a quiet dining experience.

399 Embarcadero (at Harrison St.). ⓒ **415/284-9922.** www.waterbarsf.com. Reservations recommended. Main courses $29–$36. AE, DISC, MC, V. Daily 11:30am–2pm and 5:30–10pm. Valet parking $15 lunch, $10 dinner. Bus: 1, 12, 14, or 41. Streetcar: F. BART: Embarcadero.

MODERATE

AsiaSF ★ ASIAN/CALIFORNIAN   Part restaurant, part gender-illusionist musical revue, AsiaSF manages to be both entertaining and satisfying. As you're entertained by mostly Asian men dressed as women (who lip-sync show tunes when they're not waiting on tables), you can nibble on superb grilled shrimp and herb salad; baby back pork ribs with honey tamarind glaze, pickled carrots, and sweet-potato crisps; or filet mignon with Korean dipping sauce, miso eggplant, and fried potato stars. The full bar, *Wine Spectator* award–winning wine list, and sake list add to the festivities. Fortunately, the food and the atmosphere are as colorful as the staff, which means a night here is more than a meal—it's a very happening event.

201 Ninth St. (at Howard St.). © **415/255-2742.** www.asiasf.com. Reservations recommended. Main courses $9–$20. AE, DISC, MC, V (Mon–Wed $25 minimum). Sun 7–10pm; Tues–Thurs 7–11pm; Fri 7pm–2am; Sat 5pm–2am; cocktails and dancing until 2am on weekends. Bus: 9, 12, or 47. Streetcar: Civic Center on underground streetcar. BART: Civic Center.

Yank Sing ★★ CHINESE/DIM SUM   Loosely translated as "a delight of the heart," Yank Sing is widely regarded as the best dim sum restaurant in the downtown area. The servers are good at guessing your gastric threshold as they wheel stainless-steel carts carrying small plates of exotic dishes around the vast dining room; if they whiz right by your table, there's probably a good reason. If you're new to dim sum (which, translated, means "to touch the heart"), stick with the safe, recognizable classics such as spare ribs, stuffed crab claws, scallion pancakes, shrimp balls, pork buns, and steamed dumplings filled with delicious concoctions of pork, beef, fish, or vegetables. A second location, open Monday through Friday from 11am to 3pm, is at 49 Stevenson St., off First Street (© **415/ 541-4949**) in SoMa, and has outdoor seating for fair-weather dining.

101 Spear St. (at Mission St. at Rincon Center). © **415/957-9300.** www.yanksing.com. Dim sum $3.65–$10 for 2–6 pieces. AE, DC, MC, V. Mon–Fri 11am–3pm; Sat–Sun and holidays 10am–4pm. Validated parking in Rincon Center Garage. Bus: 1, 12, 14, or 41. Streetcar: F. Cable car: California St. line. BART: Embarcadero.

INEXPENSIVE

Manora's ★ THAI   Manora's has been cranking out some of the best Thai food in town for 20 years and is well worth a jaunt to SoMa. But this is no relaxed affair: It's perpetually packed (unless you come early), and you'll be seated sardinelike at one of the cramped but well-appointed tables. During the dinner rush, the noise level can make conversation almost impossible, but the food is so darn good, you'll probably prefer to ignore people and stuff your face anyway. Start with a Thai iced tea or coffee and tangy soup or chicken satay, which comes with decadent peanut sauce. Follow these with any of the wonderful dinner dishes—which should be shared—and a side of rice. There are endless options, including a vast array of vegetarian plates. Every remarkably flavorful dish arrives seemingly seconds after you order it, which is great if you're hungry, a bummer if you were planning a long, leisurely dinner. *Tip:* Come before 7pm or after 9pm if you don't want a loud, rushed meal.

1600 Folsom St. (at 12th St.). © **415/861-6224.** www.manorathai.com. Reservations recommended for 4 or more. Main courses $7–$15. MC, V. Mon–Thurs 11:30am–2:30pm; Mon–Sat 5:30–10:30pm; Sun 5–10pm. Bus: 9, 12, or 47.

Financial District & Embarcadero

EXPENSIVE

Kokkari ★★ GREEK/MEDITERRANEAN   The funny thing is, I've been to Athens, and the food there wasn't nearly as good as what they're serving at Kokkari (Ko-*kar*-ee), one of my favorite restaurants in the city. My love affair starts with the setting: a beautifully rustic dining area with a commanding fireplace and oversize furnishings. Past the tiny bar, the other main room is pure rustic revelry, with exposed wood beams, pretty standing lamps, and a view of the glass-enclosed private dining room. Then there are the wonderful, traditional Aegean dishes. A must-order appetizer is the *Marithes Tiganites,* a beautiful platter of whole crispy smelts enhanced with garlic-potato *skordalia* (a traditional Greek dip) and lemon. Other favorites are the *pikilia* (a sampling of traditional Greek spreads served with dolmades and house-made pitas) and the fabulous mesquite-grilled octopus salad. Try not to overindulge before the main courses, which include grilled whole petrale sole with lemon, olive oil, and braised greens; to-die-for moussaka (eggplant, lamb, potato, and béchamel); and lamb chops with oven-roasted lemon-oregano potatoes. Also consider the rotisserie specialties such as roasted pork loin.

200 Jackson St. (at Front St.). ✆ **415/981-0983.** www.kokkari.com. Reservations recommended. Main courses $14–$23 lunch, $19–$39 dinner. AE, DC, DISC, MC, V. Lunch Mon–Fri 11:30am–2:30pm; bar menu 2:30–5:30pm; dinner Mon–Thurs 5:30–10pm, Fri 5:30–11pm, Sat 5–11pm. Valet parking (dinner only) $8. Bus: 12, 15, 41, or 83.

One Market ★★ CALIFORNIAN   This top-notch Embarcadero restaurant has remained popular with San Francisco's notoriously fickle dining public since it opened in 1993. Amid the airy main dining room with its open exhibition kitchen, cozy banquettes, mahogany trim, and slate flooring, a sea of diners feast from a farm-fresh menu put together by chef Mark Dommen, who has a passion for impeccably fresh local ingredients. One Market, across from the Ferry Plaza Farmers' Market, was one of its early supporters—and he shops there regularly to create its highly original dishes. During my last visit, my table was wowed by the truly divine beet carpaccio, shellfish, and seafood sampler (*not* your everyday platter), and a superb crispy-skin pork saddle with fava beans and chorizo broth. Whatever you choose, you're bound to find a perfectly accompanying wine from the "cellar," which has more than 500 selections of American vintages. Arrive early to mingle with the spirited corporate crowd that convenes from 4:30 to 7pm for happy hour at the bar—it's a fun scene.

1 Market St. (at Steuart St., across from Justin Herman Plaza). ✆ **415/777-5577.** www.onemarket.com. Reservations recommended. Lunch $16–$23; dinner $19–$29; chef's tasting menu $79 per person. AE, DC, DISC, MC, V. Mon–Fri 11:30am–2pm; daily 5:30–9pm. Valet parking $12 for lunch, $10 for dinner. Bus: All Market St. buses. BART: All BART trains.

The Slanted Door ★★ VIETNAMESE   What started in 1995 as an obscure little family-run restaurant in the Mission District has become one of the most popular and written-about restaurants in the city. Due to its meteoric rise—helped along by celebrity fans such as Mick Jagger, Keith Richards, and Quentin Tarantino—it's been relocated within a beautiful bay-inspired, custom-designed space at the Ferry Building Marketplace. What hasn't changed is a menu filled with incredibly fresh and flavorful Vietnamese dishes such as catfish clay-pot flavored with cilantro, ginger, and Thai chilies; an amazing green papaya salad with roasted peanuts; and fragrant peppercorn duck served with apples and watercress. If the cellophane noodles with fresh Dungeness crabmeat are on the menu, *definitely* order them. Be sure to start the feast with a pot of tea from their eclectic collection. If you're just looking to grab something on the go, stop by **Out the Door,** the Slanted Door's more casual—but still tasty—little sister, on the bottom floor of the Westfield Centre. It has both seating and a pickup window. Phan's latest creation, **Heaven's Dog** (Mission and Seventh sts.), offers noodles, soups, and classic Northern Chinese dishes.

1 Ferry Plaza (at the Embarcadero and Market). ✆ **415/861-8032.** www.slanteddoor.com. Reservations recommended. Lunch main courses $6–$17; dinner dishes $10–$34; 7-item fixed-price dinner $45 (parties of 7 or more only). AE, MC, V. Daily 11am–2:30pm (until 3pm Sun); Sun–Thurs 5:30–10pm; Fri–Sat 5:30–10:30pm. Bus: All Market St. buses. Streetcar: F or N-Judah line.

San Francisco has always been woefully lacking in the alfresco dining department, which may or may not have something to do with the Arctic summer fog. But **Belden Place**—an adorable little brick alley in the heart of the Financial District—defies that convention. A skinny walkway open only to foot traffic, it's a little bit of Paris just off Pine Street. Restaurants line the alley sporting big umbrellas, tables, and chairs, and, when the weather is agreeable, diners linger long after the lunch hour.

A handful of cafes line Belden Place and offer a variety of cuisines at moderate prices. There's **Cafe Bastille,** 22 Belden Place (℗ **415/986-5673**), a classic French bistro with a boho basement that serves excellent crepes, mussels, and French-onion soup; it offers live jazz on Fridays. **Cafe Tiramisu,** 28 Belden Place (℗ **415/421-7044**), is a stylish Italian hot spot serving addictive risottos and gnocchi. **Plouf,** 40 Belden Place (℗ **415/986-6491**), specializes in big bowls of mussels slathered in your choice of seven sauces, as well as fresh seafood. **B44,** 44 Belden Place (℗ **415/986-6287**), serves up a side order of Spain alongside its revered paella and other seriously zesty Spanish dishes.

At night, Belden Place takes on a Euro-speak-easy vibe—perfect for sipping aperitifs and nibbling on frites.

4

MODERATE

Sam's Grill & Seafood Restaurant ★ 🗿 SEAFOOD   Power-lunching at Sam's is a San Francisco tradition, and Sam's has done a brisk business with Financial District suits since 1867. Even if you're not carrying a briefcase, this is the place to come for time-capsule dining at its most classically San Francisco. Pass the crowded entrance and small bar to get to the main dining room—packed with virtually all men—kick back, and bask in yesteryear. (Or, conversely, slide into a curtained booth and see nothing but your dining companion.) Tuxedo-clad waiters race around, doling out big crusty cuts of sourdough bread and distributing salads overflowing with fresh crab and Roquefort vinaigrette, towering plates of seafood pasta with marinara, charbroiled fish, roasted chicken, and old-school standbys like calves' liver with bacon and onions or Salisbury steak. Don't worry—they didn't forget classic creamed spinach. The restaurant's mildly salty service and good old-fashioned character make everything on the menu taste that much better.

374 Bush St. (btw. Montgomery and Kearny sts.). ℗ **415/421-0594.** www.belden-place.com/samsgrill. Reservations recommended for dinner and for 6 or more at lunch. Main courses $12–$29. AE, DC, DISC, MC, V. Mon–Fri 11am–9pm. Bus: 15, 45, or 76.

Chinatown

INEXPENSIVE

Brandy Ho's Hunan Food ★ CHINESE   Fancy black-and-white granite tabletops and a large, open kitchen give you the first clue that the food at this casual restaurant is a cut above the usual Hunan fare. Take my advice and start immediately with fried dumplings (in sweet-and-sour sauce) or cold chicken salad, and then move on to fish ball soup with spinach, bamboo shoots, noodles, and other goodies. The best main course is Three Delicacies, a combination of scallops, shrimp, and chicken with onion, bell pepper, and bamboo shoots, seasoned with ginger, garlic, and wine, and served with black-bean sauce. Most dishes are quite hot and spicy, but the kitchen will adjust the level to meet your specifications. A full bar includes Asian food–friendly libations like plum wine and sake from 11:30am to 11pm. *Note:* There's a second location in the Castro at 4068 18th St. (at Castro St.; ☎ **415/252-8000**).

217 Columbus Ave. (at Pacific Ave.). ☎ **415/788-7527.** www.brandyhos.com. Reservations recommended. Main courses $8–$13. AE, DISC, MC, V. Sun–Thurs 11am–11pm; Fri–Sat 11am–midnight. Paid parking available at 170 Columbus Ave. Bus: 15 or 41.

House of Nanking ★ CHINESE   This place would be strictly a tourist joint if it weren't for the die-hard fans who happily wait—sometimes up to an hour—for a coveted seat at this inconspicuous spot for Shanghai-style cuisine. Order the requisite potstickers, green-onion-and-shrimp pancakes with peanut sauce, or any number of pork, rice, beef, seafood, chicken, or vegetable dishes from the menu, but I suggest you trust the waiter when he recommends a special (even if you do specify your order, the waiter may tell you to get something else; roll with it, it's a longtime Chinatown tradition). Even with an expansion that doubled the available space, seating is tight, so prepare to be bumped around a bit and don't expect perky or attentive service—it's all part of the Nanking experience.

919 Kearny St. (at Columbus Ave.). ☎ **415/421-1429.** Reservations accepted for groups of 8 or more. Main courses $6–$12. MC, V. Mon–Fri 11am–10pm; Sat noon–10pm; Sun noon–9pm. Bus: 9, 12, 15, or 30.

R&G Lounge ★ CHINESE   It's tempting to take your chances and duck into any of the exotic restaurants in Chinatown, but if you want a sure thing, go directly to the three-story R&G Lounge. During lunch, all three floors are packed with hungry neighborhood workers who go straight for the $6 rice-plate specials. Even then, you can order from the dinner menu, which features legendary deep-fried salt-and-pepper crab (a little greasy for my taste); and wonderful chicken with black-bean sauce. A personal favorite is melt-in-your-mouth R&G Special Beef, which explodes with the tangy flavor of the accompanying sauce. I was less excited by the tired chicken salad, house-specialty noodles, and bland spring rolls. But that was just fine, since I saved room for generous and savory seafood in a clay pot and classic roast duck.

631 Kearny St. (at Clay St.). ☎ **415/982-7877.** www.rnglounge.com. Reservations recommended. Main courses $9.50–$30. AE, DC, DISC, MC, V. Daily 11:30am–9:30pm. Parking validated across the street at Portsmouth Sq. garage 24 hr. or Holiday Inn after 5pm. Bus: 1, 9AX, 9BX, or 15. Cable car: California.

Nob Hill & Russian Hill

VERY EXPENSIVE

La Folie ★★★ 🎁 FRENCH   I call this unintimidating, cozy, intimate French restaurant "the house of foie gras." Why? Because on my first visit, virtually every dish overflowed with the ultrarich delicacy. Subsequent visits proved that foie gras still reigns here, but more than that, it reconfirmed La Folie's long-standing reputation as one of the city's very best fine-dining experiences—and without any stuffiness to boot. Chef/owner Roland Passot, who unlike many celebrity chefs is actually in the kitchen each night, offers melt-in-your-mouth starters such as seared foie gras with caramelized pineapple and star anise vanilla Muscat broth.

Generous main courses include rôti of quail and squab stuffed with wild mushrooms and wrapped in crispy potato strings; butter-poached lobster with glazed blood oranges and *shiso,* scallion, carrot, and toasted almond salad; and roast venison with vegetables, quince, and huckleberry sauce. The staff is extremely approachable and knowledgeable, and the new surroundings (think deep wood paneling, mirrors, long, rust-colored curtains, and gold-hued Venetian plaster) are now as elegant as the food. Best of all, the environment is relaxed, comfortable, and intimate. Finish with any of the delectable desserts. If you're not into the three-, four-, or five-course tasting menu, don't be deterred; the restaurant tells me they'll happily price out individual items.

2316 Polk St. (btw. Green and Union sts.). ℂ **415/776-5577.** www.lafolie.com. Reservations recommended. 3-course tasting menu $70; 4-course tasting menu $80; 5-course chef's tasting menu $90; vegetarian tasting menu $70. AE, DC, DISC, MC, V. Mon–Sat 5:30–10:30pm. Valet parking $15. Bus: 19, 41, 45, 47, 49, or 76.

MODERATE

Nob Hill Cafe ★ 🍴 ITALIAN/PIZZA   Considering the steep cost and formality of most Nob Hill restaurants, it's no wonder that residents don't mind waiting around for a table to open up at this cozy neighborhood bistro. This is the kind of place where you can come wearing jeans and sneakers, tuck into a large plate of linguine with clams and a glass of pinot, and leave fulfilled without blowing a wad of dough (pastas are in the humble $9–$15 range). The dining room is split into two small, simple rooms, with windows looking onto Taylor Street and bright local art on the walls. Service is friendly, and one of the owners is almost always on hand to make sure everyone's content. When the kitchen is "on," expect hearty Northern Italian comfort fare worth at least twice its price; even on off days, it's still a bargain. Start with a salad or the decadent polenta with pesto and parmigiano, and then fill up on the veal piccata, any of the pastas or pizzas, or petrale sole. If you're into "celebrity" sightings, keep your eyes peeled for the original Doublemint twins, who dress alike and dine here frequently. *Tip:* Parking can be difficult in Nob Hill; fortunately, they offer valet parking a block away at the corner of Washington and Taylor streets.

1152 Taylor St. (btw. Sacramento and Clay sts.). ℂ **415/776-6500.** www.nobhillcafe.com. Reservations not accepted. Main courses $7–$17. DC, MC, V. Daily 11am–3pm and 5–10pm. Bus: 1.

Swan Oyster Depot ★★ 🍴 SEAFOOD   Turning 98 years old in 2010, Swan Oyster Depot is a classic San Francisco dining experience you shouldn't miss. Opened in 1912, this tiny hole in the wall, run by the city's friendliest servers, is little more than a narrow fish market that decided to slap down some bar stools. There are only 20 or so stools here, jammed cheek by jowl along a long marble bar. Most patrons come for a quick cup of chowder or a plate of oysters on the half shell with an Anchor Steam beer. The menu is limited to fresh Dungeness crab, shrimp, oyster, clam cocktails, a few types of smoked fish, Maine lobster, and Boston-style clam chowder, all of which are exceedingly fresh. *Note:* Don't let the lunchtime line dissuade you—it moves fast.

1517 Polk St. (btw. California and Sacramento sts.). ℂ **415/673-1101.** Reservations not accepted. Seafood cocktails $7–$15; clams and oysters on the half shell $7.95 per half-dozen. No credit cards. Mon–Sat 8am–5:30pm. Bus: 1, 19, 47, or 49.

North Beach
MODERATE

Piperade ★★ BASQUE   Chef Gerald Hirigoyen takes diners on a Basque adventure in this charming, small, and superbly authentic restaurant. Surrounded by a low wood-beamed ceiling, oak floors, and soft sconce lighting, it's a casual affair where diners indulge in small and large plates of Hirigoyen's flavorful Basque cuisine. Your edible odyssey starts with small plates—or plates to be shared—like my personal favorites: piquillo peppers stuffed with goat cheese; and a bright and simple salad of garbanzo beans with calamari, chorizo, and piquillo peppers. Share entrees too. Indulge in New York steak with braised shallots and french fries, or sop up every drop of the sweet and savory red-pepper sauce with the braised seafood and shellfish stew. Save room for orange-blossom beignets: Light and airy, with a delicate and moist web of dough within and a kiss of orange essence, the beignet is dessert at its finest. There's a communal table for drop-in diners and front patio seating during warmer weather.

1015 Battery St. (at Green St.). ℂ **415/391-2555.** www.piperade.com. Reservations recommended. Main courses $18–$30. AE, DC, DISC, MC, V. Mon–Fri 11:30am–3pm and 5:30–10:30pm; Sat 5:30–10:30pm; closed Sun. Bus: 10, 12, 30, or 82x.

INEXPENSIVE

Capp's Corner ★ 🍴 ITALIAN   Capp's is a place of givens: It's a given that high-spirited regulars are hunched over the bar and that you'll be served huge portions of straightforward Italian fare at decent prices in a raucous atmosphere that prevails until closing. The waitresses are usually brusque and bossy, but always with a wink. Long tables are set up for family-style dining: bread, soup, salad, and choice of around 20 classic main dishes (herb-roasted leg of lamb, spaghetti with meatballs, *osso buco* with polenta, fettuccine with prawns and white-wine sauce)—all for $18 or $20 or so per person, around $13 for kids. You might have to wait awhile for a table, but if you want fun and authentic old-school dining without pomp or huge prices, you'll find the wait worthwhile.

1600 Powell St. (at Green St.). ℂ **415/989-2589.** www.cappscorner.com. Reservations accepted. Complete dinners $15–$17. AE, DC, MC, V. Daily 11:30am–2:30pm; Mon–Fri 4:30–10:30pm; Sat–Sun 4–11pm. Bus: 15, 30, or 41.

Il Pollaio ★ 🍴 ITALIAN/ARGENTINE   Simple, affordable, and consistently good is the winning combination at Il Pollaio. When I used to live in the neighborhood, I ate here at least once a week and I still can't make chicken this good. Seat yourself in the tiny, unfussy room; order; and wait expectantly for the fresh-from-the-grill lemon-infused chicken, which is so moist it practically falls off the bone. Each meal comes with a choice of salad or fries. If you're not in the mood for chicken, you can opt for rabbit, lamb, pork chop, or Italian sausage. On a sunny day, get your goods to go and picnic across the street at Washington Square.

555 Columbus Ave. (btw. Green and Union sts.). ℂ **415/362-7727.** Reservations not accepted. Main courses $8–$15. DISC, MC, V. Mon–Sat 11:30am–9pm. Bus: 15, 30, 39, 41, or 45. Cable car: Powell–Mason line.

L'Osteria del Forno ★★ ITALIAN   L'Osteria del Forno might be only slightly larger than a walk-in closet, but it's one of the top three authentic Italian restaurants in North Beach. Peer in the window facing Columbus Avenue, and you'll probably see two Italian women with their hair up, sweating from the heat of the oven, which cranks out the best focaccia (and focaccia sandwiches) in the city. There's no pomp or circumstance here: Locals come strictly to eat. The menu features a variety of superb pizzas, salads, soups, and fresh pastas, plus a few daily specials and a roast of the day (pray for the roast pork braised in milk). Small baskets of warm focaccia keep you going until the arrival of the entrees, which should always be accompanied by a glass of Italian red (this tiny place actually has a full bar, with a nice selection of grappa). Good news for folks on the go: You can get pizza by the slice. Note that it's cash only.

519 Columbus Ave. (btw. Green and Union sts.). ✆ **415/982-1124.** www.losteriadelforno.com. Reservations not accepted. Sandwiches $6–$7; pizzas $10–$18; main courses $6–$16. No credit cards. Sun–Mon and Wed–Thurs 11:30am–10pm; Fri–Sat 11:30am–10:30pm. Bus: 15, 30, 41, or 45.

Mario's Bohemian Cigar Store ★ 🎁 ITALIAN   Across the street from Washington Square is one of North Beach's most venerable neighborhood hangouts. The century-old corner cafe—small, well worn, and perpetually busy—is one of the oldest and best original cappuccino cafes in United States. I stop by at least once a month for a meatball or eggplant focaccia sandwich and a slice of Mario's house-made ricotta cheesecake, and then recharge with a cappuccino as I watch the world stroll by the picture windows. And no, they don't sell cigars.

566 Columbus Ave. (at Union St.). ✆ **415/362-0536.** Sandwiches $7.75–$11. MC, V. Daily 10am–10pm. Bus: 15, 30, 41, or 45.

Fisherman's Wharf

EXPENSIVE

Restaurant Gary Danko ★★★ FRENCH   James Beard Award–winning chef Gary Danko presides over my top pick for fine dining. Eschewing the white-glove formality of yesteryear's fine dining, Danko offers impeccable cuisine and perfectly orchestrated service in an unstuffy environment of wooden paneling and shutters and well-spaced tables (not to mention spa-style restrooms). The three- to five-course fixed-price seasonal menu is freestyle, so whether you want a sampling of appetizers or a flight of meat courses, you need only ask. I am a devoted fan of his trademark buttery-smooth glazed oysters with lettuce cream, salsify, and Osetra caviar; the seared foie gras, which may be accompanied by peaches, caramelized onions, and *verjus* (a classic French sauce); and juniper-crusted venison with braised red cabbage, cranberries, cipollini onions, and chestnut gnocchi. Truthfully, I've never had a dish here that wasn't wonderful. And wine? The list is stellar, albeit expensive. If you pass on the glorious cheese cart or flambéed dessert of the day, a plate of petits fours reminds you that Gary Danko is one sweet and memorable meal. *Tip:* If you can't get a reservation, slip in and grab a seat at the bar, where you can also order a la carte.

800 North Point St. (at Hyde St.). ✆ **415/749-2060.** www.garydanko.com. Reservations required except at walk-in bar. 3-course fixed-price menu $68, 4-course menu $85, 5-course menu $102. AE, DC, DISC, MC, V. Daily 5:30–10pm. Bar daily 5–10pm. Valet parking $10. Bus: 10. Streetcar: F. Cable car: Hyde.

Scoma's ★ SEAFOOD   A throwback to the dining of yesteryear, Scoma's eschews trendier trout preparations and fancy digs for good old-fashioned seafood served in huge portions with lots of sauce and a windowed waterfront setting. If your idea of heaven is straightforward seafood classics—fried calamari, raw oysters, pesto pasta with rock shrimp, crab cioppino, lobster thermidor—served with a generous portion of old-time hospitality, then Scoma's is as good as it gets. Unfortunately, a taste of tradition will cost you big-time. Prices are as steep as those at some of the finest restaurants in town. Personally, I'd rather splurge at Gary Danko, but many of my out-of-town guests insist we meet at Scoma's—which is fine by me, since it's a change of pace from today's überchic spots, and the parking's free.

Pier 47 and Al Scoma Way (btw. Jefferson and Jones sts.). © **800/644-5852** or 415/771-4383. www.scomas.com. Reservations not accepted. Most main courses $16–$36. AE, DC, DISC, MC, V. Sun–Thurs 11:30am–10pm; Fri–Sat 11:30am–10:30pm. Bar opens 30 min. prior to lunch daily. Free valet parking. Bus: 10 or 47. Streetcar: F.

MODERATE

Fog City Diner ★ AMERICAN   When it opened, Fog City Diner was the "it" spot for locals in search of upscale California chow. These days, it gets a lot of mixed reviews for service and food, but I've always had a satisfying experience here. The restaurant looks like a genuine American metallic railroad diner—but only from the outside. Inside, dark polished woods, inspired lighting, and a well-stocked raw bar tell you this is no hash-slinger. Dressed-up diner dishes include juicy gourmet burgers with house-made pickles, huge salads, "warm breads," soups, sandwiches, cioppino, macaroni and Gouda cheese, and pork chops. Fancier fish and meat meals include grilled catches of the day and thick-cut steaks. Light eaters can make a meal out of the long list of small plates, which include crab cakes, quesadillas with asparagus and leeks, and their famous red-curry mussel stew. They've recently opened for weekend brunch as well. The food is fine, but if your heart is set on coming here, do so at lunch or early-evening cocktails and appetizers—you'll be better off elsewhere if you want a special dinner.

1300 Battery St. (at the Embarcadero). © **415/982-2000.** www.fogcitydiner.com. Reservations recommended. Main courses $14–$24. DC, DISC, MC, V. Mon–Thurs 11:30am–10pm; Fri 11:30am–11pm; Sat 10:30am–11pm; Sun 10:30am–10pm. Bus: 42.

INEXPENSIVE

Bistro Boudin at the Wharf DELI/AMERICAN   This industrial-chic Fisherman's Wharf shrine to the city's famous tangy French-style bread is impossible to miss. Even if you're not hungry, drop in to see bakers at work making 3,000 loaves daily, or take the tour and learn about the city sourdough bread's history (Boudin is the city's oldest continually operating business). Good, strong coffee is served at **Peet's Coffee** (another Bay Area great), and at **Bakers Hall** you'll find picnic possibilities such as handcrafted cheeses, fruit spreads, and chocolates, as well as a wall map highlighting the town's best places to spread a blanket and feast. There's also a casual **self-serve cafe** serving sandwiches, clam chowder bowls, salads, and pastries, and the more formal **Bistro Boudin** restaurant, which offers Alcatraz views with its Dungeness crab Louis, pizza, crab cakes, and burgers on sourdough buns.

160 Jefferson St., near Pier 43½. © **415/928-1849.** www.boudinbakery.com. Reservations recommended at bistro. Main courses cafe $6–$10, bistro $11–$33. AE, DC, DISC, MC, V. Daily 11:45am–9pm. Bus: 10, 15, or 47. Streetcar: F.

Marina District & Cow Hollow

VERY EXPENSIVE

Spruce ★ CONTEMPORARY AMERICAN   If you haven't heard of San Francisco's Pacific Heights neighborhood, it's where most of the city's old money lives, and now the ladies-who-lunch have a new place to hang their cloches:

Spruce. In a beautifully restored 1930s-era auto barn, Spruce consists of a restaurant, cafe, bar, and lounge under a single roof, making it both a destination restaurant and a neighborhood hangout. As you enter, there's a library nook on one side filled with newspapers, cookbooks, and so on, and a cafe on the other side offering gourmet take-away items. Farther inside is an elegant bar to the right and a 70-seat restaurant to the left, both topped with a vast cathedral ceiling highlighted by a glass-and-steel skylight. With mohair couches, faux-ostrich chairs, and a black-and-chocolate decor, it's all quite visually appealing, but, alas, the cuisine isn't quite as impressive. The organic, locally sourced produce is wonderfully fresh, but many of the dishes I tried—spearmint and nettle ravioli, leek and fennel soup with salt-cod dumplings, honey-lacquered duck breast—were lacking in flavor, and the service suffered from mysteriously long spells of absence. Spruce is still one of the exciting new restaurants in San Francisco, but it's best enjoyed from a seat at the bar while tucking into their fantastic all-natural burger and fries while pondering which wine to choose from their 70 by-the-glass selections.

3640 Sacramento St. (at Spruce St.). ✆ **415/931-5100.** www.sprucesf.com. Reservations recommended. Main courses $26–$40. AE, DC, DISC, MC, V. Mon–Fri 11:30am–10pm; Sat–Sun 5–10pm. Valet parking $12 dinner only. Bus: 1, 2, or 4.

EXPENSIVE

Baker & Banker ★★★ CONTEMPORARY AMERICAN   In my opinion, Baker & Banker is the most impressive restaurant to open in San Francisco in the past few years. Moving into the old Quince spot at the end of 2009, Baker & Banker never saw a lull period once it opened, thanks to the power duo behind it—co-owners and spouses Jeff Banker (who mans the kitchen) and Lori Baker (the pastry chef who whips up such divine desserts)—who kept the cozy booths full thanks to their winning combination of superb cuisine and inviting atmosphere. (When Quince occupied the same digs, it was far too stuffy for my liking.)

Jeff's signature dishes include the smoked trout, draped over a celery root latke and served with a horseradish crème fraîche with pickled beets and shaved fennel, and a black cod with foie gras–shiitake sticky rice accompanied by charred bok choy. But really you can't go wrong with anything you order, whether you opt for the butternut squash and cavolo nero–filled crepes or the scallops with Dungeness crab, Sardinian couscous, Pernod-saffron sauce, and Satsuma mandarin salad. Just don't forget to save room for dessert, as that's one of Baker & Banker's specialties, thanks to Lori's penchant for the sweet. The hot spiced butterscotch with homemade vanilla marshmallows and olive oil–*fleur de sel* biscotti is particularly mouthwatering. The restaurant offers a very affordable chef's tasting menu for $55 a person, plus $35 for wine pairings. Baker & Banker also has a bakery component open during the day on the Bust Street side of the restaurant.

1701 Octavia St. (at Bush St.). ✆ **415/351-2500.** www.bakerandbanker.com. Reservations recommended. Main courses $20–$28. AE, MC, V. Tues–Sat 5:30am–10pm; Sun 5:30–9:30pm. Valet parking $10 dinner. Bus: 1, 2, 3, 47, 49, 76, or 90.

MODERATE

A16 ★★ ITALIAN   This sleek, casual, and wonderfully lively spot is one of San Francisco's best and busiest Italian restaurants, featuring thin-crust Neapolitan-style pizza and cuisine from the region of Campania. Named after the motorway that traverses the region, the divided space boasts a wine-and-beer bar up front, a larger dining area and open kitchen in the back, and a wall of wines in between. But its secret weapon is the creative menu of outstanding appetizers, pizza, and entrees—with ingredients sourced fresh from local farms. Even if you must hoard the insanely good roast Berkshire pork ribs and shoulder for yourself, start by sharing roasted Monterey sardines with citrus, fennel, and green olives; or artichoke and tuna conserva with dried favas, braised bitter greens, and house-made croccantini. If meatballs are on the menu, don't ask questions—get 'em. Co-owner and wine director Shelley Lindgren guides diners through one of the city's most exciting wine lists, featuring 40 wines by the half-glass, glass, and carafe.

2355 Chestnut St. (btw. Divisadero and Scott sts.). ✆ **415/771-2216.** www.a16sf.com. Reservations recommended. Main courses $10–$16 lunch, $11–$25 dinner. AE, DC, MC, V. Wed–Fri 11:30am–2:30pm; Sun–Thurs 5–10pm; Fri–Sat 5–11pm. Bus: 22, 30, or 30X.

Dosa ★★ SOUTHERN INDIAN   This favorite locals' spot has been dubbed the city's best Indian by the media for a reason. Dosa offers fresh, organic ingredients, reasonable prices, and a much more authentic cuisine than its Americanized competitors. This new outpost is more dressed up (read: swankier) than its casual Mission location (995 Valencia St.; ✆ **415/642-3672**) but serves the same winning dishes. The southern Indian menu has an entire section devoted to its namesake, dosa (a savory rice-and-lentil crepe with sambar and tomato-and-coconut chutney), as well as several uttapam dishes (a thicker pancakelike variation on the dosa). Order a couple of kinds to share, family-style. For an entree, opt for the vegetable korma and paratha (cauliflower, green beans, peas, potatoes, poppy seeds, fennel, and coconut), or cilantro and chili fish with a side of basmati rice (aromatically flavored with either jasmine or lemon). Don't pass on dessert: The banana uttapam (layered with strawberries, chocolate, and white shrikand) is divine. Drinks are creatively named and concocted. A signature four-course tasting menu is $39 and the best way to adequately sample the cuisine. Tack on $20 for wine pairings.

1700 Fillmore St. (at Post St.). ✆ **415/441-3672.** www.dosasf.com. Reservations recommended. Main courses $7–$28. AE, DISC, MC, V. Daily 11:30am–3pm and 5:30pm–midnight. Bus: 2, 3, 4, 22, 38, or 38L.

Ella's ★★ AMERICAN/BREAKFAST   Well-known throughout town as the undisputed queen of breakfasts, this restaurant's acclaim means you're likely to wait in line up to an hour on weekends. But midweek and in the wee hours of morning, it's possible to slide onto a counter or table seat in the colorful split dining room and lose yourself in outstanding and generous servings of chicken hash, crisped to perfection and served with eggs any way you like them, with a side of fluffy buttermilk biscuits. Pancakes, omelets, and the short list of other breakfast essentials are equally revered. Service can be woefully slow, but at least the busboys and -gals are quick to fill coffee cups. Come lunchtime, solid entrees like salads, chicken potpie, and grilled salmon with mashed potatoes remind you what's great about American cooking.

500 Presidio Ave. (at California St.). ✆ **415/441-5669.** www.ellassanfrancisco.com. Reservations accepted for lunch. Main courses $5.50–$11 breakfast, $9.75–$12 brunch, $9–$13 lunch. AE, DISC, MC, V. Mon–Fri 7am–3pm; Sat–Sun 8:30am–2pm. Bus: 1, 3, or 43.

Greens Restaurant ★★ VEGETARIAN   In an old waterfront warehouse, with enormous windows overlooking the Golden Gate, boats, and the bay, Greens reigns over gourmet vegetarian—a pioneer in the city and one of the most renowned vegetarian restaurants in the country. Executive chef Annie Somerville (author of *Fields of Greens*) cooks with the seasons, using produce from local organic farms. Brunch is a boisterous affair, but on a weeknight, the dining room is quiet and romantic, especially when the fog is in. Dinner might feature such appetizers as grilled asparagus with meyer lemon vinaigrette, shaved Andante cheese, and warm butter beans, or grilled portobello and endive salad. Entrees run the gamut from pizza with wilted escarole, red onions, lemon, and Parmesan to wild mushroom ravioli with chanterelle, hedgehog and maitake mushrooms, savoy spinach, and spring onions. Those interested in the whole shebang should make reservations for the $49 four-course dinner served on Saturday only. Lunch and brunch are equally fresh, tasty—and crowded. The adjacent Greens To Go sells sandwiches, soups, salads, and so on.

Building A, Fort Mason Center (enter Fort Mason opposite the Safeway at Buchanan and Marina sts.). ✆ **415/771-6222.** www.greensrestaurant.com. Reservations recommended. Main courses $11–$18 lunch, $15–$20 dinner; fixed-price dinner $48; Sun brunch $11–$17. AE, DISC, MC, V. Tues-Sat noon-2:30pm; Sun 10:30am–9pm; Mon–Sat 5:30–9pm. Greens To Go Mon–Thurs 8am–8pm; Fri–Sat 8am–5pm; Sun 10:30am–4pm. Parking in hourly lot $4 for up to 2½ hr. Bus: 28 or 30.

Isa ★★ FRENCH   Luke Sung, who trained with some of the best French chefs in the city, has captured many locals' hearts by creating the kind of menu we foodies dream of: a smattering of small dishes, served a la carte family-style, that allow you to try numerous items in one sitting. It's a good thing that the menu, considered "French tapas," offers small portions at reasonable prices. After all, it's asking a lot to make a diner choose from mushroom ragout with veal sweetbreads, seared foie gras with caramelized apples, potato-wrapped sea bass in brown butter, and rack of lamb. Here a party of two can choose all of these plus one or two more and not be rolled out the door afterward. Adding to the allure is the warm boutique dining environment—70 seats scattered amid a small dining room in the front, and a large tented and heated patio out back that sets the mood with a warm yellow glow. Take a peek at the "kitchen," a shoebox of a cooking space, to appreciate Sung's accomplishments even more. Cocktail-drinkers, take note: You'll find only beer, wine, and *shoju* cocktails (a smooth alcohol made from sweet potato and used like vodka).

3324 Steiner St. (btw. Lombard and Chestnut sts.). ✆ **415/567-9588.** www.isarestaurant.com. Reservations recommended. Main courses $9–$16. MC, V. Mon–Thurs 5:30–10pm; Fri–Sat 5:30–10:30pm. Bus: 22, 28, 30, 30X, 43, or 76.

INEXPENSIVE

The Grove ★ CAFE   The Grove is the kind of place you go just to hang out and enjoy the fact that you're in San Francisco. That the heaping salads, lasagna, pasta, sandwiches, and daily specials are predictably good is an added bonus. I like coming here on weekday mornings for the easygoing vibe, strong coffee, and friendly, fast service. Inside you can sit at one of the dark-wood tables on the scuffed hardwood floor and people-watch through the large open windows, but on sunny days the most coveted seats are along the sidewalk. It's the perfect place to read the newspaper, sip an enormous mug of coffee, and be glad you're not at work right now. A second Pacific Heights location is at 2016 Fillmore St. between California and Pine streets (✆ **415/474-1419**).

2250 Chestnut St. (btw. Scott and Pierce sts.). ✆ **415/474-4843.** Most main courses $6–$7. MC, V. Mon–Fri 7am–11pm; Sat–Sun 8am–11pm. Bus: 22, 28, 30, 30X, 43, 76, or 82X.

Mel's Drive-In ★ ☺ AMERICAN   Sure, it's contrived, touristy, and nowhere near healthy, but when you get that urge for a chocolate shake and banana cream pie at the stroke of midnight—or when you want to entertain the kids—no other place in the city comes through like Mel's Drive-In. Modeled after a classic 1950s diner, right down to the jukebox at each table, Mel's hearkens back to the halcyon days when cholesterol and fried foods didn't jab your guilty conscience with every greasy, wonderful bite. Too bad the prices don't reflect the '50s; a burger with fries and a Coke costs about $12.

Another Mel's at 3355 Geary St., at Stanyan Street (☎ **415/387-2244**), is open from 6am to 1am Sunday through Thursday and 6am to 3am Friday and Saturday. Additional locations are 1050 Van Ness (☎ **415/292-6357**), open Sunday through Thursday 6am to 3am and Friday through Sunday 6am to 4am; and 801 Mission St. (☎ **415/227-4477**), open Sunday through Wednesday 6am to 1am, Thursday 6am to 2am, and Friday and Saturday 24 hours.

2165 Lombard St. (at Fillmore St.). ☎ **415/921-2867.** www.melsdrive-in.com. Main courses $6.50–$12 breakfast, $7–$10 lunch, $8–$15 dinner. MC, V. Sun–Wed 6am–1am; Thurs 6am–2am; Fri–Sat 24 hr. Bus: 22, 30, or 43.

Japantown

Takara ★ JAPANESE/SUSHI   When I'm in the mood for sushi, I often head to this unassuming restaurant tucked at the eastern end of Japantown. Not only is it large enough that you don't have to wait in a long line (unlike other local sushi spots), but the fish is extremely fresh and affordable and the other offerings are fantastic. Along with standard nigiri, I always go for the seaweed with fabulously tangy vinegar and a floating quail egg. On the occasions that I can curb my sushi craving, I get more than my fill with their *yosenabe*. A meal for two that's under $20, it's a giant pot of soup brought to the table on a burner accompanied by a plate of fresh raw meat or seafood and vegetables. After you push the food into the liquid and briefly let it cook, you ladle it out and devour it. Even after serving two hungry people, there are always leftovers. Other favorites are anything with shrimp—pulled live from the tank—and sukiyaki, another tableside cooking experience. Bargain hunters should come for a lunch plate.

22 Peace Plaza no. 202 (in Japan Center Miyako Mall). ☎ **415/921-2000.** www.takararestaurant.com. Reservations recommended. Main courses $15–$23. MC, V. Daily 11:30am–2:30pm and 5:30–10pm.

Civic Center

EXPENSIVE

Jardinière ★★ CALIFORNIA/FRENCH   Jardinière is a pre- and post-symphony favorite, and it also happens to be the perfect setting for enjoying a cocktail with your significant other. A culinary dream team created the elegant dining room and sophisticated menu: owner-designer Pat Kuleto, who created the beautiful champagne-inspired decor, and owner-chef Traci Des Jardins, one of the city's most popular chefs. On most evenings the bi-level brick structure is abuzz with an older crowd (including ex-mayor Brown, a regular) who sip cocktails at the centerpiece mahogany bar or watch the scene discreetly from the circular balcony. The restaurant's champagne theme extends to twinkling lights and clever ice buckets built into the balcony railing, making the atmosphere conducive to splurging in the best of style—especially when live jazz is playing (7:30pm

🎁 SWEET nothings

Hayes Valley will woo you with its cutesy boutiques, littering of sidewalk cafes, and specialty stores like **Flight 001,** a visually striking display of designer travel gear. But perhaps our favorite stop in the new "it" neighborhood is for a perfect macaroon at sweet shop **Miette ★★**, 449 Octavia St. (at Linden St.; ✆ **415/626-6221**)—and maybe a bag of brightly colored, homemade candies to go, you know, since we've already come all this way—followed by a cup of joe across the way at **Blue Bottle Coffee ★★**, 315 Linden St., a well-hidden kiosk down a side alley that serves some of the city's best organic, gourmet, brewed-to-order coffee. Second locations for both can be found in the Ferry Building. A third Miette branch is at 2109 Chestnut St. (btw. Steiner and Pierce sts.; ✆ **415/359-0628**). You'll find two other Blue Bottle locations at 66 Mint St. at Jessie Street (✆ **415/495-3394**), which is home to a fancy $25,000 Japanese coffeemaker; and the new rooftop sculpture garden at SFMOMA.

nightly). The daily changing menu might include seared scallops with truffled potatoes and truffle reduction; sautéed petrale sole with Alsatian cabbage and Riesling sauce; or venison with celery root, red wine, braised cabbage, and juniper sauce. There's also an outstanding cheese selection and superb wine list—many by the glass, and more than 500 bottles.

300 Grove St. (at Franklin St.). ✆ **415/861-5555.** www.jardiniere.com. Reservations recommended. Main courses $26–$40; 6-course tasting menu $99. AE, DC, DISC, MC, V. Sun–Wed 5–10:30pm; Thurs–Sat 5–11:30pm. Valet parking $10. Bus: 19 or 21.

MODERATE

Absinthe ★ FRENCH   This Hayes Valley hot spot is sexy, fun, reasonably priced, and frequented by everyone from the theatergoing crowd to the young and chic. Decor is all brasserie, with French rattan cafe chairs, copper-topped tables, a pressed-tin ceiling, soft lighting, period art, and a rich use of color and fabric, including leather and mohair banquettes. It's always a pleasure to unwind at the bar with a Ginger Rogers—gin, mint, lemon juice, ginger ale, and a squeeze of lime. The lengthy lunch menu offers everything from oysters and caviar to Caesar salad and croque monsieur, but I always end up getting their outstanding open-faced smoked-trout sandwich on grilled Italian bread. In the divided dining room, main courses are equally satisfying, from coq au vin and steak frites to roasted whole Dungeness crab with poached leeks in mustard vinaigrette, salt-roasted potatoes, and aioli. The best item on the weekend brunch menu is the creamy polenta, with mascarpone, maple syrup, bananas, and toasted walnuts.

398 Hayes St. (at Gough St.). ✆ **415/551-1590.** www.absinthe.com. Reservations recommended. Brunch $8–$14; most main courses $12–$20 lunch, $14–$30 dinner. AE, DC, DISC, MC, V. Tues–Fri 11:30am–midnight; Sat 11am–midnight; Sun 11am–10pm. Bar Tues–Fri 11:30am–midnight (until 2am Fri); Sat 11am–2am; Sun 11am–midnight. Valet parking (Tues–Sat after 5pm) $10. Bus: 21.

Suppenküche ★★ GERMAN   It's a challenge to create a German beer hall anywhere outside of Germany and not come off as a bit tawdry. But this Hayes Valley favorite proved all of my preconceived notions wrong. Diners sit at long wooden tables, often right next to other parties, and the food is as authentic as it comes, with Wiener schnitzel, spaetzle, potato pancakes, bratwurst and sauerkraut, and other familiar Bavarian fare served heartily. The drink menu is full of German, Austrian, and Belgian brews and wine, and those with supreme thirst to quench should consider ordering Das Boot: 2 liters of your favorite beer served in a boot-shaped glass—if nothing else, it sure is fun to say. Drinks also come in 3-liter and 5-liter beer glasses, as well as the standard pint.

525 Laguna St. (at Hayes St.). ✆ **415/252-9289.** www.suppenkuche.com. Reservations recommended for parties of 6 or more. Main courses $14–$20. AE, DC, DISC, MC, V. Daily 5–10pm; Sun brunch 10am–2:30pm. Valet parking $7. Bus: 19, 21, 31, or 38.

Zuni Café ★★ 🎁 MEDITERRANEAN   Zuni Café embodies the best of San Francisco dining: Its clientele spans young hipsters to hunky gay guys, the cuisine is consistently terrific, and the atmosphere is electric. Its expanse of windows overlooking Market Street gives the place a sense of space, despite the fact that it's always packed. For the full effect, stand at the bustling, copper-topped bar and order a glass of wine and a few oysters from the oyster menu (a dozen or so varieties are on hand at all times). Then, because *of course* you made advance reservations, take your seat in the stylish exposed-brick two-level maze of little dining rooms or on the patio. Then do what we all do: Splurge on chef Judy Rodgers's Mediterranean-influenced menu. Although the ever-changing menu always includes meat (such as hanger steak), fish (grilled or braised on the kitchen's wood grill), and pasta (tagliatelle with nettles, applewood-smoked bacon, butter, and Parmesan), it's almost sinful not to order her brick-oven-roasted chicken for two with Tuscan-style bread salad. I rarely pass up the polenta with mascarpone and a proper Caesar salad. But then again, if you're there for lunch or after 10pm, the hamburger on grilled rosemary focaccia bread is a strong contender for the city's best. Whatever you decide, be sure to order a stack of shoestring potatoes.

1658 Market St. (at Franklin St.). ✆ **415/552-2522.** www.zunicafe.com. Reservations recommended. Main courses $10–$19 lunch, $15–$29 dinner. AE, MC, V. Tues–Thurs 11:30am–11pm; Fri–Sat 11:30am–midnight; Sun 11am–11pm. Valet parking $10. Bus: 6, 7, or 71. Streetcar: All Market St. streetcars.

Haight-Ashbury

INEXPENSIVE

Cha Cha Cha ★★ 🍴 CARIBBEAN   This is one of my all-time favorite places to get festive, but it's not for everybody. Dining at Cha Cha Cha is not about a meal; it's about an experience. Put your name on the waiting list, crowd into the minuscule bar, and sip sangria while you wait. When you do get seated (it can take up to two pitchers of sangria, but by then you really don't care), you'll dine in a loud—and I mean *loud*—dining room with Santería altars, banana trees, and plastic tropical-themed tablecloths. The best thing to do is order from the tapas menu and share the dishes family-style. Fried calamari, fried new potatoes, Cajun shrimp, and mussels in saffron broth are all bursting with flavor and accompanied by luscious sauces—whatever you choose, you can't go wrong. This is the kind of place where you take friends in a partying mood and make an evening of it. If you want the flavor without the festivities, come during lunch. Their second, larger location, in the Mission District, at 2327 Mission St., between 19th and 20th streets (✆ **415/824-1502**), is open for dinner only and has a full bar specializing in mojitos.

1801 Haight St. (at Shrader St.). ✆ **415/386-7670.** www.cha3.com. Reservations not accepted. Tapas $4–$9; main courses $12–$15. MC, V. Daily 11:30am–4pm; Sun–Thurs 5–11pm; Fri–Sat 5–11:30pm. Bus: 6, 7, or 71. Streetcar: N.

TOP CHEF'S YIGIT PURA PICKS
YOUR NEXT dessert

The winner of Top Chef Just Desserts *Season 1, Yigit Pura (pronounced "Yeet") started cooking in his hometown of Ankara, Turkey, worked with Daniel Boulud in New York and Las Vegas, and now lives here in San Francisco, where he works as Executive Pastry Chef for Taste Catering (www.tastecatering.com). We posed a question slightly less taxing than a Quickfire Challenge: "Which local bakeries and desserts excite you?"*

Acme Bread: Their breads are by far some of the best I've had in the United States, especially their rustic country loaves—great crunchy crust with the perfect tender chewy texture inside!

Bi-Rite Creamery: The Lavender Honey Ice Cream here is so satisfying. It's creamy, without having too much of an egg flavor, and instead, the bright flavors of the European honey shines in a very masculine manner. I love it with their berry compote and gingersnap croutons.

Boulette's Larder: I love everything in this space. It is all made with such precision and love. I especially love their fresh house-made English muffins, which they have on Saturdays at 10am. If you get up early enough to go to the Ferry Building Farmers' Market, treat yourself to one.

Kika's Treats (various retailers; http://kikastreats.com): Kika (Cristina Besher) is only sweeter than her desserts. She makes wholesale baked goods here in SF, and you can find her products in most retail stores. I am addicted to her caramelized graham crackers enrobed in milk chocolate. I'm certain she puts sea salt in the base, which makes it so addictive!

Tartine Bakery: Every once in a blue moon they will make "Bostoc," which in essence is a slice of thick brioche soaked in light orange flower syrup, baked with almond cream and sliced almonds. Tartine takes this and adds kumquat jam, and they bake it super dark. It's heaven. Sweet, bitter, chewy goodness!

Kan Zaman ★ 🎁 MIDDLE EASTERN   An evening dining at Kan Zaman is one of those quintessential Haight-Ashbury experiences that you can't wait to tell your friends about back home. As you pass through glass-beaded curtains, you're led by the hostess to knee-high tables under a billowed canopy tent. Shoes removed, you sit cross-legged with your friends in cushioned comfort. The most adventurous of your group requests an *argeeleh*, a large hookah pipe filled with fruity honey or apricot tobacco. Reluctantly at first, everyone simultaneously sips the sweet smoke from the cobralike tendrils emanating from the hookah; then dinner arrives—inexpensive platters offering a variety of classic Middle Eastern cuisine: smoky baba ghanouj, kibbe (cracked wheat with spiced lamb) meat pies, Casablanca beef couscous, spicy hummus with pita bread, succulent lamb and chicken kabobs. The spiced wine starts to take effect, just in time for the beautiful, sensuous belly dancers who glide across the dining room, mesmerizing the rapt audience with their seemingly impossible gyrations. The evening ends, the bill arrives: $17 each. Perfect. **Note:** Belly dancing starts at 9pm Thursday through Saturday only.

1793 Haight St. (at Shrader St.). ✆ **415/751-9656.** Main courses $4–$14. MC, V. Mon–Thurs 5pm–midnight; Fri 5pm–2am; Sat noon–2am; Sun noon–midnight. Bus: 6, 7, 66, 71, or 73. Metro: N.

Uva Enoteca ★★ ITALIAN   The Haight has seen a recent resurgence in its dining scene, which can largely be attributed to the arrival of gems like Uva Enoteca. The narrow wine bar with its exposed brick and intimate setting could easily be found in New York's West Village and is a breath of fresh air among Haight Street's other shoddy offerings. Start with a speck and apple purée bruschette and meat-and-cheese assortment; if you're unsure of which of the local varieties to order, ask Boris, and he'll bring you out a delectable pairing. If you still have stomach space to spare, follow that with a panini or *piadine* (flatbread sandwich), like my favorite, the pine-nut butter, raisins, bitter greens, and balsamic selection, and pasta or pizza. The wine selection changes weekly, with 80 or so types—all Italian, all the time—always on tap, which you can order by the bottle, 2 ounces, 6 ounces, or 8 ounces. The gelato, made special for the restaurant by a local company, is a can't-miss, with flavors like avocado, honey granola, bergamot, and kiwi (alongside more normal types like chocolate and vanilla). One thing's for sure: You'll want to make repeat visits to Uva Enoteca to be able to taste everything on the menu and feel as if you've done it justice.

568 Haight St. (btw. Fillmore and Steiner sts.). ✆ **415/829-2024.** www.uvaenoteca.com. Reservations recommended. Panini $8; pasta $14; pizza $13. DISC, MC, V. Sun–Thurs 5–11pm; Fri–Sat 5–11:30pm; brunch Sat–Sun 11am–2:30pm. Bus: 7, 22, or 71.

Richmond & Sunset Districts

MODERATE

Aziza ★★ MOROCCAN   If you're looking for something really different—or a festive spot for a large party—head deep into the Avenues for an exotic taste of Morocco. Chef-owner Mourad Lahlou creates an excellent dining experience through colorful and distinctly Moroccan surroundings combined with a modern yet authentic take on the cuisine of his homeland. In any of the three opulently adorned dining rooms (the front room features private booths, the middle room is more formal, and the back has lower seating and a Moroccan lounge feel), you can indulge in the seasonal five-course tasting menu ($62) or individual treats such as kumquat-enriched lamb shank; saffron guinea hen with preserved lemon and olives; or Paine Farm squab with wild mushrooms, bitter greens, and a *ras el hanout* reduction (a traditional Moroccan blend of 40 or so spices). Consider finishing off with my favorite dessert (if it's in season): rhubarb galette with rose-and geranium-scented crème fraîche, vanilla aspic, and rhubarb consommé.

5800 Geary Blvd. (at 22nd Ave.). ✆ **415/752-2222.** www.aziza-sf.com. Reservations recommended. Main courses $15–$28. MC, V. Wed–Mon 5:30–10:30pm. Valet parking $8 weekdays, $10 weekends. Bus: 29 or 38.

Beach Chalet Brewery & Restaurant ★ AMERICAN   While Cliff House (see below) has more historical character and better ocean views, the Beach Chalet is where the locals go. The Chalet occupies the upper floor of a restored historic public lounge adorned with WPA frescoes that originally opened in 1900. Dinner is pricey, and the ocean view disappears with the sun, so come for lunch or an early dinner, when you can eat your hamburger, buttermilk-fried calamari, or grilled Atlantic salmon with one of the best vistas around. In the evening, it's a more local crowd, especially on Tuesday through Sunday evenings, when live bands accompany the cocktails and house-brewed ales. Breakfast is served here as well. In early 2004, owners Lara and Greg Truppelli added the adjoining **Park Chalet** restaurant to the Beach Chalet. The 3,000-square-foot glass-enclosed extension behind the original landmark building offers more casual fare—with entrees ranging from $11 to $23—including rib-eye steak, fish and chips, roasted chicken, and pizza. *Note:* Be careful getting into the parking lot (accessible only from the northbound side of the highway)—it's a quick, sandy turn.

1000 Great Hwy. (at west end of Golden Gate Park, near Fulton St.). ✆ **415/386-8439.** www. beachchalet.com. Main courses $8–$17 breakfast, $11–$27 lunch/dinner. AE, MC, V. Beach Chalet: Breakfast Mon–Fri 9–11am; lunch daily 11am–5pm; dinner Sun–Thurs 5–10pm, Fri–Sat 5–11pm; brunch Sat–Sun 9am–2pm. Park Chalet: Lunch Mon–Fri noon–9pm; dinner Sun–Thurs 5–9pm, Fri–Sat 5–11pm; brunch Sat–Sun 11am–2pm. Bus: 18, 31, or 38. Streetcar: N.

Cliff House ★ CALIFORNIAN/SEAFOOD   In the old days (we're talking way back), Cliff House was *the* place to go for a romantic night on the town. Nowadays, the revamped San Francisco landmark caters mostly to tourists who arrive to gander at the Sutro Baths remains next door or dine at the two remodeled restaurants. The more formal (and pricey) **Sutro's** has contemporary decor, spectacular panoramic views, and a fancy seafood-influenced American menu that showcases local ingredients. The food, while nothing revolutionary, is well prepared and features the likes of roasted organic beet salad; lobster and crab cakes with shaved fennel, romesco sauce, and caramelized Meyer lemon; and a mighty fine grilled lamb sirloin sandwich (at lunch). The same spectacular views in less dramatic but still beautiful surroundings can be found at the **Bistro,** which offers big salads, sandwiches, burgers, and other soul-satisfiers. For the most superb ocean views, come for sunset, so long as it looks like the fog will let up. Alternatively, overindulge to the tune of live harp music at the Sunday champagne buffet in the **Terrace Room.** (Reserve well in advance; it's a popular event.)

1090 Point Lobos (at Merrie Way). ✆ **415/386-3330.** www.cliffhouse.com. Reservations accepted for Sutro's only. Bistro main courses $9–$26 breakfast/lunch, $13–$26 dinner. Sutro main courses $19–$32 lunch, $29–$39 dinner; 3-course prix-fixe $25 lunch and $35 dinner (Mon–Fri only). AE, DC, DISC, MC, V. Bistro: Mon–Sat 9am–9:30pm; Sun 8:30am–9:30pm. Sutro: Daily 11:30am–3:30pm and 5–9:30pm; brunch Sun 10am–3:30pm. Bus: 18 or 38.

INEXPENSIVE

Burma Superstar ★★ 🍽 BURMESE   Despite its gratuitous name, this basic dining room garners two-star status by offering exceptional Burmese food at rock-bottom prices. Unfortunately, the allure of the tea-leaf salad, Burmese-style curry with potato, and sweet-tangy sesame beef is one of the city's worst-kept secrets. Add to that a no-reservations policy, and you can count on waiting in line for up to an hour. (Parties of two are seated more quickly than larger groups, and it's less crowded at lunch.) On the bright side, you can pencil your cellphone number onto the waiting list and browse the Clement Street shops until you receive a call—or else, head 2 blocks east to the sister restaurant, **B Star Bar** (127 Clement St.; ✆ **415/933-9900**), which essentially serves the same dishes for the same prices, but in a prettier, more polished setting without nearly the wait.

309 Clement St. (at Fourth Ave.). ☎ **415/387-2147.** www.burmasuperstar.com. Reservations not accepted. Main courses $8–$16. MC, V. Sun–Thurs 11am–3:30pm; Mon–Thurs 5–10pm; Fri–Sat 5–10:30pm. Bus: 2, 4, 38, or 44.

Ton Kiang ★★ CHINESE/DIM SUM   Ton Kiang is probably the number-one place in the city to have dim sum (served daily), only partially due to the fact that they make all their sauces, pickles, and other delicacies in-house. The experience goes like this: Wait in line (which is out the door 11am–1:30pm on weekends), get a table on the first or second floor, and get ready to say yes to dozens of delicacies, which are rolled past the table for your approval. From stuffed crab claws, roast Beijing duck, and a gazillion dumpling selections (including scallop and vegetable, shrimp, and beef), to the delicious and hard-to-find *doa miu* (snow pea sprouts flash-sautéed with garlic and peanut oil) and a mesmerizing mango pudding, every tray of morsels coming from the kitchen is an absolute delight. Though it's hard to get past the dim sum, which is served all day every day, the full menu of Hakka cuisine is worth investigation as well—fresh and flavorful soups; an array of seafood, beef, and chicken; and clay-pot specialties.

5821 Geary Blvd. (btw. 22nd and 23rd aves.). ☎ **415/387-8273.** www.tonkiang.net. Reservations accepted for parties of 8 or more. Dim sum $2–$6.50; main courses $9–$25. AE, DC, DISC, MC, V. Mon–Thurs 10am–9pm; Fri 10am–9:30pm; Sat 9:30am–9:30pm; Sun 9am–9pm. Bus: 38.

The Castro

INEXPENSIVE

Café Flore ✦ CALIFORNIAN   Because of its large and lively patio overlooking a busy section of Market Street intersection, Café Flore is the top sunny-day meet-me-for-coffee spot within the Castro community. And boy, is the people-watching good here—leather-wrapped bears, drag queens, trannies (Dad, is that you?), gym bunnies, and other antiestablishment types saunter down Market Street in full glory. As for dining at the cafe, here's how it works: You order drinks and desserts inside at the bar, then find a seat indoors or outside on the patio or sidewalk, and claim a spot. Next, go to the kitchen counter (there are no waiters), place your meal order and get a number, and the food will be delivered to your table. Many of the menu items are composed of mostly organic ingredients and include a succulent version of roasted chicken over rice, Niman Ranch hamburgers, soups, salads, and pastas. Breeders are always welcome as long as they behave, and breakfast is served until 3pm.

2298 Market St. (at Noe St.). ☎ **415/621-8579.** www.cafeflore.com. Reservations not accepted. American breakfast $5.95; main courses $4.50–$10. MC, V. Daily 7am–2am (kitchen closes at 10pm). Metro: F.

Chow ★ ✦ AMERICAN   Chow claims to serve American cuisine, but the management must be thinking of today's America, because the menu is not exactly meatloaf and apple pie. And that's just fine for eclectic and cost-conscious diners. After all, what's not to like about starting with a Cobb salad before moving on to Thai-style noodles with steak, chicken, peanuts, and spicy lime-chili garlic broth, or cioppino? Better yet, everything except the fish of the day costs under $15, especially the budget-wise daily sandwich specials, which range from meatball with mozzarella (Sun) to grilled tuna with Asian-style slaw, pickled ginger, and a wasabi mayonnaise (Mon); both come with salad, soup, or fries. Although the food and prices alone would be a good argument for coming here, beer on tap, a great inexpensive wine selection, and the fun, tavernlike environment clinch the deal. A second location, **Park Chow,** is at 1240 Ninth Ave. (✆ **415/665-9912**). You can't make reservations unless you have a party of eight or more, but if you're headed their way, you can call ahead to place your name on the wait list (recommended).

215 Church St. (near Market St.). ✆ **415/552-2469.** www.chowfoodbar.com. Reservations not accepted except for parties of 8 or more. Main courses $7–$15. DISC, MC, V. Sun–Thurs 8am–11pm; Fri–Sat 8am–midnight. Bus: 8, 22, or 37. Streetcar: F, J, K, L, or M.

Mission District

MODERATE

Bar Tartine ★★ AMERICAN   You've probably passed Bar Tartine a dozen times and not even noticed it's there—it flies under the radar like that. But once you discover it, you won't forget it anytime soon. Sister to the ever-popular Tartine Bakery down the street, from where it gets its delicious homemade bread, Bar Tartine opened in 2005 and quickly became a beloved Mission staple. Chef Chris Kronner recently took over kitchen duties and has been garnering high praise from diners and critics alike—especially for tantalizing signature starters like marrow bones with herb salad and savory bread pudding. Main courses run the surf-to-turf gamut from sand dabs in brown butter to a rib steak for two with salt-roast russet potatoes. Even if you're a dedicated chocoholic like me, you'd be wise to pass and sample some of the other, more inventive desserts, such as Meyer lemon pot de crème with huckleberries and biscotti, and coconut rice pudding with rum raisins and gingersnaps. The wildly popular **bakery and cafe** is located at 600 Guerrero St. and is open Monday 8am to 7pm, Tuesday and Wednesday 7:30am to 7pm, Thursday and Friday 7:30am to 8pm, Saturday 8am to 8pm, and Sunday 9am to 8pm.

561 Valencia St. (btw. 16th and 17th sts.). ✆ **415/487-1600.** www.bartartine.com. Reservations recommended. Main courses $14–$38. AE, DISC, MC, V. Tues–Wed and Sun 6–10pm; Thurs–Sat 6–11pm; Sat–Sun 11am–2:30pm. Parking lot at 18th and Valencia sts., $8. Bus: 26 or 33. Streetcar: J.

Beretta ★★ ITALIAN   Beretta is one of those restaurants that opened to so much buzz, it would be hard *not* to be let down. And yet, I wasn't. Its casual vibe and well-thought-out small bites have kept the place packed since its debut in early 2008. Pizzas are one-of-a-kind and what the place is known for: Choose one with baccala, potato, panna, onions, and capers; or the broccolini, pancetta, tomato, and mozzarella combo. If you're heading here after work for happy hour, nosh on antipasti plates like roasted beets with ricotta salata, meatballs in spicy tomato sauce, or eggplant caponatina with burrata. Need a heartier meal? Try one of the risotto dishes, like asparagus and *robiola* (Italian soft-ripened cheese) or saffron with *osso buco,* or a daily main course special like the herb-crusted halibut with fennel and olives. Don't feel guilty sampling an array of the unique cocktails, either: Beretta has numerous mixology titles—it would be a shame to let the drinks go untasted. *An added bonus:* If you forget to make a reservation in advance—and on most nights, this place is hopping—you can call 45 minutes prior to your arrival and have your name added to the list.

1199 Valencia St. (at 23rd St.). ✆ **415/695-1199.** www.berettasf.com. Reservations recommended. Pizzas $11–$15; main courses $12–$18. AE, DISC, MC, V. Mon–Fri 5:30pm–1am; Sat–Sun noon–1pm. Parking garage at 21st St. (btw. Mission and Valencia sts.). Bus: 26 or 33. BART: 24th St. station.

Delfina ★★ ITALIAN Unpretentious warehouse-chic atmosphere, reasonable prices, and chef/co-owner Craig Stoll's superb seasonal Italian cuisine have made this family-owned restaurant one of the city's most cherished. Stoll, who was one of *Food & Wine*'s Best New Chefs in 2001 and a 2005 James Beard Award nominee, changes the menu daily, while his wife, Annie, works the front of the house (when she's not being a mom). Standards include Niman Ranch flatiron steak with french fries, and roasted chicken with Yukon Gold mashed potatoes and royal trumpet mushrooms. The winter menu might include slow-roasted pork shoulder or gnocchi with squash and chestnuts, while spring indulgences can include sand dabs with frisée, fingerling potatoes, and lemon-caper butter; or lamb with polenta and sweet peas. Trust me—order the buttermilk *panna cotta* (custard) if it's available. *A plus:* A few tables and counter seating are reserved for walk-in diners. Delfina also has a heated and covered patio that's used mid-March through November—and don't miss **Pizzeria Delfina** next door (✆ **415/437-6800;** www.pizzeriadelfina.com), where you can enjoy the same high-quality ingredients in a more casual, less expensive setting. *Note:* A second pizzeria is at 2406 California St. (at Fillmore St.; ✆ 415/440-1189) in Pacific Heights.

3621 18th St. (btw. Dolores and Guerrero sts.). ✆ **415/552-4055.** www.delfinasf.com. Reservations recommended. Main courses $18–$26. MC, V. Mon–Thurs 5:30–10pm; Fri–Sat 5:30–11pm; Sun 5–10pm. Parking lot at 18th and Valencia sts., $8. Bus: 26 or 33. Streetcar: J.

Foreign Cinema ★★ MEDITERRANEAN This place is so chic and well hidden that it eludes me every time I drive past it on Mission Street. (*Hint:* Look for the valet stand.) The "cinema" here is a bit of a gimmick: It's an outdoor dining area (partially covered and heated, but still chilly) where mostly foreign films are projected onto the side of an adjoining building, with tableside minispeakers for audio. What's definitely not a gimmick, however, is the superb Mediterranean-inspired menu created by husband-and-wife team John Clark and Gayle Pirie. Snackers like me find solace at the oyster bar with a half-dozen locally harvested Miyagi oysters and a devilishly good *brandade* (fish purée) gratin. Heartier eaters can opt for grilled halibut with chanterelles and roasted figs in a fig vinaigrette; fried Madras curry-spiced chicken with gypsy peppers; or grilled natural rib-eye with Tuscan-style beans and rosemary-fried peppercorn sauce—all made from seasonal, sustainably farmed, organic ingredients when possible. Truth be told, even if the food weren't so good, I'd still come here—it's just that cool. If you have to wait for your table, consider stepping into their adjoining bar, Laszlo.

2534 Mission St. (btw. 21st and 22nd sts.). ✆ **415/648-7600.** www.foreigncinema.com. Reservations recommended. Main courses $18–$26. AE, MC, V. Mon–Thurs 6–10pm; Fri–Sat 5:30–11pm; Sun 5:30–10pm; brunch Sat 11am–3pm, Sun 11am–3:30pm. Valet parking $10. Bus: 14, 14L, or 49.

INEXPENSIVE

Taquerias La Cumbre MEXICAN If San Francisco commissioned a flag honoring its favorite food, we'd probably all be waving a banner of the Golden Gate Bridge bolstering a giant burrito—that's how much we love the mammoth tortilla-wrapped meals. Taquerias La Cumbre has been around forever and still retains its "Best Burrito" title, each deftly constructed using fresh pork, steak, chicken, or vegetables, plus cheese, beans, rice, salsa, and maybe a dash of guacamole or sour cream. The fact that it's served in a cafeteria-like brick-lined room with overly shellacked tables featuring a woman with overflowing cleavage makes it taste even better.

Alcatraz.

515 Valencia St. (btw. 16th and 17th sts.). ℭ **415/863-8205.** Reservations not accepted. Tacos and burritos $3.50–$6.50; dinner plates $5–$7. No credit cards. Mon–Sat 11am–9pm; Sun noon–9pm. Bus: 14, 22, 33, 49, or 53. BART: Mission.

Ti Couz ★ CREPES   At Ti Couz (pronounced "Tee Cooz"), one of the most architecturally stylish and popular restaurants in the Mission, the headliner is simple: the delicate, paper-thin crepe. More than 30 choices of fillings make for infinite expertly executed combinations. The menu advises you how to enjoy these wraps: Order a light crepe as an appetizer, a heftier one as a main course, and a drippingly sweet one for dessert. Recommended combinations are listed, but you can build your own from the 15 main-course selections (such as smoked salmon, mushrooms, sausage, ham, scallops, and onions) and more than 15 dessert options (caramel, fruit, chocolate, Nutella, and more). Soups and salads are equally stellar; the seafood salad, for example, is a delicious and generous compilation of shrimp, scallops, and ahi tuna with veggies and five kinds of lettuce.

3108 16th St. (at Valencia St.). ℭ **415/252-7373.** Reservations not accepted. Crepes $2–$12. MC, V. Mon and Fri 11am–11pm; Tues–Thurs 5–11pm; Sat–Sun 10am–11pm. Bus: 14, 22, 26, 33, 49, or 53. BART: 16th or Mission.

THE TOP ATTRACTIONS
Top San Francisco Sights

Alcatraz Island ★★★ ☺   Visible from Fisherman's Wharf, Alcatraz Island (also known as the Rock) has seen a checkered history. Juan Manuel Ayala was the first European to discover it in 1775 and named it after the many "alcatraces," or pelicans, that nested on the island. From the 1850s to 1933, it served as a military fortress, protecting the bay's shoreline, as well as a military prison. In 1934, the government converted the buildings of the military outpost into a maximum-security civilian penitentiary. Given the sheer cliffs, treacherous tides and currents,

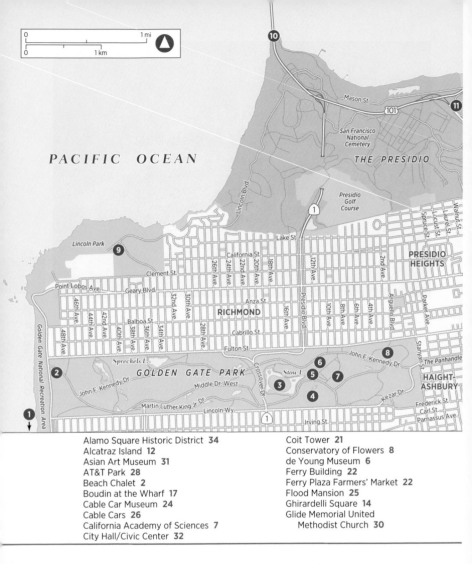

and frigid water temperatures, it was believed to be totally escape-proof. Among the famous gangsters who occupied cellblocks A through D were Al Capone; Robert Stroud, the so-called Birdman of Alcatraz (an expert in ornithological diseases); Machine Gun Kelly; and Alvin "Creepy" Karpis, a member of Ma Barker's gang. It cost a fortune to keep them imprisoned here because all supplies, including water, had to be shipped in. In 1963, after an apparent escape in which no bodies were recovered, the government closed the prison. It moldered abandoned until 1969, when a group of Native Americans chartered a boat to the island and symbolically reclaimed the island for the Indian people. They occupied the island until 1971—the longest occupation of a federal facility by Native Americans to this day—but eventually were forcibly removed by the U.S. government (see www.nps.gov/archive/alcatraz/indian.html for more information on the

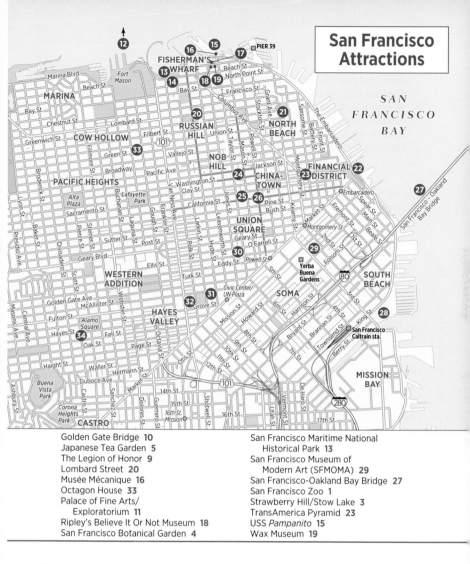

San Francisco
Attractions

SAN
FRANCISCO
BAY

PIER 39

FISHERMAN'S WHARF

Marina Blvd
Fort Mason
Beach St.
MARINA
Bay St.
Chestnut St.
Greenwich St.
COW HOLLOW
Lombard St.
Filbert St.
Green St.
Broadway
Pacific Ave.
PACIFIC HEIGHTS
Alta Plaza
Lafayette Park
Sacramento St.
Sutter St.
Post St.
Geary Blvd.
Ellis St.
WESTERN ADDITION
Turk St.
Golden Gate Ave.
McAllister St.
Fulton St.
Alamo Square
Hayes St.
HAYES VALLEY
Oak St.
Page St.
Haight St.
Waller St.
Hermann St.
Buena Vista Park
Duboce Ave.
14th St.
Corona Heights Park
15th St.
16th St.
CASTRO
17th St.

RUSSIAN HILL
NOB HILL
NORTH BEACH
CHINATOWN
FINANCIAL DISTRICT
UNION SQUARE
Civic Center/ UN Plaza
SOMA
Yerba Buena Gardens
SOUTH BEACH
MISSION BAY
San Francisco Caltrain sta.
Embarcadero
The Embarcadero
San Francisco-Oakland Bay Bridge

Golden Gate Bridge **10**
Japanese Tea Garden **5**
The Legion of Honor **9**
Lombard Street **20**
Musée Mécanique **16**
Octagon House **33**
Palace of Fine Arts/
Exploratorium **11**
Ripley's Believe It Or Not Museum **18**
San Francisco Botanical Garden **4**

San Francisco Maritime National
Historical Park **13**
San Francisco Museum of
Modern Art (SFMOMA) **29**
San Francisco-Oakland Bay Bridge **27**
San Francisco Zoo **1**
Strawberry Hill/Stow Lake **3**
TransAmerica Pyramid **23**
USS *Pampanito* **15**
Wax Museum **19**

Native American occupation of Alcatraz). The next year, the island was given over to the National Park Service, natural habitats were restored, and the wildlife that was driven away during the prison years began to return. Today you can see black-crested night herons and other seabirds here on a trail along the island's perimeter. Tours of the former prison, including an audio tour narrated by former guards and inmates, are offered daily.

Allow about 2½ hours for the round-trip boat ride and the tour. Wear comfortable shoes (the National Park Service notes that there are a lot of hills to climb) and take a heavy sweater or windbreaker, because even when the sun's out, it's cold and windy on Alcatraz. You should also bring snacks and drinks with you if you think you'll want them. Although there is a beverage-and-snack bar on the ferry, the options are limited and expensive, and only water is available on the

When asking for directions in San Francisco, be careful not to confuse numerical avenues with numerical streets. Numerical avenues (Third *Ave.* and so on) are in the Richmond and Sunset districts in the western part of the city.

Numerical streets (Third *St.* and so on) are south of Market Street in the eastern and southern parts of the city. Get this wrong, and you'll be an hour late for dinner.

island. The excursion to Alcatraz is very popular and space is limited, so purchase tickets as far in advance as possible (up to 90 days) via the **Alcatraz Cruises** website, at www.alcatrazcruises.com. You can also purchase tickets in person by visiting the Hornblower Alcatraz Landing ticket office at Pier 33. The first departure, called the "Early Bird," leaves at 9am, and ferries depart about every half-hour afterward until 4pm. Two night tours (highly recommended) are also available, offering a more intimate and wonderfully spooky experience.

For those who want to get a closer look at Alcatraz without going ashore, two boat-tour operators offer short circumnavigations of the island (see " Organized Tours" on p. 136 for complete information).

Pier 33, near Fisherman's Wharf. ℰ **415/981-7625.** www.alcatrazcruises.com or www.nps.gov/alcatraz. Admission (includes ferry trip and audio tour) $26 adults, $25 seniors 62 and over, $16 children 5–11. Night tours $33 adults, $31 seniors 62 and over, $20 children 5–11. Arrive at least 20 min. before departure time.

AT&T Park ★ ★ 📷   If you're a baseball fan, you'll definitely want to schedule a visit to the magnificent AT&T Park, home of the San Francisco Giants and hailed by the media as one of the finest ballparks in America. From April to October, an often sellout crowd of 40,800 fans pack the $319-million ballpark—which has a smaller, more intimate feel than Candlestick Park (where the 49ers play), as well as prime views of San Francisco Bay—and root for their National League's Giants.

During the season, tickets to the game can be hard to come by (and expensive when you find them), but you can try to join the Bleacher Bums by purchasing one of the 500 bleacher-seat tickets sold every day before the game. They make you work for it: You have to show up at the ballpark 4 hours early and then come back 2 hours before the game to get your tickets (maximum four per person). The upside is that the tickets are only $9 to $10.

If you can't even get bleacher seats, you can always join the "knothole gang" at the Portwalk (located behind right field) to catch a free glimpse of the game through cutout portholes into the ballpark. In the spirit of sharing, Portwalk peekers are encouraged to take in only an inning or two before giving way to fellow fans.

One guaranteed way to get into the ballpark is to take a **guided tour of AT&T Park** and go behind the scenes, where you'll see the press box, the dugout, the visitor's clubhouse, a luxury suite, and more. All tours run daily at 10:30am and 12:30pm. Ticket prices are $13 for adults, $11 for seniors 56 and over, and $7.50 for kids 12 and under. There are no tours on game days, and limited tours on the day of night games. To buy tickets online, log on to www.sfgiants.com, and then click on "AT&T Park" and "Ballpark Tours" from the drop-down list. You can also buy tour tickets at any Giants Dugout Store or Tickets.com outlet. For more tour information, call ℰ **415/972-2400.**

At the southeast corner of SoMa at the south end of the Embarcadero (bounded by King, Second, and Third sts.). (*) **415/972-2000.** www.sfgiants.com. Bus: 10, 15, 30, 45, or 47. Metro: N line.

Boudin at the Wharf ★ After more than 30 years of being an inconspicuous bread shop in the heart of Fisherman's Wharf, the Boudin Bakery was supersized a few years ago. The new, ultramodern, 26,000-square-foot flagship baking emporium is now nearly half a block long, housing not only their demonstration bakery, but also a museum, a gourmet marketplace, a cafe, an espresso bar, and a restaurant. The Boudin (pronounced Bo-*deen*) family has been baking sourdough French bread in San Francisco since the gold rush, using the same simple recipe and original "mother dough" for more than 150 years. About 3,000 loaves a day are baked within the glass-walled bakery; visitors can watch the entire process from a 30-foot observation window along Jefferson Street or from a catwalk suspended directly over the bakery (it's quite entertaining). You'll smell it before you see it: The heavenly aroma emanating from the bread ovens is purposely blasted out onto the sidewalk.

The best time to arrive is in the morning when the demo bakery is in full swing. Catch the action along Jefferson Street; then when your appetite is stoked, head to the cafe for an inexpensive breakfast of sourdough French toast or their Bread Bowl Scrambler filled with eggs, bacon, cheddar, onions, and bell peppers. After breakfast, spend some time browsing the museum and marketplace. On the upper level is **Bistro Boudin,** a full-service restaurant serving lunch, dinner, and weekend brunch. Tours of the bakery are available as well. *Tip:* If the line at the cafe is too long, walk across the parking lot to the octagon-shaped building, which serves the same items—Boudin chowder bowls, salads, pizzas—in a serve-yourself setting.

160 Jefferson St. (btw. Taylor and Mason sts.). (*) **415/928-1849.** www.boudinbakery.com. Bakery/cafe/marketplace daily 10am–7pm.

Cable Cars ★★★ ☺ ▣ Although they may not be San Francisco's most practical means of transportation, cable cars are certainly the best loved and are a must-experience when visiting the city. Designated official moving historic landmarks by the National Park Service in 1964, they clank up and down the city's steep hills like mobile museum pieces, tirelessly hauling thousands of tourists each day to Fisherman's Wharf at the brisk pace of 9 mph.

As the story goes, London-born engineer Andrew Hallidie was inspired to invent the cable cars after witnessing a heavily laden carriage pulled by a team of overworked horses slip and roll backward down a steep San Francisco slope, dragging the horses behind it. Hallidie resolved to build a mechanical contraption to

---

The Secret to Catching Cable Cars

Here's the secret to catching a ride on a cable car: Don't wait in line with all the tourists at the turnaround stops at the beginning and end of the lines. Walk a few blocks up the line (follow the tracks) and do as the locals do: Hop on when the car stops, hang on to a pole, and have your $5 ready to hand to the brakeman (hoping, of course, that he'll never ask). On a really busy weekend, however, the cable cars often don't stop to pick up passengers en route because they're full, so you might have to stand in line at the turnarounds.

Coit Tower.

replace horses, and in 1873, the first cable car made its maiden voyage from the top of Clay Street. Promptly ridiculed as "Hallidie's Folly," the cars were slow to gain acceptance.

Even today, many visitors have difficulty believing that these vehicles, which have no engines, actually work. The cars, each weighing about 6 tons, run along a steel cable, enclosed under the street on a center rail. You can't see the cable unless you peer straight down into the crack, but you'll hear its characteristic clickity-clacking sound whenever you're nearby. The cars move when the gripper (not the driver) pulls back a lever that closes a pincerlike "grip" on the cable. The speed of the car, therefore, is determined by the speed of the cable, which is a constant 9½ mph—never more, never less.

The two types of cable cars in use hold a maximum of 90 and 100 passengers, and limits are rigidly enforced. The best view (and the most fun) is from a perch on the outer running boards—but hold on tightly, especially around corners.

Hallidie's cable cars were imitated and used throughout the world, but all have been replaced by more efficient means of transportation. San Francisco planned to do so, too, but met with so much opposition that the cable cars' perpetuation was actually written into the city charter in 1955. The mandate cannot be revoked without the approval of a majority of the city's voters—a distant and doubtful prospect.

San Francisco's three existing cable car lines form the world's only surviving system, which you can experience for yourself, should you choose to wait in the often long lines (up to a 2-hr. wait in summer).

Powell–Hyde and Powell–Mason lines begin at the base of Powell and Market sts.; California St. line begins at the foot of Market St. at the Embarcadero. $5 per ride.

Coit Tower ★★   In a city known for its great views and vantage points, Coit Tower is one of the best. Atop Telegraph Hill, just east of North Beach, the round stone tower offers panoramic views of the city and the bay.

Completed in 1933, the tower is the legacy of Lillie Hitchcock Coit, a wealthy eccentric who left San Francisco a $125,000 bequest "for the purpose of adding beauty to the city I have always loved." Though many believe the tower is a fire-hose-shaped homage to San Francisco firefighters (Coit had been saved from a fire as a child and became a lifelong fan and mascot for Knickerbocker Engine Co. #5), the tower is merely an expression of Coit's esteem; a memorial to firefighters is down below in Washington Square Park.

Inside the base of the tower are impressive and slightly controversial (by 1930s standards) murals entitled *Life in California* and *1934,* which were completed under the Depression-era Public Works Art Project. Depicting California agriculture, industry, and even its leftist leanings (check out the socialist references in the library and on the newsstands), the murals are the collaborative effort of more than 25 artists, many of whom had studied under Mexican muralist Diego Rivera.

The only bummer: The narrow street leading to the tower is often clogged with tourist traffic. If you can, find a parking spot in North Beach and hoof it (or go green and walk the whole way). The Filbert and Greenwich steps leading up to Telegraph Hill are one of the most beautiful walks in the city (p. 140).

Telegraph Hill. ✆ **415/362-0808.** Admission is free to enter; elevator ride to the top is $5 adults, $3.50 seniors and youth 13–17, $1.50 children 6–12. Daily 10am–5pm. Bus: 39 (Coit).

Ferry Building Marketplace ★★★ 🎁 There's no better way to enjoy a San Francisco morning than strolling this gourmet marketplace in the Ferry Building and snacking your way through breakfast or lunch. San Franciscans—myself included—can't get enough of this place; we're still amazed at what a fantastic job they did renovating the interior. The Marketplace is open daily and includes much of Northern California's best gourmet bounty: Cowgirl Creamery's Artisan Cheese Shop, Recchiuti Confections (amazing chocolate), Acme Breads, Hog Island Oysters, gourmet fast food from Napa's Gott's Roadside Tray Gourmet (formerly Taylor's Refresher), famed Vietnamese restaurant the Slanted Door, and myriad other restaurants, delis, gourmet coffee shops, specialty foods, and wine bars. Check out the Imperial Tea Court, where you'll be taught the traditional Chinese way to steep and sip your tea; nosh on premium sturgeon roe at Tsar Nicoulai Caviar, a small Parisian-style "caviar cafe"; buy fancy cooking items at the Sur La Table shop; grab a bite and savor the bayfront views from in- and outdoor tables; or browse the Farmers' Market when it's up and running (see below). Trust me, you'll love this place.

The Embarcadero, at Market St. ✆ **415/693-0996.** www.ferrybuildingmarketplace.com. Most stores daily 10am–6pm; restaurant hours vary. Bus: 2, 7, 12, 14, 21, 66, or 71. Streetcar: F. BART: Embarcadero.

Ferry Plaza Farmers' Market ★★★ If you're heading to the Ferry Building Marketplace or just happen to be in the area at the right time (especially a sunny Sat), make a point of visiting the Farmers' Market, which is held in the outdoor areas in front of and behind the marketplace. This is where San Francisco foodies and many of the best local chefs—including the famed Alice Waters of Chez Panisse—gather, hang out, and peruse stalls hawking the finest Northern California fruits, vegetables, breads, meats, dairy, flowers, ready-made snacks, and to-go meals by local restaurants. You'll be amazed at the variety and quality, and the crowded scene itself is something to behold. Drop by on Saturday from 9am to noon for a serious social fest, including tours of the market and culinary demos by city chefs.

The Embarcadero, at Market St. ☎ **415/291-3276.** www.cuesa.org. Year-round Tues 10am–2pm, Sat 8am–2pm. Bus: 2, 7, 12, 14, 21, 66, or 71. Streetcar: F. BART: Embarcadero.

Fisherman's Wharf ☺   Few cities in America are as adept at wholesaling their historical sites as San Francisco, which has converted Fisherman's Wharf into one of the most popular tourist attractions in the world. Unless you come early in the morning to watch the few remaining fishing boats depart, you won't find many traces of the traditional waterfront life that once existed here—the only trolling going on at Fisherman's Wharf these days is for tourist dollars. Nonetheless, everyone always seems to be enjoying themselves as they stroll down PIER 39 on a sunny day, especially the kids.

Originally called Meigg's Wharf, this bustling strip of waterfront got its present moniker from generations of fishermen who used to dock their boats here. A small fleet of fewer than 30 fishing boats still set out from here, but mostly it's one long shopping and entertainment mall that stretches from Ghirardelli Square at the west end to PIER 39 at the east.

Accommodating a total of 300 boats, two marinas flank PIER 39 and house the sightseeing ferry fleets, including departures to Alcatraz Island. Twenty years ago, hundreds of California sea lions took up residence on the floating docks, attracted by herring (and free lodging). They can be seen most days sunbathing, barking, and belching in the marina—some nights you can hear them all the way from Washington Square. Weather permitting, the **Marine Mammal Center** (☎ **415/289-SEAL** [7325]) offers an educational talk at PIER 39 on weekends from 11am to 5pm that teaches visitors about the range, habitat, and adaptability of the California sea lion.

Some people love Fisherman's Wharf; others can't get far enough away from it. Most agree that, for better or for worse, it has to be seen at least once in your lifetime. Some traces of old-school San Francisco character still remain here, particularly the convivial seafood street vendors who dish out piles of fresh Dungeness crab and clam chowder from their steaming stainless-steel carts. Also

Fisherman's Wharf.

FUNKY favorites AT FISHERMAN'S WHARF

The following attractions clustered on or near Fisherman's Wharf are great fun for kids, adults, and kitsch lovers of all ages. My favorite is the ominous-looking World War II submarine **USS *Pampanito,*** Pier 45, Fisherman's Wharf (✆ **415/775-1943;** www.maritime.org), which saw plenty of action in the Pacific. It has been completely restored, and visitors are free to crawl around inside and play *Das Boot.* Admission is $10 for ages 13 and older, $6 for seniors 62 and older, $4 for children 6 to 12, and free for children 5 and under; the family pass (two adults, up to four kids) costs $20. The *Pampanito* is open daily at 9am.

Ripley's Believe It or Not! Museum, 175 Jefferson St. (✆ **415/771-6188;** www.ripleysf.com), has drawn curious spectators through its doors for over 30 years. Inside you'll experience a world of improbabilities: a ⅓-scale matchstick cable car, a shrunken human torso once owned by Ernest Hemingway, a dinosaur made from car bumpers, a walk through a kaleidoscope tunnel, and video displays and illusions. Robert LeRoy Ripley's infamous arsenal may lead you to ponder whether truth is, in fact, stranger than fiction. What it won't do is blow your mind or feel truly worth the money. That said, with the right attitude, it's easy to enjoy an hour here playing amid the goofy and interactive displays, with lots of laughs included in the admission price, which is $17 for adults, $10 for children 5 to 12, and free for children 4 and under. The museum opened with new exhibits in May 2011; hours are Sunday through Thursday 9am to 11pm, and 9am until midnight on Friday and Saturday (open 10am in winter months).

Conceived and executed in the Madame Tussaud mold, San Francisco's **Wax Museum,** 145 Jefferson St. (✆ **800/439-4305** or 415/202-0402; www.waxmuseum.com), has long been a kitschy-fun tourist trap. The museum has more than 270 lifelike figures, including Oprah Winfrey, Johnny Depp, Marilyn Monroe, John Wayne, former president George W. Bush, former Giants baseball star Barry Bonds, rap artist Eminem, and "Feared Leaders" such as Fidel Castro. The Chamber of Horrors features Dracula, Frankenstein, and a werewolf, along with bloody victims hanging from meat hooks. Other galleries include King Tut's tomb, the Palace of Living Art, and, for all you geeks out there, Nobel Prize–Winning Scientists. Admission is $14 for adults, $10 for juniors 12 to 17 and seniors 55 and older, $7 for children 6 to 11, and free for children 5 and under. The complex is open from 10am to 9pm every day of the year.

worth a look-see is the wonderful **Musée Mécanique** at Pier 45, an antique arcade featuring dozens of old-fashioned coin-operated amusements, including fortunetellers, an enormous mechanical carnival, and "Laffing Sal," the guffawing bust that once terrified children outside Playland at the Beach. A walk-through aquarium, a real World War II submarine, a blues bar, and the **Rain Forest Café** offer enough entertainment to amuse everyone here, even us snobby locals.

At Taylor St. and the Embarcadero. ✆ **415/674-7503.** www.fishermanswharf.org. Bus: 15, 30, 32, 39, 42, or 82X. Streetcar: F. Cable car: Powell–Mason to the last stop and walk to the wharf. If

The California Academy of Sciences.

you're arriving by car, park on adjacent streets or on the wharf btw. Taylor and Jones sts. for $16 per day, $8 with validation from participating restaurants.

Ghirardelli Square   This National Historic Landmark property dates from 1864, when it served as a factory making Civil War uniforms, but it's best known as the former chocolate and spice factory of Domingo Ghirardelli (pronounced "*Gear*-ar-delly"), who purchased it in 1893. The factory has since been converted into an unimpressive three-level mall containing 30-plus stores and five dining establishments. Street performers entertain regularly in the West Plaza and fountain area. Incidentally, the Ghirardelli Chocolate Company still makes chocolate, but its factory is in a lower-rent district in the East Bay. Still, if you have a sweet tooth, you won't be disappointed at the mall's fantastic (and expensive) old-fashioned soda fountain, which is open until midnight. Their "world famous" hot-fudge sundae is good, too. (Then again, have you ever had a bad hot-fudge sundae?) As if you need another excuse to laze the day away in this sweet spot, the square now boasts free wireless Internet.

900 North Point St. (btw. Polk and Larkin sts.). ✆ **415/775-5500.** www.ghirardellisq.com. Stores generally open daily 10am–9pm in summer; Sun–Fri 10am–6pm, Sat 10am–9pm rest of year. Parking $2.25 per 20 min. (1–1½ hr. free with purchase and validation, max. $30).

Golden Gate Bridge ★★★ ☺   The year 2007 marked the 70th birthday of possibly the most beautiful, and certainly the most photographed, bridge in the world. Often half veiled by the city's trademark rolling fog, San Francisco's Golden Gate Bridge, named for the strait leading from the Pacific Ocean to the San Francisco Bay, spans tidal currents, ocean waves, and battering winds to connect the City by the Bay with the Redwood Empire to the north.

With its gracefully suspended single span, spidery bracing cables, and zooming twin towers, the bridge looks more like a work of abstract art than one of the 20th century's greatest practical engineering feats. Construction was completed

GoCar Tours of San Francisco

If the thought of walking up and down San Francisco's brutally steep streets has you sweating already, consider renting a talking GoCar instead. The tiny yellow three-wheeled convertible cars are easy and fun to drive—every time I see one of these things, the people riding in them are grinning from ear to ear—and they're cleverly guided by a talking GPS (Global Positioning System), which means that the car always knows where you are, even if you don't. The most popular computer-guided tour is a 2-hour loop around the Fisherman's Wharf area, out to the Marina District, through Golden Gate Park, and down Lombard Street, the "crookedest street in the world." As you drive, the talking car tells you where to turn and what landmarks you're passing. Even if you

stop to check something out, as soon as you turn your GoCar back on, the tour picks up where it left off. Or you can just cruise around wherever you want (but not across the Golden Gate Bridge). There's a lockable trunk for your things, and the small size makes parking a breeze. Keep in mind, this isn't a Ferrari—two adults on a long, steep hill may involve one of you walking. You can rent a GoCar from 1 hour (about $49) to a full day. You'll have to wear a helmet, and you must be a licensed driver at least 18 years of age. The GoCar rental shop is at 2715 Hyde St., between Beach and North Point streets at Fisherman's Wharf. For more information, call *©* **800/91-GoCar** (914-6227) or 415/441-5695, or log on to their website at www.gocarsf.com.

in May 1937 at the then-colossal cost of $35 million (plus another $39 million in interest financed entirely by bridge tolls).

The 1¾-mile bridge (including the approach), which reaches a height of 746 feet above the water, is awesome to cross. Although kept to a maximum of 45 miles an hour, traffic usually moves quickly, so crossing by car won't give you too much time to see the sights. If you drive from the city, take the last San Francisco exit, right before the toll plaza, park in the southeast parking lot, and make the crossing by foot. Back in your car, continue to Marin's Vista Point, at the bridge's northern end. Look back, and you'll be rewarded with one of the finest views of San Francisco.

Millions of people visit the bridge each year, gazing up at the tall orange towers, out at the vistas of San Francisco and Marin County, and down into the stacks of oceangoing liners. You can walk out onto the span from either end, but be prepared—it's usually windy and cold, and the traffic is noisy. Still, walking even a short distance is one of the best ways to experience the immense scale of the structure and the perfect place to sing "San Francisco . . . open your Golden Gate."

Hwy. 101 N. www.goldengatebridge.org. $6 cash toll collected when driving south. Bridge-bound Golden Gate Transit buses ((*©* **511**) depart hourly during the day for Marin County, starting from Mission and First sts. (across the street from the Transbay Terminal and stopping at Market and Seventh sts., at the Civic Center, along Van Ness Ave., at Lombard and Fillmore sts., and at Francisco and Richardson sts.).

Lombard Street ★ Known (erroneously) as the "crookedest street in the world," this whimsically winding block of Lombard Street draws thousands of visitors each year (much to the chagrin of neighborhood residents, most of whom would prefer to block off the street to tourists). The angle of the street is so steep that the road has to snake back and forth to make a descent possible. The brick-lined street zig-zags around the residences' bright flower gardens, which explode with color during warmer months. This short stretch of Lombard Street is one-way, downhill, and fun to drive. Take the curves slowly and in low gear, and expect a wait during the weekend. Save your film for the bot-tom, where, if you're lucky, you can find a parking space and take a few snapshots of the silly spectacle. You can also take staircases (without curves) up or down on either side of the street. In truth, most locals don't understand what the fuss is all about. I'm guessing the draw is the combination of seeing such a

Lombard Street.

famous landmark, the challenge of negotiating so many steep curves, and a clas-sic photo op. *FYI:* Vermont Street, between 20th and 22nd streets in Potrero Hill, is even more crooked, but not nearly as picturesque.

Btw. Hyde and Leavenworth sts.

Golden Gate Park

The 1,017-acre Golden Gate Park consists of dozens of gardens and attractions connected by wooded paths and paved roads. While many worthy sites are clearly visible, there are infinite hidden treasures, so pick up information at **McLaren Lodge and Park Headquarters** (at Stanyan and Fell sts.; ✆ **415/831-2700;** open daily; park maps $3) if you want to find the more hidden spots. Of the doz-ens of special gardens in the park, most recognized are **McLaren Memorial Rhododendron Dell,** the **Rose Garden, Strybing Arboretum,** and, at the western edge of the park, a springtime array of thousands of tulips and daffodils around the **Dutch windmill.**

In addition to the highlights described in this section, the park contains lots of recreational facilities: tennis courts; baseball, soccer, and polo fields; a golf course; riding stables; and fly-casting pools. The Strawberry Hill boathouse han-dles boat rentals. Enter the park at Kezar Drive, an extension of Fell Street; bus riders can take no. 5, 6, 7, 16AX, 16BX, 66, or 71.

BEACH CHALET   Listed on the National Register of Historic places in 1981, the Spanish-Colonial Beach Chalet, 1000 Great Hwy., at the west end of Golden Gate Park near Fulton Street (✆ **415/386-8439**), was designed by Willis Polk in 1925. In the 1930s, the Works Progress Administration (WPA) commissioned Lucien Labaudt (who also painted the Coit Tower frescoes) to create frescoes, mosaics, and wood carvings of San Francisco life. Today, after a renovation several years back, the chalet houses the fres-coes and other historic artifacts and details downstairs, a restaurant upstairs, and a great cafe in the back. Stop upstairs for a house-made brew and a glimpse of the expansive Pacific, or head to the back dining room for glorious park views. There's even live music with some regularity.

CONSERVATORY OF FLOWERS ★★   Opened to the public in 1879, this glorious Victorian glass structure is the oldest existing public conservatory in the Western Hemisphere. After a bad storm in 1995 and delayed renovations, the conservatory was closed and visitors could only imagine what wondrous displays existed within the striking glass assemblage. Thankfully, a $25-million renovation, including a $4-million exhibit upgrade, was completed in 2003, and now the Conservatory is a cutting-edge horticultural destination with more than 1,700 species of plants. You can check out the rare tropical flora of the Congo, Philippines, and beyond within the stunning structure. As one of only four public institutions in the U.S. to house a highland tropics exhibit, its five galleries also include the lowland tropics, aquatic plants, the largest Dracula orchid collection in the world, and special exhibits. It doesn't take long to visit, but make a point of staying awhile; outside there are good sunny spots for people-watching, as well as paths leading to impressive gardens begging to be explored. If you're around during summer and fall, don't miss the Dahlia Garden to the right of the entrance in the center of what was once a carriage roundabout—it's an explosion of colorful Dr. Seuss–like blooms. The conservatory is open Tuesday through Sunday from 9am to 5pm, closed Mondays. Admission is $7 for adults; $5 for youth 12 to 17 years of age, seniors, and students with ID; $2 for children 5 to 11; and free for children 4 and under and for all visitors the first Tuesday of the month. For more information, visit www.conservatoryofflowers.org or call ✆ **415/831-2090.**

Dutch windmill, Golden Gate Park.   Buffalo paddock, Golden Gate Park.

JAPANESE TEA GARDEN   John McLaren, the man who began landscaping Golden Gate Park, hired Makoto Hagiwara, a wealthy Japanese landscape designer, to further develop this garden originally created for the 1894 Midwinter Exposition. It's a quiet place with cherry trees, shrubs, and bonsai crisscrossed by winding paths and high-arched bridges over pools of water. Focal points and places for contemplation include the massive bronze Buddha (cast in Japan in 1790 and donated by the Gump family), the Buddhist wooden pagoda, and the Drum Bridge, which, reflected in the water, looks as though it completes a circle. The garden is open daily November through February from 8:30am to 5pm (teahouse 10am–4:30pm), March through October from 8:30am to 6pm (teahouse 10am–5:30pm). For information on admission, call ✆ **415/752-4227.** For the **teahouse,** call ✆ 415/752-1171.

STRAWBERRY HILL/STOW LAKE   Rent a paddle boat or rowboat and cruise around the circular Stow Lake as painters create still lifes, joggers pass along the grassy shoreline, ducks waddle around waiting to be fed, and turtles sunbathe on rocks and logs. Strawberry Hill, the 430-foot-high artificial island and highest point in the park that lies at the center of Stow Lake, is a perfect picnic spot; it boasts a bird's-eye view of San Francisco and the bay. It also has a waterfall and peace pagoda. For the **boathouse,** call ✆ **415/752-0347.** Boat rentals are available daily from 10am to 4pm, weather permitting; four-passenger rowboats go for $19 per hour, and four-person paddle boats run $24 per hour; fees are cash only.

SAN FRANCISCO BOTANICAL GARDEN AT STRYBING ARBORETUM   More than 7,000 plant species grow here, among them some ancient plants in a special "primitive garden," rare species, and a grove of California redwoods. Docent tours begin at 1:30pm daily, with an additional 10:30am tour on weekends. Strybing is open daily from 9am to 6pm April through October, and daily from 10am to 5pm November through March. Admission is $7 for adults, $5 for seniors and youth ages 12 to 17, $2 for children. For more information, call ✆ **415/661-1316** or visit www.sfbotanicalgarden.org.

EXPLORING THE CITY
Architectural Highlights

The **Alamo Square Historic District** has one of the largest concentrations of the city's 14,000 **Painted Ladies,** or Victorian homes restored and ornately painted by residents. The area is small and easy to walk—bordered by Divisadero Street on the west, Golden Gate Avenue on the north, Webster Street on the east, and Fell Street on the south, about 10 blocks west of Civic Center. From Alamo Square at Fulton and Steiner streets, you'll see one of the most famous views of San Francisco, reproduced on postcards and posters around town—sharp-edged Financial District skyscrapers towering above a row of Victorians.

 City Hall and the **Civic Center** are part of a "City Beautiful" complex built in 1881, in the Beaux Arts style, designed by Brown and Bakewell. The newly renovated City Hall dome rises to 308 feet outside, ornamented with *oculi* (round windows) and topped by a lantern. The rotunda, which soars 112 feet, is finished in oak, marble, and limestone, with a marble staircase leading to the second floor.

The Painted Ladies of Alamo Square.

The **Flood Mansion,** 1000 California St., at Mason Street, was built between 1885 and 1886 for James Clair Flood—who, thanks to the Comstock Lode, rose from being a bartender to one of the city's wealthiest men. The house cost $1.5 million; the fence alone was $30,000. It was designed by Augustus Laver and modified by Willis Polk to accommodate the Pacific Union Club.

The **Octagon House,** 2645 Gough St., at Union Street (© **415/ 441-7512**), an unusual eight-sided, cupola-topped house, dates from 1861 and is maintained by the National Society of Colonial Dames of America. Its design was based on a past theory that people living in a space of this shape would live longer, healthier lives. Inside is a small museum where you'll find Early American furniture, portraits, silver, pewter, looking glasses, and English and Chinese ceramics. There are also some historic documents, including signatures of 54 of the 56 signers of the Declaration of Independence. Even if you're not able to visit the inside, this atypical structure is worth a look from the outside. It's open February through December on the second Sunday, and the second and fourth Thursdays, of each month from noon to 3pm; it's closed January and holidays.

The **Palace of Fine Arts,** on Baker between Jefferson and Bay streets, is the only building to survive from the Pan-Pacific Exhibition of 1915. Constructed by Bernard Maybeck, it was rebuilt in concrete using molds taken from the original in the 1950s. It now houses the **Exploratorium** (p. 132).

The **TransAmerica Pyramid,** 600 Montgomery St., between Clay and Washington streets, is the tallest structure in San Francisco's skyline. It's 48 stories tall, capped by a 212-foot spire.

Although the **San Francisco–Oakland Bay Bridge** is less famous than the Golden Gate Bridge, it's more spectacular in many ways. Opened in 1936 (a year before the Golden Gate), it's one of the world's longest steel bridges, at 8¼ miles long. A dovetailed series of spans joined midbay by one of the world's widest tunnels, at Yerba Buena Island, it's not really a single bridge: West of Yerba Buena, it's two separate suspension bridges, joined at a central anchorage; east of the island, it's a 1,400-foot cantilever span, followed by a succession of truss bridges.

Harvey Milk bust, City Hall.　　　　Palace of Fine Arts.

A Rousing Church Experience

Glide Memorial United Methodist Church ★★ 📷　The best way to spend a Sunday morning in San Francisco is to visit this Tenderloin-area church to witness the exhilarating and lively sermons accompanied by an amazing gospel choir. Rev. Cecil Williams's enthusiastic and uplifting preaching and singing with the homeless and poor of the neighborhood has attracted nationwide fame over the past 40-plus years. In 1994, during the pastor's 30th-anniversary celebration, singers Angela Bofill and Bobby McFerrin joined comedian Robin Williams, author Maya Angelou, and Oprah Winfrey to honor him publicly. Even former president Clinton has joined the crowd. Cecil Williams now shares pastor duties with Douglas Fitch and alternates presiding over the roof-raising Sunday services in front of a diverse audience that crosses all socioeconomic boundaries. Go for an uplifting experience and some hand-clapping, shoulder-swaying gospel choir music—it's an experience you'll never forget. *Tip:* Arrive about 20 minutes early to make sure you get a seat; otherwise, it's SRO.

330 Ellis St. (west of Union Sq.). ✆ **415/674-6000.** www.glide.org. Services Sun at 9 and 11am. Bus: 27. Streetcar: Powell. BART: Powell.

Museums

Asian Art Museum ★　Previously in Golden Gate Park and reopened in a stunning space that was once the Beaux Arts–style main library, San Francisco's Asian Art Museum is one of the Western world's largest devoted to Asian art. Its collection boasts more than 15,000 art objects, including world-class sculptures, paintings, bronzes, ceramics, and jade items, spanning 6,000 years of history and regions of south Asia, west Asia, Southeast Asia, the Himalayas, China, Korea, and Japan. Inside you'll find 40,000 square feet of gallery space showcasing 2,500 objects at any given time. Add temporary exhibitions, live demonstrations,

When Eric Kipp, a certified yogi, conceptualized his wildly popular concept of Hiking Yoga, he aimed to bring tourists and locals alike out and about for some fresh air, intense cardio, and fantastic city views. Kipp's 90-minute urban treks, which take place several times a day, most days of the week, depart from the clock tower at the Ferry Building and wind their way up to Coit Tower and around Telegraph Hill. Routes vary, but the formula is always the same: Participants enjoy intense and fast-paced hill hiking—this is no leisurely walk in the park—while stopping at four stations throughout the city for a series of yoga poses. The program, which originated in San Francisco in 2007, was such a hit, Kipp has now taken it to more than a dozen cities. For information or a schedule of hikes, visit **www.hikingyoga.com** or call ✆ **415/261-3641.** Reservations are required, and each session costs $20. Package deals are available.

learning activities, the very good Cafe Asia, and a store, and you've got one very good reason to head to the Civic Center.

200 Larkin St. (btw. Fulton and McAllister sts.). ✆ **415/581-3500.** www.asianart.org. Admission $12 adults, $8 seniors 65 and over, $7 youths 13–17 and college students with ID, free for children 12 and under, $10 flat rate for all (except children 12 and under, who are free) after 5pm Thurs. $5 1st Sun of the month. Tues-Wed and Fri-Sun 10am–5pm; Thurs 10am–9pm. Bus: All Market St. buses. Streetcar: Civic Center.

Cable Car Museum ★ ☺ 🎯 If you've ever wondered how cable cars work, this nifty museum explains (and demonstrates) it all. The Cable Car Museum is no stuffed shirt; it's the living powerhouse, repair shop, and storage place of the

Asian Art Museum.

Cable Car Museum.

cable car system and is in full operation. Built for the Ferries and Cliff House Railway in 1887, the building underwent an $18-million reconstruction to restore its original gaslight-era look, install an amazing spectators' gallery, and add a museum of San Francisco transit history.

The exposed machinery, which pulls the cables under San Francisco's streets, looks like a Rube Goldberg invention. Stand in the mezzanine gallery and become mesmerized by the massive groaning and vibrating winches as they thread the cable that hauls the cars through a huge figure eight and back into the system using slack-absorbing tension wheels. For a better view, move to the lower-level viewing room, where you can see the massive pulleys and gears operating underground.

Also on display here is one of the first grip cars developed by Andrew S. Hallidie, operated for the first time on Clay Street on August 2, 1873. Other displays include an antique grip car and trailer that operated on Pacific Avenue until 1929, and dozens of exact-scale models of cars used on the various city lines. The shop sells a variety of cable car gifts. You can see the whole museum in about 45 minutes, and, best part—it's free.

1201 Mason St. (at Washington St.). ✆ **415/474-1887.** www.cablecarmuseum.org. Free admission. Apr–Sept daily 10am–6pm; Oct–Mar daily 10am–5pm. Closed Thanksgiving, Christmas, and New Year's Day. Cable car: Both Powell St. lines.

California Academy of Sciences ★★★ ☺ San Francisco's California Academy of Sciences has been entertaining locals and tourists for more than 150 years, and with the grand opening of the all-new Academy in 2008, it's now going stronger than ever. Four years and $500 million in the making, the new Academy is the "greenest" museum in the world, and the only institution in the world to combine an aquarium, a planetarium, a natural history museum, and a scientific research program under one roof. The spectacular new complex has literally reinvented the role of science museums in the 21st century, a place where visitors interact with animals, educators, and biologists at hands-on exhibits such as a four-story living rainforest dome complete with flitting butterflies and birds, and the world's deepest living coral reef display. Even the Academy's 2½-acre undulating living garden roof is an exhibit, planted with 1.7 million native California plants, including thousands of flowers.

More than 38,000 live animals fill the new Academy's aquarium and natural history exhibits. Highlights include the **Morrison Planetarium,** the world's largest all-digital planetarium, which takes you on a guided tour of the solar system and beyond using current data from NASA to produce the most accurate and interactive digital universe ever created; the **Philippine Coral Reef,** the world's deepest living coral reef tank where 4,000 sharks, rays, sea turtles, giant clams, and other aquatic creatures live in a Technicolor forest of coral; and the **Rainforests of the World,** a living rainforest filled with mahogany and palm trees, croaking frogs, chirping birds, leaf cutter ants, bat caves, chameleons, and hundreds of tropical butterflies. You can climb into the treetops of Costa Rica, descend in a glass elevator into the Amazonian flooded forest, and walk along an acrylic tunnel beneath the Amazonian river fish that swim overhead.

Even the dining options here are first-rate, as both the **Academy Café** and **Moss Room** restaurant are run by two of the city's top chefs, Charles Phan and Loretta Keller, and feature local, organic, sustainable foods. The only thing you won't enjoy here is the entrance fee—a whopping $25 per adult—but it includes access to all the Academy exhibits *and* the Planetarium shows, and if you arrive by public transportation, they'll knock $3 off the fee (how very green). Combined with a visit to the spectacular de Young Museum across the Concourse, it makes for a very entertaining and educational day in Golden Gate Park.

55 Concourse Dr., Golden Gate Park. ℂ **415/379-8000.** www.calacademy.org. Admission $30 adults, $25 seniors 65 and over, $25 youths 12–17, $20 children 7–11, free for children 6 and under. Free to all 3rd Wed of each month. Mon–Sat 9:30am–5pm; Sun 11am–5pm. Closed Thanksgiving and Christmas. Bus: 5, 16AX, 16BX, 21, 44, or 71.

California Palace of the Legion of Honor ★★   Designed as a memorial to California's World War I casualties, this neoclassical structure is an exact replica of the Legion of Honor Palace in Paris, right down to the inscription HONNEUR ET PATRIE above the portal. The exterior's grassy expanses, cliffside paths, and incredible view of the Golden Gate and downtown make this an absolute must-visit attraction before you even get in the door. The inside is equally impressive: The museum's permanent collection covers 4,000 years of art and includes paintings, sculpture, and decorative arts from Europe, as well as international tapestries, prints, and drawings. The chronological display of 4,000 years of ancient and European art includes one of the world's finest collections of Rodin sculptures. The sunlit Legion Cafe offers indoor and outdoor seating at moderate prices. Plan to spend 2 or 3 hours here.

In Lincoln Park (34th Ave. and Clement St.). ℂ **415/750-3600** or 415/863-3330 (recorded information). www.famsf.org. Admission $10 adults, $7 seniors 65 and over, $6 youths 13–17 and college students with ID, free for children 12 and under. Fees may be higher for special exhibitions. Free 1st Tues of each month. Free admission with same-day tickets from the de Young Museum. Tues–Sun 9:30am–5:15pm. Bus: 18.

de Young Museum ★★★   After closing for several years, San Francisco's oldest museum (founded in 1895) reopened in late 2005 in its state-of-the-art Golden Gate Park facility. Its vast holdings include one of the finest collections of American paintings in the United States from Colonial times to the 20th century, as well as decorative arts and crafts; Western and non-Western textiles; and arts from Africa, Oceania, and the Americas. Along with superb revolving exhibitions, the de Young has long been beloved for its educational programs for both children and adults, and now it's equally enjoyed for its stunning architecture and sculpture-graced garden. The striking facade consists of 950,000 pounds of textured and perforated copper that's intended to patinate with age, while the northeast corner of the building features a 144-foot tower that slowly spirals from the ground floor and culminates with an observation floor offering panoramic views of the entire city (from a distance, it has the surreal look of a rusty aircraft carrier cruising through the park). Surrounding sculpture gardens and lush, grassy expanses are perfect for picnicking. Adding to the allure is surprisingly good and healthy organic fare at the grab-and-go or order-and-wait cafe/restaurant. **Note:** Underground parking is accessed at 10th Avenue and Fulton Street. Also, admission tickets to the de Young may be used on the same day for free entrance to the Legion of Honor (see above).

50 Hagiwara Tea Garden Dr. (inside Golden Gate Park, 2 blocks from the park entrance at Eighth Ave. and Fulton). ℂ **415/750-3600** or 415/863-3330. www.famsf.org. Adults $10, seniors $7, youths 13–17 and college students with ID $6, children 12 and under free. Free 1st Tues of the month. $2 discount for Muni riders with Fast Pass or transfer receipt. AE, MC, V. Tues–Thurs and Sat–Sun 9:30am–5:15pm; Fri 9:30am–8:45pm (excluding Dec). Closed New Year's Day, Thanksgiving, and Christmas. Bus: 5, 16AX, 16BX, 21, 44, or 71.

The Exploratorium ★★★ ☺

Exploratorium.

Scientific American magazine rated the Exploratorium "the best science museum in the world"—and I couldn't agree more. Inside you'll find hundreds of exhibits that give you hands-on access to everything from giant-bubble blowing to Einstein's theory of relativity. It's like a mad scientist's penny arcade, an educational fun house, and an experimental laboratory all rolled into one. Touch a tornado, shape a glowing electrical current, or take a sensory journey in total darkness in the **Tactile Dome** ($3 extra, and call ☎ 415/561-0362 to make advance reservations)—even if you spent all day here, you couldn't experience everything. Every exhibit at the Exploratorium is designed to be interactive, educational, safe, and, most important, fun. And don't think it's just for kids; parents inevitably end up being the most reluctant to leave. I went here recently and spent 3 hours in just one small section of the museum, marveling at all the mind-blowing hands-on exhibits related to light and eyesight. On the way out, be sure to stop in the wonderful gift store, which is chock-full of affordable brain candy.

The museum is located in the Marina District at the beautiful **Palace of Fine Arts ★★**, the only building left standing from the Panama Pacific Exposition of 1915. The adjoining park with lagoon—the perfect place for an afternoon picnic—is home to ducks, swans, sea gulls, and grouchy geese, so bring bread.

3601 Lyon St., in the Palace of Fine Arts (at Marina Blvd.). ☎ **415/EXPLORE** (397-5673) or 561-0360 (recorded information). www.exploratorium.edu. Admission $15 adults; $12 seniors, youth 13–17, visitors with disabilities, and college students with ID; $10 children 4–12; free for children 3 and under. AE, MC, V. Tues–Sun 10am–5pm. Free parking. Closed Mon except Martin Luther King, Jr., Day; Presidents' Day; Memorial Day; and Labor Day. Bus: 28, 30, or Golden Gate Transit.

San Francisco Maritime National Historical Park ★ ☺

This park includes several marine-themed sites within a few blocks of each other. Although the park's signature Maritime Museum—on Beach Street at Polk Street, shaped like an Art Deco ship, and usually filled with seafaring memorabilia—has been undergoing renovations for the past few years, it's worth walking by just to admire the building. The building is empty of exhibits until 2013 or 2014. In the interim, the Works Progress Administration history of the building is being highlighted. Head 2 blocks east to the corner of Hyde and Jefferson, and you'll find SFMNHP's state-of-the-art Visitor's Center, which offers a fun, interactive look at the city's maritime heritage. Housed in the historic Haslett Warehouse building, the Center tells the stories of voyage, discovery, and cultural diversity. Across the street, at the park's Hyde Street Pier, are several historic ships, which are moored and open to the public.

Visitor's Center: Hyde and Jefferson sts. (near Fisherman's Wharf). ☎ **415/447-5000.** www.nps. gov/safr. No fee for Visitor's Center. Tickets to board ships $5, free for children 15 and under. Visitor's Center: Memorial Day to Sept 30 daily 9:30am–5:30pm; Oct 1 to Memorial Day daily 9:30am–5pm. Ships on Hyde St. Pier: Memorial Day to Sept 30 daily 9:30am–5:30pm; Oct 1 to Memorial Day daily 9am–5pm. Bus: 19, 30, or 47. Cable car: Powell–Hyde St. line to the last stop.

San Francisco Museum of Modern Art (SFMOMA) ★   Swiss architect Mario Botta, in association with Hellmuth, Obata, and Kassabaum, designed this $65-million museum, which has made SoMa one of the more popular areas to visit for tourists and residents alike. The museum's permanent collection houses the West Coast's most comprehensive collection of 20th-century art, including painting, sculpture, photography, architecture, design, and media arts. The collection, including a new infusion of some 1,100 pieces from Don Fisher (the late founder of the Gap), features master works by Ansel Adams, Bruce Conner, Joseph Cornell, Salvador Dalí, Richard Diebenkorn, Eva Hesse, Frida Kahlo, Ellsworth Kelly, Yves Klein, Sherrie Levine, Henri Matisse, Piet Mondrian, Pablo Picasso, Robert Rauschenberg, Diego Rivera, Cindy Sherman, Alfred Stieglitz, Clyfford Still, and Edward Weston, among many others, as well as an ever-changing program of special exhibits. Unfortunately, few works are on display at one time, and for the money, the experience can be disappointing—especially compared to museums in New York. However, this is about as good as it gets in our boutique city, so take it or leave it. Docent-led tours take place daily. Times are posted at the admission desk. Phone or check SFMOMA's website for current details of upcoming special events and exhibitions.

151 Third St. (2 blocks south of Market St., across from Yerba Buena Gardens). ℂ **415/ 357-4000.** www.sfmoma.org. Admission $18 adults, $12 seniors, $9 students 13 and over with ID, free for children 12 and under. Half-price for all Thurs 6–9pm; free to all 1st Tues of each month. Thurs 11am–8:45pm; Fri–Tues 11am–5:45pm. Closed Wed and major holidays. Bus: 15, 30, or 45. Streetcar: J, K, L, or M to Montgomery.

SFMOMA.

Neighborhoods Worth Seeking Out

For self-guided walking tours of San Francisco's neighborhoods, pick up a copy of *Frommer's Memorable Walks in San Francisco.*

THE CASTRO   Castro Street, between Market and 18th streets, is the center of the city's gay community, as well as a lovely neighborhood teeming with shops, restaurants, bars, and other institutions that cater to the area's colorful residents. Among the landmarks are **Harvey Milk Plaza** and the **Castro Theatre** (www.castrotheatre.com), a 1930s movie palace with a Wurlitzer. The gay community began to move here in the late 1960s and early 1970s from a neighborhood called Polk Gulch, which still has a number of gay-oriented bars and stores. Castro is one of the liveliest streets in the city and the perfect place to shop for gifts and revel in free-spiritedness. Check **www.castroonline.com** for more info.

CHINATOWN   San Francisco has one of the largest communities of Chinese people in the United States. More than 80,000 people live in Chinatown, but the majority of Chinese people have moved out into newer areas like the Richmond and Sunset districts. Although frequented by tourists, the area continues to cater to Chinese shoppers, who crowd the vegetable and herb

The city celebrates Gay Pride the last weekend in June.

markets, restaurants, and shops. Tradition runs deep here, and if you're lucky, through an open window you might hear women mixing mah-jongg tiles as they play the centuries-old game.

THE MISSION DISTRICT   Once inhabited almost entirely by Irish immigrants, the Mission—an oblong area stretching roughly from 14th to 30th streets between Potrero Avenue in the east and Dolores on the west—is now the center of the city's Latino community. The heart of the community lies along 24th Street between Van Ness and Potrero, where dozens of ethnic restaurants, bakeries, bars, and specialty stores attract a hip crowd from all over the city. Some of San Francisco's finest Victorians still stand in the outer limits. By day, the neighborhood is quite safe and highly recommended; at night, stroll through the Mission District with caution.

NOB HILL   When the cable car started operating in 1873, this hill became the city's exclusive residential area. Newly wealthy residents who had struck it rich in the Gold Rush built their mansions here, but they were almost all destroyed by the 1906 earthquake and fire. The only two surviving buildings are the Flood Mansion, which serves today as the **Pacific Union Club,** and the **Fairmont Hotel,** which was under construction when the earthquake struck and was damaged but not destroyed. Today the burned-out sites of former mansions hold the city's luxury hotels—the InterContinental **Mark Hopkins,** the **Stanford Court,** the **Huntington Hotel,** and the spectacular **Grace Cathedral,** which stands on the Crocker mansion site. Nob Hill is worth a visit if only to stroll around **Huntington Park,** attend a Sunday service at the cathedral, or *ooh* and *aah* your way around the Fairmont's spectacular lobby.

NORTH BEACH In the late 1800s, an enormous influx of Italian immigrants to North Beach firmly established this aromatic area as San Francisco's "Little Italy." Dozens of Italian restaurants and coffeehouses continue to flourish in what is still the center of the city's Italian community. Walk down **Columbus Avenue** on any given morning, and you'll be bombarded by the wonderful aromas of roasting coffee and savory pasta sauces. Although there are some interesting shops and bookstores in the area, it's the dozens of eclectic little cafes, delis, bakeries, and coffee shops that give North Beach its Italian-bohemian character.

Flora & Fauna

In addition to **Golden Gate Park** and **Golden Gate National Recreation Area** and the **Presidio,** San Francisco boasts more than 2,000 additional acres of parkland, most of which is perfect for picnicking. **Lincoln Park,** at Clement Street and 34th Avenue, on 270 acres in northwestern San Francisco, is home to both the California Palace of the Legion of Honor (see "Museums," above) and an 18-hole municipal golf course. The park's most dramatic features, however, are the 200-foot cliffs overlooking the Golden Gate Bridge and San Francisco Bay. Take bus no. 38 from Union Square to 33rd and Geary streets, and then transfer to bus no. 18 into the park.

San Francisco Zoo (& Children's Zoo) ☺ Founded at its present site near the ocean in 1929, the zoo is spread over 100 acres and houses more than 930 animals, including some 245 species of mammals, birds, reptiles, amphibians, and invertebrates. Exhibit highlights include the Lipman Family Lemur Forest, a forest setting for five endangered species of lemurs from Madagascar; Jones Family Gorilla World, a tranquil setting for a family group of western lowland gorillas; Koala Crossing, which connects to the Australian Walkabout exhibit with its kangaroos, wallaroos, and emu; Penguin Island, home to a large breeding colony of Magellanic Penguins (join them for lunch at 2:30pm daily); and the Primate Discovery Center, home to rare and endangered monkeys. Puente al Sur (Bridge to the South) has a pair of giant anteaters and some capybaras. The Lion House is home to rare Sumatran and Siberian tigers and African lions. You can watch the big cats get fed every day at 2pm (except Mon). African Savanna is a 3-acre mixed-species habitat with giraffes, zebras, antelope, and birds.

The 6-acre Children's Zoo offers kids and their families opportunities for close-up encounters with domestic rare breeds of goats, sheep, ponies, and horses in the Family Farm. Touch and feel small mammals, reptiles, and amphibians along the Nature Trail and gaze at eagles and hawks stationed on Hawk Hill. Don't miss a visit to the fascinating Insect Zoo or the Meerkat and Prairie Dog exhibit, where kids can crawl through tunnels and play in sand, just like these amazing burrowing species.

Great Highway btw. Sloat Blvd. and Skyline Blvd. ☎ **415/753-7080.** www.sfzoo.org. Admission $15 adults, $12 seniors 65 and over and youth 12–17, $9 children 3–11, free for children 2 and under. San Francisco residents receive a discount. Free to all 1st Wed of each month, except $2 fee for Children's Zoo. Carousel $2. Daily 10am–5pm, 365 days a year. Bus: 18 or 23. Streetcar: L from downtown Market St. to the end of the line.

ORGANIZED TOURS
Orientation Tours
THE 49-MILE SCENIC DRIVE ★★

The self-guided, 49-mile drive is an easy way to get oriented and to grasp the beauty of San Francisco and its extraordinary location. It's also a flat-out stunning and very worthy excursion. Beginning in the city, it follows a rough circle around the bay and passes virtually all the best-known sights, from Chinatown to the Golden Gate Bridge, Ocean Beach, Seal Rocks, Golden Gate Park, and Twin Peaks. Originally designed for the benefit of visitors to San Francisco's 1939 and 1940 Golden Gate International Exposition, the route is marked by blue-and-white seagull signs. Although it makes an excellent half-day tour, this miniexcursion can easily take longer if you decide, for example, to stop to walk across the Golden Gate Bridge or to have tea in Golden Gate Park's Japanese Tea Garden.

The **San Francisco Visitor Information Center,** at Powell and Market streets (p. 60), distributes free route maps, which are handy since a few of the Scenic Drive marker signs are missing. Try to avoid the downtown area during the weekday rush hours from 7 to 9am and 4 to 6pm.

Boat Tours

One of the best ways to look at San Francisco is from a boat on the bay. There are several cruises to choose from, and many of them start from Fisherman's Wharf.

Blue & Gold Fleet, PIER 39, Fisherman's Wharf (✆ **415/705-8200;** www.blueandgoldfleet.com), tours the bay year-round in a sleek, 350-passenger sightseeing boat, complete with food and beverage facilities. The fully narrated, 1-hour cruise passes beneath the Golden Gate Bridge and comes within yards of Alcatraz Island. Don a jacket, bring the camera, and make sure it's a clear day for the best bay cruise. Frequent daily departures from PIER 39's West Marina begin at 10:45am daily during winter and 10am daily during summer. Tickets cost $24 for adults, $20 for seniors 63 and over and juniors 12 to 18, and $16 for children 5 to 11; children 4 and under are admitted free. There's a $2.25 charge for ordering tickets by phone; discounts are available on their website.

The **Red & White Fleet,** Pier 43½ (✆ **415/673-2900;** www.redandwhite.com), offers daily "Bay Cruises" tours that leave from Pier 43½. The tour boats cruise along the city waterfront, beneath the Golden Gate Bridge, past Angel Island, and around Alcatraz and are narrated in eight languages. Prices are $24 for adults, $16 for seniors and children 5 to 17. Discounts are available through online purchase.

Bus Tours

Gray Line (✆ **888/428-6937** or 415/434-8687; www.sanfranciscosightseeing. com) is San Francisco's largest bus-tour operator. It offers numerous itineraries daily (far too many to list here). Free pickup and return are available between centrally located hotels and departure locations. Advance reservations are required for all tours except motorized cable car and trolley tours. Day and evening tours depart from Pier 43½ at Fisherman's Wharf; motorized cable car tours depart from PIER 39 and Pier 41.

GOLDEN GATE NATIONAL PARK & THE PRESIDIO

Golden Gate National Recreation Area

The largest urban park in the world, GGNRA makes New York's Central Park look like a putting green, covering three counties along 28 miles of stunning, condo-free shoreline. Run by the National Park Service, the Recreation Area wraps around the northern and western edges of the city, and just about all of it is open to the public, with no access fees. The Muni bus system provides transportation to the more popular sites, including Aquatic Park, Cliff House, Fort Mason, and Ocean Beach. For more information, contact the **National Park Service** (© 415/561-4700; www.nps.gov/goga). For more detailed information on particular sites, see the "Outdoor Pursuits" section, later in this chapter.

Here is a brief rundown of the salient features of the park's peninsula section, starting at the northern section and moving westward around the coastline:

Aquatic Park, adjacent to the Hyde Street Pier, has a small swimming beach, although it's not that appealing (and darn cold). Far more entertaining is a visit to the San Francisco Maritime National Historical Park's Visitor Center a few blocks away (p. 132).

Fort Mason Center, from Bay Street to the shoreline, consists of several buildings and piers used during World War II. Today they hold a variety of museums, theaters, shops, organizations, and Greens vegetarian restaurant (p. 102), which affords views of the Golden Gate Bridge. For information about Fort Mason events, call © **415/441-3400** or visit www.fortmason.org. The park headquarters is also at Fort Mason.

Farther west along the bay at the northern end of Laguna Street is **Marina Green,** a favorite local spot for kite flying, jogging, and walking along the Promenade. The St. Francis Yacht Club is also here.

Next comes the 3½-mile paved **Golden Gate Promenade ★**, San Francisco's best and most scenic biking, jogging, and walking path. It runs along the shore past **Crissy Field** (www.crissyfield.org) and ends at Fort Point under the Golden Gate Bridge (be sure to stop and watch the gonzo windsurfers and kite surfers, who catch major wind here, and admire the newly restored marshlands). The Crissy Field Café and Bookstore is open from 9am to 5pm Wednesday through Sunday and offers yummy organic soups, salads, sandwiches, coffee drinks, and a decent selection of outdoor-themed books and cards.

Fort Point ★ (© **415/556-1693**; www.nps.gov/fopo) was built in 1853 to 1861 to protect the narrow entrance to the harbor. It was designed to house 500 soldiers manning 126 muzzle-loading cannons. By 1900, the fort's soldiers and obsolete guns had been removed, but the formidable brick edifice remains. Fort Point is open Friday through Sunday only from 10am to 5pm, and guided tours and cannon demonstrations are given at the site once or twice a day on open days, depending on the time of year.

Lincoln Boulevard sweeps around the western edge of the bay to **Baker Beach,** where the waves roll ashore—a fine spot for sunbathing, walking, or fishing. Hikers can follow the **Coastal Trail** (www.coastwalk.org) from Fort Point along this part of the coastline all the way to Land's End.

A short distance from Baker Beach, **China Beach** is a small cove where swimming is permitted. Changing rooms, showers, a sun deck, and restrooms are available.

A little farther around the coast is **Land's End ★**, looking out to Pyramid Rock. A lower and an upper trail offer hiking amid wind-swept cypresses and pines on the cliffs above the Pacific.

Still farther along the coast lie **Point Lobos,** the ruins of **Sutro Baths** (www.sutrobaths.com), and the **Cliff House ★**. The Cliff House (www.cliff house.com), which recently underwent major renovations, has been serving refreshments to visitors since 1863. It's famed for its views of Seal Rocks (a colony of sea lions and many marine birds) and the Pacific Ocean. Immediately northeast of Cliff House are traces of the once-grand Sutro Baths, a swimming facility that was a major summer attraction accommodating up to 24,000 people until it burned down in 1966.

A little farther inland at the western end of California Street is **Lincoln Park,** which contains a golf course and the spectacular Legion of Honor museum (p. 131).

At the southern end of Ocean Beach, 4 miles down the coast, is **Fort Funston** (© 415/561-4700), where there's an easy loop trail across the cliffs. Here you can watch hang gliders take advantage of the high cliffs and strong winds. It's also one of the city's most popular dog parks.

Farther south along Route 280, **Sweeney Ridge** affords sweeping views of the coastline from the many trails that crisscross its 1,000 acres. From here the expedition led by Don Gaspar de Portolá first saw San Francisco Bay in 1769. It's in Pacifica; take Sneath Lane off Route 35 (Skyline Blvd.) in San Bruno.

The GGNRA extends into Marin County, where it encompasses the Marin Headlands, Muir Woods National Monument (see p. 184), and Olema Valley behind the Point Reyes National Seashore.

The Presidio

In October 1994, the Presidio passed from the U.S. Army to the National Park Service and became one of a handful of urban national parks that combines historical, architectural, and natural elements in one giant arboreal expanse. (It also contains a previously private golf course and a home for George Lucas's production company.) The 1,491-acre area incorporates a variety of terrains—coastal scrub, dunes, and prairie grasslands—that shelter many rare plants and more than 200 species of birds, some of which nest here.

This military outpost has a 220-year history, from its founding in September 1776 by the Spanish under José Joaquin Moraga to its closure in 1994. From 1822 to 1846, the property was in Mexican hands.

During the war with Mexico, U.S. forces occupied the fort, and in 1848, when California became part of the Union, it was formally transferred to the United States. When San Francisco suddenly became an important urban area during the gold rush, the U.S. government installed battalions of soldiers and built Fort Point to protect the entry to the harbor. It expanded the post during the Civil War and during the Indian Wars of the 1870s and 1880s. By the 1890s, the Presidio was no longer a frontier post, but a major base for U.S. expansion into the Pacific. During the war with Spain in 1898, thousands of troops camped here in tent cities awaiting shipment to the Philippines, and the Army General Hospital treated the sick and wounded. By 1905, 12 coastal defense batteries were built along the headlands. In 1914, troops under the command of Gen. John Pershing left here to pursue Pancho Villa and his men. The Presidio expanded during the 1920s, when Crissy Army Airfield (the first airfield on the West Coast) was established, but the major action was seen during World War II, after the attack on Pearl Harbor. Soldiers dug fox-holes along nearby beaches, and the Presidio became the head-quarters for the Western Defense Command. Some 1.75 million men were shipped out from nearby Fort Mason to fight in the Pacific; many returned to the Presidio's hospital, whose capac-ity peaked one year at 72,000 patients. In the 1950s, the Presi-dio served as the headquarters for the Sixth U.S. Army and a missile defense post, but its role slowly shrank. In 1972, it was included in new legislation establishing the Golden Gate National Recreation Area; in 1989, the Pentagon decided to close the post and transfer it to the National Park Service.

El Presidio Coastal Trail.

Today the area encompasses more than 470 historic buildings, a scenic golf course, a national cemetery, the Walt Disney Family Museum, several good res-taurants, 22 hiking trails (to be doubled over the next decade), and a variety of terrain and natural habitats. The National Park Service offers walking and biking tours around the Presidio (reservations are suggested), as well as a free shuttle, "PresidioGo." For more information, call the **Presidio Visitors Center** at ✆ **415/561-4323.** Take bus no. 28, 45, 76, or 82X to get there.

OUTDOOR PURSUITS

BEACHES Most days it's too chilly to hang out at the beach, but when the fog evaporates and the wind dies down, one of the best ways to spend the day in the city is oceanside. On any truly hot day, thousands flock to the beach to worship the sun, build sandcastles, and throw the ball around. Without a wet suit, swimming is a fiercely cold endeavor. In any case, dip at your own risk—there are no lifeguards on duty and San Francisco's waters have strong undertows. On the South Bay, **Baker Beach** is ideal for picnicking, sun-ning, walking, or fishing against the backdrop of the Golden Gate (though pollution makes your catch not necessarily worthy of eating).

Ocean Beach, at the end of Golden Gate Park, on the westernmost side of the city, is San Francisco's largest beach—4 miles long. Just offshore, at the northern end of the beach, in front of Cliff House, are the jagged Seal Rocks, inhabited by various shorebirds and a large colony of barking sea lions (bring binoculars for a close-up view). To the left, Kelly's Cove is one of the more challenging surf spots in town. Ocean Beach is ideal for strolling or sunning, but don't swim here—tides are tricky, and each year bathers drown in the rough surf.

Stop by Ocean Beach bus terminal at the corner of Cabrillo and La Playa to learn about San Francisco's history in local artist Ray Beldner's whimsically historical sculpture garden. Then hike up the hill to explore **Cliff House** and the ruins of the **Sutro Baths,** once able to accommodate 24,000 bathers.

BIKING The San Francisco Parks and Recreation Department maintains two city-designated bike routes. One winds 7½ miles through Golden Gate Park to Lake Merced; the other traverses the city, starting in the south, and continues over the Golden Gate Bridge. These routes are not dedicated to bicyclists, who must exercise caution to avoid crashing into pedestrians. Helmets are recommended for adults and required by law for kids 17 and under. A bike map is available from the San Francisco Visitor Information Center, at Powell and Mason streets, for $3 (p. 60), and from bicycle shops all around town.

Ocean Beach has a public walk- and bikeway that stretches along 5 waterfront blocks of the Great Highway between Noriega and Santiago streets. It's an easy ride from Cliff House or Golden Gate Park.

Avenue Cyclery, 756 Stanyan St., at Waller Street, in the Haight (© **415/387-3155;** www.avenuecyclery.com), rents bikes for $8 per hour or $30 per day. It's open daily April through September from 10am to 7pm and October through March from 10am to 6pm. For cruising Fisherman's Wharf and the Golden Gate Bridge, your best bet is **Blazing Saddles** (© **415/202-8888;** www.blazingsaddles.com), which has five locations around Fisherman's Wharf. Bikes rent for $32 per day, including maps, locks, and helmets; tandem bikes are available as well.

BOATING At the **Golden Gate Park Boat House** (© **415/752-0347**), on Stow Lake, the park's largest body of water, you can rent a rowboat or pedal boat by the hour and steer over to Strawberry Hill, a large, round island in the middle of the lake, for lunch. There's usually a line on weekends. The boathouse is open daily from 10am to 4pm, weather permitting.

Cass' Marina, 1702 Bridgeway, Sausalito (© **800/472-4595** or 415/ 332-6789; www.cassmarina.com), is a certified sailing school that rents sailboats measuring 22 to 38 feet. Sail to the Golden Gate Bridge on your own or with a licensed skipper. In addition, large sailing yachts leave from Sausalito on a regularly scheduled basis. Call or check the website for schedules, prices, and availability of sailboats. The marina is open Wednesday through Monday from 9am to sunset.

CITY STAIR CLIMBING ★★ Many health clubs have stair-climbing machines and step classes, but in San Francisco, you need only go outside. The following city stair climbs will give you not only a good workout, but seriously stunning neighborhood, city, and bay views as well. Check www.sisterbetty. org/stairways for more ideas.

Filbert Street Steps, between Sansome Street and Telegraph Hill, are a particular challenge. Scaling the sheer eastern face of Telegraph Hill, this 377-step climb winds through verdant flower gardens and charming 19th-century cottages. Napier Lane, a narrow, wooden plank walkway, leads to Montgomery Street. Turn right and follow the path to the end of the cul-de-sac, where another stairway continues to Telegraph's panoramic summit and Coit Tower.

The **Lyon Street Steps,** between Green Street and Broadway, were built in 1916. This historic stairway street contains four steep sets of stairs, totaling 288 steps. Begin at Green Street and climb all the way up, past manicured hedges and flower gardens, to an iron gate that opens into the Presidio. A block east, on Baker Street, another set of 369 steps descends to Green Street.

FISHING   **Berkeley Marina Sports Center,** 225 University Ave., Berkeley (℃ **510/237-3474;** www.berkeleysportfishing.com), offers daily trips for ling cod, rockfish, and many other types of game fish year-round; salmon trips are April through October. Fishing equipment is available; the cost, including boat ride and bait, is about $95 per person. Reservations are required, as are licenses for adults. One-day licenses can be purchased for $12 before departure. Excursions run daily from 6am to 3:30pm. Fish are cleaned, filleted, and bagged on the return trip for a small fee (free for salmon fishing).

GOLF   San Francisco has a few beautiful golf courses. One of the most lavish is the **Presidio Golf Course** (℃ **415/561-4661;** www.presidiogolf.com). Greens fees are $125 for nonresidents (Mon–Thurs; $145 Fri–Sun). Twilight rates drop to $85 and $93, respectively, and then to $49 after 3pm. Carts are included.

There are also two decent municipal courses in town. The 18-hole **Harding Park,** Skyline Boulevard at Harding Road (℃ **415/664-4690;** www.harding-park.com), charges greens fees of $135 per person Monday through Thursday, $155 Friday through Sunday. Opened in 1925, it was completely overhauled in 2002, and the new Harding has been getting rave reviews ever since. In 2004, it was named by *Golf* magazine as the number-two best municipal golf course in America; in 2009, it hosted the President's Cup. The course, which skirts the shores of Lake Merced, is a 6,743-yard par 72. You can also play the easier Fleming executive 9. The 18-hole **Lincoln Park Golf Course,** 34th Avenue and Clement Street (℃ **415/221-9911;** www.lincolnparkgc.com), charges greens fees of $34 per person Monday through Thursday, $38 Friday through Sunday, with rates decreasing after 4pm in summer, 2pm in winter. It's San Francisco's prettiest municipal course, with terrific views and fairways lined with Monterey cypress and pine trees. The 5,181-yard layout plays to par 68, and the 17th hole has a glistening ocean view. This is the oldest course in the city and one of the oldest in the West. It's open daily at daybreak.

SKATING   Although people skate in Golden Gate Park all week, Sunday is best, when John F. Kennedy Drive, between Kezar Drive and Transverse Road, closes to cars. Disco skaters gather near the Eighth Avenue park entrance on weekends.

SHOPPING

Store hours vary, but most are open Monday through Saturday from 10am to 6pm, and Sunday from noon to 5pm. Most department stores stay open later, as do shops around Fisherman's Wharf. Sales tax in San Francisco is 8.5%. If you live out of state and buy an expensive item, consider asking the store to ship it home for you. You'll have to pay for transport, but you'll evade the sales tax.

UNION SQUARE & ENVIRONS San Francisco's most popular, congested shopping mecca centers on Union Square. Most of the big department stores and many high-end specialty shops are in this area. Be sure to venture to Grant Avenue, Post and Sutter streets, and Maiden Lane.

If you're into art, pick up *The San Francisco Gallery Guide,* a comprehensive, bimonthly publication listing the city's current shows (most of which are downtown). It's available free by mail; send a self-addressed stamped envelope to San Francisco Bay Area Gallery Guide, 1369 Fulton St., San Francisco, CA 94117 (© **415/921-1600**). You can also pick one up at the San Francisco Visitor Information Center at 900 Market St. (at Powell St.).

The **Catharine Clark Gallery,** on the ground floor of 150 Minna St., between Third and New Montgomery sts. (© **415/399-1439;** www. cclarkgallery.com), exhibits the work of up-and-coming, pop culture–inspired artists (mainly from California), and nurtures novice collectors through an unusual interest-free purchasing plan.

Century-old **Gump's,** 135 Post St., between Kearny Street and Grant Avenue (© **800/766-7628;** www.gumps.com), is a must-visit. A virtual treasure-trove of household items and gifts, the shop purveys a collection of Asian antiquities, contemporary art glass, exquisite jade and pearl jewelry, and more.

While the department stores have plenty of clothes, real fashion fiends will want to check out the boutiques. For men, **Cable Car Clothiers,** 200 Bush St., at Sansome Street (© **415/397-4740;** www.cablecarclothiers. com), is popular for traditional attire, such as three-button suits with natural shoulders, Aquascutum coats, McGeorge sweaters, and Atkinson ties.

Union Square shopping.

Wilkes Bashford, 375 Sutter St., at Stockton Street (© **415/986-4380;** www.wilkesbashford.com), is one of the most well-known, expensive clothing boutiques in the city, with fashions for both sexes. It stocks only the finest garb, including men's Kiton and Brioni suits (some of the most expensive in the world, at $2,500 and up).

For fabulous, expensive women's fashions, check out **Métier,** 355 Sutter St., between Grant and Stockton streets (© **415/989-5395;** www.metiersf.com). Its inventory of European ready-to-wear lines is in the best taste; featured designers include Italian designer Anna Molinari Hache and Blue Marine, as well as a distinguished collection of antique-style, high-end jewelry from L.A.'s Cathy Waterman and ultrapopular custom-designed poetry jewelry by Jeanine Payer.

SOMA Although this area is too big and shops are too scattered to be suitable for strolling, you'll find good discount shopping, along with a few great regular retail shops, in warehouse spaces south of Market. Most major hotels carry discount-shopping guides. Many buses pass through this area, including nos. 9, 12, 14, 15, 19, 26, 27, 30, 42, 45, and 76.

The **SFMOMA MuseumStore,** 151 Third St., 2 blocks south of Market Street, across from Yerba Buena Gardens (© **415/357-4000;** www.sfmoma.org), is a favorite among locals. The shop's art cards and books, as well as jewelry, housewares, and knickknacks, are well designed. For visitors, the San Francisco mementos here are much more tasteful than those sold in Fisherman's Wharf.

Fashionable bargain hunters head to **Jeremys,** 2 S. Park, at Second Street between Bryant and Brannan streets (© **415/882-4929;** www.jeremys.com), where top designer fashions, from shoes to suits, sell at rockbottom prices. Another worthy stop is the **Wine Club San Francisco,** 953 Harrison St., between Fifth and Sixth streets (© **415/512-9086**), with bargain prices on more than 1,200 domestic and foreign wines; bottles run from $4 to $1,100.

HAYES VALLEY Most neighborhoods cater to either trendy or conservative shoppers, but lower Hayes Street, between Octavia and Gough, celebrates anything vintage, artistic, and funky. The neighborhood is still in transition, but it's definitely the most interesting place to shop—with modern and retro furniture stores, trendy shoe stores, and hip clothiers. For fashionable classic clothing for men and women, check out **MAC,** 387 Grove St., at Gough Street (© **415/863-3011**). Nearby, **RAG,** 541 Octavia St. at Hayes Street (© **415/621-7718;** www.ragsf.com), showcases very affordable trendy fashions from upcoming local designers. **Propeller,** 555 Hayes St., between Laguna and Octavia streets (© **415/701-7767**), is my favorite contemporary furniture store. Lots of great antiques shops are south on Octavia and on nearby Market Street. Bus lines include nos. 16AX, 16BX, and 21.

The Italian men's and women's shoes at **Bulo,** 418 Hayes St., at Gough Street (© **415/255-4939;** www.buloshoes.com), run the gamut from casual to dressy, reserved to wildly funky. **Gimme Shoes,** 416 Hayes St. (© **415/864-0691;** www.gimmeshoes.com), is ultrahip but expensive. Ferret out the sale items unless you're ready to drop around $200 per pair.

THE CASTRO You could spend a day wandering the Castro's housewares and men's clothing shops. Buses serving the area are nos. 8, 24, 33, 35, and 37.

Citizen Clothing, 536 Castro St., between 18th and 19th streets (☎ **415/575-3560**), is a popular shop for stylish casual clothing.

CHESTNUT STREET   Parallel to Union Street, a few blocks north, Chestnut likewise has endless shopping and dining choices—as well as a population of superfit, postgraduate singles who hang around cafes and bars that are good for flirting and "hooking up." The area is serviced by bus line nos. 22, 28, 30, 41, 42, 43, and 76.

FISHERMAN'S WHARF & ENVIRONS   The tourist-oriented malls that run along Jefferson Street—Ghirardelli Square, PIER 39, the Cannery at Del Monte Square, and the Anchorage—include hundreds of shops, restaurants, and attractions. They're not particularly impressive where merchandise is concerned.

Locals tend to avoid this part of town, but do venture to **Cost Plus World Market,** 2552 Taylor St., between North Point and Bay streets (☎ **415/928-6200**), a vast warehouse crammed to the rafters with Chinese baskets, Indian camel bells, Malaysian batik scarves, innumerable items from Algeria to Zanzibar, and a decent wine section.

FILLMORE STREET   Some of the best women's clothes shopping in town is packed into 5 blocks of Fillmore Street in Pacific Heights, from Jackson to Sutter streets. This area is also the perfect place to grab a bite and peruse the boutiques, crafts shops, and housewares stores. It's serviced by bus line nos. 1, 2, 3, 4, 12, 22, and 24. One of my favorite stops is **Zinc Details,** 1905 Fillmore St., between Bush and Pine streets (☎ **415/776-2100;** www.zincdetails.com). They ply an amazing collection of modern and contemporary handcrafted glass vases, pendant lights, ceramics, and furniture.

HAIGHT STREET   Green hair, spiked hair, no hair, or mohair—even the hippies look conservative next to Haight Street's dramatic fashion freaks. The shopping in the 6 blocks of upper Haight Street, between Central Avenue and Stanyan Street, reflects its clientele and offers everything from incense to furniture, from European street styles to vintage and übertrendy—all at reasonable prices. Bus line nos. 7, 66, 71, and 73 run down Haight Street. The Muni Metro N line stops at Waller Street and at Cole Street.

Recycled Records, 1377 Haight St., between Central and Masonic streets (☎ **415/626-4075**), is easily one of the best used-record stores in the city. This loud shop has a good selection of promotional CDs and cases of used classic-rock LPs. You can also buy sheet music, tour programs, and old *TV Guide*s here. At the west end of Haight Street is **Amoeba Music,** 1377 Haight St., at Stanyan Street (☎ **415/831-1200**), a huge store that highlights, among other things, indie labels.

NORTH BEACH   Grant and Columbus avenues cater to their hip clientele with great coffee shops and a small but worthy selection of boutiques and specialty shops. You can pick up a great gift for yourself or anyone else at **Biordi Art Imports,** 412 Columbus Ave., at Vallejo Street (☎ **415/392-8096;** www.biordi.com). Its Italian Majolica pottery is exquisite and unique. Join the funky literary types who browse **City Lights Booksellers & Publishers,** 261 Columbus Ave., at Broadway (☎ **415/362-8193;** www.citylights. com), the famous bookstore owned by Beat poet Lawrence Ferlinghetti. Its shelves are stocked with a comprehensive collection of art, poetry, and political paperbacks, as well as more mainstream books.

Amoeba Music.

Pick your fish of choice at Fisherman's Wharf.

SAN FRANCISCO AFTER DARK

For up-to-date nightlife information, turn to the *San Francisco Weekly* (www.sfweekly.com) and the *San Francisco Bay Guardian* (www.sfbg.com), both of which run comprehensive listings. They are available free at bars and restaurants and from street-corner boxes all around the city. *Where* (www.wheresf.com), a free tourist-oriented monthly, also lists programs and performance times; it's available in most of the city's finer hotels. The Sunday edition of the *San Francisco Chronicle* features a "Datebook" section, printed on pink paper, with information on and listings of the week's events. If you have Internet access, it's a good idea to check out **www.citysearch.com** or **www.sfstation.com** for the latest in bars, clubs, and events. And if you want to secure seats at a hot-ticket event, either buy well in advance or contact the concierge of your hotel and see if they can swing something for you.

GETTING TICKETS **Tix Bay Area** (also known as **TIX;** ✆ **415/430-1140;** www.tixbayarea.org) sells half-price tickets on the day of performances and full-price tickets in advance to select Bay Area cultural and sporting events. TIX is also a Ticketmaster outlet and sells Gray Line tours and transportation passes. Tickets are primarily sold in person, with some half-price tickets available on their website. To find out which shows have half-price tickets, call the TIX info line or check out their website. A service charge, ranging from $1.75 to $6, is levied on each ticket, depending on its full price. You can pay with cash, traveler's check, Visa, MasterCard, American Express, or Discover with photo ID. TIX, located on Powell Street between Geary and Post streets, is open Tuesday through Friday from 11am to 6pm, Saturday from 10am to 6pm, and Sunday from 10am to 3pm. **Note:** Half-price tickets go on sale at 11am.

You can also get tickets to most theater and dance events through **City Box Office,** 180 Redwood St., Ste. 100, between Golden Gate and McAllister streets off Van Ness Avenue (✆ **415/392-4400;** www.cityboxoffice.com).

Tickets.com (☏ **800/225-2277;** www.tickets.com) sells computer-generated tickets (with a hefty service charge of $3–$19 per ticket!) to concerts, sporting events, plays, and special events. **Ticketmaster** (☏ **415/421-TIXS** [8497]; www.ticketmaster.com) also offers advance ticket purchases (also with a service charge).

American Conservatory Theater (A.C.T.) 🎁 The Tony Award–winning American Conservatory Theater made its debut in 1967 and quickly established itself as the city's premier resident theater group and one of the nation's best. Numerous big-name actors have trod the boards here, including Annette Bening and Nicolas Cage. The A.C.T. season runs September through July and features both classic and experimental works. Its home is the fabulous **Geary Theater,** a national historic landmark that is regarded as one of America's finest performance spaces. Performing at the Geary Theater, 415 Geary St. (at Mason St.). ☏ **415/749-2ACT.** (2228). www.act-sf.org. Tickets $14–$82.

The Magic Theatre The highly acclaimed Magic Theatre, which celebrated its 40th season in 2006, is a major West Coast company dedicated to presenting the works of new plays; over the years, it has nurtured the talents of such luminaries as Sam Shepard and David Mamet. Shepard's Pulitzer prize–winning play *Buried Child* had its premiere here, as did Mamet's *Dr. Faustus.* The season usually runs October through June; performances are held Tuesday through Sunday. A perk for anyone who's been in previous years: In 2005 and 2006, they redecorated the lobby and added new seats in one of the theaters. Bldg. D, Fort Mason Center, Marina Blvd. (at Buchanan St.). ☏ **415/441-8822.** www.magictheatre.org. Tickets $20–$45; discounts for students, educators, and seniors.

Philharmonia Baroque Orchestra This orchestra of baroque, classical, and "early Romantic" music performs in San Francisco and all around the Bay Area. The season lasts September through April. Herbst Theater, 401 Van Ness Ave. Tickets are sold through City Box Office. ☏ **415/392-4400** (box office), or call 252-1288 (administrative offices). www.philharmonia.org. Tickets $30–$75.

San Francisco Ballet Founded in 1933, the San Francisco Ballet is the oldest professional ballet company in the United States and is regarded as one of the country's finest. It performs an eclectic repertoire of full-length neoclassical and contemporary ballets. The Repertory Season generally runs February through May; the company performs *The Nutcracker* in December. The San Francisco Ballet Orchestra accompanies most performances. War Memorial Opera House, 301 Van Ness Ave. (at Grove St.). ☏ **415/865-2000** for tickets and information. www.sfballet.org. Tickets $20–$205.

San Francisco Opera The second municipal opera in the United States, the San Francisco Opera is one of the city's cultural icons. All productions have English supertitles. The season starts in September, lasts 14 weeks, takes a break for a few months, and then picks up again in June and July. During the interim winter period, future opera stars are featured in showcases and recitals. Performances are held most evenings, except Monday, with matinees on Sundays. Tickets go on sale as early as June for subscribers, and in August for the general public. The best seats sell out quickly, but some less-coveted seats are usually available until curtain time. War Memorial Opera House, 301 Van Ness Ave. (at Grove St.). ☏ **415/864-3330** (box office). www.sfopera.com. Tickets $24–$235; standing room $10, cash only; student rush $15, cash only.

San Francisco Ballet.

San Francisco Symphony   Founded in 1911, the internationally acclaimed San Francisco Symphony has long been an important part of the city's cultural life under such legendary conductors as Pierre Monteux and Seiji Ozawa. In 1995, Michael Tilson Thomas took over from Herbert Blomstedt; he has led the orchestra to new heights and crafted an exciting repertoire of classical and modern music. The season runs September through June. Summer symphony activities include a Summer Festival and a Summer in the City series. Tickets are very hard to come by, but if you're desperate, you can usually pick up a few outside the hall the night of the concert. Also, the box office occasionally has a few last-minute tickets. Performing at Davies Symphony Hall, 201 Van Ness Ave. (at Grove St.). ✆ **415/864-6000** (box office). www.sfsymphony.org. Tickets $25–$114.

Comedy & Cabaret

Beach Blanket Babylon ★★ 📷   A San Francisco tradition, *Beach Blanket Babylon* evolved from Steve Silver's Rent-a-Freak service—a group of "party guests" extraordinaire who hired themselves out as a "cast of characters" complete with fabulous costumes and sets, props, and gags. After their act caught on, it moved into the Savoy-Tivoli, a North Beach bar. By 1974, the audience had grown too large for the facility, and *Beach Blanket* has been at the 400-seat Club Fugazi ever since. The show is a comedic musical sendup that is best known for outrageous costumes and oversize headdresses. It's been playing for over 30 years, and almost every performance sells out. The show is updated often enough that locals still attend. Those 20 and under are welcome at Sunday matinees (2 and 5pm), when no alcohol is served; photo ID is required for evening performances. Get tickets at least 3 weeks in advance, through their website or by calling the box office. **Note:** Only a handful of tickets per show are assigned seating; all other tickets are within specific sections depending on price, but seating is first come, first seated within that section. Performances are Wednesday and Thursday at 8pm, Friday and Saturday at 6:30 and 9:30pm, and Sunday at 2 and 5pm. Club Fugazi, Beach Blanket Babylon Blvd., 678 Green St. (btw. Powell St. and Columbus Ave.). ℂ **415/421-4222.** www.beach blanketbabylon.com. Tickets $25–$80.

Cobb's Comedy Club Cobb's features such national headliners as Joe Rogan, Brian Regan, Tracy Morgan, Roseanne Barr, and Jake Johannsen. Comedy reigns Wednesday through Sunday, including a 15-comedian All-Pro Wednesday showcase (a 3-hr. marathon). Cobb's is open to those 18 and over, and occasionally to kids 16 and 17 when accompanied by a parent or legal guardian (call ahead). Shows are held Wednesday, Thursday, and

Comedy club performance.

Sunday at 8pm; Friday and Saturday at 8 and 10:15pm. 915 Columbus Ave. (at Lombard St.). ℂ **415/928-4320.** www.cobbscomedy.com. Cover $10–$35. 2-beverage minimum.

Punch Line Comedy Club   Adjacent to the Embarcadero One office building, this is the largest comedy nightclub in the city. Three-person shows with top national and local talent are featured here Tuesday through Saturday. Showcase night is Sunday, when 15 comics take the mic. There's an all-star showcase or a special event on Monday. Doors always open at 7pm, and shows are Sunday through Thursday at 8pm, Friday and Saturday at 8 and 10pm (18 and over; two-drink minimum). They serve a full menu—think wings, chicken sandwiches, ravioli, pizzas, appetizers, and salads. 444 Battery St. (btw. Washington and Clay sts.), plaza level. ℂ **415/397-4337** or 397-7573 for recorded information. www.punchlinecomedyclub. com. Cover Mon $7.50; Tues–Thurs $13–$15; Fri–Sat $18–$20; Sun $12. Prices are subject to change for more popular comics, maxing out at a price of $45. 2-beverage minimum.

The Club & Music Scene

ROCK & BLUES CLUBS

Bimbo's 365 Club ★★   Originally located on Market Street when it opened in 1931, this North Beach destination is a swank Ricky Ricardo–style spot to catch outstanding live rock, jazz, and smaller, eclectic acts like Flight of the Conchords. Amid glamorous leather banquettes, audiences dance and sip grown-up cocktails. Grab tickets in advance at the box office, which is open Monday through Friday, 10am to 4pm. 1025 Columbus Ave. (at Chestnut St.). ℂ **415/474-0365.** www.bimbos365club.com.

Biscuits and Blues   With a crisp, blow-your-eardrums-out sound system, New Orleans speak-easy (albeit commercial) appeal, and a nightly lineup of live, national acts, there's no better place to muse the blues than this basement-cum-nightclub. From 7pm on, they serve drink specials, along with their signature fried chicken; namesake moist, flaky biscuits; some new small-plate entrees dubbed "Southern tapas"; and a newly expanded wine list. Menu items range from $8 to $17. 401 Mason (at Geary St.). ℂ **415/292-2583.** www.biscuitsandblues.com. Cover (during performances) $15–$22.

Cafe du Nord 🎭 If you like your clubs dim, sexy, and with a heavy dose of old-school ambience, you will definitely dig Cafe du Nord. This subterranean supper club has rightfully proclaimed itself as the place for a "slightly lurid indie pop scene set in a beautiful old 1907 speak-easy." It's also where an eclectic crowd gathers to linger at the front room's 40-foot mahogany bar or dine on the likes of panko-crusted prawns and blackened mahimahi. The small stage hosts an eclectic mix of local and visiting artists ranging from Shelby Lynne (country) to the Dickdusters (punk) and local favorite Ledisi (R&B). The popular storytelling series Porchlight often calls the cafe home. 2170 Market St. (at Sanchez St.). ℂ **415/861-5016.** www.cafedunord.com. Cover $8–$20. Food $5–$15.

Great American Music Hall ★★ Built in 1907 as a restaurant/bordello, the Great American Music Hall is likely one of the most gorgeous rock venues you'll encounter. With ornately carved balconies, frescoed ceilings, marble columns, and huge hanging light fixtures, you won't know whether to marvel at the structure or watch the acts, which have ranged from Duke Ellington and Sarah Vaughan to Arctic Monkeys, the Radiators, and She Wants Revenge. All shows are all ages (6 and up), so you can bring your family too. You can buy a ticket for just the show and order bar snacks (such as nachos, black bean and cheese flautas, burgers, and sandwiches); or buy a ticket that includes a complete dinner (an extra $25), which changes nightly but always includes a salad and choice of meat, fish, or veggie entree. You can purchase tickets over the phone (ℂ **888/233-0449**) for a $2-to-$7 service fee or download a form from the website and fax it to **415/885-5075** with your Visa or MasterCard info; a service charge of $2 per ticket applies. You can also stop by the box office to purchase tickets directly the night of the performance for no charge (assuming the show isn't sold out), or buy them online at www.gamhtickets.com or www.tickets.com (ℂ **800/225-2277**). Valet parking is available for selects shows; check website for additional parking information. 859 O'Farrell (btw. Polk and Larkin sts.). ℂ **415/885-0750.** www.musichallsf. com. Ticket prices and starting times vary; call or check website for individual show information.

ZinZany Dinner Party

Hungry for dinner and a damn good time? It ain't cheap, but Teatro ZinZanni is a rollicking ride of food, whimsy, drama, and song within a stunningly elegant 1926 *spiegeltent* on the Embarcadero. Part musical theater and part comedy show, the 3-hour dinner theater includes a surprisingly decent five-course meal served by dozens of performers who weave both the audience and astounding physical acts (think Cirque du Soleil) into their wacky and playful world. Anyone in need of a night of lighthearted laughter should definitely book a table here. Shows are held Wednesday through Sunday, and tickets are $123 to $147, including dinner. The tent is located at Pier 29 on the Embarcadero at Battery Street. Call ℂ **415/438-2668** or see www.zinzanni.org for more details.

Lou's Pier 47 Club   You won't find many locals in the place, but Lou's happens to be good, old-fashioned fun. It's a casual spot where you can relax with Cajun seafood (downstairs) and live blues bands (upstairs) nightly. A vacation attitude makes the place one of the more, um, jovial spots near the wharf. There's a $3-to-$5 cover for bands that play between 4 and 8pm, and a $5-to-$10 cover for bands that play between 8 or 9pm and midnight or 1am. 300 Jefferson St. (at Jones St.). ✆ **415/771-5687.** www.louspier47.com.

Pier 23   If there's one good-time destination that's an anchor for San Francisco's party people, it's the Embarcadero's Pier 23. Part ramshackle patio spot and part dance floor, with a heavy dash of dive bar, here it's all about fun for a startlingly diverse clientele (including a one-time visit by Bill Clinton!). The well-worn box of a restaurant with tented patio is a prime sunny-day social spot for white collars, but on weekends, it's a straight-up people zoo where all ages and persuasions coexist more peacefully than the cast in a McDonald's commercial. Expect to boogie down shoulder to shoulder to 1980s hits and leave with a contagious feel-good vibe. Pier 23, at the Embarcadero (at Battery St.). ✆ **415/362-5125.** www.pier23cafe.com. Cover $5–$12 during performances.

The Saloon   An authentic Gold Rush survivor, this North Beach dive is the oldest bar in the city. Popular with both bikers and daytime pinstripers, it schedules live blues nightly and afternoons Friday through Sunday. 1232 Grant Ave. (at Columbus St.). ✆ **415/989-7666.** Cover $5–$15 Fri–Sat.

DANCE CLUBS

The Endup   This legendary party space with a huge, heated outdoor deck (complete with waterfall and fountain, no less), indoor fireplace, and eclectic clientele has always thrown some of the most intense all-nighters in town. In fact, it's practically a second home to the city's DJs. There's a different theme every night: Friday Ghettodisco, Super Soul Sundayz, and so on. The Endup is ever popular with the sleepless dance-all-day crowd that comes here after the other clubs close, hence the name. It's open Saturday morning from 6am to noon, and then nonstop from Saturday night around 10pm to Sunday night/Monday morning at 4am. The Sunday-morning t-dance, a long-held tradition, begins at 6am. Call or check the website to confirm nights—offerings change from time to time. 401 Sixth St. (at Harrison St.). ✆ **415/646-0999.** www.theendup.com. Cover free–$15.

Ruby Skye   Downtown's most glamorous and colossal nightspot led a previous life as an 1890s Victorian playhouse, and many of the beautiful Art Nouveau trimmings are still in place. Mission District clubbers won't go near the place—way too disco and full of the "bridge and tunnel" crowd—but for tourists, it's a safe bet for a dance-filled night in the city. The light and sound system here is amazing, and on weekend nights, the huge ballroom floor is packed with sweaty bodies dancing to thumping DJ beats or live music. When it's time to cool off, you can chill on the mezzanine or fire up in the smoking room. Be sure to call or check the website to make sure there isn't a private event taking place. 420 Mason St. (btw. Geary and Post sts.). ✆ **415/693-0777.** www.rubyskye.com. Cover $10–$25.

1015 Folsom   The ginormous party warehouse—total capacity is 2,000 persons—has three levels of dance floors that make for an extensive variety of dancing venues. DJs pound out house, disco, funk, acid-jazz, and more, with lots of groovy lasers and LED lights to stimulate the eye. Each night is a different club that attracts its own crowd, ranging from yuppie to hip-hop. Open Thursday through Saturday 10pm to 2am. 1015 Folsom St. (at Sixth St.). ☎ **415/431-1200.** www.1015.com. Cover varies.

SUPPER CLUBS

Yoshi's Jazz Club ★★   What started out in 1977 as a modest sushi and jazz club in Oakland has become one of the most respected jazz venues in the world. For more than 3 decades, SF locals had to cross the Bay Bridge to listen to Stanton Moore, Branford Marsalis, and Diana Krall in such an intimate setting. With the grand opening of Yoshi's in San Francisco's Fillmore District, locals can now take a taxi. The two-story, 28,000-square-foot, state-of-the-art jazz venue features the finest local, national, and international jazz artists, as well as first-rate Japanese cuisine at the adjoining restaurant. The elegant club is awash in gleaming dark and blond woods, big sculptural Japanese lanterns, and sensuously curved walls that envelop the intimate stage. Don't worry about the seating chart; there's not a bad seat in the house. It's the perfect place for a romantic date that starts with hamachi and ends with Harry Connick, Jr., so be sure to check Yoshi's website to see who's playing while you're in town and make reservations ASAP—you'll be glad you did. 1330 Fillmore St. (at Eddy St.). ☎ **415/655-5600.** www.yoshis.com.

DESTINATION BARS WITH DJ GROOVES

The Bliss Bar   Surprisingly trendy for sleepy, family-oriented Noe Valley, this small, stylish, and friendly bar is a great place to stop for a varied mix of locals, colorful cocktail concoctions, and a DJ spinning at the front window from 9pm to 2am every night except Sunday and Monday. If it's open, take your cocktail into the too-cool back Blue Room. And if you're on a budget, stop by from 4 to 7pm, when martinis, lemon drops, and cosmos are only $4. 4026 24th St. (btw. Noe and Castro sts.). ☎ **415/826-6200.** www.blissbarsf.com.

Wish Bar   Swathed in burgundy and black with exposed cinder block walls, cement floors, and red-shaded sconces aglow with candlelight, even you will look cool at this mellow SoMa bar in the popular night-crawler area around 11th and Folsom streets. With a bar in the front, DJ spinning upbeat lounge music in the back, and seating—including cushy leather couches—in between, it's often packed with a surprisingly diverse (albeit youthful) crowd. Closed Sundays. 1539 Folsom St. (btw. 11th and 12th sts.). ☎ **415/431-1661.** www.wishsf.com.

4

SAN FRANCISCO

San Francisco After Dark

The Bar Scene

Finding your idea of a comfortable bar has a lot to do with picking a neighborhood filled with your kind of people and investigating that area further. There are hundreds of bars throughout San Francisco, and although many are obscurely located and can't be classified by their neighborhood, the following is a general description of what you'll find, and where:

- **Chestnut and Union Street** bars attract a post-collegiate-type crowd.
- Young alternatives frequent **Mission District** haunts.
- **Upper Haight** is skate- and snowboarder grungy.
- Tourists mix with theatergoers and suits in **downtown** pubs.
- **North Beach** serves all types.
- **The Castro** caters mainly to gay locals.
- **SoMa** offers an eclectic mix.

Bourbon & Branch 🍸 An unmarked door on the corner of Jones and O'Farrell streets opens to unveil the dimly lit interior of Bourbon & Branch, where you're admitted only upon presenting the correct password. Anyone can make a reservation (online or by phone) to receive the code for entry, but it's often necessary to do so weeks in advance, and you're allotted a space for only 2 hours—but not a second more. Although fairly well known and wildly popular among the locals, this is one of those secrets we tend to keep to ourselves for fear we'll no longer be able to get a table. In fact, if you don't plan a few days—sometimes even a week—in advance, it's already difficult to get seating. Although if you don't have a reservation, it's not a problem if you don't mind sitting at the bar. After ringing the buzzer, give the hostess the password "books," and you'll be allowed into the hidden room accessed by way of a moving bookcase. Just don't fail to meticulously study the speak-easy's house of rules before you go—they mean business. The drinks menu is as extensive as they come, with favorites like the Old Fashioned or Sidecar mingling with more nouveau creations like a cucumber gimlet or elderflower-and-champagne concoction. 501 Jones St. (at O'Farrell St.). *C* **415/346-1735.** www.bourbonandbranch.com.

Gold Dust Lounge 🍸 If you're staying downtown and want to head to a friendly, festive bar loaded with old-fashioned style and revelry, you needn't wander far off Union Square. This classically cheesy watering hole is all that. The red banquettes, gilded walls, dramatic chandeliers, pro bartenders, and "regulars" are the old-school real deal. Add live music and cheap drinks, and you're in for a good ol' time. ***Tip:*** It's cash only, so come with some greenbacks. 247 Powell St. (at Geary St.). *C* **415/397-1695.**

Specs' 🍸 The location of Specs'—look for a tiny nook on the east side of Columbus Ave. just south of Broadway—makes it a bit tough to find but well worth the search. Specs's historically eclectic decor—maritime flags hang from the ceiling while dusty posters, photos, and oddities like dried whale penises line the walls—offers plenty of visual entertainment while you toss back a cold Bud (sans glass, of course). A "museum" collection displays memorabilia and items brought back by long-dead seamen who dropped in between voyages. There are plenty of salty and slightly pickled regulars to match the motif. 12 Saroyan Place (at 250 Columbus Ave.). *C* **415/421-4112.**

The Tonga Room & Hurricane Bar 🎁 This was the original rainforest cafe long before there was ever an enterprise of the same name. It's kitschy as all get-out, but there's no denying the goofy Polynesian pleasures of the Fairmont Hotel's tropical oasis. Drop in and join the crowds for an umbrella drink—mai tais are the house specialty—a simulated thunderstorm and downpour, and a heavy dose of whimsy that escapes most San Francisco establishments. If you're on a budget, you'll definitely want to stop by for the weekday happy hour from 5 to 7pm, when you can stuff your face at the all-you-can-eat bar-grub buffet (baby back ribs, chow mein, potstickers) for $9.50 and the cost of one drink. Settle in and you'll catch live Top-40 music after 8pm Wednesday through Sunday, when there's a $5 cover. In the Fairmont Hotel, 950 Mason St. (at California St.). ✆ **415/772-5278.** www.tonga room.com.

Toronado Gritty Lower Haight isn't exactly a charming street, but there's plenty of nightlife here, catering to an artistic/grungy/skateboarding 20-something crowd. While Toronado definitely draws in the young'uns, its 50-plus microbrews on tap and 100 bottled beers also entice a more eclectic clientele in search of beer heaven. The brooding atmosphere matches the surroundings: an aluminum bar, a few tall tables, minimal lighting, and a back room packed with tables and chairs. Happy hour runs 11:30am to 6pm every day for $1 off pints. 547 Haight St. (at Fillmore St.). ✆ **415/863-2276.** www.toronado.com.

Tosca Cafe 🎁 Open Tuesday through Saturday from 5pm to 2am, Sunday 7pm to 2am, Tosca is a low-key and large popular watering hole for local politicos, writers, media types, incognito celebrities such as Johnny Depp or Nicolas Cage, and similar cognoscenti of unassuming classic characters. Equipped with dim lights, red leather booths, and high ceilings, it's everything you'd expect an old North Beach legend to be. No credit cards. 242 Columbus Ave. (btw. Broadway and Pacific Ave.). ✆ **415/986-9651.** www.toscacafesf.com.

Vesuvio Situated along Jack Kerouac Alley, across from the famed City Lights bookstore, this renowned literary beatnik hangout is packed to the second-floor rafters with neighborhood writers, artists, songsters, wannabes, and everyone else, ranging from longshoremen and cab drivers to businesspeople, all of whom come for the laid-back atmosphere. The convivial space consists of two stories of cocktail tables, complemented by changing exhibitions of local art. In addition to drinks, Vesuvio features an espresso machine. 255 Columbus Ave. (at Broadway). ✆ **415/362-3370.** www.vesuvio.com.

Zeitgeist The front door is black, the back door is adorned with a skeleton Playboy bunny, and inside is packed to the rafters with tattooed, pierced, and hard-core-looking partyers. But forge on. Zeitgeist is such a friendly and fun punk-rock-cum-biker-bar beer garden that even the occasional yuppie can be spotted mingling around the slammin' jukebox that features tons of local bands, or in the huge back patio filled with picnic tables. (There tend to be cute girls here, too.) Along with fantastic dive-bar environs, you'll find 30 beers on draft, a pool table, and pinball machines. The regular crowd, mostly locals and bike messengers, come here to kick back with a pitcher and welcome anyone else interested in the same pursuit. And if your night turns out, um, better than expected, there's a hotel upstairs. No credit cards. 199 Valencia St. (at Duboce). ✆ **415/255-7505.**

heklina reviews **EVERY GAY BAR IN THE CASTRO**

As we go to print, roughly 25 of the city's 40-plus gay bars are in the Castro. We asked legendary drag queen Heklina to give quick takes on all of them for you. For the full list of Heklina's reviews of bars outside the Castro, search Frommers.com.

Heklina.

For more on Heklina, visit www.tranny shack.com.

Twin Peaks: Legendary Castro bar, long derided as "God's waiting room"

because of its older clientele, is actually the best bar on Castro Street for people-watching. Great martinis.

Trigger: Slick addition to the Castro at site of the late great Detour. Popular Sunday Latin event *Leche*.

Midnight Sun: Longest-running video bar in the Castro. 2-for-1 happy hour responsible for many, many hangovers.

Moby Dick: Castro institution, famous for its 250-gallon saltwater tank above the bar. Daily drink specials.

Blackbird: Extremely trendy (as in, recently opened), great ambience, great drinks. Perfect for before-dinner drinks.

The Pilsener: A slightly off-the-beaten-path neighborhood bar. Pool table, patio.

440 Castro: Booze, Music, Fun is the slogan for the Castro bar, and they live up to it with their infamous 5,4,3,2,1 drink specials.

Harvey's: Location, location! On the gayest corner on Earth, 18th and Castro. Stop here for a bite to eat before seeing

BREWPUBS

Gordon Biersch Brewery Restaurant   Gordon Biersch Brewery is San Francisco's largest brew restaurant, serving decent food and tasty beer to an attractive crowd of mingling professionals. There are always several house-made beers to choose from, ranging from light to dark. Menu items run $5.50 to $28. 2 Harrison St. (on the Embarcadero). ✆ **415/243-8246.** www.gordonbiersch.com.

San Francisco Brewing Company   The first microbrewery in the city, it's surprisingly low-key for an alehouse, serving its creations with burgers, fries, grilled chicken breast, and the like. The bar is one of the city's few remaining old saloons (ca. 1907), aglow with stained-glass windows, tile floors, skylit ceiling, beveled glass, and mahogany bar. The handmade copper brew kettle is visible

a film at the Castro Theater or heading off to a more interesting bar.

The Mix: Very laid-back, unpretentious. Pool table, jukebox. Spacious outdoor patio site of numerous fundraisers and drag shows. Quintessential Castro bar.

Last Call: Formerly known as Men's Room, perfectly located 2 blocks away from Castro St. Close, but not too close if you want to get away from the insanity. Cozy is the word; it even has a fireplace.

Toad Hall: I confess I have not given this one much of a chance, but if you think this is something more than yet another faceless, soulless new bar to pop up in the Castro, please convince me otherwise.

Badlands: I much preferred the old, seedy Badlands of lore (hay on floor, pinball machines, country vibe). The sterile "New Improved" version (now going on 10 years old) could be Anywhere, USA. Still, it's very popular, especially if you're into twinks.

The Edge: Popular neighborhood bar. Numerous charity events produced here, sometimes featuring performances on comically tiny stage.

Q Bar: Castro St. bar with younger crowd. Mondays (*Wanted*) and Wednesdays (*Booty Call*) are most popular nights. Can be twink heaven.

Café Flore: Beloved cafe in the heart of the Castro neighborhood. Outdoor seating available for people-watching. Popular Sunday brunch location.

The Lookout: Centrally located with a wrap around balcony perfect for people-watching. Great food, especially the pizza. Don't miss *JOCK* Sundays, from 3 to 9pm every week.

The Café: Another in a long line of formerly great bars that underwent a remodel and had whatever character and personality it possessed stripped away . . . but hey, that's just my opinion.

Lime: Trendy restaurant with a younger clientele. Sunday Brunch is not-to-be-missed . . . bottomless mimosas!

Lucky 13: Not a gay bar, but in the Castro so if you wander in by mistake, enjoy the free popcorn, smoking patio, and great jukebox.

Bar On Church: Pointlessly remodeled bar on cusp of Castro. Karaoke on Mondays, with other themed parties (*The Party* on Fridays, *VICE* on Saturdays).

from the street. Most evenings the place is packed with everyday folks enjoying music, darts, chess, backgammon, cards, dice, and, of course, beer. Menu items range from $3.70 for edamame to $8.70 for a shrimp-and-chips platter. The happy-hour special, a 10-ounce microbrew beer for $1 (or a pint for $1.75), is offered daily from 4 to 6pm and midnight to 1am. 155 Columbus Ave. (at Pacific St.). ✆ **415/434-3344.** www.sfbrewing.com.

ThirstyBear Brewing Company   Nine superb, handcrafted varieties of brew are always on tap at this stylish high-ceilinged brick edifice. Good Spanish food is served here, too. Pool tables and dart boards are upstairs, and live flamenco can be heard on Sunday nights. 661 Howard St. (1 block east of the Moscone Center). ✆ **415/974-0905.** www.thirstybear.com.

WINE BARS

The Bubble Lounge   This two-level champagne bar—looking ever so chic with its red-velvet sofas, brick walls, and floor-to-ceiling draperies—chills more than 300 champagnes and sparkling wines, including about 30 by the glass. As one would expect at a Financial District bubbly bar, there's a soupçon of pretentiousness emanating from the BMW-driving clientele and perpetually unshaven bartenders. If you're the type that prefers beer and free pretzels, you'll hate it here, particularly if you have to wait in line for a $20 flute of something you can't even pronounce; but the pickup scene really perks up as the bubbly flows into the night. 714 Montgomery St. (btw. Washington and Jackson sts.). ✆ **415/434-4204.** www.bubblelounge.com.

First Crush   If you're staying downtown and in the mood for a glass of fine wine, take a stroll to this popular restaurant and wine lounge. Amid a stylish and dimly lit interior, an eclectic mix of visitors and locals nosh on reasonably priced "progressive American cuisine" that's paired, if desired, with a large selection of all-California wines served by the glass. But plenty of folks also drop by just to sample flights of wine and talk shop with the wine-savvy staff. This also is a good late-night-bite spot, as it's open until midnight Thursday through Saturday. 101 Cyril Magnin St. (aka Fifth St., just north of Market St., at Ellis St.). ✆ **415/982-7874.** www.firstcrush.com.

Nectar Wine Lounge   Catering to the Marina's young and beautiful, this hip place to sip pours about 50 globally diverse wines by the glass (plus 800 choices by the bottle), along with creative small plates; pairings are optional. Soothing shades of browns lend a relaxing ambience to the lounge's industrial-slick decor that includes lots of polished woods and hexagonal highlights. 3330 Steiner St. (at Chestnut St.). ✆ **415/345-1377.** www.nectarwinelounge.com.

COCKTAILS WITH A VIEW

Harry Denton's Starlight Room 📷   If that new cocktail dress is burning a hole in your suitcase, get yourself dolled up tonight and say hello to Harry, our city's de facto party host. His celestial crimson-infused cocktail lounge and nightclub, perched on the top floor of the Sir Francis Drake hotel, is a pantheon to 1930s San Francisco, a throwback to the days when red-velvet banquettes, chandeliers, and fashionable duds were de rigueur. The 360-degree view of the city is worth the cover charge alone, but what draws tourists and locals of all ages is a night of Harry Denton–style fun, which usually includes plenty of drinking, live music, and unrestrained dancing, regardless of age. The bar stocks a pricey collection of single-malt Scotches and champagnes, and you can snack from the "Lite" menu. If you make a reservation to guarantee a table, you will also have a place to rest between songs. Early evening is more relaxed, but come the weekend, this place gets loose. *Tip:* Come dressed for success (no casual jeans, open-toed shoes for men, or sneakers), or you'll be turned away at the door. Atop the Sir Francis Drake hotel, 450 Powell St., 21st floor. ✆ **415/395-8595.** www.harrydenton.com. Cover $10 Wed–Fri after 8:30pm; $15 Sat after 8:30pm.

Top of the Mark 📷   This is one of the most famous cocktail lounges in the world, and for good reason—the spectacular glass-walled room features an unparalleled 19th-floor view. During World War II, Pacific-bound servicemen toasted their goodbyes to the States here. While less dramatic today than they were back then, evenings spent here are still sentimental, thanks to the romantic

You don't have to be gay to enjoy the free-spirited atmosphere of a gay bar. San Francisco's gay and lesbian community has a long tradition of welcoming straights to their bars, and it's pretty common to see gay, straight, male, and female revelers mix it up on the dance floor. At the **Mint Karaoke Lounge** (1942 Market St., at Laguna St.; *C* 415/626-4726; www.themint.net), no one knows or cares what your gender or sexual preferences are, as long as you clap loudly for anyone who has the guts to get up on stage. **Martuni's** (4 Valencia St., at Market St.; *C* 415/241-0205) has everything you want and expect in a piano bar: a neon martini glass on the sign, a huge bar in the front room, and a cozy little piano bar in the back room where you can sing along or listen in awe as I-shoulda-been-a-star types belt out classic show tunes.

atmosphere. Live bands play throughout the week: A jazz pianist on Tuesdays starts at 7pm; salsa on Wednesdays begins with dance lessons at 8pm, and the band starts up at 9pm. On Thursdays, Stompy Jones brings a swing vibe from 7:30pm, and a dance band playing everything from '50s hits through contemporary music keeps the joint hopping Fridays and Saturdays starting at 9pm. Drinks range from $9 to $12. A $59 three-course sunset dinner is served Friday and Saturday at 7:30pm. Sunday brunch, served from 10am to 2pm, costs $59 for adults and includes a glass of champagne; for children 4 to 12, the brunch is $30. In the Mark Hopkins InterContinental, 1 Nob Hill (California and Mason sts.). *C* **415/616-6916.** www.topofthemark.com. Cover $5–$10.

SPORTS BAR

Greens Sports Bar If you think San Francisco sports fans aren't as enthusiastic as those on the East Coast, well, you're right. These days it's pretty easy to find an empty seat at Greens during a '49ers or Giants game. The city's de facto sports bar is a classic, cozy hangout with lots of dark wood, polished brass, windows that open onto the street, and an array of elevated TVs showing various sporting events via satellite. Highlights include 18 beers on tap, a pool table, and a boisterous happy-hour scene every Monday through Friday from 4 to 7pm. Food isn't served, but you can place an order from the various restaurants along Polk Street and eat at the bar (they even provide a selection of menus). 2239 Polk St. (at Green St.). *C* **415/775-4287.**

GAY & LESBIAN BARS & CLUBS

The Café 🎁 When this place first opened, it was the only predominantly lesbian dance club on Saturday nights in the city. Once the guys found out how much fun the girls were having, they joined the party. Today it's a hugely popular mixed gay and lesbian scene with three bars; two pool tables; a steamy, free-spirited dance floor; and a small, heated patio and balcony where smoking and schmoozing are allowed. At press time, it was undergoing an extensive multimillion-dollar remodel that would render it even more upscale. An added perk: They open at 4pm weekdays and 3pm weekends (2pm on Sun). 2369 Market St. (at Castro St.). *C* **415/834-5840.** www.cafesf.com.

The Stud The Stud, which has been around for almost 40 years, is one of the most successful gay establishments in town. The interior has an antiques-shop look. Music is a balanced mix of old and new, and nights vary from cabaret to oldies to disco-punk. Check the website in advance for the evening's offerings. Drink prices range from $3 to $8. Happy hour runs Monday through Saturday 5 to 9pm, with $1 off well drinks. 399 Ninth St. (at Harrison St.). © **415/863-6623** or 415/252-STUD (7883) for event info. www.studsf.com. Cover $6–$10.

Twin Peaks Tavern Right at the intersection of Castro, 17th, and Market streets is one of the Castro's most famous (at 35 years old) gay hangouts. It caters to an older crowd but often has a mixture of patrons and claims to be the first gay bar in America. Because of its relatively small size and desirable location, the place becomes fairly crowded and convivial by 8pm, earlier than many neighboring bars. 401 Castro St. (at 17th and Market sts.). © **415/864-9470.** www.twinpeaks tavern.com.

THE SAN FRANCISCO FRANCISCO BAY AREA

by Matthew Poole

5

The City by the Bay is captivating, but don't ignore its environs, which contain a multitude of natural spectacles such as Mount Tamalpais and Muir Woods; scenic communities such as Tiburon, Sausalito, and Half Moon Bay; and diverse, culturally rich cities such as Oakland and its youth-oriented next-door neighbor, Berkeley. Farther north stretch the valleys of Napa and Sonoma, the finest wine region in the nation (see chapter 6, "The Wine Country"). To the south are high-tech Silicon Valley, San Mateo County, and San Jose, Northern California's largest city.

BERKELEY ★

10 miles NE of San Francisco

Berkeley is best known as the home of the University of California at Berkeley, which is world renowned for its academic standards, 18 Nobel Prize winners (7 are active staff), and protests that led to the most famous student riots in U.S. history. Today there's still hippie idealism in the air, but the radicals have aged; the 1960s are present only in tie-dye and paraphernalia shops. The biggest change the town is facing is yuppification; as San Francisco's rent and property prices soar out of the range of the average person's budget, everyone with less than a small fortune is seeking shelter elsewhere, and Berkeley is one of the top picks (although Oakland is quickly becoming a favorite, too). Berkeley is a lively

PREVIOUS PAGE: **Sather Tower, University of California at Berkeley.** ABOVE: **Protest in Berkeley.**

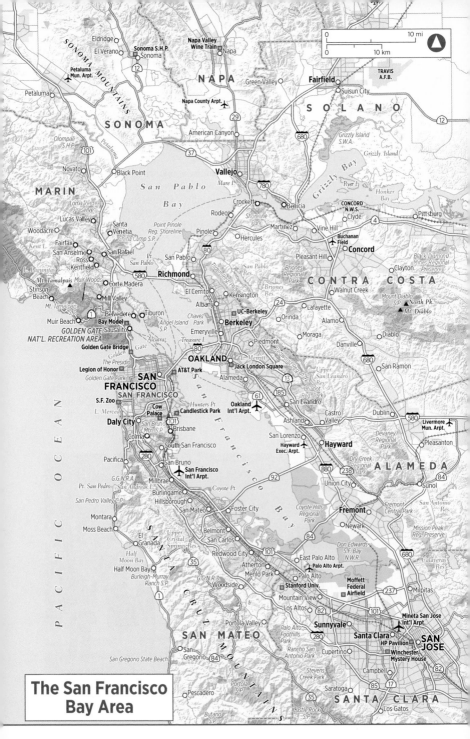

The San Francisco
Bay Area

city, teeming with all types of people, a beautiful campus, vast parks, great shopping, and some incredible restaurants.

Essentials

The Berkeley **Bay Area Rapid Transit (BART)** station is 2 blocks from the university. The fare from San Francisco is less than $4 one-way. Call ✆ **511** or visit www.bart.gov for trip info or fares, or to download trip planners to your iPod, mobile phone, or PDA.

If you are coming **by car** from San Francisco, take the Bay Bridge (go during the evening commute, and you'll think Los Angeles traffic is a breeze). Follow I-80 east to the University Avenue exit, and follow University until you hit the campus. Parking is tight, so either leave your car at the Sather Gate parking lot at Telegraph Avenue and Durant Street, or expect to fight for a spot.

What to See & Do

Hanging out is the preferred Berkeley pastime, and the best place to do it is **Telegraph Avenue,** the street that leads to the campus's southern entrance. Most of the action lies between Bancroft Way and Dwight Way, where coffeehouses, restaurants, shops, great book and record stores, and crafts booths swarm with life. Pretend you're a local: Plant yourself at a cafe, sip a latte, and ponder something intellectual or survey the town's unique residents.

UC BERKELEY CAMPUS

The University of California at Berkeley (www.berkeley.edu) is worth a stroll. It's a beautiful campus with plenty of woodsy paths, architecturally noteworthy buildings, and, of course, 33,000 students. Among the architectural highlights of the campus are a number of buildings by Bernard Maybeck, Bakewell and Brown, and John Galen Howard.

Telegraph Avenue in Berkeley.

N

1/2 mi
0
1/2 km
0

TILDEN REGIONAL PARK

Tilden Park
Golf Course

Golf Course Rd.

Grizzly Peak

Lawrence Berkeley
National Laboratory

7

6

UNIVERSITY OF
CALIFORNIA–
BERKELEY

Centennial Dr.

California
Memorial
Stadium

U.C.B.
CLARK KERR
CAMPUS

Claremont Canyon
Regional Preserve

13
13

Claremont Ave.

Warring St.
Piedmont Ave.
Derby St.
College Ave.
Benvenue Ave.
Webster St.
Prince St.

Gayley Rd.
10
11

8

Campanile

9

Hillegass Ave.
People's
Park
Hearst St.
Dana St.
Dwight Way
Willard
Park
12
Telegraph Ave.
Russell St.
Ashby Ave.

Hilgard Ave.
Le Conte Ave.
Ridge Rd.
Bancroft Way
Durant Ave.
Bowditch St.

Scenic Ave.
Arch St.
Oxford St.
Fulton St.
Carleton St.
Ellsworth St.
Stuart St.
Ward St.
Adeline St.

Visitor
Information
Center
Berkeley BART

Rose
Garden
Park
Codornices
Park
Eunice St.

Euclid Ave.

Cedar St.

Spruce St.

13

5

Shattuck Ave.
Blake St.
Milvia St.
Shattuck Ave.
Grove St.
Milvia St.
Henry St.

Live
Oak
Park
Walnut St.

Sutter St.

Los Angeles Ave.

Martin Ave.

The Alameda

Fresno Ave.

Colusa Ave.

Berryman St.
Bonita Ave.
Vine St.
Josephine St.
Edith St.
McGee Ave.
Lincoln St.

Francisco St.
Grant St.
Delaware St.
Berkeley Way

Center St.
Allston Way
Martin Luther King Jr. Way
McKinley Ave.
Roosevelt Ave.
Jefferson Ave.
California St.
Spaulding Ave.
Sacramento St.

Parker St.
McGee Ave.
Derby St.
Acton St.

San
Pablo
Park
Mabel St.
Matthews St.

Hopkins St.

Ordway St.

Peralta St.
Nelson St.

Monterey Ave.

Sonoma Ave.

Santa Fe Ave.

Curtis St.

Ramona Ave.
Pomona Ave.

Masonic Ave.

Evelyn Ave.
Talbot Ave.
Stannage Ave.
Kains Ave.
San Pablo Ave.
10th Ave.
9th St.
8th St.

Portland Ave.

Washington Ave.
Solano Ave.
San Lorenzo Ave.
Tacoma Ave.
Ventura Ave.

4

ALBANY
Cornell Ave.
Dartmouth St.
Marin Ave.

123

3

Kenney
Park
Hearst Ave.
7th St.
Page St.
Camelia St.
Jones St.

North
Berkeley
BART
Acton St.
Franklin St.
Chestnut St.
Curtis St.
Byron St.
Bonar St.
Browning St.

Virginia St.
University Ave.
Addison St.
Berkeley Way
Delaware St.

Cedar
Park
Cedar St.

Channing Way
Dwight Way

Bancroft Way
Allston Way
Carleton St.
Pardee St.
6th St.

2
1
Amtrak sta.
80
580

Harrison St.

Gilman St.

5th St.

2nd St.
Frontage Rd.

Harrison
Fields

Eastshore
State Park

Aquatic
Park

San Pablo Ave.
10th St.
9th St.

4th St.

SAN
FRANCISCO
BAY

Berkeley
Marina

Marina Blvd.

Contact the **Visitor Information Center,** 101 University Hall, 2200 University Ave., at Oxford Street (☎ 510/642-5215; www.berkeley.edu/visitors), to join a free 90-minute campus tour. Reservations are required; see website for details. Tours are available year-round Monday through Saturday at 10am and Sunday at 1pm. Weekday tours depart from the visitor center, and weekend tours start from Sather Bell Tower in the middle of campus. Electric-cart tours are available year-round for travelers with disabilities for $50 (2 weeks' advance reservations required; no tours are given the week btw. Christmas and New Year's Day). Or stop by the office and pick up a self-guided walking-tour brochure or a free Berkeley map. *Note:* The information center is closed on weekends, but you can find the latest information on their website.

The university's southern, main entrance is at the northern end of Telegraph Avenue, at Bancroft Way. Walk through the entrance into Sproul Plaza, and when school is in session, you'll encounter the gamut of Berkeley's inhabitants: colorful street people, rambling political zealots, and ambitious students. There's always something going on here, so stretch out on the grass for a few minutes and take in the Berkeley vibe.

The **Lawrence Hall of Science ★** (east of campus on Centennial Dr., just above the Botanical Gardens; ☎ 510/642-5132; www.lawrencehallof science.org) offers hands-on science exploration for kids of all ages. It's open daily from 10am to 5pm and is a wonderful place to watch the sunset. Included in the admission price is an outdoor science park called Forces That Shape the Bay, which lets visitors explore ongoing geologic forces. Admission is $12 for adults; $9 for seniors 62 and over, students, and children 7 to 18; $6 for children 3 to 6; and free for kids 2 and under. The **UC Berkeley Art Museum ★** (2626 Bancroft Way, btw. College and Telegraph aves.; ☎ 510/642-0808; www. bampfa.berkeley.edu) is open Wednesday through Sunday from 11am to 5pm. Admission is $10 for adults; $7 for seniors, non-UCB students, visitors with disabilities, and children 17 and under; and free for UCB students.

PARKS

Berkeley has some of the most extensive and beautiful parks around. If you want to wear the kids out or enjoy hiking, swimming, sniffing roses, or just getting a breath of California air, jump in your car and make your way to **Tilden Park ★.** On the way, stop at the colorful terraced WPA-era **Rose Garden ★** in north Berkeley on Euclid Avenue between Bay View and Eunice Street. Then head high into the Berkeley hills to Tilden, where you'll find plenty of flora and fauna, hiking trails, an old steam train and merry-go-round, a farm and nature area for kids, and a chilly tree-encircled lake. The East Bay's public transit system, AC Transit (☎ 511; www.actransit.org), runs the no. 67 bus line around the park on weekdays and all the way to the Tilden Visitors Center on Saturdays and Sundays. Call ☎ 888/327-2757 or see www.ebparks.org for further information.

Another worthy nature excursion is the **University of California Botanical Garden** (☎ 510/643-2755; www.botanicalgarden.berkeley.edu), which features a vast collection of native California herbage ranging from cactuses to redwoods. It's on campus in Strawberry Canyon on Centennial Drive. Unfortunately, no public bus can take you directly there, so driving is the way to go. Call for directions. Open daily from 9am to 5pm; closed the first Tuesday of every month; docent-led tours on Thursdays, Saturdays, and Sundays at 1:30pm. Admission is $9 adults, $7 seniors 65 and over, $5 for youth 13 to 17, $2 for youth 5 to 12, and free for children 4 and under and UC students.

SHOPPING

College Avenue from Dwight Way to the Oakland border overflows with eclectic boutiques, antiques shops, and restaurants. The other, more upscale option is **Fourth Street,** in west Berkeley, 2 blocks north of the University Avenue exit.

Where to Stay

Unfortunately, Berkeley is not even close to being a good hotel town. Most accommodations are extremely basic motels and funky B&Bs. The one exception (though it's overpriced) is the **Claremont Resort & Spa,** 41 Tunnel Rd., Berkeley (www.claremontresort.com; ✆ **800/551-7266** or 510/843-3000), a grand Victorian hotel, also on the border of Oakland, with a fancy spa and gym, three restaurants, a hip bar, and grandiose surroundings. But rates are nearly half of what they were prerecession, ranging from $209 to $309. Or you can contact the **Berkeley & Oakland Bed and Breakfast Network** (www.bbonline.com/ca/berkeley-oakland; ✆ **510/848-1431**), which books visitors into private homes and apartments.

MODERATE

Hotel Durant It only takes walking into the lobby of Hotel Durant to get the feeling you're living out a game of *Clue*—or else pursuing a degree of higher learning. The lobby mimics an old-fashioned library (with contemporary furnishings like a bright blue leather couch), and the rooms give the feeling that you might be enrolling in the neighboring University of California at Berkeley any day now. (The location is within spitting distance of the campus itself and 1 block off of bustling Telegraph Ave.) Shower curtains are emblazoned with dictionary entries, posters from classics like *The Graduate* adorn the walls, and even the key cards are made to look like student IDs. It's very whimsical, while being quite cool at the same time. Best of all, like other Joie de Vivre properties, Hotel Durant is pet-friendly, so you can bring your furry friend along; rooms are equipped with dog beds and food bowls, and pets are given organic treats and toy footballs.

2600 Durant Ave. (at College St.), Berkeley, CA 94704. www.hoteldurant.com. ✆ **800/238-7268** or 510/845-8981. Fax 510/486-8336. 143 units. $95–$195 double. AE, DC, DISC, MC, V. Uncovered parking $16. **Amenities:** Restaurant, bar. *In room:* TV, DVD, hair dryer, minibar, MP3 docking station, free Wi-Fi.

Rose Garden Inn Like a Merchant Ivory movie, the accommodations within this 40-room/five-building inn range from English Country to Victorian, making it a favorite for visiting grandparents and vacationing retirees. Despite your age or design sense, the stunning and expansive garden exploding with rose bushes, hydrangeas, and an abundance of flora and fauna is sure to delight, as well as erase all memories that you're on a characterless stretch of Telegraph Avenue a few blocks south of the student action. Rooms, many of which have fireplaces, cable TVs, and all the basic amenities, show some wear and tend to be a little dark, but they are spacious, updated, and very clean, despite the obvious age of some bathroom nooks and crannies.

2740 Telegraph Ave. (at Stuart St.), Berkeley, CA 94705. www.rosegardeninn.com. ✆ **800/992-9005** or 510/549-2145. Fax 510/549-1085. 40 units. $139–$235 double. Rates include breakfast, coffee, and afternoon cookies. AE, DC, DISC, MC, V. Free parking on a space-available basis. *In room:* TV, hair dryer, free Wi-Fi.

Where to Eat

East Bay dining is a relaxed alternative to San Francisco's gourmet scene. There are plenty of ambitious Berkeley restaurants and, unlike in San Francisco, plenty of parking, provided you're not near the campus.

If you want to dine student-style, eat on campus Monday through Friday. Buy something at a sidewalk stand or in the building directly behind the Student Union. There's also the **Bear's Lair Pub and Coffee House,** the **Terrace,** and the **Golden Bear Restaurant.** All the university eateries have both indoor and outdoor seating.

Telegraph Avenue has an array of small ethnic restaurants, cafes, and sandwich shops. Follow the students: If the place is crowded, it's good, supercheap, or both.

EXPENSIVE

Chez Panisse ★★★ CALIFORNIAN   California cuisine is so much a product of Alice Waters's genius that all other restaurants following in her wake should be dated A.A.W. (After Alice Waters). Most of the produce and meat comes from local farms and is organically produced, and after all these years, Alice still tends her restaurant with great integrity and innovation. In the upstairs cafe are displays of pastries and fruit and an oak bar adorned with large bouquets of fresh flowers. At lunch or dinner, the menu might feature delicately smoked gravlax or roasted eggplant soup with pesto, followed by lamb ragout garnished with apricots, onions, and spices and served with couscous.

The cozy downstairs restaurant, strewn with blossoming floral bouquets, is an appropriately warm environment in which to indulge in the fixed-price four-course gourmet dinner, which is served Tuesday through Thursday. Monday is bargain night, with a three-course dinner for $60. Every Saturday, the restaurant posts the following week's menu, which changes daily. The wine list is also excellent, with bottles ranging from $23 to $560.

1517 Shattuck Ave. (btw. Cedar and Vine). ℂ **510/548-5525** for main restaurant reservations, 548-5049 for cafe reservations. Fax 510/548-0140. www.chezpanisse.com. Reservations required for dining room and taken 1 month prior to calendar date requested. Reservations recommended for cafe, but walk-ins welcome. Restaurant fixed-price menu $75–$95; cafe main courses $15–$28. AE, DC, DISC, MC, V. Restaurant seatings Mon–Sat 6–6:30pm and 8:30–9:15pm most of the year (in slower months, like Jan–Mar, times vary; call to confirm). Cafe Mon–Thurs 11:30am–3pm and 5–10:30pm; Fri–Sat 11:30am–3:30pm and 5–11:30pm. BART: Downtown Berkeley. From I-80 N., take the University Ave. exit and turn left onto Shattuck Ave.

Meritage ★★★ CALIFORNIAN/FRENCH   In the trendy Claremont Spa & Resort, which recently underwent a very pricey remodel, this restaurant (formerly Jordan's) reopened at the close of 2009 to much acclaim and attention. With good reason—Chez Panisse aside, it's one of the only spots east of the Bay Bridge where you'll find such bold fare. Boasting contemporary California cuisine in a classy French setting (minus the pretension), Meritage has many fine attributes, but its *piece de resistance* is the world-class wine list. Crafted around the chef's menu—which largely relies on the crops and stocks of local farmers and purveyors—each wine is paired to perfection with a suggested dish. While Meritage carries 190 selections from around the world, the focal point is on Northern California wines, and 18 types are offered by the 3- or 6-ounce glass. Executive chef Josh Thomsen, who has been in the kitchen of some of the state's best dining establishments, including Yountville's French Laundry, L.A.'s Hotel Bel Air, and the Lodge at Pebble Beach, helms the restaurant. Best of all: All courses are served in either half- or full-size portions, so you can sample several, and are divided into categories by wine, such as "spicy and earthy reds" or "full-bodied whites." Do yourself a favor and check into one of the Claremont's upgraded rooms for the night so you can enjoy yourself to the fullest and not worry about stumbling home at evening's end.

41 Tunnel Rd. (inside the Claremont). ✆ **800/551-7266.** www.meritageclaremont.com. Reservations recommended. Main courses $13–$37. AE, DC, DISC, MC, V. Restaurant Mon–Sat 6:30–11am; Tues–Sat 6–11pm. Lounge Mon–Sat 5–11pm; Sat 11am–2:30pm; Sun 6:30am–1:30pm.

MODERATE

Cafe Rouge ★ MEDITERRANEAN After cooking at San Francisco's renowned Zuni Cafe for 10 years, chef-owner Marsha McBride launched her own restaurant, a sort of Zuni East. She brought former staff members with her, and now her sparse, loftlike dining room serves salads, rotisserie chicken with oil and thyme, grilled lamb chops, steaks, and homemade sausages. East Bay carnivores are especially happy with the burger; like Zuni's, it's top-notch. Tuesday, Wednesday, and Thursday are $1 oyster nights from 5:30 to 9:30pm. During warm days, outdoor dining overlooking the shopping square is ideal.

1782 Fourth St. (btw. Delaware and Hearst). ✆ **510/525-1440.** www.caferouge.net. Reservations recommended. Main courses $12–$36. MC, V. Lunch Mon–Fri 11:30am–3pm; dinner Tues–Thurs 5:30–9:30pm, Fri–Sat 5:30–10pm, Sun 5–9:30pm; brunch Sun 10am–2:30pm.

Rivoli ★★ 🏠 CALIFORNIAN One of the favored dinner destinations in the East Bay, Rivoli offers top-notch food at amazingly reasonable prices. Aside from a few house favorites, the menu changes entirely every 3 weeks to feature whatever's freshest and in season; the wine list follows suit, with around 10 by-the-glass options handpicked to match the food. While many love it, I'm not a fan of the portobello-mushroom fritter, a gourmet variation of the fried zucchini stick. However, plenty of dishes shine, including chicken cooked with prosciutto di Parma, wild mushroom chard, ricotta cannelloni, Marsala *jus*, snap peas, and baby carrots; and braised lamb shank with green garlic risotto, sautéed spinach, and oven-dried tomatoes. Finish the evening with an assortment of cheeses or a warm chocolate truffle torte with hazelnut ice cream, orange crème anglaise, and chocolate sauce.

1539 Solano Ave. ✆ **866/496-2489** or 510/526-2542. www.rivolirestaurant.com. Reservations recommended. Main courses $18–$25. AE, DC, DISC, MC, V. Mon–Thurs 5:30–9:30pm; Fri 5:30–10pm; Sat 5–10pm; Sun 5–9pm.

INEXPENSIVE

Cafe Fanny ★★ FRENCH/ITALIAN Alice Waters's (of Chez Panisse fame) cafe is one of those local must-do East Bay breakfast traditions. Don your Birkenstocks and earth-tone apparel, grab the morning paper, and head here to wait in line for a simple yet masterfully prepared French breakfast. The menu offers such items as soft-boiled farm-fresh eggs on Levain toast, buckwheat crepes with house-made preserves, cinnamon toast, and an assortment of superb pastries. Lunch is more of an Italian experience featuring seasonal selections. Sandwiches—such as Alice's baked ham and watercress on focaccia or grilled chicken breast wrapped in prosciutto, sage, and aioli on Acme bread—might convince you that maybe Berkeley isn't such a crazy place to live after all. There's also a selection of pizzettas, salads, and soup. Eat inside at the stand-up food bar (one bench) or outside at one of the cafe tables.

1603 San Pablo Ave. (at Cedar St.). ✆ **510/524-5447.** www.cafefanny.com. Breakfast items $3–$9.45; lunch $7.45–$9.45. MC, V. Mon–Fri 7am–3pm; Sat 8am–4pm; Sun 8am–3pm. Breakfast until 11am, Sun all day. Closed major holidays.

O Chamé ★★ JAPANESE   Spare and plain in its decor, this spot has a meditative air to complement the traditional, experimental, and extremely fresh Japanese-inspired cuisine. The menu, which changes daily, offers meal-in-a-bowl dishes ($13–$16) that allow a choice of soba or udon noodles in a clear soup with a variety of toppings—from shrimp and wakame seaweed to beef with burdock root and carrot. Appetizers include a flavorful melding of grilled shiitake mushrooms, as well as portobello mushrooms and green-onion pancakes. Their main entree selection always includes delicious roasted salmon, but you can also easily fill up on a bowl of soba or udon noodles with fresh, wholesome fixings (think roasted oysters, sea bass, and tofu skins).

1830 Fourth St. (near Hearst). ✆ **510/841-8783.** www.themenupage.com/ochame.html. Reservations recommended Fri–Sat dinner. Main courses $9–$19 lunch, $18–$24 dinner. AE, MC, V. Mon–Sat 11:30am–3pm; Mon–Thurs 5:30–9pm; Fri–Sat 5:30–9:30pm.

OAKLAND

10 miles E of San Francisco

Although it's less than a dozen miles from San Francisco, Oakland is worlds apart from its sister city across the bay. Originally little more than a cluster of ranches and farms, Oakland exploded in size and stature practically overnight, when the last mile of transcontinental railroad track was laid down. Major shipping ports soon followed, and, to this day, Oakland remains one of the busiest industrial ports on the West Coast.

The price for economic success, however, is Oakland's lowbrow reputation as a predominantly working-class city, forever in San Francisco's chic shadow. However, as the City by the Bay has become crowded and expensive in the past few years, Oakland has experienced a rush of new residents and businesses. As a result, Oak-town is in the midst of a renaissance, and its future continues to look brighter and brighter.

Rent a sailboat on Lake Merritt, stroll along the waterfront, explore the fantastic Oakland Museum—these are a few of many great reasons to hop the bay and spend a fog-free day exploring one of California's largest and most ethnically diverse cities.

Essentials

BART connects San Francisco and Oakland through one of the longest underwater transit tunnels in the world. Fares range from $3 to $4 one-way, depending on your station of origin; children 4 and under ride free. BART trains operate Monday through Friday from 4am to midnight, Saturday from 6am to midnight, and Sunday from 8am to midnight. Exit at the 12th Street station for downtown Oakland. Call ✆ **511** or visit www.bart.gov for more info.

By car from San Francisco, take I-80 across the San Francisco–Oakland Bay Bridge and follow signs to downtown Oakland. Exit at Grand Avenue South for the Lake Merritt area.

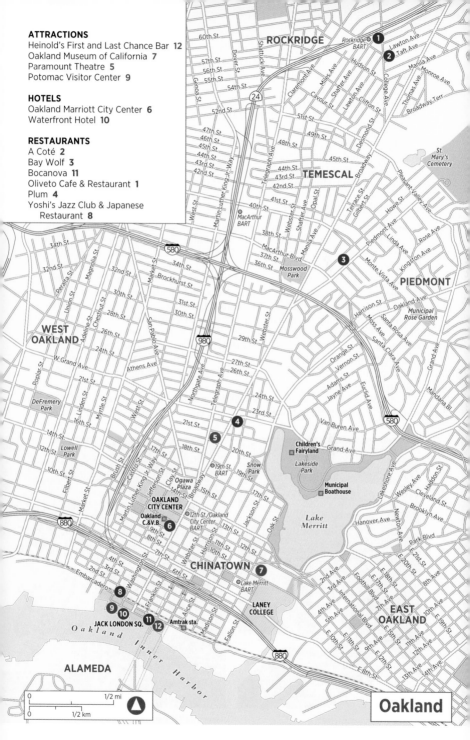

ATTRACTIONS
Heinold's First and Last Chance Bar **12**
Oakland Museum of California **7**
Paramount Theatre **5**
Potomac Visitor Center **9**

HOTELS
Oakland Marriott City Center **6**
Waterfront Hotel **10**

RESTAURANTS
A Coté **2**
Bay Wolf **3**
Bocanova **11**
Oliveto Cafe & Restaurant **1**
Plum **4**
Yoshi's Jazz Club & Japanese
    Restaurant **8**

Oakland

For a calendar of events in Oakland, contact the **Oakland Convention and Visitors Bureau,** 463 11th St., Oakland, CA 94607 (✆ **510/839-9000;** www.oaklandcvb.com). The city also sponsors eight free guided tours, including African-American Heritage and downtown tours held Wednesdays and Saturdays May through October; call ✆ **510/238-3234** or visit www.oaklandnet.com/walkingtours for details.

Downtown Oakland lies between Grand Avenue on the north, I-980 on the west, Inner Harbor on the south, and Lake Merritt on the east. Between these landmarks are three BART stations (12th St., 19th St., and Lake Merritt), City Hall, the Oakland Museum, Jack London Square, and several other sights.

What to See & Do

Lake Merritt is one of Oakland's prime tourist attractions, along with Jack London Square (see below). Three-and-a-half miles in circumference, the tidal lagoon was bridged and dammed in the 1860s and is now a wildlife refuge that is home to flocks of migrating ducks, herons, and geese. The 122-acre **Lakeside Park,** a popular place to picnic, feed the ducks, and escape the fog, surrounds the lake on three sides. Visit www.oaklandnet.com/parks for more info. At the **Municipal Boathouse ★** (✆ **510/238-2196**), in Lakeside Park along the north shore, you can rent sailboats, rowboats, pedal boats, canoes, or kayaks for $10 to $25 per hour (cash only). Or you can take an hour-long gondola ride with **Gondola Servizio** (✆ **888/737-8494;** www.gondolaservizio.com). Experienced gondoliers will serenade you June through October as you glide across the lake; the cost ranges from $45 to $225 for two, depending on the time and gondola style.

Another site worth visiting is Oakland's **Paramount Theatre ★**, 2025 Broadway (✆ **510/893-2300;** www.paramounttheatre.com), an outstanding

Municipal Boathouse rentals.

Paramount Theater.

Sailing Oakland Bay.

National Historic Landmark and example of Art Deco architecture and decor. Built in 1931 and authentically restored in 1973, it's the city's main performing arts center, hosting big-name performers like Smokey Robinson and Alicia Keys. Guided tours of the 3,000-seat theater are given the first and third Saturday morning of each month, excluding holidays. Just show up at 10am at the box office entrance on 21st Street at Broadway. The tour lasts 2 hours, cameras are allowed, and admission is $5.

If you take pleasure in strolling sailboat-filled wharves or are a die-hard fan of Jack London, you might enjoy a visit to **Jack London Square ★** (© 866/295-9853; www.jacklondonsquare.com). A relatively low-key version of San Francisco's Fisherman's Wharf, Oakland's only patently tourist area shamelessly plays up the fact that Jack London spent most of his youth along the waterfront. The square fronts the harbor, housing a mostly tourist-tacky complex of boutiques and eateries, as well as a more locals-friendly farmers' market year-round on Sundays from 10am to 2pm. Recently, a couple of top-quality restaurants—Cocina Poblana and Miss Pearl's Jam House—have been added to the mix, and a new marketplace showcasing local epicure is under construction, offering new hope for the area. Most shops are open daily from 11am to 6pm (some restaurants stay open later). One of the best reasons to come here is the live jazz at **Yoshi's Jazz Club & Japanese Restaurant ★**, 510 Embarcadero W. (© **510/238-9200**; www.yoshis.com), which attracts top international performers and serves some fine sushi in its adjoining restaurant. In the center of the square is a small, reconstructed Yukon cabin in which Jack London lived while prospecting in the Klondike during the gold rush of 1897.

In the middle of Jack London Square is a more authentic memorial, **Heinold's First and Last Chance Saloon** (© **510/839-6761**; www.heinoldsfirstandlastchance.com), a funky, friendly little bar and historic landmark. This is where London did some of his writing and most of his drinking.

Jack London Square is at Broadway and Embarcadero. Take I-880 to Broadway, turn south, and drive to the end. Or you can ride BART to 12th Street

THE USS *potomac*: FDR'S FLOATING WHITE HOUSE

It took the Potomac Association's hundreds of volunteers more than 12 years—at a cost of $5 million—to restore the 165-foot presidential yacht *Potomac*, President Franklin D. Roosevelt's beloved "Floating White House." Now a proud and permanent memorial berthed at the Port of Oakland's FDR Pier at Jack London Square, the revitalized *Potomac* is open to the public for dockside tours, as well as 2-hour History Cruises along the San Francisco waterfront and around Treasure and Alcatraz islands. Prior to departure, a 15-minute video, shown at the nearby Potomac Visitor Center, provides background on FDR's presidency and his legacy in the Bay Area.

The dockside tours are available year-round on Wednesdays and Fridays from 10am to 2:30pm, and on Sundays from noon to 3pm. Admission is $10 for ages 13 to 59, $8 for seniors age 60 and over, and free for children age 12 and under. The History Cruise runs on Thursdays and Saturdays from early May to mid-November; the departure time is 11am. History Cruise fares are $45 for ages 13 to 59, $40 for seniors 60 and older, $25 for children 6 to 12, and free for kids 5 and under. Due to the popularity of the cruises, advance purchase is strongly recommended.

Hours and cruise schedules are subject to change, so be sure to call the Potomac Visitor Center before arriving. Tickets for the Dockside Tour can be purchased at the Visitor Center upon arrival; tickets for the History Cruise can be purchased in advance via **Ticketweb** (© 866/468-3399; www.ticketweb.com) or by calling the **Potomac Visitor Center** (© 510/627-1215; www.usspotomac. org). The Visitor Center is at 540 Water St., at the corner of Clay and Water streets adjacent to the FDR pier at the north end of Jack London Square.

station and then walk south along Broadway (about half a mile). Or take bus no. 72R or 72M to the foot of Broadway.

Oakland Museum of California ★   Two blocks south of Lake Merritt, the Oakland Museum of California incorporates just about everything you'd want to know about the state and its people, history, culture, geology, art, environment, and ecology. Inside a low, modern building set among sweeping gardens and terraces, it's actually three museums in one: exhibitions of works by California artists from Bierstadt to Diebenkorn; collections of historic artifacts, from Pomo Indian basketry to Country Joe McDonald's guitar; and re-creations of California habitats from the coast to the Sierra Mountains. The museum holds major shows of California artists, as well as exhibitions dedicated to California's rich nature and history. Two new exhibit halls—the Gallery of California Art and the Gallery of California History—opened in spring of 2010, showcasing thousands of artworks and artifacts.

Forty-five-minute guided tours leave from the gallery information desks on request or by appointment. There's a fine cafe, a **Collector's Gallery** (✆ **510/834-2296**) that sells works by California artists, and a museum shop. The cafe is open Wednesday through Saturday from 10:30am to 4pm, Sunday from 1:30 to 4pm.

1000 Oak St. (at 10th St.). ✆ **510/238-2200.** www.museumca.org. Admission $8 adults, $5 students and seniors, free for children 5 and under. 2nd Sun of the month is free (special exhibitions excepted). Wed–Sat 10am–5pm (until 9pm 1st Fri of the month); Sun noon–5pm. Closed Jan 1, July 4, Thanksgiving, and Christmas. BART: Lake Merritt station; follow the signs posted in the station. From I-880 N., take the Oak St. exit; the museum is 5 blocks east. Or take I-580 to I-980 and exit at the Jackson St. ramp.

Where to Stay

Two fine midrange hotel options in Oakland are the **Waterfront Hotel,** 10 Washington St., Jack London Square (www.jdvhotels.com/hotels/waterfront; ✆ **888/842-5333** or 510/836-3800), and the **Oakland Marriott City Center,** 1001 Broadway (www.marriott.com; ✆ **800/228-9290** or 510/451-4000; fax 510/835-3466). Most major motel chains also have locations (and budget prices) around town and near the airport. If you want to stay near the fabulous shopping and dining neighborhood of Oakland's Rockridge and pamper yourself with a great gym, outdoor pools, and lit tennis courts, your best hotel bet (though it's undoubtedly overpriced) is the **Claremont Resort & Spa,** 41 Tunnel Rd., Berkeley (www.claremontresort.com; ✆ **800/551-7266** or 510/843-3000), a grand Victorian hotel (with modern rooms) that borders both Berkeley and Oakland. It ain't downtown, but it's just a quick drive to all the action, and it is one of the area's prettiest options (see p. 165 for more hotel information).

Where to Eat

EXPENSIVE

Bocanova ★★ AMERICAN   Bocanova bills itself as a "Pan-America Grill." Well, I don't know about you, but I've *never* tasted food this good south of the border. The new Jack London Square restaurant, with stellar waterfront views, can be best described as a roller coaster for your taste buds, as you'll twist and turn, dip and ride over a plethora of flavors—many of which you might never have heard of before. When you see ingredients you don't recognize on the menu—and you will, I assure you—don't hesitate to ask the knowledgeable servers for tips.

The menu is divided up by preparation: The Pantry, The Raw Bar, The Garden, The Freidora, The Stove, The Ovens, La Plancha, The Grill. Starters like Dungeness crab deviled eggs in chipotle aioli; walu crudo with mango, papaya, and rocoto pepper; and halibut ceviche are all staples. Main courses run the gamut of pork tenderloin with pineapple and chili sauce, Peruvian marinated chicken and Kobe-style bavette steak with chipotle sauce. The sweet potato and chipotle gratin, as well as the Parmesan cauliflower au gratin are must-order sides to pair with the rest of the perfect cooked-to-order meal. Don't forget to wash it all down with one of the Latin American–style cocktails like a Pisco sour. The roasted banana cake with cream cheese ice cream and cashew brittle at the end of the meal is the cherry on top.

55 Webster St. (on Jack London Sq.). ☎ **510/444-1233.** www.bocanova.com. Reservations recommended. Main courses $12–$36. MC, V. Lunch Mon–Fri 11:30am–3pm and Sat 11am–3pm; dinner Mon–Thurs 5–10pm, Fri–Sat 5–11pm, Sun 5–9:30pm; brunch Sun 11am–3:30pm.

Oliveto Cafe & Restaurant ★★★ ITALIAN   Opened 20 years ago by Bob and Maggie Klein, and now under the helm of executive chef Paul Canales (who has been with the Kleins for 11 years, working his way up through the ranks in the kitchen), Oliveto is one of the top Italian restaurants in the Bay Area (and certainly the best in Oakland). Local workers pile in at lunchtime for wood-fired pizzas, simple salads, and sandwiches served in the lower-level cafe. The upstairs restaurant—with suave neo-Florentine decor and a partially open kitchen—is more elegant and packed nightly with fans of the mind-blowing house-made pastas, sausages, and prosciutto. Oliveto has a wood-burning oven, flame-broiled rotisserie, and a full bar which sports a high-end liquor cabinet. An assortment of pricey grills, braises, and roasts anchors the daily changing menu, but the heavenly pastas, pizzettas, and awesome salads offer the most bang for your buck. Still, the Arista (classic Italian pork with garlic and rosemary and pork *jus*) is insanely good, and no one does fried calamari, onion rings, and lemon slices better than Oliveto. *Tip:* Free parking is available in the lot at the rear of the Market Hall building.

Rockridge Market Hall, 5655 College Ave. (off the northeast end of Broadway at Shafter/Keith St., across from the Rockridge BART station). ☎ **510/547-5356.** www.oliveto.com. Reservations recommended for restaurant. Main courses cafe $2.50–$12 breakfast, $4–$8 lunch, $12–$15 dinner; restaurant $13–$16 lunch, $13–$29 dinner. AE, DC, MC, V. Cafe Mon–Fri 7am–9pm; Sat–Sun 11:30am–10pm. Restaurant Mon–Fri 11:30am–2pm; Mon–Thurs 5:30–9pm; Fri–Sat 5:30–10pm; Sun 5–9pm.

Plum CALIFORNIAN   When Plum opened in 2010, it arrived to much fanfare. By the time it was 6 months old, it had already been named one of the best restaurants in the Bay Area by the *San Francisco Chronicle* and covered by every national travel magazine to pass through town. And not without cause. Its design, while aesthetically pleasing, is quite simple—communal-style wood banquettes, high loftlike ceilings, various picture collages of plums on the wall—as is the menu, at least in length. But simple doesn't have to translate to boring. The brainchild of Daniel Patterson, Plum's menu is broken up into four categories: Snacks, To Start, Vegetables and Grains, and Animal. Within each category, there are only four dishes, many of which are vegetable heavy. While the menu changes regularly, expect to see similar offerings to artichoke terrine, beet boudin noir, and turnip apple soup as smaller starters. The beef cheek and oxtail burger; slow-cooked farm egg with fried farro, chicken, and sprouts; and Manila clams are popular orders for the main event. Desserts, served in mason jars, are not only artfully presented but even more delicious than they look. For example, *panna cotta* was never my favorite—until I discovered Plum, which serves it at the perfect consistency with a glaze of quince compote and thyme on top.

2214 Broadway (at Grand Ave.). ✆ **510/444-7586.** www.plumoakland.com. Reservations recommended. Small plates $4–$13; main courses $12–$18. AE, DC, MC, V. Daily 11am–2pm; Mon–Fri 5pm–1am.

MODERATE

A Côté ★★ FRENCH TAPAS   Jack and Daphne Knowles look to chef Matthew Colgan to serve up superb rustic Mediterranean-inspired small plates at this loud, festive, and warmly lit joint. A "limited reservations" policy means there's usually a long wait during prime dining hours, but once seated, you can join locals in a noshfest featuring the likes of croque-monsieur; *pommes frites* with aioli; wood-oven cooked mussels in Pernod; grilled pork tenderloin with creamy polenta and pancetta; and cheese plates—and wash it down with Belgian ales, perky cocktails, or excellent by-the-glass or -bottle selections from the great wine list. *Note:* The heated and covered outdoor seating area tends to be quieter.

5478 College Ave. (at Taft Ave.). ✆ **510/655-6469.** www.acoterestaurant.com. Limited reservations accepted. Small plates $8–$16. MC, V. Sun–Tues 5:30–10pm; Wed–Thurs 5:30–11pm; Fri–Sat 5:30pm–midnight.

BayWolf ★ CALIFORNIAN   The life span of most Bay Area restaurants is about a year; BayWolf, one of Oakland's most revered restaurants, has, fittingly, been going strong for over 3 decades. The converted brown Victorian is a comfortably familiar sight for most East Bay diners, who have come here for years to let executive chef-owner Michael Wild do the cooking. BayWolf enjoys a reputation for simple yet sagacious preparations using only fresh ingredients. Main courses include Liberty Ranch duck three ways (grilled breast, braised leg, and crépinette) with turnips, curly endive, apples, and Calvados; flavorful seafood stew seasoned with saffron; and tender braised *osso buco* with creamy polenta and gremolata. Informal service means you can leave the tie at home. The front deck has heat lamps and a radiant heat floor, allowing for open-air evening dining year-round—a treat that San Franciscans rarely experience.

3853 Piedmont Ave. (off Broadway btw. 40th St. and MacArthur Blvd.). ✆ **510/655-6004.** www.baywolf.com. Reservations recommended. Main courses $8–$18 lunch, $10–$26 dinner. AE, MC, V. Mon–Fri 11:30am–2pm; Tues–Sun 5:30–9:30pm. Paid parking at Piedmont Ave. and Yosemite St.

SAUSALITO ★★

5 miles N of San Francisco

Just off the northeastern end of the Golden Gate Bridge is the picturesque little town of Sausalito, a slightly bohemian adjunct to San Francisco. With fewer than 8,000 residents, Sausalito feels rather like St. Tropez on the French Riviera (minus the beach). Next to the pricey bayside restaurants, antiques shops, and galleries are hamburger joints, ice-cream shops, and secondhand bookstores.

Sausalito's main strip is Bridgeway, which runs along the water; on a clear day, the views of San Francisco far across the bay are spectacular. After admiring the view, those in the know make a quick detour to Caledonia Street, 1 block inland; not only is it less congested, but it also has a better selection of cafes and shops.

Essentials

The **Golden Gate Ferry Service** fleet, Ferry Building (© **415/923-2000;** www.goldengate.org), operates between the San Francisco Ferry Building, at the foot of Market Street, and downtown Sausalito. Service is frequent, running at reasonable intervals every day of the year except New Year's Day, Thanksgiving, and Christmas. Phone for an exact schedule. The ride takes a half-hour, and one-way fares are $7.45 for adults; $3.70 for youth 6 to 18, seniors 65 plus, and passengers with disabilities (50% off full fare); and children 5 and under ride free (limit two children per full-fare adult). Family rates are available on weekends.

Ferries of the **Blue & Gold Fleet** (© **415/705-8200;** www.blueandgold fleet.com) leave from Pier 41 (Fisherman's Wharf); the one-way cost is $11 for adults, $6.75 for kids 5 to 11. Boats run on a seasonal schedule; phone or log on to their website for departure information.

By car from San Francisco, take U.S. 101 N, and then take the first right after the Golden Gate Bridge (Alexander exit). Alexander becomes Bridgeway in Sausalito.

What to See & Do

Above all else, Sausalito has scenery and sunshine, for once you cross the Golden Gate Bridge, you're out of the San Francisco fog patch and under blue California sky (we hope). Houses cover the town's steep hills, overlooking a forest of masts on the waters below. Most of the tourist action, which is almost singularly limited to window-shopping and eating, takes place at sea level on Bridgeway.

Sausalito is a mecca for shoppers seeking handmade, original, and offbeat clothes and footwear, as well as arts and crafts. Many of the town's shops are in the alleys, malls, and second-floor boutiques reached by steep, narrow staircases on and off Bridgeway. Caledonia Street, which runs parallel to Bridgeway 1 block inland, is home to more shops.

Bay Area Discovery Museum ☺ If you just can't stand the thought of one more trip to PIER 39 or Fisherman's Wharf and are looking for something else to do with your kids (infants to 8 years old), check out this museum. On 7½ acres in the Golden Gate National Recreation Area at Fort Baker, the museum offers spectacular (jaw-dropping

Bay Model Visitor Center.

even!) views of the city and Golden
Gate Bridge (you're literally at the
northern base of the bridge) and is
also the ultimate indoor-outdoor
interactive kids' adventure. Tot
Spot is tops for crawlers and toddlers (up to 42 in.); Lookout Cove
is a 2½-acre outdoor area with a
scaled-down model of the GGB
that kids can add rivets to, a shipwreck to explore, tidal pools, and
lovely site-specific art; Art Studios
splits kids into age groups 5 and
under and 6 and older; and the
Wave Workshop re-creates the habitat under the GGB. The small cafe
serves yummy, organic food far better than typical family-friendly fare.
Remi Hayashi, a California Culinary Academy grad, is at the helm
here, serving up Niman Ranch hot
dogs, fresh sandwiches, panini, and
pizzas, plus a host of snacks. *One
thing to note:* If you're here alone
with two kids of different ages, it
can be difficult to navigate, as they
do keep the little ones separate
from the older ones in the Tot Spot.
If you explain your situation, they'll
give your older one (12 and up) a
"Tot Spot Helper" sticker, and let
them in, but they won't be allowed
to play and will have to stick by you.
But if it's a nice day, you can spend
the whole time in Lookout Cove
with both kids, have lunch outside,
and still feel like you got your money's worth.

E. Fort Baker, 557 McReynolds Rd. (℃ **415/
339-3900.** www.baykidsmuseum.org.
Admission $10 adults, $8 children, free for
children under 1 and members. Discounts
available to AAA members and members
of reciprocal museum organizations (see
website). Tues–Fri 9am–4pm; Sat–Sun
10am–5pm. Closed Mon and all major
holidays. By car: Cross the Golden Gate
Bridge and take the Alexander Ave. exit.
Follow signs to E. Fort Baker and the Bay
Area Discovery Museum.

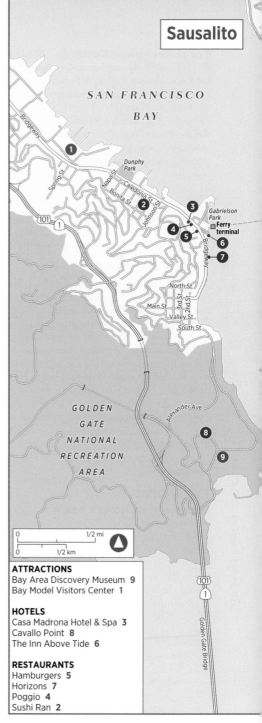

Sausalito

SAN FRANCISCO

BAY

ATTRACTIONS
Bay Area Discovery Museum 9
Bay Model Visitors Center 1

HOTELS
Casa Madrona Hotel & Spa 3
Cavallo Point 8
The Inn Above Tide 6

RESTAURANTS
Hamburgers 5
Horizons 7
Poggio 4
Sushi Ran 2

Bay Model Visitors Center ☺ The U.S. Army Corps of Engineers once used this high-tech, 1½-acre model of San Francisco's bay and delta to resolve problems and observe the impact of changes in water flow. Today the model is strictly for educational purposes and reproduces (in scale) the rise and fall of tides and the flows and currents of water. There's a 10-minute film, self-guided and audio tours ($3 donation requested), and a 1-hour tour (free; book a reservation), but the most interesting time to visit is when the model is in operation, so call ahead to inquire about the schedule.

2100 Bridgeway. ☎ **415/332-3871.** www.spn.usace.army.mil/bmvc. Free admission. Tues–Sat 9am–4pm.

Where to Stay

Sausalito is such a desirable enclave that it offers little in the way of affordable lodging. On the bright side, it's so close to San Francisco that it takes only about 15 minutes to get here, traffic permitting.

VERY EXPENSIVE

The Inn Above Tide ★★ Perched directly over the bay atop well-grounded pilings, this former luxury-apartment complex underwent a $4-million transformation in 2004 into one of Sausalito's—if not the Bay Area's—finest accommodations. The rooms aren't anything particularly special; it's the views that clinch it: Every room affords an unparalleled panorama of the San Francisco Bay, including a postcard-quality vista of the city glimmering in the distance. Should you manage to tear yourself away from your private deck, you'll find that 23 of the rooms sport romantic little fireplaces. Soothing, warm earth tones highlight the decor, which blends in well with the bayscape outside. Be sure to request that your breakfast and newspaper be delivered to your deck, and then cancel your early appointments—on sunny mornings, nobody checks out early.

30 El Portal (next to the Sausalito Ferry Landing), Sausalito, CA 94965. www.innabovetide.com. ☎ **800/893-8433** or 415/332-9535. Fax 415/332-6714. 29 units. $305–$1,025 double. Rates include continental breakfast and evening wine and cheese. AE, DC, MC, V. Valet parking $18. **Amenities:** Concierge. *In room:* A/C, TV/DVD, CD player, fridge, hair dryer, minibar, free Wi-Fi.

EXPENSIVE

Casa Madrona Hotel & Spa ★★ Sooner or later most visitors to Sausalito look up and wonder at the ornate mansion on the hill. It's part of Casa Madrona, a hideaway by the bay built in 1885 by a wealthy lumber baron. The epitome of luxury in its day, the mansion had slipped into decay when John Gallagher purchased it in 1910 and converted it into a hotel. By 1976, it was damaged and facing the threat of demolition when John Mays acquired the property and revitalized the hotel. Successive renovations and extensions added a rambling New England–style building to the hillside below the main house. Now listed on the National Register of Historic Places, the hotel offers whimsically decorated rooms, suites, and cottages, which are accessed by steep, gorgeously landscaped pathways. The 16 free-standing units, the seven cottages, and the rooms in the mansion have individual themes such as Lilac and Lace, Renoir, and the Artist's Loft. Rooms in the newer adjoining building have a chic contemporary decor, four-poster beds, marble bathrooms, and great marina views from some rooms.

801 Bridgeway, Sausalito, CA 94965. www.casamadrona.com. ☎ **415/332-0502.** Fax 415/331-3125. 63 units. $169–$389 double. AE, DC, DISC, MC, V. Valet parking $24. Ferry: Walk across the

street from the landing. From U.S. 101 N, take the 1st right after the Golden Gate Bridge (Alexander exit); Alexander becomes Bridgeway. **Amenities:** Restaurant; babysitting; concierge; room service; spa. *In room:* TV, VCR when available, hair dryer, minibar.

Cavallo Point ★★   This new über-eco lodge, which occupies Golden Gate National Park's century-old former Army quarters in Fort Baker, opened its doors in 2008 after nearly a decade in the making. The 17 red-roofed, colonial-style buildings form a horseshoe overlooking the San Francisco skyline at the bay's edge, with Adirondack chairs throughout the knee-high grassy knolls for lounging.

You have your pick of rooms: Roughly half are repurposed old officers' quarters in the historic lodging, which give off a rustic, nostalgic feel—prices start a bit lower for these than the more dressed-up rooms—while the newer buildings have a more contemporary flair. At least, that's what the hotel employees will tell you—if you ask me, there aren't too many discernible differences between the two models. The majority of rooms have unobstructed views of the Golden Gate Bridge, which practically towers over Cavallo's entities. For dinner, you needn't even head into downtown Sausalito, which is just a mile up the road; the on-site restaurant, Murray Circle, combining French, Mediterranean, and California influences in its fare, is about the finest around.

One of the four properties comprising the high-rolling Passport Resorts, Cavallo Point also offers an interesting mix of classes and activities, spanning a cooking school to sunrise yoga sessions, in its 11,000-square-foot Healing Arts Centers. Check the blackboard in the main lobby daily to see what's on tap for the coming week.

601 Murray Circle, Sausalito, CA 94965. www.cavallopoint.com. ✆ **888/651-2003** or 415/339-4700. Fax 415/339-4792. 142 units. $240–$750 double; $300–$800 suite. AE, DC, DISC, MC, V. Valet parking $20. Pets are allowed for $75 (some rooms). **Amenities:** Restaurant; concierge; room service; spa. *In room:* TV, hair dryer, minifridge, MP3 docking station, free Wi-Fi.

Where to Eat
EXPENSIVE

Horizons ★ SEAFOOD/AMERICAN   Eventually, every San Franciscan ends up at Horizons to meet a friend for Sunday bloody marys. It's not much to look at from the outside, but it gets better as you head past the 1960s-era dark-wood interior toward the waterside terrace. On warm days, it's worth the wait for alfresco seating, if only to watch dreamy sailboats glide past San Francisco's distant skyline. The food here can't touch the view, but it's well portioned and satisfying enough. Seafood dishes are the main items, including steamed clams and mussels, freshly shucked oysters, and a variety of seafood pastas. In fine Marin tradition, Horizons has an "herb tea and espresso" bar.

558 Bridgeway. ✆ **415/331-3232.** www.horizonssausalito.com. Reservations accepted weekdays only. Main courses $9–$27; salads and sandwiches $6–$11. AE, MC, V. Mon–Thurs 11:30am–9pm; Fri 11am–10:30pm; Sat 10:30am–10pm; Sun 10:30am–9pm. Valet parking $4.

Poggio ★★ ITALIAN   Poggio, which is a loose Italian translation for "special hillside place" is attached to the Casa Madrona hotel, and everything *is* special here, from the floor-to-ceiling doors opening to the sidewalk; to its interior with arches and earthen colors, mahogany accents, well-directed light, and centerpiece wood-burning oven manned by a cadre of chefs; to the wine cellar, terra-cotta-tiled floors, comfy mohair banquettes, and white-linen-draped tables. The

A picnic lunch, **SAUSALITO-STYLE**

If the crowds are too much or the prices too steep at Sausalito's bayside restaurants, grab a bite to go for an impromptu picnic in the park fronting the marina. It's one of the best and most romantic ways to spend a warm, sunny day in Sausalito. The best source for a la carte eats is the Mediterranean-style **Venice Gourmet Delicatessen,** at 625 Bridgeway, located right on the waterfront just south of the ferry landing (© **415/332-3544;** www.venicegourmet.com). Since 1964, this venerable deli has offered all the makings for a superb picnic: wines, cheeses, fruits, stuffed vine leaves, salami, lox, prosciutto, salads, quiche, made-to-order sandwiches, and fresh-baked pastries. It's open daily from 9am to 6pm.

daily menu features items like a superb salad of endive, Gorgonzola, walnuts, figs, and honey; pizzas; addictively excellent pastas (try the spinach ricotta gnocchi with beef ragout); and entrees such as whole local petrale sole deboned and served tableside, or grilled lamb chops with roasted fennel and gremolata. Special seasonal meals are offered throughout the year, including the highly anticipated white truffle dinner in November. With a full bar, well-priced wine list, and great desserts, this is Sausalito's premier dining destination—excluding the more casual Sushi Ran (see below).

777 Bridgeway (at Bay St.). © **415/332-7771.** www.poggiotrattoria.com. Italian-style breakfast a la carte $2.50–$5.50; main courses $8–$18 lunch, $13–$25 dinner. AE, DC, DISC, MC, V. Continental breakfast daily 6:30–11am; lunch 11:30am–5:30pm; dinner Sun–Thurs 5:30–10pm, Fri–Sat 5:30–11pm. Free valet parking at Casa Madrona Hotel & Spa.

Sushi Ran ★★ SUSHI/JAPANESE   San Francisco isn't exactly stellar in its Japanese food selection, but right across from the Golden Gate Bridge is a compact but fashionable destination for seriously delicious sushi and cooked dishes. All walks of sushi-loving life cram into the sushi bar, window seats, and more roomy back dining area for Nori Kusakabe's nigiri sushi and standard and specialty rolls. You'll also find a slew of creative dishes by executive chef Scott Whitman, such as generously sized and unbelievably moist and buttery miso-glazed black cod (a must-have), oysters on the half-shell with ponzu sauce and *tobiko* (fish eggs), and a Hawaiian-style ahi *poke* (Hawaiian-style minced raw fish) salad with seaweed dressing that's authentic enough to make you want to hula.

107 Caledonia St. © **415/332-3620.** www.sushiran.com. Reservations recommended. Sushi $5–$14; main courses $8.50–$16. AE, MC, V. Mon–Fri 11:45am–2:30pm; Mon–Sat 5:30–11pm; Sun 5–10:30pm. From U.S. 101 N., take the 1st right after the Golden Gate Bridge (Alexander exit); Alexander becomes Bridgeway in Sausalito. At Johnson St., turn left, and then make a right onto Caledonia.

INEXPENSIVE

Hamburgers BURGERS   Like the name says, the specialty at this tiny, narrow cafe is juicy flame-broiled hamburgers, arguably Marin County's best. Look for the rotating grill in the window off Bridgeway, and then stand in line and salivate with everyone else. Chicken burgers are a slightly healthier option. Order a side of fries, grab a bunch of napkins, and head to the park across the street.

737 Bridgeway. (✆ **415/332-9471.** www.hamburgersausalito.com. Sandwiches $4.75–$6.95. No credit cards. Daily 11am–5pm. From U.S. 101 N., take the 1st right after the Golden Gate Bridge (Alexander exit); Alexander becomes Bridgeway in Sausalito.

ANGEL ISLAND & TIBURON ★★

8 miles N of San Francisco

A California State Park, **Angel Island** is the largest of San Francisco Bay's three islets (the others are Alcatraz and Yerba Buena). The island has been, at various times, a prison, a quarantine station for immigrants, a missile base, and even a favorite site for duels. Nowadays, most visitors are content with picnicking on the large green lawn that fronts the docking area; loaded with the appropriate recreational supplies, they claim a barbecue pit, plop their fannies down on the lush green grass, and while away an afternoon free of phones, televisions, and traffic. Hiking, mountain biking, and guided tram tours are other popular activities here.

Tiburon, situated on a peninsula of the same name, looks like a cross between a fishing village and a Hollywood Western set—imagine San Francisco reduced to toy dimensions. The seacoast town rambles over a series of green hills and ends up at a spindly, multicolored pier on the waterfront, like a Fisherman's Wharf in miniature. In reality, it's an extremely plush patch of yacht-club suburbia, as you'll see by the marine craft and the homes of their owners. Ramshackle, color-splashed old frame houses line Main Street, sheltering chic boutiques, souvenir stores, antiques shops, and art galleries. Other roads are narrow, winding, and hilly, and lead up to dramatically situated homes. The view from here of San Francisco's skyline and the islands in the bay is a good enough reason to pay the precious price to live here.

Essentials

Ferries of the **Blue & Gold Fleet** (✆ **415/705-8200;** www.blueandgoldfleet.com) from Pier 41 (Fisherman's Wharf) travel to both Angel Island and Tiburon. Boats run on a seasonal schedule; phone or look online for departure

Segway tour, Angel Island.

Angel Island and Tiburon.

information. The round-trip fare is $15 to Angel Island, $8.50 for kids 6 to 12, and free for kids 5 and under. The fare includes state park fees. Tickets to Tiburon are $11 each way for adults, $6.75 for kids 5 to 11, and free for kids 4 and under. Tickets are available at Pier 41, online, or over the phone.

By car from San Francisco, take U.S. 101 to the Tiburon/Hwy. 131 exit, and then follow Tiburon Boulevard all the way downtown, a 40-minute drive from San Francisco. Catch the **Tiburon–Angel Island Ferry** (© **415/435-2131;** www.angelislandferry.com) to Angel Island from the dock at Tiburon Boulevard and Main Street. The 15-minute round-trip costs $14 for adults, $12 for children 5 to 11, and $1 for bikes. One child 4 or under is admitted free of charge with each paying adult (after that it's $3.50 each). Boats run on a seasonal schedule but usually depart hourly from 10am to 5pm on weekends, with a more limited schedule on weekdays. Call ahead or look online for departure information. Tickets can be purchased only when boarding and include state park fees. No credit cards.

What to See & Do on Angel Island

Passengers disembark from the ferry at **Ayala Cove,** a small marina abutting a huge lawn area equipped with tables, benches, barbecue pits, and restrooms. During the summer season, there's also a small store, a gift shop, the Cove Cafe (with surprisingly good grub), and an overpriced mountain-bike rental shop at Ayala Cove.

Angel Island's 12 miles of hiking and bike trails include the **Perimeter Road,** a paved path that circles the island. It winds past disused troop barracks, former gun emplacements, and other military buildings; several turnoffs lead to the top of Mount Livermore, 776 feet above the bay. Sometimes referred to as the "Ellis Island of the West," Angel Island was used as a holding area for detained Chinese immigrants awaiting admission papers from 1910 to 1940. You can still see faded Chinese characters on some of the walls of the barracks where the immigrants were held.

The 1-hour audio-enhanced open-air **Tram Tour** of the island costs $14 for adults, $13 for seniors, $9.50 for children 6 to 12, and is free for children 5 and under; schedules vary depending on the time of year. Tours generally run at

10:30am, 12:15pm, and 1:45pm on weekdays, with an additional run at 3pm on weekends and holidays. But check in at the Cove Cafe upon arrival on the island for the current day's tram schedule.

Guided **Segway tours** of the island are available as well March through November. The 2½-hour interpretive tour circles the island's paved Perimeter Trail and costs $65, plus a $3 processing fee. Tours leave at 10:30am and 12:30pm daily. All participants must be 16 years and older and sign a waiver to ride. To make tour reservations, call ✆ **415/435-3392** or visit www.angelisland.com.

During the warmer months, you can camp at a limited number of reserved sites; call **Reserve America** at ✆ **800/444-7275** or visit www.reserveamerica. com to find out about environmental campgrounds at Angel Island. Reservations are taken 2 days to 7 months in advance.

Guided **sea-kayak tours** ★ are also available. The 2½-hour trips combine the thrill of paddling stable two- or three-person kayaks in an informative, natu-ralist-led tour around the island (conditions permitting). All equipment is pro-vided (including a much-needed wet suit), kids are welcome, and no experience is necessary. Rates run $65 to $75 per person. For more information, contact the Sausalito-based **Sea Trek** (✆ **415/488-1000;** www.seatrekkayak.com). **Note:** Tours depart from Sausalito, not Angel Island.

For more information about activities on Angel Island, call ✆ **415/897-0715** or log on to www.angelisland.com.

What to See & Do in Tiburon

The main thing to do in tiny Tiburon is stroll along the waterfront, pop into the stores, and spend an easy $50 on drinks and appetizers before heading back to the city. For a taste of the Wine Country, stop at **Windsor Vineyards,** 72 Main St. (✆ **800/289-9463;** www.windsorvineyards.com)—its Victorian tasting room dates from 1888. Twenty or more choices are available for a free tasting. Wine accessories and gifts—glasses, cork pullers, carry packs (which hold six bottles), gourmet sauces, posters, and maps—are also available. Ask about per-sonalized labels for your selections. The shop is open Sunday through Thursday from 10am to 6pm, Friday and Saturday from 10am to 7pm.

Where to Eat in Tiburon

Guaymas MEXICAN   Guaymas offers authentic Mexican regional cuisine and a spectacular panoramic view of San Francisco and the bay. In good weather, the two heated outdoor patios are almost always packed with diners soaking in the sun and scene. Inside the large dining room, colorful Mexican artwork and tons of colored paper cutouts strewn overhead on string brighten the beige walls. Should you feel chilled, take advantage of the beehive-shaped adobe fireplace to the rear of the dining room.

Guaymas is named after a fishing village on Mexico's Sea of Cortez, and both the town and the restaurant are famous for their *camarones* (giant shrimp). The restaurant also features seviche; handmade tamales; and chargrilled beef, seafood, and fowl. It's not fancy, nor is it gourmet, but it is a good place to come with large parties or family. In addition to a small selection of Californian and Central American wines, the restaurant offers an exceptional variety of tequilas and Mexican beers.

5 Main St. ☎ **415/435-6300.** www.guaymasrestaurant.com. Reservations recommended. Main courses $13–$23. AE, DC, DISC, MC, V. Mon–Thurs 11:30am–9pm; Fri–Sat 11:30am–10pm; Sun 11:30am–9pm. Ferry: Walk about 10 paces from the landing. From U.S. 101, exit at Tiburon/Hwy. 131; follow Tiburon Blvd. 5 miles and turn right onto Main St. Restaurant is behind the bakery.

Sam's Anchor Café ★ 🍴 SEAFOOD   Summer Sundays are liveliest in Tiburon, when weekend boaters tie up at the docks of waterside restaurants like this one, and good-time cyclists pedal from the city to kick back here. Sam's is the kind of place where you and your cronies can take off your shoes and have a fun, relaxing time eating burgers and drinking margaritas outside on the pier. The fare is typical—sandwiches, salads, and such—but the quality and selection are inconsequential: Beer, burgers, and a designated driver are all you really need.

27 Main St. ☎ **415/435-4527.** www.samscafe.com. Main courses $12–$18 brunch, $13–$25 lunch, $21–$27 dinner. AE, DC, DISC, MC, V. Mon–Thurs 11am–9:30pm; Fri 11am–10pm; Sat 9:30am–10pm; Sun 9:30am–9:30pm. Ferry: Walk from the landing. From U.S. 101, exit at Tiburon/Hwy. 131; follow Tiburon Blvd. 4 miles and turn right onto Main St.

MUIR WOODS & MOUNT TAMALPAIS ★★

12 miles N of the Golden Gate Bridge

Muir Woods

While the rest of Marin County's redwood forests were being devoured to feed San Francisco's turn-of-the-20th-century building spree, Muir Woods, in a remote ravine on the flanks of Mount Tamalpais, escaped destruction in favor of easier pickings.

Although the magnificent California redwoods have been successfully transplanted to five continents, their homeland is a 500-mile strip along the mountainous coast of southwestern Oregon and Northern California. The coast redwood, or *Sequoia sempervirens,* is one of the tallest living things known to man; the largest known specimen in the Redwood National Forest towers 368 feet! It has an even larger relative, the *Sequoiadendron giganteum* of the California Sierra Nevada, but the coastal variety is stunning enough. Soaring toward the sky like a wooden cathedral, Muir Woods is unlike any other forest in the world and an experience you won't soon forget.

Granted, Muir Woods is tiny compared to the Redwood National Forest farther north, but you can still get a pretty good idea of what it must have been like when these giants dominated the entire coastal region. What is truly amazing is that they exist a mere 6 miles (as the crow flies) from San Francisco—close enough, unfortunately, that tour buses arrive in droves on the weekends. You can avoid the masses by hiking up the **Ocean View Trail,** turning left on **Lost Trail,** and returning on the **Fern Creek Trail.** The moderately challenging hike shows off the woods' best sides and leaves the lazy-butts behind.

To reach Muir Woods from San Francisco, cross the Golden Gate Bridge heading north on Hwy. 101, take the Stinson Beach/Hwy. 1 exit heading west, and follow the signs (and the traffic). The park is open daily from 8am to sunset, and the admission fee is $5 per person 17 and over. There's also a small gift shop, educational displays, and ranger talks. For more information, call the **National**

Parks Service at Muir Woods (☎ 415/388-2596) or visit www.nps.gov/muwo.

You can book a bus trip with **San Francisco Sightseeing** (☎ 888/428-6937 or 415/434-8687; www.sanfranciscosightseeing.com), which takes you straight to Muir Woods and makes a short stop in Sausalito on the way back. The 3½-hour tour runs twice daily at 9:15am and 2:15pm and costs $44 for adults, $42 for seniors, $20 for children 5 through 11, and free for kids 4 and under. Pickup and return are offered from select San Francisco hotels.

Mount Tamalpais

The birthplace of mountain biking, Mount Tam is the Bay Area's favorite outdoor playground and the most dominant mountain in the region. Most every local has a secret trail and scenic overlook, as well as an opinion on the raging debate between mountain bikers and hikers. The main trails—mostly fire roads—see a lot of foot and bicycle traffic on weekends, particularly on clear, sunny days when you can see a hundred miles in all directions, from the foothills of the Sierra to the western horizon. It's a great place to escape from the city for a leisurely hike and to soak in breathtaking views of the bay.

Hiking Mt. Tamalpais.

To get to Mount Tamalpais **by car,** cross the Golden Gate Bridge heading north on Hwy. 101, and take the Stinson Beach/Hwy. 1 exit. Follow the signs up the shoreline highway for about 2½ miles, turn onto Pantoll Road, and continue for about a mile to Ridgecrest Boulevard. Ridgecrest winds to a parking lot below East Peak. From there, it's a 15-minute hike up to the top. You'll find a visitor center with a small museum, video, diorama, and store, as well as informative "Mount Tam Hosts." Visitor center admission is free; it's open Saturday and Sunday from 11am to 4pm (during standard time), and Saturday and Sunday 10am to 5:30pm (when on daylight saving time). Park hours are 7am to 6pm daily in winter; 7am to 9pm for about 1 month during the height of summer. Two-hour, 2-mile moonlight hikes, among many others, are offered (☎ 415/388-2070; www.mttam.net).

Where to Stay

Pelican Inn ★★ Perhaps one of the most charming facets about the Pelican Inn is that it's beloved by locals but relatively unknown in the travel industry. The 16th-century-style English inn (which, ironically, was built in 1979) has seven rooms accessed by a tight-fitting stairwell in the back "Snug Room" (open only to inn guests and a great place for lounging at the end of a long day). Some quarters have four-poster beds and tapestry rugs; all have that quintessential old-world charm. Even if you're just rushing through, stop by the pub for a bite; it serves up some classic English fare like shepherd's pie and bangers and mash with a contemporary California spin. On sunny days, the lawn is filled with bikers and hikers—a popular coastal trail cuts in right beside the inn—and those just visiting nearby Muir Beach. The inn prides itself on being "organic," meaning service is minimal and not too attentive; also, rooms are free of outside distractions like phones, TVs, and VCRs.

10 Pacific Way (Hwy. 1), Muir Beach, CA 94965. www.pelicaninn.com. ✆ **415/383-6000.** 7 units. $190–$280 double. Rates include a full English breakfast. MC, V. **Amenities:** Restaurant.

Where to Eat

The Tavern at Lark Creek ★★ AMERICAN   It used to be the pricey Lark Creek Inn; now it's a neighborhood pub where you can grab a bite—and a damn tasty one, at that—for under $15. Housed in a stately Victorian, the interior is warm and inviting, with soaring sky-lit ceilings and ample dining space—much cozier, more convivial, and less snobby than its former state. The menu has a nice mixture of comfort fare like shrimp and grits or mac and cheese (tempura battered), as well as heartier gastro-pub eats like short ribs and wood-oven-baked, lamb-sausage moussaka. The restaurant even offers ongoing vegan options, such as quinoa-and-red-potato cakes or pumpkin risotto, and a build-your-own prix-fixe menu for $30.

234 Magnolia Ave., Larkspur, CA 94939. ✆ **415/924-7766.** www.tavernatlarkcreek.com. Reservations recommended. Main courses $8.95–$19. AE, DC, DISC, MC, V. Mon–Thurs 5:30–9:30pm; Fri–Sat 5–10pm; Sun 10am–2pm and 5–9:30pm. Free valet parking.

HALF MOON BAY ★★

28 miles SW of San Francisco

A 45-minute drive from the teeming streets of San Francisco is a heavenly little hamlet called Half Moon Bay, one of the finest—and friendliest—small towns on the California coast in charming San Mateo County. While other communities like Bolinas make tourists feel unwelcome, Half Moon Bay residents are disarmingly amicable, bestowing greetings on everyone who stops for a visit.

Half Moon Bay has only recently begun to capitalize on its beaches, mild climate, and proximity to San Francisco, so it's still not tourist-tacky. Visitors will find it a peaceful slice of classic California: pristine beaches, redwood forests, nature preserves, fishing harbors, horse ranches, organic farms, and a host of superb inns and restaurants—everything for the perfect weekend getaway.

Essentials

GETTING THERE   No public transportation runs from San Francisco to Half Moon Bay, but you can get there two ways by car. To save time, take Hwy. 92 west from I-280 or U.S. 101 out of San Francisco, which will take you over a small mountain range and drop you into Half Moon Bay. The prettier route is Hwy. 1, which starts at the south end of the Golden Gate Bridge and veers southwest to the shoreline a few miles south of Daly City. Both routes to Half Moon Bay are clearly marked, so don't worry about getting lost.

Downtown Half Moon Bay, however, is easy to miss, since it's not on Hwy. 1, but a few hundred yards inland. Head 2 blocks up Hwy. 92 from the Hwy. 1 intersection, and then turn south at the Shell gas station onto Main

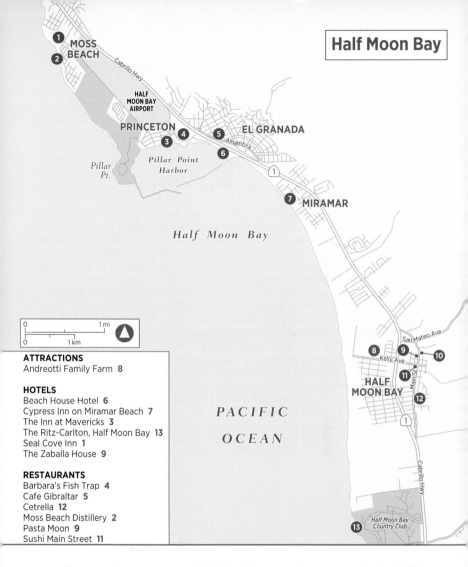

Half Moon Bay

MOSS BEACH ❶ ❷

Cabrillo Hwy.

HALF MOON BAY AIRPORT

PRINCETON ❸ ❹ ❺ EL GRANADA

Alhambra ❻

Pillar Pt.

Pillar Point Harbor

❼ MIRAMAR

Half Moon Bay

San Mateo Ave.

❽ ❾ ❿
Kelly Ave.

⓫
HALF MOON BAY
Main St.
⓬

PACIFIC OCEAN

Cabrillo Hwy.

Half Moon Bay Country Club
⓭

0 ————— 1 mi
0 ————— 1 km

ATTRACTIONS
Andreotti Family Farm **8**

HOTELS
Beach House Hotel **6**
Cypress Inn on Miramar Beach **7**
The Inn at Mavericks **3**
The Ritz-Carlton, Half Moon Bay **13**
Seal Cove Inn **1**
The Zaballa House **9**

RESTAURANTS
Barbara's Fish Trap **4**
Cafe Gibraltar **5**
Cetrella **12**
Moss Beach Distillery **2**
Pasta Moon **9**
Sushi Main Street **11**

Street until you cross a small bridge. For more information, call the **Half Moon Bay Coastside Chamber of Commerce** (*C* **866/558-6823;** www.halfmoonbaychamber.org or www.visithalfmoonbay.org).

Exploring Half Moon Bay & Environs

A wonderful **paved beach trail** winds 5 miles from Half Moon Bay to Pillar Point Harbor, where you can watch trawlers unload their catch. Be sure to keep a lookout for dolphins and whales as you walk, bike, jog, or skate along this path.

Half Moon Bay is also known for its organically grown produce, and the best place to stock up on fruits and vegetables is the **Andreotti Family Farm,** 329 Kelly Ave., off Hwy. 1 (*C* **650/726-9151**), an old-fashioned outfit in business since 1926. Every Friday, Saturday, and Sunday, a member of the Andreotti family slides open the door to their old barn at 10am sharp to reveal a cornucopia of strawberries, artichokes, cucumbers, and more. Head toward the beach and you'll see the barn on your right-hand side. It's open until 6pm year-round.

BEACHES & PRESERVES The 4-mile arc of golden sand that rings Half Moon Bay is actually three state-run beaches—Dunes, Venice, and Francis—all part of **Half Moon Bay State Beach** (© 650/726-8820). All three levy a $5-per-vehicle entrance fee. Surfing is allowed, but swimming isn't a good idea unless you happen to be cold-blooded. You can reserve campgrounds here by contacting © 800/444-PARK (7275) or visiting www.parks.ca.gov.

When the surf is really up, be sure to check out the banzai surfers at **Maverick Beach,** just south of the radar-tracking station past Pillar Point Harbor. To get there, take Westpoint Road to the West Shoreline Access parking lot and follow the trail to the beach. While you're there, keep a lookout for sea lions basking on the offshore rocks. Also adjacent to the parking lot is tiny **Pillar Point Marsh,** a unique fresh- and saltwater marsh that's home and way station to nearly 20% of all North American bird species—from great blue herons to snowy egrets, to red-winged blackbirds.

About 7 miles farther north on Hwy. 1 is the **Fitzgerald Marine Reserve** (© 650/728-3584; www.fitzgeraldreserve.org), one of the most diverse tidal basins on the West Coast, as well as one of the safest, thanks to a wave-buffering rock terrace 150 feet from the beach. Call before coming to find out when it's low tide (all the sea creatures are hidden at high tide) and to get information on the docent-led tour schedules (usually offered on Sat). Rubber-soled shoes are recommended. The reserve is at the west end of California Avenue off Hwy. 1 in Moss Beach. Reservations are required for all groups of 10 or more; call © 650/363-4021. **Note:** Dogs, open fires, and barbecue pits are prohibited, as is collecting of any kind.

Fitzgerald Marine Reserve.

Very few tourists know that the tiny **Flying Fish Grill** at the corner of Main Street and Hwy. 92 in Half Moon Bay makes a mean fish taco, each piled with fresh cod, avocado, coleslaw, lime, and jack cheese, and then wrapped in a soft corn tortilla (don't even bother ordering just one—you'll want at least two). It's open Tuesday through Sunday from 11:30am to 8pm (99 San Mateo Rd.; (✆ 650/712-1125; www.flyingfishgrill. net). Another popular local lunch spot in town is the tiny **Garden Deli Cafe**, a hole-in-the-wall lunch counter at 356 Main St. that cranks out huge, top-notch sandwiches on thick house-made bread. It's open Monday through Friday from 11am to 3pm, and Saturday and Sunday from 11am to 3:30pm ((✆ **650/726-3425**).

Sixteen miles south of Half Moon Bay on Hwy. 1 (at the turnoff to Pescadero) is the **Pescadero Marsh Natural Preserve** (see www.parks. ca.gov), one of the few remaining natural marshes on the central California coast. Part of the Pacific flyway, it's a resting stop for nearly 200 bird species, including great blue herons that nest in the northern row of eucalyptus trees. Passing through the marsh is the mile-long **Sequoia Audubon Trail,** accessible from the parking lot at Pescadero State Beach on Hwy. 1. (The trail starts below the Pescadero Creek Bridge.) Before leaving town, tour and taste at **Harley Farms Goat Dairy,** 205 North St. ((✆ **650/879-0480;** www.harleyfarms.com).

From December to March, the **Año Nuevo State Reserve** is home to one of California's most amazing animal attractions: the breeding grounds of the northern elephant seal. Every winter, people reserve tickets for a chance to witness a fearsome clash between the 2½-ton bulls over mating privileges among the females. Reservations are required for the 2½-hour naturalist-led tours (held rain or shine Dec 15–Mar 31). For tickets, which cost $5 per person (free for children 2 and under), and information, call (✆ **800/444-4445.** Even if it's not mating season, you can still see the elephant seals lolling around the shore almost year-round, particularly between April and August, when they come ashore to molt.

OUTDOOR PURSUITS   For walking, biking, jogging, and skating, a wonderful paved beach trail winds 3 miles from Half Moon Bay to Pillar Point Harbor (keep a lookout for dolphins and whales). Bicycles can be rented from the **Bike Works,** 520 Kelly St. ((✆ 650/726-6708), in downtown Half Moon Bay. The rental rate for a beach cruiser is $10 per hour or $35 per day.

Another popular tourist activity in town is horseback riding along the beach. **Sea Horse Ranch,** on Hwy. 1 a mile north of Half Moon Bay ((✆ **650/726-2362;** www.horserentals.com/seahorse.html), offers kids' pony rides and guided rides along the beach or on well-worn trails for about $60. Hours are daily from 8am to dusk.

If you're the adventurous type, you might want to consider a day of deep-sea fishing with **Huck Finn Sportfishing** ((✆ **650/726-7133;** www. huckfinnsportfishing.com). They'll take you out for a full day for about $60. You don't need experience, tackle, or even a fishing license; they provide everything and will clean, fillet, and bag your catch. December through February, they also offer whale-watching trips. The fishing boats depart from

5

THE SAN FRANCISCO BAY AREA

Half Moon Bay

Phipps Farm

Because you're already in the Half Moon Bay area, you might want to stop at **Phipps Country Store and Farm,** 2700 Pescadero Rd. (© **650/879-1032;** www. phippscountry.com), located a few miles east of Duarte's Tavern on Pescadero Road. Here's you'll find a huge assortment of fresh, organically grown fruits and vegetables, homemade jams, herbs and spices, and an amazing selection of dried beans. A popular spring and early summer pastime (and a hoot for kids) is picking your own pesticide-free olallieberries, strawberries, and boysenberries in the adjacent fields for a mere $3 a pound. It's open daily from 10am to 6pm (until 5pm in the winter), and the entrance fee is $3 for ages 5 to 59.

picturesque Pillar Point Harbor, a full-service harbor that houses more than 350 commercial fishing vessels and recreational boats. Whether you plan to go fishing or not, it's worth a gander to watch the trawlers unload their daily catch.

SHOPPING   Main Street is a browser's paradise. Dozens of small stores and boutiques line the quarter-mile strip, selling everything from feed and tack to custom furniture and camping gear. From north to south, must-see stops include **Half Moon Bay Feed & Fuel,** 331 Main St. (© **650/726-4814**), a great place to pick up a treat for your pet (and take the kids to see chicks and other cute and cuddly animals), and **Cunha's Country Store,** 448 Main St. (© **650/726-4071**), the town's beloved grocery and general store that was rebuilt in 2004 after a fire tore through the place, a mandatory stop for visitors from the Bay Area. Half Moon Bay also has a good bookstore, **Coastside Books,** 432B Main St. (© **650/726-5889;** www.coast sidebooks.com), which carries a fair selection of children's books and postcards. End your shopping spree with a stop at **Cottage Industries,** 621 Main St. (© **650/712-8078;** www.myhandmadehome.com), to marvel at the high-quality handcrafted furniture.

Where to Stay

Beach House Hotel ★★   Although the facade has a rather unimaginative Cape Cod look, the rooms at this three-story hotel are surprisingly well designed and decorated with modern prints, stylish furnishings, soothing yellow-and-blue or red-and-tan tones, and spectacular views of the bay and harbor. Every room comes fully loaded with a wood-burning fireplace, king-size bed and sleeper sofa, large bathroom, and stereo with CD player. Guests also enjoy a private patio or deck access, two color TVs, *four* telephones with dataports and voice mail, and a kitchenette with microwave and fridge. Opt for one of the corner rooms, which offer a more expansive view for the same price.

4100 N. Cabrillo Hwy. (Hwy. 1), Half Moon Bay, CA 94019. www.beach-house.com. © **800/315-9366** or 650/712-0220. Fax 650/712-0693. 54 units. $175–$375 double. Rates include continental breakfast and Fri–Sat evening wine hour. AE, DC, DISC, MC, V. From Half Moon Bay, go 3 miles north on Hwy. 1. **Amenities:** Concierge; exercise room; heated outdoor pool; oceanview whirlpool. *In room:* TV, CD player, fridge, hair dryer, free high-speed Internet, kitchenette, minibar.

Cypress Inn on Miramar Beach ★★   A favorite place to stay in Half Moon Bay, this three-building compound is free of Victorian charm (nary a lace curtain in *this* joint). Instead you have one modern, artistically designed and decorated building, infused with colorful folk art and rustic furniture made of pine and heavy wicker. Each room in the main building has a feather bed, private balcony, gas fireplace, private bathroom, and unobstructed ocean view. Adjacent is the Beach House building, which has rooms equipped with built-in stereo systems and hidden TVs, though they lack the Santa Fe–meets–California effect that I like in the main house (also a few rooms don't have ocean views and one lacks a deck). This is one of the only B&Bs right on the beach.

407 Mirada Rd., Half Moon Bay, CA 94019. www.innsbythesea.com/cypress. ℂ **800/832-3224** or 650/726-6002. Fax 650/712-0380. 18 units. $139–$279 double. Rates include breakfast, tea, wine, and hors d'oeuvres. AE, DISC, MC, V. From the junction of Hwy. 92 and Hwy. 1, go 3 miles north, then turn west and follow Medio to the end; the hotel is at Medio and Mirada. **Amenities:** Room service. *In room:* TV, CD player, hair dryer, VCR.

The Inn at Mavericks ★★ It's been a while since a new, intimate B&B came to town. (The Ritz-Carlton, a megaresort, was the last property to arrive a couple of years back.) And what a lovely one it is, too. Tucked away behind a cluster of restaurants, it's well hidden and backs the coast. You'll wake to the sound of waves crashing against the cliff below. It's especially enchanting on a stormy night when the foghorn is blowing rhythmically (which might bother some people, but I find it soothing). The inn has just six rooms, each named after an area attraction—Montara, Flat Rock, Ross' Cove, Mavericks, the Jetty, Dunes—all of which are 500 square feet, have the most amazingly comfortable beds you can imagine, and boast waterfront views. The bathrooms are spectacular, with their deep soaking tubs and rain showers, and the rooms are decked out with nautical decor and also equipped with a complimentary goodie basket of snacks. One thing to note: It's a traditional-style B&B, meaning there's no staff around after hours. The place is also dog-friendly, so you don't have to leave Fido behind. Two enthusiastic thumbs up.

346 Princeton Ave., Half Moon Bay, CA 94019. www.innatmavericks.com. ℂ **650/728-1572.** Fax 650/728-8721. 6 units. $199–$279 double. AE, DISC, MC, V. Free parking. *In room:* TV, DVD player, fridge, hair dryer, microwave, MP3 docking station, free Wi-Fi.

The Ritz-Carlton, Half Moon Bay ★★★ Set atop an ocean bluff and looking every bit like the grand seaside lodges of the 19th century is the spectacular Ritz-Carlton, Half Moon Bay. Completed in 2001, this 261-room spa and golf retreat is a popular weekend retreat for the Bay Area well-to-do. Ladies-who-lunch come for treatments at the resort's 16,000-square-foot Spa and Fitness Center, while their gents have the golf concierge squeeze them in for 36 holes on two of the finest coastal courses in the state. In typical Ritz-Carlton fashion, luxuries abound throughout the contemporary guest rooms: Egyptian cotton sheets, goose-down comforters, marble bathrooms, and personal wine cellars. Two-thirds of the rooms have ocean views, and, depending on the weather, you can opt for a fireplace or a terrace. After a day of recreating and treatments, it's de rigueur to go for a walk along the coastal path at sunset, followed by dinner at the resort's **Navio** restaurant, which serves expensive coastal cuisine prepared in a dazzling 1,000-square-foot display kitchen. Skip dessert, because the highlight of the evening is roasting s'mores at the resort's outdoor fire pit underneath a heavy wool blanket and starry skies. ***Note:*** It's often foggy and chilly throughout the year in this region, so pack warm clothing and don't be surprised if you see very little sunshine.

One Miramontes Point Rd., Half Moon Bay, CA 94019. www.ritzcarlton.com. ✆ **800/241-3333** or 650/712-7000. Fax 650/712-7070. 261 units. $399–$599 double; $799–$1,699 suite. Weekend discounts and packages available. AE, DC, DISC, MC, V. Valet parking $45. **Amenities:** 3 restaurants; airport transfer; babysitting; concierge; fitness center; outdoor Jacuzzi; room service; full-service spa. *In room:* A/C, TV w/pay movies, DVD player, hair dryer, minibar, Wi-Fi ($16 per day).

Seal Cove Inn ★★   This superior, sophisticated B&B blends California, New England, and European influences in a spectacular setting. All rooms have king beds, fireplaces, antiques, private bathroom with towel warmer, watercolors, and either a private balcony or a terrace with views of a colorful ½-acre wildflower garden, cypress trees, and the distant ocean. You'll find coffee and a newspaper outside your door in the morning; a full breakfast waiting for you; wine, appetizers, brandy, and sherry by the living room fireplace in the evening; and chocolates beside your turned-down bed at night. The ocean is just a short walk away.

221 Cypress Ave., Half Moon Bay, CA 94038. www.sealcoveinn.com. ✆ **800/995-9987** or 650/728-4114. Fax 650/728-4116. 10 units. $215–$350 double. Rates include breakfast, wine and snacks, and sherry. AE, DISC, MC, V. The inn is 6 miles north of Half Moon Bay off Hwy. 1; follow signs to Moss Beach Distillery. **Amenities:** Concierge. *In room:* TV/VCR, fridge, hair dryer, minibar, free Wi-Fi.

The Zaballa House ★   The oldest building in Half Moon Bay, this pretty pale-blue Victorian is refreshingly unpretentious—as soon as you walk through the door, you get that *mi-casa-es-su-casa* kinda vibe from the staff. The guest rooms in the main house are pleasantly decorated with understated wallpaper and country furniture; some have fireplaces, vaulted ceilings, or Jacuzzi tubs, and all have private bathrooms. Several years ago, an annex was built behind the house so the owners could add three modern suites, each equipped with a kitchenette, double Jacuzzi, fireplace, TV/VCR, fridge, and private deck (my favorite is the Casablanca room, which comes with an eponymous video). You'll like the location as well—right on Main Street next to all the shops and restaurants.

324 Main St. (at the north end of town), Half Moon Bay, CA 94019. www.zaballahouse.net. ✆ **650/726-9123.** Fax 650/726-3921. 12 units. $99–$229 double. Rates include breakfast and afternoon tea/wine/hors d'oeuvres. AE, DISC, MC, V. *In room:* TV/VCR and kitchenette in minisuites.

Where to Eat

Barbara's Fish Trap ★ SEAFOOD Fishnets on the ceilings and a wooden fisherman guarding the entrance give you an indication of what's on the menu here. Situated on stilts above the beach, with indoor and outdoor dining and panoramic bay views, this lively, popular seafood restaurant offers a wide selection of deep-fried seafood, as well as healthier broiled items such as their tangy Cajun-spiced snapper. I recommend starting with the fried calamari and a cold beer, and then moving on to the excellent rock cod fish and chips with a side of house-made clam chowder. Expect to wait in line on summer weekends, and bring cash because they don't take credit cards. **_Tip:_** A free small parking lot is across from the restaurant.

281 Capistrano Rd. (4 miles north of Half Moon Bay on Hwy. 1, west on Capistrano Rd. to Pillar Point Harbor), Princeton. © **650/728-7049.** Main courses $11–$30. No credit cards. Sun–Thurs 11am–9pm; Fri–Sat 11am–10pm.

Café Gibraltar ★★ MEDITERRANEAN The area's most creative and highly ranked restaurant is not downtown, but tucked on a nondescript side street about 5 minutes north of Half Moon Bay. This casual, romantic, and quirky spot has the kind of individual identity and personality rarely found in today's oft-too-polished restaurants. Seated at one of the well-spaced regular or low tables with seat cushions along the back wall, you'll discover that chef Jose Ugalde's menu ranges across the Mediterranean, and that each dish is made with the freshest of local coastal ingredients. The menu changes regularly. If goat-cheese-stuffed zucchini blossoms with portobello mushroom sauce are available, don't pass them up. Two other recommendations are the pan-seared sashimi-grade ahi tuna with chermoula, tomato-onion confit, capers, cured olives, and house-made preserved lemons, served with a napa cabbage relish atop a savory black beluga lentil mélange; and the wood-roasted lamb sirloin marinated with basil pesto, natural _jus,_ red wine–braised tarbais beans, and roasted wild mushrooms. A smart, affordable wine list and superb desserts round out what's sure to be a great meal.

📎 Half Moon Bay's Best Brunch

One of Half Moon Bay's biggest attractions is the stunning **Ritz-Carlton Half Moon Bay.** On a bluff above the Pacific, the six-story structure has the most luxurious guest rooms in the region, a fantastic spa, tennis courts, and all the usual five-star amenities—not to mention preferred access to the Half Moon Bay Golf Links. Most important for San Francisco day-trippers and those from farther afield, it's also the place to indulge in an outrageously opulent all-you-can-eat brunch. Held every Sunday in the stately open-kitchen restaurant Navio, which also has ocean views,

brunch includes an endless array of gourmet edibles—including sushi, dim sum, soufflés, a raw bar, classic breakfast dishes (including great blintzes), tarts, salads, cheeses, a meat-carving station, vegetables, pastas, and desserts. The feast, which has seatings at 11am and 1:30pm, costs $88 per adult (half-price for kids 5–12 and free for those 4 and under). Reservations are a must. The resort is at 1 Miramontes Point Rd., Half Moon Bay (© **650/712-7000**). Be sure to make reservations; brunch almost always sells out.

425 Ave. Alhambra (at Palma St.), El Granada. ✆ **650/560-9039.** www.cafegibraltar.com. Reservations recommended. Main courses $16–$24. AE, MC. V. Sun and Tues–Thurs 5–9pm; Fri–Sat 5–9:45pm.

Cetrella ★★ MEDITERRANEAN   Cetrella is as close as you'll come to big-city dining in Half Moon Bay. Amid warm, chic dining rooms—with a center-piece fireplace—locals and visitors mingle over dishes ranging from purée of spring onion soup, steamed Washington manila clams, white-wine-and-herb-braised Australian lamb shank, and mesquite-grilled Scottish salmon. Bonuses include an excellent cheese program and live evening jazz Friday and Saturday. If you're in the neighborhood, check it out, but make reservations first; everyone from *Gourmet* to the *San Francisco Chronicle* has trumpeted this small-town gem, so it's no secret.

845 Main St. (at Monte Vista Lane). ✆ **650/726-4090.** www.cetrella.com. Reservations recommended. Most main courses bistro dinner $19–$36, cafe dinner $10–$15; brunch $10–$16. Sun brunch 10:30am–2:30pm; Sun and Tues–Thurs 5:30–9:30pm; Fri–Sat 5:30–10pm; closed in winter months.

Moss Beach Distillery ★ 📷 CALIFORNIAN/CONTINENTAL   Ever since its bootlegging days during Prohibition almost a century ago, this old stucco dis-tillery on a cliff above Moss Beach has been a wildly popular hangout for both locals and city folk. In the 1920s, silent-film stars and San Francisco politicos frequented the distillery for drinks and the bordello next door for . . . other pas-times. Time and weather have aged it considerably, but a recent renovation spiffed things up. Although adeptly prepared, the food—blackened scallops, coastal crab cakes, panko-crusted halibut, seafood stew, seared filet mignon—has never been the main draw; rather, it's the phenomenal view of the rugged coast from the dining room windows and spacious patio. Your best bet is to come before sunset, order off the appetizer menu (the oysters are always fresh), and snuggle with your partner on the romantic patio overlooking the Pacific (they even provide blankets). Their Sunday brunch is hugely popular as well—$33 and all the bubbly you desire.

140 Beach Way (at Ocean St.), Moss Beach (6 miles north of Half Moon Bay off Hwy. 1). ✆ **650/728-5595.** www.mossbeachdistillery.com. Reservations recommended. Main courses $14–$28. DC, DISC, MC, V. Mon–Thurs noon–8pm; Fri–Sat noon–9pm; Sun 11am–8pm (Sun brunch 11am–2pm).

Pasta Moon ★★ ITALIAN   I discovered Pasta Moon nearly 20 years ago and always look forward to coming back and being greeted by the friendly, vivacious, and oh-so-Italian staff. Everything emanating from the open kitchen is made from scratch, using only fresh ingredients and always cooked perfectly. In fact, the last time I came here, I had a tortellini dish—each tender piece carefully hand cut and bursting with flavor—that was the best I have ever had on any con-tinent (I still think about that dish with fond memories). Some of my other favor-ites are the house-made linguine with Manila clams, pancetta, leeks, garlic, red-pepper flakes, and clam broth; and the semolina gnocchi with sweet peppers, *pioppini* mushrooms, and pesto. The exclusively Italian wine list features nearly 50 wines by the glass. For dessert, try the wonderful tiramisu, with its layers of espresso-soaked ladyfingers and creamy mascarpone.

315 Main St., Half Moon Bay. ✆ **650/726-5125.** www.pastamoon.com. Reservations recommended. Main courses $10–$21 lunch, $15–$34 dinner. AE, DC, DISC, MC, V. Mon–Fri 11:30am–2:30pm; Sat–Sun noon–3pm; Sun–Thurs 5:30–9:30pm; Fri–Sat 5:30–10pm.

Sushi Main Street ★ JAPANESE   Chef/owner Hirohito Shigeta started out his business more than a decade ago in a tiny space on Main Street and kept the old name when he moved into larger digs down the street. His wife, Karolynne, an interior designer with impeccable taste, decorated the new space with her vast collection of museum-quality Balinese artifacts (with beautiful results). But even if it looked like the inside of a trailer home, it would still be worth a visit for the tasty sushi, tempura, and soba dishes. Adventurous sushi warriors will want to try the New Zealand roll (mussels, radish, sprouts, avocado, and teriyaki), the *unagi* papaya, and the marinated salmon roll with cream cheese and spinach. For a traditional shoeless Japanese meal, request the knee-high table perched in the corner.

696 Mill St., Half Moon Bay. ✆ **650/726-6336.** www.sushimainstreethmb.com. Main courses $5–$10. MC, V. Mon–Sat 11:30am–2:30pm; daily 5–9pm.

SAN JOSE

45 miles SE of San Francisco

The San Jose of yesteryear—a sleepy town of orchards, crops, and cattle—is long gone. Founded in 1717, and hidden in the shadows of San Francisco, San Jose is now Northern California's largest city. Today the prosperity of Silicon Valley has transformed what was once an agricultural backwater into a thriving network of restaurants, shops, a state-of-the-art light-rail system, a sports arena (go Sharks!), and a reputable art scene. And despite all the growth, a number of surveys declare it one of the safest and sunniest cities in the nation.

Essentials

GETTING THERE   BART (✆ **510/465-2278;** www.bart.gov) travels from San Francisco to Fremont in 1¼ hours; you can take a bus from there. **Caltrain** (✆ **800/660-4287;** www.caltrain.com) operates frequently from San Francisco to San Jose's Diridon Station and takes about 1 hour and 25 minutes.

VISITOR INFORMATION   Free visitors guides, published by the **San Jose Convention & Visitors Bureau,** 408 Almaden Blvd. (✆ **800/SAN-JOSE** [726-5673] or 408/295-9600), are available at kiosks within the **San Jose Convention Center,** 150 W. San Carlos St., San Jose, CA 95113 (✆ **408/ 792-4111**). You can request information live at the visitors bureau, or log on to www.sanjose.org to receive a free visitors guide by mail.

GETTING AROUND   The **Valley Transportation Authority (VTA) light rail** (✆ **408/321-2300;** www.vta.org) is the best transportation option in town. A ticket is good for 2 hours, and stops include the Great America theme park, the convention center, and downtown museums. Fares are $2 for adults, $1.75 for children ages 5 to 17, 75¢ for seniors and travelers with disabilities, and children age 4 and under ride free. Day passes are $6 for adults, $5 for children, $2.50 for seniors.

Attractions

Children's Discovery Museum ☺   Children will find shows, workshops, and more than 150 interactive exhibitions exploring the sciences, humanities, arts, and technology. **ZOOMZone** consists of science and art activities designed by kids for kids; **Bubbalogna,** an exhibit that explores the chemistry and physics of bubbles, draws rave reviews. Smaller kids will love dressing up in costumes and playing on the firetruck.

180 Woz Way. ⓒ **408/298-5437.** www.cdm.org. Admission $10 children and adults, $9 seniors 60 and over, free for children under 1. Tues–Sat 10am–5pm; Sun noon–5pm.

Rosicrucian Egyptian Museum & Planetarium   The Rosicrucian is associated with an ancient Egyptian educational organization that strongly advocated belief in the afterlife and reincarnation. Permanent exhibitions display human and animal mummies, funerary boats, canopic jars, and a replica of a noble Egyptian's tomb. Less morbid artifacts include Egyptian jewelry, pottery, and bronze tool collections. The Planetarium features shows at 2pm daily. A second show on Saturday and Sunday begins at 3:30pm.

1660 Park Ave. ⓒ **408/947-3636.** www.egyptianmuseum.org. Museum admission $9 adults, $7 seniors and students, $5 children 5–10, free for children 4 and under. Save $1 with AAA, KQED, or military ID cards. Planetarium free admission. Mon–Wed and Fri 9am–5pm; Thurs 9am–8pm; Sat–Sun 11am–6pm. Closed major holidays.

San Jose Historical Museum   Twenty-six restored original and replica buildings, on 25 acres in Kelley Park, re-create life in 1880s San Jose. The usual cast of 19th-century characters is here—the doctor, the printer, the postmaster—with an occasional local surprise, such as the 1888 Chinese temple and the original Stevens fruit barn. If you want to peek inside, come on the weekend or during summer months, when docents offer interior tours daily.

1650 Senter Rd. ⓒ **408/287-2290.** www.historysanjose.org. Free admission. Tues–Sun noon–5pm.

San Jose Museum of Art ★   This contemporary art museum features revolving exhibitions of post-1980 works plus older 20th-century art from the permanent collection. The Historic Wing includes a cafe, a bookstore, and an education center. From Tuesday to Sunday, tours begin at 12:30 and 2:30pm; for group tours, call for reservations at least 1 week in advance. Docents will also sign tours for deaf and hearing-impaired visitors with 72 hours' notice.

110 S. Market St. ⓒ **408/271-6840.** www.sjmusart.org. Museum admission $8 adults, $5 seniors and students, free for children 5 and under. Tues–Sun 11am–5pm. Closed major holidays.

The Tech Museum ★ ☺   In a 132,000-square-foot facility, the Tech Museum allows visitors to experience a world of phenomena: Create your own virtual roller coaster ride, survive an earthquake on a giant shake table, operate an underwater ROV (remotely operated vehicle), or ride the same virtual bobsled used to train Olympic competitors. The museum also features an IMAX dome theater.

201 S. Market St., downtown at the corner of Park and Market sts. ⓒ **408/294-8324.** www.thetech.org. Admission (IMAX and museum) $10 all ages. Daily 10am–5pm.

Winchester Mystery House   The legacy of Sarah L. Winchester, widow of the son of the famous rifle magnate, the massive Winchester house is a monument to one woman's paranoia. After the deaths of her husband and baby daughter, Mrs. Winchester consulted with a seer, who proclaimed that the family had been targeted by the evil spirits of those killed with Winchester repeaters. Convinced the spirits would be appeased only by perpetual construction on the Winchester mansion, the widow used much of her $20-million inheritance to finance the construction, which started in 1884 and went on 24 hours a day, 7 days a

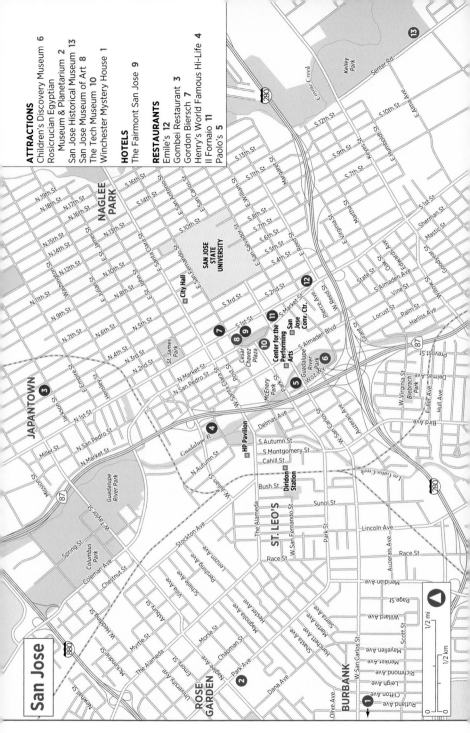

San Jose

week, 365 days a year, for 38 years. With 160 rooms, the home sprawls across a half-dozen acres and is full of disturbing features: a staircase leading nowhere, a Tiffany window with a spider-web design, and doors that open onto blank walls. There are 13 bathrooms, 13 windows and doors in the old sewing room, 13 palms lining the main driveway, 13 hooks in the séance room, and chandeliers with 13 lights. Such schemes were designed to confound the spirits that allegedly plagued the heiress.

525 S. Winchester Blvd. (near the intersection of I-280 and I-880). © **408/247-2101.** www.winchestermysteryhouse.com. Admission $28 adults, $25 seniors 65 and over, $22 children 6–12, free for children 5 and under. Tours leave every 15–30 min. Summer daily 9am–7pm; winter daily 9am–5pm.

The "Door to Nowhere" at the Winchester Mystery House.

Theme Park Thrills

It's a 10-minute drive from downtown San Jose to **California's Great America,** 100 acres of family entertainment on the Great America Parkway (off U.S. 101), in Santa Clara (© **408/988-1776;** www.cagreatamerica.com). A pretty cool place to lose your lunch, the park includes such favorites as the Flight Deck suspended jet coaster; the 3-acre Nickelodeon Central and KidZville for children; and their latest addition, FireFall, where riders are spun into 360-degree vertical arcs through fire and water effects. Check for concerts and special events too. Boomerang Bay Beach Club, a 3-acre water park with 11 slides and a "lazy river," is included in the general admission; it's $55 for adults and children ages 3 to 61, $25 for seniors age 62 and over and anyone under 48 inches tall. Kids 2 and under are free. Check the website for discounted tickets. It's open daily from Memorial Day to October but may vary according to weather, so call for details. From San Francisco, take U.S. 101 south for about 45 miles to the Great America Parkway exit.

An Excellent Shopping & Dining Excursion

Santana Row (© **408/551-4611;** www.santanarow.com), at Winchester and Stevens Creek boulevards, is *the* hotbed for dining, shopping, and strolling in San Jose. Stores range from Urban Outfitters to Gucci. Two of the many good dining bets include supercasual, fun New England seafood house **Yankee Pier** and Asian-inspired, flavorful, and creative **Strait's Café.**

Where to Stay

The Fairmont San Jose In a landmark building near the San Jose McEnery Convention Center and the Center of Performing Arts, the Fairmont is a popular spot for afternoon tea or cocktails, and the lobby attracts shoppers who are just passing through. For guests, the hotel places an emphasis on comfort: The guest rooms, located in two 13-story towers, feature high-tech amenities such as fax and high-speed modem lines. Other luxuries include a fourth-floor rooftop pool surrounded by tropical foliage. The most high-end restaurant of the four on the premises is the **Grill on the Alley.** The other options are an Asian fusion restaurant with a sushi lounge, an upscale seafood restaurant, and a coffee shop.

170 S. Market St., San Jose, CA 95113. www.fairmont.com/sanjose. © **866/540-4493** or 408/998-1900. Fax 408/287-1648. 805 units. $259–$400 double; $350–$1,800 suite. AE, DC, DISC, MC, V. **Amenities:** 4 restaurants; sushi bar; bar; concierge; health club; heated outdoor pool; room service; sauna; spa. *In room:* A/C, TV w/pay movies, hair dryer, high-speed Internet, minibar.

Where to Eat

EXPENSIVE

Emile's ★★ CONTEMPORARY EUROPEAN Since 1973, this fancy restaurant still ranks among the Bay Area's best. Mirrors, recessed lighting, and large, bold floral arrangements create an elegant atmosphere. To start, try *torchon* of foie gras with a dried fruit compote and brioche toast, or sautéed prawns Bordelaise with butter, white wine, garlic, and lemon juice over a grilled polenta crouton. Follow with beef filet in a Madagascar pepper sauce, on a bed of spinach mashed potato, served with a vegetable medley. For dessert, go with the Grand Marnier soufflé. Emile's offers "small plate" versions of entrees; a "taste" costs about two-thirds of the entree price and allows diners to snack their way through the menu.

545 S. Second St. © **408/289-1960.** www.emilesrestaurant.com. Reservations recommended. Main courses $26–$45. AE, DC, DISC, MC, V. Tues–Thurs 5:30–10pm; Fri–Sat 5:30–11pm.

Paolo's ★ NORTHERN ITALIAN Paolo's attracts a business crowd at lunchtime and a cultured crowd in the evening. The cuisine is refined northern Italian, with innovative flourishes. Appetizers include tuna carpaccio or bread-crumb-crusted prawns with white wine, garlic, lemon, parsley, and butter. The main dishes range from *pappardelle* with fresh saffron egg pasta ribbons and traditional Bolognese-style meat sauce to braised chicken with artichokes, mixed herbs, and soft polenta; and grilled dry-aged angus rib-eye chop, roasted root vegetable mash, and braised winter greens. Desserts also stretch typical Italian favorites to limits: Tuscan doughnuts, filled with chocolate, in a pomegranate glaze, for example. The extensive wine list features more than 600 selections.

San Jose.

333 W. San Carlos St. ✆ **408/294-2558.** www.paolosrestaurant.com. Reservations recommended. Main courses $15–$23 lunch, $18–$35 dinner. AE, DC, DISC, MC, V. Mon–Fri 11:30am–2:30pm; Mon–Sat 5:30–10pm.

MODERATE

Gordon Biersch ECLECTIC   This brewpub restaurant offers a little of everything. The menu features some lighter fare, ranging from a Thai satay platter and goat-cheese salads to molasses-glazed baby back ribs. Big burgers and filling pub grub are equally popular. A large outdoor patio and live music attract a youngish crowd. Four tasty home brews are always on tap.

33 E. San Fernando St. (btw. First and Second sts.). ✆ **408/294-6785.** www.gordonbiersch. com. Reservations recommended. Main courses $7.50–$14. AE, DC, DISC, MC, V. Sun–Wed 11:30am–11pm; Thurs 11:30am–midnight; Fri–Sat 11:30am–2am.

Il Fornaio ★ NORTHERN ITALIAN   Il Fornaio is always a sure thing when it comes to enjoying a satisfying meal. The specialties of the house include the mesquite-grilled fresh fish and the veal chop with sage and rosemary, as well as grilled pounded chicken breast with a purée of roasted garlic and rosemary. There are about 10 pizzas to choose from; my favorite comes topped with Maui onions, Gruyère and mozzarella cheese, smoked ham, and sage. For hearty appetites, there's an excellent and tender 22-ounce steak. Salads and appetizers, including a tasty grilled polenta with wild mushrooms and provolone, round out the menu.

302 S. Market St. (on the bottom floor of the Hyatt). ✆ **408/271-3366.** www.ilfornaio.com. Reservations recommended. Main courses $8–$11. AE, DC, MC, V. Mon–Thurs 7am–10pm; Fri 7am–11pm; Sat 8am–11pm; Sun 8am–10pm.

INEXPENSIVE

Gombei Restaurant JAPANESE   On busy nights here, the ambience is barely controlled chaos, with customers diving into big bowls of *donburi* and udon (Gombei's specialty, thick wheat noodles in a chicken broth filled with dried seaweed, green onion, and tender chunks of chicken) while the sprightly staff deftly negotiates around the crowded dining room. Be sure to check the specials board, which often lists some very esoteric Japanese entrees.

193 E. Jackson St. (btw. Fourth and Fifth sts.). ✆ **408/279-4311.** Main courses $6–$10. No credit cards. Mon–Sat 11:30am–2:30pm and 5–9:30pm.

Henry's World Famous Hi-Life BARBECUE   Harking back to the good ol' days—before "good" and "bad" cholesterol were invented—is Henry's World Famous Hi-Life. Formica tables lined with paper place mats and little fishnet-covered candles give you a pretty good indication that you probably won't need that dinner jacket and tie. A bib is more appropriate for tackling the huge servings of barbecued ribs, chicken, and steaks, all cooked in an oak barbecue pit that's big enough to roast a rhino, and then slathered in a sweet, tangy barbecue sauce.

301 W. St. John St. (at Almaden Blvd., near Calif. 87). ✆ **408/295-5414.** www.henryshilife.com. Main courses $10–$25. AE, MC, V. Tues–Fri 11:30am–2pm; Mon–Thurs 5–9pm; Fri–Sat 4–9:30pm; Sun 4–9pm.

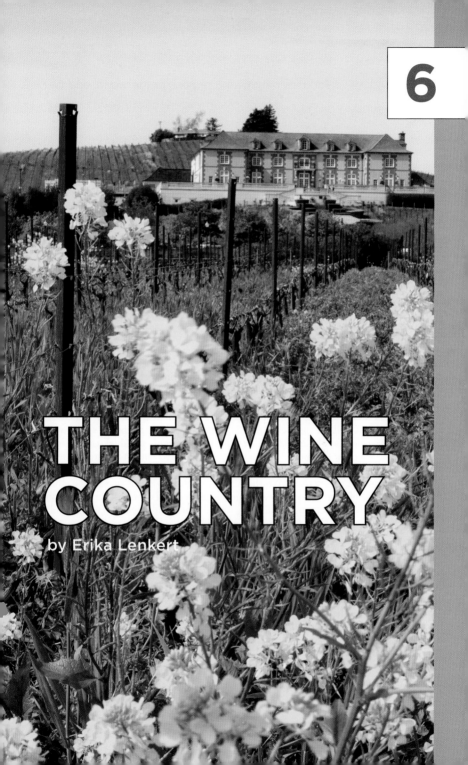

THE WINE COUNTRY

by Erika Lenkert

California's Napa and Sonoma are two of the most famous wine-growing regions in the world, and two of my favorite places to visit in the state. With wineries, hotels, and restaurants nestled among the vines, the valleys that provide a way of life for thousands of vintners, farmers, and cooks also provide the ultimate retreats for wine and food lovers and romantics. Even if you're a teetotaler, the fresh air, rolling countryside, and world-class restaurants and spas are reason enough to visit. If you can, plan to spend at least a couple of days just to get to know one of the three areas included here. No matter how long you stay, you'll probably never get enough of the good life, but be warned: A visit here does require stamina; eating and drinking to excess can seriously wear you down.

While Napa Valley, Sonoma Valley, and northern Sonoma are close to each other (about 30 min. apart by car), each is attraction packed enough that your best bet is to focus on just one of the areas, especially if your time is limited. I recommend that you read about each below and then decide which one is right for you—unless, of course, you're lucky enough to have time to explore all three.

When considering the destinations, keep in mind that Napa, while relatively rural, is still the most commercial, with fancy spas, a superior selection of restaurants and hotels, and big-business wineries offering polished winery tours. Sonoma Valley is far more laid-back and small-town, with its charming town square and a few dozen wineries—which are often family owned—dispersed amid winding country roads. Northern Sonoma, the most vast area to visit, combines a little of each valley, with extremely well-regarded wineries, genuine country charm, the outstanding Healdsburg town square (with great shopping), and a handful of destination-worthy hotels and restaurants.

NAPA VALLEY

Napa Valley is just 35 miles long, which means you can venture from one end to the other in around half an hour (traffic permitting). Most of the large wineries—as well as most of the hotels, shops, and restaurants—line a single road, Hwy. 29, which starts at the mouth of the Napa River, near the north end of San Francisco Bay, and continues north to Calistoga and the top of the growing region.

Essentials

GETTING THERE   From San Francisco, cross the Golden Gate Bridge and head north on U.S. 101. Turn east on Hwy. 37 (toward Vallejo), and then north

PREVIOUS PAGE: **Carneros District.**

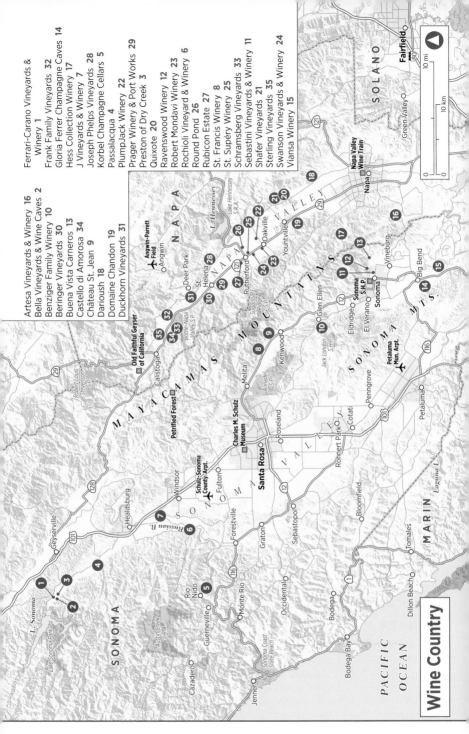

Wine Country

Ferrari-Carano Vineyards &
  Winery **1**
Frank Family Vineyards **32**
Gloria Ferrer Champagne Caves **14**
Hess Collection Winery **17**
J Vineyards & Winery **7**
Joseph Phelps Vineyards **28**
Korbel Champagne Cellars **5**
Passalacqua **4**
PlumpJack Winery **22**
Prager Winery & Port Works **29**
Preston of Dry Creek **3**
Quixote **20**
Ravenswood Winery **12**
Robert Mondavi Winery **23**
Rochioli Vineyard & Winery **6**
Round Pond **26**
Rubicon Estate **27**
St. Francis Winery **8**
St. Supéry Winery **25**
Schramsberg Vineyards **33**
Sebastini Vineyards & Winery **11**
Shafer Vineyards **21**
Sterling Vineyards **35**
Swanson Vineyards & Winery **24**
Viansa Winery **15**

Artesa Vineyards & Winery **16**
Bella Vineyards & Wine Caves **2**
Benziger Family Winery **10**
Beringer Vineyards **30**
Buena Vista Carneros **13**
Castello di Amorosa **34**
Château St. Jean **9**
Darioush **18**
Domaine Chandon **19**
Duckhorn Vineyards **31**

on Hwy. 29, the main road through Napa Valley. Or take the scenic route: Hwy. 12/121, following the signs toward Napa, and turn left onto Hwy. 29.

VISITOR INFORMATION   Once in Napa Valley, stop first at the **Napa Valley Conference & Visitors Bureau,** 1310 Town Center Mall, Napa, CA 94559 (🕾 **707/226-7459,** ext. 106; www.napavalley.com), and pick up the *Napa Valley Guide.* You can call or write in for the *Napa Valley Guidebook,* which includes information on lodging, restaurants, wineries, and other things to do, along with a winery map; the bureau charges a $6 postage fee. If you don't want to pay for the printed publication, point your browser to **www.napavalley.org**, the NVCVB's official site, which has lots of the same information free.

Another good source is **www.winecountry.com**, where you'll find tons of information on all of California's wine-producing regions.

WHEN TO GO   The beauty of the valley is striking any time of year, but it's most memorable in September and October—harvest season, when the wineries are in full production. Another great time to visit is the spring, when the mustard flowers are in full bloom and the tourist season is just beginning; you'll find less traffic and fewer crowds at the wineries and restaurants, and better deals on hotel rooms. Winter is still beautiful and wonderfully romantic. It promises the best budget rates, but the vines are dormant and rain is likely, so bring appropriate shoes and an umbrella. And in summer? Say hello to hot weather, traffic, crowds, and an expensive good time.

Touring the Valley & Wineries

Napa Valley has more than 300 wineries—each with distinct wines, atmosphere, and experience—so touring the valley takes a little planning. Decide what interests you most (a specific type of wine? atmosphere? price point?) and chart your path from there. Ask locals for their favorites and latest discoveries, too. Take my advice and don't plan to visit more than four wineries in a day; cheesy as it sounds, Wine Country, like a great glass of wine, truly is best when savored. Besides, you're bound to get sidetracked and blow any tight schedule.

Most wineries are open 10am to 4:30pm (some have extended hours during summer; most are closed on major holidays). Many offer tours daily from 10am to 4:30pm, which usually chart the entire winemaking process—from grafting and harvesting the vines, to pressing the grapes, to blending and aging the juice in oak casks. Tours vary in length and formality; most charge a small fee, which is often applied toward any wine purchase you make.

The towns and wineries below are organized geographically, from south to north along Hwy. 29, from Napa village to Calistoga. I include a handful of my favorites below; for a complete list, be sure to pick up one of the free guides to the valley (see "Essentials," above).

NAPA

55 miles N of San Francisco

The city of Napa serves as the commercial center of the Wine Country and the gateway to Napa Valley—hence the high-speed freeway that whips you right past it and on to the "tourist" towns of St. Helena and Calistoga. However, if you veer off the highway, you'll be surprised to discover a small but burgeoning community of nearly 75,000 residents with the county's most "cosmopolitan" atmosphere

shipping WINE HOME

The only thing more complex than that $800 case of cabernet you just purchased are the rules about shipping it home. Because of absurd and forever-fluctuating laws—which supposedly protect the business of the country's wine distributors—wine shipping is limited by regulations that vary in each of the 50 states. Shipping rules also vary from winery to winery.

To avoid hassles, talk to the wineries and the shipping companies below before you buy. It's technically illegal to box your own wine and send it through the U.S. mail, but people do it all the time anyway (shhh). If you go that route, you might want to disguise your box and head to a post office, UPS, or other shipping company outside the Wine Country; it's far less obvious that you're shipping wine from, say, Vallejo or San Francisco than from Napa Valley.

Shipping from Napa Valley

The UPS Store, at 3212 Jefferson St. in the Grape Yard Shopping Center (© **707/259-1398**), claims to pack and ship anything anywhere. At press time, rates for ground-shipping a case of wine were approximately $45 to Los Angeles and $79 to New York.

St. Helena Mailing Center, 1241 Adams St., at Hwy. 29, St. Helena (© **707/963-2686**), says it will pack and ship to certain states within the U.S. Rates for prewrapped shipments are around $29 per case for ground delivery to Los Angeles.

Shipping from Sonoma

The UPS Store, 19229 Sonoma Hwy., in Maxwell Village, Sonoma (© **707/935-3438**), has a lot of experience with shipping wine. It claims it will ship your wine to any state. Prices vary from $21 to Los Angeles, to as much as $75 to the East Coast and $187 to Hawaii and Alaska.

(though I use that term loosely)—and some of the most affordable accommodations in the valley (Calistoga also has good deals). Still in the process of gentrification for the past decade, and deeply affected by the economic downturn, it continues to welcome new and surprisingly fancy hotels, condos, and restaurants, including Iron Chef Masaharu Morimoto's namesake restaurant (p. 222) which opened in late 2010, while the city center's small storefront spaces remain glaringly abandoned. Heading north on either Hwy. 29 or the Silverado Trail leads you to Napa's wineries and the more quintessential Wine Country atmosphere of vineyards and wide-open country views.

One of the most popular newer attractions is **Oxbow Market ★**, 600 First St. (© **707/226-6529;** www.oxbowpublicmarket.com). A smaller version of San Francisco's Ferry Building Marketplace, the co-op features a cornucopia of tasty tenants, including organic produce vendors, an exceptional rotisserie chicken joint called RoliRoti (try the potatoes!), a wine bar, yet another outpost of Gott's Roadside Tray Gourmet (formerly Taylor's Automatic Refresher; see p. 225 for details), a food-related antiques shop, killer organic ice cream, and many other reasons to loosen your belt and your grip on your wallet. Check the website to confirm opening hours, as they are subject to change.

Anyone with an appreciation for art must visit the **di Rosa Preserve ★★**, 5200 Sonoma Hwy. (Hwy. 12/121; © **707/226-5991;** www.dirosaart.org), to explore the collection and stunning 215-acre grounds of Rene and Veronica di

Napa welcomes more than 5 million visitors a year.

Rosa, who built up a world-renowned collection of 2,000-plus works by more than 900 Greater Bay Area artists. Treasures are on display in their century-old winery-turned-residence, adjoining building, two additional galleries, and gardens, and along the shores of their 30-acre lake. Tours include a $10 1-hour overview at 10 and 11am (Wed–Fri), a $15 2-hour extended home tour at 1pm, and a $15 2-hour sculpture meadow tour. On Saturdays, you can take a guided 2½-hour tour for $15. Reservations are recommended. Drop-ins are welcome at the Gatehouse Gallery Tuesday through Friday from 9:30am to 3pm and Saturdays by appointment ($3 suggested donation).

Discount shoppers should pull off Hwy. 29 at Napa's First Street exit to find the **Napa Premium Outlets** (© **707/226-9876;** www.premiumoutlets.com), which has a Barneys New York, TSE (cashmere), Nine West, Banana Republic, BCBG, Calvin Klein, kitchenware shops, a food court, and a decent but expensive sushi restaurant. The shops are open Monday through Thursday from 10am to 8pm, Friday and Saturday 10am to 9pm, and Sunday from 10am to 6pm.

Artesa Vineyards & Winery ★★ 🎁 Views, modern architecture, seclusion, and region-specific pinot noir flights make this one of my favorite stops. On days when the wind is blowing less than 10 mph, the fountains are captivating; they automatically shut off with higher winds. Inside the winery is a very tasteful gift shop, a room outlining the history and details of the Carneros region, and a long bar with $10 to $15

Sip Tip

You can cheaply sip your way through downtown Napa without getting behind the wheel with the new "Taste Napa Downtown" wine card. For $20, you get 10¢ tasting privileges at 10 wine-centric watering holes and tasting rooms within walking distance of one another. Plus, you'll get 10% discounts at tasting rooms. Available at the **Napa Valley Conference & Visitors Bureau** (1310 Napa Town Center, off First St.; © **707/226-7459,** ext. 106). Learn more at **www.napadowntown.com.**

flights of everything from chardonnays and pinot noirs to cabernet sauvignon and zinfandel. Sorry, but Artesa's permits don't allow for picnicking.

1345 Henry Rd., Napa. ✆ **707/224-1668.** www.artesawinery.com. Daily 10am–5pm; tours daily at 11am and 2pm. From Hwy. 12/121, turn north on old Sonoma Rd. and turn left on Dealy Lane, which becomes Henry Rd.

The Hess Collection ★★ 🎁   Tucked into the hillside of rural Mount Veeder, this winery brings art and wine together like no other destination in the valley. Swiss art collector Donald Hess is behind the 1978 transformation of the Christian Brothers' 1903 property into a winery–art gallery exhibiting huge, colorful works by the likes of Frank Stella, Francis Bacon, and Andy Goldsworthy. A free self-guided tour leads through the collection and offers glimpses through tiny windows into the winemaking facilities. Newer guided tours and food-and-wine pairings, which include four wines and seasonal noshes, are available by appointment only Thursday through Saturday for $35 to $50 per person. But you can drop by the tasting room anytime, pay $10, and sample the current cabernet and chardonnay and three other featured wines; $15 to $30 gets you a reserve tasting. Current-release bottles go from $18 to $120. They've got a decent gift shop and very picturesque courtyard too.

4411 Redwood Rd., Napa. ✆ **707/255-1144.** www.hesscollection.com. Daily 10am–5:30pm, except some holidays. From Hwy. 29 north, exit at Redwood Rd. west, and follow Redwood Rd. for 6½ miles.

Darioush Winery ★   With architecture based on Persepolis, the capital city of ancient Persia, this 22,000-square-foot winery has 16 dazzling 18-foot-tall free-standing columns at the entrance, a state-of-the-art visitor center, and opulent landscaping—all in honor of Persian-American owner Darioush Khaledi's homeland. (He immigrated during the Islamic Revolution and found his fortune in a grocery chain.) Tastings include their well-regarded shiraz, merlot, cabernet sauvignon, viognier, and chardonnay, as well as addictive Persian pistachios, for $25. Opt for the appointment-only $50 private tasting with cheese pairing, and you'll get to savor local Sonoma artisan cheeses with your wine and tour the facilities. Throw down $150 (gulp!), and you're privy to an elaborate wine and food pairing featuring old-world and new-world wines.

4240 Silverado Trail (south of Oak Knoll Ave.), Napa. ✆ **707/257-2345.** www.darioush.com. Daily 10:30am–5pm. Private tasting with cheese pairing daily at 2pm and by appointment. Tours available by appointment.

Quixote ★★ 🎁   Due to zoning laws, this spectacular and truly one-of-a-kind Stag's Leap District winery welcomes no more than eight guests per day, all of whom are likely to be as awe-struck by the architecture as they are by the powerful petite Syrahs and cabernet sauvignons. The hidden hillside property owned by longtime industry power player Carl Doumani is the only U.S. structure designed by late great European artist Friedensreich Hundertwasser. Whimsical and captivating, it's a structural fantasy world with undulating lines, a gilded onion dome, and a fearless use of color. During the reservation-only, sit-down tasting, visitors can fill their agape mouths with tastes of the winery's current releases for $25 a person.

6126 Silverado Trail, Napa. ✆ **707/944-2659.** www.quixotewinery.com. Tastings by appointment only Tues–Sun.

Shafer Vineyards ★ ★  For an intimate, off-the-beaten-track wine experience, make an appointment to tour and taste at this spectacularly low-key destination producing legendary wine. Unlike many Napa wineries, this one is family owned—by John and Doug Shafer, who, along with winemaker Elias Fernandez, use sustainable farming and solar energy to make truly outstanding wines, including chardonnay, merlot, cabernet sauvignon, and Syrah. Though they produce only 32,000 cases per year, they have still managed to make their Hillside Select famous. But more important, they share it and their winemaking philosophy with you during a truly enjoyable and relaxed $45-per-person 1½-hour tour and tasting. Most wines go for $48 to $70, but their Hillside Select cabernet will cost you $215 (and, should you get your hands on some, is immediately worth more). **Tip:** Book your tasting tour 4 to 6 weeks in advance online or by phone; the tours are intimate and popular.

Quixote Winery.

6154 Silverado Trail, Napa. ☏ **707/944-2877.** www.shafervineyards.com. By appointment only Mon–Fri 9am and 4pm; closed weekends and holidays.

YOUNTVILLE

70 miles N of San Francisco

As tiny a town as it is, Yountville (pop. 3,085) is a serious power player in the world of food and wine. Why? Two words: Thomas Keller. One of the world's most revered chefs, he has not one, but four dining destinations here—and counting. But there's more to munch on than fabulous French-inspired food. TV chef Michael Chiarello (who became famous decades ago as nearby Tra Vigne's chef) has an Italian restaurant here, too, right alongside his NapaStyle shop; and several other well-established culinary legends have long given visitors reason to veer off Hwy. 29 to overindulge. The town also has lots of places to sleep off your food coma, although most are midlevel luxury resorts, which are subtly sprinkled along the thoroughfare. Case in point is the latest addition, **Hotel Luca ★ ★**, 6774 Washington St. (www.hotellucanapa.com; ☏ **707/944-8080**), a charming 20-room destination in downtown Yountville that conjures Tuscan decadence, complete with giant, opulently appointed rooms, a centerpiece courtyard with outdoor fireplace, outdoor pool, restaurant that was surprisingly polished after being open only 2 weeks, and basement spa that also delivers.

Domaine Chandon ★ ★  Founded in 1973 by French champagne house Moët et Chandon, Domaine Chandon is the valley's most renowned (and hip) sparkling winery. Manicured gardens showcase locally made sculpture, and guests linger—their glasses fizzing with bubbly—by a table loaded with snacks in the festive tasting salon or under its patio's umbrella. In the valley's only fine-dining restaurant at a winery, diners indulge in formal French-inspired meals (more casual menus are available at lunchtime). If you can pull yourself away from the salon's bubbly or still wine (tastings are $18–$25), the comprehensive tours and tastings are informative and friendly. *Note:* The restaurant is closed on Tuesday and Wednesday and has even more restricted winter hours; it usually requires reservations. Also, check the website to see if they're offering two-for-one tastings.

1 California Dr. (at Hwy. 29), Yountville. ℂ **707/944-2280.** www.chandon.com. Daily 10am–5pm; hours vary by season, so call to confirm. Call or check website for free tour schedules and seasonal hours.

OAKVILLE

68 miles N of San Francisco

Driving farther north on the St. Helena Highway (Hwy. 29) brings you to the Oakville Cross Road and the famous **Oakville Grocery Co.** (see "Gourmet Picnics, Napa-Style" on p. 225), a favorite for picnic fare.

PlumpJack Winery   If most wineries are like a Brooks Brothers suit, Plump-Jack stands out as the Todd Oldham of wine tasting: chic, colorful, a little wild, and popular with a young, hip crowd as well as aficionados. Like the franchise's PlumpJack San Francisco restaurants and wine shop, and its Lake Tahoe resort, this playfully medieval winery is a welcome diversion from the same old same old. With Getty bucks behind what was once Villa Mt. Eden winery, the budget covers far more than just atmosphere: Some serious winemaking is going on here, too. For $10 you can stand at the bar and sample sauvignon blanc, merlot, Syrah, and chardonnay. Alas, there are no tours or picnic spots.

⬡ HOT-AIR balloooning OVER THE VALLEY

Napa Valley is the busiest hot-air balloon "flight corridor" in the world. Northern California's temperate weather allows for ballooning year-round, and on summer mornings in the valley, it's a rare day when you don't see at least one of the colorful airships floating above the vineyards.

Trips depart early in the morning, when the air is cooler and the balloons have better lift. (**Note:** When weather conditions aren't optimal, balloon companies often launch flights from locations up to an hour's drive outside the valley. You won't know until the morning of the flight, but you should be able to cancel on the spot if you desire.) Flight paths vary with the direction and speed of the changing breezes, so "chase" crews on the ground must follow the balloons to their undetermined destinations. Most flights last about an hour and end with a champagne celebration and breakfast. Advance reservations are required. Prices start at about $215 per person for the basic package, which includes shuttle service from your hotel. Wedding, wine tasting, picnic, and lodging packages are also available. For more information or reservations, call Napa's **Adventures Aloft** (ℂ **800/944-4408** or 707/944-4408; www.nvaloft.com) or **Bonaventura Balloon Company** (ℂ **800/FLY-NAPA** [359-6272]; www.bonaventuraballoons.com).

620 Oakville Cross Rd. (just west of the Silverado Trail), Oakville. © **707/945-1220.** www.plump jack.com. Daily 10am–4pm. Reservations required for groups of 8 or more.

Robert Mondavi Winery ★ 🎁📷 The Mission-style Mondavi winery offers the most comprehensive tours in the valley. Basic jaunts—which last about an hour and 15 minutes and cost $25—lead you through the vineyards and winemaking facilities. (Ask the guides anything about the process; they know a lot.) After the tour, you can taste a selection of current wines. To learn even more, inquire about the in-depth tours. Mondavi offers a wide variety, including the $100 "Harvest of Joy" tour, which includes a tour of the winery and a three-course luncheon with wine pairing. Tickets to their summer series concerts are expensive, but the talent is world-class (think Buena Vista Social Club, Aimee Mann, or Chaka Kahn) and the crowd knows how to throw a picnic-party. Check the website for this season's lineup.

7801 St. Helena Hwy. (Hwy. 29), Oakville. © **888/766-6328,** ext. 2000, or 707/226-1395. www. robertmondaviwinery.com. Daily 10am–5pm. Reservations recommended for guided tour; book 1 week ahead, especially for weekend tours. Closed Easter, Thanksgiving, Christmas, and New Year's Day.

RUTHERFORD
3 miles N of Oakville

If you blink after Oakville, you're likely to overlook Rutherford, the next small town that borders on St. Helena. Rutherford has its share of spectacular wineries, but you can't see most of them while driving along Hwy. 29.

Swanson Vineyards & Winery ★ 🎁📷 Of all the valley's tasting opportunities, this one is the most fun. Chic and unique, wine tastings at Swanson's Salon aren't cheap, at $60 a pop. But with the price comes an experience more like a private party, where you and up to seven other guests sit at a round table in a refined yet whimsical parlor lingering over wine and gourmet snacks served with first-class style. Over the course of the hour-plus event, a winery host pours four to seven wines, discusses the history and fine points of each, and encourages casual banter among guests. Expect a bright pinot grigio, rich merlot, and hearty Alexis, their signature cab-Syrah blend—as well as an awesome chocolate bonbon. Newly opened in June 2010 is the adjacent Sip Shoppe (www.sipshoppe.com), for a less formal, more fun tasting experience, with tastings ranging from $15 to $25 each.

1271 Manley Lane, Rutherford. © **707/967-3500.** www.swansonvineyards.com. Tasting appointments available Thurs–Sun 11am–5pm.

St. Supéry Winery ★ 😊 The outside looks like a modern corporate office building, but inside you'll find a functional, welcoming winery that encourages first-time tasters to learn more about oenology. The self-guided tour takes you through a demonstration vineyard that explains the growing techniques, and "SmellaVision" is an interactive kid-pleasing display that teaches you how to identify different wine ingredients. Adjoining it is the Atkinson House, chronicling more than 100 years of winemaking history during public tours offered at 1 and 3pm. For $15 to $25, you can sample four wines, which hopefully includes their excellent and very well-priced sauvignon blanc. Even the prices make visitors feel at home: Bottles start at $20, although the tag on their high-end cabernet sauvignon is $85.

8440 St. Helena Hwy. (Hwy. 29), Rutherford. © **800/942-0809** or 707/963-4507. www.stsupery. com. Daily 10am–5pm.

Rubicon Estate ★ Hollywood meets Napa Valley at Francis Ford Coppola's spectacular 1880s ivy-draped historic stone winery and grounds. Originally known as Inglenook Vineyards, then Niebaum-Coppola, it's now named after its most prestigious wine. You'll have to pay $25 to visit the estate, but that includes valet parking, a tasting of five wines (they make dozens of different kinds under various labels), a tour of the impeccably renovated grounds, and access to the giant wine bar, retail center, and room showcasing Coppola film memora-

Rubicon Winery.

bilia, from Academy Awards to trinkets from *The Godfather* and *Bram Stoker's Dracula.* Wine, food, and gift items dominate the cavernous tasting area, where wines such as an estate-grown blend, cabernet franc, merlot, and zinfandel made from organically grown grapes are sampled. Bottles range from around $19 to more than $100. Along with the basic tour, you can pay extra for more exclusive, specialized tours as well.

1991 St. Helena Hwy. (Hwy. 29), Rutherford. © **800/782-4266** or 707/968-1100. www.rubicon estate.com. Daily 10am–5pm. Tours daily.

Round Pond ★★ Surrounded by imported blue agave, palm, and olive trees, Round Pond's sleek and minimalist digs are a truly stunning stage for the annual production of a minuscule 3,000 cases of cabernet sauvignon and about 100 cases of Nebbiolo. (Here only the best grapes make the cut, and bottle prices, ranging from $26 to $100, reflect as much.) The estate also grows Spanish and Italian olives, which has resulted in award-winning oils, and red-wine vinegars. Book an appointment and you can soak up some seriously chic atmosphere; choose from three tastings, which range from the $25 estate tasting to the very sexy (and pricey) $200 twilight tasting and dinner.

875 Rutherford Rd., btw. the Silverado Trail and Hwy. 29, Rutherford. © **888/302-2575.** www. roundpond.com. Winery daily 11am–3:30pm. Tours and tastings by appointment only. Olive mill open 7 days a week by appointment.

ST. HELENA

73 miles N of San Francisco

This quiet little town, 17 miles north of Napa on Hwy. 29, is home to many beautiful old houses and first-rate restaurants, accommodations, and shops. The former Seventh-Day Adventist village manages to maintain a pseudo Old West feel while catering to upscale shoppers with deep pockets: It's *the* destination for retail-therapy seekers. (Don't get too excited, though; St. Helena is still a boutique, 4-block town.) On St. Helena's **Main Street** ★, between Pope and Pine streets, you'll find trendy fashions, chic pet gifts, estate jewelry, and European home accessories. Most stores are open 10am to 5pm Monday through Sunday.

Shopaholics should also take the sharp turn off Hwy. 29, 2 miles north of downtown St. Helena, to the **St. Helena Premier Outlets** (© **707/963-7282**). Featured designers include Escada, Brooks Brothers, and Tumi. The stores are open daily from 10am to 6pm.

One last favorite stop is the **Napa Valley Olive Oil Manufacturing Company,** 835 Charter Oak Ave. (© **707/963-4173**), at the end of the road behind Tra Vigne restaurant. The tiny market presses and bottles its own oils and sells them at a fraction of the price you'd pay elsewhere. It also has an extensive selection of Italian cooking

Downtown St. Helena.

ingredients, imported snacks, great deals on dried mushrooms, and a picnic table in the parking lot. You'll love the age-old method for totaling the bill—which you must discover for yourself.

If you'd like to go **bicycling,** the quieter, northern end of the valley is an ideal place to rent a set of wheels and pedal the Silverado Trail. **St. Helena Cyclery,** 1156 Main St. (© **707/963-7736;** www.sthelenacyclery.com), rents bikes for $10 per hour or $35 a day, including rear rack, helmet, and picnic bag.

Prager Winery & Port Works 🛍 If you want an off-the-beaten-track experience, Prager's can't be beat. Turn the corner from Sutter Home winery and roll into the small gravel parking lot; you're on the right track, but when you pull open the creaky old wooden door to this shack of a wine-tasting room, you'll begin to wonder. Don't turn back! Pass the oak barrels, and you'll quickly come upon the clapboard tasting room, made homey with a big Oriental rug, some of the most interesting "wallpaper" you've ever seen, and a Prager family host. Fork over $10 (includes a complimentary glass), and they'll pour you five samples of their wines and ports (which cost $28–$80 per bottle). Also available is "Prager Chocolate Drizzle," a chocolate liqueur sauce that tops ice creams and other desserts. If you're looking for a special gift, consider their bottles, which can be custom etched in the design of your choice for around $85, plus the cost of the wine.

1281 Lewelling Lane (just west of Hwy. 29, behind Sutter Home), St. Helena. © **800/969-7678** or 707/963-7678. www.pragerport.com. Mon–Sat 10:30am–4:30pm; Sun 11am–4:30pm. Appointment required for groups of four or more.

Joseph Phelps Vineyards ★ Visitors interested in intimate, comprehensive tours and a knockout tasting should schedule a tour at this winery founded in 1973 by major wine world player Joseph Phelps. A favorite stop for serious wine lovers, primarily due to their ever-popular and expensive Insignia wine, this modern, state-of-the-art winery and big-city vibe are proof that Phelps's annual 80,000 cases prove fruitful in more ways than one. While at first meeting it seems seriousness hangs heavier than harvest grapes, the mood lightens during the hour-plus $25 informal tasting or any of the $40 "seminars" (think blending or wine appreciation), which include tastings of five or six wines. The three excellently located picnic tables, on the terrace overlooking the valley, are available on a first-come, first-served basis, with preference given to Phelps wine club members (join and get wine shipped a certain number of times per year), who are also able to make a reservation.

200 Taplin Rd. (off the Silverado Trail), P.O. Box 1031, St. Helena. ℭ **800/707-5789** or 707/963-2745. www.jpvwines.com. Mon–Fri 10am–5pm; Sat–Sun 10am–4pm. $40 seminars and tastings by appointment only weekends at 10am and 2pm, weekdays at 10am and 2:30pm. $15 per person for 1-oz. pour of Insignia.

Beringer Vineyards ★   You won't have the most personal experience at this tourist-heavy stop, but you will find a regal 1876 estate, founded by brothers Jacob and Frederick, and hand-dug tunnels in the hillside. The oldest continually operating winery in Napa Valley, Beringer managed to stay open even during Prohibition by making "sacramental" wines. White zinfandel is the winery's most popular seller, but plenty of other varietals—including some highfalutin options—are available. Tastings of current vintages, which range from $15 to $25, are conducted in newer facilities. Reserve wines are available for tasting in the remarkable Rhine House for $25 (applied toward purchase), and tours range from the $20 standard to the $30 "Taste of Beringer Tour."

2000 Main St. (Hwy. 29), St. Helena. ℭ **707/963-7115.** www.beringer.com. Oct–May 10am–5pm (last tour 4pm, last tasting 4:45pm); June–Sept 10am–6pm (last tour 5:15pm, last tasting 5:30pm).

CALISTOGA

81 miles N of San Francisco

This last tourist town in Napa Valley was named by Sam Brannan, entrepreneur extraordinaire and California's first millionaire. After making a bundle supplying miners during the Gold Rush, he took advantage of the natural geothermal springs at the north end of Napa Valley by building a hotel and spa in 1859. Flubbing up a speech in which he compared this natural California wonder to New York State's Saratoga Springs resort, he serendipitously coined the name "Calistoga," and it stuck. With less than 6,000 residents and an old-time main street (no building along the 6-block stretch is more than two stories high), this small, simple resort town is popular with city folk who come here to unwind. Calistoga is a great place to relax and indulge in mineral waters, mud baths, Jacuzzis, massages, and, of course, wine. The vibe is more casual—and a little funkier—than you'll find in towns to the south.

Want an active tour of the area? Cycling enthusiasts can rent bikes from **Getaway Adventures/Wine Country Adventures** (www.getawayadventures.com; ℭ **800/499-2453** or 707/568-3040). Full-day group tours cost $149 per person, including lunch and a visit to four or five wineries, $195 per person for private groups of six or more. Bike rental without a tour costs $30 per day plus a $45 delivery fee to Napa Valley locations. You can also inquire about the company's kayaking and hiking tours.

Frank Family Vineyards ★ 👥   "Wine dudes" Dennis, Tim, Jeff, Rick, and Pat will do practically anything to maintain their rightfully self-proclaimed reputation

Schramsberg Winery.

as the "friendliest winery in the valley." Here it's all about down-home fun: no muss, no fuss, no intimidation. At Frank Family, you're part of their family—no joke. They'll greet you like a long-lost relative and serve you all the free bubbly tastings you want (three to four varieties: blanc de blanc, blanc de noir, and reserve rouge, for example, at $13–$32 a bottle). Still-wine lovers can sample well-received chardonnay and a cabernet sauvignon in the casual back room. Behind the tasting room, a picnic area is situated under the oaks, overlooking the vineyards.

1091 Larkmead Lane (just off the Silverado Trail), Calistoga. © **707/942-0859.** www.frank familyvineyards.com. Daily 10am–5pm. No tours offered.

Castello di Amorosa ★ 🎁   For a taste of medieval Europe in Napa, head to this impressive new 121,000-square-foot stone castle. The eight-level structure, with 90 feet of caves, a dungeon, and a torture chamber, is surprisingly authentic (as evidenced by achy legs and feet after tromping on cobblestones). It's $10 to sample a variety of wines, including chardonnay, merlot, cabernet, and dessert wines (bottles range in price from $30 to $75), and $25 to $30 for the 2-hour tour ($15 for children 10 or older; children 9 and under are not permitted). Though the castle is a far cry from quintessential Wine Country (some liken it to Disneyland), it is fun to browse this stunning architectural accomplishment.

4045 N. St. Helena Hwy., Calistoga. © **707/942-8200** or 707/286-7273 (for events). www.castello diamorosa.com. Tasting daily 9:30am–6pm. Tours by reservation only: on the hour weekdays 9:30am–4:30pm, and on the half-hour weekends and holidays 9:30am–5pm.

Schramsberg ★★ 🎁   One of the valley's all-time best places to explore, this 217-acre landmark champagne estate has a wonderful old-world feel. Schramsberg is the label that presidents serve when toasting dignitaries from around the globe—with a bevy of historic memorabilia in the front room to prove it. But the real mystique begins when you enter the champagne caves, partly hand-carved by Chinese laborers in the 1800s, which wind for 2 miles—reputedly making them the longest in North America. The caves have a Tom Sawyer feel, complete with dangling cobwebs and seemingly endless passageways; you can't help but feel you're on an adventure. The comprehensive, unintimidating tour ends in the tasting room, where you'll sit around a big table and sample four surprisingly varied selections of bubbly. Tastings are $35 per person, but it's money well spent. They are offered only to those who take the free tour, and you must make reservations in advance.

1400 Schramsberg Rd. (off Hwy. 29), Calistoga. ℂ **707/942-2414.** www.schramsberg.com. Daily 10am–4pm. Tours and tastings by appointment only, at 10, 11am, 1, and 2:30pm.

Sterling Vineyards ★ ☺ 🎁   One of the more commercial wine-tasting experiences in the area, Sterling has one thing going for it that no other winery can boast: an aerial tram offering stunning valley views while en route to its white Mediterranean-style winery perched 300 feet up on a rocky knoll. The ride, which costs $25 ($10 for kids) and includes wine tasting, leads to a self-guided tour of the winemaking process and a panoramic tasting room offering samples of five varietals. However, more sophisticated sips—limited releases or reserve flights—cost from $5 to $25, respectively. Expect to pay from $14 to $100-plus for a souvenir bottle.

1111 Dunaweal Lane (off Hwy. 29, just south of downtown Calistoga), Calistoga. ℂ **707/942-3344.** www.sterlingvineyards.com. Daily 10:30am–4:30pm.

Duckhorn Vineyards   With quintessential pastoral surroundings (think meadow views), Victorian farmhouse surroundings (hello verandas!), and a selection of extremely good wines, Duckhorn Vineyards has much to offer visitors interested in a bit of relaxation. The tasting room, complete with cafe tables and a centerpiece bar, is a surprisingly modern place. You'll pay $25 for a flight of four current-release wines, or $35 for a semiprivate estate-wine tasting, the latter of which you can book in advance. The fee may be a bit high, but this is not your run-of-the-mill drink and dash. You'll get plenty of attention and information on their current releases of sauvignon blanc, merlot, and cabernet sauvignon.

1000 Lodi Lane (at the Silverado Trail), St. Helena. ℂ **707/963-7108.** www.duckhorn.com. Daily 10am–4pm. Reservations recommended.

Where to Stay

Accommodations in Napa Valley run the gamut—from standard motels and floral-and-lace Victorian-style B&Bs to world-class luxury retreats—and all are easily accessible from the main highway that stretches across the valley and leads to its attractions. Most of the romantically pastoral options (think hidden hillside spots with vineyard views or quaint small-town charmers) are found on the outskirts of historic St. Helena, which boasts the best walking/shopping street, and the equally storied but more laid-back and affordable hot-springs-heavy Calistoga, which also promises some of the region's most affordable options. The area of the few commercial blocks of pastoral Yountville has become a destination in itself thanks to a number of famous restaurants (including world-renowned French Laundry) as well as a handful of high-end hotels and middle-end B&Bs. The most "reasonably priced" (a relative term in this high-priced area) choices are the B&Bs, small hotels, and national chain options in downtown Napa, the closest thing you'll find to a city in these parts. Fortunately, no matter where you stay, you're just a few minutes—or less—away from world-class wineries.

Winemaker Brad Warner, Sawyer Cellars.

VERY EXPENSIVE

Calistoga Ranch ★★★   Tucked into the eastern mountainside on 157 pristine hidden-canyon acres, the 46 rural-chic free-standing luxury cottages may cost more than a month's rent, but if you've got the cash, it's one of the most spectacular temporary homes in the state. Auberge's sister property boasts stunning grounds and rooms packed with every conceivable amenity (including fireplaces, patios along a wooded area, and cushy outdoor furnishings). Reasons not to leave include a giant swimming pool, a reasonably large gym, an incredibly designed indoor-outdoor spa with a natural thermal pool, and individual pavilions with private-garden soaking tubs, as well as a breathtakingly beautiful restaurant with stunning views of the property's Lake Lommel. Need more enticement? They offer free activities like watercolor painting, yoga, biking, and hiking. Add the startlingly good food (that can be experienced only by guests) to the resort architecture that intentionally tries to blend with the natural surroundings, and you've got a romantically rustic slice of Wine Country heaven.

price CATEGORIES

Very Expensive	$301 and up
Expensive	$201–$300
Moderate	$150–$200
Inexpensive	Under $150

FIND THE NEW YOU—IN mud

People in Calistoga have been taking mud baths for the past 150 years. Local volcanic ash, imported peat, and naturally boiling mineral hot springs are mulled together to produce a thick, natural mud that simmers at a temperature of about 104°F (40°C). Follow your soak with a warm mineral-water shower, a whirlpool bath, a visit to the steam room, and a relaxing blanket-wrap. Emerge rejuvenated, revitalized, and squeaky-clean.

Indulge yourself at any of these Calistoga spas: **Dr. Wilkinson's Hot Springs,** 1507 Lincoln Ave. (© 707/942-4102); **Golden Haven Hot Springs Spa,** 1713 Lake St. (© 707/942-6793); **Calistoga Spa Hot Springs,** 1006 Washington St. (© 707/942-6269); **Calistoga Village Inn & Spa,** 1880 Lincoln Ave. (© 707/942-0991); **Indian Springs Resort,** 1712 Lincoln Ave. (© 707/942-4913); or **Roman Spa Motel,** 1300 Washington St. (© 707/942-4441).

580 Lommel Rd., Calistoga, CA 94515. www.calistogaranch.com. © **707/254-2800.** Fax 707/254-2888. 46 cottages. $550–$4,000 double. AE, DC, DISC, MC, V. **Amenities:** Restaurant; concierge; gym; Jacuzzi; large heated outdoor pool; room service; spa; steam room; Wi-Fi throughout. *In room:* A/C, TV/DVD w/DVDs, fax upon request, fridge, hair dryer, minibar, outdoor fireplace, private outdoor shower, 1 lodge w/full kitchen.

Harvest Inn ★★   One of the valley's few sprawling resorts, this 74-unit property has wonderfully spacious accommodations, all of which are uniquely decorated with warm, homey furnishings and nestled into 8 acres of flora; most have fireplaces. Extensive grounds (which include two swimming pools and hot tubs, a spa, and a wine bar) and well-appointed suites make the place popular with wedding parties and families. Although you can't reserve specific rooms in advance, request an abode away from the highway upon arrival. Also, if you're not into climbing stairs, ask for a ground-level room, as some accommodations are on a second story and don't have elevator access. The inn offers free wine tastings Friday and Saturday evenings.

One Main St., St. Helena, CA 94574. www.harvestinn.com. © **800/950-8466** or 707/963-9463. Fax 707/963-5387. 74 units. $299–$599 double; $645–$799 suite. Rates include breakfast. AE, MC, V. Free parking. From Hwy. 29 N., turn left into the driveway at the large HARVEST INN sign. **Amenities:** Wine bar; mountain bike rentals; 2 heated outdoor pools; 2 hot tubs. *In room:* A/C, TV/DVD, fridge, hair dryer, free Wi-Fi.

Meadowood Napa Valley ★★★ 🛎   For a true first-class country resort experience, this spectacular spot surrounded by 250 acres of pristine mountainside is the ultimate. Here, free-standing luxury accommodations—which vary in size depending on the price and boast American-country-chic style—are scattered amid the expansive hillside grounds. Most are individual suite-lodges so far removed from the common areas that you have to drive to get to them and hoof it a bit to reach the restaurant or spa. Otherwise, folks can beckon a complimentary ride or opt for more centrally located rooms.

The resort offers a wealth of activities: golf on a challenging 9-hole course, tennis on seven championship courts, and croquet on two international regulation lawns. It has private hiking trails, a health spa, yoga, two heated pools, and two

WHAT YOU'LL really pay

The prices associated with a stay in Wine Country can be jaw-dropping. Here, luxury abodes can set you back close to $1,000 per night. But more startling, even a standard motel room can go for upwards of $250 per night over the weekend during high season. Why? Because there tends to be more people who want to visit than there are hotels to accommodate them. In other words, it's a seller's market. So, if budget travel is essential to your itinerary, definitely avoid visiting during high season—March to November—when most hotels charge peak rates, sell out completely on weekends, and often have a 2-night minimum. That said, there are still deals to be had, so when you browse the rates listed here, which are "rack rates" or the maximum possible charge per night, keep in mind that you may be able to book a room for substantially cheaper; it's always worth asking. If you need help organizing your Wine Country vacation, contact an agency. **Bed & Breakfast Inns of Napa Valley** (✆ **707/944-4444;** www.bbinv.com), an association of B&Bs, provides descriptions and lets you know who has rooms available. **Napa Valley Reservations Unlimited** (✆ **800/251-6272** or 707/252-1985; www.napavalleyreservations.com) is also a source for booking everything from hot-air balloon rides to wine-tasting tours by limousine.

whirlpools. An added bonus: Their formal restaurant has award-winning talent cranking out delicious multicourse meals based on seasonal local ingredients.

900 Meadowood Lane, St. Helena, CA 94574. www.meadowood.com. ✆ **800/458-8080** or 707/963-3646. Fax 707/963-3532. 85 units. $475–$825 double; $775–$1,250 1-bedroom suite; $1,400–$3,400 2-bedroom suite; $1,875–$4,775 3-bedroom suite; $2,350–$6,150 4-bedroom suite. Ask about promotional offers and off-season rates. 2-night minimum stay on weekends. AE, DC, DISC, MC, V. **Amenities:** 2 restaurants; concierge; golf course; health club and full-service spa; Jacuzzi; 2 large heated outdoor pools (adult and family pools); room service; sauna; 7 tennis courts; 2 croquet lawns. *In room:* A/C, TV, hair dryer, kitchenette in some rooms, minibar, free Wi-Fi.

MODERATE

Christopher's Inn ★ ☺   Renovations and expansions by architect-owner Christopher Layton turned these sweet old homes in downtown Calistoga into comfy hotel rooms. Options range from simple but tasteful quarters (colorful, with impressive antiques and small bathrooms) to huge, well-appointed abodes (with four-poster beds, rich fabrics, and sunken Jacuzzi tubs that face a gas fireplace). Most rooms have gas fireplaces, and some have flatscreen TVs (with cable) and DVD players. The two plain but very functional two-bedroom units are ideal for families, provided you're not expecting the Ritz. An extended continental breakfast is delivered to your room daily. *Tip:* For a quieter room, request one away from the street. Also be warned that they have a no-refund cancellation policy and that the entire hotel is nonsmoking.

1010 Foothill Blvd., Calistoga, CA 94515. www.christophersinn.com. ✆ **866/876-5755** or 707/942-5755. Fax 707/942-6895. 24 units. $165–$395 double; $330–$350 house sleeping 5 or 6. Rates include expanded continental breakfast. AE, MC, V. **Amenities:** Smoke-free rooms; single or couples massage in fireplace room. *In room:* TV, hair dryer, free Wi-Fi.

Maison Fleurie ★★   One of the prettiest garden-set B&Bs in the Wine Country, this property run by the ever-classy Four Sisters Inn company comprises a trio of beautiful 1873 brick-and-fieldstone buildings overlaid with ivy. The main house—a charming Provençal replica with thick brick walls, terra-cotta tile, and paned windows—holds seven rooms; the rest are in the old bakery building and the carriage house. Some feature private balconies, patios, sitting areas, Jacuzzi tubs, and fireplaces. An above-par breakfast is served in the quaint little dining room; afterward, you're welcome to wander the landscaped grounds or hit the wine-tasting trail, returning in time for afternoon hors d'oeuvres and wine.

6529 Yount St. (btw. Washington St. and Yountville Cross Rd.), Yountville, CA 94559. www.maison fleurienapa.com. © **800/788-0369** or 707/944-2056. Fax 707/944-9342. 13 units. $140–$285 double. Rates include full breakfast and afternoon hors d'oeuvres. AE, DC, DISC, MC, V. **Amenities:** Free use of bikes; Jacuzzi; heated outdoor pool. *In room:* A/C, TV, hair dryer, free Wi-Fi.

Wine Country Inn ★★ Just off the highway, behind Freemark Abbey vineyard, this attractive wood-and-stone family-run inn, complete with a French-style mansard roof and turret, overlooks a pastoral landscape of vineyards. Inside, individually decorated rooms contain antique furnishings and handmade quilts; most have fireplaces and private terraces overlooking the valley, and others have private hot tubs. Five luxury cottages include king-size beds as well as a single bed (perfect for the tot in tow), sitting areas, fireplaces, private patios, and three-headed walk-in showers. One of the inn's best features (besides the absence of TVs) is the heated outdoor pool. Another outstanding feature is the selection of suites, which come with stereos and plenty of space and privacy. The owners make every guest feel welcome, serving wine and appetizers nightly, greeting guests hospitably in the warm living room, and offering a full buffet breakfast as well.

1152 Lodi Lane, St. Helena, CA 94574. www.winecountryinn.com. © **888/465-4608** or 707/963-7077. Fax 707/963-9018. 29 units, 12 with shower only. $215–$405 double; $535–$660 for cottages. Rates include breakfast and appetizers. MC, V. **Amenities:** Concierge; Jacuzzi; heated outdoor pool; spa services; free Wi-Fi, free car service to St. Helena restaurants. *In room:* A/C, hair dryer.

INEXPENSIVE

In addition to the listings below, **Napa Valley Railway Inn ★★**, 6503 Washington St., Yountville, adjacent to the Vintage 1870 shopping complex (www.napavalleyrailwayinn.com; © **707/944-2000**), rents private railway cars converted into adorable hotel rooms.

Best Western Elm House Inn ★★ 🎁 Unlike most Napa Valley hotels, this sweet family-owned and -run downtown Napa option provides true value at surprisingly reasonable prices. While rooms may be just a step up from motel flair, their sizes are generous and are accompanied by lots of perks and thoughtful human touches—including friendly personal service, an above-par breakfast with made-to-order waffles, and freshly baked afternoon cookies. With its well-appointed lobby with a large fireplace and a garden with meticulous landscaping, this special find has all the personality and charm of a B&B with all the privacy of a hotel. It's also walking distance from Napa's downtown center and close to Hwy. 29, the region's thoroughfare.

800 California Blvd., Napa, CA 94559. www.bestwestern.com. © **888/849-1997** or 707/255-1831. Fax 707/255-8609. 22 units. $119–$279 double. Rates include full breakfast and evening cookies. AE, DISC, MC, V. From Hwy. 29 north, take the First St. exit, take a right onto California Blvd., and the hotel is on the corner of Second St. and California Blvd. **Amenities:** Atrium; garden. *In room:* A/C, hair dryer, free Wi-Fi, bathrobes.

Calistoga Spa Hot Springs ★ ☺ 🍴   Calistoga Spa Hot Springs is one of very few hotels in the Wine Country that caters specifically to families with children. This "family resort" is a great bargain, with unpretentious yet comfortable rooms and a plethora of spa facilities. All of Calistoga's best shops and restaurants are within easy walking distance, and you can use the barbecue grills near the large pool and patio.

1006 Washington St. (at Gerard St.), Calistoga, CA 94515. www.calistogaspa.com. © **866/822-5772** or 707/942-6269. 57 units. $130–$152 double. Discounted rates available weekdays Nov–Feb, excluding holidays. MC, V. **Amenities:** Exercise room; 4 heated outdoor pools and children's wading pool; spa. *In room:* A/C, TV, hair dryer, kitchenette, free Wi-Fi.

Chablis Inn ★   There's no way around it: If you want to sleep cheaply in a town where the *average* room rate tops $200 per night in high season, you're destined for a motel. Look on the bright side: Because your room is likely to be little more than a crash pad after a day of eating and drinking, a clean bed and a remote control are all you'll really need anyway. And Chablis offers much more than that. All of the motel-style rooms are superclean, and some even boast kitchenettes or whirlpool tubs. Guests have access to a heated outdoor pool and hot tub.

3360 Solano Ave., Napa, CA 94558. www.chablisinn.com. © **800/443-3490** or 707/257-1944. Fax 707/226-6862. 34 units. May to mid-Nov $99–$250 double; mid-Nov to Apr $79–$150 double. AE, DC, DISC, MC, V. **Amenities:** Jacuzzi; heated outdoor pool. *In room:* A/C, satellite TV, fridge, hair dryer, kitchenette in some rooms, free Wi-Fi.

Dr. Wilkinson's Hot Springs Resort ★   This spa/"resort," located in the heart of Calistoga, is one of the best deals in Napa Valley—and also offers all the spa treatments the town is famous for. The rooms range from attractive Victorian-style accommodations to more modern guest rooms in the main 1960s-style motel. All rooms have surprisingly tasteful textiles and basic motel-style accouterments. Larger rooms have refrigerators and/or kitchens. Facilities include three mineral-water pools (two outdoor and one indoor), a Jacuzzi, a steam room, and mud baths. All kinds of body treatments are available in the spa, including famed mud baths, steams, and massage—all of which I highly recommend. Be sure to inquire about their excellent packages, their new fantastic facial offered in the facial cottage, and hot-stone-massage therapy.

1507 Lincoln Ave. (Calif. 29, btw. Fairway and Stevenson aves.), Calistoga, CA 94515. www.dr wilkinson.com. © **707/942-4102.** 42 units. $149–$299 double; $164–$600 for the Hideaway cottages. Weekly discounts and packages available. AE, MC, V. **Amenities:** Jacuzzi; 3 pools; spa; free Wi-Fi in lobby; mud baths; steam room. *In room:* A/C, TV, hair dryer.

El Bonita Motel ★ ☺ 🍴   This 1940s Art Deco motel is a bit too close to Hwy. 29 for comfort, but the awesome price and 2½ acres of beautifully landscaped gardens behind the building (away from the road) help even the score. The rooms, while small and nothing fancy (think motel basic), are spotlessly clean and decorated with newer furnishings and kitchenettes; some have a whirlpool bathtub. It ain't heaven, but it is cheap for St. Helena.

195 Main St. (at El Bonita Ave.), St. Helena, CA 94574. www.elbonita.com. © **800/541-3284** or 707/963-3216. Fax 707/963-8838. 41 units. $100–$280 double. Rates include continental breakfast. AE, DC, DISC, MC, V. **Amenities:** Free high-speed Internet access in lobby; Jacuzzi; heated outdoor pool; sauna. *In room:* A/C, TV, fridge, hair dryer, microwave, free Wi-Fi.

Roman Spa Hot Springs Resort ★ Reasonable prices, a central location just a block off Calistoga's main drag, trusty accommodations, a garden setting, and mineral pools make this low-key destination a sure thing for luxury lovers on a budget. Like most old-school "resorts" (a term used loosely in these parts) in the area, the focus is on the spa, which includes three mineral pools—one indoor pool, one outdoor pool, and one outdoor whirlpool—dry "Finnish" saunas, and mud-bath and massage facilities. Accommodations are clean, comfortable, and, depending on what you get, somewhat outdated, and upgrades include a whirlpool tub, full kitchen, or two-room "family" suite.

1300 Washington St., Calistoga, CA 94515. www.romanspahotsprings.com. © **800/914-8957** or 707/942-4441. 60 units. $140–$250 double; $230–$450 suite. AE, DC, DISC, MC, V. **Amenities:** 3 mineral pools; sauna; massage. *In room:* AC, TV, fridge.

Where to Eat

To best enjoy Napa's restaurant scene, keep one thing in mind: You'll need reservations—especially for tables in renowned establishments.

VERY EXPENSIVE

The French Laundry ★★★ CLASSIC AMERICAN/FRENCH The world-famous French Laundry is unlike any other dining experience. Part of its appeal has to do with intricate preparations, often finished tableside and always presented with uncommon artistry and detail, from the food itself to the surface it's delivered on. Other strengths are the service (superfluous, formal, and attentive) and the sheer length of time it takes to ride chef Thomas Keller's culinary magic carpet. The atmosphere is as serious as the diners who quietly swoon over the parade of bite-size delights. Seating ranges from downstairs to upstairs to seasonal garden tables. Technically, the prix-fixe menu offers a choice of nine courses (including a vegetarian menu), but after several presentations from the kitchen, everyone starts to lose count. Signature dishes include Keller's "tongue in cheek" (a marinated and braised round of sliced lamb tongue and tender beef cheeks) and "macaroni and cheese" (sweet butter-poached Maine lobster with creamy lobster broth and orzo with mascarpone cheese). The experience defies description, so if you absolutely love food, you'll simply have to try it for yourself. Portions are small, but only because Keller wants his guests to taste as many things as possible. Trust me, nobody leaves hungry.

The staff is well acquainted with the wide selection of regional wines; there's a $50 corkage fee if you bring your own bottle, which is only welcome if it's not on the list. *Hint:* If you can't get a reservation, try walking in—no-shows are rare but possible, especially during lunch on rainy days. Reservations are accepted 2 months in advance of the date, starting at 10am. Anticipate hitting redial many times. Also, insiders tell me that fewer people call on weekends, so you have a better chance at getting beyond the busy signal. You can also try www.opentable.com, though online reservations are still taken 2 months in advance.

6640 Washington St. (at Creek St.). © **707/944-2380.** www.frenchlaundry.com. Reservations required. Dress code: no jeans, shorts, or tennis shoes; men should wear jackets; ties optional. 9-course tasting menu (including vegetarian option) $250. AE, MC, V. Fri–Sun 11am–1pm; daily 5:30–9:15pm.

EXPENSIVE

Morimoto Napa ★★ JAPANESE/SUSHI   The biggest restaurant opening of 2010 is also one of the most exciting places to dine in the region. Sure, the famed owner, Iron Chef Masahara Morimoto, is the initial draw (even though he's not always here), but there's more to this spot's celebrity. The sprawling industrial-chic interior has a front lounge, surprisingly hopping bar, and spacious dining areas accented with glass, rich wood, and gnarled grapevines. Then there's the food. Skip the sushi, which is expensive and, during my visit, perched atop too-cold rice. And perhaps even consider skipping the entrees, such as whole roasted lobster with Indian spices and lemon crème fraîche, which are good but can't contend with the downright awesome appetizers. Toro tartare—with a presentation you must see for yourself—the buttery goodness that is wagyu beef carpaccio, and foie gras chawan mushi (a savory custard with duck breast) are pure edible glamour. Add a couple of Morimotinis and you've got a night well spent.

610 Main St., Napa. ✆ **707/252-1600.** www.morimotonapa.com. Reservations recommended. Main courses $26–$45. AE, DC, MC, V. Mon–Tues 5–10pm; Wed–Thurs and Sun 11:30am–2:30pm and 5–9:30pm; Fri–Sat 11:30am–2:30pm and 5pm–1am.

Terra/Bar Terra ★★ CONTEMPORARY AMERICAN   In 2011, Terra doubled its destination-worthy fun, offering two entirely different experiences—one a festive bar area with more casual (but still excellent) dining and one highlighting the fine dining that made it one of the valley's most renowned restaurants. Conceptualized by Lissa Doumani and her husband, Hiro Sone, a Japanese master chef (who are also behind San Francisco's famed Ame restaurants), the new relaxed-dining menu offers seasonal cocktails made from fruits and herbs grown by the owners (plus a full bar) and a menu featuring a broad range of dishes and prices that allows diners to mix and match a meal to suit their appetites as well as their pocket books. Hiro's fine-dining menu continues to reflect Sone's full use of the region's bounty and his formal training in classic European and Japanese cuisine. But now the affair is a 3-, 4-, 5-, or 6-course extravaganza, with options ranging from understated and refined (two must-tries: rock shrimp salad, or broiled sake-marinated cod with shrimp dumplings and shiso broth) to rock-your-world flavorful. I cannot express the importance of saving room for dessert (or forcing it even if you didn't save room). Doumani's recipes, which include to-die-for tiramisu, are heavenly.

1345 Railroad Ave. (btw. Adams and Hunt sts.). ✆ **707/963-8931.** www.terrarestaurant.com. Reservations recommended. Bar: Plates $6–$25. Dining room: 3-course $57, 4-course $66, 5-course $81, 6-course $92, chef's-menu price changes nightly. AE, DC, MC, V. Wed–Mon dinner starting at 6pm. Closed 2 weeks in early Jan.

MODERATE

BarBersQ ★ BARBECUE   Located in a Napa strip mall, this extremely crowded eatery has garnered three stars from San Francisco's most persnickety critic and a fiercely loyal following for its "American Heritage cuisine" (think Memphis-style barbecue, classic comfort foods, and meat, meat, and more meat). The menu covers all the grease and gristle faves, from legendary fried chicken (served only on Sun) to ribs, brisket, whole roast chicken for two, beans and ham, and mac and cheese. Add chocolate bourbon pecan pie, Key lime pie, or a hot-fudge sundae, and you'll be hard-pressed to get out the door with your pants buttoned. Like most Napa Valley restaurants, this one does decadence with a "healthy" twist, employing fresh, local, organic ingredients when possible. While this effort doesn't cut calories, it may mitigate any potential guilt attached to unabashed indulgence. Also, FYI, service is uneven—also a Napa norm—and takeout is a popular option.

3900 D Bel Aire Plaza. © **707/224-6600.** www.barbersq.com. Reservations recommended. Main courses $8–$30. AE, MC, V. Sun–Thurs 11:30am–8:30pm; Fri–Sat 11:30am–9pm.

Bistro Don Giovanni ★★ 🍴 REGIONAL ITALIAN This bright, bustling, cheery Italian restaurant is one of my favorites in Napa Valley. The menu alone is reason to come—it features ne'er-changing favorites, from pastas (try the duck Bolognese!) to risottos, to an awesome wood-burning-oven-baked pizza margarita, to a half-dozen other main courses, such as seared salmon filet on buttermilk mashed potatoes and steak frites. But the atmosphere within the huge, colorful, and perky dining room is a winner, too. No matter the occasion, it always feels like a party at Don Gio. On warm, sunny days, dining alfresco on the vineyard-front patio is the way to go, although indoor table and bar service always rock, too. No matter what, order the trifle for dessert. Seriously. *Note:* Service ranges from inattentive to brisk but efficient.

4110 Howard Lane (at St. Helena Hwy.). © **707/224-3300.** www.bistrodongiovanni.com. Reservations recommended. Main courses $20–$38. AE, DC, DISC, MC, V. Sun–Thurs 11:30am–9:30pm; Fri–Sat 11:30am–11pm.

Bistro Jeanty ★★ FRENCH BISTRO This veteran bistro—with muted buttercup walls, patio seats, and two dining rooms divided by the bar—is French chef Philippe Jeanty's ode to rich French comfort food. The all-day menu includes tomato soup in puff pastry, foie gras pâté, steak tartare, and house-smoked trout with potato slices. No meal should start without a paper cone filled with fried smelt, and none should end without the crème brûlée, made with a thin layer of chocolate cream between classic vanilla custard and a caramelized sugar top. In between, prepare yourself for a rib-gripping free-for-all, including coq au vin, cassoulet, and juicy thick-cut pork chop with *jus,* spinach, and mashed potatoes.

6510 Washington St. © **707/944-0103.** www.bistrojeanty.com. Reservations recommended. Appetizers $8.75–$16; most main courses $17–$38. AE, MC, V. Daily 11:30am–10:30pm.

Bottega Ristorante ★ ITALIAN Decorated in the Italian equivalent of the steakhouse—dark leather, pin lights, and brick walls—this sexy Italian hot spot is owned and operated by Food Network star Michael Chiarello, which at least partially explains its popularity. But Chiarello has more going for him than a smile that's made for TV. The guy is a good cook, and evidence can be found in dishes like wood-oven-roasted whole fish with meyer lemon and shaved fennel, and pumpkin and fontina risotto with meat Bolognese. Not everything wows, but no matter. With (relatively) reasonable prices, an awesome scene, and the famed chef himself regularly schmoozing the tables, even on the occasion you do get a just-okay dish, there's much to enjoy here.

6525 Washington St., behind the NapaStyle store. © **707/945-1050.** www.botteganapavalley. com. Reservations recommended. Main courses lunch and dinner $15–$28. AE, DC, DISC, MC, V. Tues–Sun 11:30am–2pm; Mon–Thurs 5:30–9:30pm; Fri–Sat 5–10pm; Sun 5–9:30pm.

Mustards Grill ★ CALIFORNIAN Here the promise is simple: Hyper-flavored (and undeniably tasty) comfort classics with exotic spins in heaping portions. As a popular valley standard for more than 20 years, you should also expect to wait for a table within the convivial, barn-style space—even, annoyingly, if you have a reservation. But once you're settled in with a selection from the 300 New World wine list and raise fork to mouth, all is easily forgiven. Do start with seared *ahi* tuna or moist and meaty crab cakes, and broaden your culinary horizons (not to mention your waistline) with favorites such as Mongolian-style pork chop with hot mustard sauce, or sautéed lemon-garlic half-chicken with mashed potatoes and fresh herbs. And definitely end with their famed lemon-lime tart, which is easily identified by its Bart Simpson hairdo–like meringue topping.

7399 St. Helena Hwy. (Hwy. 29). ✆ **707/944-2424.** www.mustardsgrill.com. Reservations recommended. Main courses $11–$25. AE, DC, DISC, MC, V. Mon–Thurs 11:30am–9pm; Fri 11:30am–10pm; Sat 11am–10pm; Sun 11am–9pm.

Tra Vigne Restaurant ★ ITALIAN   With lots of chef changes over the years and meals that range from totally rockin' to barely so-so, Tra Vigne may not be the culinary mecca it used to be, but it's still the very best outdoor dining venue in the valley. Sit in the Tuscany-evoking courtyard and you'll likely enjoy yourself regardless of whether the kitchen is on the money or missing the mark. The bustling, cavernous dining room and happening bar are fine for chilly days and eves, but they're not nearly as magical. You can also count on wonderful bread (served with house-cured olives), a menu of robust California dishes cooked Italian-style, a daily oven-roasted pizza special, lots of pastas, and such tried-and-true standbys as short ribs and *fritto misto.*

1050 Charter Oak Ave. ✆ **707/963-4444.** www.travigicnerestaurant.com. Reservations recommended. Main courses $16–$25. DC, DISC, MC, V. Summer daily 11:30am–10pm; winter Mon–Thurs 11:30am–9pm, Fri–Sat 11:30am–10pm, Sun 11am–9:30pm.

Ubuntu ★ VEGETARIAN   Named one of the best eateries in the country by multiple sources under its previous chef, this swank downtown Napa spot offers decadent vegetarian cuisine made from sustainably, locally grown ingredients (often plucked from owner Sandy Lawrence's biodynamic garden). The edible action takes place in an eco-friendly room characterized by high stone walls, a large centerpiece community table, and a partitioned upstairs that acts as a yoga studio. Far from familiar vegetarian food, nothing here is mushy, boring, or expected. Don't miss the roast cauliflower—a creamy, dreamy classic—mushroom pizza with homemade goat's-milk ricotta. The best part: You don't need to be crunchy to dine here. Everything about this place is grown-up and elegant.

1140 Main St., near Pearl, Napa. ✆ **707/251-5656.** www.ubuntunapa.com. Reservations recommended. AE, DC, DISC, MC, V. Lunch Sat–Sun 11:30am–2:15pm; dinner Thurs–Mon 5:30–9pm.

INEXPENSIVE

Gott's Roadside Tray Gourmet ✋ DINER   Yet another winner to slip from sublime status to buyer beware, this gourmet roadside burger shack built in 1949 and previously known as "Taylor's Refresher" still draws huge lines of tourists who love the notion of ordering at the counter and feasting alfresco. But truth be told, its burgers, onion rings, and fries are overrated, especially considering the inflated prices. However, it's still the only outdoor burger joint in St. Helena (it also offers ahi tuna burgers and various sandwiches, tacos, soups, and salads), and its everbustling status proves everyone knows it. A second location in Napa at 644 First St. (near Soscal Ave.) is open daily 10:30am to 9pm.

You could plan your entire trip around Napa restaurants, but the valley is also an ideal place for a picnic. One of the finest gourmet food stores in the Wine Country, if not the state, the **Oakville Grocery Co.,** 7856 St. Helena Hwy., at Oakville Cross Road (✆ **707/944-8802;** www.oakvillegrocery.com), is the best place to fill a basket. The store is crammed with the very best breads, cheeses, pâtés, cold cuts, fresh foie gras, smoked Norwegian salmon, fresh caviar (beluga, sevruga, osetra), and prepared foods; its selection of California wines is also exceptional. Assemble your own picnic or let the staff prepare a basket for you, with 24 hours' notice. The Grocery Co. is open daily from 9am to 6pm; it also has an espresso bar (Mon–Fri 7am–6pm; Sat–Sun 8am–6pm), with breakfast and lunch fare, including homemade pastries.

A Manhattan import, **Dean & DeLuca,** 607 S. Main St. (Hwy. 29), north of Zinfandel Lane and south of Sulphur Springs Road, in St. Helena (✆ **707/967-9980;** www.deananddeluca.com), is like a world's fair of beautifully displayed foods, often painfully pricey. Check out the 300 domestic and imported cheeses; tapenade, pastas, oils, hand-packed dried herbs and spices, chocolates, sauces, and cookware; an espresso bar; one heck of a bakery section; and more. The wine shop boasts a 1,200-label collection. It's open daily from 9am to 8pm (the espresso bar opens daily at 7am).

933 Main St. ✆ **707/963-3486.** www.gottsroadside.com. Main courses $7–$14. AE, MC, V. Daily 10:30am–9pm.

Market AMERICAN   If you're in expensive St. Helena and want some casual glamour with your burger, you'll find it here with fancy stone-wall and Brunswick bar surroundings paired with clunky steak knives and simple white-plate presentations. Food, which focuses on classics like meatloaf, fish and chips, and chopped salad, is solid and it's guaranteed to be accompanied by atmospheric surroundings, a reasonable price tag, and a local clientele. At lunch, you can also opt for a three-course meal—one of the valley's best bargains, at a measly $20.

1347 Main St. ✆ **707/963-3799.** www.marketsthelena.com. Most main courses $13–$24. AE, MC, V. Mon–Thurs 11:30am–9pm; Fri–Sat 11:30am–10pm; Sun 10am–3pm and 5–9pm.

Norman Rose Tavern ★ AMERICAN   Despite its unsavory name, Napa's favorite stop for good pub grub is a very welcome departure from the region's pervasive French and Italian menus. Here, within a handsome yet relaxed dining room, it's all about dressed-up classic American comfort foods. All the standbys are present and accounted for—from a build-your-own burger with optional fixin's like an organic fried egg, thyme roasted mushrooms, or smoked bacon, to four types of fries (including chili 'n' cheese!), to grilled flat-iron steak. Equally uncommon for the area are the moderate prices, which is why locals have been instant loyalists since the doors opened in late 2009. FYI, this joint is owned and operated by the folks behind Pizza Azzurro (✆ **707/255-5552;** www.azzurropizzeria.com).

1401 First St. (at Franklin St.), Napa. ✆ **707/258-1516.** www.normanrosenapa.com. Main courses $9.95–$19 lunch and dinner. AE, MC, V. Mon–Thurs 11:30am–10pm; Fri–Sun 11:30am–11pm.

ZuZu ★★ TAPAS   ZuZu lures neighborhood regulars with its no-reservations policy, its cramped but friendly wine and beer bar, and its affordable Mediterranean small plates, meant to be shared. The comfortable, warm atmosphere is anything but corporate. Equally casual and personal, the menu includes sizzling miniskillets of tangy, fantastic paella; addictive prawns with pimento dipping sauce for bread; light and delicate sea scallop seviche salad; and Moroccan barbecued lamb chops with a sweet-and-spicy sauce. Desserts aren't as good, but with more tasty plates than you can possibly devour, who cares?

829 Main St. ✆ **707/224-8555.** www.zuzunapa.com. Reservations not accepted. Tapas $3–$13. AE, MC, V. Mon–Thurs 11:30am–10pm; Fri 11:30am–11pm; Sat 4–11pm; Sun 4–9pm.

SONOMA VALLEY

Sonoma County is often regarded as the "other" Wine Country, forever in the shadow of Napa Valley. The truth, however, is that it's a distinct experience. Sonoma, divided in this book and on most itineraries into two distinct areas— Sonoma Valley, covered here, and Northern Sonoma, covered next—still manages to feel like backcountry, thanks to its lower density of wineries, restaurants, and hotels; because it's far less traveled than Napa, it offers a more genuine escape. Small, family-owned wineries are its mainstay—as in the early days of California winemaking, when everyone started with the intention of going broke and loving every minute of it. Unlike the rigidly structured tours at many of Napa Valley's corporate-owned wineries, tastings and tours on the Sonoma side of the Mayacamas Mountains are usually low-key, with plenty of friendly banter between staff and guests.

Essentials

GETTING THERE   From San Francisco, cross the Golden Gate Bridge and head north on U.S. 101. Exit at Hwy. 37; after 10 miles, turn north onto Hwy. 121. After another 10 miles, turn north onto Hwy. 12 (Broadway), which will take you directly into the town of Sonoma.

VISITOR INFORMATION   While you're in Sonoma, stop by the **Sonoma Valley Visitors Bureau,** 453 First St. E. (✆ **866/996-1090** or 707/996-1090; www.sonomavalley.com). It's open Monday through Saturday from 9am to 5pm (6pm in the summer Fri–Sat) and Sunday 10am to 5pm. If you prefer advance information from the bureau, contact them to order the free *Sonoma Valley Visitors Guide,* which lists almost every lodge, winery, and restaurant in the valley. An additional **Visitors Bureau** is a few miles south of the square at **Cornerstone Festival of Gardens ★,** a cool place to shop for home items and browse dramatically designed gardens at 23570 Arnold Dr. (Hwy. 121; ✆ **866/996-1090**); it's open daily from 9am to 4pm, till 5pm during summer.

Touring the Valley & Wineries

Sonoma Valley is currently home to about 45 wineries (including California's first, Buena Vista, founded in 1857) and 13,000 acres of vineyards, which produce more than five million cases a year of 25 types of wine.

The towns and wineries below are organized geographically from south to north, starting at the intersection of Hwy. 37 and Hwy. 121 in the Carneros District and ending in Kenwood. The wineries here are a little more spread out than they are in Napa, so devise a touring strategy before you set out, to avoid backtracking a lot.

I review some my favorite Sonoma Valley wineries here—more than enough to keep you busy tasting wine for a long weekend. For a complete list, pick up one of the free guides to the valley available at the Sonoma Valley Visitors Bureau (see "Visitor Information," above).

THE CARNEROS DISTRICT

As you approach the Wine Country from the south, you must pass through the Carneros District, a cool, wind-swept region that borders the San Pablo Bay and marks the entrance to both Napa and Sonoma valleys. Until the latter part of the 20th century, this mixture of marsh, sloughs, and hills was mainly used as sheep pasture (*carneros* means "sheep" in Spanish). After experimental plantings yielded slow-growing yet high-quality grapes—particularly chardonnay and pinot noir—several Napa and Sonoma wineries expanded here, eventually establishing the Carneros District as an American Viticultural Appellation.

Viansa Winery and Italian Marketplace ★ 🎁 A sprawling and extremely romantic Tuscan-style villa that overlooks the entire lower valley, Viansa is the brainchild of Sam and Vicki Sebastiani, who left the family dynasty to create their own temple to food and wine. (*Viansa* is a contraction of "Vicki and Sam.") Here you'll find gorgeous views along with a large tasting room crammed with a

Viansa Winery and Italian Marketplace.

cornucopia of high-quality mustards, olive oils, pastas, salads, breads, desserts, Italian tableware, cookbooks, and wine-related gifts.

The winery, which does extensive mail-order business through the Tuscan Club, features Italian varietals. Tastings cost $5 per person and are offered at the east and west end of the marketplace. The self-guided tour includes a trip through the underground barrel-aging cellar, adorned with colorful hand-painted murals.

Viansa is also one of the few wineries in Sonoma Valley that sell deli items; the focaccia sandwiches are delicious.

25200 Arnold Dr. (Calif. 121), Sonoma. © **800/995-4740** or 707/935-4700. www.viansa.com. Daily 10am–5pm. Daily self-guided tours.

Gloria Ferrer Champagne Caves ★ 👜 Gloria Ferrer, the grande dame of the Sonoma Valley's sparkling-wine producers, is named after José Ferrer's wife, whose family has made sparkling wine for 5 centuries. The family business, Freixenet, is the world's largest producer of sparkling wine. That legacy amounts to big bucks, and certainly a good chunk of change went into building this palatial estate. It glimmers like Oz, high atop a gently sloping hill, overlooking the verdant Carneros District. On a sunny day, enjoying a glass of dry *brut* while soaking in the magnificent views is a must.

If you're unfamiliar with the term *méthode champenoise,* take the $10, 30-minute tasting tour of the fermenting tanks, bottling line, and caves brimming with racks of yeast-laden bottles. Afterward, retire to the elegant tasting room, order a glass of one of seven sparkling wines ($5–$10 a glass) or tastes of their eight still wines ($2–$3 per taste), find an empty chair on the veranda, and say, "Ahhh. *This* is the life." There are picnic tables, but it's usually too windy for comfort. You must buy a bottle (around $20–$50) or glass of sparkling wine to reserve a table.

23555 Carneros Hwy. (Calif. 121), Sonoma. © **707/996-7256.** www.gloriaferrer.com. Daily 10am–5pm. Tours daily 11am, 1, and 3pm, $10.

SONOMA

Sonoma, at the northern boundary of the Carneros District along Hwy. 12, is the centerpiece of the valley. The midsize town owes much of its appeal to Mexican general Mariano Guadalupe Vallejo, who fashioned this pleasant, slow-paced community after a typical Mexican village—right down to its central plaza, Sonoma's geographical and commercial center. The plaza sits at the top of a T formed by Broadway (Hwy. 12) and Napa Street. Most of the surrounding streets form a grid pattern around this axis, making Sonoma easy to negotiate. The plaza's Bear Flag Monument marks the spot where the crude Bear Flag was raised in 1846, signaling the end of Mexican rule; the symbol was later adopted by the state of California and placed on its flag. The 8-acre park at the center of the plaza, complete with two ponds populated by ducks and geese, is perfect for an afternoon siesta in the cool shade.

The best way to see the town is to follow the **Sonoma Walking Tour** map, provided by the Sonoma League for Historic Preservation. Highlights include General Vallejo's 1852 Victorian-style home; the Sonoma Barracks, erected in 1836 to house Mexican army troops; and the Blue Wing Inn, an 1840 hostelry built to accommodate new settlers and travelers such as John Fremont, Kit Carson, and Ulysses S. Grant. You can purchase the $3 map at the Mission (see below).

The **Mission San Francisco Solano de Sonoma,** on Sonoma Plaza, at the corner of First Street East and Spain Street (✆ **707/938-9560**), was founded in 1823. It was the northernmost mission built in California. It was also the only one established on the Northern Coast by Mexican rulers, who wished to protect their territory from Russian fur traders. It's now part of Sonoma State Historic Park. Admission is $2 for adults, free for children 16 and under. It's open daily from 10am to 5pm except Thanksgiving, Christmas, and New Year's Day.

Sebastiani Vineyards & Winery ★   The name Sebastiani is practically synonymous with Sonoma. What started in 1904, when Samuele Sebastiani began producing his first wines, has in three generations grown into a small empire, producing some 350,000 cases a year. The original 1904 property is open to the public, with educational tours ($5–$7.50 per person), an 80-foot S-shaped tasting bar, and lots of gift-shopping opportunities. In the contemporary tasting room's minimuseum area, you can see the winery's original turn-of-the-20th-century crusher and press, as well as the world's largest collection of oak-barrel carvings, crafted by bygone local artist Earle Brown. You can sample seven Sonoma County wines for $10. Bottle prices are reasonable, ranging from $13 to $75. A picnic area adjoins the cellars; a far more scenic spot is across the parking lot in Sebastiani's Cherryblock Vineyards.

389 Fourth St. E., Sonoma. ✆ **800/888-5532** or 707/933-3200. www.sebastiani.com. Daily 11am–5pm. Tours daily at 11am, 1, and 3pm.

Buena Vista Carneros Winery ★   Count Agoston Haraszthy, the Hungarian émigré universally regarded as the father of California's wine industry, founded this historic winery in 1857. A close friend of General Vallejo, Haraszthy returned from Europe in 1861 with 100,000 of the finest vine cuttings, which he made available to all growers. Although Buena Vista's winemaking now takes place at an ultramodern facility in the Carneros District, the winery maintains a tasting

---

Garden Detour

Garden lovers should pull over for a gander at the **Cornerstone Festival of Gardens ★**, 23570 Arnold Dr., Sonoma (✆ **707/933-3010**; www.cornerstone gardens.com). Modeled in part after the International Garden festival at Chaumont-sur-Loire in France's Loire Valley and the Grand-Métis in Quebec, Canada, the 9-acre property is the first gallery-style garden exhibit in the United States and includes a series of 22 ever-changing gardens created by famed landscape architects and designers. With a children's garden featuring a brightly colored water tower surrounded by a sand moat and buckets, shovels, and plastic plumbing fittings, this is a great spot for the whole family. The garden's cafe offers light breakfasts, pastries, and espresso drinks, along with a seasonal lunch menu including soups, salads, and huge, fancy sandwiches. It's all served on nifty metal trays, perfect for carrying out to the gardens. If you need some inspiration, you can load up on gardening loot at one of the shops. Open 10am to 5pm daily (gardens close at 4pm) year-round (cafe opens at 9am). Admission to the gardens is free. You can take a self-guided tour anytime; installations are marked with descriptive plaques. Docent tours are available for groups of 10 or more by appointment.

WANNABE WINEMAKERS PACK UP FOR SONOMA'S "grape camp"

It's called **"Grape Camp"** but it's a decidedly adult experience—with much more potent bug juice this time. In September 2009, I joined this tour group of the Sonoma region, led by the Sonoma Winegrape Commission's friendly, boundlessly energetic Larry Levine—our de facto camp counselor, complete with a whistle around his neck. Around 25 of us (mostly couples) were bused around to enjoy extravagant, private dinners overlooking vineyards, and saw every step of the winemaking process at a half dozen wineries, including **Gloria Ferrer** (p. 228), **Marimar Estate** (www.marimarestate.com), and **Stonestreet Winery** (www.stonestreetwines.com), which let us blend wines the way their winemakers do. We learned that this is a difficult task, considering that the wines are blended while they're young and still slightly bitter. A wine-pairing course at **Relish Culinary Adventures** (www.relish culinary.com) divided us into teams and let us whip up pizzas to pair with our assigned wine. My team fumbled for ideas at first but won by matching a full-bodied merlot with our own pie of béchamel sauce, jack cheese, Italian sausage, pear, and sweet basil—so we had bragging rights for the afternoon.

The schedule was jampacked, starting with a 7am bus trip to the vineyards to pick grapes for an hour or so. This prompted a few jokes about tourists paying to pick grapes, but the scenery—in the heart of the Valley, with the mountains visible in the distance—was exhilarating. I chatted up the vineyard reps for winemaking tips while I picked pinot noir.

Dinners were extravagant over-the-top treats: Our first meal at **Arista Winery** (www.aristawinery.com) included a succulent *sous vide*–cooked steak, whipped up for us on-site by Charlie Palmer himself, while we sat outdoors at a long table dotted with 50 bottles of wine from the Russian River Valley. We were happy campers by the time we boarded the bus back to the inn. The second night's meal was set in the gorgeous backyard of winemaker Tom Klein's mansion and had the lively theme of a cook-off between two chefs, Josh Silvers and Jeff Mall; each course included two anonymous dishes, and we voted for "right" chef or "left" chef at the end.

The tour's only downside: The long hours tired some campers. "Who wouldn't cut off their left pinky for an extra hour of sleep tomorrow morning?"

room inside the restored 1862 Press House. The beautiful stone-crafted room brims with wines, wine-related gifts, and accessories. Tastings are $10 for a flight of seven wines. You can take the free self-guided tour anytime during operating hours, but their $20 "Carneros Experience" requires a reservation and pairs five wines with a small plate of food, including cheeses. Various cheeses, salami, bread, and spreads are all available in the tasting room.

18000 Old Winery Rd. (off E. Napa St., slightly northeast of downtown), Sonoma. ℂ **800/926-1266** or 707/265-1472. www.buenavistacarneros.com. Daily 10am–5pm.

Ravenswood Winery   The first winery in the United States to focus primarily on zinfandel—the versatile red grape known here for being big, ripe, juicy, and powerful—Ravenswood underscores its zest for zin with their motto, "No Wimpy Wines." While zins make up about three-quarters of their astonishing

one man commented on the bus after the second dinner, close to midnight.

But it's clear that the itinerary is packed to give customers their money's worth. Of course, it's also in the tourism board's interests to show off the best of Sonoma—they do, and you benefit at every turn. If they were secretly trying to convince us all to move to Sonoma to make wine, I was sold. No, really: In 2011 I moved from New York to San Francisco.

Grape Camp is held at the end of September, with varying dates and itinerary stops. Rates are $1,750 per person (with $150 single supplement fee). Optional third-night stay and lavish group dinner with a winemaker are $250 and $125 extra, respectively. Visit **www.sonomagrapecamp.org** or contact Larry.Levine@sonomagrapecamp.com for more details.

—*Stephen Bassman*

one-million-case production, they also make merlot, cabernet sauvignon, Rhone varietals, and a small amount of chardonnay.

The winery is smartly designed—recessed into the hillside to protect its treasures from the simmering summers. Tours ($15 per person) follow the wine-making process from grape to glass and include a visit to the aromatic oak-barrel aging rooms. You're welcome to bring your own picnic basket to any of the tables, and don't forget to check their website or call to find out if they're having one of their famous ongoing barbecues or winter celebrations. Regardless, tastings are $10 for five Sonoma County wines to $15 for the Vineyard Designate series. Bottles average around $35.

18701 Gehricke Rd. (off Lovall Valley Rd.), Sonoma. ℂ **888/669-4679** or 707/933-2332. www.ravenswoodwinery.com. Daily 10am–4:30pm. Tours at 10:30am; reservations recommended.

GLEN ELLEN

Glen Ellen is a fraction of the size of Sonoma, 7 miles to the south, but it's home to several of the valley's finest wineries, restaurants, and inns. Aside from the addition of a few new restaurants, this charming Wine Country town hasn't changed much since the days when Jack London settled on his Beauty Ranch, a mile west. If you haven't yet decided where you want to set up camp during your visit to the Wine Country, I highly recommend this lovable little town.

Hikers, horseback riders, and picnickers will enjoy **Jack London State Historic Park,** 2400 London Ranch Rd., off Arnold Drive (© **707/938-5216; www.jacklondonpark.com**). Within its 800 acres, which were once home to the renowned writer, you'll find 9 miles of trails, the remains of London's burned-down dream house, a museum, and many ideal picnic spots. The park is open daily from 10am to 5pm; but if you want to see everything, come on the weekend when the cottage is open and docents are available (the cottage is closed and the staff is short-handed during the week due to state budget cutbacks). Admission is $8 per car or $7 per seniors' car.

Benziger Family Winery ★ 🎁 Two generations of Benzigers (*Ben*-zig-ger) run this pastoral, user-friendly property featuring one of the region's most exceptional self-guided tours, gorgeous gardens, a spacious tasting room staffed by amiable folk, and an art gallery. The fun, informative 45-minute tram tour ($15 for adults, $5 for ages 20 and under), pulled by a beefy tractor, winds through the estate vineyards and into caves, and ends with a tasting of one estate wine. Tastings for standard-release wines are $10. Tastes of limited-production, reserve, or estate wines cost $20. The winery has several picnic spots. *Tip:* Tram tickets—a hot item in the summer—are available on a first-come, first-served basis, so arrive early or stop by in the morning to pick up tickets for the afternoon.

1883 London Ranch Rd. (off Arnold Dr., on the way to Jack London State Historic Park), Glen Ellen. © **888/490-2739** or 707/935-3000. www.benziger.com. Tasting room daily 10am–5pm. Tram tours daily (weather permitting) $15 adults, $5 children, every half-hour 11am–3:30pm (except noon).

Benziger Family Winery.

KENWOOD

A few miles north of Glen Ellen along Hwy. 12 is the tiny town of Kenwood, the northernmost outpost of the Sonoma Valley. The town consists of little more than a few restaurants, wineries, and modest homes in the wooded hillsides.

Château St. Jean ★ 🍴 Château St. Jean is notable for its exceptionally beautiful buildings, expansive landscaped grounds, gourmet market–like tasting room, and tasty wines. Among California wineries, it's a pioneer in *vineyard designation*—the procedure of making wine from, and naming it for, a single vineyard. A private drive takes you to what was once a 250-acre country retreat built in 1920; a well-manicured lawn overlooking the meticulously maintained vineyards is now a picnic area, complete with a fountain and picnic tables.

In the huge tasting room—with a charcuterie shop and housewares for sale—you can sample Château St. Jean's bounty, from chardonnays and cabernet sauvignon to fumé blanc, merlot, Johannesburg Riesling, and Gewürztraminer. Tastings are $10 per person, $20 per person for reserve wines.

8555 Sonoma Hwy. (Calif. 12), Kenwood. 🕾 **800/543-7572** or 707/833-4134. www.chateau stjean.com. Tasting daily 10am–4:30pm. At the foot of Sugarloaf Ridge, just north of Kenwood and east of Hwy. 12.

St. Francis Vineyards and Winery Although St. Francis Winery makes commendable chardonnay, zinfandel, and cabernet sauvignon, they're best known for their highly coveted merlot. In fact, Winemaker Tom Mackey, a former high-school English teacher from San Francisco, has been hailed as the "Master of Merlot" by *Wine Spectator* for his uncanny ability to craft the finest merlot in California.

Tastings at the chic tasting room are $10 per person for a choice of five wines from a selection of nationally known brands and wines available only at the winery. For $30 you can try their wine and food pairing that includes a flight of four wines paired with seasonal hors d'oeuvres. Now that St. Francis is planning more special activities, it's worthwhile to call or check their website for their calendar of events.

100 Pythian Rd. (Calif. 12/Sonoma Hwy.), Santa Rosa (at the Kenwood border). 🕾 **800/543-7713,** ext. 242, or 707/833-4666. www.stfranciswinery.com. Daily 10am–5pm.

Where to Stay

If you are having trouble finding a room, call the **Sonoma Valley Visitors Bureau** (🕾 **866/996-1090** or 707/996-1090; www.sonomavalley.com). The staff will try to refer you to a lodging that has a room to spare but won't make reservations for you. Another option is the **Bed and Breakfast Association of Sonoma Valley** (🕾 **800/969-4667;** www.sonomabb.com), which can refer you to a B&B that belongs to the association.

VERY EXPENSIVE

Fairmont Sonoma Mission Inn & Spa ★★★ Set on 12 meticulously groomed acres just blocks from a ramshackle stretch of commercial businesses, the Fairmont Sonoma Mission Inn is the only choice for visitors looking for a world-class resort. The inn consists of a massive three-story replica of a California mission built in 1927, an array of satellite wings housing numerous super-luxury suites, and world-class spa facilities. "Heritage Rooms" in the original building are understated country elegant, and the annexes include more modern, new, and sizable rooms, including their ultraposh Wine Country rooms, featuring king-size beds and huge limestone and marble bathrooms; some units have wood-burning fireplaces, and most have balconies or patios. For the ultimate in luxury, the opulently appointed Mission Suites are the way to go. Golfers will be glad to know the resort is also home to the Sonoma Golf Club.

101 Boyes Blvd., corner of Boyes Blvd. and Calif. 12, P.O. Box 1447, Sonoma, CA 95476. www. fairmont.com/sonoma. ℂ **800/441-1414** or 707/938-9000. Fax 707/938-4250. 226 units. $149–$1,259 double. AE, DC, MC, V. Valet parking is free for day use (spagoers) and $25 for overnight guests. From central Sonoma, drive 3 miles north on Hwy. 12 and turn left on Boyes Blvd. **Amenities:** 2 restaurants; babysitting; bike rental; concierge; golf course; health club and spa; Jacuzzi; 3 large, heated outdoor pools; room service; sauna; free wine tasting (4:30–5:30pm). *In room:* A/C, TV, hair dryer, high-speed Internet access ($14 per day), minibar, free bottle of wine upon arrival.

MODERATE

The Renaissance Lodge at Sonoma ★★   Downtown Sonoma's only large-scale resort is also one of my favorites. Why? It's well equipped, well located, and chic in its country decor, and it has a killer spa. At its center is a U-shaped building with modern and spacious accommodations (all with balconies or patios, and some with fireplaces and tubs with shutters that open from the bathroom to the bedroom), a classic big-hotel lobby, and a large courtyard swimming pool with plenty of lounge chairs. Surrounding the main hotel are luxe one- and two-story cottages. The Raindance Spa, where I've consistently had exceptional massages, makes excellent use of its outdoor public space, with a number of small pools surrounded by lush plants. And as a bonus after your treatment, you get to hang around the pool all day if you want to. Another perk: The on-property restaurant cranks out surprisingly good food—and is extremely accommodating of youthful palates. The only bummer: The place seems a bit short-staffed—as evidenced by lagging response times to maintenance requests and painfully long waits to speak to reception and order room service.

1325 Broadway, Sonoma, CA 95476. www.thelodgeatsonoma.com. ℂ **888/710-8008** or 707/935-6600. Fax 707/935-6829. 182 units. $249–$449 double. AE, MC, V. **Amenities:** Restaurant; concierge; health club and spa; Jacuzzi; large heated outdoor pool; limited room service. *In room:* A/C, TV w/pay movies, hair dryer, MP3 docking station, wet bar in suites and some rooms.

INEXPENSIVE

Beltane Ranch ★★ 🎁   The word *ranch* conjures up a big ol' two-story house in the middle of hundreds of rolling acres, the kind of place where you laze away the day in a hammock watching the grass grow or in the garden pitching horseshoes. Well, friend, you can have all that and more at the well-located Beltane Ranch, a century-old buttercup-yellow manor that's been everything from a bunkhouse to a brothel to a turkey farm. You simply can't help but feel your tensions ease away as you prop your feet up on the shady wraparound porch overlooking the quiet vineyards, sipping a cool, fruity chardonnay. Each room is uniquely decorated with modest American and European antiques; all have sitting areas and separate entrances. A big country breakfast is served in the garden or on the porch overlooking the vineyards. For exercise, you can play tennis on the private court or hike the trails meandering through the 105-acre estate. The staff here is knowledgeable and helpful. *Tip:* Request one of the upstairs rooms for the best views.

11775 Sonoma Hwy./Hwy. 12, P.O. Box 395, Glen Ellen, CA 95442. www.beltaneranch.com. ℂ **707/996-6501.** 5 units, 1 cottage. $150–$240 double. Rates include full breakfast. DISC, MC, V; personal checks accepted. **Amenities:** Outdoor, unlit tennis court. *In room:* No phone, free Wi-Fi.

Best Western Sonoma Valley Inn ☺ Perfect for the traveling family, this simple inn offers plenty of diversions for kids on the road. There's room to run around, plus a large heated outdoor saltwater pool, gazebo-covered spa, and sauna to play in. The rooms come with a lot of perks, such as continental breakfast delivered to your room each morning, a gift bottle of white Sonoma Valley wine (chilling in the fridge), and satellite TV with HBO. Most rooms have a balcony or a deck overlooking the inner courtyard. An added bonus: If you need someone to help you get the kinks out, you can reserve one of the two spa rooms and have the staff book someone from an outside company to come in and give you a massage. The inn is also in a good location, just a block from Sonoma's plaza.

550 Second St. W. (1 block from the plaza), Sonoma, CA 95476. www.sonomavalleyinn.com. ℭ **800/334-5784** or 707/938-9200. Fax 707/938-0935. 80 units. $114–$369 double. Rates include continental breakfast. AE, DC, DISC, MC, V. **Amenities:** Exercise room; Jacuzzi; heated outdoor pool; steam room. *In room:* A/C, TV, fridge, hair dryer, Wi-Fi.

El Pueblo Inn ★ On Sonoma's main east-west street, 8 blocks from the center of town, this isn't Sonoma's fanciest hotel, but it is well cared for and offers some of the best-priced accommodations around. The rooms here are pleasant enough, with individual entrances, post-and-beam construction, exposed brick walls, light-wood furniture, down comforters, recliners, and geometric prints. A new addition in 2002 resulted in 20 new larger rooms with high ceilings, DVDs, and fireplaces (in some). They also recently made each room open onto a courtyard with a fountain. Their new reception area doubles as a breakfast room for their continental breakfast and leads to a small meeting room. Reservations should be made at least a month in advance for the spring and summer months.

896 W. Napa St., Sonoma, CA 95476. www.elpuebloinn.com. ℭ **800/900-8844** or 707/996-3651. Fax 707/935-5988. 53 units. Apr–Nov $184–$299 double; Dec–Mar $109–$169 double. AE, DC, DISC, MC, V. Corporate, AAA, and senior discounts available. **Amenities:** Fitness room; Jacuzzi; seasonal heated outdoor pool. *In room:* A/C, TV, DVD (newer rooms only), fridge, hair dryer, high-speed Internet access.

Where to Eat

Though Sonoma Valley has far fewer visitors than Napa Valley, its restaurants are often equally crowded, so be sure to make reservations in advance.

EXPENSIVE

the girl & the fig ★★ COUNTRY FRENCH French-influenced nouveau country cuisine and magical outdoor surroundings are the prime draws to this well-loved restaurant owned by Sondra Bernstein (the girl). And, yes, figs are sure to be on the menu in one form or another. The chef uses garden-fresh produce and local meats, poultry, and fish whenever possible, in dishes such as sautéed bay scallops with parsnip purée, local chanterelle mushrooms, green garlic, and veal reduction; or roasted Sonoma County half-chicken with honey-roasted root vegetables, house-made bacon, and chestnut ragout. For dessert, try lavender crème brûlée, a glass of Botrytis Late Harvest Roussanne, and a sliver of something delicious from the cheese list. The wine list features Rhone varietals, and the staff is happy to help you choose the best accompaniment for your meal. Sunday brunch, served until 3pm, is a worthwhile endeavor.

GOURMET picnics, SONOMA STYLE

Sonoma's central plaza, with its many picnic tables, is an optimal spot to set up your own lunch spread. The venerable **Sonoma Cheese Factory,** on the plaza at 2 Spain St. (© **707/996-1000;** daily 8:30am–5:30pm), sells award-winning house-made cheeses and imported meats and cheeses; a few are set out for tasting every day. Caviar, gourmet salads, pâté, and homemade Sonoma jack cheese are also for sale. You can pick up some good, inexpensive sandwiches too—such as the fire-roasted pork loin or New York steak.

110 W. Spain St. © **707/938-3634.** www.thegirlandthefig.com. Reservations recommended. Main courses $13–$24. AE, DISC, MC, V. Daily 11:30am–10pm; Sun brunch 10am. Late-night brasserie menu until 11pm Fri–Sat.

MODERATE

Cafe La Haye ★★ ECLECTIC   Everything about this cafelike restaurant is charming. The small split-level dining room is smart and intimate, the vibe is boutique, and the straightforward, seasonally inspired cuisine from the tiny open kitchen is delicious and wonderfully well priced. Although the menu is small, it offers just enough options. Expect a risotto special; pasta such as fresh *tagliarini* with butternut squash, prosciutto, sage, and garlic cream; and pan-roasted chicken breast, perhaps with goat cheese–herb stuffing, caramelized shallot *jus,* and fennel mashed potatoes. Meat eaters are sure to be pleased with the perfectly cooked filet of beef seared with black pepper and lavender and served with Gorgonzola-potato gratin.

140 E. Napa St. © **707/935-5994.** www.cafelahaye.com. Reservations recommended. Main courses $17–$27. AE, MC, V. Tues–Sat 5:30–9pm.

Della Santina's ★ TUSCAN   For those who just can't swallow another chichi California meal, follow the locals to this friendly, traditional Italian restaurant. How traditional? Ask father-and-son team Dan and Robert, who proudly point out Signora Santina's hand-embroidered linen doilies and discuss her Tuscan recipes. Their pride is merited: Dishes are authentic and well flavored, without overbearing sauces or one hint of California pretentiousness. Start with traditional antipasti, particularly sliced mozzarella and tomatoes; move on to one of the nine authentic pasta dishes; or opt for spit-roasted chicken, pork, turkey, rabbit, or duck—or a selection of three. **Perk:** You can guiltlessly order a bottle of wine, since many choices here go for under $40. Portions are huge, but save room for dessert, like the creamy *panna cotta.* Though the inside's small, a huge back patio covered in blooming trellises is full practically every night in the summer (the wait's never too bad), and they've recently tented part of it, so you can eat back there in winter too, weather permitting.

133 E. Napa St. (just east of the square). © **707/935-0576.** www.dellasantinas.com. Reservations recommended. Main courses $12–$18. AE, DISC, MC, V. Daily 11:30am–3pm and 5–9:30pm.

El Dorado Kitchen ★ CALIFORNIAN   Downtown Sonoma's most hip and contemporary restaurant, which has sexy seating indoors and out, entices with a seasonal menu ("Mediterranean-inspired bistro cuisine") of familiar items with unfamiliar twists—think griddled prosciutto and Vermont cheddar sandwiches with San Marzano tomato soup or curry *fritto misto* (lightly battered and fried apples, cauliflower, and fall squash served with curry salt and aioli). Entrees might include Pacific salmon with white-bean cassoulet, prosciutto, and sage; or lamb loin with rosemary polenta, *piquillo* peppers, Swiss chard, and Niçoise olive sauce. Don't hesitate to order the white truffle and Parmesan french fries and one of their house drinks.

405 First St. W. ℂ **707/996-3030.** www.eldoradosonoma.com. Reservations recommended. Lunch $15–$25; dinner $12–$29; brunch $10–$20. AE, MC, V. Mon–Sat 11:30am–2:30pm and 5:30–9pm; Sun 11am–2:30pm and 5:30–9pm.

Glen Ellen Inn Oyster Grill & Martini Bar ★ CALIFORNIAN   Christian and Karen Bertrand have made this place so quaint and cozy you feel you're dining in their home, and that's exactly the place's charm. Garden seating is the favored choice on sunny days, but the covered, heated patio is also always welcoming. Courses from Christian's open kitchen are exotic—think ginger tempura calamari with wasabi or brie fondue with sourdough toast points for starters. Entrees, which change with the seasons, range from pumpkin ravioli with roasted butternut squash sauce to grilled salmon with tomatillo sauce and corncake. And let's not forget the eponymous oyster grill and martini bar, which includes half-size martinis (genius!) and oysters any way you want 'em. If that doesn't do it for you, the 550-plus wine list offers numerous bottles from Sonoma, as well as more than a dozen wines by the glass. *Tip:* A small parking lot is behind the restaurant.

13670 Arnold Dr. (at O'Donnell Lane). ℂ **707/996-6409.** www.glenelleninn.com. Reservations recommended. Main courses $14–$25. AE, DISC, MC, V. Fri–Tues 11:30am–9pm (dinner from 5pm); Wed–Thurs 5:30–9pm. Brunch Sat–Sun 10:30am–5pm. Closed 1 week in Jan.

Harvest Moon Cafe ★★ REGIONAL SEASONAL AMERICAN   If great food is essential to your experience, don't miss this restaurant run by chef/owner Nick Demarest, whose experience at Berkeley's world-famous Chez Panisse is evidenced by his use of outstanding ingredients combined into dishes of clean, pure, and glorious flavors. His chicory salad with mustard vinaigrette, house-cured pancetta, and Gruyère is a case-in-point appetizer that's easily backed up by entrees such as grilled lamb with saffron risotto and olive tapenade. Sweetening the already-delicious deal, his wife, Jen, is a pedigreed pastry chef. The interior is awkward, with the chef hard at work within the shoebox-size open kitchen and a quirky scattering of tables tucked within a cramped and warm historic adobe room. But seats at the wine bar are great, and, weather permitting, the back-garden dining is spacious and relaxed. Regardless, if it's a good meal you're after, you will not find a better one this side of the Mayacamas.

487 First St. W. ℂ **707/933-8160.** www.harvestmooncafesonoma.com. Reservations recommended. Main courses $17–$26. AE, DISC, MC, V. Sun–Thurs 5:30–9pm; Fri–Sat 5:30–9:30pm; Sun brunch 10am–2pm.

INEXPENSIVE

Black Bear Diner ☺ DINER   When you're craving a classic American breakfast, with all the cholesterol and the fixings, make a beeline to this old-fashioned diner. One, it's fun, with its over-the-top bear paraphernalia, gazette-style menu listing local news from 1961 and every possible diner favorite, and absurdly friendly waitstaff. Two, it's darned cheap. Three, helpings are huge. Four, it appeals to all ages: Kids get a kick out of the coloring books, old-timers reminisce over Sinatra on the jukebox, and everyone leaves stuffed on omelets, scrambles, and pancakes. Lunch and dinner feature steak sandwiches, salads, and comfort foods such as barbecued pork ribs, roast beef, fish and chips, and spaghetti with meat sauce. You can fill up here on the cheap, especially since dinners come with salad or soup, bread, and two sides; seniors can order from a specially discounted menu.

201 W. Napa St. (at Second St.). (C) **707/935-6800.** www.blackbeardiner.com. Main courses breakfast $5–$8.50; lunch and dinner $5.50–$17. AE, DISC, MC, V. Daily 6am–9:30pm (closing varies on weekends, depending on business).

Taste of the Himalayas ★ NEPALESE/INDIAN   If you're looking for something other than the usual pizzas, pastas, and burritos, this is your spot. Just what does a Nepalese meal entail? Start with crisp *samosas* (a mild blend of potatoes and peas served with mint sauce) or *momos* (small steamed dumplings stuffed with either lamb or veggies). Move on to entrees such as curry or Tandoori dishes, which wash down nicely with Indian Taj Mahal beer. All entrees come with a delicious bowl of mild *daal bhat,* the traditional Indian lentil soup; your choice of basmati rice or *naan;* and casual but attentive service.

464 First St. E. (C) **707/996-1161.** Reservations recommended, but walk-ins welcome. Main courses $10–$18. AE, MC, V. Daily 11am–2:30pm and 5–10pm.

NORTHERN SONOMA

Most visitors to Northern California Wine Country relegate their vacation time to Napa Valley or Sonoma Valley. But insiders have long known that the best of both worlds can be found in Northern Sonoma. Here, amid hundreds of acres of vineyards, are family-owned wineries, adorable B&Bs, charming towns, friendly residents, classic river fun in summertime, and, of course, more than your share of outstanding food and wine experiences. Add to that the best shopping (in Healdsburg) and less traffic on the charming country roads and in the tasting rooms, and you might begin to understand why this region is now a bona fide hot spot.

Essentials

GETTING THERE   From San Francisco, cross the Golden Gate Bridge and head north on U.S. 101. It's around 1½ hours to Healdsburg, the wine area's commercial and social hub.

VISITOR INFORMATION   Northern Sonoma doesn't have one major convention and visitors bureau representing the entire region. Fortunately, if you visit **www.sonomacounty.com**, it will direct you to the various visitors bureaus. However, there's plenty of information available if you contact the following sources. The **Santa Rosa Convention & Visitors Bureau,** 9 Fourth St., Santa Rosa, CA 95401 ((C) **800/404-7673** or 707/577-8674), can give you the scoop on all things Santa Rosa, as well as a bit about the areas and wineries to the north. Or you can get information by visiting **www.visitsanta rosa.com**.

   Farther north, if you roll into downtown Healdsburg off of Hwy. 101, you'll pass the **Healdsburg Chamber of Commerce and Visitors Bureau** (217 Healdsburg Ave., Healdsburg; (C) **800/648-9922** from within California or 707/433-6935; www.healdsburg.com). It's definitely worth a pit stop to get brochures and answers to any questions from their very helpful staff.

Touring the Valley & Wineries

Touring Northern Sonoma is very different from the winery-hopping in Napa and Sonoma valleys. Sipping destinations are scattered over a vast landscape of tiny towns surrounded by open land, miles of vineyards, and great destinations for outdoor fun. And they're tucked away on one-lane roads that would be impossible to find if it weren't for the periodic white arrow signs pointing you in the right direction. They are also far more mom and pop, which means it's very likely you'll rub elbows with winemaker/owners as you taste at their bars. Alas, this piece of paradise has become more known as *the* hot vacation spot, but it's still less crowded than the alternatives. Of course, you should chart your path—or, at least, attempt to—before going. But keep in mind that the diversions you'll stumble upon along the way are likely to slow you down—in a good way.

GUERNEVILLE

69 miles N of San Francisco

The town closest to the Russian River may be slightly short on wineries, but it's long on outdoor fun.

One of my all-time favorite summertime excursions—canoeing—can be embarked upon from the tiny area of Forestville, adjacent to Guerneville. At **Burke's Canoes ★★**, 8600 River Rd., at Mirabel Rd. (© **707/887-1222;** www.burkescanoetrips.com), it's an all-day adventure. You simply pack a lunch (ideally, wrapped in a waterproof bag); park the car; leave anything you don't want to get wet in the trunk (and all your valuables, at the hotel); pay $60 (cash only) for a canoe that can comfortably fit three adults (the minimum required is two adults) or two adults plus one to two children between the ages of 5 and 11; throw on a bathing suit, sunscreen, and a life vest (included); and launch yourself onto the Russian River. It's a leisurely paddle downstream, with the occasional tricky turn—especially during early summer when the water is higher. During the 10-mile journey, you'll pass beaches that beg for you to pause and bask, redwood trees, and kids jumping off rocks and rope swings, before arriving at a well-marked beach where Burke's staff will pick you up and take you back to your car. Though you can make the journey in about 3 hours, you're more likely to spend 4 or 5 with pit stops to swim, eat, and laze. Definitely reserve your canoe in advance. This is a popular activity. Also, Burke's welcomes confident swimmers only—and children over 5 years of age. One more thing: Burke's also rents kayaks ($40 per person) and offers campsites (BYO tent and equipment) on the beach or in a wooded area for $10 per person per night, and the property includes hot showers and picnic tables.

Should you be more of a landlubber, you can also simply spread a towel and picnic feast at **Johnson's Beach ★** (near downtown Guerneville, off Church St.; © **707/869-2022;** www.johnsonsbeach.com), a river resort with a big stretch of pebbly sand and snack bar that's popular with frolicking families. You can also rent a kayak, canoe, or paddle boat here from May to October. Don't come for an early-morning or evening dip—the resort is open only from 10am to 6pm daily.

Another exceptional way to experience the natural beauty of this region is on **horseback.** Longtime residents Laura and Jonathan Ayers are behind the **Armstrong Woods Pack Station** ★★ (✆ **707/887-2939;** http://redwood horses.com), which offers guided trail rides through old-growth redwood forests. All rides include instruction and a rest or lunch stop on top of a ridge with fabulous valley views. You can saddle up year-round, weather and trail conditions permitting. Prices start at $80 per adult and $75 per child for a 2½-hour ride.

To find out more about the Russian River area and its activities, contact the **Russian River Chamber of Commerce Visitors Center** (16209 First St., at the historic bridge, Guerneville; ✆ **877/644-9001** or 707/869-9000; www. russianriver.com).

Korbel Champagne Cellars ★ Okay, so technically they don't manufacture—or cellar—"champagne," since they're not located in the region of the same name in France. But that doesn't stop visitors from sipping bubbly, getting a good buzz, and having a great time here. Set in a redwood grove at the eastern edge of the town of Guerneville, Korbel is a winemaking relic with more than 120 years of history under its grape-growing belt. You can peruse the ivy-draped brick winery and its stunning gardens, take an informative tour that explains their production process, and grab picnic snacks at their Delicatessen and Market. A bottle of bubbly will set you back $10 to $25, while tastes and tours are free. May through mid-October, flower lovers should detour to browse the Antique Rose Gardens' 250 varieties of antique roses. To confirm tour times, call ✆ **707/824-7316.**

13250 River Rd. (at the eastern entrance of downtown), Guerneville. ✆ **707/824-7000.** www. korbel.com. Tasting room May 1–Sept 30 9am–5pm; Oct 1–Apr 30 10am–4:30pm. Tours in winter are daily, every hour on the hour 11am–3pm; in summer, Mon–Fri every 45 min. 10am–3:45pm; weekends and holidays at 10, 11am, and noon, and then every 45 min. until 3:45pm. Rose Garden tours May through mid-Oct Tues–Sun at 1 and 3pm. From Hwy. 101, take the River Rd. exit, turn left (westbound) onto River Rd., and follow it for 13 miles.

HEALDSBURG

65 miles N of San Francisco

A mere 30- to 45-minute drive from either valley and just north of the burgeoning suburb of Santa Rosa, Healdsburg's centerpiece historic square, which has been the heart of the town since its inception in 1857, captures the quaint shopping and dining experiences of downtown Sonoma—only better. Meanwhile, a few blocks away, rural roads lead to country B&Bs, homey wineries, and an abundance of Victorian architecture that gives the region an old-world charm. Adding to its intrinsic allure, the town is surrounded by all the premier viticultural areas, allowing for easy access to Russian River, Dry Creek, Alexander Valley, and Chalk Hill.

Rather than driving from winery to winery, consider maneuvering on two wheels along the quiet country roads. **Wine Country Bikes** (✆ **866/ 922-4537;** www.winecountrybikes.com) offers day rentals (with maps) and guided tours. A road bike goes for $55 per day and includes a helmet, lock, bag, and route suggestions. You can also rent a tandem (two-person) road bike for $125 per day. An all-day tour goes for $129 per person and includes a picnic lunch, wine tasting, and a van to lug any goodies you buy along the way.

Passalacqua ★ A romantic rural vision with a white wisteria-draped trellis, rows of old vines, umbrella-shaded tables on a patio overlooking vineyards, and a

Biking in Wine Country.

modest, welcoming tasting room pouring free samples, this family-owned winery, which was previously Pezzi King, has long been a vision of idyllic Wine Country. But since young Jason Passalacqua bought it some years ago, a lot has changed, especially regarding winemaking, since Margaret Davenport, a veteran from Clos du Bois, was appointed winemaker. Along with overseeing the development of on-site production facilities, she garnered recognition for the winery when her 2002 Dry Creek Old Vine zinfandel made the *San Francisco Chronicle*'s top 100 wine list for 2004. Drop by, absorb the afternoon sun on the patio, and see for yourself why I consider this a worthy stop.

3805 Lambert Bridge Rd. (at Dry Creek Rd.), Healdsburg. ✆ **877/825-5547.** www.passalacquawinery.com. Daily 11am–5pm. From Hwy. 101, take Dry Creek Rd. west, and turn left on Lambert Bridge Rd.

Rochioli Vineyard & Winery ★ Here it's all about the wine—no fancy logo shirts for sale, no tours, and no hard-selling or snobby staff. In fact, the only extra embellishments the simple room and its surroundings have are rotating local art and crafts and a few picnic tables on the patio. And rightly so. Rochioli (pronounced *Ro*-kee-*o*-lee) makes excellent sauvignon blanc, chardonnay, and pinot noir. It's so good that, at certain times of year, they must limit the sales of their total annual production of 12,000 cases of wine to make sure people like you get to buy a bottle when you visit. Accordingly, the staff will sell you only a limited amount (ranging from one bottle to a case) of what's currently available; prices range from $20 to $52 per bottle.

6192 Westside Rd. (near Sweetwater Springs Rd.), Healdsburg. ✆ **707/433-2305.** www.rochioli winery.com. Thurs–Mon 11am–4pm. Tues–Wed by appointment only.

Ferrari-Carano Vineyards & Winery ★ The hands-down winner for most stunning landscaping goes to this vineyard known for producing everything from fumé blanc to zinfandel. Come during spring, when the air is sweet with aromas drifting from the abundant wisteria and the grounds are in bloom with literally thousands of tulips. Come any time of year to meander the formal Asian garden, abounding with rhododendron, Japanese arched bridges, boxwood, maples, magnolia, and roses—and, of course, to taste wines and enjoy quintessential Wine Country views. Alas, the tasting room and gift shop is more big-business than country, with plenty of logo items and fine wines to taste and carry. If you're interested in the tour, which previews the winery and its production process and is offered Monday through Saturday at 10am only, make a reservation; it's required and can be made by calling ✆ **800/831-0381,** ext. 251. Tasting prices are $5 for a selection of four current releases and are refunded with a $25 purchase.

8761 Dry Creek Rd., Healdsburg. © **707/433-6700.** www.ferrari-carano.com. Daily 10am–5pm. Tours Mon–Sat 10am with a reservation. From Hwy. 101, take Dry Creek Rd. exit headed west and go 9 miles.

Bella Vineyards & Wine Caves ★★   Do yourself a favor—make a point of winding your way over to this ridiculously charming-chic winery specializing in hearty, spicy, old-vine zinfandel and red Rhone varieties. Though when you step out of the car, don't head toward the quaint barnlike building flanked by century-old olive trees. Instead, beeline through the mysterious arched doors built into the hillside to enter their too-cool cave tasting room, complete with cafe tables, chic hanging lamps, and a small casual area where staff will serve you tastes for a $5 fee. Or book a $20 cave tour (with advance notice) or reserve a picnic table plus delivered box lunches (arranged in advance by Bella). Regardless, you're destined for a very unique, scenic, and tasty experience.

9711 W. Dry Creek Rd., Healdsburg. © **866/572-3552** or 707/473-9171. www.bellawinery.com. Daily 11am–4:30pm. Appointment necessary for groups of 8 or more. Appointment recommended for cave tours and picnics; call for times.

Preston of Dry Creek ★★   Preston's wines are fine, but what makes this one of my favorite stops in all of Northern Sonoma is everything else about the place—the winding dirt road that leads to the parking lot; the rustic grassy area outside with picnic tables, well-established wisteria, games of bocce; and the supercute tasting room and store, which is located in a farmhouse and comes complete with all the charm you'd expect. Follow the neon sign's instruction and "drink zin," but also dabble in the broad selection of Rhone varietals made here—including mourvedre, viognier, roussanne, Barbera, and Syrah ($10 per tasting, which is refundable with purchase). By the way, you can taste more of owner Lou Preston's passions here: Organic vegetables grown on the property, and bread baked in the property's custom wood-fired brick oven, are sold here daily. The bread sells out quickly, so arrive early to indulge.

9282 W. Dry Creek Rd. (about 1 mile west of Yoakim Bridge Rd.), Healdsburg. © **707/433-3372.** www.prestonofdrycreek.com. Daily 11am–4:30pm.

J Vineyards & Winery ★   J is best known for its sparkling wines (hence the popularity of its "Bubble Room") but has also found a niche in the pinot noir and chardonnay markets. J hosts a variety of sexy winery experiences, from basic tastings to private wine and food pairings, on its 274 acres of Russian River Valley vineyards. Tastings aren't cheap, but food and bubbly lovers shouldn't balk at the expense, which ranges from $20 per person for a flight of five wines to $60 per person for a flight of six wines paired with six exquisite food preparations (which might include butternut squash soup served in a hollowed pumpkin, or foie gras).

11447 Old Redwood Hwy., Healdsburg. © **888/JWINECO** (594-6326) or 707/431-3646. www.jwine.com. Daily 11am–5pm. Bubble Room Fri–Sun 11am–4pm. Reservations recommended.

Where to Stay

For more lodging options, check **http://Sonoma.com** and **http://winecountry.com**.

VERY EXPENSIVE

The Farmhouse Inn & Restaurant ★   The Farmhouse Inn, located in a speck of a town just outside of Guerneville, may be more famous for its destination restaurant than its rooms, but that doesn't mean the accommodations here aren't praiseworthy. In fact, the inn has been named one of the nation's top 30 by *Travel + Leisure* magazine. Run by the Bartolomei family, who are fourth-generation Forestvilleans, the 6-acre rural property is lined with superbly spacious and charming cottages. Each looks English-country from the outside and creatively cozy from within. Exceedingly spacious rooms are individually decorated with colorful walls adorned with whimsical sayings; surprise amenities such as saunas, whirlpool tubs, or steam showers; a fireplace; quality bath products; and a good dose of solitude. Common areas include a truly beautiful and superb European country–style restaurant complete with excellent wine list, polished service, and Michelin-star ranking; a heated outdoor pool; a "farm to table" luxury spa that incorporates fresh products grown on the ranch property into fabulous treatments; and a demonstration vineyard and rose garden. Smokers should book elsewhere; this piece of paradise is all nonsmoking.

7871 River Rd., Forestville, CA 95436. www.farmhouseinn.com. © **800/464-6642** or 707/887-3300. 18 units. $325–$745 double. AE, DISC, MC, V. **Amenities:** Restaurant; concierge; heated outdoor pool (May 1–Oct 31); spa; Wi-Fi. *In room:* Flatscreen TV w/cable, DVD player, fridge, hair dryer.

Healdsburg Inn on the Plaza ★★   As the name suggests, this quaint 12-room abode run by Four Sisters boutique hotels is smack in the middle of Healdsburg's downtown center. But what the title won't tell you is that this posh little place offers spacious, well-appointed rooms with high ceilings, contemporary-chic decor in soothing colors, fireplaces, and private bathrooms (many with large jetted tubs). Pampering perks include complimentary afternoon wine, cheese, and fruit in the upstairs lounge and a scrumptious breakfast in bed for a mere $10 per room (or free buffet breakfast in the lounge); the price of a night here comes with the polished hospitality that has made Four Sisters a name in Northern California. *Tip:* Just say no to the "homey" first-floor corner room. It looks onto a dark alley and doesn't have the luminous, warm quality of other rooms.

112 Matheson St. (btw. Healdsburg Ave. and Center St.), Healdsburg, CA 95448. www.healdsburg inn.com. © **800/431-8663.** 12 units. $275–$360 double. Rate includes full breakfast and afternoon wine and hors d'oeuvres. AE, DISC, MC, V. **Amenities:** Video library; free Wi-Fi. *In room:* A/C, TV/VCR or DVD, hair dryer.

Hotel Healdsburg ★★   The first "upscale" property to debut in Healdsburg when it opened in 2001, this home-away-from-home across the street from the plaza is a visitor favorite not only for its spacious, comfortable rooms adorned with country-chic furnishings (think Pottery Barn), but also for its amenities. A spa, an outdoor heated pool, and a lobby flush with oversize couches are only the beginning. Add famed chef Charlie Palmer's **Dry Creek Kitchen** (© **707/431-0330;** www.charliepalmer.com/dry_creek) and rooms with big fluffy beds, oversize bathrooms with glass walk-in showers (some with soaking tubs), and, in many cases, balconies. An added bonus for the business-minded traveler (or anyone who wants to send an e-mail), each floor has a computer with free Internet access. FYI, the property is completely nonsmoking.

25 Matheson St. (at the square), Healdsburg, CA 95448. www.hotelhealdsburg.com. © **800/ 889-7188** or 707/431-2800. Fax 707/431-0414. 55 units. $275–$510 double; $440–$820 junior and 1-bedroom suite. Rates include a "country harvest" breakfast. AE, MC, V. Free valet parking. **Amenities:** Restaurant; cafe; bar; concierge; Jacuzzi; heated outdoor pool; room service; spa; free Wi-Fi. *In room:* A/C, TV/DVD, CD player, fridge, hair dryer.

MODERATE

Best Western Dry Creek Inn   It's not exactly a romantic Wine Country get-away, but anyone looking for a wonderfully clean and affordable place to crash after a day of wining and dining will be very happy here—especially considering all the extras. The basic motel rooms come equipped with small fridges for chilling your wine and picnic items, and the property has a tiny fitness room for working off the extra calories you're inevitably getting. If you're willing to fork over a little extra cash, definitely opt for one of the 60 newer rooms in their brand-new adjoining building. Each has a king-size bed, fireplace, Jacuzzi, and flatscreen TV. Add to that free high-speed Internet access and the great promotions featured on their website, and you've found one of the Wine Country's best bargains. It's still expensive, but that's Healdsburg for you.

198 Dry Creek Rd., Healdsburg, CA 95448. www.drycreekinn.com. ℂ **800/222-5784** or 707/433-0300. 163 units. $89–$359 double. AE, DC, DISC, MC, V. **Amenities:** Exercise room; small heated outdoor pool. *In room:* A/C, TV w/pay movies, fridge, hair dryer, free high-speed Internet.

Boon Hotel + Spa ★★   Nestled in a sunny clearing amid towering redwoods, this gloriously laid-back green-minded resort makes it impossible not to relax and enjoy. Its top selling point (well, one of them) is its heated outdoor saline pools (one swimming pool and one hot tub) flanked with comfy-chic Thai lounge furnishings—and an outdoor bar. Soothing, modern-minimal accommodations feature organic bedding, eco-friendly EO bath products, and fluffy organic cotton robes; most have fireplaces, and all but one have private backyards. Free bikes are available for hotel guests, and there's good news for dog parents: Owners Crista Luedtke and Jill McCall, who named the resort after their dog—Boon can be found roaming the property—encourage four-legged canine guests.

14711 Armstrong Woods Rd., Guerneville, CA 95446. www.boonhotels.com. ℂ **707/869-2721.** 14 units. $145–$290 double. Rates include continental breakfast. AE, MC, V. **Amenities:** Poolside bar; concierge; outdoor saline solar-heated pool; saline hot tub; room service; Wi-Fi. *In room:* TV/DVD, fridge in some rooms, hair dryer.

Piper Street Inn   This 1882 Victorian home, located about 5 blocks from the Healdsburg Plaza, is about as homey as Wine Country digs get. With only two rental options—a one-room suite in the house and the cottage in the garden—the Piper Street Inn is a good place to get away from the Wine Country whirlwind. At $195 per night, the Garden Suite (located in the main house), adorned with old photos and antiques, provides guests with a cozy queen-size bed, a down comforter, a fridge, an electric fireplace, and a small sitting area and private bathroom. The cottage behind the house promises more privacy, a fireplace, a kitchenette, and a two-person whirlpool tub. Either way, you'll enjoy a continental breakfast each morning, complimentary wine in the evening, and affordable accommodations mere blocks from the heart of Healdsburg. Another bonus: Children and pets are welcome.

402 Piper St., Healdsburg, CA 95448. www.piperstreetinn.com. ℂ **877/703-0570** or 707/433-8721. AE, MC, V. $195 1-room suite; $265 private cottage. Rates include continental breakfast and wine evenings. **Amenities:** Video library; Wi-Fi. *In room:* A/C, TV/VCR.

Where to Eat

No area in Wine Country has seen more culinary growth over the past few years than Northern Sonoma. But even before the true destination restaurants arrived, this region was still a fantastic place to dine—thanks to sweet little country restaurants and a few more contemporary staples. But now you've got even more options. Outstanding sushi, chic small plates, truly world-class experiences, excellent baked goods—they're all available, provided you make a reservation.

VERY EXPENSIVE

Cyrus ★★★ 🎁 FRENCH/INTERNATIONAL   Cyrus is characterized by a romantic Burgundy, France–inspired interior and friendly yet somewhat formal atmosphere, and to-die-for two-Michelin-star-rated seasonal "contemporary luxury" cuisine. This fine dining room run by veteran San Francisco maitre d' Nick Peyton and 2009 James Beard Award–winning chef Douglas Keane is truly a gastronome's dream destination. The intimate vaulted room is warmly lit, with colors of deep chocolate and gold brightened by ruffled white curtains. An evening appropriately starts, if your heart desires, with selections from carts showcasing caviar (measured to order on a scale against tiny gold bars and served with an excitingly postmodern take on traditional trimmings) and champagne. It continues with a five- or eight-course build-your-own menu, which might include heavenly seared foie gras with pineapple and *pain pardu* and star anise ginger broth; duck breast with scallion rice cake and ponzu; and lamb roulade with celery root, parsnip, and turnip. Everything is as stunning to look at as it is to taste. *Note:* The small bar, where the specialty drinks are as creative and revered as the food, is perfect for impromptu snacking and sipping.

29 North St. (at Healdsburg Ave.). ☎ **707/433-3311.** www.cyrusrestaurant.com. Reservations required. 5 courses $102, 8 courses $130. AE, MC, V. Thurs–Mon 5:30–9:30pm.

MODERATE

Bistro Ralph ★ CALIFORNIAN   On the square, industrial-chic Bistro Ralph is the locals' longtime standby for fresh, tasty, and familiar comfort foods and an upbeat, casual environment. Whether seated in the narrow dining room with high ceilings, concrete floors, and stainless-steel embellishments around the open kitchen and bar, or on the small sidewalk patio, diners who come to feast on chef/owner Ralph Tingle's chicken paillard (a personal fave), Caesar salad, or pan-roasted salmon with lemon risotto and pea shoots will be wholly satisfied. Lunch goes lighter, with upscale salads and sandwiches.

109 Plaza St. (at Healdsburg Ave.). ☎ **707/433-1380.** www.bistroralph.com. Reservations recommended. Main courses $8.75–$15 lunch, $18–$36 dinner. MC, V. Mon–Thurs 11:30am–2:30pm and 5:30–9pm; Fri–Sat 11:30am–2:30pm and 5:30–9:30pm. Sun brunch 10am–3pm.

Willi's Seafood & Raw Bar ★ SEAFOOD/LATIN-INSPIRED AMERICAN   Festive, modern, and city-slick with urban-Caribbean decor, this hot spot is jumping, thanks to sexy environs, a tasty exotic selection of international small plates (think seviche, skewers, and New England–style "rolls"), and 40 mostly local wines (all of which are available by the glass, carafe, and full bottle). Grab a spot at the heated sidewalk seating or at the friendly bar to try the flash-fried calamari appetizer with orange chili *gremolata,* or the outstanding sliced hanger steak drizzled with *chimichurri* sauce atop a bed of cucumber salad.

403 Healdsburg Ave. (at North St.). ☎ **707/433-9191.** www.willisseafood.net. Reservations recommended for parties of 8 or more; no reservations for Fri–Sun after 4pm, except for parties of 8 or more. Small plates $7–$15. AE, DISC, MC, V. Sun–Thurs 11:30am–9:30pm; Fri–Sat 11:30am–10pm.

Zazu ★★ AMERICAN/ITALIAN   You'll feel like you're on the road to nowhere while driving here, but chefs/owners Duskie Estes and John Stewart take road-house dining to gastronomic heights at this destination restaurant. The cozy, warmly lit room with comfy banquettes and myriad strategically placed mirrors is the perfect setting for the couple's creative and playful American and northern Italian–inspired menu, featuring extremely generous portions of homey comfort foods such as red-wine braised rabbit with mushroom risotto and rapini, or balsamic pork shoulder with creamy buttermilk mashed potatoes. Save room for dessert—you won't want to miss the messy and fun chocolate fondue with homemade Nutter Butter–like cookies. An added bonus is the well-priced Sonoma-centric wine list.

3535 Guerneville Rd. (about 5 miles west of Hwy. 101), Santa Rosa. ℂ **707/523-4814.** www. zazurestaurant.com. Reservations recommended. Main courses $17–$28. AE, DISC, MC, V. Wed-Mon 5:30–9:30pm; Sun brunch 9am–2pm.

Zin Restaurant & Wine Bar WINE BAR   Locals and visitors flock to this downtown Healdsburg hot culinary outpost, where talented and innovative young chefs fuse big-city ideas with country-comfort dishes. The seasonal menu pairs a top-notch wine list with local foods and produce, much of which is grown by the restaurant staff. For starters, try Mexican beer-battered green beans, then move to apple-wood smoked and grilled pork chops with applesauce, sautéed greens, and house-made andouille sausage-cornbread stuffing—or red-bean cassoulet with duck leg confit. Vegetarians can usually make a decent meal out of a few apps, and you'll have plenty of choices when you get to their exceptional wine list focusing on Dry Creek, Russian River, and Alexander Valley vintages (15–17 picks by the glass, around 100 by the bottle).

344 Center St., Healdsburg. ℂ **707/473-0946.** www.zinrestaurant.com. Main courses $15–$26. AE, DISC, MC, V. Mon–Fri 11:30am–2pm; daily 5:30–9pm; slower nights close earlier.

INEXPENSIVE

Jimtown Store ★★ DELI   Full of Wine Country character, this retro-hip country store promises strong coffee, a seasonal menu—focused on local farm fare—and incredible gourmet picnic grub, and charming low-key tables for on-the-spot noshing. The store, owned by cookbook author and chef Carrie Brown, sells its own brand of condiments. (Try the artichoke, caper, or fig-and-olive spreads.) In addition, bottles of local wine share shelf space with candy, antiques, and an assortment of wares they describe as "gifts that are different."

6706 State Hwy. 128, Healdsburg. ℂ **707/433-1212.** www.jimtown.com. Box lunches $12–$15. AE, MC, V. Mon–Fri 7am–5pm; Sat–Sun 7:30am–5pm.

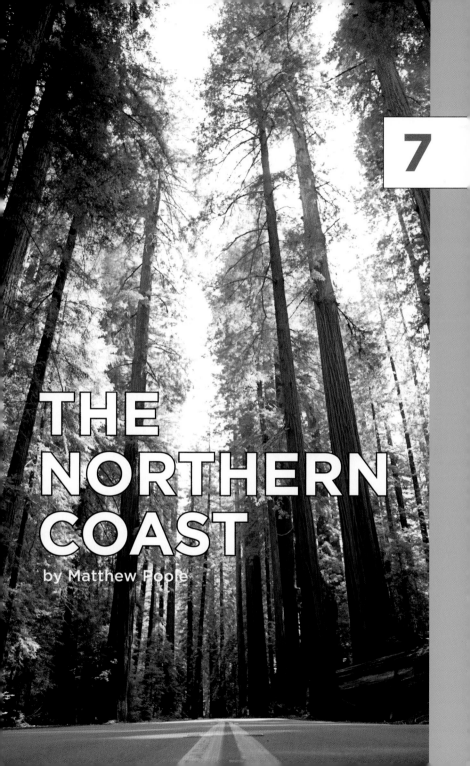

THE NORTHERN COAST

by Matthew Poole

North from San Francisco, the coast bears little resemblance to the southern part of the state. The landscape, climate, flora, and fauna are distinct, and you can forget about surfing and bikinis; instead, you'll find miles of rough shoreline with broad beaches and tiny bays harboring fantastic rock chimneys, blowholes, and bridges carved by the ocean waves.

You may think you've arrived in Alaska when you hit the beaches of Northern California. Take a dip, and you'll agree with the locals: The Arctic waters on the Northern Coast are best left to sea lions. That doesn't mean you can't enjoy the beaches, though, whether by strolling along the water or taking in the views of towering cliffs and seascapes. And unlike their southern counterparts, the beaches here are not likely to be crowded, even during summer months.

The best season to visit is spring, when wild poppy, iris, and sea foam carpet the headlands, or fall, when the sun shines clear and bright. Summers are typically cool and windy, and the ubiquitous fog burns off by afternoon.

The most scenic way to reach Stinson Beach, Mendocino, and points north is to drive Hwy. 1 along the coast. U.S. 101 runs inland much more quickly, through Healdsburg and Cloverdale, but it doesn't provide the spectacular coastal views. A good compromise if you're headed to, say, Mendocino, is to take U.S. 101 to Cloverdale and then cut over to the coast on Hwy. 128.

POINT REYES NATIONAL SEASHORE ★★★

35 miles NW of San Francisco

The government created the national seashore system to protect rural and undeveloped stretches of coastline from population growth and soaring real estate values. Nowhere is the success of this system more evident than at Point Reyes. Residents of the surrounding towns—Inverness, Point Reyes Station, and Olema—have steadfastly resisted runaway development. You will find laid-back coastal towns with cafes and country inns where gentle living prevails.

The park—a 71,000-acre hammer-shaped peninsula jutting 10 miles into the Pacific and backed by Tomales Bay—abounds with wildlife, ranging from tule elk, birds, and bobcats to gray whales, sea lions, and great white sharks. Aside from its scenery, it also boasts historical treasures that open a window into California's coastal past, including lighthouses, dairies and ranches, the site of Sir Francis Drake's 1579 landing, plus a replica of a coastal Miwok Indian village.

Though the peninsula's people and wildlife live in harmony above the ground, the situation beneath the soil is more volatile. The San Andreas Fault separates Point Reyes—the northernmost landmass on the Pacific Plate—from the rest of California, which rests on the North American Plate. Point Reyes is

PREVIOUS PAGE: **Avenue of the Giants (Hwy. 254).**

making its way toward Alaska at a rate of about 2 inches per year, but it has moved faster at times. In 1906, Point Reyes jumped north almost 20 feet in an instant, leveling San Francisco and jolting the rest of the state. The half-mile **Earthquake Trail,** near the Bear Valley Visitor Center, illustrates this geological drama with a loop through an area torn by the fault.

Essentials

GETTING THERE Point Reyes is 30 miles northwest of San Francisco, but it takes at least 90 minutes to reach by car (the small towns slow you down). The easiest route is Sir Francis Drake Boulevard from U.S. 101 south of San Rafael; it takes its time to Point Reyes, but it's without detours. For a longer, more scenic route, take the Stinson Beach/Hwy. 1 exit, off U.S. 101 south of Sausalito, onto Hwy. 1 north.

VISITOR INFORMATION As soon as you arrive at Point Reyes, stop at the **Bear Valley Visitor Center** (✆ **415/464-5100;** www.nps.gov/pore), on Bear Valley Road (look for the small sign just north of Olema on Hwy. 1), and pick up a free Point Reyes trail map. It's open Monday through Friday from 9am to 5pm, Saturday and Sunday and holidays from 8am to 5pm. Websites with information about Point Reyes include **www.pointreyes.net** and **www.pointreyes.org**.

FEES & PERMITS Entrance to the park is free. Camping is $15 per site per night all year (up to six people), and permits

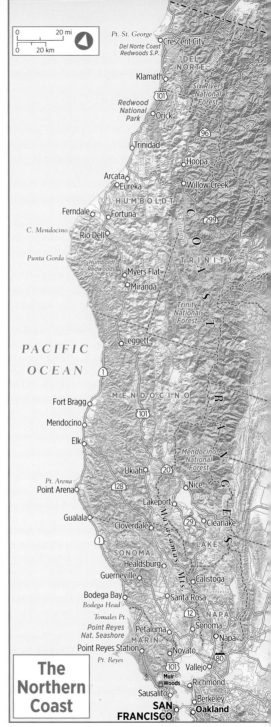

The Northern Coast

are required; reservations can be made up to 3 months in advance at ✆ **415/663-8054,** Monday through Friday from 9am to 2pm.

What to See & Do

When heading out to any part of the Point Reyes coast, expect to spend the day surrounded by nature. The park encompasses several surf-pounded beaches, bird estuaries, open swaths of land with roaming elk, and the Point Reyes lighthouse. As beautiful as the wilderness can be, however, it's also untamable. Waters in these areas are bone chilling; home to a vast array of sea life, including sharks; and dangerously unpredictable, with strong waves and riptides, and untended by lifeguards. In other words, swimming is inadvisable. Pets are not permitted on any local trails.

The most popular attraction is the venerable **Point Reyes Lighthouse ★,** at the westernmost tip. Even if you plan to forgo the 308 steps down to the lighthouse, it's worth the visit just to marvel at the scenery, which includes thousands of common murres and prides of sea lions basking on the rocks far below. The lighthouse visitor center (✆ **415/669-1534**) is open Thursday through Monday from 10am to 4:30pm, weather permitting; admission is free.

The lighthouse is also the top spot on the California coast to see **gray whales** as they make their southward and northward migrations along the coast from January to April. The annual round-trip is 10,000 miles—one of the longest mammal migrations known. The whales head south in December and January and return north in March. During the southern migration (Jan), the lighthouse affords the best view. During the northern migration (Mar), you can see the whales from any of the area's beaches. **_Tip:_** If you plan to drive out to the lighthouse to whale-watch, arrive early, as parking is limited. If possible, come on a weekday. On a weekend or holiday from December to April (weather permitting), it's wise to park at the Drake's Beach Visitor Center and take the shuttle bus to the lighthouse, which is $5 for adults and free for kids age 12 and under. Dress warmly—it's often quite cold and windy—and bring binoculars.

Rangers conduct many different tours on weekends: You can walk along the **Bear Valley Trail** and spot the wildlife at the ocean's edge; see the waterfowl at **Fivebrooks Pond;** explore tide pools; view some of North America's most beautiful ducks in the wetlands of **Limantour;** hike to the promontory overlooking **Chimney Rock** to see sea lions, elephant seals, harbor seals, and seabirds; or take a self-guided walk along the **San Andreas Fault** to observe the epicenter of the 1906 earthquake and learn about the regional geology. Tours vary seasonally; for up-to-date details, call the **Bear Valley Visitor Center** (✆ **415/464-5100**) or visit the National Park Service's website (www.nps.gov/pore). Many of the tours are suitable for travelers with disabilities.

North and South **Point Reyes beaches** face the Pacific and withstand the full brunt of ocean tides and winds—so much so that the water is far too rough for even wading. Until a few years ago, entering the water was illegal, but persistent surfers went to court for their right to shred the mighty waves. Along the southern coast, the waters of **Drake's Beach ★** can be as tranquil and serene as Point Reyes's are turbulent. Locals come here to sun and picnic; occasionally a hearty soul ventures into the cold waters. Keep in mind, though, that storms generally come inland from the south and almost always hit Drake's before moving north or south.

Alamere Falls, Point Reyes.

Some of the park's best and least crowded highlights are accessible only on foot, such as **Alamere Falls** ★, a freshwater stream that cascades down a 40-foot bluff onto Wildcat Beach, or **Tomales Point Trail** ★, which passes through the Tule Elk Reserve, a protected haven for roaming herds of tule elk that once numbered in the thousands. Hiking most of the trails usually ends up being an all-day outing, however, so it's best to split a 2-day trip within Point Reyes National Seashore into a "by car" day and a "by foot" day.

One of my favorite things to do in Point Reyes is paddle through placid Tomales Bay, a haven for migrating birds and marine mammals. **Blue Waters Kayaking** ★ (✆ 415/669-2600; www.bwkayak.com) organizes nature tours and hiking and kayak trips, including 3-hour morning or sunset outings, oyster tours, day trips, and longer excursions. Instruction, private groups and classes, clinics, and boat rental are available, and all ages and levels are welcome. Prices for tours start at $68. Rentals begin at $45 per person. Don't worry—the kayaks are very stable, and there aren't any waves to contend with. There are two launching points: One is on Hwy. 1 at the Marshall Boatworks in Marshall, 8 miles north of Point Reyes Station, and the other is on Sir Francis Drake Boulevard, in Inverness, 5 miles west of Point Reyes Station. The Marshall site is open, weather permitting, on weekends from 9am to 5pm and by appointment. Call or visit their website to confirm.

If you're into bird-watching, you'll definitely want to visit the **Point Reyes Bird Observatory** (✆ 415/868-0655; www.prbo.org), one of the few full-time ornithological research stations in the United States. It's at the southeast end of the park on Mesa Road. This is where ornithologists keep an eye on more than 400 feathered species. Admission to the visitor center and nature trail is free, and the observatory is open daily from 9am to 5pm. Banding hours vary, so call the field station for exact times.

Just north of Point Reyes National Seashore, near the small coastal town of Bolinas, is the **Audubon Canyon Ranch's Bolinas Lagoon Preserve.** From March to mid-July, this 1,000-acre preserve is the annual nesting location for great egrets, snowy egrets, and great blue herons, who set up temporary shop atop 100-foot-tall redwoods, as they've been doing for the past century or so. The 2- to 4-foot birds, with wingspans of up to 6 feet, are mesmerizing to watch as they engage in their daily courtship routines, such as plume displaying, twig shaking, crooning, and bill clappering. The flailing and crash-landing of young chicks embarking on their first flights in June or July is also entertaining. The preserve is open to the public from 10am to 4pm on weekdays and holidays from March 15 to July 13, and 2 to 4pm Tuesday through Friday by appointment. It's free, but donations are suggested. The address is 4900 State 1, just north of Stinson Beach; for more information, see **www.egret.org/bolinas_lagoon.html** or call ✆ **415/868-9244.**

One of Northern California's most popular beaches, this 3-mile-wide stretch of sand at the western foot of Mount Tamalpais is packed with Bay Area residents (and their dogs) on those rare, fog-free summer weekends. Swimming is allowed, with lifeguards on duty from May to mid-September, but notices about riptides and the cold water usually discourage beachgoers from swimming. Adjoining the beach is the small town of Stinson Beach, where you can have an enjoyable alfresco lunch at the numerous cafes along Hwy. 1. To reach Stinson Beach from San Francisco, cross the Golden Gate Bridge heading north on U.S. 101, take the Stinson Beach/Hwy. 1 exit heading west, and follow the signs (it's a winding 20 miles). The beach is free, open daily from 9am to 10pm. For more information, log on to **www. stinsonbeachonline.com**.

Where to Stay

Inns of Marin (www.innsofmarin.com; © **800/887-2880** or 415/663-2000), **Point Reyes Lodging Association** (www.ptreyes.com; © **800/539-1872** or 415/663-1872), and **West Marin Network** (© **415/663-9543**) are reputable services that will help you find accommodations, from one-room cottages to inns and vacation homes. The **West Marin Chamber of Commerce** (www.point reyes.org; © **415/663-9232**) is also a good source for lodging and visitor information. Keep in mind that many places here require a 2-night minimum stay, but in slow season they may make exceptions.

EXPENSIVE

Blackthorne Inn ★★   This redwood home, with its octagonal widow's walk, spiral staircase, turrets, and multiple decks, looks more like a deluxe treehouse than a B&B. My favorite unit (also the priciest) is the Eagle's Nest, an octagonal room enclosed by glass and topped with a sun deck, with a catwalk leading to the bathroom. The largest room is the Forest View, a two-room suite with a deck, a private entrance, and a sitting area facing the woods. All units have private bathrooms. The main sitting room in the house features a stone fireplace, skylight, wet bar, and stained-glass windows, and it's surrounded by a huge deck. A country buffet breakfast, included in the room rate, is served on the large upper deck when the sun's out.

266 Vallejo Ave. (off Sir Francis Drake Blvd., south of Inverness), Inverness Park (P.O. Box 712), Inverness, CA 94937. www.blackthorneinn.com. © **415/454-5515.** Fax 415/454-7676. 4 units. $195–$250 double. Rates include buffet breakfast. MC, V. **Amenities:** Nearby golf course; Jacuzzi.

Manka's Inverness Lodge ★★★ 🎁   If ever there was a reason to pack your bags and leave San Francisco, this wondrous collection of estates from the early

1900s is it. The main property holds two redwood cabins, an annex, and an old hunting and fishing lodge, all of which look like something out of a Hans Christian Andersen fairy tale. Sixteen-foot ceilings, wide plank floors, views over Tomales Bay, and a luxurious amount of space lend rooms in the converted 1991 boathouse a loftlike feel; the cabins have double-ended tubs and private outdoor showers opening up to the sky. Guests are invited to indulge in a three- or four-course fireside supper or a private chef's meal (in their own accommodations) that consists of seven or eight small courses. All ingredients are grown, fished, gathered, or farmed within reach of the lodge. A newly refurbished dining room is used during the holidays and for special events.

30 Callendar Way (at Argyle St., off Sir Francis Drake Blvd., ¼ mile north of downtown Inverness), P.O. Box 1110, Inverness, CA 94937. www.mankas.com. ⓒ **415/669-1034.** Fax 415/669-1598. 10 units. $285–$385 double; $235–$615 suite or cabin; $665–$815 Boathouse. 2-night minimum stay on weekends. AE, MC, V. Dogs are welcome. **Amenities:** Restaurant; room service; free Wi-Fi; movies on request; personal music library. *In room:* Fireplace, library, MP3 docking station.

MODERATE

Bear Valley Inn Bed & Breakfast ★   This two-story 1910 farmhouse has survived everything from a major earthquake to a recent forest fire, but you'd be hard-pressed to find a better B&B for the price in Point Reyes. Loaded with charm, down to the profusion of flowers and vines outside and comfy chairs fronting a toasty wood stove inside, it's in a great location too, with good restaurants within walking distance and the seashore at its doorstep. One unit is a private dog-friendly cottage with a small kitchen and bunk beds that are suitable for children. The cottage comes loaded with milk and basics, but for a little bit extra you can receive a deluxe breakfast basket.

88 Bear Valley Rd., Olema, CA 94950. www.bearvinn.com. ⓒ **415/663-1777.** 3 units, 1 cottage. $120–$180 double; $160–$250 cottage for 2 ($25 per extra person, up to 6 people). Rates include breakfast (house only). AE, DISC, MC, V. *In room:* A/C, TV, hair dryer, kitchen in cottage, free Wi-Fi.

Nick's Cove & Cottages ★★★   After driving through a lot of nothingness on Hwy. 1, reaching Nick's Cove is like finding an oasis in the middle of the Sahara. With all the amenities of a boutique stay disguised in the form of rustic bayside cottages, the Pat Kuleto enterprise has been a smash success with all looking to sample the northern coast's ruggedness. Each cabin has a wood-burning stove, a

DRAKE'S BAY oyster farm

On the edge of Drakes Estero (a uniquely pristine and nutrient-rich saltwater lagoon on the Point Reyes peninsula that produces some of the finest oysters in the world), **Drake's Bay Oyster Farm** doesn't look like much, but California has no better place to buy delicious fresh-out-of-the-water oysters by the sack full. They have picnic tables and bottled oyster sauce, so you can enjoy your recently purchased bivalves immediately (though I prefer to drive down to Point Reyes Beach), but bring your own oyster knife. Drake's Bay Oyster Farm is at 17171 Sir Francis Drake Blvd., about 6 miles west(ish) of Inverness on the way to the Point Reyes Lighthouse. It's open daily 8:30am to 4:30pm (ⓒ **415/669-1149;** www.drakesbayfamilyfarms.com).

well-stocked kitchenette, and heated bathroom floors. Yet, with Wi-Fi, satellite TV, and a DVD player, you won't feel too out of touch with the world. Cabins on the water boast private decks with Adirondack chairs for enjoying Tomales Bay's stunning sunsets. While every bit as spacious as the waterfront digs, the creek-side cottages—like Uncle Andy's cabin, which is, incidentally, bigger than the aforementioned two—are the more budget-friendly of the accommodations.

23240 Hwy. 1, Marshall, CA 94940. www.nickscove.com. © **866/63-NICKS** (636-4257) or 415/663-1033. Fax 415/663-9751. 12 units. $455–$745 cottage. 2-night minimum stay on weekends. AE, DISC, MC, V. **Amenities:** Restaurant. *In room:* A/C, TV, DVD player, kitchen, minibar, free Wi-Fi.

Olema Inn & Restaurant ★★   The pretty Olema Inn opened on July 4, 1876, as a gathering place for farmers and ranchers, was lost in gambling debt, and survived the 1906 earthquake. It still retains much of its period charm, combining modern luxuries such as down comforters and large tub/shower combinations with antique furniture and Victorian-style white porcelain—and those great high ceilings you find in old Bay Area buildings. Views are of the beautiful back garden and Olema Valley. The inn's candlelit restaurant features local produce and meats such as Bellwether Farms ricotta gnocchi with pine nuts and sage brown butter, duck confit and apple ravioli in a sherry reduction, and a Niman Ranch pork chop with cider glaze and a side of crispy corncake. Much of the restaurant's produce is grown at the inn's organic garden and orchard. *Tip:* Try to reserve room no. 3, the quietest, overlooking the garden.

10000 Sir Francis Drake Blvd., Olema, CA 94950. www.theolemainn.com. © **415/663-9559.** Fax 415/663-8783. 6 units. $174–$222 double. Rates include continental breakfast. AE, MC, V. Dogs welcome at no extra charge. **Amenities:** Restaurant.

Point Reyes Country Inn & Stables ★   Are you and your horse dreaming of a country getaway? Then book a room at Point Reyes Country Inn & Stables, a ranch-style home on 4 acres with pastoral accommodations for two- and four-legged guests (horses only), plus access to plenty of hiking and riding trails. Each of the six B&B rooms has a private bathroom and either a balcony or a garden. The innkeepers have also added two studios (with kitchens) above the stables, plus they rent out two cottages on Tomales Bay, with decks, stocked kitchens, fireplaces, and a shared dock.

12050 Hwy. 1 (P.O. Box 501), Point Reyes Station, CA 94956. www.ptreyescountryinn.com. © **415/663-9696.** Fax 415/663-8888. 10 units. $115–$180 double; $185–$225 cottage. $10–$15 per horse. Rates include breakfast in the B&B rooms, breakfast provisions in the cottages. MC, V. **Amenities:** Nearby golf course. *In room:* No phone.

INEXPENSIVE

Motel Inverness ☺   Homey, well maintained, and fronting Tomales Bay, this is the perfect pick for the spendthrift or the outdoor adventurer who plans to spend as little time indoors as possible. (Those seeking romance should dig deeper into their pockets and opt for Manka's; see above.) All guest rooms, except one twin-bed option, have queen-size beds and skylights. Attached to Inverness is a giant great room, complete with fireplace and pool table to distract the kids; parents can relax and children can play on the back lawn overlooking the bay. The hotel offers a pair of two-bedroom suites, one with wheelchair access and a deck to take in the views. The other is billed as the "luxury" suite and has a king-size bed, Jacuzzi, and kitchenette. Both are ideal for families, as is the Bird's Eye View

How's this for a great deal? For $75, you and four of your best friends can stay the night in a redwood cabin on a bluff overlooking the ocean with nearby access to hiking trails and a small, secluded beach. Mount Tamalpais State Park rents 10 cabins that were once the private retreats of Bay Area politicians. All have gorgeous ocean views, available to anyone stubborn enough to get a reservation. Wood-burning stoves, platform beds, running water, and outhouses are provided, but you must bring your own sleeping bag and lantern, there's no electricity, and firewood costs extra. Each cabin sleeps five, but only one car per cabin is allowed. Off Hwy. 1, a mile south of Stinson Beach, look for a paved turnout and a brown metal sign. The cabins are very popular, so reserve one as far in advance as possible (you can book them up to 7 months before). For reservations, call © **800/444-7275** or reserve online at **www.reserve america.com**. For more information, call the Mount Tamalpais State Park at © **415/388-2070**.

House, with two bedrooms, two bathrooms, a bonus room, and full kitchen. *Note:* The motel is nonsmoking.

12718 Sir Francis Drake Blvd., Inverness, CA 94937. www.motelinverness.com. © **866/453-3839** or 415/236-1967. 7 units, 1 cottage. $99–$190 double; $170–$290 suite; $250–$300 Bird's Eye View House. MC, V. *In room:* TV.

Point Reyes Hostel ☺ Deep within Point Reyes National Seashore, this beautiful old ranchlike complex has 44 dormitory-style accommodations, including one room reserved for families (with at least one child 5 years old or younger). The two common rooms are warmed by wood-burning stoves on chilly nights, and guests can share a fully equipped kitchen, barbecue (BYO charcoal), and patio. If you don't mind sharing your sleeping quarters with strangers, this deal can't be beat. Reservations (and earplugs) are strongly recommended.

Off Limantour Rd. (P.O. Box 247), Point Reyes Station, CA 94956. www.norcalhostels.org. © **415/663-8811.** 44 bunks, 1 private unit. $22 per adult, $10 per child 16 and under with parent. 5 nights out of 30 maximum stay. MC, V. Reception hours 7:30–10am and 4:30–9:30pm daily.

Where to Eat

Nick's Cove Restaurant ★★★ NORTH COAST CUISINE A product of celebrity restaurateur Pat Kuleto, Nick's Cove is unsurprisingly one of the best eateries around. With many of the ingredients plucked directly from the Bay, the food is sublimely fresh. Like elsewhere in the region, oysters top the menu; start your meal off right by ordering the barbecue variety in garlic butter, accompanied by a bowl of Tomales Bay clam chowder. For mains, the Bandit's Cioppino—Dungeness crabs, mussels, clams, shrimp, tomatoes, anchovy butter, and chili flake—is a popular dish, but my personal favorite is the braised lamb shank with gremolata, red-wine *jus,* and heirloom polenta. On a clear night, try to score a table on the covered deck overlooking the bay. Tuesday is Local Nights, with live music and drink and food deals, and happy hour is daily from 3 to 6pm.

23240 Hwy. 1, Marshall, CA 94940. © **866/63-NICKS** (636-4257) or 415/663-1033. www.nicks cove.com. Breakfast $8–$18; lunch $12–$25; dinner $14–$38. AE, DISC, MC, V. Daily 8am–10pm.

POINT REYES MOUNTAIN biking

Mountain biking was born in Marin, so it's no surprise that miles of meandering mountain-bike trails crisscross Point Reyes National Seashore. The challenge level varies from easy to daunting, with mostly fire roads and a few single-track trails winding through densely forested knolls and sunny meadows with pretty ocean views. Because many of the hiking trails are off-limits to bikes, you'll need a bike map to figure out which ones are bike-legal; they're available free at the Bear Valley Visitor Center (p. 249). To rent a bike, call **Point Reyes Outdoors** (☎ 415/663-8192; www. pointreyesoutdoors.com).

Station House Café ★ AMERICAN   For more than 2 decades, the Station House Café has been a favorite pit stop for Bay Area residents headed to and from Point Reyes. It's a friendly, low-key place with a full bar, an open kitchen, an outdoor garden dining area (key on sunny days), and live music. Breakfast dishes include a Hangtown omelet with local oysters and bacon, and eggs with creamed spinach and mashed-potato pancakes. Lunch and dinner specials (such as fettuccine with fresh local mussels steamed in white wine and butter sauce, two-cheese polenta served with fresh spinach sauté and grilled garlic-buttered tomato, or a daily fresh salmon special) are all made from locally sourced produce, seasonal vegetables harvested from their kitchen garden, and organically raised Niman Ranch beef. The cafe has an extensive list of fine California wines and locally brewed beers.

11180 Hwy. 1, at Point Reyes Station. ☎ **415/663-1515.** www.stationhousecafe.com. Reservations recommended. Breakfast $6.95–$11; lunch and dinner entrees $8.95–$19. AE, DISC, MC, V. Thurs–Tues 8am–9pm.

ALONG THE SONOMA COAST
Bodega Bay

Beyond the tip of the Point Reyes peninsula, the road curves around toward the coastal village of Bodega Bay, which supports a fishing fleet of around 300 boats. It's a good place to stop for lunch or a stroll. Despite the droves of tourists on summer weekends, Bodega Bay is mostly a working-class fishing town, where most locals start their day before dawn mending nets, rigging fishing poles, and talking shop. Several shops and galleries are interesting, but the best show in town—especially for kids—is at **Tides Wharf,** where the fishing boats dock, unload their catch, gut it, and pack it in ice.

Bodega Head State Park ★ is a great vantage point for whale-watching during the migration from January to April. At **Doran Beach,** a large bird sanctuary is home to willets, curlews, godwits, and more. Next door, the **UC Davis Bodega Marine Laboratory** (☎ **707/875-2211;** www.bml.ucdavis.edu) conducts guided tours of its lab projects on Friday afternoons between 2 and 4pm (suggested donation is $2).

The **Bodega Harbour Golf Links,** at 21301 Heron Dr. (*✆* **866/ 905-4657** or 707/875-3538; www. bodegaharbourgolf.com), is an 18-hole, seaside Scottish-style course designed by Robert Trent Jones, Jr. A warm-up center and practice facility is free for registered golfers. Rates range from $60 with cart Monday through Thursday, $70 on Friday, and $90 on weekends. You can also ride horseback through spectacular scenery through **Chanslor Ranch** (*✆* **707/875-2721;** www.chanslor. com), which also has pony rides for kids. It's open daily from 9am to 5pm.

One of the bay's major events is the **Fisherman's Festival** in April.

Sonoma Coast.

Local fishing boats, decked with ribbons and banners, sail out for a Blessing of the Fleet, while up to 25,000 landlubbers partake of music, a lamb-and-oyster barbecue, and an arts-and-crafts fair. For details about this festival and other events, consult the **Bodega Bay Visitors Center,** 850 Hwy. 1, Bodega Bay, CA 94923 (*✆* **707/875-3866;** www.bodega bay.com or www.visitsonomacoast.com). Open daily, it has lots of brochures, and maps of the Sonoma Coast State Beaches and the best fishing spots.

A few miles inland on Hwy. 1 (toward Petaluma) is the tiny town of **Bodega** (pop. 100), famous as the setting of Alfred Hitchcock's *The Birds,* filmed here in 1961. Fans will want to visit the Potter School House and St. Teresa's Church.

WHERE TO STAY

Expensive

Bodega Bay Lodge & Spa ★★
Near Doran Beach State Park, this is Bodega Bay's best hotel. Each room has plush furnishings, a fireplace, and a private balcony with sweeping views of the bay and bird-filled marshes. If you can afford it, opt for a large luxury suite. Guests have complimentary access to a fitness center and sauna, heated pool above the bay, and full-service oceanview spa offering an array of massages and body/facial treatments. The lodge's **Duck Club Restaurant** enjoys a reputation as Bodega Bay's finest. Picture windows show off the bay view, a romantic setting for Sonoma

Terror on Bodega Bay in Alfred Hitchcock's *The Birds.*

HORSEBACK riding ON THE SONOMA COAST

An exceptional way to experience the natural beauty of the Sonoma Coast region is on horseback with longtime residents Laura and Jonathan Ayers, who run the **Armstrong Woods Pack Station** (**707/887-2939;** www.redwoodhorses.com). Their guided trail rides through a beautiful old-growth redwood forest near Guerneville is an experience you'll never forget. You can saddle up year-round, weather and trail conditions permitting, and they even offer overnight camping rides.

County cuisine such as roasted Petaluma duck and fresh fish caught by the Bodega fleet.

103 Hwy. 1, Bodega Bay, CA 94923. www.bodegabaylodge.com. ✆ **888/875-2250** or 707/875-3525. Fax 707/875-2428. 84 units. $180–$245 double; $290–$395 suite. 2-night minimum on weekends. Rates include a complimentary wine hour 5–6pm. AE, DC, DISC, MC, V. **Amenities:** Restaurant; babysitting; concierge; nearby golf course; heated outdoor pool w/ocean view; room service; full-service spa and fitness center. *In room:* A/C, TV w/pay movies, fax, fridge, hair dryer, minibar.

Moderate

The Inn at the Tides ★ The larger of Bodega Bay's two upscale lodgings (the other being Bodega Bay Lodge), the Inn at the Tides consists of a cluster of condolike wood complexes on the side of a gently sloping hill. The selling point is the view; each unit is staggered just enough to guarantee a view of the bay across the highway. The rooms are modern and the inn's amenities are first-rate, such as the attractive indoor-outdoor pool, but I would stay here only if I couldn't get a room at the Bodega Bay Lodge. The **Bay View Restaurant** is open Wednesday through Sunday for dinner only, with ocean views, a well-prepared albeit traditional choice of entrees, and a romantic and somewhat formal ambience. Be sure to check the website for special package deals.

800 Coast Hwy. 1 (P.O. Box 640), Bodega Bay, CA 94923. www.innatthetides.com. ✆ **800/541-7788** or 707/875-2751. Fax 707/875-2669. 86 units. Summer Sun–Thurs $179, Fri–Sat $199; winter rates drop about 20%. Rates include continental breakfast. Golf packages available. AE, DC, DISC, MC, V. **Amenities:** Restaurant; babysitting (w/notice); nearby golf course; exercise room; Jacuzzi; indoor-outdoor heated pool; room service; Finnish sauna. *In room:* TV w/pay movies, hair dryer, minibar.

Hitchcock Haunt

Alfred Hitchcock fans will want to make the pilgrimage to Bodega, off Hwy. 1 a few miles southeast of Bodega Bay. Drive past the roadside shops, turn the corner, look right, and *voilà:* **a bird's-eye view of the hauntingly familiar Potter School House and St. Teresa's Church, both immortalized in Hitchcock's** *The Birds,* **filmed here in 1961.**

St. Teresa's Church, location for *The Birds.*

Inexpensive

Bodega Harbor Inn ★ 🏄 Thank Poseidon for the Bodega Harbor Inn, with some of the North Coast's best lodging bargains. On a small bluff over the bay, the inn has four single-story clapboard buildings surrounded by well-maintained lawns and gardens. The rooms are small but impeccably neat and tastefully decorated with unpretentious antiques; double beds, private bathrooms, and cable TV are standard. (The best rooms are 12 and 14, which come with small decks and partial ocean views.) The clincher is the inn's private lawn area overlooking the water. On sunny days, there's no better way to enjoy an afternoon in Bodega Bay than parking in one of the lawn chairs and watching the fishing boats bring in their daily catch. Families should inquire about the vacation homes the inn rents for as little as $125 per night.

1345 Bodega Ave., Bodega Bay, CA 94923. www.bodegaharborinn.com. ℂ **707/875-3594.** 16 units, 5 houses. $80–$155 double; $125–$375 house. Rates include continental breakfast. MC, V. *In room:* TV.

WHERE TO EAT

In addition to the following, see the Duck Club Restaurant in the listing for Bodega Bay Lodge & Spa in "Where to Stay," above.

Tides Wharf Restaurant SEAFOOD/PASTA   In summer, as many as 1,000 diners a day pass through the Tides Wharf. In the early '60s, it was a set for Hitchcock's *The Birds*, but don't expect the weather-beaten, board-and-batten luncheonette you saw in the movie—a $6-million renovation gentrified, enlarged, and redecorated the place beyond recognition. The best tables have ocean views,

---

SECRET SONOMA COAST seafood SPOTS

To be honest, my favorite seafood spots in Bodega Bay aren't the big restaurants, but the little roadside shacks that most tourists overlook, such as Tony and Carol's **Spud Point Crab Company** (1860 Westshore Rd., Bodega Bay; ℂ **707/875-9472;** www. spudpointcrab.com), a tiny takeout stand where everything's made on-premises, including their smoked salmon, crab cakes, and crab sandwiches. I'm going to start an argument here and claim that they make the best clam chowder in California (and people, I've tasted a lot of clam chowders).

Another favorite is the **Island Style Deli** (599 Hwy. 1, Bodega Bay; ℂ **707/875-8881**), which is located next to the Lucas Wharf Restaurant. It's gone through several name changes over the past 2 decades, but that little deli still cranks out the best fish and chips I've ever had, made from caught-that-day fish brought in straight from the wharf.

My other top seafood dining secret on the Sonoma Coast is **Cape Fear Cafe** (25191 Main St., Duncans Mills; ℂ **707/ 869-2659;** www.duncansmills.net), in a town you've never heard of called Duncans Mills, located a few miles inland from Hwy. 1 near Jenner. It's so damn cute and the service so friendly that it almost seems fake, like a movie set from *On Golden Pond.* I discovered the Cape Fear Cafe on a motorcycle trip about 10 years ago and have been making regular day trips there from Mill Valley just for breakfast—it's that good (their Hangtown Fry and Poor Boys made with fresh Tomales Bay oysters are wonderful). The cafe is open for dinner and brunch as well.

and the fare is what you might expect: oysters on the half shell, clam chowder, and all the fish that the owners can dredge up from the cold blue waters (they send their own boat out into the Pacific daily). Prime rib, pasta, and poultry are available as well. A fish-processing plant, snack bar, and gift shop are next door.

835 Hwy. 1. © **707/875-3652.** www.innatthetides.com. Main courses $15–$43. AE, DISC, MC, V. Sun–Thurs 7:30am–9:30pm; Fri 7:30am–10pm; Sat 7am–10pm.

The Sonoma Beaches, Jenner & Fort Ross Park ★★

Along 13 winding and picturesque miles of Hwy. 1—from Bodega Bay to Goat Rock Beach in Jenner—stretch the Sonoma Coast State Beaches. These beaches are ideal for walking, tide pooling, abalone picking, fishing, and bird-watching for species such as great blue heron, cormorant, osprey, and pelican. Each beach is clearly marked from the road, and numerous pullouts are available for parking. Even if you don't stop at a beach, the drive alone is spectacular.

At **Jenner,** the Russian River empties into the ocean. **Penny Island,** in the river's estuary, is home to otters and many species of birds; a colony of harbor seals lives out on the ocean rocks. **Goat Rock Beach** is a popular breeding ground for the seals; pupping season begins in March and lasts until June.

From Jenner, an 11-mile dramatic coastal drive brings you to **Fort Ross State Historic Park** (© **707/847-3286;** www.fortrossstatepark.org), a reconstruction of the fort established in 1812 by the Russians as a base for seal and otter hunting (a post they abandoned in 1842). At the visitor center, you can view the Russians' samovars and table services. The compound contains several buildings, including the first Russian Orthodox church on the North American continent outside Alaska. A short history lesson takes place daily at various times between Memorial Day and Labor Day, and at noon and 2pm the rest of the year. Call ahead to be sure. The park also offers beach trails and picnic grounds on more than 1,000 acres. Admission is $6 per car per day.

North from Fort Ross, the road continues to **Salt Point State Park** (© **707/847-3221**). This 3,500-acre expanse encompasses 30 campsites, 14 miles of trails, dozens of tide pools, and old Pomo village sites. Your best bet is to pull off the highway at any place that catches your eye and start exploring. At the north end of the park, head inland on Kruse Ranch Road to the **Kruse Rhododendron Reserve** (© **707/847-3221**), a forested grove of wild pink and purple flowers, where the *Rhododendron californicum* grow up to a height of 18 feet under the redwood-and-fir canopy.

WHERE TO STAY

Jenner Inn & Cottages   The worst-kept secret on the Northern Coast is Jenner Inn, a gallimaufry of individually designed and decorated houses and cottages along the coast and inland on the Russian River. Most of the houses are subdivided into suites, while second honeymooners vie for the ultraprivate oceanfront cottages. Wicker furniture, wood paneling, and private bathrooms are standard, though each lodging has its own personality: Some have kitchens, while others have fireplaces, hot tubs, or private decks. The private cottages overlooking the Pacific are the priciest, but for about $180 or so, most people are content with one of the smaller suites. A complimentary breakfast is served in the main lodge. In addition to the B&B accommodations, the inn rents vacation homes within Jenner Canyon or overlooking the ocean.

10400 Hwy. 1 (P.O. Box 69), Jenner, CA 95450. www.jennerinn.com. © **800/732-2377** or 707/865-2377. 24 units (plus several vacation homes). $118–$348 double. Rates include continental breakfast. AE, MC, V. *In room:* Kitchen in some units, no phone except in cottages.

WHERE TO EAT

River's End ★ INTERNATIONAL Established in 1927, this romantic little seaside restaurant in Jenner has sunset views to swoon over, with big windows overlooking the coast (seals and sea lions might happen to be cavorting offshore). It's owned and operated by Bert Rangel, whose passion for locally harvested seafood is equaled only by his desire to make sure all of his guests are having a wonderful dining experience (you'll love this guy). The eclectic menu offers everything from filet mignon to wild halibut, seared duck, and fresh Dungeness crab (in season). Whenever possible, the chef uses local Sonoma products—seafood, game, lamb, poultry, vegetables, microbrews, and wines. In fact, his wine list is so comprehensive it's a recipient of *Wine Spectator*'s "Award of Excellence." After dinner, take the remainder of your wine to the deck and watch the sun set. **Note:** The hours tend to vary as much as the menu, so call ahead if you're planning to dine here.

11048 Hwy. 1, Jenner. © **707/865-2484,** ext. 111. www.ilovesunsets.com. Reservations recommended. Main courses $13–$37. MC, V. Fri–Mon noon–3:30pm and 5–9pm.

Gualala & Point Arena

Back on Hwy. 1 heading north, you'll pass through Sea Ranch, a series of condominium beach developments, before you reach the small coastal community of Gualala (pronounced Wah-*la*-la). In the old days, Gualala was a vivacious logging town. A few real-life, suspender-wearing lumberjacks still end their day at the Gualala Hotel's saloon, but for the most part the town's chief function is to provide gas, groceries, and hardware for area residents. Several parks, hiking trails, and about 10 ideal sunbathing beaches lie just outside town.

The **Gualala River,** adjacent to the town of the same name, is suitable for canoeing, rafting, and kayaking, because powerboats and jet skis are forbidden. Along its banks you're likely to see ospreys, herons, egrets, and ducks; steelhead, salmon, and river otters make their homes in the waters. You can rent canoes and kayaks in Gualala for 2 hours, a half-day, or a full day from **Adventure Rents** (© **888/881-4386** or 707/884-4386; www.adventurerents.com), in downtown Gualala on Hwy. 1 behind Century 21 Realty. Prices range from $35 for a couple of hours on a kayak to $90 for a full day on a tandem ocean kayak; canoes are available as well.

Point Arena is a few miles north of Gualala. Stop here for the view at the **Point Arena Lighthouse & Museum** ★ (© **877/725-4448** or 707/882-2777; www.pointarenalighthouse.com), built in 1870 after 10 ships ran aground here one night in a storm. An $8-per-person fee ($1 for children 11 and under) covers parking, entrance to the lighthouse museum, and an interesting tour of the six-story, 145-step lighthouse (the view through the dazzling 6-ft.-wide, lead-crystal lens is worth the hike). The lighthouse is open daily 10am to 3:30pm; half-hour tours run every 20 minutes.

WHERE TO STAY

St. Orres ★★ 🏨 An extraordinary Russian-style building—complete with two onion-domed towers—St. Orres lies 1½ miles north of Gualala. The complex was

Point Arena Lighthouse.

built in 1972 with century-old timbers salvaged from a nearby mill. It offers cottage-style accommodations on 42 acres and eight rooms in the main building (these rooms share three bathrooms decorated in brilliant colors). Other units are very private. Some have wet bars, sitting areas with Franklin stoves, and French doors leading to decks with a distant ocean view. Seven cottages border St. Orres Creek and have exclusive use of a spa facility that includes a hot tub, sauna, and sun deck. The Black Chanterelle is as exotic as it sounds, with domes, a sauna and Jacuzzi, a fireplace, and an ocean view. Full breakfast is delivered to the cottages. The hotel's restaurant (see review below), open for dinner only, is in a dramatic setting below one of the main building's domes.

36601 Hwy. 1 (P.O. Box 523), Gualala, CA 95445. www.saintorres.com. ✆ **707/884-3303.** Fax 707/884-1840. 8 units (sharing 3 bathrooms), 13 cottages. Hotel $95–$135 double; cottage $140–$350 double. Rates include full breakfast. MC, V. **Amenities:** Restaurant; bar; bike rental; nearby golf course; Jacuzzi; sauna. *In room:* Fridge, hair dryer, kitchenette in some units.

Whale Watch Inn ★★ Ninety feet above the water, in five contemporary buildings on two cliffside acres, this inn has one of the best views of the Northern Coast. Private guest rooms all have ocean views, decks, and fireplaces. Room styles range from traditional bed-and-breakfast style to French Provençal to contemporary casual; check out the pictures on the website before you reserve one. For a closer encounter with nature, take the private stairway that leads to a half-mile-long beach with tidal pools. The Whale Watch building has a common room with a circular fireplace, floor-to-ceiling windows, and a wraparound deck for prime viewing.

35100 Hwy. 1, Gualala, CA 95445. www.whalewatchinn.com. ✆ **800/942-5342** or 707/884-3667. Fax 707/884-3667. 18 units. $180–$280 double. Rates include full breakfast delivered to room at prearranged time. AE, MC, V. Pets accepted for $40 to $50 per stay. **Amenities:** Nearby golf course. *In room:* Kitchen, fridge in some units, phone upon request.

WHERE TO EAT

St. Orres Restaurant ★★ NORTH COAST CUISINE Self-taught chef Rosemary Campiformio has been wowing fans and food writers for years with her version of North Coast cuisine, which favors local organic meats and produce and wild game in dark, fruity sauces. Every day fishermen and farmers deliver their best goods to Rosemary, so you never know what will be on her prix-fixe dinner menu, but it could be Stilton cheese in phyllo with smoked wild boar and tomato, followed by a garden-fresh salad and an entree of grilled veal chop with garlic mashed potatoes, foie gras, and truffle Madeira sauce. For dessert, it's a tossup between the bread pudding with homemade nutmeg ice cream and caramel sauce, and the freshly baked individual apple pie with St. Orres cinnamon ice cream. The wine cellar stores a suitable selection of reds that pair well with the hearty entrees.

36601 Hwy. 1 (St. Orres Inn), Gualala. *C* **707/884-3335.** www.saintorres.com. Reservations recommended. Prix-fixe dinner menu $45; appetizers and desserts a la carte. Beer and wine only. MC, V. Daily 6–9:30pm (winter schedule varies).

North from Point Arena

Driving north from Point Arena, you'll pass Elk (a good place to stop for lunch), Manchester, Albion, and Little River on your way to Mendocino.

WHERE TO STAY

Elk Cove Inn & Spa ★★★ It's hard to imagine a more idyllic coastal retreat than the Elk Cove Inn. Situated on 1½ acres of secluded oceanside property about 15 miles south of Mendocino, the 15-room inn offers a variety of room types, ranging from modern and spacious cottages and luxury suites to cozy guest rooms within the 1883 "Victorian Mansion." The suites are heavenly—each luxuriously appointed with a private balcony or porch, Jacuzzi tub, high ceilings, custom-made fixtures, and Arts and Crafts furniture. Most rooms have ocean views and fireplaces, and all have feather beds and fluffy comforters. But you'll be spending most of your time luxuriating at the inn's European-style day spa, exploring the nearby driftwood-strewn beach (via the inn's private beach access), watching the sunset from the gazebo, or relaxing at the full bar and restaurant,

---

✎ RENTING A home AT THE BEACH

If you're taking the family for a vacation along the coast—or if you really want to impress your partner—consider renting a furnished home at the Sea Ranch, one of the most beautiful seaside communities around. All the low-swept buildings are designed to blend in with the surrounding forest, meadows, and ocean bluffs; many have outdoor hot tubs, and most have wood-burning fireplaces or stoves. About 300 homes are available as rentals, with prices starting at about $140 per night. Rentals include use of the community's three outdoor heated swimming pools, tennis courts, and recreation center. The Sea Ranch also has a Scottish-style 18-hole public golf course, a fine-dining restaurant, and private access to 10 miles of coastline and several secluded beaches. For more information, log on to **www.searanchrentals.com** or call **Beach Rentals** at *C* **707/884-4235.**

which serves a full buffet breakfast (you can take it back to your room, if you prefer).

6300 S. Hwy 1, Elk, CA 95432. www.elkcoveinn.com. ✆ **800/275-2967** or 707/877-3321. Fax 707/877-1808. Rates include buffet breakfast for 2 and cocktail reception. 14 units. Winter $100–$375; summer $155–$395. AE, MC, V. **Amenities:** Restaurant; bar; spa. *In room:* Free Wi-Fi.

Greenwood Pier Inn & Cafe ★   On the edge of a dramatic bluff, the Greenwood Pier Inn is a New Age complex encompassing a cafe, country store, garden shop, and accommodations ranging from cabins to rooms in the main inn building. It's the unique domain of owner-operator Kendrick Petty, an artist and gardener whose collages, tiles, and marble work are on display throughout the premises, including the gardens. All rooms are within 100 feet of the cliff edge, with private decks, fireplaces, or wood burners. A beautiful building called the Tower has three levels: a two-person Jacuzzi at the bottom, a deck overlooking the ocean on the second level, and, up a library ladder, a full-size bed facing an ocean view. A continental breakfast is delivered to your room; breakfast, lunch, and dinner—filet mignon, grilled rack of lamb, and flambéed prawns—are served in the Greenwood Pier Cafe (dinner Apr–Oct Wed–Sun, Nov–Mar Sat–Sun and holidays).

5928 Hwy. 1 (P.O. Box 336), Elk, CA 95432. www.greenwoodpierinn.com. ✆ **800/807-3423** or 707/877-9997. Fax 707/877-3439. 12 units. $185–$335 double. Rates include continental breakfast. AE, MC, V. Pets accepted in some units for $20 per night. **Amenities:** Restaurant; nearby golf course; oceanview Jacuzzi. *In room:* CD player (w/CDs on loan from the Country Store), hair dryer in some units, no phone.

Griffin House Inn ★★ 🎁   I love this unpretentious, peaceful little inn with its seven cozy cottages, friendly tavern, reasonable rates, and gorgeous views of the rugged coastline. The tiny village of Elk isn't as gentrified as Mendocino up the coast, but those yearning for a calmer commune with nature will love it here. The inn's most coveted cottages are cliffside, with private decks for soaking in the splendor of Greenwood Cove (the Greenwood Cottage is my favorite). The cottages in the garden setting—sans ocean view—are less expensive but still pleasant. The cottages are individually decorated in a sort of austere Cape Cod style with stained glass, French doors, and claw-foot tubs; all have private bathrooms and wood-burning stoves. On the premises is Bridget Dolan's Pub, which serves good, hearty comfort food and plenty of fine wine and cold beer. A full hot breakfast is even delivered to your door.

5910 Hwy. 1, P.O. Box 172, Elk, CA 95432. www.griffinn.com. ✆ **707/877-3422.** Fax 707/877-1853. 8 cottages. $138–$325 cottage. Rates include full breakfast and small carafe of wine. AE, DISC, MC, V. **Amenities:** Restaurant. *In room:* Hair dryer, no phone, Wi-Fi.

Harbor House Inn & Restaurant ★★   Built in 1916 by the president of the Goodyear Redwood Lumber Co. as a hideaway for corporate executives, this beautiful redwood-sided, two-story inn offers 3 acres of gardens, access to a private beach, and views overlooking the Pacific. None of the units has a TV or phone, and that's how guests like it. All six of the rooms in the traditional main building have their own gas fireplaces, many are furnished with antiques purchased by the lumber executives, and all have private bathrooms. The four cottages tend to be small but have fireplaces and private decks. Set dinners, included in the rates, change nightly and feature California and Pacific Northwest cuisines, making use of seafood harvested from local waters, local herbs, freshly baked breads, and vegetables from the inn's gardens.

5600 S. Hwy. 1 (P.O. Box 369), Elk, CA 95432. www.theharborhouseinn.com. ✆ **800/720-7474** or 707/877-3203. Fax 707/877-3452. 6 units, 4 cottages. $360–$490 double; $315–$450 cottage (winter rates considerably less). Extra person $100. Rates include full breakfast and 4-course dinner. AE, MC, V. **Amenities:** Restaurant; nearby golf course. *In room:* Hair dryer, no phone, fireplace.

KOA Kamping Kabins ☺ "What? You expect me to stay at a Kampgrounds of America?!" You bet. Once you see these neat little log "kabins," you'll admit they're a great way to spend a weekend on the coast. The cabins sleep four to six, with one or two bedrooms and log-frame double beds or bunk beds for the kids. Mattresses, a heater, and a light bulb are your standard amenities. Beyond that, you're on your own; you'll need bedding or a sleeping bag, cooking and eating utensils, and a bag of charcoal for the barbecue in front. Enjoy your meal at the picnic table or on the front porch in the log swing. If this is a little too spartan for you, opt for one of the fully furnished "kottages," both decked out with private bathrooms, fireplaces, comfy beds, and other creature comforts. Hot showers, bathrooms, laundry facilities, a small store, and a swimming pool are a short walk away, as is Manchester Beach.

On Kinney Rd. (off Hwy. 1, 5 miles north of Point Arena). www.manchesterbeachkoa.com. ✆ **707/882-2375.** Fax 707/882-3104. 24 cabins, 2 cottages. $62–$84 cabin (up to 6 people); $152–$168 cottage (up to 4 people). AE, DISC, MC, V. **Amenities:** Children's center and playground; heated outdoor pool (seasonal); hot tub; spa; bocce ball courts; (limited) free Wi-Fi. *In room:* TV and kitchenette in cottages, no phone.

WHERE TO EAT

Ledford House Restaurant ★ MEDITERRANEAN If James Beard were alive, he'd feel at home at this innovative but simply decorated restaurant overlooking the pounding surf of the Pacific from a bluff above. The kitchen offers self-styled Mediterranean cuisine, experimenting with the bounty of the Golden State to fashion rich combinations and harmonious flavors using organic Northern California produce whenever possible. The bistro part of the menu is reserved primarily for the pastas and hearty stews suitable to this far-northern setting, such as their award-winning Antoine's cassoulet, a jumble of pork, lamb, garlic sausage, and duck confit slowly cooked with white beans. Although the menu changes seasonally, for a taste of California, try the salmon primavera with lemon-caper butter, or the crisp-roasted duckling with wild-huckleberry sauce. The cocktail lounge has live jazz in the evening.

3000 N. Hwy. 1, Albion. ✆ **707/937-0282.** www.ledfordhouse.com. Reservations recommended. Main courses $22–$30. AE, MC, V. Wed–Sun 5–9pm.

MENDOCINO ★★★

166 miles N of San Francisco

Mendocino is *the* premier destination on California's Northern Coast. Despite (or because of) its relative isolation, it emerged as one of Northern California's major centers for the arts in the 1950s. It's easy to see why artists were—and still are—attracted to this idyllic community, a cluster of New England–style captains' homes and stores on headlands overlooking the ocean.

Mendocino.

At the height of the logging boom, Mendocino was an important and active port. Its population was about 3,500 residents, who constructed eight hotels, 17 saloons, and more than a dozen bordellos. Today it has only about 1,000 residents, and most reside on the north end of town. On summer weekends, the population seems more like 10,000, as hordes of tourists drive up from the Bay Area. Despite the crowds, however, Mendocino manages to retain its charm.

Essentials

GETTING THERE   The fastest route from San Francisco is via U.S. 101 north to Cloverdale. Then take Hwy. 128 west to Hwy. 1, and then go north along the coast. It's about a 4-hour drive. (You could also take U.S. 101 all the way to Ukiah or Willits and cut over to the west from there.) The most scenic route, if you have the time and your stomach doesn't mind the twists and turns, is to take Hwy. 1 north along the coast the entire way; it's at least a 5- to 6-hour drive.

VISITOR INFORMATION   You can stock up on lots of free brochures and maps at the **Fort Bragg/Mendocino Coast Chamber of Commerce,** 217 N. Main St. (P.O. Box 1141), Fort Bragg, CA 95437 (© **707/961-6300;** www. mendocinocoast.com). Pick up a copy of the center's monthly magazine, *Arts and Entertainment,* which lists upcoming events throughout Mendocino. It's available at numerous stores and cafes, including the Mendocino Bakery, Gallery Bookshop, and Mendocino Art Center. You can also do some pretrip research on Mendocino at **MendocinoFun.com,** a nifty online events and activities website/blog to the region that's hosted by local outdoor enthusiasts, artists, and writers.

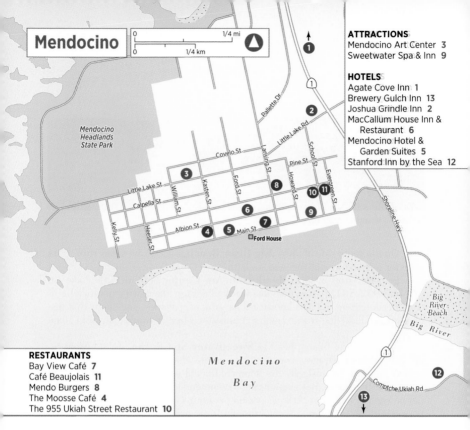

Mendocino

0   1/4 mi
0   1/4 km

ATTRACTIONS
Mendocino Art Center **3**
Sweetwater Spa & Inn **9**

HOTELS
Agate Cove Inn **1**
Brewery Gulch Inn **13**
Joshua Grindle Inn **2**
MacCallum House Inn &
    Restaurant **6**
Mendocino Hotel &
    Garden Suites **5**
Stanford Inn by the Sea **12**

RESTAURANTS
Bay View Café **7**
Café Beaujolais **11**
Mendo Burgers **8**
The Moosse Café **4**
The 955 Ukiah Street Restaurant **10**

Mendocino
Headlands
State Park

Ford House

Mendocino

Bay

*Big
River
Beach*

Big River

Exploring the Town

Stroll through town, survey the architecture, and browse through the dozens of galleries and shops. My favorites include the **Highlight Gallery,** 45052 Main St. (© **707/937-3132;** www.thehighlightgallery.com), for its handmade furniture, pottery, and other craft work; and the **Gallery Bookshop & Bookwinkle's Children's Books,** at Main and Kasten streets (© **707/937-2665;** www. gallerybooks.com), one of the best independent bookstores in Northern California, with a wonderful selection of books for children and adults. Another popular stop is **Mendocino Jams & Preserves,** 440 Main St. (© **800/708-1196;** www.mendojams.com), which offers free tastings on little bread chips of its natural, locally made gourmet fruit spreads.

After exploring the town, walk out onto **Mendocino Headlands State Park ★**, which wraps around the town. (The visitor center is in the Ford House on Main St.; © **707/937-5397.**) Three miles of trails, with panoramic views of sea arches and hidden grottoes, wind through the park. At the right time of year, wildflowers blanket the area, and blackberries grow beside the trails. The headlands are home to many unique bird species, including black oystercatchers. Behind the Mendocino Presbyterian Church on Main Street, a trail leads to stairs that take you down to the beach, a small but picturesque stretch of sand where driftwood has washed ashore.

Mendocino Headlands State Park.

On the south side of town, **Big River Beach** is accessible from Hwy. 1; it's good for picnicking, walking, and sunbathing.

In town, stop by the **Mendocino Art Center,** 45200 Little Lake St. (*©* **707/937-5818;** www.mendocinoartcenter.org), the town's unofficial cultural headquarters. It's also known for its gardens, galleries, and shops that display and sell local fine arts and crafts. Admission is free; it's open daily from 10am to 5pm.

After a day of hiking, head to **Sweetwater Spa & Inn,** 44840 Main St. (*©* **800/300-4140;** www.sweetwaterspa.com), which offers group and private saunas and hot tub soaks by the hour. Additional services include Swedish or deep-tissue massages. Reservations are recommended. Private tub prices are $15 per person per half-hour, $18 per person per hour. Group tub prices are $10 per person with no time limit. Special discounts are available on Wednesdays. The spa is open daily from noon to 9pm and Saturday from noon to 10pm.

Outdoor Pursuits

Explore the Big River by renting a canoe, a kayak, or an outrigger from **Catch a Canoe & Bicycles Too** (*©* **707/937-0273;** www.stanfordinn.com), open daily from 9am to sunset, on the grounds of the Stanford Inn by the Sea (see "Where to Stay," below). If you're lucky, you'll see osprey, blue herons, harbor seals, deer, and wood ducks. These same folks will also rent you a mountain bike (of higher

MENDOCINO'S secret SINKHOLE

Known by locals as the **Little River Cemetery Sinkhole,** this almost perfectly circular (and massive!) sinkhole is simply amazing. At low tide you can walk through the wave-cut tunnel to the tide pools at the bottom of the bluff; at high tide, you can sit on the tiny sandy beach and look at the tunnel as the waves blast through. Either way, the feeling of being within this natural phenomenon is almost eerie. To get here, park across from the Little River Cemetery on Hwy. 1, walk to the southwest corner of the cemetery, and look for a small opening in the chain-link fence. The sinkhole is only a few dozen yards down the trail, but be prepared to enter and exit the hole on all fours or you might end up buried alongside it.

quality than a standard rental), so you can head up Hwy. 1 and explore the nearby state parks on two wheels.

Visitors can ride horseback (both English- and Western-style) on the beach and into the woods through **Ricochet Ridge Ranch,** 24201 N. Hwy. 1, Fort Bragg (© **888/873-5777** or 707/964-7669; www.horse-vacation.com). Prices range from $45 for a 1½-hour beach ride to $295 for an all-day private beach-and-redwoods trail ride.

In addition to Mendocino Headlands State Park (see "Exploring the Town," above), several other state parks are within an easy drive or bike ride from Mendocino. The brochure *Mendocino Coast State Parks,* available from the visitor center in Fort Bragg, has information on all the parks, with maps of each. These areas include **Manchester State Park,** where the San Andreas Fault sweeps to the sea; **Jughandle State Reserve;** and **Van Damme State Park ★**, with a sheltered, easily accessible beach.

My favorite, on Hwy. 1 just north of Mendocino, is **Russian Gulch State Park ★★**. It's one of the region's most spectacular parks, where waves crash against the cliffs that protect the park's California coastal redwoods. The most popular attraction is the **Punch Bowl,** a collapsed sea cave that forms a tunnel through which waves crash, creating throaty echoes. Inland, visitors can pedal along a scenic, paved bike path or hoof it on miles of hiking trails, including a gentle, well-marked 3-mile **Waterfall Loop** that winds past tall redwoods and damp green foliage to a 36-foot-high waterfall. Admission is $6 and camping is $25 per night. Call © **800/444-7275** or log on to **ReserveAmerica** at **www.reserveamerica.com** for camping reservations; for general state park information, call © **707/937-5804** or visit **www.cal-parks.ca.gov**.

Deep-sea fishing charters are available from Fort Bragg, which is just a short ride up the coast.

Where to Stay

EXPENSIVE

Stanford Inn by the Sea ★★   Just south of Mendocino, this rustic but sumptuous lodge is on 11 acres of land abutting the Big River. The grounds are captivating, with tiers of gardens; a pond for ducks and geese; and fenced pastures of horses, llamas, and old gnarled apple trees. The solarium-style indoor hot tub and pool surrounded by tropical plants are gorgeous. The luxurious rooms come with thick robes, down comforters, fresh flowers, and works by local artists. All units have fireplaces or stoves and private decks from which you can gaze on the Pacific. Second honeymooners should inquire about the romantic River Cottage; families will want the big renovated barn. Pets are welcome and receive the royal treatment. The inn also has a small massage studio, individual and group yoga lessons, and the **Raven's Restaurant,** the only totally vegetarian restaurant on the Mendocino coast offering a full bar and award-winning wine list.

N. Hwy. 1 and Comptche Ukiah Rd. (P.O. Box 487), Mendocino, CA 95460. www.stanfordinn.com. © **800/331-8884** or 707/937-5615. Fax 707/937-0305. 33 units. $178–$308 double; $295–$816 suite. 2-night minimum stay on weekends. Rates include breakfast. AE, DC, DISC, MC, V. Pets accepted for $25. **Amenities:** Vegetarian restaurant; complimentary bikes; canoe and kayak rental; concierge; nearby golf course; exercise room; solarium-style pool; room service; sauna and spa. *In room:* TV/VCR w/pay movies, DVD player, hair dryer, kitchenette, free high-speed Internet.

Mendocino Nightlife

The nightlife in Mendocino is like molasses in winter. Visitors have three options: (1) have a casual cocktail in the elegant bar and lounge at the **Mendocino Hotel** (see review below); (2) knock down a few beers with the locals at **Dick's Place** (45080 Main St.; ℂ **707/937-6010**), the town's oldest bar; or (3) get in the car and head up Hwy. 1 a bit to the **Caspar Inn,** the best nightclub on the North Coast. Everything from rock and jazz to reggae and blues is played live every night starting at 9:30pm. Check its website calendar for upcoming shows and bring a designated dancer and driver. It's located at 14957 Caspar Rd. (take the Caspar Rd. exit off Hwy. 1, ¼ mile north of Mendocino; ℂ **707/964-5565; www.casparinn.com**).

MODERATE

Agate Cove Inn ★★   Good luck trying to find an accommodation with a more beautiful coastal setting than Agate Cove Inn's. Words can barely convey the splendor of the view from the front lawn—a sweeping, unfettered vista of the sea and its surging waves crashing onto the bluffs. Situate yourself on one of the Adirondack chairs with a good book, and you'll never want to leave. The inn consists of a main house trimmed in blue and white, surrounded by a bevy of single and duplex cottages. Nine of the 10 spacious units have views of the ocean, king- or queen-size beds, down comforters, fireplaces, and private decks. In the morning, a fantastic country breakfast is served in the main house's enclosed porch (yes, with the same ocean view).

11201 N. Lansing St. (P.O. Box 1150), Mendocino, CA 95460. www.agatecove.com. ℂ **800/527-3111** or 707/937-0551. Fax 707/937-0550. 10 units. $159–$329 double. Rates include full breakfast and complimentary sherry. MC, V. **Amenities:** Concierge; nearby golf course; laptop computer to use in main house. *In room:* TV/VCR w/complimentary videos, DVD player, CD player, fridge in some, hair dryer, Jacuzzi tub, no phone, free Wi-Fi.

Brewery Gulch Inn ★★   Built almost entirely from century-old redwood logs, the Brewery Gulch Inn is a three-story inn set high on a bluff overlooking Mendocino's Smuggler's Cove. You don't need to be a connoisseur of woodworking to marvel at the subtle red, purple, and blond tones that swirl throughout the inn's redwood finishes. The inn was constructed in an Arts and Crafts style, with a massive steel-and-glass central fireplace and 11 soundproofed guest rooms (including one ultra-Zen suite). Most guest rooms have Jacuzzis or soaking tubs for two, as well as private decks with expansive views of the ocean and hundreds of acres of unoccupied meadow and forest. An in-house chef prepares the gourmet country breakfast with herbs and fruit from exclusively local sources, and hearty hors d'oeuvres and Mendocino County wines are offered in the evening. *Tip:* Check the website for tempting packages such as the "Romantic Escape!" and "Ocean Kayaking" deals.

9401 Coast Hwy. 1 N., Mendocino, CA 95460. www.brewerygulchinn.com. ℂ **800/578-4454** or 707/937-4752. Fax 707/937-1279. 11 units. $210–$465 double. Rates include organic gourmet country breakfast and evening wine tasting with hors d'oeuvres. AE, MC, V. **Amenities:** Concierge; common room w/fireplace; library w/wide selection of books, CDs, and videos. *In room:* TV/DVD, CD player, hair dryer, fireplace, soaking tub for 2.

Joshua Grindle Inn ★★   When it was built in 1879, this stately Victorian was one of the most impressive houses in Mendocino, owned by the town's wealthiest banker. Now the oldest B&B in town, it features redwood siding, a wraparound porch, and emerald lawns. From its prettily planted gardens, the view across the village reaches all the way to the distant bay. The main house has five rooms, with two more in the cottage, and three in the water tower. Each is individually decorated: The Library Room has a New England feel, with its four-poster pine bed, floor-to-ceiling bookcase, and 19th-century tiles around the fireplace depicting Aesop's fables. Sherry, sweets, and tea are served in the parlor in front of the fireplace; breakfast is in the dining room. The proprietors also have a beautiful two-bedroom, two-bathroom oceanview rental home, the Grindle Guest House, with floor-to-ceiling windows, a large kitchen, and a wood-burning fireplace.

44800 Little Lake Rd. (P.O. Box 647), Mendocino, CA 95460. www.joshgrin.com. ✆ **800/GRIN-DLE** (474-6353) or 707/937-4143. 12 units. $150–$359 double. Rates include full breakfast, afternoon tea, and wine. MC, V. **Amenities:** Concierge; nearby golf course. *In room:* TV/DVD in some units, hair dryer, no phone.

MacCallum House Inn & Restaurant ★★ ☺   A historic 1882 gingerbread Victorian mansion, MacCallum House is one of Mendocino's top accommodations. Originally owned by Daisy MacCallum, the daughter of the town's richest lumber baron, the inn remained in the family until 1974, when it became a B&B. With the occasional Tiffany lamp or Persian carpet, each uniquely decorated suite is furnished with original pieces—a Franklin stove, a handmade quilt, a cushioned rocking chair, or a child's cradle. The inn offers a variety of vacation rentals and even two separate inns, the historic 1882 Mendocino Village Inn and the MacCallum House Suites. The restaurant on the premises serves North Coast cuisine ranging from pan-seared Sonoma duck breast with Mendocino wild huckleberry Syrah sauce, to pan-roasted halibut with Dungeness crab and black trumpet mushrooms. Lighter fare is served at the inn's Grey Whale Bar & Cafe. And unlike most in the area, pets and children are welcome.

45020 Albion St. (P.O. Box 206), Mendocino, CA 95460. www.maccallumhouse.com. ✆ **800/609-0492** or 707/937-0289. Fax 707/937-2243. 44 units. $149–$399 double. Extra person or pet $40. Rates include full breakfast, $14 daily tokens per couple for food or bar use. DC, DISC, MC, V. **Amenities:** Restaurant; cafe; bar; bike rentals; concierge; spa services; DVD library; hot tub. *In room:* TV, DVD/CD player, hair dryer, high-speed Internet.

Mendocino Hotel & Garden Suites ★   In the heart of town, this 1878 hotel evokes California's Gold Rush era. Beveled-glass doors open into a Victorian-style lobby and parlor. Furnishings include antiques and reproductions, such as the oak reception desk from a demolished Kansas bank, Remington paintings, stained-glass lamps, and Persian carpets. Guest rooms feature hand-painted French porcelain sinks with floral designs; old-fashioned wallpaper, beds, and armoires; and memorabilia of historic Mendocino. About half the rooms are in four handsome small buildings behind the main house. Many of the deluxe rooms have fireplaces, modern bathrooms, and good views. Suites have an additional parlor, as well as a fireplace or balcony.

45080 Main St. (P.O. Box 587), Mendocino, CA 95460. www.mendocinohotel.com. ✆ **800/548-0513** or 707/937-0511. Fax 707/937-0513. 51 units, 37 with private bathroom. $100–$120 double with shared bathroom; $115–$295 double with private bathroom; $335–$395 suite. Extra person $20. AE, MC, V. **Amenities:** 2 restaurants; 2 bars; nearby golf course; access to nearby health club ($8); room service; spa services; free Wi-Fi in lobby. *In room:* TV, hair dryer.

IN NEARBY ALBION & LITTLE RIVER

Albion River Inn and Restaurant ★★   A quarter-mile north of Albion (or 6 miles south of Mendocino), this modern, beautiful inn overlooks the mouth of the Albion River from a bluff some 90 feet above the Pacific. The view, of course, is spectacular. The rooms are decorated in a contemporary style with comfortable furnishings; all have ocean views, and most have decks. You'll find wingbacks in front of the fireplaces, down comforters on the queen- and king-size beds, well-lit desks, binoculars for wildlife viewing, and bathrobes. **_Insider tip:_** If you really want to impress, reserve one of the rooms with a spa tub for two, which has a picture window with dazzling views of the coast. The menu at the on-site restaurant changes daily, but the view from the tables remains the same: stellar. The award-winning wine list is also impressive. In the evening, piano music adds to the romantic atmosphere.

3790 N. Hwy. 1 (P.O. Box 100), Albion, CA 95410. www.albionriverinn.com. ✆ **800/479-7944** or 707/937-1919. Fax 707/937-2604. 22 units. $195–$275 double; $325 spa suite. Rates include full breakfast. AE, DC, DISC, MC, V. **Amenities:** Restaurant. _In room:_ CD player, fridge, hair dryer, free Wi-Fi, fireplace (in most).

Glendeven ★★   This 1867 farmhouse is a place of exceptional style and comfort. Accommodations spread across 2½ acres, encompassing the main house, the Carriage House Suite, and an addition known as Stevenscroft. Each room is individually decorated with a balanced mix of antiques, contemporary pieces, and original art. Most have ocean views, fireplaces, and porches. Etta's Suite in the Farmhouse has an antique walnut bed, while the Eastlin and Carriage House suites have king-size feather beds. The four rooms in the Stevenscroft annex are also spacious and beautifully furnished. A vacation rental house, the Barn Loft, has two bedrooms, a loft bathroom, and a kitchen, and the Sea Ridge Cottage is a roomy 1,400 square feet perfect for honeymooners. Adjacent to the inn, numerous fern-lined canyon trails lead to the ocean and beaches of Van Damme State Park.

8205 N. Hwy. 1, Little River, CA 95456. www.glendeven.com. ✆ **800/822-4536** or 707/937-0083. 10 units; 2 cottages. $148–$310 double; $268–$335 Carriage House Grand Suite. Rates include full breakfast. Ask about off-season midweek specials. AE, DISC, MC, V. **Amenities:** Free Wi-Fi. _In room:_ CD player, hair dryer, no phone.

Where to Eat

In addition to the following, see "Where to Stay," above, for hotel restaurants.

EXPENSIVE

Café Beaujolais ★★ AMERICAN/FRENCH   This is one of Mendocino's top dining choices and one of the most celebrated restaurants on the Northern Coast. They pride themselves on using locally grown organic produce, meat from humanely raised animals, and fresh locally caught seafood. The French-style cafe is set in an early-1900s house with a modern decor featuring black-and-white photos of the local purveyors. Café Beaujolais is open for lunch and dinner, with the menu changing seasonally and usually offering six to

Bread Winner

Few tourists know that Café Beaujolais's renowned "brickery breads" are sold daily from 11am to around 5pm at its Brickery bakery on Ukiah Street, just east of the restaurant.

seven main courses. Their signature dish is the pan-seared sturgeon filet, prepared with truffle emulsion sauce and served with house-made tagliatelle, wild mushrooms, beets, and snap peas. For dessert, try the melting chocolate lava cake served with homemade hazelnut ice cream. On a warm night, request a table in the atrium overlooking the gardens.

961 Ukiah St. ✆ **707/937-5614.** www.cafebeaujolais.com. Reservations recommended. Main courses $24–$42. DISC, MC, V. Wed–Sun 11:30am–2:30pm; daily 5:30–9pm.

The Moosse Café ★★ CALIFORNIA BISTRO   This petite cafe in a New England–style home is another one of Mendocino's most popular. The menu changes seasonally and features many items made from locally grown organic herbs and vegetables, such as the wonderful organic Rosie chicken and shiitake mushroom potpie with a chive buttermilk biscuit crust and spring vegetables. I also enjoyed the pan-roasted natural pork chop with a sweet-onion-hazelnut crust, and the braised beef short ribs with Little River organic shiitake mushroom and yellow Finn mashed potatoes. If the cioppino is on the menu—an aromatic stew of fresh fish and shellfish simmered in a saffron-fennel-tomato broth—you're in luck. Service is friendly; my only complaint is that the tables are a bit too close together, especially if it's crowded.

390 Kasten St. (at Albion St.). ✆ **707/937-4323.** www.themoosse.com. Reservations recommended for dinner. Main courses $8–$15 lunch, $22–$30 dinner. MC, V. May–Oct daily noon–3pm and 5:30–9pm; Feb-April Thurs–Mon noon–3pm and 5:30–9pm. Closed Nov-Jan.

The 955 Ukiah Street Restaurant ★★ NORTH COAST CUISINE   Shortly after this building's construction in the 1960s, Emmy Lou Packard commandeered the premises as an art studio for the creation of a series of giant murals. Today it's a spacious yet cozy restaurant, accented with railway ties and vaulted ceilings, accessed through a long ramp amid a verdant garden; ask for a window table overlooking the greenery. The cuisine is creative and reasonably priced, a worthy alternative to the perpetually booked Café Beaujolais next door. It's hard to pick a favorite dish, although the phyllo-wrapped red snapper with pesto and lime has a zesty tang, and the crispy duck with ginger, apples, and Calvados sauce would garner enthusiasm in Normandy.

955 Ukiah St. ✆ **707/937-1955.** www.955restaurant.com. Reservations recommended. Main courses $13–$36. MC, V. Thurs–Sun 6–10pm.

MODERATE

Bay View Café ★ AMERICAN   This reasonably priced cafe is one of the most popular in town—mainly for the vistas, not necessarily the food. The second-floor dining area affords a sweeping view of the Pacific and faraway headlands; to reach it, climb a flight of stairs outside the town's antique water tower and then detour sideways. You'll find a menu with southwestern selections, an array of sandwiches, fish and chips, and fresh catch of the day. Breakfast ranges from the basic bacon and eggs to eggs Florentine and honey-wheat pancakes.

45040 Main St. ✆ **707/937-4197.** Reservations not accepted. Main courses $6–$15. No credit cards. Summer daily 8am–9pm; winter Mon–Thurs 8am–3pm, Fri–Sun 8am–9pm.

INEXPENSIVE

Mendo Burgers (✆ **707/937-1111**) is arguably the best burger joint on the Northern Coast, with patties of all stripes—beef, chicken, turkey, or veggie. A side of thick, fresh-cut fries is mandatory, as is a pile of napkins. Hidden behind the Mendocino Bakery and Café at 10483 Lansing St., it's a little hard to find but well worth searching out. It's open daily from 11am to 6pm, unless they run out of food first (which has been known to happen from time to time).

In the back of the **Little River Market** (© 707/937-5133), directly across from the Little River Inn on Hwy. 1, a trio of small tables overlooks the beautiful Mendocino coastline. Order a tamale, sandwich, hamburger, or whatever else is on the menu at the tiny deli inside the market, or buy a loaf of Café Beaujolais bread, sold at the front counter, and your favorite spread. The market is open daily until 7pm.

FORT BRAGG

10 miles N of Mendocino; 176 miles N of San Francisco

As the Mendocino coast's commercial center—hence the site of most of the area's fast-food restaurants and supermarkets—Fort Bragg is far more down-to-earth than Mendocino. Inexpensive motels and cheap eats used to be its only attractions, but over the past few years, gentrification has spread throughout the town, as the logging and fishing industries have steadily declined. With no room left to open new shops in Mendocino, many gallery, boutique, and restaurant owners have moved up the road. The result is a huge increase in Fort Bragg's tourist trade, particularly during the Whale Festival in March and Paul Bunyan Days over Labor Day weekend.

To explore the town properly, get a free walking-tour map from the **Fort Bragg/Mendocino Coast Chamber of Commerce,** 217 N. Main St. (P.O. Box 1141), Fort Bragg, CA 95437 (© 707/961-6300; www.mendocinocoast. com). The friendly staff can answer most questions about Mendocino, Fort Bragg, and the surrounding region.

Shopping & Exploring the Area

Fort Bragg doesn't have as many high-end stores and galleries as its dainty cousin to the south, but it does have some worthwhile shopping spots. **Antiques shops** line Franklin Street between Laurel and Redwood (also known as Antiques Row), and several boutiques are housed within the **Union Lumber Company Store,** an impressive edifice built almost entirely with handcrafted redwoods (on the corner of Main and Redwood sts.).

The **Hot Pepper Jelly Company,** 330 N. Main St. (© 866/737-7379; www.hotpepperjelly.com), is famous for its assortment of Mendocino food products—dozens of pepper jelly varieties, plus local mustards, syrups, and biscotti; hand-painted porcelain bowls; baskets; and more. The **Mendocino Chocolate Company,** 232 N. Main St. (© 800/722-1107 or 707/964-8800; www. mendocino-chocolate.com), makes and sells homemade chocolates and truffles, which it ships all over the world. Painters, jewelers, sculptors, weavers, potters, woodworkers, and other local artists display their works at **Northcoast Artists,** 362 N. Main St. (© 707/964-8266; www.northcoastartists.org).

Fort Bragg is also the home of the **Mendocino Coast Botanical Gardens,** 18220 N. Hwy. 1 (© 707/964-4352; www.gardenbythesea.org), about 7 miles north of Mendocino. This cliff-top public garden, set among the pines along the coast, nurtures rhododendrons, fuchsias, azaleas, and a multitude of flowering shrubs. The area has bridges, streams, canyons, dells, picnic areas, and trails for easy walking. Admission is $10 for adults, $7.50 for seniors ages 60 and over, $2 for youth 13 to 17, $2 for children 6 to 12, and free for children 5 and under. (Children 17 and under must be accompanied by an adult.) The gardens are open daily March through October from 9am to 5pm, November through February from 9am to 4pm.

The **North Coast Brewing Company,** 455 N. Main St. (© **707/964-2739;** www.northcoastbrewing.com), is also worth investigating. Free tours are offered every Saturday at noon and reservations aren't required—just show up. Across the street, the Brewing Company's pub is open for lunch and dinner (see "Where to Eat," below).

Outdoor Pursuits

Fort Bragg is the county's sport-fishing hub. South of town, **Noyo Fishing Center,** 32440 N. Harbor, Noyo (© **707/964-3000;** www.fortbraggfishing.com), is a good place to buy tackle and is the best source of information on local fishing boats. Lots of party boats leave from the town's harbor, as do whale-watching tours.

Lost Coast Kayaking, in Van Damme State Park (© **707/964-7480;** www.lostcoastkayaking.com), offers guided kayak tours of the numerous sea caves on the coast. All the necessary equipment is provided; all you need to bring is a bathing suit and $50 for the 2-hour tour (closed in winter).

Three miles north of Fort Bragg, off Hwy. 1, **MacKerricher State Park** (© **707/964-9112**) is a popular place for biking, hiking, and horseback riding. This 1,700-acre park has 142 campsites and 8 miles of shoreline. For a true biking or hiking venture, travel the 8-mile-long "Haul Road"—an old logging road (partly washed out, but safe) with fine ocean vistas all the way to Ten Mile River. Harbor seals make their home at the park's Laguna Point Seal Watching Station.

Catching fresh oysters.

A train ride THROUGH THE REDWOODS

Built as a logging railroad in 1885, the North Coast's vintage Skunk Train line was originally used for moving massive redwood logs from the rugged back country to the Mendocino Coast sawmills. Today it's one of the North Coast's largest tourist attractions, taking visitors on a scenic route through the redwood forest, crossing 31 bridges and trestles, cutting through two deep tunnels, and chugging past giant trees that are more than 1,000 years old, before reaching a secluded, forested glen accessible only by train.

The trains run daily from the Fort Bragg Depot at the foot of Laurel Avenue from March 1 to November 31, and on Saturdays December through February. Schedules vary, particularly during holidays; call for details. In summer, it's a good idea to make reservations. Tickets cost from $47 to $75 for adults and $22 to $40 children ages 3 to 11, depending on the day, time, and train. The 4½-hour Sunset Dinner Barbecue ride includes an elaborate barbecue dinner with huge baskets and trays of homemade bread, barbecue chicken and ribs, baked beans, garden salads, and a "surprise" dessert. For more information, call ✆ **866/457-5865** or 707/459-1060, or see **www.skunktrain.com**.

Where to Stay

Grey Whale Inn ★ ☺ In downtown Fort Bragg, a short walk from the beach, this B&B was built as a hospital in 1915—hence the wide hallways and large guest rooms. The redwood building is now a well-run, relaxed inn, with antiques, handmade quilts, and plenty of local art. Each room is unique: Two have ocean views, four have fireplaces, one has a whirlpool tub, three have private decks, and one has a shower with wheelchair access. My favorite is the spacious, elegant Campbell Suite, with a king bed and gas-log fireplace. The buffet breakfast, served in the Craftsman-style breakfast room (with trays for carrying your food back to bed, if you prefer), includes a hot entree made from farm-fresh eggs, homemade bread or coffeecake, and fresh fruit. Kids will appreciate the game room with a pool table and foosball.

615 N. Main St., Fort Bragg, CA 95437. www.greywhaleinn.com. ✆ **800/382-7244** or 707/964-0640. Fax 707/964-4408. 13 units. $150–$225 double. Rates include buffet breakfast. AE, MC, V. **Amenities:** Access to nearby health club. *In room:* TV, DVD/VCR player in some units, hair dryer, kitchenette.

Old Coast Hotel ✦ Smack downtown just off the main drag, this quaint little charmer is one of the most delightful in all of the county. It's kitschy, sure, which lends it even more character; its themed rooms channel such icons as Elvis, Lucille Ball, or Marilyn Monroe (my favorite, with soaring ceilings). Accommodations surround a central garden, where you can enjoy the sun on the odd day Fort Bragg isn't foggy. Some rooms have fireplaces; each is one of a kind. Ask the innkeeper about the series of strange coincidences that led her to believe the old place is haunted.

101 N. Franklin St., Fort Bragg, CA 95437. www.oldcoasthotel.com. ✆ **888/468-3550** or 707/961-4488. 15 units. $120–$205 double. Rates include continental breakfast. AE, DISC, MC, V. **Amenities:** Restaurant and bar (open only in spring and summer months); pool table. *In room:* TV.

Where to Eat

Egghead's ★ AMERICAN   It's tough to find a quality breakfast joint in Fort Bragg; each seemed a greasy spoon with poor service and even worse food. Then I stumbled upon this Main Street gem. It's nothing fancy, but if the long line and patrons bursting out of the doors are any indicators, it's beloved by the residents. The menu didn't disappoint, either, offering dozens of omelets, a to-die-for pumpkin Belgian waffle topped with almond cream and fruit, and the strongest, most delicious cup of joe for miles. Like the **Old Coast Hotel,** Egghead's is all about a central theme—in this case, *The Wizard of Oz,* with menu items including the Munchkin Marvel, Dorothy's Delight, Cyclone Special, and Flying Monkey Potatoes—and, while a bit out of the ordinary, it oddly enough only adds to the experience. In a nod to the excellent service, Egghead's abides by a love-our-food-or-it's-free policy.

326 N. Main St. ✆ **707/964-5005** or 707/964-8543. www.eggheadsrestaurant.com. Main courses $6–$14. AE, DISC, MC, V. Thurs–Tues 7am–2pm.

North Coast Brewing Company ★ AMERICAN   Since it opened in 1988, this homey brewpub has been the most happening place in town—especially during happy hour, when boisterous locals take over the bar and dark-wood tables. The building that houses the pub is a century-old redwood structure, which in previous lives functioned as a mortuary, an annex to the local Presbyterian church, an art studio, and administration offices for the College of the Redwoods. Twelve types of beer are available (to go, even) year-round, in addition to seasonal brews. Standard fare, such as fish and chips and burgers, are supplemented by more substantial dishes, ranging from pork tenderloin Dijon with garlic mashed potatoes and fresh vegetables to pasta with seafood in a light herb sauce. After your meal, browse the shop or take a free tour of the brewery (see "Shopping & Exploring the Area," above).

455 N. Main St. ✆ **707/964-2739.** www.northcoastbrewing.com. Reservations accepted for large parties only. Main courses $17–$25. DISC, MC, V. Daily noon–9pm.

The Restaurant ★ ☺ PACIFIC NORTHWEST/CALIFORNIAN   One of the oldest family-run restaurants on the coast, this unpretentious Fort Bragg landmark is known for its jovial atmosphere and cuisine made from scratch from local produce, seafood, meats, and wines. The menu includes dishes from just about every corner of the planet: New York strip steak, a Provençal-style seafood stew, and a few less expensive options such as the Asian noodle bowl filled with bay shrimp and fresh vegetables. My favorites are the fresh blackened rockfish and crab cakes made from local Dungeness crab. A few vegetarian specialties include grilled polenta with melted mozzarella and sautéed mushrooms, topped with tomato-herb sauce and Parmesan cheese. A nicely priced kids' menu is available as well. The booth section is the best place to sit if you want to keep an eye on the kitchen entertainment, provided by ebullient chef Jim Larsen, who has been running things here for more than 30 years.

418 N. Main St. ✆ **707/964-9800.** www.therestaurantfortbragg.com. Reservations recommended. Dinner main courses $17–$30 (includes soup or salad); $10–$15 a la carte items. AE, DISC, MC, V. Thurs–Mon 5–10pm.

THE AVENUE OF THE GIANTS ★★

From Fort Bragg, Hwy. 1 continues north along the shoreline for about 30 miles before turning inland to Leggett and the Redwood Highway (U.S. 101), which runs north to Garberville. Six miles beyond Garberville, the **Avenue of the Giants** (Hwy. 254) begins around Phillipsville. The Avenue of the Giants is one of the most spectacular routes in the West, cutting along the Eel River through the 51,000-acre Humboldt Redwoods State Park. It roughly parallels U.S. 101, with about a half-dozen interchanges between the two roads, in case you don't want to drive the entire thing. The avenue ends just south of Scotia; from here, it's only about 10 miles to the turnoff to Ferndale, about 5 miles west of U.S. 101.

For more information or a detailed map of the area, go to the **Humboldt Redwoods State Park Visitor Center** in Weott (© **707/946-2263;** www. humboldtredwoods.org), in the center of the Avenue of the Giants.

Touring the Avenue

Thirty-three miles long, the Avenue of the Giants was left intact for sightseers when the freeway was built. The giants are the majestic coast redwoods *(Sequoia sempervirens);* more than 50,000 acres of them make up the most outstanding display in the redwood belt. Their rough-bark columns alone climb 100 feet or more and branches soar to more than 340 feet. With their fire-resistant bark and immunity to insects, they have survived for thousands of years. The oldest dated coast redwood is more than 2,200 years old.

Sadly, the route has several tacky attractions that attempt to turn the trees into some kind of freak show. My suggestion is to skip these and take advantage of the trails and campgrounds off the beaten path. As you drive along, you'll see many parking areas with short loop trails leading into the forest. From south to north, the first of these "attractions" is the **Chimney Tree,** where J. R. R. Tolkien's Hobbit is rumored to reside. This living, hollow redwood is more than 1,500 years old. A gift shop and burger place are nearby. Then there's the **One-Log House,** a small apartment-like dwelling built inside a log. You can also drive your car through a living redwood at the **Shrine Drive-Thru Tree,** at Myers Flat, midway along the avenue.

A few miles north of Weott is **Founders Grove,** named in honor of those who established the Save the

Avenue of the Giants.

Redwoods League in 1918. Farther north, close to the end of the avenue, stands the 950-year-old **Immortal Tree,** just north of Redcrest. Near Pepperwood at the end of the avenue, the **Drury Trail** and the **Percy French Trail** are two great short hikes. The park itself is also good for mountain biking. Ask the rangers for details. For more information, contact **Humboldt Redwoods State Park** (📞 **707/946-2409;** www.humboldtredwoods.org).

The state park has three **campgrounds** with 248 campsites: Hidden Springs, half a mile south of Myers Flat; Burlington, 2 miles south of Weott, near park headquarters; and Albee Creek State Campground, 5 miles west of U.S. 101 on the Mattole Road north of Weott. Reservations are advised in summer; you can make them by calling 📞 **800/444-7275** or online via **ReserveAmerica** at **www.reserveamerica.com**. Remaining sites are on a first-come, first-served basis. You'll also come across picnic and swimming facilities, motels, resorts, restaurants, and rest areas with parking lots.

WHERE TO STAY & EAT NEAR THE SOUTHERN ENTRANCE

Benbow Inn ★   This elegant National Historic Landmark, overlooking the Eel River and surrounded by gardens, has housed notable guests such as Eleanor Roosevelt, Herbert Hoover, and Charles Laughton. Constructed in 1926 in a mock-Tudor style, it's named after the family who built it. Rooms vary in size and amenities, though all are decorated with period antiques; the deluxe units have fireplaces, Jacuzzis, private entrances, and patios. The Honeymoon Cottage is the most popular accommodation, with vaulted ceilings, a canopy bed, wood-burning fireplace, and private patio overlooking the river. Beautiful Benbow Lake State Park is right out the front door. Complimentary afternoon tea and scones are served in the lobby at 3pm and hors d'oeuvres in the lounge at 5pm—all very proper, of course. The dramatic, high-ceilinged dining room opens onto a spacious terrace and offers internationally inspired (and expensive) main courses. **Note:** There's talk of a $28-million project to renovate the inn along with its surrounding amenities and turn it into a destination resort, but as of press time there's been no confirmation.

445 Lake Benbow Dr., Garberville, CA 95542. www.benbowinn.com. 📞 **800/355-3301** or 707/ 923-2124. Fax 707/923-2897. 55 units. $99–$550 double; $99–$695 cottage. Rates include complimentary decanter of sherry. AE, DISC, MC, V. **Amenities:** Restaurant; bar; babysitting (w/ advance notice); complimentary bikes; nearby golf course; pool; spa. *In room:* A/C, hair dryer, free Wi-Fi.

Ferndale ★

The village of Ferndale, beyond the Avenue of the Giants and west of U.S. 101, is a National Historic Landmark because of its Victorian homes and storefronts, including a smithy and saddlery. About 5 miles inland from the coast and close to the redwood belt, Ferndale is one of the best-preserved Victorian hamlets in Northern California. Despite its unbearably cute shops, it is nonetheless a vital part of the Northern Coastal tourist circuit.

What's less known about this small town is that it has a number of artists in residence. It's also home to one of California's oddest happenings, the **World Championship Great Arcata to Ferndale Cross-Country Kinetic Sculpture Race** (www.kineticuniverse.com), which draws more than 10,000 spectators every Memorial Day weekend. For 38 miles, over land, sand, mud, and water, participants race in whimsically designed, handmade, people-powered vehicles that have to be seen to be believed—dragons, Christmas trees, flying saucers, and pyramids, to mention but a few. Awards range from Best Art to Best Engineering to Best Bribe. And as the grand prizes are worth about $15, inspired madness is the only incentive. Stop at the museum at 780 Main St. if you want to see a few past race entries, but bear in mind it's nothing like seeing these contrivances in glorious action.

WHERE TO STAY

Shaw House Inn Bed and Breakfast ★★ Modeled after Hawthorne's House of the Seven Gables, this gorgeous B&B is the oldest structure in Ferndale, the oldest B&B in California, and one of the prettiest Victorian homes I've ever seen (and I've seen a *lot* of B&Bs). It was built in 1854 by Ferndale founder Seth Louis Shaw, who had a penchant for jutting gables, bay windows, balconies, and gazebos. Each of the eight individually decorated guest rooms is handsomely furnished with period antiques, plush fabrics, and private bathrooms (rare for a 19th-c. B&B). Four rooms have private entrances, and three have private balconies overlooking the 1-acre garden. My favorite is the romantic Fountain Family Suite, with its own fireplace, parlor, and claw-foot tub. The immaculate 1-acre park is shaded by 25 varieties of 100-plus-year-old trees and rhododendrons, and the restaurants and shops along Main Street are a short walk away. Small pets are accepted on a case-by-case basis.

703 Main St., Ferndale, CA 95536. www.shawhouse.com. (✆ **800/557-SHAW** (7429) or 707/786-9958. Fax 707/786-9758. 8 units, all with private bathroom. $95–$150 double; $205–$275 suite. Additional guest $35. Rates include breakfast and afternoon tea. DISC, MC, V. *In room:* TV/DVD in some, Wi-Fi.

EUREKA & ENVIRONS ★

296 miles N of San Francisco

Eureka

At first glance, Eureka (pop. 27,000) looks unappealing: Fast-food restaurants, cheap motels, and shopping malls predominate on the main thoroughfare. But if you turn west off U.S. 101 anywhere between A and M streets, you'll discover **Old Town Eureka** along the waterfront, which is worth exploring. It has a large number of Victorian buildings, a museum, and some good-quality stores and restaurants.

The city's newest development is a waterfront boardwalk between C and F streets, adjacent to the Old Town historic district. This section of the waterfront, previously closed to the public, now offers sweeping views of the harbor and bay.

For more visitor information, contact or visit the **Eureka/Humboldt County Convention and Visitors Bureau,** 1034 Second St., Eureka, CA 95501 (✆ **800/346-3482** or 707/443-5097; www.redwoodvisitor.org), or the **Eureka Chamber of Commerce,** 2112 Broadway, Eureka, CA 95501 (✆ **800/356-6381;** www.eurekachamber.com).

WHAT TO SEE & DO

The **Clarke Historical Museum,** 240 E St. (✆ **707/443-1947;** www.clarke museum.org), has a fine collection of Native American baskets and other artifacts.

The other popular attraction is the **Carson Mansion** ★ (on the corner of Second and M sts.), built from 1884 to 1886 for lumber baron William Carson. A three-story conglomeration of ornamentation, its design is a mélange of styles—Queen Anne, Italianate, Stick, and Eastlake. It took 100 men more than 2 years to build it. Today it's a private club, so you can only marvel at the exterior of this 18-room mansion, said to be the most photographed Victorian home in the U.S. Across the street stands the **Pink Lady,** designed for William Carson as a wedding present for his son. Both buildings testify to the wealth that was once made in Eureka's lumber trade. As early as 1856, seven sawmills produced 2 million board feet of lumber per month. A restored building now houses the **Morris Graves Museum of Art,** 636 F St. (© **707/442-0278;** www.humboldtarts.org), with four galleries showcasing local artists as well as traveling exhibitions.

The Clarke Historical Museum in Eureka.

For a good read, drop in at the **Booklegger,** 402 Second St., at E Street (© **707/445-1344**), a fantastic bookstore in Old Town with thousands of used paperbacks (especially mysteries, Westerns, and science fiction), children's books, and cookbooks.

Humboldt Bay, where the town stands, was discovered by settlers in 1850. To protect the fledgling community from local Native Americans, the government established Fort Humboldt 3 years later. Ulysses S. Grant was stationed here for 5 months until he resigned after disputes with his commanding officer about his drinking. Troops abandoned the fort in 1870. Today a self-guided trail takes visitors past a series of logging exhibits, a reconstructed surgeon's quarters, and a restored fort hospital, now a museum of Native American artifacts and military and pioneer paraphernalia. **Fort Humboldt State Historic Park** is at 3431 Fort Ave. (© **707/445-6567**). Admission is free; it's open daily from 8am to 5pm.

OUTDOOR PURSUITS

Humboldt Bay supplies a large portion of California's fish, and Eureka has a fishing fleet of about 200 boats. For an optimal view of the bay and surrounding waters, board skipper Leroy Zerlang's 1910 *Madaket*—a state historic landmark and the oldest passenger-carrying vessel in continuous service in the United States—for a 75-minute narrated **Humboldt Bay Harbor Cruise.** Tours depart from the foot of F Street in downtown Eureka Thursday through Saturday at 1, 2:30, and 4pm, and Sunday through Tuesday at 1 and 2:30pm. Tickets are $18 per person for adults, $16 for seniors, $10 for kids 5 to 12, and free for kids 4 and under. There's also a $10 cocktail cruise offered in the summer. Call © **707/445-1910** for a recorded departure schedule, or log on to **www.humboldtbay maritimemuseum.com**.

For more water recreation, you can rent kayaks, canoes, and sailboats from **Humboats** Friday through Monday from 9am to 5pm on Dock A, Woodley

Island Marina (℗ **707/443-5157;** www.humboats.com). Tours and lessons are also available.

Humboldt County is suitable for biking because it's relatively uncongested. You can rent bikes from **Pro Sport Center,** 1600 Fifth St. (℗ **707/443-6328**). Fishing, diving, biking, and hiking information are also available here.

Humboldt Bay, an important stopover point along the Pacific Flyway, is the winter home for thousands of migratory birds. South of town, the **Humboldt Bay National Wildlife Refuge ★**, 1020 Ranch Rd., Loleta (℗ **707/733-5406**), provides an opportunity to see many of the 200 or so species that live in the marshes and willow groves. The egret rookery on the bay, best viewed from Woodley Island Marina across the water, is spectacular. Peak viewing for most water birds and raptors is between September and March. The entrance is off U.S. 101 north at the Hookton Road exit. Cross the overpass and turn right onto Ranch Road.

WHERE TO STAY

Moderate

Abigail's Elegant Victorian Mansion Bed & Breakfast ★   For owners Doug and Lily Vieyra, the restoration and upkeep of this 1888 house, a National Historic Landmark, is a labor of love. They combed the country for the fabrics and designs that provide the most authentic Victorian atmosphere I have encountered in the U.S. The wallpapers are extraordinary—brilliant blues, golds, jades, and reds in patterns that feature peacocks and mythological figures. Doug pays attention to every detail, from the butler who greets you in morning dress, to the silent movies, to period music on the phonograph. Each unit is individually furnished: The Van Gogh room contains the Belgian bedroom suite of Lily's mother. The Lillie Langtry room, named after the actress and king's mistress who stayed here when she performed locally, features a four-poster bed and Langtry memorabilia. Guests can play croquet on the beautifully manicured lawn, where the staff serves ice-cream sodas and lemonade in the afternoon.

1406 C St. (at 14th St.), Eureka, CA 95501. www.eureka-california.com. ℗ **707/444-3144.** 4 units. $105–$125 double. MC, V. **Amenities:** Complimentary bikes; sauna. *In room:* A/C.

Hotel Carter, Carter House, Bell Cottage, and Carter Cottage ★★★   At the north end of Eureka's Old Town, the Carter House launched Mark Carter's renowned hostelry empire. Though Mark Carter built this copy of an 1884 San Francisco Victorian as a family home in 1982, he and his wife, Christi, began taking guests and then built the stately hotel across the street, the Hotel Carter. Later they acquired the pretty Victorian Bell Cottage and the ultraluxurious Carter Cottage as well.

The 23 rooms in the large, full-service Hotel Carter have beautiful modern furnishings and pine four-posters. The suites have luxury appointments such as fireplaces and Jacuzzis with distant views of the waterfront. The original Carter House has seven rooms, furnished with antiques, Oriental rugs, and modern artwork. Rooms in the Bell Cottage are also individually decorated in grand Victorian fashion. If you want to splurge, reserve the Carter Cottage, a small home that was converted into one of the most luxurious lodgings in Northern California—a minimansion with a chef's kitchen, two fireplaces, a grand bathroom with a whirlpool tub for two, and a private deck. The Carters offer an array of luxury accommodations, ranging from classic Victorian in the house and cottage to a softer, brighter, more contemporary look in the hotel. The ground level of the Hotel Carter houses **Restaurant 301** (see "Where to Eat," below), where a full breakfast (included in the room rate) is served each morning.

301 L St., Eureka, CA 95501. www.carterhouse.com. ✆ **800/404-1390** or 707/444-8062. Fax 707/444-8067. 32 units. $155–$238 double; $300–$385 suite; $615 Carter Cottage. Rates include full breakfast. Packages available. AE, DC, DISC, MC, V. From U.S. 101 north, turn left onto L St. to Third St. **Amenities:** Restaurant; babysitting; nearby golf course. *In room:* A/C, TV/VCR w/pay movies, hair dryer, kitchen in some units.

Inexpensive

Bayview Motel ✦ Although it's not nearly as opulent as Abigail's Elegant Victorian Mansion, the modern Bayview Motel soundly takes the prize for price and privacy. In fact, it's one of the cleanest, most meticulously landscaped motels I've ever seen. Atop a small knoll on the south side of Eureka, it *does* have a bay view, but you have to peer through a seedy industrial area to see it; the gardens actually make for the better view. All rooms are minisuites with standard motel amenities, including queen-size beds. If you feel like splurging, request a Romantic Getaway room complete with a Jacuzzi and fireplace. Family units are also available, and small pets are welcome.

2844 Fairfield St. (corner of Hwy. 1 and Henderson St.), Eureka, CA 95501. www.bayviewmotel. com. ✆ **866/725-6813** or 707/442-1673. Fax 707/268-8681. 17 units. $91–$170 double. AE, DISC, MC, V. Small pets accepted. *In room:* TV, fridge, hair dryer, free Wi-Fi.

WHERE TO EAT

Ramone's Bakery & Cafe ✦ BAKERY Ramone's has a bakery on one side and a small dining room on the other. The baked items are extraordinary—croissants, danishes, cinnamon rolls, truffles, and muffins made from scratch every morning without preservatives or dough conditioners. The bakery also prepares soups, salads, and huge sandwiches, plus a few lunch specials such as lasagna and quiche. Any time of the day, it's a great place to stop for a light, inexpensive meal and cup of coffee. Ramone's has other locations, at 2223 Harrison St., in Eureka, and in Arcata at 747 13th St., at Wildberries Marketplace.

209 E St. (in Old Town). ✆ **707/445-2923.** www.ramonesbakery.com. Main courses $4–$8. No credit cards. Mon–Sat 7am–6pm; Sun 7am–4pm.

Restaurant 301 ★★★ CALIFORNIAN This is the best restaurant in the area. The large, airy dining room adjacent to the hotel lobby has tall windows overlooking the waterfront. At dinner, patrons may order a la carte or off the highly recommended Discovery Menu—a five-course, prix-fixe feast that pairs each course with suggested wines by the glass. The chef picks most of the herbs and many of the vegetables fresh from organic gardens across the street. If you love oysters, start with a few Humboldt Bays roasted with barbecue sauce. Courtesy of the hotel's 301 Wine Shop, the wine bar features an excellent, extensive list that garnered *Wine Spectator*'s Grand Award.

In the Hotel Carter, 301 L St. ✆ **800/404-1390** or 707/444-8062. www.carterhouse.com. Reservations recommended. Main courses $18–$29. AE, DC, DISC, MC, V. Daily 6–9:30pm.

Samoa Cookhouse ★ 🏠 AMERICAN During the lumber industry's heyday, cookhouses like this one—the last of its kind in the West, dating from 1885—were common, serving as community centers. The mill men and longshoremen chowed down on three hot meals before, during, and after their 12-hour workday.

The food is still hearty (though not necessarily healthy by today's standards), served family-style at long tables covered with red-checkered cloths. The price includes soup, salad, fresh-baked bread, the main course, and dessert (usually pie). And the lunch-and-dinner menu still features a daily dish—roast beef, fried or barbecued chicken, ham, or pork chops. Breakfast typically includes eggs, potatoes, sausage, bacon, pancakes, and unlimited orange juice and coffee. Adjacent to the dining room, a small museum features memorabilia from the lumbering era. Bring the kids before this place vanishes into history.

Cookhouse Rd., Samoa. ✆ **707/442-1659.** www.samoacookhouse.net. Reservations accepted for large groups only. Main courses $7.45–$12. AE, DISC, MC, V. Mon–Sat 7am–3:30pm and 5–9pm; Sun 7am–10pm (closes 1 hr. earlier in winter). From U.S. 101, take Samoa Bridge to the end and turn left on Samoa Rd.; then take the 1st left.

Arcata ★

From Eureka, it's 7 miles to Arcata, one of my favorite towns on the Northern Coast. Sort of a cross between Mayberry and Berkeley, it has an undeniable small-town flavor—right down to the bucolic center square—yet it possesses that intellectual and environmentally conscious esprit de corps so characteristic of university towns (Arcata is the home of Humboldt State University).

Family-type activities abound. On Wednesday, Friday, and Saturday evenings between June and July, Arcata's semipro baseball team, the **Humboldt Crabs,** plays at Arcata Ballpark (✆ **707/826-2333;** www.humboldtcrabs.com), at Ninth and F streets. Also check out the kid-friendly **Humboldt State University Natural History Museum,** 1315 G St. (✆ **707/826-4479**), open Tuesday through Saturday from 10am to 5pm; **Tin Can Mailman,** at 10th and H streets (✆ **707/822-1307;** www.tincanbooks.com), a used-book store with more than 130,000 titles; and **Redwood Park** (east end of 11th St.), with an outstanding playground for kids and miles of forested hiking trails.

Home to Northern California's indigenous people, the Hoopa Indian Reservation is some 40 miles east of Eureka and a few miles north of Willow Creek. In the Hoopa Shopping Center, the **Hoopa Tribal Museum** (✆ **530/625-4110**)

Kinetic Sculpture Race, Arcata.

archives Hoopa culture and history, including ceremonial regalia, basketry, canoes, and tools. By appointment, the museum organizes guided tours of Hoopa Valley historic sites, including the traditional village of Takimildiñ. Hours are Monday through Friday from 8am to 5pm year-round, and in summer on Saturday from 10am to 4pm.

OUTDOOR PURSUITS

The **Arcata Marsh and Wildlife Sanctuary ★**, at the foot of South I Street (© **707/826-2359**), is a thought-provoking excursion. The 154-acre sanctuary—which doubles as Arcata's integrated wetland wastewater treatment plant—is a stopover for marsh wrens, egrets, and other waterfowl, including the rare Arctic loon. Every Saturday at 8:30am and 2pm, free 1-hour guided tours start at the cul-de-sac at the foot of South I Street. Or just pick up a free self-guided walking-tour map of the preserve, available at the **Arcata Chamber of Commerce,** 1635 Heindon Rd. (© **707/822-3619;** www.arcatachamber.com).

WHERE TO STAY

Fairwinds Motel ♂ Just off Hwy. 101, just a few blocks from Humboldt State University, the Fairwinds has simple yet spotless rooms with small balconies overlooking nothing in particular. Although the motel has been in operation since 1962 and its age lines are showing, the rooms have been completely remodeled in recent years with new beds and modernish furnishings and prints. I recommend it only if you can't get a room at the Hotel Arcata or you're looking to save a few bucks on lodging.

1674 G St. at 17th St., Arcata, CA 95521. www.fairwindsmotelarcata.com. © **866/352-5518** or 707/822-4824. 26 units. $71–$104 double. AE, DISC, MC, V. *In room:* TV, free Wi-Fi.

Hotel Arcata ♂ This is the town's most prominent hotel, with many guests visiting their children at Humboldt State University. If you're not inclined to stay at the fancier Lady Anne B&B (see review below), this is definitely the next best choice. Located on the northeast corner of the town plaza, the Hotel Arcata has a handsome early-1900s brick facade. The individually decorated rooms range from small, inexpensive singles to large executive suites that overlook the plaza. The minisuites are the quietest—a bargain at about $100. **Tomo,** the Japanese restaurant on the premises, is under different management.

708 Ninth St., Arcata, CA 95521. www.hotelarcata.com. © **800/344-1221** or 707/826-0217. 32 units. $85–$136 double. Rates include continental breakfast. AE, DC, DISC, MC, V. Pets accepted for $5 per day and a $50 deposit. **Amenities:** Restaurant; nearby indoor pool and health club. *In room:* TV.

The Lady Anne ★ Among Arcata's finest lodgings, this beautiful Queen Anne–style inn is kept in top-notch condition. The large, cozy guest rooms are individually decorated with antiques, lace curtains, Oriental rugs, and English stained glass. For second honeymooners, the Union Suite is ideal, with a four-poster bed and bay view. On summer afternoons, you can lounge on the veranda or play croquet on the front lawn. Several good dining options are only a few blocks away at Arcata Plaza.

902 14th St., Arcata, CA 95521. www.humboldt1.com/ladyanne. © **707/822-2797.** 5 units. $125–$140 double. MC, V. *In room:* Hair dryer, no phone.

WHERE TO EAT

Abruzzi ★ ITALIAN   Abruzzi is considered the best Italian restaurant in town. It's also romantic, with dark woods and dim lighting. Meals begin with a basket of warm breadsticks, focaccia, and a baguette from a local bakery. Specialties include range-fed veal piccata, well-seasoned filet steaks, and sea scallops with langoustines tossed with cheese tortellini. The standout dessert is the chocolate *paradiso,* a dense chocolate cake in a pool of champagne *mousseline.*

Jacoby's Storehouse (at the corner of Eighth and H sts.). © **707/826-2345.** Reservations recommended. Main courses $9–$26. AE, DISC, MC, V. Daily 5:30–9pm.

Folie Douce ★★ BISTRO   Humboldt hip meets cuisine chic at Folie Douce, the most energized, inventive restaurant in town. Designer wood-oven-fired pizza is its mainstay, like the grilled duck sausage fennel, chèvre, and Roquefort cheese with caramelized red onions, walnuts, and arugula, or the Mexican white shrimp with honey. The highlight of your vacation may well be the artichoke-heart and pancetta cheesecake appetizer. Other heartier menu items range from wasaabruzbi steak with scallions and sesame, to lamb loin chops sauced with local artichokes in minted *jus.* Everything on the menu is 100% organic, natural, free-range, and free of hormones or antibiotics. The restaurant has a serious wine list as well. This small, festive eatery is extremely popular, so make reservations.

1551 G St. (btw. 15th and 16th sts.). © **707/822-1042.** www.holyfolie.com. Reservations suggested. Main courses $12–$37. AE, DISC, MC, V. Tues–Thurs 5:30–9pm; Fri–Sat 5:30–10pm.

Plaza Grill ☺ AMERICAN   If the prices at Abruzzi are a bit more than you care to spend, consider the Plaza Grill, directly upstairs. Despite efforts to make it more upscale, it can't seem to shake its image as a college-student burger joint, albeit a nice one. The menu is more substantial than you'd think, with a choice of salads, sandwiches, burgers, fish platters, chicken specialties, steaks, and all kinds of coffee drinks. The children's menu is very reasonably priced.

Jacoby's Storehouse (at the corner of Eighth and H sts.). © **707/826-0860.** Main courses $7–$17. AE, DISC, MC, V. Mon–Thurs 5–9:30pm; Fri–Sat 5–10pm.

Trinidad & Patrick's Point State Park ★

Back on U.S. 101 north of Arcata, you'll come to **Trinidad,** a tiny coastal fishing village of 400 people. One of the smallest incorporated cities in California, it's on a peninsula 25 miles north of Eureka. If you're not into fishing, there's little to do in town except poke around at the handful of shops, walk along the busy pier, and wish you owned a house here.

Five miles north of Trinidad takes you to the 640-acre **Patrick's Point State Park** ★, 4150 Patrick's Point Dr. (© **707/677-3570**), which has one of the finest ocean access points in the north, at **Agate Beach.** It's suitable for driftwood picking, rock hounding, and camping on a sheltered bluff. The park contains a re-creation of a Sumeg village, which is used by the Yurok people and neighboring tribes.

WHERE TO STAY

The Lost Whale Bed & Breakfast Inn ★★ ☺   This modern version of a blue-and-gray Cape Cod–style house sits on 9 acres of seafront studded with firs, alders, spruces, and redwoods with a private trail leading down to Abalone Cove and a private beach. The friendly owners welcome children (there's a game room, and a playground on the lawn) as much as romantically inclined couples (a very inviting Jacuzzi on the back deck offers a view of the sea). They claim their hotel is the only one in California with a private beach featuring tide pools and sea lions. The inn's eight soundproof rooms have private balconies or sitting alcoves with views of the ocean or garden, two rooms have separate sleeping lofts, and all have private bathrooms and queen-size beds. In the morning, you'll marvel at the

Trinidad.

huge breakfasts, prepared by the resident cook: casseroles, quiches, home-baked muffins, fresh fruit, and locally smoked salmon.

3452 Patrick's Point Dr., Trinidad, CA 95570. www.lostwhaleinn.com. *©* **800/677-7859** or 707/677-3425. Fax 707/677-0284. 8 units. Summer $250–$295 double, $375 suite; winter $200–$230 double, $375 suite. Rates include country breakfast and afternoon tea. AE, DISC, MC, V. **Amenities:** Oceanview Jacuzzi; free Wi-Fi. *In room:* No phone.

Trinidad Bay Bed & Breakfast ★★ 🏠   Perched 175 feet above the ocean, this charming Cape Cod–style B&B is the best place to stay on Trinidad Bay. On a clear day, you can see up to 65 miles of rugged coastline and shimmering ocean. All the bright, colorful guest rooms are individually decorated and come with king beds, ocean views, and private bathrooms. The price is the same for all four rooms, so if it's available, opt for the Tide Pool room—it offers an amazing panoramic view from the wraparound windows, as well as a private entrance. Second choice is the Trinity Alps Room, which also has a private entrance, a small kitchenette, and wonderful bay views (also, both of these rooms have a small dining area so breakfast can be delivered to your room, if you prefer). The town shops and restaurants are a short walk away, along with numerous hiking trails, beaches, and picnic spots.

560 Edwards St. (P.O. Box 849), Trinidad, CA 95570-0849. www.trinidadbaybnb.com. *©* **707/677-0840.** 4 units. $200–$300 double. Rates include breakfast. AE, MC, V. *In room:* Fridge, hair dryer, free Wi-Fi.

Trinidad Inn 🏄   You'll find a bevy of inexpensive motels in these parts, but the Trinidad Inn is the best of the lot. It's 2 miles north of Trinidad on a serene stretch of road dwarfed by redwoods. Both the motel's exterior—trimmed in shades of white and blue—and the guest rooms are impeccably maintained. Each room is unique: Some are family units that hold up to four persons, while others offer a comfortable queen bed and private bathroom. A good room for couples is no. 10, an adorable little cottage complete with a full kitchen, living room, private bathroom, bedroom, and small patio. Each morning fresh coffee, tea, and homemade raspberry scones and muffins are served under the gazebo in the flower-filled garden. Guests are free to use the picnic table and barbecue, or wander through the adjacent forest to the beaches a short stroll away.

1170 Patrick's Point Dr., Trinidad, CA 95570. www.trinidadinn.com. *©* **707/677-3349.** 10 units. $75–$175 double. Rates include continental breakfast. AE, DC, DISC, MC, V. From U.S. 101, take the Trinidad exit and head 2 miles north on Patrick's Point Dr. Pets accepted for $15 and $20 deposit. *In room:* TV, no phone, free Wi-Fi.

WHERE TO EAT

Larrupin Café ★★ AMERICAN   On a quiet country road 2 miles north of Trinidad, this popular, beautifully decorated restaurant sports a blend of Indonesian and African artifacts mingled with colorful urns full of exotic flowers and candlelit tables. The patio with a reflecting pool and bamboo fencing is a charmer, as is the wood-burning fireplace in winter. Dinner starts with an appetizer board of gravlax, pâté, dark pumpernickel, and apple slices, followed by a red- and green-leaf salad tossed with a Gorgonzola vinaigrette. Many menu items are barbecued over mesquite fires, such as the hefty cut of halibut basted with lemon butter and served with mustard-flavored dill sauce, or pork ribs with a side of sweet-and-spicy barbecue sauce. Another recommended dish is the barbecued Cornish game hen with an orange-and-brandy glaze. **Note:** They don't take credit cards and the hours tend to vary seasonally, so be sure to call ahead and bring plenty of cash.

1658 Patrick's Point Dr. ✆ **707/677-0230.** www.larrupincafe.com. Reservations recommended. Main courses $15–$22. No credit cards. Thurs–Mon 5–9pm (hours may vary seasonally, so call ahead).

The Seascape Restaurant ★ 🍴 CALIFORNIAN   Established in the 1940s, the Seascape is an unpretentious cross between a cafe and a diner, with three dining rooms, ocean views, overworked but cheerful waitresses, and a nostalgic aura. People pop in for coffee or snacks from early morning to after sundown, but by far the biggest seller here is the Trinidad Bay Platter. Heaped with halibut, scallops, and shrimp, and accompanied by salad and rice pilaf, it's even more popular than the excellent prawn brochette. How fresh is the fish? As the menu states, "Availability of seafood depends on season, weather conditions, regulations, and luck." Halibut, rock cod, sole, and other local catches come charbroiled; sautéed in garlic, onions, and mushrooms; or prepared in four other styles. For you late risers, breakfast is served until 4pm.

Beside the pier at the foot of Bay St. ✆ **707/677-3762.** Full dinners $11–$30. DISC, MC, V. Daily 7am–9pm.

REDWOOD NATIONAL & STATE PARKS ★★

40 miles N of Eureka; 336 miles N of San Francisco

It's difficult to explain the feeling you get in the old-growth forests of Redwood National and State Parks without citing *Alice in Wonderland.* Like a jungle, the redwood forest is a multistoried affair, and the tall trees are just the top layer. Everything seems big and misty, from another era—flowering bushes cover the ground, 10-foot-tall ferns line the creeks, and the smells are rich and musty.

When Archibald Menzies first noted the botanical existence of the coast redwood in 1794, more than 2 million acres of redwood forest carpeted California and Oregon. By 1965, heavy logging had reduced that to 300,000 acres, and it was obvious something had to be done if any were to survive. The state created several parks around individual groves in the 1920s, and in 1968 the federal government created Redwood National Park. In May 1994, the National Park Service and the California Department of Parks and Recreation signed an agreement to manage these conservation areas cooperatively.

Redwood National Park.

Essentials

GETTING THERE The southern gateway to the Redwood National and State Parks is the town of Orick. Even though U.S. 101 runs right through the middle of town, you can't miss it anyway: Look for the dozens of burl stands along the road. Carved with chisels and chain saws, these former redwood logs have been transformed into just about every creature you can imagine. The northern gateway to the park is Crescent City near the Oregon border. It's your best bet for a cheap motel, gas, fast food, and outdoor supplies.

VISITOR INFORMATION In Orick you'll find the **Redwood Information Center,** P.O. Box 7, Orick, CA 95555 (☎ **707/464-6101**), one of California's rare examples of well-placed tax dollars. Stop here and pick up a free map; it's open daily from 9am to 5pm. If you missed the Orick center, don't worry: About 10 miles farther north on U.S. 101 is the **Prairie Creek Visitor Center** (☎ **707/465-7347**), which carries all the same maps and information. It's open daily from 9am to 5pm in summer, daily from 10am to 4pm (sometimes later) in winter.

Before touring the park, pick up a free guide at the **Redwood National and State Parks Headquarters and Information Center,** 1111 Second St. (at K St.), Crescent City, CA 95531 (☎ **707/464-6101**). It's open daily from 9am to 5pm.

If you happen to be arriving via U.S. 199 from Oregon, the rangers manning the **Hiouchi Information Station** (☎ **707/458-3294**) and **Jedediah Smith Visitor Center** (☎ **707/458-3018**) can also supply you with the necessary maps and advice. Both are open daily in summer from 9am to 5pm, and in winter when staffing is available. For more information about the Redwood National and State Parks, visit the website at **www.nps. gov/redw**.

FEES & PERMITS Admission to the national park is free, but to enter any of the three state parks (which contain the best redwood groves), you'll pay a $6 day-use fee, which gains you entry into all three. The camping fee is $20 per night for drive-in sites. (Reservations are highly recommended in summer.) Walk-in sites are free, though a permit is required.

RANGER PROGRAMS   The park service runs interpretive programs—covering phenomena from trees to tide pools, legends to landforms—at the Hiouchi, Crescent Beach, and Redwood information centers in summer months, and year-round at the park headquarters in Crescent City. State rangers lead campfire programs and other activities throughout the year as well. Call **Parks Information** (✆ **707/464-6101**) for information on current schedules and events.

Exploring the Parks by Car

If you're approaching the park from the south, take the detour along U.S. 101 called the **Newton B. Drury Scenic Parkway ★**, which passes through groves of redwoods and elk-filled meadows before leading back onto the highway 8 miles later. Another spectacular route is the **Coastal Drive ★**, which winds through stands of redwoods and offers grand views of the Pacific.

The most amazing car-friendly trail in the Redwood National and State Parks is the hidden, well-maintained gravel **Howland Hill Road ★★**, which winds for 12 miles through Jedediah Smith Redwoods State Park. It's an unforgettable journey through spectacular old-growth redwoods—considered by many to be one of the most beautiful areas in the world. To get here from U.S. 101, keep an eye out for the 76 gas station at the south end of Crescent City; just before the station, turn right on Elk Valley Road, and follow it to Howland Hill Road, which will be on your right. After driving through the park, you'll end up at U.S. 199 near Hiouchi, and from here it's a short jaunt west to get back to U.S. 101. Plan at least 2 to 3 hours for the 45-mile round-trip, or all day if you want to do some hiking or mountain biking. This drive is not recommended for trailers and RVs.

Sports & Outdoor Pursuits

BEACHES, WHALE-WATCHING & BIRD-WATCHING   The park's beaches vary from long, white-sand strands to cobblestone pocket coves. The water temperature is in the high 40s to low 50s (low 10s Celsius) year-round; it's often rough, so swimmers and surfers should be prepared for adverse conditions.

Crescent Beach is a long sandy beach 2 miles south of Crescent City that's popular with beachcombers, surf fishermen, and surfers. Just south of Crescent Beach is **Endert's Beach,** a protected spot with a hike-in campground and tide pools at the southern end of the beach.

High coastal overlooks (such as Klamath and Crescent Beach) make great whale-watching outposts during the southern migration in December and January and the return migration in March and April. The northern sea cliffs also provide valuable nesting sites for such marine birds as auklets, puffins, murres, and cormorants. Birders will thrill at the park's freshwater lagoons as well.

HIKING   The park's official map and guide, available at any of the information centers, provides a fairly good layout of hiking trails within the park. Regardless of how short or long your hike may be, dress warmly and bring plenty of water and sunscreen. Pets are prohibited on all of the park's trails.

The most popular walk is the short, heavily traveled **Fern Canyon Trail ★**, which leads to a lush grotto of lady, deer, chain, sword, five-finger, and maidenhair ferns clinging to 50-foot-high vertical walls divided by a brook. It's only about a 1.5-mile walk from Gold Bluffs Beach, but be prepared to scramble across the creek several times on your way via small footbridges.

The **Lady Bird Johnson Grove Loop** ★ is an easy, 1-hour self-guided tour that loops 1 mile around a glorious lush grove of mature redwoods. It's the site where Mrs. Johnson dedicated the national park in 1968. The **Yurok Loop Nature Trail** at Lagoon Creek is also an easy trek. The 1-mile self-guided trail gradually climbs to the top of a rugged sea bluff (with wonderful panoramic views of the Pacific) before looping back to the parking lot. If someone's willing to act as shuttle driver, have him or her meet you at the Requa Trail Head and take the 4-mile coastal trail to the mouth of the Klamath. And for the whiner in your group, there's **Big Tree Trail,** a .25-mile paved trail leading to a big tree.

Tall Trees Trail leads to one of the world's tallest trees—perhaps 365 feet tall, 14 feet in diameter, and more than 600 years old. It was once touted as the world's tallest tree, but new candidates keep getting discovered, and this proud giant has lost a couple of feet to time. Go to the Redwood Information Center near Orick (see "Essentials," above) for a free map and permit to drive to the trail head. The park issues 50 permits per day, on a first-come, first-served basis. After driving to the trail head, walk a steep 1.3 miles down into the grove. The trail is 3.3 miles round-trip.

WILDLIFE VIEWING   One of the most striking aspects of Prairie Creek Redwood State Park is its 200- to 300-strong herd of **Roosevelt elk** ★, usually found in the Elk Prairie, at the southern end of the park. These beasts can weigh 1,000 pounds, and the bulls carry huge antlers from spring to fall. You can also spot elk at Gold Bluffs Beach; it's a rush to come upon them out of the fog or after a turn in the trail. Nearly 100 **black bears** also call the park home, but they're seldom seen. Unlike the bears at Yosemite and Yellowstone, these are still afraid of people. Keep them that way by giving them a wide berth, observing food-storage etiquette while camping, and disposing of garbage properly.

Where to Stay

The national park proper has five small campgrounds. Four of the walk-in (more like backpack-in) camps are free—Little Bald Hills, Nickel Creek, Flint Ridge, and Butler Creek. Only one (the Redwood Creek Gravel Bar) requires a permit from the visitor center in advance.

Most car campsites are in the **Prairie Creek** and **Jedediah Smith state parks,** entirely inside the national park. Prairie Creek has two campgrounds, at Elk Prairie and Gold Bluffs Beach. Sites are $15 per night and can be reserved via ReserveAmerica (✆ **800/444-7275;** www.reserveamerica.com). It helps to know which campground and, if possible, which site you would like.

You'll find a number of bed-and-breakfasts and funky roadside motels in the surrounding communities of Crescent City, Orick, and Klamath. The **Crescent City–Del Norte Chamber of Commerce** (✆ **800/343-8300**) can probably steer you toward the proper match.

CRESCENT CITY

Crescent City has little to offer, but it makes a good base for exploring Redwood National Park and the Smith River, one of the great recreational rivers of the West. The **Battery Point Lighthouse,** at the foot of A Street (© **707/464-3089;** www.lighthousefriends.com), which is accessible on foot only at low tide, houses a museum with exhibits on the coast's history. Tours of the lighthouse ($2 for adults, 50¢ for children 12 and under) are offered Saturday and Sunday from 10am to 4pm, tides permitting, April through September.

Another draw is the **Smith River National Recreation Area ★**, east of Jedediah Smith State Park and part of Six Rivers National Forest. Headquarters is at 10600 U.S. 199, Gasquet (© **707/457-3131**), reached via U.S. 199 from Crescent City (about a 30-min. drive). You can get maps of the forest at the Supervisor's Office in Eureka, or at either of the Redwood National Park centers in Orick and Crescent City.

The 300,000-plus acres of wilderness have five small campgrounds (with fewer than 50 sites) along the Smith River. Sixteen trails draw hikers from across the country. The easiest short trail is the **McClendon Ford,** which is 2 miles long and drops from 1,000 to 800 feet in elevation to the river. Other activities include mountain biking, white-water rafting, kayaking, and fishing for salmon and trout.

For information, contact the **Crescent City–Del Norte County Chamber of Commerce,** 1001 Front St., Crescent City, CA 95531 (© **800/343-8300;** www.northerncalifornia.net).

Where to Stay

Crescent Beach Motel ⚡ Crescent City doesn't have any fancy hotels or B&Bs, but it does have lots of modestly priced motels—the best of which is the Crescent Beach, which is also the only one on the bay. Near the highway, about a mile south of town, this single-story structure is freshly remodeled, with clean and simple refurbished rooms. Four of the units face the highway; try to get one of the others, all of which have sliding glass doors to decks and a small lawn area overlooking the water.

1455 Redwood Hwy. S. (U.S. 101), Crescent City, CA 95531. www.crescentbeachmotel.com. © **707/464-5436.** Fax 707/464-9336. 27 units. Summer $77–$90 double; winter $55–$64 double. AE, DISC, MC, V. *In room:* TV, no phone.

Curly Redwood Lodge ⚡ This is a blast from the past, the kind of place where you might have stayed as a kid during a cross-country vacation in the family station wagon. It was built in 1957 on grasslands across from the harbor, and it's trimmed with lumber from a single ancient redwood. Although they're not full of high-tech gadgets, the bedrooms are among the largest and best-soundproofed in town, and certainly the most evocative of a bygone age. In winter, about a third of the rooms are locked and sealed. I still prefer the rooms on the beach at the Crescent Beach Motel, but the Curly is a solid bet for a clean, comfortable, and inexpensive hotel room.

701 Redwood Hwy. S. (U.S. 101), Crescent City, CA 95531. www.curlyredwoodlodge.com. © **707/464-2137.** Fax 707/464-1655. 36 units. Summer $65–$90 double; winter $54–$79 double. AE, DC, MC, V. *In room:* TV, Wi-Fi.

Where to Eat

Beachcomber SEAFOOD   The decor is as nautical as this restaurant's name, with rough-cut planking and a scattering of driftwood, fishnets, and buoys dangling above a dimly lit space. The restaurant is beside the beach, 2 miles south of Crescent City's center. The cuisine is a joy for fish lovers who prefer not to mask the flavor of their seafood with complicated sauces. Most of the dishes are grilled over madrone-wood barbecue pits. Freshly harvested Pacific salmon, halibut, lingcod, shark, sturgeon, Pacific snapper, oysters, and steamer clams have visitors lining up. The Beachcomber also serves great flame-broiled steaks.

1400 U.S. 101, Crescent City, CA 95531. © **707/464-2205.** Reservations recommended. Main courses $6–$15. MC, V. Fri–Tues 5–9pm. Closed Dec–Jan and part of Feb.

Harbor View Grotto Restaurant & Lounge SEAFOOD/STEAKS   This friendly local restaurant has been specializing in fresh seafood at market prices since 1961. The food is not as good as the Beachcomber's, but it's a little less expensive, it's open for lunch, and it's far less crowded on weekend nights. The "light eaters" menu includes a cup of white chowder (made fresh daily) or a salad, a main course, and vegetables; heartier eaters can choose from among three different cuts of prime rib. Menu items include fresh, locally caught fish such as Pacific snapper and salmon. Crab or shrimp Louis, as well as crabmeat or shrimp sandwiches, are popular in season.

150 Starfish Way, Crescent City, CA 95531. © **707/464-3815.** Reservations recommended. Main courses $4–$9 lunch, $6–$20 dinner. DISC, MC, V. Daily 11am–9pm (later in the summer months).

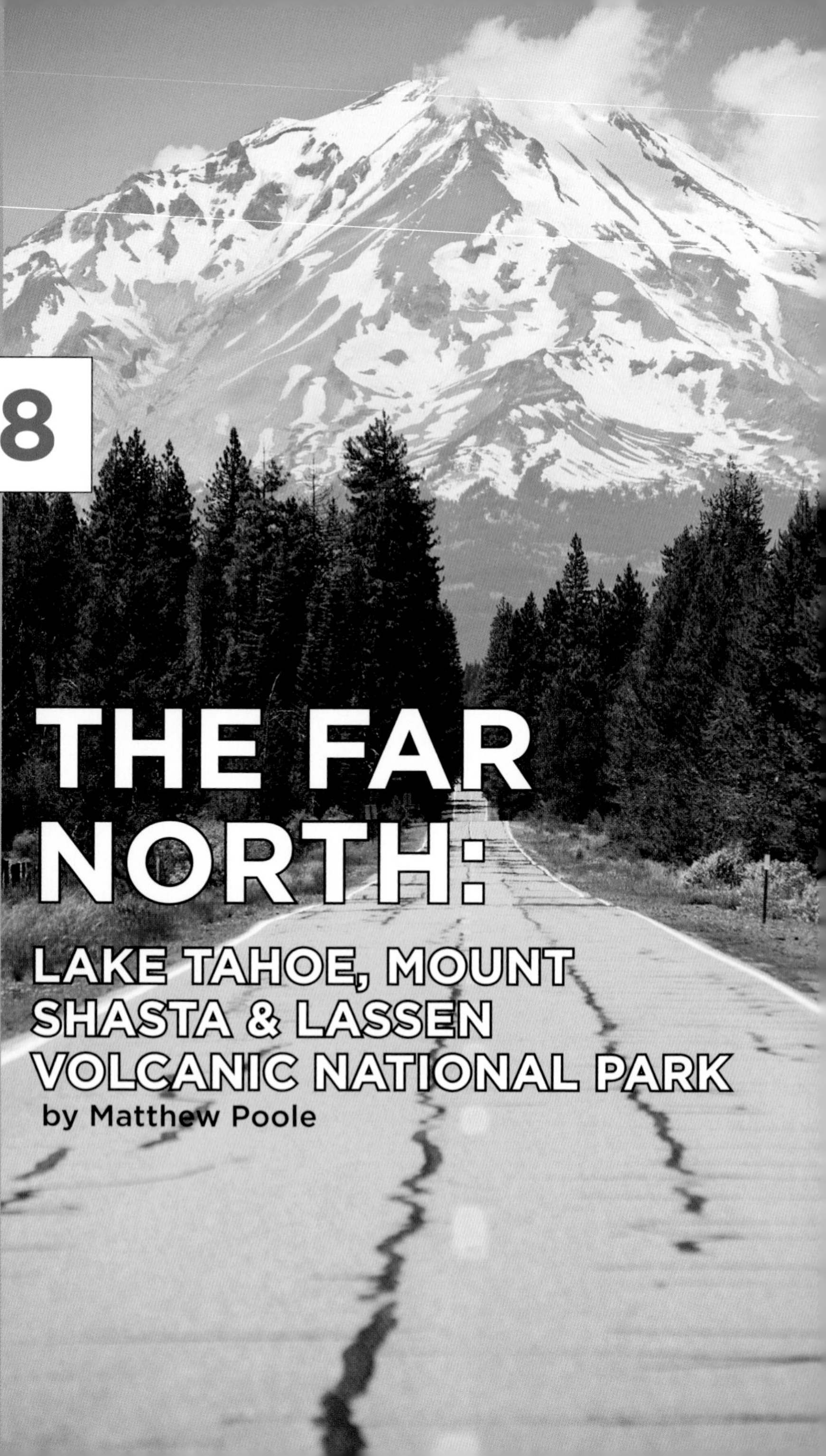

THE FAR NORTH:

LAKE TAHOE, MOUNT SHASTA & LASSEN VOLCANIC NATIONAL PARK

by Matthew Poole

Dominated by snowcapped Mount Shasta, visible for 100 miles on a clear day, California's upper northern territory is among the least-visited parts of the state. Often called "the Far North," this region stretches from the rice fields north of Sacramento to the Oregon border. The area is so immense that the state of Ohio would fit comfortably within its borders.

For the adventurous traveler, the Far North is a superlative destination for outdoor sports such as hiking, climbing, skiing, white-water rafting, and mountain biking. Other attractions, both artificial and natural, range from the Shasta Dam, the highest overflow dam in the world; to Lava Beds National Monument, which has dozens of caves to explore; to Lassen Volcanic National Park, a towering laboratory of volcanic phenomena.

South of the Cascade Range is one of the most popular recreational regions in the Golden State: Lake Tahoe, straddling the border between California and Nevada, at 6,225 feet above sea level. Although the lake has been marred by overdevelopment—particularly along the casino-riddled southern shore—the western and eastern coastlines are still quiet havens for hiking, cycling, and watersports. The surrounding Sierra Nevada mountains offer some of the best skiing in the United States, with more than a dozen resorts.

LAKE TAHOE ★★★

107 miles E of Sacramento; 192 miles E of San Francisco; 45 miles SW of Reno, NV

It's hard to imagine how captivating Lake Tahoe can be until you see it. Mark Twain declared it "the fairest picture the whole earth affords." Surrounded by the imperious peaks of the Sierra Nevada, its waters soak up the colors of the sky and the mountains, creating a kaleidoscope of sparkling blues, greens, and purples—a display that will fill your camera with screen-saver moments. The view is only a fraction of Tahoe's enchantments: Nearly every outdoor activity that exists is done here, and the lakeside casinos provide 24-hour indoor entertainment.

Things to Do   Think of Lake Tahoe as the most awesome summer camp for adults ever. Just lounging on a deck under the pines with a book and a warm summer breeze is heaven. Float down serene **Truckee River** in an inner tube, take a leisurely bike ride along the **Truckee River Bike Trail,** or soak in the sun on a **gold-sand beach.**

Active Pursuits   In summer, you can partake of **boating** and **watersports, mountain biking, golf, tennis, hiking, camping, rafting, ballooning, horseback riding, rock climbing, bungee jumping, parasailing, skating,** and so on, with seemingly endless possibilities. In winter, Lake Tahoe is one of the nation's premier ski destinations, with **15 downhill ski resorts, snowmobiling,** and other snow play.

PREVIOUS PAGE: **Snowcapped Mount Shasta.**

Nightlife & Entertainment   Nearly half of Lake Tahoe belongs to Nevada, the state that never sleeps. Casinos abound on both north and south sides of the lake, but true night owls will prefer the South Shore's big-name entertainment at **Harrahs, Horizon, Harvey's, MontBleu,** and more. If casino's aren't your thing, there are plenty of pubs lining the lake: micro-brews at **The Bridgetender,** legendary Rum Runners at **The Beacon,** and margaritas on the lakeside deck at **Sunnyside** are just a few of our favorites.

Summer in Tahoe.

Restaurants & Dining   When San Francisco's chefs need a change of scenery, they often bring their knives to Tahoe: Moroccan tagine and wine-braised short ribs at **Manzanita,** a juicy grilled rib-eye at **Gar Woods Grill & Pier,** and Real Tahoe Turkey sandwiches at **Sprouts Natural Foods Café.** And you would think sushi in the mountains makes no sense, but **The Naked Fish** in South Lake holds its own with any San Francisco sushi joint. But more important than the food is the view, so beg or bribe for a table overlooking the lake.

Essentials

GETTING THERE   It's a 4-hour drive from San Francisco; take I-80 east to Sacramento, and then U.S. 50 to the South Shore, or I-80 east to Hwy. 89 or Hwy. 267 to the North Shore. Be prepared for snow in the winter. During heavy

A TALE OF TWO shores

Before you visit Tahoe, it's important to understand the distinction between the North and the South shores. Don't let the "City" in the North Shore's "Tahoe City" fool you; you can drive through it in a couple of minutes. To the contrary, South Lake Tahoe brims with high-rise casinos, motels, and mini-malls. Where you choose to stay is important because driving from one end of the lake to the other takes an hour or more in summer and can be treacherous in winter.

So which side is for you? If you're here for gambling or entertainment, go south: The selection of casinos is better, with more action and more lodgings, often at better rates. If you seek a relaxing, outdoor retreat, head to the North Shore, which has a better selection of high-quality resorts and vacation rentals. The woodsy West Shore has the most camping spots, and the East Shore, protected from development, has no commercial activity.

Wherever you stay, you'll find plenty of water and mountain sports. The lake is crowded during summer and ski season, so plan far ahead. It's much easier to get reservations for the spring and fall, and rates drop significantly. Many vacation homes and condominiums are rentable; call the visitor center bureaus or visit the websites below under "Visitor Information" for a list of rental agents.

The Far North

storms, you won't be permitted to pass the CHP (California Hwy. Patrol) checkpoints without four-wheel-drive or chains. From Los Angeles, it's a 9-hour drive; take I-5 through the Central Valley to Sacramento, and then follow the directions above.

Reno–Tahoe International Airport (45 min. to North Shore, 90 min. to South Shore; www.renoairport.com) runs regular service by 10 major airlines, including **American** (© 800/433-7300), **Delta** (© 800/221-1212), and **United** (© 800/241-6522). Rent a car or take a shuttle up to the lake: **North Lake Tahoe Express** (© 866/216-5222; www.northlaketahoeexpress.com) serves the North and West shores; **South Tahoe Express** (© 866/898-2463; www.southtahoeexpress.com) serves the South Shore (1-day advance reservations recommended). To get to the lake, take U.S. 395 South to Rte. 431 for the North Shore or U.S. 50 for the South Shore. All the roads leading to the lake are scenic, but the panorama as you descend into the Lake Tahoe Basin from Rte. 431 is spectacular. Pull into the overlook and enjoy the view.

Amtrak (✆ **800/USA-RAIL** [872-7245]; www.amtrak.com) stops in Truckee, 10 miles north of the lake. Public transportation (TART or Truce Trolley) is available from the train depot, or you can take a taxi to the North Shore. **Greyhound Bus Lines** (✆ **800/231-2222;** www.greyhound.com) serves both Truckee and South Lake Tahoe with daily arrivals from San Francisco and Sacramento.

VISITOR INFORMATION   In Tahoe City, stop by the **Tahoe City Visitor Information Center,** 380 N. Lake Blvd. (✆ **888/434-1262;** www.gotahoe north.com). In Incline Village, go to the **Incline Village/Crystal Bay Visitors Center,** 969 Tahoe Blvd. (✆ **888/434-1262** or 775/831-4440; www.gotahoenorth.com). Go to the **South Lake Tahoe Chamber of Commerce,** 3066 Lake Tahoe Blvd. (✆ **530/541-5255;** www.tahoeinfo. com). Many other websites offer information about Lake Tahoe, including www.virtualtahoe.com, www.skilaketahoe.com, www.laketahoeconcierge. com, and www.tahoevacationguide.com.

What to See & Do

SKIING & SNOWBOARDING

With the largest concentration of ski resorts in North America, Lake Tahoe is California's best skiing destination. The ski season typically lasts from November to May and frequently extends into the summer. Lift tickets range from $44 to $82 per day for adults, and from free to $39 for children, with special rates for seniors. Ticket prices rise every year, but bargains are available, particularly midweek. Many resorts, hotels, and motels offer ski packages. Contact the visitor centers or visit the websites listed under "Visitor Information," above, to look for these values. The resorts offer instruction for adults and children, equipment rental, special courses for snowboarding, and restaurants. Most have free shuttles.

Skiing Tahoe.

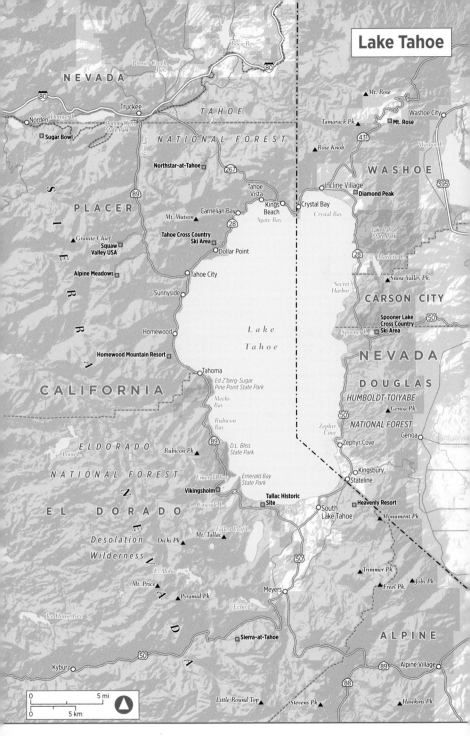

Lake Tahoe

NEVADA

Boca Res.

Prosser Creek Res.

TAHOE

I-80

Truckee

Norden
Donner L.

Donner Mem. State Park

Sugar Bowl

Mt. Rose

Tamarack Pk.

Mt. Rose

Washoe City

NATIONAL FOREST

Truckee R.

Rose Knob

WASHOE

I-395

PLACER

Mt. Watson

Northstar-at-Tahoe

267

Tahoe Vista

Incline Village

Diamond Peak

SIERRA

Granite Chief

Squaw Valley USA

Tahoe Cross Country Ski Area

Carnelian Bay

28

Kings Beach

Agate Bay

Crystal Bay

Crystal Bay

431

Washoe L.

Lake Tahoe State Park

Marlette L.

28

Alpine Meadows

Dollar Point

Tahoe City

Sunnyside

Secret Harbor

Snow Valley Pk.

CARSON CITY

Homewood

Lake Tahoe

Spooner L.

Spooner Lake Cross Country Ski Area

50

Homewood Mountain Resort

Tahoma

Ed Z'berg-Sugar Pine Point State Park

NEVADA

CALIFORNIA

Meeks Bay

DOUGLAS

HUMBOLDT-TOIYABE

Rubicon Bay

Genoa Pk.

ELDORADO

Loon L.

Rubicon Pk.

89

D.L. Bliss State Park

50

Zephyr Cove

Zephyr Cove

NATIONAL FOREST

Genoa

NATIONAL FOREST

Emerald Bay

Kingsbury

EL DORADO

Vikingsholm

Emerald Bay State Park

Stateline

Cascade L.

Tallac Historic Site

Heavenly Resort

Desolation

Dicks Pk.

Mt. Tallac

Fallen Leaf L.

South Lake Tahoe

Monument Pk.

Wilderness

L. Aloha

Mt. Price

Pyramid Pk.

Meyers

50

Trimmer Pk.

Freel Pk.

Jobs Pk.

Ice House Res.

Echo L.

ALPINE

Sierra-at-Tahoe

Kyburz

50

89

Alpine Village

88

0   5 mi

0   5 km

Little Round Top

Stevens Pk.

Hawkins Pk.

299

Alpine Meadows ★★ ☺   With more than 100 runs over 2,400 acres, Alpine has something for everyone: kids' programs, a family zone, and its "wild side" for the double-black-diamond crowd. In addition to its 14 lifts, this low-key resort has a beginner surface lift designed for children, novice skiers, and snowboarders. You can get a great bargain through its Lift & Lodging packages, which provide lift tickets and lodging (✆ **800/949-3296**). Alpine also offers ski and snowboard instruction for all ages, excellent snowboarding-terrain parks, snowshoe rentals, and snow-play areas.

2600 Alpine Meadows Rd., Tahoe City, CA 96145. ✆ **530/583-4232.** www.skialpine.com.

Diamond Peak ★ ☺ 🗲   In the heart of quiet, upscale Incline Village, this is a great choice for a low-key, less crowded, less expensive, nonetheless beautiful skiing adventure, with spectacular lake views. Smaller than most resorts in the area, it's a premier destination for families. Skiing and snowboarding options for kids abound, with a snowboard park and sledding area, a Burton Learn to Ride center for snowboarders, and a snow-play program to entertain the younger ones who aren't quite ready to hit the slopes. The Diamond Peak Cross Country and Snowshoe Center (same telephone number), east of Incline Village on NV Rte. 431, is gorgeous and even allows dogs to share in the fun in the afternoon.

1210 Ski Way, Incline Village, NV 89451. ✆ **775/832-1177.** www.diamondpeak.com.

Heavenly Resort ★★ ☺   This hugely popular resort—the only one on the South Shore—has the highest elevation (10,067 ft.) of any resort at the lake and the most vertical feet (3,500) of any West Coast resort. Skiers and snowboarders of all levels will find something to challenge them, including four terrain parks, 4,800 skiable acres, 29 lifts (including a 50-passenger aerial tram), 94 runs, and a series of tubing lanes to race your friends. Heavenly is also the only resort with day care for infants as young as 6 weeks (up through 6 years of age), child-care and ski combinations for toddlers 3 to 5, and full-day ski programs for older kids. With arcades, recreation centers, bowling alleys, and movie theaters nearby, it's a great choice if you have teenagers or if you want to visit the big casinos at night. The **Heavenly Gondola** has multiple cars that can transport up to eight passengers from the South Shore casino area up to an observation deck at 9,200 feet on Heavenly Mountain. The 2-mile journey ends at Adventure Peak, which is home to a multitude of winter and summer activities, including tubing, snow biking, and snowshoeing in the winter; and hiking, rock climbing, and the children's Spyder Climber in the summer. The resort also recently invested nearly $30 million in improvements to the mountain, including two new high-speed lifts, six new trails, a new tubing facility, expanded snowmaking, a 15-acre beginner's area, and the new fine-dining experience, the Tamarack Lodge.

4080 Lake Tahoe Blvd., South Lake Tahoe, CA 96150. ✆ **775/586-7000.** www.skiheavenly.com.

Homewood Mountain Resort ★ ☺ 🗲   Homewood is one of my favorite small ski areas, a homey little resort with 1,260 acres, 56 runs, 8 lifts, and spectacular lake views. It's a good family resort with child-care for ages 2 to 6 and ski schools for ages 4 to 12. Lift tickets were only $45 last winter on weekdays ($55 on weekends), and children 9 and under skied free when accompanied by an adult.

5145 W. Lake Blvd., Homewood, CA 96141 (6 miles south of Tahoe City and 19 miles north of South Lake Tahoe on Hwy. 89). ✆ **530/525-2992.** www.skihomewood.com.

Kirkwood ★★ ☺ Kirkwood's only drawback is that it's 30 miles south of South Lake Tahoe; otherwise, it's one of the top ski areas in Tahoe, with lots of snow and excellent spring skiing. It has 2,300 skiable acres, 12 lifts, and 65 trails. Many programs cater to children, including child-care for the younger ones (ages 2–6). The **High Alpine Adventure Center** (© **209/258-7248**) enables guests to snowshoe and cross-country ski directly from the resort; it offers lessons for all ages and spectacular scenery. Kirkwood is also ideal for summertime hiking, horseback riding, mountain biking, and rock climbing. A year-round zipline, **Zip Tahoe** (© **209/258-7330;** www.ziptahoe.com), with nine tour options, suspension bridges, and a floating step, is a recent addition to the resort; most tours are 2 hours and an additional charge. With ample lodging (© **800/967-7500**) and dining options, this is a great year-round destination. The shuttle service to South Lake Tahoe is $5 each way.

Off Hwy. 88 at Carson Pass (P.O. Box 1), Kirkwood, CA 95646. © **209/258-6000.** www.kirkwood.com.

Mt. Rose ★ 🎒 Although Mt. Rose has been open since 1964, I've never skied it until recently. Why? Because it wasn't challenging enough. But since they opened "The Chutes," Mt. Rose has become the new darling of the Tahoe ski scene. Just 22 miles from Reno and about a 20-minute drive from the lake, Mt. Rose has always been popular with beginner and intermediate skiers, offering 1,300 acres of mostly groomed slopes with the highest base elevation (7,900 ft.) in Lake Tahoe. Now that the wickedly steep and long chutes—with names such as Chaos and Nightmare—are officially open, it's attracting skiers of all levels. The ski area has seven lifts, including two high-speed detachables, as well as three snowboard terrain parks. Money-saving specials include Two-for-One Tickets on Tuesday, and Ladies Day Thursday, when gals get a full-day ticket for only $29 (holidays excepted).

22222 Mt. Rose Hwy. (Hwy. 431), Reno, NV 89511. © **800/SKI-ROSE** (754-7673) or 775/849-0704. www.skirose.com.

Northstar-at-Tahoe ★★ ☺ With 70 runs covering 2,420 acres on two mountains, Northstar is consistently rated among the top western resorts. Its sophisticated series of lifts, including an express gondola, ensures speedy access to the slopes and short lift lines. Whatever your age or experience level, you'll find what you're looking for here. Backcountry terrain on Saw Tooth Ridge will test the skills of expert skiers and snowboarders on 200 acres of ungroomed, out-of-boundary terrain. The Learning Center offers coaching in skiing, snowboarding, cross-country, and the new snow toys. Child-care (ages 2–6) is available, as well as instruction—including the "magic carpet" lift and special Paw Parks, Northstar's pint-size obstacle courses. Other outdoor pastimes include cross-country skiing, telemarking, snowshoeing, sleigh rides, tubing, and ice skating in the heart of Northstar's new Village. Check out the snow toys, such as the snowscoot, the skifox, the snowbike, and the snowskate, a skateboard deck without wheels. See p. 317 for a full review of Northstar-at-Tahoe.

100 Northstar Dr., Truckee, NV 96161 (6 miles north of Kings Beach). © **800/466-6784** or 530/562-1010. www.northstarattahoe.com.

Sierra-at-Tahoe ★ ☺ Tahoe's third-largest ski area is a great all-around resort, with slightly lower rates than most comparable places in the area. With more than 2,000 acres of slopes, from bunny to expert, Sierra-at-Tahoe features

The Village at Squaw Valley USA.

four terrain parks for both boarders and skiers, and 200 acres of backcountry terrain for steeps and deeps. The runs are very wide and well groomed, giving skiers plenty of room to fly down the mountain. On a powder day, don't miss skiing the trees. If you're staying on the South Shore, it's a good alternative to Heavenly Ski Resort. Free ski shuttle service is available from about 40 locations in South Lake Tahoe.

1111 Sierra at Tahoe Rd., Twin Bridges, CA 95735 (off Hwy. 50, 12 miles west of South Lake Tahoe). *© **530/659-7453.** www.sierraattahoe.com.

Squaw Valley USA ★★★ ☺ Site of the 1960 Olympic Winter Games, Squaw is one of the world's finest year-round resorts. Skiing is spread across six peaks with one of the most advanced lift systems on earth, providing access to more than 4,000 acres of skiable terrain—70% geared toward beginners and intermediates and 30% for the advanced, expert, and/or insane. For nonskiers and skiers alike, High Camp, at the top of the cable car, has the Olympic Ice Pavilion (year-round ice skating), a swimming lagoon and spa (spring and summer), snow tubing, snowboarding school, restaurants, and bars. Squaw also has an arcade, a climbing wall, and Central Park for snowboarders. The Nordic Center (*© **530/583-6300**) has 400 acres of groomed trails for cross-country skiing and snowshoeing. Squaw also offers free night skiing with the purchase of a full-day lift ticket. Children ages 12 and under ski for only $5. See p. 318 for a full review of the Resort at Squaw Creek.

Olympic Valley, CA 96146 (6 miles north of Tahoe City). *© **800/403-0206** or 530/583-6985. www.squaw.com.

Sugar Bowl ★★ ☺ Sugar Bowl is excellent for skiers of all levels—especially if you are driving from the Bay Area or Sacramento on I-80 and don't want to go all the way to Tahoe. This medium-size resort (13 lifts, 1,500 skiable acres) offers child-care, ski school, snowboard parks, and lodging at the foot of the mountains.

P.O. Box 5, Norden, CA 95724 (3 miles east of the Soda Springs/Norden exit of I-80). *© **530/426-9000.** www.sugarbowl.com.

MORE WINTER FUN

CROSS-COUNTRY SKIING   In addition to the major resorts, here are some excellent establishments: **Royal Gorge Cross-Country Ski Resort ★★★**, Soda Springs, near Sugar Bowl (*(℗)* **800/500-3871** or 800/666-3871), is one of the largest and best cross-country resorts anywhere, with 90 trails, including 28 novice trails and four ski lifts. For North Shore visitors, **Tahoe Cross Country Ski Area ★**, 925 Country Club Dr., Tahoe City (*(℗)* **530/583-5475;** www.tahoexc.org), is a small (14 trails) full-service ski center run by a nonprofit community group. A quiet, full-service ski center off the beaten path, **Spooner Lake Cross Country Ski Area ★**, near the intersection of Hwy. 28 and U.S. 50 on the East Shore (*(℗)* **775/749-5349;** www.spoonerlake.com), offers some of the most scenic skiing at the lake.

ICE SKATING   Accessible only by a tram ride up the mountain, **Squaw Valley's High Camp ★★** (*(℗)* **530/583-6985**) has an ice rink that's open year-round, with one of the world's most beautiful views for a skating rink. On the North Shore, there are also ice rinks at the **Northstar-at-Tahoe** resort (*(℗)* **530/562-0321;** p. 317), and the **Resort at Squaw Creek** (*(℗)* **800/327-3353;** p. 318). South Lake Tahoe has two rinks: the **South Tahoe Ice Arena** (1176 Rufus Allen Blvd.; *(℗)* **530/542-6262**), open year-round, and the **Heavenly Village Ice Rink,** at Heavenly Village on Hwy. 50 (*(℗)* **530/543-4230;** www.theshopsatheavenlyvillage.com).

SNOWMOBILING   Snowmobile rental and tours are available at several locations in the Lake Tahoe Area. Call ahead for reservations and directions. The **Zephyr Cove Snowmobile Center ★**, 760 U.S. 50, about 4 miles northeast of the casinos (*(℗)* **800/23-TAHOE** [238-2463] or 775/589-4906; www.laketahoesnowmobiles.com), offers several exhilarating tours daily for all experience levels. The cost for a 2-hour tour is about $119 for a single rider, $159 for two. **Lake Tahoe Snowmobile Tours** (*(℗)* **530/546-4280;** www.laketahoesnowmobiling.com) offers 90-minute to 4-hour

Snowmobiling the mountains high above Lake Tahoe.

backcountry tours from Brockway Summit, about 3 miles north of Kings Beach on Hwy. 267; prices start at $120 for one, $150 for two.

SNOW PLAY   For snow play beyond the resorts, try the **North Tahoe Regional Park,** at the top of National Avenue off Hwy. 28, Tahoe Vista (📞 **530/546-0605**). This ultimate snow-play hill charges a $5 fee for a choice of sled, tube, or saucer. **Taylor Creek SNO-PARK** off Hwy. 89 in South Lake Tahoe is run by the U.S. Forest Service. Bring your own equipment for sledding and tubing. For information about California Sno Park locations, call the **SNO-PARK Hot Line** at 📞 **916/324-1222.**

SUMMER ACTIVITIES

BALLOONING   See the lake and mountains from 8,000 to 10,000 feet above, with **Lake Tahoe Balloons** (📞 **800/872-9294** or 530/544-1221; www.laketahoeballoons.com) in South Lake Tahoe. A 4-hour tour costs about $250 per person.

BEACHES   Here are a few popular spots around the lake. All have sandy beaches, picnic areas, and restrooms; many have playgrounds. Remember that this is an alpine lake, so the water is *very* cold.

- **Baldwin Beach:** Hwy. 89, 4 miles north of South Lake Tahoe
- **Commons Beach Park:** Downtown Tahoe City; free movie (Fri at dusk; 📞 **530/583-3348**)
- **Connolly Beach:** U.S. 50 at Timber Cove Lodge; boat launches
- **D. L. Bliss State Park:** South of Meeks Bay on Hwy. 89; camping, trails
- **El Dorado Beach:** Between Rufus Allen and Lakeview in South Lake Tahoe
- **Kings Beach State Recreation Center:** Hwy. 28 in Kings Beach
- **Pope Beach:** Hwy. 89, 2 miles north of South Lake Tahoe
- **Sand Harbor:** 4 miles south of Incline Village on Hwy. 28; lifeguards
- **Sugar Pine Point:** Hwy. 89, just south of Tahoma; camping, trails, pier
- **Zephyr Cove Beach:** U.S. 50 at Zephyr Cove

BICYCLING   Miles of paved bicycle paths surround the lake. Incline Village has a scenic, easy 2½-mile path along Lakeshore Boulevard (a safe choice for younger children). In Tahoe City you can follow the path in three directions. The one that follows Truckee River is a relaxing, beautiful ride. On the South Shore, the Pope-Baldwin bike path runs parallel to Hwy. 89 through Camp Richardson and the Tallac Historic Site. Nearby, in South Lake Tahoe, a paved pathway runs from El Dorado Beach along the lake, paralleling U.S. 50. The Tahoe City trails are my favorites, especially the Truckee River section. You can rent a bicycle from any of the shops listed below.

A dizzying choice of mountain biking trails awaits mountain bikers in Lake Tahoe. For maps and information, check with one of the bicycle-rental shops. In North Lake Tahoe, try the **Olympic Bike Shop,** 620 N. Lake Blvd., Tahoe City (📞 **530/581-2500**); or **Tahoe Bike & Ski,** 8499 N. Lake Blvd., Kings Beach (📞 **530/546-7437;** www.tahoebikeski.com). In South Tahoe, try **Anderson's Bike Rental,** 645 Emerald Bay Rd. (📞 **530/541-0500;** www.andersonsbicyclerental.com), or **Lakeview Sports,** 3131 Hwy. 50, at El Dorado Beach (📞 **530/544-0183**).

LAKE TAHOE'S BEST cheap THRILLS

Nothing beats a cheap thrill, and the Lake Tahoe region is loaded with them. Your most affordable adventures will inevitably involve getting outside and taking in the area's natural wonders. In spring, summer, and fall, take a drive around the lake, hike to a scenic spot for a picnic lunch, or soak up some rays on the beach. In winter, inexpensive outdoor fun can be had with just a sled and a slope. Here are some other offbeat things to do in and around Tahoe:

Three miles north of South Lake Tahoe off Hwy. 89 is the Forest Service Visitor Center's **Stream Profile Chamber ★** (✆ **530/573-2674**), a series of submerged windows that allow an up-close-and-personal study of one of nature's stranger rites: the annual spawning display of red kokanee salmon as they battle their way up Taylor Creek to lay their eggs. Although the salmon run takes place during October, the chamber and visitor center are open from Memorial Day to the end of October. When the salmon aren't stealing the show, you can watch rainbow trout, crayfish, and minnows in their natural habitat through the viewing windows.

On the north side of the lake is the popular **Fanny Bridge** (at the intersection of Calif. 28 and Calif. 89). While everybody's at the railing admiring the huge rainbow trout that congregate below the bridge, take a step back and you'll see how the bridge got its name. Rent a bike for about $8 an hour at the **Olympic Bike Shop,** 620 N. Lake Blvd., Tahoe City (✆ **530/581-2500**), and ride along the beautiful **Truckee River Bike Trail.** Helmets are included in the price, and for another small fee you can rent a trailer or a tandem attachment to include your kids.

For the ultimate cheap sunset thrill, ride the **Squaw Valley cable car** (✆ **800/545-4350**; www.squaw.com). It's only $12 after 5pm (that's half the regular price). Then hang out at the High Camp, a miniresort near the top of the mountain that has an ice-skating rink, five restaurants, hiking trails, and gorgeous views of the lake basin. The 8-minute ride also offers incredible vistas as you rise 2,000 feet above the valley floor.

Another great choice is **Cyclepaths Mountain Bike Adventures,** 1785 W. Lake Blvd. in Truckee (✆ **800/780-BIKE [2453]** or 530/581-1171; www.cyclepaths.com), where you can arrange a guided off-road tour. Whether you're into hard-core downhill single track or easy-going scenic outings, the expert guides will provide you with the necessary gear, food, and transportation. The shop has a second outpost at 10200 Donner Pass Rd. (✆ **530/582-1890**) in Truckee.

BOATING, KAYAKING, PARASAILING & WATERSPORTS   Nothing beats getting out on the lake and seeing the 360-degree view of Lake Tahoe—either by taking a guided tour or by going off on your own to motor, sail, or paddle around. And plenty of companies around the lake would love your business. **Zephyr Cove Marina** (✆ **800/238-2463**; www.zephyrcove.com) is the lake's largest marina and home of the paddle-wheeler MS *Dixie II* (see "Lake Cruises," on p. 309). Here you can parasail, charter sport-fishing trips, or take guided tours. You can also rent motorized boats, pedal boats, kayaks, canoes, water-ski equipment, and jet skis. **Tahoe City Marina** (✆ **530/583-1039**; www.tahoecitymarina.com), at 700 N. Lake Blvd. in Tahoe City, rents motorized boats, sailboats, and fishing boats. This is also

A sailing TOUR OF LAKE TAHOE

I can't imagine a better way to spend an afternoon in Lake Tahoe than relaxing on a beautiful sailing yacht, sipping a cold beer or chardonnay while soaking in the sunshine and incredible scenery. That's why I think you should call **Tahoe Sailing Charters** and join them on one of their scenic 2-hour afternoon or sunset cruises aboard the *Tahoe Cruz*, a sleek 50-foot Santa Cruz–class yacht with a 12-foot beam and plenty of elbowroom. Guests can take turns at the helm or relax and let captain and crew sail the deep blue. Complimentary refreshments and snacks are included. The *Tahoe Cruz* sails daily from the Tahoe City Marina on Lake Tahoe's North Shore; rates are $50 for the afternoon sail and $60 for the sunset cruise. For departure times, reservations, and information, call ✆ **530/583-6200** or log on to **www.tahoesail.com**.

the location for **Lake Tahoe Parasailing** (✆ **530/546-7698**). **Tahoe Paddle and Oar,** North Lake Beach Center, 8299 N. Lake Blvd., Kings Beach (✆ **530/581-3029;** www.tahoepaddle.com), is a good place to rent kayaks, canoes, pedal boats, and windsurfing equipment. Paddling around in the clear waters of Crystal Bay is great fun. Other companies that rent kayaks and provide a variety of guided tours—Emerald Bay tours, East Shore tours, sunset tours, moonlight/astronomy tours, to name a few—include the **Tahoe Adventure Company** (✆ **866/830-6125;** www. tahoeadventurecompany.com) and **Tahoe City Kayak** (✆ **530/581-4336;** www.tahoecitykayak.net).

Action Water Sports rents boats, kayaks, jet skis, paddle boats, and other water toys; parasailing and guided tours are also available. Action Water Sports has two locations: 3411 Lake Tahoe Blvd. at Timber Cove Marina, South Lake Tahoe (✆ **530/544-5387;** www.action-watersports.com); and across from the Hyatt in Incline Village (✆ **775/831-4386**). **Camp Richardson Marina,** 1900 Jameson Beach Rd., off Hwy. 89 on the South Shore (✆ **530/542-6570;** www.camprichardson.com), on a long, sandy beach, rents power- and ski boats, jet skis, kayaks, and paddle boats. It also offers fishing charters, ski school, and raft and kayak tours to Emerald Bay. **SunSports,** 3564 Lake Tahoe Blvd., South Lake Tahoe (✆ **530/541-6000**), provides rentals, tours, and lessons for kayaking, rafting, sailing, and scuba diving.

CAMPING If you have an appetite for the great outdoors, here are a few of the many good campgrounds at Tahoe:

D. L. Bliss State Park, on the western shore (✆ **530/525-7277**), has 168 campsites, fine beaches, and hiking trails.

Sugar Pine Point State Park, open year-round on the western shore (✆ **530/525-7982**), has 175 campsites, a picnic area, beach, nature center, and cross-country skiing.

Campground by the Lake, 1150 Rufus Allen Blvd., South Lake Tahoe (✆ **530/542-6096**), features 170 campsites, a boat ramp, a gym, and a history museum.

Zephyr Cove RV Park and Campground, at Zephyr Cove Resort on U.S. 50 (✆ **775/589-4907;** www.zephyrcove.com), has a beach, a marina, and complete facilities.

FISHING   The cold, clear waters of Lake Tahoe are home to massive kokanee salmon and rainbow, brown, and Mackinaw trout. Fishing here is a challenge in the deep water, so most anglers opt to use a guide or charter boat. Dozens of charter companies offer daily excursions. Rates run about $65 for a half-day to $95 for a whole day (bait, tackle, fish cleaning, and food included). On the North Shore, try **Mickey's Big Mack Charters** at the Sierra Boat Company in Carnelian Bay (© 800/877-1462 or 530/546-4444; www.mickeysbigmack.com). On the South Shore, try **Blue Ribbon Fishing Charters,** Tahoe Keys Marina (© 530/544-6552; www.blue ribbonfishing.com), or **Tahoe Sportfishing,** 900 Ski Run Blvd. (© 800/696-7797 or 530/541-5448; www.tahoesportfishing.com). If you'd rather try your hand at fly-fishing, the **Northstar-at-Tahoe** resort (© 530/582-5393; www.northstarattahoe.com) has a private 10-acre reservoir stocked with hundreds of rainbow trout, reserved for catch-and-release fly-fishing only. Equipment is available for guests at no extra cost, and there's a guide on-site daily to provide helpful hints.

FITNESS CENTERS   The **Incline Recreation Center,** 980 Incline Way, Incline Village (© 775/832-1310; www.inclinerecreation.com), is impressive, with a heated indoor Olympic-size swimming pool, aerobics, basketball, cardiovascular fitness room, lounge, fireplace, and on-site child-care. It's $15 for adults and $9 for children.

GOLF   With its world-class golf courses, mild summer weather, and magnificent scenery, Lake Tahoe is a golfer's paradise. All of the following courses are very busy in the summer, so call *far* in advance for tee times. For more information about Tahoe-area golf courses, log on to **www.tahoesbest.com/Golf**.

The north end of the lake has six highly rated courses: **Incline Village Championship Course,** 955 Fairway Blvd., and the smaller **Incline Village Mountain (Executive) Course,** 690 Wilson Way (© 866/925-GOLF [4653] for both; www.golfincline.com); **Old Greenwood** and **Coyote Moon** at the new **Ritz-Carlton Highlands** (© 530/562-3000; p. 319); **Northstar-at-Tahoe** (© 530/562-3290; p. 317); and the **Resort at Squaw Creek** (© 800/327-3353; p. 318).

In the south, **Edgewood,** U.S. 50 at Lake Parkway, Stateline (© 775/588-3566; www.edgewood-tahoe.com), is home of the Celebrity Golf Championship; **Lake Tahoe Golf Course,** 2500 Emerald Bay Rd., South Lake Tahoe (© 530/577-0788; www.laketahoegc.com), also has some good 9-hole municipal courses. There's also **Old Brockway Golf Course,** 7900 N. Lake Blvd., Kings Beach (© 530/546-9909; www.old brockway.com); **Tahoe City Golf Course,** 251 N. Lake Blvd., Tahoe City (© 530/583-1516); and **Bijou Municipal Golf Course,** 3464 Fairway Ave., South Lake Tahoe (© 530/542-6097).

HIKING   Hiking trails for all levels of experience crisscross the mountains surrounding Lake Tahoe. Before setting out, you may wish to contact the local visitor centers or sporting-goods shops for a map and more in-depth information on particular trails, or hire a guide. Try **Tahoe Trips & Trails** (© 800/581-HIKE [4453] or 530/583-4506; www.tahoetrips.com) for short and long guided hikes. Everything is provided: food, drinks, transportation, and information about the lake. Going on your own? Some of the most popular short hikes in the area are listed here:

- **Eagle Falls/Eagle Lake:** This moderately easy trail is well marked and begins at Eagle Picnic Area, across Hwy. 89 from Emerald Bay. It's only about a third of a mile to the steel footbridge overlooking the falls and 2 miles round-trip (1½–2 hr.) to Eagle Lake. Be sure to sign in at the self-registration station at the trail head.

- **Emerald Bay/Vikingsholm:** The trail starts at the parking area on the north side of Emerald Bay, on Hwy. 89. It's a wide, well-maintained trail but fairly steep, about 2.5 miles round-trip. At the bottom of the trail is a picnic area, as well as world-famous Vikingsholm, a replica of a Scandinavian castle.

- **Nevada Shoreline:** Begin at the paved parking lot on the west side of Hwy. 28, 3 miles south of Sand Harbor. The trail drops to the beach and follows the shoreline, passing Chimney Beach, Secret Harbor, and Whale Beach. The trail eventually connects to a service road that can be followed back up to the parking area. It's an easy 4-mile hike, with a vertical climb of only 300 feet.

- **Shirley Lake:** This trail leads to Shirley Lake and then down to Shirley Canyon. Take the tram at Squaw Valley up to High Camp and hike down, or vice versa. The trail begins at the end of Squaw Creek Road, next to the cable car building. It's a 4-mile hike, easy to moderate in difficulty, with some steep sections.

HORSEBACK RIDING Most stables offer a variety of guided trail rides and lessons for individuals, families, and groups. Choose the one that appeals to your sense of adventure: 1- to 2-hour trail rides; breakfast, lunch, or dinner rides; or half-day, full-day, overnight, and extended pack trips. Expect to pay $25 to $35 for a 1-hour ride, $6 for a half-hour pony ride. Saddle up and savor the scenery. Try **Alpine Meadows Stables,** 355 Alpine Meadows Rd., Tahoe City (© 530/583-3905); **Squaw Valley Stables,** 1525 Squaw Valley Rd., north of Tahoe City (© 530/583-7433); **Camp Richardson Corral,** Hwy. 89, South Lake Tahoe (© 530/541-3113); or **Zephyr Cove Stables,** Zephyr Cove Resort, U.S. 50 at Zephyr Cove (© 775/588-5664; www.zephyrcove.com).

RIVER RAFTING For a swift but gentle ride down the Truckee River (the lake's only outlet), try **Truckee River Raft Rental,** 185 River Rd., Tahoe City (© 530/583-0123; www.truckeeriverraft.com). It's available only in the summer, and the rates are $35 for adults and $30 for children 6 to 12 (kids 5 and under are free). If you prefer a more exciting whitewater experience, **Tributary Whitewater Tours** (© 800/672-3846; www.whitewatertours. com) offers daily excursions (in season) down the Truckee River amid Class 2 to 3-plus rapids. It's the perfect trip for neophyte rafters and families—exciting but not dangerously so. For a half-day trip, rates range from $68 to $98 for adults and $60 to $70 for kids 7 and older.

TENNIS The mild summer weather at Lake Tahoe is perfect for great tennis. If you want to sharpen your skills, **Northstar-at-Tahoe** (© 530/562-0321; p. 317) offers several excellent tennis packages for its guests only. **Squaw Creek** (© 530/581-6694; p. 318) tennis courts are open to the public for $14 an hour. **Kirkwood** (© 209/258-6000; p. 301), **MontBleu Resort Casino & Spa** (© 775/588-3515; p. 313), and **Harveys Lake Tahoe Casino & Resort** (© 775/588-2411; p. 313) all feature tennis courts for a fee.

Budget-minded players should visit Tahoe Lake School on Grove Street in Tahoe City, or Tahoe Regional Park, at the end of National Avenue in Tahoe Vista. South Tahoe Intermediate School on Lyons Avenue has eight lighted courts and charges $3 per hour. South Tahoe High School, 1735 Lake Tahoe Blvd., has free courts.

LAKE CRUISES

If you can fit a lake cruise into your vacation plans, you won't regret it—it's one of the best ways to see the lake. The **MS *Dixie II,*** located at Zephyr Cove Marina (4 miles north of the South Lake casinos on U.S. 50; ℂ **800/238-2463;** www.zephyrcove.com), is a 570-passenger paddle-wheeler with bars, a dance floor, and a full dining room. Emerald Bay scenic cruises cost $39 for adults, $15 for children. They also offer dinner cruises ($75 adults, $41 children).

The ***Tahoe Queen*** (ℂ 800/238-2463; www.zephyrcove.com), which departs from the Marina Village at Ski Run Boulevard in South Lake Tahoe, is also an authentic paddle-wheeler offering Emerald Bay sightseeing tours ($39 adults, $15 children) and dinner/dance cruises ($75 adults, $41 children). Live music, buffet breakfast, dinner, and appetizers are all available onboard.

The ***Tahoe Gal*** (ℂ **800/218-2464** or 530/583-0141; www.tahoegal.com), departing from the Lighthouse Marina (behind Safeway) in Tahoe City, is the only cruise boat on the North Shore. Cruises include the Scenic Brunch Cruise ($35 adults, $16 children), Emerald Bay ($39 adults, $19 children), Happy Hour (4:30–6pm; $28 adults, $15 children), and Sunset Dinner ($35 adults, $16 children). ***Note:*** Prices are for the cruise only; food and beverages cost extra.

Woodwind Sailing Cruises (ℂ 888/867-6394) runs daily sightseeing tours ($35 adults, $15 children 3–12) and a Sunset Champagne Cruise ($45). ***Woodwind I,*** a 30-passenger Searunner trimaran, sails to Emerald Bay from Camp Richardson Marina in South Lake Tahoe. The ***Woodwind II,*** a 50-passenger Searunner catamaran, sails from Zephyr Cove Marina.

A DRIVE AROUND THE LAKE

Overwhelmed by the choices? Get in your car and take a leisurely drive around the lake. It's only 72 miles, but plan on expending several hours, even in the best of weather. In the worst of weather, don't try it! Parts of the road, if not closed, can be icy and dangerous. On a mild day, it will be a memorable experience. If your car has a CD player, consider buying a self-guided CD audio tour that contains facts, legends, places of interest, and just about everything else you might want to know about the lake. You'll find them at many gift shops and bookstores around the lake.

We'll start at the California–Nevada border in South Lake Tahoe and loop around the western shore on Hwy. 89 to Tahoe City and beyond. U.S. 50, which runs along the South Shore, is an ugly, overdeveloped strip that obliterates any view of the lake. Keep heading west and you will be free of this boring stretch.

First stop is the **Tallac Historic Site,** site of the former Tallac Resort and a cluster of 100-year-old mansions that provide a fascinating glimpse into Tahoe's past. In its heyday, the resort included two large hotels, a casino, and numerous outbuildings. Throughout the summer, the **Valhalla Festival of Arts and Music** (ℂ **530/541-4975;** www.valhallatahoe.com) showcases jazz, bluegrass, rock, mariachi, and classical music. Summer highlights include June's Valhalla

Renaissance Festival, July's Native American Fine Arts Festival, and August's Great Gatsby Festival.

From here the highway winds north along the shore until you reach **Cascade Lake** on the left and **Emerald Bay** ★★ on the right. The Emerald Bay Lookout is a spectacular picture-taking spot. Emerald Bay's deep green water is the site of the only island in Lake Tahoe, Fannette Island. The small structure atop the island is the teahouse, built by Ms. Lora Knight, who also constructed **Vikingsholm** ★ (www.vikingsholm.com), a 38-room Scandinavian castle built in 1929, at the head of Emerald Bay. Tours of this unique structure are available from mid-June to Labor Day every half-hour from 10am to 4pm. Even if you don't want to take the tour, it's a pleasant walk from the parking area down to the beach and the mansion's grounds. Just remember that you have to walk back up. Across the highway, there's another parking area. From here, it's a short, steep .25-mile hike to a footbridge above **Eagle Falls.** Then it's about a mile farther up to **Eagle Lake.**

It's only about 2 more miles to **D. L. Bliss State Park** (✆ 530/525-7277), with one of the lake's best beaches. It fills up in summer, so arrive early for a parking place. The park also has 168 campsites and several trails, including one along the shoreline.

In about 7 miles you will reach **Sugar Pine State Park** (✆ 530/525-7982), the largest (2,000 acres) of the lake's parks and also the only one that has year-round camping. In summer, you can visit its beaches, plus a nature center and miles of trails; in winter, you can cross-country ski on well-maintained trails.

Continuing on through the town of **Homewood** (site of the ski resort), **Sunnyside,** on the right, is a great place to stop for a lakeside lunch. Or, if you feel like taking a stroll, drive on to Tahoe City, with its beautiful paved path along the Truckee River. Check out the big trout at **Fanny Bridge** ★ (p. 305) first. If you would like to see **Squaw Valley** and **Alpine Meadows,** take a left at Hwy. 89. A ride on the Squaw Valley cable car (✆ 530/583-6985) will reward you with incredible vistas from 2,000 feet above the valley floor. It runs year-round and costs $24 for adults, $18 for seniors and youth 13 through 18, and $6 for children 12 and under. Back on Hwy. 28, as you leave **Tahoe City,** you will pass a string of small malls at 700–850 N. Lake Blvd. If you like to wander around, this is a good area to stop and eat, watch the activity at the **Tahoe City Marina** (parasailing, cruises on the *Tahoe Gal,* and boat rental), or visit the shops.

Gondola to Heaven

If you want a preview of heaven, take a ride on the **Heavenly Mountain Resort gondola** (www.skiheavenly.com). State-of-the-art "cars" whisk you from South Shore's downtown area up the mountain to Heavenly Resort's 14,000-square-foot observation deck, complete with telescopes and a cafe. The 2½-mile ride rises to an elevation of 9,123 feet, offering passengers shore-to-shore views of Lake Tahoe, Carson Valley to the east, and Desolation Wilderness to the west (all best seen at sunset). The gondola is a half-block west of Stateline, an easy walk from downtown. It's open in the summer 7 days a week from 10am to 5pm; winter hours are Monday through Friday from 9am to 4pm; Saturday, Sunday, and holidays from 8:30am to 4pm. Tickets are $32 for adults, $26 for teens ages 13 to 18, $20 for children ages 5 to 12, and free for kids 4 and under.

The Thunderbird Lodge.

Continuing around the lake on Hwy. 28, you'll reach Carnelian Bay, Tahoe Vista, and Kings Beach before crossing the state line into Nevada. **Kings Beach State Recreation Area ★** (✆ **530/546-4212**), a long, wide beach and picnic area, is jammed in the summer with sunbathers and swimmers. As you approach **Crystal Bay,** you will know, from the string of small casinos, that you have crossed the state line. The **Cal-Neva Resort, Spa & Casino** (p. 319), on the right, was once owned by Frank Sinatra and has a celebrity-studded history. The state line goes right through the lodge, and gambling is allowed only on the Nevada side (it's worth stopping to see).

Your journey next takes you to woodsy Incline Village, arguably the most beautiful community on the lake. Take a right on Lakeshore Boulevard to view the elegant estates. Lunch or dinner time? The **Lone Eagle Grille** (p. 317), at the Hyatt Regency Lake Tahoe, offers gorgeous panoramic lake views, as well as superb food.

The east shore of the lake is largely undeveloped and very scenic. Drive about 4 miles south of Incline Village to **Sand Harbor ★** (✆ **775/831-0494**), one of the lake's best-loved beaches, and home to the very popular **Lake Tahoe Shakespeare Festival** (✆ **800/747-4697;** www.laketahoeshakespeare.com) every mid-July through August. In addition to turquoise blue water dotted with big boulders and a wide sandy beach, you'll find nature trails, picnic areas, and boating.

Going south, you will come to an outcropping called **Cave Rock,** where the highway passes through 75 feet of solid stone. The historic **Thunderbird Lodge** (✆ **800/GO-TAHOE** [468-2463]; www.thunderbirdlodge.org), former home to the eccentric and wealthy George Whittell, is available for tours by reservation. Farther along is **Zephyr Cove Resort and Marina,** home to the MS *Dixie II* and a beehive of watersports activity. You'll then return to Stateline and South Lake Tahoe, your original starting point.

Where to Stay

SOUTH SHORE & SOUTH LAKE TAHOE

Expensive

Black Bear Inn Bed & Breakfast ★★   Within a wooded acre near Heavenly Ski Resort, this beautiful neorustic lodge offers luxury accommodations in a tranquil setting and convenient location (though not the prettiest in town). The great room, with its beamed ceilings, grand piano, Early American antiques, three-story rock fireplace, and complimentary evening hors d'oeuvres, offers a relaxing environment after a long day of outdoor activities. Or better yet, soak your tired body in the sheltered Jacuzzi. Breakfast—included in the room rate—is an event, with fresh-baked muffins, eggs Benedict, omelets, and other hearty fare. Each of the spacious guest rooms has an artful blend of modern and authentic Old West furnishings, including a king-size bed, private bathroom, and gas fireplace. For additional privacy, request one of the three cabins behind the inn, and ask for breakfast to be delivered to your door.

1202 Ski Run Blvd., South Lake Tahoe, CA 96150. www.tahoeblackbear.com. ℂ **877/232-7466** or 530/544-4451. 5 lodge rooms, 3 cabins. $210–$315 lodge room; $270–$485 cabin. Rates include full breakfast. AE, MC, V. **Amenities:** Nearby golf course; Jacuzzi. *In room:* A/C, TV/VCR/DVD, fridge, hair dryer in cabins, kitchenette, free Wi-Fi.

Embassy Suites Lake Tahoe Hotel & Ski Resort ★ ☺   On the edge of the state line, steps away from the Heavenly Gondola, this is the only major noncasino hotel on Tahoe's South Shore. It earns its keep by luring the upscale gambling crowd and the convention business with uncommonly large suites. The nine-story château-style hotel has a roofline pierced with a double layer of dormers; equally impressive are the three massive inner atriums featuring a collection of fine art, live plants, and a waterfall feature reminiscent of the Comstock Lode mining era. The two-room suites all have a separate living room with sofa bed, armchair, a well-lit dining/work table, a microwave, two TVs, a small refrigerator, and a wet bar. The resort's fine-dining restaurant, **Echo,** serves New American cuisine for lunch and dinner with large-screen TVs to view the latest sports activities. In the summer, guests have access to a private beach, watersports equipment rental, and a multitude of outdoor recreational activities.

4130 Lake Tahoe Blvd., South Lake Tahoe, CA 96150. www.embassytahoe.com. ℂ **877/497-8483** or 530/544-5400. Fax 530/544-4900. 400 suites. $169–$399 suite. Rates include full breakfast and evening cocktail reception. Special packages available. Children 18 and under stay free in parent's room. AE, DC, DISC, MC, V. **Amenities:** Restaurant; lounge; babysitting; concierge; health club; Jacuzzi; indoor pool; room service; dry sauna; watersports equipment rental; Wi-Fi in public areas. *In room:* A/C, TV, fridge, hair dryer.

Harrah's Lake Tahoe ★ ☺   Understatement is not a word that crosses your mind at Harrah's, the glitziest, most luxurious of Tahoe's casinos. Harrah's takes great pride in its special blend of luxury, beauty, unparalleled guest service, and casino entertainment. Large rooms have two bathrooms, each with a TV and telephone, with those thick, fluffy, white towels Sinatra always demanded. Most have bay windows overlooking the lake or the mountains. The casino has an enormous fun center for kids, with the latest in video and arcade games, virtual reality, and an indoor "playscape" for young children. Weddings and parties can be scheduled aboard the private yacht, the *Tahoe Star.* The **South Shore Room** hosts showbiz stars, and last, but by no means least, the casino is a gambler's dream.

P.O. Box 8, Stateline, NV 89449. www.harrahslaketahoe.com. ✆ **800/427-7247** or 775/588-6611. Fax 775/586-6601. 525 units. $159–$349 double; $396–$596 suite. Packages available. AE, DC, DISC, MC, V. **Amenities:** 8 restaurants; cafe; deli; coffeehouse; full-service health club/spa; indoor pool; room service. *In room:* A/C, TV/VCR, hair dryer.

Harveys Lake Tahoe Casino & Resort ☺

With its two massive towers and 740 rooms, Harveys is the largest (and possibly the ugliest) hotel in Tahoe. It features an 88,000-square-foot casino, seven restaurants, and a cabaret with some of the most glittering, bespangled shows in town. Harveys is like a city unto itself, with a children's day camp, salons and barbershops, and even a wedding chapel, should you get the urge. Heck, you never have to see the real world again. *Tip:* Try to get a room between the 15th and 19th floors in the Lake Tower, where every unit has a view of Lake Tahoe and the surrounding Sierra, or a newer room on the remodeled fifth or sixth floors. *Note:* Harrah's Entertainment owns Harveys, which is why they share the same toll-free number, and an underground tunnel connects the two buildings.

U.S. 50 at Stateline Ave. (P.O. Box 128), Stateline, NV 89449. www.harveystahoe.com. ✆ **800/427-7247** or 775/588-2411. Fax 775/588-6643. 740 units. $129–$299 double; $299–$699 suite. AE, DC, DISC, MC, V. **Amenities:** 7 restaurants; 10 bars; concierge; nearby golf course; health club; Jacuzzi; outdoor heated pool; room service; sauna; spa; watersports equipment rental. *In room:* A/C, TV w/pay movies, hair dryer, minibar.

MontBleu Resort Casino & Spa ★★

Following the bandwagon of casinos offering a resort experience, the MontBleu is selling itself as "the" park-'n'-play destination in South Lake. Recent makeovers in years past include a chic new lobby that makes other hotels on the strip look frumpy, and seven stylin' new restaurants (tapas anyone?), two hip new nightclubs, the 1,500-seat MontBleu Theatre that features celebrity performers, and a new outdoor sports arena hosting pro volleyball tournaments. The 40,000-square-foot casino floor includes a new race and sports book (also known as The Zone) and a poker room offering eight tables of the popular Texas Hold 'Em at various buy-in levels. The guest rooms, many of which offer beautiful lake views, are furnished with contemporary hardwood pieces and equipped with signature Bleu Cloud Beds and extra-large tubs. Suites range from executive-style quarters to lavish suites for high rollers. Other highlights include a lagoon-style indoor pool, a Starbucks, and the Onsen Spa.

55 U.S. 50 (P.O. Box 5800), Lake Tahoe, NV 89449. www.montbleuresort.com. ✆ **888/829-7630** or 775/588-3515. 437 units. $99–$330 double; $390–$950 suite. Packages available. AE, DC, MC, V. **Amenities:** 7 restaurants; health club; Jacuzzi; indoor pool; room service; sauna; spa; 3 outdoor tennis courts; ski rental. *In room:* A/C, TV, fridge upon request, hair dryer, kitchenette and minibar in suites, Wi-Fi.

968 Park Hotel ★★

This is the newest—not to mention greenest—hotel to open along the South Shore. Opened in 2009, 968 Park's rooms are pristine and spacious, and a suitable alternative to the pricey (and, dare I say, sometimes tacky) casinos that litter the South Shore. Everything is eco-modern and fits in seamlessly with its Tahoe surroundings (lots of wood decor constructed from all-natural materials). Service is stellar, and you're presented with a complimentary beer or glass of wine upon arrival. And for those ski bunnies, the location couldn't be more ideal: It's directly across the street from the Heavenly Gondola, as well as South Lake's central shopping area. Free parking and free Internet are further added perks.

968 Park Ave., South Lake Tahoe, CA 96150. www.968parkhotel.com. ✆ **877/544-0968.**
58 rooms. $89–$229 room; $199–$259 suite. AE, MC, V. **Amenities:** Hot tub (indoor); outdoor
pool (seasonal); sauna; spa; Zen garden. *In room:* TV, fridge, MP3 docking station, free Wi-Fi.

Tahoe Seasons Resort   Big, modern, and loaded with luxuries, the Tahoe
Seasons lies in a relatively uncongested residential neighborhood at the base of
the Heavenly Valley Ski Resort, 2 miles from Tahoe's casinos. Every unit here is
a spacious, attractive suite, sleeping up to four in the smaller one and six in the
larger one. Most have gas fireplaces, and all have huge whirlpool spas complete
with shoji screens (in case you plan to lose your shirt in more ways than one).
Skiing isn't the only activity around here: Play a round of tennis on the roof or hop
aboard the free casino shuttles.

3901 Saddle Rd., off Ski Run Blvd. (P.O. Box 5656), South Lake Tahoe, CA 96157. www.tahoe
seasons.com. ✆ **800/540-4874** or 530/541-6700. Fax 530/541-0653. 160 suites. Summer
$170–$240 double; winter $180–$250 double; spring and fall $122–$200 double. Seasonal
packages available. AE, MC, V. **Amenities:** Restaurant; pub; concierge; nearby golf course; complimentary health club use at Harveys Resort; outdoor heated pool; room service; 2 rooftop
tennis courts. *In room:* A/C, TV/VCR, fridge, hair dryer on request.

Moderate

Best Western Station House Inn 🍴   Ensconced amid towering pines but
just 3 blocks from the casinos, the Best Western Station House Inn, built in the
late 1970s, is one of the few hotels in town that still has its own private "gated"
beach on the lake. The decor is corporate dull, but the location is ideal; the large
swimming pool and hot tub are a huge bonus; and **LewMarNel's,** the on-site
restaurant, won a *Wine Spectator* award. The complimentary breakfast, cooked to
order, and free shuttle service make staying here a particularly good value.

901 Park Ave., South Lake Tahoe, CA 96150. www.stationhouseinn.com. ✆ **800/822-5953** or
530/542-1101. Fax 530/542-1714. 100 units. $74–$138 double; $135–$165 suite; $200–$300 cabin.
Rates include full breakfast. Packages available. AE, DC, DISC, MC, V. **Amenities:** Restaurant;
Jacuzzi; heated outdoor pool. *In room:* A/C, TV, hair dryer.

Camp Richardson Resort ★ ☺   If you're planning a family vacation, a
reunion, or just a weekend getaway, Camp Richardson has it all. On a long sandy
beach on the southwest shore, this woodsy retreat offers a wide array of activities
and several lodging and dining options. Its two restaurants offer lakeside dining;
there's also a general store, a candy store, and an ice-cream parlor. The sports
center rents all the seasonal equipment you'll need. You can ski right along the
shore, scale the rock-climbing wall, or visit the stable for horseback riding. The
full-service marina rents ski boats, jet skis, kayaks, and paddle boats, and offers
guided tours, cruises, and chartered fishing trips. Lodging options include a
hotel, cabins, a beachside inn, a marina duplex, tent campgrounds, and an RV
park. Cabins rent only by the week in summer and fill up quickly. *Tip:* Check
their website for seasonal money-saving packages.

Jameson Beach Rd. (P.O. Box 9028), South Lake Tahoe, CA 96158. www.camprichardson.com.
✆ **800/544-1801** or 530/541-1801. Fax 530/541-1802. $95–$195 hotel; $145–$250 cabin per day
winter, $745–$2,265 per week summer. Camping or RV hookup $25–$40 per day. DISC, MC, V.
Amenities: 2 restaurants; ice-cream parlor; cafe; children's program; Jacuzzi; bike, snowshoe,
and ski rental. *In room:* TV in inn and duplex rooms, kitchen in cabin, no phone in hotel and
cabin units.

VILLAGE people

That sprawling "alpine village" next to the casinos is the 464-room **Marriott Grand Residence Club** (4100 Lake Tahoe Blvd.; ✆ **800/845-5279** or 530/542-8400; www. marriott.com). It's the first phase of a massive redevelopment project slated for Stateline that will level most of the old, inexpensive motels with nickel-slotters and replace them with that expensive corporate faux-village thing that's taking over the world's tourist destinations. The two adjacent vacation ownership resorts also sell rooms on a per-night basis, but it's a good deal only if your family takes full advantage of the resort amenities: restaurants, bars, an ice-skating rink, two pools, a movie theater, a ski gondola, an arcade, and an alpine-style retail mini-mall. The silver lining? The new building codes are fiercely pro-environment: Holding and treatment ponds are now required to prevent polluted snowmelt and rainwater from dumping straight into the lake, and the central ski gondola and high-tech bus system are two new eco-friendly means of luring people away from their SUVs.

Deerfield Lodge at Heavenly ★★   When Robin and Eric Pels purchased the Deerfield Lodge (formerly the Dream Inn) in 2005, it was little more than a run-down roadside motel at the base of the mountain. Not anymore. The couple invested millions of dollars into making it the most high-end lodging experience on the South Shore. It looks massive from the outside—that's because the rooms are so large—yet features only 12 accommodations; 10 well-appointed suites are 750 square feet with a bedroom, two bathrooms, a living room, and a kitchenette, while the remaining two have a bedroom and bathroom each. Guests are given a generous welcome basket with breakfast staples, snacks, and sweet treats upon check-in. There are also delectable complimentary snacks, coffee, and tea always available in the lobby. Best of all: Deerfield Lodge is located in the charming, up-and-coming Ski Run Boulevard—just a mile from the Heavenly Ski Resort aerial tram and the Gunbarrel Express chairlift (where there's free parking).

As if it already didn't have such mass appeal, the lodge allows dogs of all sizes. (It's particularly popular with Bernese mountain dog owners, who I imagine must have difficulty finding a hotel that welcomes such large canines.) In fact, Robin and Eric's own polite pooches, Bentley and Baylor, are on hand to ensure their canine friends have a good time.

1200 Ski Run Blvd., South Lake Tahoe, CA 96150. www.tahoedeerfieldlodge.com. ✆ **800/757-3337** or 530/544-3337. 12 units. $169–$279 double. Rates include breakfast basket. AE, MC, V. Pets accepted; the owners ask you make a donation to the South Lake Tahoe Humane Society in lieu of a fee. **Amenities:** Ski butler valet service; concierge service; free Wi-Fi in lobby. *In room:* TV, DVD, fridge, microwave, fireplace, Jacuzzi tubs.

Horizon Casino Resort ☺ 🔥   This massive resort hotel, next to the even larger Harveys, charges less for basically the same facilities. The lobby is a cheesy sea of white marble and mirrors, and the standard rooms are bland but innocuous (although the suites are far racier). The upper floors of the two towers naturally open onto the best views of mountains and the lake. Besides the 42,000-square-foot gaming room, the resort has a multiplex movie theater, cabaret, lounge, nightclub, the largest outdoor pool in Tahoe, and restaurants ranging from buffet to gourmet.

U.S. 50 (P.O. Box C), Lake Tahoe, NV 89449. www.horizoncasino.com. ✆ **800/648-3322** or 775/588-6211. Fax 775/588-0349. 539 units. $125–$188 double summer, $99–$169 double winter; $250–$500 suite. Children 11 and under stay free in parent's room. Packages available. AE, DC, DISC, MC, V. **Amenities:** 3 restaurants; bike and ski rental; concierge; nearby golf course; health club; 3 Jacuzzis; large heated outdoor pool; room service. *In room:* A/C, TV w/pay movies, fridge, hair dryer, minibar.

Lakeland Village Beach & Mountain Resort ★ ☺   With a children's play area and summer kids' activity club, this 1970s condominium/hotel resort is a good choice for families. Clustered on 19 lightly forested acres of shoreline property is a labyrinth of redwood buildings that blend into the surrounding landscape. The only drawback is the proximity to traffic headed into Lake Tahoe, although some units are quieter than those in the main lodge, adjacent to the road. The units—ranging from studios and suites in the lodge to multibedroom lakeside town homes—have streamlined California architecture, and many have upstairs sleeping lofts. All accommodations come with fully equipped kitchens and fireplaces. Perks include a large private beach directly on the lake, access to a boat dock, and free private shuttle service to Heavenly and the casinos.

3535 Lake Tahoe Blvd., South Lake Tahoe, CA 96150. www.lakeland-village.com. ✆ **800/822-5969** or 530/544-1685. Fax 530/541-6278. 209 condo units. $99–$300 double; $165–$1,500 for a 1- to 5-bedroom town house. Includes free continental breakfast for skiers (winter only). Children stay free in parent's room. AE, DISC, MC, V. **Amenities:** Nearby golf course; fitness room; 2 Jacuzzis; 2 heated outdoor pools; children's wading pool; sauna; 2 outdoor tennis courts. *In room:* TV/VCR/DVD, hair dryer, kitchen, Wi-Fi.

Zephyr Cove ★ 🐾 ☺   Like historic Camp Richardson Resort (see review above), this place is great for families. A lakeside bargain in a shady grove of tall pines, this Nevada-side resort has everything you need for a relaxing vacation: volleyball courts, horseback riding, sailing, a beautiful gold-sand beach, a beachside bar with strong mai tais, and water toys for rent: pedal boats, kayaks, canoes, and ski boats. Zephyr Cove's pier is also the launching point for cruises on the MS *Dixie II* paddle-wheeler and the *Woodwind II* catamaran. The resort's 28 cabins range in size from studios and cottages to four-bedroom cabins sleeping up to 10. Even in the winter, it's fun to stay here: The resort's snowmobile tours are exhilarating, and the Heavenly ski resort is only a 10-minute drive away. The Zephyr Cove Restaurant serves hearty American fare for breakfast, lunch, and dinner daily. A free shuttle runs to the restaurants and casinos down the road.

750 Hwy. 50, at Zephyr Cove, NV 89448. www.zephyrcove.com. ✆ **800/23-TAHOE** (238-2463) or 775/589-4906. 28 cabins. Summer $129–$479 cabin; off season $79–$409. AE, DISC, MC, V. Pets are allowed for $15 per pet, per night. **Amenities:** Restaurant; bar; watersports equipment rental. *In room:* TV w/cable and HBO, Internet access, full kitchen.

Inexpensive

Big Pines Mountain House of Tahoe 🐾   It's nothing fancy, but you get a lot for your money here: agreeable accommodations, access to a private beach, and an easy walk to the casinos and the Heavenly Gondola. The rooms are clean and pleasant, with all the standard conveniences. If you're traveling with kids, you may want one of the units with a kitchen. Be sure to inquire about the ski and lake cruise packages.

4083 Cedar Ave., South Lake Tahoe, CA 96150. www.bigpinesmountainhouse.com. ✆ **800/288-4083** or 530/541-5155. Fax 530/541-5643. 76 units. $56–$119 double. Rates include continental

SKIING TAHOE, squaw VALLEY STYLE

The fancy new **Village at Squaw Valley** looks expensive, but it's actually one of the best deals in Tahoe. For as little as $150 per night, you can score a fully furnished condominium—fireplace, full kitchen, deck, huge TV, sofa bed, DVD player—right next to the ski lifts. And the free perks are superb: covered underground parking, eight whirlpool spas, ski and snowboard lockers, a billiards lounge, and three fitness centers with saunas. You'll never need your car because the best restaurants, bars, and shops are within walking distance. After a full day of skiing, there's no better way to finish off the day than with a Deluxe Deep Tissue massage at the Village's **Trilogy Spa** (✆ 530/584-6125; www.trilogyspa.com), followed by a drink at **Auld Dubliner** (✆ 530/584-6041; www.aulddubliner.com), an authentic Irish Pub from Ireland (literally—the pub was built in Ireland, dismantled, shipped over, and reassembled). The Dubliner has Squaw's best après-ski bar scene and serves great Irish fare. Combine all of this with Tahoe's best skiing, and you have my top resort choice for a Tahoe ski vacation. For more information, log on to **www.thevillageatsquaw.com** (be sure to check out the money-saving package deals) or call ✆ 866/818-6963.

breakfast. Children 11 and under stay free in parent's room. Packages available. AE, DC, DISC, MC, V. **Amenities:** Nearby golf course; Jacuzzi; outdoor heated pool. *In room:* TV, fridge on request, hair dryer, kitchen in 14 units.

NORTH SHORE/TAHOE CITY

Expensive

Hyatt Regency Lake Tahoe Resort, Spa & Casino ★ ☺ If you like gambling but hate gauche, glitzy casinos, you'll like the Hyatt in Incline Village. Amid towering pines and mountains on the lake's pristine northeast shore, it's far classier and quieter than the casino hotels in Stateline. The private beach, loaded with water toys—catamaran cruises, boat rentals, jet skis, parasailing—is available only to guests. The adjoining Lakeside Cottages are heaven for travelers who want beachfront access and comfortable rooms with unobstructed panoramas of the lake. Popular Camp Hyatt affords kids age 3 to 12 a break from their parents for the day. The **Lone Eagle Grille** has one of the most beautiful dining rooms on the lake and superb cuisine. Take a walk down Lakeshore Boulevard to see the magnificent estates fronting the water. The latest addition is a 15,000-square-foot Stillwater Spa facility with a multitiered swimming pool and an entire 150-room wing of Spa Terrace guest rooms.

Country Club at Lakeshore, 111 Country Club Dr., Incline Village, NV 89451. www.laketahoehyatt. com. ✆ **888/899-5019** or 775/832-1234. Fax 775/831-2171. 422 units. $160–$330 double; $405–$1,385 cottage. Packages available. AE, DC, DISC, MC, V. **Amenities:** 4 restaurants; 4 lounges; bike rental; children's program; concierge; nearby golf course; room service; watersports equipment rental. *In room:* A/C, TV w/pay movies, fridge, hair dryer, minibar.

Northstar-at-Tahoe ★★ ☺ The owners of Northstar continue to come up with more ways to have fun year-round—the list of activities here is mind-boggling. Northstar prides itself on being the ultimate self-contained family destination, and it's even better now, since completion of the new Village—seven buildings, with 213 new luxury ski-in/ski-out condominium residences, stylish boutiques, outdoor restaurants, an ice rink, and a pedestrian plaza. The Village is surrounded by a honeycomb of fully equipped redwood condos and vacation homes, all nestled among the pines, and a brand-new, midmountain Ritz-Carlton resort offers ski-in, ski-out access to the lifts. Lodging options range from a hotel room in the lodge to a five-bedroom house, with every size in between. Summer activities include golf, swimming, tennis, mountain biking, hiking, fly-fishing, rock climbing, rope courses, and horseback riding. See "Skiing & Snowboarding," earlier in this chapter, for winter activities.

Off Hwy. 267, Box 129, Northstar-at-Tahoe, CA 96160. www.northstarattahoe.com. © **800/466-6784** or 530/562-1010. Fax 530/562-2215. 250 units. $209–$349 double in lodge; $165–$989 condo, home. Packages available. AE, DISC, MC, V. **Amenities:** 2 restaurants; cafe; deli; bar; babysitting; bike rental; golf course; health club; 3 outdoor Jacuzzis; 3 pools (outdoor heated, indoor heated, children's); sauna; 10 tennis courts. *In room:* TV/DVD and HBO in select rooms, hair dryer.

PlumpJack Squaw Valley Inn ★★   Part ski chalet, part boutique hotel, PlumpJack Squaw Valley Inn is among Tahoe's most refined, elegant lodgings. It lacks the fancy toys offered by its competitor across the valley, the Resort at Squaw Creek (see below), but the PlumpJack is unquestionably more genteel, a tribute to the melding of artistry and hostelry. The hotel is done in muted, earthy tones, with swirling sconces and sculpted metal accents. Rooms have thick hooded robes, terry-cloth slippers, down comforters on expensive mattresses, and mountain views. One unit has a kitchenette. The inn's fine restaurant, **PlumpJack Café,** is reviewed on p. 326.

1920 Squaw Valley Rd. (P.O. Box 2407), Olympic Valley, CA 96146. www.plumpjack.com. © **800/323-7666** or 530/583-1576. Fax 530/583-1734. 61 units. Summer $169–$379 double; winter $199–$549 double. AE, DISC, MC, V. **Amenities:** Restaurant; bar; bike rental; concierge; nearby golf course; 2 Jacuzzis; heated outdoor pool (seasonal); room service. *In room:* TV w/pay movies, fridge, hair dryer, minibar.

The Resort at Squaw Creek ★★★ ☺   The most deluxe resort on the lake is the Resort at Squaw Creek, a paradise for skiers, golfers, and tennis players. You can't beat the resort's ski-in/ski-out access to Squaw Valley slopes; the chairlift lands just outside the door. Don't ski? Don't worry. Lots of other sports facilities will divert you, including 20 miles of groomed cross-country skiing trails (marked for hiking and biking in the summer); snowshoeing; dogsled rides; an ice-skating rink; and, in summer, a world-class golf course, guided hikes, on-property fly-fishing, and the newly renovated Spa at Squaw Creek, a full-service spa and salon. Trained counselors lead a Mountain Buddies Kids Kamp program for children ages 4 to 13, with different activities every day year-round. The standard guest rooms are not particularly spacious, but they're well equipped with attractive furnishings, original artwork, and windows that open, with beautiful views. Suites come in all different sizes and configurations. *Tip:* Be sure to ask about the money-saving midweek package deals.

400 Squaw Creek Rd., Olympic Valley, CA 96146. www.squawcreek.com. © **800/327-3353** or 530/583-6300. Fax 530/581-6632. 405 units. $179–$399 double; $259–$2,900 suite. Packages available. AE, DC, DISC, MC, V. Free valet parking. **Amenities:** 4 restaurants; deli; 2 bars; babysitting; bike rental; children's program; concierge; golf course; health club; indoor and outdoor Jacuzzis; 3 pools (1 heated); room service; dry saunas; region's largest spa; 2 outdoor tennis courts. *In room:* A/C, TV w/pay movies, hair dryer, kitchen in some units, minibar.

The Ritz-Carlton Highlands ★★★ As the most anticipated opening of the past few years in all of the state, the Ritz-Carlton Highlands managed to live up to all the fanfare when it began welcoming visitors at the end of 2009. The wait was worth it, as—in typical Ritz fashion—every last detail was perfectly planned, and the service is unsurpassed. The Ritz-Carlton Highlands, which is perched mid-mountain and quite resembles a castle high up in the Alps, is not merely a resort, but an experience. With a gondola that connects it directly to the village and ski-in, ski-out access to the Northstar-at-Tahoe lifts—not to mention an amazing 17,000-square-foot state-of-the-art spa and fitness center, a restaurant helmed by celebrity San Francisco chef Tracy Des Jardins, and a kids' program and teen arcade so you can check your young'uns at the door—why would you possibly need to ever leave the grounds? The property also has access to the snowshoe and cross-country trails at the Northstar Cross Country Center for those who don't dig downhill. During ski season, the Ritz partners with Northstar to offer stay-and-ski packages for as little as $399 a night, including room and two adult lift tickets.

The hotel boasts 170 guest rooms and suites, as well as 23 Ritz-Carlton Residences and 25 fractional ownership units. All accommodations have fireplaces and the standard first-class Ritz amenities. To sweeten the deal even further, it was built with LEED standards in mind; at press time, the resort was undergoing the rigorous environmental certification process. Other planned and executed "green" endeavors include a Living Roof, a seasonal garden for Des Jardins, the use of recycled steel in its construction, and incorporation of energy-efficient heating and cooling systems. Can you tell I kinda dig this new Tahoe staple?

13031 Ritz-Carlton Highlands Court, Truckee, CA 96146. www.ritzcarlton.com/LakeTahoe. ✆ **530/562-3000.** Fax 530/562-3001. 170 units. $249–$349 double; from $499 suite. Resort fee $25, including Internet, access to the spa and fitness center. Packages available. AE, DC, DISC, MC, V. Valet parking $35. **Amenities:** 3 restaurants; children's program; concierge; preferred tee times at nearby golf courses; fitness center; heated swimming pool, children's wading pool, and hot tubs; room service; sauna; spa; steam room; Pilates classes. *In room:* TV, hair dryer, minibar, fireplace, humidifier.

The Shore House at Lake Tahoe ★★ This romantic little bed-and-breakfast inn, right on the lake, is a real charmer. Each individually decorated room has its own entrance, handmade log furniture, knotty-pine walls, a gas-log fireplace, and a blissfully comfortable feather bed. Guests have access to a private beach and landscaped lawn that overlook the lake and an in-house spa. If you're planning to tie the knot, the charming hosts will provide everything you need for a beautiful ceremony, including an outdoor lakeside setting and a honeymoon cottage with a two-person spa tub.

7170 N. Lake Blvd. (P.O. Box 499), Tahoe Vista, CA 96148. www.shorehouselaketahoe.com. ✆ **800/207-5160** or 530/546-7270. Fax 530/546-7130. 8 units, 1 cottage. $205–$290 double; $275–$325 cottage. Rates include full breakfast. DISC, MC, V. **Amenities:** Jacuzzi. *In room:* A/C, TV, fridge, hair dryer, no phone (phone available in dining room).

Moderate

Cal-Neva Resort, Spa & Casino ★ You might (accurately) guess from the name of this place that the state line literally runs right through it, but you might never imagine its colorful, sometimes scandalous history. It's here that Marilyn Monroe allegedly had her rendezvous with John F. Kennedy (you can even see the secret tunnel), and ownership passed around to moguls with names like Pretty Boy, Babyface, and Sinatra, who built the famed Celebrity Room. Respectability has since laid claim to the Cal-Neva, however, and it's now a popular, reputable lakeside resort. Almost all the elegantly decorated rooms have lake views. Besides the casino (on the Nevada side of the hotel, of course), the Cal-Neva offers a full array of sport and spa options, a complete wedding-planning service, and two wedding chapels. Even if you don't stay here, stop by and take a look.

2 Stateline Rd. (Box 368), Crystal Bay, NV 89402-0368. www.calnevaresort.com. © **800/225-6382** or 775/832-4000. Fax 775/831-9007. 188 units, 9 chalets, 3 bungalows. $109–$209 double; $199–$289 suite, chalet, or bungalow. Packages available. AE, DC, DISC, MC, V. **Amenities:** Lakeview restaurant; bar; concierge; nearby golf course; Jacuzzi; heated outdoor pool; room service; full-service European health spa; 2 outdoor tennis courts. *In room:* A/C, TV, hair dryer.

Cedar House Sport Hotel ★★ Epitomizing the term *eco-chic*, Cedar House Sport Hotel is unlike anything else you'll find in Truckee. It's intimate with contemporary European flair—like simplistic, low-to-the-ground, modern furniture—yet features a lodgelike exterior: Rough-hewn timbers, exposed girders, and flying buttresses intermix with oversized logs. The rooms' leather-flanked platform beds and merlot-and-camel color palette are a nice deviation from the same ol' boutique interior that's cropping up everywhere. The hotel is conveniently located on the road to Northstar-at-Tahoe—about $7\frac{1}{2}$ miles away—and one of Truckee's best restaurants, Stella (see review below), also happens to be on-site, so you needn't wander far for a fine-dining experience after a long day on the slopes.

Cedar House Sport Hotel will especially appeal to the pet-toting crowd; it allows dogs of all sizes—and even gives them their own bed, toys, food bowls, and gourmet treats—so Fido doesn't have to miss out on the après-ski scene either.

10918 Broadway Rd., Truckee, CA 96161. www.cedarhousesporthotel.com. © **866/582-5655** or 530/582-5665. Fax 530/582-5665. 42 units. $170–$220 double; $220–$300 suite. Rates include full breakfast for 2 at Stella's. AE, DC, DISC, MC, V. Pets allowed for a $50 fee. **Amenities:** Restaurant; bar; concierge; outdoor hot tub; room service. *In room:* TV w/pay movies, hair dryer, free Wi-Fi.

Meeks Bay Resort ★ Ten miles south of Tahoe City, rustic Meeks Bay Resort is one of the oldest hostelries on the lake and something of a historical landmark. Opened as a public campground in 1920, its sweeping lakefront location has one of the finest beaches on the lake. Acquired by the U.S. Forest Service in 1974, the property is open during summers only. Most rentals are weekly and consist of motel lodging or modest wood cabins near the lake. Facilities include a full marina with boat rentals, a campground with RV access ($25 a night, 4-night minimum), a beachfront snack bar, a playground, and a visitor center with a cultural display, coffee bar, and retail store. The Kehlet Mansion, on a rock that juts into the lake, is the resort's prime accommodation. Owned at one time by William Hewlett, cofounder of Hewlett-Packard, and later the summer residence of billionaire Gordon Getty, it has seven bedrooms, three bathrooms, a large kitchen, a living room, and water on three sides. The entire house is rented by the week, sleeps a dozen, and costs $6,000. Make all reservations here early.

P.O. Box 787, Tahoma, CA 96142. www.meeksbayresort.com. © **877/326-3357** or 530/525-6946. Fax 530/525-4028. 21 units, 34 campsites. $90–$240 double per night, $1,350–$1,825 per week. AE, MC, V. May–Nov only. **Amenities:** Watersports equipment rental. *In room:* Kitchen in cabins.

River Ranch Lodge & Restaurant ★★ The River Ranch Lodge has long been one of my favorite places to stay in Lake Tahoe. Alongside the Truckee River, the lodge is minutes away from Alpine Meadows and Squaw Valley ski resorts, and a short drive (or ride along the bike path) into Tahoe City. The best rooms have balconies overlooking the river. All have a handsome mountain-home decor, lodge-pole pine furniture, and down comforters. Room nos. 9 and 10, the farthest from the road, are my top choices. In summer, guests relax under umbrellas on the huge patio overlooking the river, working down burgers and beer while watching the rafters float by. During ski season, the River Ranch's spectacular circular cocktail lounge and dining area, which cantilevers over the river, is a popular après-ski hangout. Another big hit is the handsome **River Ranch Lodge Restaurant,** which serves creations by its new executive chef, Julia Walter. Dishes range from fresh seafood—think seared sesame-coated *ahi* tuna or the diver-scallop pasta—to such thick meats as a ranch rib-eye with a wild mushroom demiglacé, or the filet mignon in a California cabernet and roasted garlic sauce.

On Hwy. 89, at Alpine Meadows Rd. (P.O. Box 197), Tahoe City, CA 96145. www.riverranchlodge.com. © **866/991-9912** or 530/583-4264. Fax 530/583-7237. 19 units. $115–$200 double. Rates include continental breakfast. Packages available. AE, MC, V. **Amenities:** Restaurant; bar; concierge; golf course nearby. *In room:* TV.

Sunnyside Lodge ★★   Built as a private home in 1908, this hotel and restaurant is one of the few grand old lodges left on the lake. Two miles south of Tahoe City, it looks very much like a giant, sophisticated wood cabin, complete with dormers, steep pitched roofs, and natural-wood siding. Stretching across the building, a large deck fronts a tiny marina and gravel beach. The Lakefront rooms (suite nos. 30–31 and room nos. 32–39) are the most desirable and go for about $40 more than the others—well worth the added expense. Five units have rock fireplaces. Most of the lodge's ground floor is dominated by the popular **Sunnyside Restaurant** (p. 326).

1850 W. Lake Blvd. (P.O. Box 5969), Tahoe City, CA 96145. www.sunnysideresort.com. © **800/822-2754** or 530/583-7200. Fax 530/583-2551. 23 units. $135–$295 double. Rates include continental breakfast and afternoon tea. Packages available. $10 for each additional guest. AE, MC, V. **Amenities:** Restaurant; bar; nearby golf course; room service; watersports equipment rental. *In room:* TV/VCR, fridge in some units, hair dryer.

Tahoma Meadows Bed & Breakfast ★ ☺   This historic bed-and-breakfast consists of cute red cabins nestled on a gentle forest slope surrounded by flowers and sugar pines. The units have a private bathroom and a comfy king- or queen-size bed, and are individually decorated with paintings of bucolic settings; four units have gas-log fireplaces. The largest cabins, Treehouse and Sugar Pine, sleep up to six, ideal for families. For guests staying in the B&B cottages, a family-style breakfast is served in the main lodge's common room every morning from 8 to 10am. Nearby activities include skiing at Ski Homewood (including shuttle service) and sunbathing at the lakeshore across the street. The friendly owners, Ulli and Dick White, will happily give advice on the best nearby hiking and fishing spots (Dick's an avid fly fisherman).

6821 W. Lake Blvd. (P.O. Box 810), Homewood, CA 96141. www.tahomameadows.com. © **866/525-1553** or 530/525-1553. 14 units. $109–$375 double. Rates include full breakfast. AE, DISC, MC, V. 8½ miles from Tahoe City. Pets accepted in some units for $15. **Amenities:** Nearby golf course. *In room:* TV, kitchen in some units, no phone.

Inexpensive

Ferrari's Crown Resort ✦   If you're looking for convenient lakefront accommodations at a reasonable price, this family-operated motel is a great choice. The Ferraris have proudly extended a warm welcome to guests, children included, since 1957. Family suites, completely equipped with kitchenettes and gas fireplaces, can sleep up to seven. It's nothing fancy, but it's well run, the rooms are very inviting, and you can't beat the location, which includes access to a private beach. Plan a trip during the off season to take advantage of their great bargain rates.

8200 N. Lake Blvd. (P.O. Box 845), Kings Beach, CA 96143. www.tahoecrown.com. © **800/645-2260** or 530/546-3388. Fax 530/546-3851. 72 units. $65–$139 double; $99–$235 2-bedroom suite or lakefront room. Rates include continental breakfast. Packages available. AE, DISC, MC, V. **Amenities:** Nearby golf course; 2 Jacuzzis; 2 heated outdoor pools (seasonal). *In room:* A/C, TV, hair dryer, high-speed Internet, stocked kitchenette.

Lake of the Sky Motor Inn   This remodeled 1960s-style A-frame motel in the heart of Tahoe City offers clean, quiet, inexpensive accommodations in a central location—only steps away from shops and restaurants and a main stop for the ski shuttles. You'll get just the basics here—TV, phone, bathroom—so plan on spending most of your time outdoors. Some rooms have lake views, and the land-scaped picnic and barbecue area is attractive.

955 N. Lake Blvd. (P.O. Box 227), Tahoe City, CA 96145. www.lakeoftheskyinn.com. © **530/583-3305.** Fax 530/583-7621. 23 units. $89–$167 double. Rates include continental breakfast. Children 11 and under stay free in parent's room. AE, DC, DISC, MC, V. **Amenities:** Nearby golf course; heated outdoor pool (seasonal). *In room:* TV, fridge in some units.

Pepper Tree Inn   If you're the kind of person who dislikes both frills and big bills, the Pepper Tree Inn is for you. Two people can share a perfectly comfortable room for about $50 each (considerably less in the off season). All guests have access to a redwood hot tub, heated outdoor pool with sun deck, free shuttle service to the major ski resorts, and most of the cable channels you could want, served up on 27-inch TVs. The location—right in the middle of Tahoe City with views of the lake—is great, but where the Pepper Tree Inn really shines is with its generous ski packages; be sure to inquire when you make a reservation.

645 N. Lake Blvd. (P.O. Box 29), Tahoe City, CA 96145. www.peppertreetahoe.com. © **800/624-8590** or 530/583-3711. 50 units. $99–$120 double. AE, DC, DISC, MC, V. **Amenities:** Outdoor heated pool; indoor spa. *In room:* TV, hair dryer.

Tamarack Lodge ★   Tamarack is one of the oldest lodges on the North Shore—so old it was a favorite haunt of Clark Gable and Gary Cooper. Now it's one of the best bets for the frugal traveler. Hidden among a 4-acre cadre of pines just east of Tahoe City, the Tamarack Lodge consists of a few old cabins, five "poker rooms," and a modern (and far less nostalgic) motel unit. The rooms in the motel unit are the least appealing, but they're certainly clean and comfortable. The cabins all have kitchenettes and can hold up to four guests, but the most popular rooms by far are the original poker rooms (where Gable and Cooper used to play cards) lined with gleaming knotty pine. Complimentary coffee and tea are served in the lobby, Wi-Fi access is free, and rollaway beds are available for only $8 extra. The beach is within walking distance, but to get into town, you'll need to rent a car or take the Tahoe Trolley (the lodge will provide free trolley tickets).

2311 N. Lake Blvd. (P.O. Box 859), Tahoe City, CA 96145. www.tamarackattahoe.com. © **888/824-6323** or 530/583-3350. Fax 530/583-3531. 17 units, 4 cabins. $52–$148 double. DISC, MC, V. *In room:* TV, free Wi-Fi.

Where to Eat

SOUTH SHORE & SOUTH LAKE TAHOE

Expensive

Evan's American Gourmet Café ★★ AMERICAN/CONTINENTAL   This restaurant's impeccable service, award-winning wine list, and unyielding attention to detail serve as a perfect backdrop for the creative culinary artistry of returning chef Jimi Lasquete. Lasquete reunited with the restaurant in 2007, bringing his accomplished techniques and creative flair that are clearly evident in the cuisine. For appetizers, typical choices are *mille-feuille* of goat cheese–hummus spread layered with spinach, tomato, and phyllo layers, topped with truffle honey. Entrees might include grilled filet of beef with foie gras butter and Syrah reduction, served with white-cheddar gratin potatoes and broccoli, or prosciutto-crusted veal loin chop and wild mushroom ragout in a pearl glaze with tarragon-laced mashed potatoes. The desserts are luscious and beautiful. Seats are limited in this cozy little restaurant, so be sure to call ahead for reservations.

536 Emerald Bay Rd., South Lake Tahoe. ✆ **530/542-1990.** www.evanstahoe.com. Reservations required (must confirm by 4pm). Main courses $20–$32. AE, DISC, MC, V. Daily 5:30–9:30pm.

Fresh Ketch ★ SEAFOOD   In a small marina at the foot of Tahoe Keys Boulevard, Fresh Ketch has long been regarded as South Lake's premier seafood restaurant. Try for a window table so you can watch the marina activities. For starters, I always order half a dozen oysters and the seared ahi tuna with garlic, soy, wasabi, and sesame seaweed salad. Then it's on to the fresh catch of the day, such as big Alaskan king crab, steamed in the shell and served with drawn butter. The menu also includes a modest selection of meat and poultry dishes, such as the great surf and turf of petite mignon and lobster. Prices are a bit steep, but you can also belly up with the locals and order from the extensive bar menu, with everything from blackened mahimahi to fresh-fish tacos and fish and chips for under $13. They've recently added a sushi bar as well. Live music acts perform Tuesday, Thursday, Friday, and Saturday evenings.

2433 Venice Dr. ✆ **530/541-5683.** www.thefreshketch.com. Reservations recommended. Main courses $16–$35; market price for crab and lobster. AE, DC, DISC, MC, V. Daily 11:30am–9pm (bar until 10pm).

Stella ★★ ECLECTIC   In keeping with the Cedar House Sport Hotel's European vibe, Stella concocts a mix of delightful French, Italian, Greek, and Spanish cuisine. Most of the meats, like the provolone-and-prosciutto-stuffed pork chop or the petite rack of lamb, are prepared using a sous-vide method of cooking (employing an airtight plastic bag in a tub of water), and the chef bakes mouth-watering artisan bread and pizzas in the wood-fire oven daily. The fish selections, such as the crispy fried basa filet all the way from Vietnam (served alongside Thai slaw, red onions, kaffir lime, and spicy lobster broth), are a smash hit. If you want to learn Chef Jacob Burton's detailed, yet creative styles, Stella frequently offers cooking classes where you can do just that—or else steal a peek as he whips up your dinner and take mental notes; there are no walls between the kitchen and dining room. The restaurant is pretty casual despite its fancy fare and highly knowledgeable staff; you'll often see other patrons dining in their ski apparel.

In the Cedar House Sport Hotel, 10918 Broadway Rd., Truckee, CA 96161. ✆ **866/582-5655** or 530/582-5665. Fax 530/582-5665. www.cedarhousesporthotel.com. Main courses $18–$30. AE, DC, DISC, MC, V. Wed–Sun 6–9pm.

Moderate

Aprés Wine Company ✦ CALIFORNIAN   I wasn't expecting much from this unassuming wine bar in a strip mall off Tahoe's main drag, but appearances can be deceiving. You'll enter the restaurant, tucked away toward the back of the shopping center, through its wine shop, where you can pick up a bottle (of the 300 selections for sale) on your way back out or test the Enomatic, a wine-dispensing machine that allows you to insert your prepaid Aprés Wine Pass and pour your own samples. The restaurant is small but great for tapas like mozzarella-stuffed figs wrapped in bacon, strawberry bruschetta, or hummus dip and tapenade, or a full meal of grilled pork loin, beef sliders, or wild Alaskan sockeye salmon.

Not shockingly, the drink menu is well-stocked with a variety of 50-something champagnes and wines, many available by the taste, glass, or carafe. A generous happy hour runs daily from 4 to 6pm and again from 9 to 10pm. The owner and employees rotate hosting wine tastings on Sunday and Thursday nights, a popular venue for tourists to mingle with locals.

3668 Lake Tahoe Blvd., Ste. G (in Ski Run Center), South Lake Tahoe, CA 96161. ✆ **530/544-9463.** www.apreswineco.com. Main courses $8–$18. AE, DC, DISC, MC, V. Mon–Thurs 11am–10pm; Fri–Sat 11am–11pm; Sun noon–10pm.

The Blue Angel Cafe CAFE   It may look like just a cozy coffee shop, but the Blue Angel Cafe wears a couple of different hats, popular lunch and dinner joint included. If you'd prefer to forgo the pricy dining options on Heavenly Mountain, this is the perfect spot to grab a bite en route to or from the slopes; you get a whole lot more bang for your buck. Dressed-up pub food—like sweet potato and Dungeness crab cakes or spicy Portuguese chicken wings—mix with fancier fare like beef bourguignon, coq au vin, and swordfish Wellington. Or skip the night scene entirely, and bring your laptop down for the afternoon—there is free Wi-Fi, after all—as you keep cozy by the crackling fire, steaming mug of hot chocolate in hand.

1132 Ski Run Blvd., South Lake Tahoe, CA 96150. ✆ **530/544-6544.** Fax 530/544-6543. www.theblueangelcafe.com. Main courses $10–$16. AE, DC, MC, V. Daily 8am–10pm.

Cantina Bar & Grill ★ MEXICAN   The Cantina Bar & Grill is a favorite local hangout and serves the best Mexican food in South Lake. With friendly service, sports on three TVs, and 30 kinds of beer, joviality reigns. The menu is well priced and extensive, offering Cal-Mex specialties such as tacos, burritos, and enchiladas along with a half-dozen Southwestern dishes, such as smoked chicken polenta and blue corn salmon. The steak fajitas get a thumbs up, as do the barbecued baby back ribs. To demonstrate their sense of whimsy and ethnic appeal, they offer an Oriental chicken salad and a Southwestern Reuben sandwich, as well as a few vegetarian selections.

765 Emerald Bay Rd. ✆ **530/544-1233.** www.cantinatahoe.com. Main courses $9–$17. AE, MC, V. Daily 11:30am–10:30pm. Bar daily 11:30am–midnight.

The Naked Fish ★★ SUSHI   The Naked Fish in South Lake is the best sushi bar in Tahoe. I can never understand a word the Japanese chefs are saying to me, but I'm not paying much attention; the warm-butter-soft *hamachi* nigiri (yellowtail) has made my toes curl again. The colorful aquamarine theme with mermaids floating across the walls adds to the laid-back atmosphere of this locally owned Japanese restaurant. Before you open the menu, read the "specials" board above the sushi bar—this is the *really* fresh stuff, such as the deftly shelled live octopus sashimi. In the spirit of an authentic sushi bar, the chefs are friendly and talkative, particularly if you buy them a beer. Wimps can order cooked dinners such as sesame-crusted ahi and teriyaki chicken, but it's the flavorful rolls, tender cuts of nigiri, and festive bar that sushi hounds will appreciate.

3940 Lake Tahoe Blvd. (at the junction of Hwy. 50 and Pioneer Trail). (℃ **530/541-3474.** www. thenakedfish.com. Reservations recommended for parties of 6 or more. Main courses $14–$21; sushi $4–$12. AE, DC, DISC, MC, V. Sat–Sun noon–3pm; daily 5–9pm.

Inexpensive

Ernie's Coffee Shop DINER   The undisputed king of coffee shops in South Lake Tahoe is Ernie's, which has been serving huge plates of good old American, cholesterol-laden grub to locals since the Nixon administration. The food is far from original (omelets, bacon and eggs, pancakes), so it must be the perpetually friendly service, low prices, and huge portions that attract the steady stream of customers. Another good reason to come here is that Ernie's is located next to the cheapest gas station in town, so you can top off your appetite and your tank in one stop. The milkshakes are great, too.

1207 Emerald Bay Rd./Hwy. 89. (℃ **530/541-2161.** www.erniescoffeeshop.com. Main dishes $7–$11. No credit cards. Daily 6am–2pm.

Sprouts Natural Foods Café ✦ HEALTH FOOD/JUICES   Sprouts owner Tyler Cannon has filled a much-needed niche in South Lake, serving wholesome food that looks good, tastes good, and *is* good. Most everything is made in-house, including the soups, smoothies, and fresh-squeezed juices. Menu items range from rice bowls to sandwiches (try the Real Tahoe Turkey), huge burritos, coffee drinks, muffins, fresh-fruit smoothies, and a marvelous mayo-free tuna sandwich made with yogurt and packed with fresh veggies. Order from the counter, and then scramble for a vacant seat (outdoor tables are coveted). This is also an excellent place to pack a picnic lunch.

3123 Harrison Ave. (at U.S. 50 and Alameda St., next to Lakeview Sports). (℃ **530/541-6969.** Meals $4.50–$6.75. No credit cards. Daily 8am–9pm.

Yellow Submarine ✦ SANDWICHES   When it comes to picnic supplies, the competition is stiff in South Lake Tahoe; this block alone has three sandwich shops. Still, my favorite is Yellow Sub, voted best deli sandwich shop by readers of the *Tahoe Daily Tribune* for 9 years straight. It sells 21 versions of overstuffed subs—made in 6-inch and 12-inch varieties—as well as several kinds of wraps. The shop is in a small shopping center across from the El Dorado Campground.

983 Tallac Ave. (at U.S. 50). (℃ **530/541-8808.** Sandwiches and wraps $3.20–$7.15. No credit cards. Daily 10:30am–8pm.

NORTH SHORE/TAHOE CITY

Expensive

Manzanita ★★ MODERN AMERICAN/FRENCH   At last, a fancy Tahoe eat that isn't PlumpJack. (I adore PlumpJack, but it's often crowded in peak season, and having other options is always nice.) Enter Traci Des Jardins, a celebrity whiz in the kitchen who has been on such shows as *Iron Chef* and helms San Francisco's popular, eponymous Jardinière. Celebrating Des Jardins' signature fare—French-inspired Californian cuisine—Manzanita sources primarily organic, sustainable, and locally grown meat and produce. Starters comprise oysters on the half shell, Maine diver scallops, and warm bread salad (baby artichokes and crescenza cheese); entrees might run the gamut from Moroccan tagine to red-wine-braised short ribs with horseradish potato purée and herb salad. Desserts are oh-so-sweet, from the chocolate lava cake erupting with champagne-passion-fruit sorbet to the warm bread pudding with kumquat marmalade and bourbon crème Anglaise. In keeping with the hotel's traditional hospitality, the servers bend over backward to ensure you have the best possible dining experience.

In the Ritz-Carlton Highlands resort, 13031 Ritz-Carlton Highlands Court, Truckee, CA 96146. ✆ **530/562-3050.** www.manzanitalaketahoe.com. Reservations recommended. Main courses $24–$36. AE, MC, V. Daily 11am–2pm; Sun–Thurs 5–9pm; Fri–Sat 5–10pm.

PlumpJack Café ★★ MODERN AMERICAN   Squaw Valley investors have spent oodles of money trying to turn the ski resort into a world-class destination, and one big step in the right direction is the sleek, sexy PlumpJack Café. Although dinner prices have dropped slightly (guests balked at the original rates), none of PlumpJack's standards have diminished. Expect impeccable service regardless of your attire (this is, after all, a ski resort). Menu choices range from Agave-glazed prawns, or a Sonoma duckling duo with roasted celery root in a black-cherry sauce, to grilled lamb rack served in a cracked-mustard sauce with an avocado roll. There's also a more casual bar menu, and those familiar with PlumpJack in San Francisco know that the reasonably priced wine list is among the nation's best.

In the PlumpJack Squaw Valley Inn, 1920 Squaw Valley Rd., Squaw Valley. ✆ **530/583-1578.** www.plumpjack.com. Reservations recommended. Main courses $14–$45. AE, MC, V. Mon–Fri 7:30–10:30am (7am Sat–Sun) and daily 11:30am–10pm.

Moderate

Gar Woods Grill & Pier ★ AMERICAN   Named after the builder of those beautiful mahogany race boats that used to grace the lake in the 1930s and 1940s, Gar Woods attempts to evoke and pay homage to that era. Whether folks are watching *Monday Night Football* or drinking a famous Wet Woody, it seems as though something is always going on in the bar. On a sunny day, it's great fun to sit on the lakeside deck to enjoy the good food and good cheer. The menu is wide ranging, covering everything from a shrimp-and-lobster bisque to beer-battered coconut prawns, blackened chicken sandwich, and grilled rib-eye—nothing out of the ordinary, but the preparation is solid and the service is friendly.

5000 N. Lake Blvd., Carnelian Bay. ✆ **800/BY-TAHOE** (298-2463) or 530/546-3366. www. garwoods.com. Lunch $9–$18; dinner $14–$30. AE, DISC, MC, V. Mon–Fri noon–5pm and 5:30–9:30pm; Sat–Sun 11:30am–10pm.

Sunnyside Restaurant ★ CALIFORNIAN   In summer, when the sun's shining, the most highly coveted tables in Tahoe are those on Sunnyside's lakeside veranda. Guests can also dine in the lodge's more traditional Lakeside Dining Room, with its 1930s aura. Nothing is extraordinary here: The lunch menu has burgers, chicken, and fish sandwiches, together with a variety of soups and salads. Dinners are fancier, with main courses such as lobster tail, lamb chops with raspberry mango sauce, and fresh salmon oven baked on a cedar plank. In the winter, the bar has a lively après-ski scene where both tourists and locals come to watch ski flicks on the big screen and refuel on inexpensive appetizers.

At the Sunnyside Lodge, 1850 W. Lake Blvd., Tahoe City. ✆ **800/822-2754** or 530/583-7200. www.sunnysideresort.com. Main courses $11–$36. AE, DISC, MC, V. Oct–June daily 4–9:30pm; July–Sept Sun–Thurs 11am–9:30pm, Fri–Sat 11am–10pm; year-round Sun brunch 9:30am–2pm.

Inexpensive

Bridgetender Tavern and Grill 🍴 AMERICAN   Although it's located in one of the most popular tourist areas in North Lake, the Bridgetender has been a locals' hangout since 1977. Still, they're surprisingly tolerant of out-of-towners, who come for the cheap grub, sunny patio, and huge selection of draft beers (21). Big and burly burgers, salads, hot and cold sandwiches, tacos, and hot dogs round out the menu, and the daily specials are definitely worth a taste. In summer, dine outside among the pines.

65 W. Lake Blvd. (across from Fanny Bridge), Tahoe City. ✆ **530/583-3342.** Main courses $5–$7.25. MC, V. Daily 11am–2am.

Fire Sign Café ★ 🍴 AMERICAN   Choosing a place to have breakfast in North Tahoe is a no-brainer. Since the late 1970s, the Fire Sign Café has been the locals' choice—which explains the lines out the door on weekends. Just about everything is made from scratch, such as the delicious coffeecake that accompanies the big plates of bacon and eggs, or blueberry pancakes. Even the salmon for chef and owner Bob Young's legendary salmon omelet is smoked in-house. Lunch—burgers, salads, sandwiches, burritos, and more—is also quite popular, particularly when the outdoor patio is open.

1785 W. Lake Blvd., Tahoe City. ✆ **530/583-0871.** Breakfast and lunch $6–$8. MC, V. Daily 7am–3pm.

Rosie's Café ★ ☺ AMERICAN   Two floors' worth of tables usually ensures a short wait—if one at all—at this shingled, lodge-style restaurant in the heart of downtown Tahoe City. Family owned and operated, Rosie's has been serving quality comfort food to legions of vacationers since it opened in 1980. It's noisy and casual, perfect for families (with children's menus and free balloons, even), and servings are plentiful. A big menu offers breakfasts designed to carbo-load skiers, as well as hamburgers, grilled chicken sandwiches, and chef-type salads for lunch. The two-course dinners mostly star fish and meat (the Yankee pot roast with mashed potatoes and gravy is hard to resist on a cold night). You won't mistake it for gourmet, but you'll like the value and ethos.

571 N. Lake Blvd., Tahoe City. ✆ **530/583-8504.** www.rosiescafe.com. Reservations accepted for dinner. Main courses $7–$10 lunch, $15–$20 dinner. DISC, MC, V. Daily 6:30am–10pm.

Tahoe After Dark

Tahoe is not known for its nightlife, although something is always going on in the showrooms of the major casinos on the South Shore. Call **Harrah's** (✆ **775/588-6611**), **Harveys** (✆ **775/588-2411**), **MontBleu** (✆ **775/588-3515**), and the **Horizon** (✆ **775/588-6211**) for current show schedules and prices. Most cocktail shows cost $20 to $55. On the North Shore, **Sandy's Pub,** at the Resort at Squaw Creek (✆ **530/581-6617;** p. 318), hosts live music nightly. If it's just a casual cocktail you're after, my favorite spot is the cozy fireside lounge at **River Ranch Lodge,** which cantilevers over a turbulent stretch of the Truckee River, on Hwy. 89 at the entrance to Alpine Meadows (✆ **530/583-4264** or 866/991-9912; www.riverranchlodge.com).

MOUNT SHASTA & THE CASCADES ★★

274 miles N of San Francisco

Chances are, your first glimpse of Mount Shasta's majestic, snowcapped peak will result in a twinge of awe. A dormant volcano with a 17-mile-diameter base, it stands in virtual isolation 14,162 feet above the sea. When John Muir first saw Shasta from 50 miles away in 1874, he wrote: "[I] was alone and weary. Yet my blood turned to wine, and I have not been weary since." He went on to describe it as "the pole star of the landscape," which, indeed, it is.

Keep in mind, however, that dining and lodging in these parts lean more toward sustenance than indulgence: It's the fresh air, not fresh fish, that lures visitors this far north. You can leave the dinner jacket at home—all that's required when you visit the Far North are broken-in hiking boots, binoculars (the bald eagle is a common sight in these parts), warm clothing, and an adventurous spirit.

John Muir.

Essentials

GETTING THERE   From San Francisco, take I-80 to I-505 to I-5 to Redding. From the coast, pick up Hwy. 299 East north of Arcata, to Redding.

Redding Municipal Airport, 6751 Woodrum Circle (✆ **530/224-4320**), is serviced by **United Express** (✆ **800/241-6522;** www.united.com) and **Horizon Air** (✆ **800/252-7522;** horizonair.alaskaair.com). **Amtrak** (✆ **800/USA-RAIL** [872-7245]) stops in Dunsmuir and Redding.

VISITOR INFORMATION   Regional information can be obtained from the following organizations: **Shasta Cascade Wonderland Association,** 1699 Hwy. 273, Anderson, CA 96007 (✆ **800/474-2782** or 530/365-7500; www.shastacascade.org); **Mount Shasta Visitors Bureau,** 300 Pine St., Mount Shasta, CA 96067 (✆ **800/926-4865** or 530/926-4865; www.mtshastachamber.com); **Redding Convention & Visitors Bureau,** 777 Auditorium Dr., Redding, CA 96001 (✆ **800/874-7562** or 530/225-4100; www.visitredding.org); and **Trinity County Chamber of Commerce,** 210 N. Main St., P.O. Box 517, Weaverville, CA 96093 (✆ **800/487-4648** or 530/623-6101; www.trinitycounty.com).

The Republic of California

En route to Mount Shasta from the south, you may want to stop near Red Bluff at **William B. Ide Adobe State Historic Park,** 21659 Adobe Rd. (✆ **530/529-8599**), for a picnic along the Sacramento River and a visit to an adobe home dating from 1852. The 4-acre park commemorates William B. Ide, the Republic of California's first and only president. (The Republic of California was proclaimed on June 14, 1846, following the Bear Flag Rebellion, and lasted only 3 weeks.) In summer, the park is open from 8am to sunset, and the house from noon to 4pm; call ahead in winter. Parking is $5 per vehicle.

Redding

The major town and gateway to the area is Redding, the hub of the panoramic Shasta–Cascade region, at the top of the Sacramento Valley. From here, you can turn westward into the wilderness forest of Trinity and the Klamath Mountains, or north and east into the Cascades and Shasta Trinity National Forest.

In Redding, with its fast-food joints, gas stations, and cheap motels, summer heat generally hovers around 100°F (38°C). A city of some 80,000, Redding is the transportation hub for the upper reaches of Northern California. It has little of interest; it's mainly useful as a base for exploring the natural wonders nearby. Information is available from the **Redding Convention & Visitors Bureau,** 777 Auditorium Dr., Redding, CA 96001 (© **800/874-7562** or 530/225-4100; www.visitredding.org), west of I-5 on Hwy. 299. It's open Monday through Friday from 9am to 5pm. Ahead and northeast, Mount Shasta rises to a height of more than 14,000 feet. From Redding, I-5 cuts north over the Pit River Bridge, crossing Lake Shasta and leading eventually to the mount itself. Before striking north, however, you may want to explore **Lake Shasta** and see **Shasta Dam.** Another option is to take a detour west of Redding to Weaverville, Whiskeytown–Shasta Trinity National Recreation Area, and Trinity Lake (see "Whiskeytown National Recreation Area," below).

The $15-million, 34,000-square-foot **Turtle Bay Exploration Park** (© **800/TURTLEBAY [887-8532]** or 530/243-8850; www.turtlebay.org) is often a visitor's first stop. From there, wander over the Sundial Bridge, an architectural marvel built by Spanish artist Santiago Calatrava. The 710-foot-long, 21-story-tall pylon bridge with a translucent glass surface is the largest sundial structure in the world and connects the 10-mile-long Sacramento River Trail. Free live musical performances are held by the bridge on Friday nights in summer from 7 to 10pm.

One of the best ways to truly see the area is by way of a full-guided Segway tour from **Shasta Glide 'n Ride** (© **866/466-4111** or 530/242-1150; www.shastaglidenride.com). No experience is needed, and tours are 1, 2, or 3 hours in length, departing several times a day and passing over the Sun Dial Bridge, through the arboretum, and by the turtle pond. Night Glides are offered on Friday and Saturday nights in summer months. On "Free 'fer Fridays," all daytime tours are buy-one-get-one-free (call a few weeks in advance during summer). Bike rentals are available, too.

This section of the river also offers good year-round urban fishing of steelhead, trout, and salmon; for information about where to cast your line, call Redding's world-class fly-fishing store, the **Fly Shop** (© **800/669-3474** or 530/222-3555; www.flyshop.com). Whiskeytown Lake, west of Redding, offers great beaches, windsurfing, and sailings; for information, call the lake's **Visitor Center** (© **530/246-1225**).

About 3 miles west, stop at the old mining town of **Shasta,** which has been converted into a state historic park (© **530/243-8194**). Founded on gold, Shasta was the "Queen City" of the northern mines in the Klamath Range. Its life was short, and it expired in 1872, when the Central Pacific Railroad bypassed it

Shasta vs. Mount Shasta

Don't confuse the old mining town Shasta, a few miles west of Redding, with the much larger community Mount Shasta, a major tourist destination on I-5, near the base of Mount Shasta.

in favor of Redding. Today the business district is a ghost town, complete with a restored general store and a Masonic hall. The **1861 courthouse** is now a museum, where you can view the jail and a gallows out back, as well as a remarkable collection of California art assembled by Mae Helen Bacon Boggs. The collection includes works by Maynard Dixon, Grace Hudson, and many others. Continue along Hwy. 299 west to Hwy. 3 north, which will take you to Weaverville and then to the west side of the lake and Trinity Center.

WHERE TO STAY

In addition to the Bridgehouse and Tiffany House inns (see below), Redding has a **Red Lion Hotel,** 1830 Hilltop Dr., Redding (www.redlion.com; ✆ **800/733-5466** or 530/221-8700), and a **La Quinta Inn,** 2180 Hilltop Dr., Redding (www.laquinta.com; ✆ **530/221-8200**). Both are fine choices.

Bridgehouse Bed and Breakfast ★★   Designing the perfect B&B was always a dream of Janelle Pierson's, and once she shipped her trio of kids off to college, she did just that. With the eye of a decorator, Janelle procured all the furnishings herself, and her confidence in the kitchen translates to gourmet breakfasts like stuffed French toast strata or Belgian-waffle bananas foster (her mother was a home ec teacher). Little touches like 500-thread-count sheets and Ghirardelli chocolates on your pillow push the hospitality over the edge. The two suites upstairs are quieter, with views of the Sacramento River. Spring for the Sundial Bridge Room, with its king bed, double pedestal sink, thermo massage tub, and balcony. Country music fans will be delighted by Janelle's hallway of paraphernalia, with photographs of her alongside the likes of Keith Urban. (Some musical celebs have even slept at the inn.) Bottom line: Nicest place in Redding, by a mile.

1455 Riverside Dr., Redding, CA 96003. www.reddingbridgehouse.com. ✆ **530/247-7177.** 4 units. $119–$179 double. Rates include full breakfast. AE, MC, V. **Amenities:** Small exercise room. *In room:* TV, hair dryer.

Tiffany House Bed and Breakfast Inn   On a hill above town, this beautifully refurbished Cape Cod–style inn has a sweeping view of the Lassen Mountain Range, visible from every guest room and cottage, as well as from the oversize deck above the garden in back. Common areas include the music room with a piano and the Victorian parlor with a fireplace, games, and puzzles. Each guest room is appointed with a queen-size bed and antique furnishings, and all have private bathrooms and soft robes. Lavinia's Cottage is our top choice, with a 7-foot spa tub, sitting area, and magnificent laurel-wreath iron bed.

1510 Barbara Rd., Redding, CA 96003. www.tiffanyhousebb.com. ✆ **530/244-3225.** 4 units. $125–$170 double. Rates include full breakfast. AE, DISC, MC, V. **Amenities:** Nearby golf courses; Jacuzzi; outdoor pool. *In room:* A/C, hair dryer, no phone.

WHERE TO EAT

Buz's Crab Seafood Restaurant, Market & Deli ★★ 🍴 SEAFOOD   Don't let the Naugahyde booths and Formica tables fool you: This funky fish joint is one of the best roadside seafood stands in Northern California. What's been drawing fans here from all over the state for more than 30 years are the "seafood baskets," packed with crisp potato rounds, fresh-baked sourdough bread, and whatever's in season: prawns, oysters, scallops, clam strips, calamari, catfish, even Cajun halibut. The fish and chips is also excellent. From December to May, crab's the hot ticket, served freshly boiled from the crab pots on the patio and served with drawn butter and cocktail sauce. ***Tip:*** Visit Buz's website and print the fantastic cioppino recipe—I've slain 'em at dinner parties with this one.

2159 East St., at Cypress Ave. ☎ **530/243-2120.** www.buzscrab.com. Main courses $2.50–$14. MC, V. Daily 11am–9pm.

Jack's Grill ★ STEAKHOUSE   This building was originally constructed in 1835 as a secondhand clothing store. The second floor served as a brothel in the late 1930s, and an entrepreneur named Jack Young set up the main floor as a steakhouse (his establishment serviced all of a body's needs, you might say). Today it's a local favorite. Waiting for a table over drinks in the bar is part of the fun. Good old-fashioned red meat—thick 1-pound steaks, tender brochettes, fat steak sandwiches—is supplemented by a couple of seafood dishes, such as deep-fried jumbo prawns and ocean scallops. It's a very fetching spot, with good, honest tavern food and a jovial crowd. Be prepared to wait on weekends.

1743 California St. ☎ **530/241-9705.** www.jacksgrillredding.com. Reservations not accepted. Main courses $12–$31. AE, DISC, MC, V. Mon–Sat 5–11pm. Bar Mon–Sat 4–11:30pm.

Weaverville

Weaverville was a gold mining town in the 1850s, and the **Jake Jackson Memorial Museum–Trinity County Historical Park,** 508 Main St. (www.trinity museum.org; ☎ **530/623-5211**), captures part of its history. The collection, from firearms to household items, tells an interesting story about the residents—Native Americans, miners, pioneers, especially the Chinese. In the Gold Rush era, the town was half Chinese, with a Chinatown of about 2,500 residents. Admission is free, but a donation of $1 is suggested.

Across the parking lot, you can view the oldest continuously used Taoist temple in California at the **Joss House State Historic Park** (☎ **530/623-5284**). This well-preserved temple was built by immigrant Chinese miners in 1874. Admission is $1 for adults, free for children ages 16 and under.

WHERE TO EAT

LaGrange Café ★★ 🏛 CREATIVE TRADITIONAL CUISINE   Weaverville isn't exactly a star in the culinary firmament, but there is one bright spot, far and away the best food in town. Heck, it would be considered really good in Redding, Sacramento, or Tahoe. In Weaverville's historic district, two adjoining buildings were combined and stripped to the original brick walls to make a spacious, attractive dining area with a sit-down bar. Chef and owner Sharron Heryford's menu includes the local favorite—chicken enchiladas with marinated tri-tip—plus seasonal items such as the local rabbit braised with mushrooms, fresh herbs, and white wine. The interesting menu includes other things, such as buffalo steaks, venison bratwurst, and wild-boar sausages. Heryford's buffalo ragout won third place in a national contest. The 135-plus selections on the wine list make it one of the strongest in Northern California. Desserts, such as a sinfully rich banana cream pie, are all made on the premises.

226 Main St. ☏ **530/623-5325.** Main courses $10–$25. AE, DISC, MC, V. Mon–Thurs 11:30am–9pm; Fri–Sun 11:30am–10pm (hours vary seasonally—be sure to call ahead to confirm).

The Trinity Alps

West of Weaverville stretch the Trinity Alps, with Thompson Peak rising to more than 9,000 feet. The second-largest wilderness area in the state is between the Trinity and Salmon rivers and contains more than 55 lakes and streams. Its alpine scenery makes it popular among hikers and backpackers. You can access the **Pacific Crest Trail** west of Mount Shasta at Parks Creek, South Fork Road, or Whalen Road, and also from Castle Crags State Park. For trail and other information, contact the forest service at Weaverville (☏ **530/623-2121**).

The **Fifth Season,** 300 N. Mount Shasta Blvd. (☏ **530/926-3606;** www.thefifthseason.com), offers mountaineering and backpack rentals and will provide trail maps and other information concerning Shasta's outdoor activities.

Living Waters Recreation (☏ **800/994-RAFT** [994-7238] or 530/926-5446; www.livingwatersrec.com) offers half-day to 4-day rafting trips on the Upper Sacramento, Klamath, Trinity, and Salmon rivers. **Trinity River Rafting Company,** on Hwy. 299W, in Big Flat (☏ **800/30-RIVER** [307-4837] or 530/623-3033; www.trinityriverrafting.com), also operates local white-water trips.

For additional outfitters and information, contact the **Trinity County Chamber of Commerce,** 210 N. Main St. (P.O. Box 517), Weaverville, CA 96093 (☏ **800/487-4648** or 530/623-6101; www.trinitycounty.com).

Whiskeytown National Recreation Area

In adjacent Shasta County, Whiskeytown National Recreation Area is on the eastern shore of quiet, relatively uncrowded Trinity Lake, with 157 miles of shoreline. This reservoir was originally named Clair Engle, after the politician who created it. Locals insist on calling it Trinity, however, after the river that used to rush through the region past the towns of Minersville, Stringtown, and an earlier Whiskeytown. When they dammed the river, however, they also destroyed the three towns, which now lie submerged beneath the lake's glassy surface.

Both Trinity Lake and the Whiskeytown National Recreation Area are in the Shasta Trinity National Forest, 1.3 million acres of wilderness with 1,269 miles of hiking trails. For information on trails, contact **Shasta Trinity National Forest** (☏ **530/226-2500;** www.fs.fed.us/r5/shastatrinity).

Lake Shasta

Heading north on I-5 from Redding, travel about 12 miles and take the Shasta Dam Boulevard exit to the **Shasta Dam and Power Plant ★** (☏ **530/275-4463;** www.shastalake.com/shastadam/index.html), which has an overflow spillway that is three times higher than Niagara Falls. The huge dam—3,460 feet long, 602 feet high, and 883 feet thick at its base—holds back the waters of the Sacramento, Pit, and McCloud rivers. A dramatic sight indeed, it is a vital component of the Central Valley water project. At the visitor center is a series of photographs and displays covering the dam's construction. You can walk or drive over the dam, but it's far more interesting to take the **free 1-hour tours** that run on the hour daily from 9am to 5pm in summer, and at 9, 11am, 1, and 3pm Labor Day to Memorial Day. The guided tour takes you deep within the dam's many chilly corridors (not a good place for claustrophobics) and below the spillway. It's an entertaining way to beat the summer heat. ***Note:*** Tours may be canceled due to security reasons, so call ahead first.

Lake Shasta has 370 miles of shoreline and attracts anglers (bass, trout, and king salmon), water-skiers, and other boating enthusiasts—two million, in fact, in summer. The best way to enjoy the lake is aboard a houseboat; you can rent them from several companies, including **Antlers Resort & Marina,** P.O. Box 140, Antlers Road, Lakehead, CA 96051 (© **800/238-3924;** www.shastalakevacations.com); and **Packers Bay Marina,** 16814 Packers Bay Rd., Lakehead, CA 96051 (© **800/331-3137** or 530/275-5570; www.packersbay.com). There is a 1-week minimum during the summer, and a 3- to 4-day minimum during the off season.

While you're here, you can visit **Lake Shasta Caverns** (© **800/795-CAVE** [2283] or 530/238-2341; www.lakeshastacaverns.com). These caves contain 20-foot-high stalactite and stalagmite formations—60-foot-wide curtains of them adorn the great Cathedral Room. To see the caves, drive about 15 miles north of Redding on I-5 to the O'Brien/Shasta Caverns exit. A ferry will take you across the lake, and a short bus ride will follow to the cave entrance for a 2-hour-long tour. Admission is $22 for adults, $13 for children ages 3 to 15, and free for kids 2 and under. The caverns are open daily from 9am to 4pm in the summer; 9am to 3pm April, May, and September; and from 10am to 2pm October through March.

For information about the Lake Shasta region, contact the **Redding Convention & Visitors Bureau,** 777 Auditorium Dr., Redding, CA 96001 (© **800/874-7562** or 530/225-4100; www.visitredding.org), west of I-5, on Hwy. 299. It's open Monday through Friday from 8am to 5pm.

Mount Shasta ★★★

A volcanic mountain with eight glaciers, **Mount Shasta** is a towering peak of legend and lore. It stands alone, always snowcapped, unshadowed by other mountains—visible from 125 miles away. Although it has been dormant since 1786, eruptions cannot be ruled out, and hot sulfur springs bubble at the summit. The springs saved John Muir on his third ascent of the mountain in 1875. Caught in a severe snowstorm, he and his partner took turns submersing themselves in the hot mud to survive.

Many New Agers are convinced that Mount Shasta is the center of an incredible energy vortex. These devotees flock to the foot of the mountain. In 1987, the foothills were host to the worldwide Harmonic Convergence, calling for a planetary union and a new phase of universal harmony. Yoga, massage, meditation, and metaphysics are all the rage here. These New Agers seem to coexist harmoniously with those whose metaphysical leanings begin and end with Dolly Parton song lyrics.

Those who don't want to climb can drive up to about 7,900 feet. From the town of Mount Shasta, drive 14 miles up the Everitt Memorial Highway to the end of the road near Panther Meadow. At the **Everitt Vista**

Ascending Mt. Shasta.

Turnout, you'll be able to stop and see the Sacramento River Canyon, the Eddy Mountains to the west, and glimpses of Mount Lassen to the south. You can also take the short hike through the forests to a lava outcrop overlooking the McCloud area.

Continue on to **Bunny Flat,** a major access point for climbing in summer and also for cross-country skiing and sledding in winter. The highway ends at the Old Ski Bowl Vista, providing panoramic views of Mount Lassen, Castle Crags, and the Trinity Mountains.

While in Mount Shasta, visit the **Fish Hatchery,** at 3 N. Old Stage Rd. (© **530/926-2215**), which was built in 1888. Here you can observe rainbow and brown trout being hatched to stock rivers and streams statewide—millions are born here annually. You can feed them with food purchased from the coin-operated food dispensers and observe the spawning process on certain Tuesdays during the fall and winter. Admission is free; hours are daily from 8am to sunset. Adjacent to the hatchery is the **Sisson Museum** (© **530/926-5508;** www. mountshastasissonmuseum.org), which displays a smattering of local-history exhibits. It's open daily year-round, from 10am to 4pm in summer, from 1 to 4pm in winter; admission is free.

OUTDOOR PURSUITS

GOLF & TENNIS   Golfers should head for the 27-hole Robert Trent Jones, Jr., golf course at **Lake Shastina Golf Resort,** 5925 Country Club Dr., Weed (© **800/358-4653** or 530/938-3201; www.lakeshastinagolf.com); or the 18-hole course at **Mount Shasta Resort,** 1000 Siskiyou Lake Blvd., Mount Shasta (© **800/958-3363** or 530/926-3030; www.mountshasta resort.com). The Mount Shasta resort also has tennis courts.

MOUNTAIN CLIMBING   Mount Shasta attracts thousands of hikers from around the world each year, from timid first-timers to serious mountaineers who search for the most difficult paths up. The hike isn't technically difficult, but it's a demanding ascent that takes about 8 hours of continuous exertion, particularly when the snow softens up. (**Tip:** Start early, while the snow is still firm.) Before setting out, hikers must secure a permit by signing in at the trail head or at the **Mount Shasta Ranger District** office, which also gives out plenty of good advice for amateur climbers. The office is at 204 W. Alma St., off North Mount Shasta Boulevard in Mount Shasta (© **530/926-4511**). Be sure to wear good hiking shoes and carry crampons and an ice ax, a first-aid kit, a quart of water per person, and a flashlight, in case it takes longer than anticipated. Sunblock is an absolute necessity. All the requisite equipment can be rented at the **Fifth Season,** 300 N. Mount Shasta Blvd. (© **530/926-3606;** www.thefifthseason.com). Mere mortals who don't feel compelled to summit can merely hike on the various low-elevation trails.

Weather can be extremely unpredictable, and every year hikers die on this dormant volcano, usually from making stupid mistakes. For **weather and climbing conditions,** call © **530/926-5555** for recorded information. Traditionally, climbers make the ascent from the Sierra Lodge at Horse Camp, accessible from the town of Mount Shasta via Alma Street and the Everitt Memorial Highway, or from Bunny Flat.

For more information, as well as supervised trips, contact **Shasta Mountain Guides,** 1938 Hill Rd. (© **530/926-3117;** www.shastaguides. com). This outfitter offers a 2-day climb along the traditional John Muir route for $450. It also offers a glacier climb and rock climbing in Castle Crags State Park, backpacking trips, plus cross-country and telemark skiing. The basic rock-climbing course is $150, the mountaineering course is $125, and each of the 3-day ski and snowboard descents is $550.

Also nearby is **Castle Crags State Park** (© **530/235-2684;** www.parks.ca.gov), a 4,300-acre park with 64 campsites and 28 miles of hiking trails. Here granite crags formed 225 million years ago tower more than 6,500 feet above the Sacramento River. The

Lake Siskiyou.

park is filled with dogwood, oak, cedar, and pine, as well as tiger lilies, azaleas, and orchids in summer. You can walk the 1-mile Indian Creek nature trail or take the easy 1-mile Root Creek Trail. The entrance fee is $6 per vehicle per day. Castle Crags is off I-5, about 50 miles north of Redding.

OTHER WARM-WEATHER ACTIVITIES Mount Shasta offers some excellent **mountain biking.** In the summer, ride the chairlifts to the top of Mount Shasta Ski Park and bike down the trails. An all-day chairlift pass is about $25 (© **530/926-8600;** www.skipark.com).

For fishing information or guided trips, call **Jack Trout Fly Fishing Guide** (© **530/926-4540;** www.jacktrout.com). Two other recommended sources are **Mount Shasta Fly Fishing** (© **530/926-6648**) and **Hart's Guide Service** (© **530/926-2431**).

SKIING In winter, visitors can ski at **Mount Shasta Board & Ski Park,** 104 Siskiyou Ave., Mount Shasta (© **800/SKI-SHASTA** [754-7427] or 530/926-8610; www.skipark.com), which has 31 runs with 80% snowmaking, three triple chairlifts, and a surface lift. Lift tickets are $39. The Nordic ski center has 16 miles of groomed trails, and Terrain Park is geared toward snowboarders. The Learning Center offers instruction for adults and children. In summer you can ride the chairlifts to scenic views, mountain-bike down the trails (an all-day pass is about $15), or practice on the two-story climbing wall. Access to the park is 10 miles east of Mount Shasta (the town) on Hwy. 89.

WATERSPORTS The source of the headwaters of the Sacramento River accumulates in **Lake Siskiyou,** a popular spot for boating, swimming, and fishing—and a great vantage point for photographs of Mount Shasta and its reflection. Water-skiing and jet-skiing are not allowed, but windsurfing is, and boat rentals are available at **Lake Siskiyou Camp Resort,** 4239 W. A. Barr Rd., Mount Shasta (© **888/926-2618** or 530/926-2618; www.lakesis.com).

WHERE TO STAY

Best Western Tree House Motor Inn Just off the main highway, this motor inn is one of the better places to stay in the town of Mount Shasta, and it keeps its prices low. The lobby and refurbished rooms, some with decks and fridges, are pleasant enough, and the huge indoor pool is usually deserted, making this a family favorite. Downhill and cross-country ski areas are 10 miles away.

111 Morgan Way (at I-5 and Lake St.), Mount Shasta, CA 96067. www.bestwestern.com. © **800/780-7234** or 530/926-3101. Fax 530/926-3542. 95 units. $119–$169 double. Rates include breakfast buffet. AE, DC, DISC, MC, V. **Amenities:** Restaurant; bar; nearby golf course; exercise room; Jacuzzi; indoor pool. *In room:* A/C, TV w/HBO, fridge, hair dryer, free Wi-Fi.

Mount Shasta Ranch B&B ★ ☺ One of the country's most famous horse trainers and racing tycoons, H. D. ("Curley") Brown, conceived and built the Mount Shasta Ranch as the centerpiece of a private retreat and thoroughbred horse ranch. Despite the encroachment of nearby buildings, the main two-story house and its annex are a cozy B&B with touches of nostalgia, the occasional antique, and spectacular views of Mount Shasta. Three bedrooms with private bathrooms are in the main house; the remaining five share two bathrooms, in the carriage house. It's a 3-minute trek to the shores of nearby Lake Siskiyou (15 min. to the ski slopes), or you could stay here to enjoy the Ping-Pong tables, pool table, darts, and horseshoes. Unlike at most B&Bs, kids are welcome.

1008 W. A. Barr Rd., Mount Shasta, CA 96067. www.stayinshasta.com. © **877/926-3870.** Fax 530/926-3870. 10 units, 5 with private bathroom; 1 cottage. $60–$80 double with shared bathroom; $110 double with private bathroom; $115 cottage for 2. Rates include country breakfast (except cottage). AE, DISC, MC, V. Take Central Mount Shasta exit off I-5 to W. A. Barr Rd. Pets accepted for $10. **Amenities:** Nearby golf course. *In room:* A/C, TV, kitchen in 2 units, no phone.

Railroad Park Resort ☺ A quarter of a mile from the Sacramento River, this is an offbeat place kids will love. It's at the foot of Castle Crags, with a campground and RV park, four rustic cabins, and the Caboose Motel. The guest rooms are railroad cabooses from the Southern Pacific, Santa Fe, and Great Northern railroads, with their pipes, ladders, and lofts left in place. Surrounding the fenced-in, kidney-shaped pool, they're furnished with modern king- or queen-size brass beds, table and chairs, and dressers; most have small bay windows or rooftop cupolas. The restaurant and lounge are also in vintage railroad cars.

100 Railroad Park Rd., Dunsmuir, CA 96025. www.rrpark.com. © **800/974-RAIL** (7245) in California, or 530/235-4440. 27 units. $99–$125 double. Extra person $8. AE, DISC, MC, V. Take Railroad Park exit off I-5, 1 mile south of Dunsmuir. Pets accepted for $15. **Amenities:** Restaurant; lounge; Jacuzzi; outdoor pool. *In room:* A/C, TV, fridge, microwave in some units, minibar (in some units).

Stewart Mineral Springs Resort 📷 Stewart Mineral Springs is one of the most unusual health spas in California, rich with lore and legends. Above coldwater springs that Native Americans valued for their healing powers, the place is deliberately primitive, with as few intrusions from the urban world as possible. Don't expect anything approaching a European spa or big-city luxury here. Designed in a somewhat haphazard compound of about a dozen buildings, 4 miles west of a town called Weed, it occupies a 37-acre site of sloping, forested land accented with ponds, gazebos, and decorative bridges. The grounds are riddled with hiking and nature trails, freshwater streams, and a swimming hole.

Activities revolve around hiking, nature-watching, and the healing waters of the legendary springs. The bathhouse is the resort headquarters, with 13 private rooms where spring water is heated and run into tubs for soaking. A staff member will describe the rituals for you: A 20-minute soak is followed by a visit to a nearby wood-burning sauna and an immersion in the chilly waters of Parks

Creek, just outside the bathhouse (bath price $25, sauna price $17). Other options include massages ($45 per 30-min. session, $70 for 1 hr., and $95 for 1½ hr.). On Saturdays, medicine man Walking Eagle guides guests on a spiritual journey within the Native American Purification Sweat Lodge. They even have a juice bar. If you opt for treatment and R&R here, you won't be alone. The place is popular with young Hollywood types, including soap actors, San Francisco 49ers football players, and local newscasters.

4617 Stewart Springs Rd., Weed, CA 96094. www.stewartmineralsprings.com. ✆ **530/938-2222.** Fax 530/938-4283. 5 tepees (for up to 4 persons), 4 motel rooms, 6 apt units, 4 cabins with kitchens, and a large A-frame house (suitable for 10 persons). $35 double tepee; $50–$110 double in motel, apts., and cabins; $360 for house. Each extra person $5. DISC, MC, V. Leashed pets accepted for $20 per day to stay in pet-designated rooms. **Amenities:** Restaurant (closed in winter); sauna; spa. *In room:* Kitchen in cabins and some units, no phone.

Strawberry Valley Inn   This modest mountaintop lodge is kitschy and cute and will get the job done if you're looking for somewhere cozy to crash on the cheap. While not extravagant in the slightest, guest rooms are comfortable enough, and two-room suites are available should you require more space. A generous breakfast buffet is laid out each morning with fresh fruit, granola, oatmeal, waffles, and pastries; you can dine in the main building's living room or take a tray back to your room. Rooms look pretty motelish from the outside but are nice enough (for the price) within, sporting plush beds and flatscreen TVs.

1142 S. Mount Shasta Blvd., Mount Shasta, CA 96067. www.mtshastahotels.net. ✆ **530/926-2052.** 17 units. $89–$189 double with shared bathroom. Rates include continental breakfast and wine-and-cheese hour. AE, DISC, MC, V. Take Central Mount Shasta exit off I-5 to W. Mount Shasta Blvd. Pets accepted for $10. **Amenities:** Concierge. *In room:* A/C, TV, MP3 docking station.

WHERE TO EAT

Café Maddalena ★★ 🍴 WORLD CUISINE   The smells wafting from this restaurant are enough to draw you into the refurbished old railroad quarter of Dunsmuir. The seasonal menu features authentic dishes from southern France, Spain, and North Africa: roasted beet and chèvre salad with hazelnut dressing; tagine of chicken in North African curry sauce with couscous; ricotta-stuffed ravioli with truffle sauce; and herb-roasted lamb rack with ratatouille. Everything is fresh, including the breads and desserts. During the summer months, request a table outside under the grape arbor. *Tip:* Call to confirm the menu, which changes frequently.

5801 Sacramento Ave., Dunsmuir. ✆ **530/235-2725.** www.cafemaddalena.com. Reservations recommended. Main courses $17–$25. DISC, MC, V. Thurs–Sun 5–10pm. Closed Jan 1 to mid-Mar.

Lily's ★ WORLD CUISINE   In a white-clapboard, early-1900s house, in a residential neighborhood south of the town center, this friendly little restaurant has a front porch, a picket fence, a back garden, and dining in two rooms inside and two patios out. It's popular for breakfast, with chunky breads and delicious omelets. Lunch and dinner dishes—tamale pie, Mediterranean pasta, and Kung Pao chicken salad—span the globe. Popular dishes include the chicken enchiladas with cheese, olives, and onions; and Chicken Rosie, a tender breast of chicken simmered with raspberries, hazelnut liqueur, and cream.

1013 S. Mount Shasta Blvd., Mount Shasta. ✆ **530/926-3372.** www.lilysrestaurant.com. Reservations recommended. Breakfast $7–$12; lunch $8–$12; dinner $11–$23. AE, DISC, MC, V. Mon–Fri 8am–9:30pm; Sat–Sun 8am–2:30pm and 4–9:30pm.

McArthur–Burney Falls Memorial State Park ★

On its way to Lassen Volcanic National Park (see below) from Mount Shasta, Hwy. 89 east loops back south to the 910-acre **McArthur–Burney Falls Memorial State Park** (✆ **530/335-2777**). One of its most spectacular features is **Burney Falls ★★**, an absolutely gorgeous waterfall that cascades over a 129-foot cliff. Theodore Roosevelt once called the falls "the eighth wonder of the world." Giant springs a few hundred yards upstream feed the falls and keep them flowing—100 million gallons every day—even during California's dry spells.

The .5-mile **Headwater Trail** will take you to a good vantage point above the falls. If you're lucky, you can observe the black swifts that nest in the mossy crevices behind the cascade. Other birds to look for include barn and great horned owls, the belted kingfisher, the common

McArthur–Burney Falls Memorial State Park.

flicker, and even the Oregon junco. The year-round park also has 5 miles of nature trails, 128 campsites, picnicking grounds, and good fishing for bass, crappie, and brown, rainbow, and brook trout. For **camping reservations,** call ✆ **800/444-PARK** (7275).

From here, Lassen Volcanic National Park is about 40 miles south.

LASSEN VOLCANIC NATIONAL PARK ★

45 miles E of Redding; 255 miles NE of San Francisco

In the far northeastern corner of California, Lassen Volcanic National Park is a remarkable reminder that North America is still forming, and that the ground below is alive with the forces of creation and sometimes destruction. Lassen Peak is the southernmost in a chain of volcanoes (including Mount St. Helens) that stretches all the way from British Columbia.

Although it's dormant, 10,457-foot **Lassen Peak** is still very much alive. It last awakened in May 1914, beginning a cycle of eruptions that spit lava, steam, and ash until 1921. The eruption climaxed in 1915 when Lassen blew its top, sending a cloud of ash 7 miles high, visible from hundreds of miles away. The peak has been dormant for more than three-quarters of a century now, but the area still boils with a ferocious intensity: Hot springs, fumaroles, geysers, and mud pots are all indicators that Lassen hasn't had its last word. Monitoring of geothermal features in the park shows that they are getting hotter, not cooler, and some scientists take this as a sign that the next big eruption in the Cascades is likely to happen here.

Until then, the park gives visitors an interesting chance to watch a landscape recover from the massive destruction brought on by an eruption. To the north of Lassen Peak is the aptly named **Devastated Area,** a huge swath of volcanic destruction steadily repopulating with conifer forests. Forest botanists have revised their earlier theories that forests must be preceded by herbaceous growth after watching the Devastated Area immediately revegetate with a diverse mix of eight different conifer species, four more than were present before the blast.

The 108,000-acre park is a place of great beauty. The flora and fauna are an interesting mix of species from the Cascade Range, which stretches north from Lassen, and species from the Sierra Nevada Range, which stretches south. The blend accounts for an enormous diversity of plants: 715 species have been identified in the park. Although it is snowbound in winter, Lassen is a summer feeding ground for transient herds of mule deer and numerous black bears.

In addition to the volcano and all its geothermal features, Lassen Volcanic National Park includes miles of hiking trails, 50 beautiful alpine lakes, large meadows, cinder cones, lush forests, cross-country skiing, and great backcountry camping. In fact, three-quarters of the park is designated wilderness.

And crowds? Forget it. Lassen is one of the least-visited national parks in the Lower 48, so crowd control isn't as big a consideration here as in other places. Unless you're here on the Fourth of July or Labor Day weekend, you won't encounter anything that could rightly be called a crowd. Even then, you can escape the hordes simply by skipping such popular sites as Bumpass Hell or the Sulphur Works and heading a few miles down any of the backcountry trails.

Essentials

GETTING THERE   One of the reasons Lassen Volcanic National Park is one of the least-visited national parks is its remote location. The most foolproof route here is Hwy. 44 east from Redding, which leads directly to the northern gateway to the park. A shortcut if you're coming from the south along I-5 is Hwy. 36 in Red Bluff, which leads to the park's southern gateway. If you're arriving from the east via I-80, take the U.S. 395 turnoff at Reno and head to Susanville. Depending on which end of the park you're shooting for, take either Hwy. 44 (to the northwest entrance) or Hwy. 36 (to the southwest entrance) from Susanville. The $10-per-car entrance fee, valid for a week, comes with a copy of the *Lassen Park Guide,* a handy little newsletter listing activities, hikes, and points of interest. Camping fees range from $10 to $25.

Only one major road, Hwy. 89 (also known as the Park Rd.), crosses the park, in a 39-mile half-circle with entrances and visitor centers at either end.

Most visitors enter the park at the southwest entrance station, drive through the park, and leave through the northwest entrance, or vice versa. Two other entrances lead to remote portions of the park. Warner Valley is reached from the south on the road from Chester. The Butte Lake entrance is reached by a cutoff road from Hwy. 44 between Hwy. 89 and Susanville.

VISITOR INFORMATION   **Ranger stations** are clustered near each entrance and provide the full spectrum of interpretive displays, ranger-led walks, informational leaflets, and emergency help. The largest **visitor center** is located just inside the northwest entrance station at the Loomis Museum.

Bumpass Hell, Lassen Volcanic National Park.

The park information number for all requests is ℂ **530/595-4480,** or you can visit **www.nps.gov/lavo** or write Lassen Volcanic National Park, P.O. Box 100, Mineral, CA 96063-0100.

Because of the dangers posed by the park's thermal features, rangers ask that you remain on the trails at all times. Fires are allowed in campgrounds only; please make sure they're dead before leaving. Mountain bikes are prohibited on all trails.

WEATHER   Lassen Volcanic National Park is in one of the coldest places in California. Winter begins in late October and doesn't release its grip until June. Even in the summer, you should plan for possible rain and snow. Temperatures at night can drop below freezing at any time. Winter, however, shows a different and beautiful side of Lassen that more people are starting to appreciate. Since most of the park is over a mile high and the highest point is 10,457 feet, snow accumulates in incredible quantities. Don't be surprised to find snowbanks lining the Park Road into July.

Exploring the Park

The highlight of Lassen is, of course, the volcano and all of its offshoots: boiling springs, fumaroles, mud pots, and more. You can see many of the most interesting sites in a day, making it possible to visit Lassen as a short detour from I-5 or U.S. 395 on the way to or from Oregon. Available at park visitor centers, the *Road Guide to Lassen Park* is a great traveling companion that will explain a lot of the features you'll see as you traverse the park.

Bumpass Hell ★, a 1.5-mile walk off the Park Road in the southern part of the park, is Lassen's largest single geothermal site—16 acres of bubbling mud pots reeking with the rotten-egg-like stench of sulfur. The hike leads you through a quiet, peaceful meadow of wildflowers and birds before it reaches the geothermal site—the name of which derives from an early Lassen hunter who lost a leg after he took a shortcut through the area and plunged into a boiling pool. Stay on the wooden catwalks that safely guide visitors past the pyrite pools, steam vents, and noisy fumaroles, and you won't follow in Bumpass's footsteps.

Sulphur Works ★ is another stinky, steamy example of Lassen's residual heat. Two miles from the southwest park exit, the ground roars with seething gases escaping from the ground.

Boiling Springs Lake and **Devil's Kitchen** are two of the more remote geothermal sites; they're located in the Warner Valley section of the park, which can be reached by hiking from the main road or entering the park through Warner Valley Road from the small town of Chester.

Outdoor Pursuits

In addition to the activities below, free naturalist programs are offered daily in the summer, highlighting everything from flora and fauna to geologic history and volcanic processes. For more information, call the **park headquarters** at ✆ **530/595-4480.**

CANOEING & KAYAKING   Paddlers can take canoes, rowboats, and kayaks on any of the park lakes except Reflection, Emerald, Helen, and Boiling Springs. Motors, including electric motors, are strictly prohibited on all park waters. Park lakes are full of trout, and fishing is popular. You must have a current California fishing license, which you can obtain just outside the north entrance of the park in Burney at **Vaughns Sporting Goods** (37307 Main St.; ✆ **530/335-2381**).

CROSS-COUNTRY SKIING   The Park Road usually closes due to snow in November, and most years it doesn't open until June, so cross-country skiers have their run of the park. Snowmobiles were once allowed but are now forbidden. Marked trails of all skill levels leave from Manzanita Lake at the north end of the park and Lassen Chalet at the south. Most visitors come to the southwest entrance, where the ski chalet offers lessons, rental gear, and a warm place to stay. Popular trips are the beginners' trails to Lake Helen or Summit Lake. More advanced skiers can make the trek into Bumpass Hell, a steaming valley of sulfuric mud pots and fumaroles.

You can also ski the popular 30-mile course of the Park Road in an overnight trek, but doing this involves a long car shuttle. For safety reasons, the park requires all skiers to register at the ranger stations before heading into the backcountry, whether for an overnight or just for the day. For more information, contact the **park headquarters** at ✆ **530/595-4480.**

HIKING   Most Lassen visitors drive through in a day or two, see the geothermal hot spots, and move on. That leaves 150 miles of trails and expanses of backcountry to the few who take the time to get off-road. The *Lassen Trails* booklet at the visitor centers gives good descriptions of some of the most popular hikes and backpacking destinations. Anyone spending the night in the backcountry must have a wilderness permit, issued at the ranger stations. And don't forget to bring plenty of water, sunscreen, and warm clothing.

The most popular hike in the park is the **Lassen Peak Trail** ★, a 2.5-mile climb from the Park Road to the top of the peak. The trail may sound short, but it's steep and covered with snow until late summer. At an elevation of 10,457 feet, though, you'll get a view of the surrounding wilderness that's worth every step of the way. On clear days, you can see south all the way to Sutter Buttes near Yuba City and north into the Cascades. The round-trip takes about 4 to 5 hours.

Running a close second in popularity is **Bumpass Hell Trail.** This 1.5-mile walk off the Park Road in the southern part of the park deposits you right in the middle of the largest single geothermal site in the park. (See "Exploring the Park," above.)

The **Cinder Cone Trail,** in the northeast corner of the park, is another worthy hike, best reached from Butte Lake Campground at Lassen's far northeast corner. If 4 miles seems too short, you can extend the hike (and shorten the drive) by walking in about 8 miles from Summit Lake on the Park Road. Now dormant, Cinder Cone is generally accepted as the source of mysterious flashing lights that were seen by early settlers in the 1850s. Black and charred looking, Cinder Cone is bereft of any life and surrounded by dunes of multihued volcanic ash.

SNOWSHOEING From January to March, park naturalists give free 2-hour eco-adventure snowshoe hikes across Lassen's snow-packed hills. The tours take place on Saturdays at 1:30pm at the Lassen Chalet, at the park's southwestern entrance. You must be at least 8 years old, dress warmly, and wear boots. Snowshoes are free of charge on a first-come, first-served basis, although a $1 donation is requested for upkeep. For more details, call park headquarters (⏃ **530/595-4480**).

Camping

Car campers have their choice of seven park campgrounds with 375 sites, more than enough to handle the trickle of visitors who come to Lassen every summer. In fact, so few people camp in Lassen that the park is without a reservations system, except at the **Lost Creek Group Campground,** and stays there are granted a generous 14-day limit. Sites fill up on weekends, so get to the park early on Friday to secure a place. If the park is packed, the surrounding Lassen National Forest has 43 campgrounds, so you're bound to find a site somewhere.

By far the most "civilized" campground in the park is at **Manzanita Lake,** where you can find hot showers, electrical hookups, flush toilets, and a camper store. When Manzanita fills up, rangers open the **Crags Campground** overflow camp—about 5 miles away and much more basic. Farther into the park along Hwy. 89 is **Summit Lake Campgrounds,** on the north and south ends of Summit Lake. It's a pretty spot, often frequented by deer, and it's a launching point for some excellent day hikes.

On the southern end of the park, you'll find **Southwest Campground,** a walk-in camp directly adjacent to the Lassen Chalet parking lot.

The two remote entrances to Lassen and Warner Valley have their own primitive campgrounds with pit toilets and no water, but the price is right—free.

Backcountry camping is allowed almost everywhere, and traffic is light. Ask about closed areas when you get one of the wilderness permits, which are issued at the ranger stations and required for anyone spending the night in the backcountry.

Where to Stay

INSIDE THE PARK

Drakesbad Guest Ranch ★★★ Lassen Park's only lodge is Drakesbad Guest Ranch, hidden in a high mountain valley surrounded by meadows, lakes, and streams. It's famous for its rustic cabins, lodge, and steaming thermal swimming pool fed by a natural hot spring and open 24 hours a day. Drakesbad is as deluxe as a place with some electricity and no phones can be, with handmade quilts on every bed and kerosene lamps for reading. Full meal service is available, and it's very good. Because the lodge is very popular and open only from June to mid-October, reservations are booked as far as 2 years in advance (although May and June are good times to call to take advantage of cancellations).

c/o California Guest Services, 2150 N. Main St., no. 5, Red Bluff, CA 96080. www.drakesbad.com. ✆ **866/999-0914.** Fax 530/529-4511. 19 units. $155–$201 per person, double occupancy. Rates include meals. DISC, MC, V. **Amenities:** Restaurant; hot-spring-fed pool. *In room:* No phone.

NEAR THE PARK

The Bidwell House Bed and Breakfast Inn ★★ ☺   In 1901, Gen. John Bidwell, a California senator who made three unsuccessful bids for the U.S. presidency, built a country retreat and summer home for his beloved young wife, Annie. After her death, when Chester had developed into a prosperous logging hamlet, the building, with its farmhouse-style design and spacious veranda, was converted into the headquarters for a local ranch. Today it's one of the most charming B&Bs in the region, with a yard of aspens and cottonwoods and sprawling views of mountain meadows and pretty Lake Almanor. The 14 individually decorated guest rooms are furnished with antiques, most have private bathrooms, a few have wood-burning stoves, and seven have Jacuzzi tubs. A cottage that sleeps up to six is ideal for families. Breakfast is presented with fanfare and many gourmet touches, including home-baked breads and delicious omelets.

1 Main St. (P.O. Box 1790), Chester, CA 96020. www.bidwellhouse.com. ✆ **530/258-3338.** 14 units, 12 with private bathroom. $85–$165 double; $175 suite or cottage (sleeps 6). Rates include full breakfast. MC, V. **Amenities:** Nearby golf course; beach; biking; boat launch; fishing; gold panning; hiking; horseback riding; snowmobile trails. *In room:* TV/DVD, free Wi-Fi.

Lassen Mineral Lodge ☺   A mere 9 miles south of Lassen Volcanic National Park's southern entrance, the Lassen Mineral Lodge offers 20 motel-style accommodations in a forested setting. In summer, the lodge is almost always bustling with guests and customers who venture into the gift shop, ski shop, general store, and full-service restaurant and bar. This is probably the best lodging option for families in the Lassen area.

On Hwy. 36E (P.O. Box 160), Mineral, CA 96063. www.minerallodge.com. ✆ **530/595-4422.** Fax 530/595-4452. 20 units. $72–$90 double. AE, DISC, MC, V. **Amenities:** Restaurant; saloon. *In room:* Kitchens in some units, no phone.

Mill Creek Resort ★   Deep in the forest next to ol' Mill Creek, the Mill Creek Resort is that rustic mountain retreat you've always dreamed of while slaving away in the office. A homey country general store and coffee shop serve as the resort's center, a good place to stock up on food while exploring Lassen Volcanic National Park. Nine housekeeping cabins, available on a daily or weekly basis, are clean, cute, and outfitted with vintage 1930s and 1940s furniture, including kitchens (a good thing, since restaurants are scarce in this region). Pets are welcome, too. *Note:* They don't take credit cards.

1 Hwy. 172 (3 miles south of Hwy. 36), Mill Creek, CA 96061. www.millcreekresort.net. ✆ **888/595-4449.** 6 cabins. $70–$95 cabin. No credit cards. Pets accepted. **Amenities:** Bike rental; fishing. *In room:* Kitchen, no phone.

Where to Eat

NEAR THE PARK

When you're this far into the wilderness, the question isn't *which* restaurant to choose, but *whether* there is a single restaurant at all. If bacon and eggs, sandwiches, steaks, chicken, burgers, pizza, and salads aren't part of your diet, you're in big trouble unless you packed your own grub.

Deciding where you're going to eat near Lassen Volcanic National Park depends mostly on which side you're on, north or south. At the south entrance to the park, the closest restaurant is the **Lassen Mineral Lodge** (see "Where to Stay," above) in the town of Mineral, which serves the usual uninspired American fare. The best approach, however, is

Lava Beds National Monument.

to stay at a B&B or lodge that offers meals to its guests—such as the **Bidwell House** or **Drakesbad Guest Ranch**—or at least provides a kitchen to cook your own meals, such as the **Mill Creek Resort** (see above). Food and camping supplies are available at the **Lassen Mineral Lodge,** on Hwy. 36 in Mineral, at the southern end of the park (✆ 530/595-4422; www.minerallodge.com). They also sell or rent just about every outdoor toy you'd ever want to play with in Lassen Park, including cross-country and alpine ski equipment.

LAVA BEDS NATIONAL MONUMENT

324 miles NE of San Francisco; 50 miles NE of Mount Shasta

Lava Beds takes a while to grow on you. It's a seemingly desolate place with high plateaus, cinder cones, and hills covered with lava cinders, sagebrush, and twisted junipers. Miles of land just like it cover most of this corner of California. So why, asks the first-time visitor, is this a national monument? The answer lies underground.

The earth here is like Swiss cheese, so porous in places that it actually makes a hollow sound. When lava pours from a shield volcano, it doesn't cool all at once; the outer edges cool first and the core keeps flowing, forming underground tunnels like a giant pipeline system.

More than 330 lava-tube caves lace the earth at Lava Beds—caves open to the public to explore on their own or with park rangers. Whereas most caves fuel visitors' fear of getting lost within their huge chambers, multiple entrances, and bizarre topography, these tunnels are simple and relatively easy to follow. Once inside, you'll feel that this would be a great place for a game of hide-and-seek.

Essentials

GETTING THERE   The best access to the park is from Hwy. 139, 4 miles south of Tulelake.

VISITOR INFORMATION   Call the **Lava Beds National Monument** (✆ 530/667-8100; www.nps.gov/labe) for information on ranger-led hikes, cave trips, and campfire programs. The visitor center is at the southern end of the park.

ENTRY FEES The entry fee is $10 per vehicle for 7 days, $5 per bike or walk-in, and $10 a day for camping.

WHEN TO GO Park elevations range from 4,000 to 5,700 feet, and this part of California can get cold any time of year. Summer is the best time to visit, with average temperatures in the 70s Fahrenheit (20s Celsius); winter temperatures plunge down to about 40°F (4°C) in the day and as low as 20°F (−7°C) by night. Summer is also the best time to participate in ranger-led hikes, cave trips, and campfire programs.

Exploring the Park

A hike to **Schonchin Butte** (.75 mile each way) will give you a good perspective on the stark beauty of the monument and nearby Tule Lake Valley. Wildlife lovers should keep their eyes peeled for such terrestrial animals as mule deer, coyote, marmots, and squirrels, while watching overhead for bald eagles, 24 species of hawks, and enormous flocks of ducks and geese headed to the Klamath Basin, one of the largest waterfowl wintering grounds in the Lower 48. Sometimes the sky goes dark with ducks and geese during the peak migrations.

The caves at **Lava Beds** are open to the public with little restriction. All you need to see most of them are a good flashlight or headlamp, sturdy walking shoes, and a sense of adventure. Many of the caves are entered by ladders or stairs, or by holes in the side of a hill. Once inside, walk far enough to round a corner, and then shut off your light—a chilling experience, to say the least.

One-way **Cave Loop Road,** just southwest of the visitor center, is where you'll find many of the best cave hikes. About 15 lava tubes have been marked and made accessible. Two are ice caves, where the air temperature remains below freezing year-round and ice crystals form on the walls. If exploring on your own gives you the creeps, check out **Mushpot Cave.** Almost adjacent to the visitor center, this cave has been outfitted with lights and a smooth walkway; you'll have plenty of company.

Hardened spelunkers will find enough remote and relatively unexplored caves to keep themselves busy. Many caves require specialized climbing gear.

Aboveground, several trails crisscross the monument. The longest of these, the **Lyons Trail** (8.25 miles one-way), spans the wildest part of the monument, where you are likely to see plenty of animals. The **Whitney Butte Trail** (3 miles one-way) leads from Merrill Cave along the shoulder of 5,000-foot Whitney Butte to the edge of the Callahan Lava Flow and monument boundary.

Picnicking, Camping & Accommodations

The 43-unit **Indian Well Campground,** near the visitor center, has spaces for tents and small RVs year-round, with water available only during the summer. The rest of the year, you'll have to carry water from the nearby visitor center. Two **picnic grounds,** Fleener Chimneys and Captain Jacks Stronghold, have tables but no water; open fires are prohibited.

The monument grounds have no hotels or lodges, but many services are available in nearby Tulelake and Klamath Falls. For more information, call or write **Lava Beds National Monument,** 1 Indian Well Headquarters, Tulelake, CA 96134 (© **530/667-8100;** www.nps.gov/labe).

9

THE HIGH SIERRA:

YOSEMITE, MAMMOTH LAKES, SEQUOIA & KINGS CANYON

by Matthew Poole

T

he national parks of California's Sierra lure travelers from around the globe. The big attraction is Yosemite, of course, but the region abounds with other natural wonders as well. John Muir found in Yosemite "the most songful streams in the world . . . the noblest forests, the loftiest granite domes, the deepest ice-sculpted canyons." Few visitors would disagree with Muir's early impressions as they explore this land of towering cliffs, alpine lakes, river beaches, and dazzling fields of snow in winter.

Yosemite Valley, lush with waterfalls and regal peaks, is the most central and accessible part of the park, stretching for some 7 miles from Wawona Tunnel in the west to Curry Village in the east. If you visit during spring or early fall, you'll encounter fewer problems with crowds and have a more intimate experience of Yosemite's splendors.

Across the heart of the Sierra Nevada, in east-central California, Sequoia and Kings Canyon national parks comprise a vast, mountainous region that stretches some 1,300 square miles, taking in the giant sequoias for which they're fabled. This is a land of alpine lakes, deep canyons, and granite peaks, including Mount Whitney—at 14,495 feet, the highest point in the Lower 48.

Another big attraction is Mammoth Lakes, a popular playground for California residents. Glaciers carved out much of this panoramic region, where you can partake of all sorts of recreational activities against a backdrop of lakes, streams, waterfalls, and meadows.

Because of the vast popularity of the parks, facilities can be strained at peak visiting times. Always make your reservations in advance, if possible (for camping as well as for hotel stays).

YOSEMITE'S GATEWAYS

The three most popular entrances to Yosemite (there are five total) are **Big Oak Flat** (via Hwy. 120), the west entrance, 88 miles east of Manteca and the best passage in from San Francisco; **Arch Rock** (via Hwy. 140), 75 miles northeast of Merced and the easiest route from central California; and the **South Entrance** at Wawona (via Hwy. 41), 64 miles north of Fresno and the best inroad from Southern California. Should you need to reserve accommodations outside Yosemite, it's wise to book a place near the gateway that affords you easiest access to the park.

Towns on the periphery of each gateway are built around the tourism industry, with plenty of places to stay and eat, and natural wonders of their own. The drawback is that if you stay outside Yosemite, reaching any point within the park requires at least a half-hour drive, which is especially frustrating during high season, when motor homes and congestion slow traffic to a snail's pace.

PREVIOUS PAGE: **Yosemite National Park.**

A controversial park plan would restore 180 acres to their natural state and eliminate a 3¼-mile section of road to make way for a foot-and-bike trail, but it would do so by cutting the number of day-use parking spots in Yosemite from 1,600 to 550, encouraging bus and shuttle usage, and reducing guest rooms from 1,260 to 981.

The plan is still under debate, but various public transportation options are already in effect, allowing you to leave your car behind. You can enter Yosemite on convenient, inexpensive buses and move around the valley floor on free shuttles. The **Yosemite Area Regional Transit System (YARTS; ℂ 877/989-2787;** www.yarts.com) runs round-trip transit from communities within Mariposa, Merced, and Mono counties to Yosemite. The Merced route along Hwy. 140 operates year-round, although the winter schedule is limited. Fares for riding YARTS vary but generally range from $7 to $25 round-trip for adults, including park entrance, with discounts for children and seniors. Summer routes originate at Coulterville, Mammoth Lakes and Lee Vining, and Wawona. For information on the Hwy. 120 east service (Mammoth Lakes to Yosemite Valley), call ℂ **877/989-2787** from May until it snows (Sept or Oct).

Big Oak Flat Entrance

The Big Oak Flat entrance is 150 miles east of San Francisco and 130 miles southeast of Sacramento. Among the string of small communities along the way is **Groveland** (24 miles from the park's entrance)—a throwback to gold-mining days, with some semblance of a town and the oldest saloon in the state. It will take around an hour to reach the park entrance from Groveland, but at least you'll find extracurricular activity there if you're planning to stay in the area for a while. Big Oak Flat has a few hotels as well, but no town. Call the visitor information number below for details.

GETTING THERE   If you're driving from San Francisco, take I-580 (which turns into I-205) to Manteca, and then Hwy. 120 east.

VISITOR INFORMATION   Contact the **Yosemite Chamber of Commerce** (ℂ **800/449-9120** or 209/962-0429; www.groveland.org) for an exhaustive list of hotels, motels, cabins, RV parks, and campsites in the area.

WHERE TO STAY & EAT

Great dining options are scarce in these parts. For options beyond the places mentioned below, ask around town for further recommendations—just don't expect to discover the next Chez Panisse.

Berkshire Inn Bed & Breakfast ★   The secret to vacationing at Yosemite National Park during the crowded summer months is to stay outside the park at a quiet B&B and then make day trips in. It's less expensive, and the quality of lodgings and cuisine is usually far better as well. Ergo, consider a stay at the Berkshire Inn, a sprawling open-beam lodge built in 1988 on 20 wooded acres just outside Groveland. The owners expect you to treat the inn as your own house in the woods: Enjoy breakfast on the large deck overlooking the mountains, play cards in the sunny gazebo, watch TV on the couch in the family room, or warm up by the wood stove with some complimentary wine. An extended continental breakfast is included in the rate, and the innkeepers are happy to help you arrange outdoor activities, such as rafting, fishing, golfing, bicycling, gold panning, snow skiing, horseback riding, or wine tasting.

The High Sierra

19950 Hwy. 120, Groveland, CA 95321. www.berkshireinn.net. © **888/225-2064** or 209/962-6744. 10 units. $135–$180 double. Rates include continental breakfast. AE, DISC, MC, V.

Evergreen Lodge ★★ 🎁 ☺   For the classic Yosemite experience at any time of the year, this affordable and refreshingly crowd-free 22-acre resort has it all: cozy cabins in the woods, a historic and lively tavern, a great restaurant serving a diverse menu, even a recreation center and library. Scattered throughout groves of towering pines, the cabins come with private bathrooms, decks, Sirius Satellite Radio, and quilted beds. In the evenings, you can enjoy a pitcher of beer or bottle of fine wine; play a game of Ping-Pong, pool, or horseshoes; or sit around the campfire roasting marshmallows. During the day, you'll have easy access to all parts of Yosemite—particularly the beautiful and crowd-free Hetch Hetchy

BURGERS & bullets: THE IRON DOOR SALOON

Walk through the English iron doors that were shipped around the Horn, and step into a bar that has been serving whiskey to thirsty travelers for more than 150 years. Built from solid blocks of granite, the Iron Door Saloon is a must-stop on your way to Yosemite. They say Black Bart enjoyed a tumbler or two here and put a few bullets in the walls to keep the locals jumpy (keep looking). Thousands of dollar bills are tacked to the ceiling, and a stuffed buffalo's head hangs on the wall to remind guests of the house special—a thick, juicy, charbroiled buffalo burger served with pickles, tomato, onions, and house-made coleslaw. Espressos, cappuccinos, and lattes are available as well. At 18761 Main St. in downtown Groveland, it's open daily for lunch and dinner (℗ **209/962-8904;** www.iron-door-saloon.com). Live music acts (with both local and national artists) regularly play at the saloon—a remnant perk from the days when the owners used to work for concert promoter Bill Graham.

area—as well as numerous hiking trails and swimming holes. Be sure to book one of Evergreen's guided recreation and activities programs, which include fly-fishing trips for all levels, hikes throughout the park, and bike trips (the road biking around here is excellent).

33160 Evergreen Rd. (at Hwy. 120), Groveland, CA 95321. www.evergreenlodge.com. ℗ **800/935-6343** or 209/379-2606. Fax 209/391-2390. 66 units. Open year-round. Rates vary with season and cabin size: $90–$350 for 1- and 2-bedroom cabins. AE, DISC, MC, V. From San Francisco, take I-580 east (which turns into I-205) to Manteca; take Hwy. 120 east through Groveland; turn left at Hetch Hetchy/Evergreen Rd. **Amenities:** Restaurant w/indoor-outdoor dining; tavern; children's areas; lake, pool, and tennis courts at neighboring Camp Mather for day-use fee (summer only); sun deck; theater; free Wi-Fi. *In room:* Satellite radio, DVD, hair dryer, minifridge.

The Groveland Hotel ★ Constructed in 1849 from adobe, this California landmark is one of the oldest buildings in the region and loaded with 19th-century character. The Victorian-style guest rooms are cozily appointed with feather beds, down comforters, private bathrooms, and attractive European antiques. The best rooms are the two-room suites equipped with spa tubs and fireplaces. Along with an authentic Gold Rush–era saloon, the hotel has a restaurant serving baby back ribs, rack of lamb, fresh fish, and pasta, and a wine list that's a recipient of *Wine Spectator*'s Award of Excellence. Be sure to visit the hotel's website for money-saving package deals.

18767 Main St. (P.O. Box 289), Groveland, CA 95321. www.groveland.com. ℗ **800/273-3314** or 209/962-4000. Fax 209/962-6674. 17 units. $145–$285 double. Rates include extended continental breakfast. AE, DC, DISC, MC, V. Pets accepted for $10 per night. **Amenities:** Restaurant; babysitting; concierge; nearby golf course; room service. *In room:* A/C, TV/VCR in some units, CD player, hair dryer, minibar, free Wi-Fi.

Hotel Charlotte Built in 1918 by an Italian immigrant, and listed on the National Register of Historic Places, the Charlotte is warm, comfortable, and no-nonsense—a quintessential historic Western hotel. On the outside, it looks like a gentrified saloon. Inside, the 10 individually decorated rooms are cheerily wallpapered and wainscoted. Rooms are small, quaint, and basic, with twin or queen-size beds and air-conditioning. Several units adjoin one another with connecting bathrooms (perfect for families). Two units have showers only; the rest have claw-foot tub/shower combos. The guest salons include a television, computer with Internet access (Wi-Fi also on-site), games, and a piano for impromptu singalongs. The pancake buffet is great, featuring strong coffee, eggs, yogurt, cereals, fruit, breads, and juices.

18736 Main St. (Hwy. 120), Groveland, CA 95321. www.hotelcharlotte.com. © **800/961-7799** or 209/962-6455. Fax 209/962-6254. 10 units. $119–$189 double. Extra person $20. Rates include buffet breakfast. AE, MC, V. 1 room accepts pets, for $20. **Amenities:** Restaurant; full bar; free Wi-Fi. *In room:* AC, TV.

Arch Rock Entrance

This is the most heavily used park entrance, offering easy access to the valley.

GETTING THERE   Arch Rock is 75 miles northeast of Merced. If you're driving from central California, take I-5 to Hwy. 99 to Merced, and then Hwy. 140 east through El Portal.

Greyhound (© **800/231-2222;** www.greyhound.com) and **Amtrak** (© **800/USA-RAIL** [872-7245]; www.amtrak.com) have routes to Fresno from many cities. **VIA Adventures** (© **800/VIA-LINE** [842-5463] or 209/384-1315; www.via-adventures.com) offers service from Merced Amtrak Passenger Station to Yosemite Valley Visitor Center and Yosemite Lodge. Coaches, which can be wheelchair lift equipped with advance notice, provide several round-trips daily between Merced and Yosemite.

WHERE TO STAY

Yosemite Bug Rustic Mountain Resort ☺   Twenty-five miles from Yosemite Valley, this former children's camp is closer to a hostel than a "rustic mountain resort," but if you're more interested in saving money and hiking Yosemite than in good service and fine linens, the Bug delivers. Accommodations come in multiple configurations: private cabins with bathrooms, B&B-style private rooms with shared bathrooms in the main lodge, Yosemite-style wood-frame tent cabins, and cottages for families or small groups. The on-site **Cafe at the Bug** serves California–American fare like seared grilled salmon in a lemon-herb sauce with mashed potatoes, vegan dishes, and box lunches to go. The cafe also doubles as the lodge's communal lounge. Other perks include a '70s vintage spa facility with an outdoor hot tub, big sun deck, swimming hole, hammocks, and hot-rock sauna, as well as yoga classes, a game room with a pool table, a kitchen for hostel guests, and organized outings.

6979 Hwy. 140 (P.O. Box 81), Midpines, CA 95345. www.yosemitebug.com. © **866/826-7108** or 209/966-6666. Fax 209/966-6667. Private rooms with private bathroom $75–$155; family and private rooms with semiprivate bathroom $50–$85; dorm beds with semiprivate bathroom $20; tent cabins $35–$55; cottages $255–$335. DISC, MC, V. **Amenities:** Restaurant; bike rentals; free Wi-Fi (in lodge). *In room:* A/C, no phone.

Yosemite View Lodge ☺   It's shocking to drive onto this gargantuan compound, practically at the park gate, amid otherwise pristine natural surroundings. But the bus loads of tourists need to stay somewhere, and this 335-room mega-motel along the Merced River is ground zero. The motel-style units include fridges, microwaves, and HBO; some have kitchenettes, river views, balconies, and fireplaces. The indoor and outdoor pools and pizza restaurant are a big hit with the kids, though if I were a kid, I'd rather stay at the Tenaya Lodge (p. 354). There's also a general store, spa, coin-op laundry, and cocktail lounge. The restaurant food is decent but pricey for a family. If this place is booked, ask about Yosemite Resort's other properties, although they're not so close to the park entrance. In the winter, call ahead for information about weather and road conditions.

11156 Hwy. 140 (P.O. Box D), El Portal, CA 95318. www.yosemiteresorts.us. ⓒ **209/379-2681.** Fax 209/379-2818. 335 units. $104–$209 double. 2-night minimum on holidays. MC, V. Pets accepted for $13 per night. **Amenities:** Restaurant; pizza parlor; lounge; 4 Jacuzzis; 1 indoor and 3 outdoor heated pools. *In room:* A/C, TV, fridge, hair dryer, kitchenette in some units.

South Entrance

The South Entrance is 332 miles north of Los Angeles, 190 miles east of San Francisco, 59 miles north of Fresno, and 33 miles south of Yosemite Valley. Fish Camp and Oakhurst are the closest towns to the South Entrance at Wawona. This entrance to the valley leads through the Wawona Tunnel to the **Tunnel View,** where you *must* stop to admire the panorama; if you've never been to Yosemite, I promise you that this is a view you'll never forget.

GETTING THERE If you're driving from Los Angeles, take I-5 to Hwy. 99 north, and then Hwy. 41 north. **Fresno–Yosemite International Airport** (ⓒ **559/621-4500;** www.fresno.gov/discoverfresno/airports/default.htm), in nearby Fresno, is 93 miles south of Yosemite Village. The airport is served by Alaska Airlines, America West, American, Continental, Delta, Horizon, United, and all the major car-rental companies. From the airport, take Hwy. 41 north to the South Entrance.

VISITOR INFORMATION Ask the **Yosemite Sierra Visitors Bureau,** 40637 Hwy. 41, Oakhurst, CA 93644 (ⓒ **559/683-4636;** www.yosemitethisyear. com), for a helpful brochure on the area, and check out its excellent online guide.

WHERE TO STAY & EAT

Big Creek Inn ★★ Two miles from the South Entrance to Yosemite National Park, this immaculate B&B is run by owner/innkeeper Pamela Salisbury. Near the banks of Big Creek, it has everything you could want from a mountain lodging: easy access to Yosemite, great fishing outside the front door, a balcony for reading, creek sounds from every room, a state-of-the-art telescope for stargazing, an outdoor spa tub overlooking the creek, and even in-room facials, body wraps, and foot care. The game room is filled with books, maps, and board games; Internet access is free; and more than 500 movies are available for in-room viewing. The three guest rooms have private balconies with French doors and forest views, large bathrooms with Neutrogena bath products, and cozy comforters; two come with gas fireplaces and bistro-style dining tables. A hearty, homemade buffet breakfast is served in the dining room.

1221 Hwy. 41 (P.O. Box 39), Fish Camp, CA 93623. www.bigcreekinn.com. ⓒ **559/641-2828.** 3 units. $115–$239 double. Rates include buffet breakfast and self-serve hot and cold refreshments. MC, V. **Amenities:** Nearby golf course and ski areas; spa services. *In room:* TV/VCR/DVD, CD player, Wi-Fi.

Château du Sureau ★★★ Its kudos say it all: five diamonds, five stars, hailed by *Zagat* as one of the top small hotels in the United States. The domain of Vienna-born Erna Kubin-Clanin, the Elderberries estate (*sureau* is French for "elderberry") is the sine qua non of luxurious lodging, decadent dining, and exclusivity. From the renowned restaurant, a pathway leads through gardens to the house, which resembles a French château, with turret and terra-cotta-tile roof. Each individually decorated room has a wood-burning fireplace and a wrought-iron balcony. Celebrities fleeing Los Angeles are fond of the $2,950-per-night Villa Sureau, a two-bedroom, two-bathroom luxury villa with a library, a full kitchen, and 24-hour butler service. The restaurant, **Erna's Elderberry House** (© **559/683-6800**), is known for its impeccable French-influenced cuisine and service—the $95 six-course prix-fixe menu changes daily—and the **Spa du Sureau** pampers guests from head to toe with a wide selection of treatments.

48688 Victoria Lane (P.O. Box 577), Oakhurst, CA 93644. www.chateaudusureau.com. © **559/683-6860.** Fax 559/683-0800. 10 units. $445–$575 double. Extra person $75. Rates include full breakfast. AE, DISC, MC, V. **Amenities:** Restaurant; bar; concierge; nearby golf course; outdoor pool; room service; spa services. *In room:* A/C, TV/VCR on request, CD player, hair dryer.

The Homestead Cottages ★ Secluded on 160 acres of woodland with plenty of trails, this establishment off the beaten path is a gem. The wonderful hand-built cottages are rustic yet modern, with four-poster log beds, saltillo tile floors, vaulted ceilings, stone fireplaces, and separate sitting and dining areas, with the convenience of TV and air-conditioning. Each cabin has a unique bent, and they are all spaced far apart enough to guarantee privacy. Each cottage has a kitchen stocked with coffee, teas, fruit, muffins, and such, and a gas barbecue and picnic table are available to guests as well. Families should inquire about the Ranch House, a two-bedroom/two-bathroom accommodation that sleeps up to six guests. The top-rated River Creek Golf Club is just a mile away.

41110 Rd. 600, Ahwahnee, CA 93601. www.homesteadcottages.com. © **800/483-0495** or 559/683-0495. Fax 559/683-8165. 5 cottages, 1 guesthouse. $119–$374 double. Extra person $25. DISC, MC, V. 4½ miles north of Oakhurst on Hwy. 49, and then south on Rd. 600 for 2½ miles. *In room:* A/C, TV, hair dryer, kitchen, no phone.

Hound's Tooth Inn ★ This immaculate bed-and-breakfast is just 12 miles from Yosemite's South Entrance. It has comfortable, pretty rooms (some with spas or fireplaces), individually decorated in a Victorian style with a mix of reproductions and antiques, wallpaper, lace valances, and original art. My favorite rooms are the Hounds Tooth, with a king-size bed, fireplace, and view of the Sierra; and the Victorian Tower, with rattan chairs and a spa. Kids are welcome by prior arrangement (rooms are set up for two people, so additional bedding must be brought in). The private garden area is the ideal spot for a relaxing read.

42071 Hwy. 41, Oakhurst, CA 93644. www.houndstoothinn.com. © **888/642-6610** or 559/642-6600. Fax 559/658-2946. 12 units, 1 cottage. $84–$179 double; $199–$225 cottage. Extra person $20. Rates include full breakfast. AE, DC, DISC, MC, V. *In room:* A/C, TV/VCR, fridge and minibar in some units, kitchenette.

The Narrow Gauge Inn & Restaurant If you want to stay in a place that celebrates its mountainous surrounds, book a room at this friendly inn, 4 miles south of the park entrance. All of the motel-style units have a luxury cabin feel, with A-frame ceilings, little balconies or decks, antiques, quilts, and lace curtains; some have wood paneling. The higher the price of the room, the cuter it gets (nos. 40–51 are the best and most secluded; they look directly into forest). Hiking trails run through the property, and the old-fashioned, lodge-style restaurant and

WHITE-WATER rafting ADVENTURES

Zephyr Whitewater Expeditions (☎ **800/431-3636** or 209/532-6249; www.zrafting. com) offers one of the most direct ways to interact with nature in Yosemite—especially if you're not an experienced backpacker. The half- to 3-day trips are ideal for white-water fans in the spring (when melting snow makes the ride most exciting) and for families later in the season. Although the trip doesn't go through the park, it's still an all-wilderness adventure and an experience you'll never forget. Be sure to reserve a spot well in advance, particularly in the spring.

Zephyr Whitewater Expeditions.

buffalo bar serves Angus beef, fresh seafood, chicken, and wild game; it's open Wednesday through Sunday in season from 5:30 to 9pm.

48571 Hwy. 41, Fish Camp, CA 93623. www.narrowgaugeinn.com. ☎ **888/644-9050** or 559/683-7720. Fax 559/683-2139. 26 units. Apr–Oct $140–$195 double; Nov–Mar $79–$109 double. Extra person $10. Rates include continental breakfast. DISC, MC, V. Pets accepted for $25. **Amenities:** Restaurant (seasonal); bar; Jacuzzi (seasonal); outdoor heated pool (seasonal). *In room:* TV.

Tenaya Lodge ★★ ☺   Two miles from Yosemite National Park's southern gate, the Tenaya Lodge is a large, full-service resort that's particularly idyllic for families. The three- and four-story complex is set amid 35 acres of forest a few miles outside the park. Inside, the decor is a cross between an Adirondack hunting lodge and a Southwestern pueblo, with a lobby dominated by a three-story river-rock fireplace. The modern guest rooms have tasteful Southwestern decor with quality furnishings and roomy, well-appointed bathrooms. At the Guest Experience Center on the premises, you can sign up for tours of Yosemite, white-water rafting, mountain-bike rentals, rock climbing, horseback riding, and other outdoor activities. The lodge's Adventure Club program for kids offers nature hikes, arts and crafts, games, and music for children ages 5 to 12. Babysitting for infants and children is also available. *Tip:* Check their website for package deals and Internet specials.

1122 Hwy. 41, Fish Camp, CA 93623. www.tenayalodge.com. ☏ **888/514-2167** or 559/683-6555. Fax 559/683-8684. 244 units. Winter from $129 double; summer from $255 double. Buffet breakfast $15 per person. Children 17 and under stay free in parent's room. AE, DC, DISC, MC, V. Pets accepted for $75. **Amenities:** 2 restaurants; deli; babysitting; bike rental; children's program; 2 nearby golf courses; exercise room; indoor and outdoor Jacuzzis; indoor and outdoor pools; room service; full-service spa; Wi-Fi. *In room:* A/C, TV w/pay movies, fridge on request, hair dryer, minibar.

YOSEMITE NATIONAL PARK ★★★

Yosemite is a place of record-setting statistics: the highest waterfall in North America and 3 of the world's 10 tallest waterfalls (Upper Yosemite Fall, Ribbon Fall, and Sentinel Falls), the tallest and largest single granite monolith in the world (El Capitan), the most recognizable mountain (Half Dome), one of the world's largest trees (the Grizzly Giant in the Mariposa Grove), and thousands of rare plant and animal species. But trying to explain its majesty is impossible; you simply must experience it firsthand.

What sets the valley apart is its geology. The Sierra Nevada formed between 10 million and 80 million years ago, when a tremendous geological uplift pushed layers of granite beneath the ocean up into a mountain range. Cracks and rifts in the rock gave erosion a start at carving canyons and valleys. During the last ice age, at least three glaciers flowed through the valley, shearing vertical faces of stone and hauling away the rubble. The last glacier retreated 10,000 to 15,000 years ago, but it left its legacy in the incredible number and size of the waterfalls pouring into the valley from hanging side canyons. From the 4,000-foot-high valley floor, the 8,000-foot tops of El Capitan, Half Dome, and Glacier Point look like the top of the world, but they're small compared to the park's highest mountains, which exceed 13,000 feet. The 7-square-mile valley acts like a huge drain for runoff from hundreds of square miles of snow-covered peaks (which explains why the valley flooded during the great storm of 1997).

High-country creeks flush with snowmelt catapult over the abyss left by the glaciers and form an outrageous variety of falls, from tiny ribbons that never reach the ground to the torrents of Nevada and Vernal falls. With the shadows and lighting of the deep valley, the effect of all this falling water is mesmerizing. Hundreds of visitors flock to the park for some of the finest climbing anywhere.

The valley is also home to beautiful meadows and the Merced River. When the last glacier retreated, its debris dammed the Merced and formed a lake. Eventually, sediment from the river filled the lake and created the rich, level valley floor we see today. Tiny Mirror Lake was created later by rock fall that dammed up Tenaya Creek; the addition of a man-made dam in 1890 made it more of a lake than a pond. Rafters and inner-tubers enjoy the slow-moving Merced during the heat of summer.

Deer and **coyote** frequent the valley, often causing vehicular mayhem as one heavy-footed tourist slams on brakes to whip out the camera while another rubbernecker drives right into him. Metal crunches, tempers flare, and the deer daintily hop away.

Bears, too, are at home in the valley. Grizzlies are gone from the park now, but black bears abound, hungry for your food. Bears will rip into cars for even the smallest treats, including things you think are safe in your trunk. Each year as many as 500 bear-eats-car incidents occur, and several bears have had to be

Coyote in Yosemite.

killed when they became too aggressive and destructive. Park officials levy a fine of up to $5,000 for feeding park animals, and they can also impound your car. Food storage lockers are available throughout the park—please use them.

In the middle of the valley's thickest urban cluster is the **Yosemite Valley Visitor Center** (© **209/372-0200;** www.nps.gov/yose), with exhibitions about the park's glacial geology, history, and flora and fauna. Check out the **Yosemite Museum** next door for insight into what life in the park was once like; excellent exhibits explore the Miwok and Paiute cultures that thrived here. The **Ansel Adams Gallery** (© **209/372-4413;** www.anseladams.com) features the famous photographer's prints, as well as the work of other artists. You'll also find much history and memorabilia regarding nature writer John Muir, one of the founders of the conservation movement.

It's easy to let the beauty of the valley monopolize your attention, but remember that 95% of Yosemite is wilderness. Of the four million visitors who come to the park each year, few venture more than a mile from their cars. That leaves most of Yosemite's 750,000 acres open for anyone adventurous enough to hike a few miles. Even though the valley is the hands-down winner for drama, the high country offers a more subtle kind of beauty: glacial lakes, rivers, and miles of granite spires and domes. In the park's southwest corner, the Mariposa Grove is a forest of rare sequoias, the world's largest trees, as well as several meadows and the south fork of the Merced River.

Tenaya Lake and Tuolumne Meadows are two of the most popular high-country destinations, as well as the starting points for many trails to the backcountry. Since this area is under snow November through June, summer is more like spring. From snowmelt to the first snowfall, the high country explodes with wildflowers and wildlife trying to make the most of the short season.

Essentials

ENTRY POINTS   The park has four main entrances. Most valley visitors enter through the **Arch Rock Entrance** on Hwy. 140. The best entrance for Wawona is the **South Entrance** on Hwy. 41 from Oakhurst. If you're going to the high country, you'll save a lot of time by coming in through the **Big Oak Flat Entrance,** which puts you straight onto Tioga Road without forcing you to deal with the congested valley. The **Tioga Pass Entrance** is open only in summer, and it's relevant only if you're coming from the east side of the Sierra (in which case, it's your only option). A fifth, little-used entrance is the **Hetch Hetchy Entrance** in the euphonious Poopenaut Valley, on a dead-end road.

FEES   It costs $20 per car per week to enter the park, or $10 per person per week (15 and younger free). Annual Yosemite Passes are a steal, at $40. Wilderness permits are free, but reserving them requires a $5 fee per person. If you are 62 or older, you may purchase a lifetime Golden Age Passport for $10. With reasonable proof of age, you can apply for this passport here (or at any other national park or national forest).

GAS   Yosemite Valley has no gas stations, so fill up before entering.

VISITOR CENTERS & INFORMATION   For general information, you can either call the central, 24-hour recorded information line for the park (© **209/372-0200**) or log on to the park's main website (www.nps.gov/yose). All visitor-related service lines, including hotels and information, can be accessed by phone at © **209/372-1000,** or at **www.yosemitepark.com**. Another good resource is **Yosemite Area Travelers Information** (© **209/723-3153;** www.yosemite.com). For details on lodgings within Yosemite National Park, contact **Yosemite Reservations,** P.O. Box 578, Yosemite National Park, CA 95389 (© **801/559-5000;** www.yosemitepark.com).

The biggest visitor center is the **Valley Visitor Center** (© **209/372-0200**). For trail advice and biological and geological displays about the High Sierra, the **Tuolumne Meadows Visitor Center** (© **209/372-0263**) is great (closed in winter). Each center can provide you with maps and more newspapers, books, and photocopied leaflets than you'll ever read.

REGULATIONS   Rangers in the Yosemite Valley spend more time being cops than rangers. They even have their own jail, so don't do anything you wouldn't do in your hometown. Park regulations are pretty simple: Permits are required for overnight backpacking trips; fishing licenses are required; utilize proper food-storage methods in bear country; don't collect firewood in the valley; no off-road bicycle riding; dogs are allowed in the park but must be leashed and kept off trails; and *don't feed the animals.*

SEASONS   Winter is my favorite time to visit the valley. It isn't crowded, as it is in summer, and a dusting of snow provides a stark contrast to all that granite. To see the waterfalls at their best, come in spring, when snowmelt is at its peak. Fall can be cool, but it's beautiful and much less crowded than summer. Sunshine seekers will love summer—if they can tolerate the crowds. The high country is under about 20 feet of snow November through May, so unless you're snow camping, summer is pretty much the only season to pitch a tent. Even in summer, thundershowers are a frequent occurrence, sometimes with a magnificent lightning show. Mosquitoes can be a plague during the peak of summer, but the situation improves after the first freeze.

ORGANIZED TOURS & RANGER PROGRAMS   The park offers a number of ranger-guided walks, hikes, and other programs. Check at one of the visitor centers or in the *Yosemite Guide* for current topics, start times, and locations. Walks may vary from week to week, but you can always count on nature hikes, evening discussions on park anomalies (floods, fires, or critters), and the sunrise photography program aimed at replicating some of Ansel Adams's works. The sunrise photo walk always gets rave reviews from the early risers who venture out at dawn. All photo walks require advance registration. (Get details at the visitor centers.) The living-history evening program outside at Yosemite Lodge is great for young and old alike.

Several recommended organizations host guided trips. **Southern Yosemite Mountain Guides** ★★ (© 800/231-4575; www.symg.com) leads tours to lesser-known areas of the park, fly-fishing trips for all levels, and other excursions like mountaineering and rock climbing. The **Yosemite Institute** ★ (© 209/379-9511; www.yni.org/yi) is a nonprofit group with a unique environment for learning about nature and the history of the Sierra Nevada. **Incredible Adventures** (© 800/777-8464; www.incadventures.com) runs 3-day hikes in Yosemite from San Francisco.

Yosemite & Beyond (© 559/658-6789; www.yosemiteandbeyond.com) conducts scheduled as well as customized trips. Tours are operated on air-conditioned buses with picture windows and cost $85 to $105. The sightseeing includes Mariposa Grove, Yosemite Valley, and Glacier Point. Guides point out geology, flora, and fauna and schedule stops for lunch, shopping, and photo opportunities. Pickup can be arranged from various motels throughout Oakhurst, Fish Camp, Mariposa, and Bass Lake, as well as in Fresno.

A variety of **guided tram and bus tours** are also available. You can buy tickets at Yosemite Lodge, the Ahwahnee, Curry Village, or beside the Village Store in Yosemite Village. Advance reservations are suggested for all tours; space can be reserved in person or by phone (© 209/372-1240). Always double-check for updated departure schedules and prices. Most tours depart from Yosemite Lodge, the Ahwahnee, or Curry Village, and most tours are about $75 for adults for full-day trips. Children's rates are usually 40% to 50% less, and most tours offer discounts for seniors.

The 2-hour **Valley Floor Tour** is a great way to get acclimated to the park, with a good selection of photo ops, including El Capitan, Tunnel View, and Half Dome. This ride is also available on nights when the moon is full or near full. It's an eerie but beautiful scene when moonlight illuminates the valley's granite walls. Blankets and hot cocoa are included, but dress warmly, because it can get mighty chilly after the sun goes down. Purchase tickets at valley hotels, or call © 209/372-1240 for reservations.

The **Glacier Point Tour** is a 4-hour scenic bus ride through the valley to Glacier Point. Tours also depart from Yosemite Valley to **Mariposa Grove.** The Mariposa Grove trip takes 6 hours, includes the Big Trees tram tour that winds through the grove, and stops for lunch at Wawona (lunch is not provided). You can combine the trip to Glacier Point and Mariposa Grove in an 8-hour bus ride.

Giant sequoias, Yosemite.

If you're staying in the valley, the **Park Service** and **Yosemite Concession Services** present evening programs on park history and culture. Past summer programs have included discussions on early expeditions to Yosemite, the park's flora and fauna, geology, global ecology, and the legends of the American Indians who once lived here. Other programs have focused on Mark Wellman's courageous climb of El Capitan—he made the ascent as a paraplegic—and threats to Yosemite's environment.

AVOIDING THE CROWDS   Popularity isn't always the greatest thing for wild places. Over the past 20 years, Yosemite Valley has set records for the worst crowding, noise, crime, and traffic in any California national park.

The park covers more than 1,000 square miles, but most visitors flock to the floor of Yosemite Valley, the 1-mile-wide, 7-mile-long glacial scouring that tore a deep and steep valley from the solid granite of the Sierra Nevada. It becomes a total zoo between Memorial Day and Labor Day. Cars line up bumper to bumper on almost any busy weekend, and Yosemite's superintendent has been known to close the entrances to the park occasionally between Memorial Day and mid-August when the number of visitors reaches the park's quota.

My advice is to visit before Memorial Day or after Labor Day. If you must go in summer, do your part to help out. It's not so much the numbers of people that are ruining the valley, but their insistence on driving through it. Once you're here, park your car and then bike, hike, or ride the shuttle buses. You can rent bicycles at **Curry Village** (© **209/372-8319**) and **Yosemite Lodge** (© **209/372-1208**) in summer. It may take longer to get from point A to point B, but you're in one of the most beautiful places on Earth—so why hurry?

Exploring the Park

THE VALLEY

First-time visitors are often dumbstruck as they enter the valley from the west. The first two things you'll see are the delicate and beautiful **Bridalveil Fall ★★** and the immense face of **El Capitan ★★**, a stunning 3,593-foot-tall solid-granite rock. A short trail leads to the base of Bridalveil, which, at 620 feet tall, is only a medium-size fall by park standards, but one of the prettiest.

This is a perfect chance to get those knee-jerk tourist impulses under control early: Resist the temptation to rush around seeing everything. Take your time. Look around. One of the best things about the valley is that many of its most famous features are visible from all over. Instead of rushing to the base of every waterfall or famous rock face and getting a crick in your neck from staring straight up, go to the visitor center and spend a half-hour learning something. Buy the excellent *Map and Guide to Yosemite Valley* for $2.50; it describes many hikes and short nature walks. Then go take a look. Walking and biking are the best ways to get around. To cover longer distances, the park shuttles run frequently around the east end of the valley.

Three-quarters of a mile from the visitor center is the **Ahwahnee Hotel** (p. 367). Unlike other park lodgings, the Ahwahnee lives up to its surroundings. The native granite-and-timber lodge, built in 1927, reflects an era when grand hotels were, well, grand. Fireplaces bigger than most Manhattan studio apartments warm the immense common rooms. Parlors and halls are filled with antique Native American rugs. Don't worry about your attire unless you're going to dinner—this is Yosemite, after all.

The best view in the valley is from **Sentinel Bridge ★** over the Merced River. At sunset, Half Dome's face functions as a projection screen for the many hues of the sinking sun—from yellow to pink to dark purple, and the river reflects it all. Ansel Adams took one of his most famous photographs from this very spot.

The **Nature Center at Happy Isles ★** has great hands-on nature exhibitions for kids, plus a wheelchair-accessible path along the banks of the Merced River.

VALLEY WALKS & HIKES Yosemite Falls is within a short stroll of the visitor center. You can see it better elsewhere in the valley, but it's impressive to stand at the base of all that falling water. The wind, noise, and spray generated when millions of gallons catapult 2,425 feet through space onto the rocks below are sometimes so overwhelming you can barely stand on the bridge.

The **Upper Yosemite Fall Trail ★** zigzags 3.5 miles from

El Capitan, Yosemite.

Sunnyside Campground to the top of Upper Yosemite Fall. This trail gives you an inkling of the weird, vertically oriented world that climbers enter when they scale Yosemite's sheer walls. As you climb this narrow switchback, the valley floor drops away until people below look like ants, but the top doesn't appear any closer. It's unnerving at first, but rewarding in the end. Plan on spending all day on this 7-mile round-trip trail because of the incredibly steep climb.

Rock climbing, Yosemite.

A mile-long trail leads from the Valley Stables (take the shuttle; no car parking) to **Mirror Lake ★**. The already-tiny lake is gradually becoming a meadow as it fills with silt, but the reflections of the valley walls and sky on its surface remain one of the park's most unforgettable sights.

Also accessible from the Valley Stables or nearby Happy Isles is the best valley hike of all—the **John Muir Trail ★★** to Vernal and Nevada falls. It follows the Sierra crest 200 miles south to Mount Whitney, but you need go only 1.5 miles round-trip to get a great view of 317-foot Vernal Fall. Add another 1.5 miles and 1,000 vertical feet for the climb to the top of Vernal Fall on the **Mist Trail ★**, where you'll get wet as you climb alongside the falls. On top of Vernal and before the base of Nevada Fall is a beautiful valley and deep pool. For an outrageous view of the valley and one heck of a workout, continue up the Mist Trail to the top of Nevada Fall. From 2,000 feet above Happy Isles, where you began, it's a dizzying view straight down the face of the fall. To the east is an interesting profile perspective of Half Dome. Return by either the Mist Trail or the slightly easier John Muir Trail for a 7-mile round-trip hike.

Half Dome ★★★ may look insurmountable to anyone but an expert rock climber, yet thousands take the strenuous yet popular cable route up the backside every year. It's almost 17 miles round-trip and a 4,900-foot elevation gain from Happy Isle on the John Muir Trail. Many do it in a day, starting at first light and rushing home to beat nightfall. A more relaxed strategy is to camp in the backpacking campground in Little Yosemite Valley just past Nevada Fall. From here, the summit is within easy striking distance of the base of Half Dome. If you plan to spend the night, you need a Wilderness Pass (see "Camping," below). You must climb up a very steep granite face using steel cables installed by the park service. In summer, rangers also install boards as crossbeams, but they're still far apart. Wear shoes with lots of traction and bring your own leather gloves for the cables (your hands will thank you). Given any chance of a thunderstorm, the trail closes; that cable turns into a lighting rod, so they don't take any risks. The summit yields unbeatable views of the high country, Tenaya Canyon,

SOUTHERN YOSEMITE MOUNTAIN guides

Of the dozens of outdoor recreation companies that offer guided hiking and backpacking trips throughout the Yosemite region, the best is **Southern Yosemite Mountain Guides.** For nearly 2 decades, the professional guides from SYMG have been leading visitors to the most spectacular wilderness regions throughout Yosemite National Park and the High Sierra. SYMG founder and president Ian Elman and his staff are among the top outdoor guides in the nation and are masters at providing a fun, thrilling, and safe experience for all their clients, whether it's a casual naturalist-led day hike through the Giant Sequoias or a 7-day backpacking odyssey through Southern Yosemite's Ansel Adams Wilderness (one of the best-kept secrets of the region). SYMG also offers guided fly-fishing and mountaineering trips, as well as half-day and 1-day clinics on fly-fishing and rock climbing. Check out the wide variety of trips they offer on their website at **www.symg.com**, and then give Ian a call at ✆ **800/231-4575.**

Glacier Point, and the awe-inspiring abyss of the valley. When you shuffle up to the overhanging lip for a look down the face, be extremely careful not to kick rocks or anything else onto the climbers below, who are earning this view the hard way.

THE SOUTHWEST CORNER

This corner of the park is densely forested and gently sculpted, in comparison to the stark granite that makes up so much of Yosemite. Coming from the valley, Hwy. 41 takes you to **Tunnel View ★★★**, site of a famous Ansel Adams photograph, and the best scenic outlook of the valley accessible by car. Virtually the entire valley is laid out below: Half Dome and Yosemite Falls straight ahead in the distance, Bridalveil to the right, and El Capitan to the left.

A few miles past the tunnel, Glacier Point Road turns off to the east. Closed in winter, this winding road leads to a picnic area at **Glacier Point ★★**, site of another fabulous view of the valley, this time 3,000 feet below. Schedule at least an hour to drive here from the valley and an hour or two to absorb the view. This is a good place to study the glacial scouring of the valley; the Glacier Point perspective makes it easy to picture the landscape below filled with sheets of ice.

Some 30 miles south of the valley on Hwy. 41 are the **Wawona Hotel** (p. 368) and the **Pioneer Yosemite History Center.** The Wawona, built in 1879, is the oldest hotel in the park. Its Victorian architecture evokes a time when travelers spent days in horse-drawn wagons to get here. The Pioneer Center is a collection of early homesteading log buildings across the river from the Wawona.

One of the primary reasons Yosemite was set aside as a park was the **Mariposa Grove ★** of giant sequoias. (Many trails lead through it.) These huge trees have personalities to match their gargantuan size. Single limbs on the biggest tree in the grove, the Grizzly Giant, are 10 feet thick. The tree itself is 209 feet tall, 32 feet in diameter, and more than 2,700 years old. Totally out of scale with the size of the trees are the tiny sequoia cones. Smaller than a baseball and tightly closed, the cones won't release their cargo of seeds until opened by fire.

THE HIGH COUNTRY ★★★

Yosemite's high country is stunning. Dome after dome of crystalline granite reflects the sunlight above deep-green meadows and icy-cold rivers.

Tioga Pass is the gateway to the high country. At times, it clings to the side of steep rock faces; in other places, it weaves through canyon bottoms. Several good campgrounds make it a pleasing overnight escape from summertime crowds in the valley, although use is increasing here, too. **Tenaya Lake ★** is popular for windsurfing, fishing, canoeing, sailing, and swimming, but the water is chilly. Many good hikes lead into the high country from here, and the granite domes surrounding the lake are popular with climbers. Fishing varies greatly from year to year.

Tuolumne Meadows ★★ is near the top of Tioga Pass. Covering several square miles, this meadow is bordered by the Tuolumne River on one side and granite peaks on the other. The meadow is cut by many trout streams, and herds of mule deer are almost always present. The **Tuolumne Meadows Lodge** and store are a welcome counterpoint to the overdeveloped valley. In winter, they remove the canvas roofs and the buildings fill with snow. You can buy last-minute backpacking supplies here, or grab burgers and fries at the on-site cafe.

TUOLUMNE MEADOWS HIKES & WALKS   So many hikes lead from here into the backcountry that it's impossible to do them justice. A good trail passes an icy-cold spring and traverses several meadows.

On the far bank of the Tuolumne from the meadow, a trail leads downriver, eventually passing through the grand canyon of the Tuolumne and exiting at Hetch Hetchy. Shorter hikes will take you downriver past rapids and cascades.

An interesting geological quirk is the **Soda Springs,** on the far side of Tuolumne Meadow from the road. This bubbling spring gushes carbonated water from a hole in the ground; a small log cabin marks its site.

For a selection of Yosemite high-country hikes and backpacking trips, consult some of the guidebooks to the area. Two of the best are published by Wilderness Press: *Tuolumne Meadows,* a hiking guide by Jeffrey B. Shaffer and Thomas Winnett; and *Yosemite National Park,* by Thomas Winnett and Jason Winnett.

Sports & Outdoor Pursuits

BICYCLING   With 10 miles of bike paths in addition to the valley roads, biking is an ideal way to get around the park. You can rent bikes at the **Yosemite Lodge** (✆ **209/372-1208**) or **Curry Village** (✆ **209/372-8319**) for about $7.50 per hour or $24 per day. You can also rent bike trailers for little kids at $14 per hour or $42 per day. All hiking trails in the park are closed to mountain bikes.

FISHING   Trout season begins on the last Saturday in April and continues through November 15. The Merced River from Happy Isles downstream to the Pohono Bridge is catch-and-release only for native rainbow trout, and barbless hooks are required. Everyone 16 years old or more must display a California license to fish. Get licenses at the Yosemite Village Sport Shop (✆ **209/372-1286**). Guided fly-fishing trips in Yosemite for all levels are available from **Southern Yosemite Mountain Guides** (✆ **800/231-4575;** www.symg.com). ***Note:*** Yosemite Valley has special fishing regulations; get information at the visitor centers.

GOLF   The park has one golf course and several others nearby. **Wawona** (☎ **209/375-6572**) sports a 9-hole, par-35 course that alternates between meadows and fairways. Just outside the park is the 18-hole **Sierra Meadows Ranch Course** (☎ **559/642-1343**) in Oakhurst. Call for current fees and other information.

HORSEBACK RIDING   Three stables offer day rides and multiday excursions in the park. **Yosemite Valley Stables** (☎ **209/372-8348**) is open spring through fall. The other two—**Wawona** (☎ **209/375-6502**) and **Tuolumne Stables** (☎ **209/372-8427**)—operate only in summer. Day rides run from about $60 to $119, depending on length. Multiday backcountry trips cost roughly $100 per day and must be booked almost a year in advance. The park wranglers can also be hired to make resupply drops at any of the High Sierra Camps, if you plan an extended trip. Log on to **www.yosemitepark tours.com** (click on "Activities") for more information.

ICE-SKATING   The **Curry Village Ice Rink** (☎ **209/372-8319**) is fun in winter. It's outdoors, however, and melts quickly when the weather warms up. Rates are $8 for adults and $6 for children 11 and under. Skate rentals are $3.

RAFTING   Rafting 3 leisurely miles down the Merced River is one of the most refreshing ways to see Yosemite Valley's spectacular scenery. At the raft rental shop in Curry Village (☎ **209/372-8319**), daily fees are a mere $26 for adults and $16 for children 12 and under. Fees include a raft, paddles, mandatory life preservers, and transportation from Sentinel Beach to Curry Village. Swift currents and cold water can be deadly to young kids, so children less than 50 pounds are not permitted in rental rafts. Log on to **www. yosemiteparktours.com** (click on "Activities") for more information. Also read the "White-Water Rafting Adventures" sidebar on p. 354.

ROCK CLIMBING   Much of the most technical advancement in rock climbing grew out of the highly competitive Yosemite Valley climbing scene of the 1970s and 1980s. Other places have since stepped into the limelight, but Yosemite is still one of the most desirable climbing destinations in the world.

The **Yosemite Mountaineering School** (☎ **209/372-8344;** www. yosemitepark.com) runs classes for beginning through advanced climbers. Considered one of the best climbing schools in the world, it offers private lessons that will teach you basic body moves and rappelling, and will take you on a single-pitch climb. Classes run from early spring to early October in the valley, and during summer in Tuolumne Meadows.

SKIING & SNOWSHOEING   Opened in 1935, **Badger Pass** (☎ **209/372-8430;** www.yosemitepark.com) is the oldest operating ski area in California and great for families. Four chairs and one rope tow cover a compact mountain, with beginner and intermediate runs. At $42 for adults, $37 for youths from 13 to 17, and $20 for children from 7 to 12 (kids 6 and under free with adult), it's a great place to learn how to ski or snowboard. Naturalists lead special winter children's programs, and the facility provides babysitting.

Yosemite is also popular with **cross-country skiers and snowshoers.** Both the Badger Pass ski school and the mountaineering school run trips and lessons for all abilities, ranging from basic technique to trans-Sierra crossings. Two ski huts can accommodate anyone taking guided cross-country tours, including the spiffy **Glacier Point Hut** (✆ **209/372-8444**), with its massive stone fireplace, beamed ceilings, and bunk beds; and the **Ostrander Hut** (✆ **209/379-2646;** www.ostranderhut.com), with 25 bunks. You have to pack in your own supplies, however. If you're on your own, Crane Flat is a good place to go, as is the groomed track up to Glacier Point, a 20-mile round-trip self-guided tour.

Camping

Campgrounds in Yosemite can be reserved up to 5 months in advance through the **National Park Reservation Service** (✆ **877/444-6777;** www.recreation. gov). *Be warned:* During busy season, all valley campsites sell out within hours of becoming available on the service.

Backpacking into the wilderness and camping there is the least crowded option and takes less planning than reserving a campground. If you plan to camp in the wilderness, you must get a free **Wilderness Pass** (and pay the park entrance fee). At least 40% of each trail-head quota is allocated up to 24 hours in advance; the rest is available by mail. Write to the Yosemite Association, P.O. Box 545, Yosemite, CA 95389. Specify the dates and trail heads of entry and exit, the destination, number of people, and any accompanying animals; include a $5-per-person advance-registration fee. You may also call ✆ **209/372-0740** for a pass.

VALLEY CAMPGROUNDS

Until January 1997, the park had five car campgrounds that were always full except in the dead of winter. Now the park has half the number of campsites, and getting a reservation on short notice takes a minor miracle. (Yosemite Valley lost almost half of its 900 camping spaces in a freak winter storm in 1997; it washed several campsites downstream and buried hundreds more beneath a foot of silt.)

The two-and-a-half remaining campgrounds—**North Pines, Upper Pines,** and half of **Lower Pines**—charge $20 to $30 per night. All have drinking water, flush toilets, pay phones, fire pits, and heavy ranger presence. Showers are available for a small fee at Curry Village. Upper Pines, North Pines, and Lower Pines allow small RVs (less than 40 ft. long). If you're expecting a real nature experience, skip camping in the valley unless you like doing so with 4,000 strangers.

Custom Camping

If you want to experience the fun of camping without the hassle, the **Evergreen Lodge (p. 349)** might have the perfect solution for you. It's called Custom Camping, where guests sleep in spacious and fully furnished mesh-topped tents that are already set up and ready to go. Each tent includes a comfy air bed, sleeping bags and liners, pillows, towels, quality toiletries, camping chairs, and a battery-powered lantern. Perks include a communal fire pit for roasting marshmallows, picnic tables, a spotless his-and-hers bathhouse offering private hot showers 24 hours a day, and full access to the resort's restaurant, tavern, and recreational activities. Tent rates range from $70 to $95 per night for one to four people and are available from May to October. Space is limited, so be sure to book in advance. For more information, call ✆ **209/379-2606** or log on to **www.evergreenlodge.com.**

All hotel reservations can be made exactly 366 days in advance. Call **Yosemite Concessions Services** at 📞 **801/559-4884** in the morning 366 days before your intended arrival for the best chance of securing a spot. If you don't plan that far in advance, it's still worth calling, because cancellations may leave new openings. You may also book reservations online through **www. yosemitepark.com**. Reservations without-out a deposit must be confirmed on the scheduled day of arrival by 4pm. Other-wise, you'll lose your reservation.

Camp 4 (previously named Sunnyside campground) is a year-round, walk-in campground that fills quickly since it's only $5 per night. Hard-core climbers used to live here for months at a time. The park service has stopped them, but this site still has a more bohemian atmosphere than any of the other campgrounds.

CAMPGROUNDS ELSEWHERE IN THE PARK

Outside the valley, things open up for campers. Two car campgrounds near the South Entrance of the park, **Wawona** and **Bridalveil Creek,** offer a total of 210 sites with all the amenities. Wawona is open year-round, and reservations are required May through September; otherwise, it's first-come, first-served. Family sites at Wawona are $20 per night, and group sites, which hold up to 30 people, are $40 per night. Because it sits well above the snow line, at more than 7,000 feet, Bridalveil is open only in summer. Rates are $14 per night for first-come, first-served sites, and $40 for group sites.

Crane Flat, Hodgdon Meadow, and Tamarack Flat are all in the western corner of the park near the Big Oak Flat Entrance. **Crane Flat** is the nearest to the valley, about a half-hour drive away, with 166 sites, water, flush toilets, and fire pits. Its rates are $20 per night, and it's open July through September. **Hodg-don Meadow** is directly adjacent to the Big Oak Flat Entrance at 4,800 feet elevation. It's open year-round, charges $20 per night, and requires reservations May through September through the National Park Reservation Service. Facili-ties include flush toilets, running water, a ranger station, and pay phones. It's one of the least crowded low-elevation car campgrounds, but you won't find lots to do here. **Tamarack Flat** is a waterless, 52-site campground with pit toilets. Open June through October, it's a bargain, at $10 per night.

Tuolumne Meadows, White Wolf, Yosemite Creek, and Porcupine Flat are all above 8,000 feet, open only in summer. **Tuolumne Meadows ★** is the park's largest campground, with more than 300 spaces. It absorbs the crowd well and has all the amenities, including campfire programs and slide shows in the out-door amphitheater. You, however, will feel sardine-packed between hundreds of other visitors. Half of the sites are reserved in advance; the rest are set aside on a first-come, first-served basis. Rates are $20 per night.

White Wolf, west of Tuolumne Meadows, is the other full-service camp-ground in the high country, with 74 sites available for $14 per night for family sites. It offers a drier climate than the meadow and doesn't fill up as quickly. Sites are available on a first-come, first-served basis.

Two primitive camps, **Porcupine Flat** and **Yosemite Creek,** are the last to fill up in the park. Both have pit toilets but no running water, and charge $10 per night on a first-come, first-served basis.

Where to Stay in the Park

Yosemite Concessions Services, P.O. Box 578, Yosemite National Park, CA 95389 (☏ **801/559-4884**), operates all accommodations within the park and accepts all major credit cards. The reservations office is open Monday through Friday from 7am to 7pm, Saturday and Sunday from 8am to 5pm (PST). For more lodging options and information, or to make an online reservation request, visit **www.yosemitepark.com**.

Yosemite's five backcountry **High Sierra Camps** (☏ **559/253-5674**) bridge the gap between backpacking and hotel stays. The camps are good individual destinations. Or you can link several together, because they're arranged in a loose loop about a 10-mile hike from one another. Guests bunk dormitory-style in canvas tents; each camp has bathrooms and showers. Due to the huge popularity of these camps, management books reservations by lottery. They accept applications from October 15 to November 30, hold the lottery in December, and notify winners by the end of March.

The Ahwahnee Hotel ★★★ A National Historic Landmark noted for its granite-and-redwood architecture, the six-story Ahwahnee is one of the most romantic and beautiful hotels in California. With its soaring lobby, cathedral-like dining room, outstanding views, and steep prices, it's definitely worthy of the most special occasions. Try to reserve one of the more spacious cottages, which cost the same as rooms in the main hotel. For the price, the guest rooms—though pleasant—are simple to the point of austerity. On the other hand, you can look right out your window and see Half Dome, Yosemite Falls, or Glacier Point. The **Ahwahnee Restaurant** is a colossal, impressive chamber with 50-foot-tall, floor-to-ceiling leaded windows. It's more noteworthy for its ambience, however, than for its expensive cuisine.

www.yosemitepark.com. ☏ **209/372-1489.** 99 units, 24 cottages. $239–$984 double. Children 12 and under stay free in parent's room. AE, DC, DISC, MC, V. Pets are not accepted, but they can board in the kennel at the park stables. **Amenities:** Restaurant and lounge; babysitting (need 2 weeks' notice; child must be potty trained and at least 2 years old); concierge; nearby golf course; Jacuzzi; heated outdoor pool; room service; 2 tennis courts. *In room:* A/C (ceiling fan in cottages), TV, fridge in cottages, hair dryer.

Curry Village ☺ Celebrating its 110th birthday in 2009, Curry Village is best known as a mass of more than 400 white canvas tents tightly packed together on

---

A Cottage in the Woods

Yosemite West Reservations (www.yosemitewestreservations.com; ☏ **559/642-2211**) rents a variety of privately owned accommodations, ranging from fairly simple rooms with one queen-size bed and kitchenette (suitable for one or two people) to luxurious vacation homes with full-size kitchens, two bathrooms, living rooms, and beds for as many as eight people. Kitchens and kitchenettes are fully equipped, all bedding is provided, TVs and VCRs are on hand, and outdoor decks allow you to soak up the verdant views. All units also have gas or wood-burning fireplaces. The homes are in a forested section of the park, about 10 miles from Yosemite Valley and 8 miles from Badger Pass. Most units range from $195 to $495 per night.

the valley's south slope. It was founded in 1899 to provide inexpensive lodgings at a mere $2 a day, and it's still an economical place to crash. One downside is that these tents are basically canvas affairs, and this is bear country, so you'll need to lock up all foodstuffs and anything that bears might think is food (even toothpaste) in bear-proof lockers. They're free, but they may be a healthy walk from your tent-cabin. Curry Village also has more than 100 attractive wood cabins with private bathrooms, and about 80 wood cabins that, like the tent-cabins, share a large bathhouse. There are a number of motel rooms as well. Canvas tents have wood floors and sleep two to four people, with beds, bedding, dressers, and electrical outlets. The wood cabins and motel rooms are much more substantial and comfortable, but cost more than twice the price. **Note:** If Curry Village is full, inquire about available canvas tents-cabins at Tuolumne Meadows Lodge or White Wolf Lodge.

www.yosemitepark.com. © **801/559-5000.** 628 units. $85–$207 double. Extra person $10–$14. Children 12 and under stay free in parent's room. AE, DC, DISC, MC, V. **Amenities:** Buffet-style dining from spring to fall; fast-food court; bike rental; nearby golf course; heated outdoor pool. *In room:* No phone.

Wawona Hotel ★   Six stately white buildings, set near towering trees in a green clearing, make up this classic, Victorian-style hotel. Don't be surprised if a horse and buggy round the driveway by the fishpond—it's that kind of place. What makes it so wonderful? Maybe it's the wide porches, the nearby 9-hole golf course, or the vines of hops cascading from one veranda to the next. The entire place was designated a National Historic Landmark in 1987. Clark Cottage is the oldest building, dating from 1876, and the main hotel was built in 1879. Rooms are comfortable and quaint, with a choice of a double and a twin bed, a king bed, or one double bed. (Most of the latter share bathrooms.) All rooms open onto wide porches and overlook green lawns. Clark Cottage is the most intimate. The main hotel has the widest porches and plenty of Adirondack chairs, and at night a pianist performs in the downstairs sunroom. **Note:** Nonguests attend the Saturday-evening summer **lawn barbecues** or Sunday brunch.

www.yosemitepark.com. © **801/559-5000.** 104 units, 52 with private bathroom. $126 double without private bathroom; $198 double with private bathroom. Extra person $16. Children 12 and under stay free in parent's room. AE, DC, DISC, MC, V. **Amenities:** Restaurant; golf course; swimming tank; tennis court. *In room:* No phone.

Yosemite Lodge at the Falls   The next step down in valley accommodations, Yosemite Lodge is not actually a lodge, but a large, more modern complex with two types of accommodations: standard rooms and more spacious Lodge rooms with outdoor balconies that have striking views of Yosemite Falls. Indeed, the largest bonus—and curse—is that every Lodge room's patio or balcony has a view of the valley floor, which means you're near glorious, larger-than-life natural attractions and equally gargantuan crowds.

www.yosemitepark.com. © **801/559-5000.** 249 units. $113–$180 double. Extra person $10–$12. Children 12 and under stay free in parent's room. AE, DC, DISC, MC, V. **Amenities:** 2 restaurants; food court; bar; bike rental; nearby golf course; Internet access; heated outdoor pool.

Where to Eat

IN THE PARK

You certainly won't go hungry here; you'll find plenty of dining options in or near the park. There aren't many bargains, however, so bring a full wallet.

IN THE VALLEY

Ahwahnee Dining Room ★★ AMERICAN/INTERNATIONAL   Even if you are a dyed-in-the-wool, sleep-under-the-stars backpacker, the Ahwahnee Dining Room will not fail to impress you. With understated elegance, the cavernous dining room, with its candelabra chandeliers hanging from the 34-foot beamed ceiling, seems intimate once you're seated. The menu changes frequently, with a good variety of creative yet recognizable dishes. The dinner menu includes suggested wines (from an extensive wine list) for each entree. An evening dress code requires men to wear a jacket and long pants (ties are optional).

Ahwahnee Hotel, Yosemite Valley. ✆ **209/372-1489.** Dinner reservations required. Breakfast $8–$20; lunch $8–$15; dinner $25–$40; Sun brunch $32 adults, $17 children. DC, DISC, MC, V. Mon–Sat 7–10:30am, 11:30am–3pm, and 5:30–7pm; Sun 7am–3pm and 5:30–9pm. Shuttle bus stop: 3.

Curry Taqueria Stand MEXICAN   A good place for a quick bite, this taco stand peddles spicy tacos, burritos, taco salads, beans, and rice.

Curry Village. No phone. $3–$6. No credit cards. Daily 11am–5pm. Closed in winter. Shuttle bus stops: 12, 13, 14, or 19.

Curry Village Ice Cream & Coffee Corner COFFEE SHOP   Specialty coffees and fresh-baked pastries are the fare here. You can buy coffee after 11am at the Pizza Deck and Taqueria.

Curry Village, Yosemite Valley. No phone. Most items $1–$3. DC, DISC, MC, V. Daily 7–11am. Shuttle bus stops: 12, 13, 14, or 19.

Curry Village Pavilion ☺ AMERICAN   The Pavilion is a good spot for the very hungry. All-you-can-eat breakfast and dinner buffets offer a wide variety of well-prepared basic American selections at fairly reasonable prices.

Curry Village. No phone. Breakfast $9.25 adults, $5.50 children; dinner $12 adults, $6.25 children. DC, DISC, MC, V. Daily 7–10am and 5:30–8pm. Shuttle bus stops: 12, 13, 14, or 19.

Curry Village Pizza Deck ★ ☺ PIZZA   Need to watch ESPN? This is the place, but you may have to wait in line. One of the park's few big screens awaits inside, and if you're a sports buff, this is the place to be. The scenic outdoor patio offers large umbrellas, table service, and a great view of Mother Nature, plus or minus 100 kids. The lounge also taps a few brews—nothing special, but a mix aimed to please. This is a great place to chill after a long day.

Curry Village, Yosemite Valley. No phone. Pizza $8–$16. DC, DISC, MC, V. Mon–Fri 5–9pm; Sat–Sun noon–9pm. Shuttle bus stop: 12, 13, 14, or 19.

Degnan's Cafe AMERICAN   Adjacent to Degnan's Deli, this cafe offers specialty coffee drinks, fresh pastries, wrap sandwiches, and ice cream. It's a good place for a quick bite when you're in a hurry.

Yosemite Village. ✆ **209/372-0200.** Most items $1–$4. DC, DISC, MC, V. Daily 11am–5pm. Shuttle bus stop: D, 2, or 8.

Degnan's Deli ★★ ✦ DELI   A solid delicatessen with a large selection of generous sandwiches made to order, this is our top choice for a quick, healthy lunch or supper. Sometimes the line gets long, but it moves quickly. Half market and half deli, Degnan's also sells a selection of prepared items such as soups, salads, sandwiches, desserts, and snacks. The beer and wine selection is also good.

9

THE HIGH SIERRA | Yosemite National Park

Yosemite Village. ☎ **209/372-0200.** $3–$8. DC, DISC, MC, V. Daily 7am–5pm. Shuttle bus stops: D, 2, or 8.

Degnan's Loft ☺ ITALIAN   This cheery restaurant, with a central fireplace and high-beamed ceilings, is adjacent to Degnan's Deli and Degnan's Cafe. It's a good choice for families, with a kid-friendly atmosphere and a menu that features pizza, calzones, lasagna, salads, and desserts.

Yosemite Village. ☎ **209/372-0200.** Entrees $4.25–$21. DC, DISC, MC, V. Mon–Fri 4–9pm; Sat–Sun noon–9pm. Shuttle bus stop: D, 2, or 8.

Mountain Room Restaurant AMERICAN   The best thing about this restaurant is the view. The food's good too, but the floor-to-ceiling windows overlooking Yosemite Falls are spectacular, and there's not a bad seat in the house. Try the chicken *champignon,* which is flavorful and moist, as are the mountain trout and the Pacific yellowfin tuna. Meals come with vegetables and bread. Soup or salad is extra. The menu includes entrees for vegetarians, and the dessert tray is amazing. The Mountain Room also has a good wine list, and the Mountain Room Bar and Lounge (4–10pm Mon–Fri and noon–10pm Sat–Sun) has an a la carte menu.

Yosemite Lodge. ☎ **209/372-0200.** Entrees $17–$30. DC, DISC, MC, V. Daily 5:30–9pm. Shuttle bus stop: 6.

Village Grill AMERICAN   The Village Grill is a decent place to pick up fast food. It offers burgers, chicken sandwiches, and the like, and has outdoor seating.

Yosemite Village. ☎ **209/372-0200.** Most items $3.75–$5.25. No credit cards. Daily 11am–5pm. Closed in winter. Shuttle bus stop: 1, 2, or 8.

Yosemite Lodge Food Court AMERICAN   You'll find breakfast, lunch, and dinner at this busy restaurant, which serves about 2,000 meals each day. A vast improvement over the traditional cafeteria, it's set up with a series of food stations, where you pick up your choices before heading to the centralized cashier. You can eat inside or in the outside seating area, which features good views of Yosemite Falls.

Yosemite Lodge. ☎ **209/372-0200.** Entrees $5–$14. DC, DISC, MC, V. Daily 6:30–10am, 11:30am–2pm, and 5–8:30pm. Shuttle bus stop: 8.

ELSEWHERE IN THE PARK

Tuolumne Meadows Lodge AMERICAN   One of the two restaurants in the high country, this lodge has something for everyone. The breakfast menu features the basics, including eggs, pancakes, fruit, oatmeal, and granola. Dinners always include a beef, chicken, fish, pasta, and vegetarian special, all of which change frequently. The quality can vary, but the prime rib and New York steak are consistently good.

Tuolumne Meadows. ☎ **209/372-8413.** Reservations required for dinner. Breakfast $3.55–$6.95; dinner $8.65–$19. DC, DISC, MC, V. Daily 7–9am and 6–8pm.

Wawona Hotel Dining Room ★★ AMERICAN   Like the hotel, the Wawona dining room is wide open, with lots of windows and sunlight, and the food is great. For breakfast, choose from a variety of items, including the Meadowloop Special, a combo of French toast, eggs, and bacon, ham, or sausage—to fuel you up before you hit the golf course. Lunch features a variety of sandwiches and salads. Dinner appetizers are amazing, and a number of entrees are exceptional—such as Vietnamese shrimp lettuce wraps or a roasted eggplant, lemon, herb, and garlic dip served with pita chips.

Wawona Hotel, Wawona Rd. © **209/375-1425.** Breakfast $3–$13; lunch $5–$17; dinner $20–$25. Sun buffet $9.95 breakfast, $16 brunch. DC, DISC, MC, V. Mon–Sat 7:30–10am, 11:30am–1:30pm, 5:30–9pm; Sun 7:30–10am (breakfast buffet), 10:30am–1:30pm (brunch buffet), and 5:30–9pm.

White Wolf Lodge AMERICAN   This casual restaurant has a mountain lodge atmosphere and a changing menu, serving generous portions of American standards. Breakfast choices include eggs, pancakes, omelets, or biscuits and gravy; and dinner always includes beef, chicken, fish, pasta, and vegetarian dishes. Takeout lunches are also available from noon to 2pm.

White Wolf, Tioga Rd. © **209/372-8416.** Reservations required for dinner. Breakfast $4–$8; dinner $7–$19. DC, DISC, MC, V. Daily 7:30–9:30am and 5–8:30pm.

MAMMOTH LAKES ★★

40 miles SE of Yosemite; 319 miles E of San Francisco; 325 miles NE of Los Angeles

High in the Sierra, southeast of Yosemite, Mammoth Lakes is surrounded by glacier-carved, pine-covered peaks that soar up from flower-filled meadows. It's an alpine region of sweeping beauty and one of California's favorite playgrounds for hiking, biking, fishing, horseback riding, skiing, and more. It's also home to one of the world's top-rated ski resorts. At an elevation of 11,053 feet, Mammoth Mountain is higher than either Squaw or Heavenly, so the snow stays firm longer into the year for spring skiing. You won't find Tahoe's long lift lines, either—just more mountain and fewer people.

Essentials

GETTING THERE   It's a 6-hour drive from San Francisco via Hwy. 120 over the Tioga Pass in Yosemite (closed in winter); 5 hours north of Los Angeles via Hwy. 14 and U.S. 395; and 3 hours south of Reno, Nevada, via U.S. 395. In winter, Mammoth is accessible via U.S. 395 from the north or the south.

Mammoth Air Charter (© **888/934-4279**) offers charter flights to the area. It services Mammoth Lakes Airport on U.S. 395. As of late

Mammoth Mountain.

2009, **Alaska Airlines** (© **800/252-7522;** www.alaskaair.com) operates daily flights into the airport from Los Angeles—nonstop twice daily during the winter, once daily during the summer. During winter months Alaska Airlines offers nonstop daily flights from San Jose and direct from Portland, Oregon. **United Airlines** (**800/864-8331;** www.united.com) has daily nonstop flights from San Francisco. Even better, you'll receive a free lift ticket the day you fly with presentation of your boarding pass at the ski resort. Flights operate from mid-December to mid-April. The closest international airport is Reno–Tahoe Airport (📞 **775/328-6400**). See "Lake Tahoe," in chapter 8, for some airlines that service the Reno–Tahoe International Airport.

VISITOR INFORMATION   Contact the **Mammoth Lakes Tourism,** 2510 Main St./Hwy. 203 (P.O. Box 48), Mammoth Lakes, CA 93546 (📞 **888/466-2666** or 760/934-2712; www.visitmammoth.com).

Outdoor Pursuits

At the heart of several wilderness areas, Mammoth Lakes is cut through by the San Joaquin and Owens rivers. Mammoth Mountain overlooks the Ansel Adams Wilderness Area to the west and the John Muir Wilderness Area to the southeast, and beyond to the Inyo National Forest.

The **Mammoth Mountain Ski Area** ★★ (📞 **800/626-6684** or 760/934-2571; www.mammothmountain.com) is the central focus for summer and winter activities. Visitors can ride the lifts just to see panoramic vistas, but those who want an active adventure have many options. If you do hit the slopes in winter, you can use the free **Mammoth Area Shuttle** (📞 **760/934-3184**) or **Sierra Express** taxi service (📞 **760/934-8294**) for transportation between town and the ski area. The shuttle makes many stops and eliminates the long wait that may befall you if you drive yourself.

The state-of-the-art **Gondola** provides great viewing every day, in winter or summer, weather permitting. The gondola carries eight passengers and stops midway up the mountain and at the summit with 360-degree views. In summer, you can use it to access the hiking and biking trails on the mountain. Tickets are $23 for adults, $17 for youths 13 to 18, $12 kids 7 to 12, and kids 6 and under ride free.

In addition to the most popular activities listed below, adventurers can go hot-air ballooning with **Mammoth Balloon Adventures** (📞 **760/937-UPUP** [8787]; www.mammothballoonadventures.com). And golfers can play at **Snowcreek Golf Course,** Old Mammoth Road (📞 **760/934-6633;** www.snowcreek resort.com).

HIKING   Trails abound in the Mammoth Lakes Basin area. They include the half-mile **Panorama Dome Trail,** past the turnoff to Twin Lakes on Lake Mary Road, leading to the top of a plateau with a view of the Owens Valley. The 5-mile **Duck Lake Trail** starts at the end of the Coldwater Creek parking lot with switchbacks across Duck Pass past several lakes to Duck Lake. The head of the **Inyo Craters Trail** is accessible via a gravel road, off the Mammoth Scenic Loop Road. It leads you to the edge of these craters, where a sign explains how they were created.

For additional trail information and maps, contact the **California Welcome Center, Mammoth Lakes** (📞 **760/924-5500**). For equipment and maps, go to **Kittredge Sports** (3218 Main St., 📞 **760/934-7566**), which also hosts a website of employee-suggested hikes—ranked from easy to advanced—throughout the Mammoth Lakes Region: www. kittredge.net/hiking/hiking.php.

HORSEBACK RIDING & PACKING TRIPS   The region is great for horseback riding, and numerous outfitters offer day rides and pack trips. Among them are **Mammoth Lakes Pack Outfit,** on Lake Mary Road past Twin Lakes

CAT GOT YOUR lunch?

Want a really cool après-ski experience you can't find every day? Then hop aboard a snowcat and explore the backcountry from the comfort of your heated plow, visiting mountain peaks you wouldn't be able to reach by a chairlift. Once you're at the viewing area to view the jagged Sierra skyline, your driver will pull over to an area of (often snow-covered) picnic tables and set up a scrumptious feast, complete with wine. You get bonus points if it's snowing profusely and you leave saying you had a picnic in a blizzard. Lunch tours run at 11:30am on weekends and holidays; sunset tours with appetizers and champagne are available on Fridays, Saturdays, and Sundays, as well as holidays. Full dinners at 9,600 feet occur on Friday and Saturday nights and holidays. Tour costs are $82–$89 for adults, $42–$49 for children. Reservations are required. To book, call ✆ **800/MAMMOTH** (626-6684).

(✆ **888/475-8747** or 760/934-2434; www.mammothpack.com), offering day rides, multiday riding trips, and semiannual horse drives; **Red's Meadows Pack Station** at Red's Meadows, past Minaret Vista (✆ **800/292-7758** or 760/934-2345; www.redsmeadow.com); and **McGee Creek Pack Station,** McGee Creek Road at Crowley Lake (✆ **800/854-7407** or 760/935-4324; www.mcgeecreekpackstation.com).

KAYAKING Kayaks are available at Crowley Lake from **Caldera Kayaks** (✆ **760/934-1691;** www.calderakayak.com), starting at $40 per day for a single, $60 for a double. This outfitter offers guided tours on Crowley and Mono lakes for $60 and provides instruction as well.

MOUNTAIN BIKING In summer, Mammoth Mountain becomes one huge bike park and climbing playground. The bike park is famous for its **Kamikaze Downhill Trail,** an obstacle arena and slalom course where riders can test their balance and skill. Plenty of other trails accommodate gentler folk who just want to commune with nature and get a little exercise, and one area is designed for kids. Bike shuttles will haul you and your bike to the lower mountain trails if you want to skip the uphill part, or the gondola will take you to the summit and let you find your own way down. The park operates daily from 9am to 6pm, during summer months. A 1-day pass with unlimited access to the gondola, bike shuttle, and trail system is $42 for adults, $21 for kids ages 12 and under. A variety of rent-and-ride packages is available; for more information, call ✆ **800/MAMMOTH** (626-6684) or log on to **www.mammothmountain.com**.

In town, the **Footloose Sports Center** rents mountain bikes (and stand-up paddle boards) at the corner of Main Street and Old Mammoth Road (✆ **760/934-2400;** www.footloosesports.com). The **NORBA National Mountain Bike Championships** take place here in summer.

SNOW SPORTS In winter, Mammoth Mountain has more than 3,500 skiable acres, a 3,100-foot vertical drop, 150 trails (32 with snow making), and 30 lifts, including 7 high-speed quads. The terrain is 30% beginner, 40% intermediate, and 30% advanced. It's known for power sun, ideal spring skiing conditions, and anywhere from 8 to 12 feet of snow.

Tamarack Cross Country Ski Center (✆ **760/934-2442**; www. tamaracklodge.com/xcountry) runs a cross-country ski center, and snowshoeing for nonskiers.

If you're renting equipment, you'll save money if you do it in town instead of at the resort. We recommend **Footloose Sports Center,** at the corner of Main Street and Old Mammoth Road (✆ **760/934-2400;** www. footloosesports.com), and **Wave Rave Snowboard Shop,** on Main Street (Hwy. 203; ✆ **866/3-BOARDS** [326-2737] or 760/934-2471; www.wave ravesnowboardshop.com), for snowboards and accessories. And be sure to look for the "Mammoth Coupons" booklet in town for additional discounts at local rental shops.

The **June Mountain Ski Area** ★ (✆ **888/JUNEMTN** [586-3686] or 760/648-7733; www.junemountain.com), 20 minutes north of Mammoth, is smaller but offers many summer activities, as well as 500 skiable acres, a 2,590-foot vertical drop, 35 trails, and eight lifts, including high-speed quads. The terrain is 35% beginner, 45% intermediate, and 20% advanced. It's at the center of a chain of lakes—Grant, Silver, Gull, and June—visible from the scenic driving loop around Hwy. 158. It's especially beautiful in the fall, when the aspens are ablaze with gold.

Fancy a different kind of snowplowing? Book yourself on a snowmobile tour through **Mammoth Snowmobile Adventures** (Main Lodge; ✆ **800-MAMMOTH** [626-6684] or 760/934-9645), where you'll blaze groomed trails, zipping in and out of wooded canopies. The machines (complete with hand warmers) are suitable for beginners to operate, though they take some getting used to unless you're well versed on a motorcycle (the concept of

WINTER driving IN THE SIERRA

Winter driving in the Sierra Nevada Range can be dangerous. The most hazardous roads are often closed, but others are negotiable only by vehicles with four-wheel-drive or tire chains. Be prepared for sudden blizzards, and protect yourself by taking these important precautions:

○ Check road conditions before you set out by calling ✆ **800/427-7623.**

○ Let the rental-car company know you're planning to drive in snow, and ask whether the antifreeze is prepared for cold climates.

○ Make sure your heater and defroster work.

○ Always carry chains. In a blizzard, the police will not allow vehicles without chains on some highways. If you don't know how to put them on, you'll have to pay about $40 to have someone

"chain up" your car at the side of the road.

○ In your trunk, stow an ice scraper, a small shovel, sand or burlap for traction if you get stuck, warm blankets, and an extra car key (motorists often lock their keys in the car while chaining up).

○ Don't think winter ends in March. Snow can pile up high as late as April on the sides of the roads leading to the valley, and cold temperatures make additional snowfall more than plausible.

turning is similar). Prior to switching course and beginning your trip back to the lodge, you'll be able to visit a snow park, where you can race around a snowmobile track and test out some untouched powder on the outskirts. Just be sure to wear clothes you don't mind getting mucky: The gasoline fumes leave behind a stench. Walk-ins are welcome, but it's smart to make a reservation in advance. Tours run from mid-December to mid-April and cost $95 to $130 for a 1½-hour tour, $210 to $290 for 3 hours.

TROUT FISHING   Mammoth Lakes Basin sits in a canyon a couple of miles west of town, with lakes that have made the region known for trout fishing: Mary, Mamie, Horseshoe, George, and Twin. Southeast of town, Crowley Lake is also famous for trout fishing, as are the San Joaquin and Owens rivers. For more fishing information and guides, contact **Rick's Sport Center,** at 3241 Main St. (✆ **760/934-3416**); **Trout Fitter,** in the Shell Mart Center at Main Street and Old Mammoth Road (✆ **760/934-2517;** www.thetroutfitter.com); or **Kittredge Sports,** Main Street and Forest Trail (✆ **760/934-7566;** www.kittredgesports.com), which rents equipment, supplies, and guides; teaches fly-fishing; and offers backcountry trips.

Exploring the Surrounding Area

Bodie ★ (www.visitbodie.com), one of the most authentic ghost towns in the West, is about an hour's drive north of Mammoth, past the Tioga Pass entrance to Yosemite. In 1870, more than 10,000 people lived in Bodie, mining $32 million in gold; today it's an eerie shell full of ghost stories. En route to Bodie, you'll pass **Mono Lake** ★ (pronounced *Mow*-no), near Lee Vining, which has startling tufa towers arising from its surface—limestone deposits formed by underground springs. About 300 bird species nest or stop here during their migrations. Right off Hwy. 395 is the **Mono Basin Scenic Area Visitors Center** (✆ **760/647-3044;** www.monolake.

org; daily in summer, Thurs–Mon in winter), with scheduled guided tours and a terrific environmental and historical display of this hauntingly beautiful 60-square-mile desert salt lake. After touring the visitor center, head for the **South Tufa Area,** at the lake's southern end, for a closer look at the tufa formations and briny water. *Tip:* *Mono* means "flies" in the language of the Yokuts, the Native Americans who live south of this region; get to the lake's edge, and you'll see why the nickname is suitable.

Where to Stay

If you stay at the resort, you'll be steps from the lifts. If you opt for the town, you're closer to the restaurants and nightlife. Regardless, they're within a 5-minute drive of one another, so you can never be too far from the action.

Bodie.

More than 700 campsites service the area. They open on varying dates in June, depending on the weather. The largest are at Twin Lakes and Cold Water (both in the Mammoth Lakes Basin), Convict Lake, and Red's Meadow. For additional information, call the **Mammoth Ranger Station** (☎ **760/924-5500**).

Fern Creek Lodge 🎣   The best lodging deal in the region is 25 miles north of Mammoth. Less than a mile from the June Mountain ski areas, the Fern Creek Lodge is a spread of simple, fully furnished cabins on the sunrise side of the Eastern High Sierra. Built in 1927, it has seen its ups and downs, but thanks to the latest owners—the Hart family—the year-round fishing and skiing resort is better than ever. The least expensive cabins are small, with just enough room for a bed, a table and chairs, and a bathroom. All have fully equipped kitchens, and most have fireplaces. The units are all so different, your best bet is to call and tell them what you're looking for. Rooms don't have phones, but guests may use a pay phone on the premises.

4628 Hwy. 158, June Lake, CA 93529. www.ferncreeklodge.com. ☎ **800/621-9146** or 760/648-7722. 10 cabins, 4 apts. $75–$85 cabin for 2; $145–$200 cabin for 6; $295 cabin for 8. Extra person $10. AE, DISC, MC, V. Certain pets allowed, for $10. **Amenities:** Common barbecue area. *In room:* TV w/HBO, full kitchen.

Juniper Springs Resort ★★★ ☺   Conveniently located alongside the Eagle Express lifts, Juniper Springs is comparable in terms of style and amenities to the other large resorts/condo rentals nearby, but it's far more convenient. The location and handy lockers on the ground floor mean you can leave your belongings, strap on your equipment, and ski straight out of the hotel to the lifts. Since it's 1,000 feet or so down the mountain from Mammoth Mountain Inn and other lodging, some travelers find it easier to acclimate to the altitude than they do staying elsewhere. With a range of rooms—from studios to one- or two-bedroom condos to fancy town homes with three bedrooms—Juniper Springs is a great choice for families and groups. All units have kitchens, fireplaces, dining rooms, and ample space for extra bodies. Ask for a room in the Sunstone building; it's always a fan favorite. Bear in mind: Since the resort lacks air-conditioning, units have been known to get unbearably steamy in summertime. If you're flying into Mammoth Airport, there's a free shuttle to the resort.

4000 Meridian Blvd. (P.O. Box 2129), Mammoth Lakes, CA 93546. www.mammothmountain. com. ☎ **800/626-6684** or 760/924-1102. 170 units. Winter $249–$419 double; summer $155–$235 double. AE, MC, V. **Amenities:** 2 restaurants; heated outdoor pools; room service; outdoor whirlpool spas. *In room:* TV/DVD and DVD rentals, free high-speed Internet (except Eagle Run suites), kitchen and dining area, fireplace.

Mammoth Mountain Inn ★ ☺   Opposite the ski lodge at the base of the ski resort, this inn opened in 1954 as only one building but was expanded a decade later into a larger, glossier complex. Though it was remodeled in the early 1990s, it retains the ruggedness you'd expect from a mountain resort. Guest rooms are well equipped and pleasantly furnished. The best are the junior suites with a view of the ski area. Families love this place for its large condo units, day-care activities, cribs, playground, box lunches and picnic tables, and game room. An array of sports facilities includes bike rentals, downhill skiing, snowboarding, rock climbing, and ziplining. Extras include free airport shuttle and occasional entertainment. The downside is the 10-minute drive into town, but skiers can't get any closer to the slopes. *Tip:* If you can get a similar or better rate at the new Westin Monache (see below), take it.

1 Minaret Rd. (P.O. Box 353), Mammoth Lakes, CA 93546. www.mammothmountain.com. ✆ **800/626-6684** or 760/934-2581. Fax 760/934-0701. 173 units, 40 condos (some suitable for up to 13 people). Winter $165–$315 double, $325–$545 condo; summer $125–$179 double, from $170 condo. Ski and mountain-biking packages available. AE, MC, V. **Amenities:** Restaurant; bar; babysitting; concierge; nearby golf course; heated outdoor pool; room service; 2 indoor and 1 outdoor whirlpool spas; Wi-Fi (in bar and lobby). *In room:* TV/DVD, high-speed Internet, kitchen in some units.

Sherwin Villas Outside the center of town on Old Mammoth Road, this cluster of woodsy condos is perfect for families or groups of friends traveling together. You'll find one- to four-bedroom units, each with a fully stocked kitchen, fireplace, linens, and access to a free shuttle to the slopes (a 5-min. drive away). Considering how many people you can pack into these apartments, it's a good deal—and if you stay 4 weekday nights, the fifth night is free. When making reservations, specify exactly what you're looking for: Condos are independently owned and vary dramatically in both decor and quality; you can view a few photos of each condo on the website.

362 Old Mammoth Rd. (P.O. Box 2249), Mammoth Lakes, CA 93546. www.sherwinvillas.com. ✆ **888/626-6684.** 70 condos. 1-bedroom unit for up to 4 people $100–$120 winter, from $95 summer; 2-bedroom loft for up to 6 people $140–$190 winter, from $115 summer; 3-bedroom unit for up to 8 people $155–$220 winter, from $135 summer; 4-bedroom unit for up to 10 people $195–$260 winter, from $155 summer. Extra person $10. MC, V. **Amenities:** 2 Jacuzzis; outdoor pool; Finnish sauna; tennis courts. *In room:* TV, kitchen, phone on request.

Sierra Lodge In the heart of Mammoth Lakes, this two-story inn offers contemporary lodgings without a trace of rusticity. The large guest rooms are pleasantly decorated with framed blond-wood furnishings, modern prints, track lighting, big beds, kitchenettes, and small patios or balconies with partial mountain views. The two-bedroom suite—equipped with two queen beds and a full-size pullout sofa—is ideal for groups or families. Facilities include an outdoor Jacuzzi and a fireside room for relaxing. Other perks include ski lockers, free covered parking, continental breakfast, free shuttle service right out front, and a short walk to Mammoth's best restaurant, **Nevados** (see review below).

3540 Main St. (Hwy. 203; P.O. Box 9228), Mammoth Lakes, CA 93546. www.sierralodge.com. ✆ **800/356-5711** or 760/934-8881. Fax 760/934-7231. 36 units. $79–$189 double. Rates include continental breakfast. AE, DISC, MC, V. Pets accepted for $10 per night, with $100 deposit. **Amenities:** Nearby golf course. *In room:* TV, hair dryer, kitchenette.

Tamarack Lodge & Resort ★ The lodge and cabin accommodations at this lakeside retreat aren't fancy, but that's what has kept guests coming here since the 1920s. The cabins dotted around the 6-acre property accommodate two to nine people, and they come in a variety of configurations: from rustic studios with wood-burning stoves and showers to deluxe two-bedroom/two-bathroom quarters with fireplaces. The best units are the lakefront cabins; try to request one with a lake view. The least expensive rooms, in the main lodge, come with private or shared bathrooms. **The Lakefront Restaurant** is romantic, with a seasonally changing menu. Entrees include grilled medallions of elk filet and seared sea scallops. In the winter, the lodge opens its popular cross-country ski

CAN'T FIGHT THE moonlight

Up for a moonlight stroll? Head over to the **Tamarack Cross Country Ski Center** at Twin Lakes Road, just off Lake Mary Road (✆ **800/MAMMOTH** [626-6684] or 760/934-2442; www.tamaracklodge.com), strap on your snowshoe rentals, and join in on an organized trek over the mountain and through the woods. Snowshoeing takes no prior knowledge or skill; it's essentially hiking in snow-friendly, Eskimo-like footwear that flattens the fluff and creates a packed path for an easier journey. Guided tours climb up, up, up, and then continue along a steep ridge, where all of Mammoth Village is lit up below like a Christmas tree, before returning through a tree canopy to the lodge in a 2-mile, 2-hour loop. Planned trips coincide with the full moon—the mountain lights up in a spectacular manner—and usually occur in the months of December, January, and February (call the lodge for specific times, which depend on the cycle of the moon). Just be sure to carry a tripod with you if you plan on getting any night shots with your camera. Once you're through with your physical activity, exercise your stomach with a sweet treat and a glass of mulled wine or cider in the Tamarack's cozy fireside lounge. Tours are $40 per person, including rentals, a guide, dessert, and a nonalcoholic beverage.

center with more than 25 miles of trails and skating lanes, ski rentals, and a ski school. Boat and canoe rentals are also available.

Twin Lakes Rd., off Lake Mary Rd. (P.O. Box 69), Mammoth Lakes, CA 93546. www.tamarack lodge.com. ✆ **800/MAMMOTH** (626-6684) or 760/934-2442. Fax 760/934-2281. 11 units, 6 with private bathroom; 32 cabins. $94–$300 double; $135–$485 cabin. AE, MC, V. **Amenities:** Restaurant; bar; nearby golf course; Wi-Fi. *In room:* Fridge, kitchen in cabins.

The Village Lodge ★★ ☺   Choose from one-, two-, and three-bedroom condos at this sprawling family-friendly resort located front and center in Mammoth Village, a 2-minute walk to the gondola and all the bars and restaurants at the mountain's base. All rooms have pullout sofas so you can maximize the number of people who stay in each unit and spacious balconies where you can grab a breath of fresh mountain air. A soak in one of the five whirlpools provides a perfect release after a day on the trails; three are hidden among snowbanks at the opposite end of the courtyard from the main building and reception area (check those out first, as they're often empty). Service is over-the-top friendly—in a genuine way, as if you were being invited into the staff's own home (which you are, in a sense). If you prefer peace and quiet, request a room away from the courtyard, where the noise reaches rowdy levels late at night. A complimentary shuttle transfers guests from the resort to the airport and back.

1111 Forest Trail. (P.O. Box 3459), Mammoth Lakes, CA 93546. www.mammothmountain.com. ✆ **800/626-6684** or 760/934-1982. 189 units. Winter $229–$539 double; summer $175–$259 double. $30 resort fee. AE, MC, V. **Amenities:** Concierge; 3 workout rooms; heated outdoor pool; 5 outdoor whirlpool spas; Wi-Fi; media room. *In room:* TV/DVD, free high-speed Internet, kitchen and dining area, fireplace.

Westin Monache Resort ★★   Don't worry, I didn't pronounce it right the first time, either. It's *Mon*-ah-she. In the Village at Mammoth adjacent to a 15-passenger express gondola, this 230-unit condo-hotel was Mono County's first upscale full-service resort hotel, featuring 24-hour room service, concierge, and bell staff; ski valet and rental shop; and a pool, hot tubs, a fitness center, and underground parking. Accommodations consist of one- and two-bedroom suites (most with panoramic mountain views), Westin's signature Heavenly Beds, kitchens or kitchenettes, gas fireplaces, and 32-inch flatscreen TVs. The two-bedroom suites are big enough for the entire family, with two private bedrooms, two full bathrooms, and a queen sofa bed in the living room. The hotel's **Whitebark** restaurant serves contemporary cuisine such as grilled steaks, seafood, and pizzas, or you can walk over to the numerous other restaurants in the village.

50 Hillside Dr., Mammoth Lakes, CA 93546. www.westin.com/mammoth. © **866/716-8132** or 760/934-0400. 230 units. $199–$395 double. Ski and golf packages available. AE, DC, DISC, MC, V. **Amenities:** Restaurant; bar; children's programs; concierge; fitness center; heated outdoor pool; hot tub; room service. *In room:* TV/DVD, kitchen or kitchenette, Wi-Fi, fireplace.

Where to Eat

Burgers Restaurant ☺ 🍴 AMERICAN   If, after a full day of skiing, you need a hearty American meal at a fair price, head down the mountain to Berger's. Its cabinlike interior, with local photos on the wooden walls, suits the surroundings. Portions are huge and include an array of burgers, steak, ribs, chicken, sandwiches, and hefty salads. Entrees come with salad, garlic bread, and either fries or a baked potato. Sandwiches, which cost up to $8 and come with salad and fries, will also easily fill you up without emptying your wallet. The children's menu is the ultimate bargain, offering a selection of kid-friendly feasts for under $6. The daily lunch specials are most coveted by locals, but if you want to try one, come early—they almost always sell out.

6118 Minaret Rd. © **760/934-6622.** Reservations recommended. Main courses $8.25–$15. MC, V. Daily 11:30am–8:30pm. Extended summer hours.

Grumpy's Saloon and Eatery ★ ☺ AMERICAN   For more than 2 decades, Grumpy's has been Mammoth's main "sports restaurant"—a log building with 35 TVs, pool tables, pinball machines, video games, and foosball tables. The bar has a great selection of tap beers, and the hearty, affordable grub features burgers (go for the Grumpy Burger), tasty barbecued ribs, homemade chili, a few Mexican items, and the famous quarter-pound Dogger, an unbelievably enormous hot dog. Everything on the menu comes with a choice of fries, coleslaw, or barbecued baked beans. Stop by for happy hour, which usually features a free buffet of hors d'oeuvres that may include Buffalo wings, cheese and crackers, or miniature quesadillas.

361 Mammoth Rd. © **760/934-8587.** www.grumpysmammoth.com. Main courses $6.25–$16. AE, MC, V. Mon–Sun 11am–10pm; bar until 2am.

Hyde Lounge ★★ AMERICAN/ASIAN FUSION   A new and different take on Mammoth dining, this scene-y, LA-type joint—it was introduced by the same people who helm such Beverly Hills hot spots as SLS Hotel and Bazaar—is hopping with dance tunes playing loudly in the background. It's definitely a deviation from the other dining establishments in the Village, but in a good way. The food is perfect for refueling after a long day on the slopes, with mouthwatering starters like pigs in a blanket, lollipop wings, grilled short-rib tacos in peanut dressing, and glazed barbeque pork buns with hot mustard sauce. Mains range from Chinese-style bass to rigatoni Bolognese, though the burger and sweet potato fries in spicy ketchup aioli is my favorite dish. And the double-chocolate Mammoth brownie with toasted marshmallow, peanut brittle, and coffee gelato is a no-brainer when the dessert menu comes around. The cocktail menu is interesting, with selections like a white grapefruit cosmopolitan and watermelon chili margarita.

6201 Minaret Rd., across from the gondola. © **760/934-0669.** www.mammothmountain.com. Main courses $13–$24. AE, MC, V. Mon–Fri 4–10pm; Sat–Sun noon–11pm; bar daily until 2am.

Nevados ★★ EUROPEAN/CALIFORNIAN   Nevados is one of Mammoth Lakes' best restaurants and a longtime favorite with the locals and Los Angelenos on their annual ski or summer holiday. Owner/host Tim Dawson is usually on hand nightly to ensure that everyone's satisfied with the innovative cuisine and house-baked breads. Most everyone orders the prix-fixe, three-course meal, which may consist of a strudel appetizer of wild mushrooms and rabbit with roasted shallots and grilled scallions; a main course of braised Provimi veal shank with roasted tomatoes and garlic mashed potatoes; and a warm pear-and-almond tart sweetened with caramel sauce and vanilla-bean ice cream for dessert. With its casual, sweet ambience (white tablecloths and candles) and broad choice of wines and single-malt scotches, it's no wonder this is the hangout of choice for ski instructors and race coaches.

Main St. (at Minaret Rd.). © **760/934-4466.** Reservations recommended. Main courses $21–$30; fixed-price meal $40. AE, DC, DISC, MC, V. Daily 5:30–9:30pm.

Petra's Bistro ★★ MEDITERRANEAN   A delightful and friendly little restaurant with an eight-person bar tucked on a busy street just across from one of the main access points to the mountain, Petra's Bistro offers up some of the finest dining in the area and an excellent wine selection. The wild mushroom soup and baked brie are house favorites; begin with them, before following up with the scallops or prosciutto-wrapped pork, paired with a fine vino by the knowledgeable staff. When making reservations (which you should always do on weekends in the winter), ask for a table near the huge fireplace.

6080 Minaret Rd. (located in the Alpenhof Lodge). © **760/934-3500.** www.petrasbistro.com. Reservations recommended. Main courses $25–$40. AE, DC, DISC, MC, V. Tues–Sun 5–9pm.

The Restaurant at Convict Lake ★★ COUNTRY FRENCH   For years, this restaurant on the edge of Convict Lake was a local secret, but the word got out when *Wine Spectator* featured it. Now you'd better make reservations if you want to enjoy a meal in this plank-sided cabin with an open-beam ceiling, wood floors, copper-hooded free-standing fireplace, and mountain views. Five miles south of Mammoth Lakes, it's well worth the drive to spend a romantic evening feasting on Long Island duckling breast with fresh blackberries, panko-crusted Hawaiian sunfish in a lime-ginger-tamari-sesame Thai chili vinaigrette, or curried lamb shank served with basmati rice. Linger a bit longer to savor the bananas Foster flambé or a cheese wedge served with dry fruit. During the summer months, you can even lunch under the aspens.

Convict Lake Rd. © **760/934-3803.** www.convictlake.com. Reservations recommended. Main courses $22–$50. AE, MC, V. Summer daily 11am–2pm; year-round daily 5:30–9:30pm; Sun brunch 10:30am–2:30pm.

Side Door Café ★★ AMERICAN/FRENCH   A perfect breakfast stop en route to the mountain, Side Door Café whips up an amazing array of both sweet and savory crepes and serves bottomless mimosas at weekend brunch time. (I have to say it: Just don't drink and ski!) Paninis, salads, and tapas round off the lunchtime fare; gourmet coffee and Mighty Leaf tea are always on tap. On weekends, the place turns into a bar and dessert spot after dinnertime, though food is served continuously until closing. If you want an intimate bar-going experience where you can actually hear what your friends have to say (vs. the louder, more rambunctious Hyde Lounge), Side Door is your place. It's tiny, though, and fills up quickly, so arrive before peak times if you want a table.

100 Canyon Blvd., the Village. ℂ **760/934-5200.** www.sidedoormammoth.com. Main courses $6–$12. AE, MC, V. Sun–Thurs 7am–9pm; Fri–Sat 7am–midnight.

Skadi ★★ ECLECTIC Suitably named after the Viking goddess of skiing and hunting, Skadi is the domain of chef/owner Ian Algerøen, a former chef at Nevado's. It's the perfect place for an après-ski cocktail at the 14-seat bar, a snack from the substantial selection of appetizers and desserts, or a full dinner. Skadi's big-city, postmodern aura is a welcome change after all that local alpine simplicity. Main courses include roasted maple leaf duck with Arctic lingonberries, or braised lamb shanks with rosemary-garlic mashed potatoes and garlic comfit. Finish with lemon *panna cotta* with fresh berries or frozen caramelized macadamia nut and vanilla-bean parfait topped with chocolate sauce.

587 Old Mammoth Rd. ℂ **760/934-3902.** www.skadirestaurant.com. Reservations recommended. Main courses $22–$32. AE, MC, V. Wed–Mon 5:30–9:30pm.

Whiskey Creek Mountain Bistro ★ AMERICAN If you favor surf-and-turf fare in an alpine atmosphere with a swinging nightlife scene, make a reservation here. Whiskey Creek's wraparound windows proffer a pretty view of the snow-clad mountains, and the menu is known for its excellent South Carolina pork chops, bacon-wrapped meatloaf, and barbecued pork spareribs, all served with a heaping side of roasted garlic mashed potatoes. The dining room may be peaceful, but the upper-level brewpub is a different world. If you're not too stuffed, head upstairs for music every night from 9pm to at least 1am, making it the number-one spot in town to hear cheesy pickup lines.

24 Lake Mary Rd. (at Minaret Rd.). ℂ **760/934-2555.** Reservations recommended. Main courses $16–$28. AE, DC, DISC, MC, V. Daily 4–9pm. Bar until 2am on Wed, Fri, and Sat.

The Yodler ★★ AMERICAN/BAR FOOD If you need a midday break from the slopes, this is where you should head. With excellent beer selection and delightful nibbles—like a heaping mountain of nachos or an array of artisan pizzas—that aren't your typical exorbitant ski-lodge prices, you can't go wrong with resting your tootsies while delighting your stomach. There are tables and fire pits on the deck surrounding the restaurant, should you not yet have had your fill of the Great Outdoors.

Yodler Building, adjacent to the Main Lodge. ℂ **760/934-8587.** www.mammothmountain.com. Main courses $8–$20. AE, MC, V. Daily; call for hours (they vary seasonally).

DEVILS POSTPILE NATIONAL MONUMENT ★

10 miles W of Mammoth; 50 miles E of Yosemite's eastern boundary

Just a few miles outside Mammoth Lakes, Devils Postpile National Monument is home to one of nature's most curious geological spectacles. Formed when molten lava cracked as it cooled, the 60-foot-high, blue-gray basalt columns that form the postpile look more like an enormous, eerie pipe organ or a jumble of string cheese than anything you'd expect to see made from stone. The mostly six-sided columns formed underground and were exposed when glaciers scoured the valley during the last ice age, some 10,000 years ago. Similar columnar basalt is found in Ireland and Scotland.

Because of its high elevation (7,900 ft.) and heavy snowfall, the monument is open only from summer to early fall. Summer weather is usually clear and warm, but afternoon thundershowers are common. Nights are cold, so bring good tents and sleeping bags if you're camping. Unfortunately, all those beautiful lakes attract lots of mosquitoes. Plan for them.

Devils Postpile National Monument.

Essentials

GETTING THERE   From late June to early September, cars are banned in the monument between 7:30am and 5:30pm, because the roads can't handle the traffic. Visitors must take a shuttle bus to and from locations in the monument. Although it takes some planning, the resulting peace and quiet warrant the trouble and make you wonder why the park service hasn't implemented similar programs at Yosemite Valley and other traffic hot spots.

VISITOR INFORMATION   For information before you go, call ✆ **760/934-2289** during open season, or ✆ **760/872-4881** from November to May. You'll also find plenty of info at **www.nps.gov/depo**.

Outdoor Pursuits

CAMPING   While most visitors stay in or around Mammoth Lakes, the monument does maintain a 21-site campground with piped water, flush toilets, fire pits, and picnic tables on a first-come, first-served basis. Rates are $8 per night. Bears are common in the park, so take proper food-storage measures. Leashed pets are permitted on trails and in camp. Call the **National Park Service** (✆ **760/934-2289,** or 760/872-4881 Nov–May; www.nps. gov/depo) for details. Other nearby U.S. Forest Service campgrounds include **Red's Meadow** and **Upper Soda Springs.**

HIKING   Devils Postpile is more than an impressive bunch of rocks. On the banks of the San Joaquin River, amid granite peaks and crystalline mountain lakes, the 800-acre park is a gateway to a hiker's paradise. Short paths lead from here to the top of the postpile and to **Soda Springs,** a spring of cold carbonated water.

A longer hike (about 1.3 miles) from the separate Rainbow Falls Trail head will take you to spectacular **Rainbow Falls ★**, where the middle fork of the San Joaquin plunges 101 feet from a lava cliff. From the trail, a stairway and short trail lead to the base of the falls and swimming holes below.

The **Pacific Crest Trail** and the **John Muir Trail** (which connects Yosemite National Park with Kings Canyon and Sequoia national parks) run through here. Named after the conservationist and author who is largely credited with saving Yosemite and popularizing the Sierra Nevada as a place worth preserving, the 211-mile John Muir Trail traverses some of the most difficult, remote parts of the Sierra. You can access it from two points in Devils Postpile, either near the ranger station or from the Rainbow Falls trail head. From here, you can hike as far as your feet will take you north or south. **Note:** Mountain bikes are not permitted on trails.

SEQUOIA & KINGS CANYON NATIONAL PARKS ★★

30 miles E of Visalia

Only 200 road miles separate Yosemite from Sequoia and Kings Canyon national parks, but they're worlds apart. While the National Park Service has taken every opportunity to modernize, accessorize, and urbanize Yosemite, resulting in a frenetic tourist scene, at Sequoia and Kings Canyon, they've treated the wilderness with respect and care. Only one road, the Generals Highway, loops through the area, and no road traverses the Sierra here. The park service recommends that vehicles over 22 feet long avoid the steep and windy stretch between Potwisha Campground and the Giant Forest in Sequoia National Park. Generally speaking, the park is much less accessible by car than most, but spectacular for those willing to head out on foot.

The Sierra Nevada tilts upward as it runs south. **Mount Whitney,** at 14,494 feet (the highest point in the Lower 48), is just one of many high peaks in Sequoia and Kings Canyon. The **Pacific Crest Trail** also reaches its highest point here, crossing north to south through both parks. In addition to snow-covered peaks, Sequoia and Kings Canyon are home to the largest groves of giant sequoias in the Sierra Nevada, as well as the headwaters of the Kern, Kaweah, and Kings rivers. A few high-country lakes are home to some of the only remaining pure-strain golden trout. Bears, deer, and numerous smaller animals and birds depend on the parks' miles and miles of wild habitat for year-round breeding and feeding grounds.

Mt. Whitney.

Technically, Sequoia and Kings Canyon are two separate but contiguous parks, managed jointly from the park headquarters at Ash Mountain, just past the entrance on Hwy. 198 east of Visalia.

Essentials

Most visitors make a loop through the parks by entering at Grant Grove and leaving through Ash Mountain, or vice versa.

VISITOR INFORMATION   The parks have three major visitor centers open year-round, some seasonal facilities, and a museum where you can buy books and maps and discuss your plans with park rangers. In Sequoia National Park, the largest is **Foothills Visitor Center** (✆ 559/565-3135), inside the Ash Mountain Entrance on Hwy. 198. Exhibits focus on the Sierra foothills, a biologically diverse ecosystem. The **Giant Forest Museum** (✆ 559/565-4480) is housed in a historic building and offers exhibits on giant sequoias. **Lodgepole Visitor Center** (✆ 559/565-4436) includes exhibits on geology, wildlife, air quality, and park history. It's 4½ miles north of Giant Forest Village, and it's closed Tuesday through Thursday in winter. The visitor center in **Grant Grove,** Kings Canyon National Park (✆ 559/565-4307), includes exhibits on logging and the role of fire in the forests. Open only in summer, a small visitor center at **Cedar Grove** in Kings Canyon and a ranger station at Sequoia's **Mineral King** dispense backcountry permits as well as information.

> ### 📎 Fill It Up
>
> Note that neither park has a gas station, so fill up your tank before you enter.

To research before you go, see www.nps.gov/seki, www.sequoia-kings canyon.com, www.sequoiahistory.org, or www.visitsequoia.com, or call ✆ 559/565-3341.

FEES & PERMITS   A $20 fee per car or $10 per person on foot, bike, motorcycle, or bus is good for 7 days' entry at any park entrance. An annual pass costs $30. Wilderness permits are required for overnight backpacking in the parks. You can reserve the $15 permits in advance by downloading an application from the national park website at **www.nps.gov/seki** and mailing or faxing it to the **Wilderness Permit Office,** 47050 Generals Hwy. #60, Three Rivers, CA 93271 (✆ 559/565-3766; fax 559/565-4239).

REGULATIONS   Mountain bikes and dogs are forbidden on all park trails (dogs are permitted in developed areas but must be leashed). The park service allows firewood gathering at campgrounds, although supplies can be scarce. Removing wood from living or standing trees is forbidden.

THE SEASONS   In the high altitudes, where most Sequoia and Kings Canyon visitors are headed, summers are short and winters are cold. Snow in July and August is rare but not unheard of. At midelevations, where the sequoias grow, spring can come as early as April or as late as June. Afternoon showers are occasional. In winter, only the main roads into the parks are usually open; the climate ranges from bitter cold to pleasant and can change by the minute. The Generals Highway, between Sequoia and Kings Canyon, closes for plowing during and after snowstorms. Be ready for anything if you head

Marmot Invasion

Check under your hood before leaving a parking lot. Marmots, especially in the Mineral King area, love munching on car hoses and wiring, leaving a trail of disabled vehicles in their wake. A good number of them have stowed away in a car's engine compartment and hitched rides with unsuspecting drivers to other parts of the parks; several have ridden as far as Southern California.

into the backcountry on skis. In summer, poison oak and rattlesnakes are common in lower elevations, and mosquitoes abound in all wet areas.

AVOIDING THE CROWDS   To escape the crowds and see less-used areas of the parks, enter on one of the dead-end roads to Mineral King or Cedar Grove (both open only in summer), or South Fork. Without traffic, these parts of the parks are incredibly peaceful, even at full capacity, and gateways to some of the best hiking.

Exploring the Parks

The second-oldest national park in the U.S., Sequoia National Park was created in 1890 at the request of San Joaquin Valley residents concerned with the conservation of giant redwoods. The park has some 75 groves of giant sequoias, but the best places to see them are **Grant Grove ★**, in Kings Canyon, near the park entrance on Hwy. 180 from Fresno, and **Giant Forest ★**, a huge enclave of trees with 40 miles of footpaths, 16 miles from the entrance to Sequoia National Park on Hwy. 198.

The 2-mile **Congress Trail** loop in Giant Forest starts at the base of the **General Sherman Tree ★**, reputedly the largest living tree in the world. Single branches are more than 7 feet thick. Each year it grows enough wood to make a 60-foot-tall tree of normal dimensions. Other trees in the grove are nearly as large; many of them, however peaceful-looking they may be, bear militaristic and political monikers such as General Lee. Longer trails lead to remote reaches of the grove and nearby meadows.

Unlike the coast redwoods, which reproduce by sprouting or by seeds, giant sequoias reproduce only by seed. Adult sequoias rarely die of diseases and are protected from most fire by thick bark. The huge trees have surprisingly shallow roots, and most die from toppling when their roots are damaged and can no

General Sherman Tree on Congress Trail.

Until recently, the National Park Service claimed that the General Sherman Tree was the largest living thing on earth. Technically, though, this may not be true; now the claim is that it's the largest living *tree*—which is still quite a distinction. The reason for the change? Park officials say some underground fungi may actually be larger, and groves of aspen trees share a common root system, making them one living thing, also bigger than the General.

longer support them. These groves, like the ones in Yosemite, were explored by conservationist and nature writer John Muir, who named the Giant Forest.

Besides the sequoia groves, Sequoia and Kings Canyon are home to the Sierra Nevada's most pristine wilderness. At **Road's End** on the Kings Canyon Highway (late May to early Nov), you can stand by the Kings River and stare up at granite walls rising thousands of feet above the river, the deepest canyon in the United States.

Near Giant Forest Village, **Moro Rock** is a 6,725-foot-tall granite dome formed by the exfoliation of rock layers. A ¼-mile trail scales the dome for a spectacular view of the adjacent Canyon of the Middle Fork of the Kaweah. The trail gains 300 feet in 1,200 feet, so be ready for a climb.

Crystal Cave ★ is 15 miles from the Hwy. 198 park entrance; cave parking is another 7 miles. Here you can take a 45-minute tour of Crystal's beautiful marble interior. The tour is $13 for adults, $12 for seniors, $6.50 for children ages 6 to 12, and free for kids 5 and under. Tickets are not sold at the cave. Purchase them at the Lodgepole or Foothills visitor centers at least 1½ hours in advance. Wear sturdy shoes and bring a jacket. For information, call 📞 **559/565-3759** or see **www.sequoiahistory.org**. The cave is open mid-May to late October daily from 11am to 4pm.

Boyden Cavern, on Hwy. 180 in neighboring Sequoia National Forest, is a cave where you can take an $11 45-minute tour to see stalactites and stalagmites. Call 📞 **559/338-0959** for details, or see **www.kingscanyoneering.com**. The cave is open April through November daily from 10am to 5pm.

Crystal Cave.

Hiking the Parks

Hiking and backpacking are what these parks are all about. Some 700 miles of trails connect canyons, lakes, and high alpine meadows and snowfields.

When traveling overnight inside parks boundaries, overnight and/or day-use permits are required.

If you want to do serious overnight backpacking, see "Fees & Permits" under "Essentials," above.

Some of the park's most impressive hikes start in the **Mineral King** section in the southern end of Sequoia. Beginning at 7,800 feet, trails lead onward and upward to destinations such as Sawtooth Pass, Crystal Lake, and the old White Chief Trail to the now-defunct White Chief Mine. Once an unsuccessful silver-mining town in the 1870s, Mineral King was the center of a battle in the late 1970s when developers sought to build a huge ski resort. They were defeated when Congress added Mineral King to Sequoia National Park, and the wilderness remains.

The **John Muir Trail,** which begins in Yosemite Valley, ends at Mount Whitney. For many miles it coincides with the **Pacific Crest Trail** as it skirts the highest peaks in the park. This is the most difficult part of the Pacific Crest, above 10,000 feet most of the time and crossing 12,000-foot-tall passes.

Other hikers like to explore the northern part of Kings Canyon from **Cedar Grove** and **Road's End.** The **Paradise Valley Trail,** leading to beautiful Mist Falls, is a fairly easy day trip by park standards. The **Copper Creek Trail** immediately rises into the high wilderness around Granite Pass at 10,673 feet, one of the most strenuous day hikes in the parks.

If the altitude and steepness are too much for you at these trail heads, try some of the longer hikes in **Giant Forest** or **Grant Grove.** These forests are woven with interlocking loops that allow you to take as short or as long a hike as you want. The 6-mile **Trail of the Sequoias** in Giant Forest will take you to the grove's far-eastern end, where you'll find some of the finest trees. In Grant Grove, a 100-foot walk through the hollow trunk of the **Fallen Monarch** makes a fascinating side trip. The tree has been used for shelter for more than 100 years and is tall enough inside that you can walk through without bending over.

Perhaps the most traversed trail to the park is the **Whitney Portal Trail.** It runs from east of Sequoia near Lone Pine, through Inyo National Forest, to Sequoia's boundary, the summit of Mount Whitney. Though it's a straightforward walk to the summit and it's possible to do it in a long day hike, you'd better be in tiptop shape before attempting it. Almost half the people who attempt Whitney, including those who camp partway up, don't reach the summit. Weather, altitude, and fatigue can stop even the most prepared party. For more information, contact the **Mount Whitney Ranger Station** at © **760/876-6200.** For wilderness permits, see "Fees & Permits" near the beginning of this section.

The official park map and guide has good road maps for the parks, but for serious hiking you'll want to check out *Sierra South: 100 Back-Country Trips,* by Thomas Winnett and Jason Winnett (Wilderness Press). Another good guide is *Kings Canyon Country,* a hiking handbook by Ginny and Lew Clark (Western Trails Publications). The Grant Grove, Lodgepole, Cedar Grove, Foothills, and Mineral King visitor centers sell a complete selection of maps and guidebooks. Books and maps are also available by mail through the **Sequoia Natural History Association** (© **559/565-3759;** www.sequoiahistory.org).

Other Outdoor Pursuits

FISHING   The **Kaweah** drainage, the parks' lakes, and a section of the south fork of the **Kings River** are open all year for trout fishing (rainbow, brook, German brown, and golden). Most other waters are open for trout fishing from late April to mid-November, and for other species year-round. California fishing licenses (available at stores in the park) are required for anglers

16 and older, and you should also get a copy of the National Park Service's fishing regulations, available at visitor centers.

HORSEBACK RIDING   Concessionaires in both parks and the adjacent national monument during the summer run guided horseback and mule rides and overnight pack trips. In Kings Canyon, **Cedar Grove Pack Station** (© 559/565-3464 summer, 559/337-3231 winter) is a mile east of Cedar Grove Village, and **Grant Grove Stables** (© 559/335-9292 summer, 559/337-1273 winter) is near Grant Grove Village. In Giant Sequoia National Monument, **Horse Corral Pack Station** is on Big Meadows Road, 10 miles east of Generals Highway (© 559/565-3404 summer, 209/742-6400 winter; www.highsierrapackers.org). The pack stations offer hourly rides as well as overnight treks, while the stables offer day rides only. Rates range from $45 for a half-day ride to $75 for a full day in the saddle; call for current charges for pack trips.

RAFTING & KAYAKING   Only fairly recently have professional outfitters begun taking experienced rafters and kayakers down the Class 4 and 5 Kaweah and Upper Kings rivers outside the parks. Check the **Reservation Center** website at **www.rescentre.com** for a good list of companies running trips. Rafting and kayaking here are only for the very adventurous.

SKIING & SNOWSHOEING   **Wolverton,** 2 miles north of the General Sherman tree, has a snow-play and cross-country ski area. You can rent skis and snowshoes at the Lodgepole Market. About 50 miles of marked, cross-country trails run through the **Giant Forest** and **Grant Grove** areas. Rangers offer naturalist talks and snowshoe walks some weekends. Rental equipment (including snowshoes) and lessons are available at the Grant Grove Market. For more information on cross-country skiing, sledding, or snowshoeing at Grant Grove, call the visitor center at © **559/565-4307;** for Wolverton, call © **559/565-3435.** Kids can sled and play in the snow-play areas near Wolverton and at Big Stump, Columbine, and Azalea in Grant Grove.

The Sequoia Natural History Association operates the **Pear Lake Ski Hut** for snowshoers and cross-country skiers, which can accommodate up to 10 people. Use of the facility is by lottery. For further information, call © **559/565-3759.**

WHITE-WATER BOATING   The **Kaweah** and **Upper Kings** rivers in the parks are not open to boating (neither kayaks nor inflatable rafts), but several companies run trips just outside the parks. You're guaranteed to get wet, but this roller coaster ride through the rapids is thrilling, and a great way to experience these scenic rivers. **Kaweah White Water Adventures** (© **800/229-8658** or 559/740-8251; www.kaweah-whitewater.com) runs Class 3, 4, and 5 trips (rated moderate to difficult) on the Kaweah River from spring to early fall. Prices range from about $40 to $90 per person for a half-day trip (depending on skill level) to $130 (with lunch) for the day. **Whitewater Voyages** (© **800/400-7238;** www.whitewatervoyages.com) runs trips on the Kaweah, Kings, Kern, and Merced rivers, with rates around $120 to $219 (including lunch) for full-day trips; multiday trips are also available (call for rates). **Kings River Expeditions** (© **800/846-3674** or 559/233-4881; www.kingsriver.com) specializes in rafting trips on the Kings. For 1-day trips, they charge $99 to $199. Overnight trips are also available (call for rates).

Camping

Backpackers will find numerous camping opportunities in and around Sequoia and Kings Canyon national parks. It's important to remember, when camping in this area, that proper food storage is *required*—for the sake of the black bears as well as your safety. See local bulletin boards for instructions.

IN SEQUOIA NATIONAL PARK

The only national park campgrounds that accept reservations are Dorst and Lodgepole (📞 **800/365-2267**), which will do so up to 5 months in advance; the other campgrounds are first-come, first-served. Additional information on the national park campgrounds (but not reservations) can be obtained by calling the general Sequoia/Kings Canyon information line at 📞 **559/565-3341.**

The two biggest campgrounds in the park are in the Lodgepole area. The **Lodgepole Campground,** with flush toilets, is often crowded, but it's pretty and near some spectacular big trees. Nearby backcountry trails offer some solitude. Close to the ground are a grocery store, restaurant, visitor center, children's nature center, evening ranger programs, and gift shop. From Giant Forest, drive 5 miles northeast on the Generals Highway.

Dorst Campground, 14 miles northwest of Giant Forest via the Generals Highway, is a high-elevation campground with easy access to Muir Grove and some pleasant backcountry trails. It has flush toilets and evening ranger programs. Group campsites are also available here by reservation.

In the Foothills, **Potwisha Campground** is small, with well-spaced sites tucked beneath oak trees along the Marble Fork of the Kaweah River. The campground has flush toilets, but it gets very hot in summer. From the Ash Mountain Entrance, drive 3 miles northeast on the Generals Highway to the campground entrance. The **Buckeye Flat Campground ★**, open to tents only, is also set among oaks along the Middle Fork of the Kaweah River. It also gets hot in summer, but it's among our favorites for its scenery and flush toilets. From the Ash Mountain Entrance, drive about 6 miles northeast on the Generals Highway to the Hospital Rock Ranger Station. From there, follow signs to the campground, which is several miles down a narrow, winding road. **South Fork Campground** is the smallest and most remote campground in the park, just inside Sequoia's southwestern boundary. It is set along the South Fork of the Kaweah River and has pit toilets only. From the town of Three Rivers, go east on South Fork Road 23 miles to the campground.

The two campgrounds in the Mineral King area are open to tents only—no RVs or trailers. **Atwell Mill Campground** is a pretty, small campground, near the East Fork of the Kaweah River, at Atwell Creek, with pit toilets. From Three Rivers, take Mineral King Road east for 20 miles to the campground. **Cold Springs Campground,** which also has pit toilets, is beautiful but not very accessible. Once you get there, however, you'll be rewarded with beautiful scenery. It's also a good starting point for many backcountry hikes, given its proximity to the Mineral King Ranger Station. From Three Rivers, take Mineral King Road east for 25 miles to the campground.

IN KINGS CANYON NATIONAL PARK

All the campgrounds in Kings Canyon are first-come, first-served (no reservations), and all have flush toilets. More information can be obtained by calling the general Sequoia/Kings Canyon information line at 📞 **559/565-3341.**

The Grant Grove area has three attractive campgrounds near the big trees—**Azalea, Crystal Springs,** and **Sunset.** All have a nice woodsy feel, they're close to park facilities, and they offer evening ranger programs. To get to them from the Big Stump Entrance, take Hwy. 180 east about 1¾ miles.

The Cedar Grove Village area has several campgrounds, all accessed from Hwy. 180. All are fairly close to the facilities in Cedar Grove Village. **Sentinel,** the first to open for the season, fills up quickly. **Moraine** is the farthest from the crowds. **Sheep Creek,** along picturesque Sheep Creek, opens as needed.

Where to Stay in the Parks

Cedar Grove Lodge ★   This motel offers comfortable rooms on the bank of the Kings River. Getting here is half the fun—it's a 36-mile drive down a winding highway with beautiful vistas along the way. The rooms here are standard motel accommodations—clean and comfortable, but nothing special. What you're really paying for is the location, surrounded by tall trees with a pretty river running by. Most of the rooms are above the Cedar Grove Café, with communal decks with river views. I prefer the three smaller, less attractively appointed rooms on the ground level, with private patios looking onto the river.

Hwy. 180, Cedar Grove, Kings Canyon National Park (mail: Sequoia Kings Canyon Park Services Co., 5755 E. Kings Canyon Rd., Ste. 101, Fresno, CA 93727). www.sequoia-kingscanyon.com. *(C)* **866/522-6966** or 559/522-6966. Fax 559/335-5507. 18 units. $119–$180 double. AE, DISC, MC, V. *In room:* A/C, fridge and microwave (ground-floor rooms only), no phone.

Grant Grove Cabins ✇   Although all the accommodations here are cabins, they offer a wide range of amenities and prices, from handsomely restored cabins that ooze history, with private bathrooms, to primitive tent-cabins that simply provide a comfortable bed and shelter at a very low price. Those who want to "rough it" in style should reserve one of the 9 cabins, built in the 1920s, that have electricity, indoor plumbing, and full private bathrooms. A bit less modern, but still quite comfortable, the 43 basic cabins have kerosene lanterns for light and a shared bathhouse. Some are wooden; others, available in summer only, have wood floors and walls but canvas roofs. All cabins have full linen service. It's a 10-minute walk from the cabins to the Grant Grove visitor center, and the Grant Grove Restaurant is also nearby.

Hwy. 180, Grant Grove Village, Kings Canyon National Park (mail: Sequoia Kings Canyon Park Services Co., 5755 E. Kings Canyon Rd., Ste. 101, Fresno, CA 93727). www.sequoia-kingscanyon.com. *(C)* **866/522-6966** or 559/522-6966. Fax 559/335-5507. 53 units, 9 with private bathroom. $62–$140 cabin. AE, DISC, MC, V. Register at Grant Grove Village Registration Center, btw. the restaurant and gift shop. **Amenities:** Free Wi-Fi. *In room:* No phone.

John Muir Lodge ★★   This handsome log lodge, built in 1998, looks perfect in its beautiful national park setting. It's an excellent choice for visitors who want quiet, comfortable, modern rooms, with full bathrooms and coffeemakers, in a forest environment. Standard rooms have two queen-size beds and wonderful views of the surrounding forest. A mountain lodge atmosphere prevails. Suites consist of two connecting standard rooms, but one of the rooms has a queen bed and a queen sofa sleeper instead of two queens.

Hwy. 180, Grant Grove Village, Kings Canyon National Park (mail: Sequoia Kings Canyon Park Services Co., 5755 E. Kings Canyon Rd., Ste. 101, Fresno, CA 93727). www.sequoia-kingscanyon.com. *(C)* **866/522-6966** or 559/522-6966. Fax 559/335-5507. 36 units. $89–$180 standard room; $270 suite. AE, DISC, MC, V. Register at Grant Grove Village Registration Center, btw. the restaurant and gift shop. **Amenities:** Free Wi-Fi.

Silver City Mountain Resort ★   Three types of cabins are available here, with a variety of bed combinations (some cabins sleep up to eight) and wood stoves for heat. Wood is provided, along with blankets and pillows, but guests need to bring their own sheets, pillowcases, bathroom and kitchen towels, paper towels, and tall trash bags. The top-of-the-line Swiss Chalets are finished in knotty pine with completely equipped kitchens, full bathrooms, Internet access, and an outdoor barbecue. The midlevel units, dubbed Comfy Cabins, are two-bedroom units with complete kitchens, propane wall lamps and electric lights, small restrooms with toilets but no showers (you'll have to make do with the centrally located bathhouse), and decks with barbecue grills. Rustic Cabins, which were built in the 1930s, are the most basic units, with light from propane lamps, a camp kitchen with a gas stove and an oven, a cold-water sink, and an outdoor deck with barbecue.

Mineral King, Sequoia National Park (mail: P.O. Box 56, Three Rivers, CA 93271). www.silvercity resort.com. (✆ **559/561-3223,** or 559/734-4109 in winter. Fax 559/561-2606. 14 cabins, 7 with shared central bathhouse. $130–$395 double (2–8 guests). Discounts June 1–15 and after Sept 18. MC, V. Closed Nov–May. Take Hwy. 198 through Three Rivers to the Mineral King turnoff. Silver City is a little more than halfway btw. Lookout Point and Mineral King. **Amenities:** Restaurant; bakery.

SACRAMENTO & THE GOLD COUNTRY

by Matthew Poole

10

O n the morning of January 24, 1848, carpenter James Marshall was working on John Sutter's mill in Coloma when he stumbled upon a gold nugget on the south fork of the American River. Despite Sutter's wishes to keep the discovery a secret, word leaked out—a word that would change the fate of California almost overnight: *Gold!*

The news spread like wildfire, and a frenzy seized the nation: The Gold Rush was on. Within 3 years, the population of the state exploded, from 15,000 to more than 265,000. Most newcomers were single men under the age of 40, and not far behind were the merchants, bankers, and women who made their fortunes catering to the miners, most of whom went bust in their search for wealth.

Sacramento quickly grew as a supply town at the base of the gold fields. The Gold Country boom lasted less than a decade; the supply was quickly exhausted, and many towns shrank or disappeared. Sacramento, however, continued to grow as the fertile Central Valley south of it exploited another source of wealth, becoming the vegetable-and-fruit garden of the nation.

A trip along Hwy. 49 from the northern mines to the southern mines conveys a sense of what life was like on the mining frontier. Many of the towns along this route seem frozen in time, down to Main Street, with its raised wooden sidewalks, double porches, saloons, and Victorian storefronts. Each town tells a similar story of sudden wealth and explosive growth, yet each has also left behind its own unique imprint. Any fan of movie Westerns will recognize the setting, given that hundreds, perhaps even thousands, of films have been shot in these parts.

At the base of the Gold Country's hills is the sprawling, flat Central Valley. Some 240 miles long and 50 miles wide, it's California's agricultural breadbasket, the source of bounty shipped across the nation and overseas. A lot of state history has revolved around the struggle for control of the water used to irrigate the valley and make this inland desert bloom. Yes, despite its aridity, a breathtaking panorama of orange and pistachio groves, grapevines, and strawberry fields stretches uninterrupted for miles.

SACRAMENTO ★

90 miles E of San Francisco; 383 miles N of Los Angeles

Sacramento, with a metro-area population of nearly 1.8 million, is one of the state's fastest-growing areas. Visitors and locals alike enjoy a day spent walking through Old Sacramento, floating down the American River, or biking the shady paths along the Sacramento and American rivers. In addition to being the state capital, it's a thriving shipping and processing center for the fruit, vegetables, rice, wheat, and dairy goods produced in the Central Valley. It's also become a receptacle of spillover from Silicon Valley, and a suburb for Bay Area workers

PREVIOUS PAGE: **Sacramento State Capitol.**

seeking affordable homes. As such, the quantity and quality of downtown restaurants, such as the Esquire Grill and the Waterboy, have greatly improved.

Visitors are often surprised by how pretty the River City's downtown area is, with its tree-shaded streets lined with some impressive Victorians and well-crafted bungalows. And at its heart sits the majestic capitol building—Sacramento's most visible attraction—situated within a large park, replete with flower gardens, memorial statuary, and curious squirrels. Inside the capitol, visitors strain to get a glimpse of California's reborn Governor Jerry Brown and his unpaid Chief of Staff, Anne Gust Brown, as they walk their corgi, Sutter.

Essentials

GETTING THERE If you're driving from San Francisco, Sacramento is about 90 miles east on I-80. From Los Angeles, take I-5 through the Central Valley directly into Sacramento. From North Lake Tahoe, get on I-80 west; from South Lake Tahoe, take U.S. 50.

Sacramento International Airport (© **916/929-5411**), 12 miles northwest of downtown Sacramento, is served by about a dozen airlines, including Alaska Airlines, American, America West, Continental, Delta, Northwest, Southwest, and United. **SuperShuttle** (© **800/258-3826**) runs from the airport to downtown for a flat rate of $13 to the capital, a bargain compared to the $25 a conventional taxi would cost.

Amtrak (© **800/USA-RAIL** [872-7245]; www.amtrak.com) trains serve Sacramento daily. The Greyhound terminal is at Seventh and L streets.

VISITOR INFORMATION The **Sacramento Convention and Visitors Bureau,** 1608 I St., Sacramento, CA 95814 (© **916/808-7777;** www.discovergold.org), provides plenty of information for travelers. It's open Monday through Friday from 8am to 5pm. Once in the city, you can also stop by the **Old Sacramento Visitor Center,** 1002 Second St. (© **916/442-7644**), in Old Sacramento; it's usually open daily from 10am to 5pm. The city's major daily paper is the **Sacramento Bee** (www.sacbee.com).

ORIENTATION Suburbia sprawls around Sacramento, but its downtown area is relatively compact. Getting around the city is made easy by a gridlike pattern of streets designated by numbers or letters. The capitol, on 10th Street between N and L streets, is the key landmark. From the front of the capitol, M Street—at this point called Capitol Mall—runs 10 straight blocks to Old Sacramento, the oldest section of the city.

What to See & Do

In town, you'll want to stroll around **Old Sacramento ★**, 4 square blocks at the foot of the downtown area that have become a major tourist attraction. These blocks contain more than 100 restored buildings (California's largest restoration project), including restaurants and shops. Although the area has cobblestone streets, wooden sidewalks, and authentic Gold Rush–era architecture, the high concentration of T-shirt shops and other gimmicky stores has turned it into a sort of historical amusement park. Nonetheless, there are interesting things to see, such as where the Pony Express ended and the transcontinental railroad—and the Republican Party—began. The **California State Railroad Museum** (see below) is loved by railroad buffs, and the **Sacramento Jazz Festival,** mostly

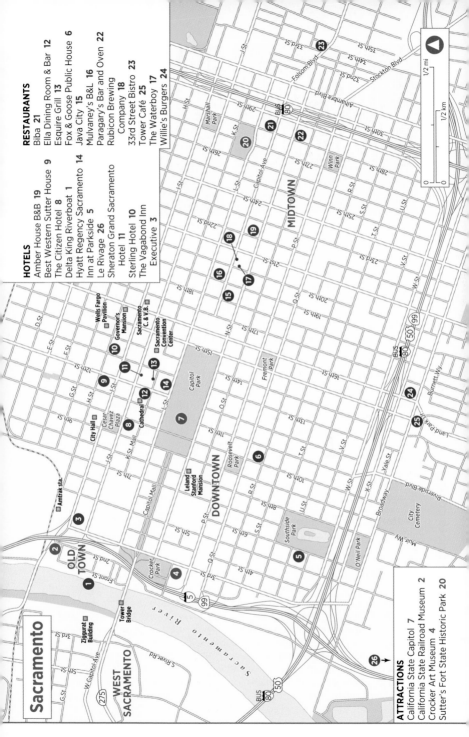

Sacramento

WEST SACRAMENTO

OLD TOWN

DOWNTOWN

MIDTOWN

Sacramento River

Tower Bridge

Ziggurat Building

Amtrak sta.

City Hall

Cesar Chavez Plaza

Wells Fargo Pavilion

Governor's Mansion

Sacramento C. & V.B.

Sacramento Convention Center

Cathedral

Capitol Park

Leland Stanford Mansion

Roosevelt Park

Fremont Park

Marshall Park

Winn Park

Southside Park

O'Neil Park

City Cemetery

Railroad Museum.

Discovery Museum.

Dixieland, draws more than 100 bands from around the world for 4 days of madness over Memorial Day weekend. While you're meandering, stop at the **Discovery Museum: Science and Space Center ★**, 3615 Auburn Blvd. (© **916/575-3941;** www.thediscovery.org), which houses exhibits of California's history, highlighting the valley's agricultural Gold Rush and the real one in 1849. It's open Tuesday through Sunday from 10am to 5pm (daily July–Aug). Entry is $5 for adults, $4 for seniors over 60 and kids ages 13 to 17, $3 for kids 4 to 12, and free for kids 3 and under ($1 more on all weekends and holidays).

THE MAIN ATTRACTIONS

California State Capitol ★★★   Closely resembling a scale model of the U.S. Capitol in Washington, D.C., the beautiful, domed California state capitol was built in 1869 and renovated in 1976. Sacramento's most distinctive landmark, the capitol has been the stage of many political dramas in California history. The 1-hour guided tours provide insight into the architecture and the workings of the government it houses. *Note:* Security will ask you to put your purse or backpack through a metal detector.

10th St. (btw. N and L sts.). © **916/324-0333.** www.capitolmuseum.ca.gov. Free admission. Daily 9am–5pm. Tours offered every hour on the hour until 4pm. Closed Thanksgiving, Dec 25, and Jan 1.

California State Railroad Museum ★★★ ☺   With its 105 shiny antique locomotives and rail cars, this museum is the highlight of Old Sacramento. Over

☺ WHERE THE wild things ARE

The best place to take little kids to let them tear around on a sunny afternoon is **Fairytale Town,** at William Land Park, Land Park Drive and Sutterville Road (© **916/808-5233;** www.fairytaletown.org). Although the slides and other climbing toys are pretty basic and show their age, kids seem to think it's the best place in the world. Across the street, at the **Sacramento Zoo** (© **916/808-5888;** www.saczoo.com), buy some cotton candy and see the animals. Adjacent to Fairytale Town, there's also the small but pleasant **Funderland** amusement park (© **916/456-0115;** www.funderlandpark.com), with kid-size rides, open all week in summer months and on spring and fall weekends, weather permitting.

half a million people visit each year, and even the hordes of schoolchildren that typically mob this place shouldn't dissuade you from visiting one of the largest and best railroad museums in the country. Allow about 2 hours to see it all. From April to September, on weekends and holidays from 11am to 5pm, **steam locomotive rides** carry passengers 6 miles along the Sacramento River. Trains depart on the hour from the Central Pacific Freight Depot in Old Sacramento, at K and Front streets. Fares are $8 for adults, $3 for children 6 to 17, and free for children 5 and under.

125 I St. (at Second St.). ℭ **916/445-6645.** www.californiastaterailroadmuseum.org. Admission $9 adults, $4 children 6–17, free for children 5 and under. Daily 10am–5pm. Closed Thanksgiving, Christmas, and New Year's Day.

Crocker Art Museum ★★ One hundred twenty-six years after Margaret Crocker, widow of railroad magnate E. B. Crocker, established the first art museum west of the Mississippi, a new, $100-million addition and renovation has tripled the museum's space. The Classic/Contemporary addition by the architectural firm that did the renovation of Manhattan's Guggenheim has propelled the museum back into the ranks of major metropolitan art museums.

The Crocker boasts one of the state's premier collections of Californian art dating from the Gold Rush to the present day, a world-renowned collection of master drawings, European paintings, one of the largest and most comprehensive international ceramics collections in the U.S., and growing collections of Asian, African, and Oceanic art. In addition to its impressive collections, the Crocker will be hosting changing exhibitions from around the world. Visiting the Crocker is a must for all Sacramento visitors. Allow at least an hour to see the new Teel Family Pavilion and the restored Crocker mansion.

216 O St. (at Third St.). ℭ **916/808-7000.** www.crockerartmuseum.org. Admission $10 adults; $8 seniors, military, and college students; $5 children 7–17; free for children 6 and under. Tues–Wed 10am–7pm; Thurs 10am–9pm; Fri–Sun 10am–5pm. Every 3rd Sun of the month is "Pay What you Wish Sunday" sponsored by Bank of America. Closed major holidays.

Crocker Art Museum.

Sutter's Fort State Historic Park ★ John Sutter established this outpost in 1839, and the park, restored to its 1846 appearance, aims to recapture the spirit of 19th-century California. Exhibits include a blacksmith's forge, cooperage, bakery, and jail—and a self-guided audio tour is available. Demonstrations and reenactments in costume are staged daily Memorial Day to Labor Day.

2701 L St. ✆ **916/445-4422.** www.parks. ca.gov. Admission $5 adults, $3 children 6–16, free for children 5 and under. Daily 10am–5pm.

OUTDOOR PURSUITS

BICYCLING One good thing about a town that's as flat as a tortilla: It's perfect for exploring on a bike. One of the best places to ride is Old Sacramento, along the

Sutter Gold Mine.

paved 32-mile American River Parkway, through town. If you didn't bring your own wheels, the friendly guys at **City Bicycle Works,** 2419 K St., at 24th Street (✆ **916/447-2453;** www.citybicycleworks.com), will rent you one for $5 to $10 an hour or $20 to $40 a day.

RIVER RAFTING Sacramento lies at the confluence of the American and Sacramento rivers, and rafting on the clear blue water of the American is popular, especially on warm weekends. Several Sacramento-area outfitters, such as **American River Raft Rentals,** 11257 S. Bridge St. (at Sunrise Ave.), Rancho Cordova (✆ **888/338-RAFT** [7238] or 916/635-6400; www.raftrentals. com), rent rafts for 4 to 15 persons, along with life jackets and paddles for $12 to $24 per person. Their shuttles drop you upstream and meet you 3 to 4 hours later at a predetermined point downstream.

Where to Stay

EXPENSIVE

Amber House Bed & Breakfast ★★ Just 8 blocks from the capitol on a quiet street, Amber House offers individually decorated, antiques-filled rooms named for famous musicians and writers. The accommodations are located within historic houses: the Poet's Refuge, a 1905 Craftsman-style home with five rooms, and an 1895 Dutch colonial home called the Musician's Manor. Its Mozart Room is the B&B's best, with a four-poster queen bed, a heart-shaped Jacuzzi, a private patio, and three bay windows overlooking the tree-shaded street. A living room and library are available for guests' use. A full breakfast is served at the time and location you request—in your room, in the large dining room, or outside on the veranda. Coffee and a newspaper are brought to your door each morning, as are freshly baked cookies every afternoon; and nonalcoholic beverages are offered all day.

1315 22nd St., Sacramento, CA 95816. www.amberhouse.com. ☏ **800/755-6526** or 916/444-8085. Fax 916/552-6529. 10 units. $169–$279 double. Rates include breakfast. AE, DC, DISC, MC, V. **Amenities:** Concierge. *In room:* A/C, TV/DVD, hair dryer, high-speed Internet.

The Citizen Hotel ★★ Citizen Hotel is Sacramento's newest and swankiest boutique hotel, and Joie de Vivre's newest addition to its family of hotels does not disappoint. Built in the 1920s, this vintage hotel was renovated with exceptional period detail and unique charm. Vaulted ceilings and original woodwork frame immaculately decorated rooms of bold-striped wallpaper, simple yet opulent furnishings, marble sinks, and fluffy bed linens. The Citizen does not miss a beat when it comes to details: Make sure to take notice of a common political theme running throughout the hotel. Rooms facing the north are recommended not only for the view of City Hall but to avoid late-night noise from the bar across the street. Room service offers impeccable cuisine (including a kids' menu) from Grange, Citizen's five-star restaurant, which offers not only some of Sacramento's best cuisine but also the chance to spot the mayor, a senator or two, and perhaps even a local celebrity.

926 J St., Sacramento, CA 95814. www.citizenhotel.com. ☏ **916/447-2700.** Fax 916/447-2701. 198 units. $149–$249 double. AE, DC, DISC, MC, V. Valet parking $25. **Amenities:** Restaurant; bar; concierge, fitness center; room service; movie library. *In room:* Flatscreen TV, hair dryer, MP3 docking station, Wi-Fi ($9.95).

Hyatt Regency Sacramento ★★ Sacramento's top hotel is in the heart of downtown, across from the state capitol and adjacent to the convention center. It's the high-status address for visiting politicos and is popular with conventioneers as well, as its facilities and services are unmatched in the city. While the rooms themselves are not terribly distinctive, they conform to a high standard and come with all the amenities you expect from Hyatt. The best are the corner units with views facing the state capitol.

1209 L St., Sacramento, CA 95814. www.sacramento.hyatt.com. ☏ **800/233-1234** or 916/443-1234. Fax 916/321-3779. 503 units. $149–$300 double; from $375 suite. AE, DC, DISC, MC, V. Self-parking $17; valet parking $25. **Amenities:** 2 restaurants; bar; concierge; nearby golf course; health club; Jacuzzi; heated outdoor pool; room service. *In room:* A/C, TV w/pay movies, fridge upon request, hair dryer, minibar, Wi-Fi.

Inn at Parkside ★★★ Sterling Hotel aside, Sacramento has long been lacking a small, independently owned charmer. Enter the Inn at Parkside, which opened a couple years ago in the former Chinese ambassador's quarters, the Fong Mansion. Owners Diane Gorker and Dan Sedlock enhanced the hotel with a few small additions, like flatscreen TVs, DVR players, and a handful of upgrades to the popular Spa Bloom. All accommodations are well appointed, but the delightfully romantic Kiss suite is particularly enticing, with its striking red color scheme, spa shower for two, and in-room Jacuzzi soaking tub by a crackling fireplace. Perhaps the grandest part of the stay is the epicurean spread you'll be treated to in the morning: gourmet coffee and tea, freshly squeezed orange juice, a fruit plate, pastries right out of the oven, and a hot dish such as eggs Benedict and country potatoes served when and where you like it.

2116 Sixth St., Sacramento, CA 95818. www.innatparkside.com. ☏ **800/995-7275** or 916/658-1818. Fax 916/659-1809. 11 units. $169–$339 double. Rates include full breakfast and cheese and wine reception. AE, DC, DISC, MC, V. **Amenities:** Concierge; spa. *In room:* A/C, TV/DVD w/DVD library, DVR, hair dryer, minibar, free Wi-Fi.

10

Le Rivage ★   While driving to this sprawling riverside hotel, you'll surely think you're lost. Its location just off the interstate in a residential, rarely visited part of Sacramento is surely perplexing. But those with boats will love the situation on the water and the ability to launch their boats directly from the hotel's backyard. Rooms are fancy but rather bland—it's quite obvious Le Rivage is aiming for a business clientele. Select suites have private balconies, fireplaces, and deep Jacuzzi tubs. Despite the lack of character, Le Rivage has everything you could possibly need to survive away from home and more—like bocce courts, a marina, and a state-of-the-art spa and fitness center. Several nights of the week, you'll find live jazz in the lounge.

4800 Riverside Blvd., Sacramento, CA 95822. www.lerivagehotel.com. © **888/760-5944** or 916/443-8400. Fax 916/706-3384. 101 units. $159–$339 double; $319–$459 suite. AE, DC, DISC, MC, V. Valet parking $21. **Amenities:** Restaurant; lounge; cafe; wine bar; bike rental; concierge; golf course and tennis courts nearby; fitness center; pool; room service; spa; boccie courts; jet ski rental. *In room:* A/C, TV, hair dryer, minibar, MP3 docking station, Wi-Fi.

Sheraton Grand Sacramento Hotel ★   This convention hotel, which opened in 2001, is praised for its high-tech amenities, a million-dollar public art collection, and the preservation of a beloved landmark. The hotel's 503 rooms are in a new 26-story building adjoining a three-story building that was originally Sacramento's public market from 1920 to the 1960s. This historic structure, designed by Julia Morgan, architect for Hearst Castle, was a favorite gathering place for three generations of Sacramentans. Now housing the lobby, bar, and two restaurants, the site is again a downtown focal point for residents and travelers alike. The accommodations are convention-type hotel rooms—a mite anonymous, but not unpleasant.

1230 J St., Sacramento, CA 95814. www.sheraton.com. © **800/325-3535** or 916/447-1700. Fax 916/477-1701. 503 units. $146–$294 double; from $375 suite. AE, DC, DISC, MC, V. Self-parking $13; valet parking $25. Dogs welcome (beds available). **Amenities:** 2 restaurants; bar; babysitting; concierge; health club; heated outdoor pool; room service. *In room:* A/C, TV w/pay movies and video games, hair dryer, minibar, Wi-Fi.

Sterling Hotel ★★   In the heart of Sacramento, 3 blocks from the capitol, this inn occupies a white-fronted Victorian mansion built in the 1890s but in stellar condition for its age. The Sterling has all the charm of a small, well-managed, sophisticated inn, with a carefully tended flowering yard, tasteful decor, designer furnishings, Italian marble, and a Jacuzzi in every room. The hotel's popular restaurant, **Restaurant THIR13EN,** serves lunch and dinner in their elegant dining room and sunny patio.

1300 H St., Sacramento, CA 95814. www.sterlinghotelsacramento.com. © **916/448-1300.** 16 units. Sun–Thurs $149–$199 double, $335 suite; Fri–Sat $209–$257 double, $335 suite. Rates include continental breakfast. AE, DISC, MC, V. **Amenities:** Restaurant; salon; tea and coffee served all day. *In room:* A/C, TV w/pay movies, fridge in most units, hair dryer, free Wi-Fi.

MODERATE

Delta King **Riverboat** ★   The *Delta King* carried passengers between San Francisco and Sacramento in the 1930s. Permanently moored in Sacramento since 1984, the riverboat is now a somewhat gimmicky but charming hotel. Staying here can be a novelty, but the staterooms are rather small and may bother landlubbers. All units have private bathrooms and typical low shipboard ceilings.

The captain's quarters, a fancy suite, is a unique, mahogany-paneled stateroom, complete with an observation platform, private deck, and wet bar.

The riverboat's **Pilothouse Restaurant** has unparalleled river views. When the weather is nice, many patrons dine on outside decks. Live entertainment is presented below decks in two venues Thursday through Saturday in the evening. The Mark Twain Salon hosts "Suspect's Murder Mystery Dinner Theatre," an interactive whodunit ($40 per person; drinks, tax, and gratuity extra).

1000 Front St., Old Sacramento, CA 95814. www.deltaking.com. © **800/825-5464** or 916/444-5464. 44 units. Sun–Thurs $99–$149 double, $550 captain's quarters; Fri–Sat $99–$179 double, $550 captain's quarters. Riverside rooms $15 extra. Rates include continental breakfast. AE, DC, DISC, MC, V. **Amenities:** Restaurant; lounge. *In room:* A/C, TV, hair dryer, Wi-Fi.

INEXPENSIVE

Best Western Sutter House 🌢   Its plain, motel-like exterior disguises one of the best values in Sacramento. Rooms here are as up-to-date as any offered by upscale hotels such as the Hilton or the Hyatt, including well-coordinated furnishings and lots of amenities. There's a pool in the courtyard, guest passes to a nearby fitness center, free covered parking, and complimentary coffee and pastries each morning.

1100 H St., Sacramento, CA 95814. www.thesutterhouse.com. © **888/256-8040** or 916/441-1314. Fax 916/441-5961. 98 units. $79–$139 double. Rates include continental breakfast. AE, DC, DISC, MC, V. **Amenities:** Access to fitness center; solar-heated outdoor pool; room service; Wi-Fi. *In room:* A/C, TV w/HBO, hair dryer, high-speed Internet.

The Vagabond Inn Executive 🌢   A reliable choice within walking distance of the state capitol and 1 block from historic Old Sacramento, the Vagabond Inn has many free features, including local phone calls, weekday newspapers, and continental breakfast. Bedrooms are clean and comfortable. There's an adjoining 24-hour Denny's restaurant.

909 Third St., Sacramento, CA 95814. www.vagabondinns.com. © **800/522-1555** or 916/446-1481. Fax 916/448-0364. 108 units. $69–$109 double. Extra person $10. Rates include continental breakfast. Children 18 and under stay free in parent's room. AE, DC, DISC, MC, V. **Amenities:** Restaurant; free airport shuttle service; nearby golf course; exercise room; heated pool; spa. *In room:* A/C, TV, fridge, hair dryer, high-speed Internet, microwave.

Where to Eat

EXPENSIVE

Biba ★★★ ITALIAN   Locals flock to this Art Deco restaurant to sample the classical Italian cuisine of Bologna-born owner Biba Caggiano, who has published nine cookbooks and also has a syndicated television show called *Biba's Italian Kitchen*. Although the menu changes seasonally, you can expect to find about 10 pastas and an equal number of main courses. There might be a delicate *pappardelle* with a fresh seafood sauce, or linguine with clams and mussels in a butter, saffron, and white-wine sauce. For a main course, the classic *osso buco* Milanese served with a soft, creamy polenta is excellent.

2801 Capitol Ave. © **916/455-2422.** www.biba-restaurant.com. Reservations recommended. Entrees $15–$30. AE, DC, MC, V. Mon–Fri 11:30am–2pm; Mon–Thurs 5:30–9:30pm; Fri–Sat 5:30–10pm.

Ella Dining Room & Bar ★★ CALIFORNIA SEASONAL   Ella is the latest entry in Sacramento's campaign to play culinary catch-up with the Bay Area. Just a block from the Capitol, the designer and architects have created an award-winning space that is smart, chic, suffused with light, and very inviting. The bar, looking over the mall, has tables outside for the alfresco-inclined. The selection of cocktails is innovative, and the wine list is exceptional. The dinner menu changes daily with entrees ranging from Sonoma duck breast with roasted pears and warm lentil salad, to ricotta gnocchi with braised porcini mushrooms, pancetta, and artichokes. Meat eaters will want to tuck into Ella's double cut pork chop with lacinato kale, black-eyed peas, and an apple-onion puree. A seafood bar has a good selection of fresh Pacific Coast oysters and other fruits *de mer*.

1131 K St. ✆ **916/443-3772.** www.elladiningroomandbar.com. Main courses $15–$38. AE, DC, DISC, MC, V. Mon–Fri 11:30am–10pm; Sat 5:30–10pm.

MODERATE

Esquire Grill ★ AMERICAN GRILL   Next door to Sacramento's convention center and a short walk from the capitol, Sheraton Grand, and the Hyatt Regency, the Esquire Grill was a hit as soon as it opened its handsome doors. Sacramento has been struggling for years to revive its downtown area, and this urbane place is one giant step toward creating the revitalized scene the city planners are hoping for. The bar is always lively, with well-dressed folks sipping martinis and mojitos, and the restaurant's food is classic American grill. Dinner specialties might include a mixed fry of calamari, fennel, and onions; or spit-roasted pork chops with buttermilk onion rings and house-made applesauce. Though it's considered one of the city's best sites for politician-watching, some folks come just for the onion rings.

1213 K St. ✆ **916/448-8900.** www.paragarys.com. Main courses $11–$34. AE, DC, DISC, MC, V. Mon–Thurs 11am–9pm; Fri–Sat 11am–10pm; Sun 11am–9pm. Limited menu Mon–Fri 2:30–5pm.

Mulvaney's B&L ★★ 🍴 NEW AMERICAN   Sacramento's downtown restaurant scene rose a notch with the quiet arrival of Mulvaney's B&L (the name refers to the Bailey Society Building & Loan from *It's a Wonderful Life*) in a historic firehouse just east of the state capitol a few years back. The restaurant's classy, understated decor evokes the feel of an upscale dinner house, with original brick walls, an open kitchen, and an inviting bar. Owner and executive chef Patrick Mulvaney's eclectic entrees spring from the bounteous local fare. Specialties include spinach ravioli with portobello mushroom; wild mushroom risotto cakes; and herb-crusted rack of lamb with roasted potatoes. The cuisine is complemented by a diverse wine list, and the waitstaff was handpicked by Patrick to make sure your experience will be flawless. Patrick himself patrols the restaurant floor, meeting and greeting with patrons in his jovial way, and thus bridging the gap between the behind-the-scenes and the public.

1215 19th St. (off L St.). ✆ **916/441-6022.** www.mulvaneysbl.com. Reservations recommended. Main courses $15–$30. AE, MC, V. Wed–Sat 5–10pm.

Paragary's Bar and Oven ★★ MEDITERRANEAN   Paragary's is widely considered one of the best moderately priced restaurants in Sacramento's trendy midtown scene. In good weather, the best seats are outside amid the gorgeous fountains and plantings of the courtyard; other seating options include the formal fireplace room and the brightly lit cafe. The same menu is served no matter where you sit, with some of the best dishes coming from the kitchen's wood-burning pizza oven. But this is more than a gourmet pizza parlor, as evidenced by the grilled skirt steak with Yukon Gold mashed potatoes, grilled broccoli rabe, and spicy salsa verde; or the hand-cut rosemary noodles with seared chicken, pancetta, artichokes, leeks, and garlic.

1401 28th St. ⓒ **916/457-5737.** www.paragarys.com. Main courses $11–$22. AE, DC, DISC, MC, V. Mon–Thurs 5–9pm; Fri–Sat 4:30–10pm; Sun 4:30–9pm. Limited menu Mon–Fri 2:30–5pm.

33rd Street Bistro ★ BISTRO   What was once an old brick building has been transformed into a hugely successful bistro. The food is good (and priced right), the staff is friendly, and the ambience is cheerful. Selections might include a variety of Italian grilled sandwiches and house favorites such as shrimp ravioli with spinach and sun-dried tomato, Uncle Bum's Jerk Ribs with Jamaican barbecue sauce and Key lime crème fraîche, and a variety of wood-fired pizzas and calzone.

3301 Folsom Blvd. (at 33rd St.). ⓒ **916/455-2233.** www.33rdstreetbistro.com. Main courses $9–$19. AE, MC, V. Sun–Thurs 8am–10pm; Fri–Sat 8am–11pm.

The Waterboy ★★ COUNTRY FRENCH/ITALIAN   Until recently, Sacramento had a slim list of really good restaurants, but no more. At the top of everybody's list is the Waterboy. It's got everything going for it: an appealing, airy but unpretentious atmosphere; friendly and knowledgeable servers; and outstanding food cooked perfectly. Chef/owner Rick Mahan uses Niman Ranch naturally raised meats and local organic produce, and he offers a fine selection of wines. Main courses change every 4 weeks but include dishes such as saffron risotto; or boneless squab with a very crispy skin, served on sautéed greens with a squash polenta, figs, and a reduction of squab stock. Rick always has a traditional American favorite on the menu. On my last visit, it was a great chili cheese dog.

2000 Capitol Ave. ⓒ **916/498-9891.** www.waterboyrestaurant.com. Main courses $16–$29. AE, DC, DISC, MC, V. Mon–Fri 11:30am–2:30pm; Tues–Thurs 5–9:30pm; Fri–Sat 5–10:30pm; Sun–Mon 5–9pm.

INEXPENSIVE

Fox & Goose Public House ★★ 🍴 ENGLISH PUB   The Fox is your classic British pub, down to the dartboard, picture of the queen, and numerous beers from across the pond. The soups at lunch are excellent, and the specials often include bangers and mash, Welsh rarebit, and Cornish pasties. The burnt-cream dessert is famous. Arrive early for lunch or be prepared for a wait, as locals love this place (no reservations are taken and they won't seat you until all members of your party have arrived). Equally popular breakfasts include kippers, crumpets, waffles, omelets, and French toast. There's live entertainment by local bands 6 nights a week, and pub grub is served Monday through Friday from 2:30 to 9:30pm.

1001 R St. (at 10th St.). ⓒ **916/443-8825.** www.foxandgoose.com. Reservations not accepted. Main courses $5–$10. AE, MC, V. Breakfast daily 7am–2pm; lunch Mon–Fri 11am–2pm; pub grub Mon–Fri 2:30–9:30pm and Sat 5:30–9:30pm. Bar until midnight Mon–Thurs, until 2am Fri–Sat.

Tower Café INTERNATIONAL   In a grand 1939 movie house with a tall Art Deco spire, the Tower Café's multicultural decor is a feast for the eyes. Dishes reflect a variety of international flavors, from the Jamaican jerk chicken to Chinese chicken salad. Usually the food is good, especially the desserts, but once in a while you get something that makes you wonder what's going on in the kitchen. On warm days, it seems as if everyone in the city is lunching here on the large outdoor patio (past patrons have included Bill Clinton), so people-watching can be a real treat.

1518 Broadway. ✆ **916/441-0222.** www.towercafe.com. Main courses $9–$18. AE, MC, V. Sun–Thurs 8am–11pm; Fri–Sat 8am–midnight.

THE GOLD COUNTRY ★★

Cutting a serpentine swath for nearly 350 miles along Hwy. 49, the Gold Country's mining sites, horse ranches, ghost towns, Gold Rush architecture, and Wild West saloons stretch from Sierra City to the foothills of Yosemite. The town of Placerville, 44 miles east of Sacramento at the intersection of U.S. 50 and Hwy. 49, is in the approximate center of the region. To the north are the old mining towns of Grass Valley and Nevada City, while in the central and southern Gold Country are such well-preserved towns as Amador City, Sutter Creek, Columbia, and Jamestown.

The Gold Country is so immense that it would take weeks to thoroughly explore. So I have narrowed my coverage to include three of my favorite regions, each of which can be explored in just 2 or 3 days: the charismatic side-by-side towns of Nevada City and Grass Valley; the Gold Rush communities of Amador City, Sutter Creek, and Jackson; and the wonderfully authentic neighboring mining towns of Angels Camp, Murphys, Columbia, Sonora, and Jamestown.

Whether you're intent on panning for gold, exploring old mines and caverns, or rafting the area's many white-water rivers, the Gold Country is one of the most underrated and least congested tourist destinations in California, a winning combination of Old West ambience, affordable bed-and-breakfasts (many have a 2-night minimum on weekends), and outdoor adventures galore.

The Northern Gold Country: Nevada City & Grass Valley

About 60 miles northeast of Sacramento, Nevada City and Grass Valley are far and away the top tourist destinations of the northern Gold Country.

These two historic towns were at the center of the hard-rock mining fields of Northern California. Grass Valley was California's richest mining town, producing more than a billion dollars' worth of gold. Both are attractive, although smaller Nevada City's wealth of Victorian homes and storefronts makes it one of the most appealing small towns in California, particularly in the fall, when the maple trees are ablaze

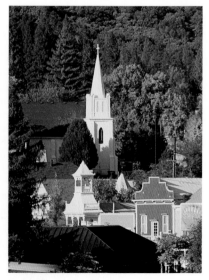

Nevada City.

Gold Country

with color. (Its entire downtown has been designated a National Historic Landmark.)

From San Francisco, take I-80 to the Hwy. 49 turnoff in Auburn and follow the signs heading north. For information about the area, contact the **Grass Valley & Nevada County Chamber of Commerce,** 248 Mill St., Grass Valley (𝒸 **800/655-4667** in California, or 530/273-4667; www.grassvalleychamber. com), or the **Nevada City Chamber of Commerce,** 132 Main St., Nevada City (𝒸 **800/655-6569** or 530/265-2692; www.nevadacitychamber.com).

NEVADA CITY ★★

Rumors of miners pulling a pound of gold a day out of Deer Creek brought thousands of fortune seekers to the area in 1849. Within a year, Nevada City was a boisterous town of 10,000, the third-largest city in California. In its heyday, everyone visited this rollicking Western outpost with its busy red-light district: Mark Twain lectured here in 1866, and former president Herbert Hoover lived and worked here as a gold miner.

Pick up a walking-tour map at the **Chamber of Commerce,** 132 Main St., and stroll the streets lined with impressive Victorian buildings; the **National Hotel** (built 1854–56) is here (the Gold Rush–era bar serves a spicy bloody mary), as is the **Nevada Theatre** (1865), one of the oldest theaters in the nation still operating as such. Today it's home to the Foothill Theatre Company.

If you want to see the source of much of the city's wealth, visit **Malakoff Diggins State Historic Park ★,** 23579 N. Bloomfield Rd. (𝒸 **530/265-2740;** www.parks.ca.gov), 28 miles northeast of Nevada City. Once the world's largest hydraulic gold mine, it's an awesome (some say environmentally disturbing) spectacle of hydraulic mining: Nearly half a mountain has been washed away by powerful jets of water, leaving behind a 600-foot-deep canyon of exposed rock. In the 1870s, North Bloomfield, then located in the middle of this park, had a population of 1,500. Some of the buildings have been reconstructed and refurnished to show what life was like then. The 3,000-acre park also offers several hiking trails, swimming at Blair Lake, and 30 campsites that can be reserved through **ReserveAmerica** (𝒸 **800/444-7275;** www.reserveamerica.com). The museum is open daily in summer from 11am to 4pm; on winter weekends the

Nevada City Shop.

Malakoff Diggins State Historic Park.

museum opens at 11:30am. To reach the park, take Hwy. 49 toward Downieville for 11 miles. Turn right onto Tyler-Foote Crossing Road for 17 miles. Turn right onto Derbec Road and then right on North Bloomfield Road, which takes you to the park entrance. The fee is $8 per car, $6 for seniors.

Another 6 miles up Hwy. 49 from the Malakoff Diggins turnoff brings you to Pleasant Valley Road, the exit that will take you (in about 7 miles) to one of the nation's most impressive **covered bridges.** Built in 1862, it's 225 feet long and was crossed by many a stagecoach (in fall, it makes for a spectacular photo opportunity).

Covered bridge, Grass Valley.

Where to Stay

Deer Creek Inn Bed & Breakfast ★   An 1860 three-floor Victorian overlooking Deer Creek and within walking distance of downtown Nevada City, this inn feels like a warm home-away-from-home. Most of the individually decorated rooms have private verandas facing the creek or town. Three bathrooms have claw-foot tubs. A stay at Deer Creek includes a three-course gourmet breakfast, served either on the deck or in the formal dining room. Guests are invited to their wine tasting, or to try a little gold panning or fishing—or simply to relax and enjoy the lawn and landscaped rose gardens along the creek.

116 Nevada St., Nevada City, CA 95959. www.deercreekinn.com. ⓒ **800/655-0363** or 530/265-0363. Fax 530/265-0980. 6 units. $160–$230 double. Rates include breakfast. MC, V. **Amenities:** Bike rental; nearby golf course. *In room:* A/C, TV/DVD, Wi-Fi.

Emma Nevada House ★★   This picture-perfect Victorian was the childhood home of 19th-century opera star Emma Nevada. You'll like everything about it: the quiet location, sun-drenched decks, wraparound porch, understated decor, and breakfast served in the hexagonal Sun Room. The guest rooms range from small and intimate to large and luxurious; all have private bathrooms and queen- or king-size beds. Top choice for honeymooners is the Empress Chamber, with its wall of windows, ivory and burgundy tones, and—of course—the Jacuzzi tub for two. You'll also like the fact that the shops and restaurants of Nevada City's Historic District are only a short walk away.

528 E. Broad St., Nevada City, CA 95959. www.emmanevadahouse.com. ⓒ **800/916-EMMA** (3662) or 530/265-4415. Fax 530/265-4416. 6 units. $169–$249 double. Rates include breakfast. AE, DISC, MC, V. **Amenities:** Concierge. *In room:* A/C, hair dryer, phone on request, free Wi-Fi.

Nevada City Inn 🛥   Surely no forty-niner had it this good: his own cabinlike motel room cooled by the shade of a small tree-lined park equipped with barbecues and picnic tables. Granted, the rooms are small and simple at this restored 1940s motor lodge, but considering that you get all the standard amenities for a really low price, the cash-conscious traveler could hardly ask for more. The inn also rents seven fully furnished cottages with kitchens, popular with families and groups. They're a good deal for such a prime location, about a half-mile from Nevada City's historic district.

760 Zion St., Nevada City, CA 95959. www.nevadacityinn.net. © **800/977-8884** or 530/265-2253. Fax 530/265-3310. 20 units, 7 cottages. $69–$139 double; $130–$189 cottage. Rates include continental breakfast. AE, DC, DISC, MC, V. *In room:* A/C, TV, hair dryer, free Wi-Fi.

Red Castle Inn Historic Lodgings ★   This elegant, comfortable hillside inn occupies a four-story Gothic Revival brick house built in 1860 in a secluded spot with a panoramic view of the town. The house retains its original woodwork, plaster moldings, ceiling medallions, and much of the handmade glass. It lacks modern intrusions such as TVs and phones. Guests enjoy five-course buffet breakfasts and relax on the verandas that encircle the first two floors of the house and overlook the rose gardens. My favorite rooms are the Garden Room, with a canopy bed and French doors leading into the gardens, and the three-room Garret Suite tucked under the eaves, with sleigh beds and Gothic arched windows.

109 Prospect St., Nevada City, CA 95959. www.redcastleinn.com. © **800/761-4766** or 530/265-5135. 7 units. $120–$185 double. Rates include breakfast. MC, V. *In room:* A/C, no phone.

Where to Eat

New Moon Café ★★ AMERICAN/INTERNATIONAL   Nevada City's favorite chef, Peter Selaya, offers a menu of imaginatively prepared items that feature free-range and antibiotic-free meats and poultry, house-baked breads, house-made pastas using organic flours and grains, and local organic vegetables, when available—which is often, in this hotbed of natural foodstuffs. Not only is the food healthy, but it tastes great. Dinner entrees include a Niman Ranch loin chop grilled with spring onion-port confit and Yukon gold mashed potatoes, or large prawns sautéed with fresh mussels, fennel, tomato, and andouille sausage. The ravioli and desserts are made fresh daily (the fresh strawberry Napoleons are beyond delicious). Nevada City's balmy climate makes the front deck a great place to dine and people-watch.

203 York St. © **530/265-6399.** www.thenewmooncafe.com. Reservations recommended. Main courses $15–$28. DC, MC, V. Tues–Fri 11:30am–2pm; Tues–Sun 5–8:30pm (or later).

GRASS VALLEY

In contrast to Nevada City's "tourist town" image, nearby Grass Valley is the commercial and retail center of the region. Although it's lacking in high-quality restaurants and B&Bs, its wealth of historical attractions makes it a worthwhile day trip. The **Empire Mine State Historic Park ★**, 10791 E. Empire St., Grass Valley (© **530/273-8522;** www.empiremine.org), the oldest, largest, and richest gold mine in California, is just outside of town. The mine once had 367 miles of shafts and produced an estimated 5.8 million ounces of gold between 1850 and 1956. You can look down the shaft of the mine, walk around the mine yard, and stroll through the owner's gardens. Tours are conducted and a mining-technique movie is shown year-round, but check the schedules at www.empiremine.org or call in advance. You can also enjoy picnicking, cycling, mountain biking, or hiking in the 854-acre park. It's open year-round except for Thanksgiving, Christmas, and New Year's Day. Admission to the park and museum costs $5 for adults over 16 and $3 for children 6 and over (children 5 and under are free). Guided tours of the mine yard and grounds are $1.50 per person.

Visitors can pick up a walking-tour map at the **Chamber of Commerce,** 248 Mill St. (© **530/273-4667;** www.grassvalleychamber.com), and explore the historic area along Mill and Main streets. Two museums will appeal to California-history and gold-mining buffs: the **Grass Valley Museum,** 410 S. Church St., adjacent to St. Joseph's Cultural Center (✆ **530/273-5509**), and the **North Star Mining Museum,** at the south end of Mill Street at Allison Ranch Road (✆ **530/273-4255;** May–Oct).

Grass Valley was, for a time, the home of **Lola Montez,** singer, dancer, and paramour of the rich and famous. A fully restored home that she bought and occupied in 1853 can be viewed at 248 Mill St., now the site of Grass Valley's chamber of commerce. **Lotta Crabtree,** Montez's famous protégée, lived down the street at 238 Mill St., now an apartment house. Also pop into the **Holbrooke Hotel,** 212 Main St., to see the signature of Mark Twain, who stayed here, as did four U.S. presidents. The saloon has been in continuous use since 1852, and locals still come for tall cold ones.

The surrounding region offers many recreational opportunities on its rivers and lakes and in the Tahoe National Forest. You can enjoy fishing, swimming, and boating at **Scotts Flat Lake** near Nevada City (east on Hwy. 20) and at **Rollins Lake** on Hwy. 174, between Grass Valley and Colfax. **Tributary Whitewater Tours,** 20480 Woodbury Dr., Grass Valley, CA 95949 (✆ **800/672-3846** or 530/346-6812; www.whitewatertours.com), offers half- to 3-day whitewater rafting trips March through October. The chambers of commerce publish a trail guide for mountain biking, but you must bring your own wheels. For regional hiking information, contact **Tahoe National Forest Headquarters,** at Coyote Street and Hwy. 49 in Nevada City (✆ **530/265-4531**).

Where to Stay

Grass Valley Courtyard Suites   If you like to lounge poolside with a good book, you'll appreciate the Courtyard Suites, and if you have your little dog Toto with you, he'll appreciate the canine cuddler (fuzzy little blanket) he's provided when you check in. In a quiet neighborhood, a block from downtown Grass Valley, this place offers enough amenities to cover your every need, including a spa, fitness facility, sauna, and seasonally heated pool. There's a generous continental breakfast in the morning, and wine and hors d'oeuvres in the evening. Some suites have fully equipped kitchens and fireplaces, and there's also a coin-operated guest laundry facility.

210 N. Auburn St., Grass Valley, CA 95945. www.gvcourtyardsuites.com. ✆ **530/272-7696.** Fax 530/272-1203. 33 units. $150–$180 double; $195–$325 suite. Rates include continental breakfast. AE, DISC, V. Covered parking. **Amenities:** Fitness facility; outdoor seasonal heated pool; sauna; spa. *In room:* A/C, TV w/HBO, DVD player, fridge, hair dryer.

Holbrooke Hotel ★   This Victorian-era white-clapboard building was a saloon during the Gold Rush days and then evolved into a place for miners to "rack out." The oldest and most historic hotel in town, it's hosted a number of legendary figures: Mark Twain and presidents Ulysses Grant, Benjamin Harrison, and Grover Cleveland, among others. Seventeen of the rooms lie within the main building. The remainder are in an adjacent annex, a house occupied long ago by the hotel's owner. Each guest room is decorated with a collection of Gold Rush–era furniture and antiques. All have cable TVs in armoires, and most bathrooms have claw-foot tubs. If you can, reserve one of the larger Veranda rooms that face Main Street and have access to the balconies; it's well worth the few extra dollars. A continental breakfast is served in the library.

212 W. Main St., Grass Valley, CA 95945. www.holbrooke.com. ☏ **800/933-7077** or 530/273-1353. Fax 530/273-0434. 28 units. $109–$239 double. Rates include continental breakfast. AE, DC, DISC, MC, V. **Amenities:** Restaurant; saloon. *In room:* A/C, TV, hair dryer, Wi-Fi.

Where to Eat

Tofanelli's 🍴 INTERNATIONAL   The venerable Tofanelli's restaurant continues to satisfy Grass Valley locals, as it has for decades, by serving large portions of good food at reasonable prices for lunch, dinner, and Sunday brunch. You'll like the setting—a bright, cheery trio of dining areas (atrium, outdoor patio, and dining room) separated by exposed brick walls. Specials on the menu, such as Gorgonzola ravioli topped with garlic-cream sauce, or pad Thai noodles with fresh ginger and marinated beef, change quarterly. Perennial mainstays include lasagna, burgers, steaks, and chocolate cake.

302 W. Main St. (across from the Holbrooke Hotel). ☏ **530/272-1468.** www.tofanellis.com. Main courses $12–$26. AE, DISC, MC, V. Sun–Thurs 8am–9pm; Fri–Sat 8am–10pm.

The Central Gold Country: Amador City, Sutter Creek, Jackson & Environs

Though Placerville is technically the center of the Gold Country, it's the small trio of towns a few miles to the south—Amador City, Sutter Creek, and Jackson—that are the most appealing destination in this region of rolling hills, dotted with solitary oaks and granite outcroppings. Since the mining boom went bust, most of these restored Gold Rush towns rely solely on tourism (hence the conversion of many Victorian homes into B&Bs), though a few mines have reopened recently.

One of the advantages of staying in this area, 55 miles southeast of Sacramento, is that both the northern and the southern regions of the Gold Country are only a few hours' drive away (via very winding roads).

To reach Amador City, Sutter Creek, or Jackson from Placerville, head south along Hwy. 49 past Plymouth and Drytown. If you're coming straight here from Sacramento, take U.S. 50 to Placerville and head south on Hwy. 49; Hwy. 16 from Sacramento is another option, but only slightly faster. For more information about any of these towns, contact the **Amador County Chamber of Commerce,** 517 S. Hwy. 49, Jackson Street (☏ **209/223-0350;** www.amadorcounty chamber.com).

AMADOR CITY ★

Once a bustling mining town, Amador City is now devoted mostly to dredging up tourist dollars. Although Amador City sounds impressive, it's the smallest incorporated city in California. Local merchants have made the most of a refurbished block-long boardwalk, converting the historic false-fronted buildings into a gallery of sorts; the stores sell everything from early-1900s antiques and folk art to handcrafted furniture, Gold Rush memorabilia, rare books, and Native American crafts. Parking can be difficult, however, especially in summer.

Where to Stay & Dine

Imperial Hotel ★★   At the foot of Main Street overlooking Amador City, this stately 1879 brick hotel and restaurant has been beautifully restored and manages to be both elegant and whimsical. The individually decorated rooms, all with private bathrooms, are furnished with wicker, iron, or pine beds and numerous

Jackson.

Sutter Creek.

antiques. Room no. 6 is the quietest, but room no. 1—with its high ceiling, queen-size canopy bed, comfortable seating area, and French doors that open onto the balcony overlooking Main Street—is the most requested. The smart and chic Oasis Bar is stocked with a large selection of spirits and California and imported wines and beers. Gourmet breakfast is served downstairs in the dining room, with French doors opening onto the native stone patio. The **Imperial Hotel Restaurant,** serving California cuisine such as Sonoma Liberty duck breast with a port reduction and thick-cut pork chops with sautéed apples in a maple brandy sauce, has a sterling reputation.

14202 Hwy. 49, P.O. Box 212, Amador City, CA 95601. www.imperialamador.com. © **209/ 267-9172.** Fax 209/267-9249. 9 units. $105–$205 double. Rates include breakfast. AE, MC, V. **Amenities:** Restaurant; bar. *In room:* A/C, hair dryer, no phone.

SUTTER CREEK ★

The self-proclaimed "nicest little town in the Mother Lode," Sutter Creek was named after sawmill owner John Sutter, employer of James Marshall (whose discovery of gold triggered the 1849 Gold Rush). Railroad baron Leland Stanford made his fortune at Sutter Creek's Lincoln Mine and then invested his millions to build the transcontinental railroad and fund his successful California gubernatorial campaign.

The town is a charmer, lined with beautiful 19th-century buildings in pristine condition, including **Downs Mansion,** the former home of the foreman at Stanford's mine (now a private residence on Spanish St., across from the Immaculate Conception Church), and the landmark **Knight's Foundry,** 81 Eureka St., off Main Street, the last water-powered foundry and machine shop in the nation. There are also numerous shops and galleries along Main Street, though finding a free parking space can be a real challenge on summer weekends.

Where to Stay

The Foxes ★★   This 1857 clapboard house is Sutter Creek's most elegant hostelry. The six rooms are all unique, each with a queen-size bed, down comforters, and 1,200-count linens. Four rooms, including the Garden Room and the Fox Den, have gas-burning fireplaces. The Fox Den has a little library of its own, while the Anniversary Room features a 9-foot-tall Renaissance Revival bed and a sitting room. All have private bathrooms. Breakfast, cooked to order and delivered on silver service, can be served in your room or in the gazebo in the flower-filled garden. Located on Main Street, the inn is only steps away from Sutter Creek's shops and restaurants.

77 Main St. (P.O. Box 159), Sutter Creek, CA 95685. www.foxesinn.com. ℂ **800/987-3344** or 209/267-5882. Fax 209/267-0712. 7 units. $160–$325 double. Rates include breakfast. AE, DISC, MC, V. **Amenities:** Concierge; Wi-Fi. *In room:* A/C, TV/DVD/VCR w/video library, CD player, fridge w/complimentary beverages, hair dryer.

Grey Gables Inn ★   The Grey Gables Inn is a postcard-perfect replica of a Victorian manor. The two-story B&B is surrounded by terraces of gardens and embellished with fountains and vine-covered arbors. Each of the plushly carpeted guest rooms is named after a British poet; the Byron Room features hues of deep green and burgundy, dark-wood furnishings, and a four-poster king bed. All rooms have queen or king beds, gas-log fireplaces, armoires, and private bathrooms (a few with claw-foot tubs). Breakfast, delivered on English bone china, is served in the formal dining room adjacent to the Victorian parlor or in your room. The only flaw is the proximity to heavily traveled Hwy. 49, but once inside, you'll hardly notice. The shops and restaurants of Sutter Creek are within walking distance.

161 Hanford St., Sutter Creek, CA 95685. www.greygables.com. ℂ **800/473-9422** or 209/267-1039. Fax 209/267-0998. 8 units. $115–$200 double. AE, DC, DISC, MC, V. *In room:* A/C, hair dryer, no phone, free Wi-Fi.

What to Do

Sutter Gold Mine   One of the most entertaining and educational attractions in the Gold Country, the Sutter Gold Mine tours lead visitors on an hour-long excursion into the bowels of a modern hard-rock gold mine. After a ride on a mining shuttle to the mine, visitors "tag in" and go through the safety training room, as the miners once did. Wearing your hard hat, you'll proceed deep into the mine, learning about geology and history while marveling at the gems and gold embedded in the quartz of the Comet Vein (you'll even learn to distinguish real gold from "fool's gold").

After the tour, be sure to buy a bag of mining ore—about $5 per bag—head over to the wood sluice, grab one of the gold pans or sluice boxes, and pan for real gold. Each bag is guaranteed to hold either gold or gemstones (emeralds, amethysts, topaz, and many other birthstones), and an assistant is on hand to show you how it's done. Other diversions include the Company Store gift shop filled with inexpensive semiprecious gems and minerals, and a 1-hour documentary about the Gold Rush and a half-hour movie about modern gold mining (a heavy-machinery flick that kids will love).

13660 Hwy. 49, about ½ mile south of Amador City, just north of Sutter Creek. ℂ **866/762-2837** or 209/736-2708. www.suttergold.com. 1-hr. Family Tour $18 for adults, $12 for children 4–13; children 3 and under are not allowed on the tour. Summer daily 9am–5pm; Oct–May daily 10am–5pm.

COLOMA ★

On Hwy. 49 between Auburn and Placerville, the town of **Coloma ★** is so small and unpretentious that it's hard to imagine the significant role it played in the rapid development of California and the West. It was here that James Marshall first discovered that there was gold aplenty in the foothills of California. Over the next 50 years, 125 *million* ounces of gold were taken from the Sierra foothills, an amount worth a staggering $50 billion today.

Although Marshall and Sutter tried to keep the discovery secret, word soon leaked out. Sam Brannan, who ran a general store at Fort Sutter, secured some gold samples himself— as well as some choice real estate— and headed for San Francisco, where he ran through the streets shouting, "Gold! Gold! Gold! From the American River!" San Francisco rapidly emptied as men rushed off to seek their fortunes at the mines.

Coloma was quickly mined out, but its boom brought 10,000 people to the settlement and lasted long enough for residents to build a schoolhouse, a gunsmith, a general store, and a tin-roofed post office.

Rafting in Coloma.

The miners also planted oak and mimosa trees that shade the street during hot summers. About 70% of this quiet, pretty town lies in the **Marshall Gold Discovery State Historic Park** (ⓒ **530/622-3470;** www.coloma.com/gold or www.parks.ca.gov), which preserves the spot where Marshall discovered gold on the banks of the south fork of the American River.

Farther up Main Street is a replica of the mill Marshall was building when he made his discovery. The largest building in town, the mill is powered by electricity during the summer. Other attractions include the **Gold Discovery Museum,** which relates the story of the Gold Rush, and a number of Chinese stores, all that remain of the once-sizable local Chinese community. The park also has three picnic areas, four trails, recreational gold panning, and a number of buildings and exhibits relating the way of life that prevailed here in the 19th century. Admission is $5 per vehicle, $4 for seniors; hours are daily from 10am to 3pm, except on major holidays.

Folks also visit for white-water thrills on the American River. (Coloma is a popular launching point.) **White Water Connection,** in Coloma (ⓒ **800/336-7238** or 530/622-6446; www.whitewaterconnection.com), runs half- to 2-day trips down the forks of the American River. It's one of the state's most exciting outdoor adventures.

JACKSON ★

Jackson, the county seat of Amador County, is far livelier than its neighboring towns to the north. (It was the last place in California to outlaw prostitution.) Be sure to stroll through the center of town, browsing in the stores and admiring the Victorian architecture. Although the Kennedy and Argonaut mines ultimately produced more than $140 million in gold, Jackson initially earned its place in the Gold Rush as a supply center. That history is apparent in the town's wide Main Street, lined by tall buildings adorned with intricate iron railings.

The **Amador County Museum,** a huge brick building at 225 Church St. (✆ **209/223-6375**), is where Will Rogers filmed *Boys Will Be Boys* in 1920. Today the former home of Armistead Calvin Brown and his 11 children is filled with mining memorabilia and information on two local mines, the Kennedy and the Argonaut, which were among the deepest and richest in the nation. Within the museum is a working large-scale model of the Kennedy. The museum is open Wednesday through Sunday from 10am to 4pm; admission is pay-as-you-wish. Tours of the Kennedy Mine model cost $1 and are offered Saturday and Sunday on the hour from 11am to 3pm.

To see the real thing, head to the **Kennedy Tailing Wheels Park,** site of the Kennedy and Argonaut mines, the deepest in the Mother Lode. The mines have been closed for years, but the tailing wheels and head frames used to convey debris over the hills to a settling pond remain. To reach the park, take Main Street to Jackson Gate Road, just north of Jackson (no phone).

A few miles south of Jackson, on Hwy. 49, is one of the most evocative towns of the region: **Mokelumne Hill ★**. The town consists of one street overlooking a valley with a few old buildings, and somehow its sad, abandoned air has the mark of authenticity. At one time, the hill was dotted with tents and wood-and-tar-paper shacks, and the town housed a population of 15,000, including an old French quarter and a Chinatown. But now many of its former residents are memorialized in the town's Protestant, Jewish, and Catholic cemeteries.

Where to Stay & Eat

The Gate House Bed & Breakfast Inn   About a mile from downtown Jackson and a short walk to the Kennedy Tailing Wheels park, the Gate House offers an assortment of accommodations in a historic mansion surrounded by landscaped lawns, garden, and open fields. Besides the two rooms and two suites in the main house, decorated with Victorian furnishings, there's a small cottage with a gas-log stove and a Jacuzzi for two. Ping-Pong, darts, a swimming pool, and newly completed boccie ball court offer fun diversions. The three- to four-course candlelit champagne breakfast is served on fine china, and in the afternoon, wine and appetizers are served. The inn is within walking distance of two fine restaurants and close to Amador County wineries, gold mines, caverns, and Daffodil Hill.

1330 Jackson Gate Rd., Jackson, CA 95642. www.gatehouseinn.com. ✆ **800/841-1072** or 209/223-3500. 5 units. $145–$215 double. Rates include breakfast. AE, DISC, MC, V. **Amenities:** Pool (solar heated). *In room:* A/C, hair dryer.

Mel and Faye's Diner 🍴 AMERICAN   How can anybody not love a classic old roadside diner? In business since 1956, Mel and Faye have been cranking out the best diner food in the Gold Country for so long that it's okay not to feel guilty for salivating over the thought of a sloppy double Moo Burger smothered with onions and special sauce and washed down with a chocolate shake. And could you please add a large side of fries with that? And how much is a slice of pie? It's a time-honored Jackson tradition, so forget about your diet.

31 Hwy. 49 (at Main St.). www.melandfayesdiner.com. ✆ **209/223-0853.** Menu items $4–$10. MC, V. Daily 5am–10pm.

VOLCANO

About a dozen miles east of Jackson on Hwy. 88 is the enchantingly decrepit town of **Volcano ★**, one of the most authentic ghost towns in the central Sierra. The town got its name in 1848, after miners mistook the origins of the craggy boulders that lie in the center of town. The dark rock and the blind window frames of a few backless, ivy-covered buildings give the town's main thoroughfare a haunted look. Sprinkled between boarded-up buildings, about 100 residents do business in the same sagging storefronts that a population of 8,000 frequented nearly 150 years ago.

The tiny, now-quiet burg has a rich history: Not only was this boomtown once home to the state's first lending library and astronomical observatory, but Volcano gold also supported the Union during the Civil War. Residents smuggled a huge cannon to the front lines in a hearse (it was never used). The story goes that had the enthusiastic blues actually fired it, it was so overcharged that "Old Abe" would have exploded. The cannon sits in the town center today, under a rusting weather vane.

Looming over the small buildings is the stately **St. George Hotel** ★ (www.stgeorgehotel.com; ✆ **209/296-4458**), a three-story, balconied building that testifies to the $90 million in gold mined in and around the town. Its ivy-covered brick and shuttered windows will remind you of colonial New England. In 1998, new owners took over the run-down 20-room hotel and have totally turned it around. The restaurant serves brunch on Sunday and dinner Thursday through Sunday. Even if you're not hungry, stop in for a libation at the classic old bar, the Whiskey Flat Saloon.

In summer, the **Volcano Theatre Company** performs locally written and produced comedies and mysteries at the town's outdoor amphitheater, hidden behind stone facades on Main Street, a block north of the St. George Hotel. It's a wonderful Gold Country experience. For information on performances, call ✆ **209/296-2525** or visit **www.volcanotheatre.org**. In early spring, people come from all around to picnic amid the nearly half-million daffodils in bloom on **Daffodil Hill,** a 4-acre ranch 3 miles north of Volcano (follow the sign on Ram's Horn Grade).

Volcano is also the site of one of the National Park Service's National Natural Landmarks—the **Black Chasm** (✆ **866/762-2837**), a cave with stalactites, stalagmites, flowstones, and rare helictite crystals. The 50-minute Landmark Family Tour leaves every 45 minutes throughout the day, open year-round, adults $14, children $7.15. It follows a series of platforms, stairs, and walkways to preserve the cave environment. Aboveground, kids can mine for gemstones at a mining flume, guaranteed to find some real gemstones, $5 for a small bag. The new Visitors Center provides information on the cave's history and contents, as well as on Black Chasm's connection to the *Matrix* trilogy. The cave site is at 15701 Pioneer–Volcano Rd.

Black Chasm.

The Southern Gold Country: Angels Camp, Murphys, Columbia, Sonora & Jamestown

No other region in the Gold Country offers more to see and do than these towns in the south, 86 miles southeast of Sacramento. From exploring caverns to riding in the stagecoach and panning for gold, the neighboring towns of Angels Camp, Murphys, Columbia, Sonora, and Jamestown offer a cornucopia of Gold Rush–related sites, museums, and activities. It's a great place to bring the family (kids love roaming around the dusty, car-free streets of Columbia), and the region offers some of the best lodgings and restaurants in the Gold Country. In short, if you're the Type A sort who needs to stay active, the southern Gold Country is for you. For information about lodging, dining, events, and the arts and entertainment in the area, contact the **Tuolumne County Visitors Bureau,** 542 W. Stockton Rd., P.O. Box 4020, Sonora, CA 95370 (© **800/446-1333** or 209/533-4420; www.tcvb.com).

To reach any of these towns from Sacramento, head south on Hwy. 99 to Stockton, and then take Hwy. 4 east into Angels Camp. (From here, it's a short, scenic drive to the other towns.) For a longer but more scenic route, take U.S. 50 east to Placerville, and then head south on Hwy. 49, which takes you to Angels Camp.

ANGELS CAMP ★

You've probably heard of Angels Camp, the town that inspired Mark Twain to pen "The Celebrated Jumping Frog of Calaveras County." This pretty, peaceful community is built on hills honeycombed with tunnels. In the 1880s and 1890s, five mines were located along Main Street—Sultana, Angel's, Lightner, Utica, and Stickle—and the town echoed with noise as more than 200 stamps crushed the ore. Between 1886 and 1910, the mines generated close to $20 million.

But a far more lasting legacy than the town's gold production is the **Jumping Frog Jubilee,** started in 1928 to mark the paving of the town's streets. The ribbiting competition takes place every third weekend in May. The record, 21 feet, 5¾ inches, was set in 1986 by Rosie the Ribbiter, beating the old record by 4½ inches. Livestock exhibitions, pageants, cook-offs, arm-wrestling tournaments, live music, carnival rides, a rodeo, and plenty of beer and wine keep the thousands of spectators entertained between jumpoffs. (You can even rent a frog if you forgot to pack one.) For more information and entry forms (around $5 per frog), call the Jumping Frog Jubilee headquarters at © **209/736-2561,** or check **www.frogtown.org**.

Where to Stay

Best Western Cedar Inn & Suites ★ ☺   If you're looking for the classic, romantic B&B experience, you'll want to reserve a room at the beautiful Dunbar House in Murphys (see below), just a few miles up the road. But if all you need is a pleasant place to stay with plenty of free perks, reasonable rates, and a central location, you can't do better than the Cedar Inn. With its cheery yellow facade, river-stone trim, and wraparound porch, it looks more like a sprawling two-story house than a hotel. The guest rooms are all large, comfy, and loaded with amenities such as free Internet access, four HBO channels, business desks, and double granite vanities. And on a typical sweltering summer day, that outdoor pool looks mighty inviting. Families will also appreciate the hotel's 12-and-under-stay-free policy, as well as the two-room suites with refrigerators and microwaves.

444 S. Main St., Angels Camp, CA 95222. www.bestwesternangelscamp.com. ✆ **800/767-1127** or 209/736-4000. 38 units. $80–$189 double. Rate includes continental breakfast. AE, DC, DISC, MC, V. Pets allowed. **Amenities:** Concierge; exercise room; Jacuzzi; outdoor heated pool; room service; free Wi-Fi. *In room:* TV/DVD, fridge, hair dryer, high-speed Internet.

Where to Eat

Camps ★★ ☺ CALIFORNIAN On the edge of a golf resort on the western fringes of Angels Camp is Camps, the culinary feather in the cap of Greenhorn Creek golf resort. The restaurant's architects have integrated the building into its natural surroundings by constructing the outer walls with locally mined rhyolite and painting it in natural earth tones. The interior is furnished with leather armchairs, wicker, and antique woods. The best seats in the house are on the veranda overlooking the golf course, particularly on warm summer nights. Though the menu changes seasonally, a typical dinner may start with house salad with field greens, toasted almonds, and champagne vinaigrette, followed by macadamia-crusted halibut with lemon whipped potatoes or crisp roasted duck with truffled risotto and port-braised vegetables.

711 McCauley Ranch Rd. (½ mile west of Hwy. 4/Hwy. 49 junction off Angel Oaks Dr.). ✆ **209/729-8181.** www.greenhorncreek.com. Reservations recommended. Main courses $12–$31. AE, MC, V. Wed–Thurs and Sun 11:30am–8pm; Fri–Sat 11:30am–9pm; bistro menu Wed–Fri noon–9pm; Sun brunch 10am–2pm.

Crusco's Ristorante ★ ITALIAN The sign at the entrance says it all: RELAX AND ENJOY. THIS IS NOT FAST FOOD. The overall experience is as important as the cuisine at Crusco's, a family-run restaurant headed by Celeste Lusher, the amiable chef/owner who oversees the kitchen along with her daughter, Sarah, while her husband and son-in-law cater to their customers. In the heart of old-town Angels Camp, the restaurant's decor is an attractive balance of 19th-century Gold Rush architecture—wood beams, 1½-foot-thick stone walls, dark-wood furnishings—and old-world Mediterranean objets d'art such as faux columns and bas-relief sculptures. It's an apropos setting for Lusher's classic Italian menu, made from scratch using generations of family recipes. Each meal begins with house-made focaccia, served with olive oil and balsamic vinegar; then come the tough choices: pan-seared tenderloin steak finished with a sweet brandy demi-glacé, sautéed apples and prunes, the creamy polenta, or the popular penne *rigate*. For lunch, Celeste recommends the New York steak with garlic french fries. Sampling a few of the house-made desserts is highly advised as well.

1240 S. Main St. ✆ **209/736-1440.** www.cruscos.com. Reservations recommended. Main courses $15–$23. DISC, MC, V. Thurs–Mon 11:30am–3pm and 5–9pm (closed occasional weeks in June; call ahead).

MURPHYS ★

From Angels Camp, a 20-minute drive east along Hwy. 4 takes you to Murphys, one of my favorite Gold Country towns. Legend has it Murphys started as a former trading post set up by brothers Dan and John Murphy in cooperation with local Indians (John married the chief's daughter). These days, tall locust trees shade gingerbread Victorians on narrow streets. Be sure to stroll down Main Street, stopping in **Grounds** (✆ **209/728-8663;** www.groundsrestaurant.com) for a bite, or a cool draft of Grizzly Brown Ale—direct from the **Snowshoe Brewing Company** (✆ **209/795-2272;** www.snowshoebrewing.com) in nearby Arnold—at the saloon within Murphys Historic Hotel and Lodge at 457 Main St.

While you're here, you might also want to check out **Ironstone Vineyards,** 1894 Six Mile Rd., 1 mile south of downtown Murphys (📞 **209/728-1251;** www.ironstonevineyards.com), a veritable wine theme park built by the Kautz family. It's open daily from 10am to 6pm.

Also in the vicinity—just off Hwy. 4, 1 mile north of Murphys off Sheep Ranch Road—are the **Mercer Caverns** (📞 **209/728-2101;** www.mercer caverns.com). These caverns, discovered in 1885 by Walter Mercer, contain a variety of geological formations—stalactites and stalagmites—in a series of chambers. Tours of the well-lit caverns take nearly an hour. From Memorial Day to September, hours are Sunday through Thursday from 9am to 5pm, Friday and Saturday from 9am to 6pm; from October 1 to Memorial Day, hours are 10am to 4:30pm daily. Admission is $12 for adults, $7 for children ages 5 to 12, and free for children 4 and under.

Fifteen miles east of Murphys up Hwy. 4 is **Calaveras Big Trees State Park** ★ (📞 **209/795-2334;** www.parks.ca.gov), where you can see giant sequoias that are among the biggest and oldest living things on Earth. It's a popular summer retreat that offers camping, swimming, hiking, and fishing along the Stanislaus River. It's open daily; admission is $6 per car for day use.

Where to Stay

Dunbar House, 1880 ★★   This Italianate home, built in 1880 for the bride of a local businessman, is one of the finest B&Bs in the Gold Country. The front porch, which overlooks the exquisite gardens, is decorated with wicker furniture and hanging baskets of ivy. Inside, the emphasis is on comfort and elegance. The guest rooms are furnished with quality antiques and equipped with every possible amenity. Beds have Egyptian cotton linens and down comforters, and each room has a fridge stocked with mineral water and a complimentary bottle of local wine. My favorite room, the Cedar, is a fabulous two-room suite with a private sun porch, whirlpool tub, and chilled bottle of champagne. I also like the Sugar Pine suite, with its private balcony in the trees. Lemonade and cookies are offered in the afternoon, appetizers and wine in the early evening. Breakfast is served in your room, the dining room, or the garden.

271 Jones St., Murphys, CA 95247. www.dunbarhouse.com. 📞 **800/692-6006** or 209/728-2897. Fax 209/728-1451. 5 units. $190–$280 double. Rates include breakfast and afternoon appetizers. AE, DISC, MC, V. *In room:* A/C, flatscreen TV/DVD, hair dryer, Wi-Fi.

Where to Eat

Firewood ★ 🍴 AMERICAN   Local restaurateur River Klass opened this order-at-the-counter cafe just down the street from his Grounds restaurant (see below). The open-air establishment specializes in fast, inexpensive, and darn good dishes such as Baja-style fish tacos; drippingly juicy, "not healthy" burgers; baby back ribs with house-made barbecue sauce; and superb gourmet pizzas baked in a wood-burning oven (the prosciutto and arugula, shrimp and feta, and sausage and pepperoni versions are all big hits). Good microbrew and local wine selections are available as well.

420 Main St. 📞 **209/728-3248.** www.firewoodeats.com. Reservations not accepted. Main courses $5–$10. MC, V. Daily 11am–9pm.

Grounds ★★ ECLECTIC   When River Klass moved here from the East Coast to open his own place, Murphys's restaurant-challenged residents heaved a sigh of relief. Its nickname is the "Rude Boy Cafe," after Klass's acerbic wit, but you'll find happy smiles and friendly service. The majority of Grounds's business is with locals addicted to the potato pancakes that come with every made-to-order omelet. For lunch, try the killer BLT with avocado on a house-baked French roll or the grilled eggplant sandwich stuffed with smoked mozzarella and fresh basil. Typical dinner choices include fresh breaded halibut with house-made lentil salsa served over garlic mashed red potatoes, or a roasted end-bone pork chop with demiglacé, cannellini beans, and grilled vegetables. The wine list is impressive (and reasonably priced). The long, narrow dining rooms are bright and airy, with pine-wood furnishings, wood floors, and an open kitchen. On sunny days, request a table on the back patio.

402 Main St. (C) **209/728-8663.** Reservations recommended. Main courses $14–$29. AE, DISC, MC, V. Mon–Fri 7am–10:30pm; Sat 7am–11:15pm; Sun 8am–11:15pm.

COLUMBIA

Though a little hokey, **Columbia State Historic Park** ★★ ((C) **209/588-9128;** www.columbiacalifornia.com or www.parks.ca.gov) is the best-maintained Gold Rush town in the Mother Lode (and one of the most popular, so expect crowds in the summer). At one point, this boisterous mining town was the state's second-largest city (and only two votes shy of becoming the state capital). When gold mining no longer panned out in the late 1850s, most of the town's 15,000 residents departed, leaving much of the mining equipment and buildings in place. In 1945, the entire town was turned into a historic park.

As a result, Columbia has been preserved and functions much as it did in the 1850s, with stagecoach rides, Western-style Victorian hotels and saloons, a newspaper office, a blacksmith's forge, a Wells Fargo express office, and numerous other relics of California's early mining days. Cars are banned from its streets, giving the shady town an authentic feel. Merchants still do business behind some storefronts, as horse, stagecoach, and pedestrian traffic wanders by.

If Columbia's heat and dust get to you, pull up a stool at the **Jack Douglass Saloon** on Main Street ((C) **209/533-4176**), open daily from 10am to 6pm (till 7pm on Fri). Inside the swinging doors of the classic Western bar, you can sample homemade sarsaparilla and wild cherry, drinks the saloon has been serving since 1857. The saloon has sandwiches and various snacks; it serves dinners on Friday night and has live music every weekend afternoon from May to September. The storefront's large shuttered windows open onto a dusty main street, so put up your boots, relax awhile, and watch the stagecoach go by.

Free historical tours of the park depart from the Main Museum Saturday and Sunday at 11am. Every second Saturday, the park presents Gold Rush Days from 1 to 4pm, when costumed docents take you down Main Street and into dusty old structures that are off-limits to the general public. Special docent-led tours are available by reservation for $2 per person.

SONORA

A few miles south of Columbia, Sonora is the largest town in the southern Gold Country. (You'll know you've arrived when traffic starts to crawl.) In Gold Rush days, Sonora and Columbia were the two richest towns in the Mother Lode. Dozens of stores and cafes line the main thoroughfare. If you find parking, it's worth an hour or two to check out the sites, like the 19th-century **St. James Episcopal Church,** at the top of Washington Street, and the **Tuolumne County Museum and History Center,** 158 W. Bradford Ave. ((C) **209/532-1317;** www.tchistory.org), in the 1857 County Jail. Admission is free, and it's open daily.

Where to Stay

Gunn House Hotel ★ 🏊 Built in 1850 by Dr. Lewis C. Gunn, the Gunn House was the first two-story adobe structure in Sonora, built to house his family, who sailed around Cape Horn from the East Coast to join him in the Gold Rush. Painstakingly restored, it's now one of the best moderately priced hotels in the Gold Country. It's easy to catch the forty-niner spirit here, as the entire hotel and grounds are brimming with quality antiques and turn-of-the-20th-century artifacts. Rare for a building this old, each guest room has a private bathroom and air-conditioning. What really makes the Gunn House one of my favorites, though, is the hotel's beautiful pool and patio, surrounded by lush vegetation and admirable stonework. It's in a convenient location as well, right in downtown Sonora.

286 S. Washington St., Sonora, CA 95370. www.gunnhousehotel.com. ✆ **209/532-3421.** 20 units. $69–$109 double. Rates include breakfast. AE, MC, V. **Amenities:** Outdoor heated pool. *In room:* A/C, TV.

Where to Eat

Diamondback Grill 🏊 AMERICAN For more than a decade, this modest family-owned diner has whipped up the Gold Country's best burger: the Diamondback—a grilled-to-order half-pounder that comes with the works, including fries. There are about a dozen other burgers, as well as gourmet sandwiches (go for the grilled eggplant with fresh tomato and mozzarella), house-made soups and pecan pies, a zesty black-bean-and-steak chili, and great daily specials listed. There's also a good selection of beer and wine by the glass.

93 S. Washington St. ✆ **209/532-6661.** www.thediamondbackgrill.com. Main courses $5–$10. No credit cards. Mon–Thurs 11am–9pm; Fri–Sat 11am–9:30pm; Sun 11am–8pm.

JAMESTOWN ★

About 4 miles southwest of Sonora on Hwy. 49 is Jamestown, a 4-block-long town of old-fashioned storefronts and two rustic turn-of-the-20th-century hotels. There's gold in these parts, too, as the marker commemorating the discovery of a 75-pound nugget attests (panning nearby Woods Creek is a popular pastime among both locals and tourists). If Jamestown looks eerily familiar to you, that's probably because you've seen it in the movies or on television. It's one of Hollywood's favorite Western movie sets; scenes from such films as *Butch Cassidy and the Sundance Kid* were shot here.

> ### Pan for Gold
>
> You can learn to pan for gold through Jamestown's **Gold Prospecting Adventures** (✆ **800/596-0009** or 209/984-4653; www.goldprospecting.com). The hour-long class is about $20, plus you get to keep any gold you might find.

Jamestown's most popular attraction is the **Railtown 1897 State Historic Park** ★, a train buff's paradise featuring three Sierra steam locomotives. These great machines were used in many a movie and television show, including *High Noon, Little House on the Prairie, Bonanza,* and *My Little Chickadee.* The trains at the roundhouse are on display daily year-round. Call for information on weekend rides and guided tours. The Depot Store and Museum are open daily from 9:30am to 4:30pm (10am–3pm Nov–Mar). The park is located near the center of town, on Fifth Avenue at Reservoir Road (✆ **209/984-3953;** www. csrmf.org/railtown or www.parks.ca.gov).

Where to Stay & Eat

Jamestown Hotel ★ The most worked-over building in town, the Jamestown was originally built in 1858; it burned down and was rebuilt twice before 1915. To achieve the old-fashioned, brick-fronted Victorian look it sports today, a lot of stucco and Spanish-revival paraphernalia had to be removed. Most of the lower floor is devoted to the front office and the bar. The second floor contains a cadre of cozy bedrooms outfitted with antiques. All of the spacious rooms are loaded with nostalgic charm; a few have sitting rooms and TVs with VCRs, and all have private bathrooms (some with claw-foot tubs, several with spa tubs).

18153 Main St. (P.O. Box 539), Jamestown, CA 95327. www.jamestownhotel.com. ✆ **800/205-4901** or 209/984-3902. Fax 209/984-4149. 8 units. $90–$175 double. Rates include full breakfast. AE, MC, V. **Amenities:** Bar. *In room:* A/C, TV/VCR, hair dryer.

National Hotel & Restaurant ★ In the center of town, this two-story classic Western hotel has been operating since 1859, making it one of the 10 oldest continuously operating hotels in the state. The saloon has its original 19th-century redwood bar, and you can imagine what it must have been like when miners traded gold dust for drinks. The guest rooms blend 19th-century details (handmade quilts, oak furnishings, lace curtains, brass beds) with 20th-century comforts such as private bathrooms. All guests have access to the authentic Soaking Room, a private room equipped with a sort of 1800s claw-foot Jacuzzi for two (when cowboys longed for a good, hot soak). Brunch, lunch, and dinner are served to the public in the handsome old-fashioned dining room or pretty garden courtyard. Dishes, many with a Mediterranean flavor, range from steak, veal, and prime rib to chicken, seafood, pasta dishes, and house-made desserts.

18183 Main St. (P.O. Box 502), Jamestown, CA 95327. www.national-hotel.com. ✆ **800/894-3446** or 209/984-3446. Fax 209/984-5620. 9 units. $100–$140 double. Rates include large buffet breakfast. AE, DC, DISC, MC, V. Pets accepted for $25 per night. **Amenities:** Restaurant; saloon; concierge; nearby golf course; room service. *In room:* A/C, TV, hair dryer, free Wi-Fi.

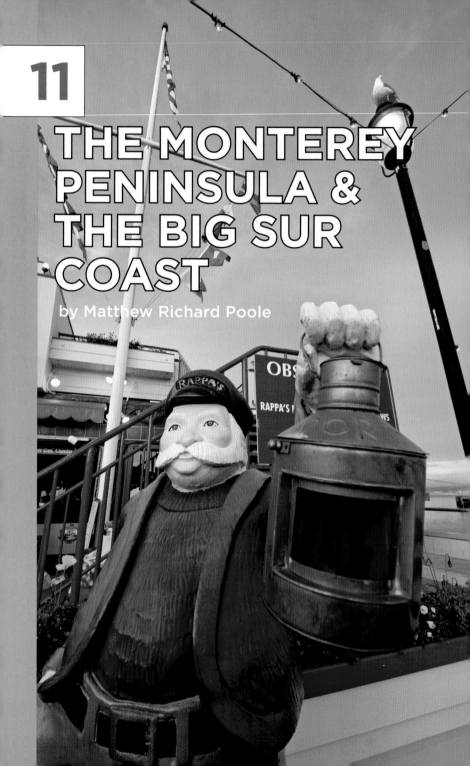

THE MONTEREY PENINSULA & THE BIG SUR COAST

by Matthew Richard Poole

The Monterey Peninsula and the Big Sur coast comprise one of the world's most spectacular shorelines, skirted with cypress trees, rugged shores, and crescent-shaped bays. Monterey reels in visitors with its world-class aquarium and array of outdoor activities. Pacific Grove is so peaceful that the butterflies choose it as their yearly mating ground. Pebble Beach attracts the golfing elite. Tiny Carmel-by-the-Sea is romantic and sweet, despite the throngs of tourists who come for the beaches, shops, and restaurants. Big Sur's dramatic and majestic coast, backed by pristine redwood forests and rolling hills, is one of the most breathtaking, tranquil environments on Earth. If you're traveling Hwy. 1 (which you should be), the coastline will guide you all the way through the region.

This chapter begins with Santa Cruz, at the northwestern end of Monterey Bay—one of my favorite destinations on the coast, and home of the Santa Cruz Beach Boardwalk. Across Monterey Bay at the northern tip of the Monterey Peninsula are the seaside communities of Monterey and Pacific Grove, while Pebble Beach and Carmel-by-the-Sea hug the peninsula's south coast along Carmel Bay. Between the north and south coasts, which are only about 5 miles apart, are many golf courses, some of the state's most stunning homes and hotels, and 17-Mile Drive, one of the most scenic coastal roads in the world.

Inland lies Carmel Valley, with its elegant inns and resorts, golf courses, and guaranteed sunshine, even when the coast is socked in with fog. Farther down the coast along Hwy. 1 is Big Sur, a stunning 90-mile stretch of coast south of the Monterey Peninsula and west of the Santa Lucia Mountains.

SANTA CRUZ ★★

77 miles SE of San Francisco

For a small bayside city, Santa Cruz has a lot to offer. The main show, of course, is the Beach Boardwalk, which attracts millions of visitors each year. But past the arcades and cotton candy is a surprisingly diverse and energetic city with a little something for everyone: Shopping, hiking, mountain biking, sailing, fishing, kayaking, surfing, wine tasting, golfing, whale-watching—the list of things to do here is almost endless, making Santa Cruz one of the premier family destinations on the California coast.

Essentials

GETTING THERE Santa Cruz is 77 miles southeast of San Francisco. The most scenic route to Santa Cruz is along Hwy. 1 from San Francisco, which, aside

PREVIOUS PAGE: **Fisherman's Wharf, Monterey.**

from the "you fall, you die" stretch called Devil's Slide, allows you to cruise at a steady 50 mph. Faster but less romantic is Hwy. 17, which is accessed near San Jose from I-280, I-880, or U.S. 101, and ends at the foot of the boardwalk. The exception to this rule is on weekend mornings, when Hwy. 17 tends to be a logjam with beachgoers while Hwy. 1 remains relatively uncrowded.

VISITOR INFORMATION For information, contact the **Santa Cruz County Conference and Visitors Council,** 1211 Ocean St., Santa Cruz, CA 95060 (© **800/833-3494** or 831/425-1234; www.santacruzca.org), open Monday through Saturday from 9am to 5pm, Sunday from 10am to 4pm.

SPECIAL EVENTS Special events include **Shakespeare Santa Cruz** in July and August (© **831/459-2159;** shakespearesantacruz.org), and the **Cabrillo Music Festival** in August (© **831/426-6966;** www.cabrillomusic.org).

What to See & Do
BEACHES, HIKING & FISHING IN SANTA CRUZ

One of the few old-fashioned amusement parks left in the world, the **Santa Cruz Beach Boardwalk ★★** (© 831/423-5590; www.beachboardwalk.com) draws more than three million visitors a year to its 30 rides and arcades, shops, and restaurants. The park has two national landmarks—a 1924 wooden Giant Dipper roller coaster and a 1911 carousel with hand-carved wooden horses and a 342-pipe organ band. It's open daily in the summer (Memorial Day weekend to Labor Day) and on weekends and holidays throughout the spring and fall, from 11am (noon sometimes in winter). Admission to the boardwalk is free, but an all-day "unlimited rides" pass is $30. See **www.beachboardwalk.com** for discounts, concerts and events, and up-to-date schedules, which can often vary.

Here, too, is **Neptune's Kingdom,** 400 Beach St. (© **831/423-5590;** www.beachboardwalk.com), an enormous indoor family recreation center with a two-story miniature golf course. Also on Beach Street is the shop- and restaurant-lined **Municipal Wharf** (© **831/420-6025**), a beachfront strip serenaded by

Natural Bridges beach.

The Monterey Peninsula & The Big Sur Coast

Santa Cruz Surfing Museum.

Santa Cruz boardwalk.

the sea lions below. You can also crab and fish from here. Most shops are open daily from 7am to 9pm; the wharf is open daily from 5am to 2am. **Stagnaro's** (© **831/427-2334;** www.stagnaros.com) runs fishing and whale-watching trips year-round, and hour-long narrated bay cruises ($16 for adults, $10 for kids 13 and under).

Farther down on West Cliff Drive, you'll come to a favorite surfing spot, **Steamer Lane,** where you can watch pro surfers shredding the waves. If you want to learn more about surfing, practiced here for more than 100 years, go to the **Santa Cruz Surfing Museum,** at the lighthouse (© **831/420-6289;** www.santacruzparksandrec.com), open Wednesday through Sunday from 10am to 5pm in the summer, Thursday through Monday from noon to 4pm in the winter. Antique surfboards, videos, photos, and other memorabilia depict the history and evolution of surfing worldwide.

Continue along West Cliff and you'll reach **Natural Bridges State Beach,** 2531 W. Cliff Dr. (© **831/423-4609;** www.scparkfriends.org), a large sandy beach with nearby tide pools and hiking trails. It's also home to a large colony of monarch butterflies that cluster and mate in the nearby eucalyptus grove.

Other Santa Cruz beaches worth noting are **Bonny Doon,** at Bonny Doon Road and Hwy. 1, an uncrowded sandy beach and a major surfing spot accessible by a steep walkway; **Pleasure Point Beach,** East Cliff Drive at Pleasure Point Drive; and **Twin Lakes State Beach,** which is ideal for sunning and also provides access to Schwann Lagoon, a bird sanctuary.

In addition to cultural and sporting events, the University of California at Santa Cruz features the **Seymour Marine Discovery Center** at the Long Marine Laboratory, 100 Shaffer Rd., at the northwest end of Delaware Avenue (© **831/459-3800;** www2.ucsc.edu/seymourcenter), where you can observe marine scientists at work with aquatic species, in tide-pool touch tanks and

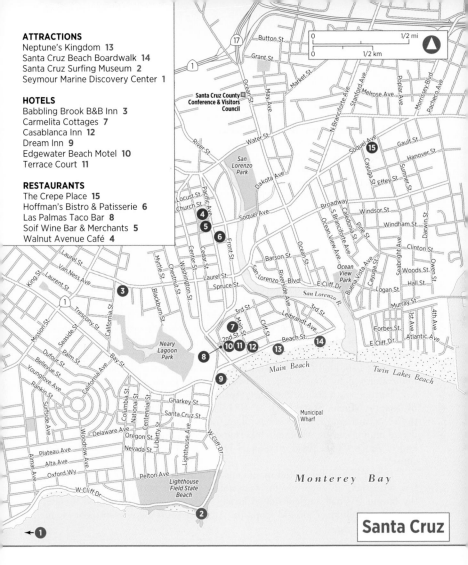

ATTRACTIONS
Neptune's Kingdom **13**
Santa Cruz Beach Boardwalk **14**
Santa Cruz Surfing Museum **2**
Seymour Marine Discovery Center **1**

HOTELS
Babbling Brook B&B Inn **3**
Carmelita Cottages **7**
Casablanca Inn **12**
Dream Inn **9**
Edgewater Beach Motel **10**
Terrace Court **11**

RESTAURANTS
The Crepe Place **15**
Hoffman's Bistro & Patisserie **6**
Las Palmas Taco Bar **8**
Soif Wine Bar & Merchants **5**
Walnut Avenue Café **4**

Santa Cruz

aquariums, and learn how marine research aids ocean conservation. Hours are Tuesday through Saturday from 10am to 5pm, and Sunday from noon to 5pm; admission is $6 for adults; $4 for students, seniors, and children ages 4 to 16; and free for kids 3 and under (free admission the first Tues of each month).

The **Santa Cruz Harbor,** 135 Fifth Ave. (© **831/475-6161;** www.santa cruzharbor.org), has boat rentals, open-boat fishing (cod, shark, and salmon), and whale-watching trips.

Bikes—mountain, kids', tandem, hybrid—are available by the hour, day, or week from various bike-rental shops in convenient locations around town. For a list of shops, call the **Santa Cruz Visitors Council** at © **800/833-3494** or see **www.santacruzca.org.**

The **Pasatiempo Golf Club,** at 18 Clubhouse Rd. (© **831/459-9155;** www.pasatiempo.com), is rated among the top 100 courses in the U.S. Greens fees are $220.

Kayaking is also an option. Outfitters include **Kayak Connection,** 413 Lake Ave., No. 103 (© **831/479-1121;** www.kayakconnection.com); and **Venture Quest Kayaking** (© **831/427-2267;** www.kayaksantacruz.com), which rents single, double, and triple kayaks at Building No. 2 on the wharf and at 125 Beach St. Classes, wildlife tours, and moonlight paddles are also available.

You can rent surfing equipment at **Cowell's Beach Surf Shop,** 30 Front St. (© **831/427-2355;** www.cowellssurfshop.com), and from the **Club Ed Surf School** (© **800/287-SURF** [7873] or 831/464-0177; www.club-ed.com), on Cowell Beach in front of the West Coast Santa Cruz Hotel. Both offer lessons: Club Ed's are $85 for a 2-hour group session and $110 per hour for private lessons (equipment included); Cowell's are $80 for 2-hour group lessons, including a board and wet suit.

IN NEARBY CAPITOLA & APTOS

South along the coast, the small community of **Capitola** ★, at the mouth of the Soquel Creek, is a spawning ground for steelhead and salmon. You can fish without a license from the **Capitola Wharf,** 1400 Wharf Rd., or rent a boat from **Capitola Boat and Bait** (© **831/462-2208;** www.santacruzboatrentals.net).

Capitola Beach fronts the bustling Esplanade. Surf fishing, clamming, and camping are popular pastimes at Capitola's **New Brighton State Beach,** 1500 State Park Dr. (© **831/464-6330**). Another popular activity is **antiquing** in the stores along Soquel Drive between 41st and Capitola avenues.

Farther south around the bay is **Aptos** ★, home to the 10,000-acre **Forest of Nisene Marks State Park** (© **831/763-7062**). This was the epicenter of the 1989 earthquake, and now has hiking trails through redwoods and past abandoned mining camps. Mountain bikers and leashed dogs are welcome. It's at the end of Aptos Creek Road off Soquel Drive, open year-round from sunrise to sunset.

In the redwood-forested mountains behind Santa Cruz, there are quite a few **wineries,** although visitors may not be familiar with the labels because the output is small and consumed locally. Most are clustered around Boulder Creek and Felton or around Capitola. All offer tours by appointment; some

---

A WALK AMONG THE redwoods

The perfect antidote to an overdose of pavement is a walk through the redwoods at **Henry Cowell Redwoods State Park.** Only a few miles from downtown Santa Cruz on Highway 9, this 1,800-acre park has 15 miles of trails through thick, cool forests and golden meadows. Top pick for a leisurely walk is the ¾-mile **Redwood Grove Trail,** a wide and flat loop around an ancient stand of giant redwoods. On summer weekends docent-led tours of the Grove Trail start from the Nature Center, but call ahead first. (**Secret Tip:** About 1½ miles south of the main entrance on Hwy. 9 is the Ox Road Parking Lot. Park here free, then take the short trail down to the locals' favorite swimming hole, the **Garden of Eden.**) Dogs are welcome in the park but must be on a leash at all times.

SEVEN money-saving TIPS FOR SANTA CRUZ TOURISTS

- On Friday nights in summer, head to the Santa Cruz Beach Boardwalk's Beach Bandstand for **free concerts** with live music from the '60s, '70s, and '80s—Greg Kihn, Eddie Money, the Fixx, Survivor—at 6:30 and 8:30pm.

- On Mondays and Tuesdays after 5pm in summer, the Santa Cruz Beach Boardwalk holds **1907 Nights,** celebrating the year it opened by reducing prices to 65¢ a ride (that's $2.50 off). Hot dogs, sodas, and cotton candy are also just 75¢. The special typically runs from late June to the end of August.

- Great Mexican food at cheap prices is served daily from 10am to 9pm at the **Las Palmas Taco Bar** at 55 Front St. near the wharf (© **831/429-1220**). This grimy little corner cafe has been a local favorite since 1955. You can smell the frijoles frying from the beach. Get a couple of beef-tongue soft tacos brimming with *pico de gallo* and salsa verde.

- To skip the entrance fee to **Henry Cowell Redwoods State Park,** drive 1½ miles south of the main entrance on Calif. 9 to the Ox Road parking lot.

- Park free and then follow the trail into the park, which takes you past a popular swimming hole called the Garden of Eden.

- A far better walk than the boardwalk is along the 2-mile oceanside paved path on **West Cliff Drive** (west of the wharf). The scenery is spectacular, particularly at sunset, and it won't cost a cent.

- **Carmelita Cottages,** 321 Main St. (www.hi-santacruz.org; © **831/423-8304**), is a hostel in Santa Cruz that will rent you a bunk bed for $22 to $25. The gaggle of white-washed Victorian cottages is a few blocks north of the Boardwalk, in a quiet residential neighborhood. The hostel also reserves a few rooms for couples and families. (It's not exactly Romance Central, but for $50 a night for your own room at such a prime location, it's hard to complain.)

- Don't pay to park in downtown Santa Cruz. Along Cedar and Front streets are three parking garages and 13 surface lots that offer 3 hours of **free parking.**

feature tastings, including the **Bargetto Winery,** 3535 N. Main, Soquel (© **800/422-7438** or 831/475-2258; www.bargetto.com), which has a courtyard wine-tasting area overlooking the creek. For information, contact the **Santa Cruz Mountains Winegrowers' Association** (© **831/685-VINE** [8463]; www.scmwa.com).

Where to Stay

If you have trouble finding a vacancy, consider the **Terrace Court** (125 Beach St.; www.terracecourt.com; © **831/423-3031**), a plain but practical motel on a hill overlooking the wharf, with ocean views and easy beach access. Santa Cruz has plenty of chain motels as well. Two **Travelodges** (www.travelodge.com; © **800/578-7878**), two **Best Westerns** (www.bestwestern.com; © **800/780-7234**), two **Super 8s** (www.super8.com; © **800/800-8000**), and an **Econo**

Lodge (www.choicehotels.com; ✆ **877/424-6423**) provide moderate- and budget-priced accommodations in addition to the nonchain recommendations below.

EXPENSIVE

Babbling Brook Bed & Breakfast Inn ★★   With charm to spare, the rooms in this popular inn are like treehouses over and around a brook running through an acre of gardens, pines, and redwoods. It's on a busy street, but what you hear from your room is running water cascading over falls and a water wheel. Rooms are tasteful and simple, with lots of windows, skylights, open-beam ceilings, balconies, and decks; most have gas fireplaces and spa tubs. The inn is within a mile of the beach and boardwalk and a short walk from downtown Santa Cruz. Breakfast and evening wine and snacks are served in the comfortable lobby.

1025 Laurel St., Santa Cruz, CA 95060. www.babblingbrookinn.com. ✆ **800/866-1131** or 831/427-2437. Fax 831/427-2457. 13 units. $209–$279 double. Rates include full country breakfast buffet. AE, DISC, MC, V. **Amenities:** Nearby golf. *In room:* TV, VCR (in some units).

Chaminade Resort & Spa ★★   If you're looking for a quiet, peaceful sanctuary, staying at a hotel that used to be a religious retreat is probably not a bad idea. High above Santa Cruz on 300 acres of native woodland, the Chaminade is a sprawling yet secluded mission-style resort. It's not the Four Seasons, but it's not trying to be. Rather, it's a down-to-earth "Green Certified" spa resort offering upscale lodgings and amenities at a reasonable price point. The well-appointed guest rooms have contemporary Spanish furnishings, very comfortable beds, and woodland views; and the perks go on: a large heated pool, four tennis courts, 3 miles of private hiking trails, a fitness center, and a newly renovated full-service spa with a knockout view from their outdoor hot tub (complete with menu service). Two restaurants offer great cuisine—the view from the outdoor dining patio is wonderful—and the best-rated brunch in Santa Cruz, and at night you can sip cocktails by the romantic fire pit. The only caveat? You'll have to drive about 10 minutes to reach the beaches, but at least you'll be above the coastal fog line and basking in the sun.

1 Chaminade Lane, Santa Cruz, CA 95065. www.chaminade.com. ✆ **800/283-6569.** 156 units. $159–$209 double; from $229 suite. AE, DC, DISC, MC, V. **Amenities:** 2 restaurants; bar; concierge; fitness center; Jacuzzi; heated outdoor pool; room service; spa; tennis courts; badminton; volleyball. *In room:* A/C, TV, hair dryer, minibar, Wi-Fi ($9.95).

Dream Inn ★★   Finally, a decent-sized hotel within Santa Cruz that we *want* to stay in. Owned by San Francisco–based hospitality group Joie de Vivre, Dream Inn's exterior blends in with the Boardwalk and Santa Cruz beachfront effortlessly, while its rooms combine the comfort and class of a boutique hotel with stellar oceanfront views. The decor has a bit of a 1970s flair, in keeping with the overall Santa Cruz feel, and every room has a patio or balcony overlooking the beach. On warm, fogless days, it doesn't get much better than laying out at the pool, a sea of surfers bobbing in the distance. The inn's location is pretty dreamy too—just a 5-minute walk puts you on the wharf or in downtown along the main drag, Pacific Avenue.

175 W. Cliff Dr., Santa Cruz, CA 95060. www.dreaminnsantacruz.com. ✆ **866/774-7735** or 831/426-4330. Fax 831/427-2025. 165 units. $149–$389 double; $399–$529 suite. AE, DISC, MC, V. **Amenities:** Restaurant; poolside bar; concierge; Jacuzzi; heated pool. *In room:* A/C, TV, hair dryer, minibar, MP3 docking station, free Wi-Fi.

The Inn at Depot Hill ★★★ A few blocks from the bay front, this converted 1910-era railroad station in nearby Capitola has been designed and decorated with such artful attention to detail that it's been ranked one of the top inns in the nation—which explains why Martha Stewart chose to stay here during her coastal tour a few years ago. All rooms and suites have fine fabrics and linens, wood-burning fireplaces, stereos, two-person showers, and full bathrooms. Most have private patios with Jacuzzis (other rooms share a common Jacuzzi). Perhaps you'll check in to the Portofino Room, patterned after an Italian villa, or the Stratford-on-Avon, a replica of an English cottage. The evening wine and hors d'oeuvres and breakfast are also of prime quality, served either in your room or out back in the garden courtyard on wrought-iron tables shaded by market umbrellas.

250 Monterey Ave. (near Park Ave.), Capitola, CA 95010. www.innatdepothill.com. ✆ **800/572-2632** or 831/462-3376. Fax 831/462-3697. 12 units. $259–$349 double. Rates include breakfast, afternoon tea or wine, hors d'oeuvres, and after-dinner dessert. AE, DC, DISC, MC, V. **Amenities:** Jacuzzi; room service. *In room:* A/C, TV/VCR, hair dryer.

Pleasure Point Inn ★★ 🏨 With the amenities of a modern hotel and the casual atmosphere of a B&B, the four-room Pleasure Point Inn has all you might want in a romantic coastal getaway: a beautiful ocean view overlooking Monterey Bay, a quiet neighborhood location, contemporary design and decor, and a roof-top deck. The Pleasure Point beach and surf break are right across the street, where local longboarders provide viewing entertainment from sunrise to sunset. Each guest room is impeccably clean, with custom furnishings, wood flooring, hand-painted tiles, private bathrooms, down comforters, a gas fireplace, and private entrances. An expanded continental breakfast is served in the oceanview dining/lounge area (I spotted a gray whale while munching on a bagel); after breakfast, guests can stroll the paved coastal path down to Capitola, walk to the beach, or relax on the sunny rooftop deck (topside toys include an eight-person hot tub, chaise longue chairs, and surround-sound music).

23665 E. Cliff Dr., Santa Cruz, CA 95062. www.pleasurepointinn.com. ✆ **831/475-4657.** 4 units. $150–$220 double. Rates include continental breakfast. MC, V. **Amenities:** Hot tub. *In room:* TV, fridge, Wi-Fi.

Seascape Resort ★★ You'll think you've surely gotten lost—particularly at night—after veering off the highway at Aptos and winding through a host of residential neighborhoods to reach your final destination. But once you've checked in and gotten situated, you'll be glad for Seascape's remoteness. Seascape is full of longer-stay vacationers, as opposed to those just passing through for the weekend. And with so much to do—from golfing and countless sports to beach activities and surfing—it's no wonder; 2 days simply isn't enough to make the most of this sprawling resort, particularly if you're just in need of a little R&R. Choose from a range of suites—studios, one-bedroom, or spa—or the fanciest option in the house, the two-bedroom beach villa. Room decor is just your usual kitschy beach condo furnishings, but all suites are massive, outfitted with nice living rooms and kitchenettes. You'll wake up to the sound of the Pacific far below, and a quick walk down a path puts you oceanfront and center.

One Seascape Resort Dr., Aptos, CA 95003. www.seascaperesort.com. ✆ **800/929-7727.** 285 units. $139–$672 suite. AE, DISC, MC, V. **Amenities:** Restaurant; bar; children's program; concierge; golf course; pool; sports club. *In room:* TV w/pay movies, DVD/VCR, free Wi-Fi.

MODERATE

Casablanca Inn   Across from the wharf in a heavily trafficked area, this aging waterfront inn and motel was once the Mediterranean-style Cerf Mansion dating from 1918. Other motel-style accommodations have grown up around the main building. Originally the home of a federal judge, it has individually decorated bedrooms, some with brass beds and velvet draperies. Some units have fireplaces and terraces, and all have microwaves. Most have ocean views. Casablanca Restaurant serves California–Continental cuisine in an oceanview setting. The Casablanca wouldn't be my first choice of lodging in Santa Cruz, but in a pinch it'll do if you can get a room well below rack rate.

101 Main St. (at the corner of Beach St.), Santa Cruz, CA 95060. www.casablanca-santacruz.com. ✆ **800/644-1570** or 831/423-1570. Fax 831/423-0235. 39 units. High season $116–$320 double. AE, DC, DISC, MC, V. **Amenities:** Restaurant; bar; nearby golf course; room service. *In room:* TV, fridge, hair dryer, kitchen in some units, minibar.

Edgewater Beach Motel ⚑   If you're nostalgic for the good ol' days when the family took road trips to the beach in the wood-paneled station wagon, you'll find a fondness for the Edgewater Beach Motel. It looks like a time capsule from the 1960s; how they kept the furnishings in such prime condition is a mystery. The motel has a range of accommodations, from family suites with kitchens to rooms with fireplaces; most have microwaves. The Edgewater also sports a nice pool, sun deck, and barbecue area, a block from the Santa Cruz boardwalk.

525 Second St., Santa Cruz, CA 95060. www.edgewaterbeachmotel.com. ✆ **888/809-6767** or 831/423-0440. 18 units. Winter $85–$219 double; summer $139–$299 double. AE, DC, DISC, MC, V. **Amenities:** Outdoor heated pool. *In room:* TV/VCR, fridge, fully equipped kitchen in suites, Wi-Fi.

INEXPENSIVE

Fern River Resort ★ 🎁   This nifty mountain retreat is 4 miles from Santa Cruz down a curvy redwood-lined road. The "resort" consists of 13 furnished and equipped cabins on 4 forested acres with lawn, garden, or river views. Outdoor toys will keep you amused, including badminton, Ping-Pong, tetherball, horseshoes, and 20 miles of hiking and mountain-biking trails in nearby Henry Cowell Park. You'll also find an enclosed spa tub and a small beach on the San Lorenzo River for sunning, swimming, and fishing. The cabins range in size from studios to some that sleep up to six. Some have equipped kitchens, but if you plan to cook, bring some pots and pans.

5250 Hwy. 9, Felton, CA 95018. www.fernriver.com. ✆ **831/335-4412.** 16 units. High season $69–$155 double; low season $75–$130 double. AE, MC, V. **Amenities:** Jacuzzi. *In room:* TV.

Where to Eat

Bittersweet Bistro ★★ CALIFORNIAN   Once a tiny operation in a small strip development, this restaurant has grown into one of the most popular around Santa Cruz. Its relocation to bigger digs in Rio Del Mar hasn't tarnished chef-owner Thomas Vinolus's reputation for serving exceptional cuisine. Carefully crafted dishes range from wood-oven pizzas to grilled lamb noisettes in a rosemary cabernet demiglacé. Co-proprietor and wine director Elizabeth Vinolus created an exceptional wine list and often hosts winemaker dinners. Bistro Hour, from 3 to 6pm daily, features two-for-one specials on gourmet pizzas and special pricing on all by-the-glass wines, beer, and spirits.

787 Rio Del Mar Blvd., Aptos (10 miles southeast of Santa Cruz on Hwy. 1). © **831/662-9799.**
www.bittersweetbistro.com. Reservations recommended. Main courses $17–$30. AE, MC, V. Daily
5:30–10pm.

The Crepe Place 🍴 CREPES/ECLECTIC   Beloved by locals, particularly as
a late-night hangout, the Crepe Place has been in business for more than 30
years. Choose from more than 15 styles of crepes (Spinach Supreme, Salsa, and
Jambalaya are local favorites), served in the wood-paneled dining room or outdoor garden area. Other menu items include soups (good clam chowder), salads,
oven-baked whole-wheat honey bread, and a popular dessert called a Tunisian
Doughnut. On weekends, egg dishes are also served, at brunch.

1134 Soquel Ave. (at Seabright Ave.). © **831/429-6994.** www.thecrepeplace.com. Main courses
$5–$17. AE, MC, V. Mon–Thurs 11am–midnight; Fri 11am–1am; Sat–Sun 9am–midnight.

Hoffman's Bistro & Patisserie ★★★ CALIFORNIAN/FRENCH   You
won't find a restaurant that epitomizes the term "family owned and operated"
quite like Hoffman's. Friendly owner June Hoffman manages the place, while
her husband, Ed, works behind the scenes as the master baker, and children and
niece are servers and hostesses. Brunch portions are hearty and delicious, from
the sweet—like the sourdough French toast with crème brûlée bananas, or the
cheese blintzes with mascarpone and berry compote—to the savory, such as the
Mexican *chilaquiles* or the eggs Benedict served on artichoke hearts in lieu of a
muffin. The lunch menu is full of light fare and salads to more filling bites like
the baked brie sandwich with sliced pears, caramelized onions, and apricot jalapeño jelly. For dinner, Hoffman's mixes game and seafood with comfort plates
like June's Homemade Meatloaf or buttermilk fried chicken breast.

1102 Pacific Ave. (at Cathcart St.). © **831/420-0135.** www.hoffmansbakery.net. Breakfast $8.95–
$12; lunch $8.50–$15; dinner $11–$20. AE, MC, V. Daily 8am–9pm.

Shadowbrook ★ AMERICAN/CONTINENTAL   One of Capitola's most
romantic restaurants has a serene setting above Soquel Creek. To reach it, diners
take a cable-driven "hillavator" down, or walk the long, steep steps beside a running waterfall. At the bottom, a log cabin built in the 1920s has been enlarged to
house Shadowbrook's wood-paneled Wine Cellar, airy Garden Room, Fireplace
Room, and creekside Greenhouse. The menu is unsurprising, with thick-cut
prime rib and steaks, seafood such as scampi and fresh halibut, and pasta dishes
such as the eggplant parmigiana. Appetizers include prawn cocktail, deep-fried
artichoke hearts, and baked brie. Standout desserts are the mud pie and the
Shadowbrook chocolate meltdown. If you're not ready to dine, grab a seat in the
lounge and nosh on appetizers and light entrees from the wood-fired oven.

1750 Wharf Rd., Capitola. © **800/975-1511** or 831/475-1511. www.shadowbrook-capitola.com.
Reservations recommended. Main courses $19–$32. AE, DC, DISC, MC, V. Mon–Thurs 5–8:45pm;
Fri 5–9:15pm; Sat 4–9:45pm; Sun 4–8:45pm.

Soif Wine Bar & Merchants ★★ FRENCH   This trendy wine bar in downtown Santa Cruz seems better suited for a culinary-conscious city like San
Francisco. Tapaslike appetizers such as roasted baby beets with orange and
hazelnuts, or Dungeness crab cakes with caper aioli and ginger cilantro vinaigrette are served to share. A mix of game and seafood—pan-roasted grouper
with sweet potato purée, confit of veal with flageolet beans and glazed spring

vegetables—round out the entrees. Be sure to save room for dessert: The bananas Foster is to die for. Every dish is paired with a suggested wine, served by the glass, bottle, or 2-ounce sample. Before leaving, pop by the merchant side of the restaurant and grab a bottle of wine to take home. Soif also has a sister restaurant, **La Posta** (538 Seabright Ave.; ☎ **831/457-2782;** www.laposta restaurant.com), a couple of blocks away; its Italian cuisine has received much praise during the eatery's 2 years in existence.

105 Walnut Ave. ☎ **831/423-2020.** www.soifwine.com. Reservations recommended. Small plates $4–$13; main courses $21–$23. AE, MC, V. Sun–Thurs 5–10pm; Fri–Sat 5–11pm.

Walnut Avenue Café ★★ AMERICAN   Nary a Santa Cruz resident has a bad thing to say about this downtown staple. The cafe serves breakfast and lunch only, and its creative substitutions—for example, eggs Benedict can be served with shrimp and tomato or blackened *ahi* tuna—will make you wish you could sample the entire menu at once. You won't find heavy entrees on the lunch menu, other than the daily pasta special, but the salad, soup, sandwich, and burger offerings are many. If you request to dine alfresco on a sunny day, you'll likely incur a lengthy wait (and the restaurant doesn't take reservations). So head there before the lunchtime rush, or else be prepared to settle for indoor seating.

106 Walnut Ave. ☎ **831/457-2307.** www.walnutavenuecafe.com. Breakfast $5–$12; lunch $8–$14. AE, MC, V. Mon–Fri 7am–3pm; Sat–Sun 8am–4pm.

A Side Trip to Mission San Juan Bautista

On U.S. 101, **San Juan Bautista** ★ is a mission town that retains the flavor of a 19th-century village. The mission complex sits in a picturesque farming valley, surrounded by the restored buildings of the original city plaza.

From U.S. 101, take Hwy. 156 east (south) to the town center to the mission itself, founded in 1797. The largest church in the mission chain, San Juan Bautista is the only one in continuous service. The padres here inspired many Native Americans to convert, creating one of the largest congregations in California. The mission once boasted a formidable Native American boys' choir, and the small museum exhibits many musical instruments and transcriptions. Mission San Juan Bautista is open daily year-round from 9:30am to 4:45pm. The suggested donation is $1 per person. For more information, call ☎ **831/623-4528** or see **www.oldmissionsjb.org** or **www.san-juan-bautista.ca.us**.

East of the church, at the edge of an abrupt drop created by the San Andreas Fault, a marker notes the path of the old **El Camino Real.** Seismographic measuring equipment and an earthquake science exhibit accompany the marker.

There's much to see on the restored city plaza as well. The **San Juan Bautista State Historic Park** comprises the old Plaza Hotel, with its frontier barroom and furnished rooms; the Plaza Hall, its adjoining stables, and blacksmith shop; and the Castro House, where the Breen family lived after traveling here with the ill-fated Donner Party in 1846. Allow 1½ to 2 hours to see the entire plaza. Admission to the park buildings is $2 for adults, $1 for children ages 6 to 12 (separate from the mission admission). Hours are daily from 10am to 4:30pm. For more information, call ☎ **831/623-4881.**

MONTEREY ★★

45 miles S of Santa Cruz; 116 miles S of San Francisco; 335 miles N of Los Angeles

Local hero John Steinbeck captured the gritty lives of the working class in *Cannery Row,* when Monterey was the sardine capital of the Western Hemisphere. After the sardines disappeared, Monterey was forced to fish for tourist dollars instead; hence, an array of boutiques, knickknack stores, and theme restaurants now reside in converted sardine factories along the bay. Distance yourself from the Row, however, and you'll discover Monterey is a serene seaside community with magnificent vistas, stately Victorians, and a number of quality lodgings and restaurants.

Things to Do   When visiting Monterey, it has to be done: Stroll down **Cannery Row** for a historical journey in search of Steinbeck's muse (and a stuffed sea otter for your niece). Then sashay over to **Fisherman's Wharf** to nosh on little cups of ceviche, crab, clam chowder and shrimp. Journey inside the **Monterey Bay Aquarium,** the no. 1 aquarium in the world.

Active Pursuits   We beg of you: Take a **sea kayak tour** of placid Monterey Bay and get eye-to-eye with a sea otter. Next, rent some bikes and cruise the **Coastal Bike Trail** while keeping an eye out for sea otters, sea lions, dolphins, and whales. After **scuba diving, paddle boarding, deep sea fishing,** and **whale watching,** take a **scenic drive** to nearby Carmel, Pebble Beach, and Big Sur.

Nightlife & Entertainment   Monterey host's the world's longest-running **jazz festival,** so there's always **live music** somewhere in town. Pubs include **Mucky Duck** and **Crown & Anchor.** A nightcap at **Schooners Bistro** overlooking the Monterey Bay is always a pleasure. Or join the spirited crowd at the piano bar at **Restaurant at Mission Ranch.**

Restaurants & Dining   You'll find everything from greasy **(Bubba Gump's)** to gourmet **(Montrio Bistro).** By day nothing beats lunching at the seaside cafes atop Fisherman's Wharf. By night, it's **Papá Chano's** for chilies rellenos and local fave **Tarpy's Roadhouse** for meatloaf and mash. Rise and shine at **Rosine's** for belly-filling breakfast plates.

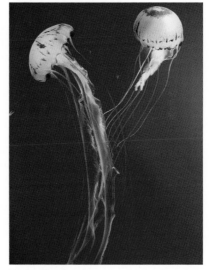

Monterey Bay Aquarium.

Essentials

GETTING THERE   The region's most convenient runway, at the **Monterey Peninsula Airport** (© **831/648-7000;** www.montereyairport.com), is 3 miles east of Monterey on Hwy. 68. American Eagle, Northwest, United, and US

Airways run daily flights into and out of Monterey. Many nearby hotels offer free airport shuttle service. If you take a taxi, it will cost about $14 to $20 to get to a peninsula hotel. Several national car-rental companies have airport locations, including **Dollar** (© **800/800-3665;** www.dollar.com) and **Hertz** (© **800/654-3131;** www.hertz.com).

VISITOR INFORMATION The **Monterey Peninsula Visitors and Convention Bureau** (© **831/649-1770;** www.seemonterey.com) has two visitor centers: one in the lobby of the Maritime Museum at Custom House Plaza near Fisherman's Wharf, the other at Lake El Estero on Camino El Estero. Both locations, open daily, offer good maps and free pamphlets and publications, including an excellent visitors' guide and the magazine *Coast Weekly.* Another good source for Monterey information is the **Monterey Peninsula On-Line Guide** at **www.monterey.com**.

GETTING AROUND The free **Waterfront Area Visitor Express (WAVE)** trolley takes passengers to and from the aquarium and other waterfront attractions from Memorial Day to Labor Day. It departs the downtown parking garages at Tyler Street and Del Monte Avenue every 10 to 12 minutes from 10am to 7pm Monday to Friday and 10am to 8pm Saturday to Sunday. Other WAVE stops include many hotels and motels in Monterey and Pacific Grove. For further information, call **Monterey Salinas Transit** at © **831/ 899-2555** or visit www.mst.org.

What to See & Do

The **National Steinbeck Center** ★ isn't in town, but fans of the author may want to make the 20-mile drive northeast from Monterey on Hwy. 68 to 1 Main St. in Salinas (© **831/775-4721;** www.steinbeck.org). The modern $11-million, 37,000-square-foot museum features interactive exhibits, a gallery of changing exhibitions, an orientation theater with a short video on Steinbeck's life, educational programs, a gift shop, and a cafe. Admission is $11 for adults, $9 for seniors over 62, $8 for children ages 13 to 17, $6 for children 6 to 12, and free for children 5 and under. Hours are daily from 10am to 5pm.

If you're passing through Monterey on a Tuesday afternoon, check out the **Old Monterey Marketplace** on Alvarado Street, from Pearl to Del Monte streets (© **831/655-8070;** www.oldmonterey.org), from 4 to 8pm (7pm in winter), rain or shine. More than 100 vendors contribute food, music, crafts, and entertainment.

Cannery Row ✋ Once the center for an industrial sardine-packing operation immortalized by John Steinbeck as "a poem, a stink, a grating noise, a quality of light, a tone, a habit, a nostalgia, a dream," this area today is a strip congested with tourists, tacky gift shops, overpriced seafood restaurants, and a parking nightmare. What changed it so dramatically? The sardines disappeared in 1948, from overfishing, changing currents, and pollution. Fishermen left, canneries closed, and the Row fell into disrepair. Curious tourists continued to visit the area. Steinbeck himself wrote, after visiting in the 1960s, "The beaches are clean where they once festered with fish guts and flies. The canneries that once put up a sickening stench are gone, their places filled with restaurants, antique shops, and the like. They fish for tourists now, not pilchards, and that species they are not likely to wipe out." I couldn't put it any better.

Btw. David and Drake aves. www.canneryrow.com.

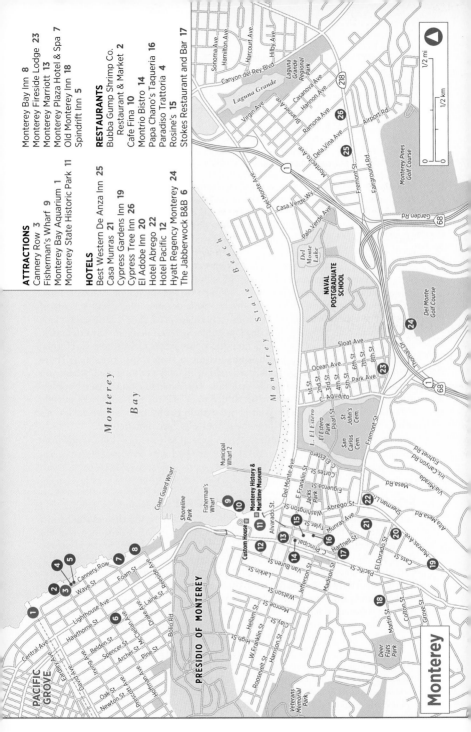

Monterey

Fisherman's Wharf   Like its counterpart in San Francisco, this wooden pier is crammed with crafts and gift shops, boating and fishing operations, fish markets, and seafood restaurants—all trawling for tourist dollars. But if you cast your view toward Monterey's stupendous view, with bobbing boats and sea lions, you might not notice the hordes of tourists. Grab some clam chowder in a sourdough bowl and find a seaside perch on the pier, or a bayfront seat at a seafood restaurant (see "Where to Eat," p. 444). Seafaring tour boats depart regularly from Fisherman's Wharf. See "Outdoor Pursuits," below, for details.

99 Pacific St. ☎ **831/649-6544.** www.montereywharf.com.

Monterey Bay Aquarium ★★★ ☺   Ranked one of the nation's top family attractions, Monterey's aquarium draws nearly two million visitors a year. On the border of one of the largest underwater canyons on Earth (wider and deeper than the Grand Canyon), it's surrounded by incredibly diverse marine life. One of the world's best and largest exhibit aquariums, it's home to more than 350,000 marine animals and plants, and about 550 species. A three-story, 335,000-gallon tank with clear acrylic walls offers stunning views of leopard sharks, sardines, anchovies, and other creatures swimming through a towering kelp forest. The 1.2-million-gallon Outer Bay tank houses open-ocean life, including yellowfin tuna, large green sea turtles, barracuda, sharks, giant ocean sunfish, and schools of bonito. The Giant Octopus exhibit is also amazing. Splash Zone (designed for kids up to 9) runs daily programs and displays of black-footed penguins, invertebrates, and other inhabitants of coral reefs and the cooler waters of Northern California. Everyone falls in love with the sea otters playing in their two-story exhibit. There are also coastal streams, tidal pools, a sand beach, and a petting pool, where you can touch living bat rays and handle sea stars. *Tip:* Avoid lines at the gate by ordering tickets in advance by calling ☎ **800/756-3737** (or 831-648-4937 outside CA) or online through TicketWeb at **www.ticketweb.com.** On weekdays, it's best to arrive in the afternoon after the school kids have departed.

886 Cannery Row. ☎ **831/648-4800** or 831/648-4888 for 24-hr. info line. www.montereybay aquarium.org. Admission $30 adults, $28 students and seniors 65 and over, $18 visitors with disabilities and children 3–12, free for children 2 and under. AE, MC, V. Daily 10am–6pm (9:30am–6pm May 28–Sept 5 and holidays).

FOLLOWING THE PATH OF HISTORY

The dozen historic buildings around Fisherman's Wharf and the adjacent town constitute the "Path of History" tour, which examines the 19th-century way of life and its architecture. Many buildings are part of the **Monterey State Historic Park ★**, 20 Custom House Plaza (☎ **831/649-7118**). Highlights include the **Custom House,** the state's oldest government building (built ca. 1827), and the **Monterey History & Maritime Museum,** 5 Custom House Plaza (☎ **831/ 372-2608;** www.montereyhistory.org), with ship models and other artifacts of the area's seafaring history—including a two-story, 10,000-pound Fresnel lens, used for nearly 80 years at the Point Sur lighthouse. At press time, the museum is closed for renovation, so call before going to visit.

You can go the self-guided route by picking up a free tour booklet at the Monterey Peninsula Visitors and Convention Bureau (see above), the Cooper Molera Adobe (at the corner of Polk St. and Munras Ave.), and various other locations. You may also opt to take the free guided tour, which departs several times daily. Call ☎ **831/649-7118** for details.

MONTEREY WINE COUNTRY

The congestion and price of Napa and Sonoma vineyards and the increasing popularity of winemaking have forced newcomers to plant their grapes elsewhere. Fortunately, much of the California coast offers ideal growing conditions. Any area between Monterey and Santa Barbara affords easy access to new appellations and a variety of boutique vintners making respectable wines. Stop by **A Taste of Monterey,** 700 Cannery Row (© **888/646-5446** or 831/646-5446; www.tastemonterey.com), daily between 11am and 6pm, to learn about local wines and taste them in front of huge bayfront windows. The site also distributes maps and winery touring information.

Outdoor Pursuits

Excellent for scuba diving, the waters off Monterey are also teeming with game fish. Among the public fishing boats are **Chris' Fishing Trips,** 48 Fisherman's Wharf (© **831/375-5951;** www.chrissfishing.com). Cod and salmon are the main catches, with separate boats leaving daily. Call or log on to the website for a price list and departure schedule. Check-in is 45 minutes before departure, and equipment rental costs a bit extra.

Several outfitters rent kayaks for a spin around the bay. Contact **Monterey Bay Kayaks,** 693 Del Monte Ave. (© **800/649-5357** or 831/373-5357; www.montereykayaks.com), on Del Monte Beach north of Fisherman's Wharf, which offers instruction as well as natural history tours that introduce visitors to the Monterey Bay National Marine Sanctuary and nearby Elkhorn Slough, one of the last remaining estuaries in California (see "The Otters, Seals & Birds of the Elkhorn Slough," below). Prices start at $45 for the tours, from $25 for rentals.

For bike rentals and kayak tours and rentals, contact **Adventures by the Sea,** 299 Cannery Row (© **831/372-1807;** www.adventuresbythesea.com). Bikes cost $7 per hour or $24 per day, and kayaks are $30 per person or $50 for

MONTEREY BAY'S COASTAL bike trail

If your kids are spending way too much time playing video games, drag them kicking and screaming to ride bikes along the **Monterey Bay Coastal Trail.** The paved waterfront trail, which was once the tracks of the Southern Pacific Railroad, stretches 18 miles from Castroville in the north to Pacific Grove in the south, then continues as a bike lane to the entrance of the fabled **17-Mile Drive,** rated one of the top bicycle rides in the nation (and there's no entrance fee for bicyclists).

The scenery all along the Coastal Trail is spectacular, and there's a very good chance you'll spot numerous sea lions and sea otters (blue whales even). There are several places to stop and get a bite to eat on the trail, or you can pack a picnic and spread out a blanket on one of the trail's many grassy areas. Even dogs are allowed on a leash. If you can't bring your own bikes, I recommend renting 24-speed hybrid bikes in Monterey at **Adventures by the Sea** (299 Cannery Row, Monterey; © **831/372-1807;** www.adventuresbythesea.com) for $25 per day, which includes a lock and helmet. Believe me, folks—a day spent cruising along this wonderful trail will be one of the highlights of your summer.

One of my favorite coastal stops is Moss Landing, 25 minutes north of Monterey on Hwy. 1, home of Captain Yohn Gideon's **Elkhorn Slough Safari** (🕿 831/633-5555; www.elkhornslough.com). For $32 for adults or $24 for children 3 to 14, friendly Cap'n Gideon loads guests onto a safe, 27-foot pontoon boat and embarks on a 2-hour tour of the Elkhorn Slough Wildlife Reserve. It's not uncommon to see a "raft" of up to 50 otters, feet up and sunning themselves; harbor seals; and hundreds of species of waterfowl and migratory shorebirds. An onboard naturalist answers questions, Cap'n Gideon educates on the surroundings, and binoculars are available.

a 2½-hour tour. Adventures by the Sea has another location at 210 Alvarado St. (🕿 **831/648-7235**), by the Portola Plaza Hotel.

Experienced scuba divers can contact **Monterey Bay Dive Charters** (🕿 **831/383-9276;** www.montereyscubadiving.com), which arranges personal dives with a dive master and has scheduled weekend dives. **Aquarius Dive Shop,** 2040 Del Monte Ave. (🕿 **831/375-1933;** www.aquariusdivers.com), also has regularly scheduled trips and dive masters. Certification cards are required.

If the kids need to let off some steam, take them to the **Dennis the Menace Playground ★**, at Camino El Estero and Del Monte Avenue, near Lake Estero (🕿 **831/646-3860**), an old-fashioned playground created by Pacific Grove resident and cartoonist Hank Ketcham. It has bridges, tunnels, and an authentic Southern Pacific Railroad engine teeming with wannabe conductors. There's also a hot-dog-and-burger stand, and a big lake where you can rent paddle boats or feed the ducks. The park is open daily from 10am to sunset.

Where to Stay

Monterey has three types of lodgings: lace-and-flower B&Bs, large corporate hotels, and run-of-the-mill motels. Consider where you'd like to be and how much you want to spend, and then check out the options below or contact **Resort 2 Me** (🕿 **800/757-5646;** www.resort2me.com), a local reservations service that offers free recommendations of Monterey Bay–area hotels in all price ranges.

EXPENSIVE

In addition to the choices below, two chain hotels are popular with business travelers and conventioneers, near Fisherman's Wharf: The **Monterey Marriott,** 350 Calle Principal, at Del Monte Boulevard (www.marriott.com; 🕿 **888/236-2427** or 831/649-4234), offers some rooms with bay views, an outdoor pool, a health club, a Jacuzzi, and saunas. Less central but great for families and golfers, the **Hyatt Regency Monterey** resort, 1 Old Golf Course Rd. (www.hyatt.com; 🕿 **800/233-1234** or 831/372-1234), adjoins the Del Monte Golf Course, with three pools, two Jacuzzis, a gym, tennis courts, and two restaurants.

Hotel Pacific ★★ The all-suite Hotel Pacific isn't waterfront (it's near the wharf, across from the Monterey Conference Center), but it's still one of the better upscale choices in Monterey. Beyond the Spanish-Mediterranean architecture in the common areas, each unit is in one of 16 buildings clustered around courtyards and gardens with spas and fountains. All of the suites have feather beds with down comforters, stylish Spanish Colonial decor, hardwood floors, fireplaces surrounded by cushy couches and seats, separate dining areas, and French doors that open onto private patios or terraces overlooking the gardens. *Tip:* Ask for a room on the fourth level with a panoramic view of the bay.

300 Pacific St., Monterey, CA 93940. www.hotelpacific.com. © **800/554-5542** or 831/373-5700. Fax 831/373-6921. 105 suites. $130–$350 suite for 2. Rates include continental breakfast and afternoon tea. AE, DC, DISC, MC, V. Parking $16. **Amenities:** Nearby golf course; 2 Jacuzzis; room service. *In room:* TV/DVD.

Monterey Bay Inn ★★ Among the tourist shuffle of Cannery Row are the quaint and quiet quarters of Monterey Bay Inn. The beds are exquisitely comfortable, and the 310-thread-count Pima cotton linens are an added bonus. Book a Bay View room for the best scenery in the house: The sound of the waves lapping against the building is the perfect wake-up call, and you can have your morning cup of joe from your private waterfront balcony. Though the hotel has no restaurant, an artfully arranged breakfast is brought to you at your request, and a handful of decent eateries are right at your doorstep. After a long day of seeing the sights, soak your weary muscles in the rooftop Jacuzzi, or book a Sanctuary Massage at the hotel spa.

242 Cannery Row, Monterey, CA 93940. www.montereybayinn.com. © **800/424-6242** or 831/373-6242. Fax 831/373-7603. 47 units. $259–$599 double. Rates include breakfast served in room. Packages available. AE, DISC, MC, V. **Amenities:** Room service; spa. *In room:* TV/DVD, CD player, Wi-Fi.

Monterey Plaza Hotel & Spa ★★ One of the most formal hotels in town, the Monterey Plaza comprises three buildings—two on the water and one across the street—connected by a second-story enclosed "skywalk." The public areas are elegantly decorated with marble, Brazilian teak, and attractive artwork. The bedrooms are more upscale-corporate than most around town and have double or king beds, decor reminiscent of 19th-century Biedermeier, and Italian marble bathrooms. Many have balconies overlooking the water (sea otters included in the view). The least desirable rooms are across the street from the ocean. There's also an 11,000-square-foot European-style spa with a fitness room and ocean views, the **Duck Club Grill** serving American regional cuisine by the sea, and the adjacent **Schooner's Bistro,** which serves lighter fare.

400 Cannery Row, Monterey, CA 93940. www.montereyplazahotel.com. © **800/334-3999** or 831/646-1700. Fax 831/646-0285. 290 units. $215–$760 double; $595–$3,200 suite. Children 17 and under stay free in parent's room. Packages available. AE, DC, DISC, MC, V. Parking $25 per day. From Hwy. 1, take the Soledad Dr. exit and follow the signs to Cannery Row. **Amenities:** 2 restaurants; concierge; nearby golf course; full fitness center; Jacuzzi; room service; dry sauna; full-service European-style spa. *In room:* TV w/pay movies, fridge, hair dryer.

Old Monterey Inn ★★★ This three-story, vine-covered, Tudor-style country inn is one of the nation's top B&Bs and one of my favorites. It's away from the surf but a perfect choice for romantics, with rose gardens aplenty, a bubbling brook, and oak-shaded brick-and-flagstone walkways. Many rooms have private bathrooms, plush feather beds, and down duvets, and many have wood-burning fireplaces; two open onto private patios. All guest rooms are unique and wonderful, but my top picks are the cozy Library, with its book-lined walls and stone fireplace; and the Stoneleigh, for its private entrance, whirlpool for two, and fireplace facing the huge bed. The private cottage is English country, with a double Jacuzzi, magnificent king-size bed, wood-burning fireplace, sitting area, and private patio. Breakfasts are stellar and served in your room or in the dining room. From 4:30 to 6pm, guests can retire to the living room for fireside wine and hors d'oeuvres. The innkeeper also provides blankets and towels for the beach. If you want to impress your sweetie, reserve a firelight Swedish massage for two at the inn's **SpaRetreat Salon.**

500 Martin St. (off Pacific Ave.), Monterey, CA 93940. www.oldmontereyinn.com. © **800/350-2344** or 831/375-8284. Fax 831/375-6730. 9 units, 1 cottage. $250–$365 double; from $430 cottage. Rates include full breakfast, tea and cookies in the afternoon, and evening wine and hors d'oeuvres. MC, V. Free parking. From Hwy. 1, take the Soledad Dr. exit and turn right onto Pacific Ave., then left onto Martin St. **Amenities:** Concierge; nearby golf course; passes to nearby health club; Jacuzzi; spa. *In room:* TV/VCR, hair dryer, Wi-Fi.

Sanctuary Beach Resort ★★   The ultimate in romantic retreats, Sanctuary Beach Resort occupies the most enviable stretch of coastline in the greater Monterey area, backing a vacated beach and just steps from the Monterey Bay National Marine Sanctuary. Book an oceanside room, where you can watch the fog roll in fireside from your living room, or the undulating sand dunes as they change course. The resort boasts 19 acres of oceanfront property, among which rooms are organized in two- or four-unit plexes, and a Serenity Spa that will make your stay even more relaxing. And what could be more fun than having your own complimentary golf cart to use for the duration of your stay? If you're visiting on a weekday, rates are a true steal, beginning at just $149—sometimes even lower when the resort's running a special (check the website for deals).

3295 Dunes Dr., Marina, CA 93933 (9 miles north of Monterey). www.thesanctuarybeachresort. com. © **877/944-3863** or 831/883-9478. Fax 831/883-9477. 60 units. $149–$475 double. AE, DC, DISC, MC, V. **Amenities:** Jacuzzi; heated outdoor pool; spa. *In room:* TV, CD player, hair dryer, minibar, MP3 docking station, Wi-Fi.

Spindrift Inn ★★   In the middle of honky-tonk Cannery Row, on a narrow stretch of beach, this four-story hotel is an island of Continental style in a sea of commercialism. It's elegant and well maintained, and the rooms are decorated with goose-down feather beds (a few with canopies), hardwood floors, wood-burning fireplaces, and cushioned window seats or private balconies. The bathrooms have marble and brass fixtures. Extras include terry robes and two phones. The ocean views are worth the extra cost, particularly from one of the corner rooms with cushioned window seats.

652 Cannery Row, Monterey, CA 93940. www.spindriftinn.com. © **800/841-1879** or 831/646-8900. Fax 831/646-5342. 42 units. $279–$339 double with Cannery Row view; $339–$469 double with ocean view. Rates include continental breakfast delivered to your room and afternoon wine and cheese. AE, DC, DISC, MC, V. Parking $16. **Amenities:** Nearby golf course; room service. *In room:* TV/DVD, CD player, hair dryer, minibar, Wi-Fi.

MODERATE

Munras Avenue and northern Fremont Avenue are lined with moderate and inexpensive family-style motels, some independently owned and some chains. They're not as central as the downtown options, and atmosphere is seriously lacking on Fremont, but if transportation isn't an issue, you can save a bundle by staying in one of these areas. If the following places are full, try calling the **Cypress Gardens**

Inn, 1150 Munras Ave. (www.cypressgardensinn.com; © **831/373-2761**), with a pool, Jacuzzi, free movie channels, and continental breakfast (dogs are welcome); the **Monterey Fireside Lodge,** 1131 10th St. (www.firesidemonterey. com; © **800/722-2624** or 831/373-4172), near Fisherman's Wharf and downtown; or the **El Adobe Inn,** 936 Munras Ave. (www.el-adobe-inn.com; © **831/ 372-5409**), a 26-room motor lodge close to downtown with distant bay views from several rooms.

Best Western De Anza Inn 🖋 The common areas of this north Monterey motel are more modern and elaborate than most Best Westerns I've seen, but the rooms are your generic, reliable motel style. Amenities include in-room coffee, free local calls, and free wireless Internet; microwaves and refrigerators are available upon request. There's also a heated pool and Jacuzzi on the premises. The only drawback is the location, a few miles north of all of Monterey's action, but it's only a 10-minute drive and well worth the money you'll save by staying here.

2141 N. Fremont St., Monterey, CA 93940. www.bestwestern.com. © **800/780-7234** or 831/646-8300. Fax 831/646-8130. 43 units. $89–$159 double; $139–$289 suite. Extra person $8. Senior discounts available. AE, DC, DISC, MC, V. **Amenities:** Restaurant; Jacuzzi; outdoor pool. *In room:* TV, in-room movies, hair dryer, Wi-Fi.

Casa Munras Casa Munras was built around the original hacienda of Don Esteban Munras, the last Spanish ambassador to California. Accommodations are scattered among 11 one- and two-story buildings along the 4½-acre landscaped property. Each is decorated with pine-wood furnishings and blue-and-white fabrics, and perks include Lather bath and body products and complimentary wireless Internet access. *Tip:* Spend a few extra bucks and get a deluxe room with a gas fireplace—it gets chilly at night in Monterey.

700 Munras Ave., Monterey, CA 93940. www.hotelcasamunras.com. © **831/375-2411.** Fax 831/ 375-1365. 171 units. $159–$229 double. AAA and Entertainment Book discounts available. AE, DC, MC, V. **Amenities:** Concierge; complimentary DVD library; access to nearby health club; outdoor pool; spa. *In room:* TV/DVD, hair dryer, free Wi-Fi.

Hotel Abrego ★ The newest hotel in town, Abrego (formerly the Sand Dollar Inn) opened in the summer of 2009, bringing Monterey posh lodging at a reasonable price—and away from the kitschy Cannery Row, at that. It's a great alternative for those who want a quieter escape (which you won't find nearer the water). Rooms are cozy and decorated in warm hues and earth tones to reflect the city's coastal feel; most have fireplaces. Request one of the new rooms; the older ones from the Sand Dollar days could still use a little TLC. The Abrego Lounge serves small bites in the lobby and on an outdoor patio.

755 Abrego St., Monterey, CA 93940. www.hotelabrego.com. © **800/982-1986** or 831/372-7551. Fax 831/372-0916. 93 units. $99–$159 double. Rates include a buffet breakfast. AE, MC, V. Free parking. **Amenities:** Concierge; Jacuzzi; pool. *In room:* TV, fridge, hair dryer, MP3 docking station, free Wi-Fi.

The Jabberwock Bed & Breakfast ★ One of the better B&Bs in the area, the Jabberwock (from Lewis Carroll's *Through the Looking Glass & What Alice Found There*) is 4 blocks from Cannery Row. It's centrally located but tranquil; its ½-acre garden with waterfalls is a respite from downtown. The seven rooms are individually furnished, some more elegantly than others; all have full bathrooms and goose-down comforters and pillows, and three have Jacuzzi tubs for two, fireplaces, and king beds. The Toves Room has a huge walnut Victorian bed and secret garden, the spacious Borogrove has a fireplace and a fine view of Monterey Bay, the Mimsy has an ocean view, and the Wabe has an Austrian carved bed. Full breakfast is served in the dining room or in guest rooms. Evening hors d'oeuvres are offered on the veranda, and a wooden Vorpal rabbit dispenses homemade chocolate chip cookies, served with milk.

598 Laine St., Monterey, CA 93940. www.jabberwockinn.com. © **888/428-7253** or 831/372-4777. Fax 831/655-2946. 7 units. $179–$299 double. Rates include full breakfast, afternoon aperitifs, and bedtime cookies. MC, V. **Amenities:** Concierge; nearby golf course; Jacuzzi; free Wi-Fi. *In room:* Hair dryer, no phone.

INEXPENSIVE

If you're still having trouble finding an inexpensive vacancy, try calling Monterey's chain gang: **Motel 6** (www.motel6.com; © **800/4-MOTEL-6** [466-8356]), **Comfort Inn** (www.choicehotels.com; © **877/424-6423**), **Travelodge** (www.travelodge.com; © **888/515-6375**), or **Super 8** (www.super8.com; © **800/889-9698**).

Cypress Tree Inn 🦅   It's 2 miles from downtown, but if you're on a budget and have transportation, this inn offers a great value for such an expensive region. The staff is friendly, the large guest rooms are in decent shape, all but one have a tub/shower combination, and nine even have Jacuzzis. You won't get designer soaps or other in-room treats, but the hostelry does have a handy coin-op laundry. RV spaces are also available.

2227 N. Fremont St., Monterey, CA 93940. www.cypresstreeinn.com. © **800/446-8303** or 831/372-7586. Fax 831/372-2940. 55 units. $69–$149 double. AE, DC, DISC, MC, V. **Amenities:** Jacuzzi; sauna; free Wi-Fi. *In room:* TV, fridge, hair dryer, kitchen or kitchenette in some units.

Where to Eat

If I had all the money in the world, I'd still have lunch the same way every day in Monterey. I'd walk down **Old Fisherman's Wharf** and snack on all those small cups of fresh seafood at the numerous faux fish markets. Priced at a couple of bucks each, fresh mussels, octopus, shrimp, crab, oysters, ceviche, and clam chowder cost a fraction of what you'd pay at a restaurant. You can either eat on foot as you head down the wharf or cart your cups to the benches at the end of the pier (to the left of Rappa's).

EXPENSIVE

Montrio Bistro ★★ AMERICAN BISTRO   Big-city sophistication meets old Monterey in this converted 1910 firehouse. The enormous dining room is the sharpest in town, a playfully chic expanse with clouds hanging from the ceiling and curvaceous walls. Order anything cooked in the open kitchen's oak-fired rotisserie grill, such as the crispy Dungeness crab cakes with spicy rémoulade or a roasted portobello mushroom with polenta and ragout of vegetables. The wine list, which received *Wine Spectator* magazine's Award of Excellence, includes numerous vintages by the glass.

414 Calle Principal (at Franklin). © **831/648-8880.** www.montrio.com. Reservations recommended. Main courses $9–$30. AE, DISC, MC, V. Sun–Thurs 4:30–10pm; Fri–Sat 4:30–11pm.

Paradiso Trattoria ★ ITALIAN   Formerly Blue Moon, this restaurant was renovated and transformed to Paradiso a couple of years back. Reverting to its original Mediterranean cuisine, the menu offers favorites such as lobster, crab risotto, eggplant Parmesan, linguine and clams, and chicken scaloppine. *Though be warned:* It's not the healthiest place to dine if you're on a diet, since many of the dishes come doused in butter or cream sauce. While the food is dependably good, Paradiso's greatest offering is its waterfront seating that overlooks the bay. *Tip:* At dinnertime, request a table by the window to enjoy the sunset.

654 Cannery Row, Monterey, CA 93940. © **831/375-4155.** www.paradisomonterey.com. Reservations recommended. AE, MC, V. Lunch $13–$19; dinner $16–$80. Daily 11:30am–9pm.

Stokes Restaurant and Bar ★★ CALIFORNIAN/MEDITERRANEAN This historic adobe and board-and-batten house, built in 1833 for the town doctor, has been converted into one of Monterey's finest restaurants. It's a handsome establishment, consisting of a bar and several large dining rooms, all outfitted with terra-cotta floors, bleached-wood-plank ceilings, and Southwestern-style wood chairs and tables. It's the perfect rustic-yet-contemporary showcase for chef Brandon Miller's California-Mediterranean fare, such as grilled local swordfish with marinated young beets, snap peas, and salsa verde; and duck confit with warm spinach salad. Everything from Miller's wood-burning oven—chicken, fish, pizza—is recommended. Desserts are dreamy, and the wine list is excellent.

500 Hartnell St. (at Madison St.). © **831/373-1110.** www.stokesrestaurant.com. Reservations recommended. Main courses $8–$24. AE, DC, DISC, MC, V. Daily 5:30pm–closing.

MODERATE

Bubba Gump Shrimp Co. Restaurant & Market ✋AMERICAN Culinary cognoscenti will flee at the sight of this tourist haven, but lots of people love it. It could be the boatyard decor or location—near the aquarium, with a million-dollar, unobstructed bayfront view—that attracts visitors in droves. More likely, it's the entertainment value, because Gump's (as in *Forrest Gump*) is packed with movie gimmicks and memorabilia. You're in for greasy, fried, and buttered-up seafood, suggested by the roll of paper towels at each table. The Bucket of Boat Trash, for example, is shrimp and lobster tails cooked and served in a bucket with a side of fries and coleslaw. There are also pork chops, a veggie dish, salads, and burgers. The "market" is a gift shop with T-shirts, caps, and, of course, boxes of chocolate.

720 Cannery Row (at Prescott). © **831/373-1884.** www.bubbagump.com. Main courses $8–$25. AE, DC, DISC, MC, V. Sun–Thurs 10am–11pm; Fri–Sat 10am–midnight.

Cafe Fina ★ 🔪ITALIAN/SEAFOOD Other pierside restaurants lure tourists with little more than a sea view, but Cafe Fina's mesquite-grilled meats, well-prepared fresh fish, brick-oven pizzas, and delicious salads and pastas give even locals a reason to head here. Betrayed by the facade of a pizza-to-go counter, the specialties are the seafood and pasta dishes, but anything that comes out of the wood broiler or wood-fired brick oven is a winner. Be sure to request a table by the back window to watch the sea otters and sea lions play in the kelp.

47 Fisherman's Wharf. © **800/THE-FINA** (843-3462) or 831/372-5200. www.cafefina.com. Reservations recommended. Main courses $16–$30. AE, DC, DISC, MC, V. Mon–Fri 11am–2:30pm; Sat–Sun 11am–3pm; daily 5–9:30pm.

Tarpy's Roadhouse ★★ AMERICAN Worth the detour a few miles east of downtown, this lively Southwestern-style restaurant is a mandatory stop when I'm in Monterey. The welcoming dining room has stylish yet rustic decor. On sunny afternoons, patrons relax under market umbrellas on the outdoor patio, sip margaritas, and munch on Tarpy's locally renowned Caesar salad. Come nightfall, the place fills with tourists and locals who pile in for the hefty plate of bourbon-molasses pork chops or Dijon-crusted lamb loin. There's a modest selection of fresh fish, shellfish, and vegetable dishes, but it's the good ol' meat-'n'-potato mainstays that sell the best, such as the juicy meatloaf on garlic whipped potatoes.

2999 Monterey–Salinas Hwy. (at Hwy. 68 and Canyon del Rey near the Monterey Airport). ℂ **831/647-1444.** www.tarpys.com. Reservations recommended for dinner. Most main courses $9–$45. AE, DISC, MC, V. Sun–Thurs 11:30am–9pm; Fri–Sat 11:30am–10pm.

INEXPENSIVE

Papá Chano's Taquería MEXICAN   Don't expect cloth napkins, a formal waiter (or any server, for that matter), or ambient music, but rather jumbo burritos and other Mexican specialties made from fresh ingredients. Forget about atmosphere—the cavernous ceilings, unadorned walls, and plain wooden tables and brick floors are anything but cozy. But the quesadillas, tacos, nachos, and *platillos especiales* (steak, pork, chicken, or chilis rellenos plates with rice, beans, cheese, lettuce, tomatoes, salsa, sour cream, guacamole, and tortillas) lure me back every time I'm in town.

462 Alvarado St. (at Bonifacio Place near Franklin). ℂ **831/646-9587.** Mexican plates $4–$8. No credit cards. Daily 10am–10pm.

Rosine's 🍴 AMERICAN   Everything served at Rosine's is filling and fairly priced, which explains why this local favorite is always busy. Aside from the large, airy window seats, the place has an upscale cafeteria feel, but its menu, filled with standard entrees, aims to please all tastes. The breakfast plates are so packed, they'll keep you full until dinner. Lunch features an extensive list of salads and sandwiches, and dinner offers an array of pastas, burgers, and more expensive items such as charbroiled pork chops with applesauce and mashed potatoes ($17) and prime rib ($20, Fri–Sat only). Other than steak and seafood, most entrees hover around $10 and include side salads and/or potatoes. Sugar fiends will appreciate the huge cakes behind glass as you walk in the front door (yes, you can buy them by the slice).

434 Alvarado St. (at Franklin St.). ℂ **831/375-1400.** www.rosinesmonterey.com. Breakfast $4–$10; lunch $6–$10; most dinner dishes $8–$20. AE, DC, DISC, MC, V. Sun–Thurs 8am–9pm; Fri–Sat 8am–10pm.

PACIFIC GROVE ★★

42 miles S of Santa Cruz; 113 miles S of San Francisco; 338 miles N of Los Angeles

Some compare 2½-square-mile Pacific Grove—the locals call it "PG"—to Carmel as it was 20 years ago. Plenty of tourists wind their way through here on oceanfront trails and dining excursions, but the town remains quaint and peaceful—amazing, considering that Monterey is a stone's throw away (a quarter of the Monterey Bay Aquarium is actually in Pacific Grove). While Monterey is comparatively congested and cosmopolitan, Pacific Grove is sprinkled with historic homes, flowers, butterflies fluttering about, and deer meandering fearlessly from yard to yard.

ATTRACTIONS
Pacific Grove Museum of
  Natural History **9**

HOTELS
The Centrella Inn **8**
Gosby House **3**
Green Gables Inn **11**
Martine Inn **12**
Pacific Grove Inn **5**
Seven Gables Inn **10**

RESTAURANTS
Fandango **6**
First Awakenings **14**
The Fishwife at
  Asilomar Beach **1**
Joe Rombi's **4**
Peppers Mexicali Café **7**
Thai Bistro II **13**
Toasties Café **2**

Pacific Grove

Essentials

VISITOR INFORMATION   The **Pacific Grove Chamber of Commerce** is on
the corner of Forest and Central avenues (© **800/656-6650** or 831/373-
3304; www.pacificgrove.org).

ORIENTATION   Lighthouse Avenue is the Grove's principal thoroughfare, running from Monterey to the lighthouse at the point of the peninsula. Lighthouse Avenue is bisected by Forest Avenue, which runs from Hwy. 1 (where
it's called Holman Hwy., or Hwy. 68) to Lover's Point, an extension of land
that sticks out into the bay in the middle of Pacific Grove.

What to See & Do

Pacific Grove is best strolled, so park the car, don walking shoes, and spend the
day meandering around George Washington Park and the waterfront around the
point. The **Point Pinos Lighthouse ★**, at the tip of the peninsula on Ocean
View Boulevard (© **831/648-5716;** www.pgmuseum.org), is the oldest working
lighthouse on the West Coast. Its 50,000-candlepower beacon has illuminated
the rocky shores since 1855, when Pacific Grove was little more than a pine forest. The museum and grounds are open and free to visitors Thursday through
Monday from 1 to 4pm.

Point Pinos Lighthouse.

Marine Gardens Park ★, a stretch of shoreline along Ocean View Boulevard on Monterey Bay and the Pacific, is renowned for ocean views, flowers, and tide-pool seaweed beds. Walk out to **Lover's Point** (named after lovers of Jesus, not groping teenagers) and watch sea otters play and crack open an occasional abalone.

An excellent shorter alternative, or complement, to 17-Mile Drive (see "Pebble Beach & 17-Mile Drive," later in this chapter) is the scenic drive or bike ride along Pacific Grove's **Ocean View Boulevard ★**. This coastal stretch starts near Monterey's Cannery Row and follows the Pacific around to the lighthouse point. Here it turns into Sunset Drive, which runs along secluded **Asilomar State Beach ★** (© 831/646-6442). Park on Sunset and explore the trails, dunes, and tide pools of this sandy shoreline. You might find purple shore crabs, green anemone, sea bats, starfish, limpets, and all kinds of kelp and algae. The 11 buildings of the conference center established here by the YWCA in 1913 are landmarks, designed by noted architect Julia Morgan. If you follow this route during winter, a furious sea rages and crashes against the rocks.

To learn more about the region, stop in at the **Pacific Grove Museum of Natural History,** 165 Forest Ave. (© 831/648-5716; www.pgmuseum.org). It has displays on monarch butterflies and their migration, stuffed examples of the local birds and mammals, and temporary exhibits and special events. Admission is free; hours are Tuesday through Saturday from 10am to 5pm.

Pacific Grove is widely known as "Butterfly Town, USA," a reference to the thousands of **monarchs** that migrate here from November to February, traveling from as far away as Alaska. Many settle in the Monarch Grove sanctuary, a eucalyptus stand on Grove Acre Avenue off Lighthouse Avenue. George Washington Park, at Pine Avenue and Alder Street, is famous for its "butterfly trees." To get here, the butterflies may travel as far as 2,000 miles, covering 100 miles a day at an altitude of 10,000 feet. *Collectors beware:* The town imposes strict fines for disturbing the butterflies.

Just as Ocean View Boulevard serves as an alternative to 17-Mile Drive, the **Pacific Grove Municipal Golf Course,** 77 Asilomar Ave. (© 831/648-5775; www.ci.pg.ca.us/golf), serves as a reasonable alternative to the high-priced courses at Pebble Beach. The back 9 of this 5,500-yard, par-70 course overlook the sea and offer the added challenge of coping with the winds. Views are panoramic, and the fairways and greens are better maintained than most semiprivate courses. There's a restaurant, pro shop, and driving range. Eighteen holes start at $40 Monday through Thursday and $45 Friday through Sunday and holidays; twilight rates are available. Optional carts cost $34.

The **American Tin Cannery Factory Premium Outlets,** 125 Ocean View Blvd., around the corner from the Monterey Bay Aquarium ((*C*) **831/372-1442;** www.americantincannery.com), is a converted warehouse with 40 factory-outlet shops, including Bass Shoes, OshKosh B'gosh, Samsonite, and Izod. It's open daily from 10am to 6pm.

Where to Stay

If you're having trouble finding a vacancy, try calling **Resort 2 Me** ((*C*) **800/757-5646;** www.resort2me.com), a local reservations service that offers free recommendations of Monterey Bay–area hotels in all price ranges.

EXPENSIVE

Martine Inn ★★ One glance at the lavish Victorian interior and the bay views, and you'll know why this Mediterranean-style inn is one of the best B&Bs in the area. Built in 1899 for James and Laura Parke (of Parke-Davis Pharmaceuticals fame), each room has a view of the ocean or garden courtyard; most have wood-burning fireplaces. Request a room with a tub if it matters to you; some have only a shower. The inn maintains an adjacent Victorian cottage, which has been converted into a luxury suite. A full breakfast is served at lace-covered tables in the front room; hors d'oeuvres are served in the evening. Guests also have access to

Asilomar State Beach.

Pebble Beach, 17-Mile Drive.

two additional common rooms: a room downstairs overlooking the ocean and a larger room with shelves of books.

255 Ocean View Blvd., Pacific Grove, CA 93950. www.martineinn.com. © **800/852-5588** or 831/373-3388. Fax 831/373-3896. 24 units. $169–$469 double. Rates include full breakfast, evening hors d'oeuvres, coffee, bottled water, and soda. AE, DISC, MC, V. **Amenities:** Babysitting; concierge; nearby golf course; Jacuzzi; room service. *In room:* Fridge, hair dryer, Wi-Fi.

Seven Gables Inn ★★★   This is one of the most opulent B&Bs I've ever seen. Named after the seven gables that cap the inn, the compound of seven Victorian buildings was built in 1886 by the Chase family (as in Chase Manhattan Bank). Outside is the coastal road overlooking the sea; inside is a collection of mostly European antiques. Everything here is luxurious and gilded, including all of the 25 guest rooms situated among the main house, Carriage House, three cottages, Guest House, and the newly acquired Beach House (formerly the Grand View Inn). Paths through the rose gardens link the satellite accommodations to the main house. All guest rooms come with ocean views, private bathrooms, down comforters, Gilchrist & Soames bath amenities, and incredibly comfortable custom-made beds (some of which are California kings, in case you like to spread out when you sleep). A full breakfast is included in all room rates.

555 Ocean View Blvd., Pacific Grove, CA 93950. www.pginns.com. © **831/372-4341.** 25 units. $175–$405 double. Rates include breakfast and afternoon wine and cheese service. 2-night minimum on weekends. AE, MC, V. **Amenities:** Nearby golf course. *In room:* Fridge in some units, hair dryer, kitchenette in 1 unit, no phone, Wi-Fi.

MODERATE

The Centrella Inn ★   A couple of blocks from the waterfront and from Lover's Point Beach, the two-story Centrella is a turreted Victorian built as a boarding-house in 1889. Today the rooms are still decorated in Victorian style with iron beds, armoires, and authentic Victorian-era antiques—even the bathrooms have claw-foot tubs. Behind the main house and connected by walkways are several cottages and suites that have fireplaces, separate bedrooms, and bathrooms. Two have private decks; the others offer decks facing the rose garden and patio, which is set with umbrella tables and chairs.

Imagine waking into a private bungalow to find a cheetah sleeping on your porch and then having an elephant deliver your breakfast basket with its trunk. That's just another morning for guests at the **Vision Quest Safari Bed & Breakfast** (www.wild thingsinc.com; © **800/228-7382**), one of the nation's most unique B&Bs. Amid the ranch's pride of exotic animals are deluxe Africa-style tent cabins with wild-animal-theme decors, full bathrooms, sitting areas, and views that overlook a 5-acre elephant playpen and the Salinas Valley. Those are real lions and tigers roaring through your canvas walls, and guests can join trainers on their evening walks among the animals. Monterey's restaurants are a short drive away. Okay, so it's not for everyone, but at least take a look at their website and see if you might want to spend a night doing the wild thing.

612 Central Ave., Pacific Grove, CA 93950. www.centrellainn.com. © **800/233-3372** or 831/372-3372. Fax 831/372-2036. 21 units, 5 cottages. $139–$269 double; $209–$320 suite and cottage. Rates include buffet breakfast. AE, DISC, MC, V. **Amenities:** Nearby golf course. *In room:* TV in cottage, fridge, hair dryer, free Wi-Fi.

Gosby House ★   Originally a boardinghouse for Methodist ministers, this Victorian was built in 1888, 3 blocks from the bay. It's one of the most charming Victorians in town, with individually decorated rooms, floral-print wallpapers, lacy pillows, and antiques. Twelve guest rooms have fireplaces, and all come with teddy bears (available for purchase if you want to keep yours). Especially noteworthy are the two Carriage House rooms, which come with a fridge and coffeemaker, fireplace, balcony, and bathroom with spa tub. The house has a separate dining room and parlor, where guests gather for breakfast and complimentary wine and hors d'oeuvres in the afternoon. Other amenities include a complimentary newspaper, twice-daily maid service, and bicycles.

643 Lighthouse Ave., Pacific Grove, CA 93950. www.gosbyhouseinn.com. © **800/527-8828** or 831/375-1287. Fax 831/655-9621. 22 units. $120–$225 double. Rates include full breakfast and afternoon wine and hors d'oeuvres. AE, DC, MC, V. From Hwy. 1, take Hwy. 68 to Pacific Grove, where it turns into Forest Ave.; continue on Forest to Lighthouse Ave., turn left, and go 3 blocks. **Amenities:** Complimentary bike use; nearby golf course. *In room:* TV, hair dryer.

Green Gables Inn ★   This 1888 Queen Anne–style mansion, decorated like an English country inn, forgoes opulence (and, in some cases, private bathrooms) to allow for reasonable rates and less formal accommodations. The rooms are divided between the main building and the carriage houses behind it. The Carriage House rooms, which are better for families, have large private bathrooms with Jacuzzi tubs. All accommodations are individually decorated with period furnishings, including some antiques and an occasional poster bed. Most rooms in the original home have ocean views and private bathrooms. Complimentary wine, tea, and hors d'oeuvres are served each afternoon in the parlor, with an antique carousel horse.

301 Ocean View Blvd., Pacific Grove, CA 93950. www.greengablesinnpg.com. © **800/722-1774** or 831/375-2095. Fax 831/375-5437. 11 units, 9 with bathroom. $135–$300 double. Rates include

full breakfast and afternoon wine and hors d'oeuvres. AE, MC, V. From Hwy. 1, take the Pacific Grove exit (Hwy. 68) and continue to the Pacific Ocean; turn right on Ocean View Blvd. and drive ½ mile to Fifth St. **Amenities:** Complimentary bike use.

Pacific Grove Inn ★   Five blocks from the beach, this beautifully renovated 1904 Queen Anne–style inn has a sort of Victorian-charm-meets-21st-century practicality. For example, all of the light, airy guest rooms are individually decorated with antiques and varying color schemes, yet come with private bathrooms, queen- or king-size beds, Wi-Fi, telephones, and cable television. Several are furnished with fireplaces and have ocean views, and unique color schemes. Rates include a buffet-style breakfast along with the morning paper, and afternoon tea and refreshments served in the parlor.

581 Pine Ave., Pacific Grove, CA 93950. www.pacificgroveinn.com. ☎ **800/732-2825** or 831/375-2825. Fax 831/375-0752. 16 units. $149–$259. Rates include buffet breakfast and afternoon tea. AE, DC, DISC, MC, V. From Calif. 1, take the Pacific Grove exit (Calif. 68) to the corner of Pine and Forest aves. *In room:* TV/VCR w/video library, fridge, hair dryer, Wi-Fi.

Where to Eat
EXPENSIVE

Fandango ★★ MEDITERRANEAN   Provincial Mediterranean specialties from Spain to Greece to North Africa spice up the menu with offerings such as seafood paella with North African couscous (a 200-year-old family recipe), *cassoulet maison,* and Greek-style lamb chops. The five dining rooms are European in feel, made cozy with roaring fires, wood tables, and antiqued walls. The international wine list has won awards. In winter, request the fireplace dining room, and in summer, ask for the terrace. Any time of year, expect everything here, from the decor to the owner, to be lively and colorful.

223 17th St. ☎ **831/372-3456.** www.fandangorestaurant.com. Reservations recommended. Main courses $17–$34. AE, DC, DISC, MC, V. Daily 11:30am–2:30pm and 5–9:30pm. From Hwy. 1, take the Pacific Grove exit (Hwy. 68), turn left on Lighthouse Ave., and continue a block to 17th St.

Joe Rombi's ★ ITALIAN   In an area where most restaurants pack 'em in, the 11-table dining room here is refreshingly intimate, with dimmed lights and antique French posters. The menu is limited to appetizers, soups, salads, pastas, and five main courses, but the food is ultrafresh. Ravioli and pastas are made fresh daily, and a basket of fresh house-made focaccia arrives upon guests' seating. Ask about the fish of the day: The last time I dined here, the halibut was excellent.

208 17th St. (at Lighthouse Ave.). ☎ **831/373-2416.** www.joerombi.com. Reservations recommended. Main courses $18–$25. AE, MC, V. Wed–Sun 5–10pm.

MODERATE

The Fishwife at Asilomar Beach ★★ ☺ SEAFOOD   The restaurant dates from the 1830s, when a sailor's wife started a small food market that became famous for its Boston clam chowder. Today locals still return for the soup as well as some of the finest seafood in Pacific Grove (everyone raves about this casual, affordable place). Two bestsellers are calamari steak sautéed with shallots, garlic, tomatoes, and white wine; and Cajun catfish topped with salsa brava. All main courses come with vegetables, bread, black beans, and rice or potatoes.

1996½ Sunset Dr. (at Asilomar Beach). ℂ **831/375-7107.** www.fishwife.com. Main courses $13–$19. AE, DISC, MC, V. Mon–Sat 11am–10pm; Sun 10am–10pm. From Hwy. 1, take the Pacific Grove exit (Hwy. 68) and stay left until it becomes Sunset Dr.; the restaurant is on your left about 1 mile ahead as you approach Asilomar Beach.

Peppers Mexicali Café ★ MEXICAN/LATIN AMERICAN Peppers is a casual, festive place with good food at reasonable prices. The inviting dining room has wooden floors and tables, lots of pepper art, and a perpetual crowd of regulars who come to suck up beers and savor spicy but well-balanced seafood tacos and fajitas or house-made tamales and chilis rellenos. Other fire starters include the snapper Yucatán, cooked with chiles, citrus, cilantro, and tomatoes; and grilled prawns with lime-cilantro dressing. More than a dozen daily specials include Mexican seafood paella and grilled swordfish. The chips and salsas are addictive, and the staff is exceptionally friendly.

170 Forest Ave. ℂ **831/373-6892.** www.peppersmexicalicafe.com. Reservations recommended. Main courses $7–$17. AE, DC, DISC, MC, V. Mon and Wed–Thurs 11:30am–9:30pm; Fri–Sat 11:30am–10pm; Sun 4–9:30pm.

INEXPENSIVE

First Awakenings ★ ⬧ AMERICAN This formerly dank canning factory is now a bright, huge, open restaurant with one of the cheapest and healthiest breakfasts in the area. Eye-openers include eight varieties of omelets; granola with nuts, fruit, and yogurt; walnut and wheat pancakes; and raisin French toast. At lunch there's a fine choice of salads and a slew of sandwiches ranging from albacore to zucchini. On sunny days, try snagging an outdoor patio table.

In the American Tin Cannery, 125 Ocean View Blvd. ℂ **831/372-1125.** www.firstawakenings.net. Reservations not accepted. Breakfast $3–$9; lunch $5–$9. AE, DISC, MC, V. Mon–Fri 7am–2pm; Sat–Sun 7am–2:30pm. From Hwy. 1, take the Pacific Grove exit (Hwy. 68) and turn right onto Lighthouse Ave.; after a mile, turn left onto Eardley Ave. and take it to the corner of Ocean View.

Thai Bistro II ★ THAI This small white house with blue trim is one of the most popular local Thai restaurants. Inside, the modern, congenial dining room is usually filled with locals. The menu is a minimanifesto, with more than 60 options. Some of the most popular plates are Panang curry (with your choice of meat or seafood), *tom kha gai* soup (chicken in coconut milk), and pad Thai. There's a full vegetarian menu as well. It's all accompanied by local wines and French desserts.

159 Central Ave. (btw. David Ave. and Eardley St.). ℂ **831/372-8700.** www.thaibistropg.com. Reservations required on weekends. Most main courses $8–$12. AE, DISC, MC, V. Daily 11:30am–3pm and 5–9:30pm.

Toasties Cafe AMERICAN Toasties draws customers with good old-fashioned meals despite the no-frills casual dining room. Some rave about the eggs Benedict with roasted potatoes. Others swear by the hefty, sinful waffles. One thing's agreed: This place serves what everyone wants from breakfast—lots of choice, good service, endless coffee refills, and heaping plates. Weekend dinner is also a homey affair, with chicken and prawn Marsala, teriyaki steak, seafood pasta, and stuffed chicken.

702 Lighthouse Dr. ℂ **831/373-7543.** Breakfast and lunch dishes $5.95–$7.25; dinner main courses $9–$12. MC, V. Mon–Sat 6:30am–3pm; Sun 7am–2pm; Fri–Sat 5–8pm.

PEBBLE BEACH & 17-MILE DRIVE ★★★

Pebble Beach is a world unto itself. Polo shirts, golf shoes, and big bankrolls are standard, and if you have to ask how much accommodations and greens fees cost, you definitely can't afford them. In this elite golfers' paradise, endless grassy fairways are interrupted only by luxury resorts and cliffs where the ocean meets the land. In winter it's also the site of the AT&T Pebble Beach National Pro-Am, a celebrity tournament originally launched in 1937 by crooner Bing Crosby.

17-Mile Drive ★★

Set aside an afternoon, pack a picnic, fork over the $9 entrance fee, and prepare to see some of the most exclusive real estate in California. The drive is accessible from any of five gates: two from Pacific Grove to the north, one from Carmel to the south, or two from Monterey to the east. The most convenient entrance from Hwy. 1 is off the main road at the Holman Highway exit. You may beat traffic by entering at the Carmel Gate and doing the tour backward. Admission to the drive includes an informative map with 26 points of interest. Other highlights include **Seal and Bird Rocks,** where you can see countless gulls and cormorants, as well as seals and sea lions; and **Cypress Point Lookout,** with a 20-mile view to the Big Sur Lighthouse. From afar, you can also admire the famous **Lone Cypress** tree that has inspired many artists and photographers (although it's no longer accessible on foot). The drive also traverses the **Del Monte Forest,** thick with tame black-tailed deer and often described as some "billionaire's private game preserve." *Note:* One of the best ways to see 17-Mile Drive is by bike. For more information on 17-Mile Drive and an interactive map, see **www.pebble beach.com** and click on "17-Mile Drive" at the bottom of the page.

The Lone Cypress.

Great Golf Courses

Locals tell me it's almost impossible to get a tee time unless you're staying at the golf resort. If you're one of the lucky few, you can choose from several famous courses along 17-Mile Drive.

PEBBLE BEACH GOLF LINKS ★★★   The most famous course is Pebble Beach Golf Links (✆ **800/654-9300** or 831/622-8723; www.pebblebeach.com), at the Lodge at Pebble Beach (p. 456). It's home each year to the AT&T Pebble Beach National Pro-Am, a celebrity-laden tournament televised worldwide. Jack Nicklaus has said, "If I could play only one course for the rest of my life, this would be it." He should know: He won the 1961 U.S. Amateur and the 1972 U.S. Open here. Indeed, 10 national championships have been decided here. Herbert Warren Wind, dean of 20th-century golf writers, said, "There is no finer seaside golf course in creation"—and that includes the Old Course at St. Andrews. Built in 1919, this 18-hole course is 6,799 yards and par 72. It's precariously perched over a rugged ocean. Greens fees are a staggering $495, and that doesn't include the cart fee for nonguests.

SPYGLASS HILL GOLF COURSE ★★   Also frequented by celebrities is this course at Stevenson Drive and Spyglass Hill Road (✆ **800/654-9300** or 831/625-8563; www.pebblebeach.com). Its slope rating of 147 means it's one of the state's toughest courses. It's justifiably famous, at 6,859 yards and par 72 with five oceanfront holes. The rest reach deep into the Del Monte Forest. Greens fees are $340 plus cart. Reservations for nonguests should be made a month in advance. The excellent Grill Room restaurant is on the grounds.

POPPY HILLS ★★   This 18-hole, 6,219-yard course on 17-Mile Drive (✆ **831/622-8239;** www.poppyhillsgolf.com) was named one of the world's top 20 by *Golf Digest*. It was designed by Robert Trent Jones, Jr., in 1986. One golf pro said the course is "long and tough on short hitters." Fees are $200, plus $36 for the cart rental. You can make reservations 30 days in advance.

THE LINKS AT SPANISH BAY ★★   On the north end of 17-Mile Drive at the Inn at Spanish Bay, Pebble Beach Resorts (✆ **800/654-9300** or 831/647-7495; www.pebblebeach.com), this is the most easily booked course. Serious golfers say it's the most challenging of the Pebble Beach links. Robert Trent Jones, Jr., Tom Watson, and Frank Tatum (former USGA president) designed it to duplicate a Scottish links course. Its fescue grasses and natural fairways lead to rolls and unexpected bounces. Greens fees are $260 plus a cart fee. Reservations accepted 60 days in advance.

DEL MONTE GOLF COURSE ★   At 1300 Sylvan Rd. (✆ **831/373-2700;** www.pebblebeach.com) lies the oldest course west of the Mississippi, charging some of the most "reasonable" greens fees: $110 per player, plus a cart rental of $20. The course, often cited in magazines for its "grace and charm," is relatively short—only 6,339 yards. This seldom-advertised course, at the Hyatt east of Monterey, is part of the Pebble Beach complex but is not along 17-Mile Drive.

Where to Stay & Eat

Casa Palmero Resort ★★★   The Casa Palmero is a small, ultraluxury resort on the first tee of the Pebble Beach Golf Links. The two-story villa is the newest gem in the sister properties, which include the Inn at Spanish Bay and the Lodge at Pebble Beach. The most intimate and private of the three, Casa Palmero is fashioned as a European villa with stucco walls, window boxes dripping bougainvillea, every modern comfort, and a staff to anticipate your every wish. It has 24 cottages and suites with amenities that include French doors opening onto private garden spas, oversize window-box sofas, wood-burning fireplaces, and soaking tubs that open to the main room. "Convivial" areas, where you can hang out, include a trellised patio, library, billiards parlor, living room, private dining room, executive boardroom and small conference room, intimate courtyards with fountains, and lavish outdoor pool pavilion.

1518 Cypress Dr. (on 17-Mile Dr.), Pebble Beach, CA 93953. www.pebblebeach.com. © **800/654-9300** or 831/647-5700. Fax 831/622-6655. 24 units. $580–$2,650 cottage or suite. Rates include continental breakfast and evening hors d'oeuvres and cocktails. AE, MC, V. From Hwy. 1 south, turn west onto Hwy. 68 and south onto 17-Mile Dr., and follow the coastal road to the hotel. **Amenities:** 3 restaurants; babysitting; bike rental; concierge; golf course; health club; Jacuzzi; outdoor heated pool; room service; sauna; full-service spa; tennis courts. *In room:* TV/VCR w/pay movies, fridge, hair dryer, minibar.

The Inn at Spanish Bay ★★★ Surrounded by the renowned Links at Spanish Bay golf course, the Inn at Spanish Bay is a plush three- and four-story lowrise on 236 manicured acres 4 miles north of the Lodge at Pebble Beach and Pebble Beach Golf Links. Approximately half the rooms face the ocean. Their less expensive counterparts overlook the forest. Each unit has about 600 square feet of floor space, a fireplace, and an outdoor deck or a patio. Bathrooms are finished in Italian marble. Custom-made furnishings include four-poster beds with down comforters and comfortable couches and easy chairs. My favorite time here is dusk, when a bagpiper strolls the terrace with a skirling tribute to Scotland.

2700 17-Mile Dr., Pebble Beach, CA 93953. www.pebblebeach.com. © **800/654-9300** or 831/647-7500. Fax 831/644-7960. 260 units. $595–$965 double; from $1,075 suite. AE, DC, MC, V. From Hwy. 1 south, turn west onto Hwy. 68 and south onto 17-Mile Dr.; the hotel is on your right, just past the gate entrance. **Amenities:** 3 restaurants; bar/lounge; babysitting; bike rental; concierge; 4 world-class golf courses; health club; Jacuzzi; heated outdoor pool; room service; sauna; full-service spa; 8 outdoor tennis courts (2 night-lit). *In room:* TV w/pay movies, fridge, hair dryer, minibar.

The Lodge at Pebble Beach ★★ For the combined cost of greens fees and a room here, you could easily create a professional putting green in your own backyard—and still have money left over. But even if you're a dedicated hacker, you've got to play here at least once. Look on the bright side—at least you can expect ultraplush rooms with every amenity, including wood-burning fireplaces. Most are in two-story cottage clusters, with anywhere from 8 to 12 units in each. Those opening onto the ocean have the highest prices.

1700 17-Mile Dr., Pebble Beach, CA 93953. www.pebblebeach.com. © **800/654-9300** or 831/624-3811. Fax 831/625-8598. 169 units. $695–$1,225 double; from $1,200 suite. AE, MC, V. From Hwy. 1 south, turn west on Hwy. 68, turn south onto 17-Mile Dr., and follow the coastal road to the hotel. **Amenities:** 6 restaurants; bar/lounge; babysitting; bike rental; concierge; golf course; health club; Jacuzzi; heated outdoor pool; room service; sauna; full-service spa; 12 tennis courts. *In room:* TV w/pay movies, fridge, hair dryer, minibar.

CARMEL-BY-THE-SEA ★★

5 miles S of Monterey; 121 miles S of San Francisco; 33 miles N of Big Sur

Carmel began as a seaside artists' colony that attracted luminaries such as Sinclair Lewis, Robert Louis Stevenson, and Ansel Adams. Residents resisted assigned street numbers and lighting and carried lanterns, which they considered more romantic. The town is still intimate enough that addresses remain unnumbered—Carmel's inns, restaurants, boutiques, and galleries identify their locations by cross streets—but that ragtag bohemian village is a thing of yesteryear. Carmel is now a tourist hot spot, weekend traffic can be intolerable, and lodging rates are grossly inflated. But thousands of annual visitors are taken nonetheless with its eclectic dwellings, quaint cafes, majestic cypresses, and silky white beaches.

Essentials

The **Carmel Business Association,** P.O. Box 4444, Carmel (*©* **831/624-2522;** www.carmelcalifornia.org), is on San Carlos Street between Fifth and Sixth streets. It distributes local maps, brochures, and publications. You'll want to pick up the *Guide to Carmel* and a schedule of events. Hours are from 10am to 5pm daily.

What to See & Do

A wonderful stretch of white sand backed by cypress trees, **Carmel Beach City Park ★★** is a bit of heaven on Earth (though the jammed parking lot can feel more like a car rally). There's room for families, surfers, and dogs with their owners (they can run off-leash). If the parking lot is full, try Ocean Avenue. It has some spaces, though they're mostly good for 90 minutes, and you will get a ticket if you park all day.

Farther south around the promontory, **Carmel River State Beach ★** is less crowded, with white sand and dunes, plus a bird sanctuary with brown pelicans, black oystercatchers, cormorants, gulls, curlews, godwits, and sanderlings.

Carmel Beach City Park.

Carmel.

Father Serra's room, Carmel mission.

The **Mission San Carlos Borromèo del Carmelo ★★**, on Basilica Rio Road at Lasuen Drive, off Hwy. 1 (© **831/624-1271;** www.carmelmission.org), is the burial ground of Father Junípero Serra and the second-oldest of the 21 Spanish missions he established. Founded in 1771 on a site overlooking the Carmel River, it's one of the largest and most interesting of California's missions. The stone church, with its Moorish bell tower and curving walls covered with a lime plaster made of burned seashells, was begun in 1793. The kitchen, the first library in California, the high altar, and the flower gardens are all worth visiting. More than 3,000 Native Americans are buried in the adjacent cemetery; their graves are decorated with seashells. The mission is open Monday through Saturday from 9:30am to 5pm, Sunday from 10:30am to 5pm. Admission is $6.50 for adults, $4 for seniors, $2 for youth, and free for children 6 and under. Docent-led tours are $7. Call the tour office (© **831/624-1271,** ext. 213) for schedules.

One of Carmel's prettiest homes and gardens is **Tor House ★**, 26304 Ocean View Ave. (© **831/624-1813;** www.torhouse.org), built by poet Robinson Jeffers. On Carmel Point, the house dates from 1918. Its 40-foot tower has stones embedded in the walls from around the world (including the Great Wall of China). Inside, an old porthole is reputed to have come from the ship on which Napoleon escaped from Elba in 1815. No photography is allowed. Admission is by guided tour only on Friday and Saturday from 10am to 3pm, and reservations are requested. It's $7 for adults, $4 for college students, and $2 for high-school students (no children 11 and under).

If the tourists aren't lying on the beach in Carmel, then they're probably **shopping**—the sine qua non of Carmel activities. This small town is home to more than 500 boutiques plying unique fashions, baskets, housewares, imported goods, and a veritable cornucopia of art galleries. Most of the commercial action is packed along the small stretch of Ocean Avenue between Junipero Street and San Antonio Avenue.

If you want to tour the **galleries,** pick up a copy of the *Carmel Gallery Guide* from the Carmel Business Association (see "Essentials," above). Serious shoppers should also head south a few miles to the **Crossroads Shopping Center** (from Hwy. 1 south, take the Rio Rd. exit west for 1 block and turn right

Carmel

PACIFIC

OCEAN

onto Crossroads Blvd.). As malls go, this one's a doozy, with oodles of shopping and a few good restaurants.

Carmel Walks offers 2-hour guided walks through gardens, hidden pathways, fairy-tale-like cottages, and the homes of famous writers, artists, and washed-up movie stars. You'll learn about Carmel's seemingly endless spirits, strange customs, and juicy gossip. The $25 tours run Saturdays at 10am and 2pm, and Tuesday through Friday at 10am. Call ✆ **831/642-2700** or see **www.carmelwalks.com** for reservations.

Where to Stay

Most Carmel lodgings are booked solid from May to October, so make reservations as far in advance as possible. If you're traveling with pets, try the moderately priced **Cypress Inn,** Lincoln and Seventh (P.O. Box Y), Carmel-by-the-Sea, CA 93921 (www.cypress-inn.com; ✆ **800/443-7443** or 831/624-3871), owned by actress Doris Day.

EXPENSIVE

Carriage House Inn ★★
Luxurious atmosphere and pampering make this one of my top picks downtown. Each room has a wood-burning fireplace and king-size bed with a down comforter. Most of the second-floor rooms have sunken tubs and vaulted beam ceilings; first-floor rooms have single whirlpool tubs. Staff members deliver breakfast to guests' rooms and serve wine and hors d'oeuvres in the afternoon and cappuccino, wine, and cheese in the evening. Most lodgings in this area are about frill and lace, but the Carriage House is a more mature, formal, yet cozy environment.

Junipero St., btw. Seventh and Eighth aves. (P.O. Box 1900), Carmel, CA 93921. www.ibts-carriage house.com. ✆ **800/433-4732** or 831/625-2585. Fax 831/624-0974. 13 units. $279–$349 double. Rates include continental breakfast and afternoon wine and hors d'oeuvres. AE, DISC, MC, V. Free parking. From Hwy. 1, exit onto Ocean Ave. and turn left onto Junipero St. **Amenities:** Concierge; nearby golf course. *In room:* TV/VCR, fridge, hair dryer, minibar.

Highlands Inn, Park Hyatt Carmel ★★
Four miles south of Carmel on a 12-acre cliff above Point Lobos, this inn has attracted honeymooners, business executives, and celebrities, including Madonna, Walt Disney, and Marlon Brando. It's rustic yet luxurious, with wildflowers gracing its pathways, plenty of character, and an exclusive atmosphere. The old-style main lounge, from 1916, affords panoramic coastal vistas. Guest rooms are distributed throughout a cluster of buildings terraced into the hillside; most units have decks or balconies and wood-burning fireplaces. The suites come with Jacuzzi tubs and fully equipped kitchens; four rooms have showers only.

120 Highlands Dr., Carmel, CA 93923. www.highlandsinn.hyatt.com. ✆ **800/633-7313** or 831/620-1234. Fax 831/626-1574. 142 units. $220 double; $280–$735 spa suite; $510–$1,050 2-bedroom, full oceanview spa suite. AE, DC, DISC, MC, V. **Amenities:** 2 restaurants; lounge; babysitting; complimentary bike use; concierge; nearby golf course; exercise room; 3 outdoor Jacuzzis; outdoor heated pool; room service. *In room:* TV/DVD w/pay movies, CD player, fridge, hair dryer, kitchen in suites.

La Playa ★
The four-story La Playa is a romantic, Mediterranean-style villa 2 blocks from the beach and within walking distance of town. In 1904, Norwegian artist Christopher Jorgensen ordered its construction for his bride, an heiress of the Ghirardelli chocolate dynasty. The stylish lobby is elegant, with terra-cotta

floors, Oriental rugs, and marble fireplace. In the courtyard, walkways lead through beautifully landscaped grounds surrounding a heated pool. Compared to the lobby and grounds, the standard guest rooms are disappointing, with thin walls and uninspiring furnishings. The luxury cottages—newly renovated in partnership with Restoration Hardware—are a vast (and costly) improvement—with kitchens, wet bars, garden patios, limited room service, and, in most cases, wood-burning fireplaces.

Camino Real and Eighth Ave. (P.O. Box 900), Carmel, CA 93921. www.laplayahotel.com. ✆ **800/ 582-8900** or 831/624-6476. Fax 831/624-7966. 80 units. $190–$375 double; $425–$775 suite or cottage. AE, DC, MC, V. Complimentary valet parking. **Amenities:** Restaurant; bar; babysitting; bike rental; concierge; nearby golf course; outdoor heated pool; room service. *In room:* TV, fridge, hair dryer.

Mission Ranch ★★   If you want to stay off the beaten track, consider this converted 1850s dairy farm, restored by Clint Eastwood to preserve the vista of the nearby wetlands stretching to the bay. Accommodations are scattered amid different structures, both old and new, and surrounded by wetlands and grazing sheep. Guest rooms range from "regulars" in the main barn (less desirable) to meadowview units with a vista across the fields to the bay. Rooms are decorated in a provincial style, with carved wooden beds bedecked in handmade quilts. Most are equipped with whirlpool bathtubs, fireplaces, and decks or patios. The Martin Family farmhouse has six units, all arranged around a central parlor, while the Bunkhouse (the oldest structure on the property) contains separate living and dining areas, bedrooms, and a fridge. Even if you're not staying here, call for a table at the **Restaurant at Mission Ranch** (p. 464).

26270 Dolores St., Carmel, CA 93923. www.missionranchcarmel.com. ✆ **800/538-8221** or 831/ 624-6436. Fax 831/626-4163. 31 units. $120–$300 double. Rates include continental breakfast. AE, MC, V. **Amenities:** Restaurant; babysitting; exercise room; 6 tennis courts. *In room:* TV, fridge in some units, hair dryer.

Tradewinds ★★★   Tucked away on a residential block just off the main drag, Tradewinds is a quiet Asian-inspired escape from the throngs of tourists milling about Ocean Avenue. I felt instantly more relaxed upon stepping foot on the Zen property with its peaceful gardens, so imagine my content when I entered my room and found the inside just as charming as the out: bamboo touches, a fresh orchid, kimono-style red-and-gold robes, simple but abstract art, stone floors, a fireplace, and a small trickling fountain. Most rooms have balcony views of Carmel's red rooftops and the ocean in the distance. From the chocolate-covered strawberries left out for your arrival to the leaf and peace prayer placed bedside at night, if ever there was a place that knew hospitality is in the details, it's Tradewinds. Tradewinds is also pet-friendly ($25 nightly fee), which is unusual for a hotel of its caliber.

Camino Real and Eighth Ave. (P.O. Box 900), Carmel, CA 93921. www.tradewindscarmel.com. ✆ **800/624-6665** or 831/624-2776. Fax 831/624-0634. 28 units. $325–$375 double; $450– $550 suite. Rate includes continental breakfast and complimentary in-room snacks. AE, DC, MC, V. **Amenities:** Concierge. *In room:* TV, hair dryer, free Wi-Fi.

MODERATE

Cobblestone Inn ★   The first floor of the Cobblestone Inn was built of stones from the Carmel River (hence the inn's name), and the cobblestone theme runs throughout this faux-English-country charmer. The guest rooms encircle a slate courtyard and vary in size; some are small, and only the Junior Suite comes with a bathtub, but all come with a queen or king bed, fireplace, television, and refrigerator with complimentary soft drinks. The largest units have a wet bar, sofa, and separate bedroom. Guests may use the comfortable living room with a large stone fireplace (cobblestone, of course). Extras include a breakfast buffet served on the patio or sitting room, afternoon wine and hors d'oeuvres, daily maid and turn-down service, and a morning newspaper.

Junipero St. (btw. Seventh and Eighth aves., ½ blocks from Ocean Ave.; P.O. Box 3185), Carmel, CA 93921. www.cobblestoneinncarmel.com. (*) **800/833-8836** or 831/625-5222. Fax 831/625-0478. 24 units. $155–$270 double. Rates include full breakfast, soda and water, and afternoon wine and hors d'oeuvres. AE, DC, MC, V. *In room:* Flatscreen TV/DVD, fridge, hair dryer.

Normandy Inn ★
Three blocks from the beach, this French Provençal–style hotel is like something out of a storybook, with an array of colorful flowers. Some guest rooms are showing their age a little, but they're well appointed with French country decor, feather beds, and down comforters. Some have fireplaces and/or kitchenettes. The tiny heated pool is banked by a flower garden. The three large family-style units are an especially good deal and accommodate up to eight; each has three bedrooms, two bathrooms, a fully equipped kitchen, a dining room, a living room with a fireplace, and a back porch. Reserve well in advance, especially in summer.

Ocean Ave., btw. Monte Verde and Casanova sts. (P.O. Box 1706), Carmel, CA 93921. www.normandyinncarmel.com. (*) **800/343-3825** or 831/624-3825. Fax 831/624-4614. 48 units. $98–$220 double; $165–$500 suite or cottage. Extra person $10. Rates include continental breakfast and afternoon sherry. AE, DC, MC, V. From Hwy. 1, exit onto Ocean Ave. and continue straight for 5 blocks past Junipero St. **Amenities:** Nearby golf course; outdoor pool (seasonal). *In room:* TV, hair dryer, kitchenette in some units.

Sandpiper Inn by the Sea ★
A flower garden welcomes visitors to this quiet, relaxing, midscale Carmel standby, in business for more than 80 years. The inn's rooms, from which you can hear the surf, offer a range of well-kept options. Corner rooms are often costliest, with four-poster beds and many windows framing the ocean view. All rooms are decorated with handsome country antiques and fresh flowers in the deluxe rooms; three have fireplaces. Carmel's white-sand beaches are 300 feet away. The complimentary buffet-style breakfast is a hit with guests. While it's not appropriate for all families, children older than age 12 are welcome.

2408 Bay View Ave., Carmel, CA 93923. www.sandpiper-inn.com. (*) **800/590-6433** or 831/624-6433. Fax 831/624-5964. 17 units. $99–$219 double. Rates include extended continental breakfast and afternoon sherry and tea. AE, DISC, MC, V. **Amenities:** Concierge; nearby golf course. *In room:* No phone.

Vagabond House ★
In typical Carmel style, doting attention has been paid to every element of this English Tudor inn—from the lobby adorned with knick-knack antiques and a welcoming decanter of sherry, to the wonderfully lush garden courtyard draped with greenery and dotted with blooms. Each room is warm and homey, with country decor and a private entrance; all but two have wood-burning fireplaces, which means the least-expensive rooms book quickly; call ahead if you want one. Guests are welcomed with a basket of fruit, and the extended continental breakfast is delivered to your room, though you'll most likely enjoy it best on the garden patio.

Fourth and Dolores (P.O. Box 2747), Carmel, CA 93921. www.vagabondshouseinn.com. ✆ **800/262-1262** or 831/624-7738. Fax 831/626-1243. 12 units. $145–$325 double. 2-night minimum on weekends. Rates include continental breakfast. AE, DISC, MC, V. Pets allowed ($30 per night). *In room:* TV, fridge, hair dryer.

INEXPENSIVE

Carmel Lodge ★   This modest hotel is a motor lodge, but it's decorated better than most, on a quiet street in Carmel. Modern rooms have pretty bedspreads and updated furnishings; some have fireplaces and wet bars. There's a small pool, but it's practically in the center courtyard parking lot. Several restaurants are nearby. I like this quiet location better than that of the comparable Carmel Village Inn (see below).

San Carlos and Fifth (P.O. Box 951), Carmel, CA 93921. www.carmellodge.com. ✆ **800/252-1255** or 831/624-1255. Fax 831/624-2576. 38 units. $85–$199 double. AE, DC, DISC, MC, V. From Ocean Ave., turn right onto San Carlos and go 2 blocks. **Amenities:** Restaurant; nearby golf course; heated outdoor pool (seasonal). *In room:* TV, fridge, hair dryer in some units, minibar.

Carmel Village Inn 🖋   Efficiently run and centrally located, the Village Inn is basically a well-kept old-school motor lodge. The rooms are always spotless, arranged around a courtyard and parking lot lined with potted geraniums, and outfitted with that ubiquitous flowery decor. The Deluxe Kings with gas fireplaces offer plenty of elbowroom for the price. Continental breakfast, accompanied by the morning newspaper, is served in the downstairs lounge.

Ocean Ave. and Junipero St. (P.O. Box 5275), Carmel, CA 93921. www.carmelvillageinn.com. ✆ **800/346-3864** or 831/624-3864. Fax 831/626-6763. 48 units. $105–$245 double. Rates include continental breakfast. AE, MC, V. From Calif. 1, exit onto Ocean Ave. and continue straight to Junipero St. **Amenities:** Babysitting. *In room:* TV, kitchenette, Wi-Fi.

Where to Eat

EXPENSIVE

Anton & Michel ★ CONTINENTAL   This elegant restaurant, across from Carmel Plaza, serves traditional French cuisine in one of the most formal rooms in town. By day, it's best to dine fountainside or on the glass-encased terrace. The view is equally alluring in the evening, when the courtyard is lit and the fountain's water sparkles. Decorated with French chandelier lamps and oil paintings, the main dining room is formal, but patrons' attire need not match it. Appetizers include crab cakes with sweet corn and tomato oil or delicate ravioli filled with wild mushrooms. Specialties include rack of lamb with herb-Dijon mustard *au jus* and more eclectic items such as a chicken breast Jerusalem, sautéed with olive oil, white wine, cream, and artichoke hearts. The wine list is impressive.

At Court of the Fountains, Mission St. (btw. Ocean and Seventh aves.). ✆ **831/624-2406.** www.antonandmichel.com. Reservations recommended. Main courses $15–$36. AE, DC, DISC, MC, V. Daily noon–2:30pm and 5–9:30pm.

Aubergine ★★★ FRENCH   The most top-notch restaurants know better than to be pretentious, which is likely why every last server and host at Aubergine is not only a culinary encyclopedia but also someone you'd like to hang out with. Dining in Aubergine is best described as a journey, with most meals taking 3 hours—or longer. Executive chef Justin Cogley (taking over for Christophe Grosjean) procures most of his produce from nearby farmer's markets, and every last dish is an exploration for the taste buds. Courses run the gamut from a white asparagus, scallop, kumquat, and almond soup; to a potato, truffle, onion, foie gras, and duck breast ravioli; and a strawberry *tres leches* cake with basil ice cream. While the underground cellar stocks 4,500 bottles from around the world, the menu's primary focus is on wines from Monterey County and France. With just 12 tables and one seating a night, you'll never have to raise your voice to be heard. In its 5-year run, Aubergine has garnered just about every accolade in the industry, consistently named as one of the best restaurants in the country by top magazines like *Gourmet, Bon Appétit, Condé Nast Traveler,* and *Robb Report,* and, really, it comes as no surprise.

Monte Verde at Seventh St. © 831/624-8578. www.laubergecarmel.com. Reservations recommended. Most main courses $15–$35. DC, MC, V. Daily 6–9:30pm.

Flying Fish Grill ★★ PACIFIC RIM/SEAFOOD   I feel more confident when a restaurant's owner runs the kitchen—and dinner here confirms that chef/proprietor Kenny Fukumoto is in the house. Dark, romantic, and Asian influenced, the 40-seat dining room has an intimate atmosphere with redwood booths (built by Kenny) and fish hanging from the ceiling. The cuisine features fresh seafood with exquisite Japanese accents. Start with *shabu-shabu,* sushi, tempura, or any of the other exotic taste teasers. Main courses include a rare peppered ahi (tuna), blackened and served with mustard-and-sesame-soy vinaigrette and angel-hair pasta; and a pan-fried almond sea bass with whipped potatoes, Chinese cabbage, and rock shrimp stir-fry.

In Carmel Plaza, Mission St. (btw. Ocean and Seventh aves.). © **831/625-1962.** www.flyingfish grill.com. Reservations recommended. Main courses $15–$28. AE, DISC, MC, V. Wed–Mon 5–10pm.

Grasing's Coastal Cuisine ★ CALIFORNIAN   Chef Kurt Grasing and renowned Bay Area restaurateur Narsai David teamed up here and opened one of Carmel's best restaurants. The bright, split-room dining area is simple yet stylish, with buttercup-yellow walls, beaded lamps, and colorful artwork. Grasing's menu reflects the decor's stylish simplicity; ultrafresh ingredients gleaned from California's coast and Central Valley are displayed modestly, belying an intense combination of textures and flavors. The warm Napa salad (with bacon, garlic, and blue cheese), for example, appears ordinary enough, but "when I took it off the menu," says Grasing, "I still made 30 a night." The Grasing's "paella" (made with prawns, clams, mussels, and sausage with saffron- and fennel-infused orzo pasta) and roast rack of pomegranate-marinated lamb with crispy polenta are also standouts. Even the bread, fresh from Gail's Bakery in Aptos, is fantastic. When the sun's out, request a table at the dog-friendly patio, and be sure to inquire about the very reasonable prix-fixe meal.

Sixth St. (at Mission St.). © **831/624-6562.** www.grasings.com. Reservations recommended. Main courses $18–$36. AE, MC, V. Daily 11am–3pm and 5–9pm.

The Restaurant at Mission Ranch ★★ AMERICAN   Former Carmel Mayor Clint Eastwood bought this rustic property in 1986 and restored the ranch-style building to its original integrity. The chance of seeing him brings in some folks, but it's the views, quality food, and merry atmosphere that make the place special. The wooden building is encased in large windows that accentuate the wonderful view of the marshlands, grazing sheep, and bay. Warm days make the patio the prime spot, but the key time to come is at sunset, when the sky is transforming and happy hour is in full swing. You'll find some of the cheapest drinks around, and Clint often stops by when he's in town. As you'd expect from the ranch motif, meat is king here: New York steak and baby back ribs. Seafood, chicken, and vegetarian options are also wonderful, and all dinners include soup or salad. Entertainment is provided at the piano bar, where locals and tourists have also been known to croon their favorites. Sunday buffet brunch, with live jazz piano, is also hugely popular; be sure to reserve a table.

At Mission Ranch, 26270 Dolores St. ✆ **831/624-6436.** www.missionranchcarmel.com. Reservations recommended. Most main courses $15–$35. DC, MC, V. Daily 5–9:30pm; Sun jazz brunch 10am–1:30pm. Bar until midnight.

MODERATE

Club Jalapeño ★★ MEXICAN Follow the divine aroma wafting down San Carlos Avenue and you'll end up at Club J, tearing into a plate of Oaxacan enchiladas drizzled with rich mole sauce. The fried and battered Baja fish tacos are just like the ones in Tijuana (love that salsa and lime-cilantro dressing). The coconut-encrusted fish is lightly fried, then topped with spicy chipotle sauce and fruit salsa. A righteous meal for two is Club J's spicy shrimp fajitas with a side of fresh-fruit salsa. The decor is faux-hacienda-rustic with dark-wood floors, exposed beams, iron furnishings, textured walls, soft lighting, hanging chilies, and a sexy corner bar with pure agave tequila.

San Carlos (btw. Fifth and Sixth aves. in the courtyard). ✆ **831/626-1997.** www.clubjalapeno. com. Main courses $8–$25. AE, MC, V. Wed–Mon noon–closing; Tues 5pm–closing.

The Hog's Breath Inn AMERICAN Clint Eastwood's involvement with this restaurant made it famous, but it's a rare day that he visits (better odds are at the Mission Ranch restaurant). No matter: The patio with tree-trunk tables and plastic chairs is ideal for taking in beer and good ol' American standbys—if you don't mind the usual wait. (Tables in the dark-wood-paneled dining room also fill up, but they're not as lively as outdoor seats.) The food—New York steak, crab cakes, chicken Marsala—is unremarkable, but the small, dark sports bar is the best place to kick back on a rainy day (or a sunny one, for that matter). Come for lunch, when it's more affordable.

San Carlos St. (btw. Fifth and Sixth aves.). ✆ **831/625-1044.** www.hogsbreathinn.net. Reservations not accepted. Main courses $10–$24. AE, DC, MC, V. Daily 11:30am–10pm. From Hwy. 1, take the Ocean Ave. exit and turn right onto San Carlos St.

Rio Grill ★★ AMERICAN Serious food and a festive atmosphere (with vibrant art, including a cartoon mural of famous locals Clint Eastwood and the late Bing Crosby) have kept this place hugely popular with the locals for years. The whimsical nature of the modern Santa Fe–style dining room belies the kitchen's ambitious preparations, which include homemade soups; a rich quesadilla with almonds, cheeses, and smoked-tomato salsa; barbecued baby back ribs from a wood-burning oven; and fresh fish from an open oak grill. The good wine selection includes some rare California vintages and covers a broad price range.

Crossroads Shopping Center, 101 Crossroads Blvd. ✆ **831/625-5436.** www.riogrill.com. Reservations recommended. Main courses $8–$25. AE, DISC, MC, V. Sun–Thurs 11:30am–9pm; Fri–Sat 11:30am–10pm. From Hwy. 1, take the Rio Rd. exit west for 1 block and turn right onto Crossroads Blvd.

Tommy's Wok ★★ ✔ CHINESE Far be it for Carmel to have an ordinary Chinese restaurant. Chef/owner Tommy Mao has eschewed the typical red-and-gold color scheme for a far more austere, almost Japanese decor. The small 12-table restaurant—with its soothing pastel hues, rice-paper posters, semiopen kitchen, and glossy wood floor—is an apt setting for Mao's stylish presentations and unique combinations of Szechuan, Hunan, and Mandarin dishes. Mao makes everything from scratch: Potstickers are made with fresh Napa cabbage, moo shu vegetables with house-made pancakes; tea-smoked duck is marinated for 48 hours. The hot and spicy string beans, pine nut chicken, marinated Lover's Prawns, and Mongolian lamb are also winners. The combo lunch plates are a bargain, and a modest dim sum menu is offered for lunch as well.

Mission (btw. Ocean and Seventh, next to the Wells Fargo ATM). ☎ **831/624-8518.** Main courses $7–$16. AE, DISC, MC, V. Tues–Sun 11:30am–2:30pm and 4:30–9:30pm.

INEXPENSIVE

Carmel Bakery BAKERY/DELI   This fancy bakery along this main street leading down to the beach serves espresso, soup, sandwiches, and pastries. It's festive and well decorated, with a few tables and chairs, and music playing from speakers overhead. Most customers grab their goods and go. For a more formal (and a mite more expensive) encounter with espresso and the like, head down the block to the Il Fornaio bakery (Ocean Ave. at Monte Verde; ☎ **831/622-5100**).

Ocean (btw. Dolores and Lincoln). ☎ **831/626-8885.** www.carmelbakery.com. Sandwiches $4–$6. No credit cards. Daily 7am–8pm.

Little Swiss Cafe CONTINENTAL   This quirky little spot looks like a Swiss cottage. Kids may love the decor, but the grown-ups come for the best homemade blintzes and pancakes in town. Breakfast is served all day. Lunch is affordable and features sandwiches, served with potato salad, mixed green salad, or soup ($6–$9); salads; and an array of unusual entrees such as Swiss sausage with smothered onions, calves' liver sauté, and filet of red snapper with a rémoulade sauce.

Sixth Ave. (btw. Lincoln and Mission). ☎ **831/624-5007.** Reservations not accepted. $5–$10. No credit cards. Mon–Sat 7:30am–3pm; Sun 8am–2pm.

Nielsen Brothers Market DELI   Why squander precious midday vacation minutes indoors when you can dine alfresco on Carmel Beach? A few blocks off the main drag, Nielsen Brothers market has what you need to fill a picnic basket, including sandwiches, barbecued chicken and ribs, pasta salads, and a vast selection of cheeses. You can even get french fries or veggie and meat burgers (noon–6pm), but expect a 10-minute wait—they cook to order. Call and order by phone or drop in.

San Carlos St. (at Seventh). ☎ **831/624-6441.** www.nielsenmarket.com. Picnic items $3–$5. MC, V. Daily 8am–7pm.

CARMEL VALLEY

3 miles SE of Carmel-by-the-Sea

Inland from Carmel stretches Carmel Valley, where the wealthy retreat beyond the reach of the coastal fog and mist. It's a scenic, perpetually sunny valley of rolling hills dotted with manicured golf courses and many a tony pony ranch.

Hike the trails in **Garland Regional Park,** 8 miles east of Carmel on Carmel Valley Road (dogs are welcome off-leash). The sun bakes you here, so bring lots of water. Several resorts and courses in the valley offer golf—notably **Quail Lodge** (now golf-only; the hotel portion closed), 8205 Valley Green Dr. (📞 **831/620-8886;** www.quaillodge.com), and **Rancho Cañada Golf Club,** Carmel Valley Road (📞 **800/536-9459** or 831/624-0111; www.ranchocanada.com).

While you're in the area, taste the wines at the **Château Julien Winery,** 8940 Carmel Valley Rd. (📞 **831/624-2600;** www.chateaujulien.com), open Monday through Friday from 8am to 5pm, Saturday and Sunday from 11am to 5pm. Tours are available by reservation.

Where to Stay

Bernardus Lodge ★★★   On the top-20 list of just about every luxury travel publication is this 57-room boutique "lodge" in scenic Carmel Valley. Bernardus Pon, who owns the Bernardus Winery and Vineyard, must have spent a small fortune to build his eponymous resort, which consists of a main lodge, nine adobe-style guest houses, two restaurants, a meditation garden, a croquet lawn and bocce court, two tennis courts, and a pool. The gorgeous main lodge resembles a French country home, with heavy wood beams, hand-plastered walls, copper chandeliers, antique wrought iron, and limestone fireplaces. The guest suites are similar, with stone wood-burning fireplaces, vaulted ceilings, arched windows, feather beds with Italian linens, and French doors that open to private decks with mountain or garden views. Carmel is only a 15-minute drive, but your time is far better spent indulging in the resort's full-service spa, playing golf at nearby Carmel Valley courses, or having a leisurely breakfast or lunch at the outdoor terrace, followed by an impromptu wine tasting. For dinner, chef Cal Stamenov offers exquisite California natural cuisine and a *Wine Spectator* Award–winning wine list at the lodge's Marinus restaurant.

415 Carmel Valley Rd., Carmel Valley, CA 93924. www.bernardus.com. 📞 **888/648-9463** or 831/648-3400. Fax 831/659-3529. 57 units. $415–$805 double; $1,065–$1,235 suite. AE, DC, DISC, MC, V. **Amenities:** 2 restaurants; concierge; exercise room; heated outdoor pool; room service; sauna; full spa; 2 tennis courts. *In room:* A/C, TV/DVD, CD player, fridge, hair dryer, minibar (w/complimentary wine and snacks).

Stonepine Estate   Flanked by lush meadows, placid ponds, and cascading waterfalls, the 330-acre Stonepine Estate resort hidden deep in the valley, tucked away from all other civilization, is about as secluded as it gets while still vacationing in California's confines. A registered Historic Hotel of America, Stonepine is not a new property: Built in 1928, it was once the private estate of a notable banking family and the biggest thoroughbred breeding farm in the West—the sprawling equestrian center is still in operation today—but recently was the recipient of a huge upgrade and began inviting guests to rent out its 20 rooms just this fall. Now, it seeks to give visitors a "Gatsby-esque" experience, dating back to the days of its conception.

While the rooms are comfortable and well-appointed, they're not the selling point. Rather, it's all the activities available on the premises. You won't be lacking in things to do, from an educational visit to the Greenhouse—where guests can learn horticulture and even pot a few plants on their own—to a movie in the Screening Room to a game of shuffleboard, a round of archery, and a leisurely horseback ride around the property. Breakfast is served in the dining room; lunch is often a picnic by the pool; and private dinners are arranged in various locations, such as the outdoor loge.

150 E. Carmel Valley Rd., Carmel Valley, CA 93924. www.stonepineestate.com. ☎ **831/659-2245.** Fax 831/659-5160. 12 units, 3 cottages. $300–$375 double; $500–$1,500 suite; $750–$3,000 cottage. Packages available. AE, DC, DISC, MC, V. Turnoff is 1½ miles east of Carmel Village on E. Carmel Valley Rd. **Amenities:** Golf practice range; outdoor pool; tennis court; equestrian center; organized hikes; mountain biking; shuffleboard. *In room:* TV/DVD, hair dryer, Wi-Fi.

THE BIG SUR COAST ★★★

3 miles S of Carmel-by-the-Sea; 123 miles S of San Francisco; 87 miles N of Hearst Castle

Big Sur is more than a drive along one of the most dramatic coastlines on Earth or a peaceful repose amid a forest of California redwoods. It's a stretch of wilderness so overwhelmingly beautiful—especially when the fog glows in the moonlight—that it enchants everyone who visits. It's one of the most romantic, relaxing places in California. There's little more to do than explore the mountains and beaches, and take in the sea air—but spend a few days here and you won't need to do much else.

Towns   Although there is an actual town of Big Sur located 25 miles south of Carmel (and it's more a pit stop for snacks than a town), "Big Sur" generally refers to the entire 90-mile stretch of coastline between Carmel and San Simeon. Just about everything there is to see and explore in Big Sur is right off of Hwy. 1, which runs its entire length, hugging the coastline the whole way. Be sure to arrive with full tank of gas, because stations here are few and far between (and expensive).

Countryside   The entire stretch of Big Sur consists of the Santa Lucia Range to the east and the rocky Pacific coast to the West. Heading south from Carmel you'll encounter numerous places to pull over and pull out the camera: **Point Lobos State Reserve, Bixby Bridge** (one of the world's highest single-span concrete bridges), **Point Sur Lighthouse, Pfeiffer Beach, Sand Dollar Beach,** and **Jade Cove** are just a few of the Kodak moments that Big Sur provides.

Eating & Drinking   The restaurants and hotels of Big Sur are easy to spot—most are situated directly on or just off the highway. A must-stop along the way is at **Nepenthe** to admire the view (but not the price—walk over to **Café Kevah** instead). Everyone loves the down-home **Big Sur River Inn,** which has something for all tastes. For romance, nothing tops the view at **Sierra Mar** restaurant at the Post Ranch Inn. Better yet, create your own oceanview dining experience courtesy of the **Big Sur Center Deli** and Big Sur's numerous **picnic spots.**

State Parks   Big Sur's tranquillity and natural beauty are ideal for hiking, picnicking, camping, fishing, and beachcombing at the four state parks that border Hwy. 1. **Garrapata State Park** offers 4 miles of rugged coastline to explore. The 4,800-acre **Andrew Molera State Park** is the largest state park in Big Sur coast, with miles of trails meandering through meadows, beaches, and bluffs. **Julia Pfeiffer Burns State Park** is the most popular park in Big Sur and offers the best photo opportunities, including 80-foot-high McWay Waterfall dropping into the ocean. **Pfeiffer–Big Sur State Park** is popular with campers, with 218 camping sites along the Big Sur River, as well as picnicking, fishing, and hiking.

Essentials

VISITOR INFORMATION   Contact the **Big Sur Chamber of Commerce** (© 831/667-2100) for specialized information on places and events in Big Sur.

ORIENTATION   Most of this stretch is state park, and Hwy. 1 runs its entire length, hugging the ocean the whole way. Restaurants, hotels, and sights are easy to spot—most are situated directly on the highway—but without major towns as reference points, their addresses can be obscure. For the purposes of orientation, I use the River Inn as a mileage guide. Located 29 miles south of Monterey on Hwy. 1, the inn is generally considered to mark the northern end of Big Sur.

Exploring the Big Sur Coast

Big Sur's tranquillity and natural beauty are ideal for hiking, picnicking, camping, fishing, and beachcombing. The first settlers arrived only a century ago, and the present highway, built in 1937, first made the area accessible by car. (Electricity followed in the 1950s, but it's still not available in the remote inland mountains.) Big Sur's mysterious, misty beauty has inspired several modern spiritual movements (the Esalen Institute was the birthplace of the human potential movement). Even the tourist bureau bills the area as a place in which "to catch up with your soul."

The region affords bountiful wilderness adventure opportunities. The inland **Ventana Wilderness,** run by the U.S. Forest Service, has 167,323 acres straddling the Santa Lucia Mountains. Steep ridges separated by V-shaped valleys characterize it. The streams throughout the area have waterfalls, deep pools, and thermal springs. The wilderness offers 237 miles of hiking trails that lead to 55 designated trail camps—a backpacker's paradise. One of the easiest trails to access is the **Pine Ridge Trail** at Big Sur station (© 831/667-2315).

From Carmel, the first stop along Hwy. 1 is **Point Lobos State Reserve ★★** (© 831/624-4909; www.pointlobos.org), 3 miles south of Carmel. Sea lions, harbor seals, sea otters, and thousands of seabirds reside in this 1,276-acre reserve. Between December and May, you can also spot migrating California gray whales offshore, and in late April I've spotted numerous mama seals with their newly born pups. Trails follow the shoreline and lead to hidden coves. Note that parking is limited; on weekends especially, you need to arrive early to secure a place.

From here, cross the Soberanes Creek, passing **Garrapata State Park** (© 831/624-4909), a 2,879-acre preserve with 4 miles of coastline. It's unmarked and undeveloped, but the trails are maintained. To explore them, park at one of the turnouts on Hwy. 1 near Soberanes Point and hike in.

Ten miles south of Carmel, you'll find North Abalone Cove. From here, Palo Colorado Road leads back into the wilderness to the first of the Forest Service camping areas at **Bottchers Gap** ($12 to camp, $5 to park overnight; © 805/434-1996; www.campone.com).

Continuing south, about 13 miles from Carmel, you'll cross the **Bixby Bridge** and see the **Point Sur Lighthouse** off in the distance. The Bixby Bridge, one of the world's highest single-span concrete bridges, towers nearly 270 feet above Bixby Creek Canyon, with canyon and ocean views from observation alcoves at intervals along the bridge. The lighthouse, which sits 361 feet above the surf on a volcanic rock promontory, was built in 1889, when only a horse trail provided access to this part of the world. Tours, which take 2 to 3 hours and involve a steep half-mile hike each way, are scheduled on weekends year-round and Wednesday and Thursday during the summer. For information, call ✆ **831/625-4419** or visit **www. pointsur.org**. Moonlight tours are offered as well, for $5 more than the normal price; check the website for specific dates. Admission is $10 for adults, $5 for youths ages 6 to 17, and free for kids 5 and under.

Point Sur Lighthouse.

About 3 miles south of the lighthouse is **Andrew Molera State Park** (✆ **831/667-2315;** www.parks.ca.gov), the largest state park on the Big Sur coast, at 4,800 acres. It's much less crowded than Pfeiffer–Big Sur (see below). Miles of trails meander through meadows and along beaches and bluffs. Hikers and cyclists use the primitive trail camp about a third of a mile from the parking area. The 2½-mile-long beach, sheltered from the wind by a bluff, is accessible via a mile-long path flanked in spring by wildflowers, and offers excellent tide pooling. You can walk the length of the beach at low tide; otherwise, take the bluff trail above the beach. Trails run through the park for horseback riders of all levels. **Molera Big Sur Trail Rides** (✆ **800/942-5486** or 831/625-5486; www.molerahorsebacktours.com) offers coastal trail

Big Sur.

Henry Miller Library.

rides daily from April to December, or until the rains come. The cost varies but starts at about $40 for a 1-hour ride along the beach. The park also has campgrounds.

Back on Hwy. 1, you'll reach the village of Big Sur, with commercial services. At **Big Sur Station** (© 831/667-2315), you can pick up maps and information about the region. It's located a quarter-mile past the entrance to **Pfeiffer–Big Sur State Park** ★ (© 831/667-2315; www.parks.ca.gov), an 810-acre park with 218 camping sites along the Big Sur River (call © **800/444-7275** for camping reservations), as well as picnicking, fishing, and hiking. It's a scenic park of redwoods, conifers, oaks, and meadows, and it gets very crowded. **The Big Sur Lodge** in the park has cabins with fireplaces and other facilities. Admission is $5 per car, and it's open daily from dawn to dusk.

Just over a mile south of the entrance to Pfeiffer–Big Sur State Park is the turnoff to Sycamore Canyon Road (unmarked), which will take you 2 winding miles down to beautiful **Pfeiffer Beach** ★, a great place to soak in the sun on the wide expanse of golden sand. It's open for day use only, there's no fee, and it's the only beach accessible by car (but not motor homes).

Back on Hwy. 1, the road travels 11 miles past Sea Lion Cove to Julia Pfeiffer Burns State Park. High above the ocean is the famous **Nepenthe** restaurant (p. 476), the retreat bought by Orson Welles for Rita Hayworth in 1944. A few miles farther south is the **Coast Gallery** (© **800/797-6869;** www.coast galleries.com), the premier local art gallery which displays lithographs of works by the late writer and, yes, artist Henry Miller; it's open daily from 9am to 5pm. The gallery also has a small cafe that offers simple self-serve lunches of soup, sandwiches, baked goods, and coffee. Miller fans will also want to stop at the **Henry Miller Memorial Library** (© 831/667-2574; www.henrymiller.org), on Hwy. 1, 30 miles south of Carmel and a quarter-mile south of Nepenthe restaurant. The library displays and sells books and artwork by Miller and houses a permanent collection of first editions. It also serves as a community art center, hosting concerts, readings, and art exhibitions (check for upcoming events on the website). The rear gallery room is a video-viewing space where films about Henry Miller can be seen. There's a sculpture garden, plus tables on the adjacent lawn where visitors can rest and enjoy the surroundings. Admission is free; hours are from 11am to 6pm daily in the summer and 11am to 6pm Thursday through Sunday winter.

Julia Pfeiffer Burns State Park ★★ (✆ **831/667-2315;** www.parks. ca.gov) encompasses some of Big Sur's most spectacular coastline. To get a closer look, take the trail from the parking area at McWay Canyon, which leads under the highway to a bluff overlooking the 80-foot-high McWay Waterfall dropping directly into the ocean. It's less crowded here than at Pfeiffer–Big Sur, and there are miles of trails to explore in the 3,580-acre park. Scuba divers can apply for permits to explore the 1,680-acre underwater reserve.

From here, the road skirts the Ventana Wilderness, passing Anderson and Marble Peaks and the Esalen Institute before crossing the Big Creek Bridge to Lucia and several campgrounds farther south. **Kirk Creek Campground** ★, about 3 miles north of Pacific Valley, offers camping with ocean views and beach access. Beyond Pacific Valley, the **Sand Dollar Beach** ★ picnic area is a good place to stop and enjoy the coastal view and take a stroll. A half-mile trail leads down to the sheltered beach, with a fine view of Cone Peak, one of the coast's highest mountains. Two miles south of Sand Dollar is **Jade Cove,** a popular spot for rock hounds. From here, it's about another 27 miles past the Piedras Blancas Light Station to San Simeon.

Where to Stay

Only a handful of Big Sur's accommodations offer the kind of pampering and luxury you'd expect in a fine urban hotel; even direct-dial phones and TVs (often considered gauche in these parts) are rare. Big Sur hotels are especially busy in summer, when advance reservations are required. There are more accommodations than those listed here, so if you're having trouble securing a room or a site, contact the chamber of commerce (listed in the "Essentials" section above) for other options.

Big Sur Lodge ☺   A family-friendly place, the Big Sur Lodge is *in* the park and sheltered by towering redwoods, sycamores, and maples. The rustic motel-style cabins are spacious, with high peaked cedar- and redwood-beamed ceilings. They're clean and heated, and have private bathrooms and reserved parking spaces. Some have fireplaces and others kitchenettes. All offer porches or decks with views of the redwoods or the Santa Lucia Range. An advantage to staying here is that you're entitled to free use of all park facilities, including hiking, barbecue pits, and picnic areas. In addition, the lodge has its own grocery store. *Note:* Winter rates are significantly cheaper.

In Pfeiffer–Big Sur State Park, Hwy. 1 (P.O. Box 190), Big Sur, CA 93920. www.bigsurlodge.com. ✆ **800/424-4787** or 831/667-3100. Fax 831/667-3110. 62 cottages. $199–$249 cottage; $259–$319 kitchen suite; $289–$359 kitchen suite with fireplace; park entrance fee included. AE, MC, V. From Carmel, take Hwy. 1 south 26 miles. **Amenities:** Restaurant; heated outdoor pool in season. *In room:* Kitchen in some units, no phone.

Deetjen's Big Sur Inn ★   In the 1930s, before Hwy. 1 was built, this homestead in a redwood canyon was an overnight stopping place on the coastal wagon road. Norwegian homesteader Helmuth Deetjen built the original units from

BIG SUR LODGING AT low rates

If you want to stay in Big Sur but can't afford it, consider **Treebones Resort ★★** (www.treebonesresort.com; ✆ **877/424-4787** or 805/927-2390). This new minire-sort, on a secluded bluff, shelters guests in oceanside yurts—circular fabric structures on a wooden frame. Half-tent, half-cabin, Treebones's yurts are spacious and taste-fully furnished with polished pine-wood floors, queen-size beds with cozy comforters, electric lighting, gas-burning fireplaces, and French doors that open to a redwood deck with Adirondack chairs and spectacular coastal views. The yurts don't have bathrooms, but shower and restroom facilities are within a short stroll. The main lodge has a heated, oceanview pool and hot tub, and a restaurant that serves nightly dinner by a crackling fire in a casual, community setting. Private, in-yurt massage treatments are also available. Rates start at $145 for two guests, with a 2-night mini-mum April to October, including a self-service waffle breakfast with coffee and orange juice. Treebones is at 71895 Hwy. 1, 65 miles south of Monterey.

hand-hewn logs and lumber. Folks either love or hate them. They're cozy and adorable, with old-fashioned furnishings and a down-home feel (the hand-hewn doors don't have locks), but those who want creature comforts should go else-where, or at least reserve a cabin with a private bathroom. Single-wall construc-tion rooms aren't soundproof, so children 11 and under are allowed only if families reserve both rooms of a two-room building. They're not insulated, so prepare to crank up the fire or wood-burning stove. *Tip:* Cabins by the river are the most private. If you stay in one of the two-story units, request the quieter upstairs rooms. The restaurant (p. 476) is a local favorite and consists of four intimate, English country inn–style rooms lit by candlelight.

Hwy. 1, Big Sur, CA 93920. www.deetjens.com. ✆ **831/667-2377.** 20 units, 15 with bathroom. $75–$180 double with shared bathroom; $95–$200 double with private bathroom. MC, V. **Ame-nities:** Restaurant. *In room:* No phone.

Post Ranch Inn ★★★ 📷 This is one of my very favorite places to stay on the planet. Perched on 98 acres of seaside ridges 1,200 feet above the Pacific, this romantic resort opened in 1992 and was instantly declared one of the world's fin-est retreats. Wood-and-glass guest cottages are built around existing trees—some are elevated to avoid damaging the delicate redwood root structures—and the ultraprivate Ocean and Coast cottages are so close to the edge of the Earth, you get the impression that you've joined the clouds (imagine that from your private spa tub). Other cottages that face the woodlands are as impressive in design. Each room has a king-size bed, wood-burning fireplace, private deck, digital music system with 45 channels, and wet bar with complimentary goodies. The bathrooms, fashioned out of slate and granite, have luxurious spa tubs. The best Jacuzzi I've ever encountered is here and seems to join the sky on a cliff. There is also an infinity pool and sun decks. The only drawback is that the vibe can be stuffy, which is due more to the clientele than to the staff. The **Sierra Mar** res-taurant and bar is open to outside guests for lunch, afternoon appetizers, and dinner (reservations required for dinner). It, too, has floor-to-ceiling views of the ocean and offers an opportunity for people who can't afford the steep rack rates to ooh and aah at one of the most beautiful hotel settings in the world.

Hwy. 1 (P.O. Box 219), Big Sur, CA 93920. www.postranchinn.com. ☎ **800/527-2200** or 831/667-2200. Fax 831/667-2512. 30 units. $550–$1,485 double. Rates include buffet breakfast. AE, MC, V. **Amenities:** Restaurant; bar/lounge; concierge; exercise room; cliffside Jacuzzi; outdoor heated pool; room service; spa services. *In room:* A/C, CD player, hair dryer, minibar.

Ventana Inn and Spa ★★★   Luxuriously rustic and utterly romantic, Ventana has been a popular wilderness outpost for more than 30 years. On 243 mountainous oceanfront acres, this is one of the best retreats in the area, if not the state. Ventana has an elegance that's atypical of the region and has attracted famous guests such as Barbra Streisand, Goldie Hawn, and Francis Ford Coppola since opening in 1975.

The accommodations, in 12 one- and two-story natural-wood buildings along winding wildflower-flanked paths, blend in with the magical Big Sur countryside. The extensive grounds are dotted with hammocks and hand-carved benches under shady trees and at vista points. The guest rooms are divinely decorated in warm, cozy luxury, with private terraces or balconies overlooking the ocean or forest. Most rooms offer wood-burning fireplaces, and some have Jacuzzis and cathedral ceilings. A small fitness center offers the basics—but you'll be more inspired to hike the grounds, where you'll find pastoral respite plus a pool, a rustic library, and clothing-optional tanning decks and spa tubs. I prefer the rooms at Post Ranch (see above), but the laid-back energy and the grounds at Ventana (and the spa). *Tips:* Be sure to check their website for seasonal specials. The **Restaurant at Ventana** is a romantic and first-rate dining experience. For nibbles, grab a bite at the intimate on-site **Bistro.** Children are permitted in the restaurant but not encouraged.

Hwy. 1, Big Sur, CA 93920. www.ventanainn.com. ☎ **800/628-6500** or 831/667-2331. Fax 831/667-0573. 62 units. $500–$1,100 double; from $925 cottage. Rates include continental breakfast and afternoon wine and cheese. AE, DC, DISC, MC, V. **Amenities:** Restaurant; concierge; exercise room; 2 heated outdoor pools; room service; sauna; full spa w/2 Japanese hot baths. *In room:* A/C, TV/DVD, fridge, hair dryer, minibar.

CAMPING

Big Sur is one of California's most spectacular camping destinations. One of the most glorious settings is **Pfeiffer–Big Sur State Park,** on Hwy. 1, 26 miles south of Carmel (☎ **831/667-2315**). The 810-acre state park has 218 secluded sites amid hundreds of acres of redwoods. Hiking trails, streams, and the river are steps from your sleeping bag, and the most modern amenities are the 25¢ showers (for 3 min.) and water faucets between sites. Each spot has a picnic table and fire pit, but no RV hookups or electricity. Riverfront sites are most coveted, but others promise more privacy among the shaded hillsides. Campfire programs and nature walks are available. A store, gift shop, restaurant, and cafe are near the entrance. Fees are $25 per night for family sites; see **www.reserveamerica.com** or call ☎ **800/444-7275** for reservations.

The entrance to the **Ventana Campground,** on Hwy. 1, 28 miles south of Carmel and 4¼ miles south of the River Inn (www.ventanawilderness campground.com; ☎ **831/667-2712**), is adjacent to the Ventana Resort entrance, but the comparison stops there. This is pure rusticity. The 80 campsites, on 40 acres of a redwood canyon, are spaced well apart on a hillside and shaded by towering trees. Each has a picnic table and fire ring, but no electricity, RV hookups, or river access. Three conveniently located bathhouses have hot showers (25¢ fee). Reserve a space with a credit card (MasterCard or Visa) for 1 night's deposit. Or mail a deposit check, the dates you'd like to stay, and a stamped, self-addressed envelope at least 2 weeks in advance (earlier during peak months). Rates are $35 for a site for two with one vehicle. An additional person is $5 extra, and it'll cost you $5 to bring Fido. Rates include the entrance fee for your car. Open March through October.

Big Sur Campground and Cabins is on Hwy. 1, 26 miles south of Carmel (© **831/667-2322;** www.bigsurcamp.com). Sites are cramped, so the feel is more like a camping village than an intimate retreat (romantic, it ain't). However, it's very well maintained and perfect for families, who love the playground, river swimming, and inner tube rentals. Each campsite has its own wood-burning fire pit, picnic table, and freshwater faucet within 25 feet of the pitching area. There are also RV water and electric hookups. Facilities include bathhouses with hot showers, laundry facilities, an aged volleyball/basketball court, and a grocery store. There are 81 tent sites (30 RV-ready with electricity and water hookup), plus 13 cabins (all with shower). The all-wood cabins are adorable, with stylish country furnishings, wood-burning ovens, patios, and full kitchens. Rates are $35 to $50 for a tent site for five people (plus $4 extra for electricity and water), $45 to $60 for an RV site for up to five people, $88 to $98 for a tent cabin (bed, but no heat or plumbing) for three, or $125 to $360 for a cabin for six. Rates include the entrance for your car. MasterCard and Visa are accepted. Pets cost $4 for campsites and $12 for tent cabins; pets are not allowed in the other cabins. It's open year-round.

Where to Eat

In addition to the following choices, you should try the **Big Sur Bakery and Restaurant** on Hwy. 1, just past the post office and a mile south of Pfeiffer–Big Sur State Park (© **831/667-0520;** www.bigsurbakery.com). It offers friendly service and healthy fare, including wood-fired pizzas and portobello-mushroom burgers at lunch, and salmon, tuna, and chicken selections at dinner. All the pastries are freshly baked on the premises, along with hearth-baked breads. It's open Tuesday through Sunday from 8am to 10pm; they close early on Monday.

Big Sur River Inn CALIFORNIAN/AMERICAN Popular with everyone from families to bikers, the River Inn is an unpretentious, rustic, down-home restaurant that has something for all tastes. Trying to seat a small army? No problem. Want to watch sports on TV at a local bar? Pull up a stool. Looking to snag a few rays from a deck right beside the Big Sur River? Break out the suntan lotion. In winter, the wooden dining room is the prime spot; on summer days, some folks grab their patio chairs and cocktails and hang out literally midstream. Along with the local color, attractions include a full bar and good ol' American breakfasts (steak and eggs, omelets, pancakes, and so on, plus espresso, with most dishes for around $6), lunches (an array of salads, sandwiches, and baby back ribs, or fish and chips), and dinners (fresh catch, pastas, burgers, or ribs). I usually order the Black Angus Burger with a side of beer-battered onion rings, or a big platter of the Roadhouse Ribs served with cowboy beans.

On Hwy. 1, 2 miles north of Pfeiffer–Big Sur State Park. © **831/667-2700.** www.bigsurriverinn. com. Main courses $6–$13 breakfast, $8.75–$18 lunch, $8.95–$36 dinner. AE, DC, MC, V. Daily 8am–10pm; 8am–9pm in winter.

Café Kevah SOUTHWEST/CALIFORNIAN   One level below Nepenthe (see below), Café Kevah offers the same celestial view at a fraction of the price, a more casual environment, and—depending on your taste—better food. Seating is outdoors—a downside when the biting fog rolls in, but perfect on a clear day. You can order breakfast (served all day) or lunch from the shack of a kitchen and then grab an umbrella-shaded table. Fare here is more eclectic than Nepenthe's, with such choices as homemade granola, baby greens with broiled salmon and papaya, chicken brochettes, omelets, and new-potato hash. It ain't cheap, but innovative cuisine, the view, and a decent mocha make it worthwhile. Don't forget your coat.

On Hwy. 1, 29 miles south of Carmel (5 miles south of the River Inn). © **831/667-2345.** www. nepenthebigsur.com. Appetizers $6.25–$12; main courses $11–$18. AE, MC, V. Daily 9am–4pm; closes when it rains.

Deetjen's Big Sur Inn Restaurant ★ AMERICAN   With the feel of an English farmhouse—white-painted wood walls, wood-burning stove, dimly lit old-fashioned lamps, country antiques—this cozy country setting is the perfect venue for delicious comfort food and friendly service. Mornings start with a cup of strong coffee and breakfast: omelets and eggs Benedict piled high with potatoes, pancakes, and granola. Dinner might include grilled chicken with mushrooms and a garlic Marsala sauce; roasted rack of lamb with a panko crust; prime New York steak with macadamia nut risotto; and roast duckling with brandy, peppercorn, and molasses sauce.

On Hwy. 1. © **831/667-2377.** www.deetjens.com. Reservations recommended. Main courses $4.25–$12 breakfast, $17–$29 dinner. MC, V. Mon–Fri 9:30am–4pm; Sat noon–4pm.

Nepenthe AMERICAN   Stop by Nepenthe if only to admire the view and pay homage to Henry Miller, who wrote some of his most significant works here. At 808 feet above sea level along the cliffs overlooking the ocean, the view is celestial—especially when fog lingers above the water. On a warm day, join the crowds on the terrace. On colder days, stay indoors. The redwood-and-adobe structure—with a wood-burning fireplace, redwood ceilings, and bayfront windows—has been a sanctuary for writers, artists, and travelers since 1949. Unfortunately, the food is another story; elsewhere, I would scoff at a $13 burger and $19 swordfish sandwich. Here, though, I consider it a nominal admission to dine at heights only birds usually enjoy. For the most part, the food is industrial fare (big-box-store-style hamburger patties for the grown-ups and Kraft macaroni and cheese on the kids' menu). Come for lunch or just a drink to see the view, and save your dinner bucks for elsewhere.

> ## Gourmet to Go
>
> The **Big Sur Center Deli** sells fresh baked goods, salads, wine, and beer, as well as fettuccine, calzones, enchiladas, and barbecue chicken—all made on-site. Sandwiches are prepared to order, or you can grab a ready-made hoagie or vegetarian portobello mushroom on a roll. Pastries and coffee drinks are available as well. It's located on Hwy. 1 next to the Big Sur Post Office and is open daily from 7:30am to 8:30pm (© **831/667-2225**).

Hwy. 1, 29 miles south of Carmel (5 miles south of the River Inn). © **831/667-2345.** www. nepenthebigsur.com. Reservations accepted only for parties of 5 or more. Main courses $14–$35. AE, MC, V. Daily 11:30am–10pm.

PINNACLES NATIONAL MONUMENT ★

58 miles SE of Monterey

A little-known outpost 10 years ago, the 24,000-acre Pinnacles National Monument is now one of central California's most popular weekend hiking and climbing spots. In Steinbeck Country, southeast of Salinas, the mild-winter climate and plentiful routes make it an ideal off-season training ground for climbers. It's also a haven for campers, bird-watchers, and nature lovers. One of the world's most unusual chaparral ecosystems, it supports a community of plants and animals, including six endangered California condors—the largest bird in North America, with a wingspan of nearly 10 feet—and one of California's largest breeding populations of raptors. Bring binoculars!

The Pinnacles—hundreds of towering crags, spires, ramparts, and hoodoos—seem out of place amid the rolling hills of the coast range. Part of the eroded remains of a volcano that formed 23 million years ago, 195 miles south in the middle of the Mojave Desert, they were brought here by the movement of the San Andreas Fault, which runs just east of the park. (The other half of the volcano remains in the Mojave.)

You could spend days here, but it's possible to cover the most interesting features in a weekend. With a single hike, you can go from the oak woodland around the Bear Gulch Visitor Center to the dry, desolate crags of the high peaks and then back down through a half-mile-long cave with underground waterfalls.

Essentials

GETTING THERE   Two entrances lead to the park: The **West Entrance** from Soledad and U.S. 101 is a dusty, winding single-lane road (not suitable for trailers) with the best drive-up view. Exit at Front Street in Soledad, turn

Pinnacles National Monument.

right, and then turn left onto Hwy. 46 heading east (it doesn't connect with the east side entrance). The west gate is open daily from 7:30am to 8pm (until 6pm in winter).

The alternative route is via the **East Entrance.** Unless you're coming from nearby, take the longer drive on Hwy. 25 through Gilroy and Hollister to enter through the east. Because most of the peaks of the Pinnacles face east and the watershed drains east, most of the interesting hikes and geologic features are on this side. The east gate is open 24 hours a day. No road crosses the park.

FEES   Park entrance fees, good for 7 days, are $3 per person or $5 per car.

VISITOR CENTER   The first place you should go when entering from the east is the **Bear Gulch Visitor Center** (© 831/389-4485), open daily from 9am to 5pm. This small center is rich with exhibits on the park's history, wildlife, and geology, with a great selection of nature handbooks and climbing guides for the Pinnacles. Climbers should check with rangers about closures and other information before heading out: Many routes are closed during hawk- and falcon-nesting season, and rangers like to know how many climbers are in the park.

Adjacent to the visitor center, the Bear Gulch picnic ground is a great place to fuel up before setting out on a hike. Don't leave before gazing up at the dramatic spires of the high peaks (the ultimate spot is from the west side).

For more information, log on to the park's website at **www.nps.gov/pinn**.

REGULATIONS & WARNINGS   Beware of poison oak, particularly in Bear Gulch. Rattlesnakes are common but rarely seen. Bikes and dogs are prohibited on all trails, and no backcountry camping is allowed in the park.

Hiking through this variety of landscapes demands versatility. Come prepared with a good pair of hiking shoes, snacks, lots of water, and a flashlight.

Daytime temperatures often exceed 100°F (38°C) in summer, so the best time of year to visit is spring, when the wildflowers are blooming, or in the fall. Crowds are common during spring weekends.

Hiking & Exploring the Park

To see most of the park in a single, moderately strenuous morning, take the **Condor Gulch Trail** from the visitor center. As you climb out of the parking area, the Pinnacles' wind-sculpted spires seem to grow taller. In less than 2 miles, you're among them, and Condor Gulch intersects with the **High Peaks Trail.** The view from the top spans miles: the Salinas Valley to your west, the Pinnacles below, and miles of coast to the east. And it's the most likely place to spot the elusive California condor. (Look for the white-triangle markings on the undersides of their wings.) After traversing the high peaks (including stretches of footholds carved in steep rock faces) for about a mile, the trail drops back toward the visitor center via a valley filled with eerie-looking hoodoos.

In another 1.5 miles, you'll reach the reservoir marking the top of **Bear Gulch Cave,** which closes occasionally; in 1998, it closed due to storm damage and to accommodate migrating Townsend bats, who in the past several years have come here to have their babies. It's usually open, but if you want to explore, you'll need your flashlight and you might get wet; still, this half-mile-long talus cave is a thrill. From the end of the cave, you're just a short walk (through the most popular climbing area of the park) away from the visitor center. It's also possible to hike just Bear Gulch and the cave, and then return via the **Moses Spring Trail.** It's about 2 miles round-trip, but you'll miss the view from the top.

If you're coming from the West Entrance, the **Juniper Canyon Trail** is a short (1.25 miles), but very steep, blast to the top of the high peaks. You'll definitely earn the view. Otherwise, try the short **Balconies Trail** to the monument's other talus cave, **Balconies Cave.** Flashlights are required here too.

Where to Stay

The Inn at the Pinnacles ★ 🎁   Unless you intend to camp, the only place to stay at the Pinnacles National Monument is this sprawling hacienda-style inn a half-mile from the west park entrance. Built in 2002 in the heart of a working vineyard—Brousseau Vineyards in the Chalone Appellation—the six-room inn has unblemished vistas of rolling vineyards and the Gabilan Mountain Range. Each of the individually decorated guest rooms has a private entrance, ceramic tile flooring, private patio with a gas grill and vineyard views, and a sitting area with gas fireplace; all but one have a two-person whirlpool tub (heaven after a long day of hiking). The inn's sprawling patio is a popular spot to sip wine under a shade umbrella with panoramic views of the surrounding hillsides and Pinnacles National Monument. The innkeepers serve a full breakfast each morning (in the dining room, patio, or guest rooms), and wine and cheese every evening. The nearest restaurants are 10 miles away, so you can either bring your own food to grill or ask if the innkeepers can make advance arrangements for dinner service.

32025 Stonewall Canyon Rd., Soledad, CA 93960. www.innatthepinnacles.com. © **831/678-2400.** 6 units. $200–$290 double. Rates include continental breakfast and afternoon wine and cheese. MC, V. *In room:* A/C, fridge, Jacuzzi (in 5 rooms).

Camping

The park's campground on the west side was demolished by El Niño storms in 1997 and 1998, and it's not scheduled for repair. Now the only campground is the privately run **Pinnacles Campground, Inc.,** on the east side (www.nps.gov/pinn/planyourvisit/camp.htm; © **877/444-6777**), which charges $23 per tent and $36 per RV. It's just outside the park (off Hwy. 25, 32 miles south of Hollister), with lots of privacy and space between sites, plus showers, a store, and a large pool. It's close enough so you can hike into the park from the campground, though it will add a few miles to your outing. Surroundings here are natural rather than overdeveloped.

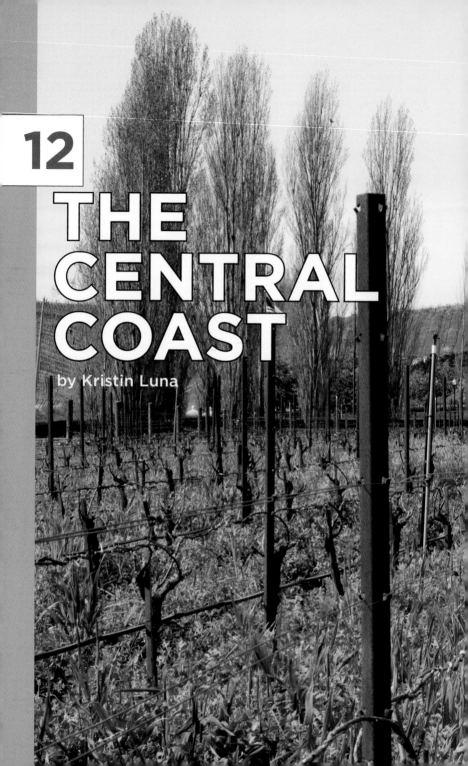

12

THE CENTRAL COAST

by Kristin Luna

C alifornia's Central Coast—an amalgam of beaches, lakes, rolling hills, and mountains—is the state's most diverse region. The narrow strip that runs for more than 100 miles from San Simeon to Ventura spans several climate zones and supports an eclectic mix of college students, middle-class workers, wealthy retirees, winemakers, strawberry farmers, ranchers, immigrant laborers, and fishermen. The ride along Hwy. 1, which follows the ocean cliffs, is almost always packed with rental cars, RVs, and bicycles on summer weekends, but the scenery is so gorgeous nobody seems to mind a little traffic.

The Central Coast is also coming into its own as a major wine region and offers another excuse to visit some of the state's most scenic countryside. Wine snobs might tell you that Central Coast wines cannot compare to those from the northern appellations, where vintages can age to sublime flavor and astronomical price, but if you're in the market for bottles in the $20-to-$30 range that are ready to drink within a couple of years, you'll love what this up-and-coming wine destination has to offer.

Whether you're driving up from Los Angeles or down from San Francisco, Hwy. 1 is the most scenic and leisurely route. (U.S. 101 is faster but less picturesque.) Most bicyclists pedal from north to south, the direction of the prevailing winds. Those in cars may prefer to drive south to north so they can get a better look at the coastline as it unfolds toward the west. No matter which direction you drive, break out the camera—you're about to experience unparalleled beauty, California-style.

SAN SIMEON: HEARST CASTLE ★★★

250 miles S of San Francisco (via Hwy. 1); 250 miles NW of Los Angeles

Few buildings on Earth are as elaborate as **Hearst Castle.** The 165-room estate of publishing magnate William Randolph Hearst, high above the village of San Simeon atop a hill he called La Cuesta Encantada (the Enchanted Hill), is an ego trip par excellence. One of the last great estates of America's Gilded Age, it's an over-the-top monument to wealth—and to the power that money brings.

Hearst Castle is a sprawling compound, constructed over 28 years in a Mediterranean Revival style and never fully completed. The focal point of the estate is **Casa Grande,** a 100-plus-room mansion filled with art and antiques that you have to see to believe. Hearst acquired most of his collection via New York auction houses, where he bought entire rooms (including walls, ceilings,

William Hearst and Marion Davies.

Hearst Castle.

and floors) and shipped them here. The result is an old-world-style castle in a mix-and-match style. You'll see 400-year-old Spanish and Italian ceilings, 500-year-old mantels, 16th-century Florentine bedsteads, Renaissance paintings, Flemish tapestries, and innumerable other treasures.

Three opulent "guesthouses" also contain magnificent works of art. A lavish private movie theater was used to screen first-run films twice nightly—once for employees, and again for the guests and host.

And then there are the swimming pools. The Roman-inspired indoor pool has intricate mosaic work, Carrara-marble replicas of Greek deities, and alabaster globe lamps that create the illusion of moonlight. The breathtaking outdoor Greco-Roman Neptune pool, flanked by marble colonnades that frame the distant sea, is one of the mansion's most memorable—and photographed—features.

In 1957, in exchange for a massive tax write-off, the Hearst Corporation donated the estate to the state of California (while retaining ownership of approximately 80,000 acres). The California Department of Parks and Recreation now administers it as a State Historic Monument and officially refers to it as the rather unpoetic Hearst San Simeon State Historical Monument.

Essentials

GETTING THERE   Hearst Castle is on Hwy. 1, about 42 miles north of San Luis Obispo, 94 miles south of Monterey, 250 miles north of Los Angeles, and 250 miles south of San Francisco. From San Francisco or Monterey, take U.S. 101 south to Paso Robles, then Hwy. 46 west to Hwy. 1, and Hwy. 1 north to the castle. From Los Angeles, take U.S. 101 north to San Luis Obispo, then Hwy. 1 north to the castle. Park in the visitor center lot; a bus takes guided-tour guests up the hill to the estate.

VISITOR INFORMATION   To get information about Hearst Castle, call © **800/ 444-4445,** or log on to **www.hearstcastle.org**. For more information on nearby Cambria (see below), check out **www.cambria-online.com** or visit

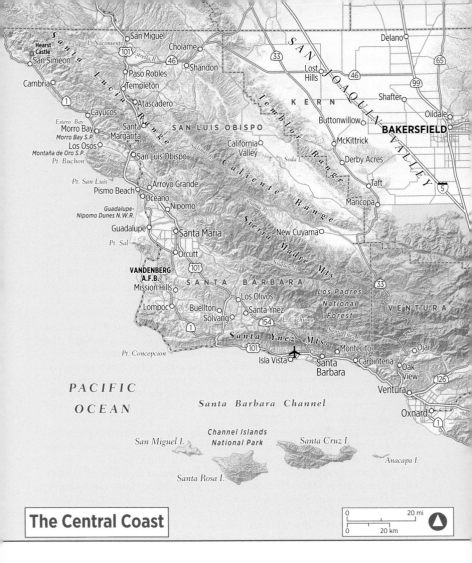

The Central Coast

PACIFIC OCEAN

Santa Barbara Channel

Channel Islands National Park

San Miguel I.

Santa Rosa I.

Santa Cruz I.

Anacapa I.

| 0 | 20 mi |
| 0 | 20 km |

the **Cambria Chamber of Commerce**'s visitor center at 767 Main St., in the west village (*℃* **805/927-3624;** www.cambriachamber.org).

Touring the Estate

Hearst Castle can be visited only by guided tours, conducted daily beginning at 8:20am, except on New Year's Day, Thanksgiving, and Christmas. Two to six tours leave every hour, depending on the season. Allow 2 hours between starting times if you plan on taking more than one tour. You can buy tickets right at the visitor center, but a day's slate of tours can easily sell out. You pay no fee for advance reservations, and you can make them from 1 hour to 8 weeks in advance. Tickets can be purchased from California Reservations (*℃* **800/444-4445;**

www.hearstcastle.org). If you're ordering tickets from outside the United States, call ☎ **916/414-8400,** ext. 4100.

Four different daytime tours run on a daily basis, each lasting 1 hour, 45 minutes, including the 15-minute bus ride to and from the castle. Docents dress in 1930s period costume and assume a variety of roles, enhancing the living-history experience.

I strongly recommend setting aside 2 full days to enjoy the castle at a leisurely pace. If you're just coming to see the castle, 1 day will do, but expect it to be a longish one and sandwich it between a 2-night stay.

Tickets for the daytime tours are $24 for adults and $12 for kids 6 to 17. The Evening Tour is $30 for adults and $15 for kids. Children 5 and under are free, though they may find walking and climbing steps for almost 2 hours a bit overwhelming.

The Experience Tour (Tour 1) is ideal for first-time visitors and is the first to get filled up. In addition to the swimming pools, this tour visits several rooms on the ground floor of Casa Grande, including Hearst's private theater, where you'll see some home movies taken during the castle's heyday. **Tour 2** focuses on Casa Grande's upper floors, including Hearst's opulent library, private suite of rooms, and lots of fabulous bathrooms. **Tour 3,** which delves into the construction and subsequent alterations of Hearst Castle, is fascinating for architecture buffs and detail hounds. From April to October, **Tour 4** is dedicated to the estate's gardens, terraces, and walkways, the Casa del Mar guesthouse, the wine cellar of Casa Grande, and the dressing rooms at the Neptune Pool.

Evening tours are held most Friday and Saturday nights during spring and fall, and usually nightly around Christmas (when the house, decked out for the holidays, is magical). Thirty minutes longer than the daytime tours, they visit highlights of the main house, the most elaborate guesthouse, and the illuminated pools and gardens.

No matter how many tours you take in a day, you must return to the visitor center each time and ride the bus back to the top of the hill with your tour group, so allow at least 2 hours between tours when you buy your tickets.

You can visit the giant-screen **Hearst Castle Theater** regardless of whether you take a tour. Larger-than-life films include the 40-minute *Hearst Castle: Building the Dream* and other films in five-story-high iWERKS format (just like IMAX) with seven-channel surround sound. Shows begin every 45 minutes throughout the day. The movie is included in the price of Tour 1; by itself it's $8 for adults, $6 for kids 6 to 17. For current information, call ☎ **805/927-6811** or visit their website at **www.hearstcastletheater.com**.

Wear comfortable shoes—you'll walk about a half-mile per tour, each of which includes 150 to 400 steps. (Wheelchair tours are available by calling ☎ **800/444-4445,** with 10 days' notice.)

What to See & Do in Nearby Cambria ★

After driving for close to an hour without passing anything but lush green hills (especially from Hwy. 46 off U.S. 101), it's a pleasant surprise to roll into the endearing coastal town of Cambria (pronounced *Cam*-bree-uh), 6 miles south of San Simeon. Not quite Northern California and not quite Southern California, not quite coastal and not quite inland, this charming artists' colony is so appealing that the town itself is reason enough to make the drive. With little more than 4 blocks' worth of shops, restaurants, and a handful of B&Bs, Cambria is the perfect place to escape the everyday, enjoy the endless expanses of pristine coastal terrain, and meander through little shops selling local artwork and antiques.

Cambria has three distinct parts. Along Main Street is "the Village," which is divided into two sections: the **West Village** and the **East Village.** The West Village is the newer, somewhat more touristy end of town, where you'll find the visitor information center. The more historic East Village is a bit quieter, more locals oriented, and a tad more sophisticated than the West Village. If you cross Hwy. 1 to the coastal side at the far west end of town (or the north end, if you're considering how the freeway runs), you'll reach Cambria's third part, **Moonstone Beach.** Lined with motels, inns, and a few restaurants on the inland side of the street, ocean-facing Moonstone Beach Drive is my favorite place to stay in Cambria.

Before you set out, pick up the Cambria Historical Society's brochure at your hotel and take a simple, fun **self-guided tour** of the historical buildings in the East Village. You'll not only get a history lesson about this picturesque village, but also discover a few places you may have overlooked otherwise, such as the **blacksmith shop** at 4121 Burton Dr. or the **Santa Rosa Chapel and Cemetery** at 2353 Main St.

An overnight stay in Cambia also allows visitors to see the coastal region's "new" attraction: a spring (yes, that's the correct term—I looked it up) of elephant seals sunning themselves on the beaches year-round. Once thought to be extinct, since 1990 these 3,000-pound mammals have returned to Piedras Blancas, an **elephant seal rookery** 12 miles north of Cambria. Today more than 2,000 of these magnificent, prehistoric-looking beasts are counted here annually. Breeding takes place here December through March; molting occurs August through September. Keep your distance from the elephant seals: They're a

Moonstone Beach.

Moonstone Beach in Cambria, California.

protected species and can be dangerous if approached. Finding the beach is easy: Just stop at the packed parking lot 4½ miles north of Hearst Castle and follow the crowds along the short, sandy walk. The beaches and coves are also great places for humans to cavort. For more information, see **www.beachcalifornia.com/ piedras.html**.

SHOPPING

Shopping is a major pastime in the village. Boutique owners are hypersavvy about keeping their merchandise current—and priced just a hair lower than in L.A. or San Francisco. This close-knit community has always attracted artists and artisans. For the finest handcrafted glass artworks, from affordable jewelry to investment-scale sculpture, head to **Seekers Collection & Gallery,** 4090 Burton Dr. (✆ **800/ 841-5250;** www.seekersglass.com). Nearby, at **Moonstones Gallery,** 4070 Burton Dr. (✆ **800/424-3827;** www.moonstones.com), you'll find a selection of works ranging from woven crafts to jewelry and an exceptional collection of wood-carvings and other crafts. The shopping highlight of the West Village is **Home Arts,** 727 Main St. (✆ **805/927-2781;** www.home-arts.com), which offers an appealingly eclectic mix of country and contemporary home fashions and gifts. **Fermen-tations,** 4056 Burton Dr. (✆ **800/ 446-7505;** www.fermentations.com), has wines, wine accessories, and gifts, plus Wine Country gourmet goodies open for tasting. **Heart's Ease,** 4101 Burton Dr. (✆ **805/927-5224**), is inside a historic cottage and is packed with an abundance of garden delights, apothecary herbs, and custom-blended potpourris.

If Cambria has aroused your artistic instincts, a few miles south is another tiny artists' colony, called **Harmony.**

Piedras Blancas, and elephant seal rookery 12 miles north of Cambria.

Where to Stay

Cambria's popularity in summertime and on holiday weekends makes advance planning necessary. If my favorites are full, try one of these alternatives: **Captain's Cove Inn,** 6454 Moonstone Beach Dr. (www.captainscoveinn.com; ✆ **800/781-COVE** [2683] or 805/927-8581), is a small beachfront B&B whose motel-style exterior belies the array of creature comforts provided by the family owners. The **Ragged Point Inn,** 19019 Hwy. 1 (www.raggedpointinn.com; ✆ **805/927-4502**), is 21 miles north of Cambria, with ocean views from every room. It's a great choice if you're planning to explore both Hearst Castle and the Big Sur Coast from one perch.

If you want a cheaper choice, try the **Creekside Inn,** 2618 Main St., Cambria (www.creeksidecambria.com; ✆ **800/269-5212** or 805/927-4021). It's basic, but the village location is extremely convenient and the rates are considerably lower—$69 to $159 double, year-round. Still too expensive? One mile north is **San Simeon State Beach** (✆ **800/444-7275** or 805/927-2020), a 133-site beachfront campground.

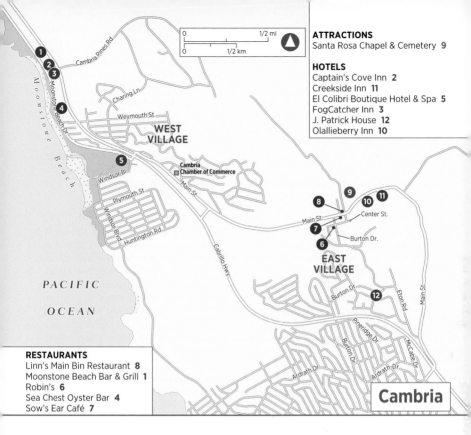

Cambria

Note: If you can't find a vacancy anywhere in Cambria, the tiny town of San Simeon, 6 miles north, has numerous run-of-the-mill motels lining both sides of Hwy. 1, but I recommend staying here only as a last resort.

Best Western Cavalier Oceanfront Resort ★ ☺   Of the dozen or so budget and midrange motels along Hwy. 1 near Hearst Castle, this surprisingly nice chain is the only one that's oceanfront. Sprawled across a slope, the family-owned hotel invites guests to huddle around cliffside bonfires each evening. Every room—whether you choose a basic double or opt for a fireplace, ocean view, wet bar, or oceanfront terrace—features an array of amenities. On-site extras include a whirlpool spa, an exercise room, a restaurant with room service, and a coin-op laundry. The motel welcomes pets, and it's a terrific choice for castle-bound families.

9415 Hearst Dr. (Hwy. 1), San Simeon, CA 93452. www.cavalierresort.com. ✆ **800/826-8168** or 805/927-4688. Fax 805/927-6472. 90 units. $99–$219 double. AE, DC, DISC, MC, V. Pets accepted. **Amenities:** 2 restaurants; exercise room; heated pool; room service; whirlpool spa. *In room:* TV/DVD, fridge, hair dryer, free high-speed Internet, minibar.

El Colibri Boutique Hotel & Spa ★★   El Colibri was a breath of fresh air to a tired lodging scene when it arrived in town in 2010. Steps away from the Moonstone Beach boardwalk, it provides convenient access for a day at the beach. If you strain, you can see the Pacific in the distance from your room, and you'll definitely hear the waves crashing against the shore at night when all is silent. The exterior is Tuscan-inspired, but the rooms' interiors are more modern with granite and marble furnishings. Several have separate stand-alone glass showers, and all boast deep soaking tubs (some with Jacuzzi jets). The fireplace will keep you warm at night as you cozy up under the plush bedding of your sleigh bed. This place is perfect for a serene, relaxing getaway, which is precisely what attracts people to this stretch of the coast in the first place.

5620 Moonstone Beach Dr., Cambria, CA 93428. www.elcolibrihotel.com. (℃) **805/924-3003.** Fax 805/924-3008. 34 units. $169–$216 double; $199–$269 suite. Rates include continental breakfast. AE, DC, DISC, MC, V. **Amenities:** Wine bar; outdoor Jacuzzi; spa. *In room:* A/C, TV, CD player, fridge, hair dryer, minibar in most rooms, free Wi-Fi, fireplace.

FogCatcher Inn ★ You'll spot the FogCatcher by its faux–English Tudor architecture (though it's a contemporary hotel) that fits right in with the mishmash of styles on funky Moonstone Beach. The U-shaped building is situated so many rooms have unencumbered views of the crashing waves across the street; some gaze oceanward over a sea of parked cars, and others are hopelessly landlocked—be sure to inquire when reserving. Rates vary wildly according to view, but each room interior has identical amenities and comforts. Immaculately maintained and furnished in a comfy cottage style with pine furniture, each room is made cozier by a gas fireplace and also has a microwave oven. Unlike many comparably priced Moonstone Beach lodgings, the FogCatcher has a heated swimming pool and Jacuzzi. Stop by the breakfast room in the morning for basic coffee, juice, and muffins to start the day.

6400 Moonstone Beach Dr., Cambria, CA 93428. www.fogcatcherinn.com. (℃) **800/425-4121** or 805/927-1400. Fax 805/927-0204. 60 units. $129–$269 double. Rates include continental breakfast. AE, DISC, MC, V. Pets accepted in select rooms for $25 per night. **Amenities:** Jacuzzi; outdoor heated pool. *In room:* TV, fridge, hair dryer, minibar, free Wi-Fi.

J. Patrick House ★ Hidden in a pine-filled neighborhood overlooking Cambria's village, this B&B is cozy, elegant, and welcoming. The main house is a two-story log cabin, where every afternoon the innkeepers host wine and hors d'oeuvres next to the living room fireplace, and each morning serve breakfast by windows overlooking a hummingbird-filled garden. Most guest rooms are in the adjacent carriage house, and all feature wood-burning fireplaces; feather duvets; bedtime milk and cookies; and knotty pine, bent-twig furniture, calico prints, and hand-stitched quilts. Amenities such as a phone and guest fridge are in the common area.

2990 Burton Dr., Cambria, CA 93428. www.jpatrickhouse.com. (℃) **800/341-5258** or 805/927-3812. Fax 805/927-6759. $139–$205 double. Rates include full breakfast, afternoon wine and hors d'oeuvres, and evening milk and cookies. Seasonal discounts and packages available. DISC, MC, V. *In room:* CD player/radio, hair dryer, no phone.

Olallieberry Inn ★★ This 1873 Greek Revival house is the area's true gem. In the afternoon, the aromas of baked brie and homemade bread (served during the wine hour) waft through the main house, and the staff does everything imaginable to make your stay special. They also have a passion for cooking and gardening, but the decor doesn't fall by the wayside: A countrified berry motif reigns, and the guest rooms are lovingly and individually appointed. Each has its own fireplace and private bathroom, although some are across or down the hall. Accommodations in an adjoining building overlook a creek; each room has a fireplace and private deck. The full breakfast—accompanied by olallieberry jam, of course—is gourmet all the way. Amenities like phone, fax, and guest fridge are available in the common area. The inn is walking distance to fine restaurants and shops.

2476 Main St., Cambria, CA 93428. www.olallieberry.com. (✆ **888/927-3222** or 805/927-3222. Fax 805/927-0202. 9 units. $135–$225 double. Rates include full breakfast and evening wine and hors d'oeuvres. AE, MC, V. **Amenities:** Massage. *In room:* Hair dryer, no phone, Wi-Fi.

Where to Eat

Tiny Cambria boasts an unusual concentration of superb restaurants. In addition to the restaurants listed below, consider **Moonstone Beach Bar & Grill,** 6550 Moonstone Beach Dr. (✆ **805/927-3859;** www.moonstonebeach.com), whose incredible view must be what accounts for prices on the expensive side for this tasty but casual restaurant—stick to breakfast or lunch—or local institution **Linn's Main Bin Restaurant,** 2277 Main St. (✆ **805/927-1499;** www.linns fruitbin.com), a casual all-day farmhouse restaurant/bakery/gift shop featuring homemade potpies, fresh-from-the-farm salads, breakfast treats, and Linn's famous olallieberry fruit pies.

Robin's ★ INTERNATIONAL   Robin's has something for everyone, from exotic dishes from Mexico, Thailand, India, and beyond to more straightforward preparations such as a tasty salad, a juicy steak, and a nightly vegetarian dish, along with tofu and tempeh specials. Offerings include a salmon bisque appetizer; artichoke and Gorgonzola ravioli in a spinach-cream sauce; other combinations such as tandoori prawns with basmati brown rice, fruit chutney, and chapati; and *rogan josh,* Indian lamb curry mixed with yogurt, almonds, and toasted coconut. Don't miss dessert—try the espresso-soaked cake with mascarpone mousse and shaved chocolate or vanilla-custard bread pudding.

4095 Burton Dr., Cambria. (✆ **805/927-5007.** www.robinsrestaurant.com. Reservations recommended. Main courses $8–$15 lunch, $17–$30 dinner. MC, V. Daily 11am–3:50pm; Sun–Thurs 5–9pm; Fri–Sat 5–9:30pm.

Sea Chest Oyster Bar ★ SEAFOOD   Feeling like a dozen other seaside old-salt hangouts, the strangely familiar Sea Chest is a must for seafood lovers. Sporting nautical kitsch and a warm, welcoming atmosphere, this gray clapboard cottage even has a game-filled lounge complete with cribbage, checkers, and chess to keep you amused during the inevitable wait for a table. Oysters are the main attraction: on the half-shell, oyster stew, oysters casino, oysters Rockefeller, or "devils on horseback" (with wine, garlic, and bacon). The menu is also filled with fresh seafood from local and worldwide waters: steamed New Zealand green-lipped mussels, clams in several preparations, halibut, salmon, lobster, scampi, plus whatever looked good off the boats that morning. There's a respectable list of microbrewed and imported beers, along with a selection of Central Coast wines. **Note:** If you don't enjoy seafood, dine elsewhere—there's not even a token steak on this menu, though pasta primavera is an option.

6216 Moonstone Beach Dr. (✆ **805/927-4514.** www.seachestrestaurant.com. Reservations not accepted. Main courses $13–$48. No credit cards. Daily 5:30–9pm (closed Tues Sept–May).

Sow's Ear Café ★★ AMERICAN/SEAFOOD   Despite the porcine moniker, this tiny old cottage at the center of the village is a rather warm and romantic hideaway. The best tables are in the fireside front room, lit just enough to highlight its rustic wood-and-brick decor. Pigs appear everywhere, in oil paintings and as ceramic or cast-iron models, and the logo is a woodcut sow. Though the menu features plenty of contemporary California cuisine, the most popular dishes are American favorites given a contemporary lift; these include a warmly satisfying chicken-fried steak with gravy, chicken and dumplings, and zesty baby pork ribs. Other standouts are parchment-wrapped salmon, and pork loin glazed with chunky olallieberry chutney. Every meal begins with the restaurant's signature marbled bread baked in terra-cotta flowerpots, and the wine list is among the area's best. *Tip:* Early birds (5–6pm nightly) choose from eight dinners priced from $13 to $20.

2248 Main St. © **805/927-4865.** www.thesowsear.com. Reservations recommended. Main courses $11–$29. DISC, MC, V. Daily 5–9pm (later in summer).

MORRO BAY

124 miles S of Monterey; 235 miles S of San Francisco (via Hwy. 1); 220 miles N of L.A.

Morro Bay is separated from the ocean by a long peninsula of towering sand dunes. It's best known for dramatic **Morro Rock,** an enormous egg-shaped monolith that juts 576 feet above the water at the entrance to Morro Bay. Across from the rock, a huge oceanfront electrical plant mars the visual appeal of the otherwise pristine bay, which is filled with birds, sea mammals, and calm water offering plenty of recreational activities such as fishing, surfing, kayaking, bird-watching (Morro Rock is a protected falcon sanctuary), and beachcombing.

Besides the "Gibraltar of the Pacific," the town itself doesn't offer all that much to see. Tourist-trade motels, shops, and seafood restaurants line the water-front Embarcadero and adjacent blocks, but the town's best feature is its setting: The beaches, bay, and wildlife sanctuaries are the main reason to visit.

Essentials

Morro Bay is on U.S. 101 (itself only four lanes on this stretch). The **Morro Bay Visitors Center & Chamber of Commerce,** 845 Embarcadero Rd., Morro Bay, CA 93442 (© **800/231-0592** or 805/772-4467; www.morrobay.org), offers lots of information on their website. The visitor center is open Monday through Friday from 9am to 5pm, Saturday from 10am to 4pm. For additional online information, log on to **www.morrobay.com**.

Exploring the Area

Most visitors come to Morro Bay to ogle **Morro Rock,** the much-photographed Central Coast icon that anchors the mouth of the waterway. This ancient land-mark, whose name comes from the Spanish word for a Moorish turban, is a vol-canic remnant inhabited by the peregrine falcon and other migratory birds.

BEACHES Popular **Atascadero State Beach,** just north of Morro Rock, has gentle waves and pretty views. Restrooms, showers, and dressing rooms are available. Just north of Atascadero is **Morro Strand State Beach,** a long, sandy stretch with normally gentle surf. Restrooms and picnic tables are available. Morro Strand has its own campgrounds; for information, call © **805/772-2560,** or reserve through **ReserveAmerica** (© **800/444-7275;** www.reserveamerica.com).

IN TOWN The Embarcadero is also home to the **Giant Chessboard,** whose 3-foot-tall, 18- to 20-pound redwood pieces were inspired by open-air

Morro Bay.

boards in Germany. If you're up for a game, contact the recreation and parks department for reservations at ℂ **805/772-6278.** Nearby is the **Morro Bay Aquarium,** 595 Embarcadero (ℂ **805/772-7647**), a modest operation notable for the injured or abandoned sea otters, seals, and sea lions it rescues and rehabilitates. Admission is $2 for adults, $1 for children 5 to 11.

ON THE WATER   You can rent sea kayaks or take a guided kayak tour around the bay with **Kayak Horizons of Morro Bay,** 551 Embarcadero (ℂ **805/772-6444;** www.kayakhorizons.com). Rentals start at $9 per hour and tours cost $55.

STATE PARKS   Cabrillo Peak, in the **Morro Bay State Park** (ℂ **805/772-2560**), makes a terrific day hike and offers 360-degree views from its summit. There's a zigzagging trail, but the best way to reach the top is by bushwhacking straight up the gentle slope—a hike that takes about 2 hours round-trip. To reach the trail head, take Hwy. 1 south and turn left at the Morro Bay State Park/Montana de Oro State Park exit. Follow South Bay Boulevard for ¾ mile, and then take the left fork another half-mile to the Cabrillo Peak dirt parking lot on your left. The park also offers camping and the oceanside **Morro Bay Golf Course** (also known as Poor Man's Pebble Beach), which charges only $51 for weekend greens fees (ℂ **805/782-8060;** www.centralcoastgolf.com).

South of Morro Bay in Los Osos is **Montana de Oro State Park** ("Mountain of Gold"), known as "petite Big Sur" because of its stony cliffs and rugged terrain. There's great swimming at Spooner's Cove and lots of easy hiking trails, including some that lead to coastal vistas or forest streams. The Hazard Reef Trail will take you up on the Morro Bay Sandspit dunes. The park's campground is in the trees, across from the beach, and is worth the detour, if you have a reservation in summer. For information or to reserve a spot, contact **ReserveAmerica** (ℂ **800/444-7275;** www.reserveamerica.com).

Where to Stay

Baywood Bed & Breakfast Inn 🎁   South of Morro Bay in Baywood Park, facing out onto Morro's "back bay," this two-story gray inn is a 1970s garden-style office building that's been converted into an all-suite B&B, with each suite furnished in a distinctive (and perhaps a bit over-the-top, in some cases) theme. Every room has a private outside entrance, gas fireplace, and microwave (plus a fridge stocked with complimentary sodas and snacks); all but a few have bay views. Included in your stay is a full breakfast each morning and a late-afternoon wine-and-cheese reception highlighted by a room tour. If you're looking for solitude, Baywood Park fits the bill, but I would visit their website before booking to find a room decor that suits you. A couple of decent restaurants are on the block, and pretty Montana de Oro is close by.

1370 Second St. (2½ blocks south of Santa Ysabel Ave.), Baywood Park, CA 93042. www.baywoodinn.com. ✆ **805/528-8888.** Fax 805/528-8887. 18 units. $80–$200 double; $300–$400 Bayfront Home. Extra person $15. Rates include full breakfast and afternoon wine and cheese. MC, V. *In room:* TV/VCR, hair dryer, kitchenette, minibar.

Cass House Inn and Restaurant   Just 6 miles north of Morro Bay in the charming beach town of Cayucos, this historic inn features five well-appointed guest rooms, each with a unique palette. Built in 1867 and restored in 2007, the design exudes Victorian elegance without feeling too stuffy or overly cluttered. Colors such as sea foam, butter, and bright teal pay homage to the inn's 19th-century beginnings, and each room has its own selling point. Opt for the Captain's Room, with its large cast-iron soaking tub or the Ocean Terrace Room featuring a private outside terrace with views of the ocean and the garden below. Don't miss the full gourmet breakfast included with your stay. And if you can, splurge on dinner at the Cass House restaurant, which features a seasonally driven, locally sourced prix-fixe menu of four courses for $62. Be sure to make a reservation, as the intimate 34-seat dining room fills quickly.

222 N. Ocean Ave., Cayucos, CA. www.casshouseinn.com. ✆ **805/995-3669.** 5 guest rooms. $165–$225 double; $275–$325 suite. Discounts available. AE, DISC, MC, V. Free self-parking. **Amenities:** Restaurant. *In room:* TV/DVD, free Wi-Fi, fireplaces and/or terraces in some rooms.

The Inn at Morro Bay   This comfortable, moderately priced resort is smart enough to let its natural surroundings be the focus. Right on the water, the inn's two-story Cape Cod–style buildings have contemporary interiors amid a quiet garden setting. Rates vary according to view; the best rooms have unobstructed views of Morro Rock; additional upgrades include private balcony Jacuzzis and bayfront sun decks. Those in back face the swimming pool, gardens, and eucalyptus-forested golf course at Morro Bay State Park (see above). The hotel has a bayside lounge and California/Mediterranean restaurant, and a full-service spa. Beach cruiser bicycles are lent out free to guests, and even the range balls are complimentary.

60 State Park Rd., Morro Bay, CA 93442. www.innatmorrobay.com. ✆ **800/321-9566** or 805/772-5651. Fax 805/772-4779. 98 units. $189–$339 double; from $449 cottage. Midweek and seasonal discounts available. AE, DISC, MC, V. Take Main St. south, past park entrance. **Amenities:** 2 restaurants; lounge; complimentary bikes; nearby golf and water recreation; outdoor heated pool; room service; full-service spa. *In room:* TV, CD player, fridge, hair dryer, high-speed Internet.

Where to Eat

Hofbrau ☺ 🍴 GERMAN/AMERICAN   *Jawohl!* When you're hungry in Morro Bay and want something other than fish and chips, Hofbrau is the place. Although they do serve the standard wharfside fare, the star here is the roast-beef French dip (their strategically placed carving station ensures its popularity). Those in the know order the minisandwich, which is a dollar less and just an inch shorter. As the name would suggest, they have a good selection of beers, as well as a kids' menu.

901 Embarcadero, Morro Bay. ℂ **805/772-2411.** www.hofbraumorrobay.com. Reservations not accepted. Most items $5–$11. AE, DISC, MC, V. Daily 11am–9pm.

Windows on the Water ★ CALIFORNIAN   If you're looking for a special meal in town, your best bet is this seaside restaurant that takes full advantage of prime waterfront views with its airy, high-ceilinged, multilevel space. The cuisine emanating from the open kitchen is a California/French/Mediterranean hybrid that incorporates local fresh seafood and produce. On a given evening, the menu might include maple-leaf duck breast, shellfish braised in champagne and tossed with house-made fettuccine, or Jamaican jerk shrimp served with coconut lime rice. The first-rate wine list includes choice Central Coast vintages and select French bottles. *Tip:* Tuesday is oyster night: Fresh, fried, or "shootered," they're 65¢ each all evening.

699 Embarcadero (in Marina Sq.), Morro Bay. ℂ **805/772-0677.** www.windowsonthewater.net. Reservations recommended. Main courses $11–$35. AE, DC, DISC, MC, V. Daily 5–8:30pm.

SAN LUIS OBISPO ★

38 miles S of Cambria; 226 miles S of San Francisco; 198 miles N of L.A.

Because the town of San Luis Obispo is not visible from U.S. 101, even many Californians don't know that it's more than another fast-food-and-gasoline stopover on the highway. But its "secret" location is part of what helps this relaxed yet vital college town keep its charm and character intact—it has much of the appeal that defined Santa Barbara a few decades ago.

Sometimes referred to as "little Santa Barbara," San Luis Obispo (SLO to locals) is tucked into the mountains halfway between San Francisco and Los Angeles. It's surrounded by green, pristine mountain ranges and filled with a mix of college kids attending California Polytechnic University (Cal Poly, for short), big-city transplants, and agricultural folk.

The town grew up around an 18th-century mission, and its dozens of historic landmarks, Victorian homes, shops, and restaurants are its primary attractions for visitors. Today it's still quaint, almost undiscovered, and best ventured around on foot. It also makes a good base for exploration of the region as a whole. To the west of town, a short drive away, are some of the state's prettiest swimming beaches; to the north and south you'll find the Central Coast's wine country.

Essentials

GETTING THERE   U.S. 101, one of the state's primary north-south roadways, runs through San Luis Obispo; it's the fastest land route here from anywhere. If you're driving down along the coast, Hwy. 1 is the way to go for its natural beauty and oceanfront cliffs. If you're entering the city from the east, take Hwy. 46 or Hwy. 41 to U.S. 101, and then go south. **Amtrak** (✆ **800/USA-RAIL** [872-7245]; www.amtrak.com) offers daily service into SLO from Oakland and Los Angeles.

VISITOR INFORMATION   At the **San Luis Obispo Visitors Center,** 1039 Chorro St. (✆ **805/781-2777;** www.visitslo.com), downtown between Monterey and Higuera streets, you can pick up the colorful, comprehensive *Visitors Guide* and self-guided *Points of Interest Walking Tour.* It's open Sunday to Wednesday from 10am to 5pm, Thursday to Saturday from 10am to 7pm.

ORIENTATION   San Luis Obispo is about 10 miles inland, at the junction of Hwy. 1 and U.S. 101. The downtown is laid out in a grid, roughly centered on the historic mission and its Mission Plaza (see below). Most of the main tourist sights are around the mission, within the small triangle created by U.S. 101 and Santa Rosa and Marsh streets.

Exploring the Town

Before heading downtown, make a pit stop at the perpetually pink **Madonna Inn,** 100 Madonna Rd., off U.S. 101 (✆ **805/543-3000;** p. 497), if for no other reason than to use its unique public restrooms (the men's has a waterfall urinal; the women's is a barrage of crimson and pink). Every inch of this place is an exercise in excess, from the dining room, complete with pink leather booths, pink table linens, and colored sugar that's—you guessed it—piquantly pink, to the rock-walled, cavelike guest rooms. And if you think it's as gaudy as it gets, you should see it around Christmastime.

Once downtown, you can ride the free trolley that repeats a loop through downtown every 15 minutes daily from noon to 5pm. (Stops are well marked.)

Madonna Inn.

San Luis Obispo

Farmers Market ★   If you're in town on a Thursday, be sure to take an evening stroll down Higuera Street, when the county's largest weekly street fair fills 4 downtown city blocks. You'll find much more here than fresh-picked produce—there's an ever-changing array of street entertainment, open-pit barbecues, food stands, and market stalls selling flowers, cider, and other seasonal farm-fresh items. Surrounding stores typically stay open until 9pm.

Higuera St. (btw. Osos and Nipomo sts.). ✆ **805/781-2777.** Thurs 6–9pm (weather permitting).

Mission San Luis Obispo de Tolosa   Founded by Father Junípero Serra in 1772, California's fifth mission was built with adobe bricks by Native American Chumash people. Serra chose this valley for the site of his fifth mission based on tales of friendly natives and bountiful food. The traditional red-tile roof was first used atop a California mission, after the original thatched tule roofs repeatedly fell to hostile Native Americans' burning arrows. The fifth mission remains one of the prettiest, most interesting structures in the Franciscan chain. The former padres' quarters are now an excellent museum chronicling both Native Americans and missionaries. Allow about 30 to 45 minutes to tour the mission and its grounds.

Mission Plaza, a garden with brick paths and park benches fronting a creek in which children love to wade, still functions as San Luis Obispo's town square. It's the focal point for local festivities and activities, from live concerts to poetry readings and dance and theater productions. Check at the visitor center (see "Essentials," above) to find out what's on when you're in town.

At the south end of Mission Plaza, the **San Luis Obispo Art Center**'s (*C* **805/543-8562;** www.sloartcenter.org) galleries display and sell an array of California-made art. Admission is free; hours are 11am to 5pm Wednesday through Monday (daily July–Aug).

751 Palm St. www.missionsanluisobispo.org. *C* **805/781-8220.** Free admission ($2 donation requested). Daily 9am–5pm.

Attractions Outside Town

Dozens of **wineries** offer tastings and tours daily and make for a fun diversion. See "The Central Coast Wine Country," later in this chapter, for further details. If you don't have time to tour the wineries or would like more information before heading out to taste, you can visit **Central Coast Wines,** 712 Higuera St. in downtown SLO (*C* **805/784-9463;** www.ccwines.com), a wine shop specializing in Central Coast wines, and offering daily wine tastings and weekly winemaker pourings.

Where to Stay

In addition to what's listed below, there's a pristine branch of **Holiday Inn Express** (*C* **877/863-4780** or 805/544-8600) and a reliable **Motel 6** (*C* **800/4-MOTEL-6** [466-8356] or 805/549-9595).

Apple Farm Inn ★★   This popular Victorian-style farmhouse offers a peaceful getaway in a Disney-plantation kind of way. Every square inch of the immaculate inn is adorable, with fresh flowers and sugar-sweet colorful touches. No two rooms are alike, although each has a gas fireplace, pine antiques, lavish country decor, and either a canopy four-poster or a brass bed. Some bedrooms open onto cozy turreted sitting areas with romantic window seats; others have bay windows and a view of San Luis Creek, where a mill spins its huge wheel to power an apple press. Other features include complimentary cribs and train and airport shuttle service, as well as a full-service spa. The hotel shares a name with their on-site restaurant, one of Hwy. 101's best-loved pit stops.

Budget travelers can opt for the adjoining motel-style **Apple Farm Trellis Court;** rooms are smaller, but rates start at $79 and include continental breakfast.

2015 Monterey St., San Luis Obispo, CA 93401. www.applefarm.com. *C* **800/255-2040** or 805/544-2040. Fax 805/546-9495. 104 units. $89–$279 double; $279–$409 suite. Rates include complimentary morning coffee/tea and afternoon wine. AE, DISC, MC, V. **Amenities:** Restaurant; Jacuzzi; outdoor heated pool; room service; spa. *In room:* A/C, TV w/pay movies, hair dryer, free high-speed Internet.

Garden Street Inn ★   SLO's prettiest (and most-polished) bed-and-breakfast is this gracious Italianate/Queen Anne downtown. Built in 1887 and restored in 1990, the house is a monument to gentility and good taste. Each bedroom and suite is decorated with well-chosen antique armoires, fabric or paper wallcoverings, and vintage memorabilia, and all have private bathrooms. Choose one with a claw-foot tub, fireplace, whirlpool tub, or private deck—whatever suits your fancy. Breakfast is served in the stained-glass morning room, and each evening wine and cheese are laid out for guests. The well-stocked Goldtree Library is always available.

1212 Garden St. (btw. Marsh and Pacific), San Luis Obispo, CA 93401. www.gardenstreetinn.com. ② **800/488-2045** or 805/545-9802. Fax 805/545-9403. 13 units. $149–$215 double. Rates include full breakfast and evening wine and cheese. AE, MC, V. *In room:* A/C.

Madonna Inn ★ ◨ This one you've got to see for yourself. The creative imaginations of the owners gave birth to the wildest fantasy world this side of Graceland. For more than 50 years, the only consistency throughout the hotel has been its color scheme: perpetual pink. Beyond that, the decor is a whimsical free-for-all. The "Rock Rooms," with zebra- or tiger-patterned bedspreads and cascading waterfall showers, conjure up thoughts of a Flintstones *Playboy* palace. There are also blue rooms, red rooms, and over-the-top Spanish, Italian, Irish, Alps, Currier and Ives, Native American, Swiss, and hunting rooms. One guest room even features a trapezoidal bed—it's 5 feet long on one side and 6 feet long on the other. The Silver Bar cocktail lounge and Gold Rush Steak House are also outlandishly ornate. Even if you don't stay here, stop by for a liquid refresher and check it out, particularly around Christmastime.

100 Madonna Rd. (off U.S. 101), San Luis Obispo, CA 93405. www.madonnainn.com. ② **800/543-9666** or 805/543-3000. Fax 805/543-1800. 108 units. $179–$269 double; $299–$499 suite. AE, DISC, MC, V. **Amenities:** 2 restaurants; coffee shop; lounge; pool; full spa. *In room:* A/C, flatscreen TV, fridge in most rooms, hair dryer.

Petit Soleil Bed et Breakfast ★ 🎁 Owners John and Dianne Conner have taken what was once an ordinary motor inn and—in the French country spirit of their other *BetB* in France—converted it into a wonderful little B&B, complete with a sunny cobblestone courtyard with cafe-style umbrellas and warm colors of Provence. Each guest room has quirky additions such as painted cupboards or a windowside reading nook; all have private bathrooms and phones for free local calls. Breakfast is served in a dining area that faces the street (coffee lovers will delight in the strong, locally roasted blend), and the hot offerings such as quiche or caramel-apple French toast are a treat. Every evening from 5 to 6:30pm there's a tasting of local and French wines paired with appetizers. You'll like the location as well—just a short walk or bike ride from downtown San Luis Obispo.

1473 Monterey St., San Luis Obispo, CA 93401. www.petitsoleilslo.com. ② **800/676-1588** or 805/549-0321. Fax 805/549-0383. 15 units. $159–$219 double; from $239 suite. Extra person $10. Rates include breakfast. AE, DISC, MC, V. **Amenities:** Complimentary bikes. *In room:* TV, CD player, Wi-Fi.

Where to Eat

Big Sky Cafe ★ AMERICAN The folk-artsy fervor of San Luis shines at this Southwestern mirage, where local art and a blue, star-studded ceiling surround diners who come for fresh, healthy food. The menu is self-classified "modern food," a category that here means a dizzying international selection including Caribbean shrimp tacos with chipotle-lime yogurt, Thai shrimp salad with mint, chilled sesame-ginger noodles, and breakfast's red-flannel turkey hash—a beet-fortified ragout topped with basil-Parmesan-glazed eggs. Big Sky's owner also runs L.A.'s funky Gumbo Pot, whose Cajun-Creole influences spice up the menu at every turn. In fact, this might be the only Central Coast outlet for decent jambalaya, gumbo, or authentically airy beignets.

1121 Broad St. ℂ **805/545-5401.** www.bigskycafe.com. Main courses $9–$19; lunch $8–$14; breakfast $5–$10. AE, MC, V. Mon–Wed 7am–9pm; Thurs–Fri 7am–10pm; Sat 8am–10pm; Sun 8am–9pm.

Buona Tavola ★★ NORTHERN ITALIAN   Most choices in town are burger-and-sandwich casual, but Buona Tavola offers well-prepared Italian food in a more upscale setting. You can stroll in wearing jeans, but the dining room, with checkerboard floors and original artwork, is warmer and more intimate than other spots in town. On the backyard terrace, you can enjoy your meal surrounded by magnolias, ficus, and grapevines. The menu boasts a number of salads on the antipasti list. Favorite pastas include *agnolotti de scampi allo zafferano,* house-made pockets filled with shrimp scampi and served in a cream-saffron sauce; *linguini fra diavolo* served with Manila clams, mussels, and river shrimp in a spicy tomato sauce; and the classic *timballo di Parma,* a vegetarian delight baked with two cheeses.

1037 Monterey St. ℂ **805/545-8000.** www.btslo.com. Reservations recommended. Main courses $9–$32. AE, DISC, MC, V. Mon–Fri 11:30am–2:30pm; Sun–Thurs 5:30–9:30pm; Fri–Sat 5:30–10pm.

Mondéo Pronto ☺ ✦ INTERNATIONAL   Mondéo Pronto pays particular attention to the presentation and freshness of their affordable wraps, which come with a variety of innovative international fillings. Choices range from American versions like the macadamia swordfish (grilled with macadamia butter, served with jasmine rice) to such Mediterranean selections as the Sicilian, with grilled portobello mushrooms, herb polenta, veggies, goat cheese, olives, capers, and sun-dried tomato pesto. "Fusion bowls" are satisfying, with such combinations as basil scampi, a shrimp dish over bowtie pasta with pesto, marinara, pine nuts, and herbs. Everything on the kids' menu is under $4, and as the menu states, "Substitutions and sides are no problem."

893 Higuera St. (in the plaza). ℂ **805/544-2956.** Most items $5–$9. MC, V. Sun–Wed 11am–9pm; Thurs–Sat 11am–10pm.

Mo's Smokehouse BBQ ★ BARBECUE   Just about everyone in SLO is a devotee of this place, whose reputation and great barbecue belie its humble ambience. It's not fancy, but you name it, they've got it—pork or baby back ribs, barbecued beef, and chicken in either a mild or hot sauce, accompanied by baked beans, bread, potato salad, or coleslaw. Practically everything on the menu is under $10.

1005 Monterey St. ℂ **805/544-6193.** www.mosbbq.com. Entrees $6–$20. AE, MC, V. Sun–Wed 11am–9pm; Thurs–Sat 11am–10pm.

PISMO BEACH

13 miles S of San Luis Obispo

Just outside San Luis Obispo, on Pismo's 23-mile stretch of prime beachfront, flip-flops are the shoes of choice and surf wear is the dominant fashion. It's all about beach life here, so bring your bathing suit, your board, and a good book.

If building sand castles or tanning isn't your idea of fun, you can explore isolated dunes, cliff-sheltered tide pools, and old pirate coves. Bring your dog (Fido's welcome here) and play an endless game of fetch. Or go fishing—it's permitted from Pismo Beach Pier, which also offers arcade entertainment, bowling, and billiards. Pismo is also the only beach in the area that allows all-terrain vehicles on the dunes.

Dune buggy, Pismo Beach.

Because the town itself consists of little more than tourist shops and surf-and-turf restaurants, nearby San Luis Obispo is a far more charming place to stay. But if all you want are a few lazy days on a beautiful beach at half the price of an oceanfront room in Santa Barbara, Pismo is the perfect choice.

Essentials

Pismo Beach Chamber of Commerce and Visitors Bureau, 581 Dolliver St., Pismo Beach, CA 93449 (✆ **800/443-7778** or 805/773-4382; www.pismo chamber.com), offers free brochures and information on local attractions, lodging, and dining. The office is open Monday through Saturday from 9am to 5pm and Sunday from 10am to 4pm. You can peruse their tourist information online at **www.classiccalifornia.com**.

What to See & Do

Beaches in Pismo are exceptionally wide, making them some of the best in the state for sunning and playing. The beach north of Grand Avenue is popular with families and joggers. North of Wadsworth Street, the coast becomes dramatically rugged as it rambles northward to Shell Beach and Pirates Cove.

Pismo Beach was once one of the most famous places in America for **clamming,** but the famed "Pismo clam" reached near-extinction in the mid-1980s due to overharvesting. If you'd like to dig for bivalves, you'll need to obtain a license and follow strict guidelines. Or come for the annual **Clam Festival:** Held at the pier each October since 1946, the celebration features a chowder cook-off, sand-sculpture contest, and Miss Pismo Beach pageant.

If **fishing** is more your style, you'll be pleased to know that no license is required to fish from Pismo Beach Pier. Catches here are largely bottom fish such as red snapper and lingcod. There's a bait-and-tackle shop on the pier.

Pacific Dunes Riding Stables, 1205 Silver Spur Place (✆ **805/489-8100;** www.pacificdunesridingstables.com), in Oceano (5 min. south of Pismo Beach), runs guided hour-long horseback rides along the beach and dunes for $40.

From late November to February, thousands of migrating **monarch butterflies** take up residence in the area's eucalyptus and Monterey-pine-tree groves. The butterflies form dense clusters on the trees, each hanging with its wings over the one below it, providing warmth and shelter for the entire group. During the monarchs' stay, naturalists at Pismo State Beach conduct 45-minute narrated walks every Saturday and Sunday at 11am and 2pm (call ✆ **805/773-4382** for tour information). The Butterfly Grove is on Hwy. 1, between Pismo Beach and Grover Beach, to the south.

12

THE CENTRAL COAST | Pismo Beach

Horseback riding on Pismo Beach.

Where to Stay

Avila la Fonda ★★   The überchic lobby of this shoddy beach town's fanciest hotel invites the question, "What's a trendy boutique like *this* doing in a town like *that?*" Re-creating a 19th-century Mexican village, the rooms' red-and-orange color scheme and terra-cotta–tiled floors are quite impressive. Each has a Jacuzzi for two in the bedroom, as well as a fireplace, plasma TV, and basket of complimentary snacks. A 24-hour hospitality room offers complimentary drinks and fresh-baked cookies, and everything in the kitchen pantry is free for the taking— just keep track of what you eat and drink, as it all operates on the honor system. If you feel like spending the night in, make use of the outdoor lanai with a barbecue kitchen, fireplace, and wet bar. If you want to walk the block to the public beach, grab a beach towel and cushy chair from the hotel to take with you.

101 San Miguel St., Avila Beach, CA 93424 (5 miles north of Pismo Beach). www.avilalafonda.com. ⓒ **805/595-1700.** Fax 805/627-1862. 30 units. $199–$549 double. AE, MC, V. Rates include nightly wine and hors d'oeuvres reception. **Amenities:** 24-hr. concierge; spa. *In room:* TV/DVD (CD, DVD, and book library), CD player, fridge, hair dryer, MP3 docking station, free Wi-Fi.

Dolphin Bay Resort & Spa ★★   An affordable luxury resort just on the outskirts of Pismo Beach? Considering its competitors, Dolphin Bay far exceeds expectations in both accommodation and communal spaces. Sleep oceanfront in a one- or two-bedroom suite—yes, all are *suites,* not mere rooms—ranging from 900 to 2,000 square feet in size. Some suites have fireplaces and Aire Jet tubs; all have private patios or terraces, not to mention brand-new, fully equipped kitchens with stainless-steel appliances. The infinity pool is pleasant, and beach access is via a staircase. The Lido Restaurant serves gourmet fare but is a bit overpriced for the area. Dolphin Bay is both family- and pet-friendly, but there's an adults-only building for those who want a little romance or simply some peace and quiet.

2727 Shell Beach Rd., Shell Beach, CA 93449. www.thedolphinbay.com. ⓒ **800/516-0112** or 805/773-4300. Fax 805/773-5200. 63 units. $325–$650 suite. AE, DC, DISC, MC, V. Take U.S. 101 to the Shell Beach Rd. exit, and turn right at Spyglass Rd. **Amenities:** Restaurant; bar; fitness center; Jacuzzi; outdoor heated pool; spa. *In room:* TV/DVD (DVDs available at front desk), hair dryer, minibar, free Wi-Fi.

The California coast was once rich in dramatic, windswept sand dunes; sheltered valleys of wildflowers and willows; and lakes full of pond turtles, red-legged frogs, muskrats, and nesting birds. San Francisco's dunes are now covered in part by Golden Gate Park, while Los Angeles's dunes were leveled to create beach towns and the airport. But travelers cruising the central coast have the chance to visit what's now a rare sight at the **Guadalupe-Nipomo Dunes Preserve** just north of the tiny agricultural hamlet of Guadalupe, about 20 minutes south of Pismo.

The preserve comprises 18 miles of the largest, most biodiverse coastal dune-lagoon ecosystem on the planet. They have been the subject of photographers such as Ansel Adams and Brett Weston; home to the Dunites, a utopian group of artists founded in 1931; and the setting for Cecil B. De Mille's spectacular 1923 film, *The Ten Commandments*. Designated by the Nature Conservancy as number one in its "Last Great Places on Earth" campaign, these dunes are now permanently protected for wildlife and passive recreation.

The **Dunes Center interpretative facility** (1055 Guadalupe St., Hwy. 1, Guadalupe; © **805/343-2455**; www.dunescenter.org), in a restored 1910 Craftsman-style home, is open Wednesdays through Sundays from 10am to 4pm, and a schedule of guided walks is available on the website.

The Dunes are accessible at the southern end by driving on West Main Street (Hwy. 166) to a parking lot just below Mussel Rock Dunes, the highest coastal dunes in the world. The middle of the dunes is accessible off Hwy. 1, 3 miles north of Guadalupe. Turn west onto Oso Flaco Lake Road, pay a small parking fee, and walk along a rare riparian corridor to a bridge that crosses Oso Flaco Lake. A 1-mile boardwalk leads you to the ocean through one of the best examples of coastal dune scrub in the country.

Kon Tiki Inn ✦ The over-the-top Polynesian architecture of this three-story gem is easy to spot from the freeway and evokes memories of 1960s Waikiki hotels. Rooms are modest, small, and simply furnished with unremarkable faux-bamboo furniture, yet each has an oceanfront balcony or patio. Outside, vast lawns slope gently toward the cliffs, broken only by the shielded, kidney-shaped swimming pool flanked by twin Jacuzzis. This humble hotel—which is privately owned and does no advertising—has a sandy beach with stairway access and lacks the highway noise that plagues many neighbors.

1621 Price St., Pismo Beach, CA 93449. www.kontikiinn.com. © **888/566-8454** or 805/773-4833. Fax 805/773-6541. 86 units. In season $150–$180 double; off season $126–$146 double. Extra person $20. Rates include continental breakfast. AE, DISC, MC, V. **Amenities:** Restaurant; free access to adjacent health club; 2 Jacuzzis; outdoor heated pool. *In room:* TV w/movie channels, fridge, Wi-Fi.

The Sea Venture Resort ★   If luxury accommodations overlooking the beach and an outdoor spa on your private deck sound like heaven, head for Sea Venture. Once in your room, you need only drag your tired feet through the thick forest-green carpeting and past the white country furnishings and feather bed, and turn on your gas fireplace to begin a relaxing stay. Rent a movie from the video library, schedule a massage, or bathe your weary bones in your own outdoor hydrother-apy spa tub. With the beach right outside your door, there's not much more you could ask for—although there is, in fact, more provided: plush robes, a wet bar, continental breakfast delivered to your room, and a restaurant on the premises with a tapas bar and Sunday brunch. Most rooms have ocean views and many have a private balcony overlooking the beach. *Tip:* Check online for specials and packages.

100 Ocean View Ave., Pismo Beach, CA 93449. www.seaventure.com. ℂ **800/760-0664** or 805/773-4994. Fax 805/773-0924. 50 units. $159–$449 double. Rates include continental bre-akfast. AE, DC, DISC, MC, V. Take U.S. 101 to the Price St. exit and turn west onto Ocean View (at the beach). **Amenities:** Restaurant; complimentary bikes; outdoor heated pool; room service. *In room:* TV/VCR, hair dryer, minibar.

Where to Eat

If you like steak and ribs served in an Old West setting, you'll love Pismo's **F. McLintocks Saloon & Dining House,** on the east side of Hwy. 101 at 750 Mattie Rd. (ℂ **800/866-6372** or 805/773-1892; www.mclintocks.com). For diners who prefer clams over *carne,* the same outfit also runs the popular **Steamers of Pismo** restaurant, at 1601 Price St. atop the bluffs of Pismo Beach (ℂ **805/773-4711**).

Giuseppe's Cucina Italiana ★ SOUTHERN ITALIAN   This is the region's best southern Italian restaurant—would you believe owner Giuseppe Difronzo started it as his senior project at Cal Poly University? It's true, and Difronzo's love of cuisine from the Pugliese region (an Adriatic seaport) continues to bring diners a taste of the Italian countryside. Along with the homemade bread baked in a wood-burning oven imported from Italy, Giuseppe's fare uses authentic recipes, imported ingredients, and organically grown produce; the large menu of anti-pasti, salads, pizzas, pastas, fish, and steak makes it easy to find something you like. Highlights of the meal include linguine with shrimp, scallops, pancetta, and garlic in a vodka cream sauce; and seared *ahi* (tuna) with a peppercorn crust and garlic-caper aioli.

891 Price St. ℂ **805/773-2870.** http://giuseppesrestaurant.com. Reservations not accepted. Main courses $8–$20 lunch, $11–$30 dinner. AE, DISC, MC, V. Daily 11:30am–3pm and 4:30–10pm.

Splash Cafe AMERICAN   This beachy burger stand, with a short menu and a few tables, gets high marks for its award-winning clam chowder in a sourdough bread bowl—more than 10,000 gallons a year are served. Fish and chips, burgers, hot dogs, and grilled ahi sandwiches are also available. Far-flung aficionados know that Splash ships its chowder frozen, overnight, anywhere in the U.S. (sourdough loaves too). There's often a line, but it usually moves quickly.

197 Pomeroy St. (near Pismo Beach Pier). ℂ **805/773-4653.** www.splashcafe.com. Most items $3–$10. MC, V. Sun–Thurs 8am–8pm; Fri–Sat until 9pm.

THE CENTRAL COAST WINE COUNTRY

When people talk about California wines, we usually assume they mean those from the Napa and Sonoma regions north of San Francisco. But here in California—and increasingly across the country, thanks to the Academy Award–winning comedy *Sideways*—wine lovers are becoming increasingly aware of quality vintages coming from the sun-drenched valleys of San Luis Obispo and Santa Barbara counties.

The truth is that the Central Coast wine country is the oldest of California's wine-growing regions. The old Franciscan missions strung along the coast and just inland by it attest to the area's heritage when early Spanish settlers planted grapevines and olive trees. But the area's wine production went into decline during Prohibition, and after it was repealed, Napa and Sonoma valleys shot ahead as the leading and best-known producers.

But in the past 25 years, the Central Coast has experienced a boom in grape production and winemaking, and with the new growth in winemaking has come general growth, much of it geared to visitors: Hotels, spas, golf courses, restaurants, art galleries, museums, antiques stores, and even a Vegas-style casino attract a mostly well-over-40 clientele who appreciate the relaxed pace and beauty of the region (little of this area—except perhaps for the bakeries in Solvang—will thrill your kids).

The principal parts of the Central Coast Wine Country are **Paso Robles** (the town of this name and the surrounding countryside), **San Luis Obispo** (again, the town of the same name plus the nearby areas of Edna Valley and Arroyo Grande), and **northern Santa Barbara County** (the Santa Maria and Santa Ynez valleys). The great news for visitors is that these areas are distinct but sufficiently close together to make visiting all of them practical on even a short timetable. And staying in Paso Robles or San Luis Obispo is also a convenient option for visiting Hearst Castle (p. 481), offering more to do (or, at least, more to drink) than quaint Cambria.

Paso Robles

Paso Robles (Pass of the Oaks) is suitably named for the clusters of oak trees scattered throughout the rolling hills of this inland region. The town has a faintly checkered past: It was established in 1870 by Drury James, uncle of outlaw Jesse James (who hid out in tunnels under the original Paso Robles Inn). In 1913, pianist Ignace Paderewski came to live in Paso Robles, where he brought zinfandel vines for his ranch—Paderewski played often in the Paso Robles Inn, which today maintains a small exhibit in his honor in the lobby. He really wasn't here for long, returning to Poland after World War I, but the town today treats Paderewski like a native son.

Arriving in downtown Paso Robles is like stepping onto a movie set. The main town square is surrounded by blocks of venerable Victorian-era buildings such as the public library, a neoclassical edifice from 1907. It's worth taking a leisurely stroll around the square before heading out into the rolling vineyards for an afternoon of wine tasting.

Paso Robles.

ESSENTIALS

GETTING THERE/ORIENTATION   Paso Robles is on U.S. 101; there's an exit for the town's main thoroughfare, Spring Street. Hwy. 46 intersects, and briefly joins, U.S. 101. **Amtrak** (© **800/USA-RAIL** [872-7245]; www.amtrak. com) offers daily service to Paso Robles from Oakland and Los Angeles.

Many wineries are on the winding roads off Hwy. 46 on either side— try to cluster your visit according to this destination, visiting one side and then the other. You'll be able to feel how the weather on the western side, which is cooler due to higher elevations and frequent coastal fog, differs from the hotter east side, on a flat plain leading inland; winemakers bicker constantly over which conditions are better for growing wine grapes.

VISITOR INFORMATION   For a list of area wineries, tasting rooms, and seasonal events, contact the **Paso Robles Vintners and Growers Association,** 744 Oak St., Paso Robles, CA 93446 (© **800/549-9463** or 805/239-8463; www.pasowine.com). Additional information on the area is offered by the **Paso Robles Chamber of Commerce and Visitors & Conference Bureau,** 1225 Park St., Paso Robles, CA 93446 (© **800/406-4040** or 805/238-0506; www.pasorobleschamber.com).

TOURING THE LOCAL WINERIES

Growers have been tending vines in Paso Robles's fertile foothills since the turn of the century—the 20th century, that is. For decades, wine aficionados overlooked the area, even though in 1983 it was granted its own "Paso Robles" appellation (the official government designation of a recognized wine-producing region; "Napa Valley" and "Sonoma County" are probably more familiar). Around 1992, wine grapes surpassed lettuce as San Luis Obispo County's primary cash crop, and the region now has at least 75 wineries and more than 100 vineyards (which grow grapes but do not produce their own wine from them).

Paso Robles is reminiscent of Napa Valley way back in the '70s before it became a major tourist destination. Because not all wine enthusiasts are wine experts, an advantage of the area is its friendly attitude and small crowds, which make it easy to learn more about the winemaking process as you go along. Enjoy the relaxed rural atmosphere along two-lane country roads, driving leisurely from winery to winery and, more often than not, chatting with winemakers while tasting their products.

Eberle Winery Owner Gary Eberle, who's been making Paso Robles wine since 1973, is sometimes called the "grandfather of Paso Robles's Wine Country," because many of the new vintners in the area honed their craft working under his tutelage. A visit to Eberle Winery includes a tour through its underground caves, where hundreds of aging barrels share space with the Wild Boar Room, site of Eberle's monthly winemaker dinners featuring guest chefs from around the country (always held on Sat nights; the prix-fixe meal is around $120, including wine). Call for current events.

3810 Hwy. 46 E. (3½ miles east of U.S. 101). ℂ **805/238-9607.** www.eberlewinery.com. Complimentary tastings daily 10am–5pm (until 6pm in summer).

Justin Vineyards & Winery ★★ At the end of a scenic country road lies Justin and Deborah Baldwin's boutique winery, and even a casual glance shows how much love and dedication the ex–Los Angelenos have put into their operation. The tasting room, dining room, offices, and even winemaking barns have a stylish Tuscan flair. Justin's flagship wine is Isosceles, a Bordeaux-style blend that—at about $60 a bottle—is pricier than most area wines but exudes sophistication—and earns *Wine Spectator* raves. Also worth a try is their port-style dessert wine, called Obtuse. Daily tours of the winery are $15, available by appointment only at 10:30am and 2:30pm, and can be arranged by calling ℂ **805/238-6932.** The winery's tasting room is open daily from 10am to 6pm; the tasting fee is $5.

The winery also has a luxurious four-suite B&B called the **JUST Inn.** Impeccably outfitted, the romantic inn has an undeniable serenity. Room rates are $350 to $395. Nightly dinners and weekend lunches are also offered to both guests and day-trippers—call ℂ **805/238-6932** for reservations.

11680 Chimney Rock Rd. (15 miles west of U.S. 101). ℂ **805/238-6932.** www.justinwine.com.

Meridian Vineyards ★ The local vintner with the largest profile is also the Central Coast's best-known label, producing more cases each year than all the other Paso wineries combined. Veteran winemaker Chuck Ortman brought a respected Napa Valley pedigree to Meridian; as a result, here's where you'll get the most Napa-like tasting experience. In addition to the beautiful natural stone winery, there's a man-made lake surrounded by rolling lawns, majestic oak trees, and landscaped herb and flower gardens. Picnicking is encouraged. There's a $5 tasting fee (refunded with wine purchase).

7000 Hwy. 46 E. (7 miles east of U.S. 101). ℂ **805/226-7133.** www.meridianvineyards.com. Tastings daily 10am–5pm.

Summerwood Winery & Inn ★★ Summerwood Winery focuses on opulent limited-edition wines—particularly cabs and Syrahs—that are available only at the West Paso Robles estate and nowhere else. With the help of award-winning winemaker Chris Cameron, Summerwood is turning out some of the best reds around, including wonderful Rhone varietals and Bordeaux-style blends. The winery also offers a gourmet deli for picnickers, plush fireside chairs for relaxed sipping, and the luxurious Summerwood Inn bed-and-breakfast set among the vines (see review below).

2175 Arbor Rd. (at Hwy. 46 W., 1 mile west of U.S. 101). ℂ **805/227-1365.** www.summerwood wine.com. Complimentary tastings daily 10am–5:30pm (till 6pm in summer).

Tobin James Cellars ★★   Winemaker Tobin James is a walking contradiction. A lifelong wine expert who claims to wear the same pair of khaki shorts every day, Toby has patterned his winery in the spirit of local bad boys, the James Gang. The tasting room has a Wild West theme and a 100-year-old saloon bar, and it plays country music, all serving to dispel the wine-snob atmosphere that prevails at so many other wineries. Tobin James's expertise lies in the production of a "user-friendly" zinfandel; the late-harvest dessert wine from zinfandel grapes is smooth and spicy.

8950 Union Rd. (at Hwy. 46 E., 8 miles east of U.S. 101). www.tobinjames.com. ℂ **805/239-2204.** Complimentary tastings daily 10am–6pm.

WHERE TO STAY

Also see **Justin Vineyards & Winery** (above) for lodging.

Adelaide Inn 🐾   Tended with loving care that's rare among lower-priced accommodations, the Adelaide Inn stands out from other motels. Although it's adjacent to gas stations and coffee shops, attention has been paid to isolate this quiet, lushly landscaped property from its surroundings. The rooms are clean and comfortable, with extra warmth, and the motel has a welcoming ambience. Unexpected comforts include complimentary newspaper and fruit and muffins. Facilities include a solar-heated outdoor pool and spa and even a putting green. Wine-tour packages are available as well.

1215 Ysabel Ave., Paso Robles, CA 93446. www.adelaideinn.com. ℂ **800/549-PASO** (7276) or 805/238-2770. Fax 805/238-3497. 108 units. $89–$129 double. Extra person $10. Rates include continental breakfast and afternoon cookies. AE, DC, DISC, MC, V. From U.S. 101, exit onto Hwy. 46 E. Turn west at 24th St.; the hotel is just west of the freeway. **Amenities:** Fitness room; Jacuzzi; heated outdoor pool; sauna. *In room:* A/C, flatscreen TV, fridge, hair dryer.

Hotel Cheval ★★★   This delightful boutique hotel with an equine bent is Paso's newest kid on the block. From the resident Clydesdale, Chester, who gives horse-drawn carriage rides on weekend nights; to the posh lounge, the Pony Club; to the names of the well-appointed rooms—Trumpator, Hanover, Darley, Rosebud—the theme is never-ending. Yet it's the details that make the interior a work of art: showers made out of luxury travertine; headboards constructed from woven leather, sea grass, and carved wood; rooms with sun decks, patios, lounges, window seats, and/or bathtubs. If you're feeling the need to relax, grab a glass of Paso Roble's finest wine in the bar downstairs and lounge in front of one of the several fire pits scattered about. There's live music downstairs Thursday, Friday, and Saturday, and a lavish breakfast spread is delivered to your door in the morning.

1021 Pine St., Paso Robles, CA 93446. www.hotelcheval.com. ℂ **866/522-6999** or 805/226-9995. Fax 805/226-9979. 16 units. $325–$400 double. AE, MC, V. **Amenities:** Restaurant/bar; room service. *In room:* A/C, TV, fridge, hair dryer, free Wi-Fi.

La Bellasera ★   This four-story hotel with boutique-style rooms and ambience couldn't have a more unfortunate location: in the parking lot of a Hampton Inn, overlooking Hwy. 101. Still, the Tuscan-like rooms are spanking new and rather posh, and if you can't swing a stay at the central Hotel Cheval (see above)—or prefer the same amenities for half the price—this is your best option in town. Rooms are spacious, ranging from 430 to 765 square feet, and beautifully decorated with spa showers and in-room Jacuzzi tubs. A well-kept swimming pool will keep you cool on those 110°F (43°C) Paso summer days.

206 Alexa Court, Paso Robles, CA 93446. www.labellasera.com. ✆ **805/238-2834.** Fax 805/238-2826. 60 units. $169–$199 double; $269–$369 suite; from $479 penthouse. AE, DISC, MC, V. **Amenities:** Restaurant; bar; concierge; fitness center; Jacuzzi; outdoor pool; room service; spa. *In room:* A/C, TV w/pay movies, fridge, hair dryer, free Wi-Fi.

Paso Robles Inn ★   This Mission Revival–style inn was built to replace the 1891 Stanford White masterpiece, El Paso De Robles Hotel, that burned down in 1940. Photos of the landmark in its heyday line the Spanish-tiled lobby and adjacent dining room and cocktail lounge. Brick-lined pathways meander through the pretty oak-shaded property, and two-story motel units are scattered across the tranquil landscaped grounds. The best rooms are worth the extra bucks: the Deluxe Spa Rooms with private Jacuzzi tubs (located either on the balcony or in the spacious bathroom) that are filled from the property's mineral springs. Carports are located behind each building. The inn also has a steakhouse, a retro-flavored coffee shop, and the Cattleman's Lounge, a local hot spot featuring live entertainment on weekends. *Tip:* The inn's new two-room suites with pullout sofas are ideal for families.

1103 Spring St., Paso Robles, CA 93446. www.pasoroblesinn.com. ✆ **800/676-1713** or 805/238-2660. 100 units. $119–$185 double. Extra person $15. AE, MC, V. **Amenities:** 2 restaurants; coffee shop; lounge; Jacuzzi; outdoor heated pool; room service. *In room:* A/C, TV w/pay movies, fridge, hair dryer, high-speed Internet.

The Summerwood Inn ★   The guest book at this elegant B&B sports more than its share of honeymooners drawn by the beautiful 46-acre vineyard estate and luxurious treatment. On the grounds of Summerwood Winery (p. 505), this three-story clapboard house looks like a cross between Queen Anne and Southern-plantation styles, but it's furnished in formal English country. It's a contemporary building, though, so rooms are spacious and bathrooms ultramodern; the main floor (including two guest rooms) is wheelchair accessible. Every room has a private balcony overlooking the vineyards, a gas fireplace, fresh flowers, terry robes, satellite television, wireless Internet, and nightly turndown service. Morning brings a selection of farm-fresh breakfast entrees prepared by the inn's full-time chef.

2130 Arbor Rd. (P.O. Box 3260), Paso Robles, CA 93447. www.summerwoodwine.com. ✆ **805/227-1111.** 9 units. $215–$299 double; $422–$469 suite. Extra person $65. Rates include full breakfast, afternoon wine and hors d'oeuvres, and evening desserts. MC, V. From U.S. 101, exit Hwy. 46 W. Continue 1 mile to Arbor Rd. *In room:* A/C, TV, hair dryer, Wi-Fi.

WHERE TO EAT

You should also consider Paso's branch of the San Luis Obispo favorite **Buona Tavola,** 943 Spring St. (✆ **805/237-0600**), whose house-made pastas and fresh-from-the-fields northern Italian cuisine are a welcome addition to town (see p. 498 for full review).

Bistro Laurent ★★ COUNTRY FRENCH   Executive chef/owner Laurent Grangien's sophisticated bistro caused quite a stir in this town unaccustomed to such innovations as a chef's tasting menu. But once the dust settled, everyone kept returning for the unpretentious neighborhood atmosphere, superb cuisine, and reasonable (at least by L.A. or San Francisco standards) prices. Whet your appetite with the crispy crab risotto hors d'oeuvre (the crispy tarts are addictive as well) and warm potato and goat-cheese salad before plunging into main dishes such as rosemary-garlic chicken or roasted pork chops with Dijon sauce and puréed potatoes.

1202 Pine St., Paso Robles. ✆ **805/226-8191.** www.bistrolaurent.com. Reservations recommended. Main courses $24–$35. MC, V. Daily 10:30am–10:30pm.

Deborah's Room ★★★ AMERICAN   While Justin wins for best winery in the region, it also boasts the finest restaurant in a 100-mile radius. Dressed-up farm fare pairs superbly with house wine in an intimate dining room with just six tables. Executive Chef Will Torres pays special attention to seasonal offerings from local sources, so the menu is an ever-evolving creation sure to please a discerning palate. The nightly four-course prix-fixe dinner (plus cheese plate) is $90 a person, with $45 each for the wine pairings. It may include an almond or pumpkin soup; foie gras torchon starter; Moroccan-spiced lamb loin or braised short ribs with truffle potato purée main; and a perfectly decadent chocolate cremeux dessert with hazelnut, Tahitian vanilla ice cream, and whipped chocolate cream. If you plan on indulging your inner oenophile, call ahead for a complimentary shuttle. An alfresco brunch is served on the pretty patio on weekends.

11680 Chimney Rock Rd., Paso Robles, CA 93446. ✆ **800/726-0049** or 805/238-6932. www.justinwine.com. Reservations required for dinner. $90 4-course dinner; $45 wine pairing. AE, DISC, MC, V. Daily breakfast for inn guests; Sat lunch noon–4pm; daily 6:30, 7, and 7:30pm dinner seatings.

McPhee's Grill ★★ ☺ CALIFORNIA GRILL   When Ian McPhee left Ian's Restaurant in Cambria and launched this one, it didn't take long for word to get out. McPhee's is worth the short drive to the historic town of Templeton. The converted old saloon features contemporary country decor, an open kitchen, and indoor and outdoor dining. The menu offers half a dozen appetizers, such as an ancho-duck quesadilla or pan-roasted black bass with artichoke pesto, roasted red pepper sauce, and fingerling potatoes. Gourmet pizza, pasta, an amazing macadamia-crusted Alaskan halibut, and four varieties of tender, juicy steaks cooked to perfection round out the Americana-with-a-twist-style menu. Especially impressive are the prices—it's rare that a restaurant "dedicated to great food and great service" offers the majority of its dishes for under $20.

416 S. Main St., Templeton. ✆ **805/434-3204.** www.mcphees.com. Reservations recommended. Main courses $13–$16 lunch, $13–$38 dinner. MC, V. Daily 11:30am–2pm and 5pm–closing.

Odyssey World Café ☺ ✦ CONTINENTAL   Odyssey offers an eclectic range of foods reflecting world influences in a cozy, casual atmosphere at affordable prices. Lunch choices include salads, pizzas, pastas, sandwiches, wraps, gyros, Asian bowls, and rotisserie chicken, with full dinners available in the evening. The kids' menu offers four choices they're sure to eat, each at $5. Odyssey is also the best place in Paso Robles to stock up on picnic foods.

1214 Pine St. (at 12th St.). ✆ **805/237-7516.** www.odysseyworldcafe.com. Reservations not accepted. Main courses $7–$16. AE, MC, V. Sun–Thurs 11am–8:30pm; Fri–Sat 11am–9pm.

The Santa Ynez Valley

ESSENTIALS

GETTING THERE   To reach the Santa Ynez Valley from the north, take Hwy. 101 to Hwy. 154 at Los Olivos. Tiny Ballard lies 3 miles south off Baseline Road. The turnoff for Solvang is just beyond, west on Hwy. 246, while a straight jaunt on Hwy. 154 will take you through the spectacular San Marcos Pass and onto Hwy. 101 toward Santa Barbara.

From the south, take Hwy. 154 off Hwy. 101 at Goleta (just north of Santa Barbara), up through the San Marcos Pass. A left turn heading west on Hwy. 246 takes you into Solvang; continuing straight along Hwy. 154 takes you through Los Olivos and onto Hwy. 101 toward San Luis Obispo.

VISITOR INFORMATION   Contact the **Santa Ynez Valley Visitors Association,** P.O. Box 1918, Santa Ynez, CA 93460 (✆ **800/742-2843;** www.syvva.com), for general visitors' information. The local and comprehensive website **www.solvangca.com** also carries information about the entire valley, as well as Santa Barbara, Lompoc, and Santa Maria. Always a definitive authority for activity in the Santa Maria and Santa Ynez valleys is the **Santa Barbara County Vintners' Association,** 3669 Sagunto St., Unit 101 (P.O. Box 1558), Santa Ynez, CA 93460 (✆ **800/218-0881** or 805/688-0881; www.sbcountywines.com), which also publishes a *Winery Touring Map.* Hours are Monday through Friday from 9am to 5pm. The **Solvang Conference & Visitors Bureau,** 1511 Mission Dr., at Fifth Street (P.O. Box 70), Solvang, CA 93464 (✆ **800/468-6765** or 805/688-6144; www.solvangusa.com), has additional information on the Santa Ynez Valley, including maps and brochures. It's open daily from 9am to 5pm (a satellite visitor information office is at 1639 Copenhagen Dr.).

ORIENTATION   U.S. 101, Hwy. 246, and Hwy. 154 form a triangle around the six towns of the Santa Ynez Valley, all residing within a 10-mile radius. Hwy. 246 becomes Mission Drive within Solvang city limits and then continues east past the mission toward Santa Ynez. Alamo Pintado Road connects Solvang with Los Olivos, whose commercial stretch is along 3 blocks of Grand Avenue. This geographic arrangement may sound confusing, but in reality it all blurs together gracefully, and the friendly residents are always handy with directions.

TOURING THE LOCAL WINERIES

Santa Barbara County has a 200-year tradition of growing grapes and making wine—an art originally practiced by Franciscan friars at the area's missions—but only in the past 20 to 30 years have wine grape fields begun to approach the size of other crops that do so well in these fertile inland valleys.

Geography makes the area well suited for vineyards: The Santa Ynez and San Rafael mountain ranges are transverse (east-west) ranges, which allows ocean breezes to flow through, keeping the climate temperate. Variations in temperature and humidity within the valley create many microclimates, and vintners have learned how to cultivate nearly all the classic grape varietals. But it's the chardonnay, pinot noir, and Syrah that draw the most acclaim, and you'll find more than 50 wineries in the Santa Ynez Valley area, most of which have tasting rooms—a few offer tours as well. If you'd like to start with a winery tour to acquaint yourself with viticulture, Gainey Vineyard is a good bet (see below). And if you'd like to sample wines without driving around, head to **Los Olivos Tasting Room & Wine Shop,** 2905 Grand Ave. (✆ **805/688-7406;** www.thelosolivostastingroom.com), in the heart of town, which offers a wide selection of vintners, including those—such as Au Bon Climat and Qupé—who don't have their own tasting rooms.

Fess Parker Winery & Vineyard ★   You loved him as a child, now visit the winery that Hollywood's Davy Crockett/Daniel Boone oversaw before his passing in 2010. Fess Parker made a name for himself in Santa Barbara County, with resort hotels, cattle ranches, and an eponymous winery (established in 1989) that's turning out some critically acclaimed Syrahs, among other varietals. Look for the Syrah and chardonnay American Tradition Reserve vintages in the tasting room. Parker's grandiose complex, shaded by the largest oak tree I've ever seen, also features picnic tables on a terrace and an extensive gift shop where you can even buy (you guessed it) coonskin caps.

6200 Foxen Canyon Rd., Los Olivos. ✆ **800/841-1104** or 805/688-1545. www.fessparker.com. Tastings daily 10am–5pm; tours daily at 11am, 1pm, and 3pm. Tasting fee $10, includes souvenir glass.

The Gainey Vineyard ★   This slick operation is one of the most visited wineries in the valley, thanks to its prime location on Hwy. 246 and its in-depth tours, offered daily. It has every hallmark of a visitor-oriented winery: a terra-cotta-tiled tasting room, plenty of logo merchandise, and a deli case for impromptu lunches at the picnic tables in a secluded vineyard garden. It bottles the most popular varietals—chardonnay, cabernet sauvignon, pinot noir, sauvignon blanc—and offers them at moderate prices.

3950 E. Hwy. 246, Santa Ynez. ✆ **888/424-6398** or 805/688-0558. www.gaineyvineyard.com. Tastings daily 10am–5pm; tours daily 11am and 1, 2, and 3pm. Tasting fee $10, includes souvenir glass.

Sunstone Vineyards and Winery ★★★   Take a rambling drive down to this locally known winery, whose wisteria-wrapped stone tasting room belies the dirt road you take to reach it. Sunstone sits in an oak grove overlooking the river, boasting a splendid view from the lavender-fringed picnic courtyard. Inside, try its flagship merlot or treasured reserve vintages; there's also a fine selection of gourmet foods, logo ware, and cigars. The pretty setting and attractive tasting room, combined with excellent products, make this a quintessentially enjoyable wine-touring experience.

125 Refugio Rd., Santa Ynez. ✆ **800/313-WINE** (9463) or 805/688-WINE (9463). www.sunstone winery.com. Tastings daily 10am–4:30pm. Tasting fee $10.

Zaca Mesa Winery ★★   One of the region's old-timers, Zaca Mesa has been in business since 1972, so one can forgive the hippie/New Age mumbo jumbo pleasantly interwoven with the well-honed vintages. Situated on a unique plateau that the Spanish named *La Zaca Mesa* (the Restful Place), this winery's 750 acres are uniquely beautiful, with two easy nature trails for visitors. You'll also find picnic tables and a giant lawn chessboard. Inside, look for the usual Syrah and chardonnay offerings jazzed up with experimental Rhone varietals such as grenache, roussanne, and viognier.

6905 Foxen Canyon Rd., Los Olivos. ✆ **805/688-9339.** www.zacamesa.com. Daily 10am–4pm (until 5pm Fri–Sat); call for tour schedule. Tasting fee $10.

SOLVANG: A TOURISTY TASTE OF DENMARK

Immortalized in the 2004 film *Sideways,* the valley's largest community is also one of the state's most popular tourist towns, hosting more than a million tourists each year. Founded in 1911 by Danish immigrants longing for plenty of sunny weather, Solvang takes a lot of flack for being a Disneyfied version of its founders' vision, where everything that *can* be Danish *is* Danish ("More Danish than Denmark!" is the oft-heard local mantra). You've never seen so many windmills, cobblestone streets, flying flags, wooden shoes, and gingerbread-trimmed bakeries. In fact, the whole town looks like a Thomas Kinkade painting, so it's no wonder that America's most populist painter has an outlet on the main drag, **Thomas Kinkade Places in the Heart Gallery,** 1576 Mission Dr. (✆ **805/693-8337**).

To reach Solvang from U.S. 101 south, turn east (left) onto Hwy. 246 at Buellton. It's a well-marked 20-minute drive along a scenic two-lane road. From Santa Barbara, take U.S. 101 north to Hwy. 154, a truly breathtaking 45-minute drive over San Marcos Pass. For a destination guide or hotel information, contact the **Solvang Conference & Visitors Bureau** (✆ **800/468-6765** or 805/688-6144; www.solvangusa.com).

One of the biggest attractions in Solvang is the conspicuous abundance of baked goods such as Danishes, Sarah Bernhardts, kringles, and *kransekage,* making walking-friendly Solvang a great place to stop for a leg stretch and a sugar rush between Hearst Castle and Santa Barbara. **Olsen's Danish Village Bakery,** 1529 Mission Dr. (✆ **805/688-6314;** www.olsensdanishbakery.com), is the town's best bakery.

Solvang is also full of Danish import shops stuffed with Royal Copenhagen collectibles, lace, and carvings. **Gerda's Iron Art Gift Shop,** 1676 Copenhagen Dr. (✆ **805/688-3750**), and the **Royal Copenhagen Shop,** 1683 Copenhagen Dr. (✆ **805/688-6660**), offer a large selection of china, cookware, potholders, and Danish gift items. **Lemos Feed and Pet Supply,** 1511-C Mission Dr. (✆ **805/693-8180**), has a great selection of gifts for pets. Antiques hounds will find plenty to admire and buy at the **Solvang Antique Center,** 486 First St. (✆ **805/688-6222;** www.solvangantiques.com), with more than 50 dealers.

Windhaven Glider Rides, Santa Ynez Airport (✆ **805/688-2517;** www. gliderrides.com), runs hang glider rides over the gorgeous valley. For a different kind of thrill, you can try your luck at the **Chumash Casino,** a huge Las Vegas–style casino on Hwy. 246 in Santa Ynez (✆ **800/CHUMASH** [248-6274]; www. chumashcasino.com).

If you want to wedge some history and culture between bites of pastries and sips of wine, the valley is the home of the historic, tragic **Mission Santa Ines,**

Solvang.

Miniature Horses & More

Miniature horses supposedly make great house pets, but you may not want to mention that to your kids until you are far, far away from **Quicksilver Miniature Horse Ranch,** 1555 Alamo Pintado Rd. (© 805/686-4002; qsminis.com). No more than 34 inches high, these four-legged Lilliputians can be petted and played with during visiting hours. If you prefer full-size equines, visit **Day Dream Arabians,** 2065 Refugio Rd.

(© 805/688-9106; daydreamarabians. com), for a presentation, a tour, and the opportunity to stroll with and feed the mares and foals. If birds are more your bag, **Ostrich Land,** 610 E. Hwy. 246, Buellton (© 805/686-9696; www. ostrichlandusa.com), lets you view the 8½-foot-tall, 350-pound bipeds from a safe distance, and then buy some low-fat ostrich meat (which, surprisingly, tastes like lean beef).

1760 Mission Dr. (© **805/688-4815;** www.missionsantaines.org; winter daily 9am–5:30pm; summer daily 9am–5pm), with its interpretive display of Chumash, religious, and Spanish artifacts, paintings, and documents. Built in 1804, the mission fell into disuse and disrepair after a series of natural and man-made disasters, but near-divine intervention—in the form of Capuchin monks—helped resurrect the mission, which now serves Mass and hosts an annual fiesta in midsummer.

Dedicated to documenting and preserving America's flora and fauna, the small yet wonderful **Wildling Museum,** 2928 San Marcos Ave., Los Olivos (© **805/688-1082;** www.wildlingmuseum.org; Wed–Sun 11am–5pm; $3 donation requested for admission) is solely supported by donations. Its three rooms offer a changing display of photographs and paintings depicting the history of our vanishing lands and wildlife, and it's truly a labor of love.

Both the **Hans Christian Andersen Museum,** 1680 Mission Dr., upstairs (© **805/688-2052;** daily 10am–5pm), and the **Elverhøj Museum,** 1624 Elverhoj Way (© **805/686-1211;** www.elverhoj.org; Wed–Thurs 1–4pm, Fri–Sun noon–4pm), cater to children—especially the Elverhøj, which is designed to stimulate children to celebrate the life of Denmark's most famous citizen. Downstairs is the Bookloft and Kaffe Hus, with a reading area for children.

LOS OLIVOS: A QUIET WINE COUNTRY TOWN

Los Olivos is a good old-fashioned country town in the middle of the Central Coast Wine Country, complete with a flagpole at the town's main intersection. If you saw TV's *Return to Mayberry,* that was Los Olivos standing in for Andy Griffith's sentimental Southern hamlet. But these days, the town's storefronts feature numerous art galleries, stylish cafes, and wine-tasting rooms. If cutesy and congested Solvang is definitely not your kind of scene, make the short, scenic drive over here along Alamo Pintado Road, spend a few hours browsing the town's 3 short blocks, and then enjoy an alfresco lunch at the Los Olivos Café or Panino gourmet sandwich shop (see "Where to Eat," below). If you're looking for a place to stay, the **Fess Parker** is a beautiful inn and spa here (p. 514).

CACHUMA LAKE: A BALD EAGLE HABITAT

Created in 1953 by the damming of the Santa Ynez River, this picturesque reservoir running along Hwy. 154 is the primary water source for Santa Barbara County. It's also the centerpiece of a 6,600-acre county park with a flourishing

Cachuma Lake, near Scenic Scenic Hwy. 154.

wildlife population and well-developed recreational facilities. Cachuma has, through agreeable climate and diligent ranger efforts, become a notable habitat for resident and migratory birds, including rarely sighted bald eagles, which migrate south from as far as Alaska in search of food.

One of the best ways to appreciate this fine-feathered bounty is to take one of the naturalist-led **Eagle Cruises** of the lake, offered between November and February. The 48-foot *Osprey* was specially designed for wildlife observation, with unobstructed views from nearly every seat. During the rest of the year, rangers lead **Wildlife Cruises** around the lake, helping you spot resident waterfowl, deer, and the elusive bobcats and mountain lions that live here. Eagle Cruises depart Wednesday, Thursday, and Sunday between 10am and noon, with additional cruises Friday and Saturday at 2pm. Wildlife Cruises run Friday and Saturday at 3pm, and Saturday and Sunday at 10am. All cruises are 2 hours long. In addition to the park day-use fee of $5 per car, the fare is $15 for adults and $7 for children 12 and under. Reservations are recommended; call the **Santa Barbara County Parks Department** (© 805/686-5050; www.sbparks.com).

The recreational opportunities also offer campers, boaters, and fishermen abundant facilities. Contact the **Lake Cachuma Recreation Area** (© 805/686-5055) for recorded information.

WHERE TO STAY

The Ballard Inn & Restaurant ★★   This two-story inn may look 100 years old, but it's actually of modern construction, offering contemporary comforts and charming country details like wicker rockers on a wraparound porch. Sumptuous wallpaper and fabrics lend a cozy touch, and hand-hooked rugs, bent-twig furniture, and vintage accessories add character to the house. The guest rooms upstairs are unique—some have fireplaces and/or private balconies, and all have well-stocked bathrooms, many featuring a separate antique washbasin in the bedroom. In addition to cooked-to-order breakfast and a wine and hors d'oeuvres reception, you'll be treated to evening coffee and tea, plus addictive chocolate cookies on your nightstand at bedtime. The inn's upscale restaurant, in a cozy room downstairs with a crackling fire, has garnered much praise since chef Budi Kazali took over a few years back.

2436 Baseline Ave., Ballard, CA 93463. www.ballardinn.com. ✆ **800/638-2466** or 805/688-7770. Fax 805/688-9560. 15 units. $245–$315 double. Rates include full breakfast, afternoon wine and hors d'oeuvres. AE, MC, V. Take Alamo Pintado Rd. to Baseline; the inn is half a block east of the intersection. **Amenities:** Restaurant; bike rental. *In room:* A/C, hair dryer.

Fess Parker's Wine Country Inn & Spa ★★   Yes, *that* Fess Parker—Daniel Boone and Davy Crockett, both. After his career playing pioneer legends, he became a big local developer. This sprawling eponymous inn is a deep lap of luxury, with each room uniquely decorated by "Mrs. Marcy Parker" herself. The rooms are certainly pristine and comfortable, and each comes with a fireplace and cushy beds with down comforters. Other welcoming perks include a complimentary full American breakfast, a bottle of Fess Parker wine upon arrival, and a free wine tasting for two at two local tasting rooms. There is also a full spa, a pool, and a Jacuzzi. And if you haven't already, buy property in these parts—this region is exploding.

2860 Grand Ave. (at Hollister St.), Los Olivos, CA 93441. www.fessparker.com. ✆ **800/446-2455** or 805/688-7788. Fax 805/688-1942. 21 units. $295–$525 double. AE, DISC, MC, V. **Amenities:** Restaurant; bike rental; pool; spa. *In room:* A/C, TV, hair dryer, free high-speed Internet.

Inn at Petersen Village ★   If you think every hotel in Solvang has a kitschy Danish theme, then step into this quiet, tasteful hotel. Rooms are decorated in a European country motif, with print wallpaper, canopy beds, and mahogany-hued furniture. But it's the little touches that impress the most, such as lighted magnifying mirrors, bathroom lights controlled by dimmers, free coffee and tea service to your room, and the complimentary food that's nearly always laid out in the hotel's friendly piano lounge. Some rooms overlook a bustling courtyard of shops, while others face Solvang's scenic hills. All are designed so everyone's happy: Smaller units have private balconies, those with noisier views are more spacious, and so on. Note that rates include a complete dinner for two and a European buffet breakfast.

1576 Mission Dr., Solvang, CA 93463. www.peterseninn.com. ✆ **800/321-8985** or 805/688-3121. Fax 805/688-5732. 42 units. $265–$380 double. Extra person $35. Rates include full dinner and breakfast buffet. AE, MC, V. **Amenities:** Restaurant; piano/wine bar; room service. *In room:* A/C, TV, hair dryer.

Solvang Gardens Lodge 🍴   Solvang's oldest motel is also one of the best values in the entire Santa Ynez Valley. The rooms are all nonsmoking and comfortably sized, with floral prints and marble bathrooms. The meticulously manicured grounds are replete with gardens and fruit trees, and ensconced in the backyard is a massage cottage that offers Swedish, deep-tissue, aromatherapy, and hot-stone massages starting at $95. Be sure to check their website for numerous money-saving package deals.

293 Alisal Rd., Solvang, CA 93463. www.solvanggardens.com. ✆ **888/688-4404** or 805/688-4404. Fax 805/688-9975. 24 units. $119–$199 double; $159–$229 suite. DISC, MC, V. **Amenities:** Billiard cottage. *In room:* A/C, TV, Wi-Fi.

WHERE TO EAT

For a quick sandwich or burger on the porch—or to select prepared salads, breads, and artisan cheeses for a picnic to go—you'll quite pleased with **Los Olivos Grocery,** 2621 W. Hwy. 154 (✆ **805/688-5115;** www.losolivosgrocery.com).

This small gourmet country store, open daily from 7am to 9pm, has a great selection of fine wine and foods made from scratch.

If you're looking for traditional Danish fare, head for **Bit o' Denmark,** 473 Alisal Rd. (© **805/688-5426**). Its smorgasbord may not be the largest in town, but it's the freshest and highest quality; you can also order from the regular menu. It's open daily from 11:30am to 9pm. **The Hitching Post,** 406 E. Hwy. 246, Buellton (© **805/688-0676;** www.hitchingpost2.com), is the valley's mecca for meat lovers and now famous as the restaurant featured in *Sideways.* Within these Western-themed surroundings, steaks are grilled to perfection over an oak-wood pit, and, fittingly, the house label wine is better than you'd expect.

Brothers Restaurant at Mattei's Tavern ★ AMERICAN/CONTINENTAL Mattei's is proud of its stagecoach past. Built in 1886 by Swiss-born Felix Mattei to service waiting stagecoach passengers, the tavern remained in business until 1914 when the Model-A Ford put the coaches out of business. Rumors abound of high-stakes poker games in Mattei's back room, where many an early rancher literally "lost the farm." As soon as you step inside this rambling white Victorian submerged in wisteria, you'll be impressed by how successfully it has retained its historic charm. The restaurant is known throughout the county for its signature reduction sauces and house-made ice cream. You'll find thick steaks on the menu, along with honey-glazed Iowa pork chops, prime rib with garlic mashed potatoes, and Australian lobster tail. Bust a pant button with the sinful fudge brownie sundae with banana ice cream, and then saddle up and mosey along.

2350 Railway Ave. (just east of Grand Ave. on Hwy. 154), Los Olivos. © 805/688-4820. www. matteistavern.com. Reservations recommended on weekends. Dinner $18–$44. AE, MC, V. Daily 5–9pm. Bar daily from 4pm.

Los Olivos Café ★ CALIFORNIAN/MEDITERRANEAN The patio is so ensconced with wisteria that it's easy to walk right past this popular cafe and not notice it (I did it twice). The sunny patio is ideal for lunch; the inside is warm and beckoning, with its massive concrete fireplace; and the food is so consistently good that even locals eat here regularly. The menu offers mostly Mediterranean-style gourmet sandwiches, salads, and pastas—think grilled eggplant and ham on hearth bread, pesto ravioli, basil pesto pizza, and butternut squash and cranberry salad. And, of course, you can sample local wines with your meal. Don't leave without a bottle of their signature olive oil.

2879 Grand Ave., Los Olivos. © 805/688-7265. www.losolivoscafe.com. Reservations recommended. Main courses $10–$24. AE, DISC, MC, V. Daily 11:30am–8:30pm. Wine tasting daily 10am–8:30pm.

Paula's Pancake House ★ ☺ AMERICAN/DANISH Morning means one thing in Solvang—Paula's three-page menu of breakfast treats. Paula's is friendly and casual, in the heart of town where patio diners can watch the world go by. So should we order the wafer-thin Danish pancakes served plain and simple or sweet and fruity? Better include some sausage and eggs with that, and a side of buttermilk pancakes. No, make that a side of whole-wheat honey pancakes, a waffle, and sourdough French toast. Hmmm, an omelet sounds pretty good, too. More coffee, please.

1531 Mission Dr., Solvang. © 805/688-2867. www.paulaspancakehouse.com. Most dishes under $10. AE, DISC, MC, V. Daily 6am–3pm.

SANTA BARBARA ★★★

45 miles S of Solvang; 105 miles S of San Luis Obispo; 92 miles NW of L.A.

Between palm-lined Pacific beaches and the sloping foothills of the Santa Ynez Mountains, this prosperous resort community presents a mosaic of white-washed stucco and red-tile roofs, and a gracious, relaxed attitude that has earned it the sobriquet American Riviera. It's ideal for kicking back on gold-sand beaches, prowling the shops and galleries that line the village's historic streets, and relaxing over a meal in one of many top-notch cafes and restaurants.

Santa Barbara mission.

Downtown Santa Barbara is distinctive for its Spanish-Mediterranean architecture. But it wasn't always this way. Santa Barbara had a thriving Native American Chumash population for hundreds, if not thousands, of years. The European era began in the late 18th century around a Spanish *presidio* (fort) that's been reconstructed in its original spot. The earliest architectural hodgepodge was destroyed in 1925 by a powerful earthquake that leveled the business district. Out of the rubble rose the Spanish-Mediterranean town of today, a stylish planned community that continues to enforce strict building codes.

Visit Santa Barbara's waterfront on a Sunday, and you're sure to see the weekly **Arts and Crafts Show,** one of the city's best-loved traditions. Since 1965, artists, craftspeople, and street performers have been lining grassy Chase Palm Park, along Cabrillo Boulevard.

Essentials

GETTING THERE   By car, U.S. 101 runs right through Santa Barbara; it's the fastest and most direct route from north or south (1½ hr. from Los Angeles, 6 hr. from San Francisco).

By train, **Amtrak** (© **800/USA-RAIL** [872-7245]; www.amtrak.com) offers daily service to Santa Barbara. Trains arrive and depart from the **Santa Barbara Rail Station,** 209 State St. (© **805/963-1015**). Fares can be as low as $32 (round-trip) from Los Angeles's Union Station.

ORIENTATION   State Street, the city's primary commercial thoroughfare, is the geographic center of town. It ends at Stearns Wharf and Cabrillo Boulevard; the latter runs along the ocean and separates the city's beaches from touristy hotels and restaurants. Electric shuttles provide frequent service along these two routes, if you'd rather leave the car behind.

ATTRACTIONS
Old Mission Santa Barbara **2**
Santa Barbara Botanic Garden **1**
Santa Barbara County Courthouse **8**
Santa Barbara Museum of Art **7**
Santa Barbara Zoo **18**
Stearns Wharf **16**

HOTELS
Canary Hotel **10**
Casa del Mar Inn at the Beach **14**
Four Seasons Resort, the Biltmore
    Santa Barbara **19**
Franciscan Inn **13**
Hotel Oceana **15**
Motel 6 **17**
Simpson House Inn **3**
The Upham Victorian Hotel and
    Garden Cottages **4**

RESTAURANTS
bouchon **5**
Brophy Bros. Clam Bar & Restaurant **12**
La Super-Rica Taqueria **11**
Palazzio **9**
Tupelo Junction Café **6**

Santa Barbara

0   1/2 mi
0   1/2 km

PACIFIC OCEAN

The **Santa Barbara Conference and Visitors Bureau,** 1601 Anacapa St. (✆ **805/966-9222;** www.santabarbaraca.com), distributes maps, brochures, an events calendar, and information. It's open Monday through Saturday from 9am to 5pm, and Sunday from 10am to 5pm.

Be sure you pick up a copy of the *Independent,* Santa Barbara's free weekly, with articles and events listings; and *Explore Santa Barbara,* a compact visitor's guide published by the local paper, the *Santa Barbara News-Press.* Both are also available at shops and sidewalk racks throughout town.

Seeing the Sights
HISTORIC DOWNTOWN

Following a devastating 1925 earthquake, city planners decreed that all new construction would follow codes of Spanish- and Mission-style architecture. In time, the adobe-textured walls, rounded archways, glazed tile work, and terra-cotta rooftops came to symbolize the Mediterranean ambience that still characterizes Santa Barbara. The architecture also gave a name to the **Red Tile Tour,** a self-guided walking tour of historic downtown. The visitor center (see "Visitor Information," above) has a map/guide of the tour, which can take anywhere from 1 to 3 hours, including time to visit some of the buildings, and covers about 12 blocks in total. Some of the highlights are destinations in their own right.

Santa Barbara County Courthouse ★ Built in 1929, this grand "palace" is considered the local flagship of Spanish colonial revival architecture (you undoubtedly saw its facade on TV during the Michael Jackson trial). It's certainly the most flamboyant example, with impressive facades, beamed ceilings, striking murals, an 85-foot-high observation clock tower, and formal sunken gardens. Free guided tours are offered on Monday, Tuesday, and Friday at 10:30am.

1100 Anacapa St. ✆ **805/962-6464.** www.santabarbaracourthouse.org. Free admission. Mon–Fri 8am–5pm; Sat–Sun and holidays 10am–4:30pm.

Santa Barbara County Courthouse.

Santa Barbara Museum of Art ★   This little jewel of a museum feels more like the private gallery of a wealthy collector. Its leaning is toward early-20th-century Western American paintings and 19th- and 20th-century Asian art, but the best displays might be the antiquities and Chinese ceramics. In addition, there are often visiting exhibits featuring small but excellent collections from other establishments.

1130 State St. ✆ **805/963-4364.** www.sbmuseart.org. Admission $9 adults; $6 seniors 65 and over, students, and children 6–17; free for children 5 and under; free for everyone every Sun. Tues–Sun 11am–5pm.

ELSEWHERE IN THE CITY

Stearns Wharf ★, at the end of State Street (www.stearnswharf.org), is California's oldest working wharf. It attracts visitors for strolling, shopping, dining, and exploring its exhibits, which include a Sea Center with aquariums and an outdoor touch-tank. Although the wharf no longer functions for passenger and freight shipping as it did when built in 1872 by local lumberman John C. Stearns, local fishing boats still dock to unload their daily catch. Consider taking a narrated sunset harbor cruise aboard the *Harbour Queen* at **Captain Don's** (✆ **805/969-5217;** www.stearnswharf.org). Public parking on the wharf is free with merchant validation.

Ganna Walska Lotusland 🎁   This secluded, lavishly landscaped 37-acre estate is renowned for exotic plants and mysterious garden paths. Named for the estate's vivacious European-born mistress and the romantic, lotus-filled ponds in her gardens, the estate reflects the late Madame Walska's eccentricity and the skill of her prestigious gardeners. She was especially fond of succulents and cactuses, interspersing them artistically among native plants and decorative objects. Assembled when money was no object and import regulations were lenient (mostly in the 1940s), the garden contains priceless rare specimens—even prehistoric plants that are extinct in the wild. Montecito is a 5-minute freeway drive south of downtown Santa Barbara. ***Note:*** Advance reservations are required and are available up to 6 months in advance.

695 Ashley Rd., Montecito. ✆ **805/969-9990.** www.lotusland.org. Admission $35 adults, $10 children 5–18, free for children 4 and under. 2-hr. guided tours mid-Feb to mid-Nov Wed–Sat 10am and 1:30pm.

Old Mission Santa Barbara ★   Established in 1786 by Father Junípero Serra and built by the Chumash Indians, this is a rare example in physical form of the blending of Indian and Hispanic spirituality. This hilltop structure is called the Queen of the Missions for its twin bell towers and beauty. It overlooks the town and the Channel Islands beyond. Self-guided tour booklets are available in six languages.

2201 Laguna St. (at Los Olivos St.). ✆ **805/682-4713.** www.santabarbaramission.org. Admission $5 adults, $4 seniors, $1 children 11 and under. Mon–Fri 9am–4:30pm.

Santa Barbara Botanic Garden 🎁   The Botanic Garden is devoted to indigenous California plants. More than 5.5 miles of meandering trails on 65 acres offer glimpses of cactuses, redwoods, wildflowers, and much more, many arranged in representational habitats or landscapes. The gardens were established in 1926. You'll catch the very best color and aroma just after spring showers.

1212 Mission Canyon Rd. (a short drive uphill from the mission). © **805/682-4726.** www.sbbg. org. Admission $8 adults, $6 seniors 60 and over and children 13–17, $4 children 2–12, free for children 1 and under. Daily 9am–5pm (till 6pm Mar–Oct).

Santa Barbara Zoo ★ ☺   When you're driving around the bend on Cabrillo Boulevard, look up—you might spot the head of a giraffe poking through the palms. This zoo is an appealing, pint-size place, where all 700 animals can be seen in about 30 minutes. Most live in natural, open settings. For more stimulation, try the Discovery Area, miniature train ride, and small carousel. The picnic areas (with barbecue pits) are underused and especially recommended.

500 Niños Dr. (off Cabrillo Blvd.). www.santabarbarazoo.org. © **805/962-5339,** or 805/962-6310 for recorded information. Admission $12 adults, $10 seniors and children 2–12, free for children 1 and under. Daily 10am–5pm; last admission 1 hr. before closing. Parking $5. Open Thanksgiving 10am–3pm. Closed Christmas.

Beaches

East Beach is Santa Barbara's favorite beach, stretching from the Santa Barbara Zoological Gardens to Chase Palm Park and the wharf. Nearer the pier you can enjoy manicured lawns, tall palms, and abundant facilities; to the east are many volleyball courts, plus the Cabrillo Pavilion, a recreational center, bathhouse, and architectural landmark dating from 1925. Picnic areas with barbecue grills, showers, and clean, well-patrolled sands make this beach a good choice for everyone.

On the other side of Santa Barbara Harbor is **Leadbetter Beach,** less sheltered than those to the south and popular with surfers. It's reached by following Cabrillo Boulevard after it turns into Shoreline Drive. This beach is also a great place to watch pleasure boats entering or leaving the harbor. Leadbetter has basic facilities, including restrooms, picnic areas, and a metered parking lot.

East Beach.

State Street nightlife.

Two miles west of Leadbetter is secluded but popular **Arroyo Burro Beach County Park,** also known as Hendry's Beach. This gem has a grassy park beneath the cliffs and a white crescent beach with great waves for surfing and bodysurfing. There are volleyball nets, picnic areas, and restrooms.

Outdoor Activities

BIKING & SURREY CYCLING   A relatively flat, palm-lined 2-mile coastal pathway, perfect for biking, runs along the beach. More adventurous riders can pedal through town (where painted bike lanes line many major routes, including one up to the mission). These routes and many more are outlined in the *Santa Barbara County Bike Map,* a free and comprehensive resource available at the visitor center or by calling **Traffic Solutions** at ℂ **805/ 963-7283.**

Wheel Fun Rentals, 23 E. Cabrillo St. (ℂ **805/966-2282;** www. wheelfunrentals.com), rents well-maintained beach cruisers, mountain bikes, tandem bikes, and an Italian four-wheel surrey that seats three adults; rates vary. It's open daily from 8am to 8pm.

BOATING   The **Santa Barbara Sailing Center,** 133 Harbor Way at the Santa Barbara Harbor (ℂ **800/350-9090** or 805/962-2826; www.sbsail.com), rents sailboats from 21 to 50 feet in length, as well as paddle boats, kayaks, and motorboats. Both skippered and bareboat charters are available by the day or the hour. Sailing instruction for all levels of experience is also available. Coastal, island, whale-watching, dinner-cruise, and adventure tours are offered on the 50-foot sailing catamaran *Double Dolphin.* Open 9am to 6pm spring and summer; 9am to 5pm fall and winter.

GOLF   At the **Santa Barbara Golf Club,** 3500 McCaw Ave., at Las Positas Road (ℂ **805/687-7087;** www.sbgolf.com), there's a great 6,009-yard, 18-hole course and a driving range. Unlike many municipal courses, the Santa Barbara Golf Course is well maintained and presents a moderate challenge for the average golfer. Greens fees are $30 to $40 Monday through Friday for 18 holes and $40 to $50 on weekends. Optional carts rent for $28.

The 18-hole, 7,000-yard **Sandpiper,** at 7925 Hollister Ave. (ℂ **805/ 968-1541;** www.sandpipergolf.com), is a scenic oceanside course that's rated as one of the top public courses in the U.S. It also has a driving range. Weekend greens fees are $159, and the cart fee is $16.

HIKING   The foothill trails in the Santa Ynez Mountains above Santa Barbara are perfect for day hikes. In general, they aren't overly strenuous. Trail maps are available at **The Travel Store,** 12 W. Anapamu St. (at State St.; ℂ **800/546-8060**); at the visitor center (see "Visitor Information," above); and from **Traffic Solutions** (ℂ **805/963-7283**).

One of the most popular hikes is the **Seven Falls/Inspiration Point Trail,** an easy trek that begins on Tunnel Road, past the mission, and skirts the edge of Santa Barbara's Botanic Garden (which contains some pleasant hiking trails itself).

SKATING   The paved beach path that runs along Santa Barbara's waterfront is perfect for in-line skating. **Wheel Fun Rentals,** 23 E. Cabrillo St. (ℂ **805/ 966-2282;** www.wheelfunrentals.com), rents skates and all the requisite protective gear. It's open daily from 8am to 8pm.

WHALE-WATCHING   Whale-watching cruises are offered between late December and late March, when Pacific gray whales pass by on migratory journeys from their breeding lagoons in Baja California, Mexico, to their Alaskan feeding grounds. **Shoreline Park,** west of the harbor, has high bluffs ideal for land-based whale-spotting. Sea excursions are offered by both **Captain Don's Harbor Tours** (② **805/969-5217;** www.stearnswharf.org), on Stearns Wharf, and the **Condor** (② **888/77-WHALE** [779-4253] or 805/882-0088; www.condorcruises.com), located at 301 W. Cabrillo Blvd. in the Santa Barbara Harbor.

Shopping

State Street from the beach to Victoria Street is the city's main thoroughfare and has the largest concentration of shops. Many specialize in T-shirts and postcards, but there are a number of boutiques as well. If you get tired of strolling, hop on one of the electric shuttle buses (25¢) that run up and down State Street.

Also check out **Brinkerhoff Avenue** (off Cota St., btw. Chapala and De La Vina sts.), Santa Barbara's "antiques alley." Most shops here are open Tuesday through Sunday from 11am to 5pm. **El Paseo** (814 State St.) is a picturesque shopping arcade reminiscent of an old Spanish street. It's built around an 1827 adobe home and is lined with charming shops and art galleries. **Paseo Nuevo,** on the other side of State Street, is a modern outdoor mall, featuring familiar chain stores and cafes, and anchored by a Nordstrom department store.

Where to Stay

Before you even begin calling around for reservations, keep in mind that Santa Barbara's accommodations are expensive—especially in summer. Then decide whether you'd like to stay beachside (even more expensive) or downtown. Santa Barbara is small, but not small enough to happily stroll between the two areas.

The free one-stop reservations service **Hot Spots** (② **800/793-7666** or 805/564-1637; www.hotspotsusa.com) keeps an updated list of availability for about 90% of the area's hotels, motels, inns, and B&Bs. Reservationists are available Monday through Saturday from 9am to 9pm, and Sunday from 9am to 4pm.

VERY EXPENSIVE

Four Seasons Resort, The Biltmore Santa Barbara ★★★   This gem of the American Riviera manages to adhere to the most elegant standards of hospitality without making anyone feel unwelcome. It's easy to sense the ghosts of golden-age Hollywood celebs such as Greta Garbo, Errol Flynn, and Bing Crosby, who used to play croquet on the hotel's perfectly manicured lawns and then head over to the private Coral Casino Beach & Cabana Club—because that's exactly what privileged guests are *still* doing. Rooms have white plantation shutters, light-wood furnishings, and full marble bathrooms. Guests can amuse themselves on the 20-acre property with a putting green or shuffleboard courts. In addition to two dining rooms, the Biltmore offers a Sunday brunch that draws folks from all over. The Spa, a multimillion-dollar, Spanish-style facility, boasts numerous treatment rooms, a swimming pool and two huge whirlpool baths, a fitness center, and 10 oceanview suites with fireplaces, in-room bars, changing rooms, and twin massage tables.

1260 Channel Dr. (at the end of Olive Mill Rd.), Santa Barbara, CA 93108. www.fourseasons.com/santabarbara. ② **800/819-5053** or 805/969-2261. Fax 805/565-8323. 207 units. $470–$8,000

THE ULTIMATE family VACATION, SANTA BARBARA STYLE

Now here's a family vacation idea you probably haven't thought of—a week of sun, sports, and fun at the University of California in Santa Barbara (my alma mater). During the months of July and August, the **Santa Barbara Family Vacation Center** offers a recreation-oriented family vacation package using vacated university dorms as lodging. It's sort of like a mini–summer camp for the entire family. One set price includes everything for a full week's vacation: all meals, lodging (with daily housekeeping service), and daily activities such as tennis, basketball, volleyball, soccer, softball, fishing, biking, hiking, and more. Evening activities include staff shows, carnivals, casino night, dancing, talent shows, bingo, arts and crafts, and campfires. There's no rigid schedule to follow, so how you want to spend your day is entirely up to you. Children up to 18 are grouped by age and cared for by UCSB student counselors from 9am to midevening, so the parents can spend the day at the beach or touring downtown Santa Barbara. They even offer child-care for infants and toddlers. Rates differ depending on age, but when you consider that you'd probably pay more just for 1 week's lodging at a Santa Barbara hotel, it's a fantastic deal. For more information, call ✆ **805/893-3123** or log on to **www.familyvacationcenter.com**.

double; from $1,250 suite. Extra person $55. Children 18 and under stay free in parent's room. Special midweek and package rates available. AE, DC, MC, V. Valet parking $20; free self-parking. **Amenities:** 4 restaurants; 2 lounges; complimentary bikes; health club; 2 outdoor heated pools; room service; spa services; 3 lit tennis courts; whirlpool. *In room:* A/C, TV/VCR w/pay movies, hair dryer, high-speed Internet, minibar.

EXPENSIVE

Canary Hotel ★★★ Formerly the Andalucia, the Canary Hotel's combination of Moroccan flair and Spanish culture fits in perfectly with downtown Santa Barbara's casual elegance. In fact, one night's visit at the centrally located establishment will make any subsequent stay in a boutique hotel pale in comparison. Every last detail has been carefully thought out and each piece of furniture finely crafted. All bedrooms boast four-poster beds, Matelasse linens, flatscreen TVs, and yoga DVDs and mats. The hotel has no spa but offers a menu of massages, facials, and other nurturing treatments performed in-room. The rooftop's heated pool and Jacuzzi offer stunning views of the surrounding Santa Ynez mountains, nearby Channel Islands, and downtown. The hotel even caters to canines with Club Canario, a pooch program that includes a cushy bed with hotel linens, dog tags, grooming kit, treats, and a Frisbee.

31 W. Carrillo, Santa Barbara, CA 93101. www.canarysantabarbara.com. ✆ **877/468-3515** or 805/884-0300. Fax 805/884-8153. 97 units. $405–$765 double. Packages available. AE, MC, V. Dogs accepted. **Amenities:** Restaurant; bar; concierge; fitness center; room service. *In room:* TV/DVD, minibar, MP3 docking station, Wi-Fi.

Simpson House Inn ★★★ The Simpson House is genuinely something special. Rooms within the 1874 Historic Landmark main house are decorated to Victorian perfection, with extras ranging from a claw-foot tub and antique brass shower to skylight and French doors opening to the manicured gardens; romantic cottages are nestled throughout the grounds. The rooms have everything you could possibly need, but most impressive are the extras: the gourmet Mediterranean hors d'oeuvres and Santa Barbara wines served each afternoon, the enormous video library, and the full gourmet breakfast (delivered on delicate china). Fact is, the Simpson House goes the distance—and then some—to create the perfect stay. Although this property is packed into a relatively small space, it still manages an ambience of country elegance and exclusivity—especially if you book one of the cottages.

121 E. Arrellaga St. (btw. Santa Barbara and Anacapa sts.), Santa Barbara, CA 93101. www.simpson houseinn.com. ℂ **800/676-1280** or 805/963-7067. Fax 805/564-4811. 15 units. $255–$615 double; $595–$605 suite and cottage. 2-night minimum on weekends. Rates include full gourmet breakfast, evening hors d'oeuvres, and wine. AE, DISC, MC, V. **Amenities:** Complimentary bikes; concierge. *In room:* A/C, TV/VCR, hair dryer, minibar.

MODERATE

Casa del Mar Inn at the Beach ♨ A half-block from the beach (sorry, no views), Casa del Mar is an excellent-value Spanish-architecture inn with one- and two-room suites in addition to standard-size rooms. All the rooms were recently remodeled with fresh modern touches while still maintaining the Mediterranean feel. The flower-sprinkled grounds are well maintained, with an attractive sun deck and Jacuzzi (but no swimming pool), and the staff is eager to please. Many rooms have kitchenettes, and a variety of different room configurations guarantee something to suit your needs (especially families). Guests may order in-room spa treatments, and golf packages can be arranged. *Tip:* Despite the hotel's multitude of rates, rooms can often be an unexpected bargain. Also check the website for Internet-only specials.

18 Bath St., Santa Barbara, CA 93101. www.casadelmar.com. ℂ **800/433-3097** or 805/963-4418. 21 units. $144–$269 double. Extra person $10. AE, DC, DISC, MC, V. Free parking. From northbound U.S. 101, exit at Cabrillo, turn left onto Cabrillo, and head toward the beach; Bath is the 2nd street on the right after the wharf. From southbound U.S. 101, take the Castillo exit and turn right on Castillo, left on Cabrillo, and left on Bath. Pets accepted for $15. **Amenities:** Jacuzzi. *In room:* TV, hair dryer, kitchen or kitchenette and fridge in some units.

Hotel Oceana ★ If you're going to vacation in Santa Barbara, you might as well stay in style and on the beach—ergo, at the Hotel Oceana, a "beach chic" hotel with an oceanfront setting and an L.A. makeover. The 2½-acre Spanish Mission–style property consists of four adjacent motels built in the 1940s that have been merged and renovated into one sprawling hotel. The result is a wide range of charmingly old-school accommodations—everything from apartments with real day beds (great for families) to courtyard rooms and deluxe oceanview suites—with bright modern furnishings. The beach and jogging path are right across the street, and the huge lawn is perfect for picnic lunches. *Note:* Yes, you will probably be paying over $250 per night for a gussied-up motel room with no air-conditioning, but that's the going rate for oceanfront accommodations in Santa Barbara.

202 W. Cabrillo Blvd., Santa Barbara, CA 93101. www.hoteloceanasantabarbara.com. ℂ **800/965-9776** or 805/965-4577. Fax 805/965-9937. 122 units. $250–$360 double. 2-night minimum for weekend reservations. AE, DC, DISC, MC, V. **Amenities:** Denny's restaurant adjacent; fitness room; 2 pools; spa; whirlpool; sun deck. *In room:* TV, CD player, fridge, hair dryer, Wi-Fi.

The Upham Victorian Hotel and Garden Cottages This conveniently located inn combines the intimacy of a B&B with the service of a small hotel. Built in 1871, the Upham is the oldest continuously operating hostelry in Southern California. Somewhere the management made time for upgrades, though, because guest accommodations are complete with all the modern comforts. The hotel is constructed of redwood, with sweeping verandas and a Victorian cupola on top. It also has a warm lobby and a cozy restaurant.

1404 De La Vina St. (at Sola St.), Santa Barbara, CA 93101. www.uphamhotel.com. ℂ **800/727-0876** or 805/962-0058. Fax 805/963-2825. 50 units. $195–$290 double; from $340 suite and cottage. Rates include continental breakfast and afternoon wine and cheese. AE, DC, MC, V. **Amenities:** Restaurant. *In room:* TV.

INEXPENSIVE

All the best buys fill up fast in the summer months, so be sure to reserve your room—even if you're just planning to stay at the reliable **Motel 6,** 443 Corona del Mar Dr. (www.motel6.com; ℂ **800/466-8356** or 805/564-1392), near the beach.

Franciscan Inn The Franciscan is situated in a quiet neighborhood just a block from the beach, near Stearns Wharf. This privately owned and meticulously maintained hotel is an affordable retreat with enough frills that you'll still feel pampered. The small but comfy rooms feature a country-tinged decor and finely tiled bathrooms. Services include free local calls and afternoon cookies with spiced cider, hot cocoa, and tea or coffee in the lobby. Most second-floor rooms have unobstructed mountain views, and some suites feature fully equipped kitchenettes. The inn stacks up as a great family choice that's classy enough for a romantic weekend too.

109 Bath St. (at Mason St.), Santa Barbara, CA 93101. www.franciscaninn.com. ℂ **800/663-5288** or 805/963-8845. Fax 805/564-3295. 53 units. Summer (mid-May to mid-Sept) $165–$180 double, $195–$230 suite; winter $125–$160 double, $145–$180 suite. Extra person $10. Rates include continental breakfast and afternoon refreshments. AE, DC, MC, V. Free parking. **Amenities:** Heated outdoor pool; whirlpool. *In room:* A/C, TV/VCR, hair dryer, Wi-Fi.

Where to Eat

EXPENSIVE

bouchon ★★ CALIFORNIAN You can tell that this warm and inviting restaurant is passionate about wine just from its name—*bouchon* is French for "wine cork." And not just any wines—those of the surrounding Santa Barbara County. Have fun by enhancing each course with a glass (or half-glass); knowledgeable servers help make the perfect match from among 50 different Central Coast vintages available by the glass. The seasonally composed and regionally inspired menu has included dishes such as smoked Santa Barbara albacore "carpaccio," arranged with a tangy vinaigrette and shaved imported Parmesan; luscious sweetbread and chanterelle ragout cradled in a potato-leek basket; local venison sliced and laid atop cumin spaetzle in a shallow pond of green peppercorn–Madeira demiglacé; and monkfish saddle fragrant with fresh herbs and accompanied by a creamy fennel-Gruyère gratin. Request a table on the heated front patio, and don't miss the signature chocolate "molten lava" cake for dessert.

9 W. Victoria St. (off State St.). ℂ **805/730-1160.** www.bouchonsantabarbara.com. Reservations recommended. Main courses $25–$35. AE, DC, MC, V. Daily 5:30–10pm.

MODERATE

Brophy Bros. Clam Bar & Restaurant ★★ SEAFOOD   This place is most known for its unbeatable view of the marina, but the dependable fresh seafood keeps tourists and locals coming back. Dress is casual, portions are huge, and favorites include New England clam chowder, cioppino, and any one of an assortment of seafood salads. The scampi and garlic-baked clams are consistently good, as is all the fresh fish, which comes with soup or salad, coleslaw, and pilaf or french fries. A great deal is the hot-and-cold shellfish combo platter for $15. Ask for a table on the narrow deck overlooking the harbor. ***Be forewarned:*** The wait at this small place can be up to 2 hours on a weekend night.

119 Harbor Way (off Cabrillo Blvd. in the Waterfront Center). ℰ **805/966-4418.** www.brophy bros.com. Reservations not accepted. Main courses $9–$19. AE, MC, V. Sun–Thurs 11am–10pm; Fri–Sat 10am–11pm.

Palazzio ★ ITALIAN   I should tell you up front: This family-style restaurant is not a good place for a first date. The fresh garlic bread, which is this State Street staple's raison d'être—and the reason so many UCSB students have no problem putting on the legendary Freshman Fifteen—is potent. Offered in half-order, "normal," or family-style sizes, the main courses aren't half bad, either, though normal dishes, such as their capellini with chicken meatballs and penne alla puttanesca, could easily feed two. (I didn't manage to plow my way through even half of my Papa Ruby's rigatoni.)

1026 State St. ℰ **805/564-1985.** www.palazzio.com. Main courses $16–$18. AE, MC, V. Mon–Thurs 11:30am–3pm and 5:30–11pm; Fri 11:30am–3pm and 5:30pm–midnight; Sat 11:30am–midnight; Sun 11:30am–11pm (kitchen closes 1 hr. before the restaurant daily).

Pane e Vino ★ ITALIAN   This popular Italian *trattoria* offers food as authentic as you'd find in Rome. The simplest spaghetti topped with basil-tomato sauce is so good, it's hard to understand why diners would want to occupy their taste buds with more complicated concoctions. But this kitchen is capable of almost anything. Pasta puttanesca, with tomatoes, anchovies, black olives, and capers, is always tops. Pane e Vino also gets high marks for its reasonable prices, service, and casual atmosphere. Although many diners prefer to eat outside on the patio, some of the best tables are in the charming, cluttered dining room.

1482 E. Valley Rd., Montecito (a 5-min. drive south of downtown Santa Barbara). ℰ **805/969-9274.** www.panevinosb.com. Reservations required. Main courses $10–$35. AE, MC, V. Mon–Sat 11:30am–9pm.

Tupelo Junction Café ★★ SOUTHERN   Most trendy restaurants have expiration dates, but the countrified Tupelo Junction has proven immune to such patterns. The unpretentious cafe, which produces Southern cuisine with a healthy California touch, is juxtaposed among the European labels and designer boutiques of State Street. Lemonade and mimosas are served in mason jars, and Jolly Ranchers are generously doled out with the bill. If you're in Santa Barbara long enough to dine at Tupelo only once, plan your pit stop for brunch: The pumpkin oatmeal waffle with candied walnuts and caramelized bananas is divine, and the apple beignets with crème anglaise aren't to be taken lightly. On Thursday nights, the venue hosts live music, with an array of alcohol and appetizer specials on tap.

1218 State St. ℰ **805/899-3100.** www.tupelojunction.com. Breakfast and lunch $5–$16; dinner $13–$29. AE, MC, V. Daily 8am–2pm and 5–9pm.

INEXPENSIVE

La Super-Rica Taqueria ★ MEXICAN   Looking at this humble street-corner shack, you'd never guess it was blessed with an endorsement by the late Julia Child. The tacos here are authentic and no-nonsense, with generous portions of filling piled onto fresh, grainy corn tortillas. My favorites are the *adobado* (marinated pork), *gorditas* (thick corn *masa* pockets filled with spicy beans), and flank steak. A dollop of house-made salsa and green or red hot sauce is the only adornment required. Sunday's special is *pozole,* a stew of pork and hominy in red-chile sauce. On Friday and Saturday, the specialty is freshly made tamales (if the Dover sole tamales are one of the specials, order them—they're incredible). **Tip:** Always check the daily specials first, and be sure to ask for extra tortillas, no matter what you order.

622 N. Milpas St. (btw. Cota and Ortega sts.). © **805/963-4940.** Most menu items $4–$10. No credit cards. Daily 11am–9pm.

Stacky's Seaside SANDWICHES   This ivy-covered shack filled with fishnets, surfboards, and local memorabilia has been a local favorite for years. A classic seafood dive, its menu of sandwiches is enormous, as are most of their pita pockets, hoagies, and club sandwiches. A sign proudly proclaims HALF OF ANY SANDWICH, HALF PRICE—NO PROBLEM, and Stacky's has made a lot of friends because of it. Choices include the Santa Barbaran (roasted tri-tip and melted jack cheese on sourdough), the Rincon pita (jack and cheddar cheeses, green Ortega chilies, onions, and ranch dressing), and a hot pastrami hoagie with Swiss cheese, mustard, and onions. Heck, they even serve a PB&J for $4. And if you like fish and chips, they nail it here. Stacky's also serves breakfast, featuring scrambled-egg sandwiches and south-of-the-border egg dishes. An order of crispy fries is enough for two.

2315 Lillie Ave., Summerland. © **805/969-9908.** Most menu items under $10. AE, DISC, MC, V. Mon–Fri 6:30am–7:30pm; Sat–Sun 7am–7:30pm. 5 min. on the freeway from Santa Barbara—take the Summerland exit, turn left under the freeway, and then take the 1st right.

THE OJAI VALLEY ★

35 miles E of Santa Barbara; 88 miles NW of L.A.

In a crescent-shaped valley between Santa Barbara and Ventura, surrounded by mountain peaks, lies Ojai (pronounced *Oh*-hi). It's a beautifully serene environment, selected by Frank Capra as Shangri-La, the legendary utopia of his 1936 classic *Lost Horizon.* The spectacularly tranquil setting has made Ojai a mecca for artists and a large population of New Age spiritualists, drawn by the area's mystical beauty.

Life is low-key in the Ojai Valley. Perhaps the most excitement generated all year happens during the first week of June, when the **Ojai Music Festival** draws world-renowned classical artists to perform in the Libbey Bowl amphitheater (for more information, call © **805/646-2094** or visit www.ojaifestival.org).

Essentials

GETTING THERE   The 45-minute drive south from Santa Barbara to Ojai is along two-lane Hwy. 150, a road that's as curvaceous as it is stunning. From Los Angeles, take U.S. 101 north to Hwy. 33, which winds through eucalyptus groves to meet Hwy. 150—the trip takes about 90 minutes. Hwy. 150 is called Ojai Avenue in the town center and is the village's primary thoroughfare.

VISITOR INFORMATION The **Ojai Valley Chamber of Commerce & Visitors Bureau,** 201 S. Signal St., Ojai, CA 93023 (*©* **805/ 646-8126;** www.ojaichamber.org), has free area maps, brochures, and the *Visitor's Guide to the Ojai Valley,* which lists galleries and events. It's open Monday through Friday from 9am to 4pm.

Exploring the Town & Valley

Ojai is home to more than 35 artists working in a variety of media; most have home studios and are represented in one of several galleries in town. The

Pink moment.

best for jewelry and smaller pieces is **HumanArts,** 246 E. Ojai Ave. (*©* **805/646-1525;** www.humanartsgallery.com). Artisans band together each October for an organized **Artists' Studio Tour** (*©* 805/646-8126; www.ojaistudioartists.org). It's fun to drive from studio to studio at your own pace, meeting artists and perhaps purchasing some of their work. Ojai's most famous artist was world-renowned Beatrice Wood, who worked until her death in 1998 at 104. Her whimsical sculpture and luminous pottery are internationally acclaimed, and her spirit is still a driving force in Ojai.

Strolling the Spanish arcade shops downtown and the surrounding area will yield a treasure-trove, including open-air **Bart's Books,** Matilija Street at Canada Street (*©* 805/646-3755; www.bartsbooksojai.com), an Ojai fixture for many years. Antiques hounds head for **Treasures of Ojai,** 110 N. Signal St. (*©* **805/ 646-2852;** www.treasuresofojai.com), an indoor antiques mall packed to the rafters with treasures, trash, and everything in between.

Residents of the Ojai Valley *love* their equine companions—miles of bridle paths are painstakingly maintained, and HORSE CROSSING signs are everywhere.

Ojai has long been a haven for several esoteric sects of metaphysical and philosophical beliefs. The **Krotona Institute and School of Theosophy,** 46 Krotona Hill (*©* 805/646-1139), has been in the valley since 1926, and visitors are welcome at their library and bookstore.

💬 Pink It Up

While in Ojai, you're bound to hear folks wax poetic about the "pink moment"—a phenomenon first noticed by the earliest Native American valley dwellers, when the brilliant sunset over the nearby Pacific is reflected onto the mountainside, creating an eerily beautiful pink glow.

Ojai Music Festival.

In the **Lake Casitas Recreation Area** (℃ **805/649-2233;** www.lakecasitas.info for visitor information), the beautiful Lake Casitas boasts nearly 32 miles of shoreline and was the site of the 1984 Olympic canoeing and rowing events. You can rent rowboats and small powerboats year-round from the **boathouse** (℃ **805/649-2043**) or enjoy picnicking and camping by the lakeside. Because the lake serves as a domestic water supply, swimming is not allowed. From Hwy. 150, turn left onto Santa Ana Road and then follow the signs to the recreation area.

When Ronald Coleman saw **Shangri-La** in *Lost Horizon,* he was really admiring the Ojai Valley. To visit the spot where he stood for his view, drive east on Ojai Avenue, up the hill, and stop at the stone bench near the top—the sight is spectacular.

Where to Stay

Blue Iguana Inn ★ ☺ 🎨   The Mission-style architecture, colorful Southwestern decor, and artwork by local artists (most of which are for sale) are just a few of the highlights of this small, charming hotel. The double rooms at the Blue Iguana are reasonably priced, and the fact that they are also equipped with clean, modern kitchens makes the inn an even bigger value for cook-at-home types. There's even a detached, private two-bedroom bungalow with one-and-a-half bathrooms and a full kitchen starting at $229. Kids can play croquet on the large open lawn while parents take a breather under the shady oaks; on hot summer days, it's straight to the pool for everyone. The icing on the cake is the friendly, helpful staff, which makes the Blue Iguana an excellent all-around choice. Heck, they even offer spa treatments. *Tip:* Be sure to visit their website for package deals.

11794 N. Ventura Ave., Ojai, CA 93023. www.blueiguanainn.com. ℃ **805/646-5277.** Fax 805/640-2866. 16 units. Rates $119–$179 double; $159–$279 suite; $219–$299 cottage. Rates include continental breakfast. AE, DISC, MC, V. Pets accepted. **Amenities:** Pool; spa services; free Wi-Fi. *In room:* A/C, TV, hair dryer, kitchen.

Emerald Iguana Inn ★★   An easy 10-minute walk from the arcades, the Emerald Iguana (the Blue Iguana's sister hotel) sits in a quiet residential neighborhood of wide streets shaded by tall trees. Accommodations range from a single room to two-bedroom bungalows. All are decorated in mellow tones with simple wood furniture and tastefully chosen Ojai artwork, complementing the lush plants and gardens that shape the grounds. Most suites have a fireplace or Jacuzzi tub. The small pool provides a welcome retreat from the Ojai heat and the setting for a wine-and-cheese gathering on spring and summer weekend nights. Whereas the Blue Iguana is geared toward families, the Emerald is a more private and romantic retreat (children age 13 and under are not allowed).

108 Pauline St., Ojai, CA 93023. www.emeraldiguana.com. ✆ **805/646-5277.** Fax 805/640-2866. 13 units. Midweek year-round $159–$289; weekend year-round $179–$369. Weekends 2-night minimum; holidays 3-night minimum. Rates include continental breakfast. Packages with spa services and meals in town available. AE, DISC, MC, V. No children age 13 and under. **Amenities:** Outdoor pool; spa services. *In room:* A/C, TV, kitchen (in suites), hair dryer, minibar, free Wi-Fi.

Ojai Valley Inn & Spa ★★★ ☺ In 1923, Hollywood architect Wallace Neff designed the clubhouse that's now the focal point of this Spanish Colonial–style resort. The inn has a sprawling Mediterranean estate ambience and provides gracious service and luxurious amenities. The jewel of the resort is 31,000-square-foot Spa Ojai, where stylish spa treatments—some modeled after Native American traditions—are administered inside an exquisitely tiled Spanish-Moorish complex. Fitness classes, art classes, nifty workout machines, and a sparkling outdoor pool complete the relaxation choices. Many guest rooms have fireplaces, and most have secluded terraces or balconies that open onto expansive views of the valley and the mountains. Take advantage of the scenery via the resort's 220 tree-shaded acres with jogging trails and horseback riding facilities. Golfers can book a tee time at the inn's oak-studded Senior PGA Tour golf course.

905 Country Club Rd. (off Hwy. 33), Ojai, CA 93023. www.ojairesort.com. ✆ **888/697-8780** or 805/646-1111. Fax 805/646-7969. 308 units. $450–$650 double; from $600 suite. AE, DC, DISC, MC, V. Free self- and valet parking. Pets accepted for $35 per night with advance notice. **Amenities:** 4 restaurants; complimentary bikes; children's camp; concierge; championship golf course; fitness center; Jacuzzi; outdoor heated 60-ft. lap pool; full-service spa; 4 tennis courts. *In room:* A/C, TV w/pay movies and Nintendo, hair dryer, minibar.

Where to Eat

EXPENSIVE

In addition to the choices below, check out "world-famous" **Deer Lodge,** 2261 Maricopa Hwy. (✆ **805/646-4256;** www.ojaideerlodge.net), the latest incarnation of Ojai's favorite hippie-biker hangout on Hwy. 33, a few minutes north of Ojai. In the valley's gorgeous foothills, the building dates back to the Depression, when it served as a country store with bait and hunting supplies for local sportsmen, but new owners have been busy sprucing up the place and expanding to include a live stage in the bar, enclosed outdoor dining, and a hearty lodge menu with enough contemporary touches to bring in an upscale yet adventuresome clientele.

The Ranch House ★★ CALIFORNIAN This restaurant has been placing an emphasis on the freshest vegetables, fruits, and herbs since opening its doors in 1965, long before this practice became a national craze. Freshly snipped sprigs from the restaurant's lush herb garden will aromatically transform your simple meat, fish, or game dish into a work of art. From an appetizer of cognac-laced liver pâté served with its own chewy rye bread to desserts such as fresh raspberries with sweet Chambord cream, the ingredients always shine through. And you'll love the setting, for the Ranch House offers alfresco dining year-round on the wooden porch facing the scenic valley, as well as in the romantic garden amid twinkling lights and stone fountains.

S. Lomita Ave. ✆ **805/646-2360.** www.theranchhouse.com. Reservations recommended. Main courses $21–$33; Sun brunch $22. AE, DC, DISC, MC, V. Tues–Fri 5:30–8:30pm; Sat 5:30–6:30pm and 8–8:30pm; Sun 12:30–7:30pm. From downtown Ojai, take Hwy. 33 north to El Roblar Dr. Turn left, and then left again at Lomita Ave.

Suzanne's Cuisine ★★ CONTEMPORARY EUROPEAN   Enjoy a great meal in a comfortably sophisticated setting at this local favorite, where every little touch bespeaks a preoccupation with quality details. Ask for a table on the covered outdoor patio, where lush greenery frames a casual setting warmed by a fireplace; when it rains, a plastic curtain descends to keep water out without losing that airy garden feel. Favorites from a seasonal menu include the lunch-only Southwest salad (wild, brown, and jasmine rice tossed with smoked turkey, feta cheese, veggies, and green chiles) and pepper-and-sesame-encrusted ahi, served at dinner sautéed or seared (your choice). From seafood specialties to Italian recipes from chef and owner Suzanne Roll's family, everything is fresh and natural. Veggies are crisply al dente, and even the occasional cream sauce tastes light and healthy. Don't skip dessert.

502 W. Ojai Ave. ✆ **805/640-1961.** www.suzannescuisine.com. Reservations recommended. Main courses $8–$16 lunch, $15–$34 dinner. MC, V. Wed–Mon 11:30am–2:30pm and 5:30pm–closing.

MODERATE

Boccali's ★ ITALIAN   This small wood-frame restaurant among citrus groves is a pastoral spot where patrons eat at picnic tables under umbrellas and oak trees, or inside at tables covered with red-and-white-checked oilcloths. Pizza is the main dish served, topped California-style with the likes of crab, garlic, shrimp, and chicken. I think Boccali's lasagna (served piping hot *en casserole*) would win a statewide contest, hands down. Fresh lemonade, from fruit plucked from local trees, is the drink of choice. Come hungry, and plan on sharing.

3277 Ojai Ave. ✆ **805/646-6116.** www.boccalis.com. Reservations recommended for dinner. Pizza $9–$23; pasta $7–$16. No credit cards. Mon–Tues 4–9pm; Wed–Sun 11:45am–9pm.

VENTURA

15 miles SW of Ojai; 74 miles NW of L.A.

Snuggled between rolling foothills and the sparkling blue Pacific Ocean, Ventura may not have the cultural and gastronomic appeal of Los Angeles or even Santa Barbara, but it does boast the picturesque setting and clean sea breezes typical of California coastal towns. Southland antiques hounds have long reveled in Ventura's quirky collectible markets, but trendy home decor shops, coffeehouses, wine bars, and fashionable restaurants are providing another lure for time-pressed vacationers who zip up from L.A. to charming bed-and-breakfasts. Ventura is also the headquarters and main point of embarkation for Channel Islands National Park (see below).

Ventura.

Most travelers don't bother exiting U.S. 101 for a closer look. But think about stopping to while away a few hours around lunchtime. Ventura's unforced charm might even convince you to spend a night.

Essentials

GETTING THERE   If you're traveling northbound on U.S. 101, exit at California Street; southbound, take the Main Street exit. If you're coming west on Hwy. 33 from Ojai, there's also a Main Street exit. By the way, don't let the directions throw you off; because of the curve of the coastline, the ocean is not always to the west, but often southward.

VISITOR INFORMATION   For a visitor's guide and genial answers to any questions you might have, stop in at the **Ventura Visitors & Convention Bureau,** 101 S. California St., Ventura, CA 93001 (✆ **800/333-2989** or 805/648-2075; www.ventura-usa.com).

Exploring the Town

Much of Ventura's recent development has taken place along **Main Street,** the town's historic center, which grew outward from the Spanish mission of San Buenaventura (see below). The best section for strolling is between the mission (to the north) and Fir Street (to the south). While many of the antiques and thrift stores are no more, you'll find plenty of window-shopping opportunities in the revitalized downtown area.

Ventura stretches south to one of California's most picturesque harbors (the departure point for the Channel Islands; see related section, below), but the town also has its own **pier** at the end of California Street. Well maintained and favored by area fishers, the picturesque wooden pier is the longest of its kind in the state.

Mission San Buenaventura   Founded in 1782 (current buildings date from 1815) and still in use for daily services, this whitewashed and red-tile church lent its style to the contemporary civic buildings across the street. Step back in time by touring the mission's inside garden, where you can examine the antique water pump and olive press once essential to daily life here. The mission is small and near the rest of Ventura's action. Pick up a self-guided tour brochure in the adjacent gift shop for the modest donation of $2 per adult, 50¢ per child.

211 E. Main St. ✆ **805/643-4318.** www.sanbuenaventuramission.org. Admission donation of $2 for adults and 50¢ for children. Mon–Fri 10am–5pm; Sat 9am–5pm; Sun 10am–4pm.

San Buenaventura City Hall   This majestic neoclassical building was built in 1912 as the Ventura County Courthouse. It sits on the hillside, overlooking old downtown and the ocean. To either side on Poli Street are some of Ventura's best-preserved and most ornate late-19th- and early-20th-century houses. Notice the carved heads of Franciscan friars adorning the facade inside and out.

501 Poli St. ✆ **805/654-7800.** www.ci.ventura.ca.us.

Ventura County Museum of History & Art   This museum is worth visiting for its Native American Room, filled with Chumash treasures, and its Pioneer Room, which contains a collection of artifacts from the Mexican-American War (1846–48). The art gallery features exhibits of local painters and photographers, and the museum has an enormous archive (20,000 and counting) of photos of Ventura County from its origins to the present. There is also a small archaeological museum across Main Street from the main building. Allow 1 to 2 hours for your visit.

89 S. California St. ⓒ **805/653-0323.** www.venturamuseum.org. Free admission. Tues–Thurs and Sat–Sun 11am–6pm; Fri 11am–8pm.

Where to Stay

Crowne Plaza Ventura Beach ★ ☺   What this former Holiday Inn lacks in cachet it more than makes up for in location and convenience. As for location, the 12-story Crowne Plaza is Ventura's only beachfront property and has ocean views from every guest room, is directly in front of a prime surf spot, and is a 5-minute walk from downtown Ventura, so you don't need to use your car to get around. As for convenience, the hotel offers perks that the whole family will enjoy, including a large heated outdoor pool, a game room, a fitness center, and instant beach access. You'll also enjoy the adjacent walking/jogging/biking that winds along the coast—great for a romantic sunset stroll. Also on the property is the **C-Street** restaurant, offering a California-inspired menu with dishes made from locally sourced organic foods, and the **AQUA Beachfront Bar** offering oceanview outdoor seating. Pets are welcome as well, and dogs receive a special welcome package upon arrival.

450 E. Harbor Blvd., Ventura, CA 93001. www.cpventura.com. ⓒ **800/842-0800** or 805/648-2100. Fax 805/653-6202. 258 units. $99–$299 double. AE, DC, DISC, MC, V. Pets accepted for $30 fee. **Amenities:** Restaurant; bar and lounge; heated outdoor pool. *In room:* A/C, TV, hair dryer, high-speed Internet.

Where to Eat

71 Palm Restaurant ★ FRENCH COUNTRY   In a beautifully restored 1910 Craftsman, this country-French restaurant is a pleasant change of pace. Upstairs tables have an ocean view, while downstairs a crackling wood fire warms diners. Chef Didier Poirier hails from Le Mans, France, and takes an earnest approach to traditional specialties such as steak au poivre with french fries, New Zealand rack of lamb Provençal style, or homemade pâté served with crusty bread and tangy pickles. Poirier also dabbles in vegetarian dishes and pastas, and every night the cuisine of a different region of France is highlighted.

71 N. Palm St. (btw. Main and Poli sts.). ⓒ **805/653-7222.** www.71palm.com. Reservations recommended. Main courses $11–$28; lunch $5–$16. AE, DC, DISC, MC, V. Mon–Fri 11:30am–2:30pm; Mon–Sat 5–9:30pm.

Taquería Vallarta 🖊 MEXICAN   There's no better place to find a snapshot of Ventura than at the Taquería Vallarta, where young, old, rich, poor, Anglo, and Latino come for Mexican-style comfort food. There's nothing fancy here—it's your standard order-at-the-counter-then-slide-into-your-Formica-booth kind of joint, but that's no problem. The *carnitas* are among the best you'll find anywhere, perfect in a burrito, and the *carne asada* is best in the enchiladas. Don't forget to dress up your dishes with the fresh salsas, limes, and chile peppers available at the condiment bar. For fans of great, cheap Mexican food, Taquería Vallarta's a must.

278 E. Main St. ⓒ **805/643-3037.** Main courses $4–$8. DC, DISC, MC, V. Mon–Fri 9:30am–9pm; Sat–Sun 7:30am–9pm.

CHANNEL ISLANDS NATIONAL PARK ★

Approximately 40 miles W (offshore) of Ventura

There's nothing like a visit to the Channel Islands for discovering the sense of awe explorers must have felt more than 400 years ago. It's miraculous what 25 miles of ocean can do, for compared to the mainland, this is wild and empty land, and only 55,000 visitors a year come to the islands. Whether you approach them by sea or air, you'll be bowled over by how untrammeled they remain despite neighboring Southern California's teeming masses.

Channel Islands National Park encompasses the five northernmost islands of the eight-island chain: Santa Barbara, Anacapa, Santa Cruz, Santa Rosa, and San Miguel. The park also protects the ocean 1 nautical mile offshore from each island, thereby prohibiting oil drilling, shipping, and other industrial uses.

The islands are the meeting point of two distinct marine ecosystems: The cold waters of Northern California and the warmer currents of Southern California swirl together here, creating an awesome array of marine life. On land, the isolation from mainland influences has allowed distinct species—including the island fox and the night lizard—to evolve and survive here. The islands are also the most important seabird-nesting area in Southern California and home to one of the biggest seal and sea lion breeding colonies in the United States.

Essentials

VISITOR INFORMATION   Each of the five islands is distinct and takes some fore-thought to reach. Odds are that you're going to visit only one island on a given trip, so it's a good idea to study your options before going. Visit the **Channel Islands National Park Headquarters and Visitor Center,** 1901 Spinnaker Dr., Ventura, CA 93001 (© **805/658-5730;** www.nps. gov/chis), to get acquainted with the programs and individual personalities of the islands through maps and displays. Rangers run interpretive programs both on the islands and at the center year-round.

GETTING THERE   **Island Packers,** near the visitor center at 1691 Spinnaker Dr. (© **805/642-1393;** www.islandpackers.com), is the park's main con-cessionaire for boat transportation to and from the islands. Daylong tours are offered daily year-round to Anacapa and Santa Cruz; the price to Ana-capa is $45 for adults, $41 for seniors, and $28 for children ages 3 to 12 (Santa Cruz is slightly higher). A half-day trip is also offered to Anacapa on Saturdays. Trips to Santa Rosa and San Miguel operate weekly May through October; boats to Santa Barbara Island are less frequent. Boats to Anacapa leave from the Channel Islands Harbor in Oxnard, 15 minutes south of Ventura. Also see Santa Barbara–based **Truth Aquatics,** under "Diving," below.

Another option, for visiting Santa Rosa Island only, is **Channel Islands Aviation,** 305 Durley Ave., Camarillo (© **805/987-1301;** www. flycia.com), which flies nine-passenger, fixed-wing aircraft. Flying time to Santa Rosa is 25 minutes. The fare is $160 per person for adults, $135 for children 2 to 12, which includes a guided island tour with a ranger via four-wheel-drive. Campers (that is, people camping) are flown over for about $250 round-trip (these flights scheduled on demand).

THE WEATHER   The climate is mild, with little variation in temperature year-round, but the weather is still unpredictable; 30mph winds can blow for days, fog banks can settle in and smother the islands for weeks, and winter rains can turn trails into mud baths. In general, plan on wind, lots of sun (bring sunscreen), cool nights, and the possibility of hot days. Water temperatures are in the 50s and 60s Fahrenheit (10–20°C) year-round. If you're camping, bring a good tent. (If you don't know the difference between a good tent and a bad tent, the island wind will gladly demonstrate it for you.)

CAMPING   Camping is legal on all the park-owned islands but limited to a certain number of campers per night, depending on the island. Fires and pets are prohibited on all the islands. You must bring everything you'll need; there are no supplies on any of the islands. To reserve camping permits, call ✆ **805/658-5711** (Santa Cruz Island) or **800/365-2267** (all other isles). The rate is about $13 per night, per site.

The Extra Mile: Exploring the Coastline & Waters off the Channel Islands

DIVING   A good portion of Channel Islands National Park is underwater. In fact, almost as many visitors come to dive the waters as ever set foot *on* the islands. Divers come from all over to explore stunning kelp forests, pinnacles, and underwater caves, all with the best visibility in California. Everything from sea snails and urchins to orcas and great white sharks calls these waters home.

  Truth Aquatics, in Santa Barbara (✆ **805/962-1127;** www.truth aquatics.com), is the best provider of single- and multiday dive trips to all the islands. They also offer single- and multiday hiking, kayaking, and fishing tours. **Ventura Dive & Sport** (✆ **805/650-6500;** www.venturadive. com) also leads trips, including a Discover Program for novice and uncertified divers accompanied by an instructor. **Channel Islands Scuba** in Thousand Oaks (✆ **805/230-9995;** www.cisdivers.com) also leads regular trips, as do boats from San Pedro and other Southern California ports.

SEA KAYAKING   Sea-kayak excursions allow you to explore fascinating sea caves and rock gardens. Fares generally run about $175 per person for full-day trips; channel crossing by charter boat, equipment, and brief lessons are included. Two- and 3-day adventures to Santa Rosa—campsite, camp gear, and guide included—are offered for $275 to $340 (you'll need to bring your own food, sleeping bag, and tent). **Aquasports** (✆ **800/773-2309** or 805/968-7231; www.islandkayaking.com) operates most trips out of Ventura Harbor, and **Paddle Sports of Santa Barbara** (✆ **888/254-2094** or 805/899-4925; www.kayaksb.com) leads similar excursions.

13

LOS
ANGELES

by Tara de Lis

T he allure of Los Angeles is undeniable. Angelenos know L.A. will never have the sophisticated style of Paris or the historical riches of Rome, but they lay claim to the most entertaining city in the United States, if not the world. It really is warm and sunny most days of the years, movie stars actually do live and dine among regular folk, and you can't swing a smartphone without hitting an in-line skater at the beach.

Things to Do   If you're going to spend any amount of time in Los Angeles, you'll need a car. How else are you going to squeeze in everything from window-shopping on **Rodeo Drive** to cruising **Pacific Coast Highway** to exploring the historic buildings of downtown L.A. to visiting world-class museums like the **Getty Center** and **LACMA?**

Relaxation   L.A. can feel like one big amusement park, as the line between fantasy and reality is often obscured. Get out among the tanned and toned at **Surfrider Beach** in Malibu, check out the **Santa Monica Pier** on a Segway or melt into the hands—or feet!—of your masseuse at one of the city's top spots for relaxation, such as **Ona Spa.**

Restaurants & Dining   Los Angeles is an international atlas of exotic cuisines: Armenian, Chinese, Japanese, Lebanese, Persian, Peruvian, Thai, Vietnamese and more. Like everything else in the city, much of L.A.'s dining culture revolves around celebrity-spotting, and places like **The Ivy** at lunch and **Koi** for dinner are usually safe bets. But in So Cal, sometimes it's the chefs themselves that are the real celebrities. Wolfgang Puck makes the rounds at **Spago** and his other fine-dining restaurants when he is in town.

Nightlife & Entertainment   Nightlife in Los Angeles is hopping. Specifically, Hollywood is the happening place to be for drinking and dancing. Storied live music venues like the **Roxy,** the **Troubadour,** and the **Whisky A Go-Go** continue to build new legacies nightly. Hotel bars across the city, from the **Standard Downtown** to the **Skybar,** still lure locals along with other guests.

ORIENTATION
Getting There
BY PLANE
LAX & the Other Los Angeles–Area Airports
There are five airports in the Los Angeles area. Most visitors fly into **Los Angeles International Airport** (✆ **310/646-5252;** www.lawa.org/lax), better known as LAX. This behemoth—ranked sixth in the world for number of passengers handled—is near the ocean, between Marina del Rey and Manhattan Beach. LAX is a convenient place to land; it's within minutes of Santa Monica and the beaches,

PREVIOUS PAGE: **Chinatown, Downtown Los Angeles.**

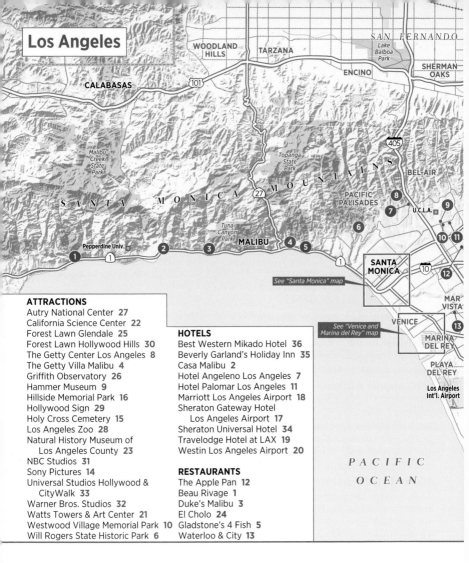

Los Angeles

WOODLAND HILLS
TARZANA
SAN FERNANDO
Lake Balboa Park
ENCINO
SHERMAN OAKS
CALABASAS
101
Malibu Creek State Park
Topanga State Park
S A N T A   M O N I C A   M O U N T A I N S
405
BEL-AIR
PACIFIC PALISADES
U.C.L.A.
27
Tuna Canyon Park
MALIBU
Pepperdine Univ.
See "Santa Monica" map
SANTA MONICA
10
MAR VISTA
VENICE
See "Venice and Marina del Rey" map
MARINA DEL REY
PLAYA DEL REY
Los Angeles Int'l. Airport
P A C I F I C   O C E A N

ATTRACTIONS
Autry National Center **27**
California Science Center **22**
Forest Lawn Glendale **25**
Forest Lawn Hollywood Hills **30**
The Getty Center Los Angeles **8**
The Getty Villa Malibu **4**
Griffith Observatory **26**
Hammer Museum **9**
Hillside Memorial Park **16**
Hollywood Sign **29**
Holy Cross Cemetery **15**
Los Angeles Zoo **28**
Natural History Museum of
   Los Angeles County **23**
NBC Studios **31**
Sony Pictures **14**
Universal Studios Hollywood &
   CityWalk **33**
Warner Bros. Studios **32**
Watts Towers & Art Center **21**
Westwood Village Memorial Park **10**
Will Rogers State Historic Park **6**

HOTELS
Best Western Mikado Hotel **36**
Beverly Garland's Holiday Inn **35**
Casa Malibu **2**
Hotel Angeleno Los Angeles **7**
Hotel Palomar Los Angeles **11**
Marriott Los Angeles Airport **18**
Sheraton Gateway Hotel
   Los Angeles Airport **17**
Sheraton Universal Hotel **34**
Travelodge Hotel at LAX **19**
Westin Los Angeles Airport **20**

RESTAURANTS
The Apple Pan **12**
Beau Rivage **1**
Duke's Malibu **3**
El Cholo **24**
Gladstone's 4 Fish **5**
Waterloo & City **13**

and not more than a half-hour drive from downtown, Hollywood, and the Westside (depending on traffic, of course). Free **shuttle buses** connect the terminals and stop in front of each ticket building under the blue sign. The shuttle letter is "A"; other shuttles exit the airport. Special minibuses accessible to travelers with disabilities are also available. Call **310/646-6402** for more information. **Travelers Aid of Los Angeles** (✆ **310/646-2270;** www.travelersaid.org) operates booths in each terminal.

Eight short-stay (and expensive) parking lots are within the main concourse building, and a long-stay park is on 96th Street and Sepulveda Boulevard. A free bus service runs between long-term parking and the terminals. For drivers picking up passengers, a free 24-hour **Cell Phone Waiting Lot** is at 9011 Airport Blvd. It can be very easy to miss, so keep an eye out for the big post office—it's

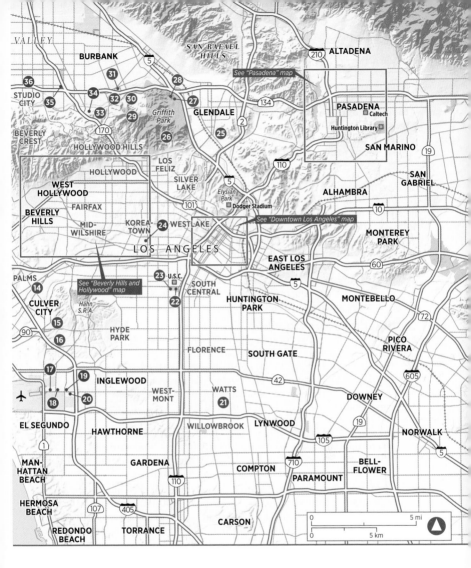

right next door. You can find extensive information about LAX—including maps, parking and shuttle-van information, and links to weather forecasts—online at **www.lawa.org**. All car-rental agencies are in the neighborhood surrounding LAX, within a few minutes' drive; each provides a complimentary shuttle to and from the airport. For more information on car rentals, see "Getting Around," in chapter 17.

For some travelers, one of the area's smaller airports might be more convenient than LAX. **Bob Hope Airport** (2627 N. Hollywood Way, Burbank; (?) **818/840-8840;** www.bobhopeairport.com) is the best place to land if you're headed for Hollywood or the valleys—and it's even closer to downtown L.A. than LAX. The small airport has especially good links to Las Vegas and other Southwestern cities. **Long Beach Municipal Airport** (4100 Donald Douglas Dr., Long

Traffic Tips

If you're renting a car at LAX, avoid arriving midweek in rush hour (now basically 3 to 7pm)—particularly if you have to drive I-405. You'll save yourself several hours of stop-and-go misery. If you're driving to or from Santa Monica and Beverly Hills, West Hollywood, or Century City, try to avoid Santa Monica Boulevard. Olympic and Pico boulevards, which run parallel to Santa Monica, are usually less congested.

Beach; ☎ **562/570-2600;** www.lgb.org), south of LAX, is the best place to land if you're visiting Long Beach or northern Orange County and want to avoid L.A. **John Wayne Airport** (18601 Airport Way, Santa Ana; ☎ **949/252-5200;** www.ocair.com) is closest to Disneyland, Knott's Berry Farm, and other Orange County attractions. **Ontario International Airport** (1923 E. Avion St., Ontario; ☎ **909/937-2700;** www.lawa.org/ont) is not a popular airport for tourists; businesspeople use it to head to San Bernardino, Riverside, and other inland communities. However, it's convenient if you're heading to Palm Springs and also a viable choice if you're staying in Pasadena.

Getting into Town from LAX

BY CAR   To reach Santa Monica and other northern beach communities, exit the airport, take Sepulveda Boulevard north, and follow the signs to Calif. 1 (Pacific Coast Hwy., or PCH) north. You *can* take the I-405 north, but you'll be sorry you did—that stretch of freeway is always heavily congested.

To reach Redondo, Hermosa, Newport, and the other southern beach communities, take Sepulveda Boulevard south and then follow the signs to Calif. 1 south.

To reach Beverly Hills or Hollywood, exit the airport via Century Boulevard and then take I-405 north to Santa Monica Boulevard east.

To reach downtown or Pasadena, exit the airport, take Sepulveda Boulevard south, and then take I-105 east to I-110 north.

BY SHUTTLE   Many city hotels provide free shuttles for their guests; ask when you make reservations. **SuperShuttle** (☎ **800/BLUE-VAN** [800/258-3826] or 310/782-6600; www.supershuttle.com) offers regularly scheduled minivans from LAX to any location in the city, as does **Prime Time Shuttle** (☎ **800/RED-VANS** [733-8267] or 310/536-7922; www.primetimeshuttle.com). Fares range from about $15 to $35 per person, depending on your destination. It's cheaper and more time-efficient to cab it to most places if you're a group of three or more, because with the shuttles you might have to stop at other passengers' destinations before you reach your own. Reservations aren't needed for your arrival but are required for a return to the airport.

BY TAXI   Taxis are at the Arrivals level under the yellow sign outside each terminal. Be sure to ask for a list of prices to various major destinations before setting off. The flat price between LAX and downtown Los Angeles is $47. Expect to pay at least $45 to Hollywood, $35 to Beverly Hills, $30 to Santa Monica, and $75 to the Valley and Pasadena. You'll also pay an airport surcharge of $2.50 for trips originating from LAX.

BY RAIL   Budget-minded travelers heading to downtown, Universal City, or Long Beach can take L.A.'s Metro Rail service from LAX. An airport shuttle can take you to the Green Line light-rail station; from there, connections on the Blue, Gold, and Red lines can get you where you're headed. It's a good idea to contact your hotel for advice on the closest station. The service operates from 5am to midnight, and the combined fare is under $3—but you should be prepared to spend 1 to 2 hours in transit. Call the **Los Angeles County Metropolitan Transit Authority (MTA)** at ✆ **323/GO-METRO** (466-3876), or see **www.mta.net** for information.

BY PUBLIC BUS   The city's MTA buses also go between LAX and many parts of the city. Phone **MTA Airport Information** (✆ **323/GO-METRO** [466-3876]; www.mta.net) for the schedules and fares. If you're arriving at LAX and your hotel is in Santa Monica, you can hop aboard the city's **Big Blue Bus** (✆ **310/451-5444;** www.bigbluebus.com). It's a slow ride, but the price, $1, is hard to beat. Bus information is available in the baggage claim area of each LAX terminal.

BY CAR   Los Angeles is well connected to the rest of the United States by several major highways—in fact, L.A. has one of the highest rates of bank robberies in the U.S. because it's so easy to make a fast getaway. Among them are I-5, which enters the state from the north; I-10, which originates in Jacksonville, Florida, and terminates in Los Angeles; and U.S. 101, a scenic route that follows the western seaboard from Los Angeles north to the Oregon state line.

If you're driving **from the north,** you have two choices: the quick route, along I-5 through the middle of the state; or the scenic route along the coast. Heading south along I-5, you'll pass a small town called Grapevine. This marks the start of the mountain pass with the same name. Once you've reached the southern end of it, you'll be in Canyon Country, just north of the San Fernando Valley, which is the start of Los Angeles County. To reach the beach communities and L.A.'s Westside, take I-405 south (hello, traffic!); to get to Hollywood, take Calif. 170 south to U.S. 101 south (this route is called the Hollywood Fwy. the entire way); I-5 will take you along the eastern edge of downtown and into Orange County.

If you're taking the **scenic coastal route** from the north, take U.S. 101 to I-405 or I-5, or stay on U.S. 101, following the instructions above.

If you're approaching **from the east,** you'll be coming in on I-10. For Orange County, take Calif. 57 south. I-10 continues through downtown and terminates at the beach. If you're heading to the Westside, take I-405 north. To get to the beaches, take Calif. 1 (PCH) north or south, depending on your destination.

From the south, head north on I-5 at the southern end of Orange County. I-405 splits off to the west; take this road to the Westside and beach communities. Stay on I-5 to reach downtown and Hollywood.

Here are some **driving times** if you're on one of those see-the-USA car trips: From Phoenix, it's about 350 miles, or 6 hours (okay, 7 if you drive the speed limit) to Los Angeles via I-10. Las Vegas is 265 miles northeast of Los Angeles (about a 4- or 5-hr. drive). San Francisco is 390 miles north of Los Angeles on I-5 (6–7 hr.), and San Diego is 115 miles south (about 2 hr.).

BY TRAIN   Amtrak (✆ **800/USA-RAIL** [872-7245]; www.amtrak.com) connects Los Angeles with about 500 American cities. As with plane travel along popular routes, fares fluctuate depending on the season and special promotions. As a general rule, heavily restricted advance tickets are competitive with similar airfares. Remember, however, that those low fares are for coach travel in reclining seats; private sleeping accommodations cost substantially more.

The L.A. train terminus is **Union Station,** 800 N. Alameda, on downtown's northern edge. Completed in 1939, this was the last of America's great train depots—a unique blend of Spanish Revival and Streamline Moderne architecture. From the station, you can take one of the taxis that line up outside; board the Metro Red Line to Hollywood or Universal City; or take the Gold Line to Pasadena. If you're headed to the San Fernando Valley or Anaheim, Metrolink commuter trains leave from Union Station; call ℂ **800/371-LINK** (5465; www.metrolinktrains.com).

Visitor Information

INFORMATION CENTERS

The **Los Angeles Convention and Visitors Bureau** (or **LA INC.;** ℂ **800/ 228-2452** or 213/624-7300; www.discoverlosangeles.com) is the city's main source for information. In addition to maintaining an informative website, answering telephone inquiries, and sending free visitors' kits, the bureau provides two **walk-in visitor centers:** downtown at 685 S. Figueroa St. at West Seventh Street (Mon–Fri 9am–5pm), and in Hollywood at the Hollywood & Highland Center, 6801 Hollywood Blvd. at Highland Avenue (daily 10am–10pm).

Many Los Angeles–area communities also have their own information centers and often maintain detailed and colorful websites that are loaded with timely information. These include the following:

- The **Beverly Hills Visitors Bureau,** 239 S. Beverly Dr. (ℂ **800/345-2210** or 310/248-1015; www.beverlyhillscvb.com), is open Monday through Friday from 8:30am to 5pm.

- The **Hollywood Arts Council,** P.O. Box 931056, Hollywood, CA 90093 (ℂ **323/462-2355;** www.discoverhollywood.com), publishes the magazine *Discover Hollywood,* a seasonal publication that contains listings and schedules for the area's many theaters, galleries, music venues, and comedy clubs; the current issue is always available online. You can also load up on visitor information at the **Hollywood Visitor Center,** 6801 Hollywood Blvd. (ℂ **323/467-6412**), on the bottom level of the Hollywood & Highland mall (across from El Capitan).

- The **West Hollywood Convention and Visitors Bureau,** 8687 Melrose Ave., M-38, West Hollywood, CA 90096 (ℂ **800/368-6020** or 310/289-2525; www.visitwesthollywood.com), is located in the Pacific Design Center and is open Monday through Friday from 8am to 6:30pm.

- The **Santa Monica Convention and Visitors Bureau,** 1920 Main St., Ste. B, Santa Monica, CA 90405 (ℂ **800/544-5319** or 310/393-7593; www. santamonica.com), is the best source for information about Santa Monica. The Palisades Park walk-up center is located near the Santa Monica Pier, at 1400 Ocean Ave. (btw. Santa Monica Blvd. and Broadway), and is open daily from 10am to 4pm. Also check out **www.malibu.org** for information about Malibu, to the northwest.

- The **Pasadena Convention and Visitors Bureau,** 300 E. Green St. (ℂ **800/307-7977** or 626/795-9311; www.pasadenacal.com), is open Monday through Friday from 8am to 5pm.

If you're the type who loves to cram as many tourist attractions as possible into one trip, then you might want to consider purchasing a **Hollywood CityPass** or **GO Los Angeles Card.** The CityPass (✆ 888/330-5008; www.citypass.com) booklet includes tickets to four attractions, all within 2 blocks of each other: **Madame Tussauds, Star Line Tour of Hollywood, Redline Tours,** and the **Kodak Theatre Guided Tour** *or* **The Hollywood Museum.** Purchase the pass at any of the above attractions, or visit the CityPass website to buy advance passes online. The pass costs $59 for adults ($39 for kids 3–11) and will expire 9 days from the first use. Is it a good deal? If you use all the tickets, you end up saving almost 45% over individual, full-price admission.

A better deal is the **GO Los Angeles Card** (✆ 866/652-3053; www.golos-angelescard.com). It offers free or discounted admission to more than 45 of L.A.'s most popular attractions, activities, and tours; has more flexibility (available in 1-, 2-, 3-, 5-, and 7-day increments over a 14-day period); and comes with a full-color guidebook that fits in your pocket. The 2-day card costs $100 for adults ($70 for kids 3–12) and doesn't need to be used on consecutive days. The 3-, 5-, and 7-day cards include admission to Universal Studios Hollywood (a great bargain). You can purchase the GO Cards via their website or at the Hollywood Visitor Information Center (6801 Hollywood Blvd. at Highland Ave.; ✆ 323/467-6412).

OTHER INFORMATION SOURCES

L.A. Weekly (www.laweekly.com), a free listings magazine, is packed with information on current events around town. It's available from sidewalk news racks and in many stores and restaurants around the city; it also has a lively website.

The *Los Angeles Times* "Calendar" section of the Sunday paper still publishes, but the old www.calendarlive.com site sadly is no more. It's been replaced by "The Guide," which still provides good coverage of the local dining and entertainment scenes. Just be sure to access it directly, via www.latimes.com/the-guide. If you want to check out L.A.'s most immediate news, the *Times'* main website is **www.latimes.com**.

Los Angeles magazine (**www.lamag.com**) is a glossy city-based monthly full of real news and pure gossip, plus guides to L.A.'s art, music, and food scenes. Its calendar of events gives an excellent overview of goings-on at museums, art galleries, musical venues, and other places. The magazine is available at newsstands around town and in other major U.S. cities; you can also access stories and listings from the current issue on the Internet. Web surfers should visit @L.A.'s website, **www.at-la.com**; its exceptional though somewhat tedious search engine provides links to more than 23,000 sites in the greater L.A. region, including destinations covered in chapter 14, "Side Trips from Los Angeles."

Neighborhoods in Brief

Los Angeles can confuse newcomers, in that downtown isn't the city center, though it is more than it used to be, thanks to an increasingly vital restaurant and nightlife scene, historic loft remodels, and the opening of the LA LIVE "entertainment campus." The city itself is more of a juxtaposition of disparate communities that loosely form a metropolis (67 suburbs searching for a city, so they say).

The best way to grasp the geography is to break it into six regions: Santa Monica and the beaches, L.A.'s Westside and Beverly Hills, Hollywood and West Hollywood, downtown, Pasadena, and—beyond the Hollywood Hills—the San Fernando Valley ("The Valley" to locals). Each encompasses a more-or-less distinctive patchwork of city neighborhoods and independently incorporated communities.

SANTA MONICA & THE BEACHES

These are many people's favorite L.A. communities and get a high recommendation as one of the premier places to book a hotel during your vacation, especially during summer, when the beaches can be a good 20 degrees cooler than the sweltering parts of the city. Fair warning, though: Especially in winter, the weather can be downright grey. The 60-mile beachfront stretching from Malibu to the Palos Verdes peninsula has milder weather and less smog than the inland communities, and traffic is nominally lighter, except on summer weekends. The towns along the coast all have a distinct mood and charm, and most are connected via a walk/bike path. They're listed below from north to south.

Malibu, at the northern border of Los Angeles County, 25 miles from downtown, was once a privately owned ranch—purchased in 1857 for 10¢ an acre and now among the most expensive real estate in L.A. Today its 27 miles of wide beaches, beachfront cliffs, sparsely populated hills, and relative remoteness from the inner city make it popular with rich recluses such as Cher and Mel Gibson. Indeed, the resident lists of Malibu Colony and nearby Broad Beach—oceanfront strips of closely packed mansions—read like a who's who in Hollywood. With plenty of green space and dramatic rocky outcroppings, Malibu's rural beauty is unsurpassed in L.A., and surfers flock to "the 'Bu" for great, if crowded, waves.

Santa Monica, Los Angeles's premier beach community, is known for its festive ocean pier, stylish oceanfront hotels, artsy atmosphere, and large population of homeless residents (I know, that's an oxymoron, but it fits). Shopping is

Venice canals.

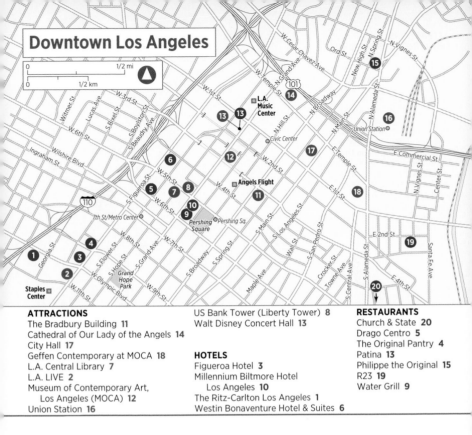

Downtown Los Angeles

0 ——— 1/2 mi
0 ——— 1/2 km

ATTRACTIONS
The Bradbury Building **11**
Cathedral of Our Lady of the Angels **14**
City Hall **17**
Geffen Contemporary at MOCA **18**
L.A. Central Library **7**
L.A. LIVE **2**
Museum of Contemporary Art,
Los Angeles (MOCA) **12**
Union Station **16**

US Bank Tower (Liberty Tower) **8**
Walt Disney Concert Hall **13**

HOTELS
Figueroa Hotel **3**
Millennium Biltmore Hotel
Los Angeles **10**
The Ritz-Carlton Los Angeles **1**
Westin Bonaventure Hotel & Suites **6**

RESTAURANTS
Church & State **20**
Drago Centro **5**
The Original Pantry **4**
Patina **13**
Philippe the Original **15**
R23 **19**
Water Grill **9**

king here, especially along the Third Street Promenade, a pedestrian-only out-door mall lined with dozens of shops and restaurants.

Venice Beach was created by tobacco mogul Abbot Kinney, who set out in 1904 to transform a worthless marsh into a resort town modeled after Venice, Italy—hence, the series of narrow canals connected by one-lane bridges that you'll see as you explore this refreshingly eclectic community. It was once infested with grime and crime, but gentrification has brought scores of great restaurants, boutiques, and rising property values for the canalside homes and apartment duplexes. Even the movie stars and pop stars are moving in: Kate Beckinsale, Anjelica Huston, and Alanis Morissette reside in this pseudo-bohemian community. Some of L.A.'s most innovative and interesting architecture lines funky Main Street. But without question, Venice Beach is best known for its Ocean Front Walk, a nonstop Mardi Gras of thong-wearing skaters, vendors, fortunetellers, street musicians, and poseurs of all ages, colors, types, and sizes.

Marina del Rey, just south of Venice, is a somewhat quieter, more upscale waterside community best known for its man-made small-craft harbor, the largest of its kind in the world. Fittingly, it offers a wide variety of public boating opportunities, including fishing trips, harbor tours, dinner cruises, boat rentals, and private sailing charters.

Manhattan, Hermosa, and **Redondo beaches** are laid-back, mainly residential neighborhoods with modest homes (except for oceanfront real estate),

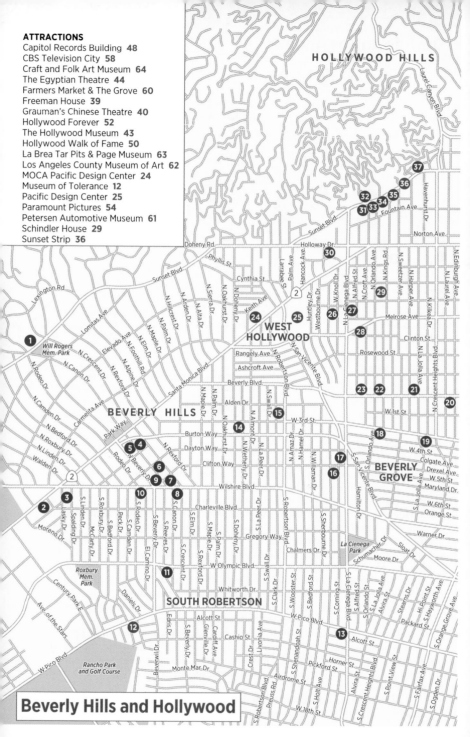

Beverly Hills and Hollywood

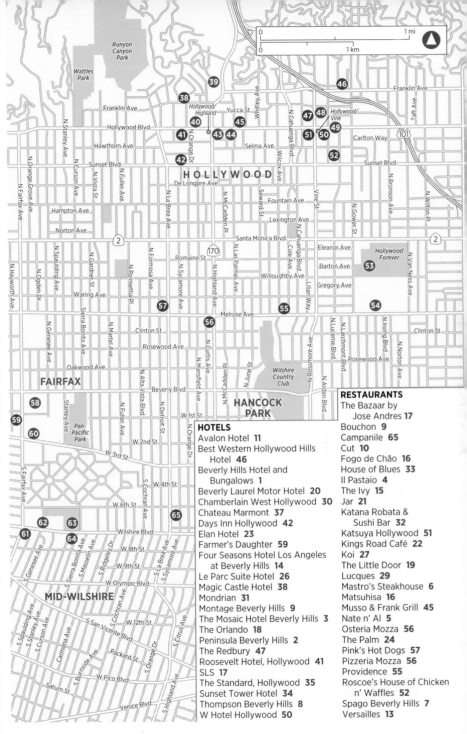

HOTELS

Avalon Hotel **11**
Best Western Hollywood Hills
　Hotel **46**
Beverly Hills Hotel and
　Bungalows **1**
Beverly Laurel Motor Hotel **20**
Chamberlain West Hollywood **30**
Chateau Marmont **37**
Days Inn Hollywood **42**
Elan Hotel **23**
Farmer's Daughter **59**
Four Seasons Hotel Los Angeles
　at Beverly Hills **14**
Le Parc Suite Hotel **26**
Magic Castle Hotel **38**
Mondrian **31**
Montage Beverly Hills **9**
The Mosaic Hotel Beverly Hills **3**
The Orlando **18**
Peninsula Beverly Hills **2**
The Redbury **47**
Roosevelt Hotel, Hollywood **41**
SLS **17**
The Standard, Hollywood **35**
Sunset Tower Hotel **34**
Thompson Beverly Hills **8**
W Hotel Hollywood **50**

RESTAURANTS

The Bazaar by
　Jose Andres **17**
Bouchon **9**
Campanile **65**
Cut **10**
Fogo de Chão **16**
House of Blues **33**
Il Pastaio **4**
The Ivy **15**
Jar **21**
Katana Robata &
　Sushi Bar **32**
Katsuya Hollywood **51**
Kings Road Café **22**
Koi **27**
The Little Door **19**
Lucques **29**
Mastro's Steakhouse **6**
Matsuhisa **16**
Musso & Frank Grill **45**
Nate n' Al **24**
Osteria Mozza **56**
The Palm **24**
Pink's Hot Dogs **57**
Pizzeria Mozza **56**
Providence **55**
Roscoe's House of Chicken
　n' Waffles **52**
Spago Beverly Hills **7**
Versailles **13**

547

mild weather, and residents happy to have fled the L.A. hubbub. There are excellent beaches for volleyball, surfing, and tanning here, but when it comes to cultural activities, pickings can be slim. The restaurant scene, while limited, has been improving steadily, and some nice new bars and clubs have opened near their respective piers.

L.A.'S WESTSIDE & BEVERLY HILLS

The **Westside,** sandwiched between Hollywood and the city's coastal communities, includes some of Los Angeles's most prestigious neighborhoods, virtually all with names you're sure to recognize:

Beverly Hills is politically distinct from the rest of Los Angeles—a famous enclave best known for its palm tree–lined streets of palatial homes, famous residents (Jack Nicholson, Warren Beatty, and Annette Bening), and high-priced shops. But it's not all glitz and glamour; the healthy mix of filthy rich, wannabes, and tourists that comprises downtown Beverly Hills creates a unique—and often snobby-surreal—atmosphere.

West Hollywood is a key-shaped community whose epicenter is the intersection of Santa Monica and La Cienega boulevards. Nestled between Beverly Hills and Hollywood, this politically independent—and blissfully fast-food-free—town is home to some of the area's best restaurants, clubs, shops, and art galleries. "WeHo," as it's come to be known, is also the center of L.A.'s gay community—you'll know you've arrived when you see the risqué billboards. Encompassing about 2 square miles, it's a pedestrian-friendly place with plenty of metered parking. Highlights include the 1½ miles of Sunset Boulevard known as Sunset Strip, the chic Sunset Plaza retail strip, and the liveliest stretch of Santa Monica Boulevard.

Bel Air and **Holmby Hills,** in the hills north of Westwood and west of Beverly Hills, are old-money residential areas featured prominently on most maps to the stars' homes.

Getty Center.

Brentwood is best known as the famous backdrop to the O. J. Simpson melodrama. If Starbucks ever designed a neighborhood, this is what it would look like—a generic, relatively upscale mix of tract homes, restaurants, and strip malls. The Getty Center looms over Brentwood from its hilltop perch next to I-405.

Westwood, an urban village founded in 1929 and home to the University of California at Los Angeles (UCLA), used to be a hot destination for a night on the town, but it lost much of its appeal in the past decade due to overcrowding and even some minor street violence. Although Westwood is unlikely to regain its old charm, the improved culinary scene has brought new life to the village. The area has been plagued by movie-theater closures of

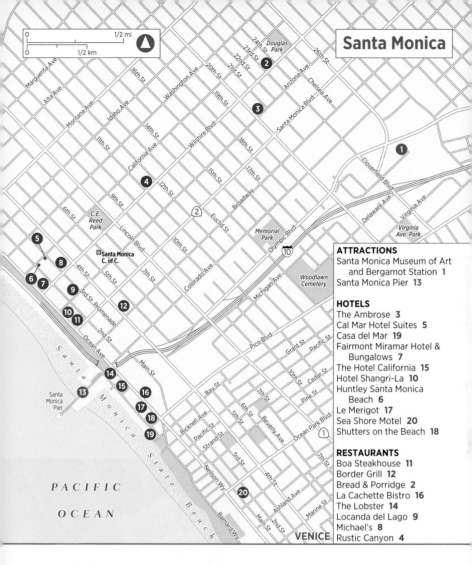

Santa Monica

ATTRACTIONS
Santa Monica Museum of Art
   and Bergamot Station **1**
Santa Monica Pier **13**

HOTELS
The Ambrose **3**
Cal Mar Hotel Suites **5**
Casa del Mar **19**
Fairmont Miramar Hotel &
   Bungalows **7**
The Hotel California **15**
Hotel Shangri-La **10**
Huntley Santa Monica
   Beach **6**
Le Merigot **17**
Sea Shore Motel **20**
Shutters on the Beach **18**

RESTAURANTS
Boa Steakhouse **11**
Border Grill **12**
Bread & Porridge **2**
La Cachette Bistro **16**
The Lobster **14**
Locanda del Lago **9**
Michael's **8**
Rustic Canyon **4**

late, but fortunately the historic Village Theater and the Bruin were both saved from the same fate, so it's still a fun destination for dinner and a flick.

Century City is a compact and rather bland high-rise area sandwiched between West Los Angeles and Beverly Hills. The primary draws here are the 20th Century Fox studios, and the Westfield Century City, a huge open-air shopping mall. Architecturally significant is the CAA building, or "Death Star," as it's referred to by locals. (CAA is one Hollywood's top agencies.) Century City's three main thoroughfares are Century Park East, Avenue of the Stars, and Century Park West.

West Los Angeles is a label that generally applies to everything that isn't one of the other Westside neighborhoods. It's basically the area south of Santa Monica Boulevard, north of Venice Boulevard, east of Santa Monica and Venice, and west and south of Century City.

HOLLYWOOD

Yes, they still come to the mecca of the film industry—young hopefuls with stars in their eyes gravitate to this historic heart of L.A.'s movie production like moths fluttering to the glare of neon lights. But today's Hollywood is more illusion than industry. Many of the neighborhood's former movie studios have moved to more spacious venues in Burbank, the Westside, and other parts of the city.

Despite the downturn, visitors continue to flock to Hollywood's landmark attractions, such as the star-studded Walk of Fame and Grauman's Chinese Theatre. And now that the city's $1-billion, 30-year revitalization project is in full swing, Hollywood Boulevard is, finally, solidly, showing signs that its ascent from a long, seedy slump is permanent. Refurbished movie houses and stylish restaurants and clubs are making a fierce comeback; a stylish W Hotel opened directly above the Hollywood and Vine Red Line Station in 2010. The centerpiece Hollywood & Highland complex anchors the more touristy part of the neighborhood, with shopping, entertainment, and a Renaissance Hotel built around the beautiful Kodak Theatre, designed specifically to host the Academy Awards (really, you'll want to poke your head into this gorgeous theater).

Melrose Avenue, scruffy but fun, is the city's funkiest shopping district, catering to often-raucous youth with secondhand and avant-garde clothing shops. There are also a number of good restaurants.

The stretch of Wilshire Boulevard running through the southern part of Hollywood is known as the **Mid-Wilshire** district, or the Miracle Mile. It's lined with tall, contemporary apartment houses and office buildings. The section just east of Fairfax Avenue, known as Museum Row, is home to almost a dozen museums, including the Los Angeles County Museum of Art, the La Brea Tar Pits, and that shrine to L.A. car culture, the Petersen Automotive Museum.

Griffith Park, up Western Avenue in the northernmost part of Hollywood, is one of the country's largest urban parks, home to the Los Angeles Zoo, the famous Griffith Observatory, and the outdoor Greek Theater.

DOWNTOWN

Despite the relatively recent construction of several major cultural and entertainment centers (such as the Walt Disney Concert Hall, L.A. LIVE, and Cathedral of Our Lady of the Angels) and a handful of trendy restaurants, L.A.'s downtown isn't the tourist hub that it would be in most cities. When it comes to entertaining visitors, the Westside, Hollywood, and beach communities are still far more popular. That said, if you haven't been in years, it's worth another look, particularly for those interested in eclectic restaurants and a sophisticated but less pretentious bar scene than Hollywood.

Walk of Fame.

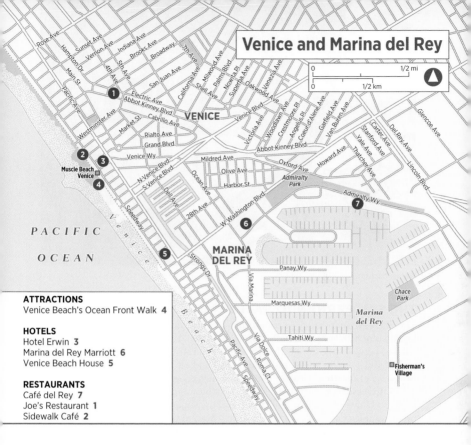

Venice and Marina del Rey

0   1/2 mi
0   1/2 km

VENICE

Muscle Beach Venice

MARINA DEL REY

PACIFIC

OCEAN

Venice Beach

Marina del Rey

Panay Wy.

Marquesas Wy.

Tahiti Wy.

Chace Park

Fisherman's Village

Rose Ave.
Hampton Dr.
Sunset Ave.
Vernon Ave.
Indiana Ave.
Brooks Ave.
Broadway
Main St.
Pacific Ave.
4th Ave.
5th Ave.
7th Ave.
San Juan Ave.
California Ave.
Shell Ave.
Milwood Ave.
Palms Blvd.
Nowita Pl.
Superba Ave.
Oakwood Ave.
Venezia Ave.
Electric Ave.
Abbot Kinney Blvd.
Cabrillo Ave.
Market St.
Westminster Ave.
Rialto Ave.
Grand Blvd.
Venice Wy.
Venice Blvd.
N. Venice Blvd.
S. Venice Blvd.
Del Ave.
Speedway
28th Ave.
Ocean Ave.
Mildred Ave.
Olive Ave.
Harbor St.
Victoria Ave.
Woodlawn Ave.
Crestmoore Pl.
Angelus Pl.
Coeur d'Alene Ave.
Abbot Kinney Blvd.
Oxford Ave.
Admiralty Park
Garfield Ave.
Van Buren Ave.
Howard Ave.
Thatcher Ave.
Carter Ave.
Stanford Ave.
Yale Ave.
Admiralty Wy.
Del Rey Ave.
Lincoln Blvd.
Glencoe Ave.
W. Washington Blvd.
Strongs Dr.
Via Marina
Via Dolce
Roma Ct.
Pacific Ave.
Speedway

ATTRACTIONS
Venice Beach's Ocean Front Walk **4**

HOTELS
Hotel Erwin **3**
Marina del Rey Marriott **6**
Venice Beach House **5**

RESTAURANTS
Café del Rey **7**
Joe's Restaurant **1**
Sidewalk Café **2**

Easily recognized by the tight cluster of high-rise offices—skyscrapers bolstered by earthquake-proof technology—the business center of the city is eerily vacant on weekends and evenings, but the outlying residential communities, such as Koreatown, Little Tokyo, and Chinatown, are enticingly ethnic and vibrant. If you want a tan, head to Santa Monica, but if you want a refreshing dose of non-90210 culture, come here.

El Pueblo de Los Angeles Historic District, a 44-acre ode to the city's early years, is worth a visit. **Chinatown** is small and touristy, but can be plenty of fun for souvenir hunting or traditional dim sum. **Little Tokyo,** on the other hand, is a genuine gathering place for the Southland's Japanese population, with a wide array of shops and restaurants with an authentic flair.

Silver Lake, a residential neighborhood just north of downtown and adjacent to Echo Park and **Los Feliz** (home to the Los Angeles Zoo and Griffith Park), just to the west, has arty areas with unique cafes, theaters, graffiti, and art galleries—all in equally plentiful proportions. The local music scene has been burgeoning of late.

Exposition Park, south and west of downtown, is home to the Los Angeles Memorial Coliseum and the L.A. Sports Arena, as well as the Natural History Museum, the African-American Museum, and the California Science Center. The University of Southern California (USC) is next door.

551

Warner back lot.

THE SAN FERNANDO VALLEY

The San Fernando Valley, known locally as "The Valley," was nationally popularized in the 1980s by the notorious mall-loving "Valley Girl" stereotype. Sandwiched between the Santa Monica and the San Gabriel mountain ranges, most of The Valley is residential and commercial and off the beaten track for tourists. But some of its attractions are bound to draw you over the hill.

Universal City, west of Griffith Park between U.S. 101 and Calif. 134, is home to Universal Studios Hollywood and the supersize shopping and entertainment complex CityWalk. About the only reason to go to **Burbank,** west of these other suburbs and north of Universal City, is to see one of your favorite TV shows being filmed at NBC or Warner Brothers Studios. There are also a few good restaurants and shops along Ventura Boulevard, in and around Studio City.

Glendale is a largely residential community north of downtown between the Valley and Pasadena. Here you'll find Forest Lawn, the city's best cemetery for very retired movie stars.

PASADENA & ENVIRONS

Best known as the site of the Tournament of Roses Parade each New Year's Day, **Pasadena** was spared from the tear-down epidemic that swept L.A., so it has a refreshing old-time feel. Once upon a time, Pasadena was every Angeleno's best-kept secret: a quiet community whose slow and careful gentrification meant nonchain restaurants and boutique shopping without the crowds, in a revitalized downtown respectful of its old brick and stone commercial buildings. Although the area's natural and architectural beauty still shines through— so much so that Pasadena remains Hollywood's favorite backyard location for countless movies and TV shows—Old Town has become a pedestrian mall similar to Santa Monica's Third Street Promenade, complete with huge crowds, midrange chain eateries, and standard-issue mall stores. It still gets our vote as a scenic alternative to the congestion of central L.A., but it has lost much of its small-town charm.

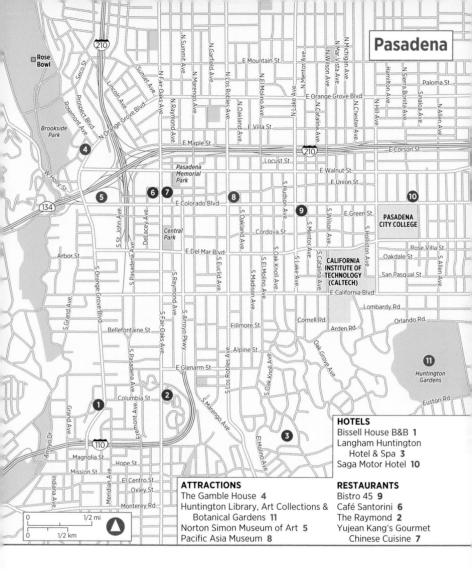

Pasadena

Rose Bowl

Brookside Park

Pasadena Memorial Park

Central Park

PASADENA CITY COLLEGE

CALIFORNIA INSTITUTE OF TECHNOLOGY (CALTECH)

Huntington Gardens

HOTELS
Bissell House B&B **1**
Langham Huntington
  Hotel & Spa **3**
Saga Motor Hotel **10**

ATTRACTIONS
The Gamble House **4**
Huntington Library, Art Collections &
  Botanical Gardens **11**
Norton Simon Museum of Art **5**
Pacific Asia Museum **8**

RESTAURANTS
Bistro 45 **9**
Café Santorini **6**
The Raymond **2**
Yujean Kang's Gourmet
  Chinese Cuisine **7**

Pasadena is also home to the famous California Institute of Technology (CalTech), which boasts 22 Nobel Prize winners among its alumni. The CalTech-operated Jet Propulsion Laboratory was the birthplace of America's space program, and CalTech scientists were the first to report earthquake activity worldwide in the 1930s.

The residential neighborhoods in Pasadena and its adjacent communities— **Arcadia, La Cañada–Flintridge, San Marino,** and **South Pasadena**—are renowned for well-preserved historic homes, from humble bungalows to lavish mansions. These areas feature public gardens, historic neighborhoods, house museums, and quiet bed-and-breakfast inns.

GETTING AROUND

By Car

Need I tell you that Los Angeles is a car-crazed city? Los Angeles is a sprawling metropolis; ergo, you're really going to need some wheels to get around easily (there *is* public transportation in L.A., but you really don't want to rely on it). An elaborate network of well-maintained freeways connects this urban sprawl, but you have to learn how to make sense of the system and cultivate some patience for dealing with the traffic—purchasing one of those plastic-covered foldout maps is a smart investment; purchasing a GPS is a better one. For a detailed view of L.A.'s freeway system, see the tear-out map tucked inside the back cover of this guide.

RENTALS   Los Angeles is one of the cheapest places in America to rent a car. Major national car-rental companies usually rent economy- and compact-class cars for about $40 per day and $130 per week, with unlimited mileage.

All the major car-rental agencies have offices at the airport and in the larger hotels; I highly recommend booking a car online before you arrive. If you're thinking of splurging on a dig-me road machine such as a Maserati, Ferrari, Rolls-Royce, Lamborghini, or Hummer, the place to call is **Beverly Hills Rent-A-Car,** 9732 Little Santa Monica Blvd., Beverly Hills (✆ **800/ 479-5996** or 310/337-1400; www.bhrentacar.com). There are additional locations in Hollywood, Santa Monica, LAX, and Newport Beach, and both offer complimentary delivery to local hotels or pickup service at LAX.

By Public Transportation

There are visitors who successfully tour Los Angeles entirely by public transportation (I've met them both), but we can't honestly recommend that plan for most readers. L.A. is a metropolis that's grown up around—and is best traversed by—the automobile, and many areas are inaccessible without one. As a result, an overwhelming number of visitors rent a car for their stay. Still, if you're in the city for only a short time, are on a very tight budget, or don't expect to be moving around a lot, public transport might be for you.

The city's trains and buses are operated by the **Los Angeles County Metropolitan Transit Authority** (**MTA;** ✆ **213/922-2000;** www.mta.net), and MTA brochures and schedules are available at every area visitor center.

BY BUS OR SHUTTLE

Spread-out stops, sluggish service, and frequent transfers make extensive touring by bus impractical. For short hops and occasional jaunts, however, buses are economical and environmentally friendly. However, I don't recommend riding buses late at night.

The basic bus fare is $1.50 for all local lines, with transfers costing 35¢. A Metro Day Pass is $6 and gives you unlimited bus and rail rides all day long; these can be purchased while boarding any Metro Bus (exact change is needed) or at the self-service vending machines at the Metro Rail stations. *Note:* Two kids under age 5 may travel free with each fare-paying adult.

The **Downtown Area Short Hop (DASH)** shuttle system operates buses throughout downtown and Hollywood. Service runs every 5 to 30 minutes, depending on the time of day, and costs just 35¢. Contact the Department of Transportation (© 213/808-2273; www.ladottransit.com) for schedules and route information (it's pretty confusing—you'll definitely need a weekday *and* weekend map).

The **Cityline** shuttle is a great way to get around West Hollywood on weekdays and Saturdays 9am–6pm). For 25¢, it'll take you from La Brea Avenue and Fountain Avenue all the way to Beverly Boulevard and the San Vicente Boulevard area near Cedars-Sinai Hospital). For more information, call © **800/447-2189.**

BY RAIL & SUBWAY

The **MetroRail** system is a sore subject around town. For years, the MTA has been digging up the city's streets, sucking in huge amounts of tax money, and pushing exhaust vents up through peaceful parkland—and for what? Let's face it, L.A. will never have New York's subway or San Francisco's BART. Today the system is still in its infancy, mainly popular with commuters from outlying suburbs. Here's an overview of what's currently in place:

The **Metro Blue Line,** a mostly aboveground rail line, connects downtown Los Angeles with Long Beach. As with all other metro rail lines, it operates daily from 5am to midnight.

The **Metro Red Line,** L.A.'s first subway, has been growing since 1993 and opened a highly publicized Hollywood–Universal City extension in 2000. The line begins at Union Station, the city's main train depot, and travels west underneath Wilshire Boulevard, looping north into Hollywood and the San Fernando Valley. The **Metro Purple Line** subway starts at Union Station, shares six stations with the Red Line downtown, and continues to the Koreatown area.

The **Metro Green Line** runs for 20 miles along the center of I-105, the Glenn Anderson (Century) Freeway, and connects Norwalk in eastern Los Angeles County to LAX and Redondo Beach. A connection with the Blue Line offers visitors access from LAX to downtown L.A. or Long Beach.

The **Metro Gold Line** is a 14-mile link between Pasadena and Union Station, in downtown L.A. Stops include Old Pasadena, the Southwest Museum, and Chinatown.

The base Metro fare is $1.50 for all lines. A Metro Day Pass is $6 and weekly passes are $20. Passes are available at Metro Customer Centers and local convenience and grocery stores. For more information on public transportation, including construction updates, timetables, and details on purchasing tokens or passes, call **MTA** at © **213/922-2000** or, better yet, log on to their handy website at **www.mta.net**.

BY TAXI

Distances are long in Los Angeles, and cab fares are high; even a short trip can cost $20 or more. Taxis currently charge $2.85 at the flag drop, plus $2.70 per mile. A service charge of $2.50 is added to fares originating from LAX. Beware, there's an additional charge of 30¢ for each 37 seconds of delay, and if you know anything about L.A. traffic, that can really add up fast.

Except in the heart of downtown, cabs will usually not pull over when hailed. Cabstands are at airports, at downtown's Union Station, and at major hotels. To ensure a ride, order a taxi in advance from **Checker Cab** (© **323/654-8400**), **L.A. Taxi** (© **213/627-7000**), or **United Taxi** (© **800/822-8294**).

[Fast FACTS] LOS ANGELES

American Express The main AmEx office is located at 327 N. Beverly Dr., Beverly Hills (✆ **310/274-8277**). To locate the one nearest you, call ✆ **800/221-7282**.

Area Codes Within the past 20 years, L.A. has gone from having a single area code (213) to a whopping seven. Even residents can't keep up. As of press time, here's the basic layout: Those areas west of La Cienega Boulevard, including Beverly Hills and the city's beach communities, use either the **310** or the **424** area code. Portions of Los Angeles County east and south of the city, including Long Beach, are in the **562** area. The San Fernando Valley has the **818** area code, while points east, including San Gabriel Valley cities like Pasadena, use the **626** code. What happened to 213, you ask? The downtown business area still uses **213**. All other numbers, including Griffith Park, Hollywood, and parts of West Hollywood (east of La Cienega Blvd.), now use the area code **323**. If it's all too much to remember, just call directory assistance at ✆ **411**.

Babysitters If you're staying at one of the larger hotels, the concierge can usually recommend a reliable babysitter. If not, contact the **Baby-Sitters Guild** in Glendale (✆ **310/837-1800** or 818/552-2229), L.A.'s oldest and largest babysitting service.

Business Hours Offices are usually open weekdays from 9am to 5pm. Banks are open weekdays from 9am to 5pm or later and sometimes Saturday mornings. Stores typically open between 9 and 10am and close between 5 and 6pm Monday through Saturday. Stores in shopping complexes or malls tend to stay open late: until about 9pm on weekdays and weekends, and many malls and larger department stores are open on Sundays.

Dentists For a recommendation in the area, call the **Dental Referral Service** (✆ **800/422-8338**).

Emergencies Call ✆ **911** to report a fire, call the police, or get an ambulance anywhere in the United States. This is a toll-free call (no coins are required at public telephones).

If you encounter traveler problems, call the Los Angeles chapter of the **Traveler's Aid Society** (✆ **310/646-2270**; www.travelersaid.org), a nationwide, nonprofit, social service organization that helps travelers in need.

Hospital The centrally located (and world-famous) **Cedars-Sinai Medical Center,** 8700 Beverly Blvd., Los Angeles (✆ **310/423-3277**), has a 24-hour emergency room staffed by some of the country's finest MDs.

Newspapers & Magazines The *Los Angeles Times* (www.latimes.com) is a high-quality daily with strong local and national coverage. Its online component, "The Guide," is an excellent road map to entertainment in and around L.A., and includes listings of what's going on and where to do it. The *L.A. Weekly* (www.laweekly.com), a free weekly listings magazine, is packed with information on current events around town. *Los Angeles* magazine (www.lamag.com) is a city-based monthly full of news, information, and previews of L.A.'s art, music, and food scenes.

World Book & News Co., at 1652 N. Cahuenga Blvd. (✆ **323/465-4352**), near Hollywood and Vine and Grauman's Chinese Theatre, stocks lots of out-of-town and foreign papers and magazines. No one minds if you browse through the magazines, but you'll be reprimanded for thumbing through the newspapers. It's open 24 hours.

Police In an emergency, dial ✆ **911**. For nonemergency police matters, call ✆ **213/485-2121;**

in Beverly Hills, dial ☎ **310/550-4951.**

Post Office Call ☎ **800/ ASK-USPS** (275-8777) to find the one closest to you.

Weather Call **Los Angeles National Weather Service** (☎ **805/988-6610**) for the daily forecast. For beach conditions, call the

Zuma Beach Lifeguard recorded information (☎ **310/457-9701**).

WHERE TO STAY

Due to space constraints, I've had to limit the number of hotels included here. For dozens of additional options, check out *Frommer's Los Angeles 2012.*

CHOOSING A LOCATION In sprawling Los Angeles, location is everything. The neighborhood you choose as a base can make or break your vacation. If you plan to spend your days at the beach but stay downtown, for example, you're going to lose a lot of valuable relaxation time on the freeway. For business travelers, choosing a location is easy: Pick a hotel near your work event—don't get on the freeways if you don't have to. For vacationers, though, the decision about where to stay is more difficult. Consider where you want to spend most of your time before you commit yourself to a base. But wherever you stay, count on doing a good deal of driving—no hotel in Los Angeles is convenient to everything.

The relatively smog-free beach communities such as **Santa Monica** and **Venice** are understandably popular with visitors—just about everybody loves to stay at the beach. Book ahead, because hotels fill up quickly, especially in summer.

If they're not at one of the beach communities, most visitors stay on the city's **Westside,** a short drive from the beach and close to most of L.A.'s colorful sights. The city's most elegant and expensive accommodations are in **Beverly Hills** and **Bel Air;** a few of the hotels in these neighborhoods, such as the Beverly Hills Hotel, have become visitor attractions unto themselves. As well as being one of the focal points of L.A. nightlife, **West Hollywood** is home to the greatest range and breadth of hotels, from $300-plus-per-night boutiques to affordably priced motels.

There are fewer hotels in **Hollywood** than you might expect. Accommodations are generally moderately priced and well maintained but unspectacular. Centrally located between downtown and Beverly Hills, just a stone's throw from Universal Studios, Hollywood makes a convenient base if you're planning to do a lot of exploring, but it has more tourists and is less visually appealing than some other neighborhoods; the trendier parts; however, are quite congested at night.

With the exception of a couple quirky boutique hotels, **downtown** lodging options are generally business-oriented, but thanks to direct Metro (L.A.'s subway) connections to Hollywood and Universal Studios, the demographic has begun to shift. The top hotels offer excellent deals on weekend packages. But chances are good that downtown doesn't embody the picture of L.A. you've been dreaming of; you need a coastal or Westside base for that.

Families might want to head to **Universal City** to be near Universal Studios, or straight to **Anaheim and Disneyland** (see chapter 14). **Pasadena** offers historic charm, small-town ambience, easy access to downtown L.A., and Stepford-Wives beauty, but driving to the beach can take forever.

To locate the hotels reviewed below, see the individual neighborhood maps in section 1, "Orientation."

RATES The **rates** quoted in the listings that follow are the rack rates—the maximum rates that a hotel charges for rooms. But rack rates are only guidelines, and there are often many ways around them. ***Always* check each hotel's website for package deals and special Internet rates.** The hotels listed in this section have provided their best estimates for 2011. **Be aware that rates can change at any time** and are subject to availability, seasonal fluctuations, and plain ol' increases.

Santa Monica & the Beaches
VERY EXPENSIVE

Casa del Mar ★★★   In a former 1920s Renaissance Revival beach club, this Art Deco stunner is a real resort hotel, equal in every respect to its sister resort, Shutters, across the street (see below). While Shutters is outfitted like a chic East Coast beach house, this impeccable, U-shape villalike structure radiates period glamour. The building's shape awards ocean views to most of the guest rooms. You're unlikely to be too disappointed, thanks to the gorgeous, summery, European-inspired decor, plus abundant luxuries such as big Italian marble bathrooms with extra-large whirlpool tubs and separate showers.

Downstairs is a big, elegant living room with ocean views, a stylish veranda lounge, and the **Catch Restaurant,** which offers a gorgeous oceanfront setting and a varied menu of small plates, salads, sushi, and fish-centric entrees. The hotel's eco-friendly Sea Wellness spa was completely renovated in 2009.

1910 Ocean Way (next to the Santa Monica Pier), Santa Monica, CA 90405. www.hotelcasadel mar.com. © **800/898-6999** or 310/581-5533. Fax 310/581-5503. 129 units. From $565 double; from $1,275 suite. AE, DC, DISC, MC, V. Valet parking $33. **Amenities:** Oceanfront restaurant; lobby lounge for cocktails and light fare; cafe for daytime dining; 24-hr. concierge; state-of-the-art health club w/spa services; Jacuzzi overlooking Santa Monica Beach; heated outdoor Roman-style pool and plunge pool; room service. *In room:* A/C, TV/DVD, hair dryer, high-speed Internet, minibar, MP3 docking station.

Fairmont Miramar Hotel & Bungalows ★★   The hidden Fairmont Miramar Hotel & Bungalows is for people who prefer their luxury hotels low-key and unobtrusive, yet within walking distance of the area's best attractions. It's almost ironic that this gem is only a block from the beach at the north end of Santa Monica's perpetually crowded Third Street Promenade. The hotel consists of two towers and a bevy of bungalows on 5 acres of grounds. The older, larger rooms in the Pacific Palisades Building are ideal for families; the more modern rooms in the taller Ocean Tower—particularly the corner rooms on the 8th through 10th floors overlooking the Santa Monica Pier or Malibu coastline—are for everyone else. All rooms are well appointed with goose-down duvets and soundproof windows, and those in the Ocean Tower have balconies. If you're in a splurging mood, get one of the über-romantic garden bungalows. **FIG,** an excellent California-style bistro named for the giant tree that fronts the hotel, opened in 2009. Take a seat at the bar and get recommendations from the fromager, or sit down to a full meal in the dining room. ***Tip:*** If you have questions, call the hotel directly—the central reservations line often has incorrect information.

101 Wilshire Blvd. (at Ocean Ave.), Santa Monica, CA 90401. www.fairmont.com/santamonica. ℭ **800/257-7544** or 310/576-7777. Fax 310/458-7912. 270 rooms, 32 bungalows. $349–$469 double; $419–$1,429 bungalow. AE, DC, DISC, MC, V. Valet parking $32. **Amenities:** Restaurant; outdoor lounge; lobby lounge; concierge; 24-hr. health and fitness center; heated outdoor pool and whirlpool; room service; Exhale Spa; Wi-Fi in lobby. *In room:* A/C, TV/DVD, hair dryer, high-speed Internet ($14 per day), minibar.

Hotel Shangri-La ★ The iconic Art Deco hotel, originally built in 1939, underwent a $30-million renovation and reopened in 2009, just in time to celebrate its 70th birthday. Additions include an elevated swimming pool with luxe cabanas, indoor/outdoor rooftop lounge suite, and a dining room, which sources much of its ingredients from the local farmers' market. Overlooking Ocean Avenue, it's not the quietest building on the block; however, a set of double windows—the outer ones remaining from the original 1930s structure—help to keep some of the noise at bay. All rooms feature kitchenettes with stainless-steel appliances and spacious bathrooms with both soaking tubs and rain shower heads. The rooftop's panoramic Suite 700 indoor/outdoor lounge, once the private domain of hotel guests, is now open to the public.

1301 Ocean Ave., Santa Monica, CA 90401. www.shangrila-hotel.com. ℭ **877/999-1301** or 310/394-2791. 71 units. $325–$395 double; from $405 suite. AE, DC, DISC, MC, V. Valet parking $33. **Amenities:** Restaurant; rooftop bar; fitness center; pool; room service. *In room:* A/C, TV/DVD, hair dryer, minibar, MP3 docking station, complimentary Wi-Fi.

Le Merigot ★★ If you want something contemporary and spacious, but not too pricey and prestigious, this low-key luxury hotel and spa fits the bill. Ideally situated on the sandy side of Ocean Avenue in the heart of Santa Monica's beach scene, the 175-room property houses a well-regarded French-California restaurant, **Cézanne,** and the 6,500-square-foot SPA Le Merigot, which offers a full range of services along with an outdoor pool and a state-of-the-art fitness center. Some of the contemporary-style guest rooms offer partial ocean views, and all are furnished with plush carpeting, oversize lounge chairs, and pillow-top beds with Italian cotton linens. Look for clever package deals such as the "California Dreamin'," which includes your choice of a convertible Porsche Boxster or a BMW 3 Series rental car; and the deluxe "California Surfin' Safari," with a 2-hour surf lesson, a rejuvenating full-session Swedish massage, and celebratory Blue Crush graduation martinis (how very L.A.).

1740 Ocean Ave., Santa Monica, CA 90401. www.lemerigothotel.com. ℭ **877/MERIGOT** (637-4468) or 310/395-9700. Fax 310/395-9200. 175 units. $405–$515 double; from $665 suite. AE, DISC, MC, V. Valet parking $34. **Amenities:** Full-service restaurant; lobby bar; concierge; fitness facilities and spa; outdoor pool; room service. *In room:* A/C, TV, minibar, high-speed Wi-Fi ($15 per day).

Shutters on the Beach ★★★ This Cape Cod–style luxury hotel is directly on the beach, a block from Santa Monica Pier. Only the Shutters' sister property—Casa del Mar (above) can compete, but Shutters is slightly better because of balconies on every guest room and a more personal boutique hotel-like ambience. The views and sounds of the ocean are the most outstanding qualities of the spacious, luxuriously outfitted rooms—and pricing is very much based on the scope of said view—some of which have fireplaces and/or whirlpool tubs; all have floor-to-ceiling windows that open. The small swimming pool and the sunny lobby lounge overlooking the sand are two great perches for spotting the celebrities who swear by Shutters as an alternative hangout to smoggy Hollywood. **One Pico,** the hotel's premier restaurant, serves modern American cuisine in a seaside setting. The hotel's **ONE** spa offers guests facials, massages, body scrubs and treatments, manicures, pedicures, and waxing. *Tip:* The beach-cottage rooms overlooking the sand are more desirable and no more expensive than those in the towers.

1 Pico Blvd., Santa Monica, CA 90405. www.shuttersonthebeach.com. © **800/334-9000** or 310/458-0030. Fax 310/458-4589. 198 units. $575–$995 double; from $1,245 suite. AE, DC, DISC, MC, V. Valet parking $33. **Amenities:** Restaurant; cafe; lobby lounge; babysitting; concierge; health club w/spa services; outdoor heated pool and Jacuzzi; room service; sauna; video library; extensive beach equipment rentals (seasonal); Wi-Fi throughout property ($13 per day). *In room:* TV/DVD, hair dryer, minibar, MP3 docking station.

EXPENSIVE

The Ambrose ★★   If being within walking distance of the ocean isn't crucial, but a soothing, peaceful environment is, I've found your hotel. In a residential Santa Monica neighborhood, the 77-room Ambrose blends the Arts and Crafts movement with soothing Asian influences—a tranquil Japanese garden, koi pond, trickling fountains, beautiful artwork, and a profusion of dark woods and mossy palates. The hotel has been designated a "green" property, in that it's committed to low-impact living to conserve the state's natural resources. Most guest rooms are on the small side but are luxuriously appointed with Matteo Italian bedding, Frette cotton kimonos and bath linens, and surround-sound CD/DVD music systems. Studio rooms come with terraces or balconies. It's the many complimentary amenities that really sold me on the Ambrose: underground parking with direct elevator access, breakfast pastries provided by local fave Urth Caffe, and even shuttle service around Santa Monica via the hotel's cute-as-all-get-out London taxi (trust me, you'll love this car).

1255 20th St. (at Arizona Ave.), Santa Monica, CA 90404. www.ambrosehotel.com. © **877-AMBROSE** (262-7673) or 310/315-1555. Fax 310/315-1556. 77 units. From $235 double. Rates include continental breakfast. AE, DC, DISC, MC, V. **Amenities:** Fitness center; room service; complimentary local shuttle. *In room:* TV/VCR, CD/DVD surround sound, hair dryer, minibar, complimentary Wi-Fi throughout property.

Huntley Santa Monica Beach ★★ 🏨   Even though it's in one of Santa Monica's tallest buildings (18 floors), the Huntley is a hidden gem—tucked away behind the Fairmont on the edge of a quiet neighborhood, yet close to Third Street Promenade dining and shopping and just a short walk from the beach. I love this hotel's strikingly stylish lobby, but the coup de grâce is the 18th-floor **Penthouse** restaurant, bar, and lounge. Combine the incredible views of the Santa Monica skyline, a lively bar scene, and good Contemporary American cuisine, and it's no surprise that hotel guests rarely venture elsewhere for drinks and light bites. The Huntley's modern, earth-toned guest rooms offer ocean or mountain views, good work desks, 42-inch flatscreen TVs, and pillow-top beds with Egyptian cotton linens. Book a room on floors 9 to 17 for ocean views. *Fun tip:* Take a thrilling ride in the streetside glass elevator (acrophobes will prefer the interior lobby elevators).

1111 Second St. (north of Wilshire Blvd.), Santa Monica, CA 90403. www.thehuntleyhotel.com. © **310/394-5454.** Fax 310/458-9776. 219 units. $489–$579 double; from $699 suite. AE, DC, DISC, MC, V. Valet parking $30. **Amenities:** Restaurant and bar; lobby cafe; concierge; fitness center; room service. *In room:* A/C, flatscreen TV w/DVD, CD player, hair dryer, MP3 docking station, Wi-Fi ($9.95 per day).

Marina del Rey Marriott ★ ★ 🏨   This is not your average Marriott. In order to attract a more L.A.-hip clientele, this Marina del Rey hotel has made some rather unorthodox modifications to your typical chain hotel. As soon as you enter the lobby, three of your senses are subliminally put at ease: Inhale the Zanzibar Mist, a subtle aromatherapy mixture that circulates throughout the hotel; hear the faint soundtrack of ambient world beats; and gaze into the hypnotic tiers of fire at Glow, their outdoor lounge (p. 662). Things get a bit more utilitarian when you enter your guest room, but each is soothingly spacious and comfortably appointed with down comforters and pillows, 32-inch HDTVs, bathrobes, Jacuzzi-style tubs, and small balconies with stress-relieving views of the marina or Pacific Ocean. Best of all, this is mainly a business hotel, so the weekend rates are often heavily discounted (check their website for deals).

4100 Admiralty Way (at the north end of the marina), Marina del Rey, CA 90292. www.marriott. com. © **800/228-9290** or 310/301-3000. Fax 310/448-4870. 370 units. $209–$279 double; from $259 suite. AE, DC, DISC, MC, V. Valet parking $26. **Amenities:** Restaurant; lobby bar; Glow outdoor lounge; concierge; fitness center; pool and whirlpool; room service. *In room:* A/C, HDTV, hair dryer, Wi-Fi ($13 per day).

MODERATE

The Hotel California ★ 🏨   On enviable real estate along Ocean Avenue— right next door to the behemoth Loews—this welcoming hacienda-style beach-front motel embodies the surfer/sun-worshiper ambience you'd expect from a Santa Monica lodging. The well-tended complex sits above and across an alley from the beach but offers excellent views and direct access to the sand via a private path. The inn offers cheery rooms with beds with down comforters, Egyptian-cotton sheets, and surfboard headboards; hardwood floors; and Spanish-tiled bathrooms. Five one-bedroom suites also have kitchenettes and trundle beds that make them great for families or longer stays; all rooms have minifridges, 27-inch TVs, and ceiling fans, as well as free wireless Internet. A handful of rooms only have showers in the bathrooms. (And no, it's not the hotel from the Eagles' hit—that hotel is rumored to be in Mexico, though the album's cover photo is actually of the Beverly Hills Hotel.) *Tip:* Pay a few bucks extra for a courtyard view, as the cheapest rooms face the parking lot and noisy Ocean Avenue. Be sure to check their website for specials.

1670 Ocean Ave. (south of Colorado Ave.), Santa Monica, CA 90401. www.hotelca.com. © **866/ 571-0000** or 310/393-2363. Fax 310/393-1063. 26 units; 9 monthly rentals. $219–$319 double or suite. AE, DISC, MC, V. Self-parking $25. **Amenities:** Jacuzzi. *In room:* TV/VCR, fridge, hair dryer, complimentary Wi-Fi.

Venice Beach House ★ 🏨   Listed on the National Register of Historic Places, this two-story, ivy-covered 1911 Craftsman bungalow is now a homey bed-and-breakfast on one of funky Venice's unique sidewalk streets, just a block from the beach. The interior has a lived-in look that adds charm for romantics but won't live up to the expectations of travelers who like designer appointments and private bathrooms. What's more, the inn hums noisily with activity when there's a full house. Still, the huge repeat clientele base doesn't seem to mind these minor caveats. My favorite room is the upstairs James Peasgood suite—light and airy, with a double-size Jacuzzi tub, king-size bed, private bathroom, and small balcony perch. An expanded continental breakfast with homemade baked goods is served in the sunroom overlooking a splendid garden.

15 30th Ave. (at Speedway, 1 block west of Pacific Ave.), Venice, CA 90291. www.venicebeach house.com. ℂ **310/823-1966.** Fax 310/823-1842. 9 units, 5 with private bathroom. $150 double with shared bathroom; $210–$255 double with private bathroom. Extra person after 2 people $20. Rates include expanded continental breakfast. AE, MC, V. On-site parking $14 a day. *In room:* A/C, TV, complimentary Wi-Fi.

INEXPENSIVE

Cal Mar Hotel Suites ★ 🔥   In a residential neighborhood 2 blocks from the ocean, this 1950s garden apartment complex delivers a lot of bang for your vacation buck. Each unit is an apartment-style suite with a living room and pullout sofa, a full-size kitchen with utensils, and a separate bedroom; most are spacious enough to accommodate four in comfort. While the furnishings aren't luxurious, they're all quite modern and very clean, and everything is well kept. It's easy to be comfortable here for stays of a week or more, especially since it's so well located, a mere block from the Third Street Promenade and a short walk to the beach. Rooms are in the process of being updated—for instance, hardwood floors have replaced carpeting in some—but it's not a full-scale renovation, just little touches here and there. The staff is attentive and courteous, and the garden courtyard has an inviting swimming pool and chaises for lounging. *Tip:* Request a room on the second floor to avoid the sound of stomping feet.

220 California Ave., Santa Monica, CA 90403. www.calmarhotel.com. ℂ **800/776-6007** or 310/ 395-5555. Fax 310/451-1111. 36 units. $164–$254 suite. Extra person $10. Children 9 and under stay free in parent's room. AE, DC, DISC, MC, V. Parking $13. **Amenities:** Heated outdoor pool. *In room:* TV, CD player, hair dryer, full kitchen, Wi-Fi ($9.95 per day).

Casa Malibu ★★ 🎒   Right on its very own beach, this leftover jewel from Malibu's golden age doesn't try to play the sleek resort game. Instead, the modest, low-rise inn has a traditional California-beach-cottage look that's cozy and time-less. Wrapped around a palm-studded inner courtyard, the 21 rooms are com-fortable and thoughtfully outfitted. Many have been upgraded, but even the older ones are in great shape and boast top-quality bedding and bathrobes. You might also find a fireplace, a kitchenette (in a half-dozen or so), a CD player (in suites), a tub (instead of shower only), and/or a private deck over the sand. The upstairs Catalina Suite (Lana Turner's old hideout) has the best view, while the gorgeous Malibu Suite is the best room in the house and, like the beachfront rooms, right on the beach. More than half have ocean views, but even those facing the court-yard offer easy beach access to the private beach. The handsome, wind-shielded sun deck extends directly over the sand, allowing everyone to enjoy the blue Pacific even in cool months. Book well ahead for summer.

22752 Pacific Coast Hwy. (about ¼ mile south of Malibu Pier), Malibu, CA 90265. ℂ **800/831-0858** or 310/456-2219. Fax 310/456-5418. 21 units. $169–$259 garden or oceanview double; $249–$299 beachfront double; $499–$529 suite. Extra person $20. Rates include continental breakfast. AE, MC, V. Free parking. **Amenities:** Access to nearby private health club for an addi-tional fee; room service. *In room:* TV/DVD, fridge, hair dryer, free Wi-Fi.

Hotel Erwin ★   Formerly Best Western Marina Pacific Hotel & Suites, this recently renovated coastal hotel is a haven of smart value just off the Venice boardwalk. The hotel's spacious rooms are brightened with beachy colors, and many rooms have at least partial ocean views (and top-floor rooms have full ocean views). Terrific for families, the one-bedroom suites offer master bedrooms with king-size beds, fully outfitted kitchens with microwave and dishwasher, dining areas, queen-size sofa sleepers, balconies, and fireplaces. Photos of local scenes and rock-'n'-roll legends, along with works by local artists, lend public spaces a cool L.A. vibe. Stay elsewhere if you need a lot in the way of service or if you don't relish the human carnival of Venice Beach. Keeping with the playful theme, the casual lobby eatery is called "Hash," and the rooftop lounge "High."

1697 Pacific Ave. (at 17th Ave.), Venice, CA 90291. www.jdvhotels.com. © **800/786-7789** or 310/452-1111. Fax 310/452-5479. 88 units. $229–$269 double; $259–$369 suite. AE, DC, DISC, MC, V. Valet parking $28. **Amenities:** Restaurant; rooftop lounge; fitness center. *In room:* A/C, flatscreen TV, hair dryer, MP3 docking station, Wi-Fi ($4.95 per day), honor bar.

Sea Shore Motel 🏄 🎁   In the heart of Santa Monica's Main Street dining and shopping sector, this small, friendly, family-run motel is one of the best bargains near the beach. The Sea Shore is such a well-kept secret that most denizens of stylish Main Street are unaware of the incredible value in their midst. Arranged around a parking courtyard, rooms are small and unremarkable from the outside, but the conscientious management has done a nice job with the interiors, installing attractive terra-cotta floor tiles, granite countertops, and conveniences such as voice mail and Internet access. Complete with a living room and full kitchen, the 800-square-foot suites that sleep up to six are a phenomenal deal; book them as far in advance as possible. With a full slate of restaurants out the front door and the Santa Monica Pier and beach just a couple of blocks away, it's a terrific bargain base for exploring the sandy side of the city.

2637 Main St. (south of Ocean Park Blvd.), Santa Monica, CA 90405. www.seashoremotel.com. © **310/392-2787.** Fax 310/392-5167. 24 units. $110–$180 double; $150–$300 suite. Extra person $5. 1 child 10 or under stays free in parent's room. AE, DISC, MC, V. Free parking. Pets accepted for $10 per night. **Amenities:** Unaffiliated deli in building; sun deck. *In room:* 27-in. flatscreen TV, fridge, free Wi-Fi.

Near LAX

If you have an early-morning flight and need an airport hotel, the **Westin Los Angeles Airport,** 5400 W. Century Blvd. (© **800/937-8461** or 310/216-5858; www.westin.com/losangelesairport), is a cut above the rest, with its patented Westin Heavenly Beds. Two other good, moderately priced choices are the **Sheraton Gateway Hotel,** 6101 W. Century Blvd., near Sepulveda Boulevard (www.sheratonlosangeles.com; © **800/325-3535** or 310/642-1111), a comfortable, California-style hotel that overlooks the runway; and the **Marriott Los Angeles Airport,** 5855 Century Blvd. (www.marriott.com; © **800/228-9290** or 310/641-5700), a reliable choice for travelers on the fly.

An inexpensive option is the **Travelodge at LAX,** 5547 W. Century Blvd. (www.travelodgelax.com; © **800/421-3939** or 310/649-4000), an otherwise standard member of the reliable chain with a beautiful tropical garden around the pool area.

L.A.'s Westside & Beverly Hills

VERY EXPENSIVE

Beverly Hills Hotel and Bungalows ★★★   Behind the famous facade (remember the Eagles' *Hotel California* album?) is this star-studded haven where legends were, and still are, made: The "Pink Palace" was center stage for both deal- and star-making in Hollywood's golden days. Today stars and industry hot-shots can still be found lounging around the Olympic-size pool (into which Katharine Hepburn once dove fully clothed) or digging into Dutch apple pancakes in the iconic **Polo Lounge,** where Hunter S. Thompson kicked off his adventure to Las Vegas.

Following a $250-million restoration about 10 years ago, the hotel's grand lobby and impeccably landscaped grounds retain their over-the-top glory, while the lavish guest rooms boast every state-of-the-art luxury. Many rooms feature private patios, Jacuzzi tubs, kitchens, fireplaces, and/or dining rooms. The 23 bungalows—with two more sizable three-bedroom suites (bye-bye tennis courts)—are more luxe than ever, and the lush, tropical-like grounds are brimming with exotic trees and flowers. Even the outdoor pathways are carpeted, to keep noise to a minimum. Adding one more layer of luxury to the hotel, the **Beverly Hills Hotel Spa by La Prairie** offers European and Asian-influenced massage and expert facials. Stop by **Bar NINETEEN12** for drinks, which are pricey, or the informal, retro-chic **Fountain Coffee Shop** for lunch or early dinner. For a truly iconic L.A. dining experience—or just a martini—the old-school vibe at the more upscale Polo Lounge can't be beat.

9641 Sunset Blvd. (at Rodeo Dr.), Beverly Hills, CA 90210. www.beverlyhillshotel.com. ✆ **800/283-8885** or 310/276-2251. Fax 310/887-2887. 210 units. $530–$760 double; from $1,150 suite or bungalow. AE, DC, MC, V. Valet parking $34. Pets accepted in bungalows only ($200 nonrefundable pet fee). **Amenities:** 3 restaurants; 2 bars; 2 lounges; babysitting; concierge; fitness center; Olympic-size outdoor heated pool; room service; full spa services; whirlpool. *In room:* A/C, TV/VCR, CD player, hair dryer, minibar, Wi-Fi ($10 per day).

Four Seasons Hotel Los Angeles at Beverly Hills ★★   This intimate-feeling 16-story hotel attracts a mix of A-list jet-setters and an L.A. showbiz crowd who cherish the hotel as an après-event gathering place. Lush gardens will help you forget you're in the heart of the city, the concierge is famously well connected, and service goes the distance. Guest rooms are sumptuously furnished, with luxuries including custom Sealy mattresses with heavenly linens and pillows, marble bathrooms, and French doors leading to private balconies. Room rates rise with the elevator, so bargain hunters need to sacrifice the view. For not much more money per night, the Premiere King rooms are on the corners of the building, and offer wraparound balconies. Along with a full-service spa, try the poolside California Cabana massage at one of the private candlelit poolside areas. The view-endowed fourth-floor deck has a lap pool, poolside grill, and glass-walled fitness center. Replacing the long-standing Gardens restaurant, Culina debuted in 2010, and serves exquisite Italian cuisine.

300 S. Doheny Dr. (at Burton Way), Los Angeles, CA 90048. ✆ **800/819-5053,** 800/332-3442, or 310/273-2222. Fax 310/859-3824. www.fourseasons.com/losangeles. 285 units. $525–$595 double; from $745 suite. AE, DC, DISC, MC, V. Valet parking $30. Pets 15 lb. and under welcomed (no charge). **Amenities:** Restaurant; lounge; poolside grill; concierge; fitness center; Jacuzzi; rooftop heated pool; room service; full-service spa. *In room:* A/C, TV/DVD, CD player, hair dryer, minibar, Wi-Fi ($10 per day).

Hotel Palomar Los Angeles ★   This 19-story property near the heart of Westwood Village oozes with elements of boutique style and exoticism, from the grand rouge marble fireplace in the shimmering lobby to velvet shams and faux snakeskin chests in each guest room, though things have been dialed back a bit since its opening in 2008. There are still higher-end perks like Aveda bath products, 42-inch

LCD flatscreen TVs, plush terry bathrobes, lighted makeup and full-length mirrors, and Fuji spa tubs in all but one of the suites. However, other amenities like personal trainers are gone, and the Lexus Hybrid town car has been replaced by third-party shuttle service, though it's still free within a limited radius. Fortunately for the eco-friendly among us, the in-room recycling bins remain. The hotel's signature restaurant, **Blvd 16,** can be hit-or-miss with food, drinks, and service.

10740 Wilshire Blvd., Los Angeles, CA 90024. www.hotelpalomar-lawestwood.com. ☏ **800/472-8556** or 310/475-8711. Fax 310/475-5220. 268 units. $209–$249 double; $269–$309 suite. AE, DC, DISC, MC, V. Valet parking $33. **Amenities:** Blvd 16 Restaurant & Lounge; evening wine reception; concierge; 24-hr. fitness center; heated pool; room service. *In room:* A/C, TV, hair dryer, minibar, MP3 docking station, Wi-Fi ($10 per day).

Mondrian ★★　Theatrical, coveted, sophisticated—this is the kind of place superhotelier Ian Schrager has created from a once-drab apartment building. Working with *enfant terrible* French designer Philippe Starck, Schrager used the Mondrian's breathtaking views (from every room) as the starting point for his vision of a "hotel in the clouds." Purposely underlit hallways lead to bright, clean rooms outfitted with simple furniture casually slipcovered in white; about three-quarters of the rooms and suites have fully outfitted kitchenettes. The accommodations themselves are only secondary to the superhip, star-studded scene. Booking a room guarantees admission to **Skybar,** one of L.A.'s hottest watering holes. (Soundproof windows on the south side of the building have eliminated a troublesome noise problem in rooms overlooking the raucous late-night scene.) In addition to its ultrahip Asian-Latin fusion restaurant, **Asia de Cuba,** light meals and sushi are served at a quirky communal table in the lobby. The elegant **Agua Spa** offers a full range of treatments in a Zen-like atmosphere. The beautiful-people staff aren't strong on service, but they look great.

8440 Sunset Blvd., West Hollywood, CA 90069. www.mondrianhotel.com. ☏ **800/697-1791** or 323/650-8999. Fax 323/650-5215. 237 units. $315–$505 double; from $385 suite. AE, DC, DISC, MC, V. Valet parking $32. **Amenities:** 2 restaurants; bar; concierge; fitness room; outdoor pool; room service; Agua Spa; video, DVD, and CD libraries. *In room:* A/C, TV/DVD player; CD player, hair dryer, minibar, MP3 docking station, Wi-Fi ($10 per day).

Montage Beverly Hills ★★★　Smack-dab in the center of the Golden Triangle, a credit-card's throw from Rodeo Drive, this relatively new resort has it all: beautiful rooms, top-notch service, an excellent spa, and a rooftop restaurant and pool with sweeping views of the city. The Mediterranean-inspired, Spanish Colonial decor is warm and inviting, serene and plush, just what you'd expect from the Montage. Because it opened only in late 2008, this definitely feels like a contemporary hotel; if you're looking for history, try the Beverly Hills Hotel. All 201 rooms have balconies, extremely comfortable beds, and ample desk space for business travelers. The suites are worth the extra dollars, especially if you like to spread out; book a Superior Suite, and you'll get a complimentary Mercedes-Benz to drive around town during your stay. Private cabanas around the pool are completely decked out with TVs, refrigerators—pretty much anything you could possibly want, they'll get it for you. Get a treatment in the two-story spa; we found that even the facials are relaxing. There's afternoon tea in the lobby, and two restaurants: **Scarpetta,** for storied Italian fare from New York–based chef/restaurateur Scott Conant adjacent to the rooftop pool, and the **Conservatory Grill,** a much more casual indoor/outdoor space with lovely views. Additionally, the lobby lounge serves afternoon tea and libations.

225 N. Canon Dr., Beverly Hills, CA 90210. www.montagebeverlyhills.com. ℂ **800/462-7899** or 310/860-7800. Fax 310/860-7801. 201 units. $475–$775 double; from $925 suite. AE, DC, DISC, MC, V. Parking $30. **Amenities:** 3 restaurants; 2 bars; concierge; state-of-the-art fitness center; rooftop heated pool; room service; terrific full-service spa. *In room:* A/C, TV, hair dryer, minibar, free Wi-Fi.

Peninsula Beverly Hills ★★★ The Peninsula is one of L.A.'s three finest hotels (along with the still-shuttered Hotel Bel-Air and the Beverly Hills Hotel). This stellar brand—like its sister Peninsula properties in exotic locales like Hong Kong, Beijing, and Bangkok—has risen above the rest by making ultraservice its hallmark. At Beverly Hills' crossroads, this gardenlike oasis is impeccable in every respect (although laid-back types will surely consider it too formal). Special features in the large, lavish, European-style guest rooms include controls for everything—lighting, climate, DO NOT DISTURB sign—as well as the luxurious Frette-made bed, and round-the-clock personal valets. The 16 private villa suites in lush gardens have fireplaces, kitchens, and individual security systems. Sure, rooms are expensive, but the 24-hour checkout policy—which allows you to keep your room for a full 24 hours, no matter what time you check in—means you get your money's worth. All guests are entitled to access the courtesy Town Car or Rolls-Royce Phantom, within a 3-mile radius. **Belvedere** is one of L.A.'s premier hotel dining rooms; breakfast is a tradition among CAA agents and their thespian clients (insiders order the nowhere-on-the-menu banana-stuffed brioche French toast), and Sunday brunch is delicious. The mahogany-paneled bar is also popular among the power suits, while the English Garden–style **Living Room** pours a splendid high tea. The renovated **Peninsula Spa** is worthy of a visit, even if you don't stay at the hotel.

9882 S. Santa Monica Blvd. (at Wilshire Blvd.), Beverly Hills, CA 90212. www.peninsula.com. ℂ **800/462-7899** or 310/551-2888. Fax 310/788-2319. 196 units. $585–$955 double; from $1,550 suite. AE, DC, DISC, MC, V. Parking $28. **Amenities:** Restaurant; bar; concierge; state-of-the-art fitness center; rooftop heated lap pool and Jacuzzi; room service; stellar full-service spa. *In room:* A/C, TV/DVD w/WebTV, hair dryer, minibar, free Wi-Fi.

SLS ★★ After a $230-million renovation, the SBE group turned the former staid Le Meridien into a whimsical tapestry of living art. Designed by Philippe Starck, the whole place is visually compelling: Life-size photographs of people decorate the elevator walls; mirrors in the rooms are bordered by the outline of human heads; the TV is projected through a glass wall. Fitness buffs might consider booking an exercise suite that comes outfitted with built-in weightlifting equipment (though the hotel gym is amazing). The hotel's restaurant, bar, and retail area, called **The Bazaar** (which is, fittingly, bizarre), is among one of the most cutting-edge eateries in town; half the menu is classic Spanish tapas, and the other half focuses on molecular gastronomy. **Ciel Spa** does a fine job living up to its name by creating the illusion that you've arrived at the pearly gates through a series of mirrors, bright lighting, and billowy, white drapings.

465 S. La Cienega Blvd., Los Angeles, CA 90048. www.slshotels.com. ℂ **310/247-0400.** Fax 310/247-0315. 297 units. $369–$649 double; from $769 suite. AE, DC, DISC, MC, V. Valet parking $35. **Amenities:** Restaurant; lounge and patisserie; concierge; fitness facility; rooftop pool w/ private cabanas; room service; DVD library. *In room:* A/C, TV/DVD, hair dryer, minibar, MP3 docking station, Wi-Fi ($13 per day).

Thompson Beverly Hills ★★ Beverly Hills just got a tad bit cooler with the spring 2008 introduction of the Thompson to the neighborhood's main drag,

Wilshire Boulevard. While all the mirrors almost make it feel like a posh fun house, the rooms are plush and dapper, with a nod to California modernism. If you want to spring for an upgrade, you can't go wrong with the signature and sexy Thompson Suite, which has a balcony with sweeping views, a kitchen, two bathrooms (one with a tub, one with a shower), a sitting area, and a bedroom. Though a stay here comes at a pretty penny, particularly on the weekend, the hotel is worth the price tag simply for access to the dual-level, mostly members-only rooftop pool and its accompanying bar, **ABH** (Above Beverly Hills), offering private cabanas and stunning panoramic views of the city. Sundays and Mondays are now locals' nights, so it's not as exclusive as it once was. The outpost of New York City's trendy **Bond Street** restaurant will be closing; the new concept has yet to be announced. *Tip:* If you want to see the Hollywood sign from your room, ask for something on floors seven through nine.

9360 Wilshire Blvd., Beverly Hills, CA 90212. www.thompsonbeverlyhills.com. ⓒ **310/273-1400.** Fax 310/859-8551. 107 units. $254–$314 double; from $349 suite. AE, DC, DISC, MC, V. Valet parking $30. **Amenities:** Restaurant; rooftop bar; 24-hr. concierge; state-of-the-art fitness center; pool; room service. *In room:* A/C, TV/DVD, hair dryer, minibar, MP3 docking station, Wi-Fi ($10 per day).

EXPENSIVE

Avalon Hotel ★ 🎁   The first style-conscious boutique hotel on the L.A. scene, this mid-20th-century-inspired gem is located in the heart of Beverly Hills. With a soothing sherbet-hued palette and classic atomic-age furnishings—Eames cabinets, Heywood-Wakefield chairs, Nelson bubble lamps—mixed with smart custom designs, every room looks as if it could star in a *Metropolitan Home* photo spread. But fashion doesn't forsake function at this beautifully designed hotel, which offers enough luxury comforts and amenities to please design-blind travelers too. The main building is the hub of a chic but low-key scene, but the quieter Canon building features rooms with kitchenettes and/or furnished terraces. All guests have easy access to the sunny courtyard, with its retro-hip amoeba-shape pool; the fitness room; and **Oliverio,** the groovy blue-hued Italian restaurant and bar. Service is friendlier than you'll find in other style-minded hotels. *Note:* If you're a light sleeper, request a room away from the pool area, where the occasional nighttime party can get loud.

9400 W. Olympic Blvd. (at Beverly Dr.), Beverly Hills, CA 90212. www.avalonbeverlyhills.com. ⓒ **800/670-6183** or 310/277-5221. Fax 310/277-4928. 84 units. $248–$400 double; from $400 1-bedroom suite. AE, DC, MC, V. Valet parking $30. **Amenities:** Restaurant and lounge; courtyard pool; room service. *In room:* A/C, TV/DVD, hair dryer, minibar, MP3 docking station, Wi-Fi ($11 per day).

Chateau Marmont ★★   Perched secretively in a curve above the Sunset Strip, the château modeled after an elegant Loire Valley castle is a landmark from 1920s-era Hollywood. Greta Garbo regularly checked in as Harriet Brown, and Jim Morrison was one of many celebrities to call this home in later years. This historic landmark built its reputation on exclusivity and privacy, which was shattered when John Belushi overdosed in Bungalow No. 2. Now under the guiding hand of boutique hotelier Andre Balazs, the funky luxury oasis is hipper and more exclusive than ever. No two of the antiques-filled standard rooms, suites, cottages, or bungalows are alike. Many units have fireplaces and CD stereos, and all but 11 have kitchenettes or full kitchens.

The Chateau Marmont is beautifully kept, eternally chic, faultlessly service-oriented, and overflowing with Hollywood and rock-'n'-roll lore (not to mention a look-at-me/don't-look-at-me clientele), but it's not for everybody. Quirkiness rules, so don't expect traditional luxuries.

8221 Sunset Blvd. (btw. La Cienega and Crescent Heights blvds.), West Hollywood, CA 90046. www.chateaumarmont.com. ℂ **800/242-8328** or 323/656-1010. Fax 323/655-5311. 63 units. From $415 double; from $500 suite; from $545 cottage; from $1,800 bungalow. AE, DC, MC, V. Valet parking $28. Pets accepted for $150 per pet. **Amenities:** Restaurant (serves in lobby, garden, and dining room); bar; 24-hr. concierge; exercise room; access to nearby health club; outdoor heated pool w/brick sun deck; room service; CD library. *In room:* A/C, TV/DVD, CD player, fridge, hair dryer, minibar, MP3 docking station, free Wi-Fi.

Le Parc Suite Hotel ★★   On a quiet, tree-lined residential street, Le Parc is a sophisticated and stylish all-suite hotel that attracts an interesting mix of clientele: Designers stay here because it's a few minutes' walk to the Pacific Design Center; celebrities in the music industry stay because of its low-key neighborhood location; patients and medical consultants check in because it's close to Cedars-Sinai; and tourists enjoy being near the Farmers Market, the Beverly Center, and Museum Row. The renovated apartment-like units are extra-large, and each has a well-outfitted kitchenette, a dining area, a living room with a fireplace, and a balcony. What the hotel lacks in views it makes up for in value and elbowroom, and the rooftop night-lit tennis court is a rare perk in this area. The hotel's intimate bistro-style restaurant, **Knoll,** offers contemporary American cuisine and romantic alfresco seating at the rooftop dining area.

733 N. West Knoll Dr., West Hollywood, CA 90069. www.leparcsuites.com. ℂ **800/578-4837** or 310/855-8888. Fax 310/659-7812. 154 units. $279–$409 junior or 1-bedroom suite. Check for tour and bed-and-breakfast packages. AE, DC, DISC, MC, V. Parking $30. Pets accepted for $75 fee. **Amenities:** Restaurant w/full bar; concierge; well-equipped exercise room w/sauna; access to nearby health club; outdoor heated pool and Jacuzzi; room service; rooftop night-lit tennis court. *In room:* A/C, TV/DVD, CD player, hair dryer, kitchenette, minibar, MP3 docking stations (upon request only; $100 deposit), free Wi-Fi.

The Mosaic Hotel Beverly Hills ★★ 🎁   The owners pumped $3 million into completely renovating this boutique hotel (formerly the Beverly Hills Inn), and the result is spectacular. The lobby is a showcase of functional art, with gleaming tile mosaics; fabrics in deep, rich tones; and a profusion of artfully arranged orchids. Continuing a trend that I'm all for, a wall has been removed to allow direct access from the check-in desk to the bar and lounge, where guests are encouraged to sample the house special—a Mosaic sake martini. The guest rooms are equally impressive, with 300-count linens, goose-down comforters and piles of pillows, windows that open onto the quiet street or garden courtyard, stocked minibars, and sparkling bathrooms with Bulgari bath products and huge rain shower heads. Other perks include free high-speed Internet access, poolside cabanas, and CD players in the suites. *Tip:* The "preferred" corner rooms are worth the extra $50 (you get an extra 50 sq. ft.).

125 S. Spalding Dr., Beverly Hills, CA 90212. www.mosaichotel.com. ℂ **800/463-4466** or 310/278-0303. Fax 310/278-1728. 49 units. From $350 double; from $700 1-bedroom suite. AE, DC, MC, V. Parking $30. Small pets accepted. **Amenities:** Restaurant; full bar; small exercise room w/sauna; heated outdoor pool; room service. *In room:* A/C, TV, CD player, DVD upon request only, fridge, hair dryer, free Wi-Fi.

Sunset Boulevard, winding through the Sunset Strip.

Sunset Tower Hotel ★★★   Standing out like an Art Deco pearl among the surrounding architectural swine, the 15-story Sunset Tower was built in 1921 as a luxury apartment for Hollywood's top movie stars: everyone from Jean Harlow and Clark Gable to Marilyn Monroe, Elizabeth Taylor, and Frank Sinatra have lived (or housed lovers) here. The building lost its luster in the '60s and was nearly demolished in the '80s. In 2005, hotelier Jeff Klein bought and meticulously restored the hotel with fine woods, muted colors of natural brown and beige, and brass fittings. Guest rooms have floor-to-ceiling windows with wonderful city views, as well as oversize tubs, Egyptian linens, and a soothing aura of old-Hollywood elegance. What better way to spend a day in L.A. than to have a massage and spa treatments at the hotel's **Argyle Spa,** spend the afternoon sunbathing at the pool while noshing on blinis and rosé from the **Terrace** poolside grill, settle into a Plymouth martini and a lobster Cobb at the beautiful **Tower Bar,** and then step out the front door and stroll along the famous Sunset Strip?

8358 Sunset Blvd. (on the Sunset Strip), West Hollywood, CA 90069. www.sunsettowerhotel. com. ⓒ **800/225-2637** or 323/654-7100. Fax 323/654-9287. 74 units. $295–$325 double; from $345 suite; from $2,500 penthouse. AE, DC, DISC, MC, V. Valet parking $32. Pets accepted ($100 fee). **Amenities:** Restaurant; poolside grill; bar and lounge; concierge; 24-hr. fitness center; heated outdoor pool; room service; full-service spa. *In room:* A/C, TV/DVD, hair dryer, minibar, MP3 docking station, free Wi-Fi.

MODERATE

Chamberlain West Hollywood ★★   This four-story boutique hotel in a tree-lined residential West Hollywood neighborhood looks and feels much like a high-quality Manhattan apartment building (probably because it used to be an apartment building). The location alone is reason enough to stay here, as it's only 2 blocks from the Sunset Strip and Santa Monica Boulevard. If you're young and hip and have plenty of room on your credit card, you won't need your car once it's parked in the underground garage (hell, you won't even need comfortable shoes). If you've been to the Viceroy in Santa Monica, you'll recognize the English Modern decor—dusky grays, greens, and blues among stark white furnishings. Each guest room is a suite with a separate living and sleeping area, and comes pleasantly equipped with a plush king-size bed with Sferra sheets, gas-log fireplace, small balcony, flatscreen TV, DVD/VCR combo, CD player, and large desk with Internet access. The rooftop pool and cabana are ideal for sunbathing, and the roof has a great view of the city. The small restaurant and bar are good for meeting friends for a drink and appetizers before you hit the town.

1000 Westmount Dr. (1 block west of La Cienega Blvd.), West Hollywood, CA 90069. www. chamberlainwesthollywood.com. (€ **800/201-9652** or 310/657-7400. Fax 310/854-6744. 114 units. $249–$369 suite. AE, DC, DISC, MC, V. Valet parking $30 with in/out privileges. **Amenities:** Concierge; newly expanded fitness center; heated rooftop pool; room service. *In room:* A/C, TV/ DVD, CD player, hair dryer, MP3 docking station, Wi-Fi ($11 per day).

Elan Hotel ★★ 🎁   The Elan is not only one of L.A.'s best boutique-style hotels; it's one of its best values as well. Rebuilt and freshly renovated from the bones of a 1969 retirement home, the modern structure blends elements from the original 1969 facade with a modern, sophisticated decor. A mod, loungey lobby leads to handsomely appointed guest rooms that are amenity-laden and surprisingly luxurious for the price. Standard rooms aren't huge but have high ceilings; thoughtfully designed custom furnishings; beautifully made beds with cushioned headboards, goose-down comforters, and high-quality cotton linens; bathrooms with cotton robes; and plush towels. On the downside, there's no view, no pool, no fitness center (although you can purchase a $14 pass to the nearby health club), and no restaurant, and this stretch of Beverly Boulevard isn't exactly the hippest. But double-paned glass ensures that rooms are quiet, and the location in central L.A. is ideal (shoppers will love the walking-distance proximity to the Beverly Center).

8435 Beverly Blvd. (btw. La Cienega Blvd. and Fairfax Ave.), Los Angeles, CA 90048. www.elan hotel.com. (€ **888/611-0398** or 323/658-6663. Fax 323/658-6640. 49 units. From $189 double. Rates include continental breakfast and manager's wine-and-cheese reception. AE, DC, DISC, MC, V. Valet parking $19 plus tax. **Amenities:** Access to nearby health club ($14). *In room:* A/C, HDTV, hair dryer, minibar, MP3 docking station, free Wi-Fi.

Hotel Angeleno Los Angeles ★   This L.A. landmark building is the last of a vanishing breed of circular hotels from the 1960s and 1970s. Formerly a Holiday Inn, it was revamped into a hip, modern destination. The location alone is a good reason to stay here: It's perched beside the city's busiest freeway, a short hop from the popular Getty Center and centrally located between the beaches, Beverly Hills, and the San Fernando Valley. Each pie-shaped room comes with a private balcony and double-paned glass to keep most of the freeway din at bay—think of it as complimentary white noise—while comfort comes in the form of 300-count Italian linens, feather duvets, and pillow-top mattresses. Little extras like 30-inch plasma TVs, free Wi-Fi, and great views add to the panache. The 17th-story, penthouse-level **West,** a supper club and cocktail lounge, is an Italian steak-house. Additional perks include an outdoor pool with cabanas and a fire pit, and complimentary transport to and from the Getty Center, UCLA, and Westwood. *Tip:* There are only 3 suites in the hotel, and they must be booked directly; they are not listed on the website.

170 N. Church Lane (at intersection of Sunset Blvd. and I-405), Los Angeles, CA 90049. www. hotelangeleno.com. © **866/ANGELENO** (264-3536) or 310/476-6411. Fax 310/472-1157. 208 units. $179–$209 double; from $249 suite. Rates include evening wine reception. AE, DC, DISC, MC, V. Valet parking free for 1 car; additional vehicles $20 each. **Amenities:** Rooftop restaurant and lounge; lobby cafe; concierge; small fitness center; heated outdoor pool; room service. *In room:* A/C, TV w/pay movies and free HBO, hair dryer, minibar, free Wi-Fi.

The Orlando ★   Not only is the Orlando situated between Beverly Hills and West Hollywood in the heart of the Third Street Shopping District, but it's also within walking distance of the Grove, the Farmers Market, the Beverly Center, and Restaurant Row. The large guest rooms are comfortably equipped with custom furnishings, 30-inch plasma TVs, MP3 docking stations, minibars, and beds with 400-thread-count Egyptian cotton sheets, but you'll probably spend most of your time at the rooftop deck, floating in the saltwater pool. If you're in a splurging mood, request one of the newly created Hollywood Premium rooms with a big ol' king-size bed, a personal iPod with surround-sound Bose speakers, and private patio. The hotel is recently renovated. There's an onsite Italian trattoria called **Minestraio.** *Tip:* Celebrities like to stay here because of the hotel's low-key location and privacy.

8384 W. Third St. (at Orlando St.), Los Angeles, CA 90048. www.theorlando.com. © **800/62-HOTEL** (624-6835) or 323/658-6600. Fax 323/653-4737. 98 units. From $189 standard room; rates for premium rooms unavailable at press time. AE, DC, DISC, MC, V. Valet parking $29. Small pets welcome ($50 per night fee). **Amenities:** Restaurant; bar; 24-hr. fitness center; saltwater-heated pool; room service; free Wi-Fi. *In room:* A/C, TV w/On Demand, CD player, hair dryer, minibar, MP3 docking station, DVD/iPods available for rental.

The Standard ★★   Designed to appeal to the under-35 "it" crowd, André Balazs's swank West Hollywood neomotel is sometimes absurd, sometimes brilliant, and always provocative (not to mention crowded). It's a scene worthy of its Sunset Strip location: shag carpeting on the lobby ceiling, blue Astroturf around the swimming pool, a DJ spinning ambient sounds while a performance artist poses in a display case behind the check-in desk. But look past the retro clutter and often-raucous party scene, and you'll find a level of service more often associated with hotels costing twice as much. Constructed from the bones of a vintage 1964 motel, it boasts comfortably sized rooms outfitted with cobalt blue indoor-outdoor carpeting, silver beanbag chairs, and Warhol's poppy-print curtains, plus private balconies and minibars whose contents include goodies like sake, condoms, and animal crackers. On the downside, the cheapest rooms face noisy Sunset Boulevard, and the relentless scene can get tiring if you're not into it. *Note:* The 12-story **Downtown Standard,** 550 S. Flower St. (© **213/892-8080**), brings a similar dose of retro-future style and cool attitude to downtown. It's worth visiting just to check out the retro-glam rooftop bar with its vibrating waterbed pleasure pods, movies projected onto neighboring buildings, and hot waitstaff.

8300 Sunset Blvd. (at Sweetzer Ave.), West Hollywood, CA 90069. www.standardhotel.com. © **323/650-9090.** Fax 323/650-2820. 139 units. $199–$230 double; from $350 suite. AE, DC, DISC, MC, V. Valet parking $29. Pets 20 lb. and under accepted for $100 per pet. **Amenities:** 24-hr. coffee shop; poolside cafe; bar/lounge; concierge; access to nearby health club ($16 per day); outdoor heated pool; room service. *In room:* A/C, large-screen TVs w/DVD, minibar, MP3 docking station, free Wi-Fi.

INEXPENSIVE

Beverly Laurel Motor Hotel ⚑   The Beverly Laurel is a great choice for wallet-watching travelers who want a central location and a room with more style than your average motel. Overlooking the parking lot, the budget-basic but well-kept rooms are smartened up with diamond-print spreads and eye-catching artwork; other features include a minifridge, microwave, and ample closet space, and a large kitchenette for an extra 55 bucks. The postage-stamp-size outdoor pool is a little public for carefree sunbathing, but it does the job on hot summer days. Best of all is the motel's own excellent coffee shop, **Swingers** (p. 665)—known for its burgers and malts—and you may even spot your favorite alt-rocker tucking into a 3pm breakfast in the vinyl booth next to yours.

8018 Beverly Blvd. (btw. La Cienega Blvd. and Fairfax Ave.), Los Angeles, CA 90048. ✆ **800/962-3824** (outside CA) or 323/651-2441. Fax 323/651-5225. 52 units. $109–$165 double. AAA and senior discounts may be available. AE, DC, MC, V. Free parking. **Amenities:** Outdoor pool. *In room:* A/C, TV, hair dryer, minifridge, Wi-Fi ($5.95 per day).

Farmer's Daughter ⚑   Most people end up at the Farmer's Daughter hotel fortuitously because they're waiting to be the next contestants on *The Price Is Right.* The CBS Studios across the street recommend the budget motel to its game show fans, but I recommend it just because I dig this chic little lodge. It's cheery from the moment you walk in the lobby. Bright yellows and cool blues mix well with the country-kitsch theme: rooster wallpaper, faded barn-wood paneling, denim bedspreads, cow-skin rugs, and a parade of inflatable animals that float around the pool. It's obvious that someone with smart fashion sense and a little money turned a dumpy motel into an oasis of stylish affordability for people like me who drive Jettas and wear flip-flops in the winter. It's also obvious that someone with a good sense a humor was behind the "No Tell" room, which is outfitted with a giant copper-framed mirror above the bed. Money-saving perks include a free DVD library and across-the-street access to an entire Farmers Market of inexpensive foodstuffs (p. 600). Since the hotel opened its own comfort food restaurant, **TART,** there's the option of staying in, though if you have only 1 day/night, it would be sad to miss the people-watching and dining experience unique to the iconic Farmers Market. *Tip:* Request a room facing the alley—the view is terrible, but you don't get the 24-hour road noise off Fairfax Avenue.

115 S. Fairfax Ave. (btw. Beverly Dr. and Third St.), Los Angeles, CA 90036. www.farmers daughterhotel.com. ✆ **800/334-1658** or 323/937-3930. Fax 323/932-1608. 66 units. From $219 double; from $269 suite. AE, DISC, MC, V. Valet parking $18 plus tax. **Amenities:** Restaurant and bar; morning coffee and tea service; pool. *In room:* A/C, TV/DVD, CD player, complimentary DVD library, minibar, MP3 docking station, free Wi-Fi.

Hollywood

EXPENSIVE

The Redbury ★   A smaller sister property to the SLS, the spacious rooms at this stylish Hollywood & Vine boutique hotel feel more like a hipster friend's loft. Owned by lifestyle-curating entertainment company SBE, subtle this is not, from its striking crimson red exterior to its iconic hallway imagery of early Hollywood film vixens like Jean Harlow to the "opa!" Greek-style plate-breaking at Mediterranean eatery **Cleo.** This is not to say it's style over substance; in fact, the rooms are quite spacious and feature lots of thoughtful touches like easy-to-operate, single-cup coffeemakers with to-go cups (including lids!); a combo washer/dryer in each unit; and record players with a section of 45s ranging from John Coltrane to Daft Punk. With the smallest "flat" starting at 750 square feet, the room is more luxurious than most affordable NYC apartments. The only surprise was the lack of a happening nightlife scene; the only bar here is the one at the restaurant.

1717 Vine St., Hollywood, CA 90028. www.theredbury.com. (*) **877/962-1717** or 323/962-1717. Fax 323/962-1710. 57 units. From $339–$739 doubles. AE, DISC, MC, V. Valet parking $33. **Amenities:** Restaurant; free passes to nearby 24-hr. fitness center; pool privileges at SLS; room service. *In room:* TV/DVD, record player, fridge, hair dryer, minibar, Wi-Fi ($10 per day).

Roosevelt Hotel, Hollywood ★★   After a $30-million face-lift, this venerable 12-story landmark became *the* place to stay in Hollywood, though lately competition has increased with the openings of the Redbury and the W. Still, it's got history, style, exclusivity, models-slash-actresses serving cocktails at the poolside bar, a raucous nightlife scene, and just the right amount of L.A. attitude from the staff. Host to the first Academy Awards in 1929—not to mention a few famous-name ghosts—this national landmark is Hollywood's only historic hotel still in operation. Much of the 1927 Spanish-influenced sunken lobby remains the same, but the guest rooms have been completely renovated with extra-large bathrooms, platform beds with luxurious Frette linens, and the latest high-tech accessories. Rooms on the upper floors have skyline views, while the individually decorated cabana rooms have a balcony or terrace overlooking the Olympic-size pool (whose mural was originally painted by David Hockney). Off the lobby, there's a popular late-night burger bar called **25 Degrees.** You'll like the location, smack-dab in the touristy section of Hollywood Boulevard, across from Grauman's Chinese Theatre and along the Walk of Fame. It's also a playground for the young, hot Hollywood set, with antics from the poolside **Tropicana** bar and exclusive **Teddy's** lounge getting gobs of press. More low-key is the small Library Bar, with its focus on mixology.

7000 Hollywood Blvd., Hollywood, CA 90028. www.hollywoodroosevelt.com. (*) **800/950-7667** or 323/466-7000. Fax 323/462-8056. 300 units. $231–$339 double; from $389 suite; from $299 poolside cabana rooms. AE, DC, DISC, MC, V. Valet parking $30. **Amenities:** 2 restaurants; 4 bars; concierge; fitness center; outdoor pool and Jacuzzi; room service. *In room:* A/C, TV/DVD, CD player, hair dryer, minibar, MP3 docking station, Wi-Fi ($10 per day).

W Hollywood Hotel ★★   One of the "It" hotels of 2011 is the W Hollywood, which opened in January 2010 at the corner of Hollywood and Vine and has been the darling of the dig-me crowd ever since. The first and largest LEED-compliant property in L.A., W Hollywood combines eco-conscious construction with stylish design, luxury finishes, dramatic views, and cutting-edge technology (all this for a mere $360 million). All of the W's 305 large studios and one-bedroom suites come with a signature bed with a feather-top mattress, 350-thread-count Egyptian-cotton sheets, and goose down comforter—all the comforts of Caligula—but most of your time will be spent striking a pose at the hotel's signature **Living Room** (essentially a large lobby-cum-lounge); at **Station Hollywood,** an outdoor lounge (preferred by smokers) with a giant TV screen; at the rooftop pool; at the enormous fitness center; at **Bliss Hollywood,** a 6,075-square-foot full-service spa; or, if you can get in (good luck), at **Drai's Hollywood,** currently one of the hottest clubs in Los Angeles, especially for summer pool parties. The hotel's signature restaurant is **Delphine,** a 6,000-square-foot indoor/outdoor French bistro.

6250 Hollywood Blvd., Hollywood, CA 90028. www.whotels.com/hollywood. (*) **877/946-8357** or 323/798-1300. 305 units. From $329–$660 double. AE, DC, DISC, MC, V. Valet parking $35.

Pets accepted ($25 per day with a $100 1-time cleaning fee). **Amenities:** 2 restaurants; 2 lounges; concierge; exercise room; outdoor heated pool; room service; spa. *In room:* A/C, TV/DVD, CD player, hair dryer, minibar, Wi-Fi ($15 per day).

INEXPENSIVE

Best Western Hollywood Hills Hotel ★   Location is a big selling point for this family-owned (since 1948) member of the reliable Best Western chain: It's just off U.S. 101 (the Hollywood Fwy.); a Metro Line stop just 3 blocks away means easy, car-free access to Universal Studios; and the famed Hollywood and Vine intersection is just a 5-minute walk away. The entire hotel has been recently renovated in a contemporary style, and all the spiffy guest rooms come with a refrigerator, coffeemaker, microwave, and wireless Internet; further renovations to the lobby and exterior were completed in early 2011. The rooms in the back building are my favorites, as they sit well back from busy Franklin Avenue, face the gleaming blue-tiled, heated outdoor pool, and have an attractive view of the neighboring hillside. A major convenience is the **101 Hills Coffee Shop** located off the lower lobby.

6141 Franklin Ave. (btw. Vine and Gower sts.), Hollywood, CA 90028. www.bestwestern.com/hollywoodhillshotel. © **800/287-1700** or 323/464-5181. Fax 323/962-0536. 80 units. $169–$199 double. AAA and AARP discounts available. AE, DISC, MC, V. Valet parking $5. Pets accepted for $75 per night. **Amenities:** Coffee shop; heated outdoor pool. *In room:* A/C, cable TV w/HBO, fridge, hair dryer, free Wi-Fi.

Days Inn Hollywood   While it's east of the prime Sunset Strip action, this renovated motel is safe and convenient, and extras like free underground parking and continental breakfast make it an especially good value. Doubles are large enough for families. Some rooms have microwaves, fridges, and coffeemakers; if yours doesn't have a hair dryer or an iron, they're available at the front desk. For maximum bang for your buck, ask for a room overlooking the pool.

7023 Sunset Blvd. (btw. Highland and La Brea aves.), Hollywood, CA 90028. www.daysinnhollywood.com. © **800/381-2935** or 323/463-7171. Fax 323/461-8259. 66 units. $75–$129 double; from $130 for Jacuzzi suite. Rates include continental breakfast. Ask about AAA, AARP, and other discounted rates. AE, DC, DISC, MC, V. Free secured parking. **Amenities:** Restaurant; outdoor pool. *In room:* A/C, TV, free Wi-Fi.

Magic Castle Hotel ★ ☺ ✦   A stone's throw from Hollywood Boulevard's attractions, this garden-style hotel/motel at the base of the Hollywood Hills offers L.A.'s best cheap sleeps and is ideal for wallet-watching families or long-term stays. You won't see the Magic Castle Hotel in *Travel + Leisure* anytime soon, but the units are spacious, comfortable, and well kept. Named for the Magic Castle, the illusionist club just uphill, the hotel was once an apartment building; it still feels private and insulated from Franklin Avenue's constant stream of traffic. The units are situated around a central swimming pool. Most are large apartments with fully equipped kitchens complete with a microwave and coffeemaker (grocery-shopping service is available as well).

7025 Franklin Ave. (btw. La Brea and Highland aves.), Hollywood, CA 90028. www.magiccastlehotel.com. © **800/741-4915** or 323/851-0800. Fax 323/851-4926. 40 units. $174 double; $214–$314 suite. Rates include continental breakfast. Off-season and other discounts available. AE, DC, DISC, MC, V. Parking $10. **Amenities:** Outdoor heated pool. *In room:* A/C, cable TV w/HBO, DVD player w/free movie rentals, CD/stereo, hair dryer, free Wi-Fi.

Downtown

VERY EXPENSIVE

The Ritz-Carlton Los Angeles ★★   Opened in February 2010, the Ritz is notable because of its location next to L.A. LIVE, a vast entertainment complex that includes the STAPLES Center, the Nokia Theatre, and more than a dozen restaurants, in a newly gentrified area of downtown L.A. The Ritz comprises floors 22 to 26 of a property that it actually shares with the JW Marriott, which represents the high-end branch of the Marriott chain. The hotel is the epitome of luxury, with sleek furnishings, professional service, and lush amenities, like a heated rooftop pool with panoramic views; a sexy Asian-fusion restaurant by Wolfgang Puck, **WP 24;** and an impressive spa and state-of-the-art fitness center. Guest rooms are modern, comfortable, and tech-savvy—check out the cool mini TV inside the bathroom mirror! Beds are firm and outfitted with 400-thread-count linens. **Note:** Though the two hotels are attached, the entrances and lobbies are separate; for the Ritz, enter off of Georgia Street.

900 W. Olympic Blvd., Los Angeles, CA 90015. www.ritzcarlton.com/en/Properties/LosAngeles. ℂ **888/275-8063** or 213/743-8800. Fax 213/743-8801. 123 units. From $299 double; from $409 suite. AE, DISC, MC, V. Valet parking $40. **Amenities:** Restaurant and lounge; concierge and club level; fitness center and spa; Jacuzzi; heated outdoor pool; room service. *In room:* TV/DVD, hair dryer, small fridge, minibar, Wi-Fi ($13 per day).

EXPENSIVE/MODERATE

Traditionally the domain of business folk and convention attendees, downtown L.A. is becoming increasingly attractive to leisure travelers for several reasons: a Rudy Giuliani–style cleanup in the late 1990s; a growing number of cultural attractions, destination dining, and a vital bar scene; excellent-value weekend packages at luxury hotels that empty out once the workweek ends; and easy, car-free access via the Metro Line to Hollywood and Universal Studios. Every freeway passes through downtown, so it's a breeze to hop in the car and head to other neighborhoods, except during rush hour. Consider yourself forewarned, however: Despite low weekend rates, parts of downtown L.A. can feel like a ghost town, particularly after dusk. And all the hoopla about urban revival? Let's just say downtown has had more comebacks than Madonna.

Figueroa Hotel ★   With an artistic eye and a heartfelt commitment to creating exotic, whimsical, and oh-so-anti-corporate accommodations, charming owner Uno Thimansson has transformed a 1925-vintage former YWCA residence into a top pick for affordable lodging. This venerable 12-story property sits in an increasingly gentrified corner of downtown, within shouting distance of the ever-growing L.A. LIVE entertainment complex. The big, airy lobby exudes a romantic Spanish Colonial–Gothic vibe, and elevators lead to equally artistic guest rooms that, although poorly lit, are very comfortable. Each comes with a firm, well-made bed with a wrought-iron headboard or canopy, a Mexican-tiled bathroom, and East Asian fabrics that double as blackout drapes. The Casablanca Suite is a Moroccan pleasure den, ideal for romance. Out back is a desert-garden deck with a mosaic-tiled pool and Jacuzzi, and the Verandah Bar, the poolside place to go on warm Southern California nights for a minty mojito.

939 S. Figueroa St. (at Olympic Blvd.), Los Angeles, CA 90015. www.figueroahotel.com. ℂ **800/421-9092** or 213/627-8971. Fax 213/689-0305. 265 units. $148-$164 double; $225–$265 suite. AE, DC, MC, V. Parking $12. **Amenities:** Restaurant; bar; outdoor pool area w/lounge chairs and Jacuzzi. *In room:* A/C, TV, minifridge, Wi-Fi ($5 per day).

Millennium Biltmore Hotel Los Angeles ★★ The Biltmore is one of those hotels that's worth a visit even if you're not staying here. Built in 1923 and encompassing almost an entire square block, this Italian-Spanish Renaissance landmark is the grande dame of L.A.'s hotels. Chances are, you've seen it in many movies, including *The Wedding Crashers, Chinatown, Ghostbusters, Bugsy, Beverly Hills Cop,* and Barbra Streisand's *A Star Is Born.* The hotel lobby—JFK's campaign headquarters during the 1960 Democratic National Convention— appeared upside-down in *The Poseidon Adventure.* The "wow" factor ends at guest rooms, however, which are a little on the small side (common for older hotels) and aren't quite as eye-popping as the public spaces, but they've recently been redecorated in a style that meshes well with the hotel's vibe. A range of dining and cocktail outlets includes Sai Sai for modern Asian cuisine and sushi. Pretty, casual Smeraldi's serves American fare during the day, but transforms into impressive Italian steakhouse La Bisteccca at night. Off the lobby is the stunning Gallery Bar. Afternoon tea and cocktails are served in the Rendezvous Court, which used to be the hotel's original lobby and resembles the interior of a Spanish cathedral. Take advantage of your complimentary access to the Art Deco health club, with its gorgeous Roman-style pool.

506 S. Grand Ave. (btw. Fifth and Sixth sts.), Los Angeles, CA 90071. www.thebiltmore.com. ☎ **800/245-8673** or 213/624-1011. Fax 213/612-1545. 683 units. $169–$239 double; from $244 suite. Leisure discount packages available. AE, DC, DISC, MC, V. Valet parking $40. **Amenities:** 3 restaurants; bar; concierge; health club w/original 1923 inlaid pool, Jacuzzi, steam, and sauna; room service; Wi-Fi ($9.95 per day). *In room:* A/C, TV w/pay movies, hair dryer, minibar.

Westin Bonaventure Hotel & Suites ★ This 35-story, 1,354-room monolith is the hotel that locals love to hate. The truth is that the Bonaventure is a terrific hotel. It's certainly not for travelers who want intimacy or personality in their accommodations—but with numerous restaurants and bars, a full-service spa, a monster health club, a business center, and much more on hand, you'll be hard-pressed to want for anything here (except maybe some individualized attention). The hotel's five gleaming glass silos encompass an entire square block and form one of downtown's most distinctive landmarks. The pie-shaped guest rooms are on the small side, but a wall of windows offering great views and Westin's unparalleled Heavenly Bed—the ultimate in hotel-bed comfort—make for a very comfortable cocoon. With executive workstation, fax, and wet bar, guest office suites are great for business travelers, while tower suites—with living room, extra half-bathroom, minifridge, microwave, and two TVs—are ideal for families. Ask about the "running concierge" program, which offers scenic jogs through historical parts of downtown.

404 S. Figueroa St. (btw. Fourth and Fifth sts.), Los Angeles, CA 90071. www.westin.com/ bonaventure. ☎ **866/716-8132** or 213/624-1000. Fax 213/612-4800. 1,354 units. $169–$289 double; from $249 suite. Ask about specials and packages. AE, DC, DISC, MC, V. Valet parking $42. **Amenities:** 5 restaurants, plus fast-food outlets; bar; concierge; access to 4,500-sq.-ft. health club; outdoor heated lap pool; room service; full-service spa; indoor running track. *In room:* A/C, TV, hair dryer, minifridge, Wi-Fi ($13 per day).

San Fernando Valley & Universal City

MODERATE

Beverly Garland's Holiday Inn ★ ☺ The "Beverly Garland" in this 258-room hotel's name is the actress who played Fred MacMurray's wife on *My Three*

Sons. Grassy areas and greenery abound at this North Hollywood Holiday Inn, a virtual oasis in the concrete jungle. The Mission-influenced buildings are a bit dated, but if you grew up with *Brady Bunch* reruns, this only adds to the charm. Southwestern-themed fabrics complement the natural-pine furnishings in the spacious (and soundproof) guest rooms, attracting your attention away from the somewhat unfortunate painted cinder block walls. On the plus side, all of the well-outfitted rooms have balconies overlooking the pleasant grounds, which include a pool and two lighted tennis courts. With Universal Studios just down the street and a free shuttle to the park, the location can't be beat for families. Since proximity to the 101 and 134 freeways also means the constant buzz of traffic, ask for a room facing Vineland Avenue for maximum quiet. *Tip:* If you're bringing the kids along, be sure to inquire about the KidSuites.

4222 Vineland Ave., North Hollywood, CA 91602. www.beverlygarland.com. ℂ **800/238-3759** or 818/980-8000. Fax 818/766-0112. 255 units. $161–$186 double; from $195 suite. Children 12 and under stay free in parent's room and eat free. Ask about AAA, AARP, corporate, military, Great Rates, weekend, and other discounted rates. AE, DC, DISC, MC, V. Self-parking $14. **Amenities:** Restaurant; bar; Jacuzzi; heated outdoor pool; lighted tennis courts. *In room:* A/C, TV, hair dryer, free Wi-Fi.

Sheraton Universal Hotel ★★ ☺   Despite the addition of the sleekly modern Hilton just uphill, the 21-story Sheraton is still considered "the" Universal City hotel of choice for tourists, businesspeople, and industry folks visiting the studios' production offices. Located on the back lot of Universal Studios, it has a spacious 1960s feel, with updated styling and amenities. Although the Sheraton does its share of convention/event business, the hotel feels more leisure oriented than the Hilton next door (an outdoor elevator connects the two properties). Choose a Lanai room for balconies that overlook the lushly planted pool area, or a Tower room for stunning views and solitude. The hotel is very close to the Hollywood Bowl, and you can practically roll out of bed and into the theme park (via a continuous complimentary shuttle). All suites include Club Level access—worth the money for the extra amenities such as concierge service and free continental breakfast and afternoon hors d'oeuvres.

333 Universal Hollywood Dr., Universal City, CA 91608. www.sheraton.com. ℂ **800/325-3535** or 818/980-1212. Fax 818/985-4980. 451 units. $249–$279 double; from $324 suite. Children stay free in parent's room. Ask about AAA, AARP, and corporate discounts; also inquire about packages that include theme-park admission. AE, DC, DISC, MC, V. Valet parking $23; self-parking $18. **Amenities:** Casual indoor/outdoor restaurant; concierge; health club; outdoor pool and whirlpool. *In room:* A/C, TV w/pay movies, hair dryer, high-speed Internet ($9.95 per day).

INEXPENSIVE

Best Western Mikado Hotel   This Asian-flavored garden hotel has been a Valley fixture for 40-plus years. The kitsch value extends from the pagoda-style exterior to the sushi bar (the Valley's oldest) across the driveway. Two-story motel buildings face two well-maintained courtyards, one with a koi pond and wooden footbridge, the other with a shimmering blue-tiled pool and hot tub. Guest rooms are suitably comfortable and well outfitted. Furnished in 1970s-era chic (leather sofas, earth tones), the one-bedroom apartment is a steal, with enormous rooms and a full-size kitchen.

12600 Riverside Dr. (btw. Whitsett and Coldwater Canyon), North Hollywood, CA 91607. www. bestwestern.com/mikadohotel. ℂ **800/780-7234** or 818/763-9141. Fax 818/752-1045. 58 units.

$119–$159 double; $250 1-bedroom apt. Rates include full breakfast. Extra person $10. Rates include full American breakfast. Children 11 and under stay free in parent's room. Ask about AAA, senior, and other discounted rates. AE, DC, DISC, MC, V. Free parking. **Amenities:** Japanese restaurant and sushi bar; cocktail lounge; outdoor pool and Jacuzzi. *In room:* A/C, TV, hair dryer, free high-speed Internet.

Pasadena & Environs

EXPENSIVE

Langham Huntington Hotel & Spa ★★★   Originally opened in 1907, the opulent Huntington Hotel was one of America's grandest hotels, but not the most earthquake-proof. No matter—the hotel was rebuilt and opened in the same spot in 1991, save its two historic ballrooms, and the astonishing authenticity (including reinstallation of many decorative features) even fools patrons from the hotel's early days. This Spanish-Mediterranean beauty sits on 23 spectacularly landscaped acres that seem a world apart from L.A., though downtown is only 20 minutes away. Langham Hotels International took over this former Ritz-Carlton in 2008 and has invested significantly in property upgrades. The hotel's dining room, bar, club lounge, and eight cottages have undergone renovations, in addition to its 11,000-square-foot full-service spa, which now offers unique services based upon traditional Chinese medicine. Each oversize guest room is conservatively dressed with Frette linens and has lots of natural light. Spend a few extra dollars on a Club Level room, which features access to the club lounge with dedicated concierge and complimentary gourmet spreads all day (including breakfast). Guests and locals enjoy the Cal-French cuisine of former Patina Group chef David Féau at the **Royce;** the more casual **Terrace** restaurant serves meals at umbrella-covered tables by the pool and hosts an award-winning Sunday brunch.

1401 S. Oak Knoll Ave., Pasadena, CA 91106. http://pasadena.langhamhotels.com. ⓒ **800/591-7481** or 626/568-3900. Fax 626/568-3700. 380 units. $279–$450 double; from $589 suite. AE, DC, MC, V. Valet parking $25. **Amenities:** 2 restaurants; 2 lounges (bar, lobby lounge for high tea); concierge; fitness center; Jacuzzi; heated outdoor pool; room service; full-service spa w/ whirlpool, sauna, and steam room; 3 tennis courts (lit for night play). *In room:* A/C, TV, CD player, hair dryer, minibar, Wi-Fi ($9.95 per day).

MODERATE

Bissell House Bed & Breakfast ★   If you enjoy the true B&B experience, you'll love the Bissell House. Hidden behind hedges that carefully isolate it from busy Orange Grove Avenue, this antiques-filled 1887 gingerbread Victorian—the former home of the vacuum heiress and now owned by the Hoyman family—offers a unique taste of life on what was once Pasadena's "Millionaire's Row." Outfitted in a traditional chintz-and-cabbage-roses style, all individually decorated rooms have private bathrooms (two with an antique claw-foot tub, one with a whirlpool tub, four with showers only), individual heating and air-conditioning (a B&B rarity), Internet access, and very comfortable beds. If you don't mind stairs, request one of the more spacious top-floor rooms. Most rooms are now equipped with flatscreen TVs—all have televisions of some sort—DVDs, and premium cable, and the downstairs library features a selection of DVDs for guest use. The beautifully landscaped grounds boast an inviting pool, Jacuzzi, and deck with lounge chairs. Included in the room rate is an elaborately prepared vegetarian breakfast served in the large dining room, as well as an afternoon dessert. A self-serve continental breakfast is also available weekdays for business guests, provided notice is given no later than the night before.

201 Orange Grove Ave. (at Columbia St.), South Pasadena, CA 91030. www.bissellhouse.com. © **800/441-3530** or 626/441-3535. Fax 626/441-3671. 7 units. $155–$295 double. Rates include full breakfast. AE, MC, V. Free parking. **Amenities:** Outdoor pool and Jacuzzi; DVD library. *In room:* A/C, cable flatscreen TV (most rooms), hair dryer, free Wi-Fi.

INEXPENSIVE

Saga Motor Hotel 🏷️ This 1950s relic of old Route 66 has far more character than most other motels in its price range. The rooms are small, clean, and simply furnished with the basics. The doubles are spacious enough for shares, but budget-minded families will prefer the extra-large configuration of the Family Suites, which have a king-size bed and two doubles. The best rooms are in the front building surrounding the gated swimming pool, shielded from the street and inviting in warm weather. The grounds are attractive and well kept, if you don't count the Astroturf "lawn" on the pool deck. The location is relatively quiet (considering it's on a busy strip of Colorado Blvd. directly across from Pasadena Community College) and very convenient, just off the Foothill (210) Freeway about a mile from the Huntington Library and within 10 minutes of both the Rose Bowl and Old Pasadena. The Saga is 100% smoke free; there's no smoking allowed anywhere on its grounds, including the pool and parking lot.

1633 E. Colorado Blvd. (btw. Allen and Sierra Bonita aves.), Pasadena, CA 91106. www.thesaga motorhotel.com. © **800/793-7242** or 626/795-0431. Fax 626/792-0559. 70 units. $92–$94 double; $135 suite. Rates include continental breakfast. AE, DC, DISC, MC, V. Free parking. Small pets under 15 lb. are allowed ($35 cleaning fee). **Amenities:** Outdoor heated pool; free laundry facilities. *In room:* A/C, cable TV w/HBO, free Wi-Fi.

WHERE TO EAT

As one of the world's cultural crossroads, Los Angeles is an international atlas of exotic cuisines: Afghan, Argentinean, Armenian, Burmese, Cajun, Cambodian, Cuban, Ethiopian, Jewish, Korean, Lebanese, Moroccan, Oaxacan, Persian, Peruvian, Spanish, Vietnamese, and so on. Whatever you're in the mood for, this town has it. All you need to join the dinner party is an adventurous palate, because half the fun of visiting Los Angeles is experiencing worldly dishes.

The famous celebrity chefs and celebrity-owned restaurants attract most of the limelight, but most of L.A.'s best dining experiences are in the kind of restaurants you'd never find unless someone let you in on the secret. For a greater selection, pick up *Frommer's Los Angeles 2012*. For additional late-night dining options, see "Late-Night Bites" under "Los Angeles After Dark," later in this chapter. To locate the restaurants reviewed below, see the individual neighborhood maps in section 1, "Orientation."

Santa Monica & the Beaches

EXPENSIVE

Boa Steakhouse ★ STEAKHOUSE It's a no-brainer: Combine high-quality steaks with a sexy decor, a lively bar, and a key corner location at the foot of Santa Monica Boulevard, and you'll do well. The sophisticated decor eschews the traditional dim steakhouse ambience in favor of a warm, sleek interior highlighted with floor-to-ceiling windows that allow natural light to filter in. Tough decisions await you: Should you order the bone-in filet mignon, Kobe filet mignon, 35-day dry-aged New York strip, bone-in rib-eye, flatiron steak, or porterhouse? Non–meat eaters may prefer the lump crab cake appetizer with heart-of-palm salad and Cajun rémoulade, or sides such as the homemade crispy fries, macaroni and cheese, and roasted garlic whipped potatoes. For a pick-me-up dessert, try the refreshing blackberry smash cocktail, a mojito-like mixture made with fresh fruit and top-shelf vodka. **Note:** The original West Hollywood Boa Steakhouse moved to fancy new Sunset Strip digs in 2009 (9200 W. Sunset Blvd; ✆ **310/278-2050**).

101 Santa Monica Blvd. (at Ocean Ave.), Santa Monica. ✆ **310/899-4466.** www.boasteak.com. Reservations recommended. Main courses $28–$44. AE, DC, DISC, MC, V. Mon–Fri noon–3pm; Sat–Sun noon–5pm; Mon–Wed 5:30–10:30pm; Thurs 5:30–11pm; Fri–Sat 5:30–11:30pm. Valet parking $7 with validation.

Cafe Del Rey ★ CALIFORNIAN   Cafe Del Rey is one of those lively restaurants where everyone seems to be celebrating something on the company's tab. There's a terrific view of the marina's bobbing sailboats, particularly in the summer when the windows facing the harbor are open, creating an indoor-outdoor dining area. The exhibition kitchen focuses on eclectic preparations of fresh and seasonal foods. Sure bets are the day boat specials like mahimahi or swordfish, which list both the boats and the captains who brought them in fresh. The *Wine Spectator* award–winning wine list offers more than 340 selections. My advice: Request a table by the window, ask your server what's good today, pair it with a nice bottle of wine, and enjoy a long, leisurely meal.

4451 Admiralty Way (btw. Lincoln and Washington blvds.), Marina del Rey. ✆ **310/823-6395.** www.cafedelreymarina.com. Reservations recommended. Main courses dinner $26–$33, lunch $12–$23. AE, DC, DISC, MC, V. Lunch Mon–Fri 11:30am–3pm, Sat 11:30am–2:30pm; dinner Mon–Thurs 5:30–10pm, Fri–Sat 5:30–10:30pm, Sun 5–9:30pm; Sun brunch 10:30am–3pm. Valet parking free for lunch, $4 for dinner.

The Lobster ★ SEAFOOD   There's been a seafood shack called the Lobster on the Santa Monica Pier since 1923—almost as long as the pier's been standing—but this incarnation is a perpetually lively favorite. You won't notice the contemporary decor much, with floor-to-ceiling windows affording a million-dollar ocean view, but the space is comfortable. The food is better than it needs to be, given the location, but not quite what it once was. Although the namesake crustacean from Maine is a good choice—get it grilled, steamed, poached—other specialties range from pan-seared crab cakes to wild Columbia River king salmon. There are a few steaks for landlubbers, and the practiced bar serves lots of bloody marys garnished with jumbo shrimp to dedicated locals. **Tip:** Request a table on the deck and enjoy the 180-degree panoramic view of the Pacific.

1602 Ocean Ave. (at Colorado Blvd.), Santa Monica. ✆ **310/458-9294.** www.thelobster.com. Reservations recommended. Main courses $21–$50. AE, DC, DISC, MC, V. Mon–Thurs 11:30am–10pm; Fri–Sat 11:30am–11pm. Valet parking $6.50 for 1st 3 hr.; $10 maximum.

Michael's ★★ CALIFORNIAN   Owner Michael McCarty, L.A.'s answer to Alice Waters, is considered by many to be the father of California cuisine. Since Michael's opened in 1979 (when McCarty was only 25), several top L.A. restaurants have caught up to it, but the market-to-table philosophy remains. Although the furniture and decor are dated, the dining room is filled with contemporary art by Michael's wife, Kim McCarty, and the restaurant's garden is one of the city's

The Old Place, Up in Them Thar Hills

In a small town in the Santa Monica Mountains, the **Old Place**, 29983 Mulholland Hwy., Cornell (✆ **818/706-9001;** www.oldplacecornell.com), is reminiscent of another time. It's no wonder, since the rustic wood building served as a post office and general store from 1908 to 1940; although it was transformed into a restaurant in 1970, it still retains an Old Western feel with its dark-wood booths, original wood bar, and dim chandeliers. The menu changes regularly, but it features hearty classic dishes that hearken back to the early 20th century—even the warm, crusty sourdough bread is like edible history. For an appetizer, try the delicious wild mushroom skillet, which is an assortment of fresh local mushrooms served over buttery toast in a cast-iron skillet. For a main, the juicy oak-grilled Black Angus sirloin steak is excellent. The rotating list of specials might include blackened Idaho trout or oak-grilled chicken potpie. Portions are large, so come hungry. *Tip:* The place is tiny, so reservations are a must—they are taken 30 days out and are available only at the following seating times: 5, 6:30, and 8:30pm. Main courses are $14 to $29. Open Thursday to Friday 4 to 10pm, Saturday and Sunday 9am to 2pm and 4 to 10pm. Free parking.

most romantic settings. The menu changes seasonally, but you might find things like grilled Mediterranean loup de mer with chorizo and mussels, oven-roasted Channel spiny lobster with garlic-fennel potato purée, or grilled pork chop with Calvados apple pan sauce. Don't miss Michael's famous warm mushroom salad, which is prepared in various styles utilizing only market-fresh ingredients. The dry-aged New York strip is also fantastic, as are the steak *frites*.

1147 Third St. (north of Wilshire Blvd.), Santa Monica. ✆ **310/451-0843.** www.michaelssanta monica.com. Reservations recommended. Main courses $18–$25 lunch, $29–$39 dinner. AE, DC, DISC, MC, V. Lunch Mon–Fri noon–2:30pm; dinner Mon–Sat 6–10pm. Valet parking $8.

MODERATE

Border Grill ★ MEXICAN   Before Mary Sue Milliken and Susan Feniger spiced up cable TV with *Too Hot Tamales*, they opened this vibrant, cavernous, and *muy* loud space that's packed every night with locals and tourists. This is not your Combo #7 kind of place: Menu items include freshly made corn masa filled with tender roast duck, *guajillo* chili sauce, and roasted sweet peppers; or plantain empanadas with *chipotle* salsa and Mexican *crema*; and übertender roasted lamb tacos with strips of poblano chilies and manchego cheese. If it's on special, order the grilled chicken *enchiladas verdes* simmered in green mole sauce with Oaxacan cheese and hand-rolled corn tortillas. To join in on the nonstop fiesta, start with one of their margaritas or mojitos. *Tip:* The happy hour menu (Mon–Fri 4–7pm, Fri–Sat after 10pm) has tasty $3 treats such as tacos, chile poppers, and ceviche shots; and margaritas are only $5.

1445 Fourth St. (btw. Broadway and Santa Monica Blvd.), Santa Monica. ✆ **310/451-1655.** www. bordergrill.com. Reservations recommended. Main courses $19–$29. AE, DC, DISC, MC, V. Sun–Thurs 11:30am–10pm; Fri–Sat 11:30am–11pm. Metered parking and parking lots.

Joe's Restaurant ★★ 🍴 CALIFORNIAN/FRENCH   This is one of L.A.'s best dining bargains. Formerly a tiny, quirky storefront, chef/owner Joe Miller gutted and completely remodeled the entire place, adding a far more spacious dining room and display wine room (though the best tables are still tucked away on the trellised outdoor patio complete with a gurgling waterfall). But don't let the upscale additions dissuade your budgeted appetite—Joe's remains a hidden treasure for those with a champagne palate but a seltzer pocketbook. For lunch, the three-course menu is only $18, featuring things like California sand dabs with cherry tomato, arugula, and Maine sweet shrimp, with a fresh mixed green salad or one of Miller's exquisite soups. Seasonal dinner entrees are equally sophisticated: beet risotto with grilled asparagus, fallow deer wrapped in bacon (served in a black currant sauce with a side of roasted root vegetables), monkfish in a saffron broth, and wild striped bass with curried cauliflower coulis. Brunch is among the best in town.

1023 Abbot Kinney Blvd., Venice. ✆ **310/399-5811.** www.joesrestaurant.com. Reservations recommended. Main courses $13–$18 lunch, $19–$31 dinner. AE, MC, V. Lunch Tues–Fri noon–2:30pm; dinner Sun and Tues–Thurs 6–10pm, Fri–Sat 6–11pm; brunch Sat–Sun 11am–2:30pm. Free street parking; valet parking $5 weekdays, $6 weekends. Closed Mon.

La Cachette Bistro ★★ FRENCH Widely considered one of the most influential French chefs in America, Jean François Meteigner literally wrote the book on this cuisine—*Cuisine Naturelle*—a revolutionary approach to French cooking that eschews heavy creams, butter, and complex recipes in favor of dishes that are simple, light, full of flavor, and 90% free of cream and butter. His flagship fine-dining restaurant in Century City, La Cachette, set the standard for 10 years, but in 2009, he closed down the upscale, elegant eatery and opened this more casual bistro in Santa Monica. Meteigner is still very much the driving force in the kitchen—and popular dishes like the in-shell "eggs and caviar" from his early days at L.A.'s once beloved L'Orangerie can still be ordered (in advance only), but now he's also serving more accessible and more affordable small plates like port-dried figs and cured duck sausage and steamed clams in ginger-garlic butter.

1733 Ocean Ave., Santa Monica, CA 90401. ✆ **310/434-9509.** www.lacachettebistro.com. Reservations recommended. Main courses $14–$22 lunch, $19–$25 dinner. AE, DC, MC, V. Lunch Tues–Fri noon–2:30pm; dinner Tues–Sun 6pm–closing. Valet parking $6.50 (dinner only).

Locanda del Lago ★ NORTHERN ITALIAN In a sea of mediocre restaurants along Santa Monica's Third Street Promenade is this corner trattoria that reminds you Italians are great cooks. Locanda del Lago (Trattoria of the Lake) specializes in cuisine from northern Italy's Lombardy region. On sunny days, there's no better place in L.A. to people-watch than at the trattoria's outdoor patio, savoring a glass of chianti while tucking into the house specialty—*osso buco alla Milanese*, a veal shank slow-cooked in white wine and vegetables, topped with traditional *gremolata* (a parsley, garlic, and lemon zest mixture) and served with saffron risotto. Other outstanding dishes include house-made whole-wheat pasta in a duck ragout, and tagliolini tossed with pink trout and escarole in a thyme-infused white-wine sauce.

231 Arizona Ave. (at Third St.), Santa Monica. ✆ **310/451-3525.** www.lagosantamonica.com. Reservations recommended. Main courses $22–$34. AE, DC, DISC, MC, V. Mon–Thurs and Sun 11am–10pm; Fri–Sat 11am–11pm. Valet parking $5 with validation; public parking garages nearby.

Rustic Canyon ★★ CALIFORNIAN/SEASONAL Locals flock to this popular restaurant for simply prepared, wine-friendly cuisine. It's a compact but

SEA BREEZES & SUNSETS: OCEANVIEW DINING IN malibu

Beau Rivage, 26025 Pacific Coast Hwy. (at Corral Canyon; ✆ **310/456-5733;** www.beaurivagerestaurant.com), is my only pick located on the *other* side of PCH from the beach, but this romantic Mediterranean restaurant (whose name means "beautiful shore") has nearly unobstructed ocean views. The baby-pink villa and its flagstone dining patio are overgrown with flowering vines. The place is prettiest at sunset; romantic lighting takes over after dark. The menu is composed of country French and Italian dishes with plenty of moderately priced pastas, many with seafood. Other main courses are more expensive; they include chicken, duck, rabbit, and lamb, all traditionally prepared. An older, nicely dressed crowd tends to dine at this special-occasion place. It's open Wednesday through Friday from 5 to 11pm, and Saturday and Sunday from 11am to 11pm. There's a large lot for free self-parking. *Tip:* The weekend brunch menu, which isn't limited to breakfast dishes, is a less pricey alternative to dinner.

Duke's Malibu ★, 21150 Pacific Coast Hwy. (at Las Flores Canyon; ✆ **310/317-0777;** www.dukesmalibu.com), allows lovers of Hawaii and all things Polynesian to thrive in this outpost of the Hawaiian chain. Imagine a South Pacific T.G.I. Fridays where the food is secondary to the decor, then add a rocky perch atop breaking waves, and you have this surfing-themed crowd pleaser. It's worth a visit for the memorabilia alone—the place is named for Hawaiian surf legend "Duke" Kahanamoku. Duke's offers pretty good food at inflated, but not outrageous, prices. You'll find plenty of fresh fish prepared in the Hawaiian regional style, hearty surf and turf, a smattering of chicken and pasta dishes, and plenty of pupus to accompany Duke's

DayGlo tropical cocktails. As the name Barefoot Bar suggests, in this area, guests can remove their footwear and curl their toes in the sand. The Sunday brunch buffet (10am–3pm) is a tasty deal, at $24 for adults and $12 for kids. It's open Monday from 3 to 9pm; Tuesday through Thursday for lunch from 11:30am to 3pm, dinner from 5 to 9pm; Friday for lunch from 11:30am to 3pm, dinner from 5 to 9:30pm; Saturday for lunch from 11:30am to 3pm, dinner from 4:30 to 10pm. Sunday brunch takes place from 10am to 3pm, and dinner from 4 to 9pm. Valet parking is $4.

Gladstone's 4 Fish, 17300 Pacific Coast Hwy. (at Sunset Blvd.; ✆ **310/454-3474;** www.gladstones.com), a local tradition, is totally immersed in the Malibu scene. It shares a parking lot with a public beach, so the restaurant's wooden deck has a constant view of surfers, bikini-clad sunbathers, and other beachgoers. At busy times, Gladstone's even sets up picnic-style tables on the sand. Prices are moderate, and the atmosphere is casual. The menu offers several pages of fresh fish and seafood, augmented by a few salads and other meals for landlubbers—quality has improved somewhat since local hospitality group SBE took over the space, but it's still mostly tourist food, though the large portions get the job done. Gladstone's is popular for afternoon/evening drinking and offers nearly 20 seafood appetizer platters; it's also known for its decadent chocolate dessert, the Mile High Chocolate Cake, large enough for the whole table. It's open Monday through Thursday from 11am to 9:30pm, Friday from 11am to 11pm, Saturday from 9am to 11pm, and Sunday from 9am to 10pm. Parking is $5.50.

comfortable room with a few tables in the bar area, and it can get deafeningly loud, but that's half the fun. The chef uses top seasonal ingredients, with an emphasis on the organic and sustainable: arugula salad with mandarin oranges and pistachios; roasted prawns with beets and spring onions; amazing handmade sweet pea ravioli with bacon confit. There's even a dynamite burger and fries that's almost big enough for two. People drive across town for Zoe Nathan's desserts, like the hot cinnamon-sugar donuts. Rustic Canyon isn't open for lunch, but the owners opened a daytime cafe and bakery called **Huckleberry,** 1014 Wilshire Blvd. (✆ **310/451-2311;** www.huckleberrycafe.com), just across the street. Get fantastic sandwiches on home-baked breads and sample some of the best pastries in town: delectable fruit crostadas, éclairs, puddings, and cookies.

1119 Wilshire Blvd., Santa Monica. ✆ **310/393-7050.** www.rusticcanyonwinebar.com. Reservations recommended. Main courses $18–$32. AE, MC, V. Daily 5:30–10:30pm. Valet parking $6.50.

INEXPENSIVE

Bread & Porridge ★ 🍴 AMERICAN/BREAKFAST   A dozen tables are all that compose this neighborhood cafe, but steady streams of locals mill outside, reading their newspapers and waiting for a vacant seat. Once inside, surrounded by the vintage fruit-crate labels adorning the walls and tabletops, you can sample the delicious breakfasts, fresh salads and sandwiches, and superaffordable entrees. There's a vaguely international twist to the menu, which leaps from breakfast quesadillas and omelets—all served with black beans and salsa—to the Southern comfort of Cajun crab cakes and coleslaw, and typical Italian pastas adorned with roma tomatoes and plenty of garlic. All menu items are truck-stop cheap, but with an inventive elegance that makes this a best-kept secret. This place thoughtfully serves breakfast all day; get a short stack of one of five varieties of pancakes with any meal.

2315 Wilshire Blvd. (3 blocks west of 26th St.), Santa Monica. ✆ **310/453-4941.** www.breadand porridge.com. Main courses $7–$18. AE, MC, V. Mon–Fri 7am–2pm; Sat–Sun 7am–3pm. Metered street parking.

Sidewalk Cafe AMERICAN/BREAKFAST   Nowhere in L.A. is the people-watching better than along Ocean Front Walk. The constantly bustling Sidewalk Cafe is ensconced in one of Venice's few remaining early-20th-century buildings. The best seats, of course, are out front, around overcrowded open-air tables, all with perfect views of the crowd, which provides nonstop entertainment. The menu is extensive, and the food is better than it has to be at a location like this. Choose from the seriously overstuffed sandwiches or other oversize, familiar American, Italian, and Mexican.

1401 Ocean Front Walk (btw. Horizon Ave. and Market St.), Venice. ✆ **310/399-5547.** www. thesidewalkcafe.com. No reservations. Main courses $8.95–$20. MC, V. Daily 8am–midnight. Pay lots, street parking.

L.A.'s Westside & Beverly Hills

EXPENSIVE

The Bazaar by José Andrés ★★★ SPANISH/TAPAS   The Bazaar is the Disneyland of culinary adventures, and it's putting L.A. on the dining map. It's a Philippe Starck–designed playground for celebrity chef José Andrés—of PBS show *Made in Spain*—who serves up avant-garde Spanish cuisine. Located in the splashy new SLS Hotel, it's four separate spaces in one open room, and it's sensory overload, from bullfighter pictures and the open kitchen in Rojo, to the calming relaxed vibe in Blanca, to the pink and glossy Patisserie. You'll get traditional tapas like garlic shrimp, codfish fritters, and impeccable Spanish *jamon,* but it's the "modern tapas" menu and Andrés' molecular gastronomy techniques that get us excited. We can't get enough of the "Philly cheesesteak," a hollowed-out bread filled with oozy cheese and topped with thinly sliced seared Kobe beef, or anything with the "spherical" olives—juice-filled olive "skin" that dissolves in your mouth like magic. Picking candies like saffron gelee in "edible paper" from jars in the Patisserie makes us giddy with delight. Even cocktails get the José treatment at **Bar Centro:** Margaritas come with salt "air," and caipirinhas are made tableside with liquid nitrogen. It's the best (and most expensive, at $20 a pop) slushy cocktail we ever tasted.

465 S. La Cienega Blvd. (in SLS Hotel), Beverly Hills. ✆ **310/246-5555.** www.thebazaar.com. Reservations required. Tapas $9–$38. AE, DC, DISC, MC, V. Daily 10am–10pm. Valet parking $12.

Bouchon ★ FRENCH BISTRO   The highly anticipated Bouchon restaurant, the third such French-style bistro created by renowned Chef Thomas Keller (of Napa Valley's the French Laundry fame), made a grand entrance in Beverley Hills in mid-November '09. The name, derived from a specific style of cafe that existed in the French province of Lyon, hints at a classic bistro menu with selections such as steak *frites,* mussels meunière, *soupe à l'oignon,* quiche Lorraine, foie gras pâté, and other French classics. It's ironic that a chef of Keller's ilk has built a high-end brand around a concept that is traditionally non–haute cuisine, and reaction to this particular outpost has been mixed. At the restaurant's Bar Bouchon, diners may choose from small-plate options or oysters from the raw bar, complemented by a glass of wine or White Apron, a Pilsener-style beer crafted especially for Bouchon.

235 N. Canon Dr. (at Dayton Way), Beverly Hills. ✆ **310/271-9910.** www.bouchonbistro.com. Reservations recommended. Main courses $18–$45. AE, DC, MC, V. Restaurant daily 11:30am–2:30pm and 5:30–10:30pm. Valet parking $8.

Cut ★★★ STEAKHOUSE   This has been a power dinner spot for entertainment industry heavyweights since it opened at the Beverly Wilshire hotel in 2006. Think of this as special-occasion—or, like most everyone else, expense-account—dining. The Richard Meier–designed room is chic, if not sparse, perfect for seeing Tom and Katie or any of the myriad celebs walk in and dine. Linen-wrapped meat is brought to the table so you can learn the difference between Japanese Kobe beef (at $120 for a 6-oz. New York strip, this is the most expensive steak in town), American Wagyu, and Illinois corn-fed USDA prime. The steaks are grilled over hard wood and charcoal and finished under a 1,200°F (649°C) broiler, ensuring a buttery, juicy cut. Everything is a heightened experience, including side dishes: creamed spinach comes topped with an organic sunny-side-up egg; mac 'n' cheese is with Quebec cheddar; and potatoes aren't simply *au gratin,* they're a beautiful *tarte tatin.* Sherry Yard's desserts are fantastic, and the wine list is exemplary, if not overpriced. Across the hall is **Sidebar,** a great spot for people-watching while sipping a martini and noshing on Kobe beef sliders.

9500 Wilshire Blvd., Beverly Hills. ✆ **310/276-8500.** www.wolfgangpuck.com. Reservations required. Main courses $40–$120. AE, DISC, MC, V. Mon–Thurs 6–10pm; Fri–Sat 5:30–11pm. Valet parking $12 with validation.

Fogo de Chão ★★ BRAZILIAN STEAKHOUSE What was started long ago by four brothers in São Paulo, Brazil, has finally made its way to California—Beverly Hills, even—and is now one of the most popular restaurants in the city. Pronounced "Fogo dee *Shown*," this enormous southern Brazilian–style steakhouse is packed nightly with fans of the *churrasco* style of cooking meat—large cuts of meat slow-roasted over an open wood flame, then deftly sliced and continuously served onto your plate until you give in and flip your disk to red (you'll see). It's a prix-fixe system where everything on the menu except alcohol is available for a flat fee, and the superb waitstaff are always hovering nearby with meat-laden platters in the off chance that you actually clear your plate. Truly, it's bacchanalia revisited as you wander wide-eyed to a dazzling salad bar (be careful not to ruin your appetite). The gluttony continues with mountains of freshly roasted meats and endless side dishes, all washed down with rich red wines from among the 10,000 bottles that surround you in two-story temperature-controlled towers of glass and steel. Dessert? Only if you somehow manage to save room; the meat is the real star here.
133 N. La Cienega Blvd. (btw. W. Third St. and Beverly Blvd.), Los Angeles. © **310/289-7755.** www.fogodechao.com. Reservations recommended. Fixed-price menu $57 adults, $28 children. AE, DC, DISC, MC, V. Lunch Mon–Fri 11:30am–2pm; dinner Mon–Thurs 5–10pm, Fri 5–10:30pm, Sat 4:30–10:30pm, Sun 4–9:30pm. Valet parking $5.50.

The Ivy ★ AMERICAN If you're willing to endure the cold shoulder to ogle L.A.'s celebrities and pay lots for a mediocre meal, the Ivy can be enjoyable. This snobby place attracts one of the most industry-heavy crowds in the city and treats celebrities and nobodies as differently as Brahmins and untouchables. Just past the cool reception lie two disarmingly countrified dining rooms filled with rustic antiques, comfortably worn chintz, and hanging baskets of fragrant flowers. Huge roses bloom everywhere, including out on the charming brick patio (where the highest-profile patrons are seated and dutifully ignore the stares). The Ivy's Caesar salad is nice, as are the plump and crispy crab cakes. Recommended dishes include spinach linguine with a peppery tomato-basil sauce, prime rib dusted with Cajun spices, and tender lime-marinated grilled chicken. There's even a good burger and fried chicken. The wine list is notable, and there's always a terrific variety of desserts (pink boxes are on hand for chocolate-chip cookies to go).
113 N. Robertson Blvd. (btw. Third St. and Beverly Blvd.), West Hollywood. © **310/274-8303.** Reservations recommended. Main courses $25–$60. AE, DC, DISC, MC, V. Daily 10am–10pm. Valet parking $5.50.

Jar ★★ MODERN CHOPHOUSE Jar offers everything you could hope for in a modern American restaurant: a warm and relaxed setting, excellent service, and generous servings of reliably good comfort food. The braised Kurobuta pork shank and a Kobe-style filet of beef—both perfectly cooked, simply seasoned—are divinely flavorful. It was always chef Suzanne Tracht's dream to open a contemporary version of a 1940s-era chophouse, and you can tell that she's putting her best into every plate that leaves the kitchen. Everything she makes is a lesson in quality and simplicity. Among her most popular dishes are the Niman Ranch char sui pork chops and, her coup de grâce, a sensational pot roast with caramelized onions and carrots. An extensive wine list and martini menu are two good reasons to arrive early and stay for a nightcap at the beautiful Parisian-style bar. *Tip:* Suzanne's Sunday brunch is one of the best in the city; try the corn pancakes or the lobster Benedict.

8225 Beverly Blvd. (at Harper Ave.), Los Angeles. ℂ **323/655-6566.** www.thejar.com. Reservations recommended. Main courses $21–$42. AE, DC, DISC, MC, V. Mon–Thurs 5:30–10pm; Fri–Sat 5:30–11pm; Sun 10am–2pm and 5:30–10pm. Valet parking $6.

Lucques ★★ FRENCH/MEDITERRANEAN   Once Los Angeles became accustomed to this restaurant's unusual name—"Lucques" is a variety of French olive, pronounced "Luke"—local foodies fell hard for this quietly and comfortably sophisticated flagship of former Campanile chef Suzanne Goin. The old brick building, once silent star Harold Lloyd's carriage house, is decorated in muted, clubby colors with subdued lighting that extends to the handsome enclosed patio. Goin cooks with bold flavors, fresh-from-the-farm produce, and an instinctive feel for the Mediterranean. The short and oft-changed menu makes the most of unusual ingredients such as salt cod and oxtails. Standout dishes include Tuscan bean soup with tangy greens and pistou, grilled duck breast served alongside braised red cabbage with chanterelle mushrooms and chestnuts, braised beef short ribs with potato purée and horseradish cream, and a perfect vanilla *pòt de crème* for dessert. Lucques's bar menu, featuring steak *frites* béarnaise, omelets, and tantalizing hors d'oeuvres (olives, warm almonds, sea salt, chewy bread), is a godsend for late-night diners, and the bartenders make a mean vodka Collins. *Tip:* On Sundays, Lucques offers a bargain $45 prix-fixe three-course dinner from a weekly changing menu.

8474 Melrose Ave. (east of La Cienega Blvd.), West Hollywood. ℂ **323/655-6277.** www.lucques. com. Reservations recommended. Main courses $27–$34. AE, DC, MC, V. Mon 6–10pm; lunch Tues–Sat noon–2:30pm; dinner Mon–Thurs 6–10pm, Fri–Sat 6–10:30pm, Sun 5–10pm. Metered street parking or valet ($5.50).

Mastro's Steakhouse ★★★ STEAKS/SEAFOOD   Down the street from Spago, this is one of the best steakhouses in Southern California. Typical of an upscale steakhouse, the dimly lit dining room on the first floor has a dark, leathery, serious men's club feel to it, so be sure to request a table on the second floor, where the bar, live music, and cool vibe are located. Slide into a plush black leather booth, order a Mastro Dry Ice Martini (which comes with the shaker, so it takes only one to get a groove on), and start off the feast with an Iced Seafood Tower—a massive pyramid of crab legs, lobster, shrimp, clams, and oysters the size of your palm. The Fred Flintstone–size slabs of hand-cut USDA beef are served on sizzling plates heated to 400°F (204°C) so your steak stays warm and juicy throughout the meal. Greens are always a good idea—but one of the most popular sides here is the decadent lobster mashed potatoes. The bad news is that a bone-in rib-eye runs about $50; the good news is that one will feed three normal-size people.

246 N. Canon Dr. (btw. Dayton Way and Wilshire Blvd.), Beverly Hills. ℂ **310/888-8782.** www. mastrosrestaurants.com. Reservations highly recommended. Main courses $32–$90. AE, DC, MC, V. Sun–Thurs 5–11pm; Fri–Sat 5pm–midnight. Lounge daily 4:30pm–1am. Valet parking $7.

Matsuhisa ★ JAPANESE/PERUVIAN   Japanese chef/owner Nobuyuki Matsuhisa arrived in Los Angeles via Peru in 1987 and opened what may be the most creative restaurant in the city. A true master of fish cookery, Matsuhisa creates unusual dishes by combining Japanese flavors with South American spices and salsas (he was the first to introduce Americans to yellowtail sashimi with sliced jalapeños). Broiled sea bass with black truffles, miso-flavored black cod, sautéed squid with garlic and soy, tempura sea urchin in a shiso leaf, and Dungeness crab tossed with chilies and cream are just a few examples of the masterfully prepared dishes available, in addition to thickly sliced nigiri and creative sushi rolls. Matsuhisa is perennially popular with celebrities and old-school foodies, so reserve well in advance. The small, crowded main dining room suffers from poor lighting and precious lack of privacy; many big names are ushered through to private dining rooms. Expect a bit of attitude from the staff as well. In short, this is a landmark eatery, but compared to others at similar price points, it's now past its prime. *Note:* Matsuhisa's very local outpost of his successful **Nobu** chain is right up the street (903 N. La Cienega Blvd., ✆ **310/657-5711**). It's more scene-y, so it tends to appeal to a younger demographic.

129 N. La Cienega Blvd. (north of Wilshire Blvd.), Beverly Hills. ✆ **310/659-9639.** www.nobu matsuhisa.com. Reservations recommended. Main courses $28–$38; sushi $6–$18 per order; full *omakase* dinner from $90. AE, DC, MC, V. Mon–Fri 11:45am–2:15pm; daily 5:45–10:15pm. Valet parking $5.50.

The Palm ★ STEAKS/LOBSTER The child of the famous New York restaurant of the same name, the Palm is one of the top traditional American eateries in the city. In both food and ambience, this West Coast WeHo apple hasn't fallen far from the tree. The restaurant is brightly lit, bustling with energy, and playfully decorated with dozens of celebrity caricatures on the walls. Live Nova Scotia lobsters are flown in almost daily and then broiled over charcoal and served with big bowls of melted butter. Most are enormous (3–7 lb.) and, although they're obscenely expensive, can be shared. The steaks and swordfish are similarly sized, perfectly grilled to order, and served a la carte by cheeky white-jacketed waiters who have been around since the Nixon administration. For dessert, stick with the Palm's perfect New York cheesecake, flown in straight from the Bronx.

9001 Santa Monica Blvd. (btw. Doheny Dr. and Robertson Blvd.), West Hollywood. ✆ **310/550-8811.** www.thepalm.com. Reservations recommended. Main courses $14–$24 lunch, $23–$68 dinner. AE, DC, MC, V. Mon–Thurs noon–10pm; Fri noon–11pm; Sat 5–11pm; Sun 5–9:30pm. Valet parking $6.

Providence ★★★ MODERN AMERICAN/SEAFOOD Chef Michael Cimarusti and his quadrilingual Italian compatriot, Donato Poto, fulfilled their dream to create the city's preeminent seafood experience. It's a pleasure to just relax at this sleek, modern space and converse with Donato at the bar, so be sure to arrive a bit early. Because Cimarusti visits the fish market daily for the choicest seafood available, I recommend asking the waiter which are the evening's best dishes—or, better yet, inquire whether Michael has time to make a brief visit to your table and offer his advice (he's a wonderful guy). Because his philosophy is to let the divine flavors of wild fish prevail, sauces are never overpowering— striped sea bass in a pea tendril broth, wild king salmon with a truffle vinaigrette, kelp-marinated fluke. Lastly, be sure to order anything Cimarusti makes with sea urchin, even if you don't like sea urchin. If you are open-minded, he might just convert you.

5855 Melrose Ave. (at N. Cahuenga Blvd.), Los Angeles. ✆ **323/460-4170.** www.providencela. com. Reservations recommended. Main courses $35–$49. AE, MC, V. Fri noon–2:30pm; Mon–Fri 6–10pm; Sat 5:30–10pm; Sun 5:30–9pm. Valet parking $5.50.

Spago Beverly Hills ★★ CALIFORNIAN Despite all the hoopla—and years of stiff competition—Spago may not be quite the pioneer it once was, but it's still very respectable. Wolfgang Puck's talented henchman, Lee Hefter, presides over the kitchen, delivering the culinary sophistication demanded by an upscale Beverly Hills crowd. This high-style indoor/outdoor space glows with the aura of big bucks, celebrities, and the well-honed California cuisine that set the standard. Men will feel most comfortable in jacket and tie (suggested, but not required). All eyes may be on the romantically twinkle-lit outdoor patio (the most coveted tables), but the food takes center stage. Highlights include the appetizer of foie gras "three ways"; crawfish salad; savory duck either honey-lacquered and topped with foie gras or Cantonese-style with a citrus tang; slow-roasted Sonoma lamb with braised greens; and rich Austrian dishes from "Wolfie's" childhood, such as spicy beef goulash and perfect veal schnitzel.

176 N. Canon Dr. (north of Wilshire Blvd.), Beverly Hills. © **310/385-0880.** www.wolfgangpuck. com. Reservations required. Jackets advised for men. Main courses $32–$45; tasting menu $140. AE, DC, DISC, MC, V. Mon–Sat noon–2:30pm; daily 6–10pm. Valet parking $8.

MODERATE

Il Pastaio ★ NORTHERN REGIONAL ITALIAN   Sicilian-born chef/owner Giacomino Drago (scion of L.A.'s well-known Drago restaurateur family) hit the jackpot with this hugely successful, value-priced trattoria, located on a busy corner in the shopping district of Beverly Hills. All day long, Giacomino's fans take a break from work or shopping and converse over glasses of chianti and plates of oh-so-authentic pasta. You'll swoon over the *arancini,* breaded rice cones filled with mozzarella cheese and peas, then fried crispy brown (highly addictive); the pumpkin tortelloni in a light sage-and-cream sauce; the *arrabbiata,* a simple penne pasta dish in a fantastic spicy tomato-and-garlic sauce; and, for dessert, the *panna cotta* (the silkiest in Southern California). There's almost always a wait—and not much room to wait in—but by meal's end, it always seems worth it.

400 N. Canon Dr. (at Brighton Way), Beverly Hills. © **310/205-5444.** www.giacominodrago. com. Main courses $12–$30 lunch, $13–$30 dinner. AE, DC, MC, V. Mon–Wed 11:30am–11pm; Thurs–Sat 11:30am–midnight; Sun 11:30am–10pm. Valet parking $7.

Koi ★ ASIAN-FUSION   Even after almost 10 years, this place still attracts Hollywood's A-list crowd—everyone from Paris Hilton to Demi and Ashton to George Clooney has dined here. Incorporating feng shui elements of trickling water, votive candles, open-air patios, and soft lighting, the minimalist earthen-hued interior has a calming ambience that is a welcome relief from the hectic La Cienega scene just outside the ornately carved gates. The chef's fusions of Japanese and California cuisine account for the repeat clientele, and—befitting a trendy restaurant like this—the food was historically overpriced though good. However, an eight-course tasting menu includes many of the restaurant's signature dishes and costs only $50 per person. The only caveat? It's served only at the sushi bar. Start with the refreshing cucumber *sunomono* tower flavored with sweet vinegar and edible flowers, followed by a baked crab roll with edible rice paper (fantastic), the tuna tartare and avocado on crispy wontons, the yellowtail carpaccio delicately flavored with grape-seed oil, and black cod bronzed with miso that's warm-butter soft and exploding with sweet flavor. ***Tip:*** Request one of the horseshoe booths on the back patio amid Buddha statues and candlelight.

730 N. La Cienega Blvd. (btw. Melrose Ave. and Santa Monica Blvd.), West Hollywood. © **310/ 659-9449.** www.koirestaurant.com. Reservations recommended. Main courses $14–$50. AE, DC, DISC, MC, V. Sun–Wed 6–11pm; Thurs 6–11:30pm; Fri–Sat 6pm–midnight. Valet parking $8.

Waterloo & City ★ BRITISH GASTROPUB   Gastropubs have come and gone in one form or another in waves since the trend first hit back in the mid-2000s, but none has had as distinctly a British take as this one. On the outskirts of Culver City near the Marina del Rey border—it's kind of in the middle of nowhere, really—sits this former coffee shop, which has been transformed into a casually chic neighborhood favorite and destination dining institution. There's a whole section of charcuterie—and not just the usual suspects. If you're adventurous enough to try a smoked tongue and carrot terrine, I highly recommend it. The Caesar salad is also far from passé; it's wrapped in a giant "crouton," beautifully dressed and topped with white anchovies. Missteps are small: The short rib is beautifully cooked, but benefits from a pinch of salt. For dessert, you may discover a new favorite triple cream cheese or try the seasonal "limey" pie with ginger sorbet and Key lime confit.

12517 Washington Blvd., Culver City. ℂ **310/391-4222.** www.waterlooandcity.com. Main courses $19–$26. AE, MC, V. Mon–Sat 6–10pm; Sun 5–9pm. Free street parking.

INEXPENSIVE

The Apple Pan ★ SANDWICHES/AMERICAN   There are no tables, just a U-shape counter, at this classic American burger shack and hugely popular L.A. landmark. Open since 1947, the Apple Pan is a diner that looks—and acts—the part. It's famous for juicy burgers, grumpy service, and an authentic frills-free atmosphere. The hickory burger is best, though the tuna sandwich also has its share of fans. Ham, egg-salad, and Swiss-cheese sandwiches round out the menu. Definitely order fries and, if you're in the mood, the house-baked apple pie. Expect to wait a bit during the lunch rush (don't worry, the honor-system line moves pretty fast).

10801 Pico Blvd. (east of Westwood Blvd.), Los Angeles. ℂ **310/475-3585.** www.applepan.com. Most menu items under $6. No credit cards. Tues–Thurs and Sun 11am–midnight; Fri–Sat 11am–1am. Free parking.

Nate 'n Al Delicatessen ★ DELI/BREAKFAST   If you want to know where old-money, rich-and-famous types go for comfort food, look no further. Despite its location in the center of Beverly Hills' "Golden Triangle," Nate 'n Al has remained unchanged since 1945, from the Naugahyde booths to the motherly waitresses, who treat you the same whether you're a house-account celebrity regular or just a visitor stopping in for an overstuffed pastrami on rye, beef brisket, or short ribs. The too-salty chicken soup keeps Nate 'n Al from being the best L.A. deli (actually, I'd be hard-pressed to choose any one deli as the city's best), but staples such as chopped liver, dense potato pancakes, blintzes, borscht, and well-dilled pickles more than make up for it. *Tip:* This is a little-known and low-rent hot spot for celebrity spying.

414 N. Beverly Dr. (at Brighton Way), Beverly Hills. ℂ **310/274-0101.** www.natenal.com. Main courses $9.50–$16. AE, DISC, MC, V. Daily 7am–9pm. Public parking lot next door; 2 hr. free; after 6pm, it's a flat rate of $5.

Versailles ★ CARIBBEAN/CUBAN   Outfitted with Formica tabletops and looking something like an ethnic IHOP, Versailles feels much like any number of restaurants in Miami that cater to the Cuban community. The menu reads like a veritable survey of Havana-style cookery and includes specialties such as "Moros y Cristianos" (flavorful black beans mixed together with white rice), *ropa vieja* (a stringy beef stew), and fried whole fish (usually sea bass). Anybody who's eaten here will tell you the same thing: "Order the shredded roast pork." Tossed with the restaurant's trademark garlic-citrus sauce, it's highly addictive. Equally fetching is the garlic chicken—succulent, slow roasted, and smothered in onions and garlic-citrus sauce. Almost everything is served with black beans and rice; wine and beer are available. Because meals are good, bountiful, and cheap, there's often a wait.

1415 S. La Cienega Blvd. (south of Pico Blvd.), Los Angeles. ☎ **310/289-0392.** www.versailles cuban.com. Main courses $11–$22. AE, MC, V. Sun–Thurs 11am–10pm; Fri–Sat 11am–10pm. Free parking.

Hollywood

EXPENSIVE

Campanile ★★ CALIFORNIAN/MEDITERRANEAN Built as Charlie Chaplin's private offices in 1928, this Tuscan-style building has a multilevel layout with flower-bedecked interior balconies, a bubbling fountain, and a skylight through which diners can see the campanile (bell tower). Often ranked as one of L.A.'s finest restaurants, a meal here might begin with fried zucchini flowers drizzled with melted mozzarella or lamb carpaccio surrounded by artichoke leaves—a dish that arrives looking like one of van Gogh's sunflowers. Spago alumnus chef/owner Mark Peel heads the kitchen and is particularly known for his grills and roasts. Try the wood-grilled prime rib smeared with black-olive tapenade; *pappardelle* with braised rabbit, roasted tomato, and collard greens; or the rosemary-charred lamb with artichokes and fava beans. One of the most popular nights is still grilled-cheese night on Thursdays, when the bar fills up with regulars seeking haute versions of the childhood treat. *Tip:* On Monday nights, chef Peel offers a $38 three-course family-style themed menu.

624 S. La Brea Ave. (north of Wilshire Blvd.). ☎ **323/938-1447.** www.campanilerestaurant.com. Reservations recommended. Main courses $26–$38. AE, DC, DISC, MC, V. Mon–Wed noon–2:30pm and 6–10pm; Thurs–Fri noon–2:30pm and 5:30–11pm; Sat 10:30am–1:30pm and 5:30–11pm; Sun 9:30am–1:30pm. Valet parking $6.50.

Hatfield's ★★★ NEW AMERICAN Foodies took notice when Quinn and Karen Hatfield opened their first eponymous eatery in 2006, but after the move to the larger Melrose location in 2010, the savory/sweet chef couple has achieved a new level of sophistication without pretention, from food and beverage to service and decor. Request one of the twin booths against the south wall in the sparsely stylish main dining room for maximum comfort and the best view of the exhibition kitchen. Quinn's signature starter, a variation on the croque madame, sandwiches yellowtail sashimi and prosciutto between brioche halves. Mains follow suit: Supple slow-baked salmon almost melts in your mouth, and oven-roasted veal loin is reminiscent of the best bockwurst. Beverage director Peter Birmingham elevates wine pairings to poetry. *Tip:* Karen's specialty dessert, a chocolate and peanut butter truffle cake—think molten meets soufflé—is an off-menu secret.

6703 Melrose Ave. (at Citrus Ave.), Los Angeles. ☎ **323/935-2977.** www.hatfieldsrestaurant. com. Reservations recommended. Main courses $28–$36. AE, MC, V. Mon–Thurs 11:45am–2:15pm and 6–10pm; Fri 11:45am–2:15pm and 6–10:30pm; Sat 6–10:30pm; Sun 6–10pm. Valet parking $7.

Katana Robata & Sushi Bar ★★ JAPANESE ROBATA In the City of Sushi, you need to stand out from the crowd if you want to run a successful Japanese restaurant. And that's just what they did at Katana. The restaurant has sex appeal, with steel beams, perforated metallic screens, exotic woods, worn brick, and a fantastic patio overlooking the Sunset Strip. Katana is known for its *robata-yaki,* a traditional Japanese style of cooking where meats, fish, and vegetables are cooked on small bamboo skewers over imported *bincho tan* coal that imparts a unique smoky essence to the food. The sushi is very good, but it's the incredibly flavorful skewers that you'll want to sample: foie gras and asparagus wrapped with filet mignon, fresh lobster with a peppercorn-miso glaze, giant seared scallops with shiitake mushrooms, Kurobuta pork, and pineapple drizzled with plum sauce. Be sure to start the adventure with an $18 Sake Sampler.

8439 W. Sunset Blvd. (near La Cienega Blvd.), West Hollywood. © **323/650-8585.** www.katana robata.com. Reservations recommended. Main courses $12–$35. AE, DC, DISC, MC, V. Sun–Mon 6–11pm; Tues–Wed 6–11:30pm; Thurs–Sat 6pm–12:30am. Valet parking $9 for 1st 3 hr. with validation; $20 max.

Katsuya Hollywood ★ JAPANESE   Anchoring the corner of Hollywood and Vine, this überhip restaurant has all the tourists and snooties agog. Capitalizing on their raging success of the original Katsuya by Starck in Brentwood, the SBE group once again partnered with designer Philippe Starck and master sushi chef Katsuya Uechi to create this shrine to sushi and high design. The decor is an intriguing mix of gleaming-white leather and chrome furniture, overblown images of a geisha's facial parts, and a sinister black banner bearing the kanji symbol for Katsuya. Katsuya's must-try signature dishes include the crispy rice with spicy tuna, the Kobe filet with foie gras and plum soy sauce, and the baked whitefish with truffle in a shell of salt. Reservations may be difficult to get, particularly on a weekend night: Call as far in advance as possible.

6300 Hollywood Blvd. (at Vine St.), Hollywood. © **323/871-8777.** www.sbe.com/katsuya. Reservations recommended. Main courses $22–$55. AE, DC, DISC, MC, V. Mon 11am–2:30pm and 5:30–11pm; Tues–Thurs 11:30am–2:30pm and 5:30pm–midnight; Fri–Sat 11am–2:30pm and 5:30pm–12:3am; Sun 4:30–11pm. Valet parking $10.

The Little Door ★★ FRENCH MEDITERRANEAN   For more than a decade, this provincial hideaway off Third Street has been voted one of L.A.'s most romantic restaurants. Four dining areas are situated throughout a converted cottage-style house, the most popular being the "Patio," with its tile fountain, koi pond, wrought-iron candelabras, and lush greenery. If you can't get a table here, ask for one in the back room by the fireplace, which is both quieter and roomier. Fittingly, the cuisine is French/Mediterranean, ranging from a terrine of duck foie gras with strawberries, to pistachio-encrusted scallops with Moroccan greens, to rosemary-encrusted rack of lamb in a parsnip purée. It's pricey ($28 for couscous?), the tables are a tad too close together, and the attitude from the servers can be a bit, er, French. But when it all comes together perfectly—the candlelit table, an attentive waiter, a warm summer night, a nice glass of wine, a soupçon of foie gras melting on your tongue—it's easy to see why the Little Door is where the locals go when they're in the mood for romance.

8164 W. Third St. (btw. Crescent Heights and La Jolla sts.), Los Angeles. © **323/951-1210.** www. thelittledoor.com. Reservations recommended. Main courses $28–$44. AE, MC, V. Sun–Thurs 6–10pm; Fri–Sat 6–11pm. Valet parking $6.75.

MODERATE

Hungry Cat ★★ SEAFOOD   Tucked away near the back entrance of Borders at the odd Sunset + Vine complex is this modern, casual, bustling place for local and regional seafood that is simple and seasonal. The raw bar has some of the freshest chilled oysters, crab legs, and Santa Barbara sea urchin; the market lettuces with pecorino cheese, egg, and avocado are a refreshing take on chopped salad; and mussels or clams simmered in chorizo-laden broth are hearty and flavorful. And for you landlubbers, there is exactly one all-meat dish: The pug burger, a towering beef patty (more like a ball) charred to perfection and served with thin, crispy fries. The annual Maryland-style crab feast (one of Lentz's childhood favorites) is one of the most anticipated events for locals. The bar puts out fresh-fruit cocktails; get the "kumquatini" if it's in season. There's a great patio for lunch, brunch, and warm summer nights.

1535 N. Vine St. (near back entrance of Sunset + Vine complex), Hollywood. ☎ **323/462-2155.** www.thehungrycat.com. Main courses $16–$25. AE, MC, V. Mon–Wed noon–11pm; Thurs–Sat noon–midnight; Sun 11am–11pm. Parking garage at Sunset + Vine complex (entrance on Morningstar Court).

Kings Road Cafe ★ AMERICAN   This is the cafe you wish was down the street from your place instead of that Starbucks. The Kings Road Cafe has the perfect combo of everything you'd want in a neighborhood eatery—sunny sidewalk seating along bustling Beverly Boulevard, excellent coffee served in big bowl-like cups, great people-watching, attitude-free service, the occasional celebrity sighting, a huge magazine stand right next door, and fresh, healthy, inexpensive food served in large portions. It's open from morning to night, so you can drop by anytime for such local favorites as banana-pecan buttermilk pancakes, fluffy French toast, spinach and shiitake mushroom omelet, blackened *ahi* with sweet mashed potatoes, and signature panini-style sandwiches. You can pretty much count on waiting for an outside table on weekends, but it gives you time to do a bit of inconspicuous star searching, pick up a few magazines, and check out the Kings Road Cafe Bakery next door (the black-currant scones are wonderful).

8361 Beverly Blvd. (at Kings Rd.), Los Angeles. ☎ **323/655-9044.** www.kingsroadcafe.com. Reservations not accepted. Main courses $7.50–$13 breakfast, $8.95–$18 lunch and dinner. AE, MC, V. Mon–Fri 6:30am–8pm; Sat–Sun 6:30am–6:30pm. Metered street parking.

Musso & Frank Grill ★ AMERICAN/CONTINENTAL   A survey of Hollywood restaurants that leaves out Musso & Frank is like a study of Las Vegas singers that fails to mention Wayne Newton. As Hollywood's oldest eatery (since 1919), Musso & Frank is the paragon of Old Hollywood grillrooms. This is where Faulkner and Hemingway drank during their screenwriting days and where Orson Welles used to hold court. The restaurant is still known for its bone-dry martinis and perfectly seasoned bloody marys. The setting is what you'd expect: oak-beamed ceilings, gruff red-coated waiters, red leather booths and banquettes, mahogany room dividers, and chandeliers with tiny shades. The extensive old-school menu is a veritable survey of American/Continental cookery. Hearty dinners include veal scaloppini Marsala, roast spring lamb with mint jelly, and broiled lobster. Grilled meats are a specialty, as is the Thursday-only chicken potpie. *Tip:* Either sit at the counter for the full M&F effect or request table no. 1 in the west room, which was Charlie Chaplin's regular table.

6667 Hollywood Blvd. (at Cherokee Ave.), Los Angeles. ☎ **323/467-7788.** Reservations recommended. Main courses $14–$45. AE, DC, MC, V. Tues–Sat 11am–11pm. Self-parking behind the restaurant, $2.25 for 2 hr. with validation.

Have mercy and say "Hallelujah!" for the Gospel Brunch at the **House of Blues** (8430 Sunset Blvd., West Hollywood; www.hob.com). For more than a decade, it's been a Sunday tradition at the HOB to feed both the body and the soul with inspiring gospel performances and heaping plates of all-you-can-eat Southern home cookin'. Every week different gospel groups from around the region perform uplifting and energetic music that invariably gets the crowd on its feet and raising the roof. Seatings are every Sunday at 10am and 1pm. Tickets are $41 for adults, $33 for seniors, and $19 for kids, and are available only through the House of Blues Sunset Strip box office; call ✆ **323/848-5100.**

Osteria Mozza ★★ ITALIAN This is the kind of place that can be so wonderful, you keep thinking about it for days afterward. The partner restaurant to the bustling Nancy Silverton and Mario Batali restaurant, Pizzeria Mozza (see below), is an airy, lively, Italianesque space with a central free-standing mozzarella bar of dark wood and marble (Nancy's helm), a full bar along the south wall with beautiful millwork, and an indoor/outdoor dining area that opens onto Melrose Avenue. Dishes gleaned from their culinary adventures in New York and Bologna are composed of only the finest and freshest ingredients. The result: small-dish heaven for the adventurous epicurean, with standouts like fresh ricotta and egg ravioli with browned butter, the grilled whole orata, the *mozzarella di bufala* with caperberry relish (sigh), and, for dessert, the *bombolini,* a huckleberry compote with vanilla gelato. The only downside is that sometimes service doesn't mirror the skill of the kitchen. Reservations are taken 1 month to the calendar day in advance, though walk-ins can be accommodated at the mozzarella and regular bars.

6602 Melrose Ave. (at N. Highland Ave.), Los Angeles. ✆ **323/297-0100.** www.mozza-la.com. Reservations required. Main courses $26–$36. AE, MC, V. Mon–Fri 5:30–11pm; Sat 5–11pm; Sun 5–10pm. Valet parking $8.50 at lunch, $10 at dinner.

Pizzeria Mozza ★★ ITALIAN   Open since 2006, this is still one of the hardest reservations to get in town. Locals call up to a month in advance for an opportunity to experience celeb chef Nancy Silverton's—she founded the famed La Brea Bakery—artisanal pies. When she partnered with Mario Batali, L.A.'s foodies swooned and surged. In contrast to the restaurant's celebrity status (everyone from Scarlett Johansson to Jake Gyllenhaal to Mario Batali himself often dines here), the ambience and decor are entirely unpretentious. The dozen tables and two first-come bars—one is in front of the pizza ovens—are always packed. The pizzas are small and inexpensive enough for everyone to order their own. Favorites are the house-made fennel sausage with *panna* and red onion; stinging nettles and salumi with cacio di Roma cheese; and the squash blossoms, tomato, and burrata. But the toppings are secondary to Nancy's complex crust—in true Italian style, each is wafer thin in the middle, yet impossibly puffy, crunchy, and flavorful on the edges. For dessert, the butterscotch budino with Maldon sea salt is a must-try; even stubborn non–sweet tooths worship it. Fittingly, the wines are all Italian, and moderately priced between $33 and $50.

641 N. Highland Ave. (at Melrose Ave.), Los Angeles. ✆ **323/297-0101.** www.mozza-la.com. Reservations required. Main courses $10–$23. AE, MC, V. Daily noon–midnight. Valet parking $8.50 at lunch, $10 at dinner.

INEXPENSIVE

El Cholo ★ MEXICAN   L.A.'s oldest Mexican restaurant (Gary Cooper and Bing Crosby were regulars, and Jack Nicholson and Warren Beatty still are), El Cholo has been serving up authentic Mexican cuisine in this pink adobe hacienda since 1925, even though the once-outlying mid-Wilshire neighborhood around it has since turned into Koreatown. El Cholo's *muy* strong margaritas, invitingly messy nachos—the first served in the U.S.—and classic combination dinners don't break new culinary ground, but the kitchen has perfected these standards over 80 years. Other specialties include seasonally available green-corn tamales and creative sizzling vegetarian fajitas that go way beyond just eliminating the meat. The atmosphere is festive, as people from all parts of town dine happily in the many rambling rooms that compose the restaurant. Westsiders head to El Cholo's Santa Monica branch at 1025 Wilshire Blvd. (at 11th St.; ℂ 310/899-1106). *Note:* Be prepared for a long wait on weekends.

1121 S. Western Ave. (south of Olympic Blvd.), Los Angeles. ℂ **323/734-2773.** www.elcholo.com. Reservations suggested. Main courses $9.95–$16. AE, DC, DISC, MC, V. Mon–Thurs 11am–10pm; Fri–Sat 11am–11pm; Sun 11am–9pm. Metered street parking; valet parking $4.50.

Pink's Hot Dogs ☺ HOT DOGS   Pink's isn't your usual guidebook recommendation, but then again, this corner stand isn't your typical hot dog shack. This L.A. icon grew around the late Paul and Betty Pink, who opened for business in 1939 selling 10¢ wieners from a used hot dog cart. Now 2,000 of them are served every day on Pink's soft steamed rolls. There are 24 varieties of dogs available, many coined by the celebrities who order them. Martha Stewart once stopped her caravan to order a 10-incher with mustard, relish, onions, chopped tomatoes, sauerkraut, bacon, and sour cream, and now you too can order a "Martha Stewart" dog. The heartburn-inducing chili dogs (made from Betty's chili formula that's still a secret) are craved by even the most upstanding, health-conscious Angelenos. There's lots of folklore emanating from this wiener shack as well: Bruce Willis reportedly proposed to Demi Moore in the parking lot, and Orson Welles holds the record for the most hot dogs consumed in one sitting (18). Even though the dogs are churned out every 30 seconds, expect to wait in line even at midnight—you'll invariably meet a true crossroads of Los Angeles cultures.

709 N. La Brea Ave. (at Melrose Ave.), Los Angeles. ℂ **323/931-4223.** www.pinkshollywood. com. Chili dog $3.30. No credit cards. Sun–Thurs 9:30am–2am; Fri–Sat 9:30am–3am. Free lot; metered street parking.

Roscoe's House of Chicken 'n' Waffles BREAKFAST/SOUTHERN   It sounds like a bad joke—fried chicken and waffles on the same plate. But Roscoe's is one of those places that you have to visit at least once to see how it works (and judging by the wait, it definitely works). A chicken-and-cheese omelet isn't everyone's ideal way to begin the day, but it's de rigueur at Roscoe's. At lunch, few calorie-unconscious diners can resist the juicy fried chicken smothered in gravy and onions, a house specialty that's served with waffles or grits and biscuits. Large chicken-salad bowls and chicken sandwiches also provide plenty of cluck for the buck. Homemade corn bread, sweet potato pie, homemade potato salad, and corn on the cob are available as side orders. Granted, the waffles are of Eggo quality and come with enough whipped butter to stop your heart, but the Southern fried chicken is addictive. *Tip:* The waffles tend to come a bit undercooked, so ask for them crispy.

1514 N. Gower St. (at Sunset Blvd.), Los Angeles. ✆ **323/466-7453.** www.roscoeschickenand
waffles.com. Main courses $6.40–$15. AE, DISC, MC, V. Sun–Thurs 8:30am–midnight; Fri–Sat
8:30am–4am. Metered street parking, pay lots, valet parking Fri–Sat only $10.

Downtown

EXPENSIVE

Church & State ★ FRENCH BISTRO   Hidden in an industrial neighborhood
downtown, in the ground floor of the Biscuit Lofts, classic dishes like garlicky
escargot topped with buttery puff pastry, nicely cooked steak *frites,* and house-
made charcuterie like rabbit galantine and foie gras terrine. The crisp, thin-crust
tarte flambé smothered with caramelized onions, bacon, and crème fraîche
should not be missed. The room is exactly what you'd imagine finding in an urban
setting: high ceilings, brick walls, mirrored columns, and an open kitchen bustling with chefs. The wine list is just as exemplary as the menu—mostly French
varietals priced right for the neighborhood. During the day, the place is crawling
with artists and loft dwellers from the building; at night it might seem a bit out of
the way and uninhabited, until you see all the expensive sedans lining the street.
1850 Industrial St. (at Matteo St.), downtown. ✆ **213/405-1434.** www.churchandstatebistro.
com. Reservations recommended. Main courses $15–$27. AE, DC, DISC, MC, V. Mon–Thurs
11:30am–2:30pm and 6–10pm; Fri 11:30am–2:30pm and 6–11pm; Sat 5:30–11pm; Sun 5:30–9pm.
Metered street parking (free after 6pm) and nearby lots.

Drago Centro ★★ ITALIAN   Celestino Drago, chef/owner of Santa Monica's
Drago and Beverly Hills' **Il Pastaio** (p. 589), and Donato Poto, the former general
manager at **Cut** (p. 585), joined forces to create one of the splashiest restaurants
downtown. On the ground floor of the City National Bank building, the room is
filled with creamy leather banquettes, stunning Murano chandeliers, and a custom-designed glass wine room that showcases bottles from the extensive collection. Expense-account office workers and Drago fans enjoy the refined Italian
cuisine, which is inspired by different regions of Italy: perfectly cooked *branzino,*
a flaky whitefish in seafood broth, and tender veal chop with sweetbreads; and we
could eat the *pappardelle* ribbons with pheasant and morel mushrooms every day.
Tip: The bar and outdoor lounge is a great spot for thin-crust pizzas (the pizza *all'
anatra* with duck and radicchio is good) and fresh-fruit cocktails, and don't forget
to check out the exhibition kitchen set up in the former bank vault.
525 S. Flower St. (at Fifth St.), downtown. ✆ **213/228-8998.** www.dragocentro.com. Reservations recommended. Main courses dinner $18–$35, lunch $17–$25. AE, DC, MC, V. Mon–Fri
11:30am–2:30pm and 5–10pm; Sat 5–10pm; Sun 5–9pm. Valet parking $5 for up to 2 hr. before
5pm, 3 hr. free after 5pm, $7 flat rate after.

Patina ★★★ FRENCH   When celebrity L.A. restaurateur Joachim Splichal
moved his flagship Patina restaurant from Melrose Avenue to the new Walt Disney Concert Hall, it raised one pertinent question: "Is it as good as the old
Patina?" If you arrived after a performance ended, you wouldn't hear the answer
anyway. Billowing walls of laser-cut walnut and floor-to-ceiling glass panels only
augment the hubbub as droves of smartly clad fans of the performing arts dine on
Splichal's signature dishes of wild game and the de rigueur ahi tuna appetizer.
The après-show performances continue with a trio of carts—mounds of caviar,
giant rib-eye steaks for two, and expensive cheeses—crisscrossing the dining
room. Vegetarian dishes and wine pairings are also available, as are prix-fixe

theater menus. Jackets are suggested but not required for dinner. *Tip:* If you want a quiet, romantic dinner, ask the hostess to schedule it at the *start* of a performance.

141 S. Grand Ave. (near First St.), Los Angeles. ℂ **213/972-3331.** www.patinagroup.com. Reservations recommended. Main courses $38–$48 dinner. AE, DC, MC, V. Tues–Sat 5–9:30pm; Sun 4–9:30pm (on L.A. Philharmonic performance evenings, last seating takes place 30 min. after concert ends). Valet parking $8 with validation. Closed Mon.

R23 ★★ 🎁 JAPANESE/SUSHI   This gallery-like space in downtown's out-of-the-way warehouse/artist-loft district has been the secret of sushi connoisseurs since 1991. At the back of R23's single, large exposed-brick dining room, the 12-seat sushi bar shines like a beacon; what appear at first to be ceramic wall ornaments are really stylish sushi platters hanging in wait for large orders. Genial sushi wizards stand at the ready, cases of fine fish before them. Salmon, yellowtail, shrimp, tuna, and scallops are among the always-fresh selections; excellent here is seared *toro,* in which the rich belly tuna absorbs a faint and delectable smoky flavor from the grill. Though R23's sublimely perfect sushi is excellent, the short but inventive menu also includes smoked salmon with melon, eel avocado dynamite, sautéed scallops with shiitake mushrooms, and deep-fried Sawagani crab, along with special creations available only here, like the "Red Sun," with tuna tartare over potatoes, topped with a quail egg. Browse a wide selection of premium wines and sakes.

923 E. Second St. (btw. Alameda St. and Santa Fe Ave.), Los Angeles. ℂ **213/687-7178.** www. r23.com. Reservations recommended. Small plates $7.50–$19; sushi $5–$14. AE, DC, DISC, MC, V. Mon–Thurs 11:30am–2pm and 5:30–10pm; Fri 11:30am–2pm and 5:30–10:30pm; Sat 5:30–10:30pm; Sun 5:30–9:30pm. Valet parking $4.

Water Grill ★ SEAFOOD   Widely considered to be the best seafood house in the city, Water Grill is popular with the suit-and-tie crowd at lunch and with concertgoers en route to the Music Center at night. The dining room is a stylish and sophisticated fusion of wood, leather, and brass, but it gets a lighthearted lift from cavorting papier-mâché fish that play against an aquamarine ceiling painted with bubbles. The restaurant is known for its outstanding raw bar selection; among the appetizers are a dozen different oysters; Nantucket Bay scallops with Queensland blue pumpkin; and crispy sweetbreads with crayfish, chanterelles, and roasted asparagus. Main courses are imaginative dishes influenced by the cuisines of Hawaii, the Pacific Northwest, New Orleans, and New England. Other selections from the menu may range from Santa Barbara spot prawns paired with fingerling potato salad to line-caught pan-roasted Alaskan halibut with Niman Ranch bacon and sweet pea tendril juice. For dessert, try the mascarpone with figs and cherries, or the chocolate bread pudding.

544 S. Grand Ave. (btw. Fifth and Sixth sts.), Los Angeles. ℂ **213/891-0900.** www.watergrill. com. Reservations recommended. Main courses $29–$41. AE, DC, DISC, MC, V. Mon–Tues 11:30am–9pm; Wed–Fri 11:30am–10pm; Sat 5–10pm; Sun 4:30–9pm. Valet parking $5 for 1st 2 hr., $3 for 3rd, $30 max.

INEXPENSIVE

The Original Pantry AMERICAN/BREAKFAST   This bastion of blue-collar cooking has been serving huge portions of comfort food round-the-clock since 1924. Owned by former L.A. mayor and botched governor contender Richard

Riordan, the cash-only Pantry is popular with politicos who come here for weekday lunches and with conferencegoers en route to the nearby L.A. Convention Center. The well-worn restaurant is also a welcoming beacon to hungry clubbers after hours. A bowl of celery stalks, carrot sticks, and whole radishes greets you at your Formica table, and creamy coleslaw and sourdough bread come free with every meal. The menu? It's a chalkboard hanging on the wall. Famous for quantity rather than quality, the Pantry serves huge T-bone steaks, densely packed hamburger loaf, macaroni and cheese, and other American favorites. A typical breakfast—served all day—consists of a huge stack of hotcakes, a big slab of sweet cured ham, home fries, and coffee.

877 S. Figueroa St. (at Ninth St.), Los Angeles. ℭ **213/972-9279.** www.pantrycafe.com. Main courses $6–$14. No credit cards. Daily 24 hr. Free parking across the street with validation.

Philippe The Original 🍴 BREAKFAST/SANDWICHES   Good old-fashioned value is what this legendary landmark cafeteria is all about. Popular with both South Central project residents, Beverly Hills elite, lawyers and jurors, and tourists, Philippe's unspectacular dining room with sawdust floors is one of the few places in L.A. where everyone can get along. Philippe's claims to have invented the French-dipped sandwich at this location in 1908; it remains the most popular menu item. Patrons watch while their choice of beef, pork, ham, turkey, or lamb is sliced and layered onto crusty French bread that's been either single- or double-dipped in meat juices. Regulars slather on the restaurant's signature spicy mustard, which is available as a condiment at most of the communal tables (take home a jar for $4). A hearty breakfast, served daily from 6 to 10:30am, is worthwhile if only for Philippe's uncommonly good cinnamon-dipped French toast. Beer and wine are available. For added entertainment, try to snag a booth in the Train Room, which houses the nifty Model Train Museum. *Tip:* A regular coffee at Philippe The Original is the same price it was when the diner opened in 1924: 9¢. That explains why they serve more than 20,000 cups per week.

1001 N. Alameda St. (at Ord St.), Los Angeles. ℭ **213/628-3781.** www.philippes.com. Most menu items under $8. No credit cards. Daily 6am–10pm. Free parking.

Pasadena & Environs
EXPENSIVE

Bistro 45 ★★ CALIFORNIAN/FRENCH   All class, yet never stuffy, Bistro 45 is a favorite among Pasadena's old guard and nouvelle riche. The restaurant's warm, light ambience and gallery-like decor are an unexpected surprise after the ornately historic Art Deco exterior (the building is a former bank) and provide a romantic backdrop for owner Robert Simon's award-winning cuisine. The seasonally inspired menu changes frequently; dishes might include braised veal short ribs with Asian five spice, rock shrimp risotto with saffron, pan-roasted monkfish with garlic polenta, roasted veal loin filled with Roquefort, Fanny Bay oyster salad, and Nebraska pork with figs. For dessert, try the "chocolate soup," a creamy soufflé served with warm chocolate sauce and vanilla ice cream. The knowledgeable waitstaff can answer questions about the excellent wine list; Bistro 45 appears regularly on *Wine Spectator*'s Best Of lists, and hosts special-event wine dinners.

45 S. Mentor Ave. (btw. Colorado Blvd. and Green St.), Pasadena. ℭ **626/795-2478.** www.bistro45.com. Reservations recommended. Main courses $16–$34 lunch, $19–$35 dinner. AE, DC, MC, V. Tues–Thurs 11:30am–2:30pm and 5–9pm; Fri 11:30am–2:30pm and 5–10pm; Sat 5–10pm; Sun 5–8:30pm. Valet parking $4.50.

The Raymond ★★ NEW AMERICAN   With its easy-to-miss setting in a sleepy part of Pasadena, the Raymond is a jewel even few locals know about. This Craftsman cottage was once the caretaker's house for a grand Victorian hotel called the Raymond. Though the city has grown to surround it, the place maintains an enchanting air of seclusion, romance, and serenity. In 2005, the classic restaurant got a face-lift, as did the haute American- and European-inspired menu, which changes seasonally. A typical dinner may start with locally grown organic lettuces simply dressed in artisan olive oil, lemon, and smoked salt or pork belly in a bourbon barrel-aged maple. Popular entrees can be straightforward American, like 48-hour braised short ribs and Prime New York steak, or more avant garde—for instance, a duck in potato-butter emulsion or Moroccan-style braised lamb shank. Tables are scattered throughout the house and in the lush English garden, and there's plenty of free parking (you won't find *that* on the Westside). *Note:* Bar 1886, named after the year the Raymond hotel opened, is an experience in and of itself—right down to its secret entrance off the parking lot. There are unique handcrafted cocktails, such as the Rose Parade punch and a horseradish egg sour, along with small plates like Kentucky fried quail and grilled octopus.

1250 S. Fair Oaks Ave. (at Columbia St.), Pasadena. ✆ **626/441-3136.** www.theraymond.com. Reservations recommended. Main courses $12–$20 lunch, $24–$39 dinner. AE, DC, DISC, MC, V. Tues–Thurs 5:30–9:30pm; Fri 11:30am–2:30pm and 5:30–9:30pm; Sat 9am–2:30pm and 5:30–9:30pm; Sun 9am–2:30pm and 5–9pm. Free parking lot; free valet parking Fri–Sun.

MODERATE

Café Santorini ★ GREEK   At ground zero of Pasadena's crowded Old Town shopping mecca, this second-story gem has a secluded Mediterranean ambience, due in part to its historic brick building with patio tables overlooking, but insulated from, the plaza below. In the evening, lighting is subdued and romantic, but ambience is casual; many diners are coming from or going to an adjacent movie-theater complex. The food is terrific and affordable, featuring grilled meats and kabobs, pizzas, fresh and tangy hummus, plenty of warm pita, and other staples of Greek cuisine. The menu includes regional flavors such as lamb, feta cheese, spinach, or Armenian sausage; the vegetarian baked butternut squash is filled with fluffy rice and smoky roasted vegetables.

64 W. Union St. (main entrance at the shopping plaza at the corner of Fair Oaks Ave. and Colorado Blvd.), Pasadena. ✆ **626/564-4200.** www.cafesantorini.com. Reservations recommended on weekends. Main courses $10–$31. AE, DC, DISC, MC, V. Mon–Thurs 11am–10pm; Fri–Sat 11am–midnight; Sun 11am–10pm. Valet parking $7 with validation; self-parking across the street $7.

Yujean Kang's Gourmet Chinese Cuisine ★ CHINESE   Many Chinese restaurants put the word *gourmet* in their name, but few really mean it—or deserve it. Not so at Yujean Kang's, where Chinese cuisine is taken to an entirely new level. A master of fusion cuisine, the eponymous chef/owner snatches bits of techniques and flavors from both China and the West, merging them in an entirely fresh way. Can you resist such provocative dishes as "Ants on Tree" (beef sautéed with glass noodles in chili and black sesame seeds), Chinese polenta with shrimp and mushrooms, or sautéed pork chop with fresh leeks? Kang is also a wine aficionado and has assembled a magnificent cellar of California, French, and particularly German wines. Try pairing a German Spätlese with tea-smoked duck salad. The red-wrapped dining room is less subtle than the food but just as elegant.

67 N. Raymond Ave. (btw. Walnut St. and Colorado Blvd.), Pasadena. ✆ **626/585-0855.** www.yujeankangs.com. Reservations recommended. Main courses $8–$10. AE, MC, V. Sun–Thurs 11:30am–2pm and 5–9pm; Fri–Sat 11:30am–2pm and 5–10pm. Valet parking $6 with validation.

L.A.'S TOP ATTRACTIONS

Farmers Market & the Grove ★ ☺   Having celebrated its 75th anniversary in 2009, the original market was little more than an empty lot with wooden stands set up by farmers during the Depression so they could sell directly to city dwellers. Eventually, permanent buildings grew up, including the trademark shingled 10-story clock tower. Today the place has evolved into a sprawling marketplace with a carnival atmosphere, a kind of "turf" version of San Francisco's Fisherman's Wharf. About 70 restaurants, shops, and grocers cater to a mix of workers from the CBS Television City complex, locals, and tourists brought here by the bus load. Retailers sell greeting cards, kitchen implements, candles, and souvenirs, but everyone comes for the food stands, which offer oysters, hot doughnuts, Cajun gumbo, fresh-squeezed orange juice, corned-beef sandwiches, fresh-pressed peanut butter, and all kinds of international fast foods. You can still buy produce here—it's no longer a farm-fresh bargain, but the selection's better than at the grocery store. Don't miss **Loteria Grill** (✆ **323/930-2211**) for

Free-spirited L.A.

cocinita pibil tacos on handmade tortillas and cool *aguas frescas,* or **Du-Par's** (✆ **323/933-8446**) for a slice of pie. The seafood gumbo and gumbo ya ya at the **Gumbo Pot** (✆ **323/933-0358**) are also very popular.

At the eastern end of the Farmers Market is the **Grove,** a massive 575,000-square-foot Vegas-style retail complex composed of various architectural styles ranging from Art Deco to Italian Renaissance. Miniature streets link the Grove to the Market via a double-decker electric trolley. Granted, it's all a bit Disney-gaudy, but the locals love it. Where else can you power-shop until noon, check all your bags at a drop-off station, see a movie at the 14-screen **Grove Theatre** (✆ **323/692-0829;** www.thegrovela.com), have a concierge secure you an early dinner reservation at **Morels French Steakhouse & Bistro** (✆ **323/965-9595**), and be home by 7pm?

6333 W. Third St. (at Fairfax Ave.), Hollywood. ✆ **888/315-8883** or 323/900-8080. www.thegrovela.com. Mon–Thurs 10am–9pm; Fri–Sat 10am–10pm; Sun 10am–8pm.

The Getty Center Los Angeles ★★ ☺   Since opening in 1997, the Richard Meier–designed Getty Center has quickly assumed its place in the L.A. landscape (literally and figuratively) as the city's cultural acropolis and international mecca. Headquarters for the Getty Trust's research, education, philanthropic, and conservation concerns, the postmodernist complex—perched on a hillside in the Santa Monica mountains and swathed in Italian travertine marble—is most frequently visited for the museum galleries displaying the Getty's enormous collection of Impressionist paintings, truckloads of glimmering French furniture and decorative arts, fine illuminated manuscripts, contemporary photography, and European drawings. As a local, I personally think there's nothing more relaxing than spending part of a pretty day just strolling through the Central Garden, which itself is actually a copyrighted work of art by Robert Irwin. The area that's open to the public consists of five two-story pavilions set around an open courtyard, and each gallery within is specially designed to complement the works on display. A sophisticated system of programmable window louvers allows many works (particularly paintings) to be displayed in the natural light in which they were created for the first time in the modern era. One of these is van Gogh's *Irises,* one of the museum's finest and most popular holdings. Trivia buffs will enjoy knowing that the museum spent $53.9 million to acquire this painting; it's displayed in a complex that cost roughly $1 *billion* to construct.

One of the more recent additions to the Getty Center is the Fran and Ray Stark Sculpture Garden. This collection of 28 modern and contemporary outdoor sculptures from the collection of the late legendary film producer Ray Stark and his wife, Fran, was donated to the Getty Museum by the Ray Stark Revocable Trust and features many of the 20th century's greatest sculptors, including works by **Elisabeth Frink, Joan Miró,** and **Isamu Noguchi.** Visitors to the center park at the base of the hill and ascend via a cable-driven electric tram. On clear days, the sensation is of being in the clouds, gazing across Los Angeles and the Pacific Ocean (and into a few chic Brentwood backyards). If you're like me and don't remember a thing from your college art-appreciation class, get one of the new GettyGuide Audio Guides at the information desk. The nifty device allows visitors to take their own guided tour through the Getty Museum. The 45-minute human-led architectural tours, offered throughout the day, are also worth looking into. Dining options include several espresso/snack carts, a cafeteria, a self-service cafe, and the elegant (though informal) "Restaurant" offering table service for lunch (Tues–Sat), dinner (Sat), and Sunday brunch with breathtaking views overlooking the ocean and mountains (restaurant reservations are recommended, though walk-ins are accepted; call ✆ **310/440-6810,** or make reservations online at www.getty.edu).

Realizing that fine-art museums can be boring for kids, the center provides several clever programs for kids, including a family room filled with hands-on activities for families, weekend family workshops, and Art Detective cards to help parents and kids explore the grounds and galleries; and some tours are geared specifically for families.

Entrance to the Getty Center is free and no reservations are required. Cameras and video cameras are permitted, but only if you use existing light (flash units are *verboten*) and limit photos to the permanent collection and outdoor areas.

1200 Getty Center Dr., Los Angeles. ✆ **310/440-7300.** www.getty.edu. Free admission. Tues–Fri 10am–5:30pm; Sat 10am–9pm; Sun 10am–5:30pm. Parking $15 (free after 5pm for special evening events and Sat). Closed Mon and major holidays.

The Getty Villa Malibu ★★ ☺ After 8 years and $275 million, the magnificent Getty Villa is receiving guests again. As the Getty Center was the cultural coup of 1997, a ticket to the renovated Villa was also once one of the most sought-after items in the city. Fortunately, it's more accessible now; while you still need to secure advance tickets, for all but busy holiday periods, it can usually be done the day before. And thankfully, the museum has upgraded to the PDF system (versus snail mail). This former residence of oil tycoon J. Paul Getty, built in 1974 on the edge of a Malibu bluff with dazzling views of the ocean, was modeled after a first-century Roman country house buried by the eruption of Mount Vesuvius in A.D. 79—the Villa dei Papiri in Herculaneum, Italy. In fact, as you enter the sun-filled inner courtyard, it's not hard to imagine toga-clad senators wandering the gardens where fountains and bronze busts occupy the same spots as the original villa.

The museum's permanent collection of Greek, Roman, and Etruscan artifacts—dating from 6,500 B.C. to A.D. 400—consists of more than 1,200 works in 23 galleries arranged by theme, and 5 additional galleries for changing exhibitions. Exhibits on display range from everyday items such as coins, jewelry, and sculpture to modern interactive exhibits that illustrate key moments in the history of the ancient Mediterranean. Highlights include *Statue of a Victorious Youth,* a large-scale bronze discovered in an Adriatic shipwreck that is kept in a special climate-controlled room to preserve the metal (it's one of the few life-size Greek bronzes to have survived to modern times), as well as a beautiful 450-seat open-air theater where visitors are encouraged to take a break. Performances of either a Greek comedy or tragedy take place here every September (a commanding rendition of *Elektra* featured Olympia Dukakis). For keeping the kids entertained, the Villa's education team created a hands-on space called the Family Forum where children can partake in art-related activities.

For a more enlightening museum experience, I strongly suggest you rent a $5 GettyGuide Audio Player, which features commentary from curators and conservators on more than 150 works (it's available at the Pick-Up Desk on Floor 1). Admission to the Getty Villa is free, but, unlike the Getty Center, advance tickets are required and can be obtained online or by phone.

17985 Pacific Coast Hwy. (1 mile north of Sunset Blvd.), Malibu. ✆ **310/440-7300.** www.getty. edu. Free admission, but tickets required. Wed–Mon 10am–5pm. Parking $15 (free for evening programs). Closed Tues and major holidays.

Grauman's Chinese Theatre ★ This is one of the world's great movie palaces and one of Hollywood's finest landmarks. The theater was opened in 1927 by impresario Sid Grauman, a brilliant promoter who's credited with originating the idea of the paparazzi-packed movie "premiere." Outrageously conceived, with both authentic and simulated Chinese embellishments, Grauman's theater was designed to impress. Original Chinese heavenly doves top the facade, and two of the theater's columns once propped up a Ming dynasty temple.

Visitors by the millions flock to the theater for its famous entry court, where stars such as Elizabeth Taylor, Paul Newman, Ginger Rogers, Humphrey Bogart, Frank Sinatra, Marilyn Monroe, and about 160 others set their signatures and hand-/footprints in concrete (a tradition started when actress Norma Talmadge "accidentally" stepped in wet cement during the premiere of Cecil B. De Mille's *King of Kings*). It's not always hands and feet: Betty Grable's shapely leg; the hoof prints of Gene Autry's horse, Champion; Jimmy Durante's and Bob Hope's

View from the Griffith Observatory.

trademark noses; Whoopi Goldberg's dreadlocks; George Burns's cigar; and even R2-D2's wheels appear in concrete.

6925 Hollywood Blvd. (btw. Highland and La Brea Ave.). ☏ **323/464-8111.** www.manntheaters. com/chinese. Ticket prices vary. Call for showtimes.

Griffith Observatory ★★   Made world-famous in the film *Rebel Without a Cause,* Griffith Observatory's bronze domes have been Hollywood Hills landmarks since 1935. Closed for renovation for what seemed like forever, it finally reopened in November 2006 after a $93-million renovation. The central dome houses the 300-seat **Samuel Oschin Planetarium,** where hourly screenings of a narrated half-hour projection show called "Centered in the Universe" reveals the stars and planets that are hidden from the naked eye by the city's ubiquitous lights and smog.

The Observatory also features 60 space-related exhibits designed to "sparkle your imagination," the highlight being the largest astronomically accurate image ever produced—a 20×152-foot porcelain enamel dazzler that's cleverly called "The Big Picture." It supposedly encompasses a million galaxies, but I lost count after 11. There's also the 200-seat Leonard Nimoy Event Horizon Theater (go Spock!), a Wolfgang Puck "Café at the End of the Universe," and several Zeiss and solar telescopes for public use both day and night.

Truth be told, most locals never actually go inside the observatory; they come to this spot on the south slope of Mount Hollywood for unparalleled city views. On warm nights, with the lights twinkling below, this is one of the most romantic places in L.A.

2800 E. Observatory Rd. (in Griffith Park, at the end of Vermont Ave.). ☏ **213/473-0800.** www. griffithobservatory.org. Planetarium tickets $7 adults, $5 seniors 60 and over and students with ID, $3 children 5–12. Wed–Fri noon–10pm; Sat–Sun 10am–10pm. Call or check website for planetarium showtimes.

The HOLLYWOOD Sign ★   These famous 50-foot-high white sheet-metal letters have come to symbolize the movie industry and the city itself. The sign was erected on Mount Lee in 1923 as an advertisement for a real estate development. The full text originally read HOLLYWOODLAND and was lined with thousands of 20-watt bulbs around the letters (changed periodically by a caretaker who lived in a small house behind the sign). The sign gained notoriety when actress Peg Entwistle leapt to her death from the "H" in 1932. The LAND section was damaged by a landslide, and the entire sign fell into major disrepair until the Hollywood Chamber of Commerce spearheaded a campaign to repair it (Hugh Hefner, Alice Cooper, Gene Autry, and Andy Williams were all major contributors). Officially completed in 1978, the 450-foot-long installation is now protected by a fence and motion detectors. The best view is from down below, at the corner of Sunset Boulevard and Bronson Avenue. *Tip:* It may look like it on a map, but Beachwood Drive does not lead to the sign. If you want to reach the sign on foot (you still won't be able to touch it), it requires a somewhat strenuous (depending on your level of physical fitness) 5-mile round-trip hike on the Brush Canyon Trail in Griffith Park—the trail head is at the end of Canyon Drive. You can also choose to park at the Observatory (it's the same distance either way) and combine two activities in one. For more information, call the Griffith Park headquarters at ℂ **323/913-4688.**

Hollywood Walk of Fame ★ ☺   When the Hollywood honchos realized how limited the footprint space was at Grauman's Chinese Theatre, they came up with another way to pay tribute to the stars. Since 1960, more than 2,400 celebrities have been honored along the world's most famous sidewalk. Each bronze medallion set into the center of a terrazzo star pays homage to a famous television, film, radio, theater, or recording personality. Although about a third of them are as obscure as the late **Michael Jackson's** sexual preference—you can pay your homage at the pop icon's star at **6927 Hollywood Boulevard**—millions of

The Hollywood Sign.

visitors are thrilled by the sight of famous names such as **James Dean** (1719 Vine St.), **John Lennon** (1750 Vine St.), **Marlon Brando** (1765 Vine St.), **Rudolph Valentino** (6164 Hollywood Blvd.), **Marilyn Monroe** (6744 Hollywood Blvd.), **Elvis Presley** (7080 Hollywood Blvd.)—the only star that has ever been moved—**Greta Garbo** (6901 Hollywood Blvd.), **Louis Armstrong** (7000 Hollywood Blvd.), **Barbra Streisand** (6925 Hollywood Blvd.), and **Eddie Murphy** (7000 Hollywood Blvd.). **Gene Autry** is all over the place: The singing cowboy earned five different stars (a sidewalk record), one in each category.

The sight of bikers, metal heads, homeless wanderers, and hordes of disoriented tourists all treading on memorials to Hollywood's greats makes for a bizarre and somewhat tacky tribute. But the Hollywood Chamber of Commerce has been doing a terrific job sprucing up the pedestrian experience with filmstrip crosswalks, swaying palms, and more. And at least 1 weekend a month, a group of fans calling themselves Star Polishers busy themselves scrubbing tarnished medallions.

The legendary sidewalk is continually adding new names, such as Muhammad Ali in front of the Kodak Theatre. The public is invited to attend dedication ceremonies; the honoree—who pays a whopping $25,000 for the eternal upkeep—is usually in attendance. Contact the **Hollywood Chamber of Commerce,** 7018 Hollywood Blvd., Hollywood, CA 90028 (✆ **323/469-8311**), for information.

Hollywood Blvd., btw. Gower St. and La Brea Ave.; and Vine St., btw. Yucca St. and Sunset Blvd. ✆ **323/469-8311.** www.hollywoodchamber.net.

La Brea Tar Pits & Page Museum ★ ☺ An odorous swamp of gooey asphalt oozes to the Earth's surface in the middle of Los Angeles. No, it's not a low-budget horror-movie set—it's La Brea Tar Pits, a truly bizarre primal pool on Museum Row where hot tar has been bubbling from the Earth for more than 40,000 years. The bubbling pools may look like a fake Disney set, but they're the real thing and have enticed thirsty animals throughout history. Nearly 400 species of mammals, birds, amphibians, and fish—many of which are now extinct—walked, crawled, landed, swam, or slithered into the sticky sludge, got stuck in the worst way, and stayed forever. In 1906, scientists began a systematic removal and classification of entombed specimens, including ground sloths, giant vultures, mastodons, camels, bears, lizards, and even prehistoric relatives of today's super-rats. Today it's one of the world's richest excavation sites for Ice Age fossils. The best finds are on display in the adjacent **Page Museum at the La Brea Tar Pits,** which houses the largest and most diverse collection of Ice Age plants and tar-stained skeletons in the world. Archaeological work is ongoing; you can watch as scientists clean, identify, and catalog new finds in the Paleontology Laboratory. An entertaining 15-minute film documenting the recoveries is also shown.

5801 Wilshire Blvd. (east of Fairfax Ave.), Los Angeles. ✆ **323/934-7243.** www.tarpits.org. Museum admission $7 adults; $4.50 seniors 62 and over, students with ID, and teens 13–17; $2 children 5–12; free for children 4 and under; free for everyone the 1st Tues of every month. Daily 9:30am–5pm. Parking $7 with validation, $9 without validation.

L.A. LIVE If you watched the GRAMMYs a few years ago, you probably already know about the new L.A. LIVE "entertainment campus" that is the keystone of L.A.'s downtown gentrification project. This being Los Angeles, L.A. LIVE will eventually become one of the largest and flashiest mixed-use

Carousel, Santa Monica Pier.

Ferris wheel, Santa Monica Pier.

entertainment complexes in the world, costing $2.5 billion to build and covering more than 6 city blocks (hence its nickname—Times Square West). It's anchored by the **NOKIA Theatre,** the **STAPLES Center** (where the Lakers and Clippers play their home games), and the **Los Angeles Convention Center,** and is crammed with a dozen chain restaurants and cafes, two huge nightclubs, a 14-screen Regal Cinema, the **GRAMMY Museum,** a bowling center, and **ESPN's West Coast broadcast headquarters.** The JW Marriott and Ritz-Carlton hotels opened in 2010 (both within a 54-story tower). Log on to the L.A. LIVE website to see who's playing or performing while you're in town.

Figueroa St. btw. Venice and Olympic blvds., Los Angeles. ℭ **866/548-3452** or 213/763-5483. www.lalive.com.

Santa Monica Pier ★★ 😊 📷   Piers have been a tradition in Southern California since the area's 19th-century seaside resort days. Many have long since disappeared (such as Pacific Ocean Park, an entire amusement park perched on offshore pilings), and others have been shortened by battering storms and are now mere shadows (or stumps) of their former selves, but you can still experience those halcyon days of yesteryear at world-famous Santa Monica Pier.

Built in 1908 for passenger and cargo ships, the Santa Monica Pier does a pretty good job of recapturing the glory days of Southern California. The wooden wharf is now home to seafood restaurants and snack shacks; a touristy Mexican cantina; a gaily colored 1920s indoor wooden **carousel** (which Paul Newman operated in *The Sting*); and an **aquarium** filled with sharks, rays, octopus, eels, and other local sea life. Summer evening concerts, which are free and range from big band to Miami-style Latin, draw crowds, as does the small amusement area perched halfway down. Its name, **Pacific Park** (ℭ **310/260-8744;** www. pacpark.com), hearkens back to the granddaddy pier amusement park in California, Pacific Ocean Park; this updated version has a **solar-powered Ferris wheel,** a vintage **merry-go-round,** and 10 other rides, plus a high-tech **arcade** shootout.

But anglers still head to the end to fish, and nostalgia buffs to view the photographic display of the pier's history. This is the last of the great pleasure piers, offering rides, romance, and perfect panoramic views of the bay and mountains.

The pier is about a mile up Ocean Front Walk from Venice; it's a great round-trip stroll. Parking is available for $6 to $8 on both the pier deck and the beachfront nearby. Limited short-term parking is also available. For information on twilight concerts (generally held Thurs btw. mid-June and the end of Aug), call © **310/458-8900** or visit **www.santamonicapier.org**.

Ocean Ave. at the end of Colorado Blvd., Santa Monica.

Six Flags California (Magic Mountain and Hurricane Harbor) ★ ☺

What started as a countrified little amusement park with a couple of relatively tame roller coasters in 1971 has been transformed by Six Flags into a thrill-a-minute daredevil's paradise called the Xtreme Park. Located about 20 to 30 minutes north of Universal Studios, Six Flags Magic Mountain is one of the only ones out of the 38 Six Flags parks that is open year-round. The 18 world-class roller coasters (more than any other place in the world) make it enormously popular with teenagers and young adults, and the children's playland—Bugs Bunny World—creates excitement for the pint-size set (kids under 48 in. tall). Bring an iron constitution; rides with names such as Goliath, Déjà Vu, Ninja, Viper, Colossus, and Apocalypse will have your cheeks flapping with the G-force, and queasy expressions are common at the exit. Some rides are themed to action-film characters (such as Superman: Escape from Krypton and The Riddler's Revenge); others are loosely tied to their surroundings, such as the Log Jammer and Swashbuckler. One of the newest thrill rides is TATSU, a "flying beast" that debuted as the tallest, fastest, and longest flying coaster in the world; Scream! where riders are strapped into a "flying chair" and raced upside down seven times at 65 mph; and the redesigned X2, where riders rotate 360 degrees forward and backward. Arcade games and summer-only entertainment (stunt shows, animal shows, and parades) round out the park's attractions.

Hurricane Harbor is Six Flags' tropical paradise. It's located right next door to Magic Mountain and is open mid-June through September. You really can't see both in 1 day, so plan accordingly. Bring your own swimsuit; the park has changing rooms with showers and lockers. Like Magic Mountain, areas have themes like a tropical lagoon and an African river (complete with ancient temple ruins). The primary activities are swimming, going down the 20-plus water slides, rafting, playing volleyball, and lounging; many areas are designed especially for the little "buccaneer."

Note: Be sure to check their website for money-saving discounts on admission tickets—you could save up to $25 per ticket by buying online.

Magic Mountain Pkwy. (off Golden State Fwy. [I-5 N]), Valencia. © **661/255-4100** or 818/367-5965. www.sixflags.com. Magic Mountain $60 adults, $35 children under 48 in. high, free for children 2 and under; Hurricane Harbor $33 adults, $25 children under 48 in. high, free for children 2 and under. Magic Mountain daily Mar to Labor Day, and weekends and holidays the rest of the year; Hurricane Harbor daily mid-June to Labor Day, weekends May and Sept, closed Oct–Apr. Both parks open at 10:30am, and closing hours vary btw. 6pm and midnight. Parking $15. Prices and hours are subject to change without notice, so call before you arrive.

Sunset Boulevard & the Sunset Strip ★★

Unless you were raised in a cave, you've undoubtedly heard of L.A.'s Sunset Boulevard. The most famous of the city's many legendary boulevards, it winds dozens of miles over prime real estate as it travels from downtown (where it briefly turns into Cesar Chavez Ave. btw. Spring and Figueroa sts.) to the beach, taking its travelers on both a historical and a microcosmic journey that defines Los Angeles as a whole—from tacky strip malls and historic movie studios to infamous strip clubs and some of the most coveted zip codes on Earth. In fact, driving the stretch from Hollywood to the Pacific should be required for all first-time visitors because it is such a good example of what L.A. is all about: instant gratification.

Bam! From the start, you'll see the **Saharan Motor Hotel,** of many a movie shoot; the Guitar Center's **Hollywood RockWalk,** where superstars such as Chuck Berry, Little Richard, Santana, and the Van Halen brothers left handprints or signatures; the **"Riot Hyatt"** (now the Andaz), where The Doors, Led Zeppelin, and Guns N' Roses crashed and smashed from the '60s to the '80s; and **Chateau Marmont,** where Greta Garbo lived and John Belushi died.

Phew! And you've barely even started. Once you pass the Chateau Marmont, you're officially cruising the **Sunset Strip**—a 1¾-mile stretch of Sunset Boulevard from Crescent Heights Boulevard to Doheny Drive. The tour continues with the **Comedy Store,** where Roseanne, Robin Williams, and David Letterman rose to stardom; Dan Aykroyd's ramshackle **House of Blues,** where the rock stars still show up for an impromptu show; the **Sunset Tower Hotel,** where Clark Gable, Marilyn Monroe, and John Wayne once lived; the exclusive **Skybar** within the Mondrian

> **Body Double**
>
> Here's a really cheap and easy way to get a great seat at a fancy Hollywood award ceremony: Log on to **Seatfiller.com** and sign up to be one of those people who make sure all the empty seats are occupied.

hotel; the **Viper Room,** once owned by Johnny Depp and the site of River Phoenix's overdose in 1993; the **Whisky A Go-Go,** where The Doors were once a house band; and the **Rainbow Bar & Grill,** where Jimi Hendrix, Bruce Springsteen, and Bob Marley became legends.

Once you emerge from the Strip, things calm down considerably as you drive through the tony neighborhoods of **Beverly Hills, Bel Air, Brentwood,** and **Pacific Palisades.** By the time you've reached the beaches where *Baywatch* was filmed, you'll have seen a vivid cross-section of the city and have a pretty good idea of what L.A. is all about.

Universal Studios Hollywood & CityWalk ★★ ☺ Believing that filmmaking itself is a bona fide attraction, Universal Studios began offering tours to the public in 1964. The concept worked: Today Universal is more than just one of the largest movie studios in the world—it's one of the largest theme parks as well. By integrating shows and rides with behind-the-scenes presentations on moviemaking, Universal created a new genre of theme park, stimulating a number of clone and competitor parks.

The main attraction continues to be the **Studio Tour,** a nearly 1-hour guided tram ride around the company's 420 acres that's "hosted" (via video screen) by Jimmy Fallon. En route you pass production offices before visiting the most extensive back-lot reconstruction in Universal's history, including the new New York Street, plus classic stops from *War of the Worlds* and *How the Grinch Stole Christmas.* A new feature of the tour is director Peter Jackson's **King Kong 360 3D,** the largest experience of its kind in the world.

Along the way, the tram encounters several staged "disasters," which I won't divulge here, lest I ruin the surprise (they're all very tame), and a staged street-race special effects sequence echoing the action in Universal's *Fast and Furious* movie series. Though the wait to board might appear long, don't be discouraged—each tram carries several hundred people and departures are frequent, so the line moves quickly. The "Front of the Line" ticket option renders it moot.

Other attractions are more typical of high-tech theme park fare, but all have a film- or TV-oriented slant. The newest will be **Transformers 3D: The Ride,** which opens in the spring of 2012. **The Simpsons Ride** allows guests to join Homer, Marge, Bart, Lisa, and Maggie as they soar high above the fictional "Krustyland" theme park in a "virtual roller coaster," creating the sensation of thrilling drops and turns and a full 360-degree loop. **Revenge of the Mummy** is a high-tech indoor roller coaster that whips you backward and forward through a dark Egyptian tomb filled with creepy Warrior Mummies (and ends a bit too soon). **Jurassic Park—The Ride** is short in duration as well but long on dinosaur animatronics; riders in jungle boats float through a world of five-story-tall T-rexes and airborne raptors that culminates in a pitch-dark vertical drop with a splash ending. **Terminator 2: 3D** is a high-tech cyberwar show that combines live action along with triple-screen 3-D technology, explosions, spraying mists, and laser fire (Arnold prevails, of course). **Shrek 4D** is one of the park's best attractions, a multisensory animated show that combines 3-D effects, a humorous story line, and "surprise" special effects—the flying dragon chase is wild.

Waterworld is a fast-paced outdoor theater presentation (and far better than the film that inspired it) featuring stunts and special effects performed on and around a small man-made lagoon (arrive at the theater at least 15 min. before the showtime listed in the handout park map to ensure seating). Straight ahead of the park's main entrance on Main Street is the **Hollywood Ticket Office,** where you can obtain free tickets (subject to availability) for any TV shows that are taping during your visit—including *The Tonight Show with Jay Leno*—as well as tickets and passes to other local museums, sporting events, and entertainment attractions.

Universal Studios is an exciting place for kids and teens, but just as in any theme park, lines can be brutally long; the wait for a 5-minute ride can sometimes last more than an hour. In summer, the stifling Valley heat can dog you all day. To avoid the crowds, try not to visit on weekends or during school vacations. If you're willing to pay extra money to skip the hassle of standing in line, the park offers a **"Front of Line" pass** with—obviously—front-of-the-line privileges, as well as VIP passes (essentially private tours). You can also save time standing in line by purchasing and printing your tickets online. Log on to **www.universalstudioshollywood. com** for more information. Another ticket option is the **"All You Can Eat"** pass, which allows guests to dine all day at selected in-park restaurants for one price.

The **Southern California CityPass** (© 888/330-5008; www.citypass. com) offers admission to five So Cal attractions including Universal Studios Hollywood and the Disneyland Resort.

Located just outside the gate of Universal Studios Hollywood is **Universal CityWalk** (© 818/622-4455; www.citywalkhollywood.com). If you have any money left from the amusement park, you can spend it at this 3-block-long pedestrian promenade crammed thick with flashy name-brand stores (Billabong, Fossil, Skechers, Abercrombie & Fitch), nightclubs (the Jon Lovitz Comedy Club, Howl at the Moon dueling piano bar, Rumba Room Latin dance club, and the newest outpost of San Francisco's sexy **Infusion Lounge**), restaurants

(Hard Rock Cafe, Daily Grill, Bubba Gumps, Pink's Hot Dogs, Samba Brazilian Steakhouse & Lounge, Saddle Ranch Chop House—ride the mechanical bull, we dare you!), a six-story 3-D IMAX theater, the 18-screen **CityWalk Cinemas,** a 6,200-seat amphitheater, an indoor skydiving wind tunnel, and even a bowling alley (take *that,* Disney!). Be sure to stop into the **Zen Zone** (ⓒ **818/487-7889**), where you can get an inexpensive 20-minute "aqua massage." You lay down fully clothed in what looks like a tanning bed, and strong rotating jets of water massage your backside from neck-to-toe (a blue rubber sheet keeps you dry). Entrance to CityWalk is free; it's open until 9pm on weekdays and until midnight Friday and Saturday. *Tip:* The sushi at the Wasabi at CityWalk restaurant (ⓒ **818/763-8813**) was surprisingly good and very reasonably priced.

Hollywood Fwy. (Universal Center Dr. or Lankershim Blvd. exits), Universal City. ⓒ **800-UNIVER-SAL** (864-8377) or 818/622-3801. www.universalstudioshollywood.com. Admission $74 adults, $66 children under 48 in. tall, free for children 2 and under. Winter daily 10am–6pm; summer daily 9am–7pm. Hours are subject to change. Parking $12.

Venice Beach's Ocean Front Walk ★★★ ☺
This has long been one of L.A.'s most colorful areas and a must-visit for any first-time tourist. Founded at the turn of the last century, Venice was a development inspired by its Italian namesake. Authentic gondolas plied miles of inland waterways lined with rococo palaces. In the 1950s, Venice became the stomping grounds of Jack Kerouac, Allen Ginsberg, William S. Burroughs, and other Beats. In the 1960s, this was the epicenter of L.A.'s hippie scene.

Today Venice is still one of the world's most engaging bohemian locales. It's not an exaggeration to say that no visit to L.A. would be complete without a stroll along the famous paved beach path, an almost surreal assemblage of every L.A. stereotype—and then some. Among stalls and stands selling cheap sunglasses, Mexican blankets, and medical marijuana swirls a carnival of humanity that

Venice Beach boardwalk.

Graffiti artists, Venice Beach.

includes bikini-clad in-line skaters, tattooed bikers, tan hunks pumping iron at Muscle Beach, panhandling vets, beautiful wannabes, and plenty of tourists and gawkers. On any given day, you're bound to come across all kinds of performers: mimes, break dancers, stoned drummers, chain saw jugglers, talking parrots, and the occasional apocalyptic evangelist.

On the beach, btw. Venice Blvd. and Rose Ave., Venice. www.venicebeach.com.

Walt Disney Concert Hall ★★★ The strikingly beautiful Walt Disney Concert Hall isn't just the new home of the Los Angeles Philharmonic; it's a key element in an urban revitalization effort now underway downtown. The Walt Disney family insisted on the best, and, with an initial gift of $50 million to build a world-class performance venue, that's what they got: A masterpiece of design by world-renowned architect Frank Gehry, with acoustical quality that equals or surpasses that of the best concert halls in the world. Similar to Gehry's most famous architectural masterpiece, the Guggenheim Museum in Bilbao, the concert hall's dramatic stainless-steel exterior consists of a series of undulating curved surfaces that partially envelop the entire building, presenting multiple glimmering facades to the surrounding neighborhood. Within is a dazzling 2,265-seat auditorium replete with curved woods and a dazzling array of organ pipes (also designed by Gehry), as well as Joachim Splichal's Patina restaurant, the hip Concert Hall Cafe, a bookstore, and a gift shop.

The 3½-acre Concert Hall is open to the public for viewing, but to witness it in its full glory, do whatever it takes to attend a concert by the world-class Los Angeles Philharmonic and the sensational new music director Gustavo Dudamel. Also highly recommended are the free tours, which lead visitors through the Concert Hall's history from conception to creation. The 45-minute self-guided tour is narrated by actor John Lithgow and includes interviews with Frank Gehry, former Los Angeles Philharmonic music director Esa-Pekka Salonen, and acoustician Yasuhisa Toyota, among others. One big caveat is that you see just about everything except the auditorium: There's almost always a rehearsal in progress, and the acoustics are so good that there's no discreet way to sneak a peek. The audio tours are available on most nonmatinee days from 10am to 2pm (be sure to check their website for the monthly tour schedule).

111 S. Grand Ave. (at First St.). 📞 **323/850-2000** or 213/972-7211. www.disneyhall.com, www. laphil.com, or www.musiccenter.org.

EXPLORING THE CITY

To locate the attractions discussed below, see the individual neighborhood maps in section 1, "Orientation."

Museums & Galleries

L.A.'S WESTSIDE & BEVERLY HILLS

Hammer Museum ★ Created by the former chairman and CEO of Occidental Petroleum, the Hammer Museum is ensconced in a two-story Carrara marble building attached to the oil company's offices. It's better known for its high-profile and often provocative visiting exhibits. With a reputation for championing contemporary political and experimental art, the Hammer continues to present often daring and usually popular special exhibits, and it's definitely worth calling ahead to find out what will be there during your visit to L.A. The permanent collection (Armand Hammer's personal collection) consists mostly of traditional western European and Anglo-American art, and contains noteworthy paintings by Toulouse-Lautrec, Rembrandt, Degas, and van Gogh.

10899 Wilshire Blvd. (at Westwood Blvd.). © **310/443-7000.** www.hammer.ucla.edu. Admission $7 adults; $5 seniors 65 and over; free for children 17 and under, military, and veterans; free for everyone Thurs. Tues–Wed and Fri-Sat 11am–7pm; Thurs 11am–9pm; Sun 11am–5pm. Parking $3 for 1st 3 hr. with validation.

Museum of Tolerance ★ The Museum of Tolerance is designed to expose prejudices, bigotry, and inhumanity while teaching racial and cultural tolerance. Since its opening in 1993, it's hosted four million visitors from around the world, including King Hussein of Jordan and the Dalai Lama. It's located in the Simon Wiesenthal Center, an institute founded by the legendary Nazi hunter. While the Holocaust figures prominently here, this is not a Jewish museum—it's an academy that broadly campaigns for a live-and-let-live world. *Tolerance* is an abstract idea that's hard to display, so most of this $50-million museum's exhibits are high-tech and conceptual in nature. Fast-paced interactive displays are designed to touch the heart as well as the mind, and engage everyone from heads of state to Gen Y.

9786 W. Pico Blvd. (at Roxbury Dr.). © **310/553-8403.** www.museumoftolerance.com. Admission $15 adults, $12 seniors 62 and over, $11 students with ID and youth 5–18, free for children 4 and under. Advance purchase recommended; photo ID required for admission. Mon–Thurs 10am–5pm; Sun 11am–5pm; Fri 10am–3:15pm. Closed Sat and many Jewish and secular holidays; call for schedule.

HOLLYWOOD

Craft & Folk Art Museum This gallery, housed in a prominent Museum Row building, has grown into one of the city's largest. "Craft and folk art" encompasses everything from clothing, tools, religious artifacts, and other everyday objects to woodcarvings, papier-mâché, weaving, and metalwork. The museum displays folk objects from around the world, but its strongest collection is masks from India, America, Mexico, Japan, and China. The museum is also known for its annual International Festival of Masks, held each October in Hancock Park, across the street. Be sure to stop in the funky, eclectic Museum Shop to peruse the wearable art, folk-art books, and various handmade crafts.

5814 Wilshire Blvd. (btw. Fairfax and La Brea aves.). © **323/937-4230.** www.cafam.org. Admission $7 adults, $5 seniors and students, free for children 9 and under; free to all 1st Wed each month. Tues–Fri 11am–5pm; Sat–Sun noon–6pm. Paid parking lots nearby.

The Hollywood Museum The historic Max Factor Building—Max Factor was the patriarch of the Hollywood makeup industry—has finally been restored to its original 1935 Art Deco splendor and is now the home of the Hollywood Museum, which features four floors of famous and rare props (including Hannibal Lecter's cell), costumes (Nicole Kidman's from *Moulin Rouge*), scripts, cameras, awards, and numerous vintage photos and posters from the television, stage, and recording industries. It's arranged for the visitor to experience Hollywood chronologically—from the Silent Era and Golden Era to current production technology and a glimpse into the future of the industry. The museum, located across from the Hollywood & Highland entertainment complex, also houses a library, a screening room, an education center, and a museum/studio gift shop. Private guided tours are available upon request.

LACMA.

1660 N. Highland Ave. (at Hollywood Blvd.), Hollywood. ✆ **323/464-7776.** www.thehollywood
museum.com. Admission and tour $15 adults, $12 seniors and children 11 and under. Wed–Sun
10am–5pm.

Los Angeles County Museum of Art (LACMA) ★★★ For more than 50
years, LACMA has been one of the finest art museums in the nation, housing a
100,000-piece permanent collection that includes works by Degas, Rembrandt,
Hockney, and Monet. The huge 20-acre complex—it's the largest visual-arts
museum west of Chicago—has been expanded even more with the 2008 opening
of the $56-million, three-story **Broad Contemporary Art Museum** (also
known as BCAM). Boasting 60,000 square feet of exhibition space, it's the first
new art museum built in L.A. since the Getty Center opened in 1997. BCAM is
one of the largest column-free art spaces in the U.S., and opening installations
include works by such contemporary artists as Richard Serra, Jeff Koons, Jasper
Johns, Andy Warhol, and Roy Lichtenstein.

More recently, the Lynda and Stewart Resnick Exhibition Pavilion was
added in 2010. The single-story structure is 45,000 square feet in size, and is
now the world's largest custom-built, open-plan museum with natural lighting.
Three diverse exhibits inaugurated its debut—one focused on decorative arts,
another on ancient Mexican masterworks, and the third on European fashion
from 1700 to 1915. Other highlights include LACMA's **Pavilion for Japanese
Art,** which has exterior walls made of Kalwall, a translucent material that, like
shoji screens, permits the entry of soft natural light. Inside is a collection of Japanese Edo paintings that's rivaled only by the holdings of the emperor of Japan.
The **Ahmanson Building** houses the majority of the museum's permanent collections—everything from 2,000-year-old pre-Columbian Mexican ceramics to
19th-century portraiture, to a unique glass collection spanning the centuries.
Other displays include one of the nation's largest holdings of costumes and textiles, and an important Indian and Southeast Asian art collection. Free 50-min-
ute guided tours of many of LACMA's special exhibitions are offered
weekly—check the museum's online calendar for times and locations.

5905 Wilshire Blvd. ✆ **323/857-6000.** www.lacma.org. Admission $15 adults, $10 students and
seniors 62 and over, free for children 17 and under; regular exhibitions free for everyone after
5pm, all day the 2nd Tues of each month, and all holidays that fall on Mon. Mon–Tues and Thurs
noon–8pm; Fri noon–9pm; Sat–Sun 11am–8pm. Parking $7.

Autry National Center ★★   North of downtown in Griffith Park, this is one of the country's finest and most comprehensive museums of the American West. More than 100,000 pieces of art and artifacts showcasing the history of the region west of the Mississippi River are intelligently displayed. Evocative exhibits illustrate the everyday lives of early pioneers, not only with antique firearms, tools, saddles, and the like, but with many hands-on displays that successfully stir the imagination and the heart. Displays include the Southwest Museum of the American Indian Collection and the works of western artists, as well as film clips from the silent days of early Westerns and contemporary movies. Provocative visiting exhibits usually focus on cultural or domestic regional history. Docent-led tours are generally scheduled on Saturdays at 11:30am, 1, and 3pm. Admission is free every second Tuesday of the month.

4700 Western Heritage Way (in Griffith Park). ☎ **323/667-2000.** www.autrynationalcenter.org. Admission $10 adults, $6 seniors 60 and over and students 13-18, $4 children 3-12, free for children 2 and under; free to all Thurs after 4pm. Tues–Fri 10am–4pm (Thurs until 8pm July–Aug); Sat–Sun 11am–5pm. Free parking.

Petersen Automotive Museum ★★ ☺   When the Petersen opened in 1994, many locals were surprised that it had taken this long for the city of freeways to salute its most important shaper. Indeed, this museum says more about the city than probably any other in L.A. Named for Robert Petersen, the publisher responsible for *Hot Rod* and *Motor Trend* magazines, the four-story, 300,000-square-foot museum displays more than 200 cars and motorcycles, from the historic to the futuristic. Cars on the first floor are exhibited chronologically in period settings. Other floors are devoted to frequently changing shows of race cars, early motorcycles, famous movie and TV vehicles like the Batmobile, and celebrity wheels. On the third floor is the Discovery Center, a 6,500-square-foot interactive "hands-on" learning center that teaches adults and kids the basic scientific principles of how a car works. Past shows have included a comprehensive exhibit of "woodies" and surf culture, Hollywood "star cars," and the world's fastest and most valuable cars.

6060 Wilshire Blvd. (at Fairfax Ave.). ☎ **323/930-CARS** (2277). www.petersen.org. Admission $10 adults; $5 seniors, students, and military with ID; $3 children 5-12; free for children 4 and under. Tues–Sun 10am–6pm. Parking $8.

DOWNTOWN

California Science Center ★★ ☺   A $130-million renovation—reinvention, actually—has turned the former Museum of Science and Industry into Exposition Park's most popular attraction. Using high-tech sleight of hand, the center stimulates kids of all ages with questions, answers, and lessons about the world. The museum is organized into themed worlds, and one of the museum's highlights is Tess, a 50-foot animatronic woman whose muscles, bones, organs, and blood vessels are revealed, demonstrating how the body reacts to a variety of external conditions and activities. (Appropriate for children of all ages, Tess doesn't possess reproductive organs.) Another highlight is the **Air and Space Gallery,** a seven-story space where real air- and spacecraft are suspended overhead. Ecosystems is the newest permanent exhibition wing; in it the Earth's various environments can be explored through live habitats and hands-on technology.

There are nominal fees, ranging from $2 to $5, to enjoy the science center's more thrilling attractions. You can pedal a bicycle across a high wire suspended

43 feet above the ground (demonstrating the principle of gravity and counter-weights) or get strapped into the Space Docking Simulator for a virtual-reality taste of zero gravity. There's plenty more, and plans for expansion are always in the works. The IMAX theater screen is seven stories high and 90 feet wide, with state-of-the-art surround-sound and 3-D technology. Films are screened throughout the day until 9pm and are nearly always breathtaking, even the two-dimensional ones.

700 State Dr., Exposition Park. ✆ **323/724-3623;** IMAX theater 213/744-7400. www.california sciencecenter.org. Free admission to the museum; IMAX theater $8.25 adults, $6 seniors 62 and over and children 12–17, $5 children 3–11. Multishow discounts available. Daily 10am–5pm. Parking $8. Closed Thanksgiving, Christmas, and New Year's Day.

The Museum of Contemporary Art, Los Angeles (MOCA) ★ MOCA is Los Angeles's only institution devoted to art from 1940 to the present. Displaying one of the country's finest collections of American and European art, the MOCA holds roughly 6,000 objects of various visual media—ranging from masterpieces of abstract expressionism and pop art to recent works by young and emerging art-ists—housed in three different buildings, two downtown and one in West Hol-lywood. The Grand Avenue main building (250 S. Grand Ave.), which has received numerous design accolades, is a contemporary red sandstone structure by renowned Japanese architect Arata Isozaki. Also at the Grand Avenue location is the museum's popular restaurant, **Lemonade** (open the same hours as the museum itself; ✆ **213/628-0200**), a local quick-service chain.

The museum's second space, on Central Avenue in Little Tokyo (152 N. Central Ave.), was the "temporary" Contemporary while the Grand structure was being built and now presents rotating exhibits in a warehouse-type space that's been renamed the **Geffen Contemporary at MOCA,** for entertainment mogul and art collector David Geffen. Unless there's a visiting exhibit of great interest at the main museum, I recommend that you start at the Geffen building, where it's also easier to park.

The third gallery is the **MOCA Pacific Design Center** (8687 Melrose Ave., West Hollywood)—it's the compact building next to the Pacific Design Center. Unlike the other two, admission to this gallery is free, and emphasis is on contemporary architecture and design, as well as new work by emerging and established artists.

Main MOCA information line: ✆ **213/626-6222.** www.moca.org. Admission $10 adults, $5 seniors 65 and over and students, free for children 12 and under; free admission to all MOCA galleries Thurs 5–8pm. Mon and Fri 11am–5pm; Thurs 11am–8pm; Sat–Sun 11am–6pm.

Natural History Museum of Los Angeles County ★ ☺ The "Dueling Dinosaurs" are not a high-school football team, but the trademark symbol of this massive museum: *Tyrannosaurus rex* and triceratops skeletons poised in a stance so realistic that every kid feels inspired to imitate their *Jurassic Park* bellows (think *Calvin & Hobbes*). Opened in 1913 in a beautiful domed Beaux Arts build-ing, this massive museum—it's the largest natural and historical museum in the western United States—is like a giant warehouse of Earth's history, chronicling the planet and its inhabitants from 600 million years ago to the present day, and housing more than 35 million specimens and artifacts. There's a mind-numbing array of exhibits of prehistoric fossils, bird and marine life, gems and minerals, and North American mammals. The kid-friendly **Discovery Center** entertains children via hands-on, interactive exhibits: Kids can make fossil rubbings, dig for fossils, and view live animals such as snakes and lizards. **The Dino Lab**

is a specially designed workroom where visitors can watch the actual work of paleontologists as they prepare and assemble the fossils of a 66-million-year-old *Tyrannosaurus rex.* The best permanent displays include the world's rarest shark, a walk-through vault of priceless gems (including the largest collection of gold in the United States), and an Insect Zoo.

The new **Dinosaur Hall** is a world-class permanent exhibit; of particular interest is the 30-foot-tall "Thomas" the T-rex, whose bones had previously been assembled in the on-site Dino Lab. **Age of Mammals,** which features everything from mastodons to saber-toothed cats, is also now a permanent exhibit.

The **Museum Store** sells ant farms and exploding volcano and model kits, and has one-of-a-kind folk art and jewelry from around the world, and the bookstore has an extensive selection of scientific titles and hobbyists' field guides.

900 Exposition Blvd., Exposition Park. ℂ **213/763-DINO** (3466). www.nhm.org. Admission $9 adults; $6.50 children 13–17, seniors, and students with ID; $2 children 5–12; free for children 4 and under; free for everyone 1st Tues of month. Daily 9:30am–5pm.

SANTA MONICA

Santa Monica Museum of Art and Bergamot Station ★★   One of Santa
Monica's primary cultural destinations is this campuslike art complex just off the I-10 freeway. The location dates from 1875 when it was a stop for the Red Line trolley, and it retains a quasi-industrial look. Filled with more than 20 galleries, plus the Santa Monica Museum of Art, the unique installations on display here range from photography and sculpture to interactive pieces that are both eclectic and cutting edge. Its central location allows visitors to park in the free lot and spend the day seeing art rather than driving from one gallery to the next. Most pieces are available for purchase.

2525 Michigan Ave. (off Cloverfield Blvd.), Santa Monica. ℂ **310/453-7535.** www.bergamot station.com. Free admission. Tues–Fri 10am–6pm; Sat 11am–5:30pm.

PASADENA

Norton Simon Museum of Art ★★★ 🎁   Named for a food-packing king
and financier who reorganized the failing Pasadena Museum of Modern Art, the Norton Simon displays one of the finest private collections of European, American, and Asian art in the world (and yet another feather in the cap of architect Frank Gehry, who redesigned the interior space). Comprehensive collections of masterpieces by Degas, Picasso, Rembrandt, and Goya are augmented by sculptures by Henry Moore and Auguste Rodin, including *The Burghers of Calais,* which greets you at the entrance. The "Blue Four" collection of works by Kandinsky, Jawlensky, Klee, and Feininger is impressive, as is a superb collection of Southeast Asian sculpture. *Still Life with Lemons, Oranges, and a Rose* (1633), an oil by Francisco de Zurbarán, is one of the museum's most important holdings. Perhaps the most popular piece is *The Flower Vendor/Girl with Lilies,* by Diego Rivera, followed by *Mulberry Tree,* by Vincent van Gogh. The collection of paintings, sculptures, pastels, and prints by French Impressionist Edgar Degas is among the best in the world. *Tip:* Unless you're an art expert, you'll probably want to take the "Acoustiguide" audio tour—it's $3 well spent.

411 W. Colorado Blvd., Pasadena. ℂ **626/449-6840.** www.nortonsimon.org. Admission $10 adults, $5 seniors 62 and over, free for students and children 17 and under; free for everyone 1st Fri of the month 6–9pm. Wed–Mon noon–6pm (Fri until 9pm). Free parking.

Pacific Asia Museum   The most striking aspect of this museum is the building itself. Designed in the 1920s in Chinese Imperial Palace style, it's rivaled in flamboyance only by Grauman's Chinese Theatre in Hollywood (see "L.A.'s Top Attractions," earlier in this chapter). Rotating exhibits of 15,000 rare Asian and Pacific Islands art and artifacts span the centuries, from 100 B.C. to the current day. This manageable-size museum is worth a visit, particularly if you're an adherent of Buddhism.

46 N. Los Robles Ave., Pasadena. (✆ **626/449-2742,** ext. 10. www.pacificasiamuseum.org. Admission $9 adults, $7 students and seniors, free for children 11 and under; free for everyone 4th Fri of the month. Wed–Sun 10am–6pm. Free parking.

Architectural Highlights

Los Angeles is a veritable Disneyland of architecture—home to an amalgam of styles, from Art Deco to Spanish Revival, to coffee-shop kitsch, to suburban ranch, to postmodern, and more. Over-the-top styles that would be out of place in other cities are perfectly at home here. Though it's no longer new, Angelenos are still most proud of the Frank Gehry–designed **Walt Disney Concert Hall,** at the intersection of First Street and Grand Avenue in the historic Bunker Hill area.

SANTA MONICA & THE BEACHES

When you're strolling the historic canals and streets of Venice, be sure to check out the old **Chiat/Day** offices at 340 Main St. What would otherwise be an unspectacular contemporary office building is made fantastic by a **three-story pair of binoculars** that frames the entrance. The sculpture is modeled after a design created by Claes Oldenburg and Coosje van Bruggen.

When you're on your way in or out of LAX, be sure to stop for a moment to admire the **Control Tower** and **Theme Building.** The spacey *Jetsons*-style Theme Building, which has always loomed over LAX, has been joined by a more recent silhouette. The main control tower, designed by local architect Kate Diamond to evoke a stylized palm tree, is tailored to present Southern California in its best light. You can go inside to enjoy the view from the Theme Building's observation deck, or have a space-age cocktail at the Technicolor bachelor pad that is the **Encounter at LAX** restaurant.

L.A.'S WESTSIDE & BEVERLY HILLS

In addition to the sights below, don't miss the **Beverly Hills Hotel and Bungalows** (p. 563), and be sure to wind your way through the streets of Beverly Hills off Sunset Boulevard.

Pacific Design Center   The bold architecture and overwhelming scale of the Pacific Design Center, designed by Argentine architect Cesar Pelli, aroused controversy when it was erected in 1975. Sheathed in gently curving cobalt-blue glass, the six-story building houses more than 750,000 square feet of wholesale interior-design showrooms and is known to locals as "the Blue Whale." In 1988, a second structure, more boxlike than the original building but dressed in equally dramatic Kelly green, was added to the design center and surrounded by a protected outdoor plaza. The long-delayed Red Building towers are scheduled to finally open in the summer of 2011. Visitors are welcome during regular business hours and one designated Saturday each month (except June–Aug). There are two casual Wolfgang Puck restaurants, Red 7 and Spectra.

8687 Melrose Ave., West Hollywood. ✆ **310/657-0800.** www.pacificdesigncenter.com. Mon–Fri 9am–5pm; select Sat 10am–4pm. Parking varies; daily max typically $14.

Schindler House ★   A protégé of Frank Lloyd Wright and contemporary of Richard Neutra, Austrian architect Rudolph Schindler designed this innovative modern house for himself in 1921 and 1922. It's now home to the Los Angeles arm of Austria's Museum of Applied Arts (MAK). The house is noted for its complicated interlocking spaces; the interpenetration of indoors and out; simple, unadorned materials; and technological innovations. Docent-guided tours are conducted at no additional charge on weekends only.

The MAK Center offers guides to L.A.-area buildings by Schindler and other architects, and presents original related exhibitions and creative arts programming. Call for schedules.

835 N. Kings Rd. (north of Melrose Ave.), West Hollywood. ✆ **323/651-1510.** www.makcenter. org. Admission $7 adults, $6 students and seniors, free to children 12 and under; free to all every Fri after 4pm, Sept 10 (Schindler's birthday), and May 24 (International Museum Day). Wed–Sun 11am–6pm. Street parking.

HOLLYWOOD

In addition to the buildings listed below, don't miss the **Griffith Observatory** (p. 603), **Grauman's Chinese Theatre** (p. 602), and the **Roosevelt Hotel, Hollywood** (p. 573).

Capitol Records Building   Opened in 1956, this 13-story tower, just north of the legendary intersection of Hollywood and Vine, is one of the city's most recognizable buildings. The world's first circular office building is often, but incorrectly, said to have been made to resemble a stack of 45s under a turntable stylus (it kinda does, though). Nat "King" Cole, Ella Fitzgerald, and Billie Holiday are among the artists featured in the giant exterior mural known as *Hollywood Jazz.* Look down, and you'll see the sidewalk stars of Capitol's recording artists (including John Lennon). In the lobby, numerous gold albums are on display.

> ### Not Quite SOS, but . . .
>
> The light on the rooftop spire of the Capitol Records building flashes "H-O-L-L-Y-W-O-O-D" in Morse code. Really, it does.

1750 Vine St. ✆ **323/462-6252.**

The Egyptian Theatre   Conceived by grandiose impresario Sid Grauman, the Egyptian Theatre is just down the street from his better-known Chinese Theatre, but it remains less altered from its original design, which was based on the then-headline-news discovery of hidden treasures in pharaohs' tombs—hence the hieroglyphic murals and enormous scarab decoration above the stage. Hollywood's first movie premiere, *Robin Hood,* starring Douglas Fairbanks, was shown here in 1922, followed by the premiere of *The Ten Commandments* in 1923. The building has undergone a sensitive restoration by American Cinematheque, which screens rare, classic, and independent films. *Tip:* Check the website schedule for screenings hosted by celebrity guest speakers and directors such as Ron Howard and George Clooney.

6712 Hollywood Blvd. ✆ **323/466-FILM** (3456). www.egyptiantheatre.com.

Freeman House   Frank Lloyd Wright's Freeman House, built in 1924, was designed as an experimental prototype of mass-produced affordable housing. The home's richly patterned "textile-block" exterior was Wright's invention and is the most famous aspect of the home's design. Situated on a dramatic site overlooking Hollywood, Freeman House was built with the world's first glass-to-glass corner windows. Dancer Martha Graham, bandleader Xavier Cugat, art collector Galka Sheye, photographer Edward Weston, and architects Philip Johnson and Richard Neutra all lived or spent significant time at this house, which became known as an avant-garde salon. The house is currently closed for restoration; call ahead to see if it's open.

1962 Glencoe Way (off Hillcrest, near Highland and Franklin aves.). ℭ **323/851-0671.**

DOWNTOWN

For a taste of what downtown's Bunker Hill was like before the bulldozers, visit the residential neighborhood of **Angelino Heights,** near Echo Park. Entire streets are still filled with stately gingerbread Victorian homes; most still enjoy the beautiful views that led early L.A.'s elite to build here. The 1300 block of Carroll Avenue is the best preserved. Don't be surprised if a film crew is scouting locations while you're there; these blocks appear often on the silver screen.

The Bradbury Building ★   This National Historic Landmark, built in 1893 and designed by George Wyman, is Los Angeles's oldest commercial building and one of the city's most revered architectural achievements. Legend has it that an inexperienced draftsman named George Wyman accepted the $125,000 commission after communicating with his dead brother through a Ouija board. Capped by a magical five-story skylight, Bradbury's courtyard combines glazed brick, ornate Mexican tile floors, rich Belgian marble, Art Nouveau grillwork, handsome oak paneling, and lacelike wrought-iron railings—it's one of the great interior spaces of the 19th century. The glass-topped atrium is often used as a movie and TV set; you've probably seen it before in *Chinatown* and *Blade Runner.*

304 S. Broadway (at Third St.). ℭ **213/626-1893.** Mon–Fri 9am–6pm; Sat–Sun 9am–5pm.

Cathedral of Our Lady of the Angels ★   Completed in September 2002 at a cost of $163 million and built to last 500 years, this ultracontemporary cathedral is one of L.A.'s newest architectural treasures and the third-largest cathedral in the world. It was designed by award-winning Spanish architect Jose Rafael Moneo and features a 20,000-square-foot plaza with a meditation garden, more than 6,000 crypts and niches (making it the largest crypt mausoleum in the U.S.), Mission-style colonnades, biblically inspired gardens, and numerous artworks created by world-acclaimed artists. While most Angelenos admit that the exterior of this austere, sand-colored structure is rather uninspiring and uninviting (the church doors don't face the street, but rather a private plaza in back surrounded by fortresslike walls), the view from the inside is breathtaking: Soaring heights, 12,000 panes of translucent alabaster, and larger-than-life tapestries lining the walls create an awe-inspiring sense of magnificence and serenity. The 25,000-pound bronze doors, created by sculptor Robert Graham, pay homage to Ghiberti's bronze baptistery door in Florence. Free self-guided tours are available, and there's a small cafe and gift shop as well.

555 W. Temple St. (at Grand Ave.), Los Angeles. ℭ **213/680-5200.** www.olacathedral.org. Mon–Fri 6am–6pm; Sat 9am–6pm; Sun 7am–6pm.

City Hall Built in 1928, the 27-story Los Angeles City Hall was the tallest building in the city for more than 30 years. The structure's distinctive ziggurat tower was designed to resemble the Mausoleum at Halicarnassus, one of the Seven Wonders of the World. The building has been featured in numerous films and television shows, but it is probably best known as the headquarters of the *Daily Planet* in the *Superman* TV series (or *Beverly Hills Cop,* depending on your birth date). When it was built, City Hall was the sole exception to an ordinance outlawing buildings taller than 150 feet. While you're here, be sure to take the elevator to the rarely used 27th-floor Observation Deck—on a clear day (yeah, right), you can see to Mount Wilson 15 miles away. Free docent-led tours are available from 10am to noon Monday through Thursday, and self-guided tours are available at other times. Call ✆ **213/978-1995** for tour information.

200 N. Spring St. ✆ **213/485-2121.** www.lacityhall.org. Mon–Fri 8am–5pm.

L.A. Central Library ★★ This is one of L.A.'s early architectural achievements and the third-largest library in the United States. The city rallied to save the library when arson nearly destroyed it in 1986; the triumphant restoration has returned much of its original splendor. Working in the early 1920s, architect Bertram G. Goodhue employed the Egyptian motifs and materials popularized by the discovery of King Tut's tomb, and combined them with a more modern use of concrete block to great effect. Free docent-led art and architecture tours are given daily—call ✆ **213/228-7168.** Tours last about an hour; they're led Tuesday through Friday at 12:30pm, and Saturday at 11am and 2pm. ***Warning:*** Parking in this area can involve a heroic effort. Try visiting on the weekend and using the Flower Street parking entrance; the daily max is only $8, a relative bargain for downtown.

630 W. Fifth St. (btw. Flower St. and Grand Ave.). ✆ **213/228-7000.** www.lapl.org/central. Tues, Thurs 10am–8pm; Wed, Fri, Sat 10am–5:30pm.

Union Station ★ Union Station, completed in 1939, is one of the finest examples of California Mission-style architecture and one of the last of America's great rail stations. It was built with the opulence and attention to detail that characterize 1930s WPA projects, such as its cathedral-like size and richly paneled ticket lobby and waiting area. When you're strolling through these grand historic halls, it's easy to imagine the glamorous movie stars who once boarded *The City of Los Angeles* and *The Super Chief* to journey back East during the glory days of rail travel; it's also easy to picture the many heartfelt reunions between returning soldiers and loved ones following the victorious end to World War II, in the station's heyday. Movies shot here include *Bugsy, The Way We Were,* and *Blade Runner.*

800 N. Alameda St. (at Cesar E. Chavez Ave.).

Union Station.

US Bank Tower (also known as Library Tower) Designed by renowned architect I. M. Pei, L.A.'s most distinctive skyscraper (it's the round one) is the tallest building between Chicago and Singapore. Built in 1989 at a cost of $450 million, the 76-story monolith is both square and rectangular, rising from its Fifth Street base in a series of overlapping spirals and cubes. The Bunker Hill Steps wrapping around the west side of the building were inspired by Rome's Spanish Steps. *Gee-whiz fact:* The glass crown at the top—illuminated at night—is the highest building helipad in the world.

633 W. Fifth St. (at S. Grand Ave.).

Watts Towers & Art Center Watts became notorious as the site of riots in the summer of 1965, during which 34 people were killed and more than 1,000 were injured. Today a visit to Watts is a lesson in inner-city life. It's a high-density land of gray strip malls, well-guarded check-cashing shops, and fast-food restaurants; but it's also a neighborhood of hardworking families struggling to survive in the midst of gangland. Although there's not much for the casual tourist here, the Watts Towers are truly a unique attraction, and the adjoining art gallery illustrates the fierce determination of area residents to maintain cultural integrity.

The Towers—the largest piece of folk art created by a single person—are colorful, 99-foot-tall cement-and-steel sculptures ornamented with mosaics of bottles, seashells, cups, plates, pottery, and ceramic tiles. They were completed in 1955 by folk artist Simon Rodia, an immigrant Italian tile-setter who worked on them for 33 years in his spare time. True fans of decorative ceramics will enjoy the fact that Rodia's day job was at the legendary Malibu Potteries (are those fragments of valuable Malibu tile encrusting the Towers?). Closed in 1994 due to earthquake damage, the towers were triumphantly reopened in 2001 and now attract more than 20,000 visitors annually. Tours are by request.

Note: Next to these designated Cultural Landmarks is the Art Center, which has an interesting collection of ethnic musical instruments, as well as several visiting art exhibits throughout the year.

1727 E. 107th St., Los Angeles. ℂ **213/847-4646.** http://wattstowers.us. Art Center Wed–Sat 10am–4pm; Sun noon–4pm. Free admission. Towers Thurs–Sat 10:30am–3:30pm; Sun 12:30–3:30pm. Tours $7 adults, $3 seniors 55 and over and teens 13–17, free for children 12 and under.

PASADENA & ENVIRONS

For a quick but profound architectural fix, stroll past Pasadena's grandiose and baroque **City Hall,** 100 N. Garfield Ave., 2 blocks north of Colorado Boulevard; closer inspection will reveal its classical colonnaded courtyard, formal gardens, and spectacular tiled dome.

The Gamble House ★★ The huge two-story Gamble House, built in 1908 as a California vacation home for the wealthy family of Procter & Gamble fame, is a sublime example of Arts and Crafts architecture. The interior, designed by the famous Pasadena-based Greene & Greene architectural team, abounds with handcraftsmanship, including intricately carved teak cornices, custom-designed furnishings, elaborate carpets, and a fantastic Tiffany glass door. No detail was overlooked. Every oak wedge, downspout, air vent, and switch plate contributes to the unified design. Admission is by 1-hour guided tour only, which departs every 15 to 20 minutes. Tickets go on sale on tour days in the bookstore at 10am Thursday through Saturday, and at 11:30am on Sunday. No reservations are necessary, but tours are often sold out, especially on weekends by 2pm. And don't wear high heels

> ### House Hygiene
>
> **The restoration of the Gamble House was so meticulous that workers used dental picks to scrape gunk from the home's 262 rafters.**

or they'll make you put on slippers. No interior photography is allowed either.

If you can't fit the tour into your schedule but have an affection for Craftsman design, visit the well-stocked bookstore and museum shop located in the former garage (you can also see the exterior and grounds of the house this way). The bookstore is open Tuesday through Saturday 10am to 5pm, and Sunday 11:30am to 5pm.

Additional elegant Greene & Greene creations (still privately owned) abound 2 blocks away along **Arroyo Terrace,** including nos. **368, 370, 400, 408, 424,** and **440.** The Gamble House bookstore can give you a walking-tour map ($1.50). For occasional opportunities to actually go inside the homes, there's the annual Craftsman Weekend in October, and Bungalow Heaven in April.

4 Westmoreland Place (in the 300 block of N. Orange Grove Blvd.), Pasadena. © **626/793-3334.** www.gamblehouse.org. Most tours $10 adults, $7 students and seniors 65 and over, free for children 11 and under. 2pm tours are $13 per person and reservations must be made at least 1 week in advance. Tours Thurs–Sun noon–3pm. Closed holidays.

Parks & Gardens

In addition to the two examples of urban parkland below, check out **Pan Pacific Park,** a hilly retreat near the Farmers Market and CBS Studios, named for the Art Deco auditorium that, unfortunately, no longer stands at its edge.

Griffith Park ★★ ☺   Mining tycoon Col. Griffith J. Griffith donated these 4,107 acres to the city in 1896 as a Christmas gift. Today Griffith Park is one of the largest urban parks in America. There's a lot to do here, including 53 miles of hiking trails (the prettiest is the Fern Dell trail near the Western Ave. entrance, a shady hideaway cooled by waterfalls and ferns), horseback riding, golfing, swimming, biking, and picnicking. For a general overview of the park, drive the mountainous loop road that winds from the top of Western Avenue, past Griffith Observatory, and down to Vermont Avenue. For a more extensive foray, turn north at the loop road's midsection, onto Mount Hollywood Drive. To reach the golf courses or **Los Angeles Zoo** (p. 625), take Los Feliz Boulevard to Riverside Drive, which runs along the park's western edge.

Near the zoo, in a particularly dusty corner of the park, you can find the **Travel Town Transportation Museum,** 5200 Zoo Dr. (© **323/662-5874;** www.traveltown.org), a little-known outdoor museum with a small collection of vintage locomotives and old airplanes. Kids love the miniature train ride that circles the perimeter of the museum. The museum is open Monday through Friday from 10am to 4pm, and Saturday and Sunday from 10am to 6pm; admission is free.

Hollywood; entrances are along Los Feliz Blvd., at Riverside Dr., Vermont Ave., and Western Ave. © **323/913-4688.** www.laparks.org/dos/parks/griffithpk. Free admission.

Huntington Library, Art Collections & Botanical Gardens ★★ ☺   The Huntington Library is the jewel in Pasadena's crown. The 207-acre hilltop estate was once home to industrialist and railroad magnate Henry E. Huntington (1850–1927), who bought books on the same massive scale on which he acquired land. The continually expanding collection includes dozens of Shakespeare's first editions, Benjamin Franklin's handwritten autobiography, a Gutenberg Bible

Griffith Park.

Huntington in bloom.

from the 1450s, and the earliest known manuscript of Chaucer's *Canterbury Tales*. Although some rare works are available only to visiting scholars, the library has a regularly changing (and always excellent) exhibit showcasing hundreds of different items in the collection.

If you prefer canvas to parchment, Huntington also put together a terrific 18th-century and 19-century British and French art collection. The most celebrated paintings are Gainsborough's *The Blue Boy* and *Pinkie,* by Sir Thomas Lawrence, depicting the youthful aunt of Elizabeth Barrett Browning. These and other works of Renaissance paintings and bronzes are displayed in the stately Italianate mansion on the crest of this hillside estate, so you can also get a glimpse of its splendid furnishings. American art is exhibited in an additional gallery, and includes work ranging from Edward Hopper to Andy Warhol.

But it's the vast **botanical gardens** featuring more than 14,000 species of plants that draw most locals to the Huntington. The Japanese Garden comes complete with a traditional open-air Japanese house, koi-filled stream, and serene Zen garden. There's also an exotic **Desert Garden,** intriguing **Jungle Garden, Bing Children's Garden** (designed specifically for kids ages 2–7), and the glass-and-steel **Conservatory for Botanical Science,** where visitors learn some of the fundamentals of botany via state-of-the-art science stations. The latest addition is a new 4½-acre **Chinese Garden,** one of the largest of the Huntington's 14 specialized gardens. Highlights include a lake, teahouse, pavilions, and bridges within a landscape of plants native to China.

Because the Huntington surprises many with its size and wealth of activities to choose from, first-timers might want to start with a tour. One-hour garden tours are offered daily, subject to volunteer availability; no reservations or additional fees are required. Times vary, so check at the information desk upon arrival. I also recommend that you tailor your visit to include the popular **English tea** served Monday, Wednesday, Thursday, and Friday from noon to 4:30pm, and Saturday and Sunday from 10:45am to 4:30pm (last seating at 3:30pm). The tearoom overlooks the Rose Garden (home to 1,000 varieties displayed in chronological order of their breeding), and since the finger sandwiches and desserts are served buffet-style, it's a genteel bargain even for hearty appetites, at $28 per

free CULTURE

To beef up attendance and give indigent folk like us travel writers a break, almost all of L.A.'s art galleries and museums are open free to the public 1 day of the week or month (or both), and several charge no admission. Use the following list to plan your week around the museums' free-day schedules; refer to the individual attractions listings in this chapter for more information on each museum.

FREE EVERY DAY

- J. Paul Getty Museum at the Getty Center
- The Getty Villa Malibu
- Museum of Television and Radio (donation suggested)
- Los Angeles County Museum of Art, *after* 5pm
- California African American Museum
- California Science Center
- Bergamot Arts Station & Santa Monica Museum of Art

FREE EVERY THURSDAY

- Museum of Contemporary Art (MOCA), from 5 to 8pm
- Museum of the American West, from 4 to 8pm
- UCLA Hammer Museum, from 11am to 9pm
- Japanese American National Museum, from 5 to 8pm
- Skirball Cultural Center, from noon to 9pm
- Geffen Contemporary at MOCA, from 5 to 8pm

FREE EVERY FRIDAY

- Schindler House, from 4 to 6pm

FREE EVERY FIRST TUESDAY

- Natural History Museum of Los Angeles County, from 9:30am to 5pm
- Page Museum at La Brea Tar Pits, from 9:30am to 5pm

FREE EVERY FIRST WEDNESDAY

- Craft & Folk Art Museum, from 11am to 5pm

FREE EVERY FIRST THURSDAY

- Huntington Library, Art Collections & Botanical Gardens, from noon to 4:30pm

FREE EVERY FIRST FRIDAY

- Norton Simon Museum of Art, from 6 to 9pm

FREE EVERY SECOND TUESDAY

- Museum of the American West, from 10am to 5pm
- Los Angeles County Museum of Art, from noon to 8pm

FREE EVERY THIRD TUESDAY

- Los Angeles County Arboretum and Botanic Garden, from 9am to 4:30pm
- Japanese American National Museum, from 10am to 8pm

FREE EVERY FOURTH FRIDAY

- Pacific Asia Museum, from 10am to 8pm

person (please note that museum admission is a separate required cost). Phone ☎ **626/683-8131** for tearoom reservations, which are required and should be made at least 2 weeks in advance.

1151 Oxford Rd., San Marino. ✆ **626/405-2100.** www.huntington.org. Weekday admission $15 adults, $12 seniors 65 and over, $10 students and children 12–18, $6 children 5–11, free to children 4 and under; free to all the 1st Thurs of each month. Weekend admission $20 adults, $15 seniors 65 and over, $10 students and children 12–18, $6 children 5–11, free for children 4 and under. Sept–May Mon and Wed–Fri noon–4:30pm, Sat–Sun 10:30am–4:30pm; June–Aug Wed–Mon 10:30am–4:30pm. Free parking. Closed major holidays.

Will Rogers State Historic Park   Will Rogers State Historic Park was once Will Rogers's private ranch and grounds. Willed to the state of California in 1944, the 168-acre estate is now both a park and a historic site, supervised by the Department of Parks and Recreation. Visitors may explore the grounds, the former stables, and the 31-room house filled with the original furnishings, including a porch swing in the living room and many Native American rugs and baskets. Charles Lindbergh and his wife, Anne Morrow Lindbergh, hid out here in the 1930s during part of the craze that followed the kidnap and murder of their first son. There are picnic tables, but no food is sold. Guided Ranch House tours are available as well.

Who's Will Rogers, you ask? He was born in Oklahoma in 1879 and became a cowboy in the Texas Panhandle before drifting into a Wild West show as a folksy, speechifying roper. The "cracker-barrel philosopher" performed lariat tricks while carrying on a humorous deadpan monologue on current events. The showman moved to Los Angeles in 1919, where he become a movie actor, as well as the author of numerous books detailing his down-home "cowboy philosophy." 1501 Will Rogers State Park Rd., Pacific Palisades (btw. Santa Monica and Malibu). ✆ **310/454-8212.** www.parks.ca.gov. Park entrance $12 per vehicle. Daily 8am–sunset. House opens Thurs–Fri 11am–3pm, Sat–Sun 10am–4pm; guided Ranch House tours offered every hour, on the hour, up until 1 hr. before closing. From Santa Monica, take the Pacific Coast Hwy. (Calif. 1) north, turn right onto Chautauqua Blvd., then right onto Sunset Blvd., and continue to the park entrance.

The Zoo

Los Angeles Zoo ★ ☺   The L.A. Zoo has been welcoming visitors and bus loads of school kids since 1966. In 1982, the zoo inaugurated a display of cuddly koalas, still one of its biggest attractions among 1,100 animals from around the world. Although it's smaller than the world-famous San Diego Zoo, the L.A. Zoo is far easier to explore. As much an arboretum as a zoo, the grounds are thick with mature shade trees from around the world that help cool the once-barren grounds, and new habitats are light-years ahead of the cruel concrete roundhouses originally used to exhibit animals (though you can't help feeling that, despite the fancy digs, all the creatures would rather be in their natural habitat).

The zoo's latest attraction is the **Elephants of Asia,** which tracks the history and culture of the animal through Cambodia, China, India, and Thailand. There are bathing pools, sand pits, and no fewer than five viewing areas for the public.

Among other highlights is the $19-million **Campo Gorilla Reserve,** a habitat for seven African lowland gorillas that closely resembles their native West African homeland. Visitors partake in a pseudo-African-jungle experience as they journey along a misty, forested pathway with glassed viewing areas for close-up views of the gorillas.

There's also the **Sea Lion Cliffs** habitat, where visitors can view the saltwater habitat from an underwater glass viewing area; the Jane Goodall–approved **Chimpanzees of the Mahale Mountains** habitat, where visitors can see plenty of primate activity; the **Red Ape Rainforest,** a natural orangutan habitat; the entertaining **World of Birds** show; and Dragons of Komodo, featuring a pair of the world's largest lizard species. The gargantuan Andean condor had me enthralled as well (the facility is renowned in zoological circles for the successful breeding and releasing of California condors, and occasionally some of these majestic and endangered birds are on exhibit). Kids will also enjoy the **Winnick Family Children's Zoo,** which contains a petting area, an exhibition animal-care center, Adventure Theater storytelling and puppet show, and other kid-hip exhibits and activities. *Tip:* To avoid the bus loads of rambunctious school kids, arrive after noon. The Moss Family Conservation Carousel opened in summer 2011, followed by the Living Amphibians, Insects, and Reptiles (LAIR) center in the fall of 2011.

5333 Zoo Dr., Griffith Park. ℂ **323/644-4200.** www.lazoo.org. Admission $14 adults, $11 seniors 62 and over, $9 children 2–12, free for children 1 and under. Daily 10am–5pm. Free parking. Closed Christmas.

Organized Tours

STUDIO TOURS

NBC Studios ☺ According to a security guard, John Wayne and Redd Foxx once got into a fight here after Wayne refused to ride in the same limo as Foxx, who called the movie star a "redneck." Well, your NBC tour will probably be a bit more docile than that. The guided indoor and outdoor walking tour includes a brief walk-in unstaged to the set of *The Tonight Show with Jay Leno* set (see p. 630 for info on how to get free Jay Leno tickets), and wardrobe, makeup, and prop-building departments. In fact, NBC is the only TV studio that offers the public a behind-the-scenes look at the inner workings of its television operation, and it's a lot less expensive than the competition's studio tours. Granted, it doesn't have the cachet of a major motion picture studio tour, but it's entertaining nonetheless.

Tours depart at the top of the hour Monday through Friday from 9am to 1pm, and tickets are sold at the Guest Relations Department (bring cash—they don't take credit cards). Also, this is one of the few studio tours that doesn't have a minimum age requirement. *Note:* Before you make the drive to Burbank, be sure to call the studio and make sure tours are being offered that day and aren't already sold out.

3000 W. Alameda Ave. (off California St.), Burbank. ℂ **818/840-3537.** Tours $8.50 adults, $7.50 seniors 60 and over, $5 children 5–12, free for children 4 and under. Mon–Fri 9am–1pm.

Paramount Pictures ★★ Paramount is the only major studio still located in Hollywood, which makes

Paramount Studios.

the 2-hour "cart tour" around its Hollywood headquarters far more historically enriching than the modern studios in Burbank (even the wrought-iron gates Gloria Swanson motored through in *Sunset Boulevard* are still there). The tour is both a historical ode to filmmaking and a real-life, behind-the-scenes look at working movie and television facilities in day-to-day operation; ergo, no two tours are alike, and chances of spotting a celebrity are pretty good. Visits typically include a walk-through of the soundstages of TV shows or feature films, though you can't enter while taping is taking place. The $40 tours depart Monday through Friday by advance reservations up to 1 month out, though you can occasionally get lucky with same-day tickets if you are in the neighborhood. You need to be 12 or older to take the tour, and recording equipment is *verboten* (still cameras are okay in certain areas).

5555 Melrose Ave. ✆ **323/956-1777.** www.paramountstudios.com. Tours $40 per person by advance reservation. Mon–Fri at 10, 11am, 1, and 2pm.

Sony Pictures Studio Tour Although it doesn't have quite the historical cachet as Warner Brothers or Paramount, a lot of movie history was made at this Culver City lot. The 2-hour walking tour includes stops at historical stages where famous films like *The Wizard of Oz* were shot, though the sets themselves are long gone. There are also opportunities to visit sets currently in production, and to drop in on the *Jeopardy!* or *Wheel of Fortune* sets (but not actual tapings). The main reason for the tour is the chance to catch a glimpse of the stars who work here (it's one of the busiest studio lots in the world). Tours depart from the Sony Pictures Plaza; be sure to call ahead and make a reservation.

Sony Picture Studios, 10000 W. Washington Blvd., Culver City. ✆ **310/244-8687.** www.sony picturesstudios.com. Reservations highly recommended; children 11 and under not admitted. Photo ID required. Tours $33 per person. Tours depart Mon–Fri at 9:30, 10:30am, 1:30, and 2:30pm, but are subject to change. Free parking.

Universal Studios ★ Universal offers daily 1-hour tram tours of its studio lot as part of the general admission price to the amusement park, which is open from 9am to 7pm in the summer and from 10am to 6pm in the winter. See p. 608 for more information.

Warner Bros. Studios ★ The Warner Brothers "VIP Tour" takes visitors on a 2¼-hour jaunt around the world's busiest movie and TV studio. After a brief introductory film about the history of WB, groups of 12 pile into stretch golf carts for an intimate view of the inner workings of a motion picture and television studio: back-lot streets, soundstages, sets, and craft shops. Because nothing is staged, there's no telling what or who you might encounter, and no two tours are the same. The tour also includes a visit to the Warner Bros. Museum, which contains original costumes, props, sets, scripts, and correspondence from classic WB films and television shows. Advance tickets are recommended and available online via their website, or by calling ✆ **866/777-8932;** otherwise, tickets are sold the day of the tour on a first-come, first-served basis, but they recommended arriving at the ticket office early to make sure they don't sell out. Children 7 and under are not admitted, you must bring valid photo ID, and they recommend you show up about 30 minutes before the tour starts.

3400 Riverside Dr., Burbank. ✆ **818/972-8687.** www.wbstudiotour.com. Advance reservations recommended; children 7 and under not admitted. Tours $48 per person. Tours depart Mon–Fri every 20 min. 8:20am–4pm (extended hours during spring and summer).

BUS/VAN TOURS

L.A. Tours (✆ 323/460-6490; www.latours.net) operates regularly scheduled tours of the city. Plush shuttle buses pick up riders from major hotels for morning or afternoon tours of Sunset Strip, the movie studios, the Farmers Market, Hollywood, homes of the stars, and other attractions. Different itineraries are available, from downtown and the Music Center to Disneyland or Universal Studios. Tours vary in length from a half-day Beaches & Shopping tour to a full-day Grand City tour. Advance reservations are required.

The other major tour company in L.A. is **Starline Tours ★** (✆ 800/959-3131; www.starlinetours.com)—you'll see their air-conditioned minibuses, double-decker Big Red buses, and open-air trolleys all over the city. Since 1935, Starline has been offering a wide selection of L.A. tours, including the first-ever Movie Stars' Homes tour. Its most popular tour, the 2-hour neighborhood jaunt, departs every half-hour from the front of Grauman's Chinese Theatre between 9:30am and 4pm (you'll see the Starline kiosk to the right of the theater entrance at 6925 Hollywood Blvd.). If you really like driving tours, sign up for the *pièce de résistance:* the 5½-hour Grand Tour of L.A. Check out their website for more tour information.

WALKING TOURS

If you want the classic Hollywood walking tour, **Red Line Tours** (✆ 323/402-1074; www.redlinetours.com) offers daily sightseeing expeditions to all the famous (and infamous) landmarks in Hollywood. Its unique "live-audio" system allows customers to hear the tour guide even over the city noise. Customers wear an audio headset receiver, while the tour guide wears a headset microphone transmitter (pretty clever, actually). Trips depart from the Egyptian Theatre (6708 Hollywood Blvd.) at 10am, noon, 2, and 4pm, 7 days a week. Rates are $25 for adults, $18 for students and seniors, and $15 for children ages 9 to 15. Log on to the Red Line Tour website for more information.

The **L.A. Conservancy** (✆ 213/623-2489; www.laconservancy.org) conducts about a dozen entertaining walking tours of historic downtown L.A. In Pasadena, **Pasadena Heritage** (✆ 626/441-6333; www.pasadenaheritage.org) offers a walking tour of Old Pasadena.

BICYCLE TOURS

Perry's Beach Café & Rentals in Santa Monica offers 1½-hour bicycle tours of the Santa Monica and Venice beach communities. It's a great way to explore the area while learning about its history and landmark architecture. The package costs $35 per person and includes a tour guide, a 3-hour bike rental with protective gear, water, and a bike lock. *Note:* A minimum of three people is required for the tour. For more information or to make a reservation, call ✆ 310/939-0000.

HELICOPTER TOURS

Touring L.A. from above is certainly a unique perspective. Just the thrill of riding in a helicopter is worth the price. **Celebrity Helicopters** (✆ 877/999-2099; www.celebheli.com) offers a wide array of themed trips, ranging from a 35-minute Celebrity Home Tour ($189) to a 25-minute fly-by of the L.A. coastline ($149). Other tour packages are available as well; check the website for more information.

JOGGING TOUR

Off 'N Running Tours (✆ 310/246-1418; www.offnrunningtours.com) combines sporting with sightseeing, taking joggers on guided runs through Los Angeles.

The themed tours, such as Running from the Paparazzi, are customized to take in the most entertaining areas around the city and can accommodate any skill level for 4 miles. Another popular option is the Mansion Tour, which starts at Santa Monica Boulevard and Rodeo Drive, with a midpoint break at Greystone Mansion, where runners can stroll the grounds while winding down, before taking a route through different neighborhoods on the way back. It's a fun way to get the most out of your morning jog. Tours cost about $60 and include a technical T-shirt, a bottle of water, and a cupcake at the end.

BEVERLY HILLS TROLLEY TOURS

The city of Beverly Hills offers inexpensive trolley tours that detail the city's history as well as little-known facts and celebrity tidbits. The tour takes visitors on a 40-minute docent-led tour through the tony avenues of Beverly Hills, including Rodeo Avenue and the Golden Triangle. It runs every Saturday on the hour from 11am to 4pm. The fare is a mere $10 for adults and $5 for kids 12 and under. The trolley departs at the "Trolley Stop" at the intersection of Rodeo Drive and Dayton Way. For more information, call ℂ **310/285-2442** or log on to **www.beverly hills.org**.

TV TAPINGS

Being part of the audience for the taping of a television show might be the quintessential L.A. experience. This is a great way to see Hollywood at work, to find out how your favorite sitcom or talk show is made, and to catch a glimpse of your favorite TV personalities. Timing is important—remember that most series go on hiatus between March and July. And tickets to the top shows are in greater demand than others, so getting your hands on them takes advance planning—and possibly some waiting in line.

Request tickets as far in advance as possible. Several episodes may be shot on a single day, so you may be required to remain in the theater for up to 4 hours (in addition to the recommended 1-hr. early check-in). If you phone at the last moment, you may luck into tickets for your top choice. More likely, however, you'll be given a list of shows that are currently filming, and you won't recognize many of the titles; studios are always taping pilots, few of which end up on the air. But you never know who may be starring in them—look at all the famous faces that have launched new sitcoms in the past couple of years. Tickets are always free, are usually limited to two per person, and are distributed on a first-come, first-served basis. Many shows don't admit children under the age of 10; in some cases, no one under the age of 18 is admitted.

Tickets are sometimes given away to the public outside popular tourist sites such as Grauman's Chinese Theatre in Hollywood and Universal Studios in the Valley; L.A.'s visitor information centers in downtown and Hollywood often have

---

✎ The Cold Truth About Talk Shows

The sets of most talk shows are kept at a cool temperature (the hot lights raise the temperature on stage), so be sure to bring a sweater or jacket. And if you dress well—no T-shirts or shorts—your chances of getting a front-row seat increase dramatically.

tickets as well. But if you're determined to see a particular show, contact the following suppliers:

Audiences Unlimited Inc. (www.tvtickets.com) is a good place to start. It distributes tickets for most of the top sitcoms, including *Hot in Cleveland, Rules of Engagement,* and more. This service is organized and informative (as is its website), and fully sanctioned by production companies and networks. ABC, for example, no longer handles ticket distribution directly, but refers most inquiries to Audiences Unlimited Inc. **TVTIX.COM** (📞 **323/653-4105;** www.tvtix.com) also distributes tickets for numerous talk and game shows, including *The Tonight Show with Jay Leno* and *Jeopardy!*

You also may want to contact the networks for information on a specific show, including some whose tickets are not available at the above agencies. At **ABC,** most ticket inquiries are referred to Audiences Unlimited (see above), but you may want to check out ABC's website at **www.abc.com** for a colorful look at their lineup and links to specific show sites.

For **CBS Television City,** 7800 Beverly Blvd., Los Angeles, CA 90036, call 📞 **323/575-2458** between Monday and Friday from 9am to 5pm to see what's being filmed while you're in town. Tickets for CBS tapings are distributed on a first-come, first-served basis; you can write in advance to reserve them or pick them up at the studio the day of the show. Tickets for many CBS sitcoms are also available from Audiences Unlimited (see above). For tickets to *The Price Is Right,* call the 24-hour ticket hot line at 📞 **323/575-2449** or log on to **www.cbs.com/daytime/the_price_is_right/tickets**.

For **NBC,** 3000 W. Alameda Ave., Burbank, CA 91523 (📞 **818/840-3537**), call to see what's on while you're in L.A. Tickets for NBC tapings, including *The Tonight Show with Jay Leno* (minimum age to attend this show is 16), can be obtained four ways: (1) Pick them up at the NBC ticket counter on the day of the show—two tickets per person are distributed on a first-come, first-served basis at the ticket counter off California Avenue starting at 8am (be sure to get there early); (2) at least 6 weeks before your visit, send a self-addressed, stamped envelope with your ticket request to the address above; (3) go to the Audiences Unlimited ticket booth at Universal Studios Hollywood (p. 608); (4) via the show's website at www.tonightshow/tickets.com. When writing to the studio for option 2, be sure to include show name, number of tickets (four per request), and dates desired. All the NBC shows are represented online at either **www.nbc.com** or **www.tvtickets.com**.

Paramount Studios also offers free tickets to their live-audience shows. All you need to do is call one of the friendly employees at Paramount Guest Relations (📞 **323/956-1777**) between 9am and 5pm on weekdays and make a reservation. For seating reservations for *Dr. Phil,* call 📞 **323/461-7445. Universal Studios** (📞 **800/UNIVERSAL** [864-8377]; www.universalstudios.com) also offers free tickets to their live-audience shows. At the amusement park's **Audiences Unlimited ticket booth,** you can obtain free tickets to join the audience for any TV shows that are taping during your visit (subject to availability).

BEACHES

Los Angeles County's 72-mile coastline sports more than 30 miles of beaches, most of which are operated by the **Department of Beaches & Harbors,** 13837 Fiji Way, Marina del Rey (📞 **310/305-9503; www.beaches.lacounty.gov**).

El Matador.

Point Dume.

County-run beaches usually charge for parking ($3–$12). Alcohol, bonfires, and pets are prohibited. For recorded **surf conditions** (and coastal weather forecast), call ☏ **310/457-9701.** The following are the county's best beaches, listed from north to south.

EL PESCADOR, L.A. PIEDRA & EL MATADOR BEACHES   These rugged and isolated beaches (real finds) front a 2-mile stretch of Pacific Coast Highway (Calif. 1) between Broad Beach and Decker Canyon roads, a 10-minute drive from the Malibu Pier. Picturesque coves with unusual rock formations are great for sunbathing and picnicking, but swim with caution, as there are no lifeguards. The beaches can be difficult to find; only small signs on the highway mark them. There are a limited number of parking spots atop the bluffs. Descend to the beach via stairs that cling to the cliffs.

ZUMA BEACH COUNTY PARK ★   Jampacked on warm weekends, L.A. County's largest beach park is located off Pacific Coast Highway (Calif. 1), a mile past Kanan Dume Road. While it can't claim to be the most scenic beach in the Southland, Zuma has the most comprehensive facilities: plenty of restrooms, lifeguards, playgrounds, volleyball courts, and snack bars. The southern stretch, toward Point Dume, is Westward Beach, separated from the noisy highway by sandstone cliffs. A trail leads over the point's headlands to Pirate's Cove, once a popular nude beach.

PARADISE COVE   This private beach in the 28000 block of Pacific Coast Highway (Calif. 1) charges $25 to park and $5 per person if you walk in. Changing rooms and showers are included in the price. The beach is often full by noon on weekends. *Tip:* If you dine at the restaurant, parking is only $3 for the first 4 hours.

MALIBU LAGOON STATE BEACH ★★   Not just a pretty white-sand beach, but an estuary and wetlands area as well, Malibu Lagoon is the historic home of the Chumash Indians. The entrance is on Pacific Coast Highway (Calif. 1) south of Cross Creek Road, and there's a small admission charge. Marine life and shorebirds teem where the creek empties into the sea, and the waves are always mild. The historic **Adamson House** is here, a showplace of Malibu tile now operating as a museum.

SURFRIDER BEACH Without a doubt, L.A.'s best waves roll ashore here. One of the city's most popular surfing spots, this beach is located between the Malibu Pier and the lagoon. In surf lingo, few "locals only" wave wars are ever fought here—surfing is not as territorial as it can be in other areas, where out-of-towners can be made to feel unwelcome. Surfrider is surrounded by all of Malibu's hustle and bustle; don't come here for peace and quiet, as the surf is always crowded.

Will Rogers State Beach.

TOPANGA STATE BEACH Highway noise prevents solitude at this short, narrow strip of sand located where Topanga Canyon Boulevard emerges from the mountains. Why go? Ask the surfers, who wait in line to catch Topanga's excellent right point breaks. There are restrooms and lifeguard services here, and across the street you'll find one of the best fresh fish restaurants around, the **Reel Inn,** 18661 Pacific Coast Hwy., Malibu (*©* **310/456-8221**).

WILL ROGERS STATE BEACH Three miles along Pacific Coast Highway (Calif. 1), between Sunset Boulevard and the Santa Monica border, are named for the American humorist whose ranch-turned-state-historic-park is nestled above the palisades that provide the backdrop for this popular beach. A pay parking lot extends the entire length of Will Rogers, and facilities include restrooms, lifeguards, and a snack hut in season. While the surfing is not the best, the waves are friendly for swimmers, and there are always competitive volleyball games to be found.

SANTA MONICA STATE BEACH The family-friendly beaches on either side of the Santa Monica Pier are popular for their white sands and accessibility. There are big parking lots, cafes, and well-maintained restrooms. A paved beach path runs along here, allowing you to walk, bike, or skate to Venice and points south. Colorado Boulevard leads to the pier; turn north on Pacific Coast Highway (Calif. 1) below the coastline's bluffs, or south along Ocean Avenue; you can find parking in both directions.

VENICE BEACH ★★ Moving south from the city of Santa Monica, the paved pedestrian Promenade becomes Ocean Front Walk and gets progressively weirder until it reaches an apex at Washington Boulevard and the Venice fishing pier. Although there are people who swim and sunbathe, Venice Beach's character is defined by the sea of humanity on the Ocean Front Walk, plus the bevy of boardwalk vendors and old-fashioned pedestrian streets a block away. Park on the side streets or in the plentiful lots west of Pacific Avenue.

MANHATTAN STATE BEACH The Beach Boys used to hang out at this wide, friendly beach backed by beautiful oceanview homes. Plenty of parking on 36 blocks of side streets (btw. Rosecrans Ave. and the Hermosa Beach

AVP volleyball tournament, Hermosa Beach.

border) draws weekend crowds from the L.A. area. Manhattan has some of the best surfing around, restrooms, lifeguards, and volleyball courts. Manhattan Beach Boulevard leads west to the fishing pier and adjacent seafood restaurants.

HERMOSA CITY BEACH ★★ This very wide white-sand beach is one of the best in Southern California and my favorite. Hermosa extends to either side of the pier and includes the Strand, a wide, smooth pedestrian lane that runs its entire length. Main access is at the foot of Pier Avenue, which is lined with interesting shops and cafes with outdoor seating. There's plenty of street parking, as well as restrooms, lifeguards, volleyball courts, a fishing pier, playgrounds, and good surfing.

REDONDO STATE BEACH Popular with surfers, bicyclists, and joggers, Redondo's white sand and ice-plant-carpeted dunes are just south of tiny King Harbor, along the Esplanade (South Esplanade Dr.). Get there via Pacific Coast Highway (Calif. 1) or Torrance Boulevard. Facilities include restrooms, lifeguards, and volleyball courts.

OUTDOOR PURSUITS

Bisected by the Santa Monica Mountains and fronted by long stretches of beach, L.A. is one of the world's best cities for nature and sports lovers. Where else can you hike in the mountains, skate on the beach, swim in the ocean, eat a gourmet meal, and take in a basketball, ice-hockey, or baseball game—all in the same day?

BICYCLING Los Angeles, being mostly flat, is great for biking. If you're into distance pedaling, you can do no better than the flat, paved bicycle trail that follows about 22 miles of state beaches, harbors, LAX, and laid-back beach towns such as Venice, Manhattan Beach, Hermosa Beach, and Redondo Beach. The first stretch starts at Will Rogers State Beach in Pacific Palisades and runs south through Santa Monica and Venice to Marina del Rey—about 8 miles. The second stretch—called the South Bay Bike Trail—starts at the south end of Marina del Rey and takes you all the way to Torrance Beach. If you want to ride the entire path, you'll have to detour around Marina del Rey, which takes only about 15 minutes. The bike path attracts all levels of riders and gets pretty busy on weekends, so ixnay the time trials. Don't worry about packing food and water—plenty of fountains, snack stands, and public restrooms are along the trail. For information on this and other city bike routes, log on to **www.labikepaths.com**. For **guided bicycle tours** of the Santa Monica and Venice beach communities, see "Bicycle Tours," on p. 628.

The best place to mountain-bike in the L.A. region is along the trails of **Malibu Creek State Park** (✆ **818/880-0367**), in the Santa Monica Mountains between Malibu and the San Fernando Valley in Calabasas. Fifteen miles of trails rise to a maximum of 3,000 feet and are appropriate for intermediate to advanced bikers. Pick up a trail map at the park entrance, 4 miles south of U.S. 101 off Las Virgenes Road, just north of Mulholland Highway. Park admission is $12 per car. For more information on mountain bike trails in the L.A. region, log on to **www.latrails.com**.

Spokes 'N Stuff Bike Rental has four locations, one at 4175 Admiralty Way, Marina del Rey (✆ **310/306-3332**), which is open only on weekends, and another at 1715 Ocean Front Walk, behind Loews Hotel, Santa Monica (✆ **310/395-4748**), which is open every day. They rent 10-speed cruisers and 15-speed mountain bikes for about $7.50 per hour and $22 per day. Another good Santa Monica rental shop is **Blazing Saddles Bike Rentals** (Santa Monica Pier; ✆ **310/393-9778**). The rates are about the same as those at Spokes 'N Stuff. Be sure to ask for a free **self-guided tour map** (it's really handy).

In Griffith Park, there's a bike-rental shop (✆ **323/662-6573**) on Crystal Springs Road; there's no official address, but it's two stop signs from the Los Feliz entrance. It's open daily in summer and on weekends during the off season.

In the South Bay, bike rentals—including tandem bikes—are available 1 block from the Strand at **Hermosa Cyclery,** 20 13th St. (✆ **310/374-7816;** www.hermosacyclery.com). Cruisers are $7 per hour; tandems are $13 per hour. FYI, the Strand is an excellent car-free path that's tailor-made for a leisurely bike ride.

FISHING   **Del Rey Sport Fishing,** 13759 Fiji Way, Marina del Rey (✆ **800/822-3625;** www.marinadelreysportfishing.com), has two deep-sea boats departing daily on half- and full-day ocean fishing trips. Of course, it depends on what's running when you're out, but bass, barracuda, halibut, and yellowtail are the most common catches on these party boats. Excursions start at $35 ($25 for kids 11 and under) for half-day trips; tackle rental is available for $10 as well. Phone for reservations. ***Note:*** Anyone 16 years and up needs a fishing license, which can be obtained at just about any sporting goods store.

No permit is required to cast from shore or drop a line from most public piers. Local anglers will hate me for giving away their secret spot, but the **best saltwater fishing spot** in all of L.A. is at the foot of Torrance Boulevard in Redondo Beach.

GOLF   The greater Los Angeles area has more than 100 golf courses, which vary in quality from abysmal to superb. Most of the city's public courses are administered by the Department of Recreation and Parks, which follows a complicated registration/reservation system for tee times. A new online reservation system allows any player to book a tee time up to 8 days in advance. The nonrefundable, nontransferable cost is $5 per person (https://golf reservation.lacity.org/golferla72/). You're also still welcome to play any of the courses by just showing up and getting on the call sheet (much easier for 9-hole courses versus full ones). Expect to wait for the most popular tee times, but try to use your flexible vacationer status to your advantage by avoiding the early-morning rush.

TOPANGA CANYON: nature's solution TO L.A.'S NOISE POLLUTION

When you've had enough of cellphones, cement, and Mercedes, then it's time to take the short drive from L.A. to Topanga Canyon to bargain-shop, drink margaritas, and play cowgirl for a day. Here's the game plan: Call **Los Angeles Horseback Riding** (✆ **818/591-2032;** www.losangeleshorsebackriding.com) and make a reservation for a guided horseback ride in the late afternoon. Next, take the winding drive up Topanga Canyon Boulevard to tiny **Topanga,** one of the last art communities left in Southern California—it was the former haunt of Fleetwood Mac, Neil Young, and other music legends of the '60s and '70s—and the perfect antidote to the dig-me L.A. scene. Spend an hour or so picking though the treasure-trove of vintage clothes, accessories, and antiques at **Hidden Treasures** (154 S. Topanga Canyon Blvd.; ✆ **310/455-2998**), one of the funkiest little shops I've ever seen (the custom-made sea-theme toilet seat lids are mesmerizing). After the scenic horseback ride through the boulder-strewn Topanga canyons, lined with oaks, sycamores, chaparral, and sage, finish off your relaxing day with a leisurely dinner in Topanga at **Abuelitas,** 137 S. Topanga Canyon Rd. (✆ **310/455-8788;** www.abuelitastopanga.com), a popular Mexican restaurant.

Of the city's seven 18-hole and three 9-hole courses, you can't get more central than the **Rancho Park Golf Course,** 10460 W. Pico Blvd. (✆ **310/838-7373;** www.rpgc.org), located smack-dab in the middle of L.A.'s Westside. The par-71 course has lots of tall trees, but not enough to blot out the towering Century City buildings next door. For the money, it's a real bargain (heck, even Bill Clinton golfed here). Rancho also has a 9-hole, par-3 course, as well as a driving range.

For a genuinely woodsy experience, try one of the three courses inside Griffith Park, northeast of Hollywood. The courses are extremely well maintained, challenging without being frustrating, and (despite some holes alongside I-5) a great way to leave the city behind. Bucolic pleasures abound, particularly on the 9-hole **Roosevelt,** on Vermont Avenue across from the Greek Theatre; early-morning wildlife often includes deer, rabbits, raccoons, and skunks (fore!). **Wilson** and **Harding** are each 18 holes and start from the main clubhouse off Riverside Drive, the park's main entrance.

Greens fees on all city courses range from $16 to $48 for nonresidents; 9-hole courses start at $16 on weekdays and $19 on weekends and holidays. For details on other city courses, or to contact the starter directly by phone, call the Department of Recreation and Parks at ✆ **213/625-1040,** or log on to the city's parks website at **www.laparks.org**.

If you're not a fan of crowded city courses, it's well worth the 20-minute drive north to play **Robinson Ranch,** 27734 Sand Canyon Rd., Santa Clarita (✆ **661/252-8484;** www.robinsonranchgolf.com), one of the best and least-crowded public courses in the L.A. region (my golfing buddy loves this place). Golfers can choose from two courses, Mountain or Valley, both of which offer challenging, hilly terrain—bring extra balls—and great views of the Santa Clarita Valley. The striking 25,000-square-foot clubhouse makes a nice view as well and houses a well-stocked pro shop and full-service restaurant. Greens fees for both courses are $87 Monday through Thursday, $117 Friday through Sunday. Carts and practice balls are included.

The **Trump National Golf Club,** 1 Ocean Trails Dr. ((C) **310/265-5000;** www.trumpgolf.com/trumplosangeles), recently opened in Rancho Palos Verdes. Perched on a bluff overlooking the Pacific Ocean, the course provides a spectacular view from every hole. Originally designed by Pete Dye as the Ocean Trails Golf Course, the property was purchased by developer Donald Trump, who spent more than $250 million to redesign it with elements such as lakes and waterfalls. Located on the Palos Verdes Peninsula, 30 minutes south of downtown Los Angeles, the course also offers a 45,000-square-foot clubhouse with locker rooms, a pro shop, three dining options, conference rooms, and a grand ballroom. Greens fees at the public course are $275 mornings, $215 midday, $160 for the afternoon, and after 2:30pm the price dips to $80.

Industry Hills Golf Club, 1 Industry Hills Pkwy., City of Industry ((C) **626/810-4653;** www.ihgolfclub.com), has two 18-hole courses designed by William Bell. Together they encompass eight lakes, 160 bunkers, and many long fairways. The Eisenhower Course, consistently ranked among *Golf Digest's* top 25 public courses, has extra-large undulating greens and the challenge of thick Kikuyu grass. (Kikuyu, even coarser than Bermuda's broad-leaf terrain, is often called Bermuda on steroids.) An adjacent driving range is lit for night use. Greens fees are $70 to $80 Monday through Friday and $100 to $105 Saturday and Sunday, including a cart; call in advance for tee times.

For more information on regional golf courses, log on to **www.golfcalifornia.com**.

> ### The Big Sprawl
>
> How crowded is L.A.? If the five-county area were a state, it would surpass all states in total population size, with the exception of California, New York, and Texas.

HANG GLIDING   Up and down the California coast, it's not uncommon to see people poised on the crests of hills, hanging from enormous colorful kites. **Windsports Soaring Center,** 12623 Gridley St., Sylmar ((C) **818/367-2430;** www.windsports.com), offers instruction and rentals for both novices and experts. A 1-day lesson in a solo hang glider on a bunny hill costs $120 (Wed–Sun, by advance reservation only). If it's more of a thrill you're looking for, choose the 3,000-foot-high tandem flight for $199, which is offered 7 days a week. Beginner lessons are waterside at Dockweiler State Beach Training Flight Park (near LAX), while tandem flights take off from a San Fernando Valley hilltop. Phone for reservations.

HIKING   The **Santa Monica Mountains,** a small range that runs only 50 miles from Griffith Park to Point Mugu, on the coast north of Malibu, makes Los Angeles a great place for hiking. The mountains, which peak at 3,111 feet, are part of the Santa Monica Mountains National Recreation Area, a contiguous conglomeration of 350 public parks and 65,000 acres. Many animals live in this area, including deer, coyote, rabbit, skunk, rattlesnake, fox, hawk, and quail. The hills are also home to almost 1,000 drought-resistant plant species, including live oak and coastal sage.

Hiking is best after spring rains, when the hills are green, flowers are in bloom, and the air is clear. Summers can be very hot; hikers should

Segway Rentals in Santa Monica

Those weird-looking upright electronic scooters zipping around the Santa Monica beach scene are coming from the **Segway Los Angeles** rental shop near the Santa Monica Pier. Riding these human transporters is a hoot: lean forward, go forward; lean back, go back; stand straight up, stop. Simple. After the free 25-minute lesson, it becomes intuitive, and then you're on your own to scoot around the paved shoreline path around Venice Beach and the Santa Monica Pier (*everyone* checks you out). It's the closest you'll come to being a celebrity. A 2-hour rental with lesson is $79 plus tax. Guided tours are available for groups of four or more. *Note:* You have be at least 18 to rent one solo; the minimum age for kids accompanied by a parent is 12. 1660 Ocean Ave., 1 block south of the pier, Santa Monica; (C) 310/395-1395; www.segway.la. *Note:* There's a 24-hour cancellation policy.

always carry fresh water. Beware of poison oak, a hearty shrub that's common on the West Coast. Usually found among oak trees, poison oak has leaves in groups of three, with waxy surfaces and prominent veins. If you come into contact with this itch-producing plant, you'll end up with a California souvenir that you'll soon regret.

Santa Ynez Canyon, in Pacific Palisades, is a long and difficult climb that rises steadily for about 3 miles. At the top, hikers are rewarded with fantastic views over the Pacific. At the top is **Trippet Ranch,** a public facility providing water, restrooms, and picnic tables. From Santa Monica, take Pacific Coast Highway (Calif. 1) north. Turn right onto Sunset Boulevard and then left onto Palisades Drive. Then continue for 2½ miles, turn left onto Verenda de la Montura, and park at the cul-de-sac at the end of the street, where you can find the trail head.

Temescal Canyon, in Pacific Palisades, is far easier than the Santa Ynez trail and far more popular, especially among locals. This is one of the quickest routes into the wilderness. Hikes here are anywhere from 1 to 5 miles. From Santa Monica, take Pacific Coast Highway (Calif. 1) north; turn right onto Temescal Canyon Road, and follow it to the end. Sign in with the gatekeeper, who can also answer your questions.

Will Rogers State Historic Park, Pacific Palisades, is also a terrific place for hiking. An intermediate-level hike from the park's entrance ends at Inspiration Point, a plateau from which you can see a good portion of L.A.'s Westside.

For more information on hiking in the L.A. region, log on to **www. latrails.com**.

HORSEBACK RIDING **Griffith Park Horse Rental,** 480 Riverside Dr. (in the Los Angeles Equestrian Center), Burbank ((C) **818/840-8401**), rents horses by the hour for guided rides through Griffith Park's hills; no experience is necessary. Horse rental starts at $25 for 1 hour (it's more for riders over 200 lb.), cash only. The stables are open daily from 8am to 5pm (till 6pm in the summer), and you must be at least 6 years old to ride. If you have a rider younger than 6, you can opt for either the pony rides in Griffith Park, or an on-site hand-led ride for kids ages 2 to 5. For private lessons, call (C) **818/569-3666.**

Horse riding at Sunset Ranch.

Another popular horseback-riding outfit is **Sunset Ranch,** located at 3400 Beachwood Dr. off of Franklin Avenue, just under the HOLLYWOOD sign. Horse rentals are offered daily from 9am to closing (generally, 5pm) for all levels of riders. The ranch is on the edge of Griffith Park, with access to 52 miles of trails. Also available are private night rides (very romantic), dinner rides, and riding lessons. Rates are $25 for a 1-hour ride, $40 for 2 hours, not including tip. No reservations are required. For more information, call ✆ 323/469-5450 or log on to **www.sunsetranchhollywood.com**.

Closer to the ocean in Topanga Canyon is **Los Angeles Horseback Riding** (p. 635), a small, friendly outfit that offers guided Western-style trail rides for beginners to advanced riders. It's situated at the top of an 1,800-foot ridgeline—about a 25-minute drive from Santa Monica—with panoramic views of the ocean and San Fernando Valley (best seen on one of the sunset or full-moon rides). What I like about this outfit is that if the guide feels that the group is experienced enough, she'll pick up the pace to a canter. Although same-day reservations are sometimes possible, try to book at least 3 days in advance. Kids 6 and older are welcome, and kids 17 and under must wear helmets (bring a bike helmet, if possible). Prices start at about $60 for a 1-hour guided ride, plus tip; 2-hour canyon rides and full-moon trips are available as well.

SAILING Marina del Rey, the largest man-made marina in the world, is the launching point for Paradise Bound Yacht Charters. Book Captain Alex's 42-foot sailing vessel for a minimum of 2 hours for $340 an hour for up to 6 people. The cost covers the services of captain, crew, a hostess, and soft drinks. Food can be catered, or you can bring your own. Touring options include harbor cruises, coastal and sea-life exploration, and more. Captain Alex is a retired Navy vet who commanded four warships; in the sailing business since 1990, he enjoys "taking care of and pampering his guests."

SEA KAYAKING A simple and serene way to explore the southern coastline, sea kayaking is all the rage in Southern California. **Southwind Kayak Center** (17855 Skypark Circle, Irvine; ✆ 800/768-8494 or 949/261-0200; www. southwindkayaks.com) rents a variety of kayaks, including sit-on-top, sit-inside, foot-peddled, hand-peddled, and doubles, for use in the bay or open ocean at their Newport Beach rental base. Rates start at $50 per day; instructional classes are available as scheduled on the website, and preregistration is required. The center also conducts several easygoing, guided outings, including a $55 Back to Nature trip that highlights marine life Newport. Visit their website for more details.

SKATING The 22-mile-long South Beach Trail that runs from Pacific Palisades to Torrance is one of the premier skating spots in the country. In-line skating is especially popular, but conventional skates are often seen here, too. Skating is allowed just about everywhere bicycling is, but be advised that cyclists have the right of way. **JS Rentals,** 1501 Ocean Front Walk, Venice (✆) **310/ 392-7306**), is just one of many places to rent wheels in Venice. In the South Bay, in-line skate rentals are available 1 block from the Strand at **Hermosa Cyclery,** 20 13th St. (✆ **310/374-7816;** www.hermosacyclery.com). Skates cost $6 per hour ($18 for the day); kneepads and wrist guards come with every rental.

SURFING George Freeth (1883–1918), who first surfed Redondo Beach in 1907, is widely credited with introducing the sport to California. But surfing didn't catch on until the 1950s, when CalTech graduate Bob Simmons invented a more maneuverable lightweight fiberglass board. The Beach Boys and other surf-music groups popularized Southern California in the minds of beach babes and dudes everywhere, and the rest, as they say, is history.

If you're a first-timer eager to learn the sport, contact **Learn to Surf L.A.** (✆ **310/663-2479;** www.learntosurfla.com). This highly respected school features a team of experienced instructors who will supply all necessary equipment and get you up and riding a foam board on your first day (trust me, it's a blast). Private lessons are $120, and group lessons are $75. Another great source for learning to surf is **Malibu Longboards** (✆ **310/ 467-6898** or 818/990-7633; www.malibulongboards.com), the official surf instruction for Santa Monica College (don't you wish you'd spent a semester here?). The company offers private lessons for $99 single person, about $150 double, as well as group lessons and 5-day surf camps.

If you want to try it on your own, surfboards are available for rent at shops near all top surfing beaches in the L.A. area. **Zuma Jay Surfboards,** 22775 Pacific Coast Hwy., Malibu (✆ **310/456-8044;** www.zumajays. com), Malibu's oldest surf shop, is about a half-mile south of Malibu Pier. Rentals are about $20 per day, plus $10 for wet suits in winter. For more information about surfing in Southern California, log on to **www.surfline.com**.

TENNIS While soft-surface courts are more popular on the East Coast, hard surfaces are most common in California. If your hotel doesn't have a court

---

The Surfing Rabbi

This is *so* only-in-L.A.: Surfing instructor and orthodox rabbi Nachum Shifren hosts "Surf and Soul" sermons on the sand in Santa Monica. Not only will the rabbi teach you how to surf, but his wise words will empower you to succeed in this competitive world we live in. Yes, even gentiles are welcome (✆ 310/877-1482; www.surfingrabbi.com).

and can't suggest any courts nearby, try the well-maintained, well-lit **Griffith Park Tennis Courts,** on Commonwealth Road, just east of Vermont Avenue (✆ **323/662-7772**). Call or log on to the website of the **City of Los Angeles Department of Recreation and Parks** (✆ **323/644-3536;** www.laparks.org/dos/sports/tennis.htm) to see a long list of free tennis courts or make a reservation at a municipal court near you. *Tip:* Spectators can watch free collegiate matches at the UCLA campus's L.A. Tennis Center from October to May. For a schedule of tournaments, call ✆ **310/206-6831.**

SPECTATOR SPORTS

BASEBALL   The **Los Angeles Dodgers** (✆ **866/DODGERS** [363-4377]; www.dodgers.com), winner of nine National League championships and five World Series titles, play at Dodger Stadium, located at 1000 Elysian Park near Sunset Boulevard. Watching a game at this old-school ballpark is a great way to spend the day, chomping on Dodger Dogs and basking in the sunshine. Tickets are reasonably priced too. And even if you can't score tickets, you can still take a 90-minute **"Championship Tour" of Dodger Stadium,** including access to the field, the Dodger Dugout, the Dugout Club, the press box, and the Tommy Lasorda Training Center. Tours are offered Tuesdays, Thursdays, Saturdays, and Sundays at 10 and 11:30am through October. The cost is $15 for adults, $10 for seniors (55 and up) and children 14 and under. You can reserve and purchase tour tickets online at **www.dodgers.com** (click on "Dodger Stadium," then scroll down to "Stadium Tours").

The 2002 World Series champion **Los Angeles Angels of Anaheim** (✆ **888/796-HALO** [4256]; http://losangeles.angels.mlb.com) play American League ball at Anaheim Stadium, at 2000 Gene Autry Way, in Anaheim, about 30 minutes from downtown L.A. The regular Major League Baseball season runs from April to October. Log on to either team's website for ticket information.

BASKETBALL   Los Angeles has two NBA franchises: the **L.A. Lakers** (www.lakers.com), who have won 11 NBA titles for the city, and the **L.A. Clippers** (www.clippers.com), who haven't. Both teams play in the **STAPLES Center** in downtown L.A., 1111 S. Figueroa St. Celebrity fans such as Jack Nicholson, Leonardo DiCaprio, Ice Cube, and Dyan Cannon have the best tickets, but this 20,000-seater should have room for you—that is, if you have the big bucks for a Lakers ticket or the interest in watching a Clippers game. The season runs from October to April, with 2 months of playoffs following. For tickets to see either team, call ✆ **213/742-7340** or log on to **www.staplescenter.com**.

FOOTBALL   Los Angeles suffers from an absence of major-league football, but it gets by just fine with two popular college teams. The college season runs September through November; if you're interested in checking out a game, contact **UCLA Bruins Football** (✆ **310/825-2101;** www.uclabruins.com) or **USC Trojan Football** (✆ **213/740-2311;** www.usctrojans.com).

HORSE RACING   One of the most beautiful tracks in the country, **Santa Anita Racetrack,** 285 W. Huntington Dr., Arcadia (✆ **626/574-7223;** www.santaanita.com), offers racing from late December to mid-April. Set against

polo, ANYONE?

Way back in 1930, cowboy humorist Will Rogers got a hankerin' to play some polo, so he cleared the field in front of his Pacific Palisades home for a friendly match with his ponies and celebrity pals. Shortly after, he started his famed **Will Rogers Polo Club,** and of the 25 polo organizations that existed at the time, his polo field is the only one that remains. Matches are still held on weekends May through early October, and the bucolic setting of wide green fields, whitewashed fences, and majestic oaks is ideal for a leisurely picnic lunch and a bit of respite from the city. The polo field is located at 1501 Will Rogers State Park Rd. in Pacific Palisades, off West Sunset Boulevard. For more information, call the club at ✆ **818/509-9965,** or log on to its website at **www. willrogerspolo.org** (there's a great feature, "How to Watch a Polo Game").

the majestic San Gabriel Mountains, the track was featured in the Marx Brothers' film *A Day at the Races* and in the 1954 version of *A Star Is Born.* On weekdays during the season, the public is invited to watch morning workouts from 5:30 to 10am at Clockers' Corner. Admission is free; be sure to call or check the website for exact post times. *Tip:* The infield is ideal for picnics (no glass or alcohol), as well as getting an up-close look at the horses and jockeys in action—it even has a children's playground.

Located just down the road from LAX, the scenic **Hollywood Park Racetrack,** 1050 S. Prairie Ave., in Inglewood (✆ **310/419-1500;** www. hollywoodpark.com), with its lakes and flowers, features thoroughbred racing from mid-April to July, as well as from mid-November to mid-December. Opened in 1938, it had shareholders that included movie mogul Harry Warner, Walt Disney, and Bing Crosby. Well-placed monitors project views of the backstretch, as well as stop-action replays of photo finishes. Races are usually held Thursday through Sunday. Post times are 1pm in summer (7pm Fri) and 12:30pm on weekends and holidays. General admission is $8; admission to the clubhouse is $10.

ICE HOCKEY The **L.A. Kings** (✆ **888/546-4752;** www.lakings.com) hold court at the STAPLES Center home (see above); down the road in Orange County, the **Mighty Ducks** (✆ **877/945-3946;** www.mightyducks.com) play at the Arrowhead Pond in Anaheim. The hockey season typically runs October through mid-April, with playoffs following. Tickets are available at either arena or through Ticketmaster.

SOCCER Since its inaugural season in 1996, the **Los Angeles Galaxy** (✆ **877/ 3-GALAXY** [342-5299]; www.lagalaxy.com) has already won the Major League Soccer Cup and earned a reputation as a major force in MLS. But the big news in the past couple of years is all about soccer superstar David Beckham joining the roster. He and his pop-star wife, Victoria Beckham, have made international headlines by making Los Angeles their home. In fact, within the first hour following the announcement, the LA Galaxy sold more than 500 home game tickets. Visitors can catch a game at the Home Depot Center stadium at 18400 Avalon Blvd. in Carson. Tickets for individual games are available through the Galaxy box office and Ticketmaster.

SHOPS & SPAS

Whether you're looking for trendsetting fashions or just some tourist schlock mementos, Los Angeles has your shopping needs covered like no other place in the world. Heck, Los Angeles practically *invented* the shopping mall.

But to really shop L.A.-style, you need to combine your outing with a trip to a day spa and make it an all-day event. For example, if you're planning an outing to the Grove outdoor mall (highly recommended), first make a lunch reservation at **Morels French Steakhouse & Bistro** (② 323/965-9595), then go online to buy movie tickets to the **Grove Theatres** (② 323/692-0829; www.the grovela.com). When the big day arrives, you meet your friends for coffee in the morning, hit the shops, check your packages with the Grove concierge, have lunch, see a matinee, pick up your purchases, and call it a day. Nicely done.

Here's a rundown of the primary shopping areas, with descriptions of their best stores. The sales tax in Los Angeles is 9.75%, but out-of-state shoppers know to have more expensive items shipped home, thereby avoiding the tax.

L.A.'s Westside & Beverly Hills

BEVERLY BOULEVARD ★ (from Robertson Blvd. to La Brea Ave.)   Beverly is L.A.'s premier boulevard for mid-20th-century furnishings. Expensive showrooms line the street, but the shop that started it all is **Modernica,** 7366 Beverly Blvd. (② 323/933-0383; www.modernica.net). You can still find vintage Stickley and Noguchi pieces, but Modernica has become best known for the authentic—and more affordable—replicas they offer (Eames storage units are one popular item). **Scent Bar,** 8327 Beverly Blvd. (② 323/782-8300), the sleek retail shop from the wildly popular fragrance website **www.luckyscent.com**, is the place to go for exclusive fragrances from Monyette Paris and Parfums de Nicolai.

Shoppers descending the Spanish Steps on Rodeo Drive.

British designer and rock royalty **Stella McCartney,** 8823 Beverly Blvd. (📞 **310/273-7051;** www.stellamccartney.com), opened her eponymous digs in an ivy-covered 1920s cottage. Here you'll find the entire collection, from ready-to-wear and fragrance to footwear and handbags. At nearby **Erica Courtney,** 7465 Beverly Blvd. (📞 **323/938-2373;** www.ericacourtney.com), celebs like Julia Roberts, Sandra Bullock, and Eva Longoria are all fans of Courtney's drop-dead-gorgeous diamonds. If you complain that they just don't make 'em like they used to . . . well, they do at **Re-Mix,** 7605½ Beverly Blvd. (btw. Fairfax and La Brea aves.; 📞 **323/936-6210;** www.remixvintageshoes.com). This shop sells only vintage (1920s–1950s)—as well as brand-new reproductions (as in, unworn)—shoes for women and men (though the selection is smaller for men), such as wingtips, Joan Crawford pumps, and wedge styles. It's more like a shoe-store museum. A rack of unworn vintage socks all display their original tags and stickers, and the prices are downright reasonable. Celebrity hipsters and hepcats are often spotted here.

Other vintage wares are found at **Second Time Around Watch Co.,** 8763 Rosewood Ave. (just 2 blocks north of the longtime Beverly Blvd. location; 📞 **310/271-6615;** www.secondtimearoundwatchco.com). The city's best selection of collectible timepieces includes dozens of classics from Tiffany, Cartier, and Rolex, plus rare pocket watches. Priced for collectors, but a fascinating browse for the Swatch crowd too.

When it's time to unwind and beautify, hit **Ona Spa,** 7373 Beverly Blvd. (just east of Martel Ave.; 📞 **323/931-4442**) for a tension-relieving massage (try the Ona Pada, a high-intensity technique which utilizes the therapist's feet as tools for ultimate deep-tissue pressure). The attached **Privé Salon** is one of the city's trendiest salons, where celebrity sightings are common.

LA BREA AVENUE ★ (north of Wilshire Blvd.)   This is L.A.'s artiest shopping strip. La Brea is anchored by the giant **American Rag, Maison Midi** alterna-complex and is also home to lots of great urban antiques stores dealing in Art Deco, Arts and Crafts, 1950s modern, and the like. You'll also find vintage clothiers, furniture galleries, and other warehouse-size stores, as well as some of the city's foodiest restaurants, such as Campanile (p. 591).

Upscale seekers of home decor head to **Mortise & Tenon,** 446 S. La Brea Ave. (📞 **323/937-7654;** www.mortisetenon.com), where handcrafted heavy wood pieces sit next to overstuffed velvet-upholstered sofas and even vintage steel desks. The best place for a snack is the **La Brea Bakery,** 624 S. La Brea Ave. (📞 **323/939-6813;** www.labreabakery.com), which epicureans know from gourmet markets and the attached Campanile restaurant.

Stuffed to the rafters with hardware and fixtures of the past 100 years, **Liz's Antique Hardware,** 453 S. La Brea Ave. (📞 **323/939-4403;** www.lahardware.com), thoughtfully keeps a canister of wet wipes at the register—believe us, you'll need one after sifting through bags and crates of doorknobs, latches, finials, and any other home hardware you can imagine. Perfect sets of Bakelite drawer pulls and antique ceramic bathroom fixtures are some of the more intriguing items. Be prepared to browse for hours, whether you're redecorating or not. There's a respectable collection of coordinating trendy clothing for men and women, too.

URBAN shopping ADVENTURES

Shopping may be a casual pastime in other cities, but in the urban jungle of Los Angeles, it's a competitive sport. If you're a shopping rookie at best, you might consider an outing with **Urban Shopping Adventures,** which offers custom guided shopping tours of the L.A. Fashion District—more than 100 sprawling blocks loaded with wholesale and retail venues—and celebrity-frequented boutiques in Westside neighborhoods along Rodeo Drive, Robertson Boulevard, West Third Street, and Melrose Heights. Hosted by shopping expert Christine Silvestri, the 3-hour walking tours start at just $36 per person, and merchants are often willing to provide deep discounts to her tour guests. All shopping excursions include a shopping bag, a district map, bottled water, a snack bar, and plenty of time to browse at your own pace. She also offers round-trip transportation options such as shuttle, bus, or limousine service from your hotel to your chosen location for an additional cost. Advance reservations are required for all tours, and additional shopping districts are also available upon request. Call ✆ **213/683-9715** or log on to **www.urbanshoppingadventures.com.**

ROBERTSON BOULEVARD ★ (btw. Wilshire and Beverly blvds.) If you're a fan of celeb magazines like *US Weekly,* you simply must pay a visit to one of L.A.'s most popular shopping streets. It's common to see the likes of Jessica Simpson and Paris Hilton shopping at trend-obsessed boutiques like **Kitson,** 115 S. Robertson Blvd. (✆ **310/859-2652;** www.shopkitson.com), and **Lisa Kline,** 143 S. Robertson Blvd. (✆ **310/246-0907**). A splashy **Dolce & Gabbana,** 147 N. Robertson Blvd. (✆ **310/247-1571;** www.dolce gabbana.com), flagship boutique has the full spectrum of men's and women's clothing, and must-have accessories like sunglasses and jewelry. After shopping like a celebrity, dine among them at the **Ivy** (p. 586).

Just up the street, one of L.A.'s top day spas beckons the tired, the stressed, and the famous. In fact, skin-care specialist **Kinara Spa,** 656 N. Robertson Blvd. (✆ **310/657-9188;** www.kinaraspa.com), lists among its faithful fans Halle Berry, Naomi Watts, and Jennifer Garner.

RODEO DRIVE & BEVERLY HILLS' GOLDEN TRIANGLE ★★ (btw. Santa Monica Blvd., Wilshire Blvd., and Crescent Dr., Beverly Hills) Everyone knows about Rodeo Drive, the city's most famous shopping street. Couture shops from high fashion's Old Guard are located along these 3 hallowed blocks, along with plenty of newer high-end labels. And there are two examples of the Beverly Hills version of mini-malls, albeit more insular and attractive: the **Rodeo Collection,** 421 N. Rodeo Dr. (www.rodeocollection.net), a contemporary center with towering palms; and **2 Rodeo** (www.tworodeo. com), a cobblestoned Italianate piazza at Wilshire Boulevard. The 16-square-block area surrounding Rodeo Drive is known as the Golden Triangle. Shops off Rodeo are generally not as name-conscious as those on the strip (and you might actually be able to afford something), but they're nevertheless plenty upscale. Little Santa Monica Boulevard has a particularly colorful line of specialty stores, and Brighton Way is as young and hip as relatively staid Beverly Hills gets. Parking is a bargain, with seven city-run lots offering 2 hours of free parking.

The big names to look for here are **Prada,** 343 N. Rodeo Dr. (☎ 310/278-8661); **Chanel,** 400 N. Rodeo Dr. (☎ 310/278-5500); **Bulgari,** 201 N. Rodeo Dr. (☎ 310/858-9216); **Gucci,** 347 N. Rodeo Dr. (☎ 310/278-3451); **Hermès,** 434 N. Rodeo Dr. (☎ 310/278-6440); **Louis Vuitton,** 295 N. Rodeo Dr. (☎ 310/859-0457); **Polo/Ralph Lauren,** 444 N. Rodeo Dr. (☎ 310/281-7200); and a three-story **Tiffany & Co.,** 210 N. Rodeo Dr. (☎ 310/273-8880). Other ultrachic clothiers include **Dolce & Gabbana,** 312 N. Rodeo Dr. (☎ 310/888-8701); British plaid palace **Burberry,** 9560 Wilshire Blvd. (☎ 310/550-4500); and **NikeTown,** on the corner of Wilshire Boulevard and Rodeo Drive (☎ 310/275-9998), a behemoth shrine to the reigning athletic-gear king.

Wilshire Boulevard is also home to New York–style department stores (each in spectacular landmark buildings) such as **Saks Fifth Avenue,** 9600 Wilshire Blvd. (☎ **310/275-4211**); **Barneys New York,** 9570 Wilshire Blvd. (☎ **310/276-4400**); and **Neiman Marcus,** 9700 Wilshire Blvd. (☎ **310/550-5900**).

When all that walking and gawking tires you out, do what all the Beverly Hills beauties do: Hit a spa. Aida Thibiant has been offering classic treatments at **Thibiant Beverly Hills Day Spa,** 449 N. Canon Dr. (☎ **310/278-7565;** www.thibiantspa.com), since the 1970s. Guys have a place of their own at the new high-end barbershop, the **Shave,** 230 S. Beverly Dr. (☎ **310/888-2898;** www.theshavebeverlyhills.com). You don't need to stay in one of the fabulously luxurious Beverly Hills hotels to get all the pampering services. At the **spa at the Four Seasons** (p. 564), California-flavored treatments use everything from pumpkin to caviar in decadent massages and facials. At the **Beverly Hills Hotel Spa by La Prairie** (p. 564), the facials and massages are some of the most expensive in town, but it's a great reason to spend a decadent day at the "Pink Palace" without having to drop $1,000 a night on a suite.

THE SUNSET STRIP (btw. La Cienega Blvd. and Doheny Dr., West Hollywood) The monster-size billboards advertising the latest rock god make it clear this is rock-'n'-roll territory. The Strip is lined with trendy restaurants, industry-oriented hotels, and dozens of shops offering outrageous fashions and stage accessories. One anomaly is Sunset Plaza, an upscale cluster of Georgian-style shops resembling Beverly Hills at its snootiest. You'll find **Billy Martin's,** 8605 Sunset Blvd. (☎ **310/289-5000**), founded by the legendary Yankees manager in 1978. This chic men's Western shop—complete with fireplace and leather sofa—stocks hand-forged silver and gold belt buckles, Lucchese and Liberty boots, and stable staples such as flannel shirts. **Book Soup,** 8818 Sunset Blvd. (☎ **310/659-3110;** www.book soup.com), has long been one of L.A.'s most celebrated bookshops, selling mainstream and small-press books and hosting book signings and readings.

The Sunset Strip's trendiest hotels have in-house spas and spa services—such as **Agua at the Mondrian,** 8440 Sunset Blvd. (☎ **323/203-1138;** www.mondrianhotel.com)—which offer great added amenities for hotel guests. But to feel like a real superstar on the Strip, go to the "facialist of the stars": **Ole Henriksen Face/Body,** 8622 W. Sunset Blvd. (☎ **310/854-7700;** www.olehenriksen.com), is where stunners such as Ashley Judd and Charlize Theron get glowing skin.

Market-fresh produce.

WEST THIRD STREET ★ (btw. Fairfax and Robertson boulevards)   You can shop until you drop on this trendy strip, anchored on the east end by the **Farmers Market** and the **Grove** (p. 600). Many of Melrose Avenue's shops have relocated here, along with terrific up-and-comers, several cafes, and popular restaurants such as **Loteria Grill** (p. 600), **Gumbo Pot** (p. 600), and **Dupar's** (p. 664) at the Farmers Market. *Fun* is more the catchword here than *funky,* and the shops (including the vintage-clothing stores) are a bit more refined than those along Melrose. **Traveler's Bookcase,** 8375 W. Third St. (℘ **323/655-0575;** www.travelbooks.com), is one of the best travel bookshops in the West, stocking a huge selection of guidebooks and travel literature, as well as maps and travel accessories.

There's lots more to see along this always-growing street. Refuel at **Chado Tea Room,** 8422½ W. Third St. (℘ **323/655-2056**), a temple for tea lovers. Chado is designed with a nod to Paris's renowned Mariage Frères tea purveyor; one wall is lined with nooks whose recognizable brown tins are filled with more than 250 varieties of tea from around the world. Among the choices are 15 kinds of Darjeeling, Indian teas blended with rose petals, and ceremonial Chinese and Japanese blends. You can also get tea meals here, featuring delightful sandwiches and individual pots of any loose tea in the store.

Hollywood

HOLLYWOOD BOULEVARD (btw. Gower St. and La Brea Ave.)   One of Los Angeles's most famous streets is, for the most part, a cheesy tourist strip. But along the Walk of Fame, between the T-shirt shops and greasy pizza parlors, you'll find some excellent poster shops, souvenir stores, and Hollywood-memorabilia dealers worth getting out of your car for—especially if there's a chance of getting your hands on that long-sought-after Ethel Merman autograph or *200 Motels* poster.

Some long-standing purveyors of memorabilia include **Hollywood Book and Poster Company,** 6562 Hollywood Blvd. (✆ **323/465-8764;** www.hollywoodbookandposter.com), which has an excellent collection of posters (from about $20 each), strong in horror and exploitation flicks. Photocopies of about 5,000 movie and television scripts are sold for $15 each—*Pulp Fiction* is just as good in print, by the way—and the store carries music posters and photos.

The legendary **Fredericks of Hollywood,** 6751 Hollywood Blvd. (✆ **323/957-5953;** www.fredericks.com), located just a block east of Hollywood and Highland, is worth a stop if you're looking for devilish dainties. The flagship store features lingerie once worn by celebrities such as Sharon Stone, Julianne Moore, and Halle Berry.

LARCHMONT BOULEVARD (btw. Melrose Ave. and Third St.)   Neighbors congregate on this old-fashioned street just east of busy Vine Avenue. As the surrounding Hancock Park homes become increasingly popular with artists and young industry types, the shops and cafes lining Larchmont get more stylish. Sure, chains such as Jamba Juice and the Coffee Bean are infiltrating this formerly mom-and-pop terrain, but plenty of unique shopping awaits amid charming elements such as diagonal parking, shady trees, and sidewalk bistro tables.

One of L.A.'s landmark independent bookstores is **Chevalier's Books,** 126 N. Larchmont Blvd. (✆ **323/465-1334**), a 60-year Larchmont tradition. If your walking shoes are letting you down, stop into **Village Footwear,** 248 N. Larchmont Blvd. (✆ **323/461-3619**), which specializes in comfort lines such as Josef Siebel. Or even better, stop in for a foot—or full-body—massage at **Healing Hands Wellness Center,** 414 N. Larchmont Blvd. (✆ **323/461-7876;** www.healinghandswc.com), which has affordable 1-hour massages starting at $55. An entire afternoon of pampering can be had at **Le Petite Retreat Day Spa,** 331 N. Larchmont Blvd. (✆ **323/466-1028;** www.lprdayspa.com), which offers great packages for couples or a girls' day out.

MELROSE AVENUE ★★ (btw. Fairfax and La Brea aves.)   It's showing some wear—some stretches have become downright ugly—but this is still one of the most exciting shopping streets in the country for cutting-edge fashions (and some eye-popping people-watching, to boot). Melrose is always an entertaining stroll, dotted with plenty of hip restaurants and funky shops selling the latest in clothes, gifts, jewelry, and accessories that are sure to shock. Where else could you find green patent-leather cowboy boots, a working 19th-century pocket watch, an inflatable girlfriend, and glow-in-the-dark condoms on the same block? Here are some highlights.

l.a. Eyeworks, 7407 Melrose Ave. (✆ **323/653-8255**), revolutionized eyeglass designs from medical supply to stylish accessory, and now their brand is nationwide. **Off the Wall** is filled with neon-flashing, bells-and-whistles kitsch collectibles, from vintage Wurlitzer jukeboxes to life-size fiberglass cows. The L.A. branch of a Bay Area hipster hangout, **Wasteland** has an enormous steel-sculpted facade. There's a lot of leather and denim, and some classic vintage—but mostly funky 1970s-style garb, both vintage and contemporary. An outpost of the edgy **Floyd's Barbershops,** 7300 Melrose Ave. (✆ **323/965-7600**), keeps the street's style-for-less theme by charging around $21 for men's and $24 for women's cuts. It's like a salon, funky music store, and Internet cafe all rolled into one.

MELROSE HEIGHTS ★★ (btw. La Cienega Blvd. and Fairfax Ave.)   This posh section of Melrose, anchored by the venerable favorite **Fred Segal,** 8100 Melrose Ave. (✆ **323/655-3734**), houses designer boutiques such as **Diane Von Furstenberg,** 8407 Melrose Ave. (✆ **323/951-1947**); and **Paul Smith,** 8221 Melrose Ave. (✆ **323/951-4800**). L.A. jewelry designer **Suzanne Felsen,** 8332 Melrose Ave. (✆ **323/653-5400**), is a celebrity favorite—she transformed a 1920s Spanish home to house her gold and platinum baubles lined with Peruvian opals and Mandarin garnets. Perennial fashion favorite **Marc Jacobs** has three stores, at 8400, 8409, and 8410 Melrose Ave., featuring ready-to-wear, accessories, menswear, and the less expensive Marc by Marc Jacobs collection.

Santa Monica & the Beaches

MAIN STREET ★ (btw. Pacific St. and Rose Ave., and Santa Monica and Venice blvds.)   An excellent street for strolling, Main Street is crammed with a combination of mall standards, as well as upscale, left-of-center individual boutiques. You can also find plenty of casually hip cafes and restaurants. The primary strip connecting Santa Monica and Venice, Main Street has a relaxed, beach-community vibe that sets it apart from similar strips. The stores here straddle the fashion fence between upscale trendy and beach-bum edgy. Highlights include **Obsolete,** 222 Main St. (near Rose Ave; ✆ **310/399-0024**), a hip antiques store. Collectibles range from antique carnival curios to 19th-century anatomical charts from Belgium (you'd be amazed at how much some of that junk in your attic is worth). **CP Shades,** 2937 Main St. (btw. Ashland and Pier sts.; ✆ **310/392-0949**), is a San Francisco ladies' clothier whose loose and comfy cotton and linen line is carried by many department stores and boutiques. If you're looking for some truly sophisticated, finely crafted eyewear, the friendly **Optical Shop of Aspen,** 2904 Main St. (btw. Ashland and Pier sts.; ✆ **310/392-0633**), is for you. Ask for frames by cutting-edge L.A. designers Bada and Koh Sakai. For aromatherapy nirvana, it's **Cloud's,** 2719 Main St. (✆ **310/399-2059**), where Jill Cloud (happily assisted by her lovely mom) carries the most heavenly scented candles. Then there's **Arts & Letters,** 2665 Main St. (✆ **310/392-9076**), a stationery haven that includes invitations by the owner herself, Marilyn Golin. Outdoors types will get lost in 5,600-square-foot **Patagonia,** 2936 Main St. (✆ **310/314-1776;** www.patagonia.com), where climbers, surfers, skiers, and hikers can gear up in the functional, colorful duds that put this environmentally friendly firm on the map. For a dose of beachy pampering, check out **Olivia's Organic Skin Care,** 2909 Main St. (📞 **310/422-5548;** www.beysgarden.com). Owned by Olivia, formerly of Bey's Garden, this environmentally committed shop is part aromatherapy apothecary, part gift shop, part day spa; you'll find everything from body-sugaring hair removal to detoxifying wraps.

MONTANA AVENUE (btw. 17th and 7th sts., Santa Monica; www.montanaave. com)   This breezy stretch of slow-traffic Montana has gotten a lot more pricey than in the late 1970s, when tailors and laundromats ruled the roost, but the specialty shops still outnumber the chains. Look around and you can see upscale moms with strollers and cellphones shopping for designer fashions, country home decor, and gourmet takeout.

Montana is still original enough for residents from across town to make a special trip here, seeking out distinctive shops like **Shabby Chic,** 1013 Montana Ave. (📞 **310/394-1975;** www.shabbychic.com), a much-copied purveyor of slipcovered sofas and flea market furnishings, while clothes-horses shop for designer wear at minimalist **Savannah,** 706 Montana Ave. (📞 **310/458-2095**); ultrahip **Jill Roberts,** 920 Montana Ave. (📞 **310/260-1966;** www.jillroberts.com); and sleekly professional **Weathervane,** 1209 Montana Ave. (📞 **310/393-5344**). **Leona Edmiston,** 1007 Montana Ave. (📞 **310/587-1100;** www.leonaedmiston.com), houses the Aussie designer's famed frocks. For more grown-up style, head to **Ponte Vecchio,** 702 Montana Ave. (📞 **310/394-0989;** www.pontev.com), which sells Italian hand-painted dishes and urns. If Valentine's Day is approaching, duck into **Only Hearts,** 1407 Montana Ave. (📞 **310/393-3088;** www.only hearts.com), for heart-themed gifts and seductively comfortable intimate apparel. And don't forget the one-of-a-kind shops such as **Sun Precautions,** 1601 Montana Ave. (📞 **310/451-5858;** www.sunprecautions.com), specializing in 100% UV protection apparel, and the second-largest **Kiehl's**

GR8 FINDS IN WEST L.A.'S j-town

What started off as a magazine has spawned two of L.A.'s most-talked-about stores—**Giant Robot,** 2015 Sawtelle Blvd. (📞 **310/478-1819**), and **GR2,** 2062 Sawtelle Blvd. (📞 **310/445-9276**)—and **gr/eats** restaurant, 2050 Sawtelle Blvd. (📞 **310/478-3242;** www.gr-eats.com). Across the street from each other in West L.A.'s Japantown (at Sawtelle and Olympic blvds.), both shops specialize in a wide range of Asian-American pop-culture items, including T-shirts, books, music, stationery, toys, art, and accessories (check out the Takashi Murakami pins). There are several other cool shops and restaurants along this 1½-block stretch as well. One of my favorite stores is **Happy Six,** 2115 Sawtelle Blvd. (📞 **310/479-5363**), which looks like Hello Kitty on acid and sells playful apparel and accessories for men and women. If you're hungry, my favorites along Sawtelle are **Manpuku,** 2125 Sawtelle Blvd. (📞 **310/473-0580;** www.manpuku.us); **Sawtelle Kitchen,** 2024 Sawtelle Blvd. (📞 **310/473-2222;** www.sawtellekitchen.com); and **Hurry Curry of Tokyo,** 2131 Sawtelle Blvd. (📞 **310/473-1640;** www.hurrycurryoftokyo.com). Or you can pop into **Nijiya Market,** 2130 Sawtelle Blvd. (📞 **310/575-3300**), and grab a *bento* (Japanese boxed lunch) to go.

store outside of New York City, at 1516 Montana Ave. (☏ **310/255-0055;** www.kiehls.com). Skin is taken incredibly seriously at the flagship store and spa, **Dermalogica on Montana,** 1022 Montana Ave. (☏ **310/260-8682;** www.dermalogicaonmontana.com), where "touch therapies" and "skin mapping" are just the beginning of the dynamite facials. Enjoy a meal at the local favorite, **Café Montana,** 1534 Montana Ave. (☏ **310/829-3990**), for great people-watching through its floor-to-ceiling glass windows; the original **Father's Office,** 1018 Montana Ave. (☏ **310/736-2224;** www.fathers office.com) for microbrews and one of the city's best burgers; or **R+D Kitchen,** 1323 Montana Ave. (☏ **310/395-3314**), for classic California cuisine and cocktails.

THIRD STREET PROMENADE ★ (Third St. btw. Wilshire Blvd. and Broadway; www.downtownsm.com) Packed with those ubiquitous corporate chain stores, restaurants, and cafes (gee, another Starbucks), Santa Monica's pedestrians-only section of Third Street is one of the most popular shopping areas in the city. The Promenade bustles all day and well into the evening with a seemingly endless assortment of street performers among the shoppers, bored teens, and home-challenged. There are, however, a few shopping gems squeezed between Gap, Abercrombie & Fitch, and Old Navy. You can easily browse for hours at **Hennessey & Ingalls,** 214 Wilshire Blvd. (☏ **310/458-9074**), a bookstore devoted to art and architecture. **Restoration Hardware,** 1221 Third Street Promenade (☏ **310/458-7992**), is still the retro-current leader for reproduction home furnishings and accessories. **Puzzle Zoo,** 1413 Third Street Promenade (☏ **310/393-9201**), was the original location of this now-regional chain; you'll find an array of toys and puzzles, as well as many brain-teasing challenges.

Exhale is perfect for those seeking quiet time and relief from the crowds. There's yoga and Core Fusion classes, the Healing Waters sanctuary with eucalyptus steam rooms, relaxing spa services, and the simply titled "Quiet Room" for rejuvenation. Stores stay open late (often until 1 or 2am on the weekends) for the moviegoing crowds, and there's plenty of public parking in six structures along Second and Fourth streets between Broadway and Wilshire Boulevard.

A MECCA FOR HIGH-END vintage

If your style is more Hepburn than Hilton, you won't want to miss the mother lode of high-end vintage shopping L.A. has to offer. Doris Raymond's **The Way We Wore,** 334 S. La Brea Ave. (☏ **323/937-0878;** www.thewaywewore.com), is a favorite among celebs and stylists for vintage Chanel, Balenciaga, and Fortuny. Cameron Silver's **Decades,** 8214½ Melrose Ave. (☏ **323/655-0223;** www.decadesinc.com), is an L.A. institution, where you'll find frocks from Halston, Gucci, Lilly Pulitzer, and Missoni. **Lily et Cie,** 9044 Burton Way (☏ **310/724-5757**), supplies many of the glamour gowns you see on the red carpet. Owner and vintage maven Rita Watnick has an impeccable collection of pieces from important designers such as Yves Saint Laurent, Givenchy, and Trigere.

abbot kinney BOULEVARD: L.A.'S ANTITHESIS TO RODEO DRIVE

When you're finally fed up with the Rodeo Drive attitude and megamall conformity, it's time to drive to Venice and stroll the eclectic shops along **Abbot Kinney Boulevard.** This refreshingly antiestablishment stretch of street has the most diverse array of shops, galleries, and restaurants in Los Angeles. (Locals still cheer that there are no franchises in the neighborhood.) You can easily spend the entire afternoon here poring over vintage clothing, antique furniture, vintage Vespas, local art, and amusing gifts. Or if you're looking for a unique gift, you'll want to try **Strange Invisible Perfumes,** 1138 Abbot Kinney Blvd. (✆ **310/314-1505;** www.siperfumes.com), where they can custom-make a scent to match your musk. Then there's **Firefly,** 1409 Abbot Kinney Blvd. (✆ **310/450-6288;** www.shopfirefly.com), a local favorite. It's that one store you can go into and find everything from great baby gifts, stationery, and books to quirky handbags and cool clothing. **DNA Clothing Co.,** 411 Rose Ave. (✆ **310/399-0341;** www.dnaclothing.com), is the mother lode for those in search of the coolest, most current styles for men and women at great prices (stylists and costumers often use DNA as their resource for sitcoms or feature films). You'll find all your major brands, as well as their own private-label wear, and fresh stock arrives weekly. Take a break to eat at one of the boulevard's many restaurants, including **Joe's** (among the best California cuisine in L.A.; p. 581), **Primitivo, Axe, Lilly's, Jin's Patisserie, French Market Café,** newcomers **Tasting Kitchen** and **Gjelina,** and, of course, **Hal's Bar & Grill,** with its live jazz music. Heck, there are even 2 hours of free street parking.

Downtown

Since the late lamented Bullock's department store closed in 1993 (its Art Deco masterpiece salons were rescued to house the Southwestern Law School's library), downtown has become less of a shopping destination than ever. Although many of the once-splendid streets are lined with cut-rate luggage and electronics stores, shopping here can be a rewarding—albeit gritty—experience for the adventuresome.

Savvy Angelenos still go for bargains in the garment and fabric districts; florists and bargain hunters arrive at the vast **Los Angeles Flower District,** 766 Wall St. (btw. E. Eighth St. and E. Seventh sts.; ✆ **213/622-1966;** www.laflowerdistrict.com), before dawn for the city's best selection of fresh blooms; and families of all ethnicities stroll the **Grand Central Market ★★**, 317 S. Broadway (btw. Third and Fourth sts.; ✆ **213/624-2378;** www.grandcentralsquare.com). Opened in 1917, this bustling market has watched the face of downtown L.A. change while changing little. On weekends, you'll be greeted by a mariachi band at the Hill Street entrance, near my favorite market feature, the fruit-juice counter, which dispenses 20 fresh varieties from wall spigots and blends the tastiest, healthiest "shakes" in town. Farther into the market you'll find produce sellers and prepared-food counters, spice vendors who seem straight out of a Turkish bazaar, and a grain-and-bean seller who'll scoop out dozens of exotic rices and dried legumes. It's open 9am to 6pm daily.

At the base of The Fashion Institute of Design & Merchandising's downtown campus, you'll find the **FIDM Scholarship Store,** where donated new merchandise is sold at bargain prices. All sales go toward scholarships for FIDM students, so you can shop with the karmic awareness that you're helping the fashion industry's next generation of designers with their tuition. It's located at 919 S. Grand Ave. at West Ninth Street (🕾 213/624-1200; www.fidm.edu).

Another of my favorite downtown shopping zones is **Olvera Street** ★ (🕾 213/628-1274; www.olvera-street.com), a lively brick pedestrian lane near Union Station that's been lined with stalls selling Mexican wares since the 1930s. Everything that's sold south of the border is available here, including custom leather accessories, huarache sandals, maracas, and—but of course—freshly baked *churros.* On weekends, you're bound to see strolling bolero musicians, mariachis, folk dancers, and performances by Aztec Indians. It's open daily from 10am to about 8pm.

If you're looking to find *the* best shopping deals in handbags, luggage, shoes, costume jewelry, and trendy fashions, then try your best to find a parking meter or park in one of the parking structures from Olympic Boulevard to 12th Street and explore **Santee Alley,** located in the alley between Santee Street and Maple Avenue. Often referred to as the heart of the fashion district, you'll find everything you've ever wanted at bargain prices. Go early on Saturday mornings if you want to blend in with the locals.

Okay, so you have to wake up a little early to experience the **Southern California Flower Mart,** 742 Maple Ave. between Seventh and Eighth streets (🕾 213/627-2482; www.laflowerdistrict.com), but if you do it right—wear

Treats at Grand Central Market.

Vendors, Grand Central Market.   Olvera Street vendors.

comfortable shoes, bring cash, and pick up a cup o' joe—you'll find walking through the myriad flower stalls a very tranquil experience. Besides the usual buds and stems that you see in *Sunset Magazine,* you'll be surprised to find tropicals such as torch ginger, protea, and bird of paradise. You can purchase flowers by the bundles at amazingly low prices.

LOS ANGELES AFTER DARK

The City of Angels has some of the most cutting-edge clubs and bars in the world and is the polestar for the best and brightest in the music scene. Entertainment of all stripes—from Hollywood Bowl picnic performances to cool jazz venues, retro chic bars, and rock-'n'-roll clubs—can be found in the following pages.

Your best bet for current entertainment info is the **L.A. Weekly (www. laweekly.com**), a free weekly paper available at sidewalk stands, shops, and restaurants. It has all the most up-to-date news on what's happening in Los Angeles's playhouses, cinemas, museums, and live-music venues. The Sunday **"Calendar"** and Thursday **"Weekend"** sections of the *Los Angeles Times* (**www.latimes.com/theguide/**) are also a good source of information for what's going on throughout the city.

To purchase tickets in advance, first try buying them directly from the venue to avoid paying a surcharge. If that doesn't work, log on to **Prestige Tickets'** website at www.prestigetickets.com or call ✆ **888/595-6260.** The original company, based in Hollywood for more than 30 years (now moved to Encino and merged with an East Coast company), it specializes in selling tickets to sporting, theater, concerts, and other entertainment events throughout Los Angeles—at a markup, of course. If all else fails, call **Ticketmaster** (✆ **800/745-3000;** www.ticketmaster.com), but beware of their absurdly high processing fees.

Theater

Tickets for most plays usually cost $10 to $35, although big-name shows at the major theaters can fetch up more than $100 for the best seats. **LA Stage Alliance** (✆ **213/614-0556**), a nonprofit association of live theaters and producers in Los Angeles, offers half-price tickets to more than 100 venues via their Internet-only service at **www.lastagealliance.com**. This handy site features a frequently updated list of shows and availability. Tickets can be purchased online with a credit card, and they'll be waiting for you at the box office; a service fee is applied depending on the cost of the ticket. ***Note:*** One caveat of the half-price bargain is that the seating assignments are solely at the discretion of the theater—there's no guarantee you'll be sitting next to your partner (though this is rare)—and you must bring a printed or faxed copy of your e-mail confirmation to the box office.

The all-purpose **Music Center of Los Angeles County,** 135 N. Grand Ave., downtown, houses the city's top two playhouses: the **Ahmanson Theatre** and **Mark Taper Forum.** They're both home to the Center Theater Group (www.centertheatregroup.org), as well as traveling productions (often Broadway or London bred). Each season, the Ahmanson Theatre (✆ **213/628-2772**) hosts a handful of high-profile shows, such as the Tony Award–winning *Jersey Boys* and Oprah Winfrey's musical *The Color Purple*. ***Tip:*** The best seats in the theater are in the front mezzanine section.

The **Mark Taper Forum** (✆ **213/628-2772;** www.centertheatregroup.com) is a more intimate theater with a thrust stage—where the audience is seated on three sides of the acting area—that hosts contemporary works by international and local playwrights. Neil Simon's humorous and poignant *The Dinner Party* and Tom Stoppard's witty and eclectic *Arcadia,* which has won three Pulitzer Prizes and 18 Tony Awards, are among the more popular productions performed on this internationally recognized stage.

One of L.A.'s most venerable landmarks, the **Orpheum Theatre,** 842 S. Broadway (at Ninth St.; ✆ **877/677-4386;** www.laorpheum.com), reopened after a 75-year hiatus. Built in 1926, this renowned venue has hosted an array of theatrical productions, concerts, film festivals, and movie shoots—from Judy Garland's 1933 vaudeville performance to *American Idol*. The 2,000-seat theater is home to the Mighty Wurlitzer, one of three original theater organs still existing in Southern California theaters.

Across town, the moderate-size **Geffen Playhouse,** 10886 Le Conte Ave., Westwood (✆ **310/208-5454;** www.geffenplayhouse.com), presents dramatic and comedic work by prominent and emerging writers. UCLA purchased the theater—which was originally built as a Masonic temple in 1929, and later served as the Westwood Playhouse—back in 1995 with a little help from philanthropic entertainment mogul David Geffen. This striking venue is often the West Coast choice of many acclaimed off-Broadway shows, and also attracts locally based TV and movie actors eager for the immediacy of stage work. One popular production featured the world premiere of *Wishful Drinking,* a poignant comedy written and performed by Carrie Fisher. More audience-friendly than some, the Playhouse prices tickets in the $35 to $75 range.

You've probably already heard of the **Kodak Theatre,** 6834 Hollywood Blvd. (✆ **323/308-6300;** www.kodaktheatre.com), home of the Academy Awards. The crown jewel of the Hollywood & Highland entertainment complex, this modern beauty hosts a wide range of international performances, musicals,

Kodak Theatre.

Pantages Theatre.

and concerts ranging from Alicia Keys and David Gilmour to the Moscow Stanislavsky Ballet and *Sesame Street Live*. Guided tours are given 7 days a week from 10:30am to 4pm.

The restored **Pantages Theatre,** 6233 Hollywood Blvd., between Vine and Argyle (*©* **323/468-1770;** www.pantages-theater.com), reflects the full Art Deco glory of L.A.'s theater scene. Opened in 1930, this historical and cultural landmark was the first Art Deco movie palace in the U.S. and site of the Academy Awards from 1949 to 1959. The theater recently presented *Hair, Spring Awakening,* and *Westside Story.*

At the foot of the Hollywood Hills, the 1,245-seat outdoor **John Anson Ford Amphitheatre** (*©* **323/461-3673;** www.fordamphitheatre.org) is located in a county regional park and is set against a backdrop of cypress trees and chaparral. It is an intimate setting, with no patron more than 96 feet away from the stage. Music, dance, film, theater, and family events run May through September. The indoor theater space, a cozy 87-seat space that was extensively renovated in 1998 and renamed **[Inside] The Ford,** features live music and theater year-round.

One of the most highly acclaimed professional theaters in L.A., the **Pasadena Playhouse,** 39 S. El Molino Ave., near Colorado Boulevard, Pasadena (*©* **626/356-7529;** www.pasadenaplayhouse.org), is a registered historic landmark that has served as the training ground for many theatrical, film, and TV stars, including William Holden and Gene Hackman. After an unexpected closure for most of 2010, productions are once again being staged on the main theater's elaborate Spanish Colonial revival.

For a schedule at any of the above theaters, check the listings in *Los Angeles* magazine (www.lamag.com), available at most area newsstands, or the "Calendar" section of the Sunday *Los Angeles Times* (www.latimes.com/theguide/); or call the box offices at the numbers listed above.

SMALLER PLAYHOUSES & COMPANIES

On any given night, there's more live theater to choose from in Los Angeles than in New York City, due in part to the surfeit of ready actors and writers chomping at the bit to make it in Tinseltown. Many of today's familiar faces from film and

TV spent plenty of time cutting their teeth on L.A.'s busy theater circuit, which is home to nearly 200 small and medium-size theaters and theater companies, ranging from the 'round-the-corner, neighborhood variety to high-profile, polished troupes of veteran actors. With so many options, navigating the scene to find the best work can be a monumental task. A good bet is to choose one of the theaters listed below, which have established excellent reputations for their consistently high-quality productions; otherwise, consult the *L.A. Weekly* (www.laweekly.com), which advertises most current productions, or call **LA Stage Alliance** (© **213/614-0556;** http://lastagealliance.com) for up-to-date performance listings.

In the same complex as Walt Disney Concert Hall, **REDCAT** (an acronym for the Roy and Edna Disney/CalArts Theater) is a relatively new multiuse forum for cutting-edge performance and media arts. Befitting its ultramodern location, the REDCAT is one of the most versatile and technologically advanced presentation spaces in the world. Be sure to arrive a bit early so you can visit the REDCAT lounge and bookstore for a pre-performance espresso or cocktail—wrapped in signature Frank Gehry plywood, it's one of the best-kept secret bars in the city. The REDCAT is located at 631 W. Second St. at the southwest corner of the Walt Disney Concert Hall (© **213/237-2800;** www.redcat.org).

The **Colony Studio Theatre,** 555 N. Third St., Burbank (© **818/558-7000;** www.colonytheatre.org), was formed in 1975 and has developed from a part-time ensemble of TV actors longing for their theatrical roots into a nationally recognized company. The company produces plays in all genres at the 276-seat Burbank Center Stage, which is shared with other performing arts groups.

Actors Circle Theater, 7313 Santa Monica Blvd., West Hollywood (© **323/882-6805;** www.actorscircle.net), is a 47-seater that's as acclaimed as it is tiny. Look for original contemporary works throughout the year.

Founded in 1965, **East West Players,** 120 N. Judge John Aiso St., Los Angeles (© **213/625-7000;** www.eastwestplayers.org), is the oldest Asian-American theater company in the United States. It's been so successful that the company moved from a 99-seat venue to the 200-seat David Henry Hwang Theater in downtown L.A.'s Little Tokyo.

The **L.A. Theatre Works** (© **310/827-0889**) is renowned for its marriage of media and theater and has performed more than 500 plays and logged more than 1,000 hours of on-air programming. Performances are held at the Skirball Cultural Center, nestled in the Sepulveda Pass near the Getty Center. In the past, personalities such as Richard Dreyfuss, Julia Louis-Dreyfus, Jason Robards, Annette Bening, and John Lithgow have given award-winning performances of plays by Arthur Miller, Neil Simon, Joyce Carol Oates, and more. For nearly 2 decades, the group has performed simultaneously for viewing and listening audiences in its radio theater series. Tickets are usually around $49; a full performance schedule can be found online at **www.latw.org**.

Classical Music & Opera

While L.A. is best known for its pop realms, other types of music here consist of top-flight orchestras and companies—both local and visiting—to fulfill the most demanding classical music appetites; scan the papers to find out who's performing while you're in the city.

The world-class **Los Angeles Philharmonic** (© **323/850-2000;** www.laphil.org), the only major classical music company in Los Angeles, just got a

Walt Disney Concert Hall. BELOW: Gustavo Dudamel, Walt Disney Concert Hall.

whole lot more popular with the completion of its incredible home: the **Walt Disney Concert Hall** (p. 611), at the intersection of First Street and Grand Avenue in historic Bunker Hill. Designed by world-renowned architect Frank Gehry, this addition to the Music Center of L.A. includes a breathtaking concert hall, outdoor park, restaurant, cafe, bookstore, and gift shop.

The Philharmonic's Venezuelan-born music director, Gustavo Dudamel, is known for his youthful vigor and passion for classical and Latin compositions; he does an excellent job attracting first-time audiences. In addition to performances at the Walt Disney Concert Hall, the Philharmonic plays a summer season at the **Hollywood Bowl** (see "Concerts Under the Stars," below).

Slowly but surely, the **Los Angeles Opera** (𝓒 **213/972-8001;** www.losangelesopera.com), which performs at the **Dorothy Chandler Pavilion,** is gaining respect and popularity with inventive stagings of classic pieces, modern operas, visiting divas, and the contributions from high-profile general director Plácido Domingo. The 120-voice **Los Angeles Master Chorale** sings a varied repertoire that includes classical and pop compositions. Concerts are held at the **Walt Disney Concert Hall** (𝓒 **213/972-7200**) September through May.

The **UCLA Center for the Performing Arts** (𝓒 **310/825-2101;** www.uclalive.org) has presented music, dance, and theatrical performances of unparalleled quality for more than 60 years and continues to be a major presence in the local and national cultural landscape. Presentations occur at several theaters around Los Angeles, both on and off campus. UCLA's **Royce Hall** is the Center's pride; it has even been compared to New York's Carnegie Hall. Standouts from the Center's busy calendar have included the famous Gyuto Monks Tibetan

Tantric Choir and the Cinderella story *Cendrillon*, with an original score by Sergei Prokofiev.

Concerts Under the Stars

Hollywood Bowl ★★★  Built in the early 1920s, the elegant Greek-style natural outdoor amphitheater, cradled in a small mountain canyon, is the summer home of the Los Angeles Philharmonic and Hollywood Bowl orchestras, and often hosts internationally known conductors and soloists on Tuesday and Thursday nights. Friday and Saturday concerts typically feature orchestral swing or pops concerts. The summer season also includes a jazz series; past performers have included Natalie Cole, Dionne War-

Hollywood Bowl performance.

wick, and Chick Corea. Other events, from standard rock-'n'-roll acts such as Radiohead to Garrison Keillor programs, summer fireworks galas, and the annual Mariachi Festival, are often on the season's schedule.

To round out an evening at the Bowl, many concertgoers use the occasion to prepare or purchase a picnic dinner and a bottle of wine—it's one of L.A.'s grandest traditions. Call ✆ **323/850-1885** by 4pm the day before you go to place your food order if you plan to utilize the services of on-site Patina Catering Group. Arrive a couple of hours before the show starts, in order to dine while listening to the orchestra or band tune up. 2301 N. Highland Ave. (at Pat Moore Way), Hollywood. ✆ **323/850-2000.** www.hollywoodbowl.com.

The Greek Theatre ★★ Located inside Griffith Park, this scenic outdoor amphitheater holds 5,800 guests, and has received the accolade of being North America's Best Small Outdoor Venue by trade publication *Pollstar Magazine.* Over the years, it's been the site of everything from Neil Diamond's infamous *Hot August Night* live concert album to the destination of Russell Brand's maniacal main character Aldous Snow in the 2010 film *Get Him to the Greek.* 2700 N. Vermont Ave., Los Angeles. ✆ **323/665-3125.** www.greektheatrela.com.

The Club & Music Scene

The Avalon Hollywood Formerly known as the Palace, this 1,100-capacity theater and nightclub—just across Vine from the famed Capitol Records tower—has been the site of numerous significant classical to alternative rock shows for more than 60 years; everyone from Frank Sinatra to Nirvana has performed inside this Art Deco gem. After a much-needed makeover when it became the Avalon, club nights feature famous DJs such as Felix da Housecat and Sebastian Ingrosso. 1735 N. Vine St., Hollywood. ✆ **323/462-8900.** www.avalonhollywood.com.

Fais Do-Do ★   Most nights, this New Orleans–style nightspot hosts jazz, blues, and the occasional rock combo. It's in a once-upscale suburb west of downtown, but the surrounding neighborhood has become somewhat sketchy. Originally built as a bank, the building has gone through several jazz-club incarnations. (It's even rumored that Miles Davis once graced the stage.) The club offers great music in a memorable atmosphere, as well as good Cajun and soul food from the busy kitchen. 5257 W. Adams Blvd., Los Angeles. ✆ **323/931-4636.** www. faisdodo.com.

House of Blues ★   With three great bars, signature Southern art, and a key Sunset Strip location, there are plenty of reasons music fans and industry types keep coming back to House of Blues. Night after night, audiences are dazzled by performances from nationally and internationally acclaimed acts as diverse as the Black Eyed Peas, Motorhead, and Prince. The food in the upstairs restaurant can be good (reservations are a must), and the Sunday Gospel Brunch, though a bit pricey, puts a mean raise on the roof. 8430 Sunset Blvd., West Hollywood. ✆ **323/848-5100.** www.hob.com.

Largo at the Coronet ★   In 2008, this longstanding music venue moved from its Fairfax Village home to the aging Coronet Theatre near the Beverly Center. After some major refurbishment, the main stage is a comfortable 280-seater, and there's an intimate 60-seat room aptly named The Little Room. There's an eclectic array of performances, ranging from the plugged-in folk set to vibrant trip hoppers, and pop-music archaeologist Jon Brion continues his amazing Friday-night shows (which are now monthly versus weekly). It's (thankfully) no longer a dinner theater. Everyone from Fiona Apple to Randy Newman to comedians Sarah Silverman and Will Ferrell has performed here. This is an all-ages club. 366 N. La Cienega Blvd., Los Angeles. ✆ **310/855-0350.** www.largo-la.com.

The Roxy Theatre   Veteran record producer/executive Lou Adler opened this Sunset Strip club in the mid-1970s with concerts by Neil Young and a lengthy run of the premovie *Rocky Horror Show.* Since then, it's remained among the top showcase venues in Hollywood. Although the revitalized Troubadour and such new entries as the House of Blues challenge its preeminence among cozy clubs, you can still find national acts such as the Black Crowes, who will pop in, and great local bands. 9009 W. Sunset Blvd. ✆ **310/278-9457.** www.theroxyonsunset.com.

Satellite ★   The wall-to-wall mirrors and shiny brass posts decorating the interior create the feeling that, in a past life, Satellite, formerly named Spaceland, must've been a seedy strip joint, but the club's current personality offers something entirely different. Having hosted countless performances by artists such as Pavement, Mary Lou Lord, Elliot Smith, and Beck, this hot spot on the fringe of east Hollywood has become one of the most important clubs on the L.A. circuit. 1717 Silver Lake Blvd. ✆ **323/661-4380.** www.thesatellitela.com.

The Troubadour   This West Hollywood mainstay radiates rock history—from the 1960s to the present days, the Troub really has seen 'em all. Audiences are consistently treated to memorable shows from the already-established or young-and-promising acts that take the Troubadour's stage. But bring your earplugs—this beer- and sweat-soaked club likes it loud. All ages are accepted. 9081 Santa Monica Blvd., West Hollywood. ✆ **310/276-6168.** www.troubadour.com.

Villains Tavern ★   Downtown has had a fair share of cool nightlife venues opening in Bunker Hill and South Park, but this L.A. River–adjacent property is

Satellite.

truly boundary-pushing. Done up in Steampunk style, all of the pieces fit together nicely here: from a small but satisfying pub-grub menu (juicy burger, addictive fried chickpeas) and artisanal, original cocktails to a jarringly friendly crowd and a roster of talented old-timey Americana bands. 1356 Palmetto St. ✆ **213/613-0766.** www.villainstavern.com.

Viper Room This world-famous club on the Strip has been king of the hill since it was first opened by actor Johnny Depp and co-owner Sal Jenco back in 1993. With an intensely electric and often star-filled scene, the intimate rock club is also known for unforgettable late-night surprise performances from such powerhouses as the late Johnny

Partying at Whisky A Go-Go.

Cash, Iggy Pop, Tom Petty, Slash, and Trapt (to name but a few) after headline gigs elsewhere in town. 8852 Sunset Blvd., West Hollywood. ✆ **310/358-1880.** www.viperroom.com.

Whisky A Go-Go ★ This legendary bi-level venue personifies L.A. rock 'n' roll, from Jim Morrison and X to Guns N' Roses and Beck. Every trend has passed through this club, and it continues to be the most vital venue of its kind. With the hiring of an in-house booker a few years ago, the Whisky began showcasing more local talent. All ages are welcome. 8901 Sunset Blvd., West Hollywood. ✆ **310/652-4202.** www.whiskyagogo.com.

The Wiltern ★★   Saved from the wrecking ball in the mid-1980s, this 1930s-era Art Deco showcase is perhaps the most beautiful theater in town. Countless national and international acts such as Pearl Jam and Pete Yorn have played here. In addition, plenty of non–pop music events such as Penn & Teller and Cedric the Entertainer complement the schedule. 3790 Wilshire Blvd., Los Angeles. ☎ **213/ 388-1400.** www.livenation.com/The-Wiltern-tickets-Los-Angeles/venue/73790.

Winston's   The lack of a sign gives you a pretty good indication of the type of hip, in-the-know crowd you'll encounter at this tiny West Hollywood bar opened by überhip owners Andy Fiscella (of "Dime" fame) and *GQ* editor Chris Huvane. The decor is pure 1920s Tinseltown, with DJs spinning vintage '80s and '90s for young starlets such as Lindsay Lohan, Mary Kate Olsen, and Jessica Alba. Plan on snotty service, strong drinks, and attitude in abundance. Oh, and good luck getting in on a weekend night if you don't have the right look. 7746 Santa Monica Blvd., West Hollywood. ☎ **323/654-0105.** www.winstonsla.com.

DANCE CLUBS

The Kress   This former historic department store (and Frederick's of Hollywood headquarters after that) is now a four-story entertainment complex in the heart of Hollywood. After a $7-million renovation, it's very opulent and Art Deco–y, the kind of place where Paris Hilton would want to hold a masquerade party (she did in 2008). There's a nightclub in the basement, an Asian-inspired restaurant on the ground floor—which basically turns into a club after 10pm on the weekends—and an exclusive rooftop with cabanas offering sweeping views of the city, including the Hollywood sign. The club is open only Friday and Saturday nights (unless there's a special event or private party); the cover is $20 for basement and third-floor access. *Tip:* You can skirt the entrance fee and get priority access if you have dinner at the restaurant (with a $20 minimum per person). But if you want access to the roof, you'll need to pony up for bottle service, or somehow magically get on a promoter's list (but still be prepared to wait), or just happen to be a hot girl. 6608 Hollywood Blvd., Hollywood. ☎ **323/785-5000.** www.thekress.net. Fri–Sat 6pm–2pm.

Zanzibar ★   A DJ'd musical extravaganza in Santa Monica, this club hosts an eclectic mix of hip-hop, Afro funk, boogie, nu jazz, and future soul in a

---

Dinner-&-a-Show-&-DJs-&-Dancing

For a truly surreal spin on the old dinner-and-a-movie date night, or for a fun group outing, check out **Hollywood's Supperclub.** Based on an all-in-one restaurant, DJ, performance art, and after-party dancing concept that began in Amsterdam, Hollywood's old Vogue theater has been transformed into an avant-garde party space. The evening typically begins in the lobby with an amuse-bouche and a shot, then moves to the middle staging room (in neither place are you more than a few feet from a bar), before the curtains are drawn and guests are escorted to their "beds" (more like flat couches). A multicourse meal ensues while DJs spin everything from George Michael to Afrika Bambaataa. Interactivity is key, be it with costumed performers or flirtatious neighbors. 6675 Hollywood Blvd., Hollywood. ☎ **323/466-1900.** www.supperclub.com. From $75 all-inclusive.

Moroccan-style environment with leather ottomans, low upholstered benches, and curtains that you can pull when you want a little privacy. 1301 Fifth St., Santa Monica. ✆ **310/451-2221.** www.zanzibarlive.com.

Bars & Cocktail Lounges

Bar Nineteen12 I'll take any excuse to walk through the front doors of the luscious Beverly Hills Hotel and rub shoulders with the celebs who love to hang out here. Me, I'm out on the veranda nursing a $14 Spanish Manhattan (secret ingredient: sherry!) while lounging on the golden-toned velvet sofas and high-backed leather chairs. This is the more contemporary alternative to the classic Polo Lounge, which *is* your grandfather's martini bar. ***Tip:*** Tables can be booked in advance—without having to order bottle service, which is a rarity for bars in L.A. 9641 Sunset Blvd., Beverly Hills. ✆ **310/273-1912.** www.barnineteen12.com.

Beauty Bar It's a proven concept in New York, Las Vegas, and San Francisco: a cocktail lounge/beauty salon. Decorated with vintage salon gear and sporting a hip-retro vibe, the Beauty Bar is both campy and trendy. Where else can you actually get a manicure while sipping cocktails with such names as the Shampoo (a combination of vodka, ginger, bitters, and muddled lemons) or the Platinum Blonde (Malibu rum and pineapple)? Known as the Martinis & Manicures happy hour, the special runs Thursday to Saturday from 7 to 11pm. 1638 N. Cahuenga Blvd., Hollywood. ✆ **323/464-7676.** www.thebeautybar.com/los_angeles.

The Dresden Room ★★ Hugely popular with L.A. hipsters because of its longevity, location, and elegant ambience, "The Den" was pushed into the mainstream of L.A. nightlife thanks to its inclusion in the movie *Swingers.* But it's the timeless lounge act of Marty and Elayne (the couple has been performing there up to 5 nights a week since 1982) that has proven that, fad or no fad, this place is always cool. Sidle up to the bar for a glass of the sweet house classic Blood and Sand cocktail. 1760 N. Vermont Ave., Hollywood. ✆ **323/665-4294.** www.thedresden.com.

Glow 🎁 Yes, it's at the Marriott Hotel in Marina del Rey, but I know what you're thinking and you're wrong—this place is swank. Not nearly as swank as Hollywood hotel bars like the Tropicana Bar or the Skybar, but very nice for the area, which is otherwise lacking in upscale nightlife options. The outdoor venue literally glows in shades of deep amber as post-meeting groups, young neighborhood types, and pleasantly surprised hotel guests lounge in semiprivate booths and order bottle service from the lithe staff. 4100 Admiralty Way, Marina del Rey. ✆ **310/578-4152.** www.glow-bar.com.

Good Luck Bar Until they installed a flashing neon sign outside, only locals and hipsters knew about this kung fu–themed room in the Los Feliz area. The dark red windowless interior boasts Asian ceiling tiles, fringed Chinese paper lanterns, sweet-but-deadly drinks such as the Yee Mee Loo (translated as "blue drink"), and a jukebox with selections ranging from Thelonious Monk to Cher's "Half-Breed." The spacious sitting room, furnished with mismatched sofas, armchairs, and banquettes, provides a great atmosphere for conversation or romance. Arrive early to avoid the throngs of L.A. scenesters. 1514 Hillhurst Ave. (btw. Hollywood and Sunset blvds.), Los Angeles. ✆ **323/666-3524.**

Nic's Beverly Hills ★ There's nothing like a really good martini to take the edge off, and some of the best I've ever had are poured at Nic's. Unlike the surrounding Beverly Hills establishments, there's no attitude here, just lots of retro-groovy slippery white leather, bold colorful stripes, and laid-back locals noshing on cocktail cuisine while listening to good jazz bands and big-band trios. Owner Larry Nicola takes pride in his self-anointed title as "Vodkateur," or vodka expert. In fact, he built a walk-in freezer called a VODBOX just so he could have a proper tasting room where his guests can sample the best vodkas from around the world. 453 N. Canon Dr., Beverly Hills. ✆ **310/550-5707.** www.nicsbeverlyhills.com.

Skybar ✋ Since its opening in hotelier Ian Schraeger's refurbished Sunset Strip hotel, Skybar has been a favorite among L.A.'s most fashionable of the fashionable set. This place was at one time so hot that even the agents to the stars needed agents to get in—rumor has it that one agent was so desperate to gain entrance that he promised one of the servers a contract—but this is a fickle town, and the young and hot have moved on to greener pastures. Nevertheless, the view is still spectacular and you may yet get to rub elbows with some of the faces that regularly appear on the cover of *People* (but please don't stare). 8440 W. Sunset Blvd., West Hollywood. ✆ **323/848-6025.** www.mondrianhotel.com.

The Standard Downtown ★★ This rooftop bar, located atop the Standard Hotel in downtown L.A. (formerly Superior Oil headquarters), is surrounded by high office towers and helipads, and the view is magnificent. The skyscrapers act like strangely glowing lava lamps in the night sky as exotic ladies sip exotic cocktails amid waterbeds and bent-plastic loungers. 550 S. Flower St. ✆ **213/892-8080.** www.standardhotel.com.

Whiskey Blue When ascending the dramatic backlit staircase and entering the dimly lit, seductive interior, it's hard to believe Whiskey Blue in the W Hotel is situated on UCLA's Sorority Row. The atmosphere is as chic as the decor, which features high screen partitions, low cushioned couches, sleek private rooms, and a row of carved stumps of wood where manicured martinis may be set. Patrons are encouraged to dress their best, especially on the weekends, when the Westside's glitterati come out to this scene to be seen. Hotel guests are given priority entrance. 930 Hilgard Ave., Westwood. ✆ **310/443-8232.**

Comedy Clubs

Acme Comedy Theater The Acme players provide a barrage of laughs with their improv and sketch comedy acts—a veritable grab bag of funnies. 135 N. La Brea Ave., Hollywood. ✆ **323/525-0202.** www.acmecomedy.com. Cover $8–$17.

Comedy Store ★ You can't go wrong here: New comics develop their material, and established ones work out their kinks at this landmark owned by Mitzi Shore (Pauly's mom). The Main Room, which seats 350, features professional stand-ups continuously on Friday and Saturday nights. Several comedians are always featured, each doing about a 15-minute stint. The talent is always first-rate and includes comics who regularly appear on *The Tonight Show* and other shows. The **Original Room,** which seats 150, features a dozen or so comedians back-to-back nightly, whereas the smaller Belly Room is for development. As Mitzi likes to say, "Life begins in the Belly," so you never know what you might get there. Sundays and Mondays Potluck night is amateur night: Anyone with enough guts can take the stage for 3 minutes—Lord only knows what you'll see, though celebs have been known to "pop in." 8433 Sunset Blvd., West Hollywood. ✆ **323/650-6268.** www.comedystore.com. Cover free–$20, plus 2-drink minimum. Always 21 and over.

Groundling Theater ★ L.A.'s answer to Chicago's Second City has been around for more than 25 years, yet it remains the most innovative and funny group in town. The skits change every year or so, but they take new improvisational twists every night and the satire is often savage. The Groundlings were the springboard to fame for Pee-wee Herman, Elvira, and former *Saturday Night Live* stars Jon Lovitz, Phil Hartman, and Julia "It's Pat" Sweeney. Phone for showtimes and reservations. 7307 Melrose Ave., Los Angeles. ✆ **323/934-4747.** www.groundlings. com. Tickets $10–$17.

The Improv A showcase for top stand-ups since 1975, the Improv offers something different each night. Although it used to have a fairly active music schedule, the place is now mostly doing what it does best—showcasing comedy. Owner Budd Freedman's buddies—such as Jay Leno, Billy Crystal, and Robin Williams—hone their skills here more often than you would expect. But even if the comedians on the bill are all unknowns, they won't be for long. Shows are at 8pm Sunday and Thursday, and at 8:30 and 10:30pm Friday and Saturday. 8162 Melrose Ave., West Hollywood. ✆ **323/651-2583.** www.improvclubs.com. Tickets average $14, plus 2-drink minimum.

Laugh Factory ★ Yes, this is where Michael Richards made his infamous racist comments toward two black men who were heckling him (and where Mr. Richards is no longer welcome). In fact, just about every comedian you've seen on TV—living or dead—has been a regular at the Laugh Factory: Rodney Dangerfield, Dave Chappelle, Robin Williams, Richard Pryor, Jim Carrey, Jerry Seinfeld, and others. The best night to attend is the Friday All Star Comedy show, because you never know when a celebrity guest is going to sneak onstage and try out a new routine. 8001 Sunset Blvd., Hollywood. ✆ **323/656-1336.** www.laughfactory. com. Tickets $20–$35, plus 2-drink minimum.

Late-Night Bites

Finding places to dine in the wee hours is getting easier in L.A., as each year sees the opening of more 24-hour and after-midnight restaurants and diners.

The Apple Pan ★★ This classic American burger shack, an L.A. landmark, hasn't changed much since 1947—and its burgers and pies continue to hit the spot. Open until 1am Friday and Saturday, and until midnight other nights; closed Monday. 10801 W. Pico Blvd., West L.A. ✆ **310/475-3585.**

Canter's Fairfax Restaurant, Delicatessen & Bakery This 24-hour Jewish deli has been a winner with late-nighters since it opened more than 66 years ago. If you show up after the clubs close, you're sure to spot a bleary-eyed celebrity or two alongside the rest of the after-hours crowd, chowing down on a giant pastrami sandwich, matzo-ball soup, potato pancakes, or other deli favorites. Try a potato knish with a side of brown gravy—trust me, you'll love it. 419 N. Fairfax Ave., West Hollywood. ✆ **323/651-2030.**

Dolores's One of L.A.'s oldest surviving coffee shops, Dolores's offers just what you might expect: Naugahyde, laminated counters, lots of linoleum, and comforting predictability. Expect the usual coffee shop fare of pancakes, burgers, and eggs at this 24-hour joint. 11407 Santa Monica Blvd., Los Angeles. ✆ **310/477-1061.**

Du-par's Restaurant & Bakery ★ Open 24 hours, this popular Valley coffee shop serves early-morning "beat the clock" specials from 4 to 6am, and blue-plate specials from 6 to 11am. 12036 Ventura Blvd. (1 block east of Laurel Canyon), Studio City. ✆ **818/766-4437.**

Jerry's Famous Deli ★   Valley hipsters head to 24-hour Jerry's to satiate the late-night munchies. 12655 Ventura Blvd. (east of Coldwater Canyon Ave.), Studio City. © 818/980-4245.

Kate Mantilini ★   Kate's serves stylish nouveau comfort food in a striking setting. It's open until midnight Sunday and Monday, Tuesday through Thursday until 1am, and Friday and Saturday until 2am. 9101 Wilshire Blvd. (at Doheny Dr.), Beverly Hills. © 310/278-3699.

Mel's Drive-In   Straight from an episode of *Happy Days*, this 24-hour 1950s diner on the Sunset Strip attracts customers ranging from chic shoppers during the day to rock-'n'-rollers at night. The fries and shakes here are among the more popular dishes. 8585 Sunset Blvd. (west of La Cienega), West Hollywood. © 310/854-7200.

101 Coffee Shop   This retro coffee shop right out of the early '60s has rock walls, funky colored tiles, comfy booths, and cool light fixtures, all pulled together nicely in a hip yet subdued fashion. Count on tasty grinds until 2:45am (try the breakfast burritos or the creamy mac and cheese). 6145 Franklin Ave., Hollywood. © 323/467-1175.

The Original Pantry   Owned by former Los Angeles mayor Richard Riordan, this downtown diner has been serving huge portions of comfort food round-the-clock for more than 60 years; in fact, they don't even have a key to the front door (there's no lock)! See p. 597 for a full review. 877 S. Figueroa St. (at Ninth St.), downtown. © 213/972-9279.

Pink's Hot Dogs   Many a woozy hipster has awakened with the telltale signs of a post-cocktailing trip to this greasy streetside hot dog stand—the oniony morning-after breath and chili stains on your shirt are dead giveaways. Open Friday and Saturday until 3am, and all other nights until 2am. See p. 595 for a full review. 709 N. La Brea Ave., Los Angeles. © 323/931-4223.

Swingers ★   This hip coffee shop keeps L.A. scene-stealers happy with its retro comfort food. Open daily until 4am. A second location is at 802 Broadway (at Lincoln Ave.; © 310/393-9793) in Santa Monica. 8020 Beverly Blvd. (west of Fairfax Ave.), Hollywood. © 323/653-5858.

Toi on Sunset ★   Those requiring a little more oomph from their late-night snack should come here. At this colorful and *loud* hangout, garbled pop-culture metaphors mingle with the tastes and aromas of "rockin' Thai" cuisine in delicious ways until 4am nightly. 7505½ Sunset Blvd. (at Gardner), Hollywood. © 323/874-8062.

14

SIDE TRIPS FROM LOS ANGELES

by Tara de Lis

T he area within a 100-mile radius of Los Angeles is one of the world's most diverse regions. You can find arid deserts, rugged mountains, historic towns, alpine lakes, and even an island paradise. In the following pages, I cover a variety of the best attractions beyond Los Angeles County, such as the smog-free mountain communities of Big Bear and Lake Arrowhead, Disneyland and Knott's Berry Farm amusement parks, So Cal beach towns such as Newport and Huntington Beach, and the ultimate L.A. weekend getaway, Catalina Island. From L.A., you can reach most of these scenic side trips in less than an hour by car or by boat—for an easy, refreshing diversion from the big-city scene.

LONG BEACH & THE *QUEEN MARY*

21 miles S of downtown L.A.

The fifth-largest city in California, Long Beach is best known as the permanent home of the former cruise liner *Queen Mary* and the Long Beach Grand Prix, whose star-studded warm-up race has included hipster Jason Priestly and formerly perennial racer Paul Newman burning rubber through the streets of the city in mid-April.

Essentials

GETTING THERE   See chapter 17 for airport and airline information. Driving from Los Angeles, take either I-5 or I-405 to I-710 south, which leads directly to both downtown Long Beach and the *Queen Mary* Seaport.

ORIENTATION   Downtown Long Beach is at the eastern end of the vast Port of Los Angeles; Pine Avenue is the central restaurant and shopping street, which extends south to Shoreline Park and the Aquarium. The *Queen Mary* is docked just across the waterway, gazing south toward tiny Long Beach marina and Naples Island. See the beginning of this guide for a color map of the Long Beach area.

VISITOR INFORMATION   Contact the **Long Beach Area Convention & Visitors Bureau,** 301 E. Ocean Blvd, Ste. 1900 (© **800/452-7829** or 562/436-3645; www.visitlongbeach.com). For information on the **Long Beach Grand Prix,** call © **562/981-2600** or check out **www.longbeachgp.com**.

The Major Attractions

Aquarium of the Pacific ★ ☺   This enormous aquarium—one of the largest in the U.S.—is the cornerstone of Long Beach's ever-changing waterfront.

PREVIOUS PAGE: **International Surfing Museum, Huntington Beach.**

Figuring that what stimulated flagging economies in Monterey and Baltimore would work in Long Beach, planners gave their all to this project, creating a crowd-pleasing attraction just across the harbor from Long Beach's other mainstay, the *Queen Mary*. The vast facility—it has enough exhibit space to fill three football fields—re-creates three areas of the Pacific: the warm Baja and Southern California regions, the Bering Sea and chilly northern Pacific, and faraway tropical climes, including impressive re-creations of a lagoon and barrier reef. There are more than 11,000 creatures in all, from 150 sharks (some you can touch, some you can't) prowling a 90,000-gallon habitat to delicate sea horses, moon jellies, and gaggles of tropical birds within the Lorikeet Forest. Learn little-known aquatic facts at the many educational exhibits, or come nose-to-nose with sea lions, moray eels, and other inhabitants of giant tanks up to nearly three stories high.

100 Aquarium Way, off Shoreline Dr., Long Beach. 562/590-3100. www.aquariumofpacific. org. Admission $25 adults, $22 seniors 62 and over, $13 children 3–11, free for children 2 and under. Daily 9am–6pm. Parking $8. Closed Christmas Day and Toyota Grand Prix weekend (mid-Apr).

The *Queen Mary* ★   It's easy to dismiss this old cruise ship/museum as a barnacle-laden tourist trap, but it's the only surviving example of this particular kind of 20th-century elegance and excess. From the staterooms paneled lavishly in now-extinct tropical hardwoods to the perfectly preserved crew quarters and the miles of hallway handrails made of once-pedestrian Bakelite, wonders never cease aboard this 81,237-ton Art Deco luxury liner. Stroll the teakwood decks with just a bit of imagination, and you're back in 1936 on the maiden voyage from Southampton, England. Don't miss the streamlined modern observation lounge, featured often in period motion pictures; have drinks and listen to some live jazz. Kiosk displays of photographs and memorabilia are everywhere—following the success of the movie *Titanic*, the *Queen Mary* even hosted an exhibit of artifacts from its less fortunate cousin. The Cold War–era Soviet submarine *Scorpion* resides alongside; separate admission is required to tour the sub. ***Tip:*** Buy a First Class Passage ticket to both the sub and the ship, and you'll also get a behind-the-scenes guided tour, peppered with worthwhile anecdotes and details—plus all the bells and whistles (and dramatic lighting effects) of the Ghosts and Legends Tour—well worth the extra $8.

> **Save Some Cash**
>
> If you plan on visiting the *Queen Mary* and the Aquarium the same day, you can purchase a combined ticket package at either venue for $36 ($20 for kids 5–11). You'll save about $10 (hey, that's a free lunch).

1126 Queen's Hwy. (end of I-710), Long Beach. 800/437-2934. www.queenmary.com. Admission $25 adults, $22 seniors 55 and over and military, $13 children 5–11, free for children 4 and under. First Class Passage admission $33 adults, $29 seniors ages 55 and over and military, $20 children 5–11, free for children 4 and under. Daily 10am–6pm. Parking $12.

Where to Stay

Hotel Queen Mary ★ 📠   The *Queen Mary* isn't only a piece of maritime history; it's also a hotel. But although the historic ocean liner is considered the most luxurious vessel ever to sail the Atlantic, with some of the largest rooms built aboard a ship, the quarters aren't exceptional when compared to those on terra firma today, nor are the amenities. The idea is to enjoy the novelty and charm of

The Los Angeles Area

features such as the original bathtub water faucets ("cold salt," "cold fresh," "hot salt," "hot fresh")—along with the more modern duplicate features (there are two of many things!). The beautifully carved interior is a feast for the eye and fun to explore, and the weekday rates are hard to beat. Three onboard restaurants are overpriced but convenient (though the new Chelsea Chowder House is showing promise), and the shopping arcade has a decidedly British feel (one sells great *Queen Mary* souvenirs). An elegant Sunday champagne brunch—complete with ice sculpture and a harpist—is served in the ship's Grand Salon, and it's always worthwhile to have a cocktail in the Art Deco Observation Bar. If you're too young to have traveled on the old luxury liners, this is the perfect opportunity to experience the romance of an Atlantic crossing—with no seasickness or cabin fever.

1126 Queen's Hwy. (end of I-710), Long Beach, CA 90802-6390. www.queenmary.com. © **800/ 437-2934.** 365 units. Inside cabin from $110; deluxe cabin from $164; suite from $360. Many packages available. AE, DC, MC, V. Valet parking $19; self-parking $15. **Amenities:** 3 restaurants; spa. *In room:* A/C, TV, Wi-Fi ($9.95 per day).

Where to Eat

The Sky Room ★★ CALIFORNIAN/FRENCH It takes a 40-minute drive from Los Angeles to Long Beach to get a sense of what fine dining must have been like during Hollywood's Golden Age. Built in 1926 and meticulously restored by proprietor Bernard Rosenson, the restaurant's Art Deco–period design inspires oohs and aahs among first-time guests. Awash in brilliant white, the interior's massive pillars, curvaceous ramps, glimmering brass, elevated maple-and-ebony dance floor, and classic jazz band playing enticing dance tunes all combine to create the illusion of dining on a luxury ocean liner (the view of the stately *Queen Mary* certainly enhances the effect). Opulence continues with white Frette linens, custom black-rimmed china, Villeroy & Boch tableware, and a *Wine Spectator* award–winning wine list. The Californian/French menu offers a pleasing presentation of the classics: scallops with sweet potato purée, prime rib-eye with pommes frites, and *osso buco*. Nothing groundbreaking here, but that's not what the Sky Room is about. I highly recommend that you take the advice of the experienced waitstaff and sommelier; our duo handled the task flawlessly. A night of dinner, drinking, dancing, and romance—what's not to like?

40 S. Locust Ave. (at Ocean Blvd.), Long Beach, CA 90802. © **562/983-2703.** www.theskyroom. com. Reservations recommended. Dinner main courses $27–$45. AE, DC, DISC, MC, V. Mon-Thurs 5:30–9pm; Fri–Sat 5:30pm–midnight; Sun 4:30–9pm. Valet parking $7.

Yard House ★ AMERICAN ECLECTIC Not only does it have one of the best outdoor dining venues in Long Beach, but the Yard House also features one of the *world's* largest selection of draft beers. The keg room houses more than 1,000 gallons of beer, all visible through a glass door, where you can see the golden liquids transported to a signature oval bar via miles of nylon tubing to the dozens of taps. The restaurant takes its name from the early colonial tradition of serving beer in 36-inch-tall glasses—or yards—to weary stagecoach drivers. Customers are encouraged to partake in this tradition and can drink from the glass yards, as well as half-yards and traditional pint glasses. Signature dishes range from the tortelike California roll to the crab-cake hoagie and an impressive selection of steaks and chops. There's also an extensive list of appetizers—perfect for a tapas-style meal—salads, pasta, and rice dishes, as well as sandwiches and individual pizzas (the Thai chicken pizza is excellent, as are the crab cakes and coconut-encrusted shrimp). On sunny days, be sure to request a table on the deck overlooking the picturesque harbor.

401 Shoreline Village Dr., Long Beach. ✆ **562/628-0455.** www.yardhouse.com. Reservations accepted only weekdays until 5pm. Main courses $12–$30. AE, DC, MC, V. Sun–Thurs 11am–midnight; Fri–Sat 11am–2am.

SANTA CATALINA ISLAND

22 miles W of mainland Los Angeles

After an unhealthy dose of the mainland's soupy smog and freeway gridlock, you'll appreciate an excursion to Santa Catalina Island, with its clean air, crystal-clear water, and the blissful absence of traffic. In fact, there isn't a single traffic light on the "Island of Romance." Conditions like these can fool you into thinking that you're miles away from the hustle and bustle of the city, but the reality is that you're only 22 miles off the Southern California coast and *still* in L.A. County.

Because of its relative isolation, out-of-state tourists tend to ignore Santa Catalina—which everyone calls simply Catalina—but those who do make the crossing have plenty of elbowroom to boat, fish, swim, scuba, and snorkel. There are also miles of hiking and biking trails, plus golf and tennis, but the main sport here seems to be barhopping.

Catalina is so different from the mainland that it almost seems like a different country, remote and unspoiled. In 1919, the island was purchased by William Wrigley, Jr., the chewing-gum magnate, who had plans to develop it into a fashionable pleasure resort. To publicize the new vacationland, Wrigley brought big-name bands to the Avalon Ballroom and moved the Chicago Cubs, which he owned, to the island for spring training. His marketing efforts succeeded and Catalina soon became a world-renowned playground, luring such celebrities as Laurel and Hardy, Cecil B. De Mille, John Wayne, and even Winston Churchill.

In 1975, the Santa Catalina Island Conservancy—a nonprofit operating foundation organized to preserve and protect the island's nature habitat—acquired about 88% of Catalina Island, protecting virtually all of the hilly acreage and rugged coastline that make up what is known as the interior. In fact, some of the most spectacular outlying areas can be reached only by arranged tour (see "Exploring the Island," below).

> ## Cart Culture
>
> One of the first things you'll notice when you arrive in Avalon, the only city on the island, is the abundance of golf carts in a comical array of styles and colors. Since Avalon is the only city in California authorized by the state legislature to regulate the number of vehicles allowed to drive on city streets, there are no rental cars and only a handful of privately owned vehicles. For information on renting a golf cart, see "Getting Around," below.

Essentials

GETTING THERE The most common way to get to and from the island is on the **Catalina Express** ferryboat (© **800/481-3470**; www.catalinaexpress.com), which operates up to 30 daily departures year-round from Long Beach, San Pedro, and Dana Point. High-speed catamarans make the trip in about an hour. Captain's and Commodore Lounge upgrades are available. Round-trip fares are $67 for adults, $60 for seniors 55 and over, $51 for children ages 2 to 11, and $4 for infants. Fares for Dana Point are $2 more, except for infants. In San Pedro, the Catalina Express departs from the **Sea/Air Terminal,** Berth 95;

Avalon.

take the Harbor Freeway (I-110) south to the Harbor Boulevard exit and then follow signs to the terminal. In Long Beach, boats leave from the **Catalina Landing;** take the 710 Freeway south into Long Beach. Stay to the left, follow signs to downtown, and exit Golden Shore. Turn right at the stop sign and follow around to the terminal on the right. Parking is in the parking structure on the left. In Dana Point, boats depart from Dana Wharf Sportfishing. From San Diego, take I-5 North and exit at Beach Cities Hwy. 1, left at Dana Point Harbor Drive, then left at Golden Lantern. Call ahead for reservations. **Note:** Check-in at the ticket window is required and begins 1 hour prior to each departure. Passengers must be checked in, holding tickets, and ready to board at least 15 minutes prior to departure (30 min. ahead suggested), or the reservation will be canceled and the credit card will be charged for the full amount of the round-trip fare. Luggage is limited to 70 pounds per person; reservations are necessary for bicycles, surfboards, and dive tanks; and there are restrictions on transporting pets. You can leave your car at designated lots at each departure terminal; the parking fee is around $10 per 24-hour period.

The **Catalina Flyer,** 400 Main St., Balboa (© **949/673-5245**; www.catalinainfo.com), the largest passenger-carrying catamaran on the West Coast, departs daily from Newport Beach's historic Balboa Pavilion. The boat leaves once a day at 9am and returns to Newport at 4:30pm daily. Travel time is about 75 minutes each way. Round-trip fares are $42 for adults, $39 for seniors, $25 for children 12 and under. Pets are not allowed.

Island Express Helicopter Service, 1175 Queens Way Dr., Long Beach (© **800/2-AVALON** [228-2566] or 310/510-2525; www.islandexpress.com), flies from Long Beach (regularly) or San Pedro (seasonally) to Avalon in about 15 minutes. The expense is definitely worth the thrill and convenience, particularly if you're prone to seasickness. It flies on demand between 8am and sunset year-round, charging $104 plus tax each way, or $200 round-trip. The weight limit for luggage, however, is a mere 25 pounds.

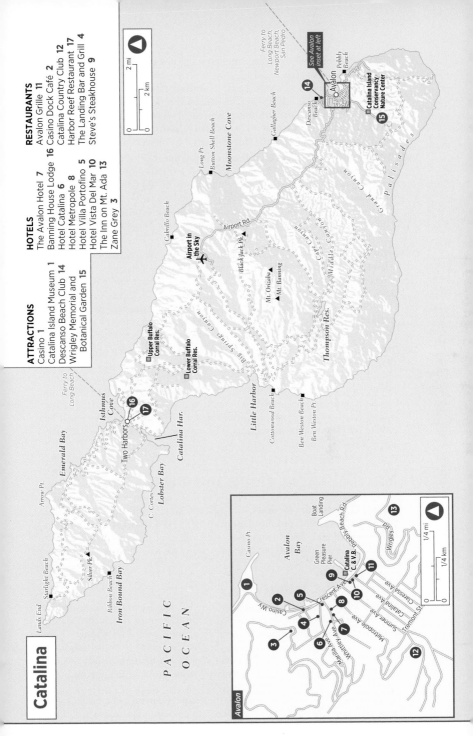

Catalina

PACIFIC OCEAN

Lands End
Starlight Beach
Arrow Pt.
Emerald Bay
Ferry to Long Beach
Isthmus Cove
Silver Pk.
Ribbon Beach
Iron Bound Bay
C. Cortes
Lobster Bay
Two Harbors
Catalina Har.

Upper Buffalo Corral Res.
Lower Buffalo Corral Res.

Little Harbor
Cottonwood Beach
Ben Weston Beach
Ben Weston Pt.

Cabrillo Beach
Airport in the Sky
Airport Rd
Black Jack Pk.
Mt. Orizaba
Mt. Banning

Long Pt.
Button Shell Beach
Moonstone Cove
Gallagher Beach

Thompson Res.

Pebble Beach Rd.

Grand Canyon
Palisades

Ferry to Long Beach, Newport Beach, San Pedro

See Avalon inset at left
Avalon
Descanso Beach
Pebbly Beach

Catalina Island Conservancy Nature Center

2 mi
2 km

Avalon

Casino Pt.
Avalon Bay
Boat Landing
Green Pleasure Pier
Casino Wy.
Crescent Ave.
Catalina C. & V.B.
Marilla Ave.
Whittley Ave.
Metropole Ave.
Sumner Ave.
Catalina Ave.
Claressa Ave.
Tremont St.
Pebbly Beach Rd.
Wrigley Rd.

1/4 mi
1/4 km

It also offers brief air tours over the island; prices vary. In Long Beach, the heliport is located a few hundred yards southwest of the *Queen Mary.*

The 149-passenger catamaran **Catalina Marina del Rey Flyer,** 13737 Fiji Way, C#2, Marina del Rey, CA 90292 (✆ **310/305-7250;** www. catalinaferries.com), departs from Fisherman's Village at Marina del Rey. Schedule varies. Travel time to Avalon is 1¾ hours. Round-trip fare is $90 for adults, $82 for seniors, $69 for children 2 to 11 years old, $5 for infants.

VISITOR INFORMATION   The **Catalina Island Chamber of Commerce and Visitors Bureau,** P.O. Box 217, Avalon, CA 90704 (✆ **310/510-1520;** fax 310/510-7606; www.catalinachamber.com), on the Green Pleasure Pier, distributes brochures and information on island activities, hotels, and transportation. Call for a free visitor's guide. Its colorful website, **www.catalina chamber.com**, offers hotel availability information and local weather, in addition to updated activities and events listings.

ORIENTATION   The picturesque town of **Avalon** is both the port of entry for the island and the island's only city. From the ferry dock, you can wander along Crescent Avenue, the main road along the beachfront, and easily explore adjacent side streets.

Northwest of Avalon is the village of **Two Harbors,** accessible by boat or shuttle bus. Its twin bays are favored by pleasure yachts from L.A.'s various marinas, so there's more camaraderie and a less touristy ambience overall.

GETTING AROUND   Once in Avalon, take **Catalina Taxi Service** (✆ **310/510-0025**) from the heliport or dock to your hotel, and enjoy the quick and colorful trip through town (don't blink or you'll miss it). Only a limited number of cars are permitted on the island; visitors are not allowed to drive cars on the island, and most residents motor around in golf carts (many of the homes have only golf cart–size driveways). Don't worry, though—you'll be able to get everywhere you want to go by renting a cart yourself or just hoofing it, which is what most visitors do.

If you want to explore the area around Avalon beyond where your feet can comfortably carry you, rent a mountain bike or tandem from **Brown's Bikes,** 107 Pebbly Beach Rd. (✆ **310/510-0986;** www.catalinabiking. com). If you'll be exploring, you'll want to rent a gas-powered golf cart from **Cartopia Golf Cart Rentals,** on Crescent Avenue at Pebbly Beach Road (✆ **310/510-2493**), or **Island Rentals** (✆ **310/510-1456**), across from the boat terminal. Both companies offer a map of town for a self-guided tour. Rates are about $50 per hour plus a deposit. You must be 25 or older to drive.

Exploring the Island

ORGANIZED TOURS   The Santa Catalina Island Company's **Discovery Tours** (✆ **800/322-3434** or 310/510-TOUR [8687]; www.visitcatalinaisland. com) has a ticket and information office at the Green Pier and the Tour Plaza, in the center of town. It offers the greatest variety of excursions from Avalon; many last just a couple of hours and don't monopolize your whole day. Tours are available in money-saving combo packs; inquire about them when you call.

Noteworthy excursions include the **Cape Canyon,** which takes you into the heart of Catalina's "outback" in an open-air four-wheel-drive

Mercedes Benz Unimog Vehicle. The tour's rugged route includes the American Bald Eagle and Catalina Island Fox habitats at Middle Ranch, lunch at Airport-in-the-Sky, and plenty of photo stops ($107 adults, $96 seniors and children). You can also try the **Undersea Tour,** a leisurely 45-minute cruise of Lover's Cove Marine Preserve in a semisubmersible vessel that allows you to sit 5 feet under the water in a climate-controlled cabin, where you comfortably observe Catalina's kelp forests by day or night ($32 adults, $23 kids, $28 seniors; discount on night rates). The **Casino Tour** is a fascinating 50-minute look at the style and inventive engineering of this elegant ballroom (see the "Catalina's Grand Casino" box, below; $19 adults, $17 seniors, $14 kids). The Casino also offers a Behind the Scenes Tour ($31 adults, $23 kids, $27 seniors) where you visit the "green rooms" used by Errol Flynn, Cary Grant, and all the big bands; walk across the stage where Benny Goodman played; visit the projection room with the original 1929 equipment on display; and gain unprecedented access to other backstage areas. Both tours include admission to the Catalina Island Museum. The nighttime **Flying Fish Boat Trips** (seasonal) are a 50-minute Catalina tradition in searchlight-equipped open boats ($24 adults, $21 seniors, $18 kids).

Newer tours include the Catalina Zip Line Eco Tour and the Sea Trek Undersea Adventure, as well as Snuba and the GPS Ranger Walking tour. Beginning almost 600 feet above Avalon, the new **Zip Line Eco Tour** ($99 per person) provides a way to see and experience Catalina like never before. The nearly 4,000-foot zipline comprises five separate zips across Descanso Canyon and ends by the seashore at Descanso Beach, with speeds reaching 45 miles per hour and heights of more than 300 feet. Each zip ends at a specially designed platform with spectacular views of the surrounding island interior and ocean. Platforms will have special interpretive signage highlighting the unique flora and fauna of the island.

Whereas the Zip Line Eco Tour provides a view of Catalina from above, the **Sea Trek Undersea Adventure** ($103 per person) and **Snuba** ($69 per person) provide a glimpse from below (no prior diving experience is necessary). Beneath the waves, participants may find themselves surrounded by teeming schools of mackerel or anchovies, observe sea lions or

14

CATALINA'S GRAND casino

No trip to Catalina is complete without taking the **Casino Tour** (see "Organized Tours," above). The Casino Building, Avalon's world-famous Art Deco landmark, is not—and never was—a place to gamble your vacation money away (*casino* is an Italian word for a place of entertainment or gathering). Rather, the incredibly ornate structure (the craftsmanship inside and out is spectacular) is home to the island's only movie theater and the world's largest circular ballroom. Virtually every big band of the '30s and '40s played in the 158-foot-diameter ballroom, carried over CBS radio beginning with its grand opening in May 1929. Today it's a coveted venue for elaborate weddings, dances, gala dinners, and the Catalina Jazz Festival. The 3-week **Jazz-Trax Festival** (✆ **866/872-9849;** www.jazztrax.com) takes place every October. To experience the festival, be sure to book your tickets and accommodations as far in advance as possible.

Instant Massaging

After a full day of island activity, why not pamper yourself with a relaxing professional massage in the privacy and comfort of your hotel room? Make a reservation with **Catalina Sea Spa** (✆ 310/510-8920; www.catalinaseaspa.com), and she'll tote her table and oils to you. Michelle specializes in sports, deep tissue, Swedish, Thai, Swede-Thai combo, and pregnancy massage. Other treatments include sugar glow, foot scrubs, peppermint scalp massage, couples massages, and lavender or honey facial massages. Michelle works in 50- to 80-minute increments, offers packages, and caters to groups. If you're just visiting for the day, Michelle offers her own pampering facility for you to visit. Prices range from $85 to $135.

a solitary bat ray gliding through the blue water, or even catch a glimpse of an octopus or California lobster hiding among the rocks.

The **GPS Walking Tour,** which meanders through the streets of Avalon, offers visitors their own personal high-tech guide to experience the sights at their own pace. The GPS-enabled multimedia units will lead the way, pointing out landmarks and historical points of interest using audio, video, and photos. The tour accommodates up to six people per unit, and guests will have ample time to complete the tour. Cost is $15 per device.

VISITING TWO HARBORS If you want to get a better look at the rugged natural beauty of Catalina and escape the throngs of beachgoers, head over to Two Harbors, the quarter-mile "neck" at the island's northwest end that gets its name from the "twin harbors" on each side, known as the Isthmus and Catalina Harbor. An excellent starting point for campers and hikers, Two Harbors also offers just enough civilization for the less-intrepid traveler.

The **Banning House Lodge** (✆ 800/626-1496; www.visittwoharbors.com) is a 12-room bed-and-breakfast overlooking the Isthmus. The clapboard house was built in 1910 for Catalina's pre-Wrigley owners and has seen duty as on-location lodging for movie stars like Errol Flynn and Dorothy Lamour. Peaceful and isolated, the simply furnished but comfortable lodge has spectacular views of both harbors. Peak-season rates range from $160 to $280, including deluxe continental breakfast, and they'll even give you a lift from the pier.

Everyone eats at the **Harbor Reef Restaurant** (✆ 310/510-4215) on the beach. This nautical, tropical-themed saloon/restaurant serves breakfast, lunch, and dinner, the latter consisting of hearty steaks, ribs, swordfish, and buffalo burgers in summer. The house drink is sweet "buffalo milk," a potent concoction of vodka, crème de cacao, banana liqueur, milk, whipped cream, and nutmeg.

WHAT TO SEE & DO IN AVALON Walk along horseshoe-shaped Crescent Avenue, past private yachting and fishing clubs, toward the landmark **Casino** building. You can see the Art Deco **theater** for the price of a movie ticket any night. Also on the ground floor is the newly renovated **Catalina Island Museum** (✆ 310/510-2414; www.catalinamuseum.org), which explores 7,000 years of island history, including fascinating exhibits of archaeology, steamships, big bands, and natural history. The museum has also been updated with more advanced technology, like flatscreen TVs, and more interactivity. Admission to the museum is $5 for adults, $4 for seniors, $2 for kids age 5 and above, free for children 4 and under; it's included in the price of Discovery's Casino Tours (see "Catalina's Grand Casino," above). The museum is open daily from 10am to 5pm.

Around the point from the Casino is the **Descanso Beach Club** (_©_ **310/510-7410**), a mini–Club Med nestled in a private cove just past the famous Casino Building. While you can get on the beach year-round, the club's facilities—an open-air restaurant and two bars, live music, beach area, volleyball lawns, dance area, fire rings on the beach, private cabana and chaise longue rentals, and thatched beach umbrellas (bring your own towels or be prepared to purchase them)—are open only from spring to October. The Descanso Beach Club also serves as an activity headquarters, where guests can rent kayaks, stand-up paddle boards, and snorkeling and scuba gear, as well as book massage and golf tee times, plus tours. Admission is $2.

About 1½ miles from downtown Avalon is **Wrigley Memorial and Botanical Garden** (_©_ **310/510-2595**). The specialized gardens, a project of Ada Wrigley, showcase plants endemic to California's coastal islands. It's open daily from 8am to 5pm; admission is $5 for adults, free for children 11 and under.

Diving, Snorkeling & Sea Kayaking ★

Snorkeling, scuba diving, and sea kayaking are among the main reasons mainlanders head to Catalina. Catalina Island's naturally clean water and giant kelp forests teeming with marine life have made it a renowned diving destination that attracts experts and beginning divers alike. **Casino Point Marine Park,** Southern California's first city-designated underwater park, was established in 1965 and is located behind the Casino. Due to its convenient location, it can get outrageously crowded in the summer (just like everything else at that time of year).

Catalina Divers Supply (_©_ **800/ 353-0330** or 310/510-0330) runs two full-service dive shops: one from a large trailer behind the Casino at the edge of Avalon's underwater park, where they offer guided snorkeling tours and introductory scuba dives; and another at the Green Pier, where they launch boat dives aboard the _Scuba Cat._ The three best locations for snorkeling are **Lover's Cove Marine Preserve, Casino Point Marine Park,** and **Descanso Beach Club. Catalina Snorkeling Adventures,** at Lover's Cove (_©_ **877/SNORKEL** [766-7535]), offers snorkel-gear rental. Snorkeling trips that take you outside of Avalon depart from **Joe's Rent-a-Boat** (_©_ **310/510-0455**), on the Green Pier.

Casino Point Marine Park.

At Two Harbors, stop by **West End Dive Center** (☎ **310/510-4272**). Excursions range from half-day introductory dives to complete certification courses; however, all are from shore, not boat. It also rents snorkel gear and offers kayak rental, instruction, and tours.

Hiking & Biking

When the summer crowds become overwhelming, it's time to head on foot for the peacefulness of the interior, where secluded coves and barren, rolling hills soothe frayed nerves. Visitors can obtain a free **hiking permit** at the Conservancy Office (125 Clarissa Ave.; ☎ **310/510-2595;** www.catalinaconservancy. org), where you'll find maps, wildlife information, and friendly assistance from Conservancy staffers who love to share their knowledge of the interior. It's open daily from 8:30am to 4:30pm and closed for lunch on weekends. Among the sights you may see are the many giant buffalo roaming the hills, scions of movie extras that were left behind in 1929 and have since flourished.

More than 200 miles of trails beckon both the "tennis shoe" hiker and the experienced trekker. The granddaddy of them all is the Trans-Catalina Trail, a 37.2-mile track that transverses the entire island.

Mountain biking is allowed on the island's designated dirt roads but requires a $35 permit that must be purchased in person at the Conservancy Office, which is located at 125 Clarissa Ave. For more details, call the office at ☎ **310/510-2595,** ext. 100, or log on to their website at www.catalinaconservancy.org.

Beaches

Unfortunately, Avalon's beaches leave much to be desired. The town's central beach, located off Crescent Avenue, is small and completely congested in the busy season. Be sure to claim your spot early in the morning before it's full. **Descanso Beach Club** (see "What to See & Do in Avalon," above) offers the best beach in town but also gets crowded very quickly. Your best bet is to kayak out to a secluded cove where you have the beach virtually to yourself.

Where to Stay

If you plan to stay overnight, be sure to reserve a room in advance because most places fill up quickly during the summer and holiday seasons. There are only a handful of hotels whose accommodations and amenities actually justify the rates that they charge. Some are downright scary, so book as far in advance as possible to get a room that makes the trip worthwhile. Don't stress too much over your accommodations, as you'll probably spend most of your time outdoors. Keep in mind that the best time to visit is in September or October, when the water is warm, the crowds have somewhat subsided, and hotel occupancy is easier to come by. If you're having trouble finding a vacancy, try calling the Catalina Chamber of Commerce & Visitors Bureau (☎ **310/510-1520**); they keep daily tabs on last-minute cancellations.

VERY EXPENSIVE

The Inn on Mt. Ada ★★ When William Wrigley, Jr., purchased Catalina Island in 1921, he built this ornate hilltop Georgian Colonial mansion as his summer vacation home; it's now one of the finest small hotels in California. The opulent inn—considered to be the best in town for its luxury accommodations and views—has several ground-floor salons, a club room with a fireplace, a formal library, and a sunroom where tea, cookies, and fruit are always available. The best guest room is the Grand Suite, fitted with a fireplace and a large private patio. Amenities include a golf cart during your stay. An early-morning continental breakfast, a hearty full breakfast, a light deli-style lunch, appetizers, fresh fruit, freshly baked cookies, soft drinks, beers, wines, and champagne are included in the rate. *Tip:* Even if you find that they're sold out or too pricey to fit your budget, make a breakfast or lunch reservation and enjoy amazing views from the inn's spectacular balcony. Reservations are taken 1 month in advance; space is limited for non-overnight guests. *Note:* The entire property shuts down every January for annual maintenance.

398 Wrigley Rd. (P.O. Box 2560), Avalon, CA 90704. www.innonmtada.com. ✆ **800/608-7669** or 310/510-2030. Fax 310/510-2237. 6 units. Nov–Apr $375–$550 double, $640 suite; May–Oct $415–$550 double, $765 suite. Rates include 2 meals daily. AE, MC, V. **Amenities:** Restaurant; free harbor/heliport transfer. In room: TV, hair dryer, no phone, free Wi-Fi.

EXPENSIVE

The Avalon Hotel The Avalon Hotel was originally developed at the turn of the last century as the Pilgrim Club, a gentleman's club that vanished in the great fire of 1915. After many incarnations, the dilapidated property was finally renovated to become one of the island's most luxurious hideaways. The cozy Craftsman-style hotel is decked out in rich, hand-carved mahogany and imported slate tastefully accented with handmade tile and local artwork. Catalina's silhouette is artfully etched into the slate, stained glass, and light fixtures, while shadow boxes showcase island memorabilia throughout the hotel's homey public space. Guest rooms, which come in a variety of sizes, feature garden or ocean views (some with balconies) and an incredibly comfy queen- or king-size Supple-Pedic memory-foam bed.

124 Whittley Ave. (P.O. Box 706), Avalon, CA 90704. www.theavalonhotel.com. ✆ **310/510-7070.** 15 units. Mid-Oct to mid-June $195–$435 double; mid-June to mid-Oct $295–$545 double. Rates include continental breakfast. AE, MC, V. **Amenities:** Free harbor/heliport transfer. *In room:* TV/DVD, fridge, hair dryer, Internet.

MODERATE

Hotel Villa Portofino ★ Enjoy European elegance on the oceanfront from your courtyard room or deluxe suite after a warm welcome from the hotel's efficient and friendly staff. The hotel boasts renovated rooms and a spacious rooftop deck overlooking the bay that is perfect for people-watching, sunbathing, cocktail sipping, or just enjoying the fantastic view. Some rooms have luxurious touches such as fireplaces, balconies, deep soaking tubs, and separate showers. The hotel is just steps away from the beach, shops, and sights.

111 Crescent Ave. (P.O. Box 127), Avalon, CA 90704. www.hotelvillaportofino.com. ✆ **888/510-0555** or 310/510-0555. Fax 310/510-0839. 35 units. May–Oct $150–$375 double, from $285 suite; winter $115–$315 double, from $225 suite. Rates include continental breakfast, beach towels, and chairs. AE, DC, MC, V. **Amenities:** Award-winning restaurant. *In room:* A/C, TV, fridge, hair dryer, free Wi-Fi.

Hotel Vista Del Mar The hotel's location smack-dab in the middle of town, lush garden atrium courtyard, lovely balcony with views of the harbor, and friendly staff make it an island favorite for families and couples alike. The ocean-view suites with double Jacuzzi tubs are fantastic but hard to secure, as the only two are booked by regulars almost year-round.

For Travelers Who Use Wheelchairs

Visitors who use wheelchairs should request a room at **Hotel Metropole** (www.hotel-metropole.com; ✆ **800/300-8528** or 310/510-1884). One of the most modern properties in Avalon, it has an elevator, a large sun deck that overlooks Avalon Bay, a shopping complex, and a very convenient location in the heart of Avalon.

417 Crescent Ave. (P.O. Box 1979), Avalon, CA 90704. www.hotel-vistadelmar.com. ✆ **800/601-6836** or 310/510-1452. 15 units. Apr–Nov $175–$265 double, $325–$495 suite; Dec–Mar $145–$185 double, $250–$400 suite. Rates include continental breakfast and freshly baked cookies and milk in the evening. AE, DISC, MC, V. *In room:* A/C, TV/VCR, fridge, minibar, free Wi-Fi.

INEXPENSIVE

Our recommended choices for inexpensive lodgings are **Hotel Catalina** (www.hotelcatalina.com; ✆ **800/540-0184** or 310/510-0027), a well-maintained Victorian-style hotel just a half-block from the beach, with tons of charm, family cottages, a courtyard with beautiful stained glass, and large verandas with bay views; **Zane Grey** (www.zanegreypueblohotel.com; ✆ **310/510-0966**), a Hopi-style pueblo built in 1926 and former home of American author Zane Grey, situated above town and equipped with a cozy living room with fireplace and piano, free shuttle service, and a swimming pool; and **Hermit Gulch Campground** (www.visitcatalinaisland.com; ✆ **310/510-8368**), one of Avalon's three campgrounds, which can be crowded and noisy in peak season. Campsites can be tough to secure, especially when hotels are booked, so it's a good idea to make reservations in advance. The walk to town and back can be draining, so hop on the red trolley that runs you back and forth to town for a couple dollars each way.

Where to Eat

Along with the choices below, recommended Avalon options include the **Avalon Grille,** a new American restaurant with patio seating and full bar. It's on the waterfront in the center of town, across from the Green Pleasure Pier (**310/510-7494**). On the Two Harbors side of the island, the **Harbor Reef Restaurant** is the place to eat; see "Exploring the Island," above.

EXPENSIVE

Catalina Country Club ★ CALIFORNIAN   You'll find some of Avalon's most elegant meals at the landmark Catalina Country Club, whose stylish Spanish-Mediterranean clubhouse was built by William Wrigley, Jr., during the 1920s. The Club exudes a chic and historical atmosphere; the menu is peppered with archival photos and vintage celebrity anecdotes. Sit outdoors in an elegant tiled Fountain Terrace courtyard, or inside the intimate, exquisite dining room. The executive chef infuses new American cuisine with creative influences from around the world, using free-range, organic meats, fresh produce, and seafood from environmentally sensitive fisheries. *Note:* The Club is only a few minutes from the waterfront but uphill.

1 Country Club Dr. (above Sumner Ave.). ✆ **310/510-7404.** Reservations recommended. Main courses $12–$30 dinner. AE, DISC, MC, V. Daily 11:30am–2:30pm and 5–9pm; summer hours Thurs–Sun 4pm–closing (varies); live music on the patio Thurs (in summer).

MODERATE

The Landing Bar and Grill AMERICAN   With a secluded, heated deck overlooking the harbor, the Landing is one of the most romantic dining spots in Avalon. It boasts beautiful Spanish-style architecture located in the historic El Encanto Center that manages to attract as many jeans-clad vacationers as dressed-up islanders. The menu is enticing, with local seafood offerings, pasta, Mexican cuisine, and gourmet pizzas that can be delivered to your hotel room if you wish.

Intersection of Crescent and Marilla aves. ✆ **310/510-1474.** Reservations recommended. Main courses $11–$22. AE, DISC, MC, V. Tues–Sun 11am–3pm and 4–10pm (subject to change in winter).

Steve's Steakhouse AMERICAN   Step up above the busy bayside promenade into a fantastic collage of museum-quality photos capturing the Avalon of old. This setting overlooking Avalon Bay feels just right for the hearty menu of steaks, seafood, and pasta—all of which can be ordered at the full bar as well as in the dining room. Catalina swordfish is their specialty, along with excellent cuts of meat. You can also make a respectable repast from the many appetizer selections, especially the fresh oysters and sashimi.

417 Crescent Ave. (directly across from the Green Pier, upstairs). ✆ **310/510-0333.** Reservations recommended on weekends. Main courses $9–$18 lunch, $20–$32 dinner. AE, DISC, MC, V. Daily 11am–3pm and 5–10pm.

INEXPENSIVE

My favorite for a low-bucks meal is the **Casino Dock Café** (✆ **310/510-2755**), with live summertime entertainment, marina views from the sun-drenched deck, breakfast burritos loaded with homemade salsa, and kicking bloody marys.

Barhopping

Note: Avalon doesn't have listed street addresses, but all these bars are within stumbling distance of each other on the main drag. The **Chi Chi Club** (✆ **310/510-9211**), the "noisy bar in Avalon" referred to in Crosby, Stills, and Nash's song "Southern Cross," is the island's only dance club and quite a scene on summer weekend evenings—the DJ spins an eclectic mix of dance tunes. **Luau Larry's** (✆ **310/510-1919**) is Avalon's signature bar that everyone must visit; its tacky Tiki theme and signature Wicky Wacker drink kicks you into island mode as soon as you step inside. Or go where the locals go and swill beers at the **Marlin Club** (✆ **310/510-0044**), Avalon's oldest drinking hole, or catch the Dodgers game at **J. L.'s Locker Room** (✆ **310/510-0258**).

Shopping

Don't worry—you won't have any trouble finding that must-have Catalina key chain or refrigerator magnet, as Crescent Avenue is lined with myriad schlocky souvenir shops. There are, however, a few stores that do offer unique and tasteful items. **C. C. Gallagher** (✆ **310/510-1278**) carries high-end gifts and also is a coffee shop; they're best for finding beautiful art, music, and jewelry created by local artists. **Buoys and Gulls** (✆ **310/510-0416**) offers men's and women's wear such as Reyn Spooner islander shirts, Nautica, Hurley, and Billabong. The **Steamer Trunk** (✆ **310/510-2600**) is loaded with unique gifts to take home to the dog sitter or neighbor who collected your mail. **Leo's Drugstore** (✆ **310/510-0189**) is the obvious spot to pick up the sunscreen that you forgot to pack. **Von's,** located on Metropole Avenue in the center of town, and **Von's Express,** on Catalina Avenue, are Avalon's main grocery stores where you'll find all your food staples.

BIG BEAR LAKE & LAKE ARROWHEAD

100 miles NE of downtown L.A.

These two deep-blue lakes, close to one another in the San Bernardino mountains, have long been favorite year-round alpine playgrounds for city-weary Angelenos.

Big Bear Lake is popular with skiers as well as boaters (it's much larger than Arrowhead, and equipment rentals abound), and in the past decade the area has received a much-needed face-lift. Big Bear Boulevard was widened to handle high-season traffic, and downtown Big Bear Lake (the "Village") was spiffed up but retains its woodsy charm. In addition to two excellent ski slopes less than 5 minutes from town, you can enjoy the comforts of a real supermarket and several video-rental shops, all especially convenient if you're staying in a cabin. Most people choose Big Bear over Arrowhead because there's so much more to do, from boating, fishing, and hiking to snow sports, mountain biking, and horseback riding. The weather is nearly always perfect at this 7,000-foot-plus elevation: If you want proof, ask CalTech, which operates a solar observatory here to take advantage of nearly 300 days of sunshine per year.

Lake Arrowhead has always been privately owned, as is apparent from the affluence of the surrounding homes, many of which are gated estates rather than rustic mountain cabins. The lake and the private docks lining its shores are reserved for the exclusive use of homeowners, but visitors can enjoy Lake Arrowhead by boat tour or use of the summer-season beach clubs, a privilege included in nearly all private-home rentals. Reasons to choose a vacation at Lake Arrowhead? The roads up are less grueling than the winding ascent to Big Bear Lake and, being at a lower elevation, Arrowhead gets little snow (you can forget those pesky tire chains). It's very easy and cost-effective to rent a luxurious house from which to enjoy the spectacular scenery, crisp mountain air, and relaxed resort atmosphere—and if you do ski, the slopes are only a half-hour away.

Essentials

GETTING THERE Lake Arrowhead is reached by taking Hwy. 18 from San Bernardino. The last segment of this route takes you along the aptly named **Rim of the World Highway,** with its breathtaking view over the valley on clear days. Hwy. 18 then continues east to Big Bear Lake, but to get to Big Bear Lake, it's quicker to bypass Arrowhead by taking Hwy. 330 from Redlands, which meets Hwy. 18 in Running Springs.

Big Bear Lake.

During heavy-traffic periods, it can be worthwhile to take scenic Hwy. 38, which winds up from Redlands through mountain passes and valleys to approach Big Bear from the other side.

Note: Nostalgia lovers can revisit legendary **Route 66** on the way from Los Angeles to the mountain resorts, substituting scenic motor courts and other relics of the "Mother Road" in place of impersonal I-10. For a complete driving tour, see "Get Your Kicks on Historic Route 66" in chapter 15.

VISITOR INFORMATION   National ski tours, mountain bike races, and one of Southern California's largest Oktoberfest gatherings are just some of the events held year-round. Contact the **Big Bear Lake Resort Association,** 630 Bartlett Rd., Big Bear Lake Village (🕽 **800/4-BIG-BEAR** [424-2327] or 909/866-7000; www.bigbearinfo.com), for schedules and information. They also provide information on sightseeing and lodging and will send you a free visitors guide.

In Lake Arrowhead, contact the **Lake Arrowhead Communities Chamber of Commerce** (🕽 **909/337-3715;** www.lakearrowhead.net). The visitor center is in the Lake Arrowhead Village lower shopping center.

ORIENTATION   The south shore of Big Bear Lake was the first resort area to be developed here and remains the most densely populated. Hwy. 18 passes first through the city of Big Bear Lake and its downtown village; then, as Big Bear Boulevard, it continues east to Big Bear City, which is more residential and suburban. Hwy. 38 traverses the north shore, home to pristine national forest and great hiking trails, as well as a couple of small marinas and a lakefront bed-and-breakfast inn (see the Windy Point Inn on p. 687).

Arrowhead's main town is Lake Arrowhead Village, on the south shore at the end of Hwy. 173. The village's commercial center is home to factory-outlet stores, about 40 chain and specialty shops, and the Lake Arrowhead Resort (p. 688). Minutes away is the town of Blue Jay (along Hwy. 189), where the Blue Jay Ice Castle skating rink is located (see "Winter Fun," below).

Enjoying the Outdoors

For up-to-date info on what outdoor activities are available in the region, call the **Big Bear Mountain Resorts Activities** hot line at 🕽 **909/866-5766,** or log on to their website at www.bigbearmountainresorts.com.

In addition to the activities described below, there's a great recreation spot for families near the heart of Big Bear Lake: **Alpine Slide at Magic Mountain,** 800 Wildrose Lane (🕽 **909/866-4626;** www.alpineslidebigbear.com), has a year-round bobsled-style Alpine Slide, a splashy double water slide open from mid-June to mid-September, and bunny slopes for snow tubing from November to Easter. The dry Alpine Slide is $4 a ride, the water slide is $12 for an unlimited pass, and snow play costs $25 per day, including tube and rope tow.

WATERSPORTS

BOATING   You can rent all kinds of boats—including speedboats, rowboats, paddle boats, pontoons, sailboats, and canoes—at a number of Big Bear Lake marinas. Rates vary only slightly from place to place: A 14-foot dinghy with an outboard runs around $30 per hour; pontoon (patio) boats that can hold large groups range in size and price from $65 to $90 per hour or $180 to $250 for a

half-day. **Pine Knot Landing** (✆ **909/866-2628;** www.pineknotlanding.
com) is the most centrally located marina, behind the post office at the foot of
Pine Knot Boulevard in Big Bear Lake. **Big Bear Marina,** 500 Paine Rd. at
Lakeview (✆ **909/866-3218;** www.bigbearmarina.com), is close to Big Bear
Lake Village and also rents a variety of watercraft.

FISHING   Big Bear Lake brims with rainbow trout, bass, and catfish in spring
and summer, the best fishing seasons. Pine Knot Landing, Gray's Landing,
and Big Bear Marina (see "Boating," above) all rent fishing boats and have
bait-and-tackle shops that sell licenses.

JET-SKIING, WATER-SKIING & WAKE BOARDING   Personal watercraft (PWCs)
are available for rent at **Big Bear Marina** (see "Boating," above). **North
Shore Landing,** on Hwy. 38, 2 miles west of Fawnskin (✆ **909/878-4-
FUN** [4386]; www.800bigbear.com), rents jet skis and two- and three-person WaveRunners at rates ranging from $90 to $115 per hour plus gas. Call
ahead to reserve your craft and check age and deposit requirements.

OTHER WARM-WEATHER ACTIVITIES

GOLF   The **Bear Mountain Golf Course,** Goldmine Drive, Big Bear Lake
(✆ **909/585-8002;** www.bigbearmountainresorts.com), is a 9-hole, par-
35, links-style course that winds through a gently sloping meadow at the
base of the Bear Mountain Ski Resort. The course is open daily April
through November. Weekend greens fees are $30 and $47 for 9 and 18
holes, respectively. Both riding carts and pull carts are available. Call ahead
for tee times.

HIKING   Hikers love the **San Bernardino National Forest.** The gray squirrel
is a popular native, so you may see them scurrying around gathering acorns
or material for their nests. You can sometimes spot deer, coyotes, and American bald eagles, which come here with their young in winter. The black-
crowned Steller's jay and the talkative red, white, and black acorn
woodpecker are the most common of the great variety of birds in this pine
forest.

The best choice for a short mountain hike is the **Woodland Trail,**
which begins near the ranger station. The best long hike is a section of the
Pacific Crest Trail, which travels 39 miles through the mountains above
Big Bear and Arrowhead lakes. The most convenient trail head is at Cougar
Crest, half a mile west of the Big Bear Ranger Station.

The best place to begin a hike in Lake Arrowhead is at the **Arrowhead
Ranger Station** (✆ **909/382-2782**), in the town of Skyforest on Hwy. 18,
a quarter-mile east of the Lake Arrowhead turnoff (Hwy. 173). The staff will
provide you with maps and information on the best area trails, which range
from easy to difficult. The **Enchanted Loop Trail,** near the town of Blue
Jay, is an easy half-hour hike. The **Heaps Peak Arboretum Trail** winds
through a grove of redwoods; the trail head is on the north side of Hwy. 18,
at an auxiliary ranger kiosk west of Running Springs.

The area is home to a **National Children's Forest,** a 20-acre area
developed so that children, people in wheelchairs, and those with visual
impairments can enjoy nature. To get to the Children's Forest from Lake
Arrowhead, take Hwy. 330 to Hwy. 18 east, past Deer Lick Station; when you
reach a road marked ɪɴ96 (open only in summer), turn right and go 3 miles.

HORSEBACK RIDING   **Baldwin Lake Stables,** southeast of Big Bear City (℃ **909/585-6482;** www.baldwinlakestables.com), conducts hourly, lunch-break, and sunset rides along a wide variety of terrains and trails—all with spectacular vistas—including the Pacific Crest Trail, which includes expansive views of the Mojave Desert. It's open year-round.

MOUNTAIN BIKING   Big Bear Lake has become a mountain biking center, with most of the action around the Snow Summit ski area (see "Winter Fun," below), where a $15 lift ticket will take you and your bike to a web of trails, fire roads, and meadows at about 8,000 feet. The lake's north shore is also a popular destination; the forest-service ranger stations (see "Hiking," above) have maps to the historic Gold Rush–era Holcomb Valley and the 2-mile Alpine Pedal Path (an easy lakeside ride).

    Bear Valley Bikes, 40298 Big Bear Blvd. (℃ **909/866-8000**), rents quality mountain bikes for about $10 an hour or $40 a day. At Lake Arrowhead, bikes are permitted on all hiking trails and back roads except the Pacific Crest Trail. See the local ranger station for an area map. Visitors can rent gear from the **Lake Arrowhead Resort** (℃ **909/336-1511**) or **Above & Beyond Sports** (℃ **909/867-5517**), 32877 Hwy. 18, Running Springs.

WINTER FUN

ICE-SKATING   The **Blue Jay Ice Castle,** at North Bay Road and Hwy. 189 (℃ **909/337-0802;** www.icecastle.us), near Lake Arrowhead Village, was a training site for world champion Michelle Kwan and boasts former "Olympic Coach of the Year" Frank Carroll on its staff. Several public sessions each day—as well as hockey, broomball, group lessons, and private parties—give nonpros a chance to enjoy this impeccably groomed "outdoor" rink, open on three sides to the scenery and fresh air.

SKIING & SNOWBOARDING   When the L.A. basin gets wintertime rain, skiers rejoice, for they know snow is falling up in the mountains. The past few seasons have seen abundant natural snowfall at Big Bear, augmented by snowmaking equipment. While the slopes can't compare with those in Utah or Colorado, they do offer diversity, difficulty, and convenience.

    Snow Summit, at Big Bear Lake (℃ **909/866-5766;** www.bigbear mountainresorts.com), is the skiers' choice, especially because it installed its second high-speed quad express from the 7,000-foot base to the 8,200-foot summit. There are also green (easy) runs, even from the summit, so beginners can enjoy the Summit Haus lodge and breathtaking lake views from the top. Advanced risk-takers will appreciate three double-black-diamond runs. The resort offers midweek, beginner, half-day, night, and family specials, as well as ski and snowboard instruction. Other helpful Snow Summit phone numbers include advance lift-ticket sales (℃ **909/866-5841**) and a snow report (℃ **800/BEAR-MTN** [232-7686]).

    The **Bear Mountain Resort,** at Big Bear Lake (℃ **909/866-5766;** www.bigbearmountainresorts.com), has the largest beginner area, but experts flock to the double-black-diamond Geronimo run from the 8,805-foot Bear Peak. Natural-terrain skiers and snowboarders will enjoy legal access to off-trail canyons, but the limited beginner slopes and kids' areas get pretty crowded in season. One of two high-speed quad expresses rises from the 7,140-foot base to 8,440-foot Goldmine Mountain; most runs from here are intermediate. Bear Mountain has a ski-and-snowboard school, abundant dining facilities, and a well-stocked ski shop.

The **Snow Valley Ski Resort,** in Arrowbear, midway between Arrowhead and Big Bear (© **909/867-2751;** www.snow-valley.com), has improved its snowmaking and facilities to compete with the other two major ski areas, and it's the primary choice of skiers staying at Arrowhead. From a base elevation of 6,800 feet, Snow Valley's 13 chairlifts (including 5 triples) can take you from the beginner runs all the way up to black-diamond challenges at the 7,898-foot peak. Children's programs, night skiing, and lesson packages are also available.

ORGANIZED TOURS

LAKE TOURS The *Big Bear Queen* (© **909/866-3218;** www.bigbearmarina. com), a small version of a Mississippi-style paddle-wheeler, cruises Big Bear Lake on 90-minute tours daily from late April to the end of November. The boat departs from Big Bear Marina (at the end of Paine Ave.). Tours are $18 for adults, $16 for seniors 65 and older, $12 for children ages 3 to 12, and free for kids 2 and under. Call for reservations and information on the special Sunday brunch, champagne sunset, and dinner cruises.

Fifty-minute tours of Lake Arrowhead are available year-round on the *Arrowhead Queen* (© **909/336-6992**), a sister ship that departs hourly each day between 10am and 6pm from Lake Arrowhead Village. Tours are $16 for adults, $14 for seniors, $10 for children 3 to 12, and free for kids 2 and under. It's about the only way to really see this alpine jewel, unless you know a resident with a boat. Highlights include celebrity homes—past and present—famous film locations, and the occasional bald eagle or two.

Where to Stay

BIG BEAR LAKE

Vacation rentals are plentiful in the area, from cabins to condos to private homes. Some can accommodate up to 20 people and can be rented on a weekly or monthly basis. For a wide range of rental properties, all pictured in detail online, contact the **Village Reservation Service** (© **800/693-0018** or 909/866-9689; www.villagereservations.net), which can arrange for everything from condos to lakefront homes, or call the **Big Bear Lake Resort Association** (© **800/4-BIG-BEAR** [442-4232]; www.bigbear.com) for referrals on all types of lodgings.

Besides the places below, I also recommend **Apples Bed & Breakfast Inn,** 42430 Moonridge Rd. (www.applesbigbear.com; © **909/866-0903**), a crab-apple-red New England–style clapboard that blends hotel-like professionalism with B&B amenities (and lots of frilly touches); and **Gold Mountain Manor,** 1117 Anita Ave. (www.goldmountainmanor.com; © **800/509-2604** or 909/585-6997), a woodsy 1920s lodge that's now an ultracozy, affordable B&B.

Best Western Big Bear Chateau ☺   This European-flavored property is one of only two traditional full-service hotels in Big Bear. Its location—just off Big Bear Boulevard at the base of the road to Bear Mountain—makes the Chateau a popular choice for skiers and families (kids 17 and under stay free in their parent's room, and there are also children's activities). The rooms are modern but more charming than your average Best Western, with tapestries, brass beds, antique furniture, gas fireplaces, and marble bathrooms with heated towel racks and many with whirlpool tubs. The compound is surrounded by tall forest. The casual Le Bistro restaurant serves a free continental breakfast each morning for guests.

42200 Moonridge Rd. (P.O. Box 1814), Big Bear Lake, CA 92315. www.bestwestern.com. ℰ **800/ 232-7466** or 909/866-6666. Fax 909/866-8988. 80 units. Winter $120–$259 double; summer $100–$150 double. Children 17 and under stay free in parent's room. Winter-ski, romance, and summer-fun packages available. AE, DISC, MC, V. **Amenities:** Restaurant; lounge; Jacuzzi; heated outdoor pool. *In room:* A/C, TV, hair dryer, free Wi-Fi.

Grey Squirrel Resort ☺   This is the most attractive of the many cabin-cluster-type motels near the city of Big Bear Lake, offering a wide range of rustic cabins, most with fireplace and kitchen. They're adequately, if not attractively, furnished—the appeal is the flexibility and privacy afforded large or long-term parties. Facilities include a heated pool that's enclosed in winter, a fire pit and barbecues, volleyball and basketball courts, and completely equipped kitchens.

39372 Big Bear Blvd., Big Bear Lake, CA 92315. www.greysquirrel.com. ℰ **800/381-5569** or 909/866-4335. Fax 909/866-6271. 18 cabins. $79–$176 1-bedroom cabin; $138–$160 2-bedroom cabin; $218–$239 3-bedroom cabin. Value rates available; higher rates on holidays. AE, DISC, MC, V. Pets accepted for $10 per day. **Amenities:** Jacuzzi; heated indoor/outdoor pool. *In room:* TV/ DVD, kitchen (some units), free Wi-Fi.

Knickerbocker Mansion Country Inn ★   Innkeepers Thomas Bicanic and Stan Miller faced quite a task reviving this landmark log house; when they moved in, it was empty of all furnishings and suffered from years of neglect. But Knickerbocker Mansion has risen to become the most charming and sophisticated inn on the lake's south side; chef Bicanic, who honed his craft in L.A.'s culinary temple Patina restaurant, is now serving intimate gourmet dinners at the Bistro at the Mansion on Friday and Saturday evenings. The pair scoured antiques stores in Big Bear and Los Angeles for vintage furnishings, creating a warm and relaxing ambience in the grand-yet-quirky house of legendary local character Bill Knickerbocker, who assembled it by hand almost 90 years ago. Today's guest rooms are a cedar-paneled dream, with luxury bed linens, cozy bathrobes, modern marble bathrooms with deluxe Australian shower heads, and refreshing mountain views. After Bicanic's memorable breakfast, you can spend the day relaxing on veranda rockers or garden hammocks; Big Bear's village is also an easy walk away.

869 Knickerbocker Rd. (P.O. Box 1907), Big Bear Lake, CA 92315. www.knickerbockermansion. com. ℰ **877/423-1180** or 909/878-9190. Fax 909/878-4248. 8 units. $125–$170 double; $225 suite. Rates include full breakfast, refreshments, and snacks. AE, DISC, MC, V. *In room:* TV/VCR/ DVD, hair dryer, free Wi-Fi.

Windy Point Inn ★   A contemporary architectural showpiece on the scenic north shore, the Windy Point is the only shorefront B&B in Big Bear; ergo, all guest rooms have a view of the lake. Hosts Val and Kent Kessler's attention to detail is impeccable: If you're tired of knotty pine and Victorian frills, here's a grown-up place for you, with plenty of romance and all the pampering you can stand. Every room has a wood-burning fireplace, feather bed, private deck, and DVD player (guests may borrow DVDs from the inn's plentiful collection); some also feature whirlpool tubs and luxurious state-of-the-art bathrooms. The welcoming great room features a casual sunken fireplace nook with floor-to-ceiling windows overlooking the lake, a telescope for stargazing, a baby grand, and up-to-date menus for every local restaurant. You might not want to leave the cocoon of your room after Kent's custom gourmet breakfast (only an option in the Coves and the Shores rooms, but if you do, you'll be pleasantly surprised to find that you are dining with your travel partner(s) only—mealtimes are staggered for privacy. There's a wintertime bald eagle habitat just up the road, and the city of Big Bear Lake is only a 10-minute drive around the lake.

39015 N. Shore Dr., Fawnskin, CA 92333. www.windypointinn.com. © **909/866-2746.** Fax 909/866-1593. 5 units. $145–$265 double. Rates include welcome cookies, full breakfast. Midweek discounts available. AE, DISC, MC, V. *In room:* TV/DVD (for movies only; no TV channel reception), CD player (some units), fridge, hair dryer, no phone.

LAKE ARROWHEAD

Arrowhead has far more private homes than tourist accommodations, but rental properties abound, from cozy cottages to mansions; many can be economical for families or other groups. Two of the largest agencies are **Arrowhead Cabin Rentals** (© **800/244-5138** or 909/337-2403; www.arrowheadrent.com) and **AAA Resorts Rentals** (© **800/743-0865** or 909/337-4413; www.lakearrowheadrentals.com). Overnight guests in rentals enjoy some resident lake privileges—ask when you reserve.

Two other options are **Chateau du Lac,** 911 Hospital Rd. (www.chateau-du-lac.com; © **909/337-6488**), an elegant and contemporary four-room B&B with stunning views of the lake; and the **Saddleback Inn,** 300 S. Hwy. 173 (www.saddlebackinn.com; © **800/858-3334** or 909/336-3571), an inn and restaurant that still boasts historic charm while offering some up-to-date amenities, all at a prime location in the center of the village.

Lake Arrowhead Resort & Spa ★★ ☺   A $20-million resortwide transformation greatly improved every part of this sprawling resort—including a new full-service, luxurious **Spa of the Pines** and **Bin 189** restaurant—but its location is still its most outstanding feature. On the lakeshore adjacent to Lake Arrowhead Village, the hotel has its own beach, plus docks that are ideal for fishing. The newly renovated rooms are decked out with 32-inch swiveling flat-panel TVs, Essential Elements body and hair-care products, and Anichini linens; most have balconies, king-size beds, and fireplaces as well. The suites are equipped with kitchen amenities and whirlpool tubs and floor heaters in the bathrooms. The hotel caters primarily to groups and sports a businesslike ambience during the week, but you'll spend most of your time on the beach anyway. A full program of supervised children's activities, ranging from nature hikes to T-shirt painting, is offered on weekends year-round.

27984 Hwy. 189, Lake Arrowhead, CA 92352. www.laresort.com. © **800/800-6792** or 909/336-1511. Fax 909/744-3088. 173 units. $179–$349 double; $309–$785 suite. AE, DC, DISC, MC, V. **Amenities:** Restaurant; babysitting; children's programs; fitness center; Jacuzzi; outdoor pool (summer only). *In room:* A/C, flat-panel TV w/pay movies, hair dryer, minibar, free Wi-Fi.

Pine Rose Cabins ★ ☺   Pine Rose Cabins is a good choice for families. On 5 forested acres about 3 miles from the lake, the wonderful free-standing cabins offer lots of privacy. Owners David and Tricia DuFour have 15 cabins, from romantic studios to a five-bedroom lodge, each decorated in a different theme: The Indian cabin has a tepeelike bed; the bed in Wild Bill's cabin is covered like a wagon. Multibedroom units have stocked kitchens and separate living areas; for all cottages, daily maid service is available at an extra charge. There are lots of diversions on hand, including swing sets, croquet, tetherball, and Ping-Pong.

25994 Hwy. 189 (P.O. Box 31), Twin Peaks, CA 92391. www.pinerose.com. ℭ **800/429-PINE** (7463) or 909/337-2341. Fax 909/337-0258. 17 units. $109–$189 studio for 2; $149–$229 1-, 2-, and 3-bedroom cabins for up to 10 people; $325–$550 large-group lodges. Ski packages available. AE, DISC, MC, V. Pets accepted for $10 per night and $100 refundable deposit. **Amenities:** Jacuzzi; outdoor heated pool. *In room:* TV/VCR, kitchen, high-speed Internet access ($5 per day).

Where to Eat

BIG BEAR LAKE

A reliable option for all-day dining is **Stillwell's,** 40650 Village Dr. (ℭ **909/866-3121,** ext. 3). You might otherwise bypass it, because Stillwell's is the dining room for convention-friendly Northwoods Resort at the edge of the village. Despite the unmistakable hotel feel, its American/Continental menu is respectable, with something for everyone, noted attention to detail, and fair prices (rare in this mountain resort town). Another in-hotel dining option is the restaurant **Bin 189** at the Lake Arrowhead Resort & Spa (see above).

Note: Hours of operation often change depending on the season and weather conditions, so be sure to call ahead to see if these restaurants are open.

The Captain's Anchorage STEAK/SEAFOOD   Historic and rustic, this knotty-pine restaurant has been serving fine steaks, prime rib, seafood, and lobster since 1947. Inside, the dark, nautical decor and fire-warmed bar are just right on blustery winter nights. It's got one of those mile-long soup-and-salad bars, plus some great early-bird and weeknight specials.

Moonridge Way at Big Bear Blvd., Big Bear Lake. ℭ **909/866-3997.** www.captainsanchorage. com. Reservations recommended. Full dinners $18–$40. AE, MC, V. Sun–Thurs 4:30–9pm; Fri–Sat 4:30–10pm.

Himalayan Restaurant ★ INDIAN/NEPALESE   To say that the Himalayan is the best Indian eatery in the Big Bear area is a self-fulfilling prophesy—in fact, it's the only one. But when an Indian expat shares this sentiment, you take notice. The simple dining room is run by casual waiters more likely to be in baseball hats than turbans, but the menu reflects the soul of the subcontinent. And they aren't afraid of spice, so think twice before ordering anything hot. Particularly good is the clay-roasted tandoori lamb sekuwa with mint sauce. There are more familiar dishes like chicken tikka masala and spinach paneer as well.

672 Pine Knot, Big Bear Lake. ℭ **909/878-3068.** www.himalayanbigbear.com. Main courses $7.95–$16. MC, V. Mon–Thurs and Sun 11am–9pm; Fri–Sat 11am–10pm. Closed Wed.

LAKE ARROWHEAD

For a mountain community, Lake Arrowhead has a few surprisingly good dining options. It's worth venturing beyond your hotel to some of the local haunts. These include the **Lake Arrowhead Sports Grille,** 27200 State Hwy. 189, Blue Jay (ℭ **909/744-8785**), a local's favorite pub; the **Royal Oak,** 27187 Hwy. 189, Blue Jay Village (ℭ **909/337-6018**), an expensive American/Continental steakhouse; and **Belgian Waffle Works,** dockside at Lake Arrowhead Village (ℭ **909/337-5222**), a bargain coffee shop with Victorian decor, known for flavorful waffles with tasty toppings.

Moderate

Casual Elegance MODERN AMERICAN 🎁 If you can make it past the unfortunate moniker (truly, what were they thinking?), you'll be glad you did; this is a restaurant that could hold its own food-wise in a much more competitive market. The bi-level space is small, and the seating can seem downright French at times. But it's worth it for exquisitely cooked cuts of lamb, among other typical entree choices of Atlantic salmon and chicken breast. *Note:* All entrees are served as part of a four-course set menu.

26848 Hwy. 189, Blue Jay. ℂ **909/337-8932.** www.casualelegancerestaurant.com. Set menu $22–$34 per person. AE, DISC, MC, V. Wed–Sun 5–9pm.

The Grill at Antlers Inn ECLECTIC AMERICAN   A rustic retreat sought out by special-occasion-celebrating locals, as well as curious tourists, both come for the friendly atmosphere and whimsical fare. It's a fun spot for folks who don't take food too seriously, meaning you can be happy with something as wild as tempura avocado with raspberry rémoulade appetizer, or a simple rib-eye steak—with purple whipped potatoes. *Tip:* In winter, the mulled wine here is exceptional.

26125 State Hwy. 189, Twin Peaks. ℂ **909/336-2600.** www.thegrillatantlersinn.com. Main courses $16–$34. DISC, MC, V. Tues–Sat 4:30pm–close; Sun 10am–2pm and 4:30pm–close.

THE DISNEYLAND RESORT ★★★

30 miles SE of downtown L.A.

There are newer and sometimes larger Disney parks in Florida, Tokyo, France and Hong Kong, but Disneyland—the original and the inspiration for them all—still opens its gates in Anaheim every day, proudly proclaiming itself "The Happiest Place on Earth." In 2001, Disney unveiled a new sister theme park, Disney's California Adventure, along with the shopping/dining/entertainment district called Downtown Disney.

Attractions & Rides   Savvy visitors know to use the FASTPASS system for the park's most popular rides—basically an appointment time so you can skip the lines. For little ones, **It's A Small World** is still timeless. Slightly older kids will love the Jack Sparrow scene in another classic, **Pirates of the Caribbean.** Thrill-seekers can count on Space Mountain, Indiana Jones Adventure, the Matterhorn Bobsleds, Big Thunder Mountain Railroad, plus the California Screamin' roller coaster at California Adventure, for a good time.

Restaurants & Dining   Kids will eat up character-dining opportunities, from Chip and Dale at the **Grand Californian's Storytellers Café** to **Lilo & Stitch's Aloha Breakfast** at the Paradise Pier Hotel, plus **Goofy's Kitchen** at Downtown Disney. For a one-of-a-kind experience, make a reservation at the dimly lit **Blue Bayou,** which is located inside the Pirates attraction. For a more upscale, adult-oriented experience, the **Napa Rose** competes with Orange County's best fine-dining establishments; **Catal Restaurant** is quite good as well, and more moderately priced.

Nightlife & Entertainment   Downtown Disney isn't just for kids. In fact, even though most shows at the **House of Blues** are all ages, unaccompanied minors aren't even allowed. The impressive live music venue regularly hosts local heroes like Social Distortion to singer/songwriters, tribute bands and club nights. **ESPN Zone** is technically a restaurant, but really a world-class sports bar with more than 175 TV screens.

CityPass Savings

If your vacation includes a visit to San Diego, look into purchasing a **Southern California CityPass** (www.citypass.com). It includes a 3-Day Park Hopper ticket to Disneyland and Disney's California Adventure, plus a 1-day admission to Universal Studios Hollywood, SeaWorld Adventure Park, and the San Diego Zoo or Wild Animal Park. It costs $276 for adults and $229 for children, and if you visit all these attractions, you'll save more than $90.

Characters & Parades   Disneyland and California Adventure are also known for sensational productions such as the seasonal **FANTASMIC!,** which takes its inspiration from *The Sorcerer's Apprentice,* and mixes magic, music, live performance, floats and special effects. California Adventure's electrifying **World of Color** is a lighting and water-feature feat, showcasing beloved Disney film characters and scenes, and takes place nightly in the Paradise Park lagoon.

Essentials

GETTING THERE   To reach the Disneyland Resort by car from LAX, take I-105 east to I-605 north, then I-5 south. From downtown Los Angeles, take I-5 south until you see signs for Disneyland. Dedicated offramps from I-5 lead to the attraction's parking lots and surrounding streets (follow signs leading to THEME PARKS). The drive from both downtown L.A. and LAX takes approximately 40 minutes with no traffic. (Right!)

To reach Anaheim from John Wayne Airport, take I-405 north to Calif. 55 north to I-5 north, and then take the Harbor Boulevard exit and follow signs to THEME PARKS. You can also catch a ride with **Yellow Cab Co.** (𝄫 877/733-3305), whose cabs queue up at the Ground Transportation Center on the airport's lower level; reservations are not necessary. Expect the fare to cost about $45.

VISITOR INFORMATION   For information on the **Disneyland Resort,** including show schedules and ride closures that apply to the specific day(s) of your visit, call 𝄫 **714/781-4565** for automated information or 𝄫 **714/781-7290** to speak to Guest Relations (but expect a long wait). Better yet, log on to the Disneyland Resort's official website at **www.disneyland.com**.

For general information on the entire Anaheim region, contact the **Anaheim/Orange County Visitor and Convention Bureau,** 800 W. Katella Ave., inside the Anaheim Convention Center (𝄫 **714/765-8888;** www.anaheimoc.org). It's open Monday to Friday from 8am to 5:30pm. Staffers can fill you in on area activities and shopping, as well as send you their *Official Visitors Guide* and information on the AdventureCard, which offers discounts at dozens of local attractions, hotels, restaurants, and shops.

You can find out everything you need to know about the Disneyland Resort online, beginning with the official site, **www.disneyland.com**, which contains the latest information on park improvements and additions, plus special offers (sometimes on airfare or reduced admission) and an interactive trip planner that lets you build a custom Disney vacation package. If you prefer human interaction, contact a Walt Disney Travel Company specialist at 𝄫 **866/60-DISNEY** (603-4763).

14

SIDE TRIPS FROM LOS ANGELES

The Disneyland Resort

There are numerous unofficial Disney websites as well, which provide very detailed—and often judgmental—information about the Disneyland Resort. The best I've found are **Disneyland: Inside & Out** (www.intercot west.com), **LaughingPlace.com, MouseInfo.com, Mouseplanet.com,** and **MouseSavers.com.**

ADMISSION, HOURS & INFORMATION   As of press time, admission to *either* Disneyland or Disney's California Adventure, including unlimited rides and all festivities and entertainment, is $76 for adults and children 10 and over, $68 for children 3 to 9, and free for children 2 and under. Parking is $14. A **1-Day Park Hopper ticket,** which allows you to go back and forth as much as you'd like, is $101 for adults and $91 for children. A **2-day Park Hopper ticket** is $161 for adults and children 10 and over, and $146 for children 3 to 9. Other multiday, multipark combination passes are available as well. In addition, many area accommodations offer lodging packages that include admission for 1 or more days. Be sure to check the Disney website, www.disneyland.com, for seasonal ticket specials.

Advance tickets may be purchased through Disneyland's website (www.disneyland.com), at Disney stores in the United States, by calling the ticket mail-order line (☏ **714/781-4043**), at any nearby Disneyland Resort Good Neighbor Hotel, or as part of your travel package.

Disneyland and Disney's California Adventure are open every day of the year, but operating hours vary, so be sure to call ☏ **714/781-7290** for information that applies to the specific day(s) of your visit. The same information, including ride closures and show schedules, can also be found online at **www.disneyland.com**. Generally speaking, the parks are open from 9 or 10am to 6 or 7pm on weekdays, fall to spring; and from 8 or 9am to midnight or 1am on weekends, holidays, and during winter, spring, or summer vacation periods.

WHEN TO GO   The Disneyland Resort is busiest in summer (btw. Memorial Day and Labor Day), on holidays (Thanksgiving week, Christmas week, Presidents' Day weekend, and Easter week), plus weekends year-round. All other periods are considered off season. Peak hours are from noon to 5pm; visit the most popular rides before and after these hours, and you'll cut your waiting times substantially. If you plan to arrive during a busy time, buy your tickets in advance and get a jump on the crowds at the ticket booths.

Attendance falls dramatically during the winter, so the park offers discounted or two-for-one admission to Southern California residents, who may buy up to five tickets per zip code verification.

Another secret timesaving tip is to enter Disneyland from the turnstile at the Monorail Station in Downtown Disney. The line is usually shorter and the Monorail will take you straight into Tomorrowland (but it doesn't stop in Disney's California Adventure). Another timesaver is booking your vacation through the Walt Disney Travel Company—those package guests can enter Mickey's Toontown and Fantasyland 1 hour before the general public.

Check out Disney's complimentary **FASTPASS** system. Here's how it works: Say you want to ride Space Mountain, but the line is long—*so* long, the current wait sign indicates a 75-minute standby. Instead, you can head to the automated FASTPASS ticket dispenser, where you pop in your park ticket to receive a free voucher listing a computer-assigned boarding time later that day. When you return at the assigned time, you enter through the

RELAX . . . THINK fun, NOT FRANTIC

It's finally here, the dream vacation to "The Happiest Place on Earth"! Whether you're 6 or 60, it's hard to keep from getting caught up in the excitement, even when you're the one responsible for the (seemingly) endless planning stage.

Once you arrive and enter the theme park(s), kids—and plenty of adults—seem to kick into warp speed. Here are just a few suggestions to avoid common pitfalls:

o **Write Down Your Car's Location:** When you're rushing to jump the tram for the park, it's easy to forget that your section/row/floor looks exactly like dozens of others in the parking lot or structure. Take a second to write down your parking location, because you'll be absorbing a lot of memories between now and the exhausted end of the day.

o **Don't Overplan:** Only the most stubbornly energetic parkgoers can manage to see everything at Disneyland in 1 day. California Adventure is more manageable but can also be time-consuming at peak capacity. Agree as a group to several must-do rides and activities each.

o **Pace Yourself:** First thing in the morning . . . why are those folks running to catch the parking lot tram? Relax, the theme parks aren't going anywhere, and trams run constantly during peak arrival and departure hours. While inside the park, stagger long waits in line with easy-entry shows and rides, and remember to sit with a refreshing drink every now and then.

o **Set a Spending Limit:** Kids should know they have a certain amount to spend on between-meal snacks and Disney souvenirs, so they'll look around and carefully decide which trinket is the one they can't live without.

o **Dress Comfortably:** We mean *really* comfortably, so you can stay that way throughout a long, hot day with lots of walking and lots of standing. Reliable walking shoes, layered clothing, and a hat and/or sunglasses to protect against sunburn are all must-haves. And be advised, there are lockers inside the park near the entrance to Main Street, so you needn't weigh yourself down by trying to carry everything you brought—and everything you bought—with you at all times.

FASTPASS gate and have to wait only about 10 minutes (to the envy of everyone in the slowpoke line).

Note: You can obtain a FASTPASS for only one attraction at a time. Also, the FASTPASS system doesn't eliminate the need to arrive at the theme park early because there's only a limited supply of FASTPASSes available for each attraction on a given day. So if you don't show up until the middle of the afternoon, you might find that all the FASTPASSes have been distributed to other guests.

DISNEYLAND ★★★

Disneyland is divided into eight subareas, or "lands," arranged around a central hub, each of which has a number of rides and attractions that are, more or less, related to that land's theme.

MAIN STREET U.S.A. At the park's entrance, Main Street U.S.A. is an idealized version of a turn-of-the-20th-century American small-town street inspired by Marceline, Missouri (Walt Disney's childhood home), and built on a seven-eighths scale. Attention to detail here is exceptional—interiors, furnishings, and fixtures conform to the period. As with any real Main Street, the Disney version is essentially a collection of shops and eating places, with a city hall, a fire station, and an old-time silent cinema. Live performances include piano playing at the Carnation ice-cream parlor and Dapper Dan's barbershop quartet along the street. A mixed-media attraction combines a presentation on the life of Walt Disney (The Walt Disney Story) with a patriotic remembrance of Abraham Lincoln. Horse-drawn trolleys, fire engines, and horseless carriages give rides along Main Street and transport visitors to the central hub (properly known as the Central Plaza).

Because there are no major rides, it's best to tour Main Street during the middle of the afternoon, when lines for rides are longest, and in the evening, when walkways can be packed with visitors viewing Disneyland's parades and shows.

ADVENTURELAND ★★ Inspired by the most exotic regions of Asia, Africa, India, and the South Pacific, Adventureland is home to several popular rides. Here's where you can cavort inside **Tarzan's Treehouse,** a climb-around attraction based on the animated film. Its neighbor is the **Jungle Cruise,** where passengers board a large, authentic-looking Mississippi River paddle boat and float along an Amazon-like river; a spear's throw away is the **Enchanted Tiki Room,** one of the most sedate attractions in Adventureland. Inside, you can sit down and watch a 20-minute musical comedy featuring electronically animated tropical birds, flowers, and "Tiki gods."

The **Indiana Jones Adventure ★★** is Adventureland's star ride. Based on the Steven Spielberg films, this ride takes adventurers into the Temple of the Forbidden Eye in joltingly realistic all-terrain vehicles. Riders follow Indy and experience the perils of bubbling lava pits, whizzing arrows, fire-breathing serpents, collapsing bridges, and the familiar tumbling boulder (an effect that's very realistic to riders in the front seats).

NEW ORLEANS SQUARE A large, grassy green dotted with gas lamps, New Orleans Square evokes the French Quarter's timeless charm. One of Disneyland's most popular rides, **Pirates of the Caribbean,** is located here; visitors still float on boats through mock underground caves, but now one of the major scenes is Captain Jack Sparrow and his cohorts from the hit film franchise doing battle with Davy Jones. The venerable **Haunted Mansion** looms here as well, where the dated effects are more funny than scary. Even in the middle of a sweltering summer day, you can dine by the cool moonlight to the sound of crickets in the **Blue Bayou** restaurant, the only eatery inside Disneyland that requires reservations (stop by early in the day to make yours).

CRITTER COUNTRY An ode to the backwoods, Critter Country is a sort of Frontierland without those pesky settlers. Older kids and grown-ups head straight for **Splash Mountain ★★**, one of the largest water-flume rides in the world. Loosely based on the Disney movie *Song of the South,* the ride is lined with about 100 characters that won't stop singing "Zip-A-Dee-Doo-Dah." Be prepared to get wet, especially if someone sizable is in the front seat of your log-shaped boat. The **Many Adventures of Winnie the Pooh**

The Disneyland Resort

SIDE TRIPS FROM LOS ANGELES

is a children's attraction based on Winnie the Pooh and his friends from the Hundred-Acre Wood—Tigger, Eeyore, Piglet, and the gang. The attraction is of the kinder, gentler sort, where you board "hunny bee-hives" and take a slow-moving journey through the Hundred-Acre Wood in endless pursuit of "hunny." The high-tech gadgetry and illusions are spellbinding for kids and mildly entertaining for adults. (*Tip:* It's a very popular attraction, so be sure to arrive early or make use of FASTPASS.) While it may not be the fastest ride in the park, **Davy Crockett's Explorer Canoes** allow folks to row around Tom Sawyer Island. It's the only ride where you actively control your boat (no underwater rails!).

FRONTIERLAND Inspired by 19th-century America, Frontierland features a raft to **Pirate's Lair at Tom Sawyer's Island,** a do-it-yourself play area with live pirates, island caverns, and rope bridges leading to buried treasure. You'll also find the **Big Thunder Mountain Railroad,** a runaway roller coaster that races through a deserted 1870s gold mine. Children will dig the petting zoo, and there's an Abe Lincoln–style log cabin; both are great for exploring with the little ones. This is also where you board one of two riverboats—*Mark Twain* and the *Sailing Ship Columbia*—that navigate the waters around Tom Sawyer Island and Fort Wilderness. As with the other river craft, the riverboats suspend operations at dusk.

When it's showing (it's a seasonal presentation), head to Frontierland's **Rivers of America** after dark to see the *FANTASMIC!* show. It mixes magic, music, 50 live performers, floats, and sensational special effects. Just as he did in *The Sorcerer's Apprentice,* Mickey Mouse battles evil and conjures good, using his magical powers to create giant water fountains, enormous flowers, and fantasy creatures.

MICKEY'S TOONTOWN ★ This is a colorful, whimsical world inspired by the film *Who Framed Roger Rabbit?*—a wacky, gag-filled land populated by 'toons. In addition to serving as a place where guests can be certain of finding Disney characters at any time during the day, Mickey's Toontown serves as an elaborate interactive playground where it's okay for the kids to run, climb, and let off steam. There are several rides and play areas, including **Roger Rabbit's CarToonSpin, Donald's Boat, Chip 'n' Dale's Treehouse, Gadget's Go Coaster,** and **Mickey's House & Minnie's House.**

FANTASYLAND With a storybook theme, this is the catchall "land" for stuff that doesn't quite fit anywhere else. Most of the rides are geared to the under-6 set, including the **King Arthur Carousel, Mad Tea Party, Dumbo the Flying Elephant ride,** and **Casey Jr. Circus Train.** Some, like **Mr. Toad's Wild Ride** and **Peter Pan's Flight,** appeal to grown-ups as well, and are original attractions from opening day in 1955. You'll also find **Alice in Wonderland, Snow White's Scary Adventures, Pinocchio's Daring Journey,** and more.

The most lauded attraction is **it's a small world,** a slow-moving indoor river ride through a saccharine scenario of all the world's children singing the song everybody loves to hate. For a different kind of thrill, try the **Matterhorn Bobsleds,** a zippy roller coaster through chilled caverns and drifting fog banks. It's one of the park's most popular rides and the world's first steel tubular-track roller coaster.

TOMORROWLAND ★ Conceived as an optimistic look at the future, Tomorrowland employs an angular, metallic look popularized by futurists like Jules Verne. Longtime Tomorrowland favorites include the revamped **Space Mountain ★** (a pitch-black indoor roller coaster that assaults your equilibrium and ears with its near constant side-to-side motions), and **Star Tours,** the original Disney–George Lucas joint venture, with a 3-D update that opened the summer of 2011. Those with queasy tendencies should sit out this ride. In the **Finding Nemo Submarine Voyage,** the famous Tomorrowland submarines have resurfaced after a hiatus and now dive the Tomorrowland Lagoon with Marlin and Dory in search of Nemo from the Disney film *Finding Nemo.*

Other Tomorrowland attractions include **Buzz Lightyear Astro Blasters,** where guests pilot their own Star Cruiser through a comical interactive space mission to conquer the Evil Emperor Zurg; *Captain EO Returns,* the 17-minute interactive film starring the late Michael Jackson as Captain EO on his quest to change the world; the **Disneyland Monorail,** a "futuristic" elevated monorail that takes you to Downtown Disney and back again (and offers the only practical opportunity for escaping the park during the crowded lunch period and early afternoon); and **Innoventions,** a huge, busy collection of industry-sponsored hands-on exhibits such as the **Dream Home**—a 5,000-plus-square-foot home belonging to the fictional Elias family—which provides a glimpse of the emerging digital advances for future high-tech homes.

DISNEY'S CALIFORNIA ADVENTURE ★★

In late 2007, Disney executives announced a multiyear expansion plan for the Disneyland Resort, largely focused on creating some new shows and attractions for Disney's California Adventure. The goal, they said, will be to bring more of Walt Disney into Disney's California Adventure, and to celebrate the hope and optimism of California that attracted Walt to the Golden State in the 1920s.

That said, guests to Disney's California Adventure will notice changes taking place around them through 2012, when the park caps its expansion with the opening of a new Cars Land. Until then, all of Disney's California Adventure's popular attractions will generally continue to operate, but expect a few construction fences guiding guests around development sites.

THE GOLDEN STATE ★★ This multidimensional area represents California's history, heritage, and physical attributes. Sound boring? Actually, the park's splashiest attractions are here. **Condor Flats** is a tribute to daring aviators; inside a weathered corrugated test pilots' hangar is **Soarin' Over California ★★★**, the simulated hang-glider ride that immediately rose to the top on everyone's "ride first" list (it's equipped with FASTPASS, and I highly recommend using it). It uses cutting-edge technology to combine elevated seats with a spectacular IMAX-style surround-movie—riders literally "soar" over California's scenic lands, feeling the Malibu ocean breeze and smelling the Central Valley orange groves and Yosemite pines.

Nearby, California Adventure's iconic Grizzly Peak towers over the **Grizzly River Run ★**, a splashy gold-country ride through caverns, mine shafts, and water slides; it culminates with a wet plunge into a spouting geyser. Kids can cavort nearby on the **Redwood Creek Challenge Trail,** a forest playground with smoke-jumper cable slides, net climbing, and swaying bridges.

Pacific Wharf was inspired by Monterey's Cannery Row and features mouthwatering demonstration attractions by **Boudin Sourdough Bakery** and **Mission Tortillas.** If you get hungry, each has a food counter where you can enjoy soup in a sourdough bowl or tacos, burritos, and enchiladas.

PARADISE PIER ★★ Journey back to the glory days of California's beachfront amusement piers—remember Santa Monica, Santa Cruz, and Belmont Park?—on this fantasy boardwalk. Highlights include **California Screamin' ★★**, a classic roller coaster that replicates the whitewashed wooden white-knucklers of the past—but with state-of-the-art steel

> **Sneak Preview**
>
> Stop by the "Blue Sky Cellar," a converted "aging room" in the Golden Wine Vinery that now hosts a terrific preview of all the changes coming to Disney's California Adventures. It's updated frequently by Disney's Imagineers and provides a behind-the-scenes look at the future development projects.

construction and a smooth, computerized ride that catapults you from 0 to 55 mph in less than 5 seconds, then takes a loop-de-loop over the boardwalk. There's also the **Silly Symphony Swings,** a wave swinger themed to Disney's Band Concert; **Goofy's Sky School,** a wacky, wild trip along L.A.'s precarious hilltop street that is way scarier than it looks (formerly Mulholland Madness); and **Mickey's Fun Wheel,** featuring unique zigzagging cars that bring a new twist to the familiar ride. Guests can don 3-D glasses as they "shrink" to the size of a toy and hop into fanciful vehicles that travel and twist along a midway-themed route in **Toy Story Mania.** Upon arriving at each game booth, you aim for animated targets using your onboard "toy cannon." The newest addition to the area is a nighttime water spectacular: **World of Color.** Disney animation comes to life by combining hundreds of fountains, dazzling LED-produced colors, and a kaleidoscope of audio and visual effects, all projected on the largest water screen.

Paradise Pier also has all the familiar boardwalk games (complete with stuffed prizes); guilty-pleasure fast foods like pizza, corn dogs, and burritos; plus a full-service ocean-themed restaurant called **Ariel's Grotto.**

HOLLYWOOD PICTURES BACKLOT ★★ If you've visited Disney in Florida, you might recognize many elements of this *trompe l'oeil* re-creation of a Hollywood movie-studio lot. Pass through a classic studio archway flanked by gigantic golden elephants and you'll find yourself on a surprisingly realistic Hollywood Boulevard. One of the resort's most anticipated attractions is the **Twilight Zone Tower of Terror ★★**. This truly scary ride has been a huge hit since its debut at Walt Disney World. Legend has it that during a violent storm on Halloween night 1939, lightning struck the Hollywood Tower Hotel, causing an entire wing and an elevator full of people to disappear. In this now eerily vacant hotel, you tour the lobby, library, and boiler room, and ultimately board the elevator to plunge 13 stories to the fifth dimension and beyond.

The Backlot's other main attraction is *Disney Channel Rocks!* featuring songs from *Hannah Montana, High School Musical,* and more. Other popular shows include ***Monsters, Inc. Mike & Sully to the Rescue!*** where guests ride taxis through Monstropolis on a mission to safely return "Boo" to her bedroom; and ***Jim Henson's MuppetVision 3D ★***, an on-screen comedy romp featuring Kermit, Miss Piggy, Gonzo, Fozzie Bear—and even hecklers Waldorf and Statler. Although it's not nearly as entertaining as ***It's Tough to Be a Bug*** (see below), it has its moments and won't scare the bejesus out of little kids.

At the end of the street, the replica movie palace **Hyperion Theater** presents Broadway-caliber live-action shows of classic Disney films. In the **Disney Animation** building, visitors can participate in different interactive galleries and learn how stories become animated features as told by Disney artists in the Drawn to Animation studio.

A BUG'S LAND ★   This bug-themed land encompasses ***It's Tough to Be a Bug ★★***, **Flik's Fun Fair,** and **Bountiful Valley Farm.** Inspired by the movie *A Bug's Life, It's Tough to Be a Bug* uses 3-D technology to lead the audience on an underground romp in the insect kingdom, with bees, termites, grasshoppers, stink bugs, spiders, and a few surprises that keep everyone hopping, ducking, and laughing along. (I could see how little kids might find the show rather terrifying, however.) The **Flik's Fun Fair** area features bug-themed rides and a water playground designed especially for little ones ages 4 to 7—but sized so their parents can ride along, too. **Bountiful Farm** pays tribute to California's agriculture.

DOWNTOWN DISNEY DISTRICT ★

Borrowing a page from central Florida's successful Disney compound, the **Downtown Disney District** is a colorful (and very sanitized) "street scene" filled with restaurants, shops, and entertainment for all ages. Options abound: Window-shop with kids in tow, have an upscale dinner for two, or party into the night. The promenade begins at the amusement park gates and stretches toward the Disneyland Hotel; there are nearly 20 shops and boutiques, and a dozen-plus restaurants, live music venues, and entertainment options.

Highlights include **House of Blues,** the blues-jazz restaurant/club that features Delta-inspired cuisine, big-name musicians, and the hand-clapping Sunday Gospel Brunch; **Ralph Brennan's Jazz Kitchen,** a spicy mix of New Orleans traditional foods and live jazz; **ESPN Zone,** the ultimate sports, dining, and entertainment experience, including an interactive game room with a rock-climbing wall; and **World of Disney,** one of the biggest Disney shopping experiences anywhere, with a vast and diverse range of toys, souvenirs, and collectibles. There is also an AMC Theatres 12-screen multiplex, the LEGO Imagination Center, a Sephora cosmetics store, and more.

Where to Stay

For vacation packages at any of the Disneyland Resort hotels, call the Walt Disney Travel Company at **866/60-DISNEY** (603-4763).

VERY EXPENSIVE

The Disneyland Hotel ★★ ☺   The Holy Grail of Disney-goers has always been this, the "Official Hotel of the Magic Kingdom." A monorail connection via Downtown Disney means you'll be able to return to your room anytime, whether to take a much-needed nap or to change your soaked shorts after riding Splash

Mountain. The theme hotel is an attraction unto itself and is the best choice for families with small children. The rooms are in the midst of a full-scale "reimagination," which will be completed in early 2012; each of the three towers will reflect a distinct "land" within the park (Adventureland, Fantasyland, and Frontierland). The look will be stylish but still family-friendly—down to headboards featuring Sleeping Beauty's Castle with illuminated fireworks. In-room amenities include movie channels (with free Disney Channel, naturally) and even Disneyland-themed toiletries and accessories such as Sneezy on the tissue box. The resort offers several restaurants (see below for a full review of **Goofy's Kitchen**), snack bars, and cocktail lounges; every kind of service desk imaginable; a video game center; and the Never Land Pool Complex with a white-sand beach and separate adult pool nearby.

1150 W. Magic Way, Anaheim, CA 92802. www.disneyland.com. ✆ **714/956-MICKEY** (6425). Reservations fax 714/956-6582. 990 units. $255–$345 double; from $750 suite. 2-night minimum stay. AE, MC, V. Valet parking $22; self-parking for up to 2 cars $15. **Amenities:** 2 restaurants; lounge; children's programs; concierge; small fitness center; Jacuzzi; 3 outdoor pools (including adults-only pool); room service. *In room:* A/C, TV, fridge, hair dryer, free Wi-Fi.

Disney's Grand Californian Hotel & Spa ★★ ☺

Disney didn't miss the details when constructing this enormous version of an Arts and Crafts–era lodge (think Yosemite's Ahwahnee and Pasadena's Gamble House), hiring craftspeople throughout the state to contribute one-of-a-kind tiles, furniture, sculptures, and artwork. Taking inspiration from California's redwood forests, mission pioneers, and plein-air painters, designers created a nostalgic yet state-of-the-art high-rise hotel that has its own private entrance into Disney's California Adventure park and Downtown Disney District.

Enter through subtle (where's the door?) stained-glass sliding panels to the hotel's centerpiece, a six-story "living room" with a William Morris–designed marble "carpet," an angled skylight seen through exposed support beams, display cases of Craftsman treasures, and a three-story walk-in "hearth" whose fire warms Stickley-style rockers and plush leather armchairs.

Guest rooms are spacious and smartly designed, carrying through the Arts and Crafts theme surprisingly well, considering the hotel's grand scale. The best ones overlook the park, but you'll pay for that view. Despite the sophisticated air of the Grand Californian, this is a hotel that truly caters to families, with a bevy of room configurations, including one with a double bed plus bunk beds with a trundle. Since the hotel provides sleeping bags (rather than rollaways) for kids, this standard-size room will sleep a family of five—but you have to share the bathroom. *Tip:* Ask for a free upgrade to a room with a view of the park when you check in—they're pretty generous about this.

The hotel's two main restaurants are the upscale **Napa Rose** and the **Storytellers Cafe,** a "character dining" restaurant that's always bustling with excited kids who pay more attention to Chip and Dale than their eggs and bacon (be sure to make a breakfast reservation). Also on the property is **Mandara Spa,** offering a complete array of spa services for men and women.

1600 S. Disneyland Dr., Anaheim, CA 92802. www.disneyland.com. ✆ **714/956-MICKEY** (6425; central reservations) or 714/635-2300. Fax 714/956-6099. 948 units. $300–$500 double; from $600 suite. AE, DC, DISC, MC, V. Valet parking $22; self-parking $15. **Amenities:** 2 restaurants; lounge; children's center; concierge; concierge-level rooms; Jacuzzi; 2 outdoor pools; room service; spa. *In room:* A/C, TV, fridge, hair dryer, free Wi-Fi.

EXPENSIVE

Disney's Paradise Pier Hotel ★ ☺   The whimsical beach-boardwalk theme of this 15-story hotel ties in with the Paradise Pier section of Disney's California Adventure park across the street. The surfer theme salutes the heyday of seaside amusement parks with nautical and beach decor in the guest rooms, nostalgic California artwork, and a water slide modeled after the wooden roller coasters of yesteryear. Book a room at this smallest Disney property only if the other two are full—it's not as "magical" as the original Disneyland Hotel and is soundly trounced by the superlative Grand Californian. It's also not as centrally located as the other two hotels, which could be a problem if you're not fond of walking. It does, however, offer "family suites" that comfortably accommodate families of six or more, as well as Lilo & Stitch's Aloha Breakfast featuring island songs and tableside visits at the hotel's **PCH Grill.** Kids even get to make their own pizzas (pseudo–breakfast pizzas with peanut butter and gummy bears and such, or, for lunch/dinner, traditional pizzas baked in the kitchen oven). *Tip:* Request a room that either overlooks the Paradise Pier section of California Adventure or has direct access to the poolside cabanas.

1717 S. Disneyland Dr., Anaheim, CA 92802. www.disneyland.com. ✆ **714/956-MICKEY** (6425). Reservations fax 714/956-6582. 489 units. $250–$350 double; from $400 suite. AE, MC, V. Valet parking $22; self-parking $15. **Amenities:** 2 restaurants; lounge; children's programs; fitness center; Jacuzzi; outdoor pool; room service. *In room:* A/C, TV, fridge, hair dryer, free Wi-Fi.

Sheraton Anaheim Hotel ★   This hotel rises to the festive theme-park occasion with its fanciful English Tudor architecture; it's a castle that lures business conventions, Disney-bound families, and local high-school proms. The public areas are quiet and elegant—intimate gardens with fountains and koi ponds, and a plush lobby and lounges—which can be a pleasing touch after a frantic day at the amusement park. The rooms are modern and unusually spacious, but otherwise not distinctive. A large swimming pool sits in the center of the complex, surrounded by attractive landscaping. Book suites well in advance; they are often the first room types to go due to the busy conference schedule during the week and families coming in on weekends.

900 S. Disneyland Dr. (at I-5), Anaheim, CA 92802. www.sheraton.com. ✆ **800/325-3535** or 714/778-1700. Fax 714/535-3889. 489 units. $149–$225 double; from $300 suite. AE, DC, MC, V. Parking $10; free Disneyland shuttle. **Amenities:** Restaurant; lounge; concierge; fitness center; Jacuzzi; outdoor pool; room service; free Wi-Fi in lobby. *In room:* A/C, TV, hair dryer, minibar, Wi-Fi ($9.95 per day).

MODERATE

The Anabella Hotel ★   Uniting several formerly independent low-rise hotels across the street from Disney's California Adventure, the developers behind the Anabella started from scratch, gutting each building to create carefully planned rooms for park-bound families and business travelers alike. The complex features a vaguely mission-style facade of whitewashed walls and red-tiled roofs, though guest room interiors are strictly contemporary in style and modern in appointments. Bathrooms are generously sized and outfitted in honey-toned granite; most have a tub/shower combo—just a few are shower-only. Though parking areas dot the grounds, you'll also find a pleasant garden around the central swimming pool and whirlpool; a separate adult pool hides out next to the streetside fitness room. Business travelers will appreciate the in-room executive desks with high-speed Internet access, while families can take advantage of "kids' suites" complete with bunk beds and separate bedrooms. There's a pleasant indoor-outdoor all-day restaurant, and the hotel is a stop on both the Disney and Convention Center shuttle routes. *Note:* Rooms and rates vary wildly in terms of room size, layout, and occupancy limits; extra time spent at the hotel's website and with the reservationist will pay off in the most comfortable room for your needs.

1030 W. Katella Ave. (at S. West St.), Anaheim, CA 92802. www.anabellahotel.com. © **800/863-4888** or 714/905-1050. Fax 714/905-1054. 360 units. $99–$209 double. AE, DC, DISC, MC, V. Parking $12. **Amenities:** Restaurant; lounge; concierge; exercise room; Jacuzzi; 2 outdoor heated pools (including adults-only pool); room service. *In room:* A/C, TV, fridge, hair dryer, Wi-Fi ($9.95 per day).

Anaheim Plaza Hotel & Suites ★ ✦ Although it's across the street from the Disneyland Resort's main gate, you'll appreciate the way this hotel's clever design shuts out the noisy world. In fact, the seven two-story garden buildings remind me more of 1960s Waikiki than busy Anaheim (maybe it's the palm trees). A key feature is the Olympic-size heated outdoor pool and adjacent whirlpool. The furnishings are motel-bland, but you won't spend much time here anyway. On the plus side, little has changed about the friendly rates, which often drop as low as $69.

1700 S. Harbor Blvd. (at Katella Ave.), Anaheim, CA 92802. www.anaheimplazahotel.com. © **800/631-4144** or 714/772-5900. Fax 714/772-8386. 300 units. $89–$129 double; from $178 suite. AE, DC, DISC, MC, V. Parking $4.60. **Amenities:** Restaurant; lounge; Jacuzzi; large outdoor heated pool; room service (only at breakfast). *In room:* A/C, TV, hair dryer, Wi-Fi ($9.95 per day).

Portofino Inn & Suites ★ ☺ Emerging from the rubble of the former Jolly Roger Hotel renovation, this complex of low- and high-rise all-suite buildings sports a cheery yellow exterior and family-friendly interior. The location couldn't be better—directly across the street from California Adventure's backside. You can either walk or take the ART (Anaheim Resort Transit) to the front gate. Designed to work as well for business travelers from the nearby Convention Center as for Disney-bound families, the Portofino offers contemporary, stylish furnishings, as well as vacation-friendly rates and suites for any family configuration. Families will want a Kids' Suite, which features bunk beds and a sleeper sofa, plus a TV, fridge, and microwave—and that's just in the kids' room; Mom and Dad have a separate bedroom with grown-up comforts like a double vanity, shower massage, and their own TV. Parking and complimentary Internet access are included in the daily resort fee of $9.50.

1831 S. Harbor Blvd. (at Katella Ave.), Anaheim, CA 92802. www.portofinoinnanaheim.com. © **800/398-3963** or 714/782-7600. Fax 714/782-7619. 190 units. $109–$169 double; $132–$259 suite. AE, DC, DISC, MC, V. Free parking. **Amenities:** Exercise room; Jacuzzi; outdoor pool. *In room:* A/C, TV, hair dryer, free Wi-Fi.

INEXPENSIVE

Candy Cane Inn ★★ ✦ Take your standard U-shaped motel court with outdoor corridors, spruce it up with cobblestone drives and walkways along with old-time street lamps, add flowering vines engulfing room balconies, and you have the Candy Cane. The face-lift worked, making this gem near Disneyland's main gate a treat for the stylish bargain hunter. The rooms are decorated in bright floral motifs with comfortable furnishings, including queen-size beds and a separate dressing and vanity area. Breakfast is served in the courtyard, where you can also splash around in a heated pool, whirlpool, or kids' wading pool. If you feel like splurging, request one of the Premium Rooms with extended checkout and nightly turndown service.

1747 S. Harbor Blvd., Anaheim, CA 92802. www.candycaneinn.net. ✆ **800/345-7057** or 714/774-5284. Fax 714/772-1305. 171 units. $95–$179 double. Rates include expanded continental breakfast. AE, DC, DISC, MC, V. Free parking and Disneyland shuttle. **Amenities:** Exercise room; Jacuzzi; outdoor heated pool and wading pool. *In room:* A/C, TV, fridge, hair dryer, free Wi-Fi.

Travelodge Anaheim   On the back side of Disneyland, this modest hotel appeals to the budget-conscious traveler who's looking for plenty of free perks, such as Wi-Fi and continental breakfast. All rooms have a refrigerator and microwave, and you can relax by the large outdoor heated pool and Jacuzzi while using the laundry room. The extra-large family rooms accommodate virtually any brood, and the public ART shuttles run regularly to the park. *Tip:* Request a Star Light room, in which "stars" appear when you turn off the lights at night (it's free!).

1057 W. Ball Rd., Anaheim, CA 92802. www.travelodge.com. ✆ **800/578-7878** or 714/774-7600. Fax 714/535-6953. 95 units. $90–$110 double; $115 family room with 3 queen beds. Rates include full breakfast. AE, DC, DISC, MC, V. Free parking. **Amenities:** Jacuzzi; outdoor heated pool. *In room:* A/C, TV, fridge, hair dryer, free Wi-Fi.

Where to Eat

There's nothing quite like an energetic family vacation to build an appetite, and sooner or later, you'll have to make the inevitable Disney dining decisions: where, when, and for how much? The expanded Disneyland Resort has something for everyone, a respectable lineup that can easily meet your needs for the duration of the typical visit. For many years, dining options were pretty sparse, limited to those inside Disneyland and some old standbys at the Disneyland Hotel. But Disney's big expansion upped the ante with national theme/concept restaurants along Downtown Disney and competitive dining options at the resort hotels. The best of the bunch are reviewed below. For dining reservations at any place throughout the Disneyland Resort, call ✆ **714/781-DINE** (3463).

EXPENSIVE

Napa Rose ★★★ CALIFORNIAN   Inside the upscale Grand Californian Hotel, Napa Rose is the first really serious (read: on "foodie" radar) restaurant at the Disneyland Resort. Its warm and light dining room mirrors the Arts and Crafts style of the hotel, down to Frank Lloyd Wright stained-glass windows and Craftsman-inspired seating throughout the restaurant and adjoining lounge. Executive chef Andrew Sutton was lured away from the Napa Valley's chic Auberge du Soleil, bringing with him a wine-country sensibility and passion for fresh California ingredients and inventive preparations. You can see him busy in the impressive open exhibition kitchen, showcasing specialty items like Sierra golden trout, artisan cheeses from Humboldt County and the Gold Country, and the Sonoma rabbit in Sutton's signature braised mushroom-rabbit tart. The tantalizing Seven Sparkling Sins starter platter (for two) features jewel-like portions of foie gras, caviar, oysters, lobster, and other exotic delicacies; the same attention to detail is evident in seasonally composed main-course standouts like grilled yellowtail with tangerine-basil fruit salsa atop savory couscous, or free-range veal *osso buco* in rich bacon–forest mushroom ragout. Leave room for dessert, to at least share one of pastry chef Jorge Sotelo's creative treats; our favorites are Sonoma goat-cheese flan with Riesling-soaked tropical fruit, and chocolate crepes with house-made caramelized banana ice cream. Napa Rose boasts an impressive and balanced wine list, with 60 by-the-glass choices (and 40-plus sommeliers, the most of any restaurant in the world); and outdoor seating is arranged around a rustic fire pit, facing a landscaped arroyo toward California Adventure's distinctive Grizzly Peak. *Tip:* My favorite place to sit is at the counter facing the exhibition kitchen. Also, you can skip all the pomp and circumstance of a full sit-down meal by dining at the restaurant's lounge, which offers full menu service.

1600 S. Disneyland Dr. (in Disney's Grand Californian Hotel). © **714/300-7170.** www.disney land.com. Reservations strongly recommended. Main courses $26–$40. AE, DC, DISC, MC, V. Daily 11:30am–2pm and 5:30–10pm.

MODERATE

Catal Restaurant/Uva Bar ★★ MEDITERRANEAN/TAPAS

Branching out from the acclaimed Patina restaurant in Los Angeles, high-priest-of-cuisine Joachim Splichal brings us this Spanish-inspired Mediterranean concept duo at the heart of Downtown Disney. The main restaurant, Catal, features a series of intimate second-floor rooms that combine rustic Mediterranean charm with fine dining. Complemented by an international wine list, the menu is a collage of flavors that borrow from France, Spain, Italy, Greece, Morocco, and the Middle East—all united in selections that manage to be intriguing but not overwhelming. Though the menu will vary seasonally, expect to find selections that range from braised lamb shoulder with spicy red lentil curry to chorizo-spiked Spanish paella or roasted half chicken with savoy cabbage and Dijon mustard *jus*.

The Uva Bar (*uva* means "grape" in Spanish) is a casual tapas bar located at an outdoor courtyard right in the middle of the Downtown Disney walkway. Martinis are a standout here; and there are also 40 different wines by the glass. The affordable menu features the same pan-Mediterranean influence, even offering many items from the Catal menu; standouts include cabernet-braised short ribs atop horseradish mashed potatoes, marinated olives, and cured Spanish ham; and Andalusian gazpacho with rock shrimp.

Note: For an even more casual Italian experience—and one that's considerably more kid-friendly—try **Naples Ristorante e Pizzeria** (1550 Downtown Disney Dr.; © **714/776-6200**), also a Patina Group restaurant. There are two dozen thin-crust pizzas, plus sandwiches and salads.

1580 Disneyland Dr. (at Downtown Disney). © **714/774-4442.** www.disneyland.com. Reservations recommended Sun–Thurs, not accepted Fri–Sat for Catal; not accepted for Uva Bar. Main courses $23–$34; tapas $8–$12. AE, DC, DISC, MC, V. Daily 8am–10pm.

Goofy's Kitchen ☺ AMERICAN

Your younger kids will never forgive you if they miss an opportunity to dine with their favorite Disney characters at this colorful, lively restaurant inside the Disneyland Hotel. Known for its entertainment and wacky and off-center Toontown-esque decor, Goofy's Kitchen features tableside visits by a rotating selection of Disney characters (always Goofy, but also may include Jasmine, Pinocchio, or Cinderella) who thrill the youngsters with dancing, autograph signing, and up-close-and-personal encounters. Meals are buffet-style and offer an adequate selection of crowd pleasers and reliable standbys, from made-to-order omelets at brunch to Prime rib, salmon, Caesar salad, and pastas at dinner. The most popular kid food is the peanut butter pizza (even for breakfast), the buffet of desserts, Mickey Mouse–shaped waffles, and Mickey ear–shaped chicken nuggets. This place isn't really about the food, though, and is definitely *not* for kidless grown-ups (unless you're trying to make up for a deprived childhood). Bring a camera and Disney autograph book for capturing the family's "candid" encounters. *Tip:* Make reservations for an early or late breakfast or dinner to avoid the mayhem.

1150 Magic Way (inside the Disneyland Hotel). ✆ **714/956-6755** or 714/781-DINE (3463). www.disneyland.com. Reservations recommended. Buffet dinner $32 adults, $14 children 3–9; buffet brunch $26 adults, $14 children 3–9. AE, DC, DISC, MC, V. Daily 7am–1pm and 5–9pm.

Sports fans may prefer to dine at the **ESPN Zone** in Downtown Disney, 1545 Disneyland Dr. (✆ **714/300-ESPN [3776]**; www.espnzone.com). More than 175 TV monitors allow you to watch just about every current sporting event in the U.S. while dining on American grill food and pub fare.

House of Blues AMERICAN/SOUTHERN   For years, fans have been comparing the House of Blues to Disneyland, so this celeb-backed restaurant/nightclub fits right into the Disney compound. Locations in Las Vegas, L.A., Orlando, and so forth all sport a calculated backwoods-bayou-meets-Country-Bear-Jamboree appearance that fits right into the Disney-fied world. The Anaheim HOB follows the formula, filled with made-to-look-old found objects, amateur paintings, uneven wood floors, seemingly decayed chandeliers, and a country-casual attitude. The restaurant features Delta-inspired stick-to-your-ribs cuisine like gumbo, pan-seared voodoo shrimp, Creole seafood jambalaya, cornmeal-crusted catfish, baby back ribs glazed with Jack Daniel's sauce, and spicy Cajun meatloaf—plus some out-of-place Cal-lite stragglers like a fresh catch of the day and wild-mushroom penne pasta. Sunday's Gospel Brunch is an advance-ticket event of hand-clapping, foot-stomping proportions. The adjacent Company Store offers logo ware interspersed with selected pieces of folk art. HOB's state-of-the-art Music Hall is a welcome addition to the local music scene (advance tickets are highly recommended for big-name bookings).

1530 S. Disneyland Dr. (at Downtown Disney). ✆ **714/778-2583**. www.hob.com. Reservations recommended (tickets required for performances). Main courses $18–$29. AE, DC, DISC, MC, V. Daily 11am–1:30am.

Rainforest Cafe ☺ INTERNATIONAL   Designed to suggest ancient temple ruins in an overgrown Central American jungle, this national-chain favorite successfully combines entertainment, retail, and family-friendly dining in one fantasy setting. There are cascading waterfalls inside and out, a canopy of lush vegetation, simulated tropical mists, and even a troupe of colorful parrots beckoning shoppers into the Retail Village. Once seated, diners choose from an amalgam of wildly flavored dishes inspired by Caribbean, Polynesian, Latin, Asian, and Mediterranean cuisines. Masquerading under exotic-sounding names like Shrimpkins (a kids' menu staple of popcorn shrimp and "Jurassic" chicken tidbits) and Mojo Bones (barbecued pork ribs), the food is really fairly familiar: A translated sampling includes Cobb salad, pita sandwiches, potstickers, shrimp-studded pasta, and charbroiled chicken. Fresh-fruit smoothies and tropical specialty cocktails are offered, as is a best-shared dessert called the Giant Chocolate Volcano. After your meal, you can browse through logo items, environmentally educational toys and games, stuffed jungle animals and puppets, straw safari hats, and other themed souvenirs in the lobby store. There's a children's menu, and the Rainforest Cafe is one of the few Downtown Disney eateries to have full breakfast service.

1515 S. Disneyland Dr. (at Downtown Disney). ☏ **714/772-0413.** www.rainforestcafe.com. Reservations recommended for peak mealtimes. Main courses $13–$20. AE, DC, DISC, MC, V. Sun–Thurs 8am–11pm; Fri–Sat 8am–midnight.

Ralph Brennan's Jazz Kitchen ★★ CAJUN/CREOLE If you always thought Disneyland's New Orleans Square was just like the real thing, wait until you see this fun Southern concept restaurant at Downtown Disney. Ralph Brennan, of the New Orleans food dynasty responsible for NOLA landmarks like Commander's Palace and a trio of Big Easy hot spots, commissioned a handful of New Orleans artists to create the handcrafted furnishings that give the Jazz Kitchen its believable French Quarter ambience. Lacy wrought-iron grillwork, cascading ferns, and trickling stone fountains enhance three separate dining choices: The upstairs Carnival Club is an elegant dining salon with silk-draped chandeliers and terrace dining that overlooks the "street scene" below; casual Flambeaux is downstairs, where a bead-encrusted grand piano hints at the nightly live jazz that sizzles in this room; and the Creole Cafe is a quick stop for necessities like muffulettas or beignets. Expect traditional Cajun-Creole fare with heavy-handed seasonings and rich, heart-stopping sauces.

1590 S. Disneyland Dr. (at Downtown Disney). ☏ **714/776-5200.** www.rbjazzkitchen.com. Reservations strongly recommended. Main courses $19–$33; cafe items $7–$10. AE, DC, DISC, MC, V. Mon–Thurs 11am–10pm; Fri–Sat 11am–11pm; Sun 10am–10pm.

INEXPENSIVE

Tortilla Jo's ☺ MEXICAN The offerings at this indoor/outdoor eatery are diverse enough to appeal to kids—they get their menu of mini soft tacos and quesadillas—and upscale enough to attract hungry adults (did I mention there are also more than 100 tequilas to choose from?). Guacamole is prepared fresh to-order; if you like it spicy, ask the kitchen to add jalapeños. As the name might suggest, the tortillas are handmade here. Fajitas are a favorite, as are citrus-braised pork carnitas.

1510 Disneyland Dr. (at Downtown Disney). ☏ **714/535-5000.** www.patinagroup.com. Main courses $12–$19. AE, DISC, MC, V. Sun–Thurs 11am–9pm; Fri–Sat 11am–10pm.

KNOTT'S BERRY FARM

30 miles SE of Downtown Los Angeles

Although destined to forever be in the shadow of Mickey's megaresort, the reality is that Knott's doesn't even attempt to compete with the Disney empire: Instead, it targets Southern California thrill-seekers (droves of them) by offering a far better selection of scream-inducing thrill rides.

Like Disneyland, Knott's Berry Farm is not without historical background. In 1920, Walter Knott began farming 20 acres of leased land on Hwy. 39 (now Beach Blvd.). When things got tough during the Depression, Mrs. Knott began selling pies, preserves, and home-cooked chicken dinners. Within a year, she was selling 90 meals a day. Lines became so long that Walter decided to create an Old West Ghost Town—America's first theme park—in 1940 as a diversion for waiting customers.

Today Knott's amusement park offers a whopping 165 shows, attractions, and state-of-the-art rides that are far more intense than most of the rides at the Disneyland Resort. Granted, it's less than half the size of the Disney Resort, but if you're more into fast-paced amusement rides than swirling teacups, it offers twice the thrill.

Essentials

GETTING THERE   Knott's Berry Farm is at 8039 Beach Blvd. in Buena Park. It's about a 10-minute ride north on I-5 from Disneyland. From I-5 or California 91, exit south onto Beach Boulevard. The park is about half a mile south of California 91.

VISITOR INFORMATION   The **Buena Park Convention and Visitors Office,** 6601 Beach Blvd., Ste. 200, Buena Park (✆ **714/562-3560;** www.buena park.com), provides specialized information on the area, including Knott's Berry Farm. To learn more about the amusement park before you arrive, call ✆ **714/220-5200** or log on to **www.knotts.com**.

ADMISSION PRICES & OPERATING HOURS   Admission to the park, including unlimited access to all rides, shows, and attractions, is $57 for Regular (ages 12 and up), $25 for Junior (ages 3–11) and Senior (62 and older), and free for children 2 and under. Admission after 4pm (on any day the park is open past 6pm) is $29 for Regular and $25 for Junior. Parking is $12. Tickets can also be purchased at many Southern California hotels, where discount coupons are sometimes available.

Like Disneyland, Knott's offers discounted admission—$47—for Southern California residents with zip codes 90000 through 93599, so if you're bringing local friends or family members along, try to take advantage of the bargain. Always check the website for Deals and Discounts, too. Also like Disneyland, Knott's Berry Farm's hours vary from week to week, so call ahead. The park generally opens daily at 10am and closes at 6 or 7pm, except Saturdays, when it stays open until 10pm. Operating hours and prices often change with seasonal promotions, so it's always a good idea to call Knott's Info at ✆ **714/220-5200** for specific hours on the day you plan to visit. Stage shows and special activities are scheduled throughout the day; pick up a schedule at the ticket booth.

Where to Stay

Knott's Berry Farm Resort Hotel ★ ☺   Within easy walking distance of Knott's Berry Farm, this nine-story hotel offers the only accommodations near the amusement park. Despite the hotel's lengthy moniker, the exterior and lobby have the look of a business hotel. There are two things I like best about this hotel: the Peanuts-themed rooms, complete with Snoopy tuck-in service and Camp Kids bedtime stories (told via the in-room phone by the bed), and free shuttle service to Disneyland, 7 miles away. There's also a large family pool with a children's water play structure, and an arcade. Be sure to inquire about special rates and Knott's multiday vacation package deals.

7675 Crescent Ave. (at Grand Ave.), Buena Park, CA 90620. www.knottshotel.com. ✆ **866/752-2444** or 714/995-1111. Fax 714/828-8590. 320 units. $179 standard room; $224 Snoopy room. Prices vary depending on date of visit and room availability. AE, DC, DISC, MC, V. Parking $12 per night; free Disneyland shuttle. **Amenities:** Restaurant; lounge; concierge; fitness center; Jacuzzi;

large outdoor pool; room service; 2 outdoor tennis and basketball courts (lit for night play). *In room:* A/C, TV, hair dryer, Wi-Fi ($10 per day).

Where to Eat

Mrs. Knott's Chicken Dinner Restaurant ☺ AMERICAN   Knott's Berry Farm got its start as a roadside diner in 1934, and you can still get a filling—albeit unhealthful—all-American meal without even entering the theme park. Cordelia Knott's down-home cooking was so popular that her husband created a few humble attractions to amuse patrons as they waited to be served. Today more than 1.5 million annual patrons line up around the building to experience Cordelia's original recipe (very similar to the Colonel's, I must admit). Looking just as you'd expect—country cute, with window shutters, old black-and-white photos of the original diner, and calico prints aplenty—the restaurant serves up its featured attraction of the original fried chicken dinner, complete with soup, salad, warm buttermilk biscuits, mashed potatoes and chicken gravy, and a slice of famous pie (the boysenberry pie is fantastic). If you're not visiting the amusement park, park in the lot that offers 3 free hours.

8039 Beach Blvd. (near La Palma Ave.), Buena Park. *©* **714/220-5080.** Reservations not accepted. Complete dinners $16. DC, DISC, MC, V. Daily at 7am; closing times vary.

THE SOUTH COAST

Seal Beach is 36 miles S of downtown L.A.; Newport Beach, 49 miles; Dana Point, 65 miles

Whatever you do, don't say "Orange County" here. The mere name evokes images of smoggy industrial parks, cookie-cutter housing developments, and the staunch Republicanism that prevails behind the so-called "orange curtain." We're talking instead about the Orange Coast, one of Southern California's best-kept secrets—a string of seaside jewels that have been compared with the French Riviera or the Costa del Sol. Forty-two miles of beaches offer pristine stretches of sand, tide pools teeming with marine life, ecological preserves, secluded coves, picturesque pleasure-boat harbors, and legendary surf breaks. My advice? Make it a day trip from L.A.—hit the road early for a scenic cruise down Pacific Coast Highway starting at Seal Beach, stop for lunch at Laguna Beach (the prettiest of all the So Cal beach towns), continue south to Dana Point where the *really* expensive resorts reside, and then take the freeway back to L.A. (I-5 to the I-405).

Essentials

GETTING THERE   See "Getting There," in chapter 17, for airport and airline information. By car from Los Angeles, take I-5 or I-405 south. The scenic, shore-hugging Pacific Coast Highway (Calif. 1, or just PCH to the locals)

A Special Arts Festival

A tradition for 60-plus years in arts-friendly Laguna, the **Festival of Arts & Pageant of the Masters** is held each summer throughout July and August.

It's pretty large now, and it includes the formerly "alternative" Sawdust Festival across the street. See **www.foapom. com.**

Laguna Beach.

Huntington Beach.

links the Orange Coast communities from Seal Beach in the north to Capistrano Beach just south of Dana Point, where it merges with I-5. To reach the beach communities directly, take the following freeway exits: **Seal Beach,** Seal Beach Boulevard from I-405; **Huntington Beach,** Beach Boulevard/Calif. 39 from either I-405 or I-5; **Newport Beach,** Calif. 55 from either I-405 or I-5; **Laguna Beach,** Calif. 133 from I-5; **San Juan Capistrano,** Ortega Highway/Calif. 74 from I-5; and **Dana Point,** Pacific Coast Highway/Calif. 1 from I-5.

Driving the Orange Coast

You'll most likely be exploring the coast by car, so the beach communities are covered in order, from north to south. Keep in mind, however, that if you're traveling between Los Angeles and San Diego, Pacific Coast Highway (Calif. 1) is a breezy, scenic detour that adds less than an hour to the commute—so pick out a couple of seaside destinations and take your time.

Seal Beach, on the border between Los Angeles and Orange counties, and a neighbor to Long Beach's Naples Harbor, is geographically isolated by both the adjacent U.S. Naval Weapons Station and the self-contained Leisure World retirement community. As a result, the beach town appears untouched by modern development—it's Orange County's version of small-town America. Take a stroll down Main Street for a walk back in time, culminating in the Seal Beach Pier. Although the clusters of sunbathing, squawking seals that gave the town its name aren't around any more, old-timers still fish, lovers still stroll, and families still cavort by the seaside, enjoying great food and retail shops or having a cold drink at Hennessey's tavern.

Huntington Beach—or Surf City, as it's known—is the largest Orange Coast city; it stretches quite a way inland and has seen the most urbanization. To some extent, this has changed the old boardwalk and pier to a modern outdoor mall where cliques of teens coexist with families and the surfers who continue to flock here, drawn by Huntington's legendary place in surf lore. Hawaiian-born George Freeth is credited with bringing the sport here in 1907, and some say the breaks around the pier and Bolsa Chica are the best in California. The world's top wave riders flock to Huntington each August for the rowdy but professional **U.S. Open of Surfing.** If you're around at Christmastime, try to see the gaily decorated marina homes and boats in Huntington Harbor by taking the **Cruise of Lights,** a 45-minute narrated sail through and around the harbor islands. The festivities generally last from mid-December to Christmas; call 🕿 **714/840-7542** for schedules and ticket information.

The name **Newport Beach** conjures comparisons to Rhode Island's Newport, where the well-to-do enjoy seaside living with all the creature comforts. That's the way it is here too, but on a less grandiose scale. From the million-dollar Cape Cod–style cottages on sunny Balboa Island to elegant shopping complexes such as Fashion Island and South Coast Plaza (an über-mall with valet parking, car detailing, limo service, and concierge; see sidebar on p. 718), this is where fashionable socialites, right-wing celebrities, and business mavens can all be found. Alternatively, you could explore **Balboa Peninsula**'s historic Pavilion and old-fashioned pier, or board a passenger ferry to Catalina Island.

Laguna Beach, whose breathtaking geography is marked by bold elevated headlands, coastal bluffs, pocket coves, and a very inviting beach, is known as an artists' enclave, but the truth is that Laguna has became so "in" (read: expensive) that it's driven most of the true bohemians out. Their legacy remains, with the annual **Festival of Arts & Pageant of the Masters** (see "A Special Arts Festival," above), as well as a proliferation of art galleries mingling with high-priced boutiques along the town's cozy streets. In warm weather, Laguna Beach has an overwhelming Mediterranean-island ambience, which makes *everyone* feel beautifully, idly rich.

San Juan Capistrano, in the verdant headlands inland from Dana Point, is defined by Spanish missions and its loyal swallows. The mission architecture is authentic, and history abounds. Think of San Juan Capistrano as a compact, life-size diorama illustrating the evolution of a small Western town—from Spanish-mission era to secular rancho period, statehood, and into the 21st century. Surprisingly, Mission San Juan Capistrano (see "Seeing the Sights," below) is

Bolsa Chica Ecological Reserve.

Balboa Peninsula.

once again the center of the community, just as the founding friars intended 200 years ago.

Dana Point, the last town south, has been called a "marina development in search of a soul." Overlooking the harbor stands a monument to 19th-century author Richard Henry Dana, who gave his name to the area and described it in *Two Years Before the Mast.* Activities generally center on yachting and Dana Point's beautiful harbor. Nautical themes are everywhere, particularly the streets named for old-fashioned shipboard lights—a hodgepodge that includes Street of the Amber Lantern, Street of the Violet Lantern, Street of the Golden Lantern, and so on. Bordering the harbor is Doheny State Beach (see "Beaches & Nature Preserves," below), one of the very best for its seaside park and camping facilities.

Enjoying the Outdoors

BEACHES & NATURE PRESERVES   The **Bolsa Chica Ecological Reserve,** in Huntington Beach (© 714/846-1114; www.bolsachica.org), is a 900-acre restored urban salt marsh that's a haven to more than 200 bird species, as well as a wide variety of protected plants and animals. Naturalists come to spot herons and egrets, as well as California horn snails, jackknife clams, sea sponges, common jellyfish, and shore crabs. An easy 1.5-mile loop trail begins from a parking lot on Pacific Coast Highway (Calif. 1) a mile south of Warner Boulevard; docents lead a narrated walk the first Saturday of every month. The trail heads inland, over Inner Bolsa Bay and up Bolsa Chica bluffs. It then loops back toward the ocean over a dike that separates the Inner and Outer Bolsa bays and traverses a coastal sand-dune system. This beautiful hike is a terrific afternoon adventure. The Bolsa Chica Conservancy has been working since 1978 on reclaiming the wetlands from oil companies that began drilling here more than 70 years ago. It's an ongoing process, and you can still see those "seesaw" drills dotting the outer areas of the reserve.

Huntington City Beach, adjacent to Huntington Pier, is a haven for volleyball players and surfers; dense crowds abound, but so do amenities such as outdoor showers, beach rentals, and restrooms. Just south of the city beach is 3-mile-long **Huntington State Beach.** Both popular beaches have lifeguards and concession stands seasonally. The state beach also has restrooms, showers, barbecue pits, and a waterfront bike path. The main entrance is on Beach Boulevard, and there are access points all along Pacific Coast Highway (Calif. 1).

Newport Beach runs for about 5 miles and includes both Newport and Balboa piers. It has outdoor showers, restrooms, volleyball nets, and a vintage boardwalk that just may make you feel as though you've stepped 50 years back in time. **Balboa Bike and Beach Stuff** (© 949/723-1516), at the corner of Balboa and Palm near the pier, rents a variety of items, from pier fishing poles to bikes, beach umbrellas, and body boards. The **Southwind Kayak Center,** 17855 Sky Park Circle, Irvine (© 800/768-8494 or 949/261-0200; www.southwindkayaks.com), rents sea kayaks for use in the bay or open ocean at rates starting at $60 per day; instructional classes are available on weekends, with some midweek classes in summer. The center also conducts several easygoing guided outings, including a $55 Back to Nature trip that highlights the marine life around Dana Point.

Crystal Cove State Park.

Crystal Cove State Park, which covers 3 miles of coastline between Corona del Mar and Laguna Beach and extends into the hills around El Moro Canyon, is a good alternative to the more popular beaches for seekers of solitude. (There are, however, lifeguards and restrooms.) The beach is a winding, sandy strip, backed with grassy terraces; high tide sometimes sections it into coves. The entire area offshore is an underwater nature preserve. There are four entrances, including Pelican Point and El Moro Canyon. For information, call **© 949/494-3539** or log on to **www.crystalcovestatepark.com**.

Salt Creek Beach Park lies below the palatial Ritz-Carlton Laguna Niguel; guests who tire of the pristine swimming pool can venture down the staircase on Ritz-Carlton Drive to wiggle their toes in the sand. The setting is spectacular, with wide white-sand beaches looking out toward Catalina Island (which explains why the Ritz-Carlton was built here). The park has lifeguards, restrooms, a snack bar, and convenient parking near the hotel.

Doheny State Beach in Dana Point, just south of Dana Point Marina (enter off Del Abispo St.), has long been known as a premier surfing spot and camping site. Doheny has the friendly vibe of beach parties in days gone by: Tree-shaded lawns give way to wide beaches, and picnicking and beach camping are encouraged. There are 121 sites that can be used for either tents or RVs, plus a state-run visitor center featuring several small aquariums of sea and tide-pool life. For more information and camping availability, call **© 949/496-6172.**

BICYCLING Biking is the most popular beach activity up and down the coast. A slower-paced alternative to driving, it allows you to enjoy the clean, fresh air and notice smaller details of these laid-back beach towns and harbors. The Newport Beach visitor center (see "Visitor Information," earlier in this chapter) offers a free map of trails throughout the city and harbor. Bikes and equipment can be rented at **Balboa Bike & Beach Stuff,** 601 Balboa Blvd., Newport Beach (**© 949/723-1516**); and at **Laguna Beach Cyclery,** 240 Thalia St. (**© 949/494-1522;** www.lagunacyclery.net).

GOLF Many golf-course architects have used the geography of the Orange Coast to its full advantage, molding challenging and scenic courses from the rolling bluffs. Most courses are private, but a few outstanding ones are open to the public. **The Links at Monarch Beach,** 50 Monarch Beach Resort North, Dana Point (**© 949/240-8247;** www.monarchbeachgolf.com), is particularly impressive. This hilly, challenging course, designed by Robert Trent Jones, Jr., offers great ocean views. Afternoon winds can sneak up, so accuracy is essential. Weekend morning greens fees are $165 to $195

($145–$175 weekdays). The rates after 1pm drop to $135 weekends and $115 weekdays.

GONDOLA RIDES   Newport Harbor's 6-mile-long stretch of luxury homes and boats provides a picturesque backdrop for mood-setting romance aboard the Venetian-style boats of **Gondola Adventures ★★**, 3101 West Coast Hwy. (*©*) **949/646-2067;** www.gondola.com). Cozy couples can bundle up beneath blankets as they cruise the canals—tradition dictates that you kiss under every bridge. If you're lucky, your gondolier will amplify the experience—literally—with song. *Tip:* Many a proposal has been accepted via the "message in a bottle" notes that your gondolier can plant for an additional fee.

Seeing the Sights

Beyond the sights listed below, one of the most popular Orange Coast attractions is **Balboa Island** (www.balboaisland.com). The charm of this pretty little neighborhood isn't diminished by knowing that the island was man-made—and it certainly hasn't affected the price of real estate (it's hard to believe that the original property lots sold for $250). Tiny clapboard cottages in the island's center and modern houses with two-story windows and private docks along the perimeter make a colorful and romantic picture. You can drive onto the island on Jamboree Road to the north or take the three-car ferry from Balboa Peninsula (www.balboaislandferry. com). It's generally more fun to park and take the 30-minute ferry ride as a pedestrian, since the island is crowded and lacks parking, and the tiny alleys they call streets are more suitable for strolling. **Marine Avenue,** the main commercial street, is lined with small shops and cafes that evoke a New England fishing village. Shaved ices sold by sidewalk vendors will relieve the heat of summer.

Balboa Pavilion & Fun Zone ★ ☺   This historic cupola-topped structure, a California Historical Landmark, was built in 1906 as a bathhouse for swimmers in their ankle-length bathing costumes. Later, during the Big Band era, dancers

Newport Harbor.

Balboa Pavilion & Fun Zone.

rocked the Pavilion doing the Balboa Hop. Now it serves as the terminal for Catalina Island passenger service, harbor and whale-watching cruises, and fishing charters. The surrounding boardwalk is the Balboa Fun Zone (© **949/673-0408;** www.thebalboafunzone.com), a collection of carnival rides, game arcades, and vendors of hot dogs and cotton candy. For Newport Harbor or Catalina cruise information, call © **949/673-5245;** for sport fishing and whale-watching, call © **949/673-1434.**

600 E. Bay Ave., Balboa, Newport Beach. © **949/675-1905.** www.balboapavilion.com. From Calif. 1, turn south onto Newport Blvd. (which becomes Balboa Blvd. on the peninsula); turn left at Main St.

International Surfing Museum Nostalgic Gidgets and Moondoggies shouldn't miss this monument to the laid-back sport that has become synonymous with California beaches. You'll find gargantuan longboards from the sport's early days, memorabilia of Duke Kahanamoku and the other surfing greats represented on the Walk of Fame near Huntington Pier, and a gift shop where a copy of the *Surfin'ary* can help you bone up on your surfer slang even if you don't know which foot is goofy.

411 Olive Ave., Huntington Beach. © **714/960-3483.** www.surfingmuseum.org. Free admission. Mon and Wed–Fri noon–5pm; Tues noon–9pm; Sat–Sun 11am–6pm (hours tend to vary, so call ahead).

Laguna Art Museum   This beloved local institution is working hard to position itself as the artistic cornerstone of the community. In addition to a small but interesting permanent collection, the museum presents installations of regional works definitely worth a detour. Past examples include a display of surf photography from the coast's 1930s and 1940s golden era, and dozens of plein-air Impressionist paintings (ca. 1900–30) by the founding artists of the original colony. The museum is also open for extended hours (until 9pm) during Laguna Beach Artwalk, the first Thursday each month, when all are admitted free from 5 to 9pm.

307 Cliff Dr., Laguna Beach. © **949/494-8971.** www.lagunaartmuseum.org. Admission $12 adults, $10 students and seniors, free for children 11 and under. Daily 11am–5pm.

Mission San Juan Capistrano   The seventh of the 21 California coastal missions, Mission San Juan Capistrano is continually being restored. The mix of old ruins and working buildings is home to small museum collections and various adobe rooms that are as quaint as they are interesting. The intimate mission chapel with its ornate baroque altar is still used for religious services, and the mission complex is the center of the community, hosting performing arts, children's programs, and other cultural events year-round.

Mission San Juan Capistrano.

This mission is best known for its **swallows,** which are said to return to nest each year at their favorite sanctuary. According to legend, the birds wing their way back to the mission annually on March 19, St. Joseph's Day, arriving at dawn; they are said to take flight again on October 23, after bidding the mission farewell. In reality, you'll probably see the well-fed birds here any day of the week, winter or summer. *Tip:* Admission for adults and seniors includes a complimentary audio tour.

Ortega Hwy. (Calif. 74), San Juan Capistrano. © **949/234-1300.** www.missionsjc.com. Admission $9 adults, $8 seniors, $5 children. Daily 8:30am–5pm. Closed Thanksgiving, Christmas Eve, Christmas Day, and Good Friday (weather conditions can close the Mission unexpectedly).

Where to Stay

VERY EXPENSIVE

Montage Resort & Spa ★★   The rich have it good when it comes to vacationing, and the investors behind this 30-acre Arts and Crafts beauty have created yet another reason for big spenders to unwind along the Orange Coast. You can barely see it from the PCH, and the front entrance is rather understated, but as you walk through the lobby and onto the balcony overlooking the . . . oh my. The change of scenery is so breathtakingly abrupt that it takes composure not to sprint down to the gorgeous mosaic-tiled pool or run barefoot along the sun-kissed beach. It's the same view from the balcony of every room, and you never tire of it.

The Montage Resort is all about style. You don't even check in at the front desk: As soon as you arrive, you're warmly greeted and given a well-rehearsed tour of the resort by attractive khaki-clad employees wearing tailored jackets. The tour ends at the neo-Craftsman-style guest rooms, which are spacious, immaculate, and tastefully decorated with muted color schemes, museum-quality plein-air artwork, huge marble bathrooms with oversize tubs and plush robes, 27-inch flatscreen TVs with DVD players, quality dark-wood furnishings, feather-top beds with goose-down pillows, and very inviting balconies. But you'll be spending very little time here as you lounge by the infinity-edged pool sipping a lemonade, spend hours exploring the tide pools, stroll through the hotel's impeccably manicured park and pristine beaches, spoil yourself rotten with skin treatments and massages at the oceanfront Spa Montage, and then feast on chef Craig Strong's imaginative cuisine at the resort's signature restaurant, **Studio.** There's plenty for kids to do as well: They have their own pool and several fun-filled programs to keep them entertained (and, of course, there's the beach).

30801 South Coast Hwy., Laguna Beach, CA 92651. www.montagelagunabeach.com. © **866/ 271-6953** or 949/715-6000. Fax 949/715-6100. 250 units. $575–$795 double; from $1,295 suite. AE, DISC, MC, V. Valet parking $30. **Amenities:** 3 restaurants and lobby lounge w/live entertainment; concierge; oceanfront fitness facilities and spa; room service. *In room:* A/C, flatscreen TV and DVD/CD player, hair dryer, minibar, Wi-Fi ($16 per day).

Pelican Hill Resort ★★   Past grand Romanesque columns on PCH, everything about this luxury resort was inspired by the 16th-century architecture of Andrea Palladio. Not just ordinary guest rooms or suites, there are only two main room categories here: bungalow and villa. Bungalows are geared more toward the casual traveler, while villas are intended to accommodate larger groups for longer-term stays. Each bungalow features its own patio (I only wish each had an umbrella to protect against sun or inclement weather—request one that does), a gas fireplace, and a gorgeous marble bathroom. The concierge gallery is its own dedicated space of first-rate, multimedia assistance and interactivity.

The two championship golf courses were designed by the celebrated Tom Fazio, and the 23,000-square-foot spa provides 22 treatment rooms for blissful escape. One of a kind, the awe-inspiring Coliseum pool features more than a million hand-laid glass tiles. The lovely Northern Italian Andrea restaurant is one of the best on the entire South Coast, making it truly unnecessary to ever leave the property. (The truffled risotto, which is finished in a giant wheel of aged Parmesan, is a must-try.) For kids, Camp Pelican provides activities for recreation and education; teens can enjoy similar amenities.

22701 Pelican Hill Rd., Newport Coast, CA 92657. www.pelicanhill.com. © **800/315-8214** or 949/467-6800. Fax 949/467-6888. 204 bungalows, 128 villas. $795–$995 double; from $1,150 suite. AE, DISC, MC, V. Valet parking complimentary. **Amenities:** 5 restaurants; concierge; children's programs; 2 championship golf course; fitness facilities and spa; 3 pools; room service. *In room:* A/C, flatscreen TV/DVD, hair dryer, minibar, free Wi-Fi.

Ritz-Carlton Laguna Niguel ★★ After a sorely needed $40-million renovation to keep up with neighboring resorts such as the Montage and St. Regis, this Dana Point grande dame has recaptured its status as one of the top resorts on the Orange Coast. From its perch on the edge of a 150-foot-high bluff overlooking an idyllic 2-mile-long beach, the view from most every window is spectacular (you can spend hours on your balcony admiring the ocean view). The most welcome change is that every guest room and public space has been completely remodeled with a much more chic and contemporary look. The spacious rooms are now outfitted with 42-inch plasma TVs with DVD players, sumptuous furnishings and fabrics, an Italian-marble bathroom equipped with a double vanity, and very comfortable feather beds. The resort's main restaurant, the surprisingly casual hallway-adjacent Raya, offers chef Richard Sandoval's flavorful pan-Latin fare, along with gorgeous ocean views. For an impressive selection of cheese, chocolate, and fine wines, the small but elegant Eno bar conjures impressive pairings. Other improvements include a new luxury spa and oceanfront fitness center. As always, lush terraces and colorful flower gardens abound throughout the well-tended property, and service—in typical Ritz-Carlton style—is unassuming and impeccable. Garden tours, beach shuttles, surf lessons, and excellent kids' programs are available as well.

1 Ritz-Carlton Dr., Dana Point, CA 92629. www.ritzcarlton.com. © **800/241-3333** or 949/240-2000. Fax 949/240-0829. 393 units. From $495 gardenview/poolview double; $645 oceanview double; from $1,050 suite. Children 17 and under stay free in parent's room. Midweek and special packages available. AE, DC, DISC, MC, V. Parking $35. **Amenities:** 2 restaurants; lounge; children's programs; concierge; health club; room service; spa; 2 outdoor tennis courts; shuttle to/from beach and golf course. *In room:* A/C, TV w/pay movies, hair dryer, minibar, Wi-Fi included in resort fee.

St. Regis Monarch Beach Resort & Spa ★★★ Let's cut to the chase: The St. Regis Monarch Beach Resort is one of the finest luxury hotels I have ever had the pleasure of reviewing. They nailed it with this one, setting a standard for all other resort hotels. Everything oozes with indulgence, from the stellar service to the striking artwork, high-tech electronics, absurdly comfortable beds, stellar restaurants, and a 30,000-square-foot spa that will blow your mind. The $240-million, 172-acre resort opened on July 30, 2001, with a massive star-studded gala, and has since been wooing the wealthy with its gorgeous Tuscan-inspired architecture and soothing ocean views.

Perfection is all in the details, and the St. Regis is full of them: a three-lane lap pool with an underwater sound system; a yoga, spinning, and "movement" studio; a full-service Vogue salon; private poolside cabanas; fantastic cuisine at Michael Mina's popular **Stonehill Tavern** restaurant ★★★; couples' spa treatment rooms with whirlpool baths and fireplaces; an 18-hole Robert Trent Jones, Jr., golf course; and even a private beach club. The guest rooms are loaded with beautiful custom-designed furniture, 32-inch Sony Vega flatscreen TVs with CD/DVD audio systems and a 300-DVD library, huge marble-laden bathrooms with glass shower doors that must weigh 100 pounds, the most comfortable bathrobe I've ever worn, and 24-hour butler service.

The resort's only drawback is that although it's near the beach, unlike the Ritz-Carlton Laguna Niguel and Montage (see above), it's not on it. The view of the terraced pool area, golf course, and shimmering ocean beyond is fantastic, however, and the hotel offers complimentary shuttle service to the 2-mile-long beach, as well as exclusive access to the **St. Regis Beach Club,** where attendants set up chairs, towels, and umbrellas, and also take food and beverage orders. You can even hire a "Surf Butler," who takes your measurements for a wet suit, brings out a board, and gives you lessons.

1 Monarch Beach Rd., Dana Point, CA 92629. www.stregismb.com. ℭ **800/722-1543** or 949/234-3200. Fax 949/234-3201. 400 units. From $512 resortview double; from $620 oceanview double; from $775 suite. Golf and spa packages available. AE, DC, DISC, MC, V. Valet parking $30. **Amenities:** 6 restaurants; lounge; wine cellar tasting room; children's club; concierge; 18-hole golf course; fitness center; 3 pools; 2 hot tubs; room service; Spa Gaucin; complimentary local shuttle. *In room:* A/C, TV w/DVD library, CD/DVD player, hair dryer, minibar, Wi-Fi ($13 per day).

Surf and Sand Resort ★   The nine-story Surf and Sand Resort has come a long way since it started in 1948 as a beachside motor lodge with 13 units. Still occupying the same fantastic oceanside location, it now features 152 guest rooms that, despite their simplicity and standard size, feel enormously decadent. They're all very bright and beachy; each has a private balcony with a dreamy ocean view, a marble bathroom accented handsomely with granite, and plush cotton terry robes. *Tip:* Try getting one of the deluxe corner rooms, with an expanded 90-degree view of the California coastline—it's well worth the additional dollars. Also, be sure to check their website for special package deals. Opened in early 2002, the hotel's Mediterranean-style **Aquaterra Spa** offers a tantalizing array of personalized massage, skincare, and body treatments. You'll find the requisite ocean-inspired treatments, but the menu also features eight different specialty massages, each with your choice of four aromatherapy oils. The spa's four Couples Rituals offer themed body treatments followed by a bubble bath for two (the tub has an ocean view) and a massage to finish. The outdoor fire-pit areas are very romantic. **Splashes** restaurant serves breakfast, lunch, and dinner daily in a beautiful oceanfront setting.

1555 South Coast Hwy. (south of Laguna Canyon Rd.), Laguna Beach, CA 92651. www.surfand sandresort.com. ℭ **888/869-7569** or 949/497-4477. Fax 949/494-2897. 165 units. $535–$700 double; from $700 suite. AE, DC, DISC, MC, V. **Amenities:** Restaurant; bar; summer children's programs; concierge; fitness room; outdoor heated pool; room service; full-service spa; whirlpool. *In room:* TV/DVD, hair dryer, minibar, MP3 docking station, free Wi-Fi.

EXPENSIVE

The Balboa Bay Club & Resort ★   Spread out over 15 acres, this bayfront resort retains late '40s charm but with many modern-day amenities; it's been a perennially popular destination for the duration. The staff is immensely helpful and takes great pride in its knowledge of the property. Ask a question that someone can't answer off the top of his head, and you just might get an unexpected call from the concierge with the information. Rooms are tastefully appointed with mostly muted tones, though the occasional too-vibrant pattern—floral curtains adjacent to striped chairs—could use a retouch.

The 1,200-square-foot Bay View suites are worth the splurge for their unobstructed waterside sightlines, two separate patios—and privacy between bedroom and living area. There's even a ½-bath in the living room. The aptly named **First Cabin** restaurant is reminiscent of a cruise ship, in terms of both the offerings—everything from tableside Caesar and dry-aged filet mignon—and the sharply dressed longtime servers.

1221 Coast Hwy., Newport Beach, CA 92663. www.balboabayclub.com. ℂ **888/445-7153** or 949/645-5000. Fax 949/630-4215. 160 units. $325–$495 double; from $565 suite. Themed packages are available. AE, DISC, MC, V. Valet parking $28. **Amenities:** Restaurant, lounge with live entertainment; concierge; fitness center; heated pool with hot tub; room service; spa. *In room:* TV/DVD, fridge, Wi-Fi ($13 per day).

MODERATE

Blue Lantern Inn ★★ A three-story New England–style gray clapboard inn, the Blue Lantern is a pleasant cross between romantic B&B and modern, sophisticated small hotel. Almost all the rooms, which are decorated with reproduction traditional furniture and plush bedding, have a balcony or deck overlooking the harbor. All have a fireplace and whirlpool tub. You can have your breakfast here in private (clad in the fluffy robe provided) for an extra $5 per person or go downstairs to the sunny dining room that also serves complimentary afternoon tea. There's also an exercise room and a cozy lounge with menus for many area restaurants, plus loaner items like movies, books, and board games. The friendly staff welcomes you with home-baked cookies at the front desk.

34343 St. of the Blue Lantern, Dana Point, CA 92629. www.bluelanterninn.com. ℂ **800/950-1236** or 949/661-1304. Fax 949/496-1483. 29 units. $175–$600 double. Rates include full breakfast and afternoon tea, wine, hors d'oeuvres, and desserts. AE, DC, MC, V. Free parking. **Amenities:** Complimentary bikes; concierge; exercise room; whirlpool. *In room:* A/C, TV/DVD, fridge w/complimentary soft drinks, free Wi-Fi.

Casa Laguna Inn & Spa ★ Once you see this romantic terraced complex of Spanish-style cottages amid lush gardens and secluded patios—which offers all the amenities of a B&B *and* affordable prices—you might wonder, *What's the catch?* Well, the noise of busy PCH wafts easily into Casa Laguna, so light sleepers may be disturbed. Still, the Casa has been a favorite hideaway since Laguna's early days and now glows under the watchful eye of a terrific owner, who has upped the ante by adding a spa. Some rooms—especially the suites—are downright luxurious, with fireplace, kitchen, bathrobes, CD player, VCR, and other in-room goodies. Throughout the property, Catalina tile adorns fountains, and bougainvillea spills into paths; each room has an individual charm. Breakfast is served in the sunny morning room of the Craftsman-style Mission House, where a cozy living room invites relaxation and conversation.

2510 South Coast Hwy., Laguna Beach, CA 92651. www.casalaguna.com. ℂ **800/233-0449** or 949/494-2996. Fax 949/494-5009. 21 units. $159–$349 double; from $279 suite. Rates include breakfast, afternoon wine, and hors d'oeuvres. Off-season and midweek discounts available. AE, DISC, MC, V. **Amenities:** Heated outdoor pool; spa; whirlpool. *In room:* TV.

Where to Eat

Options in Seal Beach are limited, but a good choice for seafood is **Walt's Wharf,** 201 Main St. (☎ **562/598-4433**), a bustling, polished restaurant featuring market-fresh selections either plain or with Pacific Rim accents.

MODERATE

Crab Cooker SEAFOOD   Since 1951, folks in search of fresh, well-prepared seafood have headed to this bright-red former bank building. Also a fish market, the Crab Cooker has a casual atmosphere of humble wooden tables, uncomplicated smoked and grilled preparations, and meticulously selected fresh fare. The place is especially proud of its Maryland crab cakes; clams and oysters are also part of the repertoire.

2200 Newport Blvd., Newport Beach. ☎ **949/673-0100.** www.crabcooker.com. Main courses $14–$30 dinner, $11–$30 lunch. AE, MC, V. Sun–Thurs 11am–9pm; Fri–Sat 11am–10pm.

Harbor Grill SEAFOOD/STEAK   Located in a business/commercial mall right in the center of the Dana Point Marina, the Harbor Grill is enthusiastically recommended by locals for mesquite-broiled ocean-fresh seafood. Hawaiian mahimahi with a mango-chutney baste is on the menu, along with Pacific swordfish, crab cakes, and beef steaks. The restaurant is particularly proud of its scratch-made sauces and homemade marinades.

34499 St. of the Golden Lantern, Dana Point. ☎ **949/240-1416.** www.harborgrill.com. Reservations recommended. Main courses $19–$29. AE, DC, DISC, MC, V. Mon–Sat 11:30am–10pm; Sun 9am–9pm.

Las Brisas 📷 MEXICAN SEAFOOD   Las Brisas's breathtaking view of the Pacific (particularly at sunset) and potent margaritas are a surefire combination for a *muy romantico* evening. In fact, it's so popular that it can get pretty crowded during the summer months, so be sure to make a reservation. Affordable during

---

Shop-and-Dine in South Beach

Leave it to designer-conscious Orange County to plop some of its best restaurants in superupscale shopping malls. It turns out all fresco **Fashion Island,** 401 Newport Center Dr. (☎ 949/721-2000; www.shopfashionisland.com), is more than a playground for the *Real Housewives of Orange County*—it's a foodie oasis. And the same can be said for luxury behemoth **South Coast Plaza** (actually in Costa Mesa), 3333 Bristol St (☎ 800/782-8888; www.southcoastplaza.com). Highlights at the former include **Brasserie Pascal** (☎ 949/263-9400), the more casual but still stylish bistro from acclaimed area chef Pascal Olhats; **Rustica** (☎ 949/706-8282), a fresh modern Italian temple of gastronomy; and **True Food Kitchen** (☎ 949/644-2400), a global fusion of healthy goodies. At South Coast Plaza, both The An Family's Crustacean-offshoot **Anqi** (☎ 714/557-5679), a Vietnamese fusion eatery and gourmet noodle bar, and **Charlie Palmer** (☎ 714/352-2525), a modern American fine-dining restaurant with an emphasis on wine, are based in Bloomingdale's alone. Nearby there's also **Hamamori** (☎ 714/850-0880) for refined Japanese cuisine, and **Seasons 52** (☎ 714/437-5252), for festive but casual American fare and nightly piano music.

The Ramos House Café

If you're anywhere near San Juan Capistrano, you *have* to stop for breakfast or lunch at the Ramos House Café, a petite restaurant within an adorable little old house in the historic Los Rios district of San Juan Capistrano. Chef John Humphreys's swoon-inducing menu changes daily, and everything—from his roast turkey hash scramble with apple cider gravy to his corn and buttermilk crab cakes and Southern fried chicken salad—is made from scratch (even the ice cream is turned by hand). And if that's not the best soju bloody mary you'll ever have, send me a better recipe. The cafe is located at 31752 Los Rios St.—the oldest remaining residential street in California—near the train depot, and is open for breakfast and lunch Tuesday through Sunday from 8:30am to 3pm (© 949/443-1342; www.ramoshouse.com).

lunch but pricey at dinner, the menu consists mostly of seafood recipes from the Mexican Riviera. Even the standard enchiladas and tacos get a zesty update with crab or lobster meat and fresh herbs. Calamari steak is sautéed with bell peppers, capers, and herbs in a garlic-butter sauce, and king salmon is mesquite-broiled and served with a creamy lime sauce. Although a bit on the touristy side, Las Brisas can be a fun part of the Laguna Beach experience. *Tip:* The patio is considered prime territory at both lunch and dinner, but the birds can detract from the experience. I much prefer an inside window table. You still get the view, without the fuss.

361 Cliff Dr. (off the PCH north of Laguna Canyon), Laguna Beach. © **949/497-5434.** www.lasbrisaslagunabeach.com. Reservations recommended. Main courses $10–$27. AE, DC, DISC, MC, V. Mon–Thurs 8am–10pm; Fri–Sat 8am–11pm; Sun 9am–10pm. Valet parking $6.

Summer House CONTEMPORARY AMERICAN Fashioned after a seaside holiday beach retreat, with lots of cream-colored walls, subtle stripes, and an overall airy vibe, the casual but fresh menu is quite affordable. An ever-popular appetizer, the Kung Pao calamari strikes the right balance of spicy-sweet; for entrees, whole-grain mustard gives a new spin on the macadamia-crusted mahimahi.

2744 East Coast Hwy., Corona Del Mar. © **949/612-7700.** www.summerhousecdm.com. Main courses $10–$18. AE, DISC, MC, V. Daily 11am–9:30pm.

Watermarc NEW AMERICAN/SMALL PLATES The newest sister restaurant to more established area favorites 230 Forest and Opah, this sleek but welcoming bistro pulls off solid small plates during both lunch and dinner service. A large front window provides fun people-watching ops, particularly in the summer during festival season. Skilled servers are as well versed with the food-portion of the menu as they are enthusiastic about the wine list—heed their advice unless you feel strongly about a particular label or varietal. Some standout dishes include the sweet and savory fried Laura Chenel goat cheese with apples and honey, and refreshing *ahi* watermelon skewers. A handful of regular-sized entrees are available as well.

448 South Coast Hwy., Laguna Beach. © **949/376-6272.** www.watermarcrestaurant.com. Reservations recommended at dinner. Main courses $21–$34. AE, MC, V. Sun–Thurs 11am–11pm; Fri–Sat 11am–11pm.

14

SIDE TRIPS FROM LOS ANGELES

The South Coast

THE
SOUTHERN
CALIFORNIA
DESERT

by Harry Basch

15

To the casual observer, the Southern California desert might seem like a desolate expanse under an unrelenting sun. Its splendor is subtle, though; its beauty unfolds over time. If it looks as though nothing but insects could survive here, look again: You're bound to see a roadrunner or a tiny gecko dart across your path. Close your eyes and listen for the cry of a hawk or an owl. Check the ground for coyote or bobcat tracks. Notice the sparkle of fish in the streams running through palm oases. Check the road signs, which warn of desert tortoise crossings (the tortoise being one of many endangered species found only here, where it's protected by the federal government in a wildlife sanctuary). Visit in spring, when the ground throughout the Lancaster area is carpeted with the brilliant golds and oranges of the poppy, California's state flower.

If the beauty you seek is that of personal renewal, you're likely to find that, too—if not in the shadow of purple-tinged mountains and otherworldly rock formations, then in a chaise longue beside a sparkling, impossibly blue swimming pool. Destinations here range from gloriously untouched national parks to luxurious resorts—united by the fact that it's a rare day when the sun doesn't shine.

EN ROUTE TO THE PALM SPRINGS RESORTS

If you're making the drive from Los Angeles via I-10, you'll spend your first hour or so extricating yourself from the L.A. sprawl. But soon enough, you'll leave the Inland Empire auto plazas behind, and edge ever closer to the snowcapped (if you're lucky) San Bernardino and San Jacinto mountain ranges (coming from San Diego via I-15 N to I-215 N, to I-60 E, to I-10; the Palm Springs resorts are east of the junction with I-10).

Hadley's Fruit Orchards   Since 1931, this friendly emporium has been a fixture here, packed with people shopping for dates, dried fruits, nuts, honey, preserves, and other regional products. A snack bar serves the beloved date shake; there are also plenty of gift-packed treats to carry home. (For more about the date mystique, see "Sweet Desert Treat: The Coachella Valley Date Gardens," on p. 736.)

48980 Seminole Dr. (off I-10), Cabazon. ☏ **888/854-5655** or 951/849-5255. www.hadleyfruit orchards.com. Mon–Thurs 9am–5pm; Fri–Sun 8am–8pm (call to verify).

PREVIOUS PAGE: **Mature Joshua Tree, Covington Flat.**

Windmill Tours 🎁 For years, travelers through the San Gorgonio Pass have been struck by an awesome, otherworldly sight: never-ending, ever-expanding fields of windmills that harness the force of the breezes gusting through this passage and convert them to electricity, to power air-conditioners throughout the Coachella Valley. If you get a charge out of them, consider a guided tour, to understand more about this effective alternative energy source. Learn how designers have improved the efficiency of wind turbines (technically, they're not windmills), and measure those long rotors against the average human height (about 10 people could lie along one span).

I-10 (Indian Ave. exit), Palm Springs. ℃ **760/320-1365.** www.windmilltours.com. Admission $30 adults, $27 seniors, $11 children 11 and under. Tours Mon–Sat 9, 11:30am, and 2:30pm (varies seasonally). Call for reservations.

GET YOUR KICKS ON HISTORIC ROUTE 66

Until the final triumph of the multilane interstate system in the early 1960s, 2,300-mile-long **Route 66** was the only automobile route between the Chicago shores of Lake Michigan and L.A.'s golden Pacific beaches. "America's Main Street" rambled through eight states, and today, in each one, organizations exist, such as Route 66 Tourism, just to preserve its remnants. California has a lengthy stretch of the original highway, many miles of which still proudly wear the designation "California State Hwy. 66." Many stretches are home to clusters of new developments, shopping centers, and fast-food chains. Pretty mundane—until you round a curve and unexpectedly see a vintage wood-frame house, from a ranch that predates the Great Depression. Other picturesque relics of that era—single-story motels, two-pump gas stations—exist beside their modern neighbors, inviting nostalgia for a time when the vacation began the moment you backed out of the driveway.

Essentials

THE ROUTE   Our drive begins in **Pasadena** and ends in downtown **San Bernardino,** 56 miles west of Palm Springs. In San Bernardino, I-215 intersects Rte. 66; take it 4 miles south to rejoin I-10 and continue east.

   Note: This detour works equally well if your destination is Lake Arrowhead or Big Bear Lake; take I-215 north 3 miles to Hwy. 30 and continue into the mountains. For more information, see chapter 14, "Side Trips from Los Angeles." The drive can take from 2 to 3 hours, depending on how many relics and photo opportunities you investigate.

VISITOR INFORMATION   For more information, contact the **National Historic Route 66 Federation,** Box 1848, Dept. WS, Lake Arrowhead, CA 92352-1848 (℃ **909/336-6131;** www.national66.org). Or check out the quarterly *Route 66 Magazine* (four issues, $25; P.O. Box 1129, Port Richey, FL 34673; ℃ **727/847-9621;** www.route66magazine.com).

Let's Hit the Road!

Rte. 66 terminated at the picturesque Pacific, but the heart of Los Angeles has very few remnants of the old road. In light of this fact, Pasadena is the best point to enter the time warp that exists along this highway.

The Southern California Desert

One of my favorite establishments in Pasadena is the **Fair Oaks Pharmacy,** on the Southwest corner of Fair Oaks Avenue at 1526 Mission St., 1½ miles south of Colorado Boulevard (✆ **626/799-1414;** www.fairoakspharmacy.net), a fixture since 1915. Try an authentic ice-cream soda, a sparkling phosphate, a "Route 66" sundae, or an old-fashioned malt (complete with the frosty mixing can), all served by fresh-faced soda jerks from behind the marble counter. They also serve soup, sandwiches, and snacks. The Fair Oaks is still a pharmacy and offers a variety of gifts, including an abundance of Rte. 66–themed items. It's open Monday through Saturday from 9am to 9pm and Sunday from 10am to 7pm. The pharmacy is closed on Sunday.

For some driving music, reverse and go north on Fair Oaks to Colorado and turn right. **Canterbury Records,** 805 E. Colorado Blvd., a block west of Lake Avenue (✆ **626/792-7184**), has L.A.'s finest selection of big bands and pop vocalists on CDs. The store is open Monday through Saturday from 9am to 9pm and Sunday from 10am to 7pm.

As you continue east on Colorado Boulevard, keep your eyes peeled for **motels** such as the Saga Motor Hotel, Vagabond, Astro (fabulous *Jetsons*-style architecture), and Hi-Way Host. Lodgings have proven the hardiest post-66 survivors, and you'll be seeing many motor courts frozen in time on the way.

Turn left on Rosemead Boulevard, passing under the freeway (boo, hiss) to Foothill Boulevard. Turning right, you'll soon be among the tree-lined streets of **Arcadia,** home to the Santa Anita Racetrack and the Los Angeles Arboretum, the picturesque former estate of "Lucky" Baldwin, whose Queen Anne cottage has been the setting for many movies and TV shows. Passing into **Monrovia,** look for the life-size plastic cow on the southeast corner of Mayflower. It marks the drive-through called **Mike's Dairy**—a splendid example of this auto-age phenomenon. Mike's has all the typical features, including the refrigerated island display case still bearing a vintage DRIFTWOOD DAIRY PRODUCTS price sign.

Next, look for Magnolia Avenue and the **Aztec Hotel** on the northwest corner. Opened in 1925, the Aztec was a local showplace, awing guests with its overscale, dark, Native American–themed lobby, Maya murals, and exotic Brass Elephant bar. Little has changed about the interior, and a glance behind the front desk reveals the original cord-and-plug telephone switchboard still in use.

Leaving the Aztec, you'll pass splendid Craftsman bungalows and other historic homes. Turn right on Shamrock Avenue and ogle the old gas station with its classic (if ornamental) gas pumps on the northwest corner of Almond Avenue; continue onward 2 more blocks, and then make a left turn on Huntington Drive. Now you're in **Duarte,** where Huntington Drive is lit by graceful and ornate double street lamps on the center median. This stretch also has many fabulous old motor courts; see if you can spot the Ranch Inn, Evergreen, Oak Park, Duarte Inn, and Capri. Check out the **Justice Brothers Racing Museum,** 2734 E. Huntington Dr., Duarte, CA 91010, in an officelike building at the east edge of town just before the river (✆ **800/835-8784** or 626/359-9174; www.justice brothers.com; free admission; Mon–Fri 8am–4:30pm).

As you cross over the wide but nearly dry San Gabriel River, glance right from the bridge to see cars streaming along the interstate that supplanted Rte. 66. In **Irwindale**—which smells just like the industrial area it is, with plants ranging from a Miller brewery to Health Valley Foods—the street resumes the Foothill Boulevard name. At Irwindale Avenue, the 30-mile "neon cruise" begins. You'll pass into **Azusa,** with its elegant 1932 **Azusa City Hall and Auditorium,** with vintage lampposts and a Moorish fountain enhancing a charming courtyard.

Our route swerves right onto Alosta Avenue at the site of the former **Foothill Drive-In Theater,** Southern California's last single-screen drive-in. As you cruise by, think of the days when our cars were an extension of our living rooms, and the outdoor theaters were filled every summer evening by dusk. Alas, the drive-in sign awaits demolition, but the new owners may donate it to the city of Los Angeles, relocate it, and refurbish the marquee.

Continuing on Alosta, you'll enter **Glendora,** named in 1887 by founder George Whitcomb for his wife, Ledora. Look for the **Palm Tropics,** one of the best-maintained old motels along the route. Farther along on the left-hand side is the **Golden Spur,** which began 70 years ago as a ride-up hamburger stand for the equestrian crowd. Unfortunately, the restaurant was remodeled in stucco, leaving only the original sign with its neon cowboy boot as a reminder of its colorful past. At the corner of Cataract Avenue, a covered wagon announces the **Pinnacle Peak** restaurant, guarded by a giant steer atop the roof. In a mile or two, you'll pass through **San Dimas,** a ranchlike community where you must heed the HORSE CROSSING street signs.

Foothill Boulevard enters **La Verne** as you pass underneath the ramps to the I-30 freeway. **La Paloma** Mexican cafe, a fixture on the route for years, is on your left as you leave town. Continue on to **Claremont,** known for its highly respected group of **Claremont Colleges.** You'll pass several of them along this eucalyptus-lined boulevard. In days gone by, drivers would cruise along this route for mile upon mile, through orchards and open fields, the scenery punctuated only by ambling livestock or a rustic wood fence.

At Benson Avenue in **Upland,** a classic **1950s-style McDonald's** stands on the southeast corner, its golden arches flanking a low, white walk-up counter with outdoor stools. The fast-food chain has its roots in this region: Richard and Maurice McDonald opened their first burger joint in San Bernardino in 1939. The brothers expanded their business, opening locations throughout Southern California, until entrepreneur Ray Kroc purchased the chain in 1955 and franchised McDonald's nationwide. Farther along, look north at the intersection of Euclid Avenue for the regal **monument to pioneer women.**

Pretty soon you'll be cruising through **Rancho Cucamonga,** whose fertile soil still yields a reliable harvest. You might see **produce stands** springing up by the side of the road; stop and pick up a fresh snack. If you're blessed with clear weather, gaze north at the gentle slope of the **San Gabriel Mountains** and you'll understand how Foothill Boulevard got its name. The construction codes in this community are among the most stringent in California, designed to respect the region's heritage and restrict runaway development. All new buildings are Spanish-Mediterranean in style and amply landscaped. At the corner of San Bernardino Road, the architectural bones of a wonderful old service station now stand forsaken. Across the street is the **Sycamore Inn,** in a grove of trees, looking like an old-style stagecoach stop. This reddish-brown wooden house, dating from 1848, has been a private home and gracious inn; today it serves the community of Cucamonga as a restaurant and civic hall.

Rancho Cucamonga has preserved two historic wineries. First you'll see the **Thomas Vineyards,** at the northeast corner of Vineyard Avenue, established in 1839. Legend holds that the first owner mysteriously disappeared, leaving hidden treasure still undiscovered on the property. The winery's preserved structures

If all this driving has made you hungry, consider the **Magic Lamp Inn,** 8189 Foothill Blvd. (📞 **909/981-8659**). It's open for lunch Tuesday through Friday from 11:30am to 2:30pm, and for dinner Tuesday through Sunday from 5pm to closing time, which varies (call first). It's closed Mondays. Built in 1957, the Magic Lamp serves excellent Continental cuisine (nothing nouvelle about Rte. 66!) in a setting that's part manor house and part *Aladdin* theme park. Dark, stately dining rooms lurk behind a funky banquette cocktail lounge punctuated by a psychedelic fountain/fire pit and a panoramic view. The genie-bottle theme is everywhere, from the restaurant's dinnerware to the plush carpeting, which would be right at home in a Las Vegas casino. Lovers of kitsch and hearty retro fare shouldn't pass up this one.

now house a restaurant, coffeehouse, country crafts store, and garden-supply boutique in the former brandy-still tower.

Continuing on to Hellman Avenue, look for the **New Kansan Motel** (on the northeast corner). With that name, it must have seemed welcoming to Dust Bowl refugees. Near the northwest corner of Archibald Avenue, you'll find remnants of a **1920s-era gas station.** Empty now, those service bays have seen many a Ford, Studebaker, and Packard in need of a helping hand. Nearby, on the left, is **Route 66 Memories,** 10150 Foothill Blvd. (📞 **909/476-3843**), open 9am to 5pm, in a three-story classic house with a collection of metallic dinosaurs in the front yard, and a gift shop for antiques and rustic furniture. Next you'll pass the **Virginia Dare Winery,** at the northwest corner of Haven Avenue, whose structures now house part of a business park/mall but retain the flourish of the original (1830s) winery logo.

Soon you'll pass the I-15 junction and drive through Fontana, whose name in Italian means "fountain city." Slow down to have a look at the **motor-court hotels** lining both sides of the road. They're of various vintages, all built to cater to the once-vigorous stream of travelers passing through. Today they're dingy, but the melody of their names conjures up those glory days: Oasis, Rose Motel, Moana, El Rey, Rex, Fiesta, Dragon, Sand & Sage, and Sunset.

As you enter **San Bernardino,** be on the lookout for Meriden Avenue, site of the **Wigwam Motel.** Built in the 1950s (along with an identical twin motor court in Holbrook, AZ), the whimsy of these stucco tepees lured in many a road-weary traveler for the night. Its catchy slogan, "Sleep in a wigwam, get more for your wampum," has been supplanted today by the more to-the-point "Do it in a tepee."

Soon Foothill Boulevard will become Fifth Street, where the San Bernardino sign must have been a welcome sight for hot and weary westbound travelers emerging from the Mojave Desert. Rte. 66 wriggled through the steep Cajon Pass into a

Wigwam Motel, San Bernardino.

land fragrant with orange groves, where agricultural prosperity earned this region a lasting sobriquet: "The Inland Empire."

The year 1928 saw the grand opening of an elegant movie palace, the **California Theatre,** 562 W. Fourth St., only a block from Rte. 66. From Fifth Street east, turn right at E Street, and then make a right on Fourth Street. Lovingly restored and still popular for nostalgic live entertainment and the rich tones of its original Wurlitzer pipe organ, the California was a frequent site of Hollywood "sneak previews." Humorist Will Rogers made his last public appearance here, in 1935. (Following his death, the highway was officially renamed the Will Rogers Memorial Hwy.) Notice the intricate relief of the theater's stone facade, and peek into the lobby to see the red-velvet draperies, rich carpeting, and gold-banistered double staircase leading up to the balcony.

The theater is the last stop on your time warp driving tour. Continue west on Fourth Street to the superslab highway only 2½ blocks away—that's I-215, your entry back to the present (see "Essentials" above).

THE PALM SPRINGS DESERT RESORTS

120 miles E of downtown L.A.; 135 miles NE of San Diego

Palm Springs had been known for years as a golf course–studded retirement mecca, invaded annually by hordes of libidinous college kids on spring break. Well, the city of Palm Springs has been quietly changing its image and attracting a whole new crowd. The late former mayor Sonny Bono's revolutionary "antithong" ordinance in 1991 halted the spring-break migration by eliminating public display of the bare derrière. However, with the Narco incidents in Mexico, some students returned to the area in spring 2009 with much less notorious activities than the '60s. The upscale fairway-condo crowd now congregates in the outlying resort cities of Rancho Mirage, Palm Desert, Indian Wells, and La Quinta.

These days, no billboards are allowed in Palm Springs; all the palm trees in the center of town are backlit at night, and you won't see the word *motel* on any establishment. Seniors are everywhere, dressed to the nines in leisure suits and plaid shorts, sustaining the retro-kitsch establishments from the days when Elvis, Liberace, and Sinatra made the desert a swingin' place. But they're not alone: Baby boomers and yuppies nostalgic for the kidney-shaped swimming pools and backyard luaus of the Eisenhower/Kennedy glory years are buying ranch-style vacation homes and restoring them to their 1950s splendor. Hollywood's young glitterati, along with upscale gays, are returning, too. Today the city fancies itself a European-style resort with a dash of small-town Americana—think *Jetsons* architecture and the crushed-velvet vibe of piano bars with the colors and attitude of a laid-back Aegean village. One thing hasn't changed: Swimming, sunbathing, golfing, and tennis are still the primary pastimes.

During the recent economic downsizing, many storefronts had empty windows. The City Council subsidized local artists to fill the spaces with artworks and portraits of Palm Springs celebrities.

Another important presence in Palm Springs has little to do with socialites and Americana. The Agua Caliente Band of Cahuilla Indians settled in this area 1,000 years before the first golf ball was ever teed up. Recognizing the beauty and spirituality of this wide-open space, they lived a simple life around the mineral springs on the desert floor, migrating into the cool canyons during the summer months. Under a treaty with the railroad companies and the U.S. government, the tribe owns half the land on which Palm Springs is built and works to preserve Native American heritage.

Essentials

GETTING THERE Airlines that service the **Palm Springs International Airport,** 3400 E. Tahquitz Canyon Way (✆ 800/433-7300 or 760/318-3800), include **Alaska Airlines** (✆ 800/426-0333; www.alaskaair.com), **Allegiant Air** (✆ 702/505-8888; www.allegiantair.com), **American** (✆ 800/433-7300; www.aa.com), **Delta** and **Delta Connection** (✆ 800/221-1212; www.delta.com), **Horizon Air** (✆ 800/547-9308; www.horizonair.com), **Sun Country Airlines** (✆ 800/359-6786; seasonal), **United Airlines** (✆ 800/241-6522; www.united.com), **US Airways** (✆ 800/428-4322; www.usairways.com), and **WestJet** (✆ 800/538-5696; www.westjet.com). Flights from Los Angeles take about 40 minutes.

If you're driving from Los Angeles, take I-10 east to the Hwy. 111 turn-off to Palm Springs. You'll breeze into town on North Palm Canyon Drive, the main thoroughfare. The trip from downtown L.A. takes 2 hours if traffic is light. If you're driving from San Diego, take I-15 north to I-215 and pick up I-10 east; it takes a bit more than 2 hours.

VISITOR INFORMATION Be sure to pick up *Palm Springs Life* magazine's free monthly, *Desert Guide.* It contains copious visitor information, including a comprehensive calendar of events. Copies are distributed in hotels and newsstands and by the **Palm Springs Desert Resorts Convention & Visitors Authority,** 70–100 Hwy. 111, Rancho Mirage, CA 92270 (✆ **800/967-3767** or 760/770-9000). The bureau's office staff can help with maps, brochures, and advice Monday through Friday from 8:30am to 5pm. They also operate a website (www.palmspringsusa.com).

The **Palm Springs Visitors Information Center,** 777 N. Palm Canyon Dr., Palm Springs, CA 92262 (✆ **800/34-SPRINGS** [347-7746] or 760/778-8418; www.palm-springs.org), offers maps, brochures, advice, souvenirs, and a free hotel reservation service. The office is open Monday through Saturday from 9am to 5pm, and Sunday from 8am to 4pm.

An offshoot of the local newspaper the Desert Sun, **www.thedesert sun.com**, has information for locals and visitors.

ORIENTATION The commercial downtown area of Palm Springs stretches about half a mile along North Palm Canyon Drive between Alejo and Ramon streets. The street is one-way southbound through the heart of town, but its northbound counterpart is Indian Canyon Drive, 1 block east. The mountains lie west and south, while the rest of Palm Springs is laid out in a grid to the southeast. Palm Canyon forks into South Palm Canyon (leading to the Indian Canyons) and East Palm Canyon (the continuation of Hwy. 111), traversing the towns of Cathedral City, Rancho Mirage, Palm Desert, Indian Wells, and La Quinta before looping up to rejoin I-10 at Indio. Desert Hot Springs is north of Palm Springs, straight up Gene Autry Trail. Tahquitz Canyon Way creates North Palm Canyon's primary intersection, tracking a straight line between the airport and the heart of town.

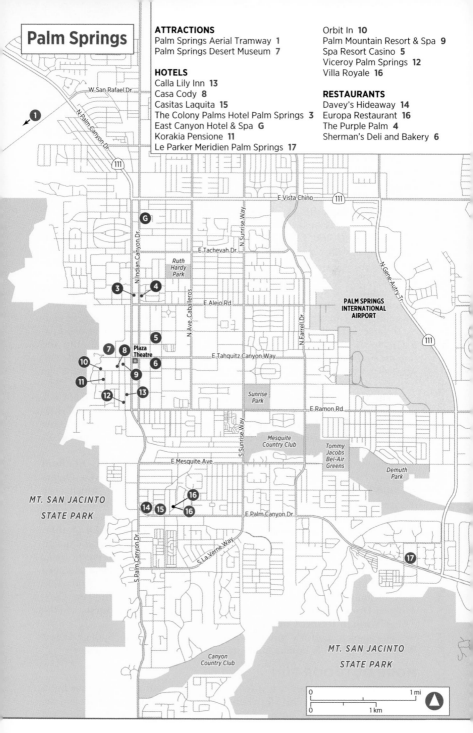

Palm Springs

ATTRACTIONS
Palm Springs Aerial Tramway **1**
Palm Springs Desert Museum **7**

HOTELS
Calla Lily Inn **13**
Casa Cody **8**
Casitas Laquita **15**
The Colony Palms Hotel Palm Springs **3**
East Canyon Hotel & Spa **G**
Korakia Pensione **11**
Le Parker Meridien Palm Springs **17**

Orbit In **10**
Palm Mountain Resort & Spa **9**
Spa Resort Casino **5**
Viceroy Palm Springs **12**
Villa Royale **16**

RESTAURANTS
Davey's Hideaway **14**
Europa Restaurant **16**
The Purple Palm **4**
Sherman's Deli and Bakery **6**

What to See & Do

GREAT GOLF COURSES

The Palm Springs Desert Resorts are a mecca for golfers (see "Fairways & Five-Irons, Desert-Style," below), with 115 public, semiprivate, and private courses in the area. If you're the type who starts polishing your irons the moment you begin planning your vacation, you're best off staying at one of the valley's many golf resorts; many offer smart package deals. If, on the other hand, you like to squeeze a round of golf into an otherwise varied trip, you don't need to stay at a hotel with its own links; many courses, of all levels, are open to the public, many in Palm Springs, with others down the valley in Cathedral City, Palm Desert, Indian Wells, La Quinta, and Indio. Call ahead to see which will rent gear on short notice. To arrange tee times for all courses, call (C) **800/727-8331.**

Beginners will enjoy **Tommy Jacobs' Bel-Air Greens,** 1001 El Cielo, Palm Springs ((C) **760/322-6062**), a 9-hole, par-32 executive course that challenges golfers with water and sand traps but fosters a few confidence-boosting successes as well. Generally flat fairways and trees characterize the relatively short (3,350-yard) course. Greens fees are $20, less for a replay.

Slightly more intermediate amateurs will want to check out the **Tahquitz Creek Golf Resort,** 1885 Golf Club Dr., Palm Springs ((C) **760/328-1005;** www.tahquitzgolfresort.com), whose two diverse courses both appeal to mid-handicappers. The **Legend's** wide, water-free holes will appeal to anyone frustrated by the "target" courses popular with many architects, while the Ted Robinson–designed **Resort** course offers all those accuracy-testing bells and whistles more common to lavish private clubs. Greens fees, including cart, range from $69 to $109, depending on the time of day.

The Classic Club (75–200 Northstar Resort Pkwy., north of I-10 at Cook St. exit, Palm Desert; (C) **760/601-3600;** www.classicclubgolf.com) is a 7,305-yard Arnold Palmer–designed course that won critical praise from the pros at the Bob Hope Classic in 2007. Greens fees in winter are $129, which includes a cart and a driving range; summer fees are half that.

One of my favorite desert courses is the **PGA West TPC Stadium Course,** La Quinta Resort & Club, 49499 Eisenhower Dr., La Quinta ((C) **800/598-3828** or 760/564-4111; www.laquintaresort.com), which once received *Golf* magazine's Gold Medal Award for the total golf-resort experience. It's one of the most difficult courses in the U.S., and greens fees are $199 to $209. Also open for semiprivate play is the **Mountain Course at La Quinta,** another Dye design that regularly appears on U.S. top-100 lists. It's set dramatically against the rocky mountains, which thrust into fairways to create tricky doglegs, and its small Bermuda greens are well guarded by boulders and deep bunkers. Greens fees for nonguests vary seasonally, from $169 to $179 on weekends, including the required cart. Also at La Quinta Resort is the Pete Dye–designed **Dunes Course,** the (Jack) **Nicklaus Tournament Course,** and the (Greg) **Norman Resort Course.**

A complete **golfer's guide** is available from the Palm Springs Desert Resorts Convention & Visitors Authority (see "Visitor Information," above).

MORE OUTDOOR FUN

The Coachella Valley Desert is a sunny playground, and what follows is but a sampling of outdoor pastimes for visitors. *Tip:* The abundant sunshine and dry air that are so appealing can also sneak up on you, in the form of sunburn and

FAIRWAYS & FIVE-IRONS, desert-style

Two hours outside of Los Angeles in the Coachella Valley, strung like ripe dates from I-10, lie the resort cities of Palm Springs, Rancho Mirage, Palm Desert, Indian Wells, and La Quinta. This all-season golfer's paradise boasts more than 100 courses, their lush fairways and velvety greens carved from the arid desert scruff. Both public and resort/semiprivate courses range in difficulty to accommodate low-handicappers and weekend duffers alike, and every imaginable service is available nearby.

In case you'd like to sharpen your game, all the principal clubs have resident pros, and there are several schools and clinics, including the **Indian Wells Golf School** at Indian Wells Resort (© **760/346-4653**), or the **1st Tee in Palm Desert** (© **760/779-1877**). If you're looking to pick up new equipment or golf attire, try **Lumpy's Discount Golf,** 67–625 Hwy. 111 in Cathedral City (© **800/553-2117** or 760/321-2437) and 46630 Washington St. in La Quinta (© **760/904-4911**); and **Lady Golf** at 42–412 Bob Hope Dr., Rancho Mirage (© **760/773-4949**).

Many fine resorts offer generous golf packages, among them **Marriott's Desert Springs Spa & Resort** in Palm Desert (© **760/341-2211**), **Marriott's Rancho Las Palmas Resort & Spa** in Rancho Mirage (© **760/568-2727**), the **Hyatt Grand Champions** in Indian Wells (© **760/341-1000**), and **La Quinta**

Resort & Club in La Quinta (© **760/564-4111**).

Tee times at many courses cannot be booked more than a few days in advance for nonguests, but **Golf à la Carte** (© **877/887-6900** or 760/397-7670; www.palmspringsgolf.com) will make arrangements several months earlier or construct a package with accommodations, golf, meals, and other extras. A valuable service for the budget traveler, **Stand-By Golf** (© **866/224-BOOK** [2665] or 760/321-2665; www.standbygolf.com) helps more than 40 area courses—including semiprivate and resort courses—fill their bookings by offering players a last-minute discount of 40% to 60%. You can book some courses in advance, but many tee times are for the same or next day; call between 7am and 9pm daily.

heat exhaustion. Especially during the summer, but even in milder times, always carry and drink plenty of water, and slather on the sunscreen.

BALLOONING   Floating above the landscape in a hot-air balloon may be the most memorable way to see the desert. Choose from such specialty themes as sunrise, sunset, or romantic champagne flights, from $165 per person. Rides are offered by **Dream Flights** leaving from Goody's Café, 40–205 Washington St., in Palm Desert (from L.A., take Washington St. exit from I-10 past light to Goody's; © **800/933-5628** or 760/321-5454), $160 per person; and **Fantasy Balloon Flights,** 74181 Parosella St., Palm Desert (© **800/GO-ABOVE** [462-2683] or 760/568-0997; www.dreamflights. com), where rates range from $170 to $185 per person for a 60- to 90-minute flight (two per day), including champagne and hors d'oeuvres. Reservations are required for both flights.

BICYCLING ★   The clean, dry desert air makes for ideal conditions for pedaling your way around town or into the desert. **Tri a Bike Rental,** 44841 San Pablo Ave., Palm Desert (© **760/340-2840**), rents road and mountain bikes for the hour ($12), the day ($30), or the week ($99), and offers children's and tandem models and helmets as well. **Off Road Rentals,** 599–511 Hwy. 111, Palm Springs, CA 92262 (© **760/325-0376**), has quads, ARVs, dune buggies, and so on. They also provide tours at $40.

HIKING ★   The most popular spot for hiking is the nearby **Indian Canyons,** at the end of South Palm Canyon Drive (© **800/790-3398** or 760/699-6800). The Agua Caliente tribe dwelt here centuries ago, and remnants of its culture can be seen among the streams, waterfalls, and palm groves in Andreas, Murray, and Palm canyons. The striking rock formations and herds of bighorn sheep and wild ponies are more appealing than the Trading Post in Palm Canyon, but the shop sells detailed trail maps. The Tribal Council charges admission of $9 per adult; $7 for students, seniors, and military; and $5 for kids ages 6 to 12. The canyons are closed to visitors from late June to early September. The canyons are open 8am to 5pm, and guided hiking tours and ranger lectures are also available.

HORSEBACK RIDING ★   Novice and advanced equestrians alike can experience the desert's solitude and quiet on horseback, at **Smoke Tree Stables** (© **760/327-1372**). South of downtown, at 2500 Toledo Ave., and ideal for exploring the nearby Indian Canyon trails, Smoke Tree offers guided rides for $50 per hour, $90 for 2 hours; the 2-hour tour includes admission to an Agua Caliente Indian reservation. But don't expect your posse leader to spew facts about the natural features you'll encounter; this is strictly a do-it-yourself experience.

JEEP EXCURSIONS ★   **Desert Adventures** (© **888/440-JEEP** [5337] or 760/340-2345; www.red-jeep.com), 74794 Lennon Place, Palm Desert, offers four-wheel-drive ecotours led by naturalist guides. Your off-road adventure may take you to a replica of an ancient Cahuilla village, the Santa Rosa Mountain roads overlooking the Coachella Valley, or picturesque

Palm Canyon.

ravines on the way to the San Andreas Fault. Tours run from 3 to 5 hours and cost from $75 to $150. Advance reservations are required. The company's red Jeeps depart from Coco's Restaurant at the Washington Street exit of I-10.

Elite Land Tours ★, 540 S. Vello Rd., Palm Springs (✆ **800/514-4866** or 760/318-1200; www.elitelandtours.com), offers a new way to visit the desert region: eco-exploration of the greater Palm Springs backcountry from the air-conditioned comfort of an all-terrain Hummer H2. Tours can include desert and mountain regions, with exploration of ancient cultures, wildlife, and geological wonders. A desert sampler travels along the San Andreas fault plus tours sand farms (2 hr.; $69 per person with a group of four). The Night Discovery Tour lets you view the desert wildlife after dark with special night-vision equipment. Tours run from $119 per person for a four-person group.

Don't miss the opportunity to explore **Tahquitz Canyon** ★★, 500 W. Mesquite, west of Palm Canyon Drive, also in Agua Caliente territory. This scenic canyon, home of the waterfall in *Lost Horizon,* was closed to the public for nearly 30 years after careless squatters suffered injuries in the canyon and hippies made it an all-night party zone, vandalizing land considered sacred. The tribe cleaned up decades' worth of dumping, and now that vegetation has regrown, they have begun offering 2½-hour ranger-led hikes into their most spiritual and beautiful place. The 2-mile round-trip hike is of moderate difficulty; hikes depart daily at 8, 10am, noon, and 2pm. The fee is $13 for adults, $6 for children ages 6 to 12; call ✆ **760/416-7044** for reservations (recommended).

Ten miles east of Palm Springs is the 13,000-acre **Coachella Valley Preserve** (✆ **760/343-2733**), open daily from sunrise to sunset. It has springs, mesas, both hiking and riding trails, the Thousand Palms Oasis, a visitor center, and picnic areas.

Tahquitz Canyon.

If you're heading up to Joshua Tree National Park (see later in this chapter), consider stopping at the **Big Morongo Canyon Preserve ★** (✆ **760/363-7190**), which was once an Indian village and later a cattle ranch. It's open daily from 7:30am to sundown. The park's high water table makes it a magnet for birds and other wildlife; the lush springs and streams are an unexpected desert treat. Admission is free, but donations are accepted.

SEEING STARS ★ The Palm Springs area has been the getaway watering hole for screen stars from the '20s to today. **Celebrity Tours,** 67-555 E. Palm Canyon Dr., Cathedral City (✆ **760/770-2700**), has a tour 2½ hours long that covers the valley and visits Desert Memorial Park Cemetery, the resting place of Sonny Bono and Frank Sinatra; it also points out the homes of Sinatra, Bob Hope, Elvis, and Liberace, among others. The stories related by the guide are worth the trip alone. Rates are $44 adults, $40 seniors, and $19 children 12 and under.

TENNIS Virtually all the larger hotels and resorts have tennis courts. If you're staying at a B&B, you might want to play at the **Plaza Racquet Club,** 1300 Baristo Rd. (✆ **760/323-8997**). It has nine courts and runs day and evening clinics for adults, juniors, and seniors, and ball machines for solo practice. USPTA pros are on hand. Rates are $20 per hour for court rental, $20 for a 1½-hour group clinic. The night-lit courts at **Palm Springs High School,** 2248 E. Ramon Rd., are free, open to the public on weekends, holidays, and in summer. Beautiful **Ruth Hardy Park,** at Tamarisk and Caballero streets, also has eight free night-lit courts.

A WATER PARK FOR THE FAMILY ★★ Knott's Soak City, off I-10 south on Gene Autry Trail between Ramon Road and East Palm Canyon Drive (✆ **760/327-0499;** www.knotts.com/soakcity/ps/index.shtml), is a 16-acre water playground with 12 water slides, bodysurfing and board surfing, a wave pool, and more. Dressing rooms, lockers, and private beach cabanas (with food service) are available. Admission is $30 for adults, $20 for seniors and kids 3 to 11, and free for kids 2 and under; rates are discounted after 3pm. The park is open Wednesday through Sunday mid-March through August, and weekends through October, from 10am to 6pm. Parking for a car is $8, for an RV $16. It's closed Mondays and Tuesdays.

EXPLORING THE AREA

The Living Desert Zoo & Gardens

★ ☺ This 1,200-acre desert reserve, museum, zoo, and educational center is designed to acquaint visitors with the Southern California desert's unique habitats. You can walk or take a tram tour through sectors that re-create life in several distinctive desert zones. See

Living Desert Zoo & Gardens.

HERE'S THE RUB: TWO BUNCH PALMS
desert spa

Since the Native American Cahuilla learned how great it felt to soak in the Coachella Valley's natural hot springs, this desert has drawn stressed-out masses seeking relaxation. My number-one choice is heavenly **Two Bunch Palms.** Posh yet intimate, this spiritual sanctuary in Desert Hot Springs (about 20 min. north of Palm Springs) has been drawing weary city dwellers since Chicago mobster Al Capone hid out here in the 1930s. Two Bunch Palms later became a playground for the movie community, but today it's a friendly and informal haven, with 56 acres of renowned spa services, well-appointed bungalows on lush grounds, and lagoons of steaming mineral water. Float in serenity at the Grotto, which consists of small mineral pools surrounded by tall, tranquil greenery. Service is famously discreet, and legions of return guests will attest that the outstanding spa treatments (including 12 varieties of massage, mud baths, body wraps, facials, salt rubs, water therapy) and therapeutic waters are what make the luxury of Two Bunch Palms irresistible. To maintain the relaxed atmosphere, guests are requested to speak softly, just above a whisper. Loud, argumentative guests will be asked to leave and denied access in the future. Room rates run from $225 to $425 (including breakfast) in high season, with substantial discounts midweek and off season. Spa treatments cost between $80 and $185 per hour, and multiday money-saving room/spa packages run from $1,049 to $1,379 for two, with double occupancy. There is a $10 resort fee. Other packages may be available. The quiet dining room serves delicious lunches and dinners, with a full bar and wine available. No one 17 and under is allowed. The resort is off Palm Drive (Gene Autry Trail) at 67-425 Two Bunch Palms Trail in Desert Hot Springs (✆ **877/839-3609** or 760/329-8791; www.twobunchpalms.com).

and learn about a dizzying variety of plants, insects, and wildlife, including bighorn sheep, mountain lions, rattlesnakes, lizards, owls, golden eagles, and the ubiquitous roadrunner, plus new exhibits featuring frogs and butterflies. It's a nonstuffy learning experience for kids and grown-ups alike in the Gecko Gulch Playland. 47-900 Portola Ave., Palm Desert. ✆ **760/346-5694.** www.livingdesert.org. Admission $14 adults, $13 seniors/military, $7.75 children 3-12, free for children 2 and under. Reduced summer rates. Daily 9am-5pm (last entrance 4pm); summer (mid-June to Aug) 8am-1:30pm.

Palm Springs Aerial Tramway ★★ To gain a bird's-eye perspective on the Coachella Valley, take this 14-minute ascent up nearly 5,900 feet to the upper slopes of Mount San Jacinto. While the Albert Frey–designed boarding stations retain their 1960s ski-lodge feel, newly installed Swiss funicular cars are sleekly modern and rotate during the trip to allow each passenger a panoramic view. Once you arrive, you will be thrust into alpine scenery, a ski-lodge-flavored restaurant and gift shop, and temperatures typically 40° cooler than the desert floor. The most dramatic contrast is during the winter, when the mountaintop is a snowy wonderland, irresistible to hikers and bundled-up kids with saucers. The excursion might not be worth the expense during the rest of the year. Guided mule rides and cross-country ski equipment are available at the top. An upscale restaurant, **Peaks,** serves contemporary California cuisine. Appetizers begin at

Palm Springs Aerial Tramway.

$10, entrees $21. Wait and take the tram to the top after 3pm for a lower rate and "Ride and Dine" at the **Pines Restaurant,** a cafeteria-style restaurant, $36 adults, $24 children, 4:30 to 8:30pm. Peaks is open 11am to 7:30pm daily, and reservations are recommended (✆ **760/325-4537**).

Tramway Rd. off Hwy. 111, Palm Springs. ✆ **888/515-TRAM** (8726) or 760/325-1391. www.pstramway.com. Tickets $23 adults, $21 seniors, $16 children 3–12, free for children 2 and under. Mon–Fri 10am–8pm; Sat–Sun 8am–8pm. Tram runs every 30 min., last tram down at 9:45pm. Tram cars and stations are accessible to travelers w/disabilities.

Palm Springs Desert Museum ★ Unlikely though it may sound, this museum is well endowed and worth a look. Exhibits include world-class Western and Native American art collections, the natural history of the desert,

SWEET DESERT treat: THE COACHELLA VALLEY DATE GARDENS

In a splendid display of wishful thinking and clever engineering, the Coachella Valley has grown into a rich agricultural region, known internationally for grapefruit, figs, and grapes—and dates. Entrepreneurs, fascinated with Arabian lore and fueled by the Sahara-like conditions of the desert around Indio, planted these date palm groves in the 1920s. Launched with a few parent trees imported from the Middle East, the groves now produce 95% of the world's date crop.

Farmers hand-pollinate the trees, and the resulting fruit is bundled in wind-protective paper while still on the tree, which makes an odd sight indeed. You'll see them along Hwy. 111 through Indio, locally known as the "Date Highway."

The most picturesque place in the valley to sample dates is **Oasis Date Gardens,** 59111 Hwy. 111 (✆ **800/827-8017** or 760/399-5665; www.oasisdate.com), started in 1912 with nine Moroccan trees and now one of the nation's largest commercial date groves. It's a 40-minute drive from downtown Palm Springs—but there's a lot to do here. Picnic tables dot an inviting lawn, videos illustrate the history and art of date cultivation, and there's a cool palm arboretum and cactus exhibit. Many varieties of dates are laid out for free tasting. Oasis also sells date shakes, ice cream, date pie by the slice, homemade chili and sandwiches, and gourmet food gifts from all over the Southwest. Open Monday to Saturday (except Christmas) from 8am to 5pm.

and an outstanding anthropology department, primarily representing the local Cahuilla tribe. Tools, baskets, and other relics illustrate traditional Indian life as it was lived for centuries. Check local schedules to find out about visiting exhibits (which are usually excellent). Plays, lectures, and other events are presented in the museum's **Annenberg Theater** (© **760/325-4490**).

101 N. Museum Dr. (just west of the Palm Canyon/Tahquitz intersection), Palm Springs, CA 92262. © **760/322-4800.** www.psmuseum. org. Admission $13 adults, $11 seniors 62 and over, $5 military and children 6–17, free for children 5 and under, free for all each Thurs after 4pm. Tues–Wed and Fri–Sun 10am–5pm; Thurs noon–8pm.

Palm Springs Desert Museum.

Shopping

Downtown Palm Springs revolves around **North Palm Canyon Drive;** many art galleries, souvenir shops, and restaurants are here, along with a couple of large-scale hotels and shopping centers. This wide one-way boulevard is designed for pedestrians, with many businesses set back from the street (don't be shy about poking around the little courtyards you'll encounter). On Thursday nights from 6 to 10pm, the blocks between Amado and Baristo roads are transformed into **VillageFest,** a town street fair. Handicrafts vendors and aromatic food booths vie for attention with wacky street performers and even wackier locals shopping at the fresh-produce stalls.

The northern section of Palm Canyon, known for collectibles, is touted as the **Antique and Heritage Gallery District.** Check out **Antiques Collector,** 798 N. Palm Canyon Dr. (© **760/323-4443**), a discriminating mall-style store with 35 dealers displaying wares that range from vintage linens to handmade African crafts, to prized Bakelite jewelry. Open hours are 10am to 4:30pm.

Serious shoppers head south to Palm Desert, with the delicious excesses of **El Paseo,** a cornucopia of high-rent boutiques, salons, and upscale restaurants reminiscent of Rodeo Drive in Beverly Hills, along with more than a dozen major shopping malls.

El Paseo.

Gay & Lesbian Life in Palm Springs

The Palm Springs area is among America's top destinations for gay and lesbian travelers. Real estate agents cater to gay shoppers for vacation properties, and year-round condo communities are also marketed toward gay residents. Advertisements for these and scores of other gay-owned businesses can be found in the **Bottom Line,** 312 N. Palm Canyon Dr. (✆ **760/323-0552;** www.psbottomline.com), the desert's free biweekly magazine of articles, events, and community guides for the gay reader, which is available at hotels, at newsstands, and from select merchants. The **Palm Springs Visitor and Hotel Information Center** publishes an *Official Gay & Lesbian Visitors Guide.* Obtain it and additional information at their office at 2901 N. Palm Canyon Dr. (✆ **800/347-7746** or 760/778-8418; www.palm-springs.org).

In March, the **Desert AIDS Walk** benefits the Desert AIDS Project, while one of the world's largest organized gathering of lesbians—the **Dinah Shore Weekend** (✆ **888/92DINAH** [923-4624]; www.clubskirts.com)—coincides with the LPGA's **Kraft Nabisco Championship** (www.kncgolf.com) in March. **Greater Palm Springs Pride** occurs the first weekend in November, with a parade and 2-day cultural fair (✆ **760/416-8711;** www.pspride.org).

Palm Springs has more than two dozen gay hotels, many concentrated on Warm Sands Drive south of Ramon. Known simply as "Warm Sands," this area is home to many of the private resorts—mostly discreet, gated inns, many of them clothing optional. Try the **East Canyon Hotel & Spa,** 288 E. Camino Monte Vista, a 15-unit luxurious hotel with a pool and an in-house spa that caters to the male guest. Clothing is not optional. Rates are $139 to $359, including breakfast buffet (✆ **877/324-6835** or 760/320-1928; www.eastcanyonps.com). **Casitas Laquita,** 450 E. Palm Canyon Dr. (✆ **877/203-3410** or 760/416-9999; www.casitaslaquita.com), is one of two all-women resorts in town. Rates are $155 to $250.

Where to Stay

The city of Palm Springs has a wide range of accommodations, but I particularly like the inns that have opened as a result of new owners renovating the many fabulous 40- to 60-year-old cottage complexes in the wind-shielded Tennis Club area west of Palm Canyon Drive. The other desert resort cities offer mostly sprawling complexes, many boasting world-class golf, tennis, or spa facilities and multiple on-site restaurants. Most are destinations in and of themselves, with activities for the whole family (including a whole lot of relaxing and pampering). If you're looking for a good base from which to shop or sightsee, Palm Springs is your best bet.

Note: Regardless of your choice, remember that the rates below are for high season (winter, generally Nov–May). During the hotter summer months, it's common to find $300 rooms going for $99 or less, as part of off-season packages. Even in high season, discounts for midweek stays are common.

PALM SPRINGS

Expensive

The Colony Palms Hotel Palm Springs ★★★ Originally built in 1936 by a head of the "Purple Gang" and later frequented by a number of Hollywood stars, this hotel within walking distance of downtown has undergone a $15-million renovation. A two-story Spanish Hacienda–style building surrounds a lush patio area with a full-size swimming pool, a large Jacuzzi, poolside cabanas, and a bevy of comfortable lounges for sunning. Along one side is the **Purple Palm** (p. 745), an inviting restaurant with indoor seating and outdoor patio tables by the pool. The 56 guest rooms are large and tastefully done in a '40s Hollywood decor with fireplaces; all are nonsmoking. Casitas set quietly behind the main building have private patios and outdoor hot tubs. The atmosphere is elegant-casual, with friendly and efficient service.

572 N. Palm Canyon Dr., Palm Springs, CA 92262. www.colonypalmshotel.com. © **800/557-2187** or 760/969-1800. 56 units. $150–$299 double; $318–$1,160 casita and suite. Discounts available in summer. AE, DISC, MC, V. **Amenities:** Poolside full-service restaurant; pool bar; gym; Jacuzzi; large heated pool; room service; spa treatments; poolside cabanas. *In room:* A/C, flatscreen plasma TV, DVD/CD player, fridge, minibar, Wi-Fi.

Le Parker Meridien Palm Springs ★★★   Well ensconced on the superluxury Palm Springs hotel scene is a $27-million renovation of the former Gene Autry Melody Ranch and then the Merv Griffin Givenchy Resort and Spa, known simply as the Parker. If you have been to either of these, you won't recognize the makeover. The 13-acre property has 131 rooms, 12 one-bedroom villas, and the original Gene Autry house. In keeping with the desert decor, the rooms are basically a relaxed white with light-wood overtones. And bathrooms include both tub and shower. Two restaurants serve your every desire: **Norma's ★★** has all-day breakfast for late sleepers, including the renowned $1,000 sevruga caviar and lobster omelet, served indoors or on an outdoor terrace open 11am to 2pm; **Mister Parker's ★★★** presents a daily changing dinner menu in an intimate atmosphere (closed Mon–Tues). A chic boutique, Veri Peri, features upscale designs. Activities center around four red-clay tennis courts, four pools (two of them heated), and the Palm Springs Yacht Club spa, to revive the jet-lagged body, and a 24-hour gym to get it back in shape. Golfers will be able to use the next-door Seven Lakes Country Club's 18-hole golf course, where President Dwight D. Eisenhower reportedly scored his only hole in one.

4200 E. Palm Canyon Dr., Palm Springs, CA 92264. www.theparkerpalmsprings.com. © **760/770-5000.** 144 units. Oct–May $255–$595 double, $995–$5,000 private villa; June–Sept $179–$459 double, $695–$3,000 private villa. $30 resort fee. Check online for current special packages. Guests 29 and under can stay in the staff quarters for much less; call for details. AE, DC, DISC, MC, V. **Amenities:** 2 restaurants; lobby bar; gym; Jacuzzi; 4 pools (2 heated); room service and free morning coffee delivery upon request; spa; steam and sauna rooms; 4 red-clay tennis courts; DVD library. *In room:* A/C, TV, CD/DVD/MP3 player, fridge, minibar, Wi-Fi.

Moderate

Korakia Pensione ★★   If you can handle the Korakia's rigid deposit-cancellation policy, you're in for a special stay at this Greek-Moroccan oasis, a few blocks from Palm Canyon Drive. This former artist's villa from the 1920s draws a hip international crowd of artists, writers, and musicians. The simply furnished rooms and spacious suites are peaceful and private, surrounded by flagstone courtyards and flowering gardens. Rooms are divided between the main house, a second restored villa across the street, and guest bungalows. Most have kitchens; many have fireplaces. All beds are blessed with thick duvets, and the windows are shaded by flowing white-canvas Mediterranean-style draperies. All rooms are nonsmoking. You also get a sumptuous breakfast served in your room or poolside. *Korakia* is Greek for "crow," and a tile mosaic example graces the pool bottom. **Note:** You must pay a deposit to book a room, there's a 2-night minimum on weekends, and you have to give at least 2 weeks' cancellation notice (45 *days'* advance notice for holidays) or you'll lose your deposit.

257 S. Patencio Rd., Palm Springs, CA 92262. www.korakia.com. ✆ **760/864-6411.** Fax 760/864-4147. 29 units. $127–$223 double; $287–$369 suite; $499–$649 house. Rates include breakfast and pool snack. MC, V. Free parking. No pets. No children 12 and under. **Amenities:** Bikes; 2 outdoor heated pools. *In room:* A/C, fridge, hair dryer, no phone, Wi-Fi on request.

Orbit In ★★ 🎒 This much-hyped renovation of a classic 1950s motel gets my vote as the grooviest digs in town. With its cocktails-by-the-pool Rat Pack aesthetic, it has exceeded everyone's expectations, with an almost scholarly appreciation of the architects and designers responsible for Palm Springs's reign as a mecca of vintage modernism. Serious connoisseurs of interior design will find a museum's worth of furnishings in these rooms, each of which adheres to a theme (Martini Room, Atomic Paradise, and so on), down to customized lounge-music CDs. Contemporary comforts abound, from cushy double pillow-top mattresses and private patios to poolside misters that create an oasis of cool even during midsummer scorchers. Kitchenettes all boast charming restored fixtures, as do the candy-pink-tiled original bathrooms, which have only stall showers but are surprisingly spacious—and naturally sunlit. Guests gather at the poolside "boomerang" bar, or in the **Albert Frey Lounge** (homage to the late, great architect whose unique home sits midway up the mountain backdrop); a central "movies, books, and games" closet encourages old-fashioned camaraderie. Nearby, the eight-unit **Hideaway** is a quieter, more secluded lodging with a large saltwater pool—no Jacuzzi, but access to the Orbit amenities is available.

562 W. Arenas Rd., Palm Springs, CA 92262. www.orbitin.com. ✆ **877/99-ORBIT** (996-7248) or 760/323-3585. Fax 760/323-3599. 10 units. $149–$259 double. Rates include deluxe continental breakfast, evening wine. AE, DISC, MC, V. Free parking. **Amenities:** Poolside bar; free bikes; Jacuzzi; outdoor heated saltwater pool; spa facilities. *In room:* A/C, TV/VCR, CD player, hair dryer, kitchenette.

Spa Resort Casino ★★ This is one of the more unusual choices in town. It's on the Indian-owned parcel of land containing the mineral springs for which Palm Springs was named. The Cahuilla claimed the springs had magical powers to cure illness. Today's travelers still come here to pamper body and soul by "taking the waters," though now the facility is sleekly modern. There are three pools on the premises: One is a conventional outdoor swimming pool; the other two are

---

OLD IS NEW again

Bring back the romance of the '50s with a vacation stay at the **Twin Palms Sinatra Estate.** Built in 1947 by Stewart Williams for Frank and his then-wife Nancy, it became the center of desert social life when Frank brought home a new bride, Ava Gardner. The 4,500-square-foot home has three bedrooms, seven bathrooms, a living room with massive glass doors that open to the patio, and the piano-shaped swimming pool. Period furniture sustains the atmosphere, with artwork, pottery, and textiles. It wasn't all peaches and cream in the Sinatra household—note the chip in the sink, from a champagne bottle tossed during one of Frank's tiffs with Ava. But if you still dote on Ol' Blue Eyes, nostalgia is your bag, and you can afford $7,800 for 3 nights' minimum stay ($2,600 for each additional night), see **www.timeandplace.com** for availability, rates, and other information.

filled from the underground natural springs brimming with revitalizing minerals. Inside the hotel's extensive spa are private sunken marble swirl-pools fed by the springs. After your bath, you can pamper yourself with one of many treatments. Despite the addition of the Vegas-style casino (a separate unit across the street), the Cahuilla have integrated modern hotel comforts with this land's ancient healing tradition and Indian spirit.

401 E. Amado Rd. (off N. Indian Canyon Dr.), Palm Springs, CA 92262. www.sparesortcasino.com. ✆ **888/999-1995** or 760/883-1000. Reservations: 800/854-1279. Fax 760/325-3344. 228 units. $199–$229 double; $369–$1,500 suite. AE, DC, MC, V. Free parking. **Amenities:** 5 restaurants; 2 bars; concierge; fitness center; Olympic-size outdoor heated pool plus an indoor pool; room service; full-service spa. *In room:* A/C, plasma flatscreen TV, fridge, hair dryer, Wi-Fi.

Viceroy Palm Springs ★★ Once the choice of Hollywood celebrities, this outstanding historic hotel, formerly the Estrella, is quiet and secluded yet close to the action. It's composed of three distinct properties from three different eras, which benefited from a chic transformation in 2002—sort of a Grecian-meets-modern Regency style popular during Palm Springs's golden era. Guest rooms vary in terms of size and amenities—some have fireplaces and/or full kitchens, others have wet bars or private balconies. The color scheme is black and white with lemon-yellow accents. The real deals are the studio bungalows, even though they have tiny 1930s bathrooms. Lavish landscaping is an elegant finishing touch. The restaurant, **Citron,** serves breakfast, lunch, and dinner (entrees $21–$32) and has a full bar. There is also pool food service.

415 S. Belardo Rd. (south of Tahquitz Way), Palm Springs, CA 92262. www.viceroypalmsprings. com. ✆ **800/670-6184** or 760/320-4117. Fax 760/323-3303. 68 units. $160–$220 double; $320 suite; $380–$550 villa. Golf Packages available. AE, DC, MC, V. Free parking. **Amenities:** Restaurant; bar; fitness room; 2 Jacuzzis; 3 outdoor heated pools (including children's pool); full-service spa. *In room:* A/C, flatscreen TV/DVD, fridge, hair dryer, high-speed Internet, daily newspaper.

Villa Royale ★★ This charming inn, 5 minutes from the hustle and bustle of downtown, evokes a European cluster of villas, complete with climbing bougainvillea and rooms filled with international antiques and artwork. Uniform luxuries (down comforters and other pampering touches) appear throughout. Rooms vary widely in size and ambience; larger isn't always better, as some of the inn's most appealing rooms are in the smaller, more affordable range. Many rooms have fireplaces, private patios, full kitchens, and a variety of other amenities. A full breakfast is served in an intimate garden setting surrounding the main pool. This is a genuine desert oasis. The hotel's romantic restaurant, **Europa** (p. 745), is a sleeper, offering some of Palm Springs's very best meals.

1620 Indian Trail (off E. Palm Canyon), Palm Springs, CA 92264. www.villaroyale.com. ✆ **800/245-2314** or 760/327-2314. Fax 760/322-3794. 30 units. $105–$230 suite; $175–$312 villa. Rates include full breakfast. Golf packages available. AE, DC, DISC, MC, V. Free parking. **Amenities:** Restaurant; Jacuzzi; 2 outdoor heated pools. *In room:* A/C, TV, hair dryer, Internet, newspaper.

Inexpensive

Calla Lily Inn With a recent extensive renovation, this nine-unit inn offers deluxe rooms with kitchens and poolside suites, all with tile floors and luxurious beds. Instead of wine at cocktail time, the Calla Lily offers a nighttime cordial or brandy. The tropical decor is enhanced by the lush landscaping with (what else?) calla lilies. A 2-day minimum is required on weekends and holidays, and pets and smoking are prohibited.

350 S. Belardo Rd., Palm Springs, CA 92262. www.callalilypalmsprings.com. ☏ **888/888-5787** or 760/323-3654. Fax 760/323-4964. 9 units. $129–$179 double; $159–$398 suite. AE, DC, DISC, MC, V. **Amenities:** Bikes; Jacuzzi; heated pool. *In room:* A/C, TV/VCR/DVD, Wi-Fi, robes, complimentary bottle of wine on arrival.

Casa Cody ★ ☺   Once owned by "Wild" Bill Cody's niece, this 1920s house with a double courtyard (each with swimming pool) has been restored to fine condition. It now sports a Southwestern decor and peaceful grounds marked by large lawns and mature, blossoming fruit trees. You'll feel more like a houseguest than a hotel client at the Casa Cody. It's in the residential, tennis-clubby part of town, a couple of easy blocks from Palm Canyon Drive. Most of the 27 units here have fireplaces and full-size kitchens. Breakfast is served poolside, as are complimentary wine and cheese on Saturday afternoons. Kids are welcome.

175 S. Cahuilla Rd. (btw. Tahquitz Way and Arenas Rd.), Palm Springs, CA 92262. www.casacody. com. ☏ **800/231-2639** or 760/320-9346. Fax 760/325-8610. 27 units. $89–$189 double; $219–$299 suite; $429 2-bedroom house; $649 4-bedroom house. Rates include expanded continental breakfast. AE, DC, DISC, MC, V. Pets accepted for $15 extra per night. **Amenities:** Jacuzzi; 2 outdoor heated pools. *In room:* A/C, TV, fridge.

Palm Mountain Resort and Spa ☺   Within easy walking distance of Palm Springs's main drag, this former Holiday Inn welcomes kids 17 and under free in their parent's room, making it a good choice for families. Rooms are in the two- or the three-story wing, and many have a patio or balcony, with a view of the mountains or the large Astroturf courtyard. Midweek and summer rates are as low as $49. For the best rates, book online or ask for "Great Rates."

155 S. Belardo Rd., Palm Springs, CA 92262. www.palmmountainresort.com. ☏ **800/622-9451** or 760/325-1301. Fax 760/323-8937. 119 units. Jan–Apr $89–$109 double; May–Sept $69–$139 double; Oct–Dec $79–$95 double. $8 resort fee. Rates include continental breakfast. Children 17 and under stay free in parent's room. AE, DC, DISC, MC, V. Free parking. **Amenities:** Restaurant; lounge; heated pool; day spa. *In room:* A/C, TV, fridge, hair dryer, microwave.

RANCHO MIRAGE

Marriott's Rancho Las Palmas Resort & Spa ★★ ☺   The early California charm of this relaxing Spanish hacienda makes Rancho Las Palmas one of the least pretentious luxury resorts in the desert. Dedicated golfers play on the adjoining country club's 27 holes, tennis buffs flock to the 25 hotel courts (3 of them red clay), and everybody enjoys the world-class health spa, plus a new aquatic adventure called Splashtopia with 200-foot water slides. Guest rooms are in a complex of low-rise, tile-roofed structures, and the public areas have an easygoing elegance, filled with flower-laden stone fountains, smooth terra-cotta tile floors, and rough-hewn wood trim. Each room has a balcony or patio.

41000 Bob Hope Dr., Rancho Mirage, CA 92270. www.rancholaspalmas.com. ☏ **866/423-1195** or 760/568-2727. Fax 760/568-5845. 466 units. $199–$319 double, $609–$759 suite. Children 17 and under stay free in parent's room. AE, DISC, MC, V. Self-parking. **Amenities:** 3 restaurants; cocktail lounge; babysitting; children's pool and programs; concierge; health club; 2 Jacuzzis; 2 outdoor heated pools; room service; 20,000 sq.-ft. full-service spa; 8 night-lit outdoor tennis courts. *In room:* A/C, TV w/pay movies, hair dryer, minibar.

Westin Mission Hills Resort ★★ ☺   Designed to resemble a Moroccan palace surrounded by pools, waterfalls, and lush gardens, this self-contained resort stands on 360 acres. It's an excellent choice for families and travelers who take their golf game seriously. (Regular desert visitors will note the Westin is situated so that Palm Springs and Palm Desert are equally accessible without driving on congested Hwy. 111.) Rooms range from basic to palatial, but all have terraces and come with an array of creature comforts befitting this price range—including the Westin trademark Heavenly Bed.

The Westin has the business demeanor of a practiced group-and-meeting hotel, but it offers a multitude of recreation options for leisure travelers, gamblers attracted to the nearby Agua Caliente Casino, or professionals after the day's business is concluded. In addition to their championship golf course, you'll find a running track, bike trails, lawn games, and the freshly expanded Spa at Mission Hills, a boutiquelike oasis whose treatments range from sports massage to pampering Hawaiian body treatments.

71-777 Dinah Shore Dr. (at Bob Hope Dr.), Rancho Mirage, CA 92270. www.starwood.com. ☎ **800/WESTIN-1** (937-8461) or 760/770-8250. Fax 760/324-6343. 512 units. $189–$575 double. Extra person $35. Children 17 and under stay free in parent's room. Golf, spa, and family packages available. AE, DC, DISC, MC, V. Free valet and self-parking. **Amenities:** 3 restaurants; 2 lounges; 3 poolside cabana bars; babysitting; bike rental; children's activity center; concierge; health club; multiple outdoor heated pools and Jacuzzis; room service; full-service spa; night-lit outdoor tennis courts. *In room:* A/C, TV w/pay movies, hair dryer, minibar.

PALM DESERT

Desert Springs—A JW Marriott Resort & Spa ★★ ☺

A tourist attraction in its own right, Marriott's Desert Springs resort is worth a peek even if you're not lucky enough to stay here. Most guests come for the golf and tennis facilities, and the luxurious, full-service spa is an added perk. The shaded marble lobby greets guests with its 60-foot bar backed by waterfalls spilling into reflecting pools. The "dock" at the end of the lobby has two gondolas to transport guests through a network of Venetian-inspired waterways to view the fairways and lush gardens.

Rooms are not as fancy as the lobby would lead you to believe, but they're exceedingly comfortable and have contemporary furnishings. All have terraces with views of the golf course and the San Jacinto Mountains. Recreational options include a jogging trail, 36 holes of golf, a driving range, a unique 18-hole putting range, basketball courts, lawn croquet, and a sunbathing "beach" with volleyball court. The spa has 47 treatment rooms and suites with private showers and patios, fireplaces, and outdoor whirlpools. You need not ever leave the premises if you don't want to.

74855 Country Club Dr., Palm Desert, CA 92260. www.desertspringsresort.com. ☎ **800/331-3112** or 760/341-2211. Reservations 888/538-9459. Fax 760/341-1872. 884 units. $199–$535 double; from $549–$759 suite. Children 17 and under stay free in parent's room. Senior discount available. AE, DC, DISC, MC, V. **Amenities:** 5 restaurants; 4 snack bars; 3 lounges; babysitting; bike rental; children's programs; concierge; 5 outdoor Jacuzzis; 5 heated outdoor pools; room service; full-service spa and health club; 20 tennis courts (hard, clay, and grass; 7 lit). *In room:* A/C, TV w/pay movies, hair dryer, minibar.

The Mod Resort ★

This 14-unit hideaway is a remembrance of the '70s as a vision in white. In fact, in the rooms, it's white on white, with accents of chrome and mirrors. The bathroom has a glass bowl sink and a glass tile shower with rainshower head. The suites have private patios, some with kitchenettes, some with full kitchens. The units flank a full-size pool set among palm trees and augments with white-and-chrome loungers and tables. Truly, a place to relax and still be a short walk to El Paseo's shopping and restaurants.

73758 Shadow Mountain Dr., Palm Desert, CA 92260. ☎ **888/MOD-1970** (663-1970) or 760/674-1966. 14 units. $159–$349 double. Rates include continental breakfast. AE, MC, V. **Amenities:** Jacuzzi; pool. *In room:* Flatscreen LCD TV/DVD, CD player, some w/kitchenette or full kitchen, Wi-Fi.

LA QUINTA

La Quinta Resort & Club ★★★   A luxury resort amid citrus trees, towering palms, cactuses, and desert flowers at the base of the Santa Rosa Mountains, La Quinta is *the* place to be if you're serious about golf or tennis. The resort is renowned for its five championship golf courses—including one of California's best, Pete Dye's PGA West TPC Stadium Course. All guest rooms are in single-story, Spanish-style buildings throughout the grounds. Each has its own patio and access to one of several dozen small pools, enhancing the feeling of privacy at this retreat. Some units have a fireplace or Jacuzzi. The tranquil lounge and library in the original hacienda hearken back to the early days of the resort, when Clark Gable, Greta Garbo, Frank Capra, and other luminaries chose La Quinta as their hideaway. The resort includes Spa La Quinta, a Mission-style complex with more than 35 treatment rooms for every pampering luxury.

49–499 Eisenhower Dr., La Quinta, CA 92253. www.laquintaresort.com. ☎ **800/598-3828** or 760/564-4111. Fax 760/564-7656. 796 units. $179–$399 double; from $599 suite. Extra person $25. $27 resort fee per night. Children 17 and under stay free in parent's room. Packages available. AE, MC, V. Free self-parking; valet parking. Pets welcome for a fee. **Amenities:** 3 restaurants; 3 bars (2 featuring entertainment); bike rental; children's programs; concierge; 53 Jacuzzis; 41 outdoor pools; room service; full-service 23,000-sq.-ft. spa; 23 outdoor tennis courts (10 lit). *In room:* A/C, flatscreen TV/VCR w/pay movies, hair dryer, minibar, Wi-Fi, private patios.

INDIAN WELLS

Miramonte Resort & Spa ★★   This collection of 215 rooms in 12 Mediterranean villas covers 11 acres of bougainvillea-filled gardens and Italian fountains. Standard rooms, all with patios, are enlarged to become luxurious minisuites adding a living room area with a second TV. Suites add one or two bedrooms. An extra-large pool has cabanas that can be rented by the day, plus whirlpools, and is the center of activity in the main area. Another pool is designated as adults only, making it a quiet respite. An $18 resort fee includes local phone calls, 24-hour fitness center, valet and self-parking, daily newspaper, and Wi-Fi. Dining is especially fine in the Grove Artisan Kitchen, with farm-to-table California cuisine. The Vineyard Lounge offers tapas and local jazz on the weekends. The WELL SPA is a 14,000-square-foot expanse with relaxation suites, mud bars, river benches, and a Watsu pool.

A La Quinta Bed & Breakfast Hideaway

Devotees of bed-and-breakfasts or boutique inns might be daunted by the La Quinta Resort's 800 rooms, but there's a way to enjoy this quiet, affluent end of the valley with a little more intimacy. Check out the hidden-secret **Lake La Quinta Inn,** 78–120 Caleo Bay (www.lakelaquintainn.com; ☎ **888/226-4546** or 760/564-7332), a 13-room Norman-style B&B on the shores of a man-made lake, blocks from the famous resort. Exquisitely outfitted rooms, Wi-Fi, delightful hosts, on-site facials and massage, and a 24-hour pool and Jacuzzi complete the fantasy. Rates are $179 to $289 (double); suites are $289 to $399, including breakfast and wine in the afternoon.

45-000 Indian Wells Lane (on Hwy. 111), Indian Wells, CA 82210. www.miramonteresort.com.
© **800/237-2926** or 760/341-2200. Fax 760/568-0541. 215 units. $159–$179 double; $229–
$544 suite; $599 1-bedroom villa. $20 resort fee per night. Children 15 and under stay free in
parent's room. All rooms are nonsmoking. AE, MC, V. Free self- and valet parking. **Amenities:**
Restaurant; bar; lounge; concierge; 2 Jacuzzis; 2 pools; room service; full spa w/fitness room and
pool. *In room:* A/C, 42-in. flatscreen TV, hair dryer, minibar, Wi-Fi.

Where to Eat

PALM SPRINGS

Expensive

Europa Restaurant ★★★ CALIFORNIAN/CONTINENTAL   Long adver-
tised as the "most romantic dining in the desert," Europa is a sentimental favorite
of many regulars, equal parts gay and straight. This European-style hideaway
exudes charm and ambience. Whether you sit under the stars on Europa's garden
patio or in subdued candlelight indoors, you'll savor dinner prepared by one of
Palm Springs's most dedicated kitchens and served by a discreetly attentive staff.
Standout dishes include a tender *osso buco* that falls off the bone, filet mignon on
a bed of crispy onions with garlic butter, and a show-stopping salmon baked in
parchment with crème fraîche and dill. And don't miss the signature chocolate
mousse—smooth and addictive.

1620 Indian Trail (at the Villa Royale). © **760/327-2314.** Reservations recommended. Main
courses $28–$42. AE, DC, DISC, MC, V. Tues–Sun 5–10pm.

The Purple Palm ★★★ FRENCH/MEDITERRANEAN   Poolside at the
Colony Palms Hotel, this fresh, innovative addition to Palm Springs dining has
quickly become *the* place to dine. Relax in the comfortable dining room or dine
by candlelight alongside the pool. Specialties include Scottish Salmon, Australian Barramundi, and Bone-in Rib Eye. Don't leave without tasting the tiramisu
with a raspberry soda shooter.

572 N. Indian Canyon Dr. (at the Colony Palms Hotel). © **800/557-2187.** www.colonypalms
hotel.com. Reservations recommended. Main courses $30–$50. AE, DISC, MC, V. Daily 9am–
10pm summer; 7:30–10pm winter.

Inexpensive

Davey's Hideaway ★ 📷AMERICAN   For a relaxed, casual, inexpensive evening, you must try Davey's Hideaway, at the beginning of East Palm Canyon.
Featuring patio dining and piano entertainment, this small cafe serves salads,
pasta, beef, rack of lamb, and their special fresh Atlantic salmon charbroiled or
Cajun-style. Nightly specials sell for $20 from 5 to 6pm, and wines are $26 to
$60 per bottle.

292 E. Palm Canyon, Palm Springs (across the street from Lyon's). © **760/320-4480.** Reservations suggested. Main courses $18–$32. MC, V. Sun–Thurs 5–9pm; Fri–Sat 5–10pm.

Murph's Gaslight ★ SOUTHERN   Join those in the know at this budget-
saving lunch-and-dinner meeting place, where the chicken just keeps coming,
with all the trimmings: black-eyed peas, mashed potatoes, corn bread, hot biscuits, country gravy, and fruit cobbler. Call ahead for takeout or join the family-
style crowd, on a first-come, first-served basis. An early-bird special starts at 5pm
for $10. If there's a wait, relax in Murph's Irish Pub.

79–860 Ave. 42, next to the airport in Bermuda Dunes near Jefferson. © **760/345-6242.** $16 for
full dinner. MC, V. Tues–Sat 11am–3pm and 5–9pm; Sun 3–9pm. Closed Mon.

Sherman's Deli and Bakery ★ KOSHER DELI   Join the locals at this indoor and outdoor-patio restaurant with 2-inch-thick deli sandwiches, lox and bagels, and a bakery with rich, delicious cakes and pastries that would put any calorie-conscious dieter into trauma if it weren't for the Lite Lunch Special: mushroom barley or matzo ball soup with half of any regular deli-variety sandwich. Iced tea is the official drink, but wine and beer are also available. Sherman's has another branch in Palm Desert (73–161 Country Club Dr.; ✆ **760/568-1350**).

401 Tahquitz, Palm Springs. ✆ **760/325-1199.** Breakfast omelets $6.75–$9.45; deli sandwich board $8.45–$13 (includes potato salad); dinner $15–$21; early-bird dinner 4–7pm $12. AE, DC, DISC, MC, V. Daily 7am–9pm.

PALM DESERT & VICINITY

Louise's Pantry ★ COFFEE SHOP/DINER   A real old-fashioned luncheon-ette, Louise's was a fixture in Palm Springs since opening as a drugstore lunch counter in 1945. The original location on Palm Canyon Drive fell victim to sky-rocketing property values, but devoted patrons—young and old—flocked to the new location in La Quinta, for premium-quality comfort foods such as Cobb salad, Reuben and French-dip sandwiches, burgers, pantry sandwiches, chicken and dumplings, hearty breakfasts with biscuits and gravy, and tasty fresh-baked pies. Beer and wine are available. The new branch is on Washington Street in La Quinta, serving the same menu through dinner.

47-150 Washington (south of Hwy. 111), La Quinta. ✆ **760/771-3330.** Reservations not accepted. Most menu items under $11. MC, V. Daily 7am–2pm; Sat 4–8pm.

Palmie ★★ 🎁 CLASSIC FRENCH   Martine and Alain Clerc's cozy bistro is filled with Art Deco posters of French seaside resorts. Chef Alain sends out mas-terful traditional French dishes such as braised lamb shank, *cassoulet des confit de canard,* and ravioli stuffed with lobster. In fact, every carefully garnished plate is a work of art. To the charming background strains of French chanteuses that can sometimes be heard over the noise of happy diners, hostess and manager Martine circulates among tables, determined that visitors enjoy their meals as much as the loyal regulars she greets by name. Don't leave without sampling dessert: My favorite is the trio of petite crème brûlées, flavored with ginger, vanilla, and Kahlúa.

44-491 Town Center Way, Ste. G, Palm Desert. Go north on Town Center Way, then take the 1st left into the mall, and a direct left to the restaurant. ✆ **760/341-3200.** Reservations recommen-ded. Main courses $17–$32. AE, DC, MC, V. Mon–Sat 5:30–9pm.

Sammy's Woodfired Pizza ★ PIZZA   In the same mall complex as Tommy Bahama's is a great inexpensive restaurant for families. The large room with booths and tables is fronted by a misted outdoor patio. Choose from 21 wood-fired pizza drizzled with chili oil, such as the N.Y. pizza: homemade tomato sauce, sautéed mushrooms, pepperoni, salami, and Italian sausage for $13. The menu also has a variety of salads and pasta. Beer and wine are available.

73595 El Paseo (at Larkspur Ave.). ✆ **760/836-0500.** Pizzas $9.75–$13; salads $9.50–$17; pastas $13–$17. AE, MC, V. Daily 11am–9pm.

Tommy Bahama's Tropical Café ★★ CARIBBEAN   If all this desert ter-rain makes you long for *de islands, mon,* step upstairs from fashionable Tommy Bahama's boutique for a dose of Caribbean relaxation, without the humidity. The decor alone is worth a visit: a fantasy port of call, around 1940, with ceiling fans, plenty of rattan and palms, and upholstery in TB's signature tropical prints. Enormous umbrellas shade patio seating with valley views, and spacious indoor booths make for easy relaxing over a series of sweet umbrella drinks. The food is a delicious change of pace, its Caribbean zing not overly spiced; check out coconut shrimp with mango dip, conch fritters, mango shrimp salad, Boca Chica chicken, Jamaican jerk pork, and Key lime pie for dessert. Diners are an entertaining mix of socialites fresh from the tennis courts, perennially vacationing retirees, and well-heeled shoppers.

73595 El Paseo (at Larkspur Ave.). ✆ **760/836-0188.** Reservations recommended in season. Main courses $8–$18 lunch, $18–$37 dinner; 3-course tasting menu $29. AE, MC, V. Daily 11am–10pm.

The Desert Resorts After Dark

Every month a different club or disco is the hot spot in the Springs, and the best way to tap into the trend is by consulting the *Desert Guide,* the *Bottom Line* (see "Gay & Lesbian Life in Palm Springs," earlier in this chapter), or one of the many other free newsletters available from area hotels and merchants. **VillageFest** (see "Shopping," earlier in this chapter) turns Palm Canyon Drive into an outdoor party every Thursday night. Below, I describe a couple of the enduring arts and entertainment attractions around the desert resorts.

The **Fabulous Palm Springs Follies,** at the Plaza Theatre, 128 S. Palm Canyon Dr., Palm Springs (✆ **760/327-0225;** www.psfollies.com), a vaudeville-style show filled with highly polished and lavishly costumed production numbers reminiscent of the Ziegfeld days, is a long-running hit in the historic Plaza Theatre in the heart of town. With a cast of retired showgirls, singers, dancers, and comedians, the revue is hugely popular. In addition, there are guest stars such as Susan Anton, The Crystals, and Leslie Gore and the Four Preps. The season runs November through May; call for exact schedule. Tickets range from $50 to $95. Matinees are at 1:30pm, evening shows at 7pm.

The **McCallum Theatre for the Performing Arts,** 73000 Fred Waring Dr., Palm Desert (✆ **866/889-2787** or 760/340-2787), offers the only cultural high road around. Frequent symphony performances feature visiting virtuosos such as conductor Seiji Ozawa or violinist Itzhak Perlman. Other recent offerings have included musicals such as *Hairspray* and *Chicago;* comedy by Norm Crosby, Tim Conway, and Kathy Griffin; and musical shows such as *A Tribute to Glenn Miller,* with the Tex Beneke Orchestra, and *Sinatra Sings,* featuring Frank, Jr. Call for upcoming events.

Casinos

Native American gaming has been part of desert life for years now, but recently the industry seems to have joined the major leagues, with a professionalism and polish that have given rise to a "virtual Vegas."

The best-known and most centrally located casino is the **Spa Resort Casino** in the heart of Palm Springs (p. 740). Gaming rooms that were once an afterthought now share the spotlight with the hot springs. Attendees at the hotel's conference center on business can often be found playing hooky at one or both.

You can't help but be impressed by the brilliant neon fireballs of the **Agua Caliente Casino,** northeast of Palm Springs at 32–250 Bob Hope Dr., Rancho Mirage (✆ **888/999-1995** or 760/321-2000; www.hotwatercasino.com), down the street from the Westin Mission Hills. The new hotel has 340 rooms, a

10,000-square-foot spa, three restaurants, and a 2,000-seat showroom; call ☎ 866/923-7244 for reservations.

The former Trump 29, now run by the owning Indian tribe, is called **Spotlight 29,** 46–200 Harrison Place, Coachella (☎ **866/377-6829** or 760/775-5566; www.spotlight.com), about a half-hour from Palm Springs. Although the land is tribal owned, this sophisticated complex is Vegas all the way, from its big-name shows and high-roller players club to its 24-hour fine dining and all-you-can-eat prime-rib buffets.

Other tribal casino/resorts flank the valley, with the **Morongo Casino, Resort and Spa** to the northwest, at 49500 Seminole Dr., Cabazon, CA 92230 (☎ **888/MORONGO** [667-6646]; www.morongocasinoresort.com), with 310 rooms, 32 suites, and six casitas by the pool. Four restaurants, food court, and full-service salon and spa augment the three nightclubs, not to mention the tables.

JOSHUA TREE NATIONAL PARK ★

40 miles NE of Palm Springs; 128 miles E of downtown L.A.

The Joshua trees in this national park are merely a jumping-off point for exploring this seemingly barren desert. Viewed from the roadside, the dry land only hints at hidden vitality, but closer examination reveals a giant mosaic of intense beauty and complexity. From lush oases teeming with life to rusted-out relics of human attempts to tame the wilderness, from low plains of tufted cactuses to mountains of exposed, twisted rock, the park is much more than a tableau of the curious tree for which it is named.

The Joshua tree is said to have received its name from early Mormon settlers traveling west, for its upraised limbs and bearded appearance reminded them of the prophet Joshua leading them to the Promised Land. Other observers were not so kind. Explorer John C. Frémont called it "the most repulsive tree in the vegetable kingdom."

That's harsh criticism for this hardy desert dweller—really not a tree, but a variety of yucca and member of the lily family. The relationship is apparent when pale-yellow, lilylike flowers festoon the limbs of the Joshuas when they bloom in March, April, or May (depending on rainfall). When Mother Nature cooperates, the park also puts on quite a wildflower display. Call the park ranger (see "Essentials," below) for an updated report on prime viewing sites.

The park, which reaches the southernmost boundary of this special tree's range, straddles two desert environments. The mountainous, Joshua tree–studded Mojave Desert forms the northwestern part of the park, while the Colorado Desert—hotter, drier, lower, and characterized by a wide variety of desert flora, including cactuses, cottonwood, and native California fan palms—comprises the southern and eastern sections of the park. Between them runs the "transition zone," displaying characteristics of each.

The area's geological timeline is fascinating, stretching back 8 million years to a time when the Mojave landscape was one of rolling hills and grasslands, when horses, camels, and mastodons abounded, preyed upon by saber-toothed tigers and wild dogs. Displays at the **Oasis Visitor Center** show how resulting climatic, volcanic, and tectonic activity created the park's signature cliffs and boulders and turned Joshua Tree into the arid desert it is today.

Mastodon Peak, Joshua Tree National Park.

Human presence has been traced back nearly 10,000 years, with the discovery of Pinto Man, and more recent habitation is suggested by Native American pictographs carved into rock faces. Miners and ranchers began coming in the 1860s, but the boom went bust by the turn of the 20th century. Then a Pasadena doctor, treating World War I veterans suffering from respiratory ailments caused by mustard gas, prescribed the desert's clean, dry air—and the town of Twentynine Palms was (re)born.

In the 1920s, cactus gardens were very much in vogue. Entrepreneurs hauled truckloads of desert plants into Los Angeles for quick sale or export, and souvenir hunters removed archaeological treasures. Incensed that the beautiful Mojave was in danger of being picked clean, Los Angeles socialite Minerva Hoyt organized a conservation movement and successfully lobbied for the establishment of Joshua Tree National Monument in 1936. The park got an unexpected boost when the first rock-climbing route was put up in 1956, near Jumbo Rock. The sport didn't take off until the late 1960s, but today the park is considered Southern California's best rock-climbing area, and in winter (when places such as Yosemite are embraced by cold weather), Joshua Tree is crawling with climbers.

In 1994, under provisions of the federal California Desert Protection Act, Joshua Tree rose to national park status and expanded to nearly 800,000 acres. The park is popular with everyone from

Load Up on Everything

Joshua Tree National Park has no restaurants, lodging, gas stations, or stores. Water is available only at five park locations: Cottonwood Springs, the Black Rock Canyon Campground, the Indian Cove Ranger Station, the West Entrance (the hamlet of Joshua Tree), and the Oasis Visitor Center. Joshua Tree, Twentynine Palms, and Yucca Valley have lots of restaurants, markets, motels, and B&Bs.

campers to wildflower lovers and even RVers. It's a must-see for nature and geology lovers visiting during temperate weather, and it's more "user-friendly" than the other two hard-core desert parks.

Essentials

GETTING THERE   From metropolitan Los Angeles, the usual route to the **Oasis Visitor Center,** 74485 National Park Dr., 92277, in Joshua Tree National Park is via I-10 to its intersection with Hwy. 62 (some 92 miles east of downtown). Hwy. 62 (the Twentynine Palms Hwy.) leads northeast for about 43 miles to the town of **Twentynine Palms.** Total driving time is around 2½ hours. In town, follow the signs at National Park Drive or Utah Trail to the visitor center and ranger station. Admission to the park is $15 per car (good for 7 days). Camping fees are $10 with no water, $15 with water.

WHEN TO GO   The park is busiest—relatively speaking, since it rarely feels crowded—in winter (Nov–Mar). Rock climbers flock to Joshua Tree in winter and spring, along with day-trippers drawn by brilliant wildflower displays (if winter rainfall was sufficient) in March, April, and May. The sizzling summer months are popular with international visitors curious about the legendary extremes of temperature, and hardy campers looking for the solitude of balmy evenings.

VISITOR CENTERS & INFORMATION   In addition to the **Oasis Visitor Center** (© 760/367-5500) at the Twentynine Palms entrance, **Cottonwood Visitor Center** is at the south entrance, and the privately operated **Park Center** is in the town of Joshua Tree, close to the West Entrance, the unofficial portal for rock climbers.

The Oasis Visitor Center is open daily (except Christmas) from 8am to 5pm. Check here for a detailed map of park roads, plus schedules of ranger-guided walks and interpretive programs. Ask about weekend tours of the Desert Queen Ranch, once a working homestead and now part of the park.

For information before you go, contact the **Park Superintendent's Office,** 74485 National Park Dr., Twentynine Palms, CA 92277 (© 760/367-5525; www.nps.gov/jotr). The **Joshua Tree National Park Association** is another good resource; reach them at © 760/367-5525 (www.joshuatree.org). Another outfit focused on the surrounding communities is **www.desertgold.com**.

Exploring the Park

An excellent first stop, outside the park's north entrance, is the main **Oasis Visitor Center,** alongside the Oasis of Mara, also known as the Twentynine Palms Oasis. For many generations, the native Serrano tribe lived at this "place of little springs and much grass." Get maps, books, and the latest in road, trail, and weather conditions before beginning your tour.

From the Oasis Center, drive south to **Jumbo Rocks,** which captures the essence of the park: a vast array of rock formations, a Joshua tree forest, and the yucca-dotted desert, open and wide. Check out Skull Rock (one of the many rocks in the area that appear to resemble humans, dinosaurs, monsters, cathedrals, or castles) via a 1.5-mile nature trail that provides an introduction to the park's flora, wildlife, and geology.

Jumbo Rocks.

At Cap Rock Junction, the main park road swings north toward the **Wonderland of Rocks,** 12 square miles of massive jumbled granite. This curious maze of stone hides groves of Joshua trees, trackless washes, and several small pools of water. To the south is Keys View Road, which dead-ends at mile-high **Keys View.** From the crest of the Little San Bernardino Mountains, enjoy grand desert views that encompass both the highest (Mt. San Gorgonio) and lowest (Salton Sea) points in Southern California.

Don't miss the contrasting Colorado Desert terrain found along Pinto Basin Road. To conserve time, you might plan to exit the park via this route, which ends up at I-10. You'll pass both the **Cholla Cactus Garden** and spindly **Ocotillo Patch** on your way to vast, flat **Pinto Basin,** a barren

Sleeping under the stars.

lowland surrounded by austere mountains and punctuated by trackless sand dunes. The dunes are an easy 2-mile round-trip hike from the backcountry camping board (one of the few man-made markers along this road and one of the only designated parking areas), or simply continue to **Cottonwood Springs,** near the southern park entrance. Besides a small ranger station and well-developed campground, Cottonwood has a cool, palm-shaded oasis that is the trail head for a tough hike to Lost Palms Oasis.

Hiking, Biking & Climbing

HIKING & NATURE WALKS   The national park has a variety of nature trails, from strenuous challenges to kid-friendly interpretive walks; two of these (**Oasis**

of **Mara** and **Cap Rock**) are paved and wheelchair accessible. A popular route, among the 11 short interpretive trails, is **Cholla Cactus Garden,** in the park's center, where you stroll through dense clusters of the deceptively fluffy-looking "teddy bear cactus."

For the more adventurous, **Barker Dam** is an easy 1-mile loop accessible by a graded dirt road east of Hidden Valley. A small man-made lake is framed by the majestic Wonderland of Rocks. It's fun to scramble atop the old dam or search out Native American petroglyphs carved into the cliffs lining your return to the trail head.

The challenging **Lost Horse Mine Trail** near Keys View leads through 4 miles of rolling hills to the ruins of a successful gold-mining operation; from here, a short, steep hike leads uphill behind the ruins for a fine view into the heart of the park.

When you're ready for a strenuous hike, try the **Fortynine Palms Oasis Trail,** accessible from Canyon Road in Twentynine Palms. After a steep, harsh ascent to a cactus-fringed ridge, the rocky canyon trail leads to a spectacular oasis, complete with palm-shaded pools of green water and abundant birds and other wildlife. Allow 2 to 3 hours for the 3-mile round-trip hike.

Another lush oasis lies at the end of **Lost Palms Oasis Trail** at Cottonwood Springs. The first section of the 7.5-mile trail is moderately difficult, climbing slowly to the oasis overlook; from here, a treacherous path continues to the canyon bottom, a remote spot that the elusive bighorn sheep find attractive.

Joshua Tree Hiking Adventures (© 760/821-3227) offers half- and full-day guided hikes in the nearby mountains and washes. Half-day costs run from $60 per person for groups of five or more to $150 for one person, full day $70 to $240.

Desert Adventures Jeep Eco-Tours (© 888/440-5337 or 760/ 340-2345; www.red-jeep.com) offers four-wheel-drive ecotours led by naturalist guides. Desert Adventures is the only outdoor adventure company that can take you to a private 1,000-acre preserve located on the San Andreas Fault. The award-winning tours feature interactive displays and offer miles of pristine desert, a private natural palm oasis, and amazing steep-walled canyons to explore. Your off-road adventure may take you to a replica of an ancient Cahuilla village filled with Indian interpretive displays, a replica Old Mining Camp where you can pan for gold, an EPICENTER Earthquake Education Center where you can learn about geology and earthquakes, or a homestead where you can discover how early Coachella Valley pioneers survived in the harsh desert. Desert Adventures also offers jeep adventures to Joshua Tree National Park. Rates are $75 to $159 per person, $750 to $850 per jeep holding up to seven persons. Check out their special Internet prices.

MOUNTAIN BIKING   Much of the park is designated wilderness, meaning that bicycles are limited to roads (they'll damage the fragile ecosystem if you venture off the beaten track). None of the paved roads have bike lanes, but rugged mountain bikes are a great way to explore the park via unpaved roads, where there aren't many cars.

Try the 18-mile **Geology Tour Road,** which begins west of Jumbo Rocks. Dry lake beds contrast with towering boulders along this sandy downhill road, and you'll also encounter abandoned mines.

A shorter but still-rewarding ride begins at the **Covington Flats** picnic area. A steep 4-mile road climbs through Joshua trees, junipers, and pinyon pines to Eureka Peak, where you'll be rewarded with a panoramic view. For other bike-friendly unpaved and four-wheel-drive roads, view the official park map.

ROCK CLIMBING From Hidden Valley to the Wonderland of Rocks, the park has emerged as one of the state's premier rock-climbing destinations. The park offers some 4,000 climbing routes, from the easiest bouldering to some of the sport's most difficult climbs. November through May is the prime season to watch lizardlike humans scale sheer rock faces with impossible grace. Beginners can get into the act with the **Joshua Tree Rock Climbing School** (✆ **800/890-4745** or 760/366-4745; www.joshuatreerock climbing.com). In business since 1988, it offers weekend and 4-day group lessons ($125 for 1 day, $270 for 2 days, and $540 for 4 days, including equipment), plus private guiding ($325 for one person per day; less if more in the group, such as $135 per person if five in the group). **Nomad Adventures** in Joshua Tree (✆ **760/366-4684**) is the local climbing store for gear sales and shoe rentals ($10 a day). Open weekdays from 8am to 6pm, weekends 8am to 8pm.

Where to Stay

If you're staying in the Palm Springs area, it's possible to visit the national park as a day trip. But if you'd like to stay close by or spend more time here, consider Twentynine Palms, just outside the north boundary of the national park on Hwy. 62, which offers budget-to-moderate lodging. There are also accommodations in Blackrock and Joshua Tree (West Entrance). For a complete listing of Twentynine Palms lodging, contact the **Twentynine Palms Chamber of Commerce,** 73484 Twentynine Palms Hwy., Joshua Tree, CA 92277 (✆ **760/367-3445;** www.29chamber.org). Blackrock information is available through the **Yucca Valley Chamber of Commerce,** 56711 Twentynine Palms Hwy., Yucca Valley, CA 92284 (✆ **760/365-6323;** www.yuccavalley.org). For Joshua Tree (West Entrance), contact the **Joshua Tree Chamber of Commerce,** 6448 Hallee Rd., Ste. #9, Joshua Tree, CA 92252 (✆ **760/366-3723;** www.joshua treechamber.org).

Near the visitor center in the Oasis of Mara is the rustic **29 Palms Inn,** 73950 Inn Ave. (www.29palmsinn.com; ✆ **760/367-3505**), a cluster of adobe cottages and old cabins from the 1920s; its garden-fresh restaurant is the best in town. The 100-room **Best Western Garden Inn,** 71487 Palm Hwy. (www.best western.com; ✆ **760/367-9141**), is also a comfortable base from which to maximize your outdoor time. Also recommended in Twentynine Palms is the 53-room **Holiday Inn Express Hotel and Suites,** 71809 Twentynine Palms Hwy. (www.hiexpress.com; ✆ **760/361-4009**).

Nine **campgrounds** scattered throughout the park offer pleasant though often spartan accommodations, with just picnic tables and pit toilets, for the most part. Only two—**Black Rock Canyon** and **Cottonwood Springs**—have potable water and flush toilets, for a $15 overnight fee. Indian Cove and West Entrance have water at the ranger station, less than 2 miles from their closest campgrounds. You can make reservations online at **http://nps.gov** or by calling ✆ **800/365-2267.**

ANZA-BORREGO DESERT STATE PARK ★

90 miles NE of San Diego; 31 miles E of Julian

The 600,000-acre Anza-Borrego Desert State Park, the nation's largest contiguous state park, lies mostly within San Diego County, and getting to it is almost as much fun as being there. From Julian, the first 20 minutes of the winding hour-long drive feel as if you're going straight downhill; in fact, it's a 7-mile drop called Banner Grade. A famous scene from the 1954 movie *The Long, Long Trailer,* with Lucille Ball and Desi Arnaz, was shot on the Banner Grade, and countless Westerns have been filmed in the Anza-Borrego Desert. An easier access is from Indio: Go south on Hwy. 86 to Salton City and west on County Road S22 into Borrego Springs.

The desert is home to fossils and rocks dating from 540 million years ago (humans arrived only 10,000 years ago). The terrain ranges in elevation from 15 feet to 6,100 feet above sea level. It incorporates dry lakebeds, sandstone canyons, granite mountains, palm groves fed by year-round springs, and more than 600 kinds of desert plants. After the spring rains, thousands of wildflowers burst into bloom, transforming the desert into a brilliant palette of pink, lavender, red, orange, and yellow. The rare bighorn sheep can sometimes be spotted navigating rocky hillsides, and an occasional migratory bird stops off on the way to the Salton Sea. A sense of timelessness pervades this landscape; it's worth slowing down to take a long look around.

When planning a trip here, keep in mind that temperatures rise to as high as 115°F (46°C) in summer. Winters days are comfortable, with temperatures in the low to mid-70s (mid-20s Celsius), but nighttime temps can drop to freezing. **Note:** Hypothermia is as big a killer out here as the heat.

Essentials

GETTING AROUND You don't need four-wheel-drive to tour the desert, but you'll probably want to get off the highways and onto the jeep trails. The Anza-Borrego Desert State Park Visitor Center staff can tell you which jeep trails are in condition for two-wheel-drive vehicles. A free Back Country Permit is required to camp or use the jeep trails in the park. The Ocotillo Wells area has been set aside for off-road vehicles such as dune buggies and dirt bikes. A vehicle must be licensed for highway use to ride the jeep trails.

ORIENTATION & VISITOR INFORMATION In Borrego Springs, the shopping center known as "The

Anza-Borrego Desert State Park.

Mall" is on Palm Canyon Drive, the main drag. Christmas Circle surrounds a grassy park at the entry to town. The **Anza-Borrego Desert State Park Visitor Center** (☎ 760/767-4205; www.parks.ca.gov) is just west of the town of Borrego Springs. It supplies information, maps, and two 15-minute audiovisual presentations, one on the desert's changing faces and the other on wildflowers. The visitor center is open October through May Thursday to Monday from 9am to 5pm, closed Tuesday and Wednesday, June through September weekends only from 9am to 5pm. The **Desert Natural History Association,** 652 Palm Canyon Dr. (☎ 760/767-3098; www.abdnha.org), runs the sleek Borrego Desert Nature Center and Bookstore with an impressive selection of guidebooks, historical resources, educational materials for kids, native plants and regional crafts, and a small museum display that includes a frighteningly real stuffed bobcat. This is also your best source for information on the nearby Salton Sea. It's open daily 9am to 5pm.

For information on lodging, dining, and activities, contact the **Borrego Springs Chamber of Commerce,** 786 Palm Canyon Dr., Borrego Springs, CA 92004 (☎ 800/559-5524 or 760/767-5555; www.borregosprings.org).

Exploring the Desert

Remember that when you're touring in this area, hydration is of paramount importance. Whether you're walking, cycling, or driving, always have a bottle of water at your side. If you will be out after dusk, or anytime during January and February, warm clothing is also essential.

You can explore the desert terrain on a trail or self-guided driving tour; the visitor center can supply maps. For starters, the **Borrego Palm Canyon self-guided hike** (1.5 miles each way) starts at the campgrounds near the visitor center. It is beautiful and easy, leading to a waterfall and massive fan palms in about 30 minutes. A day-use fee of $4 to $6 per vehicle applies.

Note: Don't miss the sunset from Font's Point (accessible via four-wheel-drive; check at the visitor center). Plan ahead and bring champagne and beach chairs for the nightly ritual.

Where to Stay

Borrego Springs is small but has enough lodgings to suit all travel styles and budgets. Peak season corresponds with the most temperate weather and wildflower viewing—mid-January through mid-May. Other decent options include **Palm Canyon Resort,** 221 Palm Canyon Dr. (www.pcresort.com; ☎ 800/242-0044 or 760/767-5341), a large complex that includes a moderately priced hotel ($89–$189), RV park ($36–$44 for full hookup), restaurant, and recreational facilities; and **Borrego Valley Inn,** 405 Palm Canyon Dr. (www.borregovalleyinn.com; ☎ 800/333-5810 or 760/767-0311), a luxury Southwestern complex featuring sand-colored pueblo-style rooms and upscale bed-and-breakfast amenities. High-season rates are $180 to $295.

15

THE SOUTHERN CALIFORNIA DESERT

Anza-Borrego State Park

Borrego Springs Resort and Country Club ★★ South of Palm Springs, Borrego Springs has had some changes. The **Borrego Ranch Resort** has closed its doors. But an excellent alternative is the Borrego Springs Resort and Country Club. Situated beside their three 9-hole golf courses is the clubhouse and hotel facing the well-manicured greens and fairways lined with local desert foliage including several hundred mature Date Palms and the Santa Rosa mountains as a backdrop. No need to leave the premises for dinner; the **Arches Restaurant** in the Clubhouse serves American fare with a southwestern flair while the **Fireside Lounge and Bar** offers nachos and appetizers.

1112 Tilting T Dr., Borrego Springs, CA 92004. www.borregospringsresort.com. (℘ **888/826-7734** or 760/767-5700. $149–$193 double; $215–$236 suites. AE, DC, DISC, MC, V. **Amenities:** Restaurant, lounge, 3 9-hole golf courses, pool, Spa Serenity w/face and body treatments. *In room:* A/C, flatscreen TV, fridge, Wi-Fi, robes.

The Palms at Indian Head ★★ 📷 It takes a sense of nostalgia and an active imagination for most visitors to appreciate Borrego Springs's only bed-and-breakfast. Its fervent owners, David Leibert and Cynthia Wood, have renovated the once-chic resort. Originally opened in 1947, then rebuilt after a fire in 1958, the Art Deco–style hilltop lodge was a favorite hideaway for San Diego's and Hollywood's elite. It hosted stars such as Bing Crosby, Clark Gable, and Marilyn Monroe. The Leiberts rescued it from disrepair in 1993, uncovering original wallpaper, light fixtures, and priceless memorabilia. The inn now has 12 rooms and a popular restaurant, the **Krazy Coyote** (see "Where to Eat," below). Also restored is the 42-by-109-foot pool, soon to be joined by the original subterranean grotto bar behind viewing windows at the deep end and solar heating. The inn occupies the most envied site in the valley—shaded by palms, next to the state park, with a view across the entire Anza-Borrego region. A hiking trail begins steps from the hotel. The Palms at Indian Head rewards you with charm, comfort, and convenience.

2220 Hoberg Rd., Borrego Springs, CA 92004. www.thepalmsatindianhead.com. (℘ **800/519-2624** or 760/767-7788. Fax 760/767-9717. 12 units. $119–$249 double. Extra person $20. Rates include continental breakfast. DC, DISC, MC, V. Take S22 into Borrego Springs; at Palm Canyon Dr., S22 becomes Hoberg Rd. Continue north ½ mile. **Amenities:** Restaurant; bar; outdoor pool; room service. *In room:* A/C, TV, fridge.

CAMPING

The park has two developed campgrounds. **Borrego Palm Canyon,** with 117 sites, is 2½ miles west of Borrego Springs, near the visitor center. Full hookups are available, and there's an easy hiking trail. **Tamarisk Grove,** at Hwy. 78 and County Road S3, has 27 sites. The overnight rate at both ranges from $20 to $29. Both have restrooms with pay showers (bring quarters!) and a campfire program; reservations are a good idea. The park allows open camping along all trail routes. For more information, check with the visitor center (℘ **760/767-4238).**

Where to Eat

Pickings are slim, but your best bet—if you're not willing to break the bank at Borrego Ranch Resort's classy dining room (dinner $25–$60)—is the surprisingly good **Krazy Coyote** (see below), which presents a new menu of steaks and seafood. Follow legions of locals into downtown mainstay **Carlee's Place,** 660 Palm Canyon Dr. (✆ **760/767-3262**), a casual bar and grill with plenty of neon beer signs, a pool table, and a fuzzy-sounding jukebox. It's easy to understand why Carlee's is the watering hole of choice for motorcycle brigades that pass through town on recreational rides—and the food is tasty, hearty, and priced just right. Open daily from 11am "till whenever," and food service stops at 9pm. If you are crying out for Mexican fare, a new addition to Borrego Springs is Carmelita's **Mexican Grill and Cantina** at 575 Palm Canyon Dr., **760/767-5666.** You'll find the usual suspects on the menu, tasty and well prepared. For a quick lunch, you'll find sandwiches and pizza at **Calicos Restaurant,** 587 Palm Canyon Dr., **760/767-7747.** And if you have a sweet tooth, check out the **Fudge Factory,** 202 Palm Canyon (✆ **760/767-7782**), for a wide variety of fudge, ice creams, pastries, and espresso. It's open Tuesday through Sunday 8am to 4pm. Closed Monday.

Assaggio ITALIAN   This addition to the Borrego Springs dining scene has daily specials to augment the inexpensive menu of seafood, pasta, veal, beef, and chicken. The decor is uninspired, but the traditional trattoria dining hits the mark. The restaurant is open for breakfast, lunch, and dinner; and beer and house wine are available.

1816 Palm Canyon Dr. (3 miles east of town near the local airport). ✆ **760/767-3388.** Main courses mostly under $16. Tues–Sun 11am–9pm. Closed Mon.

The French Corner FRENCH BISTRO   New to the Springs, the French Corner offers a menu of traditional dishes, including quiche, crepes, beef bourguignon, and coq au vin. You'll find it next to the Christmas Circle behind the *Borrego Sun* office.

721 Av. Surreste. ✆ **760/767-5713.** www.thefrenchcorner.biz. Wed–Sun 11am–2:30pm and 5–9pm. Reservations suggested.

Kendall's Cafe ★ COFFEE SHOP   Here's an economical spot to grab a bite. Buffalo burgers and Mexican dishes are popular. The best bet here is breakfast or anything that can be packed to go so you can dine overlooking the desert.

In the Mall. ✆ **760/767-3491.** Lunch $6–$10; dinner $7–$14. MC, V. Daily 6am–8pm.

Krazy Coyote Saloon & Grille ★ STEAK/SEAFOOD   The same style and perfectionism that pervades David Leibert and Cynthia Wood's bed-and-breakfast is evident in this restaurant, overlooking the inn's swimming pool and the desert beyond. The menu includes prime steaks, New Zealand rack of lamb or lobster, scampi, salmon, and chicken. The evening ambience is welcoming and romantic, as the sparse lights of tiny Borrego Springs twinkle on the desert floor below.

In the Palms at Indian Head, 2220 Hoberg Rd. ✆ **760/767-7788.** Main courses $10–$50. AE, MC, V. Daily; call for seasonal hours.

The Red Ocotillo DINER   For an old-fashioned hearty breakfast (served all day) or a casual lunch, join the crowd at the Red Ocotillo. Dining is casual indoors or in the patio. Eggs Benedict and omelets go for $9.95, and sandwiches are $8.95. Beer and wine are available.

2220 Hoberg Rd. ✆ **760/767-7400.** MC, V. Daily 7am–9pm.

MOJAVE NATIONAL PRESERVE

235 miles E of downtown L.A.; 125 miles SW of Las Vegas

Two decades of park politicking ended in 1994 when President Bill Clinton signed into law the California Desert Protection Act, which created the Mojave National Preserve. Thus far, the Mojave's elevated status has not attracted hordes of sightseers, and devoted visitors are happy to keep it that way. Unlike a fully protected national park, the "national preserve" designation allows hunting and certain commercial land uses, and the continued grazing and mining within the preserve's boundaries goad ardent environmentalists.

To most Los Angelenos, the East Mojave is that vast, bleak, interminable stretch of desert to be crossed as quickly as possible while leaving California via I-15 or I-40. Few realize that these highways are the boundaries of what some have long considered the crown jewel of the California desert.

This land is hard to get to know; unlike more developed desert parks, it has no lodgings or concessions, few campgrounds, and a handful of roads suitable for the average passenger vehicle. It takes a love of the desert to appreciate the stark, barren terrain. But gems are hidden within this natural fortress: The preserve's 1.6 million acres include the world's largest Joshua tree forest; abundant wildlife; spectacular canyons, caverns, and volcanic formations; nationally honored scenic back roads and footpaths to historic mining sites; tabletop mesas; and a dozen mountain ranges.

Essentials

GETTING THERE   I-15, the major route between the Southern California metropolis and the state line for Las Vegas–bound travelers, extends along the northern boundary of Mojave National Preserve. I-40 is the southern access route to the East Mojave. It's a 3½-hour drive from L.A. to Kelso Depot, in the center of the preserve. Well worth the visit, the Depot has been lovingly restored to its original luster, including train memorabilia from the period. The closest major airport is in Las Vegas.

WHEN TO GO   Spring and autumn are splendid times to visit this desert. From March to May, temperatures are mild, the Joshua trees are in bloom, and the lower Kelso Dunes are bedecked with yellow and white desert primrose and pink sand verbena.

VISITOR CENTERS & INFORMATION   The best source for up-to-date weather conditions and a free topographical map is the new **Kelso Visitor Center** in the Kelso Depot (✆ **760/252-6108**), open daily 9am to 5pm. Additional information and maps are available inside the preserve at the **Hole-in-the-Wall Visitor Center** (✆ **760/928-2572**), which is open 9am to 4pm Wednesday to Sunday for most of the year, Friday to Sunday in summer. You can visit the preserve online at **www.nps.gov/moja**.

Exploring the Park

One of the preserve's spectacular sights is the **Kelso Dunes,** the West's most extensive dune field. The 45-square-mile formation of magnificently sculpted sand is famous for "booming": Visitors' footsteps cause small avalanches that go "sha-boom-sha-boom-sha-boom." Geologists speculate that the extreme dryness of the East Mojave Desert, combined with the wind-polished, rounded nature of the

Kelso Dunes.

individual sand grains, has something to do with their musicality. Sometimes the low rumbling sound resembles a Tibetan gong; other times it sounds like a 1950s doo-wop musical group.

A 10-mile drive from the Kelso Dunes, **Kelso Depot,** built by the Union Pacific in 1924, now houses the visitor center, and after a nearly 2-decade hiatus, the Depot lunchroom, **The Beanery,** is back in business. Open daily 9am to 5pm. The Spanish Revival–style structure was designed with a red-tile roof, graceful arches, and a brick platform. The depot remained open for freight-train crew use through the mid-1980s, although it ceased to be a passenger railroad stop after World War II.

On and around **Cima Dome,** a rare geological anomaly, grows the world's largest and densest Joshua tree forest. Botanists say Cima's Joshuas are more symmetrical than their cousins elsewhere in the Mojave. The dramatic colors of the sky at sunset provide a breathtaking backdrop for Cima's Joshua trees, some more than 25 feet tall and several hundred years old.

Tucked into the Providence Mountains, in the southern portion of the preserve, is a treat everyone should try to see. The **Mitchell Caverns ★**, contained in a state recreation area within the national preserve, is a geological oddity exploited for tourism but still quite fascinating. Regular tours are conducted of these cool rock "rooms"; in addition to showcasing stalactites, stalagmites, and other limestone formations, the caves have proven to be rich in Native American archaeological finds.

Hole-in-the-Wall and **Mid Hills** are the centerpieces of Mojave National Preserve. Both offer diverse desert scenery, fine campgrounds, and the feeling of

Trail between Hole-in-the-Wall and Mid Hills.

being in the middle of nowhere. The preserve's best drive links the two sites. In 1989, **Wildhorse Canyon Road,** which loops from Mid Hills Campground to Hole-in-the-Wall Campground, was declared the nation's first official "Back Country Byway," an honor federal agencies bestow upon America's most scenic back roads. The 11-mile, horseshoe-shaped road crosses open country dotted with cholla and, in season, purple, yellow, and red wildflowers. Volcanic slopes and flattop mesas tower over the low desert.

Mile-high Mid Hills, named for its location between the Providence and New York mountains, recalls the Great Basin Desert topography of Nevada and Utah. Mid Hills Campground offers a grand observation point from which to gaze out at the creamy, coffee-colored Pinto Mountains to the north and the rolling Kelso Dunes shining on the western horizon.

Hole-in-the-Wall is the kind of place Butch Cassidy and the Sundance Kid would have chosen as a hideout. This twisted maze of rhyolite rocks is a form of crystallized red-lava rock. A series of iron rings aids descent into Hole-in-the-Wall; they're not particularly difficult for those who are reasonably agile.

Kelso Dunes, Mitchell Caverns, Cima Dome, and Hole-in-the-Wall are highlights of the preserve that can be viewed in a weekend. But you'll need a week to see all the major sights, and maybe a lifetime to get to know the East Mojave. And right now, without much in the way of services, the traveler to this desert must be well prepared and self-reliant. For many, this is what makes a trip to the East Mojave an adventure.

If Mojave National Preserve attracts you, you'll want to return again and again to see its wonders, including **Caruthers Canyon,** a "botanical island" of pinyon pine and juniper woodland, and **Ivanpah Valley,** which supports the largest desert-tortoise population in the California desert.

Hiking & Biking

HIKING   The free-form ambling climb to the top of the **Kelso Dunes** is 3 miles round-trip. The **Caruthers Canyon Trail,** 3 miles round-trip, wends through a cool, inviting pinyon pine/juniper woodland. The longest path, **Mid Hills to Hole-in-the-Wall Trail,** is a grand tour of basin and range tabletop mesas, large pinyon trees, and colorful cactuses; it's 8 miles one-way. The 1-mile trip from **Hole-in-the-Wall Campground** to **Banshee Canyon** and the 5-mile jaunt to **Wildhorse Canyon** are easier options. Pick up trail maps at one of the visitor centers.

MOUNTAIN BIKING   Opportunities are as extensive as the preserve's hundreds of miles of lonesome dirt roads. The 140-mile historic **Mojave Road,** a rough four-wheel-drive route, visits many of the most scenic areas in the East Mojave; sections of this road make excellent bike tours. Prepare well: These are rugged routes through desert wilderness.

Camping

The **Mid Hills Campground** is in a pinyon-pine/juniper woodland and offers outstanding views. This mile-high camp is the coolest in the East Mojave. Nearby **Hole-in-the-Wall Campground** is above two canyons. Both campgrounds have pit toilets and potable water but no utility hookups. There is a graded dirt road between the two, but it's suitable for two-wheel-drive passenger cars.

There are also some sites at **Providence Mountain State Recreation Area** (Mitchell Caverns; see "Exploring the Park," above).

One of the highlights of the East Mojave Desert is camping in the open desert all by your lonesome, but certain rules apply. Call the **Kelso Visitors Center** at ✆ **760/252-6108** for suggestions.

Nearby Towns with Tourist Services

BAKER   Lodgings and food are available in this small desert town, which is a good place to fill your gas tank and purchase supplies before entering Mojave National Preserve. Inexpensive lodging can be secured at the **Bun Boy Motel and Country Store,** 72139 Baker Blvd. (✆ **760/733-4252**). The Bun Boy Coffee Shop is open 24 hours. For a tasty surprise, hop across the street to the **Mad Greek,** 72112 Baker Blvd. (✆ **760/733-4354**), open daily 24 hours. Order a gyro, Greek salad, souvlakia, or baklava, and marvel at your good fortune for finding such tasty food and pleasant surroundings in the middle of nowhere.

BARSTOW   This sizable town has many restaurants and motels, about a 1-hour drive from the center of the preserve. On the east end of Main Street is Barstow Station, looking like a collection of railway cars, but inside is a rambling shop with an amazing collection of tacky souvenirs: everything from life-size plaster-of-Paris howling wolves to Marilyn Monroe cookie jars. The **Route 66 museum** (681 N. First St.; ✆ **760/255-1890;** www.route 66museum.org), on the other end of Main Street, at the Harvey House Casa del Desierto, is free but open only Friday through Sunday from 10am to 4pm. Of the town's dozen motels, the most reliable are **Best Western Desert Villa,** 1984 E. Main St. (✆ **760/256-1781**), and the **Ramada Inn,** 1511 E. Main St. (✆ **760/256-5673**).

NEWBERRY SPRINGS   The only reason for venturing 18 miles southeast of Barstow on Rte. 66 is to visit the **Bagdad Café** (✆ **760/257-3101**). It's noted for the location of a movie of the same name, which went unnoticed in the States but became a cult favorite among Europeans. They come in bus loads to see the site, munch on Jack Palance burgers (with bacon), and mix with some of the colorful locals.

NIPTON   This tiny (pop. 30), charming town boasts a "trading post" with snacks, maps, ice, and native jewelry; and the **Hotel Nipton** (✆ **760/856-2335;** www.nipton.com), a B&B with a sitting room, two bathrooms down the hall, and five guest rooms, each for $79 a night, including breakfast. There are also four eco-tents on platforms that sleep four for $65 per night. Owners Jerry and Roxanne Freeman—he was a former hard-rock miner who purchased the entire town in 1984—moved from Malibu to the abandoned ghost town, and brought it back to life. Nipton is on Nipton Road, a few miles from I-15 near the Nevada state line.

PRIMM VALLEY RESORT (FORMERLY STATELINE)   This town on the California–Nevada border has three hotel/casinos—Whiskey Pete's, Buffalo Bill's, and Primm Valley—each as large and garish as an amusement park, all managed by the same company. Rooms are pretty nice, cheap, and (if you have a twisted sense of humor) an ironic counterpoint to the wilderness. With a dozen restaurants, including low-cost Vegas-style buffets, Primm might also be your best dining bet. For reservations, call ✆ **800/FUN-STOP** (386-7867) or visit www.primmvalleyresorts.com.

DEATH VALLEY NATIONAL PARK ★

290 miles NE of downtown L.A.; 120 miles NW of Las Vegas

Park? Death Valley National Park? The forty-niners, whose suffering gave the valley its name, would have howled at the notion. To them, other four-letter words would have been more appropriate: *gold, mine, heat, lost, dead.* And when you trace the whole history, you can imagine a host of other four-letter words shouted by teamsters who drove the 20-mule-team borax wagons.

Americans looking for gold in California's mountains in 1849 were forced to cross the burning sands to avoid severe snowstorms in the nearby Sierra Nevada. Some perished en route, and the land became known as Death Valley.

Mountains stand naked, unadorned. The bitter waters of saline lakes evaporate into bizarre, razor-sharp crystal formations. Jagged canyons jab deep into the earth. Ovenlike heat, frigid cold, and the driest air imaginable combine to make this one of the most inhospitable locations in the world.

But, human nature being what it is, it's not surprising that people have long been drawn to challenge the power of Mother Nature, even in this, her home court. Tourism here began in 1925, a scant 76 years after the forty-niners' harrowing experiences. It probably would have begun sooner, but the valley had been consumed with lucrative borax mining since the late 1880s.

Death Valley is raw, bare earth, the way it must have looked before life began. Here, forces of the Earth are exposed to view with dramatic clarity; just looking out on the landscape, it's impossible to know what year—or what century—it is. It's no coincidence that many of Death Valley's topographical features are associated with hellish images—the Funeral Mountains, Furnace Creek, Dante's View, Coffin Peak, and the Devil's Golf Course. But it can be a place of serenity.

President Herbert Hoover signed a proclamation designating Death Valley a national monument on February 11, 1933. With the stroke of a pen, he not only authorized the protection of a vast and wondrous land but also helped transform one of the Earth's least hospitable spots into a tourist destination.

The naming of Death Valley National Monument came when Americans began to discover the romance of the desert. Land that had been considered devoid of life was now celebrated for its spare beauty; places that had been feared for their harshness were now admired for their uniqueness. In 1994, when President Clinton signed the California Desert Protection Act, Death Valley became the largest national park outside Alaska, with more than 3.3 million acres. It's remote but one of the most popular, and you're likely to hear less English than German, French, and Japanese.

Today's visitor to Death Valley drives in air-conditioned comfort, stays

Darwin Falls, Death Valley.

Trona Pinnacles, Death Valley.

in comfortable hotels or well-maintained campgrounds, orders meals and provisions at park concessions, even quaffs a beer at the local saloon. You can swim in the Olympic-size pool, tour a Moorish castle, shop for souvenirs, and enjoy the landscape while hiking along a nature trail with a park ranger.

Essentials

GETTING THERE   Several routes lead into the park, all of which involve crossing one of the steep mountain ranges that isolate Death Valley from, well, everything. Perhaps the most scenic entry is via Calif. 190, east of Calif. 178 from Ridgecrest. Another scenic drive is by way of Calif. 127 and Calif. 190 from Baker. For a first-time visitor, I recommend the road 1 mile north of Tecopa, marked to Badwater and Death Valley. It's longer and rougher, but you dip down from the hills into the valley and have the full approach into the region. Otherwise, for the shorter route, continue to 190, which will bring you into Death Valley Center. The $20-per-car entrance fee is valid for 7 days. The closest major airport is in Las Vegas. *Note:* Top off your gas tank in Tecopa—it's pricey but not as bad as in the valley.

WHEN TO GO   Death Valley is popular year-round, with the greatest number of visitors during the temperate winter and spring (Nov–Mar). The heavy rains of 2005 caused road washouts and brought forth a carpet of multicolor wildflowers, and the floor of the desert became a lake, 2 feet deep, offering rare kayak adventures. All disappeared when the summer temperatures returned. But the park is never deserted, not even in the scorching months of July, August, and September, as international visitors and extreme-heat seekers come to experience record-breaking temperatures. Even during the "cool" months (when evenings can become chilly), it's essential to wear sunscreen by day to protect against unfiltered rays, and to drink plenty of water to avoid becoming dehydrated in the ultra-arid climate.

VISITOR CENTER & INFORMATION   For camping and road information before you go, contact the Superintendent, Death Valley National Park, Death Valley, CA 92328 (© **760/786-3200** for road, camping, and weather information; www.nps.gov/deva). The **Furnace Creek Visitor Center & Museum,** 15 miles inside the eastern park boundary on Calif. 190 (✆ **760/786-3200**), offers interpretive exhibits and an hourly slide program. Ask at the information desk for ranger-led nature walks and evening naturalist programs. The center is open daily from 8am to 6pm in summer (to 5pm in winter). In November, a group called Death Valley 49ers (www.deathvalley49ers.org) gathers for 5 days to celebrate the pioneers who first traveled through this harsh environment. A $35 membership fee per family gives access to hootenannies, hoedowns, covered-wagon parades, gold panning, hiking, and four-wheel-drives in the area. *Tip:* Make your reservations months in advance.

Exploring the Park

A good first stop, after checking in at the main park visitor center in Furnace Creek, is the **Harmony Borax Works**—a rock-salt landscape as tortured as you'll ever find. Death Valley prospectors called borax "white gold," and though it wasn't exactly a glamorous substance, it was profitable. From 1883 to 1888, more than 20 million pounds (used to make laundry detergent) were transported from the Harmony Borax Works, and borax mining continued in Death Valley until 1928. A short trail with interpretive signs leads past the ruins of the old refinery and some outlying buildings. Transport of the borax was the stuff of legends, too. The famous 20-mule teams hauled the huge loaded wagons 165 miles to the rail station at Mojave. To learn more about this colorful era, visit the **Borax Museum** at Furnace Creek Ranch and the park visitor center, also located in Furnace Creek. Call for hours, **760/786-2345.**

Badwater—at 282 feet below sea level, the lowest point in the Western Hemisphere—is possibly the hottest place in the world, with regularly recorded summer temperatures of 120°F (49°C). Badwater is mostly a curiosity, and not that much hotter or more brutal than the rest of Death Valley; most folks like to make a brief detour to see the other-worldly landscape and say they were there.

Salt Creek is home to the **Salt Creek pupfish,** found nowhere else on Earth. The little fish, which has made amazing adaptations to survive in this land, can be glimpsed from a boardwalk nature trail. In spring, a million pupfish wriggle in the creek, but by summer's end only a few thousand remain.

Before sunrise, photographers set up tripods at **Zabriskie Point** and aim their cameras down at the magnificent panoramic view of Golden Canyon's pale mudstone hills and the great valley beyond. For another spectacular vista, check out **Dante's View,** a 5,475-foot viewpoint overlooking the shimmering Death Valley floor, backed by the high Panamint Mountains.

Badwater, Death Valley.

Zabriskie Point, Death Valley.

South of Furnace Creek is the 9-mile loop of **Artists Drive,** an easy must-see for visitors (except those in RVs, which can't negotiate the sharp, rock-bordered curves in the road). From the highway, you can't see the splendid palette of colors splashed on the rocks behind the foothills; once inside, though, stop and climb a hill that offers an overhead view, and then continue through to aptly named **Artists Palette,** where an interpretive sign explains the source of nature's rainbow.

Scotty's Castle & the Gas House Museum (✆ **760/786-2392**), the Mediterranean hacienda in the northern part of the park, is Death Valley's premier tourist attraction. Visitors are wowed by the elaborate Spanish tiles, well-crafted furnishings, and construction that included solar water heating. Even more compelling is the colorful history of this villa in Grapevine Canyon, brought to life by park rangers dressed in 1930s period clothing. Don't be surprised if the castle cook or a friend of Scotty's gives you a special insight into castle life.

Construction of the "castle"—more officially, Death Valley Ranch—began in 1924. It was to be a winter retreat for eccentric Chicago millionaire Albert Johnson. The insurance tycoon's unlikely friendship with prospector, cowboy, and spinner-of-tall-tales Walter Scott put the $2.3-million structure on the map and captured the public's imagination. Scotty greeted visitors and told them fanciful stories from Death Valley's early hard-rock mining days.

The 1-hour walking tour of Scotty's Castle is excellent, for its inside look at the mansion and its exploration of Johnson's and Scotty's eccentricities. Tours (9am–5pm daily) fill up quickly; arrive early for the first available spots ($11 adults, $9 seniors, and $6 children). It's open daily from 8:30am to 5:30pm.

Near Scotty's Castle is **Ubehebe Crater.** It's known as an explosion crater—one look, and you'll know why. When hot magma rose from the depths of the Earth to meet the groundwater, the resultant steam blasted out a crater.

THE SOUTHERN CALIFORNIA DESERT | Death Valley National Park

Biking & Hiking

BIKING Because most of the park is federally designated wilderness, cycling is allowed only on roads used by cars. Bikes are not allowed on hiking trails. Call ☏ **760/786-3200** for road and trail conditions.

Good routes for bikers include Racetrack (28 miles, mainly level), Greenwater Valley (30 miles, mostly level), Cottonwood Canyon (20 miles), and West Side Road (40 miles, fairly level with some washboard sections). Artists Drive is 8 miles long and paved, with some steep uphills. A favorite is Titus Canyon, a 28-mile one-way route that starts 2¾ miles east of the park boundary on Nevada Hwy. 374.

HIKING The trails in Death Valley range from the .5-mile **Salt Creek Nature Trail,** an easy boardwalk suitable for everyone in the family, to the grueling **Telescope Peak Trail** (14 miles round-trip). Telescope Peak is a daylong, 3,000-foot climb to the 11,049-foot summit. Snow-covered in winter, the peak is best climbed between May and November.

For moderate hikes, try the trail into **Mosaic Canyon,** near Stovepipe Wells, where water has polished the marble rock into mosaics. It's an easy 2.5-mile scramble through long, narrow walls that provide shade at every turn.

Romping among the **Sand Dunes** on the way to Stovepipe Wells is also fun, particularly for kids. It's a free-form adventure, and the dunes aren't particularly high—but the sun can be merciless. The sand in the dunes is actually tiny pieces of rock, most of them quartz fragments. As with all desert activities, having an adequate water supply is crucial.

Near the park's eastern border, two trails lead from the **Keane Wonder Mill,** site of a successful gold mine. The first is a steep and strenuous 2-mile challenge leading to the mine itself, passing along the way the solid, efficient wooden tramway that carried ore out of the mountain. The 2-mile **Keane Wonder Spring Trail** is much easier. The spring announces itself with a sulfur smell and piping birdcalls.

Dante's View, Death Valley.

Artists Drive, Death Valley.

If you're visiting **Ubehebe Crater,** check out the steep but plain trail leading from the parking area up to the crater's lip and around some of the contours. Fierce winds can hamper your progress, but you'll feel like you're on another planet.

Park rangers can provide topographical maps and detailed directions to these and a dozen other hiking trails within the national park.

Where to Stay

The park's nine campgrounds are at elevations ranging from below sea level to 8,000 feet. In Furnace Creek, **Sunset** has 230 spaces with water and flush toilets. **Furnace Creek Campground** has 136 similarly appointed spaces, $18 in winter, $12 in summer. **Stovepipe Wells** has 190 spaces with water and flush toilets. Make reservations online at **http://recreation.gov** or call ✆ **877/ 444-6777.**

The **Ranch at Furnace Creek** (www.furnacecreekresort.com; ✆ **760/786-2345**), a private in-holding within the park, has 224 no-frills cottage units with air-conditioning and showers ($130–$213). The swimming pool is a popular hangout. Nearby are a coffee shop, saloon, steakhouse, and general store. **Stovepipe Wells Village** (✆ **760/786-3279**) suffered a fire in 2010 that damaged part of the store and saloon. Call for the latest information. The 83 modest rooms with air-conditioning and showers were not damaged, and you'll find a swimming pool, plus a casual dining room that closes between meals ($75–$115).

The only lodging in the park not run by Xanterra Parks Resorts, the official concessionaire, is the **Panamint Springs Resort** (www.deathvalley.com; ✆ **775/482-7680**), with 10 RV sites ($20–$30), a rustic motel ($79–$149 double), a cafe, and a snack shop an hour east of Furnace Creek. Because accommodations in Death Valley are limited and expensive, you might consider the money-saving (but inconvenient) option of spending a night at one of the two gateway towns: **Lone Pine,** on the west side of the park, or **Baker,** on the south. **Beatty, Nevada,** which has inexpensive lodging, is an hour's drive from the park's center. The restored **Amargosa Hotel** (www.amargosa-opera-house.com;

Panamint Dunes, Death Valley.

© 760/852-4441) in Death Valley Junction offers 14 rooms in a historic, out-of-the-way place, 40 minutes from Furnace Creek ($60–$75).

Tip: Meals and groceries are very costly due to the park's remoteness. If possible, bring a cooler with some snacks, sandwiches, and beverages to last the duration of your visit. Ice is easily obtainable, and you'll also be able to keep water chilled.

The Inn at Furnace Creek ★★   Like an oasis in the middle of Death Valley, the inn's red-tiled roofs and sparkling blue mineral-spring-fed swimming pool hint at the elegance within. The hotel has completely renovated its 66 deluxe rooms and suites with every modern amenity while successfully preserving the charm of this 1930s resort. Stroll the palm-shaded gardens before sitting down to a meal in the elegant dining room, where the food is excellent but the formality a bit out of place. Don tennis whites for a match in the midwinter sunshine, enjoy 18 holes of golf ($55 greens fee), take an excursion on horseback—there's even a shuttle from the Furnace Creek airstrip for well-heeled clientele. The inn is open mid-October to mid-May. Reserve early: The inn is booked solid in winter with guests who appreciate a little pampering after a day in the park.

Hwy. 190 (P.O. Box 1), Death Valley, CA 92328. www.furnacecreekresort.com. *©* **800/236-7916** or 760/786-2345. Fax 760/786-2514. 66 units. $330–$435 double; $438–$460 suite. Extra person $20. AE, DISC, MC, V. **Amenities:** 4 restaurants; lounge; golf course; naturally heated outdoor pool; room service; 4 night-lit tennis courts. *In room:* A/C, TV w/pay movies, fridge, hair dryer, Wi-Fi.

Ubehebe Crater, Death Valley.

SAN DIEGO & ENVIRONS

by Mark Hiss

Higig-end nightclubs. Adventurous dining. Hypermodern architecture. What happened to that nice little Navy town of San Diego? Well, that sleepy burg has woken up and it wants to party. Growth has been fast and furious over the past two decades and this Southern California city now finds itself with a glittering skyline and a fresh attitude. With its beaches and theme parks it's still one of the most family-friendly destinations in the United States, but the nearly nightly bacchanalia in the **Gaslamp Quarter** leaves no doubt this is not your father's San Diego.

Things to Do   San Diego's shining jewel is **Balboa Park,** an 1,100-acre oasis in the heart of the city. Featuring meticulously maintained gardens, hiking trails, and recreational opportunities, it's also the nation's largest urban cultural park, the setting for 15 museums. And if that's not enough, the park is where you'll also find the world famous **San Diego Zoo.** The city's rollicking downtown **Gaslamp Quarter,** highlighted by its dazzling Victorian architecture, is where both locals and visitors go for shopping, dining, and nightclubbing.

Active Pursuits   With weather that is usually nothing less than pleasant, San Diego is a year-round beach town (though water temperatures can be downright chilly). With some 70 miles of coastline, there's a beach that's just right for you. Looking for a nonstop party? Join the parade along the **Mission Beach** and **Pacific Beach** boardwalk. Family in tow? **Coronado** is just the place. Trying surfing for the first time? **La Jolla Shores** is forgiving. *Au naturel* sunbathing? Head to **Black's Beach.**

Restaurants & Dining   The locavore movement is in high gear here, with menus featuring generous portions of San Diego–sourced products, from seafood and beef to fruits and vegetables. **Mexican food** is a high priority, too, with the humble **fish taco**—an immigrant from Baja California—solidly entrenched as the city's favorite fast food. On the tonier side are the sumptuous restaurants of **La Jolla,** including two of the area's signature spots (both featuring stupendous views): **The Marine Room** and **Georges California Modern.**

Nightlife & Entertainment   San Diego is a hotbed of serious theater, having spawned numerous productions that have gone on to Broadway acclaim. Leading the pack are the **Old Globe Theatre** and **La Jolla Playhouse,** both Tony Award winners for outstanding regional theater. Those who want to break a sweat on the dance floor need look no further than the city's nightlife nerve center, the **Gaslamp Quarter.** It offers glitzy dance and supper clubs, as well as bars (from dive to swanky) and live music venues.

PREVIOUS PAGE: **African elephant calf, San Diego Zoo.**

ORIENTATION
Getting There

BY PLANE

San Diego International Airport (✆ 619/231-2100; www.san.org; airport code **SAN**), locally known as Lindbergh Field, is just 3 miles from downtown. All the major domestic carriers fly here, plus **Air Canada** from Toronto and Vancouver, and British Airways from London (as of summer 2011). The airport has two main terminals, with short local flights departing from the Commuter Terminal, a half-mile away. The facilities are currently undergoing a build-out that is scheduled to be completed in 2013; improvements will include a two-level road providing separate pickup and drop-off locations, 10 new gates, curbside check-in, and additional shopping and dining options. **Beware of traffic delays due to construction.**

TRANSPORTATION FROM THE AIRPORT All the major car-rental agencies have offices at the airport, including **Avis** (✆ 800/331-1212; www.avis.com), **Budget** (✆ 800/527-0700; www.budget.com), **Dollar** (✆ 800/800-3665; www.dollar.com), and **Hertz** (✆ 800/654-3131; www.hertz.com). If you're driving to downtown from the airport, take Harbor Drive south to Broadway, the main east-west thoroughfare, and turn left. To reach Hillcrest or Balboa Park, exit the airport toward I-5 and follow the signs for Laurel Street. To reach Mission Bay and the beaches, take I-5 north to I-8 west. To reach La Jolla, take I-5 north to the La Jolla Parkway exit, which turns into Torrey Pines Road.

Metropolitan Transit System (**MTS;** ✆ 619/233-3004; www.transit.511sd.com) bus route no. 992 provides service between the airport and downtown San Diego, running along Broadway. Bus stops are located at each of the three terminals, and the one-way fare is $2.25. If you're connecting to another bus or the San Diego Trolley, you'll need to purchase a Day Pass; a 1-day pass is $5 and is available from the driver. The ride downtown takes 15 minutes, with buses coming at 15-minute intervals. At Broadway and First Avenue is the **Transit Store** (✆ 619/234-1060), where you can get information about San Diego's mass transit system (bus, rail, and ferry) and pick up passes, free brochures, route maps, and timetables; it's open Monday through Friday 9am to 5pm.

Shuttle services run regularly from the airport to points around the city; you'll see designated pickup areas outside each terminal. The fare is about $8 per person to downtown hotels; Mission Valley and Mission Beach are $12, La Jolla $20, and Coronado $16. Rates to a residence in these areas are about $3 to $7 more than the above rates for the first person, with discounted fares for an additional rider. One company that serves all of San Diego County is **SuperShuttle** (✆ 800/974-8885; www.supershuttle.com). Reservations can be made online, but advance notification is not needed for service from the airport or from a hotel. **Taxis** line up outside Terminals 1 and 2, and the trip downtown, usually a 10-minute ride, is about $10 (plus tip); budget $20 to $25 for Coronado or Mission Beach, and about $30 to $35 for La Jolla.

BY CAR

From Los Angeles, you'll enter San Diego via coastal route **I-5.** From points northeast of the city, you'll come down on **I-15** and **Hwy. 163** south to drive into downtown (where 163 turns into 10th Ave.), or hook up with **I-8** west for the beaches. From the east, you'll come in on I-8, connecting with Hwy. 163 south. The freeways are well marked, pointing the way to downtown streets.

BY TRAIN

Amtrak (𝒞 **800/872-7245;** www.amtrak.com) connects San Diego to the rest of the country via Los Angeles. Trains pull into San Diego's Mission-style **Santa Fe Train Depot,** 1050 Kettner Blvd. (at Broadway), within walking distance of some downtown hotels and the Embarcadero. It's $31 one-way from L.A.

BY BUS

Greyhound (𝒞 **800/231-2222;** www.greyhound.com) buses from Los Angeles, Phoenix, Las Vegas, and other points in the southwestern U.S. arrive at the station in downtown San Diego at 120 W. Broadway. The one-way fare from Los Angeles is $22, but you can whittle the price down further by purchasing nonrefundable tickets or by getting them in advance online. Local buses stop in front of the station, and the San Diego Trolley is nearby.

Visitor Information

You'll find staffed information booths at the airport, train station, and cruise ship terminal. Downtown, the Convention & Visitors Bureau's **International Visitor Information Center** (𝒞 **619/236-1212;** www.sandiego.org) is at 1040⅓ W. Broadway at Harbor Drive (across from the cruise ship terminal). Daily summer hours are from 9am to 5pm; it's open 9am to 4pm daily the rest of the year and is closed on major holidays. The bureau offers great info and deals on its website, but you can also get your hands on the glossy *Official Visitors Planning Guide* from the information center. The guide includes information on dining, activities, attractions, tours, and transportation. A walk-up-only facility (sans phone) at the **La Jolla Visitor Center,** 7966 Herschel Ave., near the corner of Prospect Street, is open daily in summer from 10am to 6pm, with more limited hours from September to May.

Specialized visitor information outlets include the **Coronado Visitor Center,** 1100 Orange Ave., Coronado (𝒞 **866/599-7242** or 619/437-8788; www. coronadovisitorcenter.com), and **Promote La Jolla,** 7734 Herschel Ave. (𝒞 **858/454-5718;** www.lajollabythesea.com). For information on San Diego's North County destinations including Del Mar, Encinitas, Carlsbad, and Oceanside, check out, respectively, www.delmar.ca.us, www.cityofencinitas.org, www. visitcarlsbad.com, and www.visitoceanside.org.

To find out what's playing in clubs and theaters, pick up a copy of the *San Diego Weekly Reader* (www.sdreader.com), a free newspaper available all over the city every Thursday; in tourist areas, it is distributed in a condensed version, called the *Weekly.* "Night & Day," the entertainment supplement in the city's main daily newspaper, the *San Diego Union-Tribune* (www.signonsandiego. com), appears on Thursday; the free alternative weekly *San Diego CityBeat* comes out on Wednesday.

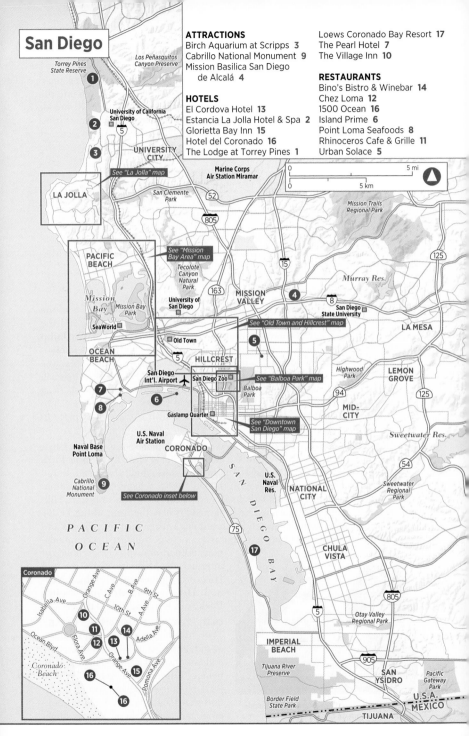

San Diego

ATTRACTIONS
Birch Aquarium at Scripps **3**
Cabrillo National Monument **9**
Mission Basilica San Diego
de Alcalá **4**

HOTELS
El Cordova Hotel **13**
Estancia La Jolla Hotel & Spa **2**
Glorietta Bay Inn **15**
Hotel del Coronado **16**
The Lodge at Torrey Pines **1**

Loews Coronado Bay Resort **17**
The Pearl Hotel **7**
The Village Inn **10**

RESTAURANTS
Bino's Bistro & Winebar **14**
Chez Loma **12**
1500 Ocean **16**
Island Prime **6**
Point Loma Seafoods **8**
Rhinoceros Cafe & Grille **11**
Urban Solace **5**

City Layout

San Diego has a clearly defined downtown, surrounded by about a dozen separate neighborhoods—each with its own personality, but all incorporated into the city. The street system is straightforward, so getting around is fairly easy: Broadway is the main street downtown, intersected by Fourth and Fifth avenues (running south and north, respectively). Harbor Drive hugs the waterfront (Embarcadero), connecting downtown with the airport to the northwest and the Convention Center to the south.

The San Diego–Coronado Bay Bridge leading to Coronado is accessible from I-5 south of downtown, and I-5 north leads to Old Town, Mission Bay, La Jolla, and North County coastal areas. Balboa Park (home of the San Diego Zoo), Hillcrest, and uptown areas lie north of downtown San Diego. The park and zoo are easily reached via Park Boulevard (which would otherwise be 12th Ave.), which leads to parking lots. Fifth Avenue takes you to the Hillcrest and uptown neighborhoods. Hwy. 163, which heads north from 11th Avenue, leads into Mission Valley.

Neighborhoods in Brief

DOWNTOWN   The business, shopping, dining, and entertainment heart of the city encompasses Horton Plaza, the Embarcadero (waterfront), and the Convention Center, sprawling over eight "neighborhoods." The **Gaslamp Quarter** is jampacked with boutiques, restaurants, and nightspots in renovated Victorian buildings; immediately southeast of the Gaslamp is the **East Village** and **PETCO Park,** home of the San Diego Padres baseball team. Northwest, **Little Italy** is another rejuvenated neighborhood, along India and Kettner streets between Cedar and Laurel. It's a great place to find Italian food and upscale shopping. Downtown is the easiest place to stay if you don't have a car.

HILLCREST & UPTOWN   First established in 1907, Hillcrest was the city's first self-contained suburb. Despite the cachet of being close to **Balboa Park** (home of the San Diego Zoo and numerous museums), the area fell into neglect in the 1960s. However, in the late 1970s, legions of preservation-minded residents—particularly its gay community—began to restore Hillcrest's charms; this gentrified neighborhood is now the heart of the LGBT social scene. Centrally located and brimming with popular restaurants and shops, Hillcrest also offers less expensive, more personalized accommoda-

Family of Klingons at Comic-Con, hosted annually at the Convention Center.

tions. Other uptown neighborhoods of interest are **Mission Hills** west of Hillcrest, **University Heights, Normal Heights, North Park, South Park,** and **Kensington,** to the east.

OLD TOWN & MISSION VALLEY These two busy areas wrap around the neighborhood of Mission Hills. On one end are Old Town State Historic Park (where California "began"), Presidio Park, Heritage Park, and several museums that focus on local history. Shopping and dining here largely target visitors. Not far from Old Town lies the congested, suburban sprawl of Mission Valley, home to gigantic shopping centers, Qualcomm Stadium, and numerous condo developments. Hotel Circle is an elongated loop road paralleling I-8, featuring a string of budget and moderately priced hotels.

MISSION BAY & THE BEACHES Here's where they took the picture on the postcard you'll send home. Mission Bay is a watery playground perfect for waterskiing, sailing, and windsurfing. The adjacent communities of **Ocean Beach, Mission Beach,** and **Pacific Beach** are known for their wide stretches of sand, nightlife, and casual dining. The boardwalk, which runs from South Mission Beach to Pacific Beach, is a popular place for skating, biking, people-watching, and sunsets. It's the best place to stay if you are traveling with beach-loving kids.

LA JOLLA Mediterranean in design and ambience, La Jolla is the Southern Californian Riviera. This seaside community of about 25,000 is home to an inordinate number of wealthy folks who could afford to live anywhere. They choose La Jolla for good reason—it has one of the state's most stunning coastlines and offers an outstanding array of restaurants, shops, and galleries, as well as a host of cultural and recreational attractions. There are really two La Jollas: the original seaside community—the so-called "village"—and the residential and business areas that have sprouted along La Jolla Village Drive east of I-5, which are of less interest. Public transportation is limited, so La Jolla is not an ideal base if you don't have a car.

CORONADO You might be tempted to think of Coronado as an island—it does have a self-contained, resort ambience, and it's most easily accessed by the sweeping Coronado Bridge or by ferry. The city is actually on a peninsula, though, connected to the mainland by a long, sandy isthmus known as the **Silver Strand.** Coronado is home to a U.S. Naval Air Station, in use since World War I, and also has a history as an elite playground for snowbirds. This charming, wealthy community is home to the iconic Hotel del Coronado as well. Built in 1888, the "Hotel Del," as it's known, sits on one of the area's finest beaches and is a major attraction for both guests and nonguests.

GETTING AROUND
By Car

San Diego traffic can be problematic; it's not L.A., by any means, but the construction of dense, outlying suburbia over the past 25 years has made morning and evening rush-hour traffic a headache. Aside from that, it's car-friendly and easy to navigate. For up-to-the-minute traffic info, dial ℂ **511.**

Downtown, many streets run one-way, and finding a parking space can be tricky. There are several centrally located parking lots, where prices fluctuate wildly according to the day, time, or any special events taking place.

RENTALS All the large, national car-rental firms have outlets at the airport (see "Getting There," above), in major hotels, and at other locations around the city. Some car-rental companies allow their cars into Mexico as far as Ensenada, provided you stop before crossing the border to buy Mexican auto insurance. Mexican insurance is also highly advised if you drive your own car over the border.

PARKING   Parking meters are common in most San Diego areas, including downtown, Hillcrest, the beaches, and La Jolla. Signs post operating hours—generally between 9am and 6pm daily except Sunday; meters devour one quarter every 12 minutes. In downtown and in Hillcrest you will also find meters that accept credit cards; there are also some multispace meters (one per block) requiring you to print out a receipt and place it on your dashboard. The Gaslamp Quarter has two large parking structures (on Sixth Ave. at Market and K sts.). Parking is free in Balboa Park and Old Town.

By Public Transportation

The **San Diego Metropolitan Transit System** (**MTS;** ☎ **619/233-3004;** www.transit.511sd.com) runs both city buses and the San Diego Trolley. The website displays timetables, maps, and fares online, and provides information for travelers with disabilities. The system's **Transit Store,** 102 Broadway at First Avenue (☎ **619/234-1060**), is an information center, supplying travelers with passes, tokens, timetables, maps, and brochures. Get a copy of the useful pamphlet *Fun Places by Bus & Trolley,* which details routes to the city's most popular tourist attractions. The store is open Monday through Friday from 9am to 5pm. If you know your route and just need schedule information—or automated answers to questions—call **Info Express** (☎ **619/685-4900**) from any touchtone phone 24 hours a day. A $5 **Regional Day Pass** allows for 1 day of unlimited rides and can be purchased from the driver. You can also buy a 2-day pass for $9, a 3-day pass for $12, or a 4-day pass for $15; they're available from the Transit Store and at all trolley ticket vending machines.

BY BUS   San Diego's bus system is adequate and will get you where you want to go—eventually. Bus stops are marked by rectangular red, white, and black signs every other block or so on local routes, farther apart on express routes. Most fares are $2.25. Buses accept dollar bills, but the driver can't give change. Transfers are not issued, so if you need to make a connection with another bus or trolley, purchase a $5 day pass from the driver, at the Transit Store, or from a trolley-station ticket vending machine. It gives you unlimited use of most bus and trolley routes for the rest of the service day. Some routes stop at 6pm, while other lines continue until 9pm, midnight, and 2am. Ask your bus driver for more specific information.

BY TROLLEY   The San Diego Trolley is great for visitors, particularly if you're staying downtown and plan to visit Tijuana, Old Town, or Mission Valley. The Blue Line travels from the Mexican border north through downtown and then on to Old Town. The trip to the border takes about 40 minutes from downtown. The Orange Line runs from downtown east through Lemon Grove and El Cajon to the city of Santee, while the Green Line heads from Old Town to San Diego State University and on to El Cajon. *Note:* The trolley system is being upgraded with new vehicles which require construction of different platforms; some stations may be closed on weekends (shuttle buses will service shuttered stations). When the upgrades are completed in 2015, the Green Line will be extended to downtown.

Riders must buy trolley tickets from machines in stations before boarding (some require exact change). It's a flat fare of $2.50 for travel between any two stations. A $5 day pass is also available, good for all trolley trips and most bus routes. Fare inspectors board trains at random to check tickets.

Trolleys run every 15 minutes during the day and every 30 minutes at night; during peak weekday rush hours, the Blue Line runs about every 10 minutes. There is also expanded service to accommodate events at PETCO Park and Qualcomm Stadium. The trolleys generally operate daily from 4 or 5am to about midnight; the Blue Line provides service until 1am.

BY TRAIN   San Diego's express rail commuter service, the **Coaster,** travels between the downtown Santa Fe Depot station and the Oceanside Transit Center, with stops at Old Town, Sorrento Valley, Solana Beach, Encinitas, and Carlsbad. Fares range from $5 to $6.50 each way and can be paid by credit card at machines at each station. Eligible seniors and riders with disabilities pay $2.50 to $3.25. The trip from downtown to Oceanside takes an hour. Trains run Monday through Friday, from about 6:30am (5:30am heading south from Oceanside) to 7pm, with four trains each direction on Saturday (no service Sun); call ✆ **800/262-7837** or 511, or visit www.transit.511sd.com, for the current schedule. The **Sprinter** rail service runs west to east alongside Hwy. 78, from Oceanside to Escondido. The Sprinter operates Monday through Friday from about 4am to 9pm daily, with service every 30 minutes in both directions. On weekends, trains run every half-hour from 9:30am to 5:30pm (westbound) and 10:30am to 6:30pm (eastbound), with hourly service before and after those times. Basic one-way fare is $2 ($1 for seniors and those with disabilities).

Amtrak (✆ **800/872-7245;** www.amtrak.com) trains run between San Diego and downtown L.A. 12 times daily each way. Trains depart from the Santa Fe Depot and stops include Solana Beach, Oceanside, San Juan Capistrano, Santa Ana, and Anaheim (Disneyland). Two trains per day also stop in San Clemente. A one-way ticket to Solana Beach is $11, to Oceanside $14, to San Clemente $17, to San Juan Capistrano $18, and to Anaheim $23.

BY FERRY & WATER TAXI   **San Diego Harbor Excursion** (✆ **800/442-7847** or 619/234-4111; www.sdhe.com) runs regularly scheduled ferry service between San Diego and Coronado. Ferries leave from the Broadway Pier (1050 N. Harbor Dr., at the intersection with Broadway) and the Fifth Avenue Landing (600 Convention Way, behind the Convention Center). Broadway Pier departures are scheduled daily on the hour from 9am to 9pm (Fri–Sat until 10pm). They return from the Ferry Landing in Coronado to the Broadway Pier every hour on the half-hour from 9:30am to 9:30pm (Fri–Sat until 10:30pm). Trips from the Convention Center depart about every 2 hours, beginning at 9:25am, with the final departure at 8:25pm (10:25pm Fri–Sat). Return trips begin at 9:17am, then run about every 2 hours until 8:17pm (10:17pm Fri–Sat). The ride takes 15 minutes. The fare is $3.75 each way; buy tickets at the San Diego Harbor Excursion kiosk on Broadway Pier, the Fifth Avenue Landing, or the Ferry Landing in Coronado. **Note:** Ferries do not accommodate cars.

Water taxis (✆ **619/235-8294;** www.sdhe.com) will pick you up from any dock around San Diego Bay and operate Sunday to Thursday 9am to 9pm, and Friday to Saturday 9am to 11pm. If you're staying in a downtown hotel, this is a great way to reach Coronado. Boats are sometimes available on the spur of the moment, but reservations are advised. Fares are $7 per person to most locations.

By Taxi

Half a dozen taxi companies serve the area. Rates are based on mileage and can add up quickly in sprawling San Diego; a trip from downtown to La Jolla, for example, will cost $30 to $35. Other than in the Gaslamp Quarter after dark, taxis don't cruise the streets as they do in other cities, so you have to call ahead for quick pickup. If you are waiting at a hotel or restaurant, the front-desk attendant or host will call one for you. Local companies include **Orange Cab** (*ⓒ* **619-291-3333**), **San Diego Cab** (*ⓒ* **619/226-8294**), **Yellow Cab** (*ⓒ* **619/444-4444**), and **Coronado Cab Company** (*ⓒ* **619/435-6211**). You can also just dial *ⓒ* **511** and say "taxi" and you will be connected to a dispatcher. There is no pickup from Coronado or at the airport with this service (but you can be dropped off at those locations).

By Bicycle

San Diego is ideal for exploration by bike and was named "one of the top 10 cities in the U.S. to bicycle" by *Bicycling* magazine.

Many major thoroughfares offer bike lanes; bikes are also allowed on the San Diego–Coronado ferry, as well as on the San Diego Trolley and most city buses (no additional charge). To request a detailed map of San Diego County's bike lanes and routes, call **San Diego iCommute** (*ⓒ* **511**), or go to www.511sd. com for a downloadable version. You might also want to look into the **San Diego County Bicycle Coalition** (*ⓒ* **858/487-6063**; www.sdcbc.org). *Cycling San Diego,* by Nelson Copp and Jerry Schad, is a good resource for bicyclists, too; the book is sold at most local bike shops. For information on rentals, see "Outdoor Pursuits," later in this chapter.

[FastFACTS] SAN DIEGO

Area Codes San Diego's main area code is **619,** used primarily by downtown, uptown, Mission Valley, Point Loma, Coronado, La Mesa, Chula Vista, and El Cajon. The area code **858** is used for northern and coastal areas, including Mission Beach, Pacific Beach, La Jolla, Del Mar, and Rancho Santa Fe. Use **760** to reach the remainder of San Diego County, including Encinitas, Carlsbad, Oceanside, Escondido, Julian, and Anza-Borrego.

Babysitters Marion's Childcare (*ⓒ* **888/891-5029** or 619/303-4379;

www.hotelchildcare.com) will send bonded babysitters to your hotel. **Panda's Domestic Service Agency** (*ⓒ* **619/295-3800**; www. sandiegobabysitters.com) is also available.

Dentists & Doctors For dental referrals, contact the **San Diego County Dental Society** at *ⓒ* **800/ 201-0244** (www.sdcds. org), or call *ⓒ* **1-800-DENTIST** (866/993-9546; www.1800dentist.com). For a doctor referral, contact the **San Diego County Medical Society** (*ⓒ* **858/ 565-8888**; www.sdcms. org) or **Scripps Health**

(*ⓒ* **800/727-4777**; www. scripps.org). In a life-threatening situation, dial *ⓒ* **911.**

Emergencies Call *ⓒ* **911** for fire, police, and ambulance; or 619/233-3323 for the hearing impaired.

Hospitals In Hillcrest, near downtown San Diego, **UCSD Medical Center– Hillcrest,** 200 W. Arbor Dr. (*ⓒ* **619/543-6222**; www. health.ucsd.edu), has the most convenient emergency room. In La Jolla, **UCSD Thornton Hospital,** 9300 Campus Point Dr. (*ⓒ* **858/657-7000**; www. health.ucsd.edu), has a good emergency room, and you'll find another in Coronado, at **Sharp Coronado Hospital,** 250 Prospect Place, opposite the Marriott Resort (© **619/522-3600;** www.sharp.com). Twenty-four-hour pharmacies include **CVS,** 8831 Villa La Jolla Dr., La Jolla (© **858/457-4480;** www.cvs.com), and **Rite Aid,** 535 Robinson Ave., Hillcrest (© **619/291-3705;** www.riteaid.com).

Police The downtown police station is at 1401 Broadway (© **619/531-2000;** www.sandiego.gov/police). From North San Diego, call © **858/484-3154.**

Post Office Downtown post offices are in Horton Plaza (Mon–Fri 9:30am to 6pm and Sat 10am–5pm), next to the Westin Hotel, and at 815 E St. (Mon–Fri 9am–5pm). For other branch locations, call © **800/275-8777** or log on to www.usps.com.

Safety Of the 10 largest cities in the United States, San Diego historically has had the lowest incidence of violent crime per capita. Virtually all areas of the city are safe during the day, but caution is advised in parts of Balboa Park not frequented by regular foot traffic. Transients are common—especially

downtown, in Hillcrest, and in beach areas. Downtown areas to the east of PETCO Park are sparsely populated and poorly lighted after dusk.

Taxes Sales tax in restaurants and shops is 8.75%. Hotel tax is 10.5%, or 12.5% for lodgings with more than 70 rooms.

Useful Telephone Numbers For the latest San Diego arts and entertainment info, call © **619/238-0700;** for half-price day-of-performance tickets, call © **858/381-5595;** for a beach and weather report, call © **619/221-8824;** for transit information, call © **619/233-3004.**

WHERE TO STAY

Rates tend to be highest in summer at beach hotels and midweek downtown when a big convention is in town. Remember to factor in the city's hotel tax—it's 10.5%, or 12.5% for lodgings with more than 70 rooms. The **San Diego Convention & Visitors Bureau** is a good place to start looking for hotel deals (© **619/232-3101;** www.sandiego.org), while the **San Diego Bed & Breakfast Guild** (© **619/523-1300;** www.bandbguildsandiego.org) is a helpful resource if you are interested in staying someplace cozy.

Downtown

San Diego's downtown is an excellent place for leisure travelers to stay. The nightlife and dining in the Gaslamp Quarter and Horton Plaza shopping are close at hand; Balboa Park, Hillcrest, Old Town, and Coronado are less than 10 minutes away by car; and beaches aren't much farther. It's also the city's public-transportation hub and, thus, very convenient for car-free visitors.

Many downtown hotels seem designed for the expense-account or trust fund crowd, but some accommodations have more moderate rates. There's the colorful, modern **Bristol Hotel,** 1055 First Ave. (www.thebristolsandiego.com; © **800/662-4477** or 619/232-6141), adjacent to the Gaslamp Quarter; and in the budget category, you can't beat the 259-room **500 West,** 500 W. Broadway (www.500westhotel.com; © **866/315-4251** or 619/234-5252). It offers small but comfortable rooms for $79 to $119 a night in a seven-story building dating from 1924. It has contemporary style, history, and a good location, but bathrooms are down the hall. Cheaper still are downtown hostels, where private rooms start at about $45 and dorm rooms are around $20: **USA Hostels** (www.usahostels.com; © **800/438-8622** or 619/232-3100) is in the Gaslamp, at 726 Fifth Ave.;

HI Downtown Hostel (www.sandiegohostels.org; ☎ **888/464-4872,** ext. 156, or 619/525-1531) is nearby, at 521 Market St.

Best For: Just about everything. There are museums, bars and nightclubs, fine dining, and shopping opportunities galore.

Drawbacks: The action goes on late and loud here, particularly on weekends, and some of the most popular nightspots are in hotels.

VERY EXPENSIVE

Andaz Hotel ★★★   The Maryland Hotel, a dowdy property built in 1914, has been artfully transformed into a world-class, high-style luxury destination (most recently known as the Ivy Hotel). The $75-million renovation at this non-smoking property was overseen by a design team that has not only worked on various W Hotels, but also made a name for itself in Hollywood, overseeing projects for such directors as Jim Jarmusch and Ridley Scott. Its unbeatable Gaslamp Quarter address ensures a steady stream of beautiful people making their way into **Ivy,** the hotel's four-level nightclub. The Andaz also boasts downtown's largest rooftop pool and entertainment area: a 17,000-square-foot playground known as **Ivy Rooftop.** *Note:* These are very popular weekend nightspots; if you don't care to play along, you may want to look for other accommodations.

650 F St. (btw. Sixth and Seventh aves.), San Diego, CA 92101. www.andaz.com. ☎ **877/489-4489** or 619/814-1000. Fax 619/531-7955. 159 units. $279–$479 double; from $999 suite. Children 12 and under stay free in parent's room. Packages available. AE, DC, DISC, MC, V. Valet parking $35. Bus: 3 or 120. Pets less than 35 lb. accepted for $150. **Amenities:** Restaurant; bar; nightclub; free local transportation; 24-hr. concierge; fitness center; outdoor pool; room service; spa services. *In room:* A/C, TV/DVD, CD player, full bar, hair dryer, MP3 docking station, free Wi-Fi.

Hard Rock Hotel San Diego ★★   A far cry from the tired burger-and-memorabilia joint over on Fourth Avenue, this 12-story condo-hotel has a sweet location—right at the gateway to the Gaslamp Quarter—and plenty of star power. The Black Eyed Peas weigh in with their million-dollar "doped-out" suite specially designed by the group; it's one of 17 Rock Star suites, some of which include private decks, fire pits, outdoor hot tubs, and 270-degree city views. Standard rooms are hip and modern, with sophisticated furnishings and widescreen TVs; accommodations are also well soundproofed from the Gaslamp hubbub. Master chef Nobuyuki Matsuhisa, who has partnered with actor Robert De Niro on restaurants around the world, adds San Diego to the list with **Nobu,** the hotel's signature eatery (p. 800). The Hard Rock, which opened in late 2007, also features a full-service spa, a retail boutique, a happening lounge, and an outdoor party space adjacent to the fourth-floor pool, where special events and concerts draw big crowds.

207 Fifth Ave. (btw. K and L sts.), San Diego, CA 92101. www.hardrockhotelsd.com. ☎ **866/751-7625** or 619/702-3000. Fax 619/702-3007. 420 units. From $259 double; from $329 suite. AE, DC, DISC, MC, V. Valet parking $35. Trolley: Gaslamp Quarter. **Amenities:** 2 restaurants; 2 bars; music venue; concierge; exercise room; pool; room service; spa. *In room:* A/C, TV, hair dryer, minibar, MP3 docking station, free Wi-Fi.

Hilton San Diego Gaslamp Quarter ★★★   At the foot of the Gaslamp Quarter, across from the Convention Center, this hotel is ideally situated for business travelers. The Hilton doesn't overwhelm with size, making it a great place for guests who want to stay near the action but out of the fray. This

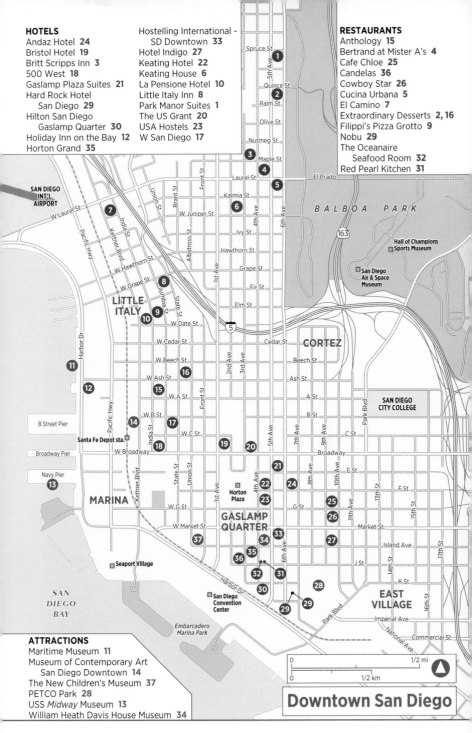

HOTELS
Andaz Hotel **24**
Bristol Hotel **19**
Britt Scripps Inn **3**
500 West **18**
Gaslamp Plaza Suites **21**
Hard Rock Hotel
   San Diego **29**
Hilton San Diego
   Gaslamp Quarter **30**
Holiday Inn on the Bay **12**
Horton Grand **35**

Hostelling International -
   SD Downtown **33**
Hotel Indigo **27**
Keating Hotel **22**
Keating House **6**
La Pensione Hotel **10**
Little Italy Inn **8**
Park Manor Suites **1**
The US Grant **20**
USA Hostels **23**
W San Diego **17**

RESTAURANTS
Anthology **15**
Bertrand at Mister A's **4**
Cafe Chloe **25**
Candelas **36**
Cowboy Star **26**
Cucina Urbana **5**
El Camino **7**
Extraordinary Desserts **2, 16**
Filippi's Pizza Grotto **9**
Nobu **29**
The Oceanaire
   Seafood Room **32**
Red Pearl Kitchen **31**

ATTRACTIONS
Maritime Museum **11**
Museum of Contemporary Art
   San Diego Downtown **14**
The New Children's Museum **37**
PETCO Park **28**
USS *Midway* Museum **13**
William Heath Davis House Museum **34**

SAN DIEGO INT'L. AIRPORT

BALBOA PARK

Hall of Champions
Sports Museum

San Diego
Air & Space
Museum

SAN DIEGO
CITY COLLEGE

Horton
Plaza

GASLAMP
QUARTER

MARINA

Santa Fe Depot sta.

B Street Pier

Broadway Pier

Navy Pier

Seaport Village

SAN
DIEGO
BAY

Embarcadero
Marina Park

San Diego
Convention
Center

LITTLE
ITALY

CORTEZ

EAST
VILLAGE

0   1/2 mi
0   1/2 km

Downtown San Diego

nonsmoking hotel opened in 2001 on the site of the old Bridgeworks building, part of San Diego's original wharf a century ago; much of the brick facade was incorporated into the hotel's polished design. Standard rooms boast upmarket furniture, down comforters, and pillow-top mattresses. There are suites and an executive floor, but the really snazzy picks are rooms in the Lofts at Fifth Avenue, a hotel within the hotel that features 30 oversize guest rooms with towering ceilings, custom furnishings, and lavish tubs. These are some of the handsomest hotel rooms available downtown.

401 K St. (at Fourth Ave.), San Diego, CA 92101. www.hilton.com. ✆ **800/445-8667** or 619/231-4040. Fax 619/231-6439. 283 units. $289 double; from $319 suite. Children 11 and under stay free in parent's room. AE, DC, DISC, MC, V. Valet parking $35. Trolley: Gaslamp Quarter or Convention Center. Pets less than 75 lb. accepted for $75. **Amenities:** Restaurant; bar; babysitting; concierge; health club; Jacuzzi; outdoor pool; room service; full-service spa. *In room:* A/C, TV, hair dryer, free Internet, minibar.

Keating Hotel ★   Pininfarina, the Italian design group that is the driving force behind Ferrari and Maserati, made its first foray into hotel design here in San Diego. The Keating is located in the heart of the Gaslamp in a gorgeous Roman-esque-style structure built in 1890. Boutique in size, with 35 rooms, this non-smoking property features sleek, ultramodern interiors and luxury amenities, such as goose-down beds, Bang & Olufsen electronics, and in-room espresso machines (gotta love those Italians). The rooms are highly contemporary—some may find them cold—and feature an interior design that does away with walls between the bed and bathroom areas. The hotel's **Sway** lounge is a Gaslamp hot spot (the pricey late-night cover charge is waived for guests), while the **MerK Bistro Italiano** keeps the style quotient high. *Note:* If you're not interested in partaking of the Gaslamp's loud and late revelry, you might want to look for quieter digs elsewhere.

432 F St. (btw. Fourth and Fifth aves.), San Diego, CA 92101. www.keatinghotel.com. ✆ **877/753-2846** or 619/814-5700. Fax 619/814-5750. 35 units. From $239 double; from $739 suite. 1 child 11 and under stays free in parent's room. Packages available. AE, DC, DISC, MC, V. Valet parking $32. Bus: 3, 120, or 992. Pets accepted for $25. **Amenities:** Restaurant; bar; babysitting; 24-hr. concierge; room service; spa services. *In room:* A/C, TV/DVD, CD player, hair dryer, minibar, MP3 docking station, free Wi-Fi.

The US Grant ★★★   Following a 20-month, $56-million renovation, one of San Diego's most historic properties reopened in the fall of 2006. Originally built in 1910 by the son of Ulysses S. Grant, this grandiose 11-story property sits at the northern edge of the Gaslamp Quarter. An impressive Beaux Arts beauty, the Grant is owned by the Sycuan Band of the Kumeyaay Nation—a nice touch of irony, as the tribe was given its sovereignty in 1875 by President Grant. Guest rooms all have 9-foot ceilings, plush wool carpets, ornate moldings, custom furniture, Italian linens, and Native American artwork in the foyer. In-room spa services incorporating local herbs and plants are also available. The **Grant Grill,** long a clubby spot for power lunches and dinners, has been given a modern Art Deco makeover, with plenty of curves, creamy white leather booths, rich mahogany, and iron filigrees.

326 Broadway (btw. Third and Fourth aves., main entrance on Fourth Ave.), San Diego, CA 92101. www.usgrant.net. ✆ **800/237-5029** or 866/837-4270. Fax 619/239-9517. 317 units. From $309 double; from $514 suite. Children 17 and under stay free in parent's room. Packages available. AE, DC, DISC, MC, V. Valet parking $32. Bus: Numerous downtown routes, including 2, 3, 7, 20, 120,

923, 929, and 992. Trolley: Civic Center. Dogs less than 40 lb. accepted for $150. **Amenities:** Restaurant; bar; babysitting; 24-hr. concierge; exercise room; room service. *In room:* A/C, TV, CD player, hair dryer, minibar, Wi-Fi ($12).

W San Diego ★★ With its dynamic restaurant and lounges, the W took San Diego by storm when it opened in 2003, delivering swanky nightlife beyond the Gaslamp Quarter. Rooms are bright and cheery—like mod beach cabanas beamed into downtown, replete with beach-ball-shaped pillows, cozy window seats, and sexy showers. The restaurant, **Rice,** has an adventurous and playful menu featuring contemporary global cuisine; the adjoining lounge, **Access,** has a menu of creative cocktails, while the airy lobby bar, **Living Room,** has turntables and board games (good luck concentrating on your chess match). The rooftop **Beach** is where the developers let it rip: The open-air bar has a sand floor (heated at night to encourage bare feet), a fire pit, and cabanas. Pets feel the love at the hotel, too, and can enjoy a "peticure" paw treatment and doggie happy hours (last Tues of the month, 5–7pm).

421 W. B St. (at State St.), San Diego, CA 92101. www.whotels.com/sandiego. © **619/398-3100.** Fax 619/231-5779. 259 units. From $299 double; from $500 suite. Children 11 and under stay free in parent's room. AE, DC, DISC, MC, V. Valet parking $32. Bus: All Broadway lines. Trolley: America Plaza. Dogs accepted, usually under 40 lb. for $100 plus $25 extra per night. **Amenities:** Restaurant; 2 lounges; free local transportation; 24-hr. concierge; exercise room; pool; room service; spa. *In room:* A/C, TV/DVD, CD player, hair dryer, minibar, Wi-Fi ($15).

EXPENSIVE

Horton Grand ★ 🎁 A cross between an elegant hotel and a charming inn, the Horton Grand combines two hotels that date from 1886—one of which was the residence of lawman Wyatt Earp during his San Diego days. Both properties were saved from demolition, moved to this spot, and connected by an airy atrium lobby filled with white wicker. The facade, with its graceful bay windows, is original. Each room at this nonsmoking property is unique, with vintage furnishings and gas fireplaces; bathrooms are lush, with reproduction floor tiles, fine brass fixtures, and genteel appointments. Rooms overlook either the city or the fig tree–filled courtyard; the suites (really just large studio-style rooms) are in a newer wing—choosing one means sacrificing historic character for a sitting area/sofa bed and minibar with microwave. If you're lonely, request room no. 309, where Roger the ghost hangs out.

311 Island Ave. (at Fourth Ave.), San Diego, CA 92101. www.hortongrand.com. © **800/542-1886** or 619/544-1886. Fax 619/239-3823. 132 units. From $229 double; from $279 suite. Extra person $20. Children 17 and under stay free in parent's room. AE, DC, MC, V. Valet parking $25. Bus: 3, 11, or 120. Trolley: Convention Center. **Amenities:** Restaurant (breakfast only); bar. *In room:* A/C, TV, hair dryer, Wi-Fi ($15).

Hotel Indigo ★★ Opened in 2009, this is San Diego's first LEED-certified hotel, meaning it was designed and built—and continues to operate—under the highest standards of sustainability. It has eco-friendly features, like a 4,000-square-foot rooftop garden for insulation, energy-efficient lighting (and floor-to-ceiling windows to maximize natural light), and in-room recycling receptacles. Best of all, this nonsmoking, pet-friendly property sees to it you don't sacrifice one little bit of style or comfort. Liberal doses of nature-inspired original art, including colorful in-room wall murals, stylish hardwood floors, and plenty of easily accessible outlets for plugging in electronics, give the accommodations a livable, residential feel. The ninth-floor **Phi Terrace** deck is a great spot for a cocktail, affording tantalizing views right into PETCO Park.

509 9th Ave. (at Island Ave.), San Diego, CA 92101. www.hotelindigo.com/sandiego. ✆ **877/846-3446** or 619/727-4000. Fax 619/727-4010. 210 units (most bathrooms have shower only). $226–$281 double; from $400 suite. Children 17 and under stay free in parent's room. AE, DC, DISC, MC, V. Valet parking $32. Bus: 3, 11, 901, or 929. Hwy. 163 S. becomes 10th Ave.; make a right on Island Ave. Pets accepted (no fees). **Amenities:** Restaurant; 2 bars; concierge; exercise room; room service. In room: A/C, TV, hair dryer, MP3 docking station, free Wi-Fi.

MODERATE

Gaslamp Plaza Suites ★★ ✦   You can't get closer to the center of the vibrant Gaslamp Quarter than this restored 11-story Edwardian beauty; built in 1913, it was San Diego's first skyscraper. Crafted (at great expense) of Australian gumwood, marble, brass, and exquisite etched glass, the splendid building originally housed the San Diego Trust & Savings. Various other businesses set up shop here until 1988, when the elegant structure was placed on the National Register of Historic Places and reopened as a boutique hotel. Most rooms are spacious and offer luxuries rare in this price range, such as pillow-top mattresses and premium toiletries, microwaves and dinnerware, and impressive luxury bathrooms. The cheapest rooms, on the back side, have no view and are uncomfortably small. The higher floors boast splendid city and bay views, as do the rooftop deck and breakfast room. Don't be surprised to hear a hum from the street below when things get rockin' on weekends.

520 E St. (corner of Fifth Ave.), San Diego, CA 92101. www.gaslampplaza.com. ✆ **800/874-8770** or 619/232-9500. Fax 619/238-9945. 64 units. From $139 double; from $279 suite. Extra person $15. Rates include continental breakfast. AE, DC, DISC, MC, V. Valet parking $28. Bus: 3 or 120, plus numerous downtown routes. Trolley: Fifth Ave. **Amenities:** Concierge. In room: A/C, TV, fridge, hair dryer, microwave, Wi-Fi ($9.95).

Holiday Inn on the Bay ★★ ☺   This better-than-average Holiday Inn is reliable and nearly always offers great deals. The three-building complex is on the Embarcadero across from the harbor and the Maritime Museum. This scenic spot is only 1½ miles from the airport (you can watch planes landing and taking off) and 2 blocks from the train station and trolley. Rooms, while basic and identical, always have clean new furnishings and plenty of thoughtful comforts. The only choice you have to make is whether you want marvelous bay views or a look at the San Diego skyline. In either case, request the highest floor possible.

1355 N. Harbor Dr. (at Ash St.), San Diego, CA 92101. www.holiday-inn.com/san-onthebay. ✆ **800/972-2802** or 619/232-3861. Fax 619/232-4924. 600 units. From $185 double; from $320 suite. Children 17 and under stay free in parent's room. AE, DC, DISC, MC, V. Valet parking $28; self-parking $22. Bus: 2, 210, 810, 820, 850, 860, 923, or 992. Trolley: America Plaza. Pets accepted for $25 per night and $100 deposit. **Amenities:** 3 restaurants; bar; babysitting; bikes; concierge; exercise room; outdoor heated pool; room service. In room: A/C, TV, hair dryer, free Wi-Fi.

INEXPENSIVE

La Pensione Hotel ★★ ✦   Made even better following a major renovation in 2010, this place has so much going for it: up-to-date amenities, remarkable value, a central location in the heart of Little Italy, a friendly staff, and free parking (a rare perk in San Diego). The four-story structure, erected in 1926 and then modernized in 1991 by one of the city's most acclaimed architects, is built around a courtyard and feels like a small European hotel. The moderately sized but comfortable rooms offer contemporary design and private bathrooms, and some have killer views; ask for room no. 422, which has floor-to-ceiling windows, or room no. 320, which has its own balcony. La Pensione is within walking distance of eateries (two restaurants are directly downstairs), nightspots, and a trolley station. Noise-sensitive travelers should note this is a very active neighborhood, though, where the cafes stay busy until midnight on weekends and trains rumble by a block away.

606 W. Date St. (at India St.), San Diego, CA 92101. www.lapensionehotel.com. © **800/232-4683** or 619/236-8000. Fax 619/236-8088. 68 units. $99 double. AE, DC, DISC, MC, V. Limited free underground parking. Bus: 83. Trolley: Little Italy. *In room:* A/C, TV, fridge, hair dryer, free Wi-Fi.

Little Italy Hotel ★   Originally a boardinghouse for Italian fishermen, this renovated 1910 property is a boutique bed-and-breakfast just steps from the galleries, delightful eateries, and hip boutiques of Little Italy. It's also just a short distance from the Gaslamp Quarter and Balboa Park. While preserving the building's historic architecture, the owner has added the latest in guest comforts, such as wireless Internet and a healthful, filling continental breakfast. The accommodations are cozy, romantic, and tastefully appointed with antiques, but are not fussy or precious; every room is unique and smoke free (smoking is allowed on the outdoor patio only). Some feature bay views, in-room Jacuzzi tubs, or kitchenettes (one has a full kitchen), as well as oversize closets, wood floors, and spacious bathrooms with plush bathrobes; some rooms have shared bathrooms. And though the inn is located at an intersection of planes, trains, and automobiles, the rooms are well insulated from the sound.

505 W. Grape St. (at India St.), San Diego, CA 92101. www.littleitalyhotel.com. © **800/518-9930** or 619/230-1600. Fax 619/230-0322. 23 units. From $99 double; from $149 suite. Extra person $15. Rates include continental breakfast. AE, DISC, MC, V. Street parking only. Bus: 83. *In room:* A/C, TV/DVD, fridge, hair dryer, free Wi-Fi.

Hillcrest/Uptown

The gentrified historic neighborhoods north of downtown are still something of a bargain. They're convenient to Balboa Park, with easy access to the rest of town. Filled with casual and upscale restaurants, eclectic shops, and upbeat nightlife, the area is also easy to navigate. All the following accommodations cater to the mainstream market but attract a gay/lesbian clientele as well.

There are bed-and-breakfasts in elegant older neighborhoods to consider, as well. **Keating House** ★★, 2331 Second Ave. (www.keatinghouse.com; © **800/995-8644** or 619/239-8585), is an 1880s Victorian mansion with period decor, between Hillcrest and downtown; **The Cottage,** 3829 Albatross St. (www.cottagevacation.us; © **619/299-1564**), is a romantic hideaway built in 1913 and tucked into a quiet cul-de-sac.

Best For: Those who want to log time at the zoo and Balboa Park, yet still want to be within striking distance of the downtown action.

Drawbacks: It lacks the glitzy wattage of downtown's Gaslamp Quarter (which is also one of the neighborhood's strengths).

VERY EXPENSIVE

Britt Scripps Inn ★★★   Built around 1887, this property was home to one of San Diego's most prominent families, the Scripps. Today the house and its grounds function as a nine-room "estate hotel"—part B&B, part luxury hotel. With first-class amenities, such as 1,000-thread-count sheets, flatscreen TVs (most hidden in antique armoires), free Wi-Fi, and heated towel racks, this gracious lady lays on the personal charm as well, with gourmet breakfasts including homemade pastries and breads, late-afternoon wine and cheese, and a vintage Steinway piano in the music alcove. Staff is always on-site but usually out of sight. Striking architectural elements include seven gables; a dramatic turret; a wraparound porch; a twisting oak staircase; and a two-story, three-paneled stained-glass window. And it's all just a block away from Balboa Park.

406 Maple St. (at Fourth Ave.), San Diego, CA 92103. www.brittscripps.com. ✆ **888/881-1991** or 619/230-1991. Fax 619/230-1188. 9 units. From $300 double. Rates include full breakfast and afternoon wine and hors d'oeuvres. AE, DC, MC, V. Bus: 3 or 120. Take the Laurel St. exit off I-5; then make a left on Laurel, a left on Fifth Ave., and a left on Maple St. *In room:* A/C, TV/DVD, CD player, hair dryer, MP3 docking station, free Wi-Fi.

MODERATE

Park Manor Suites ★ 🍸   On a prime corner overlooking Balboa Park, this hotel became a popular stopping-off point for celebrities headed for Mexican vacations in the 1920s and 1930s. Although dated, guest rooms are huge and very comfortable, featuring full kitchens, dining rooms, living rooms, and bedrooms with a separate dressing area. A few have glassed-in terraces; request one when you book. The overall feeling is that of a prewar East Coast apartment building, complete with steam heat and lavish moldings. Park Manor Suites does have its weaknesses, particularly bathrooms that have mostly original fixtures and could use some renovation. The restaurant on the ground floor also has a piano bar, and lunch is served weekdays in the penthouse banquet room (the view is spectacular). On Friday evenings, the penthouse bar becomes the launching pad for the gay party scene, drawing big crowds.

525 Spruce St. (btw. Fifth and Sixth aves.), San Diego, CA 92103. www.parkmanorsuites.com. ✆ **800/874-2649** or 619/291-0999. Fax 619/291-8844. 75 units. From $200 studio; from $289 1-bedroom suite; $341 2-bedroom suite. Extra person $15. Rates include continental breakfast. Children 11 and under stay free in parent's room. AE, DC, DISC, MC, V. Free parking. Bus: 3 or 120. Take Washington St. exit off I-5; turn right on Fourth Ave., left on Spruce. **Amenities:** Restaurant; bar; access to nearby health club ($5); room service. *In room:* TV, hair dryer, kitchen, free Wi-Fi.

INEXPENSIVE

Balboa Park Inn ★   Insiders looking for unusual accommodations head straight for this small inn at the northern edge of Balboa Park. This cluster of four Spanish Colonial–style former apartment buildings is in a mostly residential neighborhood a half-mile east from the heart of Hillcrest; the hotel has long been popular with gay travelers drawn to the area's restaurants and clubs. All the rooms and standard suites are themed (and nonsmoking), some evoking Victorian or Art Deco sensibilities, others reaching for a more elaborate fantasy, such as the Orient Express room with its red hues and Chinese wedding bed. Seven of the rooms have Jacuzzi tubs, and most have kitchens; all have private entrances,

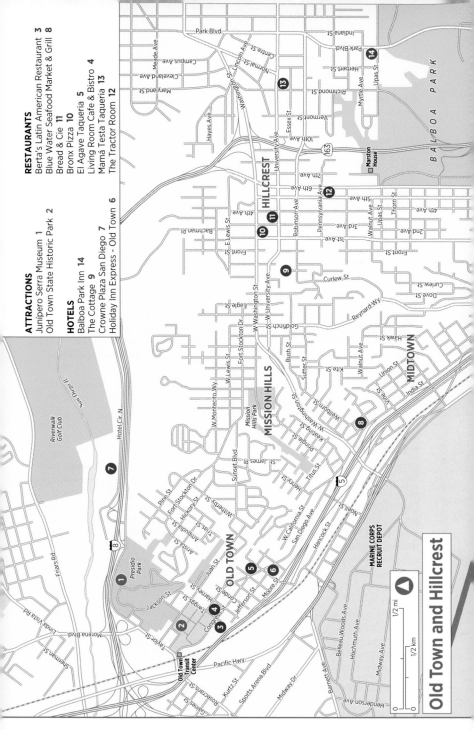

Old Town and Hillcrest

ATTRACTIONS
Junípero Serra Museum **1**
Old Town State Historic Park **2**

HOTELS
Balboa Park Inn **14**
The Cottage **9**
Crowne Plaza San Diego **7**
Holiday Inn Express - Old Town **6**

RESTAURANTS
Berta's Latin American Restaurant **3**
Blue Water Seafood Market & Grill **8**
Bread & Cie **11**
Bronx Pizza **10**
El Agave Taqueria **5**
Living Room Cafe & Bistro **4**
Mamá Testa Taqueria **13**
The Tractor Room **12**

though the front desk operates 24 hours. From here, you're close enough to walk to the San Diego Zoo and other Balboa Park attractions.

3402 Park Blvd. (at Upas St.), San Diego, CA 92103. www.balboaparkinn.com. © **800/938-8181** or 619/298-0823. Fax 619/294-8070. 26 units. $99 double; from $149 suites. Extra person $10. Rates include continental breakfast. Children 11 and under stay free in parent's room. AE, DC, DISC, MC, V. Parking available on street. Bus: 7. From I-5, take Washington St. east, follow signs to University Ave. E., and turn right at Park Blvd. *In room:* TV, fridge, microwave, free Wi-Fi.

Old Town & Mission Valley

Old Town is popular with families because of its proximity to Old Town State Historic Park and other attractions within walking distance; SeaWorld and the San Diego Zoo are within a 10-minute drive. Around the corner, in Mission Valley, you'll find the city's largest collection of hotels with rooms under $100 a night. Mission Valley lacks personality—this is the spot for chain restaurants and huge shopping malls, not gardens or water views. But it caters to convention groups and leisure travelers drawn by the lower prices and competitive facilities.

Room rates at properties on Hotel Circle are significantly cheaper than those in many other parts of the city. You'll find a cluster of inexpensive chain hotels and motels, including **Best Western Seven Seas** (www.bw7seas.com; © **800/328-1618** or 619/291-1300), **Mission Valley Travelodge** (www.travelodge.com; © **888/515-6375** or 619/297-2271), **Ramada Plaza** (www.ramada.com; © **888/298-2054** or 619/291-6500), and **Vagabond Inn-Hotel Circle** (www.vagabondhc.com; © **800/571-2933** or 619/297-1691).

Best For: Families looking for less expensive digs close to major attractions; the area is also a transportation hub.

Drawbacks: The style quotient drops considerably in the commuter corridor of Mission Valley.

MODERATE

Crowne Plaza San Diego ★   Formerly known as the Red Lion Hanalei, this Mission Valley hotel has a Polynesian theme and comfort-conscious sophistication. Most rooms are split between two eight-story towers, set back from the freeway with balconies opening onto the tropically landscaped pool courtyard or the attractive links of an adjacent golf club; a few rooms are found in a third structure, which is a little too close to the freeway. The heated outdoor pool and the oversize Jacuzzi are large enough for any luau, and there's even a waterfall in an open-air atrium. **The Islands** restaurant serves breakfast, lunch, and dinner, bringing out the sushi and pupu platters in the evening to go along with the specialty tropical cocktails. Hotel services include a free shuttle to Old Town and the Fashion Valley Shopping Center.

2270 Hotel Circle N., San Diego, CA 92108. www.cp-sandiego.com. © **800/227-6963** or 619/297-1101. Fax 619/297-6049. 417 units. From $179 double; from $275 suite. AE, DC, DISC, MC, V. Parking $12. Bus: 88. From I-8, take Hotel Circle exit and follow signs for Hotel Circle N. **Amenities:** 2 restaurants; bar; nearby golf course (packages available); exercise room; Jacuzzi; outdoor pool; room service; spa. *In room:* A/C, TV, hair dryer, Internet ($9.95).

Holiday Inn Express–Old Town ★   A couple of blocks from the heart of Old Town, this Holiday Inn's Spanish Colonial exterior suits the neighborhood. Inside, above-par contemporary furnishings and small touches make this hotel an

affordable favorite of business travelers and families alike. Adjacent streets are unspectacular, so the hotel is smartly oriented toward the interior; request a room with a patio or balcony that opens onto the pleasant courtyard. Rooms are thoughtfully, practically appointed, with extras such as microwave ovens and writing tables. The lobby, surrounded by French doors, has a large fireplace, several sitting areas, and a TV.

3900 Old Town Ave., San Diego, CA 92110. www.hiexpress.com/ex-oldtown. $\textcircled{C}$ **800/972-2802** or 619/299-7400. Fax 619/299-1619. 125 units. From $159 double; from $184 suite. Rates include continental breakfast. Children 17 and under stay free in parent's room. AE, DC, DISC, MC, V. Parking $12. Bus: 10 or 30. Trolley: Old Town. Take I-5 to Old Town Ave. exit. **Amenities:** Jacuzzi; outdoor pool. *In room:* A/C, TV, fridge, microwave, free Wi-Fi.

Mission Bay & the Beaches

If the beach and aquatic activities are the focus of your San Diego agenda, this part of town may be for you. Even though the beach communities feel removed from the city, downtown and Balboa Park are only a 15-minute drive away. Some hotels are right on Mission Bay, San Diego's water playground; they're usually good choices for families. Ocean Beach, Mission Beach, and Pacific Beach provide a total immersion in the beach lifestyle. These places can be raucous at times, especially on summer weekends, and dining options are largely limited to chains and casual restaurants. If you're looking for a more refined landing, head to La Jolla or Coronado (covered later in this chapter).

Hostelling International has a 53-bed location in **Point Loma** (www. sandiegohostels.org; $\textcircled{C}$ **888/464-4872,** ext. 157, or 619/223-4778), 3790 Udall St., about 2 miles inland from Ocean Beach; rates start at $19 per person, and private rooms that sleep two or three start at $42 and $48, respectively. The **Ocean Beach International Hostel,** 4961 Newport Ave. (www.california hostel.com; $\textcircled{C}$ **800/339-7263** or 619/223-7873), has more than 60 beds and is just 2 blocks from the beach; bunk rates start at $19 per person. Free pickup from the airport, train, or bus station is offered. U.S. residents must show current student ID, show proof of international travel within the past 6 months, or be a member of a hostelling organization in order to stay. You can truly embrace your inner beach bum at **Banana Bungalow,** 707 Reed Ave. (www.bananabungalow sandiego.com; $\textcircled{C}$ **858/273-3060**). Even the finest hotel won't get you any closer to the beach than this place—it's right on the rollicking Pacific Beach boardwalk. In summer, dorm rooms are $25, and private rooms are $105.

Best For: Families looking for fun in the sun, or anyone with a penchant for outdoor recreation.

Drawbacks: The party almost never stops (or maybe that's a good thing).

VERY EXPENSIVE

Crystal Pier Hotel ★★ 🎁☺   If historic charm is higher on your wish list than hotel-style service, head to this utterly unique cluster of cottages sitting literally over the surf on the vintage Crystal Pier in Pacific Beach. You'll get a separate living room and bedroom, a fully equipped kitchen, and a private patio with breathtaking ocean views—all within the whitewashed walls of sweet, blue-shuttered cottages that date from 1936 (the pier itself dates from 1927). Each of the Cape Cod–style cottages has a deck; the more expensive units farthest out have more privacy. Six cheaper units are not actually on the pier, but still offer sunset-facing sea views. Guests drive right out and park beside their cottages, a real boon on crowded weekends. These nonsmoking accommodations book up fast; reserve at least 4 to 6 months in advance. Or, with luck, you might be able to nab someone's cancelled reservation.

4500 Ocean Blvd. (at Garnet Ave.), San Diego, CA 92109. www.crystalpier.com. ✆ **800/748-5894** or 858/483-6983. Fax 858/483-6811. 29 units. From $300 double; $500 for larger unit sleeping 6. 3-night minimum in summer, 2-night minimum in winter. DISC, MC, V. Free parking. Bus: 8, 9, 27, or 30. Take I-5 to Grand/Garnet exit; follow Garnet to the pier. **Amenities:** Beach equipment rental. *In room:* TV, kitchen, free Wi-Fi.

Pacific Terrace Hotel ★   This modern hotel swaggers with a heavy-handed South Seas–meets–Spanish Colonial ambience. More upscale than most places nearby, it's at the north end of the Pacific Beach boardwalk; the surfer contingent tends to stay a few blocks south. Large, comfortable guest rooms each come with a balcony or terrace; bathrooms, designed with warm-toned marble and natural woods, have a separate sink/vanity area. About half the rooms have kitchenettes, and top-floor rooms in this three-story hotel enjoy particularly nice views. The lushly landscaped pool and hot tub are literally 15 feet from the boardwalk, overlooking a relatively quiet stretch of beach. Four nearby restaurants allow meals to be billed to the hotel, but there's no restaurant on the premises.

610 Diamond St., San Diego, CA 92109. www.pacificterrace.com. ✆ **800/344-3370** or 858/581-3500. Fax 858/274-3341. 73 units. From $359 double; from $465 suite. Extra person $15. 2- to 4-night minimums apply in summer. Children 12 and under stay free in parent's room. AE, DC, DISC, MC, V. Parking $20. Bus: 30. Take I-5 to Grand/Garnet exit and follow Grand or Garnet west to Mission Blvd., turn right (north) and then left (west) onto Diamond. **Amenities:** Concierge; exercise room; Jacuzzi; pool; room service; spa services. *In room:* A/C, TV/DVD, fridge, hair dryer, microwave (in some), minibar, Wi-Fi ($9.95).

Paradise Point Resort & Spa ★★ ☺   Smack-dab in the middle of Mission Bay, this hotel complex is almost as much a theme park as its closest neighbor, SeaWorld (a 3-min. drive away). Single-story accommodations are spread across 44 tropically landscaped acres of duck-filled lagoons, lush gardens, and swim-friendly beaches; all have private verandas and plenty of thoughtful conveniences. The resort was updated with refreshingly colorful beach-cottage decor, while still retaining its low-tech 1960s charm. Standard "lanai" rooms range considerably in price, based solely on view; despite daunting high-season rack rates, though, you can usually get a deal here. An upscale waterfront restaurant, **Baleen** (p. 806), offers fine dining in a contemporary, fun space. A stunning Indonesian-inspired spa is a vacation in itself and offers cool serenity and aromatic Asian treatments.

1404 Vacation Rd. (off Ingraham St.), San Diego, CA 92109. www.paradisepoint.com. ✆ **800/344-2626** or 858/274-4630. Fax 858/581-5924. 462 units. From $329 double; from $850 suite. Extra person $20. Children 17 and under stay free in parent's room. AE, DC, DISC, MC, V. Parking $25. Bus: 9. Follow I-8 west to Mission Bay Dr. exit; take Ingraham St. north to Vacation Rd. **Amenities:** 2 restaurants; 2 bars; bikes; concierge; 18-hole miniature golf course; exercise room; Jacuzzi; 5 outdoor pools; room service; full-service spa; tennis/basketball courts; marina w/watersports equipment/rentals. *In room:* A/C, TV, fridge, hair dryer, Wi-Fi ($10–$15 per day).

Tower 23 ★★   Named for a lifeguard station that once pulled duty nearby, Tower 23 is a modernist beach resort that opened in 2005. Sitting on the Pacific Beach (also known as PB) boardwalk, the hotel enjoys a sky-high people-watching quotient matched only by its first-class contemporary amenities, including

Mission Bay Area

Turquoise St.
Tourmaline St.
Opal St.
Foothill Blvd.
Beryl St.
Loring St.
Wilbur Ave.
Law St.
Chalcedony St.
Missouri St.
Diamond St.
PACIFIC BEACH
Garnet Ave.
Balboa Ave.
Emerald St.
Felspar St.
Hornblend St.
Grand Ave.
Thomas Ave.
Reed Ave.
Oliver Ave.
Pacific Beach Dr.
Fortuna Ave.

Crystal Pier

Sail Bay

Santa Clara Pt.

Santa Barbara Cove

MISSION BEACH

La Playa Ave.
Moorland Dr.
La Mancha Dr.

MISSION BAY

MISSION BAY PARK

Vacation Isle

Fiesta Island

Quivira Basin

Sea World Dr.
San Diego R.

Ocean Beach Athletic Area

Ocean Beach

Ocean Beach Pier

OCEAN BEACH

W. Point Loma Blvd.

POINT LOMA HEIGHTS

Valley View Casino Center

Sports Arena Blvd.
Midway Dr.
Kurtz St.
Hancock St.

Garnet Ave.
Brandywine St.
Ticonderoga St.
Morena Blvd.
BAY PARK

Mission Bay Dr.
Mission Bay Golf Course

De Anza Point

Fiesta Island Rd.

Chicago St.
Denver St.
Littlefield St.
Morena Blvd.

Pacific Hwy.

Pacific Ocean

Mission Beach

0   1 mi
0   1 km

ATTRACTIONS
Belmont Park **11**
SeaWorld San Diego **16**

HOTELS
Banana Bungalow **8**
The Beach Cottages **7**
Catamaran Resort Hotel **9**
Crystal Pier Hotel **4**

The Dana on Mission Bay **15**
Hostelling International -
SD Point Loma **23**
Ocean Beach International
Hostel **21**
Ocean Park Inn **6**
Pacific Terrace Hotel **2**
Paradise Point Resort & Spa **13**
Tower 23 **3**

RESTAURANTS
Baleen **14**
Bay Park Fish Co. **19**
Caffe Bella Italia **12**
The Fishery **1**
Gringo's **5**
The Mission **10**
Rubio's Fresh
Mexican Grill **18**

South Beach
Bar & Grill **20**
Sushi Ota **17**
The 3rd Corner **22**
Wahoo's Fish Taco **24**

791

wireless Internet access right on the beach. Featuring clean lines and glass-box architecture, the three-story Tower 23 has 44 rooms, all with private balconies or patios (though not all with ocean views); a guest-only second-story deck with a fire pit overlooks the beach. The hotel's **Tower Bar,** which has indoor/outdoor seating along the boardwalk, and **JRDN** restaurant, serving contemporary steak and seafood, are the most chic establishments in the area (don't miss the hypnotic 75-ft.-long "wave wall" and its morphing color scheme).

723 Felspar St., San Diego, CA 92109. www.t23hotel.com. ✆ **866/869-3723** or 858/270-2323. Fax 858/274-2333. 44 units. From $319 double; from $665 suite. Children 17 and under stay free in parent's room. AE, DC, MC, V. Valet parking $20. Bus: 8, 9, 27, or 30. Take I-5 to Grand/Garnet exit; then left on Grand Ave., right on Mission Blvd., left on Felspar St. Pets less than 25 lb. accepted for $150. **Amenities:** Restaurant; bar; room service; spa services. *In room:* A/C, TV/DVD, CD player, hair dryer, minibar, MP3 docking station, free Wi-Fi.

EXPENSIVE

Catamaran Resort Hotel ★★ ☺   Right on Mission Bay, the Catamaran has its own beach, complete with watersports facilities. Built in the 1950s, the hotel has been fully renovated to modern standards without losing its trademark Polynesian theme. Guest rooms—in either a 13-story building or one of the six two-story buildings—have subdued South Pacific decor, and each has a balcony or patio. Tower rooms on higher floors have commanding views, and studios and suites have kitchenettes; the 9,300-square-foot spa features a menu of South Pacific and Asian-inspired treatments. The Catamaran is also within a few blocks of Pacific Beach's restaurant-and-nightlife scene. During the summer, the Bahia Belle, a Mississippi River–style stern-wheeler boat, plies Mission Bay nightly (weekends only the rest of the year), and guests board free of charge. Luaus are also a part of the summer fun.

3999 Mission Blvd. (4 blocks south of Grand Ave.), San Diego, CA 92109. www.catamaranresort. com. ✆ **800/422-8386** or 858/488-1081. Fax 858/488-1387. 313 units. From $283 double; from $488 suite. Children 11 and under stay free in parent's room. AE, DC, DISC, MC, V. Valet parking $30; self-parking $25. Bus: 8. Take Grand/Garnet exit off I-5 and go west on Grand Ave., then south on Mission Blvd. **Amenities:** Restaurant; 2 bars; bikes; children's programs; concierge; exercise room; Jacuzzi; outdoor pool; room service; full-service spa; watersports equipment/rentals. *In room:* A/C, TV, fridge (in most), hair dryer, MP3 docking station, free Wi-Fi.

The Dana on Mission Bay ★   A 2004 renovation added 74 contemporary rooms to this 1960s Mission Bay stalwart, set right on the water's edge. Some rooms overlook bobbing sailboats in the recreational marina; others face the original kidney-shaped pool whose surrounding tiki-torch-lit gardens offer shuffleboard and table tennis. You'll pay a little extra for bay and marina views; if the view doesn't matter, save your money: The old rooms are plain but well maintained. The new rooms are bigger and feature water views and reclaimed redwood beam ceilings. Beaches and SeaWorld are a 15-minute walk away, or the complimentary shuttle can take you to the theme park.

1710 W. Mission Bay Dr., San Diego, CA 92109. www.thedana.com. ✆ **800/345-9995** or 619/222-6440. Fax 619/222-5916. 271 units. From $214 double; from $314 suite. AE, DC, DISC, MC, V. Parking $18. Bus: 8. Follow I-8 west to Mission Bay Dr. exit; take W. Mission Bay Dr. **Amenities:** 2 restaurants; bikes; concierge; exercise room; 2 Jacuzzis; 2 outdoor heated pools; room service; spa services; marina w/watersports equipment/rentals. *In room:* A/C, TV, fridge, hair dryer, microwave (in some), wet bar (in some), free Wi-Fi.

Ocean Park Inn ★   This oceanfront motor hotel offers simple, attractive, spacious rooms with contemporary furnishings. Although this nonsmoking property has a smidgen of sophistication uncommon in this casual, surfer-populated area, you won't find much solitude with the boisterous scene outside; but you can't beat the direct beach access. Most rooms have at least a partial ocean view; all have a private balcony or patio. Units in front are most desirable, but it can get noisy directly above the boardwalk; try for the second or third floor, or pick one of the three junior suites, which have huge bathrooms and pool views.

710 Grand Ave., San Diego, CA 92109. www.oceanparkinn.com. ℂ **800/231-7735** or 858/483-5858. Fax 858/274-0823. 72 units. From $216 double; from $289 suite. Rates include continental breakfast. AE, DC, DISC, MC, V. Parking $10. Bus: 8, 9, or 30. Take Grand/Garnet exit off I-5; follow Grand Ave. to ocean. **Amenities:** Jacuzzi; outdoor pool; room service; spa services. *In room:* A/C, TV, fridge, hair dryer, microwave, free Wi-Fi.

MODERATE

The Beach Cottages   This family-owned operation has been around since 1948 and offers a variety of guest quarters, most of them geared to the long-term visitor. It's the 17 cute detached cottages just steps from the sand that give it real appeal: Some of them lack a view (of anything), but each has a patio with tables and chairs. The cottages themselves aren't pristine, but they have a rustic charm—reserve one well in advance. Adjoining apartments are perfectly adequate, especially for budget-minded families who want to log major hours on the beach—all cottages and apartments sleep four or more and have full kitchens. The standard motel rooms are worn but cheap (most of these sleep two). The property features shared barbecue grills, shuffleboard courts, and table tennis, and is also within walking distance of shops and restaurants.

4255 Ocean Blvd. (1 block south of Grand Ave.), San Diego, CA 92109. www.beachcottages.com. ℂ **858/483-7440.** Fax 858/273-9365. 61 units, 17 cottages. From $140 double; from $285 cottages and apts for 4–6. Extra person $10. 2-night minimum on weekends. AE, DC, DISC, MC, V. Free parking. Bus: 8. Take I-5 to Grand/Garnet exit; go west on Grand Ave. and left on Mission Blvd. *In room:* TV, fridge, kitchen (in some), free Wi-Fi.

The Pearl Hotel ★ 🛍   The designers of this midcentury modernist gem took a run-down motel property dating from 1959 and let fly with the vintage cool. Accommodations are modest in size but have been refreshed with amenities such as Internet radios and contemporary chrome bathroom fixtures; thoughtful design touches include custom mosaic artwork and a pet fish in each room. The Pearl's restaurant and lounge area is cozy and features outdoor dining spaces alongside the saltwater pool (where "dive-in" movies are screened weekly). Although the closest beach is over the hill in Ocean Beach, Point Loma is a nautical neighborhood, with the marinas, bars, and restaurants of Shelter Island nearby; the airport and Cabrillo National Monument are also just minutes away. The hotel is entirely nonsmoking.

1410 Rosecrans St. (at Fenelon St.), San Diego, CA 92106. www.thepearlsd.com. ℂ **877/732-7573** or 619/226-6100. Fax 619/226-6161. 23 units. From $149 double; "Play & Stay" rate $79 after midnight (must be booked on-site, subject to availability). AE, DISC, MC, V. Parking $10. Bus: 28. Take I-5 S. to Rosecrans St. exit. **Amenities:** Restaurant; bar; bikes; outdoor saltwater pool; spa services. *In room:* A/C, TV, hair dryer, MP3 docking station, free Wi-Fi.

La Jolla

No one is quite sure, but the name "La Jolla" may be misspelled Spanish for "the jewel"—a fitting comparison for this section of the city, with its beautiful coastline and compact downtown village. You'll have a hard time finding bargain accommodations in this upscale, conservative community. But remember, most hotels—even those in our "Very Expensive" category—have occupancy-driven rates.

Best For: Those who want it all—style, luxury, fine dining, excellent shopping, sophisticated cultural attractions, and outdoor activities.

Drawbacks: All that good stuff is going to cost you; also there's not much in the way of nightlife here.

Kayaking La Jolla.

VERY EXPENSIVE

The Grande Colonial ★★★ 🎁   Possessed of an old-world European flair that's more London or Georgetown than seaside La Jolla, the Grande Colonial has earned accolades for its meticulous restorations over the past decade. The most recent involves the renovation of two adjacent properties, dating from 1925 and 1926, that add 18 more suites to the Grande Colonial; some of the new suites feature ocean views, fireplaces, and full kitchens. A large spray of fresh flowers is the focal point in the hotel lounge, where guests gather in front of the fireplace for drinks—often before enjoying dinner at the hotel's excellent **Nine-Ten** restaurant (p. 809). Guest rooms at this nonsmoking property are quiet and elegantly appointed, with beautiful draperies and traditional furnishings. Many rooms in the original building have sea views.

910 Prospect St. (btw. Fay and Girard aves.), La Jolla, CA 92037. www.thegrandecolonial.com. ✆ **888/530-5766** or 858/454-2181. Fax 858/454-5679. 93 units. From $279 double; from $395 suite. Children 11 and under stay free in parent's room. AE, DC, MC, V. Valet parking $22. Bus: 30. Take Torrey Pines Rd. to Prospect Place and turn right. Prospect Place becomes Prospect St. **Amenities:** Restaurant; bar; concierge; access to nearby health club; outdoor pool; room service. *In room:* A/C, TV, hair dryer, kitchen (in some), MP3 docking station, free Wi-Fi.

Hotel Parisi ★★★ 🎁   This intimate hotel overlooking one of La Jolla village's main intersections offers a nurturing, wellness-inspired vibe. The Italy-meets-Zen composition includes custom guest-room furnishings that are modern yet comfy; Parisi calls the spacious accommodations "suites" (some are more like junior suites), and each has an ergonomic desk, dimmable lighting, and super-luxe goose-down bedding. Each darkly cool marble bathroom boasts a shower (some with dual shower heads), a separate tub with contoured backrest, and smoothly sculpted fixtures. Less expensive rooms at this nonsmoking property are smaller, with little or no view; across the street from the hotel is **Parisi Apart**—seven luxury units available for extended stays. Though primped and elegant, Parisi is not stuffy, and the personal service stops at nothing—there's

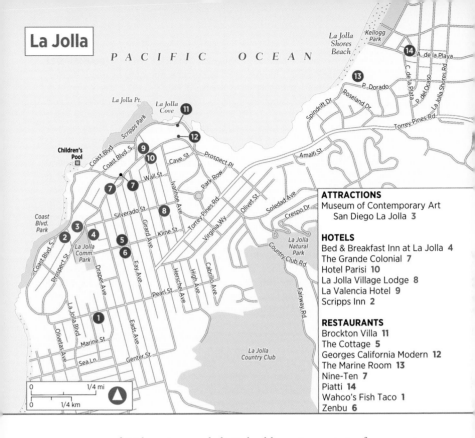

La Jolla

P A C I F I C   O C E A N

La Jolla Shores Beach

Kellogg Park

La Jolla Pt.

La Jolla Cove

Children's Pool

Coast Blvd. Park

Coast Blvd.

ATTRACTIONS
Museum of Contemporary Art
    San Diego La Jolla **3**

HOTELS
Bed & Breakfast Inn at La Jolla **4**
The Grande Colonial **7**
Hotel Parisi **10**
La Jolla Village Lodge **8**
La Valencia Hotel **9**
Scripps Inn **2**

RESTAURANTS
Brockton Villa **11**
The Cottage **5**
Georges California Modern **12**
The Marine Room **13**
Nine-Ten **7**
Piatti **14**
Wahco's Fish Taco **1**
Zenbu **6**

---

even a menu of 24-hour in-room holistic health services, ranging from yoga to psychotherapy.

1111 Prospect St. (at Herschel Ave.), La Jolla, CA 92037. www.hotelparisi.com. 📞 **877/472-7474** or 858/454-1511. Fax 858/454-1531. 29 units. From $239 double; from $359 suite; extended stay from $265. Rates include continental breakfast. AE, DC, DISC, MC, V. Parking $15. Bus: 30. Take Torrey Pines Rd. to Prospect Place and turn right; Prospect Place becomes Prospect St.; turn left on Herschel Ave. **Amenities:** Room service; spa services. *In room:* A/C, TV/DVD, CD player, hair dryer, minibar, free Wi-Fi.

La Valencia Hotel ★★★   Looking much like a Mediterranean villa, "La V" has been the centerpiece of La Jolla since it opened in 1926. Brides still pose in front of the lobby's picture window, well-coiffed ladies lunch in the dappled shade of the garden patio, and neighborhood cronies quaff libations in the clubby **Whaling Bar.** All rooms are comfortably and traditionally furnished, with lavish appointments and all-marble bathrooms with signature toiletries. Because rates vary wildly according to the view (from sweeping to *nada*), get a cheaper room and enjoy the scene from one of the many lounges, one of the serene garden terraces, or the amazing pool, which fronts the Pacific and nearby Scripps Park. Room decor, layouts, and size are all over the map, too; a few extra minutes with the reservationist will ensure a custom match for you. If you've got the bucks, spring for one of the newer villas (with fireplaces and butler service) and a meal at the hotel's 11-table **Sky Room,** one of the city's most celebrated dining rooms.

1132 Prospect St. (at Herschel Ave.), La Jolla, CA 92037. www.lavalencia.com. ☎ **800/451-0772** or 858/454-0771. Fax 858/456-3921. 113 units. From $309 double; from $595 suite and villa. Minimum stays may be required in summer and on weekends. AE, DC, DISC, MC, V. Valet parking $29. Bus: 30. Take Torrey Pines Rd. to Prospect Place and turn right. Prospect Place becomes Prospect St. Pets accepted. **Amenities:** 3 restaurants; 2 bars; babysitting; concierge; exercise room; Jacuzzi; outdoor pool; room service; sauna; spa services. *In room:* A/C, TV/DVD, hair dryer, minibar, free Wi-Fi.

The Lodge at Torrey Pines ★★★   Patterned largely after the 1908 Greene & Greene–designed Gamble House, the Lodge brims with perfectly assembled odes to Arts and Crafts style: clinker-brick masonry, art-glass windows and doors, Stickley furniture, and exquisite pottery. The least expensive rooms are an unstinting 520 square feet, lavished with Tiffany-style lamps, period wallpaper, and framed Hiroshige prints, with lots of wood accents. Views face a courtyard carefully landscaped to mimic the rare coastal environment that exists just beyond the hotel grounds. More expensive rooms overlook the Torrey Pines Golf Course and the sea in the distance; most of these have balconies, fireplaces, and giant bathrooms with separate tub and shower. The 9,500-square-foot spa specializes in treatments utilizing coastal sage and other local plants; **A. R. Valentien,** the resort's exceptional restaurant, also makes use of the region's top-quality seasonal products.

11480 N. Torrey Pines Rd., La Jolla, CA 92037. www.lodgetorreypines.com. ☎ **800/656-0087** or 858/453-4420. Fax 858/453-7464. 170 units. From $275 double; from $659 suite. Children 17 and under stay free in parent's room. AE, DC, DISC, MC, V. $27 valet parking; $22 self-parking. Bus: 101. From I-5, take La Jolla Village Dr. west; bear right (north) onto N. Torrey Pines Rd. **Amenities:** 2 restaurants; bar; concierge; preferential tee times at golf course; exercise room; Jacuzzi; outdoor pool; room service; spa. *In room:* A/C, TV, hair dryer, minibar, free Wi-Fi.

Scripps Inn ★★ 🎁   This meticulously maintained inn is hidden away behind the Museum of Contemporary Art, offering seclusion even though the attractions of La Jolla are just a short walk away. Only a small, grassy park comes between the inn and the beach, cliffs, and tide pools; the view from the second-story deck can hypnotize guests, who gaze out to sea indefinitely. Rates vary depending on ocean view (all have one, but some are better than others). Rooms have a pleasant pale cream/sand palette with new bathroom fixtures and appointments. All rooms have sofa beds; two have wood-burning fireplaces, and four have kitchenettes. The inn supplies French pastries each morning, beach towels, and firewood. Book a room here well in advance.

555 Coast Blvd. S. (at Cuvier), La Jolla, CA 92037. www.scrippsinn.com. ☎ **866/860-6318** or 858/454-3391. Fax 858/456-0389. 14 units. From $305 double; from $365 suite. Extra person $10. Rates include continental breakfast. Children 4 and under stay free in parent's room. AE, DC, DISC, MC, V. Parking $10. Bus: 30. Take Torrey Pines Rd., turn right on Prospect Place; past the museum, turn right onto Cuvier. Pets accepted with $50 fee. *In room:* Ceiling fans, TV, fridge, hair dryer, free Wi-Fi.

EXPENSIVE

Estancia La Jolla Hotel and Spa ★★★   This 9½-acre California ranchostyle property has some pretty cool neighbors: the Louis I. Kahn–designed Salk Institute, UC San Diego, the Torrey Pines Gliderport, and Black's Beach. You won't see any of those things from this self-contained retreat, but the romance created by the hacienda flavor and the meticulously maintained gardens with their native flora and bubbling fountains is diversion enough. Guest rooms face a central courtyard, so many rooms have balconies or patios; all are tastefully appointed with comfy furnishings that would be at home in an upscale residence. With its old *Californio* exterior, outdoor fireplace, and live Spanish guitar music, the **Mustangs & Burros** lounge and bar is a great place to chill out; there is also an award-winning restaurant on-site and a full-service spa offering organic-based treatments.

9700 N. Torrey Pines Rd., La Jolla, CA 92037. www.estancialajolla.com. ✆ **877/437-8262** or 858/550-1000. Fax 858/550-1001. 210 units. From $218 double; from $369 suite. Bed-and-breakfast packages available for an additional $20. AE, DC, DISC, MC, V. Valet parking $25. Bus: 101. From I-5, take the Genesee Ave. exit westbound; go left on N. Torrey Pines Rd. **Amenities:** 2 restaurants; 2 bars; babysitting; concierge; exercise room w/yoga and personal training; Jacuzzi; outdoor pool; room service; full-service spa. *In room:* A/C, TV, hair dryer, minibar, Wi-Fi ($12).

MODERATE

The Bed & Breakfast Inn at La Jolla ★★ 🎒 A house designed in 1913 by San Diego's first important architect, Irving Gill—and occupied in the 1920s by composer/conductor John Philip Sousa and his family—is the setting for this cultured and elegant B&B. Reconfigured as lodging, this nonsmoking inn features lovely enclosed gardens and a cozy library and sitting room. Some rooms feature a fireplace or an ocean view; each has a private bathroom, most of which are on the compact side. The period furnishings are tasteful and cottage-style, with plenty of old photos of La Jolla adding to the sense of history. A gourmet breakfast is served wherever you desire—dining room, patio, sun deck, or in your room. There is afternoon wine and cheese offered daily in summer, and an evening nightcap of sherry and sweets is provided in the off season.

7753 Draper Ave. (near Prospect), La Jolla, CA 92037. www.innlajolla.com. ✆ **888/988-8481** or 858/456-2066. Fax 858/456-1510. 15 units. From $199 double; from $325 suite. 2-night minimum on weekends. Rates include full breakfast; afternoon wine and cheese is served daily in summer. AE, DISC, MC, V. Limited free parking. Bus: 30. Take Torrey Pines Rd. to Prospect Place and turn right. Prospect Place becomes Prospect St.; proceed to Draper Ave. and turn left. Children 11 and under not allowed. *In room:* A/C, hair dryer, free Wi-Fi.

INEXPENSIVE

Wealthy, image-conscious La Jolla is not the best place for deep bargains, but if you're determined to stay here on a budget, try the 30-room **La Jolla Village Lodge,** 1141 Silverado St. (www.lajollavillagelodge.com; ✆ **877/551-2001** or 858/551-2001). This motel with small, basic rooms has rates that vary wildly by season and day of the week—a room going for $90 midweek in winter doubles in price for a summer weekend.

Coronado

Coronado is a great escape, featuring quiet, architecturally rich streets; a small-town, Navy-oriented atmosphere; and one of the state's most beautiful, welcoming beaches. Coronado's resorts are especially popular with Southern California and Arizona families for weekend escapes. Although downtown San Diego is just a 10-minute drive or 15-minute ferry ride away, you may feel pleasantly isolated on this peninsula, but it isn't the best choice if you plan to spend time in central parts of the city.

Best For: Families and those who want some quality beach time without the raucous partying.

Drawbacks: Things get mighty quiet here after dark.

VERY EXPENSIVE

Hotel del Coronado ★★★   Opened in 1888 and designated a National Historic Landmark in 1977, the "Hotel Del" is the last of California's stately old seaside hotels. This monument to Victorian grandeur boasts tall cupolas, red turrets, and gingerbread trim, all spread out over 28 acres. Even if you don't stay here, take a stroll through the sumptuous, wood-paneled lobby and along one of the state's finest beaches, or enjoy Sunday brunch in the amazing **Crown Room.** Guest rooms—almost no two alike—run the gamut from compact to extravagant, and all are packed with antique charm. The least expensive rooms are snug and have views of a roof or parking lot; the best are junior suites with large windows and balconies fronting the shore. Almost half the hotel's rooms are in the renovated, seven-story contemporary tower—it has more living space but none of the historical ambience. Since 2001, the Del has done nonstop restoration and upgrading, with recent additions including a state-of-the-art spa and the creation of **Beach Village.** These privately owned two- and three-bedroom rental condos feature fireplaces and oceanview balconies or terraces.

1500 Orange Ave., Coronado, CA 92118. www.hoteldel.com. © **800/468-3533** or 619/435-6611. Fax 619/522-8238. 757 rooms. From $300 double; from $545 suite; from $1,200 cottage. Extra person $25. $25-per-day resort fee. Minimum stay requirements apply most weekends. Children 17 and under stay free in parent's room. AE, DC, DISC, MC, V. Valet parking $35; self-parking $25. Bus: 901 or 904. From Coronado Bridge, turn left onto Orange Ave. **Amenities:** 5 restaurants; 4 bars; airport transfers; babysitting; bikes; children's programs; concierge; health club; 2 Jacuzzis; 2 outdoor pools; room service; full-service spa. *In room:* A/C, TV, hair dryer, minibar, free Wi-Fi.

EXPENSIVE

El Cordova Hotel ★   This Spanish hacienda across the street from the Hotel del Coronado began life as a private mansion in 1902. By the 1930s, it had become a hotel, the original building augmented by a series of attachments hosting retail shops along the ground-floor arcade. Shaped like a baseball diamond and surrounding a courtyard with meandering tiled pathways, flowering shrubs, a swimming pool, and patio seating for **Miguel's Cocina** Mexican restaurant, El Cordova pleasantly hums with activity. Each room differs from the next—some have a Mexican Colonial feel, while others evoke comfy beach cottages. Most rooms at this nonsmoking property have kitchenettes with gas stoves; all are no-frills, with ceiling fans and brightly tiled bathrooms. El Cordova's prime location makes it a popular option; make reservations well in advance of a summer stay.

1351 Orange Ave. (at Adella Ave.), Coronado, CA 92118. www.elcordovahotel.com. © **800/229-2032** or 619/435-4131. Fax 619/435-0632. 40 units. From $185 double; from $255 suite. Children 11 and under stay free in parent's room. AE, DC, DISC, MC, V. Parking in neighboring structure $8. Bus: 901 or 904. From Coronado Bridge, turn left onto Orange Ave. **Amenities:** 4 restaurants; bikes; Jacuzzi; outdoor pool; watersports equipment/rentals. *In room:* A/C, TV, free Wi-Fi.

Glorietta Bay Inn ★★   Across the street from the Hotel Del, this pretty property consists of the historic John D. Spreckels mansion (1908) and several younger—and decidedly less charming—motel-style buildings. The mansion has

11 rooms with original fixtures, a grand staircase, and a music room with a player piano; the guest rooms are decked out in antiques. Rooms and suites in the 1950s annexes are much less expensive but were upgraded from motel-plain to better match the main house; some have kitchenettes and marina views. The least expensive units are small, with parking-lot views. Glorietta Bay, with its boat rentals and excursions, is right outside your door, and the hotel is within easy walking distance of the beach, golfing, tennis, watersports, shopping, and dining. Rooms in the mansion book early but are worth the extra effort and expense. *Note:* This is a nonsmoking hotel.

1630 Glorietta Blvd. (near Orange Ave.), Coronado, CA 92118. www.gloriettabayinn.com. © **800/283-9383** or 619/435-3101. Fax 619/435-6182. 100 units. From $185 double; from $260 suite (from $425 in summer). Extra person $10. Rates include continental breakfast and after-noon refreshment. Children 17 and under stay free in parent's room. AE, DC, DISC, MC, V. Self-parking $10. Bus: 901 or 904. From Coronado Bridge, turn left onto Orange Ave. After 2 miles, turn left onto Glorietta Blvd.; the inn is across the street from the Hotel del Coronado. **Amenities:** Babysitting; concierge; access to nearby health club; Jacuzzi; outdoor pool; spa services. *In room:* A/C, TV/DVD, CD player, fridge, hair dryer, free Wi-Fi.

Loews Coronado Bay Resort ★★ ☺   The area's most removed hotel, this is the perfect place to really get away from it all. On its own private peninsula 4 miles south of downtown Coronado, across the highway from the Silver Strand State Beach, the Loews is an all-inclusive resort destination. There is a plethora of water-related activities such as sailing and jet-skiing from the private 80-slip marina; there's also direct, private access to the beach. This is a family-friendly place with special (healthy) kids' menus, supervised children's activities, and teen-themed DVDs and Game Boys to borrow; pets are always welcome at Loews, too. Adult pleasures include romantic gondola rides through the canals of the adjacent Coronado Cays, an exclusive, waterside community; fine dining at the wonderful **Mistral** restaurant (ask for table 61 or 64 for best vistas); and a full-service spa.

4000 Coronado Bay Rd., Coronado, CA 92118. www.loewshotels.com. © **800/815-6397** or 619/424-4000. Fax 619/424-4400. 439 units. From $269 double; from $489 suite. Extra person $25. Up to 2 children 17 and under stay free in parent's room. Packages available. AE, DC, DISC, MC, V. Valet parking $28; self-parking $22. Bus: 901. From Coronado Bridge, turn left onto Orange Ave., left onto Coronado Bay Rd. Pets accepted for $25. **Amenities:** 2 restaurants; 2 bars; babysitting and pet-sitting; children's programs; concierge; exercise room and classes; 2 Jacuzzis; 3 outdoor pools; room service; spa; 3 lighted tennis courts; marina w/watersports equipment/rentals. *In room:* A/C, TV/DVD, CD player, hair dryer, minibar, Wi-Fi ($13).

INEXPENSIVE

The Village Inn ⚜   Its location a block or two from Coronado's main sights—the Hotel Del, the beach, shopping, and cafes—is this inn's most appealing fea-ture. Historic charm runs a close second; a plaque outside identifies the three-story brick-and-stucco hotel as the once-chic Blue Lantern Inn, built in 1928. The vintage lobby sets the mood in this European-style hostelry; each simple but well-maintained room holds a four-poster bed and antique dressers and armoires, plus lovely Battenburg lace bedcovers and shams. Front rooms enjoy the best view, and the communal full kitchen is available day and night for guest use. The inn's only Achilles' heel is its tiny (but private) bathrooms, though some have been updated with Jacuzzi tubs.

1017 Park Place (at Orange Ave.), Coronado, CA 92118. www.coronadovillageinn.com. ☎ **619/435-9318.** 15 units. $85–$95 double. Rates include continental breakfast. AE, MC, V. Parking available on street. Bus: 901 or 904. From Coronado Bridge, turn left onto Orange Ave. and then right on Park Place. **Amenities:** Kitchen. *In room:* TV.

WHERE TO EAT

While San Diego hasn't achieved top-tier foodie status, its culinary profile is at an all-time high. Young Turk chefs, mentored by major players, have set up shop here, often incorporating the bounty of local farms and ranches into their menus. The city still clings to conservative tastes and service can often be casual to the point of indifference, but the pieces are in place and San Diego's dining renaissance is well underway.

What follows is an abbreviated sampling of highlights from the local dining scene, with an emphasis on the best of the best in all price categories, locations, and cuisines. For a greater selection of reviews, see *Frommer's San Diego 2012.*

Downtown

VERY EXPENSIVE

Nobu ★★ SUSHI/PACIFIC RIM/ASIAN FUSION   Chef Nobu Matsuhisa has earned a devoted worldwide following for his creative, celebrity-approved sushi and Asian fusion cuisine. Following a 3-year stint in Peru (hence the seviche and Pisco sours on the Nobu menu), Matsuhisa found himself in Los Angeles, where he became friends with actor Robert De Niro, now one of his partners for the Nobu franchise installed at the **Hard Rock Hotel** (p. 780). You may hear complaints about the restaurant's pricey fare, lean portions, and full-volume ambience, but you'll be hard-pressed to argue with the textures, flavors, and beautiful presentations. House specialties include the broiled black cod with miso and the Sino-Latino scallops tiradito; when in doubt, entrust yourself to the chef with the *omakase* tasting menu.

207 Fifth Ave (at L St.), Gaslamp Quarter. ☎ **619/814-4124.** www.noburestaurants.com. Reservations recommended. Main courses $29–$96; sushi $5–$15. AE, DC, DISC, MC, V. Sun–Thurs 5:30–10:15pm; Fri–Sat 5:30–11:15pm. Lounge/bar Sun–Thurs 5–10:15pm; Fri–Sat 5–11:15pm. Valet parking $25–$30 with validation. Trolley: Gaslamp Quarter.

EXPENSIVE

Anthology ★★★ MEDITERRANEAN   It's difficult to categorize Anthology: Is it a fine-dining establishment or a world-class live music venue? The answer to both is a resounding yes. Featuring a menu with Mediterranean flair (pan-seared sea bass soup, house-made fettuccine) and highlighted by local ingredients, Anthology is also a sophisticated, acoustically excellent concert hall. The music is eclectic, with an emphasis on jazz (think heavy hitters like Poncho Sanchez and Chick Corea), world music, and blues. It won't drown out the food, though—in fact, you'll know the band onstage is really jamming when you're able to tear your attention away from your meal.

1337 India St. (btw. A and Ash sts.), downtown. ☎ **619/595-0300.** www.anthologysd.com. Reservations recommended. Main courses $17–$28. AE, DISC, MC, V. Tues–Sat 5:30–11pm; open selected Sun. Valet parking $10 (Fri–Sat). Bus: 83.

Candelas ★★ MEXICAN   If you're in the mood for a sophisticated, romantic fine-dining experience, look no further than Candelas; if you're looking for tacos and burritos, go somewhere else. Owner Alberto Mestre and executive chef Eduardo Baeza are both natives of Mexico City and brought with them that city's culinary influences, which often blend Mexican and European elements. The chef's signature creation is *langosta Baeza*: fresh lobster in its shell, stuffed with mushrooms, chilies, onions, bacon, and tequila. Candelas, which also has a sexy lounge next door, may forever alter your notion of Mexican food. The restaurant has given sleepy Coronado a jolt, as well, opening a view-enhanced location at the Ferry Landing, 1201 First St. (𝄞 **619/435-4900**), serving dinner nightly, weekday lunch, and Sunday brunch.

416 Third Ave. (at J St.), Gaslamp Quarter. 𝄞 **619/702-4455.** www.candelas-sd.com. Reservations recommended. Main courses $7–$16 breakfast, $18–$53 dinner. AE, DC, DISC, MC, V. Breakfast Sat–Sun 8:30am–2pm; dinner daily 5–11pm. Bus: 11 or 120. Trolley: Convention Center.

Cowboy Star ★★ AMERICAN   This restaurant and butcher shop celebrates the Old West as seen through the squint of a celluloid cowboy. It's an unabashed homage to the Hollywood Westerns of the 1930s and 1940s, combined with an unstinting commitment to the finest products available. Specializing in dry-aged meats and game fowl, all products come from sustainable sources; everything is organic, hormone free, grass fed, or free-range. The adjacent butcher shop stocks the same cuts you get at the restaurant and sells house-made sauces and rubs too. The decor features exposed wood beams and cow skulls but never dips into kitsch; you can definitely picture Gary Cooper in one of the deep booths, sipping on one of the many specialty cocktails, unwinding after a day on the set.

650 10th Ave. (btw. G and Market sts.), East Village. 𝄞 **619/450-5880.** www.thecowboystar. com. Reservations recommended. Main courses $8–$82 lunch, $22–$82 dinner. AE, DISC, MC, V. Lunch Tues–Fri 11:30am–2:30pm; dinner Tues–Thurs 5–10pm, Fri–Sat 5–10:30pm, Sun 5–9pm; bar menu Tues–Sat from 4pm. Butcher shop Tues–Sat noon–7pm. Bus: 3, 5, 11, 901, or 929. Trolley: Park and Market.

Island Prime ★★ SEAFOOD   With its over-the-water dining, patio with fireplace, plentiful free parking, and spectacular bay and skyline views, it would be easy to understand if Island Prime didn't bother to make its food interesting. Executive chef Deborah Scott isn't just going through the motions here, though. With such dishes as shaved corn with black truffle and fresh herbs, hazelnut-crusted diver scallops, and porcini-dusted rack of Colorado lamb with Moroccan-spiced tomato jam, the views actually have some competition. The restaurant's C-Level Lounge serves lunch and has a bar menu of both food and specialty cocktails. Scott is also the mastermind behind the successful eateries **Kemo Sabe** and **Indigo Grill.** Both do mash-ups of Pacific Coast and Mexican/Southwestern cuisine to good effect and are worth a visit. Kemo Sabe is at 3958 Fifth Ave., Hillcrest (𝄞 **619/220-6802**); Indigo Grill is at 1536 India St., Little Italy (𝄞 **619/234-6802**).

880 Harbor Island Dr., Embarcadero. 𝄞 **619/298-6802.** www.cohnrestaurants.com. Reservations recommended. Main courses $11–$29 lunch, $25–$49 dinner. AE, DC, DISC, MC, V. Sun–Thurs 11:30am–10pm; Fri–Sat 11:30am–11pm. Free parking. Bus: 923 or 992.

The Oceanaire Seafood Room ★★ SEAFOOD   As you sweep up the dramatic staircase of the Oceanaire, the retro-nautical decor may evoke the grand elegance of a *Titanic*-style luxury liner. Don't worry, though; the only iceberg ahead is of the lettuce variety. A Minneapolis-based chain that opened here in 2004, Oceanaire features top local products as well as fish imported daily from around the globe. The eclectic preparations incorporate elements of Pacific Rim, Italian, classic French, and Asian cuisine, or you can have your catch-of-the-day simply grilled or broiled. Non–fish eaters can enjoy top-quality prime beef, chicken, and pork.

400 J St. (at Fourth Ave.), Gaslamp Quarter. ✆ **619/858-2277.** www.theoceanaire.com. Reservations recommended. Main courses $19–$55. AE, DISC, MC, V. Sun–Thurs 5–10pm; Fri–Sat 5–11pm. Valet parking from 5pm $15–$20. Bus: 3, 11, or 120. Trolley: Convention Center.

MODERATE

Cafe Chloe ★★ FRENCH   Creative, whimsical touches (such as a children's play area, a retail space, and a patio built for two) abound at this bistro infused with the refined tastes and joie de vivre of its proprietors. Cafe Chloe is small, it's loud when at capacity, and its tiny kitchen can get backed up. But the neighborly conviviality—combined with a short-but-sweet French-inspired menu covering breakfast, lunch, dinner, and weekend brunch—makes for a winning dining experience, and one unique enough to create a stir in ever-morphing San Diego.

721 Ninth Ave. (at G St.), East Village. ✆ **619/232-3242.** www.cafechloe.com. Reservations for parties of 5 or more, or afternoon tea (3–5pm) only. Main courses $8–$13 breakfast, $7–$18 lunch, $15–$23 dinner. AE, MC, V. Mon–Fri 7:30am–10:30pm; Sat 8:30am–10:30pm; Sun 8:30am–9:30pm. Bus: 3, 5, 11, 901, or 929.

El Camino ★ MEXICAN   Combining a lively south-of-the-border cantina ambience with a hipster aesthetic, this *"super cocina mexicana"* serves simple, traditional fare like open-face street-style tacos, enchiladas, and burritos created from local, organic products (vegetarian offerings are available, too). Adorned with bold and kitschy graphics, including a graffiti-inspired Day of the Dead mural that bursts from the restaurant's back wall, El Camino segues into a casual nightspot with DJs and live music (Wed features local jazz mainstay Gilbert Castellanos). The open-air back patio, where jets scream overhead on approach to Lindbergh Field, is a cool hangout with vintage Atari games and air hockey.

2400 India St. (at W. Kalmia St.), Little Italy. ✆ **619/685-3881.** www.elcaminosd.com. Main courses $9–$14. AE, MC, V. Mon 5–10pm; Tues–Sat 5–11pm; Sun 10am–10pm. Bar nightly until 1 or 2am. Bus: 83.

Red Pearl Kitchen ★★ CHINESE/ASIAN FUSION   Specializing in dim sum dishes with a contemporary, pan-Asian flair, this sexy Gaslamp Quarter restaurant is decorated in hues of deep red and features stone and tile accents, a cool pebbled floor, some nice deep booths, and two private dining areas. At Red Pearl, you may see a kung fu flick on one of the flatscreens over the bar while dining on your strawberry-cinnamon short ribs, duck lettuce wraps, or wok-fired Kobe beef with papaya and mint. For dessert, don't miss the airy *andagi,* the Japanese version of a donut hole. If all those reality-TV cooking shows have whetted your appetite for a glimpse of professionals in action, Red Pearl has an in-kitchen chef's table seating up to 12 people. Like any Chinese restaurant worth its noodles, Red Pearl also has takeout.

440 J St. (btw. Fourth and Fifth aves.), Gaslamp Quarter. ✆ **619/231-1100.** www.redpearl kitchen.com/sandiego. Reservations recommended. Main courses $10–$24. AE, MC, V. Daily 5–10pm. Valet parking $15. Bus: 3, 11, or 120. Trolley: Convention Center or Gaslamp Quarter.

INEXPENSIVE

Extraordinary Desserts ★★★ DESSERTS/LIGHT FARE Dozens of divine creations are available daily at this architecturally striking space, including a passion fruit ricotta torte bursting with kiwis, strawberries, and bananas, or a *gianduia* (chocolate cake lathered with hazelnut butter cream, chocolate mousse, and boysenberry preserves, sprinkled with shards of praline). The menu also includes panini, salads, and artisan cheeses, as well as organic wines, boutique beers, and more than 50 different loose-leaf teas; a light breakfast featuring pastries, granola, and smoked salmon is offered Sundays from 11am to 2pm ($17). Extraordinary Desserts also sells its own line of jams, chutneys, syrups, spices, and confections. The original location in Hillcrest, 2929 Fifth Ave. (☏ **619/294-2132**), is more cozy and intimate but serves only desserts and does not have alcohol.

1430 Union St. (at Ash St.), Little Italy. ☏ **619/294-7001.** www.extraordinarydesserts.com. Desserts $2–$9; salads and sandwiches $8–$18. AE, MC, V. Mon–Thurs 8:30am–11pm; Fri 8:30am–midnight; Sat 10am–midnight; Sun 10am–11pm. Bus: 30.

Filippi's Pizza Grotto ◢ ITALIAN When longtime locals think "Little Italy," Filippi's often comes to mind. To get to the dining area, decorated with Chianti bottles and red-checked tablecloths, you walk through a "cash and carry" Italian grocery store and deli stocked with cheeses, pastas, wines, bottles of olive oil, and salamis. You might even end up eating behind shelves of canned olives, but don't feel bad—this has been a tradition since 1950. Filippi's has more than 15 pizza varieties (including vegetarian), plus huge portions of spaghetti, lasagna, and other pasta; children's portions are available, too. The line to get in on Friday and Saturday can look intimidating, but it moves quickly. This was the first of a dozen branches throughout the county, including one in **Pacific Beach** at 962 Garnet Ave. (☏ **858/483-6222**).

1747 India St. (btw. Date and Fir sts.), Little Italy. ☏ **619/232-5094.** www.realcheesepizza.com. Reservations Mon–Thurs for groups of 8 or more. Main courses $6–$13. AE, DC, DISC, MC, V. Sun–Mon 11am–10pm; Tues–Thurs 11am–10:30pm; Fri–Sat 11am–11:30pm. Deli daily at 8am. Free parking. Bus: 83. Trolley: Little Italy.

Hillcrest/Uptown

VERY EXPENSIVE

Bertrand at Mister A's ★★★ AMERICAN/MEDITERRANEAN Since 1965, San Diegans have come to high-rise Mister A's for proms, anniversaries, power meals, and other special occasions. Mister A's star began to wane in the '80s, however, despite its unsurpassed views of Point Loma, downtown, and Balboa Park. In 2000, it finally closed—only to reopen 4 months later, after a reported $1-million makeover. The original Mister A's, with its dark, red-velvet interiors and cocktail waitresses in campy one-shouldered gowns, was reborn into Bertrand at Mister A's—an elegant, bright, sophisticated space, with an array of modern art. The seasonal menu is modern American with a French/Mediterranean twist; a bar/patio menu gives diners on a budget access to the unsurpassed vistas.

2550 Fifth Ave. (at Laurel St.), Hillcrest. ☏ **619/239-1377.** www.bertrandatmisteras.com. Reservations recommended. Main courses $18–$30 lunch, $26–$50 dinner. AE, DC, MC, V. Mon–Fri 11:30am–2:30pm and 5:30–9:30pm; Sat–Sun 5–9:30pm. Valet parking $9. Bus: 3 or 120.

EXPENSIVE

The Tractor Room ★★ AMERICAN   Dark and woody, with a touch of industrial design, this self-described "hunting lodge" is a carnivore's delight and a haven for those who like their spirits amber and peaty. Prominently featuring game meats such as bison, rabbit, venison, and boar, as well as manly cuts of steak, the Tractor Room also has a massive selection of scotch, whiskey, bourbon, and rye. Vegetarians? Well, this place even throws a stick of jerky into its Bloody Mary, so not so much. Non–meat eaters will do best contenting themselves at the bar with cocktails both classic and inventive (many of which have no meat products in them), or the weekend brunch, where you'll find flapjacks, French toast, and granola on the menu, along with the elk hash.

3687 Fifth Ave. (at Pennsylvania Ave.), Hillcrest. ✆ **619/543-1007.** www.thetractorroom.com. Main courses $15–$36. AE, DISC, MC, V. Mon–Tues 5pm–midnight (kitchen till 11:30pm); Wed–Thurs 5:30pm–close; Fri 5:30pm–1am (kitchen till midnight); Sat 9am–2pm and 5:30pm–1am (kitchen till midnight); Sun 9am–2pm and 5:30pm–midnight (kitchen till 11:30pm). Bus: 3 or 120.

MODERATE

Cucina Urbana ★★★ ITALIAN   When the recession gives you lemons, what's a restaurateur to do but make . . . Italian food? That's what Tracy Borkum has done by boldly scrapping Laurel, her French/Med bistro and opening in its place the casually cool and visually striking Cucina Urbana. The new concept has been a resounding smash, and the restaurant has become one of the city's food-scene darlings, featuring rustic Italian fare (often sourced from local and organic producers) that keeps one's pocketbook in mind while at no time sacrificing quality or creativity. No dish is more than $20, and there's a small-but-thoughtful wine-shop component that allows you to browse for a bottle and enjoy it at retail cost plus $7 corkage. Highlights include the Gorgonzola-walnut mousse with sun-dried tomato on crostini, gourmet wood-fired pizzas, the daily salami and cheese boards, and artisanal cocktails.

505 Laurel St. (at Fifth Ave.), Balboa Park. ✆ **619/239-2222.** www.sdurbankitchen.com. Reservations recommended. Main courses $12–$20. AE, DISC, MC, V. Sun–Mon 5–9pm; Tues–Thurs 5–10pm; Fri–Sat 5–10:30pm (limited menu till midnight); lunch Tues–Fri 11:30am–2pm. Valet parking $7 (Fri–Sat evenings only). Bus: 3 or 120.

Urban Solace ★★ AMERICAN   One of the bright lights along North Park's burgeoning restaurant row, this loud and cheerful spot will definitely take you to a happy place. With its New Orleans–style facade, outdoor patio, and menu of American comfort food, Urban Solace offers just that. Look for creative, contemporary takes on old standards like the lamb meatloaf with figs, pine nuts, and feta cheese; or mac 'n' cheese with duck confit and blue cheese. The bacon-wrapped trout stuffed with spinach and mushrooms is also a winner. A selection of local beer, West Coast wines, and specialty cocktails—as well as Sunday brunch served with a side of live bluegrass music—ensure that the good times keep rolling.

3823 30th St. (at University Ave.), North Park. ✆ **619/295-6465.** www.urbansolace.net. Main courses $9–$16 lunch, $14–$20 dinner. AE, DISC, MC, V. Mon–Thurs 11:30am–10pm; Fri–Sat 11:30am–11pm; Sun 10am–2:30pm and 5–9pm. Bus: 2, 6, 7, or 10.

INEXPENSIVE

Bread & Cie. ★★ LIGHT FARE/MEDITERRANEAN   The traditions of European artisan bread-making and attention to the fine points of texture and crust quickly catapulted Bread & Cie. to local stardom—they now supply bread to more than 75 local restaurants. Some favorites are available daily, like anise and fig, black olive, and jalapeño and cheese; others are available just 1 or 2 days a week. Ask for a free sample or order one of the many Mediterranean-inspired sandwiches. A specialty coffee drink perfectly accompanies a light breakfast of fresh scones, muffins, and homemade granola with yogurt; seating is at bistro-style tables in full view of the busy ovens.

350 University Ave. (at Fourth St.), Hillcrest. © **619/683-9322.** www.breadandcie.com. Reservations not accepted. Sandwiches and light meals $4–$9. DISC, MC, V. Mon–Fri 7am–7pm; Sat 7am–6pm; Sun 8am–6pm. Bus: 1, 3, 10, 11, or 120.

Bronx Pizza ★ 🍴 ITALIAN   With its red vinyl booths, checkered curtains, and pictures of boxers on the walls, the interior dining room of this pizzeria looks as if it were airlifted straight out of the boroughs of New York. Bronx Pizza makes only pizzas and calzones—no salads, no chicken wings. And if there's a line out the door (a frequent occurrence), don't hesitate to order when you get to the counter: These guys will definitely drop a little New York attitude on you, and you may find yourself living out the *Seinfeld* Soup Nazi episode. Choices are simple, though. It's all thin-crust, 18-inch pies, or by the slice, with straightforward toppings—although Bronx Pizza has made concessions to the locals by including such ingredients as marinated artichokes and pesto.

111 Washington St. (at First Ave.), Hillcrest. © **619/291-3341.** www.bronxpizza.com. Phone orders accepted for full pies. Pies $13–$20; $2.50 by the slice. No credit cards. Sun–Thurs 11am–10pm; Fri–Sat 11am–11pm. Street parking. Bus: 3, 10, or 83.

Old Town & Mission Valley

EXPENSIVE

El Agave Tequileria ★★ MEXICAN   Don't be misled by this restaurant's less-than-impressive location above a liquor store. The regional Mexican cuisine here leaves Old Town's touristy fajitas and *cerveza* joints far behind. El Agave is named for the plant from which tequila and its smoky cousin mescal are derived, and the restaurant boasts more than 850 different brands. Needless to say, El Agave serves some of the best margaritas in town. Even teetotalers, though, will enjoy the restaurant's authentically flavored mole sauces—from Taxco, rich with walnuts; tangy tomatillo from Oaxaca; and the more familiar dark mole flavored with chocolate and sesame.

2304 San Diego Ave., Old Town. © **619/220-0692.** www.elagave.com. Reservations recommended. Main courses $10–$20 lunch, $16–$32 dinner. AE, MC, V. Daily 11am–10pm. Street parking. Bus: Numerous Old Town routes, including 8, 9, 10, 28, and 30. Trolley: Old Town.

MODERATE

Berta's Latin American Restaurant ★ LATIN AMERICAN   Housed in a charming, basic cottage tucked away on a side street, Berta's faithfully re-creates the sunny flavors of Central and South America, where slow cooking mellows the heat of chilies and other spices. Mouthwatering dishes include Guatemalan *chilemal,* a rich pork-and-vegetable casserole with chilies, cornmeal *masa,* coriander, and cloves; or try the Salvadoran *pupusas* (at lunch only)—dense corn-mash turnovers with melted cheese and black beans, their texture perfectly offset with crunchy cabbage salad and one of Berta's special salsas. You can also opt for a table full of Spanish-style tapas, grazing alternately on crispy cheese or beef *empanadas* (filled turnovers), strong Spanish olives, or *pincho moruno* (skewered lamb and onion redolent of spices and red saffron).

3928 Twiggs St. (at Congress St.), Old Town. ☏ **619/295-2343.** www.bertasinoldtown.com. Main courses $7–$12 lunch, $13–$19 dinner. AE, DISC, MC, V. Tues–Sun 11am–10pm (lunch menu till 3pm). Free parking. Bus: Numerous Old Town routes, including 8, 9, 10, 28, and 30. Trolley: Old Town.

INEXPENSIVE

Living Room Cafe & Bistro COFFEE & TEA/AMERICAN   Once a humble coffeehouse, the Living Room has added "cafe and bistro" to its name and expanded its menu. Covering breakfast, lunch, and dinner, the Living Room features omelets and waffles, hearty sandwiches, burgers, salads, quiches, and personal-sized pizzas. In a nod to the neighborhood, there are also Mexican staples like fajitas, burritos, and fish tacos. Keeping true to its roots, though, plenty of specialty coffee drinks are still available, in addition to beer, wine, margaritas, and martinis. Grab a patio table in the courtyard of this lovely old house and enjoy the people-watching; there's also delivery service from 10am to 4pm Monday through Saturday. Other locations are in La Jolla at 1010 Prospect St. (☏ **858/459-1187**), in Point Loma at 1018 Rosecrans St. (☏ **619/222-6852**), and near San Diego State University at 5900 El Cajon Blvd. (☏ **619/286-8434**).

2541 San Diego Ave., Old Town. ☏ **619/325-4445.** www.livingroomcafe.com. Most menu items $6–$10. AE, DISC, MC, V. Sun–Thurs 7am–10pm; Fri–Sat 7am–midnight. Bus: Numerous Old Town routes, including 8, 9, 10, 28, and 30. Trolley: Old Town.

Mission Bay & the Beaches

VERY EXPENSIVE

Baleen ★★ ☺ SEAFOOD/CALIFORNIAN   This attractive waterfront eatery is right in the middle of Mission Bay at the **Paradise Point Resort** (p. 790). With its lush bayfront view (and a dining deck that's sublime on warm evenings), it's easy to miss the design details indoors—from a monkey motif that includes simians hanging off chandeliers to specialized serving platters for many of Baleen's artistically arranged dishes. Ocean fare takes precedence, and local fish and shellfish are featured in a chef's tasting menu; also on offer is a classic surf and turf or a selection of wood-roasted meats and seafood. ***Note:*** This is a family-oriented resort, so knee-high types may be sharing the space; a children's menu goes beyond the usual burgers-and-fries option to include items such as scampi and petit filet.

1404 Vacation Rd. (Paradise Point Resort), Mission Bay. ☏ **858/490-6363.** www.paradisepoint. com. Reservations recommended. Main courses $22–$78. AE, DC, DISC, MC, V. Sun–Thurs 5–9pm; Fri–Sat 5–10pm. Free parking. Bus: 9.

MODERATE

Caffé Bella Italia ★★ ITALIAN   It's well away from the surf, has a rather odd-looking exterior, and is in a less-than-inspiring section of PB, but this place is lovely inside—and the food can knock your socks off. It's the best spot in the area for shellfish-laden pasta, wood-fired pizzas (a selection of more than 30), and management that welcomes guests like family. Romantic lighting, sheer draperies, and warm earth tones create a Mediterranean ambience, assisted by the lilting Milanese accents of the staff (when the din of a few dozen happy diners doesn't drown them out, that is). A sister restaurant, the stylish **Solare,** is at

EATING ON THE GO: BAJA fish tacos

A native of Baja, California, fish tacos were popularized in San Diego by **Rubio's Fresh Mexican Grill** in the early 1980s. Rubio's has since grown into a sizable chain, and it's a good option if you're on the go—the original stand is still operating at the east end of Pacific Beach, 4504 E. Mission Bay Dr. (© 858/272-2801; www.rubios. com). Better yet are such retail fish market/eateries as **Bay Park Fish Co. ★**, 4121 Ashton St., Bay Park (© 619/276-3474; www.bayparkfishco.com); **Blue Water Seafood Market and Grill ★**, 3667 India St., Mission Hills (© 619/497-0914); and **Point Loma Seafoods ★**, 2805 Emerson St., Point Loma (© 619/223-1109; www.pointloma seafoods.com).

Other top choices include the **Brigantine** (www.brigantine.com), 2725 Shelter Island Dr., Shelter Island (© 619/224-2871), 1333 Orange Ave., Coronado (© 619/435-4166), and 3263 Camino del Mar, Del Mar (© 858/481-1166); **Mamá Testa ★**, 1417A University Ave., Hillcrest (© 619/298-8226; www.mamatestata-queria.com); **South Beach Bar & Grill,** 5059 Newport Ave., Ocean Beach (© 619/226-4577; www.southbeachob. com); and **Wahoo's Fish Taco** (www. wahoos.com), 639 Pearl St., La Jolla (© 858/459-0027), 1006 N. El Camino Real, Encinitas (© 760/753-5060), 2195 Station Village Way, Mission Valley (© 619/299-4550), and 3944 W. Point Loma Blvd., Sports Arena area (© 619/222-0020).

Liberty Station in Point Loma, 2820 Roosevelt Dr. (© **619/270-9670;** www. solarelounge.com).

1525 Garnet Ave. (btw. Ingraham and Haines sts.), Pacific Beach. © **858/273-1224.** www.caffe bellaitalia.com. Reservations suggested for dinner. Main courses $13–$22. AE, DC, DISC, MC, V. Daily 4:30–10pm. Free (small) parking lot. Bus: 9 or 27.

The Fishery ★ 🍴 SEAFOOD You're pretty well guaranteed seafood fresh off the boat at this off-the-beaten-track establishment: It's really a wholesale warehouse and retail fish market with a casual restaurant attached. The owners work with local, national, and global suppliers, and the wide range of bounty is reflected in an eclectic menu that ranges from sushi rolls and clam chowder, to Scottish salmon and Mexican lobster. The Fishery makes an effort to offer sustainable product, so look for owner-caught harpooned swordfish in season. In spite of its informal air, there's a surprisingly impressive wine list, including some 35 vinos served by the glass; belly up to the restaurant's Fish Bar for some Prosecco and mussels.

5040 Cass St. (at Opal St., ¾ mile north of Garnet Ave.), Pacific Beach. © **858/272-9985.** www. pacshell.com. Reservations recommended for dinner. Main courses $9–$20 lunch, $10–$38 dinner. AE, DISC, MC, V. Daily 11am–10pm. Street parking usually available. Bus: 30.

Gringo's ★ MEXICAN This upscale space features warm woods, cool flagstone, and trendy lighting; a large patio is primed with heaters and fire pits most evenings. The menu offers dishes the average gringo will recognize (quesadillas, fajitas, burritos), but flip it over and you'll find regional specialties from all over Mexico—Oaxaca, the Yucatán, and Mexico's Pacific coast. Look for chicken breast stuffed with goat cheese and corn, and then lathered in a sauce of *huitlacoche;* or a poblano chili stuffed with picadillo and draped in walnut-cream sauce with a drizzle of pomegranate reduction. The margarita options, with more than 100 tequilas available, are worth inspecting, as are the Mexican wines. Sunday brunch is available from 9am to 2pm.

4474 Mission Blvd. (at Garnet Ave.), Pacific Beach. ℂ **858/490-2877.** www.gringoscantina.com. Reservations suggested for weekends. Main courses $6–$14 lunch, $8–$31 dinner, $17–$20 brunch. AE, DC, DISC, MC, V. Mon–Fri 11am–11pm; Sat–Sun 11am–10pm. Free (small) parking lot. Bus: 8, 9, 27, or 30.

Sushi Ota ★★★ 🎁 SUSHI   Masterful chef/owner Yukito Ota creates San Diego's finest sushi. This sophisticated, traditional restaurant (no Asian fusion here) is a minimalist bento box with stark white walls and black furniture, softened by indirect diffused lighting. The sushi menu is short—discerning regulars look first to the daily specials posted behind the counter. The city's most experienced chefs, with nimble fingers and seriously sharp knives, turn the day's fresh catch into artful bundles. The rest of the varied menu features seafood, teriyaki-glazed meats, tempura, and appetizers perfect for accompanying sushi. The restaurant is in a nondescript part of Pacific Beach, adjacent to a laundromat and convenience store in a mini-mall, though none of that should discourage you from seeking it out.

4529 Mission Bay Dr. (at Bunker Hill), Pacific Beach. ℂ **858/270-5670.** Reservations strongly recommended on weekends. Main courses $6–$14 lunch, $9–$22 dinner; sushi $4–$13. AE, MC, V. Mon 5:30–10:30pm; Tues–Fri 11:30am–2pm and 5:30–10:30pm; Sat–Sun 5–10:30pm. Free parking (additional lot behind the mall). Bus: 30.

The 3rd Corner ★★ FRENCH   Set in an old beach bungalow on the outskirts of Ocean Beach, the 3rd Corner is part wine shop, part bistro, part neighborhood bar—and all intimate, convivial, and unique. You can wander through racks of wine (about 1,000 bottles are available at any given time), pick the one you like, and find yourself a spot to enjoy a menu of small plates and entrees with a French-Mediterranean flair ($5 corkage fee). Seating for dining is limited, but there's a full bar, lounge, and patio. Look for wine-friendly fare like charcuterie plates, an array of cheeses, and pâté, as well as black truffle risotto and duck confit; Sunday brunch is served 11am to 3pm. Best of all, food and drinks are served late—until 1am (except Mon). There's also an outpost in Encinitas at the Lumberyard shopping center, 897 S. Coast Hwy. (ℂ **760/942-2104**).

2265 Bacon St. (at W. Point Loma Blvd.), Ocean Beach. ℂ **619/223-2700.** www.the3rdcorner. com. Main courses $10–$21. AE, DISC, MC, V. Kitchen Tues–Sun 11:30am–1am. Wine shop Tues–Sun 10am–1:30am. Free parking. Bus: 35 or 923.

INEXPENSIVE

The Mission ★ 🍴 BREAKFAST/LIGHT FARE   Set alongside the funky surf shops and bikini boutiques of bohemian Mission Beach, this is the neighborhood's central meeting place. It attracts more than just locals, however, and it has siblings near the ballpark and east of Hillcrest. The menu features all-day breakfasts, from traditional pancakes to nouvelle egg dishes, to burritos and quesadillas; standouts include chicken-apple sausage with eggs and a mound of rosemary potatoes, and cinnamon French toast with blackberry purée. At lunch, the menu expands for sandwiches, salads, and a few Chino-Latino items such as ginger-sesame chicken tacos. The other locations are at 2801 University Ave., in North Park (ℂ **619/220-8992**), and in a historic building at 1250 J St., downtown (ℂ **619/232-7662**).

3795 Mission Blvd. (at San Jose), Mission Beach. ℰ **858/488-9060.** All items $6–$10. AE, MC, V. Daily 7am–3pm. Bus: 8.

La Jolla

VERY EXPENSIVE

The Marine Room ★★★ 📷 FRENCH/CALIFORNIAN   Since 1941, San Diego's most celebrated dining room has been this shorefront institution. Executive chef Bernard Guillas of Brittany and chef de cuisine Ron Oliver work with local produce but never hesitate to pursue unusual flavors from other corners of the globe—like pomegranate-macadamia-coated Scottish salmon with red quinoa, bok choy, and lemon verbena essence; or nectarine-glazed pompano with crab risotto and a sake emulsion. The Marine Room ranks as one of San Diego's most expensive venues, but it's usually filled to the gills on weekends; weekdays it's much easier to score a table. Ideally, schedule your reservation a half-hour or so before sunset; if you can't get in at that magic hour, experience sundown by the bar—a more wallet-friendly lounge and a happy hour menu are available.

2000 Spindrift Dr., La Jolla. ℰ **866/644-2351.** www.marineroom.com. Reservations recommended, especially weekends. Main courses $27–$48. AE, DC, DISC, MC, V. Daily 5:30–9pm. Lounge daily from 4pm. Valet parking $5. Bus: 30.

Nine-Ten ★★★ CALIFORNIAN   This warmly stylish space is the place for market-fresh cuisine, prepared by Jason Knibb, another member of San Diego's cadre of skilled chefs. Knibb, who was mentored by such culinary figures as Wolfgang Puck, Roy Yamaguchi, and Hans Rockenwagner, presides over a shape-shifting, seasonal menu that's best enjoyed via small-plate grazings—past offerings have included espresso-and-chocolate-braised boneless short ribs, Maine scallops with apple risotto, and harissa-marinated shrimp. Or better yet, turn yourself over to the "Mercy of the Chef," a five-course tasting menu for $70, or $100 with wine pairings (your whole table has to participate, though). When you're looking for a classy fine-dining experience—without the old-guard attitude—Nine-Ten, located at the Grande Colonial hotel (p. 794), fits the bill nicely.

910 Prospect St. (btw. Fay and Girard), La Jolla. ℰ **858/964-5400.** www.nine-ten.com. Reservations recommended. Main courses $6–$18 breakfast, $11–$18 lunch, $13–$40 dinner. AE, DC, DISC, MC, V. Tues–Sat 6:30am–2:30pm and 6–10pm; Sun 6:30am–2:30pm. Valet parking $5. Bus: 30.

EXPENSIVE

Georges California Modern ★★★ 📷 CALIFORNIAN   La Jolla's signature restaurant has it all: stunning ocean views, style, impeccable service, and, above all, a world-class chef. Georges closed briefly in early 2007, undergoing a $2.5-million renovation, reemerging with a slightly new name (it had been known as George's at the Cove since opening in 1984) and a new design-forward environment. The menu—overseen by chef Trey Foshee (named one of America's top-10 chefs by *Food & Wine*)—is now larger and more adventurous, but still driven by the freshest local ingredients available. Those seeking fine food and incomparable views at more modest prices can head upstairs to the **Ocean Terrace** and **George's Bar.** These two spaces offer indoor and outdoor seating, as well as food from the same kitchen as the pricey main dining room; lunch is served here daily.

1250 Prospect St., La Jolla. ☏ **858/454-4244.** www.georgesatthecove.com. Reservations strongly recommended. Main courses $28–$90. AE, DC, DISC, MC, V. Mon–Thurs 5:30–10pm; Fri–Sat 5–11pm; Sun 5–10pm. Ocean Terrace Bistro main courses $10–$15 lunch, $17–$25 dinner. Sun–Thurs 11am–9pm; Fri–Sat 11am–10:30pm. Valet parking $8. Bus: 30.

Zenbu ★★ SUSHI/SEAFOOD La Jolla native Matt Rimel loved fishing so much he bought a commercial fishing boat. He now operates four restaurants and still owns that local boat—not to mention an international fleet that trawls for his eateries as well as select clients. So many fresh, tempting things appear on the menu that decision making at Zenbu is no easy task. You can order something from the sushi bar, such as exquisite toro, creamy *uni* (sea urchin), or one of the specialty rolls. You could try an entree like steak of locally harpooned swordfish or grilled local fish of the day; there's also the fabulous lobster dynamite, a half lobster (local, naturally), and crab baked in a special sauce, given a dramatic, flaming presentation. Next door, intimate **Zenbu Lounge** (Thurs–Sat) has a sushi bar and DJs, while in North County, Zenbu has opened a second location in Cardiff-by-the-Sea, 2003 San Elijo Ave. (☏ **760/633-2223**).

7660 Fay Ave. (at Kline St.), La Jolla. ☏ **858/454-4540.** www.zenbusushi.com. Reservations not accepted. Main courses $22–$30. AE, DC, DISC, MC, V. Sun–Wed 5–9:30pm; Thurs–Sat 5–10:30pm. Happy hour all night Sun–Mon, Tues–Thurs 5–7pm. Lounge Thurs–Sat 8pm–1am. Free parking. Bus: 30.

MODERATE

Brockton Villa ★ BREAKFAST/CALIFORNIAN A restored 1894 beach bungalow, this charming cafe occupies a breathtaking perch overlooking La Jolla Cove. The biggest buzz is at breakfast, when you can enjoy inventive dishes such as soufflélike "Coast Toast" (the house take on French toast) and Greek "steamers" (eggs scrambled with an espresso steamer, and then mixed with feta cheese, tomato, and basil). Breakfasts are served till noon weekdays, till 3pm weekends. Lunch highlights include house-made soups, salads, and sandwiches like the grilled organic salmon BLT. The somewhat less successful supper menu—served summer only—includes seafood and steak dishes, plus paella, pastas, and grilled meats. ***Note:*** Steep stairs from the street limit wheelchair access.

1235 Coast Blvd. (across from La Jolla Cove), La Jolla. ☏ **858/454-7393.** www.brocktonvilla.com. Reservations recommended. Main courses $8–$15 breakfast, $11–$16 lunch, $16–$30 dinner. AE, DISC, MC, V. Daily 8am–3pm, till 9pm June–Sept. Bus: 30.

Piatti ★ ITALIAN/MEDITERRANEAN La Jolla's version of the neighborhood hangout is this pasta-centric trattoria a couple of blocks inland from La Jolla Shores. You're likely to be surrounded by a crew of regulars who pop in once or twice a week and know all the staff by name. You won't feel left out, however, and the food is well priced. The lemon herb-roasted chicken and *bistecca* (ribeye) are fantastic, but it's the pastas that parade out to most tables. Try *orecchiette* bathed in Gorgonzola with grilled chicken and sun-dried tomatoes, or *pappardelle*—shrimp-crowned ribbons of saffron pasta, primed with garlic, tomato, and white wine. The outdoor patio, beneath the sprawl of an enormous ficus tree, is ideal for dining any night.

2182 Avenida de la Playa, La Jolla. ☏ **858/454-1589.** www.piatti.com. Reservations recommended. Main courses $13–$29; Sat–Sun brunch $9–$13. AE, DC, MC, V. Mon–Thurs 11:30am–10pm; Fri 11:30am–11pm; Sat 11am–11pm; Sun 11am–10pm. Street parking usually available. Bus: 30.

INEXPENSIVE

The Cottage ★ BREAKFAST/LIGHT FARE   La Jolla's best breakfast is served at this turn-of-the-20th-century bungalow. The cottage is light and airy, but most diners opt for tables outside, where a charming white picket fence encloses the trellis-shaded brick patio. Omelets and egg dishes feature Mediterranean, Cal-Latino, and classic American touches; house-made granola is a favorite, too (it's even packaged and sold to take home). The Cottage also bakes its own muffins, rolls, and coffeecakes. While breakfast dishes are served all day, toward lunchtime the kitchen begins turning out freshly made, healthful soups, light meals, and sandwiches. Dinners (served in summer only) are a delight, particularly when you're seated before dark on a balmy night.

7702 Fay Ave. (at Kline St.), La Jolla. ✆ **858/454-8409.** www.cottagelajolla.com. Reservations accepted for dinner only. Main courses $8–$13 breakfast, $10–$16 lunch, $12–$23 dinner. AE, DISC, MC, V. Daily 7:30am–3pm; dinner (June–Sept only) Tues–Sat 5–9:30pm. Bus: 30.

Coronado

VERY EXPENSIVE

1500 Ocean ★★ CALIFORNIAN   The Hotel del Coronado's longtime fine-dining option, the **Prince of Wales,** was dethroned by 1500 Ocean, which opened to enthusiastic reviews in 2006. This smart, contemporary space eschews the Del's ever-present Victoriana for a stylish California Craftsman look. The menu is California oriented as well, featuring a Southland coastal cuisine that draws inspiration—and top-quality product—from throughout the region, from Baja to Santa Barbara. A four-course tasting menu ($75) is offered, as well as entrees like lamb porterhouse with stewed fennel and pan-seared scallops in a black truffle vinaigrette. For dessert, don't miss the spicy chipotle chocolate cake. There's also fabulous patio dining, with views of the ocean and Point Loma.

1500 Orange Ave., Coronado. ✆ **619/522-8490.** www.dine1500ocean.com. Reservations recommended. Main courses $28–$46. AE, DC, DISC, MC, V. Tues–Sat 5:30–10pm. Bar Tues–Sat 5–11pm. Bus: 901 or 904.

EXPENSIVE

Chez Loma ★ FRENCH   This intimate Victorian cottage filled with antiques and subdued candlelight makes for romantic dining. The house dates from 1889, the French restaurant from 1975. Tables are scattered throughout the building and on the enclosed garden terrace; an upstairs wine salon, reminiscent of a Victorian parlor, is a cozy spot. Among the entrees are salmon in a horseradish crust with a smoked-tomato vinaigrette; and roast duck with lingonberry, port, and burnt-orange sauce. Follow dinner with a cheese platter with berries and port sauce or a dessert sampler. California wines and American microbrews are available, in addition to a full bar. Early birds enjoy specially priced meals: $25 for a three-course dinner before 6pm and all night on Tuesday.

1132 Loma (off Orange Ave.), Coronado. ✆ **619/435-0661.** www.chezloma.com. Reservations recommended. Main courses $24–$37. AE, DC, DISC, MC, V. Tues–Sun 5–9pm. Bus: 901 or 904.

MODERATE

Rhinoceros Cafe & Grille ★ AMERICAN   This light, bright bistro is more casual than it looks from the street and offers large portions, though the kitchen can be a little heavy-handed with sauces and spices. At lunch, try the popular penne à la vodka in creamy tomato sauce; favorite dinner specials are Italian cioppino, Southwestern-style meatloaf, and salmon poached and crusted with herb sauce. Plenty of crispy fresh salads balance out the menu; wine drinkers will find a fair wine list.

1166 Orange Ave., Coronado. ✆ **619/435-2121.** www.rhinocafe.com. Main courses $7–$12 lunch, $12–$27 dinner. AE, DC, DISC, MC, V. Daily 11am–10pm. Street parking usually available. Bus: 901 or 904.

INEXPENSIVE

Bino's Bistro & Winebar 🍴 BREAKFAST/LIGHT FARE   This casual, Euro-style spot near the Hotel Del serves up sweet and savory crepes and fresh-baked pastries and bread that keep the regulars coming back for more. Owned by a husband-and-wife team with solid culinary creds (she's a native of Austria, where she attended culinary school; he's a veteran of one of San Diego's finest hotel dining rooms), the menu also includes creative omelets, deli sandwiches, and salads with house-made dressings. Specialty coffees, wine, champagne, and beer are also on hand. Service can be spotty, but you'll be happy once you get your Nutella-banana crepe.

1120 Adella Ave., Coronado. ✆ **619/522-0612.** www.binosbistro.com. Main courses $6–$11. AE, DISC, MC, V. Daily 7am–9:30pm. Bus: 901 or 904.

THE THREE MAJOR ANIMAL PARKS

San Diego Zoo Safari Park ★★★ ☺   Thirty-four miles north of San Diego, outside Escondido, this terrific "zoo of the future" will transport you to the African plains and other faraway landscapes. Originally a breeding facility for the San Diego Zoo, the 1,800-acre Zoo Safari Park (formerly known as the Wild Animal Park) now holds 3,500 animals representing more than 400 species. Many of the animals roam freely in vast enclosures, allowing giraffes to interact with antelopes, much as they would in Africa. You'll find the largest crash of rhinos at any zoological facility in the world, an exhibit for the endangered California condor, and a mature landscape of exotic vegetation. The San Diego Zoo is world famous, but many visitors end up preferring the Zoo Safari Park.

The easiest way to see critters is on the "Journey into Africa" tour (included with admission) aboard the **African Express,** an open-air, soft-wheeled tram that runs on biodiesel. Although it visits less park space than the now-retired monorail, the 2½-mile circuit, which takes about 30 minutes, brings guests much nearer to the animals—in some locations up to 300 feet closer. Depending on the crowd size, trams leave every 10 minutes or so. Lines build up by late morning, so make this your first or last attraction of the day (the animals are more active then, anyway). The **Savanna Safari** is a deluxe, 50-minute experience for up to 10 people. You can choose to visit either the Asian or the African exhibits on this personalized, intimate tour; tickets are $35 (not including admission), and no reservations are necessary.

There are also several self-guided **walking tours** that take you to various habitats, including **Elephant Overlook** and **Lion Camp;** but why walk when you can tool around the park on Segway personal transporters ($80, minimum age 13)? The commercial hub of the park is **Nairobi Village,** but even here animal exhibits are interesting, including the **nursery area,** a **petting station,** the **lowland gorillas,** and the **African Aviary.** There's an amphitheater for bird shows and other animal encounters, scheduled two or three times daily; Nairobi Village also has souvenir stores and several spots for mediocre dining. Visitors should be prepared for sunny, often downright hot weather; it's not unusual for temperatures to be 5° to 10° warmer here than in San Diego.

If you want to get really close to the animals, take one of the park's **Photo Caravans,** which shuttle groups in flatbed trucks into the open areas that are inaccessible to the general public. There are a variety of itineraries (some are seasonal with varying age requirements); prices start at $90, and you'll want to make reservations ahead of your visit (© **800/407-9534** or 619/718-3000). The park also schedules a variety of **sleepovers** year-round (except Dec–Jan); programs for families, kids, teens, and adults let you camp out next to the animal compound in spacious canvas tents. Reservations required (© **800/407-9534** or 619/718-3000). You can also get unique aerial perspectives of the park from the **Balloon Safari** ($20), a tethered hot-air balloon that soars to 400 feet, and **Flightline** ($70, minimum age 10), a zipline ride that scoots above the African and Asian enclosures.

15500 San Pasqual Valley Rd., Escondido. © **760/747-8702.** www.sandiegozoo.org. Admission $37 adults, $27 children 3–11, free for children 2 and under and active-duty military (U.S. and foreign); discounted 2-day passes can be used for both the zoo and Zoo Safari Park; children 11 and under are free in Oct. AE, DISC, MC, V. Daily 9am–4pm (grounds close at 5pm); extended hours during summer and Festival of Lights (2 weekends in Dec). Parking $9, $14 RVs. Bus: 386 (Mon–Fri). Take I-15 to Via Rancho Pkwy.; follow signs for about 3 miles.

San Diego Zoo ★★★ ☺   More than 4,000 creatures reside at this influential zoo, started in 1916 and run by the Zoological Society of San Diego. The zoo's founder, Dr. Harry Wegeforth, traveled the world and bartered native Southwestern animals such as rattlesnakes and sea lions for more exotic species. "Dr. Harry" also brought home flora, which flourishes in the zoo's botanical gardens; there are now more than 1 million plants on the zoo's 1,900 acres.

The zoo is one of only four in the U.S. with giant pandas, and many other rare species are here, including Buerger's tree kangaroos of New Guinea, longbilled kiwis from New Zealand, wild Przewalski's horses from Mongolia, lowland gorillas from Africa, and giant tortoises from the Galapagos. The Zoological Society is involved with animal preservation efforts around the world and has engineered many firsts in breeding. The zoo was also a forerunner in creating barless, moated enclosures that allow animals to roam in sophisticated environments resembling their natural ones.

Monkey Trails and Forest Tales is the zoo's largest, most elaborate habitat, re-creating a wooded forest full of endangered species such as the mandrill monkey, clouded leopard, and pygmy hippopotamus. An elevated trail through the treetops allows for close observation of the primate, bird, and plant life that thrives in the forest canopy. **Absolutely Apes** showcases orangutans and siamangs of Indonesia, while next door is **Gorilla Tropics,** where two troops of Western lowland gorillas roam an 8,000-square-foot habitat. Despite the hype, the **Giant Panda Research Center** is *not* worth the hassle when a long line is in place (lines are shortest first thing in the morning or toward the end of the day). More noteworthy is **Ituri Forest,** simulating a central African rainforest with forest buffaloes, otters, okapis, and hippos, which are viewed underwater from a glassed-in enclosure; and the renovated **Polar Bear Plunge,** which also offers below-the-waterline perspectives and interactive elements. The **Children's Zoo** features a nursery with baby animals and a petting area where kids can cuddle up to sheep, goats, and the like; there's also a **sea lion show** at the 3,000-seat amphitheater (easy to skip if you're headed to SeaWorld). **Elephant Odyssey,** which opened in 2009, features a herd of Asian elephants, as well as life-size replicas of prehistoric animals that roamed Southern California; you can also watch handlers interact with the pachyderms at the elephant care center.

A 35-minute **Guided Bus Tour** provides a narrated overview and covers about 70% of the facility; it's included with the price of admission. Since you get only brief glimpses of the enclosures, and animals won't always be visible, you'll want to revisit some areas. Also included with admission is access to the unnarrated **Express Bus,** which allows you to get on and off at one of five different stops along the same route; a park overview is available from the **Skyfari** aerial tram, though you won't see many creatures. Ideally, take the complete bus tour early in the morning, when the animals are more active (waits for the bus tour can be long on a busy day); after the bus tour, take the Skyfari to the far side of the park and wend your way back on foot or by Express Bus to revisit animals you missed. Other zoo experiences include sleepovers and **Backstage Passes** ($99), a 1½-hour, behind-the-scenes tour (ages 5 and up) that includes interacting with animals and trainers; call ✆ **800/407-9534** or 619/718-3000 for more information and reservations.

In addition to several fast-food options, **Albert's** restaurant is a beautiful oasis at the lip of a canyon and a lovely place to take a break.

2920 Zoo Dr., Balboa Park. ✆ **619/234-3153** (recorded info) or 619/231-1515. www.sandiegozoo. org. Admission $37 adults, $27 children 3–11, free for children 2 and under and active-duty military (U.S. and foreign); discounted 2-day passes can be used for both the zoo and Zoo Safari Park; children 11 and under are free in Oct. AE, DISC, MC, V. Sept to mid-Dec and mid-Jan to mid-June daily 9am–4pm (grounds close at 5 or 6pm); mid-June to Aug and mid-Dec to mid-Jan daily 9am–8pm (grounds close at 9pm). Bus: 7. I-5 S. to Pershing Dr., follow signs.

Now **That's a Deal!**

If you plan to visit both the zoo and the Zoo Safari Park, a 2-Visit Pass is $70 for adults, $50 for children ages 3 to 11; passes are valid for 1 year (and can be used twice at the same attraction, if you choose). A 3-for-1 pass gives you 1-day passes to the zoo and Zoo Safari Park, and unlimited entry to SeaWorld for 5 days from first use. The cost is $121 adults, $99 children ages 3 to 9.

Other value options include the **Southern California CityPass** (✆ **888/ 330-5008;** www.citypass.com), which covers the zoo or Zoo Safari Park, plus SeaWorld, Disneyland Resorts, and Universal Studios in Los Angeles; passes are $276 for adults, or $229 for kids age 3 to 9 (a savings of about 30%), and are valid for 14 days. The **Go San Diego Card** (✆ **866/628-9032;** www.gosandiego card.com) offers unlimited general admission to more than 50 attractions, including the zoo and LEGOLAND, as well as deals on shopping, dining, and day trips to Mexico and the local wine country. One-day packages start at $69 for adults and $58 for children (ages 3–12).

Sea World.

SeaWorld San Diego ★★ ☺ Opened in 1964, this aquatic theme park is perhaps the country's premier showplace for marine life, in a nominally informative atmosphere. At its heart, SeaWorld is a shoreside family entertainment center where the performers are whales, dolphins, otters, sea lions, walruses, and seals. The 20-minute shows run several times daily, with visitors cycling through the various open-air amphitheaters.

Several successive 4-ton, black-and-white killer whales have taken turns as the park's mascot, Shamu, who stars in *Believe,* SeaWorld's most popular show. Performed in a 5,500-seat stadium, the stage is a 7-million-gallon pool lined with plexiglass walls with magnified views of the huge performers. But think twice before you sit in the seats down front—a highlight of the act is multiple drenchings in the first 12 or so rows of spectators. A seasonal nighttime show (spring and summer), *Shamu Rocks,* features concert lighting, animation, and a rock soundtrack; *Blue Horizons* is a theatrical presentation mixing dolphins, whales, birds, and human performers. The slapstick *Sea Lions Live* and *Pets Rule!* are other performing-animal routines, all in venues seating more than 2,000; during the summer, human acrobats are added to the mix with *Cirque de la Mer.* A small collection of rides is led by **Journey to Atlantis,** a roller coaster and log flume; **Shipwreck Rapids** is a splashy adventure on raft-like inner tubes, and **Wild Arctic** is a simulated helicopter trip to the frozen north. There's also a passel of *Sesame Street*–related attractions, including rides and a "4-D" interactive movie experience. **Quick Queue** passes (an additional $20–$35) provide access to express entrances for rides and reserved seating at shows.

SeaWorld's real specialties are simulated marine environments, though, such as the **arctic research station,** surrounded by beluga whales and polar bears; other animal environments worth seeing are the **Shark Encounter** and **Penguin Encounter.**

Visitors can also sign up for various guided tours and interactive offerings. The **Dolphin** and **Beluga Interaction Programs** allow you to wade waist-deep with dolphins and beluga whales; there is some classroom time involved before participants wriggle into a wet suit and climb into the water for 20 minutes. It costs $190 per person (not including park admission); participants must be age 10 or older. Advance reservations required (✆ **800/257-4268**).

500 SeaWorld Dr., Mission Bay. ✆ **800/257-4268** or 619/226-3901. www.seaworld.com. Admission $70 adults, $60 children 3–9, free for children 2 and under; tickets are good for 7 days of unlimited admission. AE, DISC, MC, V. Hours vary seasonally, but always at least daily 10am–5pm; most weekends and during summer 9am–11pm. Parking $12, $17 RVs. Bus: 9 (route 9A does not serve the main gate). From I-5, take SeaWorld Dr. exit; from I-8, take W. Mission Bay Dr. exit to SeaWorld Dr.

BEACHES

San Diego County is blessed with 70 miles of sandy coastline and more than 30 individual beaches, probably the state's best collection. The beaches cater equally to surfers, snorkelers, swimmers, sailors, divers, walkers, volleyballers, sunbathers—you get the drift. Even in winter and spring, when water temps drop to the high 50s (teens Celsius), they are great places to walk and jog, and surfers happily don wet suits to pursue their passion. In summer, the beaches teem with locals and visitors alike—the bikinis come out, the pecs are bared, and a partyhearty atmosphere prevails. From mid-May to mid-July, however, prepare for **May Gray** and **June Gloom,** a local phenomenon caused when inland deserts heat up at the end of spring and suck the marine layer—a thick bank of fog—inland for a few miles. Expect moist mornings and evenings.

Note: In 2008, voters made permanent what originally had been a 1-year trial **ban on alcohol** at all city beaches, bay shores, and coastal parks. First offense has a maximum fine of $250.

Here's a list of San Diego's best stretches of sand, each with its own personality and devotees (you can get more details at **www.sandiego.gov/lifeguards/beaches**). They are listed geographically from south to north.

CORONADO   Lovely, wide, and sparkling, this beach is conducive to strolling and lingering, especially in the late afternoon. At the north end, you can watch fighter jets in formation flying from the Naval Air Station, while just south is the pretty section fronting Ocean Boulevard and the Hotel del Coronado. Waves are gentle here, so the beach draws many Coronado families—and their dogs, which are allowed off-leash at the northwestern end. South of the Hotel Del, the beach becomes the beautiful, often deserted, **Silver Strand.**

OCEAN BEACH   The northern end of Ocean Beach Park is officially known as **Dog Beach,** and it's one of a few in the county where your pooch can roam freely. Surfers congregate around the O.B. Pier, mostly in the water but

Mission Beach.

often at the snack shack on the end. Rip currents can be strong—check with the lifeguard stations. Facilities at the beach include restrooms, showers, picnic tables, volleyball courts, and metered parking lots. To reach the beach, take West Point Loma Boulevard to the end.

MISSION BEACH   Anchored by the **Giant Dipper** roller coaster, built in 1925, the sands and wide cement "boardwalk" sizzle with activity for most of the year. At the southern end, volleyball and basketball games are almost always underway. Parking can be tough, with your best bet being the public lots around the Giant Dipper or at the south end of Mission Boulevard. This street is the centerline of a 2-block-wide isthmus that leads a mile north to Pacific Beach.

PACIFIC BEACH   There's always action here, particularly along **Ocean Front Walk**—a paved promenade showcasing a human parade akin to the one at L.A.'s Venice Beach boardwalk. It runs along Ocean Boulevard (just west of Mission Blvd.) to the pier. Surfing is popular year-round, in marked sections, and the beach is well staffed with lifeguards. You're on your own to find street parking. A half-mile north of the pier is **Tourmaline Surfing Park,** where the sport's old guard gathers to surf waters where swimmers are prohibited.

MISSION BAY PARK   This man-made, 4,600-acre aquatic playground features 27 miles of bayfront picnic areas, playgrounds, and paths for biking, in-line skating, and jogging. The bay lends itself to kayaking, windsurfing, sailing, water-skiing, and fishing. There are dozens of access points; at the southwest corner is **Bonita Cove,** a protected inlet with calm waters, grassy picnic areas, and playground equipment. Parts of the bay have been subject to closure over the years due to high levels of bacteria—check for posted warnings. Get there from Mission Boulevard in south Mission Beach.

LA JOLLA COVE   These protected, calm waters—celebrated as the clearest along the coast—attract kayakers, snorkelers, scuba divers, and beach-loving families. The stunning setting offers a small sandy beach and a lovely park, as well as the nearby cove known as the **Children's Pool,** inhabited by a colony of harbor seals. Smaller fish huddle in the tide pools between the two beaches. La Jolla Cove is terrific for swimming, cramped for sunbathing, and accessible from Coast Boulevard; street parking is free, if sparse.

LA JOLLA SHORES   The wide, flat mile of sand at La Jolla Shores is popular with joggers, swimmers, and beginning body- and board surfers, as well as with families. Weekend crowds can be enormous, quickly claiming fire rings and occupying both the sand and the metered parking spaces in the lot. There are restrooms, showers, and picnic areas here, as well the grassy, palm-lined Kellogg Park across the street.

BLACK'S BEACH   The area's unofficial nude beach—though technically it's illegal—2-mile-long Black's lies north of La Jolla Shores, at the base of steep, 300-foot-high cliffs. It's tricky to reach, but it draws scores with its secluded beauty and excellent swimming and surfing conditions. The spectacle of hang gliders launching from the cliffs above adds to the show. To get here, take North Torrey Pines Road, park at the Gliderport, and clamber down the makeshift path. To bypass the cliff descent, you can walk to Black's from beaches north (Torrey Pines) or south (La Jolla Shores). ***Note:*** Lifeguards are usually present from spring break to October; citations for nude sunbathing are rarely issued. There are no restroom facilities.

TORREY PINES At the north end of Black's Beach, at the foot of Torrey Pines State Park, this fabulous strand is accessed by a pay parking lot at the park entrance. A visit to the park combined with a day at the beach is the quintessential outdoor San Diego experience. It's rarely crowded, though you need to be aware that, at high tide, most of the sand gets a bath. In almost any weather, it's a great beach for

Torrey Pines State Reserve.

walking. *Note:* At Torrey Pines and other bluffside beaches, never sit at the bottom of the cliffs. The hillsides are unstable and could collapse.

EXPLORING THE AREA
Balboa Park

Established in 1868, 1,174-acre Balboa Park is not only the nation's second-oldest city park (after New York's Central Park), but also the largest urban cultural park in the United States. Tree plantings began in the late 19th century, and the initial buildings were created to host the 1915–16 Panama-California Exposition; another expo in 1935–36 brought additional developments. Today Balboa Park's most distinctive features include mature landscaping, the architectural beauty of the Spanish Colonial Revival buildings lining the pedestrian thoroughfare, and a diverse collection of museums. You'll also find the **Old Globe Theatre** complex (p. 836) and the **San Diego Zoo** (p. 813) here.

Entry to Balboa Park is free, as is parking, but most of the museums have admission charges and varying hours (some closed on Mon); a free tram can transport you around the park. Get details from the **Balboa Park Visitor Center,** in the House of Hospitality (© **619/239-0512;** www.balboapark.org). The visitor center is also the starting point for several free tours of the park that focus on architecture, horticulture, and so on. Top museums include the following:

Mingei International Museum ★★ This captivating museum (pronounced *Min*-gay, meaning "art of the people" in Japanese) offers exhibitions one could generally describe as folk art. The exhibits—usually four at a time—encompass artists from countries across the globe; displays include textiles, costumes, jewelry, toys, pottery, paintings, and sculpture. The permanent collection features whimsical contemporary sculptures by the late French artist Niki de Saint Phalle, who made San Diego her home in 1993. As one of the only major museums in the United States devoted to folk crafts on a worldwide scale, it's well worth a look. It has a wonderful gift store as well.

1439 El Prado, in the House of Charm. © **619/239-0003.** www.mingei.org. Admission $7 adults; $5 seniors; $4 children 6–17, students, and military with ID; free for children 5 and under. Tues–Sun 10am–4pm. Bus: 7.

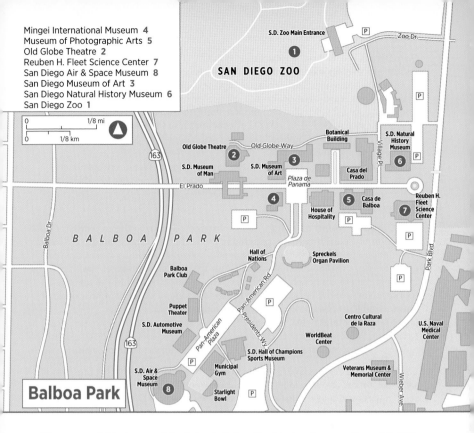

Mingei International Museum **4**
Museum of Photographic Arts **5**
Old Globe Theatre **2**
Reuben H. Fleet Science Center **7**
San Diego Air & Space Museum **8**
San Diego Museum of Art **3**
San Diego Natural History Museum **6**
San Diego Zoo **1**

0   1/8 mi
0   1/8 km

S.D. Zoo Main Entrance

Zoo Dr.

SAN DIEGO ZOO

Botanical
Building

S.D. Natural
History
Museum

Old Globe Theatre   Old Globe Way

S.D. Museum
of Man

S.D. Museum
of Art

Casa del
Prado

El Prado

Plaza de
Panama

Reuben H.
Fleet
Science
Center

Casa de
Balboa

House of
Hospitality

B A L B O A   P A R K

Hall of
Nations

Spreckels
Organ Pavilion

Balboa
Park Club

Puppet
Theater

Pan-American Rd.

S.D. Automotive
Museum

Centro Cultural
de la Raza

U.S. Naval
Medical
Center

Pan-American Plaza

Presidents Wy.

WorldBeat
Center

S.D. Hall of Champions
Sports Museum

S.D. Air &
Space
Museum

Municipal
Gym

Veterans Museum &
Memorial Center

Wieber Ave.

Balboa Park

Starlight
Bowl

Museum of Photographic Arts ★★★ Don't miss the sampling of 9,000-plus images housed by this museum—one of few in the United States devoted exclusively to the photographic arts (including cinema, video, and digital photography). Provocative traveling exhibits change every few months, and the permanent collection features photos by Alfred Stieglitz, Margaret Bourke-White, Imogen Cunningham, and Manuel Alvarez Bravo. The plush cinema hosts special screenings on an ongoing basis.

1649 El Prado. ☏ **619/238-7559.** www.mopa.org. Admission $6 adults; $4 seniors, students, and retired military; free for active-duty military and their dependents, and children 11 and under with adult. Tues–Sun 10am–5pm. Bus: 7.

Reuben H. Fleet Science Center ★ ☺ A park highlight for kids, this tantalizing collection of interactive exhibits and experiences is designed to stimulate the imagination and teach scientific principles. The Fleet also has a giant-screen IMAX Dome Theater for large-format movies, as well as planetarium shows (held the first Wed of each month). Friday nights at the Fleet feature screenings of three or four IMAX films at discounted prices.

1875 El Prado. ☏ **619/238-1233.** www.rhfleet.org. ExperienceGallery admission plus an IMAX film: $15 adults, $12 seniors and children 3–12 (exhibit gallery can be purchased individually, $10 adults, $9 seniors and children). Mon–Thurs 10am–5pm; Friday 10am–8pm; Sat 10am–7pm; Sun 10am–6pm. Bus: 7.

San Diego Air & Space Museum ★★ ☺   The other big kid pleaser, this facility provides an overview of aeronautical history, from the days of hot-air balloons to the space age, with plenty of biplanes and military fighters in between. It emphasizes local aviation history, particularly the construction here of the *Spirit of St. Louis*; you'll also find motion simulator rides and a theater screening 3-D films (with added "4-D" special effects built into the seats). The museum is housed in a cylindrical hall built by the Ford Motor Company in 1935 for the park's second international expo.

2001 Pan American Plaza. ☏ **619/234-8291.** www.sandiegoairandspace.org. Admission $17 adults; $14 seniors, retired military, and students with ID; $6 children 3–11; free for active military with ID and children 2 and under. Sept–May daily 10am–4:30pm; June–Aug daily 10am–5:30pm. Bus: 7.

San Diego Museum of Art ★   This museum is known in the art world for its collection of Spanish baroque painting and possibly the largest horde of South Asian paintings outside India. The American collection includes works by Georgia O'Keeffe and Thomas Eakins, but only a small percentage of the 12,000-piece permanent collection is on display at any given time, in favor of prestigious touring shows. SDMA also has an ongoing schedule of concerts, films, cocktail parties, and lectures, usually themed with a current exhibition.

1450 El Prado. ☏ **619/232-7931.** www.sdmart.org. Admission $12 adults, $9 seniors and military, $8 students, $4.50 children 7–17, free for children 6 and under; family 4-pack $28. Admission to traveling exhibits varies. Tues–Sat 10am–5pm; Sun noon–5pm; Thurs till 9pm in summer. Bus: 7.

San Diego Natural History Museum ☺   The main focus of this museum is the flora, fauna, and mineralogy of Southern and Baja California. There's a 300-seat large-format movie theater that boasts the latest in 3-D technology, and two or three films are screened throughout the day (included with admission). The interactive installation *Fossil Mysteries* explores the region's prehistory and includes life-size models of primeval animals, including the megalodon shark, the largest predator the world has ever known. SDNHM also leads free nature hikes and has a schedule of events and overnight expeditions for both children and adults.

1788 El Prado. ☏ **619/232-3821.** www.sdnhm.org. Admission $17 adults; $15 seniors; $12 students, youth 13–17, and active-duty military; $11 children 3–12; free for children 2 and under. Daily 10am–5pm. Bus: 7.

More Attractions in & Around San Diego
DOWNTOWN & BEYOND

Downtown, you can wander through the turn-of-the-20th-century **Gaslamp Quarter** ★★, with 17 blocks of restored historic buildings. You'll find dozens of restaurants and a vigorous nightlife scene here. More information about the Gaslamp Quarter—as well as walking tours on Saturdays at 11am—is available at the **William Heath Davis House,** a museum in downtown's oldest structure and home to the quarter's historical foundation; it's at 410 Island Ave., at Fourth Avenue (☏ **619/233-4692;** www.gaslampquarter.org). At **Horton Plaza** ★ (p. 833), notable for its colorful, jumbled architecture, you can shop, dine, see a movie or play, and people-watch.

In 2004, the city completed $474-million **PETCO Park,** home to San Diego's Major League Baseball team, the **Padres.** The 42,000-seat ballpark incorporates seven historic structures into the stadium, including the Western Metal Supply building, a four-story brick edifice dating from 1909 that now sprouts left-field bleachers from one side. The San Diego Padres play April through September; for information or tickets, call 𝓒 **877/374-2784** or 619/795-5000, or visit www.padres.com. PETCO parking is limited and costly—for a space within a couple blocks, expect to pay up to $20. Better yet, take the San Diego Trolley.

Cabrillo National Monument ★★★ 📷   Breathtaking views mingle with the history of San Diego, starting with the arrival of Juan Rodríguez Cabrillo in 1542. This tip of Point Loma is also a vantage point for viewing migrating Pacific gray whales en route from Alaska to Baja California (and back again) December through March. A tour of the restored lighthouse, built in 1855, illuminates what life was like here more than a century ago. National Park Service rangers lead walks at the monument, and tide pools at the base of the peninsula beg for exploration. Free 25-minute films on Cabrillo, tide pools, and the whales screen daily on the hour from 10am to 4pm. The drive from downtown takes 20 minutes.

1800 Cabrillo Memorial Dr., Point Loma. 𝓒 **619/557-5450.** www.nps.gov/cabr. Admission $5 per vehicle, $3 for walk-ins (valid for 7 days from purchase). Daily 9am–5pm. Bus: 84. By car, take I-8 west to Rosecrans St., turn right on Canon St. and left on Catalina, and follow signs.

Maritime Museum ★★ ☺   This flotilla of classic ships is led by the full-rigged merchant vessel *Star of India* (1863), a National Historic Landmark and the world's oldest sailing ship that still goes to sea. The gleaming white San Francisco–Oakland steam-powered ferry *Berkeley* (1898) worked round-the-clock to take people to safety after the 1906 San Francisco earthquake; it now pulls duty as a museum. The elegant *Medea* (1904) is one of the world's few remaining large steam yachts, and *Pilot* (1914) was San Diego Bay's official pilot boat for 82 years. There's also the HMS *Surprise,* a reproduction of an 18th-century Royal Navy Frigate which played a supporting role to Russell Crowe in the film *Master*

Gaslamp Quarter.

and Commander, and two submarines, including a 300-foot-long Cold War–era Soviet attack vessel. You can board and tour each ship.

1492 N. Harbor Dr. © **619/234-9153.** www.sdmaritime.org. Admission $14 adults; $11 seniors 62 and over, students 13–17, and active military with ID; $8 children 6–12; free for children 5 and under. Daily 9am–8pm (till 9pm in summer). Bus: 2, 210, 810, 820, 850, 860, 923, or 992. Trolley: County Center/Little Italy or America Plaza.

Cabrillo National Monument.

Museum of Contemporary Art San Diego Downtown ★★★ In 2007, the Museum of Contemporary Art opened a new downtown space known as the Jacobs Building. The annex is boldly grafted onto the end of historic Santa Fe Depot, built in 1915, and transforms what had been the train station's baggage building into a state-of-the-art museum and educational facility; it features site-specific work by Richard Serra, Jenny Holzer, and others. Across the street at America Plaza are MCASD's original downtown galleries (MCASD's flagship museum is in La Jolla, p. 825). Lectures and special events for adults and children are offered, and free tours are given every third Thursday at 6pm and weekends at 2pm.

1100 and 1001 Kettner Blvd. (btw. B St. and Broadway). © **858/454-3541.** www.mcasd.org. Admission $10 adults, $5 seniors and military, free for anyone 25 and under; free admission every 3rd Thurs 5–7pm; paid ticket valid for 7 days at all MCASD locations. Thurs–Tues 11am–5pm; 3rd Thurs 11am–7pm; closed Wed. Bus: 83 and numerous Broadway routes. Trolley: America Plaza.

The New Children's Museum ★ ☺ Have some restless kids on your hands? Turn them loose at this high-style, $25-million facility that opened in 2008. Industrial and angular, the museum features ever-changing artworks by local artists that can be climbed on, touched, or interacted with in some way (and which just might intrigue the adults in tow as well). There are also lots of arts-based classes and good old-fashioned play areas. Designed for kids from toddlers to teens, the New Children's Museum will appeal mostly to the under-13 set.

200 W. Island Ave. (at Front St.). © **619/233-8792.** www.thinkplaycreate.org. Admission $10 adults, $5 seniors and military, free for children under 1; free admission the 2nd Sun of the month. Mon–Tues and Fri–Sat 10am–4pm; Thurs 10am–6pm; Sun noon–4pm (2nd Sun of the month 10am–4pm); closed Wed. Parking $10. Bus: 3, 11, 120, or 992. Trolley: Convention Center.

USS *Midway* Museum The USS *Midway*'s 47-year military history began 1 week after the Japanese surrender of World War II in 1945. By the time *Midway* was decommissioned in 1991, the aircraft carrier had patrolled the Taiwan Straits in 1955, operated in the Tonkin Gulf, and served as the flagship from which Desert Storm was conducted. In all, more than 225,000 men served aboard the warship. The carrier is now moored at the Embarcadero and in 2004 became a floating naval-aviation museum. Self-guided audio tours take visitors to several levels of the ship, telling the story of life onboard; the highlight is climbing up the superstructure to the bridge and gazing down on the 1,001-foot-long flight deck, with various aircraft poised for duty. *Note:* Be prepared to climb stairs and ladders.

910 Harbor Dr. (at Navy Pier). © **619/544-9600.** www.midway.org. Admission $18 adults, $15 seniors and students, $10 retired military and children 6–17, free for children 5 and under and active-duty military. Daily 10am–5pm. Limited parking on Navy Pier, $7 for 4 hr.; metered parking available nearby. Bus: 2, 210, or 992. Trolley: Seaport Village.

OLD TOWN & BEYOND: CALIFORNIA'S BEGINNINGS

The birthplace of San Diego—indeed, of California—Old Town takes you back to the Mexican California of the mid-1800s. Today the spot undergoes a daily invasion of tourists, many of them headed to **Fiesta de Reyes,** a one-time 1930s-era motel that is now a collection of restaurants and shops (see "Shopping," later in this chapter).

Mission Valley, which starts at Presidio Park and heads straight east, is anything but old; until Hwy. 8 was built in the 1950s, it was little more than cow pastures with a couple of dirt roads. Shopping malls, motels, a golf course, condos, and car dealerships fill it today. Old Town and Mission Valley are easily accessed via the San Diego Trolley. It's also the site of **Qualcomm Stadium,** 9449 Friars Rd., where San Diego's National Football League team, the **Chargers,** play. The season runs from August to December; for information, call © **800/745-3000** or 619/280-2121, or log on to www.chargers.com.

Junípero Serra Museum ★   On the hill above Old Town, this iconic Spanish Mission–style building built in 1929 overlooks the slopes where, in 1769, the first mission, first presidio (fort), and first nonnative settlement on the West Coast of the United States and Canada were founded. The museum's exhibits introduce visitors to the Native American, Spanish, and Mexican people who

Maritime Museum.

Museum of Contemporary Art.

first called this place home. On display are their belongings, from cannons to cookware. From the 70-foot tower, visitors can compare the spectacular view with historic photos to see how this land has changed over time.

2727 Presidio Dr., Presidio Park. © **619/232-6203.** www.sandiegohistory.org. Admission $5 adults; $4 seniors, students, and military; $2 children 6–17; free for children 5 and under. Fri 11am–3pm; Sat–Sun 10am–5pm. Bus: 8, 9, 10, 28, 30, 35, 44, 83, 88, 105, or 150. Trolley: Old Town. Take I-8 to the Taylor St. exit. Turn right on Taylor and then left on Presidio Dr.

Mission Basilica San Diego de Alcalá   This was the first link in a chain of 21 California missions founded by Spanish missionary Junípero Serra (the mission was moved from Old Town to this site in 1774 for agricultural reasons, and to separate Native American converts from the fortress that included the original building). The mission was sacked by the local tribe a year after it was built—Father Serra rebuilt the structure using 5- to 7-foot-thick adobe (mud) walls and clay-tile roofs, rendering it harder to burn. In the process, he inspired a bevy of 20th-century California architects. Mass is said daily in this active Catholic parish.

10818 San Diego Mission Rd., Mission Valley. © **619/281-8449.** www.missionsandiego.com. Admission $3 adults, $2 seniors and students, $1 children 11 and under. Free Sun and for daily Masses. Museum and gift shop daily 9am–4:45pm; Mass daily 7am (except Sat) and 5:30pm, with additional Sun Mass at 8, 10, 11am, and noon. Trolley: Mission San Diego. Take I-8 to Mission Gorge Rd. to Twain Ave., which turns into San Diego Mission Rd.

Old Town State Historic Park ★   The Stars and Stripes weren't raised over Old Town until 1846, and this historic park is dedicated to re-creating the city as it was during this era of Mexican influence, from around 1821 to 1872. Seven of the park's 20 structures are original, including the adobe homes. La Casa de Estudillo represents the living conditions of a wealthy family in 1872; Seeley Stables is named after A. L. Seeley, who ran the stagecoach and mail service in these parts from 1867 to 1871. Pick up a map at Park Headquarters and peruse the model of Old Town as it looked in 1872. On Wednesdays and Saturdays from 10am to 4pm, costumed park volunteers reenact 19th-century life with cooking and crafts demonstrations, a working blacksmith, and parlor singing; there's storytelling on the green Tuesdays and Thursdays noon to 2pm and Friday from 1 to 3pm. Free 1-hour walking tours leave daily at 11am and 2pm from the Robinson-Rose House.

4002 Wallace St., Old Town. © **619/220-5422.** www.parks.ca.gov. Free admission (donations welcome). Museums daily 10am–5pm; most restaurants till 9pm. Bus: 8, 9, 10, 28, 30, 35, 44, 88, 105, or 150. Trolley: Old Town. Take I-5 to the Old Town exit and follow signs.

MISSION BAY & THE BEACHES

Opened to the public in 1949, **Mission Bay** is a 4,600-acre aquatic playground created by dredging tidal mud flats and opening them to seawater. Today it's a great area for walking, jogging, in-line skating, biking, and boating. The boardwalk connecting **Mission Beach** and **Pacific Beach** is almost always bustling and colorful. For Mission Bay recreational activities, see "Outdoor Pursuits" (p. 828).

Belmont Park ☺   This seaside amusement park was opened in 1925 as a real-estate scheme to lure people to what was then a scarcely populated area. Today Belmont Park's star attraction is the **Giant Dipper roller coaster ★**, one of two surviving fixtures from the original park and a registered National Historic

Landmark; the other holdover is **The Plunge,** Southern California's largest (175-ft.) indoor swimming pool. There are a variety of carny-style rides at Belmont Park, but something more unique awaits next door at the **Wave House ★** (🕿 **858/228-9317;** www.wavehousesandiego.com). This self-described "royal palace of youth culture" features **FlowBarrel ★,** a wave machine designed to create stand-up rides on a 10-foot wave, and **FlowRider,** which provides a less gnarly wave-riding experience for novices. You must qualify on the FlowRider before attempting the FlowBarrel. *Note:* As of this writing Belmont Park has declared bankruptcy over a lease dispute with the city. It's unknown how this will play out, but operation of the Giant Dipper will be unaffected by the proceedings.

3190 Mission Blvd., corner of W. Mission Bay Dr. 🕿 **858/488-1549.** www.giantdipper.com. Ride on the Giant Dipper $6, unlimited rides $23; FlowRider $20 for 1 hr. (plus $10 registration fee), Flow-Barrel $40 for 1 hr. Belmont Park daily 11am–8pm (weekend and summer hours later; closed Mon–Thurs Jan–Feb); FlowRider Sat–Sun 11am–7pm, FlowBarrel Mon–Fri noon–4:45pm, Sat–Sun 11am–7pm. Bus: 8. Take I-5 to the SeaWorld exit, and follow W. Mission Bay Dr. to Belmont Park.

LA JOLLA

One of San Diego's most photogenic spots is **La Jolla Cove** and the **Ellen Browning Scripps Park** on the bluff above it. Take a stroll along Coast Walk, which offers some of California's most resplendent coastal scenery. Just south is the **Children's Pool,** a beach where dozens of harbor seals laze in the sun. For a fine scenic drive, follow La Jolla Boulevard to Nautilus Street and turn east to get to 823-foot-high **Mount Soledad ★,** with a 360-degree view of the area.

Birch Aquarium at Scripps ★★ ☺   This beautiful aquarium and museum is run as the interpretive arm of the world-famous Scripps Institution of Oceanography. The aquarium affords close-up views of the Pacific Northwest, the California coast, Mexico's Sea of Cortés, and the tropical seas, presented in more than 60 marine-life tanks. The giant kelp forest is particularly impressive; other highlights include a variety of sharks and ethereal moon jellyfish. A re-created tide pool demonstrates marine coastal life and affords an amazing view of Scripps Pier and La Jolla. Off-site adventures like whale-watching are conducted year-round.

2300 Expedition Way. 🕿 **858/534-3474.** www.aquarium.ucsd.edu. Admission $12 adults, $9 seniors and college students with ID, $8.50 children 3–17, free for children 2 and under. AE, MC, V. Daily 9am–5pm. Free 3-hr. parking. Bus: 30. Take I-5 to La Jolla Village Dr. exit, go west 1 mile, and turn left at Expedition Way.

Museum of Contemporary Art San Diego ★★★   Focusing on works produced since 1950, this museum is internationally recognized for its permanent collection and thought-provoking exhibitions. The 4,000-plus holdings represent every major art movement of the past half-century, with a strong showing by California artists. The museum is on a bluff overlooking the ocean, and the views from the galleries are gorgeous; the original building was designed by Irving Gill in 1916 and was the residence of San Diego's legendary philanthropist Ellen Browning Scripps. Free docent tours are available every third Thursday at 6pm and weekends at 2pm. The bookstore is a great place for contemporary gifts, and the cafe is a pleasant stop before or after your visit.

700 Prospect St. 🕿 **858/454-3541.** www.mcasd.org. Admission $10 adults, $5 seniors and military, free for anyone 25 and under; free admission every 3rd Thurs 5–7pm; paid ticket valid for 7 days at all MCASD locations (there are two downtown galleries; p. 822). Thurs–Tues 11am–5pm; 3rd Thurs

La Jolla Coast Walk.

11am–7pm; closed Wed. Bus: 30. Take I-5 N to La Jolla Pkwy. or take I-5 S to La Jolla Village Dr. W. Take Torrey Pines Rd. to Prospect Place and turn right; Prospect Place becomes Prospect St.

Torrey Pines State Reserve ★★★ The rare Torrey pine grows only two places in the world: Santa Rosa Island, 175 miles northwest of San Diego, and here, at the north end of La Jolla. If the gnarled beauty of these trees doesn't move you, the equally rare, undeveloped coastal scenery should. This 2,000-acre reserve encompasses the 300-foot-high water-carved sandstone bluffs, which provide a precarious footing for the trees. Six trails, less than 1.5 miles long, travel from the road to the cliff edge or to the beach. Guided nature walks are offered weekends and holidays at 10am and 2pm, departing from the small visitor center, built in the adobe style of the Hopi Indians. This delicate park is truly one of San Diego's unique treasures. **Note:** The park has no food or drink facilities; picnics are allowed on the beach only.

12600 N. Torrey Pines Rd., btw. La Jolla and Del Mar. ☎ **858/755-2063.** www.torreypine.org. Admission $10 per car, $9 seniors. Daily 8am–sunset. Bus: 101. From I-5, take Carmel Valley Rd. west; turn left at Hwy. 101.

CORONADO

It's hard to miss San Diego Bay's most iconic landmark: the **San Diego–Coronado Bay Bridge ★**. Completed in 1969, this graceful five-lane bridge spans 2¼ miles and links the city and the "island" of Coronado. At 246 feet high, the bridge is tall enough to allow navy aircraft carriers to pass under it. It still looks more elegant than utilitarian, with a sweeping curve that maximizes the view, encompassing Mexico and the shipyards of National City to the south; the city skyline to the north; and Coronado, the naval station, and Point Loma before you—designated drivers are hard-pressed to keep their eyes on the road. Bus no. 901 from downtown will also take you across the bridge. The **Hotel del Coronado ★★★** is also worth checking out, even if you're not checking in. This turreted Victorian seaside resort is a national treasure (p. 798).

Sightseeing Tours

Hornblower Cruises   These 1- or 2-hour narrated tours lead passengers through San Diego harbor on tours that highlight dozens of San Diego landmarks. You'll see the *Star of India,* cruise under the San Diego–Coronado Bridge, and swing by a submarine base and an aircraft carrier or two. Guests can visit the captain's wheelhouse for a photo op, and harbor seals and sea lions on buoys are a regular sighting. Whale-watching trips (mid-Dec to late Mar) are a blast; a 2-hour Sunday champagne-brunch cruise departs at 11am, and dinner/dance cruises run nightly.

1066 N. Harbor Dr. ℰ **888/467-6256** or 619/686-8715. Harbor tours $20–$25 adults; $2 off for seniors and military; half-price for children 4–12. Dinner cruises start at $70; brunch cruise $55; whale-watching trips $34–$39 ($5 off for seniors and military), $17–$20 children. Bus: 2, 210, or 992. Trolley: America Plaza.

Old Town Trolley Tours   Not to be confused with the public transit trolley, these narrated excursions are an easy way to get an overview of the city. These vehicles gussied up like old-time trolleys do a 30-mile circular route, and you can hop off at any one of 11 stops, explore at leisure, and reboard when you please (trolleys run every half-hour). Stops include Old Town, the Gaslamp Quarter, Coronado, the San Diego Zoo, and Balboa Park. You can begin wherever you want, but you must purchase tickets before boarding (most stops have ticket kiosks, or you can get discounted tickets online). Old Town Trolley also operates **Sea and Land Adventures,** a 90-minute tour in amphibious vehicles that hold 46 passengers. After cruising along the Embarcadero, you'll dip into the bay to experience the maritime and military history of San Diego.

4010 Twiggs St., Old Town. ℰ **888/910-8687** or 619/298-8687. www.historictours.com. $34 adults, $17 children 4–12, free for children 3 and under. The route takes 2 hr. Trolleys run daily 9am–5pm Nov–Feb, 9am–6pm in summer.

San Diego–Coronado Bay Bridge.

San Diego Harbor Excursion   This company also offers daily 1- and 2-hour narrated tours of the bay. Two 1-hour itineraries each cover about 12 miles—the south bay tour includes the San Diego–Coronado Bridge and Navy shipyards, and the north bay route motors past Naval Air Station North Island and Cabrillo National Monument. The 25-mile, 2-hour tour encompasses the entire bay. Two-hour Sunday (and Sat in summer) brunch and nightly dinner cruises are also available. In winter, whale-watching excursions feature onboard naturalists from the Birch Aquarium.

1050 N. Harbor Dr. (foot of Broadway). © **800/442-7847** or 619/234-4111. www.sdhe.com. Harbor tours $20–$25, $2 off for seniors and military, half-price for children 4–12. Dinner cruises start at $67 adults, $38 children; brunch cruise $55 adults, $38 children; whale-watching trips $32–$37 adults, $27–$32 seniors and military, $16 children. Bus: 2, 210, or 992. Trolley: America Plaza.

Vizit Tours   Narrated tours aboard open-top double-decker buses run along several routes, including loops along the harbor (which includes Old Town and downtown) and through Balboa Park. There are on-and-off privileges, and each tour is about an hour; you can also combine the routes into city tours that also include admission to the zoo or a harbor cruise (all tickets are valid for 48 hr.). Tours start in Seaport Village; you can also save some cash by buying your tickets online ahead of time.

W. Harbor Dr. at Kettner Blvd. © **619/727-4007.** www.vizitsandiegotours.com. $15–$52 adults, $12–$39 children. Most tours daily 10am–5pm. Trolley: Seaport Village.

Xplore Offshore ★★ 🎁   This fleet has only two small boats, and the one to ride is the tricked-out RIB (rigid-inflatable boat), similar to the crafts used by Navy SEALs. Capable of cruising at up to 45 mph, the RIB is built for speed and comfort; there's lots of padding and straddle-seating up front, and a roomy head—not bad for a 24-foot vessel. Other special features include hot water for showering after a swim and an underwater camera for those who don't want to get wet. Trips are unscripted; you go where you want and do what you'd like: rip-roaring wave riding or serene pleasure boating; whale-watching or a booze cruise to a bayside restaurant—it's your call.

Pickup points are flexible, but usually Dana Landing in Mission Bay. © **858/456-1636.** www. xploreoffshore.com. 3-hr. rates start at $49–$79 per person. Bus: 9 (for Dana Landing).

OUTDOOR PURSUITS

BALLOONING & SCENIC FLIGHTS   A peaceful balloon ride reveals sweeping vistas of the Southern California coast, the wine country surrounding Temecula (70 min. north of downtown), or rambling estates and golf courses around Del Mar and Rancho Santa Fe (25 min. north of downtown). For a sunrise (Temecula) or sunset (Del Mar) flight, followed by a traditional champagne toast, contact **Skysurfer Balloon Company** (© **800/660-6809** or 858/ 481-6800; www.sandiegohotairballoons.com). The cost is $165 for sunrise ballooning, $205 for sunset trips. **California Dreamin'** (© **800/373-3359** or 951/699-0601; www.californiadreamin.com) has sunrise Temecula flights with rates ranging from $138 to $148; **biplane excursions** over Temecula's wine country start at $248 for two people. Check both companies' websites for special offers.

   Barnstorming Adventures (© **800/759-5667** or 760/930-0903; www.barnstorming.com) offers just about everything but wing walking.

Vintage biplane flights leave from Montgomery Field, 3750 John J. Montgomery Dr., in Kearny Mesa, taking passengers on scenic flights along the coast; rates start at $199 for one- or two-person, 20-minute rides. Air Combat flights, with you at the controls (under the guidance of active-duty fighter pilots), offer simulated dogfights. If you're bringing your own adversary, you need to reserve space 1 to 2 weeks in advance; if you need your target assigned, call 3 weeks in advance. Rates start at $298. You can also opt for a flight—with or without aerial acrobatics—in a 1941 SNJ-4 warbird ($345 and up), or a 30-minute you-fly-it experience (no pilot's license necessary; $177).

BIKING While it can get crowded when cruising along the oceanfront **boardwalk** between Pacific Beach and Mission Beach, especially on weekends, that's really half the fun; the paths around **Mission Bay** are also great for leisurely rides. The road out to **Point Loma** (Catalina Dr.) is hilly, with wonderful scenery; traveling old **State Rte. 101** (also known as the Pacific Coast Hwy.) from La Jolla north to Oceanside yields terrific coastal views, with plenty of places to refuel with coffee, a snack, or a swim.

For rentals, call **The Bike Revolution,** 522 Sixth Ave. (© **619/564-4843;** www.sandiegobiketoursinc.com), which also runs guided tours ($65–$89). Rates for a city/hybrid rental start at $25 for the day. Mission Beach rental outlets include **Cheap Rentals,** 3689 Mission Blvd. (© **800/941-7761** or 858/488-9070; www.cheap-rentals.com), which has everything from beach cruisers ($12 per day) to tandems ($24 per day) and baby trailers ($12 per day); and **Mission Beach Surf & Skate,** 704 Ventura Place, off Mission Boulevard at Ocean Front Walk (© **858/488-5050**), for one-speed beach cruisers. In Coronado, check out **Bikes and Beyond,** 1201 First St., at the Ferry Landing Marketplace (© **619/435-7180;** www. hollandsbicycles.com), for beach cruisers and hybrids. Expect to pay $7 and up per hour for bicycles, $30 for 24 hours.

Hike Bike Kayak San Diego, 2246 Avenida de la Playa, La Jolla (© **866/425-2925** or 858/551-9510; www.hikebikekayak.com), has a variety of organized bike tours, including a plunge down La Jolla's Mount Soledad (ages 14 and up; $50).

BIRD-WATCHING More than 500 bird species have been observed in San Diego county—more than anywhere else in the continental United States. The area is a haven along the Pacific Flyway—the migratory route along the Pacific Coast—and the diverse range of ecosystems helps lure a wide range of winged creatures. From the tidal marshes to the desert, it's possible for birders to enjoy four distinct bird habitats in a single day.

Among the best places for bird-watching is the **Chula Vista Nature Center** at **Sweetwater Marsh National Wildlife Refuge** (© **619/409-5900;** www.chulavistanaturecenter.org), where you may spot rare residents such as the light-footed clapper rail and the western snowy plover, as well as predatory species such as the American peregrine falcon and northern harrier. **Torrey Pines State Reserve** (p. 826) is a protected habitat for swifts, thrashers, woodpeckers, and wren-tits. Inland, the **Anza-Borrego Desert State Park** (see chapter 15) makes an excellent day trip from San Diego—with some 268 species of birds.

Get the free brochure *Birding Hot Spots of San Diego* from the Port Administration Building (3165 Pacific Hwy.), the San Diego Zoo, Zoo Safari Park, San Diego Natural History Museum, or Birch Aquarium. It's also posted online at www.portofsandiego.org/environment; click on "Birds of San Diego Bay." The **San Diego Audubon Society** is another great source of birding information (✆ **858/273-7800;** www.sandiegoaudubon. org). The Society also operates two wildlife sanctuaries that are open to the public on weekends.

FISHING   Summer and fall are ideal for boat fishing, when the waters around **Point Loma** are brimming with bass, bonito, and barracuda. The nearby **Islas los Coronados,** which belong to Mexico, are popular for yellowtail, yellowfin, and big-eyed tuna; some outfitters will take you deeper into Baja California waters on multiday trips. Fishing charters depart from Harbor and Shelter islands, Point Loma, Imperial Beach, and Quivira Basin in Mission Bay. Participants over age 16 need a California fishing license, but anglers of any age can fish free without a license off any **municipal pier** in the state, including those of Shelter Island, Ocean Beach, and Imperial Beach. *Note:* California has rolled out its Automated License Data System, an ATM-like console that issues licenses. Many small outfitters and shops will not be furnished with these machines, so call ahead. Licenses can also be purchased online; call ✆ **858/467-4201** or go to www.dfg.ca.gov for information.

San Diego's sport-fishing fleet consists of more than 75 large commercial vessels and several dozen private charter yachts. A variety of half-, full-, and multiday trips are available. Rates for trips on a large boat average $42 for half a day or $95 for three-quarters of a day. Or spring $135 to $195 for a 20-hour overnight trip to the Coronados (call around and compare prices). Rates are lower for kids, and discounts are available for twilight sailings; charters or "limited load" rates are also to be had. The following outfitters offer short or extended outings with daily departures: **H&M Landing,** 2803 Emerson St. (✆ **619/222-1144;** www.hmlanding.com); **Point Loma Sportfishing,** 1403 Scott St. (✆ **619/223-1627;** www.pointloma sportfishing.com); and **Seaforth Sportfishing,** 1717 Quivira Rd. (✆ **619/ 224-3383;** www.seaforthlanding.com).

GOLF   San Diego County has 90-plus courses, and more than 50 of them are open to the public. For a full listing of area courses, visit www.golfsd.com, or request the *Golf Guide* from the San Diego Convention and Visitors Bureau (✆ **619/236-1212**); it's also available online at www.sandiego.org. **San Diego Golf Reservations** (✆ **866/717-6552** or 858/456-8300; www.sandiegogolf.com) can arrange tee times for you.

The city's most famous links are at the **Torrey Pines Golf Course ★★★**, a pair of 18-hole championship courses on the cliffs between La Jolla and Del Mar. Home of the annual Farmers Insurance Open (formerly known as the Buick Invitational), Torrey Pines tee times are taken 8 to 90 days in advance by automated telephone system ($43 booking fee); first-come, first-served tee times are offered from 6:30am to 7:20am (Mon–Thurs) and sunup to 7:20am (Fri–Sun). Weekday greens fees on the south course are $183, $229 weekends; the north course is $100 weekdays, $125 weekends. Cart rentals are $40, and discounted twilight rates are available. You can also arrange for lessons, which ensure you a spot on the course. For automated reservations, call ℂ **877/581-7171,** option 3. For the pro shop or lessons, call ℂ **800/985-4653** or go to www.torreypinesgolfcourse.com.

Other acclaimed links include **Aviara Golf Club** in Carlsbad (ℂ 760/ 603-6900; www.parkaviara.hyatt.com), Ramona's **Mt. Woodson Golf Club** (ℂ 760/788-3555; www.mtwoodsongc.com), the **Grand Del Mar Golf Club** (guests only, ℂ 858/314-1930; www.thegranddelmar.com), Carlsbad's **La Costa Resort and Spa** (ℂ 800/854-5000; www.lacosta. com), **Maderas Golf Club** in Poway (ℂ 858/451-8100; www.maderasgolf. com), **Barona Creek Golf Club** in Lakeside (ℂ 619/387-7018; www. barona.com), **Salt Creek Golf Club** in Chula Vista (ℂ 619/482-4666; www.saltcreekgc.com), and **Sycuan Resort & Casino** in El Cajon (ℂ 800/ 457-5568; www.sycuanresort.com). More convenient for most visitors is the **Riverwalk Golf Club** (ℂ 619/296-4653; www.riverwalkgc.com), which wanders along the Mission Valley floor; humble **Balboa Park Municipal Golf Course** (ℂ 619/570-1234 for automated reservations; www.sandiego. gov/golf); or **Coronado Municipal Golf Course** (ℂ 619/435-3121; www. golfcoronado.com). The latter two feature distractingly nice views of the city skyline.

HANG GLIDING & PARAGLIDING   The windy cliffs at the **Torrey Pines Gliderport,** 2800 Torrey Pines Scenic Dr., La Jolla (ℂ **858/452-9858;** www.fly torrey.com), are one of the country's top spots for hang gliding and paragliding. A 20- to 25-minute tandem flight with a qualified instructor costs $150 for paragliding and $200 for hang gliding. Even if you don't muster the courage to try a tandem flight, sitting at the cafe here and watching the graceful aerobatics is stirring.

HIKING & WALKING   The best **beaches** for walking are Coronado, Pacific Beach, La Jolla Shores, and Torrey Pines, but pretty much any shore is a good choice. You can also walk around most of Mission Bay on a series of connected footpaths. If a four-legged friend is walking with you, head for Dog Beach in Ocean Beach or Fiesta Island in Mission Bay—two of the few areas where dogs can legally go unleashed. The **Coast Walk** offers supreme surf-line views above the bluffs of La Jolla. Other places for hikes listed elsewhere in this chapter include **Torrey Pines State Reserve** (p. 826) and **Cabrillo National Monument** (p. 821).

The **Sierra Club** sponsors many hikes in the San Diego area, and nonmembers are welcome to participate. Contact the office at ℂ **858/569-6005,** or check the website www.sandiego.sierraclub.org. Volunteers from the **Natural History Museum** (ℂ **619/232-3821;** www.sdnhm.org) also lead free nature walks throughout San Diego County.

Walkabout International, 2650 Truxton Rd., Ste. 110, Point Loma (ℂ **619/231-7463;** www.walkabout-int.org), sponsors more than 100 free walking tours every month. Led by local volunteers, they're listed on the website and hit all parts of the county, including the Gaslamp Quarter, La Jolla, and the beaches. Wilderness hikes take place most Wednesdays and Saturdays.

SAILING & MOTOR YACHTS   Sailors can choose from among the calm waters of 4,600-acre **Mission Bay,** with its 26 miles of shoreline; **San Diego Bay,** one of the most beautiful natural harbors in the world; or the open **Pacific Ocean,** where you can sail south to the Islas los Coronados (the trio of uninhabited islets on the Mexico side of the border).

Dennis Connor's America's Cup Experience (© 800/644-3454 or 619/922-6215; www.stars-stripes.com) offers bay sails aboard one of two 80-foot America's Cup Class racing yachts. The 2½-hour excursions, on either *Stars and Stripes* or *Abracadabra*, are $99. **Sail Jada Charters** (© 619/ 572-3443; www.sailjada.com) offers sunset champagne cruises on a gorgeous wooden (and truly yare) sailing yacht. Constructed of oak, cedar, and teak in 1938, *Jada* plies the bay Thursday to Sunday ($110 per person); it's also available for whale-watching and private charters.

If you have sailing or boating experience, go for a nonchartered rental. **Seaforth Boat Rental** (© 888/834-2628; www.seaforthboatrental.com) has a wide variety of boats for bay and ocean, from kayaks ($12–$20 for 1 hr.) to 240-horsepower cabin cruisers ($350, 2-hr. minimum). Sailboats start at $35 to $38 for 1 hour; jet skis begin at $90 to $99 for 1 hour. Half- and full-day rates are offered. Stand-up paddle boards, catamarans, and pedal boats are also available, as well as fishing boats and equipment. Seaforth has several locations, including Mission Bay, 1641 Quivira Rd. (© 619/223-1681); downtown at the Marriott San Diego Hotel & Marina, 333 W. Harbor Dr. (© 619/239-2628); and in Coronado at 1715 Strand Way (© 619/437-1514).

Mission Bay Sportcenter, 1010 Santa Clara Place (© 858/488-1004; www.missionbaysportcenter.com), rents sailboats (from $24 per hr.), catamarans (from $30 per hr.), sailboards ($18 per hr.), kayaks (from $13 per hr.), jet skis ($95 per hr.), pedal boats ($17 per hr.), and powerboats (from $175 per hr.). Discounts are given for 4-hour and full-day rentals. In summer, a variety of youth programs (ages 4–16) teach watersports such as surfing and sailing.

SCUBA DIVING & SNORKELING   San Diego's underwater scene ranges from the magnificent giant kelp forests of Point Loma to a nautical graveyard off Mission Beach called Wreck Alley, where a 366-foot Canadian destroyer, the *Yukon*, and other ships (and the remains of a toppled research platform) sit on the sea floor. Fishing and boating activity are banned in the 533-acre Ecological Reserve off the La Jolla Cove, but diving and snorkeling are welcome. It's a reliable place to spot garibaldi, California's state fish, as well as giant black sea bass. Shore diving here or at nearby La Jolla Shores is common, and a number of dive shops will help set you up. Boat dives are the rule, however, particularly to the Islas los Coronados, a trio of uninhabited islets off Tijuana, where seals, sea lions, and eels cavort against a landscape of boulders.

The **San Diego Oceans Foundation** (© 619/523-1903; www. sdoceans.org) is devoted to the stewardship of local marine waters; the website contains good information about local diving opportunities. Notable dive outfits include **Ocean Enterprises,** 7710 Balboa Ave. (© 858/565-6054; www.oceanenterprises.com); and **Lois Ann Dive Charters,** 1717 Quivira Way (© 800/201-4381; www.loisann.com). **OEX Dive & Kayak Centers** (www.oexcalifornia.com) has locations in La Jolla, 2132 Avenida de la Playa (© 858/454-6195), and Mission Bay, 1010 Santa Clara Place (© 619/866-6129).

SKATING   Gliding around on in-line skates, especially in the Mission Bay area, is a quintessential Southern California experience. In Mission Beach, rent a pair of in-line skates or a skateboard ($5 per hr.) from **Cheap Rentals,** 3689

Mission Blvd. (☎ **800/941-7761** or 858/488-9070; www.cheap-rentals. com). In Coronado, go to **Bikes and Beyond,** 1201 First St., at the Ferry Landing (☎ **619/435-7180;** www.hollandsbicycles.com); rates are $6 per hour.

SURFING   San Diego is a popular year-round surf destination. Some of the best spots include Black's Beach, La Jolla Shores, Windansea, Pacific Beach, Mission Beach, Ocean Beach, and Imperial Beach. In North County, there's Swami's in Encinitas, Carlsbad State Beach, and Oceanside. A word of caution, though—hazards include strong riptides and territorial locals.

Boards are available for rent at stands at many popular beaches. Many local surf shops also rent equipment and provide lessons, including **La Jolla Surf Systems,** 2132 Avenida de la Playa, La Jolla Shores (☎ **858/456-2777;** www.lajollasurfsystems.com); **Pacific Beach Surf Shop,** 4150 Mission Blvd. (☎ **858/373-1138;** www.pacificbeachsurfshop.com), and **Ocean Beach Surf & Skate,** 4976 Newport Ave. (☎ **619/225-0674;** www.obsurfandskate.com or www.oceanexperience.net). In Coronado, you can rent boards at **Emerald City: The Boarding Source,** 1118 Orange Ave. (☎ **619/435-6677;** www.emeraldcitysurf.com).

For surfing lessons in the North County, check with **Kahuna Bob's Surf School** (☎ **800/524-8627** or 760/721-7700; www.kahunabob. com), based in Encinitas; or **Surf Diva,** 2160 Avenida de la Playa (☎ **858/454-8273;** www.surfdiva.com), a surfing school for women and girls, based in La Jolla. Surf Diva has become so popular, it now does lessons for guys, as well as coed group instruction; in summer, there are coed surf camps for adults and kids ages 5 to 17.

SHOPPING

San Diegans have embraced the suburban shopping mall with vigor, and many residents do the bulk of their shopping at two massive complexes in Mission Valley. Downtown has even adopted the mall concept at Horton Plaza. Sales tax in San Diego is 8.75%, but savvy out-of-state shoppers avoid the tax by shipping larger items home at the point of purchase.

Downtown

The Disneyland of shopping malls, **Horton Plaza ★**, 324 Horton Plaza (☎ **619/239-8180;** www.westfield.com/hortonplaza), opened in 1985 to rave reviews and was a catalyst for the Gaslamp's redevelopment. The multilevel facility transcends its genre with a conglomeration of crisscrossing paths, bridges, towers, and piazzas, and has more than 130 specialty shops and kiosks. There's a 14-screen cinema, a performing arts venue, two major department stores, several restaurants, and a roster of short-order dining spots. Three hours of free parking are available from 7am to 9pm; you can self-validate your ticket at machines scattered throughout the mall. It's $8 per hour without validation. The garage is confusing (losing your car is part of the Horton Plaza experience) and is open 24 hours.

Fourteen-acre **Seaport Village,** 849 W. Harbor Dr. (☎ **619/235-4014;** www.seaportvillage.com), alongside San Diego Bay, was built to resemble a seaside community. The more than 50 shops are Southern California cutesy, but the waterfront atmosphere is pleasant, and 2 hours of parking are free with a purchase.

Seekers of serious art, design, and home furnishings should head to Little Italy. The conglomeration of hip stores and galleries along Kettner Boulevard and India Street, from Laurel to Date streets, has become known as the **Kettner Art and Design District.** Highlights include **Boomerang for Modern,** 2475 Kettner Blvd. (✆ **619/239-2040;** www.boomerangformodern.com); **Mixture,** 2210 Kettner Blvd. (✆ **619/239-4788;** www.mixturehome.com); and **DNA European Design Studio,** 750 W. Fir St. (✆ **619/235-6882;** www.dna europeandesign.com). Look for fine art at **Scott White Contemporary Art,** 939 W. Kalmia St. (✆ **619/501-5689;** www.scottwhiteart.com), and **Noel-Baza Fine Art,** 2165 India St. (✆ **619/876-4160;** www.noel-bazafineart.com).

Hillcrest/Uptown

Compact Hillcrest is an ideal shopping destination for vintage clothing, books, and home furnishings; there are plenty of cafes and wine bars as well. Start at the intersection of University and Fifth avenues. Street parking is available.

To the north and east of Hillcrest are the Uptown neighborhoods of University Heights and North Park, which are brimming with boutiques. You'll find independent-minded clothing stores and unusual gift shops along Park Boulevard and University Avenue. Running east from where Park Boulevard T-bones Adams Avenue, you'll find the area once commonly known as **Adams Avenue Antique Row.** It doesn't have the number of antiques stores it once had, but plenty of shops, restaurants, and bars still enliven the excursion. The district is best tackled by car; for more information, contact the **Adams Avenue Business Association** (✆ **619/282-7329;** www.adamsavenuebusiness.com).

Old Town & Mission Valley

Old Town State Historic Park features restored historic sites and adobe structures, a number of which now house shops that cater to tourists. Many have a "general store" theme and carry gourmet treats and inexpensive Mexican crafts alongside standard-issue souvenirs. **Fiesta de Reyes,** Juan Street, between Wallace and Mason streets (✆ **619/297-3100;** www.fiestadereyes.com), maintains the park's old *Californio* theme and has more than a dozen specialty shops and three restaurants. Costumed employees, special events and activities, and strolling musicians heighten the festive atmosphere. You'll have plenty of shopping opportunities outside the park perimeter as well.

Mission Valley is home to two giant malls: **Fashion Valley Center,** 7007 Friars Rd. (✆ **619/688-9113;** www.simon.com), and **Mission Valley Center,** 1640 Camino del Rio N. (✆ **619/296-6375;** www.westfield.com/mission valley). They provide more than enough stores to satisfy any shopper and have free parking. Both are also accessible via the San Diego Trolley from downtown.

Mission Bay & the Beaches

The beach communities offer laid-back shopping options: surf shops, recreational gear, and casual clothing stores. The best selection of bikinis is at **Pilar's,** 3745 Mission Blvd., Mission Beach (✆ **858/488-3056;** www.pilarsbeachwear.com). Across the street is **Liquid Foundation Surf Shop,** 3731 Mission Blvd. (✆ **858/488-3260**), which specializes in board shorts for guys.

In Pacific Beach, **Pangaea Outpost,** 909 Garnet Ave. (✆ **858/581-0555;** www.pangaeaoutpost.com), gathers more than 70 diverse artists and merchants under one roof; San Diego's greatest concentration of antiques stores is found in the **Ocean Beach Antique District** (www.antiquesinsandiego.com), along the 4800 block of Newport Avenue. Several stores are mall-style, with dozens of dealers. Most of the O.B. antiques stores are open daily from 10am to 6pm, with reduced hours Sunday.

La Jolla

Shopping is a major pastime in this upscale community of moneyed professionals and retirees. Women's clothing boutiques tend toward conservative and costly, such as those lining Girard Avenue and Prospect Street (**Armani Exchange, Polo Ralph Lauren, Nicole Miller,** and **Sigi's Boutique**), but you'll also find less pricey, mainstream stores such as **Banana Republic** and **Talbots.** Even if you're not in the market to buy, the many home-decor boutiques make for great window-shopping, as do La Jolla's ubiquitous jewelers. La Jolla also has more than 20 art galleries—although most won't appeal to serious collectors.

Coronado

This insular, conservative navy community doesn't have many shopping opportunities beyond the stores on Orange Avenue at the southwestern end of town. In addition to some scattered housewares and home-furnishings stores and women's boutiques, there are gift shops at Coronado's major resorts. The **Ferry Landing Marketplace,** 1201 First St., at B Avenue (✆ **619/435-8895;** www. coronadoferrylandingshops.com), is a touristy gaggle of shops, galleries, and restaurants with a sweeping view of the bay and downtown skyline.

SAN DIEGO AFTER DARK

Historically, San Diego's cultural scene has languished in the shadows cast by those of Los Angeles and San Francisco, but the go-go '90s brought new blood and money into the city, and arts organizations reaped the benefits. The San Diego Symphony, Old Globe Theatre, and Museum of Contemporary Art San Diego each received megamillions from individual donors, but don't think "after-dark" activity in this city is limited to highfalutin affairs for the Lexus crowd. Rock and pop concerts, bars (both swank and dive), and nightclubs crank up the volume on a nightly basis.

The Performing Arts

The San Diego Convention and Visitors Bureau's **Art + Sol** campaign publishes a calendar of performing and visual-arts events; check it out at www.sandiego artandsol.com. The San Diego Performing Arts League produces the *What's Playing?* guide every 2 months. You can pick one up at the ARTS TIX booth (see below) or view the calendar online (✆ **619/238-0700;** www.sdartstix.com).

Deeply discounted tickets to theater, music, and dance events are available at the **ARTS TIX** booth, in Horton Plaza Park at Broadway and Third Avenue. For a daily roster of offerings or to purchase tickets, visit www.sdartstix.com; for additional information call ✆ **858/381-5595.** The Horton Plaza kiosk is open Tuesday to Thursday noon to 6pm, Friday and Saturday 11am to 6pm, and Sunday noon to 5pm.

Thankfully, San Diego's orgy of development over the past decade has included more than just luxury condos. **NTC Promenade** (✆ **619/573-9260;**

www.ntcpromenade.org) consists of 26 historic buildings on 28 bayfront acres in Point Loma. It's the remnants of a huge navy base transformed into a flagship hub of creative activity, housing museums and galleries, educational facilities, and arts groups. The **Birch North Park Theatre,** 2891 University Ave. (© **619/239-8836;** www.birchnorthparktheatre.net), is a resurrected 1928 vaudeville and movie house. It's now the home base for Lyric Opera San Diego and hosts numerous other groups throughout the year. The **Balboa Theatre,** 868 Fourth Ave. (© **619/570-1100;** www.sdbalboa.org), opened in early 2008 following a 5-year, $27-million restoration. Originally built in 1924, the Balboa sat empty and decaying for years, barely avoiding several brushes with the wrecking ball. This Gaslamp Quarter icon is once again presenting music, dance, theater, and films. **Sushi Performance & Visual Art,** 390 11th Ave. (© **619/235-8466;** www.sushiart.org), was homeless for several years but is now settled into a cool, industrial space in the East Village. Although it's ensconced on the ground floor of a new condo tower, Sushi remains uncompromised. Since 1980, Sushi has been presenting brave, fierce, brazen, provocative works of art, dance, and performance.

THEATER

A complex of three performance venues in Balboa Park, the multifaceted **Old Globe Theatre ★★★** includes the 580-seat Old Globe Theatre (fashioned after Shakespeare's wooden-O theater), a 612-seat open-air theater, and a 250-seat arena stage. This Tony Award–winning company produces more than a dozen productions year-round, from world premieres of subsequent Broadway hits such as *Dirty Rotten Scoundrels* and *The Full Monty,* to an excellent outdoor summer Shakespeare festival. The Globe grounds underwent a massive face-lift just in time for the theater's 75th anniversary in 2010. Backstage tours are offered most weekends at 10:30am ($5 adults; $3 students, seniors, and military). Tickets range from $29 to $94. For more information, call © **619/234-5623** or see www.theoldglobe.org.

Founded in 1947 by Gregory Peck, Dorothy McGuire, and Mel Ferrer, **La Jolla Playhouse ★★★** won a 1993 Tony Award for outstanding regional theater. The Playhouse is a three-theater complex located on the campus of UC San Diego and is known for its contemporary takes on classics and commitment to commedia dell'arte style—as well as producing Broadway-bound blockbusters like *Jersey Boys* and *The Who's Tommy.* Tickets are $25 to $80, but discounted tickets ($15–$20) for seniors and students, subject to availability, are offered 1 hour before curtain. For seniors, the rush is on for the first six performances of a show; student rush is for all performances. The Playhouse is also the site of a Wolfgang Puck restaurant, **Jai.** For details, call © **858/550-1010** (www.lajollaplayhouse.org).

Also noteworthy are **San Diego Repertory Theatre ★**, which mounts plays and musicals at the Lyceum Theatre in Horton Plaza (© **619/544-1000;** www.sdrep.org); **Lamb's Players Theatre ★** (© **619/437-6000;** www.lambsplayers.org), a resident-professional company based in Coronado; and **Cygnet Theatre ★** (© **619/337-1525;** www.cygnettheatre.com), which produces work at the **Old Town Theatre,** 4040 Twiggs St.

CLASSICAL MUSIC, OPERA & DANCE

The **San Diego Symphony ★** lures top talent for its year-round programs. Under the leadership of music director Jahja Ling, the symphony presents a

Old Globe Theatre in Balboa Park.

traditional season October through May at Copley Symphony Hall, 750 B St., a baroque jewel dating from 1929, swallowed whole by a downtown financial tower. The Summer Pops series, devoted to a mix of big band, Broadway, Tchaikovsky, and sundry "pops," runs weekends from July to early September at the Embarcadero. Tickets are $20 to $100; select performances offer $10 student tickets 1 hour before curtain. For additional information, call ✆ **619/235-0804** (www.sandiegosymphony.com).

The well-respected **La Jolla Music Society ★★** has been bringing marquee names to San Diego since 1968, including Pinchas Zukerman, Emanuel Ax, and Joshua Bell. Many of the 40-plus annual shows are held October through May in La Jolla's Sherwood Auditorium at the Museum of Contemporary Art San Diego (p. 825). The annual highlight is SummerFest, a 3-week series of eclectic concerts, forums, open rehearsals, talks, and artist encounters held in August. Tickets range from $25 to $105; for more information, call ✆ **858/459-3728** (www.ljms.org).

The **San Diego Opera ★★★** is perhaps the community's most successful arts organization. The annual season runs from late January to mid-May, with five offerings at downtown's 3,000-seat Civic Theatre, 1200 Third Ave., and occasional recitals at smaller venues. Productions range from well-trod war horses such as *Carmen* to edgier works such as Alban Berg's *Wozzeck,* performed by name talent from around the world, as well as local singers. Tickets run $35 to $220; rush tickets ($20–$50) become available 2 hours before curtain. For details, call ✆ **619/533-7000** (box office) or 619/232-7636 (www.sdopera.com).

Dance Place at NTC Promenade (p. 835) has become the heart of the city's dance scene, providing studio, performance, and educational space for several of San Diego's leading companies, including **San Diego Ballet** (✆ **619/294-7311;** www.sandiegoballet.org), **Malashock Dance** (✆ **619/260-1622;** www.malashockdance.org), and **Jean Isaacs San Diego Dance Theater** (✆ **619/225-1803;** www.sandiegodancetheater.org).

The Club & Music Scene

Comprehensive listings are found in the free *San Diego Weekly Reader* (www. sdreader.com), published Thursdays and distributed all over town (in tourist areas, it's a condensed version called the *Weekly*).

LIVE ROCK, POP, FOLK, JAZZ & BLUES

San Diego's downtown **House of Blues ★★**, 1055 Fifth Ave. (© **619/299-2583;** www.hob.com/sandiego), features an eclectic lineup of rock, blues, reggae, and world music. **Anthology ★★★** (p. 800) is a fine-dining establishment masquerading as a top-notch music venue, presenting jazz, blues, world, and rock music. You'll find live music nightly at **Croce's Restaurant & Jazz Bar ★**, 802 Fifth Ave. at F Street (© **619/233-4355;** www.croces.com), a mainstream gathering place for jazz and rhythm and blues in the Gaslamp. **The Casbah ★**, 2501 Kettner Blvd. at Laurel (© **619/232-4355;** www.casbahmusic.com), is a Little Italy dive with a well-earned rep for presenting alternative bands that are, were, or will be famous. May through October, San Diegans flock to **Humphrey's ★**, 2241 Shelter Island Dr. (© **619/224-3577;** www.humphreys concerts.com), a 1,300-seat outdoor venue overlooking a marina; the lineup spans the musical spectrum. Jazz fans should look into **Dizzy's ★**, 200 Harbor Dr. (© **858/270-7467;** www.dizzyssandiego.com), conveniently located at the San Diego Wine & Culinary Center in the Gaslamp. Tickets are cash only, available at the door.

DANCE CLUBS & DISCOS

The Gaslamp Quarter is the hub of nightlife in San Diego, and high-end dance clubs where you can also enjoy a fancy sit-down meal have become popular. Options include **Stingaree ★★**, 454 Sixth Ave. at Island Street (© **619/544-9500;** www.stingsandiego.com), a three-level, 22,000-square-foot megaclub with a cool rooftop lounge; and **On Broadway ★**, 615 Broadway at Sixth Avenue (© **619/231-0011;** www.obec.tv), a converted 1925 bank building with a sushi bar and billiards parlor (Fri and Sat only). As of this writing one of San Diego's oldest clubs, **Sevilla ★★**, 353 Fifth Ave. (© **619/233-5979;** www.sevillanight club.com), is about to reopen in a new location in the heart of the Gaslamp; you can dance to salsa and merengue (lessons Tues–Thurs and Sun at 8:30pm, followed by live bands) or nibble on tapas. At **Voyeur ★★**, 755 Fifth Ave. (© **619/756-7678;** www.voyeursd.com), there's plenty to gawk at, including the Goth fun-house decor and go-go dancers embedded in a wall of pulsing LED lights. With three floors, **Tipsy Crow ★**, 770 Fifth Ave. (© **619/338-9300;** www. thetipsycrow.com), manages to be a sophisticated martini bar, dance club, concert venue, and relaxing cocktail lounge all in one. **Ivy** and **Ivy Rooftop ★★★** (© **619/814-2055;** www.envysandiego.com) are the hip and happening clubs located in the ultrastylish Andaz Hotel (p. 780). Multilevel Ivy is *très* chic, with a definite A-lister vibe; Ivy Rooftop is an open-air lounge. In an old warehouse district in Middletown, **Spin ★**, 2028 Hancock St. (© **619/294-9590;** www.spin nightclub.com), hosts DJs doing their thing into the wee after-hours.

BARS & COCKTAIL LOUNGES

The Beach ★★, the rooftop bar of the W Hotel, at 421 B St. downtown (© **619/398-3100;** www.wbeachbar.com), features a heated sand floor, cabanas, and a fire pit. Other open-air lounges taking advantage of San Diego's mild weather are

Sky Lounge ★★, 660 K St. (✆ **619/696-0234;** www.altitudeskybar.com), perched on the 22nd story of the Gaslamp Quarter Marriott; **LOUNGEsix ★**, at the Hotel Solamar, 616 J St. (✆ **619/531-8744;** www.hotelsolamar.com); the Hard Rock Hotel's **Float ★**, 207 Fifth Ave. (✆ **619/764-6924;** www.hardrock hotelsd.com); and the **Siren Pool & Uber Lounge ★★**, at the sexy Sè San Diego hotel, 1047 Fifth Ave. (✆ **619/515-3000;** www.sesandiego.com). San Diego's ulti-mate bar with a view, though, is the romantic **Top of the Hyatt ★★★**, 1 Market Place, at Harbor Drive (✆ **619/232-1234;** www.manchestergrandhyatt.com)—it's on the 40th floor of the West Coast's tallest waterfront building. Hypermod-ern **Thin ★★** and its downstairs sister club, the **Onyx Room ★★**, 852 Fifth Ave., Gaslamp Quarter (✆ **619/235-6699;** www.onyxroom.com), let you move from a contemporary vibe to a classic lounge. Glamorous **Confidential ★★**, 901 Fourth Ave. (✆ **619/696-8888;** www.confidentialsd.com), sports contem-porary design and a tasty tapas menu, while **Vin de Syrah Spirit & Wine Par-lor ★★**, 901 Fifth Ave. (✆ **619/234-4166;** www.syrahwineparlor.com), has an oddball *Alice in Wonderland* setting and morphs into a jamming club on week-ends. Whether you bowl passionately or ironically, raucous **East Village Tavern & Bowl,** 930 Market St. (✆ **619/677-2695;** www.bowlevt.com), has you cov-ered; it features colorfully lit bowling lanes, as well as a separate bar area. Off the main tourist grid is **Starlite ★★**, 3175 India St. (at Spruce St.), in Mission Hills (✆ **619/358-9766;** www.starlitesandiego.com), a nifty drinking and dining spot with a great patio.

GAY & LESBIAN CLUBS & BARS

The **Brass Rail,** 3796 Fifth Ave., Hillcrest (✆ **619/298-2233;** www.thebrass railsd.com), is San Diego's oldest gay bar but has been remodeled and refreshed. Across the street from one another in Hillcrest, **Numbers ★**, 3811 Park Blvd., near University Ave. (✆ **619/294-7583;** www.numberssd.com), and the **Flame,** 3780 Park Blvd. (✆ **619/795-8578;** www.flamesandiego.com), are popular dance emporiums. The Flame features ladies' night on Fridays; Numbers caters to the girls on Saturdays. **Bourbon Street Bar & Grill ★**, 4612 Park Blvd., University Heights (✆ **619/291-4043;** www.bourbonstreetsd.com), is a gay bar featuring karaoke, open-mic nights, and DJs; Sunday is ladies' night. **Rich's ★**, 1051 University Ave., between 10th and 11th avenues (✆ **619/295-2195;** www.richssandiego.com), is a high-energy dance club that has been an institution for years; Thursday is ladies' night. On Friday evenings from 5 to 10pm, the weekend party scene officially begins at the **Top of the Park ★★**, 525 Spruce St. (✆ **619/291-0999;** www.parkmanorsuites.com). This pent-house bar at the Park Manor Suites (p. 786) offers panoramic views of Balboa Park and beyond.

NORTH COUNTY BEACH TOWNS

The string of picturesque beach towns that dot the coast of San Diego County from Del Mar to Oceanside make great day trips. *Be forewarned:* You'll be tempted to spend the night.

Essentials

Del Mar is only 18 miles north of downtown San Diego; **Carlsbad** is about 33 miles. If you're driving, follow I-5 north; Del Mar, Solana Beach, Encinitas,

Suds City

With more than 30 breweries in town, it's no wonder *Men's Journal* declared San Diego to be America's number-one beer city. Here is just a small sampling of the places a serious beer drinker is guaranteed to love.

San Diego's most acclaimed brewery is headquartered in far-flung Escondido, but elegant **Stone Brewery World Bistro and Gardens,** 1999 Citracado Pkwy. (② **760/471-4999;** www.stonebrew. com), is worth the drive. **Pizza Port Brewing Company** (www.pizzaport. com) has three locations: 1956 Bacon St., Ocean Beach (② **619/224-4700**); 135 N. Hwy. 101, Solana Beach (② **858/ 481-7332**); and 571 Carlsbad Village Dr. in Carlsbad (② **760/720-7007**). Kids can get in on the action with Pizza Port's house-made root beer. At **Pacific Beach AleHouse,** 721 Grand Ave. (② **858/ 581-2337;** www.pbalehouse.com), you

can watch a Pacific sunset from the rooftop deck while you sip on a Pacific Sunset IPA. In Normal Heights, one of the city's great beer bars, **Blind Lady Ale House,** 3416 Adams Ave. (② **619/255-2491;** www.blindladyalehouse.com), is making a foray into brewing (one of the owners was a master brewer at Stone once upon a time). **5 Points Brewing Co.** in Middletown, 1795 Hancock St. (② **619/550-2739;** www.5pbc.com), does contract brewing for two other beer makers, meaning you can taste suds from three local breweries in one tap room.

If you'd like to do some tours and sampling without the driving, check out **Brewery Tours of San Diego** (② **619/961-7999;** www.brewerytoursofsandiego. com) or **Brew Hop** (② **858/361-8457;** www.brewhop.com).

Carlsbad, and Oceanside all have freeway exits. The farthest point, Oceanside, will take about 45 minutes. The other choice by car is the coast road, known as Camino del Mar, "PCH" (Pacific Coast Hwy.), Old Hwy. 101, and County Hwy. S21.

From downtown San Diego, the **Coaster** commuter train provides service to Solana Beach, Encinitas, Carlsbad, and Oceanside, and **Amtrak** stops in Solana Beach—just a few minutes north of Del Mar—and Oceanside. The Coaster makes the trip a number of times (6:30am–7pm) weekdays, four times on Saturday; Amtrak passes through a dozen times daily each way. Call ② **800/ 262-7837** or 511, or visit www.transit.511sd.com for transit information; for Amtrak call ② **800/872-7245** (www.amtrak.com).

Del Mar ★★

Del Mar is a small community with some 4,500 inhabitants in 2 square miles. The town has adamantly maintained its independence, eschewing incorporation into the city of San Diego. It's one of the most upscale communities in the metropolitan area, yet Del Mar maintains a casual, small-town personality and charm. The history and popularity of Del Mar are inextricably linked to the **Del Mar Racetrack & Fairgrounds,** 2260 Jimmy Durante Blvd. (② **858/793-5555;** www.sdfair.com). In 1933, actor/crooner Bing Crosby developed the Del Mar Turf Club, enlisting the help of celebrity friends. Soon Hollywood stars were seen around Del Mar, and the town became famous as the place where "the turf meets the surf." The town still swells in summer, as visitors flock to **thoroughbred horse races** (mid-July through early Sept) and the **San Diego County**

Fair (📞 **858/755-1161** or 858/793-5555; www.sdfair.com), the region's largest annual event, referred to by most locals as the Del Mar Fair (mid-June to early July).

Two excellent beaches flank Del Mar: **Torrey Pines State Beach** to the south and **Del Mar State Beach.** Both are wide, well-patrolled strands popular for sunbathing, swimming, and surfing (in marked areas). The sand stretches north to the mouth of the San Dieguito Lagoon, where people bring their dogs for a romp in the sea. The hub of activities for most residents and visitors, **Del Mar Plaza,** 1555 Camino del Mar (www.delmarplaza.com), is an open-air shopping center with fountains, sculptures, palazzo-style terraces, good restaurants and shops, and wonderful views of the sea.

For more information about Del Mar, contact or visit the **San Diego Coastal Chamber of Commerce,** 1104 Camino del Mar, Del Mar, CA 92014 (📞 **858/755-4844;** www.delmarchamber.org). There's also a helpful city-run website at www.delmar.ca.us.

WHERE TO STAY

Del Mar Motel on the Beach 🎁 The only property in Del Mar right on the beach, this simply furnished white-stucco motel has been here since 1946. The rooms are large and well kept; upstairs units have one king-size bed, downstairs rooms have two double beds. Most of them have scant views, but two oceanfront rooms, dressed up with faux plants and larger bathrooms, sit right over the sand. You can walk the shore for miles, and the popular seaside restaurants **Poseidon** and **Jake's** are right next door. The hotel offers free use of beach gear.

1702 Coast Blvd. (at 17th St.), Del Mar, CA 92014. www.delmarmotelonthebeach.com. 📞 **800/ 223-8449** for reservations, or 858/755-1534. 44 units (upper units with shower only). $259–$309 double; check for reduced Oct–May rates. AE, DISC, MC, V. Free parking. Take I-5 to Via de la Valle exit. Go west, and then south on Hwy. 101 (Pacific Coast Hwy.); veer west onto Coast Blvd. **Amenities:** Picnic and barbecue area. *In room:* A/C, TV, fridge, hair dryer.

The Grand Del Mar ★★★ ☺ A faux Tuscan villa nestled in the foothills of Del Mar, this resort features ornate, Las Vegas–style luxury and high-end comforts. Liberally accented with fountains, courtyards, terraces, sweeping staircases, and outdoor fireplaces, the hotel is so grandly European, you'll feel as if you are visiting the doge at his country estate. It has a canyonside walking path overlooking the golf course, tennis courts, four swimming pools, a tricked-out kids' activity center, and a 21,000-square-foot spa. The signature restaurant, **Addison,** is one of San Diego's most sumptuous dining rooms: plush, elegant, and refined, serving the cuisine to match. This is simply San Diego's most opulent resort. **Note:** Gay-rights activists have called for a boycott of this property in response to the owner's $125,000 contribution to Proposition 8, which, as of this writing, has outlawed same-sex marriage in California; see www.sleepwiththe rightpeople.org.

5300 Grand Del Mar Court, San Diego, CA 92130. www.thegranddelmar.com. 📞 **888/314-2030** or 858/314-2000. Fax 858/314-2001. 249 units. From $425 double; from $725 suite. Children 17 and under stay free in parent's room. Packages available. AE, DC, DISC, MC, V. Valet parking. From I-5, merge onto Hwy. 56 E., exit Carmel Country Rd., and turn right, left at Grand Del Mar Way. **Amenities:** 4 restaurants; 5 bars; live entertainment; children's activity center; concierge; 18-hole championship golf course; exercise room; Jacuzzi; 4 swimming pools; room service; spa; 2 tennis courts. *In room:* A/C, TV/DVD, CD player, hair dryer, minibar, free Wi-Fi.

L'Auberge Del Mar Resort & Spa ★★★   Sporting a French beach-château look, this classy property received a top-to-bottom, $25-million renovation in 2009. Changes include a stand-alone spa (with indoor/outdoor relaxation areas) and a handsome pool area with lattice deck, chill-out fire-pit area, and dramatic one-story water-wall feature. Not all rooms offer a view, but many have balconies or patios. Unchanged, of course, is the hotel's prime location—the beach is a 3-minute walk away down a private pathway, and Del Mar's main shopping and dining scene is just across the street. The hotel's signature eatery, **Kitchen 1540,** serves seasonal California cuisine that uses organic, sustainable products; there's also a charcuterie bar and lots of raw food designed for sharing. This is one of North County's destination dining spots; it offers some very cool outdoor dining opportunities too.

1540 Camino del Mar (at 15th St.), Del Mar, CA 92014. www.laubergedelmar.com. ✆ **800/245-9757** or 858/259-1515. Fax 858/755-4940. 120 units. From $350 double; from $600 suite. AE, DC, MC, V. Valet parking $25. Take I-5 to Del Mar Heights Rd. west, and then turn right onto Camino del Mar Rd. **Amenities:** Restaurant; 2 bars; concierge; access to nearby health club; Jacuzzi; 2 outdoor pools; room service; full-service spa; 2 tennis courts. *In room:* A/C, TV, CD player, hair dryer, minibar, MP3 docking station, free Wi-Fi.

Les Artistes 🎁   What do you get when you take a 1940s motel and put it in the hands of an owner with a penchant for prominent painters? An intriguingly funky, disarmingly informal hotel, a few blocks from downtown Del Mar. Some of the rooms at this nonsmoking property have partial ocean views, and charming touches abound, such as a lily-and-koi pond, Asian chimes, and bougainvillea (downstairs rooms have tiny private garden decks). Ten rooms are tributes to artists; two more were given a Japanese makeover. The Diego Rivera room feels like a warm Mexican painting come to life; the Japanese Furo room features a soaking tub carved into the bathroom floor. A sister B&B, the five-room **Secret Garden Inn,** is at 1140 Camino del Mar.

944 Camino del Mar (btw. 9th and 10th sts.), Del Mar, CA 92014. www.lesartistesinn.com. ✆ **858/755-4646.** 12 units. $105–$250 double. Rates include continental breakfast. DISC, MC, V. Free parking. From I-5, go west on Del Mar Heights Rd. and then left onto Camino Del Mar Rd. Pets accepted with $50 cash deposit plus $30 cleaning fee. *In room:* TV.

WHERE TO EAT

Head to the upper level of the centrally located Del Mar Plaza, at Camino del Mar and 15th Street. Here you'll find **Il Fornaio Cucina Italiana** ★ (✆ 858/755-8876; www.ilfornaio.com), for pleasing Italian cuisine and an *enoteca* (wine bar) with great ocean views; **Pacifica Del Mar** ★★ (✆ 858/792-0476; www.pacificadelmar.com), which serves outstanding seafood; and **Shimbashi Izakaya** ★★ (✆ 858/523-0479; www.shimbashi-restaurants.com), for Japanese small plates and sake. West from the plaza on 15th Street is neighborhood favorite **Sbicca** ★★, 215 15th St. (✆ **858/481-1001;** www.sbiccabistro.com), serving modern American cuisine sweetened with great wine deals. Fabulous vistas come with your meal at **Poseidon,** 1670 Coast Blvd. (✆ **858/755-9345;** www.poseidonrestaurant.com), set right on the beach. Ensconced in an uninspiring Marriott hotel, there's no view at **Arterra** ★★, 11966 El Camino Real (✆ **858/369-6032;** www.arterrarestaurant.com), but the seasonally driven menu is attractive enough—not to mention the swanky outdoor lounge.

Jake's Del Mar ★ SEAFOOD/CALIFORNIAN   This Hawaiian-owned seafood restaurant with a killer view occupies a building originally constructed in 1910. Jake's has a perfect seat beside the sand, and diners get straight-on views of the beach scene. The predictable menu can't live up to the panorama, but it's prepared competently and service is swift (sometimes too swift—don't let them rush you). At lunch, you'll find sandwiches and salads; dinner brings in the big boys: Maine lobster tails, giant scampi, rib-eye steak, and so on. Happy hour features a shorter bar/bistro menu with discounted prices.

1660 Coast Blvd. (at 15th St.), Del Mar. ⓒ **858/755-2002.** www.jakesdelmar.com. Reservations recommended. Main courses $11–$17 lunch and brunch, $14–$52 dinner. AE, DISC, MC, V. Tues-Sat 11:30am–2:30pm; Sun brunch 10am–2pm; Mon–Thurs 5–9pm; Fri 5–9:30pm; Sat 4:30–9:30pm; Sun 4:30–9pm. Valet parking $3. Bus: 101.

Market Restaurant + Bar ★★★ CALIFORNIAN   Comfortably elegant Market specializes in a regional San Diego cuisine, showcasing the best ingredients from the area's top farms, ranches, and seafood providers. The menu is printed daily, depending on what is available at the produce stands; the wine list, which is reprinted about every week, is no less quality obsessed, focusing on small and non-traditional wineries. Past Market menu items have included blue cheese soufflé with roasted pears, candied pecans, and fig-port reduction; tempura black sea bass; and a tasting of game hen served three ways. Market also has four-course tasting menus ($68) and a sushi menu. Truly fine dining in a relaxed atmosphere.

3702 Via de la Valle (at El Camino Real), Del Mar. ⓒ **858/523-0007.** www.marketdelmar.com. Reservations recommended. Main courses $25–$35; sushi $12–$22. AE, MC, V. Daily 5:30–10pm. Free valet parking. Bus: 308.

Pamplemousse Grille ★★★ FRENCH   The whimsical interior murals of pigs on parade and a slouched chef with a cigarette dangling from his lips might lead one to believe this isn't a serious restaurant. Even the name, which is French for "grapefruit," is a bit silly. But make no mistake—this is one of the county's upper-echelon dining destinations. The internationally inspired menu also has room for personal input: You can create your own entree of grilled meats (prime rib-eye, lamb chops, and so on) with a choice of sauce (wild mushroom, peppercorn, and so on), along with a selection of veggies and potatoes (truffled Parmesan fries!); a vegetarian entree is always available, too. Happy hour, Monday to Friday 4:30 to 6:30pm, features more casual fare and drink specials.

514 Via de la Valle (across from the Del Mar Fairgrounds), Solana Beach. ⓒ **858/792-9090.** www.pgrille.com. Dinner reservations recommended (and a necessity during race season). Main courses $20–$25 lunch (served Fri only), $24–$49 dinner. AE, MC, V. Daily 5–9pm; Fri 11:30am–2pm. Bus: 308.

Solana Beach, Encinitas & Carlsbad ★

North of Del Mar and about a 45-minute drive from downtown San Diego, the pretty communities of Solana Beach, Encinitas, and Carlsbad provide many reasons to linger on the California coast: good swimming and surfing beaches, small-town atmosphere, antiques and boutiques, and the region's most beautiful flowers.

Carlsbad was named after the town of Karlsbad, Czech Republic, because of the similar mineral waters (some say they're curative) each produced. Carlsbad's once-famous artesian well was capped in the 1930s but was redrilled in 1994, and the healthful water is flowing once more. Carlsbad is also a noted commercial flower-growing region, along with its neighbor, Encinitas. Each spring (Mar through early May) at **Carlsbad Ranch** (© 760/431-0352; www.theflowerfields.com), 50 acres of solid ranunculus fields bloom into a spectacular rainbow pattern and are open to the public. In December the nurseries are alive with holiday poinsettias.

The **Solana Beach Visitor Center** is near the train station at 103 N. Cedros (© 858/350-6006; www.solanabeachchamber.com). The **Encinitas Visitors Center** is at 859 Second St. (corner of H St.) in downtown Encinitas (© 760/753-6041; www.cityofencinitas.org). The **Carlsbad Visitor Information Center,** 400 Carlsbad Village Dr. (in the old Santa Fe Depot; © 800/227-5722 or 760/434-6093; www.visitcarlsbad.com), has information on flower fields, nursery touring, and attractions.

FUN THINGS TO SEE & DO

The main area of activity for **Solana Beach** is South Cedros Avenue, parallel to Pacific Coast Highway, 1 block east. A 2-block stretch known as the **Cedros Design District ★★** (www.cedrosavenue.com) is lined with many of San Diego County's best furniture and home-design shops, antiques stores, art dealers, and boutiques. The **Belly Up Tavern ★★**, 143 S. Cedros Ave. (© 858/481-9022; www.bellyup.com), is one of San Diego's most appealing concert venues.

If you've ever wanted to get a glimpse into the artistic process, get yourself to the **Lux Art Institute ★★** in **Encinitas,** 1550 S. El Camino Real (© 760/436-6611; www.luxartinstitute.com). This unique facility—a work of art in itself—allows visitors to watch as an artist-in-residence paints, sculpts, or draws in a studio environment. It's open to the public Thursday and Friday 1 to 5pm and Saturday from 11am to 5pm ($10, ticket good for two visits; ages 20 and under are free). Every third Wednesday of the month is Lux@Night, a free wine and cheese reception from 7 to 9pm. Lux also has a retail component that features local artists and products.

The **San Elijo Lagoon Ecological Reserve ★★** encompasses coastal wetlands that were nearly lost to development. This 1,000-acre preserve features 7.5 miles of hiking trails and is home to some 700 species of plants and animals; the **San Elijo Nature Center,** 2710 Manchester Ave. (© 760/634-3026; www.sanelijo.org), interprets the flora and fauna. Another popular spot is **Moonlight Beach,** where you'll find plenty of facilities, including free parking, a playground, restrooms, showers, picnic tables, and fire grates. The beach entrance is at the end of B Street (at Encinitas Blvd.). A mile south is the appropriately serene **Swami's Beach,** named for the adjacent spiritual retreat. To the north, it adjoins little-known **Boneyard Beach,** where low-tide coves shelter romantics and nudists; this isolated stretch is accessible only from Swami's Beach. Swami's has a free parking lot, restrooms, and a picnic area.

The **Self-Realization Fellowship Retreat and Hermitage ★★** was founded in 1920 by guru Paramahansa Yogananda, and these exotic-looking domes are what remain of the retreat originally built in 1937. Today the site is a sanctuary for holistic healers and their followers, featuring serene, cliffside gardens with koi ponds and beautiful flower displays. Enter the garden at 215 W. K St., at the south end of Encinitas; it's open Tuesday through Sunday, admission is free, and you won't be pitched any philosophy. Also on-site, the **Hermitage,** where Yogananda lived and worked for many years, is usually open Sundays from

2 to 5pm. There's a gift shop, as well, at 1150 S. Coast Hwy. (© **760/753-2888;** www.yogananda-srf.org).

Carlsbad is a great place for antiquing and boutique shopping. Whether you're a serious shopper or seriously window-shopping, park the car and stroll the 3 blocks of **State Street** between Oak and Beech streets. There are about two dozen shops in this part of town, which has a village atmosphere.

Carlsbad State Beach (also known as Tamarack Surf Beach) runs alongside downtown. It's a great place to stroll along a wide concrete walkway. Enter on Ocean Boulevard at Tamarack Avenue; parking is $2 per hour or $10 for the day. South of town is **South Carlsbad State Beach,** with its nearly 3 miles of cobblestone-strewn sand. A state-run campground (© **760/438-3143;** www. parks.ca.gov) at the north end is popular year-round, and the southern portion is favored by surfers. There's a $10 vehicle fee at the beach's entrance, along Carlsbad Boulevard at Poinsettia Lane.

Dedicated shoppers won't want to miss the **Carlsbad Premium Outlets,** Paseo del Norte, via Palomar Airport Road (© **888/790-7467** or 760/804-9000; www.premiumoutlets.com), a smart, upscale outlet mall featuring some 90 stores. Also of note is the **Museum of Making Music,** 5790 Armada Dr. (© **877/ 551-9976** or 760/438-5996; www.museumofmakingmusic.org), which chronicles the American music industry from Tin Pan Alley to MTV. It's open Tuesday through Sunday from 10am to 5pm. Admission is $7 for adults; $5 for seniors, military, and children ages 6 to 18; free for children 5 and under.

LEGOLAND California ★ ☺ Opened in 1999, this 128-acre theme park is the ultimate monument to the world's most famous plastic building block. This was the third LEGOLAND to open, following branches in Denmark and Britain (and now Germany and Florida). *Note:* LEGOLAND is geared toward children ages 2 to 12, and there's just enough of a thrill-ride component to amuse preteens, but teenagers will find it a snooze. There are more than 60 rides, shows, and attractions, as well as a life-size menagerie of animals and scale models of international landmarks all constructed of LEGO bricks. In 2008, a sister attraction opened just outside the LEGOLAND gates—**Sea Life Aquarium,** focusing on the creatures (real ones, not LEGO facsimiles) found in regional waters from the Sierra Mountains to the Pacific. The highlight is a 200,000-gallon tank with sharks, rays, and colorful tropical fish; a 35-foot acrylic tunnel takes you right into the depths of it. Separate admission is required; discounted two-park tickets are available. The 5½-acre **LEGOLAND Water Park**, where kids can splash down water slides, float along a lazy river, or wade at a sandy beach, opened in 2010; ticket upgrades to include the water park are $12.

1 Legoland Dr. © **877/534-6526** or 760/918-5346. www.legoland.com, www.sealifeus.com. LEGOLAND $69 adults, $59 seniors and children 3–12, free for children 2 and under; Sea Life $20 adults, $17 seniors, $13 children; discounted 1- or 2-day park-hopper tickets available. AE, DISC, MC, V. June daily 10am–5 or 6pm; July–Aug daily 10am–8pm; off season Thurs–Mon 10am–5 or 6pm. Parking $12. Closed Tues–Wed Sept–May, but open daily during winter and spring holiday periods; Water Park closed Jan to mid-Mar, weekends only early Sept–Dec. From I-5, take the Cannon Rd. exit east ½ mile, following the signs toward Legoland Dr. Bus: 321.

San Diego Botanic Garden ★ You don't need a green thumb to appreciate this wonderful botanical facility, formerly known as the Quail Botanical Gardens. It has the country's largest bamboo collection, plus more than 35 acres of California natives; exotic tropicals; palms, cactuses; and Mediterranean, Australian, and other unusual collections. Scenic walkways and trails crisscross the compound. There's also a Children's Garden, featuring a treehouse built into a 20-foot, climbable tree. The gardens are free on the first Tuesday of the month; guided tours take place Saturdays at 10:30am.

230 Quail Gardens Dr., Encinitas. ☏ **760/436-3036.** www.sdbgarden.org. Admission $12 adults; $8 students, seniors, and military; $6 children 3–12; free for children 2 and under. Daily 9am–5pm (till 8pm Thurs in summer). Parking $2. From San Diego, take I-5 north to Encinitas Blvd.; go ½ mile east, then left on Quail Gardens Dr.

WHERE TO STAY

Beach Terrace Inn ★ At Carlsbad's only beachside hostelry (others are across the road or a little farther away), almost all the rooms—as well as the pool and Jacuzzi—have ocean views. This downtown property, which was given a clean and contemporary makeover in 2009, is tucked between rows of high-rent beach cottages and touts its scenic location as its best quality. The rooms are extra-large (some with balconies), and feature fridges, wet bars, and work spaces, making this a good choice for business or pleasure. Plus, you can walk everywhere from here—except LEGOLAND, which is a 5-minute drive away.

2775 Ocean St. (at Christiansen Way), Carlsbad, CA 92008. www.beachterraceinn.com. ☏ **800/433-5415** or 760/729-5951. Fax 760/729-1078. 48 units. $269–$459 double (nonsummer rates considerably lower). Extra person $20. Rates include continental breakfast. AE, DC, DISC, MC, V. Free parking. **Amenities:** Jacuzzi; outdoor pool. *In room:* A/C, TV, fridge, hair dryer, MP3 docking station, free Wi-Fi.

La Costa Resort and Spa ★★ ☺ With a 45-foot bell tower, white stucco walls, and red-tile roofs, this California mission-style resort has a charming, campuslike setting. Families and golf and tennis enthusiasts come here for some pampering and time on the links and courts; while those in search of mind/body health and wellness flock to the acclaimed spa and the (Dr. Deepak) **Chopra Center Well-Being.** The huge spa has 42 treatment rooms, a sprawling gym, and gorgeously landscaped outdoor sunning areas; the Chopra Center offers special programs, workshops, and spa services (which are also open to nonguests). **BlueFire Grill,** the resort's stylish bar and restaurant, faces a lovely plaza and features three chic spaces; the 400-acre property also boasts two championship 18-hole golf courses and a 17-court racquet club. Dedicated areas for kids feature high- and low-tech entertainments, and several pools have theme park–style water slides. The resort has 149 privately owned luxury villas (some with kitchens) available for rental as well.

2100 Costa del Mar Rd. (at El Camino Real), Carlsbad, CA 92009. www.lacosta.com. ☏ **800/854-5000** or 760/438-9111. Fax 760/931-7585. 611 units. $379–$439 double; from $529 suite; from $589 villa with kitchen. $22 per day resort fee. Children 17 and under stay free in parent's room. Golf, spa, and tennis packages available. AE, DC, DISC, MC, V. Valet parking $25 overnight; self-parking $12. From I-5, take La Costa Ave. east; turn left on El Camino Real. **Amenities:** 5 restaurants/cafes; 4 bars; bike rentals; children's center and programs (age 6 months to 16); concierge; 2 golf courses; health club; 5 Jacuzzis; 8 outdoor pools; room service; spa; 17 tennis courts (7 lighted); free Wi-Fi in lobby, pool areas, and conference center. *In room:* A/C, TV, hair dryer, free Internet, minibar.

Park Hyatt Aviara Resort ★★★ ☺ A nasty management dispute prompted this former Four Seasons property to change over to the Park Hyatt flag in 2010. The hotel strives to maintain the high standards (and AAA 5 Diamond ranking) that longtime guests—and locals who come for special events and to dine at the exceptional signature restaurant, **Vivace**—have come to expect. The ambience here is still one of privilege, but the rooms, with their passive pastel color schemes and nature prints, are beginning to feel a bit dated. When not wielding club or racquet, you can lie by the dramatically perched pool, relax in a series of carefully landscaped gardens, or luxuriate in the spa, where treatments incorporate regional flowers and herbs. A recreation center offers everything from basketball and sand volleyball to croquet and boccie ball; there's even a surf concierge who can give lessons and a beach butler who will arrange a perfect day at the shore for you. The resort also includes an Arnold Palmer–designed golf course that maintains harmony with the surrounding wetlands, which is home to some 130 bird species.

7100 Four Seasons Point, Carlsbad, CA 92009. www.fourseasons.com/aviara. © **800/633-7313** or 760/448-1234. Fax 760/603-6801. 329 units. $395–$495 double; from $645 suite. Children 17 and under stay free in parent's room. AE, DC, DISC, MC, V. Valet parking $30. From I-5, take Poinsettia Lane east to Aviara Pkwy. S. **Amenities:** 4 restaurants; 2 bars; babysitting; bike rental; children's center and programs (ages 4–12); concierge; golf course; health club; Jacuzzi; 2 outdoor pools; room service; spa; 6 lighted tennis courts; watersports equipment/rentals. *In room:* A/C, TV/DVD, CD player, fridge, hair dryer, minibar, MP3 docking station, Wi-Fi.

Pelican Cove Inn ★ Two blocks from the beach, this Cape Cod–style bed-and-breakfast hideaway combines romance with luxury. Your hosts see to your every need, from furnishing guest rooms with feather beds and down comforters to providing beach chairs and towels or preparing a picnic basket (with 24-hr. notice). Each room features a gas fireplace and private entrance and bathroom; some have spa tubs. The Pacific Room is most spacious, while the airy La Jolla Room has bay windows and a cupola ceiling. Courtesy transportation from the Carlsbad or Oceanside train stations is available.

320 Walnut Ave., Carlsbad, CA 92008. www.pelican-cove.com. © **888/735-2683** or 760/434-5995. 10 units. $95–$215 double. Extra person $15. Rates include full breakfast. AE, MC, V. Free parking. From downtown Carlsbad, follow Carlsbad Blvd. south to Walnut Ave.; turn left and drive 2½ blocks. *In room:* TV, no phone, free Wi-Fi.

WHERE TO EAT

Sleek and sophisticated **Blanca** ★★★, 437 S. Coast Hwy. 101, Solana Beach (© **858/792-0072;** www.dineblanca.com), quickly ascended to the top of the San Diego food chain when it opened in 2006—it's foodie nirvana. Always crowded, **Fidel's Little Mexico** ★ is reliable for tasty Mexican food and kickin' margaritas; it's in Solana Beach at 607 Valley Ave. (© **858/755-5292;** www.fidelslittlemexico.com). **Claire's on Cedros** ★★, 246 N. Cedros Ave. (© **858/259-8597;** www.clairesoncedros.com), is another Solana Beach crowd pleaser, serving breakfast and lunch; it's also LEED-certifiably green. Perfect for breakfast, lunch, or dinner, **Beach Grass Café** ★★ has two locations: 159 S. Coast Hwy. 101, Solana Beach (© **858/509-0632;** www.beachgrasscafe.com), and a newer, less stylish location at 1476 Encinitas Blvd., Encinitas (© **760/942-2741**).

Also in Encinitas is **Q'ero** ★★, 564 S. Coast Hwy. 101 (© **760/753-9050;** www.qerorestaurant.com), an excellent hole-in-the-wall find that serves both exotic and familiar Latin American fare. Other local hangouts include the **Potato Shack Cafe** ★, in Encinitas, 120 W. I St. (© **760/436-1282;** www.potatoshackcafe. com), good for breakfast carbo-loading; and casual **Swami's Cafe** ★, 1163 S. Coast Hwy. 101 (© **760/944-0612;** www.swamis.signonsandiego.com). At **Siamese**

Basil ★, 527 S. Coast Hwy. 101 (✆ **760/753-3940**), the bland surroundings belie the restaurant's well-deserved reputation for zesty Thai food. Chocoholics should not miss **Chuao Chocolatier ★★**, which has several North County locations, including the Lumberyard mall, 937 S. Coast Hwy. (✆ **760/635-1444;** www. chuaochocolatier.com).

One of the county's finest dining destinations is in Carlsbad—the Aviara resort's **Vivace ★★★**, 7100 Four Seasons Point (✆ **760/603-6999;** www.park aviara.hyatt.com). The architectural centerpiece of Carlsbad is **Ocean House,** 300 Carlsbad Village Dr. (✆ **760/729-4131;** www.oceanhousecarlsbad.com), a restored Victorian mansion. Inside, there's a formal dining area in a 1920s-era pavilion, as well as a casual cafe and bar; most evenings feature live music or a DJ. In the Carlsbad Premium Outlets shopping center, **Bellefleur ★**, 5610 Paseo del Norte (✆ **760/603-1919;** www.bellefleur.com), re-creates a wine-country experience with wood-fired grills, a tasting bar, and a glassed-in aging room. Lunch, dinner, and Sunday brunch fare surpasses shopping mall standards.

JULIAN: GOLD, APPLE PIES & A SLICE OF SMALL-TOWN CALIFORNIA

60 miles NE of San Diego; 31 miles W of Anza-Borrego Desert State Park

A trip to Julian (pop. 3,000) is a trip back in time. The old gold-mining town, now best known for its apples, has a handful of cute B&Bs, but its popularity is based on the fact that it provides a chance for city-weary folks to get away from it all. It's at its best on weekdays, when things are a little quieter.

Prospectors first ventured into these fertile hills—elevation 4,225 feet—in search of gold in the late 1860s. They discovered it in 1870 near where the Julian Hotel stands today, and 18 mines sprang up like mushrooms. Four cousins—all former Confederate soldiers from Georgia, two with the last name Julian— founded the town. The mines produced an estimated $13 million worth of gold in their day.

In October 2003, Julian was engulfed by the devastating Cedar Fire, and firefighters made a valiant stand to protect the town against what seemed insurmountable odds. The central historic part of Julian was saved, though, along with the town's famed apple orchards. You can stand on Main Street again without knowing catastrophe visited just a few hundred yards away.

Essentials

GETTING THERE   The drive can be made in 90 minutes via Hwy. 78 or I-8 to Hwy. 79. Hwy. 78 traverses countryside and farmland severely burned by the Witch Fire, one of Southern California's epic wildfires in 2007, while Hwy. 79 winds through scenic Cuyamaca Rancho State Park, where you'll still see residual damage from the 2003 fire.

VISITOR INFORMATION   Contact the **Julian Chamber of Commerce,** 2129 Main St. (✆ **760/765-1857;** www.julianca.com), where staffers offer enthusiastic suggestions. The office is open daily 10am to 4pm.

Exploring the Town

This 1880s gold-mining town offers an abundance of early California history, Old West streets with apple-pie shops and antiques stores, fresh air, and friendly people. *Note:* Julian's downtown can be crowded during the fall harvest season, so consider making your trip at another time. The autumn air is crisp, and Julian often gets dusted—sometimes buried—by snow during the winter months. Don't worry, though: They bake their famous apple pies year-round.

Downtown Julian.

The best way to experience tiny Julian is on foot. The **Julian Drug Store & Miner's Diner,** 2130 Main St. (✆ 760/765-3753), is an old-style soda fountain serving sparkling sarsaparilla; the **Eagle and High Peak Mine** (ca. 1870), at the end of C Street (✆ 760/765-0036), although seemingly a tourist trap, offers an educational look at the town's one-time economic mainstay. The town's **Pioneer Cemetery,** at Main and A streets (www.juliancemetery.org), is a hilltop graveyard straight out of *Our Town.* There's more local history on view at the **Julian Pioneer Museum,** 2811 Washington St. (✆ 760/765-0227); it's open April through December Thursday through Sunday, 10am to 4pm, weekends 10am to 4pm the rest of the year.

The **California Wolf Center ★** (✆ 760/765-0030 or 619/234-9653; www.californiawolfcenter.org) is a conservation and educational facility located about 4 miles from town. It offers public programs on Saturday at 2 and 4:30pm (10am and 2pm in fall and winter), and Sunday at 10am (reservations required; $10–$20 adults, $5–$10 children); tours include a visit with the resident wolf pack. Private tours can be arranged Monday through Friday ($25 per person).

The Julian hills are rife with **roadside fruit stands** and **orchards;** in autumn, they're open all day, every day, but in the off season, many are open only on weekends. Many line Hwy. 78 between Julian and Wynola; Farmers Road, a country lane leading north from downtown, also has stands. Wineries have a presence in the area, too, including rustic **Menghini Winery,** 1150 Julian Orchards Dr. (✆ 760/765-2072; www.menghiniwinery.com), and **Witch Creek Winery,** 2000 Main St. (✆ 760/765-2023; www.witchcreekwinery.com).

Apple pie is the town's unquestioned mainstay, though, and you'll need to sample them all to judge whether the best pies come from **Mom's Pies ★,** 2119 Main St. (✆ 760/765-2472; www.momspiesjulian.com); the **Julian Pie Company ★,** 2225 Main St. (✆ 760/765-2449; www.julianpie.com); **Apple Alley Bakery ★,** a nook on Main Street between Washington and B streets (✆ 760/765-2532); or the **Julian Café & Bakery ★,** 2112 Main St. (✆ 760/765-2712). At the **Julian Cider Mill,** 2103 Main St. (✆ 760/765-1430), you can see cider presses at work October through March; it offers free tastes and sells jugs to take home.

Outdoor Pursuits

Within 10 miles of Julian, numerous hiking trails traverse rolling meadows, high chaparral, and oak and pine forests. Fire damage is visible—oaks have recovered, but pine trees have not, though seedlings have sprung up. The most spectacular hike is at **Volcan Mountain Preserve** (© 760/765-4098; www.volcanmt. org), north of town along Farmers Road; the trail to the top is a moderately challenging hike of about 5 miles round-trip, with a 1,400-foot elevation gain. From the top, hikers have a panoramic view of the desert, mountains, and sea.

The 26,000-acre **Cuyamaca Rancho State Park,** on Hwy. 79 between Julian and the I-8, was badly burned during the October 2003 forest fires but is regenerating nicely. For a map or information, stop at the **park headquarters** (© 760/765-3020; www.parks.ca.gov) or check in with the **Cuyamaca Rancho State Park Interpretive Association** (© 619/756-5354; www.cuyamaca.us).

Eight miles south of Julian, **Lake Cuyamaca** is a tiny community that is centered on lake activities, primarily boating and fishing for trout (stocked year-round), plus bass, catfish, bluegill, and sturgeon. The fishing fee is $6 per day, $3.50 per day for kids 8 to 15, free for children 7 and under; rods and reels are also available ($10). A California state fishing license is required for those over 16 ($14 for the day); as of this writing, Lake Cuyamaca has received the state's new automated licensing equipment but it's not operational yet. Call ahead to make sure the system is up and running; otherwise, purchase a license online (www.dfg.ca.gov). Rowboats are $15 per day, motorboat rentals run $45 for the day ($35 after 1pm), and pontoon boats are $150. In summer, you can rent canoes and paddle boats by the hour for $15. For boat rental, fishing information, and RV or tent sites, call © 877/581-9904 or 760/765-0515, or see www.lakecuyamaca.org.

Where to Stay

Julian is B&B country, and they fill up months in advance for the fall harvest season. The **Julian Bed & Breakfast Guild** (© 760/765-1555; www.julian bnbguild.com) has about 10 members and is a terrific resource for locating accommodations.

Julian Gold Rush Hotel ★ Built in 1897 by freed slave Albert Robinson, this frontier-style hotel is a living monument to the area's boomtown days and is one of Southern California's oldest continually operating hotels. Downtown, it isn't as secluded or plush as some of the area's B&Bs, but if you seek historically accurate Queen Anne–style lodgings, it's ideal. The 14 rooms and two cottages are authentically restored with antiques, and nicely designed private bathrooms were added where necessary. Some rooms are tiny, so claustrophobia sufferers should ask about room size before booking. An inviting private lobby is stocked with books, games, literature on local activities, and a wood-burning stove.

2032 Main St., at B St. (P.O. Box 1856), Julian, CA 92036. www.julianhotel.com. © **800/734-5854** or 760/765-0201. Fax 760/765-0327. 16 units. $135–$165 double; $170–$210 cottage. Rates include full breakfast and afternoon tea. AE, MC, V. Take I-8 E. to Hwy. 79. *In room:* A/C, no phone, Wi-Fi.

Camping in Julian.

Orchard Hill Country Inn ★★★ Hosts Darrell and Pat Straube offer the most upscale lodgings in Julian—a posh, two-story Craftsman lodge and 12 cottages on a hill overlooking town. The lodge has 10 guest rooms, a guests-only dining room (open 4 nights a week), and a great room with a massive stone fireplace; the 12 cottages are romantic hideaways, spread over 3 acres. All units have contemporary country furnishings and snacks. Rooms in the main lodge feel hotelish, but the cottage suites are secluded and luxurious, with private porches, fireplaces, wet bars, and whirlpool tubs in most. Hiking trails lead from the lodge into the adjacent woods. Check the website for specials and packages.

2502 Washington St., at Second St. (P.O. Box 2410), Julian, CA 92036. www.orchardhill.com. ⓒ **800/716-7242** or 760/765-1700. Fax 760/765-0290. 22 units. $195–$250 double; from $295 for cottages. 2-night minimum stay if including Sat. Rates include breakfast and afternoon hors d'oeuvres. AE, MC, V. From Calif. 79, turn left on Main St. and then right on Washington St. **Amenities:** Restaurant; bar; bike rental. *In room:* A/C, TV/VCR, movie library, CD player, hair dryer.

Where to Eat

In a cozy cottage with lacy draperies, flickering candles, and a warm hearth, the **Julian Grille** ★, 2224 Main St. (ⓒ 760/765-0173), is the nicest restaurant in town. It serves soups, sandwiches, large salads, charbroiled burgers, and hearty omelets for lunch; dinner (served nightly except for Mon) features grilled and broiled meats, seafood, and prime rib. In a historic home off Main Street, **Romano's Dodge House** ★, 2718 B St. (ⓒ 760/765-1003; www.romanosjulian. com), serves home-style Italian fare, with red-checkered tablecloths and straw-clad Chianti bottles. A small lounge in back sometimes stays open late.

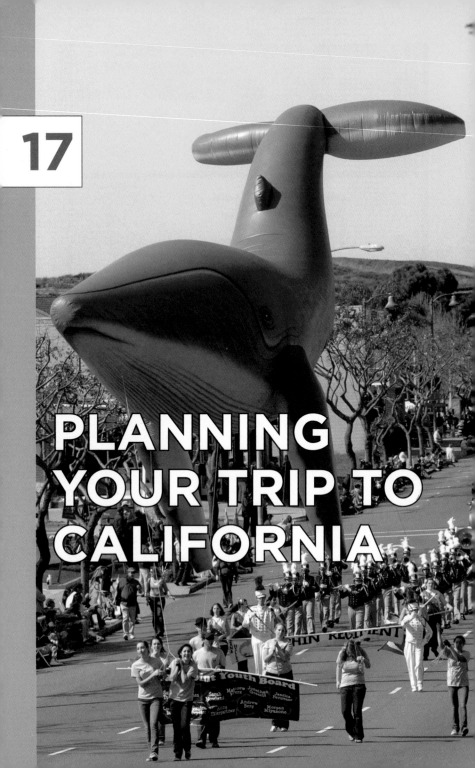

17

PLANNING YOUR TRIP TO CALIFORNIA

GETTING THERE
By Plane

All major U.S. carriers serve the San Francisco (SFO), Sacramento (SMF), San Jose (SJC), Los Angeles (LAX), John Wayne (Orange County; SNA), and San Diego (SAN) airports. They include **American** (✆ 800/433-7300; www.aa.com), **Continental** (✆ 800/523-3273; www.continental.com), **Delta** (✆ 800/221-1212; www.delta.com), **JetBlue** (✆ 800/538-2583; www.jetblue.com), **Northwest** (✆ 800/225-2525; www.nwa.com), **Southwest** (✆ 800/435-9792; www.southwest.com), **United** (✆ 800/241-6522; www.united.com), **US Airways** (✆ 800/428-4322; www.usairways.com), and **Virgin America** (✆ 877/359-8474; www.virginamerica.com). The lowest round-trip fares to the West Coast from New York fluctuate between about $200 and $450; from Chicago, they range from $200 to $300.

ARRIVING AT THE AIRPORT   International visitors arriving by air, no matter what the port of entry, should cultivate patience and resignation before setting foot on U.S. soil. U.S. airports have considerably beefed up security clearances in the years since the terrorist attacks of September 11, and clearing **Customs and Immigration** can take as long as 2 hours.

By Train

Amtrak (✆ **800/USA-RAIL** [872-7245]; www.amtrak.com) connects California with about 500 American cities. The Sunset Limited is Amtrak's regularly scheduled transcontinental service, originating in Florida and making 52 stops along the way as it passes through Alabama, Mississippi, Louisiana, Texas, New Mexico, and Arizona, before arriving in Los Angeles 2 days later. The train, which runs three times weekly, features reclining seats, a sightseeing car with large windows, and a full-service dining car. Round-trip coach fares begin at around $350; several varieties of sleeping compartments are also available for an extra charge.

GETTING AROUND
By Plane

In addition to the major carriers listed earlier in this section, several airlines provide service within the state, including **Alaska Airlines/Horizon Air** (✆ 800/252-7522), **American Eagle** (✆ 800/433-7300), **JetBlue** (✆ 800/538-2583), **Southwest** (✆ 800/435-9792), **United Express** (✆ 800/241-6522), **US Airways Express** (✆ 800/428-4322), and **Virgin America** (✆ 877/359-8474). The round-trip fare between Los Angeles and San Francisco ranges from $100 to $300. See "Orientation" or "Getting There," in some of the city chapters, for more information.

Overseas visitors can take advantage of the APEX (Advance Purchase Excursion) reductions offered by all major carriers. This system is the easiest, fastest, cheapest way to see the country. Some large airlines offer transatlantic or transpacific passengers special discount tickets under the name **Visit USA,** which allows mostly one-way travel from one U.S. destination to another at very low prices. Unavailable in the U.S., these discount tickets must be purchased abroad in conjunction with your international fare.

PREVIOUS PAGE: **Festival of Whales, Dana Point.**

By Car

Unless you plan to spend the bulk of your vacation in a city where walking is the best way to get around, the most cost-effective way to travel is by car.

Green being the thing in California, numerous carbon-conscious companies specialize in green car rentals. For example, in Southern California **Simply Hybrid Rental Cars** (☎ **888/359-0055;** www.simplyhybrid.com) rent, well, simply hybrids. **Fox Rent A Car** (☎ **800/225-4369,** ext. 1; www.foxrentacar. com) takes it a step further by offering *discount* hybrid car rentals at eight major airports in California.

In San Francisco, the epicenter of the green movement, they even reward you for going greener: Customers who rent hybrid cars—such as the Honda Civic Hybrid, Nissan Altima Hybrid, or Toyota PRIUS—from the major rental-car companies at SFO—Alamo, Avis, Budget, Dollar, Enterprise, Thrifty, Hertz, National, Fox—are given a $15 discount at the counter. By offering these incentives to customers and rental-car companies, SFO hopes to increase the total number of hybrid and alternative-fuel rental cars. (***Note:*** Foreign driver's licenses are usually recognized in the U.S., but you should get an international one if your home license is not in English.)

California's freeway signs often indicate direction by naming a town rather than a point on the compass. If you've never heard of Canoga Park, you might be in trouble—unless you have a map. The best state road guide is the comprehensive ***Thomas Guide California Road Atlas,*** a 300-plus-page book of maps with schematics of towns and cities statewide. It costs about $15, a good investment if you plan to do a lot of exploring. Smaller, accordion-style maps are handy for the entire state or for individual cities and regions; you'll find a useful one in the back of this book.

If you're heading into the Sierra or Shasta-Cascades region for a winter ski trip, stock up on antifreeze and carry snow chains for your tires. (Chains are mandatory in certain areas.)

See the full-color driving-distance chart inside the front cover of this book for an idea of the distance between the state's most popular destinations.

DRIVING RULES   California law requires drivers and passengers to wear seat belts, and specifies that a safety seat must be used for children under the age of 6 or less than 60 pounds. Motorcyclists must wear helmets at all times. Auto insurance is mandatory; the car's registration and proof of insurance must stay in the car.

You can turn right at a red light, unless otherwise indicated—but be sure to come to a complete stop first.

Many California freeways have designated car pool lanes, also known as high-occupancy vehicle (HOV) lanes or "diamond" lanes. Some require two passengers, others three. Most on-ramps are metered during even light congestion to regulate the flow of traffic onto the freeway; cars in HOV lanes can pass the signal without stopping. All other drivers are required to observe the stoplights—fines begin at $381.

If you're visiting from abroad and plan to rent a car in the United States, keep in mind that foreign driver's licenses are usually recognized in the U.S., but you may want to consider obtaining an international driver's license.

By Train

Amtrak (☎ **800/USA-RAIL** in the U.S. or Canada, or 001/215-856-7953 outside the U.S.; www.amtrak.com) operates up and down the California coast, connecting San Diego, Los Angeles, San Francisco, and points in between. Multiple trains depart each day, and rates fluctuate according to season and special promotions. One-way fares for the most popular segments can range from $16 (L.A.–Santa Barbara) to $29 (L.A.–San Diego), and from $50 to $78 (San Francisco–L.A.).

International visitors can buy a **USA Rail Pass,** good for 15, 30, or 45 days of unlimited travel on **Amtrak.** The pass is available online or through many overseas travel agents. See Amtrak's website for the cost of travel within the western, eastern, or northwestern United States. Reservations are generally required and should be made as early as possible. Regional rail passes are also available.

By Bus

Bus travel is often the most economical form of public transit for short hops between U.S. cities, but it's certainly not an option for everyone (particularly when Amtrak, which is far more luxurious, offers similar rates). **Greyhound** (☎ **800/231-2222** in the U.S., or 001/214-849-8100 outside the U.S. with toll-free access; www.greyhound.com) is the sole nationwide bus line. International visitors can obtain information about the **Greyhound North American Discovery Pass.** The pass, which offers unlimited travel and stopovers in the U.S. and Canada, can be obtained outside the United States from travel agents or through www.discoverypass.com.

TIPS ON ACCOMMODATIONS
California House Swapping

House swapping is becoming a more popular and viable means of travel: You stay in their place, they stay in yours, and you both get an authentic and personal view of the area, the opposite of the escapist retreat that many hotels offer. Try **HomeLink International** (Homelink.org), the largest and oldest home-swapping organization, founded in 1952, with more than 11,000 listings worldwide ($115 for a yearly membership). **HomeExchange.com** ($120 a year) and **Inter-Vac.com** ($100 for more than 10,000 listings) are also reliable. Many travelers find great housing swaps on Craigslist (www.craigslist.org) too, though the offerings cannot be vetted or vouched for. Swap at your own risk.

[FastFACTS] CALIFORNIA

Business Hours Offices are usually open weekdays from 9am to 5pm. Banks are open weekdays from 9am to 3pm or later and sometimes Saturday mornings. Stores typically open between 9 and 10am and close between 5 and 6pm Monday through Saturday. Stores in shopping complexes or malls tend to stay open late, until about 9pm on weekdays and weekends; many malls and department stores are open on Sundays.

Car Rental See "By Car" under "Getting Around," earlier in this chapter.

Cellphones See "Mobile Phones," later in this section.

Crime See "Safety," later in this section.

Drinking Laws The legal age for purchase and consumption of alcoholic beverages is 21; proof of age is required and often requested at bars, nightclubs, and restaurants, so it's always a good idea to bring ID when you go out. Supermarkets and convenience stores in California sell beer, wine, and liquor.

Most restaurants serve alcohol, but some serve only beer and wine. By law, all bars, clubs, restaurants, and stores cannot sell or serve alcohol after 2am, and "last call" tends to start at 1:30am. Do not carry open containers of alcohol in your car or any public area that isn't zoned for alcohol consumption. The police can fine you on the spot. And nothing will ruin your trip faster than getting a citation for DUI (driving under the influence).

Driving Rules See "Getting Around," earlier in this chapter.

Earthquakes In the rare event of an earthquake, *don't panic*. If you're in a tall building, don't run outside; instead, move away from windows and toward the building's center. Crouch under a desk or table, or stand against a wall or under a doorway. If you're in bed, get under the bed, stand in a doorway, or crouch under a sturdy piece of furniture. When exiting the building, use stairwells, *not* elevators. If you're in your car, pull over to the side of the road and stop, but wait until you're away from bridges or overpasses, as well as telephone or power poles and lines. Stay in your car. If you're outside, stay away from trees, power lines, and the sides of buildings.

Electricity Like Canada, the United States uses 110 to 120 volts AC (60 cycles), compared to 220 to 240 volts AC (50 cycles) in most of Europe, Australia, and New Zealand. Downward converters that change 220–240 volts to 110–120 volts are difficult to find in the United States, so bring one with you.

Embassies & Consulates All embassies are in the nation's capital, Washington, D.C. Some consulates are in major U.S. cities, and most nations have a mission to the United Nations in New York City. If your country isn't listed below, call for directory information in Washington, D.C. (✆ **202/555-1212**), or check **www.embassy.org/ embassies**.

The embassy of **Australia** is at 1601 Massachusetts Ave. NW, Washington, DC 20036 (✆ **202/797-3000;** www.usa.embassy.gov.au). Consulates are in New York, Honolulu, Houston, Los Angeles, and San Francisco.

The embassy of **Canada** is at 501 Pennsylvania Ave. NW, Washington, DC 20001 (✆ **202/682-1740;** www.canadainternational.gc.ca/washington). Other Canadian consulates are in Buffalo (New York), Detroit, Los Angeles, New York, and Seattle.

The embassy of **Ireland** is at 2234 Massachusetts Ave. NW, Washington, DC 20008 (✆ **202/462-3939;** www.embassyofireland.org). Irish consulates are in Boston, Chicago, New York, San Francisco, and other cities. See website for complete listing.

The embassy of **New Zealand** is at 37 Observatory Circle NW, Washington, DC 20008 (✆ **202/328-4800;** www.nzembassy.com). New Zealand consulates are in Los Angeles, Salt Lake City, San Francisco, and Seattle.

The embassy of the **United Kingdom** is at 3100 Massachusetts Ave. NW, Washington, DC 20008 (✆ **202/588-6500;** http://ukinusa.fco.gov.uk). Other British consulates are in Atlanta, Boston, Chicago, Cleveland, Houston, Los Angeles, New York, San Francisco, and Seattle.

Emergencies Call ℂ **911** to report a fire, call the police, or get an ambulance anywhere in the United States. This is a toll-free call. (No coins are required at public telephones.)

If you encounter traveler's problems, call the Los Angeles chapter of the **Traveler's Aid Society** (ℂ **310/646-2270;** www.travelersaid.org), a nationwide nonprofit social service organization.

Family Travel Family travel can be immensely rewarding, giving you new ways of seeing the world through smaller pairs of eyes. To make things easier for family vacationing, be sure to watch for the "Kids" icon throughout this guide.

Recommended family travel websites include **Family Travel Forum** (www.familytravelforum.com), a comprehensive site that offers customized trip planning; **Family Travel Network** (www.familytravelnetwork.com), an online magazine providing travel tips; and **TravelWithYourKids.com** (www.travelwithyourkids.com), a comprehensive site written by parents for parents, offering sound advice for long-distance and international travel with children.

Recommended family travel books include *Frommer's San Francisco with Kids, Frommer's Family Vacations in the National Parks,* and *The Unofficial Guide to California with Kids,* all published by Wiley Publishing, Inc.

Internet & Wi-Fi More and more hotels, resorts, airports, cafes, and retailers offer free high-speed Wi-Fi access or charge a small fee for usage. Wi-Fi is even found in campgrounds, RV parks, and sometimes entire towns. To find public Wi-Fi hot spots at your destination, go to **www.jiwire.com**; its Hotspot Finder holds the world's largest directory of public wireless hot spots. Other public Wi-Fi hot spot sites are **www.cybercaptive.com** and **www.cybercafe.com**.

For dial-up access, most business-class hotels in the U.S. offer dataports for laptop modems, and a few thousand hotels in the U.S. and Europe now offer free high-speed Internet access.

Wherever you go, bring a **connection kit** of the right power and phone adapters, a spare phone cord, and a spare Ethernet network cable—or find out whether your hotel supplies them to guests.

Legal Aid While driving, if you are pulled over for a minor infraction (such as speeding), never attempt to pay the fine directly to a police officer; this could be construed as attempted bribery, a much more serious crime. Pay fines by mail, or directly into the hands of the clerk of the court. If accused of a more serious offense, say and do nothing before consulting a lawyer. In the U.S., the burden is on the state to prove a person's guilt beyond a reasonable doubt, and everyone has the right to remain silent, whether he or she is suspected of a crime or actually arrested. Once arrested, a person can make one telephone call to a party of his or her choice. The international visitor should call his or her embassy or consulate.

LGBT Travelers California is one of the country's most progressive states when it comes to antidiscrimination legislation and workplace benefits for domestic partners. The gay and lesbian community spreads well beyond the famed enclaves of San Francisco, West Hollywood, and San Diego's Hillcrest. Gay travelers (especially men) will find a number of gay-owned inns in Palm Springs and the Russian River, north of the Bay Area.

The International Gay and Lesbian Travel Association (**IGLTA;** ℂ **954/630-1637;** www.iglta.org) is the trade association for the gay and lesbian travel industry, and offers an online directory of gay- and lesbian-friendly travel businesses and tour operators.

Many agencies offer tours and travel itineraries specifically for gay and lesbian travelers. San Francisco–based **Now, Voyager** (📞 **800/255-6951;** www.nowvoyager.com) offers worldwide trips and cruises. **Olivia** (📞 **800/631-6277;** www.olivia.com) offers lesbian cruises and resort vacations.

For more gay and lesbian travel resources, visit **Frommers.com.**

Mail At press time, domestic postage rates were 28¢ for a postcard and 44¢ for a letter. For international mail, a first-class letter of up to 1 ounce costs 98¢ (75¢ to Canada and 79¢ to Mexico); a first-class postcard costs the same as a letter. For more information go to **www.usps.com**.

If you aren't sure what your address will be in the United States, mail can be sent to you, in your name, c/o General Delivery at the main post office of the city or region where you expect to be. (Call 📞 **800/275-8777** for information on the nearest post office.) The addressee must pick up mail in person and must produce proof of identity (driver's license, passport, and so on). Most post offices will hold mail for up to 1 month, and are open Monday to Friday from 8am to 6pm, and Saturday from 9am to 3pm.

Always include zip codes when mailing items in the U.S. If you don't know your zip code, visit www.usps.com/zip4.

Medical Requirements
Unless you're arriving from an area known to be suffering from an epidemic (particularly cholera or yellow fever), inoculations or vaccinations are not required for entry into the United States.

Mobile Phones Just because your cellphone works at home doesn't mean it'll work everywhere in the U.S. Take a look at your wireless company's coverage map on its website before heading out; T-Mobile, Sprint, and Nextel are particularly weak in rural areas. If you need to stay in touch at a destination where you know your phone won't work, **rent** a phone that does from **InTouch USA** (📞 **800/872-7626;** www.intouch global.com) or a rental-car location, but beware that you'll pay $1 a minute or more for airtime.

If you're not from the U.S., you'll be appalled at the poor reach of the **GSM (Global System for Mobile Communications) wireless network,** which is used by much of the rest of the world. Your phone will probably work in most major U.S. cities; it definitely won't work in many rural areas. To see where GSM phones work in the U.S., check out **www.t-mobile.com/coverage**. And you may or may not be able to send SMS (text messages) home.

For visitors arriving via LAX, a phone-rental company called **Triptel** has a rental kiosk located on the arrival level of the international terminal. Triptel also has a San Francisco rental location at 1525 Van Ness Ave. The daily rental fee is $3, and nationwide coverage is 95¢ per minute. At the end of your stay, the phones can be dropped off at the airport or shipped back via Federal Express for an additional fee. For more information, call 📞 **877/TRIPTEL** or log on to **www.triptel.com**.

Money & Costs Beware of hidden credit card fees while traveling. Check with your credit or debit card issuer to see what fees, if any, will be charged for overseas transactions. Recent reform legislation in the U.S., for example, has curbed some exploitative lending practices. But many banks have responded by increasing fees in other

THE VALUE OF THE US$ VS. OTHER POPULAR CURRENCIES

US$	Can$	UK£	Euro (€)	Aus$	NZ$
1	C$1.03	£0.66	€0.73	A$1.09	NZ$1.42

Frommer's lists exact prices in the local currency. The currency conversions quoted above were correct at press time. However, rates fluctuate, so before departing consult a currency exchange website such as **www.oanda.com/currency/converter** to check up-to-the-minute rates.

areas. Check with your bank before departing to avoid any surprise charges on your statement.

For help with currency conversions, tip calculations, and more, download Frommer's convenient Travel Tools app for your mobile device. Go to www.frommers.com/go/mobile/ and click on the Travel Tools icon.

Passports   Virtually every air traveler entering the U.S. is required to show a passport. All persons, including U.S. citizens, traveling by air between the United States and Canada, Mexico, Central and South America, the Caribbean, and Bermuda are required to present a valid passport. **Note:** U.S. and Canadian citizens entering the U.S. at land and sea ports of entry from within the Western Hemisphere must now also present a passport or other documents compliant with the Western Hemisphere Travel Initiative (WHTI; see www.getyouhome.gov for details). Children 15 and under may continue entering with only a U.S. birth certificate, or other proof of U.S. citizenship.

WHAT THINGS COST IN CALIFORNIA	US$
Taxi from SFO or LAX to downtown	$35–$40
Moderate hotel room, double occupancy	$150–$200
Cup of coffee (Peets or Starbucks)	$1.80
1 gallon of regular gas	$3.50–$3.75
Admission to museums	$10–$25
Glass of Napa Valley red wine	$7–$15
Bus or streetcar fare for adult	$2
Cable car fare	$5
Fine for expired parking meter	$35–$60
SuperShuttle from your hotel to SFO or LAX	$17–$25
Dinner for one, without wine, expensive	$45
Dinner for one, without wine, moderate	$25
Dinner for one, without wine, inexpensive	$12
Admission to most national parks	$15–$25

Passport Offices

- **Australia**   Australian Passport Information Service (☏ **131-232;** www.passports.gov.au).

- **Canada**   **Passport Office,** Department of Foreign Affairs and International Trade, Ottawa, ON K1A 0G3 (☏ **800/567-6868;** www.ppt.gc.ca).

- **Ireland**   **Passport Office,** Setanta Centre, Molesworth Street, Dublin 2 (☏ **01/671-1633;** www.foreignaffairs.gov.ie).

- **New Zealand**   **Passports Office,** Department of Internal Affairs, 47 Boulcott St., Wellington, 6011 (☏ **0800/225-050** in New Zealand, or 04/474-8100; www.passports.govt.nz).

- **United Kingdom**   Visit your nearest passport office, major post office, or travel agency or contact the **Identity and Passport Service (IPS),** 89 Eccleston Sq., London, SW1V 1PN (☏ **0300/222-0000;** www.ips.gov.uk).

- **United States**   To find your regional passport office, check the U.S. State Department website (http://travel.state.gov/passport) or call the **National Passport Information Center** (☏ **877/487-2778**) for automated information.

Police   For any emergency, dial ☏ **911** from any phone, including cellphones and pay phones.

Safety   An unscientific survey indicates that the biggest issue on the minds of would-be visitors to California is **earthquakes,** but the incidence of earthquakes is far surpassed by the paranoia. Major quakes are rare, and they're localized enough that it is highly unlikely you will ever feel one. Refer to "Earthquakes," earlier in this chapter, for general tips on what to do in the event of an earthquake.

Driving perils in California include winter driving on mountain roads. Chains may be required in the Sierra during icy weather at elevations above 3,000 feet. The **California Department of Transportation** provides 24-hour info at ☏ **916/654-5266.**

Conversely, driving in desert areas carries its own hazards: Always be aware of the distance to the next gas station. In some areas, they may be 50 miles apart, and summer temperatures well above 100°F (38°C) can turn a scenic drive into a disaster.

Penalties in California for drunk driving are among the nation's toughest. The legal limit is .08% blood alcohol level. In some areas, freeway speed limits are aggressively enforced after dark, as a pretext for nabbing drivers who might have imbibed.

Senior Travel   Members of **AARP,** 601 E St. NW, Washington, DC 20049 (☏ **888/687-2277;** www.aarp.org), get discounts on hotels, airfares, and car rentals. AARP offers members a wide range of benefits, including *AARP The Magazine* and a monthly newsletter. Anyone 50 or over can join.

The U.S. National Park Service offers an **America the Beautiful—National Park and Federal Recreational Lands Pass—Senior Pass** (formerly the **Golden Age Passport**), which gives seniors 62 years or older lifetime entrance to all properties administered by the National Park Service—national parks, monuments, historic sites, recreation areas, and national wildlife refuges—for a one-time processing fee of $10. The pass must be purchased in person at any NPS facility that charges an entrance fee. Besides free entry, the America the Beautiful Senior Pass also offers a 50% discount on some federal-use fees charged for such facilities as camping, swimming, parking, boat launching, and tours. For more information, go to **www.nps.gov/fees_passes.htm.**

Smoking   Heavy smokers are in for a tough time in California. Smoking is illegal in public buildings, sports arenas, elevators, theaters, banks, lobbies, restaurants, offices, stores, bed-and-breakfasts, most small hotels, and bars. That's right: You can't even smoke in California bars unless drinks are served solely by the owner (though you will find that many neighborhood bars turn a blind eye and pass you an ashtray).

Student Travel A valid student ID will often qualify students for discounts on airfare, accommodations, entry to museums, cultural events, movies, and more. Check out the **International Student Travel Confederation** (**ISTC;** www.istc.org) website for comprehensive travel services information and details on how to get an **International Student Identity Card (ISIC),** which qualifies students for substantial savings on rail passes, plane tickets, entrance fees, and more. It also provides students with basic health and life insurance and a 24-hour help line. The card is valid for a maximum of 18 months. You can apply for the card online or in person at **STA Travel** (✆ **800/781-4040** in North America, 132 782 in Australia, or 0871/230-0040 in the U.K.; www.statravel.com), the biggest student travel agency in the world; check out the website to locate STA Travel offices worldwide. If you're no longer a student but are still 25 or under, you can get an **International Youth Travel Card (IYTC)** from the same people, which entitles you to some discounts. **Travel CUTS** (✆ **800/592-2887;** www.travelcuts.com) offers similar services for both Canadians and U.S. residents. Irish students may prefer to turn to **USIT** (✆ **01/602-1906;** www.usit.ie), an Ireland-based specialist in student, youth, and independent travel.

Taxes The United States has no value-added tax (VAT) or other indirect tax at the national level. Every state, county, and city may levy its own local tax on all purchases, including hotel and restaurant checks and airline tickets. These taxes will not appear on price tags. Sales tax in California is generally around 8%. Hotel tax is charged on the room tariff only (which is not subject to sales tax) and is set by the city, ranging from 12% to 17% throughout California.

Telephones Many convenience groceries and packaging services sell **prepaid calling cards** in denominations up to $50. Many public pay phones at airports now accept American Express, MasterCard, and Visa. **Local calls** made from most pay phones cost either 25¢ or 35¢. Most long-distance and international calls can be dialed directly from any phone. **To make calls within the United States and to Canada,** dial 1 followed by the area code and the seven-digit number. **For other international calls,** dial 011 followed by the country code, the city code, and the number you are calling.

Calls to area codes **800, 888, 877,** and **866** are toll-free. However, calls to area codes **700** and **900** (chat lines, bulletin boards, "dating" services, and so on) can be expensive—charges of 95¢ to $3 or more per minute. Some numbers have minimum charges that can run $15 or more.

For **reversed-charge or collect calls,** and for person-to-person calls, dial the number 0 and then the area code and number; an operator will come on the line, and you should specify whether you are calling collect, person-to-person, or both. If your operator-assisted call is international, ask for the overseas operator.

For **directory assistance** ("Information"), dial 411 for local numbers and national numbers in the U.S. and Canada. For dedicated long-distance information, dial 1, then the appropriate area code plus 555-1212.

Time The continental United States is divided into **four time zones:** Eastern Standard Time (EST), Central Standard Time (CST), Mountain Standard Time (MST), and Pacific Standard Time (PST). Alaska and Hawaii have their own zones. For example, when it's 9am in Los Angeles (PST), it's 7am in Honolulu (HST), 10am in Denver (MST), 11am in Chicago (CST), noon in New York City (EST), 5pm in London (GMT), and 2am the next day in Sydney.

Daylight saving time (summertime) is in effect from 1am on the second Sunday in March to 1am on the first Sunday in November, except in Arizona, Hawaii, the U.S. Virgin Islands, and Puerto Rico. Daylight saving time moves the clock 1 hour ahead of standard time.

For help with time translations, and more, download our convenient Travel Tools app for your mobile device. Go to www.frommers.com/go/mobile/ and click on the Travel Tools icon.

Tipping In hotels, tip **bellhops** at least $1 per bag ($2–$3 if you have a lot of luggage) and tip the **chamber staff** $1 to $2 per day (more if you've left a big mess for him or her to clean up). Tip the **doorman** or **concierge** only if he or she has provided you with some specific service (for example, calling a cab for you or obtaining difficult-to-get theater tickets). Tip the **valet-parking attendant** $1 every time you get your car.

In restaurants, bars, and nightclubs, tip **service staff** and **bartenders** 15% to 20% of the check, tip **checkroom attendants** $1 per garment, and tip **valet-parking attendants** $1 per vehicle.

As for other service personnel, tip **cab drivers** 15% of the fare; tip **skycaps** at airports at least $1 per bag ($2–$3 if you have a lot of luggage); and tip **hairdressers** and **barbers** 15% to 20%.

For help with tip calculations, currency conversions, and more, download our convenient Travel Tools app for your mobile device. Go to www.frommers.com/go/mobile/ and click on the Travel Tools icon.

Toilets You won't find public toilets, or "restrooms," on the streets in most California cities (except San Francisco), but they can be found in hotel lobbies, bars, restaurants, museums, department stores, railway and bus stations, and service stations. Large hotels and fast-food restaurants are often the best bet for clean facilities. Restaurants and bars in resorts or heavily visited areas may reserve their restrooms for patrons.

VAT See "Taxes," earlier in this section.

Visas The U.S. State Department has a **Visa Waiver Program (VWP)** allowing citizens of the following countries to enter the United States without a visa for stays of up to 90 days: Andorra, Australia, Austria, Belgium, Brunei, Czech Republic, Denmark, Estonia, Finland, France, Germany, Greece, Hungary, Iceland, Ireland, Italy, Japan, Latvia, Liechtenstein, Lithuania, Luxembourg, Malta, Monaco, the Netherlands, New Zealand, Norway, Portugal, San Marino, Singapore, Slovakia, Slovenia, South Korea, Spain, Sweden, Switzerland, and the United Kingdom. (*Note:* This list was accurate at press time; for the most up-to-date list of countries in the VWP, consult http://travel.state.gov/visa.) Even though a visa isn't necessary, in an effort to help U.S. officials check travelers against terror watch lists before they arrive at U.S. borders, visitors from VWP countries must register online through the Electronic System for Travel Authorization (ESTA) before boarding a plane or a boat to the U.S. Travelers must complete an electronic application providing basic personal and travel eligibility information. The Department of Homeland Security recommends filling out the form at least 3 days before traveling. Authorizations will be valid for up to 2 years or until the traveler's passport expires, whichever comes first. Currently, there is a US$14 fee for the online application. Existing ESTA registrations remain valid through their expiration dates. *Note:* Any passport issued on or after October 26, 2006, by a VWP country must be an **e-Passport** for VWP travelers to be eligible to enter the U.S. without a visa. Citizens of these nations also need to present a round-trip air or cruise ticket upon arrival. E-Passports contain computer chips capable of storing biometric information, such as the required digital photograph of the holder. If your passport doesn't have this feature, you can still travel without a visa if the valid passport was issued before October 26, 2005, and includes a machine-readable zone; or if the valid passport was issued between October 26, 2005, and October 25, 2006, and includes a digital photograph. For more information, go to **http://travel.state.gov/visa**. Canadian citizens may enter the United States without visas, but will need to show passports and proof of residence.

Citizens of all other countries must have (1) a valid passport that expires at least 6 months later than the scheduled end of their visit to the U.S.; and (2) a tourist visa.

For information about U.S. visas, go to **http://travel.state.gov** and click on "Visas." Or go to one of the following websites:

Australian citizens can obtain up-to-date visa information from the **U.S. Embassy Canberra,** Moonah Place, Yarralumla, ACT 2600 (✆ **02/6214-5600**), or by checking the U.S. Diplomatic Mission's website at **http://canberra.usembassy.gov/visas.html**.

British subjects can obtain up-to-date visa information by calling the **U.S. Embassy Visa Information Line** (✆ **09042-450-100** from within the U.K. at £1.20 per minute; or ✆ **866/382-3589** from within the U.S. at a flat rate of $16, payable by credit card only) or by visiting the American Embassy London's website at **http://london.us embassy.gov/visas.html**.

Irish citizens can obtain up-to-date visa information through the **U.S. Embassy Dublin,** 42 Elgin Rd., Ballsbridge, Dublin 4 (✆ 1580-47-VISA [8472] from within the Republic of Ireland at €2.40 per minute; **http://dublin.usembassy.gov**).

Citizens of **New Zealand** can obtain up-to-date visa information by contacting the **U.S. Embassy New Zealand,** 29 Fitzherbert Terrace, Thorndon, Wellington (✆ **644/462-6000;** http://newzealand.usembassy.gov).

Visitor Information For information on the state as a whole, log on to the **California Tourism** website at www.visitcalifornia.com. U.S. and Canadian residents can receive free travel planning information by mail by calling ✆ **800/862-2543.** Most cities and towns also have a tourist bureau or chamber of commerce that distributes information on the area. These are listed in the respective chapters, organized geographically.

To learn more about California's national parks, contact the **Pacific West Region Information Center,** National Park Service, 1111 Jackson St., Ste. 700, Oakland, CA 94607 (✆ **510/817-1300;** www.nps.gov). Make reservations at national park campsites—including Yosemite—via the website **www.recreation.gov**, or call ✆ **877/444-6777** within the U.S. (for international calls dial ✆ 001-518-885-3639).

For information on state parks, contact the **Department of Parks and Recreation,** P.O. Box 942896, Sacramento, CA 94296-0001 (✆ **800/777-0369;** http://cal-parks. ca.gov). Thousands of campsites are on the department's reservation system and can be booked in advance by calling **ReserveAmerica** at ✆ **800/444-7275** or logging on to their website at **www.reserveamerica.com**.

To read blogs about travel within California, try www.gocalifornia.about.com. Numerous national travel blogs cover the state, including www.localgetaways.com; www. gridskipper.com; www.realtravel.com; www.travelpost.com; www.travelblog.org; and www.worldhum.com.

Wi-Fi See "Internet & Wi-Fi," earlier in this section.

Index

INDEX

Photo Credits